America

A CONCISE HISTORY

SECOND EDITION

America
A CONCISE HISTORY

James A. Henretta
University of Maryland

David Brody
University of California, Davis

Lynn Dumenil
Occidental College

BEDFORD/ST. MARTIN'S
Boston • New York

For Bedford/St.Martin's

Publisher of History: Patricia A. Rossi
Developmental Editors: Gretchen Boger, Jessica Angell
Production Editor: Bridget Leahy
Senior Production Supervisor: Joe Ford
Marketing Manager: Jenna Bookin Barry
Copyeditor: Rosemary Winfield
Text Design: Wanda Kossak
Advisory Editor for Cartography: Michael P. Conzen, University of Chicago
Indexer: Melanie Belkin
Cover Design: Donna Lee Dennison
Cover Art: Across the Continent, Westward the Course of Empire Takes Its Way, published by Currier and Ives, 1868. Museum of the City of New York, the Harry T. Peters Collection
Composition: TechBooks
Printing and Binding: R.R. Donnelley & Sons Company

President: Charles H. Christensen
Editorial Director: Joan E. Feinberg
Director of Marketing: Karen Melton
Director of Editing, Design, and Production: Marcia Cohen
Managing Editor: Elizabeth M. Schaaf

Library of Congress Control Number: 2001087440

6   5   4   3   2
f   e   d

For information, write: Bedford/St. Martin's, 75 Arlington Street, Boston, MA 02116 (617-399-4000)

ISBN: 0–312–25612–4 (combined edition)
         0–312–25613–2 (Vol. 1)
         0–312–25614–0 (Vol. 2)

For Ellie,
Susan,
Janet, Michael, & Emily

involved, as in Chapters 18 and 19, major reordering of sections. We have also re-duced the numbers of chapters from 33 to 31 to correspond more closely with the academic calendar. Former Chapters 13 (on sectionalism) and 14 (on the crisis of union) have been combined, with much of Chapter 13's treatment of southern so-ciety, industrialization, and the West shifted to earlier chapters, while former Chapter 30 (on the politics of the 1960s) has been incorporated into the surrounding chapters. Changes of this magnitude have a bracing effect, and we are hopeful that by being forced to think hard about how to organize materials, we have come up with a stronger periodization and clearer thematic development.

The revising process is also an opportunity to incorporate new scholarship. In this second edition we have expanded the treatment of Native Americans in the colonial era, and we have been more attentive to the role of gender and the emer-gence of a distinctive southern social order before 1820. Our treatment of the com-ing of the Industrial Revolution shifts the emphasis from industrialization as such to the extension of markets, in keeping with new scholarship on the market revo-lution. We have drawn on recent Reconstruction scholarship that sees the transi-tion from slavery to freedom in large part as a battle over labor systems. We have improved our analysis of Native Americans in the Great Depression and postwar years and expanded our account of the New Right in the 1970s. The final chapter not only updates political developments but also discusses the economic prosper-ity of the late 1990s.

A new feature of this edition of *America: A Concise History* is the Epilogue, which deals with some of the open, still unresolved questions of our own time and how the historian thinks about them. The Epilogue invites the student to enter the historian's world—to participate with us in the act of interpretation that lies be-hind every historical text, including this one.

Supplements

Since the first edition of *America: A Concise History,* we have been working with in-structors from around the country to determine how we can improve our ancillary package. Instructors stress the growing demand for online resources, particularly for students, and now more than ever our supplements reflect that request.

ONLINE STUDY GUIDE FOR STUDENTS

By Michael Goldberg, University of Washington, Bothell

We are pleased to offer a new *Online Study Guide* that features up-to-date tech-nology to present students with attractive and highly effective presentations and learning tools. Written by Michael Goldberg of the University of Washington, Bothell, this interactive resource has unique self-assessment capabilities. As a stu-dent completes a practice test, the *Online Study Guide* immediately assesses her performance, targets the subject areas that need review, and refers the student back to the appropriate portions of the text. Through a series of multiple-choice, fill-in-the-blank, short-answer, and essay questions, students can gauge whether they have mastered the chapter's key events and themes. Exercises on the maps and on special features in the book encourage critical thinking. This resource is located at <www.bedfordstmartins.com/henrettaconcise>.

DOCUMENTS COLLECTION

Volume 1 by David L. Carlton (Vanderbilt University) and Volume 2 by Samuel T. McSeveny (Vanderbilt University)

This affordable two-volume *Documents Collection* offers students over 350 primary-source readings on topics covered in *America: A Concise History.* The documents emphasize contested issues in American history that will spark critical thinking and class discussions. Sets of documents highlight different perspectives on the same issue, while added attention has been given to America in the context of the larger world. Each document is preceded by a brief introduction and followed by questions for further thought.

INSTRUCTOR'S RESOURCE MANUAL

By Bradley T. Gericke (United States Military Academy)

Instructors, too, will benefit from our ancillary package. Bradley Gericke's *Instructor's Resource Manual,* provided free of charge with adoption of the book, offers an extensive collection of tools to aid both first-time and experienced teachers in structuring and customizing the American history course. The *Instructor's Resource Manual* has been revised and expanded to include informative and guiding chapter outlines, lecture strategies, questions to prompt class discussion, and writing assignments involving our American Voices features. This resource also includes map exercises, an extensive film guide, and historiographical essays on topics of particular interest.

TEST BANK

Volume 1 by Thomas L. Altherr (Metropolitan State College of Denver) and Volume 2 by Adolph Grundman (Metropolitan State College of Denver)

Our *Test Bank* now places a greater emphasis on thematic concerns within American history. What patterns in religious, cultural, political, and economic history do we see develop over time? How is a specific incident representative of a larger trend? *Test Bank* authors Thomas L. Altherr and Adolph Grundman have revised our first edition with these questions in mind. They have included multiple-choice, fill-in-the-blank, short-answer, essay, and map questions for each chapter. To provide greater ease in using this resource, it is now available on CD-ROM.

TRANSPARENCIES

An expanded set of over 150 full-color acetate transparencies, free to adopters, includes all maps and many tables, graphs, and images from the text.

CD-ROM WITH PRESENTATION MANAGER PRO

For teachers who wish to use electronic media in the classroom, this CD-ROM includes images, maps, graphs, and tables from *America: A Concise History* as well as sound recordings and a collection of supplementary images, in an easy-to-use format that allows instructors to customize their own presentations. The CD-ROM may be used with Presentation Manager Pro or with PowerPoint.

USING THE BEDFORD SERIES IN THE U.S. HISTORY SURVEY, SECOND EDITION

By Scott Hovey

Recognizing that many instructors use a survey text in conjunction with supplements, Bedford/St. Martin's has made the Bedford series volumes available at a discount to adopters of *America: A Concise History.* This short guide gives practical suggestions for using the more than fifty volumes from The Bedford Series in History and Culture and the Historians at Work series with a core text. The guide not only supplies connections between the text and the supplements but also provides ideas for starting discussions focused on a single primary-source volume.

Acknowledgments

The scholars and teachers who reviewed *America: A Concise History* made suggestions that we gratefully incorporated in the new edition. All of our reviewers have used concise texts in their courses, and their classroom experience has helped us to craft a book that meets the needs of today's diverse students. Thanks are due to Michael Goldberg, University of Washington, Bothell; David F. Krugler, University of Wisconsin–Platteville; Connie L. Lester, Mississippi State University; Carl H. Moneyhon, University of Arkansas at Little Rock; Katherine M. B. Osburn, Tennessee Technological University; Glenna R. Schroeder-Lein, University of Tennessee, Knoxville; and Nancy Shoemaker, University of Connecticut.

As the authors of *America: A Concise History,* we know how much this book is the work of other hands and minds. We are grateful to Katherine E. Kurzman and Patricia A. Rossi, who oversaw the project, and Gretchen Boger, who did a splendid job as our history editor (before departing for the Dominican Republic to serve in the Peace Corps). Elizabeth M. Welch offered invaluable insight and guidance along the way. Charles H. Christensen and Joan E. Feinberg have been generous in providing the resources we needed to produce the second edition. Elizabeth M. Schaaf, Joe Ford, and Bridget Leahy have done an outstanding job overseeing the production of the book. Karen Melton and Jenna Bookin Barry in the marketing department have been instrumental in helping this book reach the classroom. We also thank the rest of our editorial and production team for their dedicated efforts: Jessica Angell, Sarah Barrash, Rose Corbett Gordon, William Lombardo, Pembroke Herbert and Sandi Rygiel at Picture Research Consultants, Sandy Schechter, and Rosemary Winfield. Finally, we want to express our appreciation for the invaluable assistance of Patricia Deveneau, Stephanie Murvachik, Norman S. Cohen, and Anastasia Christman, whose work contributed in many ways to the intellectual vitality of this new edition of *America: A Concise History.*

James A. Henretta
David Brody
Lynn Dumenil

CONTENTS

Part Two
THE NEW REPUBLIC, 1775–1820   **156**

Part Three
ECONOMIC REVOLUTION AND SECTIONAL STRIFE, 1820–1877   **276**

Part Four
A MATURING INDUSTRIAL SOCIETY, 1877–1914   456

Part Six
AMERICA AND THE WORLD, 1945 TO THE PRESENT   774

LIST OF MAPS

ABOUT THE AUTHORS

James A. Henretta is Priscilla Alden Burke Professor of American History at the University of Maryland, College Park. He received his undergraduate education at Swarthmore College and his Ph.D. from Harvard University. He has taught at the University of Sussex, England; Princeton University; UCLA; Boston University; as a Fulbright lecturer in Australia at the University of New England; and at Oxford University as the Harmsworth Professor of American History. His publications include *The Evolution of American Society, 1700–1815: An Interdisciplinary Analysis;* *"Salutary Neglect": Colonial Administration under the Duke of Newcastle; Evolution and Revolution: American Society, 1600–1820;* and *The Origins of American Capitalism.* Recently he co-edited and contributed to a collection of original essays, *Republicanism and Liberalism in America and the German States, 1750–1850,* as part of his larger research project on "The Rise and Transformation of the Liberal State: New York, 1820–1940."

David Brody is Professor Emeritus of History at the University of California, Davis. He received his B.A., M.A., and Ph.D. from Harvard University. He has taught at the University of Warwick in England, at Moscow State University in the former Soviet Union, and at Sydney University in Australia. He is the author of *Steelworkers in America; Workers in Industrial America: Essays on the 20th Century Struggle;* and *In Labor's Cause: Main Themes on the History of the American Worker.* He has been awarded fellowships from the Social Science Research Council, the Guggenheim Foundation, and the National Endowment for the Humanities. He is past president (1991–1992) of the Pacific Coast Branch of the American Historical Association. His current research is on industrial labor during the Great Depression.

Lynn Dumenil is Robert Glass Cleland Professor of American History at Occidental College in Los Angeles. She is a graduate of the University of Southern California and received her Ph.D. from the University of California, Berkeley. She has written *The Modern Temper: American Culture and Society in the 1920s* and *Freemasonry and American Culture: 1880–1930.* Her articles and reviews have appeared in the *Journal of American History,* the *Journal of American Ethnic History, Reviews in American History,* and the *American Historical Review.* She has been a historical consultant to several documentary film projects and is on the Council of the Pacific Coast Branch of the American Historical Association. Her current work, for which she received a National Endowment for the Humanities Fellowship, is on World War I, citizenship, and the state. In 2001–2002 she will be at the University of Helsinki as the Bicentennial Fulbright Chair in American Studies.

SECOND EDITION

America

A CONCISE HISTORY

Part One

THE CREATION OF AMERICAN SOCIETY
1450–1775

T H E M A T I C   T I M E L I N E

	ECONOMY	SOCIETY	GOVERNMENT
	FROM STAPLE CROPS TO INTERNAL GROWTH	ETHNIC, RACIAL, AND CLASS DIVISIONS	FROM MONARCHY TO REPUBLIC
1450	• Native American subsistence economy • Europeans fish off North American coast.	• Sporadic warfare among Indian peoples • Spanish conquest of Mexico (1519–1521)	• Rise of monarchical nation-states in Europe
1600	• First staple crops: furs and tobacco	• English-Indian warfare • African servitude begins in Virginia (1619).	• James I rules by "divine right" in England. • Virginia House of Burgesses (1619)
1640	• New England trade with sugar islands • Mercantilist regulations: first Navigation Act (1651)	• White indentured servitude in the Chesapeake • Indians retreat inland.	• Puritan Revolution • Stuart restoration (1660) • Bacon's rebellion (1675)
1680	• Tobacco trade stagnates. • Rice cultivation expands.	• Indian slavery in the Carolinas • Ethnic rebellion in New York (1689)	• Dominion of New England (1686–1689) • Glorious Revolution (1688–1689)
1720	• Mature agricultural economy in North • Imports from Britain increase.	• Scots-Irish and German migration • Growing rural inequality	• Rise of the representative assembly • Challenge to "deferential" politics
1760	• Trade boycotts encourage domestic manufacturing.	• Uprisings by tenants and backcountry farmers • Artisan protests	• Ideas of popular sovereignty • Battles of Lexington and Concord (1775)

Societies are made, not born. They are the creation of generations of human endeavor and experience. Many centuries ago hunting and gathering peoples who migrated to the Western Hemisphere from Asia formed the first American societies. Over many generations these migrants—called the Native Americans—came to live in a wide variety of environments and cultures. In much of North America they developed kinship-based societies that relied on hunting and farming. But in the lower Mississippi Valley, Native Americans developed a hierarchical social order similar to that of the great civilizations of the Aztecs, Mayas, and Incas of Mesoamerica.

The coming of the Europeans and their diseases tore the fabric of most Native American cultures into shreds. Indian peoples increasingly confronted a new American society that included thousands of enslaved Africans and was dominated by even greater numbers of settlers of European ancestry. Most of the Europeans attempted to transplant their traditional societies to America—their farming practices, their social hierarchies, their culture and heritage, and their religious ideas. But in learning to live in the new land, the Europeans who settled Britain's North American colonies eventually created societies that were distinctly different from those of their homelands in their economies, social character, political systems, religion, and culture.

RELIGION	CULTURE
FROM HIERARCHY TO PLURALISM	THE CREATION OF AMERICAN IDENTITY
• Protestant Reformation begins (1517).	• Diverse Native American cultures in eastern Woodlands
• Persecuted English Puritans and Catholics migrate to America.	• Puritans implant Calvinism, education, and freehold ideal.
• Established churches in Virginia and Massachusetts • Roger Williams creates religious liberty in Rhode Island.	• Aristocratic aspirations in the Chesapeake
• Religious freedom in Quaker Pennsylvania	• Emergence of African American language and culture
• German and Scots-Irish Pietists in mid-Atlantic region • Great Awakening	• Emergence of regional cultures • Franklin and the American Enlightenment
• Evangelical Baptists in Virginia • Quebec Act allows Catholicism (1774).	• Emergence of "American" identity • Republican innovations in political theory

ECONOMY. Many of the new settlements compiled an impressive record of economic achievement. Traditional Europe was made up of poor and unequal societies periodically racked by famine. But in the bountiful natural environment of North America, plenty replaced poverty, and the settlers created a bustling economy and many prosperous communities of independent farm families. Indeed, England's northern mainland colonies became "the best poor man's country" for migrants from the British Isles and Germany.

SOCIETY. However, some of the new settle-ments became places of oppressive captivity for Africans. Aided by African slavers, Europeans transported hundreds of thousands of Africans, from many peoples, to the West Indies and the southern mainland colonies and forced them to work as slaves on sugar, tobacco, and rice plantations. Although their labor produced vast quantities of valuable export crops, these enslaved Africans lived from one generation to the next in abject poverty and without civil or political rights.

GOVERNMENT. At the same time the Europeans who lived in the emerging American societies created an increasingly free and competitive political system. The first English settlers brought many authoritarian institutions with them, and the English government attempted to impose tight control over their lives. But after 1689 authoritarian customs and controls gradually gave way to governments based in part on representative assemblies. Eventually, the growth of self-rule in these colonies led to demands for political independence from Britain.

RELIGION. The American experience profoundly changed religious institutions and values. Many migrants came to America in the wake of the conflicts of Europe's Protestant Reformation seeking to practice their religion without interference. The societies they created became increasingly religious, especially after the evangelical revivals of the 1740s. By this time many Americans had rejected the harshest tenets of Calvinism (a strict Protestant doctrine), and others had embraced the rationalist view of the European Enlightenment. As a result, American Protestant Christianity became increasingly tolerant, democratic, and optimistic.

CULTURE. Finally, the new American society was marked by changes in the family, the local community, and the broader culture. The first English settlers lived in patriarchal families ruled by dominant fathers and in communities controlled by men of high status. By 1750, however, many American fathers no longer strictly managed their children's lives. Geographic and economic expansion helped to create more open and diverse communities in which many white men—and some women—began to enjoy greater personal independence. These communities formed part of an increasingly pluralistic society that by the eighteenth century was composed of various European migrants—English, Scots, Scots-Irish, Dutch, and German—as well as enslaved West Africans and many different Native American peoples. As these migrants settled in distinct American environments, four regional cultures developed: in New England, the mid-Atlantic colonies, the Chesapeake, and the lower South. Consequently an American identity—based on the English language, British legal and political institutions, and shared experiences—emerged very slowly.

The story of the colonial experience is historically and morally complex—a multifaceted world that brought oppression to some and opportunity to others. The European intruders warred with Native Americans and condemned most Africans to bondage, even as their new society offered a continuing stream of European migrants rich possibilities for economic security, political freedom, and spiritual fulfillment.

Chapter 1

WORLDS COLLIDE: EUROPE, AFRICA, AND AMERICA
1450–1620

Soon there will come from the rising sun a different kind of man from any you have yet seen. . . . [After that,] the world will fall to pieces.

A SPOKANE INDIAN PROPHET

"**B**efore the French came among us," an elder of the Natchez people of Mississippi exclaimed in 1728, "we were men . . . and we walked with boldness every road." "But now," he lamented, "we walk like slaves, which we shall soon be, since the French already treat us . . . as they do their black slaves." Before the 1420s the Indian peoples of the Western Hemisphere knew absolutely nothing about the French inhabitants of Europe and the dark-skinned peoples of Africa, and those peoples knew only a little bit about each other. Then a few Europeans, hungry for the trade and riches of Asia, sailed along the west coast of Africa and were soon involved in the long-established trade in African slaves. By 1492 Christopher Columbus, another European searching for a sea route to Asia, had encountered the lands and peoples of the Americas. The destinies of three continents quickly became intertwined. In 1493, on his second voyage to the Western Hemisphere, Columbus carried a cargo of enslaved Africans, beginning the centuries-long process that created a multitude of triracial societies in the Americas.

As the Natchez elder well knew, the resulting mixture of peoples from the three continents was based not on equality but on exploitation. In 1728 he was urging his people to fight the encroachment of Europeans, but resistance by then was useless. Within a decade, 250 years after the strangers had first arrived in the Americas, Europeans and their Indian allies had killed hundreds of Natchez and sold many of the survivors into slavery in the West Indies.

The fate of the Natchez was not new. Over the course of the three centuries following Columbus's voyage, many Native American peoples came under the domination of the Europeans—Spanish, Portuguese, French, English, Dutch—who had colonized the Western Hemisphere and now worked its plantations with enslaved Africans. How did Europeans become leaders in world trade and extend their influence across the Atlantic? What was the character of the Native Americans' life and culture, and what made their societies vulnerable to conquest by European adventurers? And what led to the transatlantic trade in African slaves? In the answers to these questions lie the origins of the United States.

Native American Worlds

When the Europeans arrived, the great majority of Native Americans—about 40 million—lived in Mesoamerica (present-day Mexico and Guatemala), and another 15 million resided in lands to the north (present-day United States and Canada). Some lived in simple hunter-gatherer or agricultural communities governed by kin ties, but the majority resided in societies ruled by warrior-kings and priests. In Mesoamerica and Peru Indian peoples created civilizations whose art, religion, society, and economy were as complex as those of Europe and the Mediterranean.

THE FIRST AMERICANS

For the Navajo people, history began when their ancestors emerged from under the earth; for the Iroquois, the story of their Nations began when people fell from the sky. However, most anthropologists and historians believe that the first people to live in the Western Hemisphere were migrants from Asia. Some might have come by water, but most probably came by land. Strong archaeological evidence suggests that during the last Ice Age, which began about 30,000 years ago, small bands of hunters followed herds of game across a land bridge between Siberia and Alaska. A tale of the Tuscarora Indians, who lived in present-day North Carolina, tells of a famine in the old world and a journey over ice toward where "the sun rises," a trek that brought their ancestors to a lush forest with abundant food and game. Most anthropologists believe that this migratory stream continued for about 20,000 years, until the glaciers melted and the rising ocean waters submerged the land bridge and created the Bering Strait. Then the people of the Western Hemisphere, who by that time had moved as far south as the tip of South America and as far east as the Atlantic coast of North America, were cut off from the rest of the world for 400 generations.

For many centuries the first Americans lived as hunter-gatherers, subsisting on the abundant wildlife and vegetation. But about 3000 B.C. some Native American peoples began to develop horticulture, most notably in the area of present-day Mexico. These inventive farmers planted avocado, chili peppers, and cotton and learned how to breed maize, or Indian corn, as well as tomatoes, potatoes, and manioc—crops that would eventually enrich the food supply of the entire world. Over the centuries the Indian peoples bred maize into a much larger, extremely nutritious plant that was hardier, had more varieties, and had a higher yield per

Gold Piece from Peru

Skilled Inca artisans created gold jewelry of striking beauty. Note the intricate detail on the head-dress and the stylized treatment of the face.

(Dumbarton Oaks Research Library and Collections, Washington, DC)

acre than wheat, barley, and rye, the staple cereals of Europe. They also learned to cultivate beans and squash and plant them together with corn, creating a mix of crops that provided a nutritious diet and preserved soil fertility, allowing intensive farming and high yields. The resulting agricultural surplus laid the economic foundation for populous and wealthy societies in Mexico, in Peru, and in the Mississippi River Valley.

THE MAYAS AND THE AZTECS

The flowering of civilization in Mesoamerica began among the Mayan peoples of the Yucatan Peninsula of Mexico and the neighboring rain forests of Guatemala (see Map 1.1). The Mayas built large religious centers, urban communities with elaborate systems of water storage and irrigation. By A.D. 300 the Mayan city of Tikal had at least 20,000 inhabitants, mostly farmers who worked the nearby fields and whose labor was used to build huge stone temples. An elite class claiming descent from the gods ruled Mayan society, living in splendor on goods and taxes extracted from peasant families. Drawing on religious and artistic traditions that stretched back to the Olmec people, who had lived along the Gulf of Mexico around 700 B.C., skilled Mayan artisans decorated temples and palaces with art depicting warrior-gods and complex religious rituals. Mayan astronomers created a calendar that recorded historical events and predicted eclipses of the sun and the moon with remarkable accuracy. The Mayas also developed hieroglyphic writing to record royal lineages and noteworthy events, including wars.

Beginning around A.D. 800, Mayan civilization declined. Some evidence suggests that a two-century-long dry period caused a decline in population and an economic crisis that prompted overtaxed peasants to desert the temple cities and retreat into the countryside. By A.D. 900 many religious centers had been abandoned, but some Mayan city-states lasted until the Spanish invasion in the 1520s.

As the Mayan peoples flourished in the Yucatan, a second major Mesoamerican civilization developed in the central highlands of Mexico around the city of

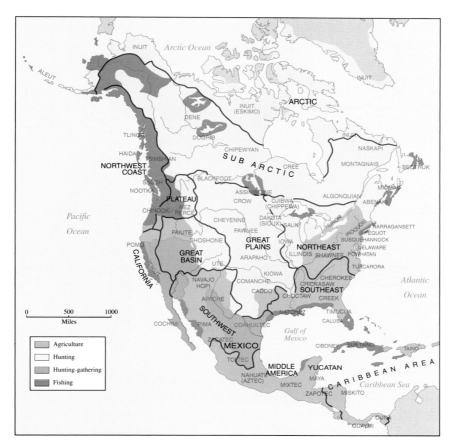

M A P   1.1
Native American Peoples, 1492

Native Americans populated the entire Western Hemisphere at the time of Columbus's arrival. Having learned how to live in many environments, they created diverse cultures that ranged from the centralized agriculture-based empires of the Mayas and the Aztecs to seminomadic tribes of hunter-gatherers. The sheer diversity among Indians—of culture, language, and tribal identity—inhibited united resistance to the European invaders.

Teotihuacán, with its magnificent Pyramid of the Sun. At its zenith about A.D. 500 Teotihuacán had more than 100 temples, about 4,000 apartment buildings, and a population of at least 100,000. By A.D. 800 Teotihuacán had also declined, probably because of a long-term drop in rainfall and recurrent invasions by seminomadic warrior peoples. Eventually one of these peoples, the Aztecs, established an even more extensive empire.

The Aztecs entered the highlands of Mexico from the north and settled on an island in Lake Texcoco. There, in A.D. 1325, they began to build a new city, Tenochtitlán (present-day Mexico City). They learned the settled ways of the resident peoples, mastered their complex irrigation systems, and established an elaborate culture with a hierarchical social order. Priests and warrior nobles ruled over twenty clans of free Aztec commoners who farmed communally owned land, and the nobles used huge numbers of non-Aztec slaves and serfs to labor on their private estates. Artisans worked in stone, pottery, cloth, leather, and especially obsidian (hard volcanic glass used to make sharp-edged weapons and tools).

The Aztecs remained an aggressive tribe and soon subjugated most of central Mexico. Their rulers demanded both economic and human tribute from scores of subject tribes, gruesomely sacrificing untold thousands of men and women to ensure agricultural fertility and the daily return of the sun. Aztec merchants created far-flung trading routes and imported furs, gold, textiles, food, and obsidian. By A.D. 1500, when the Spanish arrived in the Caribbean, Tenochtitlán had grown into a great metropolis with splendid palaces and temples and over 200,000 inhabitants. The Aztecs' wealth, strong institutions, and military power posed a formidable challenge to any adversary, at home or from afar.

THE INDIANS OF THE NORTH

The Indians who resided north of the Rio Grande were fewer in number and lived in less coercive societies. In A.D. 1500 these Indians lived in dispersed communities of a few thousand people and spoke many different languages—no fewer than sixty-eight east of the Mississippi River (see Map 1.1). Most were organized in self-governing tribes composed of clans—groups of related families that had a common identity and a real or legendary common ancestor. The tribes were led by local chiefs who, aided by the clan elders, conducted ceremonies and regulated personal life. For example, elders encouraged individuals to share food and other scarce goods, promoting an ethic of reciprocity rather than one of accumulation. "You are covetous, and neither generous nor kind," the Micmac Indians of Nova Scotia told French fur traders around 1600. "As for us, if we have a morsel of bread, we share it with our neighbor." The individual ownership of land was virtually unknown in Indian culture, although elders granted families exclusive use-rights over certain planting grounds and hunting areas. Clan leaders also resolved personal feuds, disciplined individuals who violated customs, decided whether to go to war, and banned marriage between members of the same clan, a rule that helped prevent inbreeding. However, their power was far less than that of the Mayan and Aztec nobles because their kinship-based system of government was locally based and worked by consensus, not by coercion.

Over the centuries some of these tribes exerted influence over their immediate neighbors through trade or conquest. The earliest expansive Indian cultures appeared in the eastern woodlands of North America as the inhabitants increased the food supply by domesticating plants and were thus able to settle in large villages. By A.D. 100 the vigorous Hopewell people in the area of present-day Ohio had spread their influence through trade from Wisconsin to Louisiana, importing obsidian from the Yellowstone region of the Rocky Mountains, copper from the Great Lakes, and pottery and marine shells from the Gulf of Mexico. They built large burial mounds and surrounded them with extensive circular, rectangular, or octagonal earthworks that in some cases still survive. The Hopewell people buried their dead with striking ornaments fashioned by their craftsmen: copper beaten into elaborate designs, crystals of quartz, mica cut into the shapes of serpents and human hands, and stone pipes carved to represent frogs, hawks, bears, and other animals. For unknown reasons, their elaborate trading network gradually collapsed around A.D. 400.

A second complex culture developed among the Pueblo peoples of the Southwest. By A.D. 600 Mogollon peoples in the highland region along the border of present-day Arizona and New Mexico were using irrigation to grow two crops a year, fashioning fine pottery, and worshipping their gods on platform mounds; by A.D. 1000, they were living in elaborate multiroom stone structures (or pueblos). In the north of present-day New Mexico, the Anasazi culture developed around

Casas Grandes Pot

The artistically and architecturally talented Mogollon and Anasazi peoples of Arizona and New Mexico took utilitarian objects—such as this ordinary pot—and decorated them with black-on-white designs. Their cultures flourished from 600 to 1150, after which they slowly declined.

(The Amerind Foundation, Dragoon, AZ. Photo by Robin Stancliff)

A.D. 900. The Anasazis were master architects, building residential-ceremonial villages in steep cliffs and a pueblo in Chaco Canyon that housed 1,000 people. Over 400 miles of straight roads radiated out of Chaco Canyon, making it a center for trade. But the culture of the Anasazis and the Mogollons (as well as that of the neighboring Hohokam people) gradually collapsed after A.D. 1150 as long periods of drought disrupted food production and prompted the abandonment of Chaco Canyon and other long-established communities. The descendants of these Pueblo peoples—including the Zunis and the Hopis—later built strong but smaller and more dispersed village societies.

The last large-scale culture to emerge north of the Rio Grande was the Mississippian civilization. Beginning about A.D. 700, the advanced farming technology of Mesoamerica spread into the Mississippi River Valley, perhaps carried by emigrants fleeing from warfare among the Mayas. The resident peoples planted new strains of maize and beans on fertile river bottomland, providing a protein-rich diet and creating an agricultural surplus. A robust culture based on small, fortified temple cities quickly emerged. By A.D. 1150 the largest city, Cahokia (near present-day St. Louis), had a population of 15,000 to 20,000 and more than 100 temple mounds, one of them as large as the great Egyptian pyramids. As in Mesoamerica, the tribute paid by peasant cultivators supported a privileged class of nobles and priests who waged war against neighboring chiefdoms, patronized skilled artisans, and may have been worshipped as deities.

However, by A.D. 1350 this 600-year-old Mississippian civilization was in rapid decline, undermined by warfare over fertile bottomlands and by urban diseases such as tuberculosis. Nonetheless, the values and institutions of this culture endured for centuries in the lands to the east of the Mississippi River and help to account for the fierce resistance of the inhabitants to Spanish and French invaders. When the Spanish invaded northern Florida in the 1540s, they found the Apalachee and Timucua Indians living in permanent settlements and planting and harvesting their fields twice a year. A century and a half later French traders and priests who encountered the Natchez people in the area of present-day Mississippi found a society rigidly divided among hereditary chiefs, two groups of nobles and honored people, and a bottom class of peasants. Undoubtedly influenced by Mayan or Aztec rituals, the Natchez practiced human sacrifice; the death of a chief called for the sacrifice of his wives and the enlargement of a ceremonial mound to bury their remains (see American Voices, "The Customs of the Natchez"). Like the Indians of Mesoamerica, the peoples of this region (such as the Choctaws, Creeks, Chickasaws, Cherokees, and Seminoles) developed a stable, agricultural-based way of life, prompting eighteenth-century British settlers to call them the Civilized Tribes.

Although farming in Mesoamerica was the province of both sexes, among peoples who lived in the eastern woodlands of North America it became the work of women. Over the centuries Indian women became adept horticulturists, using flint hoes and more productive strains of corn, squash, and beans to reduce the

The Customs of the Natchez

FATHER LE PETITE

B *eliefs and institutions from the earlier Mississippian culture (A.D. 1000–1450) lasted for
centuries among the Natchez, who lived in the area of present-day Mississippi. This letter was written around 1730 by Father le Petite, a Jesuit priest who lived among the Natchez
after their uprising against the French. Here, Father le Petite accurately describes many Indian
customs but misinteprets the rules governing the succession of the chief, which simply followed
the normal practice of descent and inheritance in a matrilineal society.*

My Reverend Father, The peace of Our Lord.

This Nation of Savages inhabits one of the most beautiful and fertile countries in the
World, and is the only one on this continent which appears to have any regular worship.
Their Religion in certain points is very similar to that of the ancient Romans. They have
a Temple filled with Idols, which are different figures of men and of animals, and for which
they have the most profound veneration. Their Temple in shape resembles an earthen oven,
a hundred feet in circumference. They enter it by a little door about four feet high, and
not more than three in breadth. Above on the outside are three figures of eagles made of
wood, and painted red, yellow, and white. Before the door is a kind of shed with folding-
doors, where the Guardian of the Temple is lodged; all around it runs a circle of palisades,
[pointed wooden stakes], on which are seen exposed the skulls of all the heads which their
Warriors had brought back from the battles in which they had been engaged with the enemies of their Nation. . . .

The Sun is the principal object of veneration to these people; as they cannot conceive
of anything which can be above this heavenly body, nothing else appears to them more
worthy of their homage. It is for the same reason that the great Chief of this Nation, who
knows nothing on the earth more dignified than himself, takes the title of brother of the
Sun, and the credulity of the people maintains him in the despotic authority which he
claims. To enable them better to converse together, they raise a mound of artificial soil, on
which they build his cabin, which is of the same construction as the Temple.

The old men prescribe the Laws for the rest of the people, and one of their principles
is . . . the immortality of the soul, and when they leave this world they go, they say, to live
in another, there to be recompensed or punished.

In former times the Nation of the *Natchez* was very large. It counted sixty Villages and
eight hundred Suns or Princes; now it is reduced to six little Villages and eleven Suns. [Its]
Government is hereditary; it is not, however, the son of the reigning Chief who succeeds
his father, but the son of his sister, or the first Princess of the blood. This policy is founded
on the knowledge they have of the licentiousness of their women. They are not sure, they
say, that the children of the chief's wife may be of the blood Royal, whereas the son of the
sister of the great Chief must be, at least on the side of the mother.

SOURCE: Reuben Gold Thwaites, ed., *The Jesuit Relations and Allied Documents* (Cleveland: Murrow
Brothers, 1900), vol. 68: pp. 121–35.

Timucuan Women at Work in the Field

As suggested in this engraving by the European artist De Bry, Indian women took the major responsibility for growing corn, beans, and other food crops. But there are many inaccuracies in the portrait. Indians did not use plows (and so there should be no furrows), and though men removed trees and brush from the fields, they did not usually wield hoes.

(Courtesy of the John Carter Brown Library at Brown University)

dependence of their peoples on gathering and hunting. In the summer many tribes lived in semipermanent villages of domed wigwams where women cultivated fields, passing the right to use them to their daughters. Because of the importance of farming, a matrilineal inheritance system developed among many eastern Indians, including the Five Nations of the Iroquois. The ritual lives of these peoples also focused on religious ceremonies related to the agricultural cycle, such as the Iroquois green corn and strawberry festivals. Indian peoples ate better as a result of these advances in farming, but they enjoyed few material comforts, and their populations grew slowly.

In A.D. 1500 most Indians north of the Rio Grande had resided on the same lands for generations, but the elaborate civilizations that had once flourished in the Southwest and in the great river valleys in the heart of the continent had vanished. Consequently, when the European adventurers, traders, and settlers came ashore from the Atlantic, there were no great Indian empires or religious centers that could lead a campaign of military and spiritual resistance against the invaders.

Traditional European Society in 1450

In A.D. 1450 few observers would have predicted that the European peoples would become the overlords of the Western Hemisphere. A thousand years after the fall of the Roman empire Europe remained a backward society. Most Europeans, like most Native Americans, were exploited peasants or poor farmers who had little knowledge of the wider world. Their lives and those of their descendants who would migrate to the Americas were shaped by the cultural and religious values of the traditional rural world.

THE PEASANTRY

There were only a few large cities in Western Europe before A.D. 1450—only Paris, London, and Naples had 100,000 residents and thus equaled the size of Teotihuacán at its zenith. More than 90 percent of the population consisted of peasants living in small rural communities. Peasant families usually owned or leased a small dwelling in the village center and had the right to farm strips of land in the surrounding fields. The fields were not divided by fences or hedges, making cooperative farming a necessity. Because there were few merchants or good roads, most families exchanged surplus grain and meat with their neighbors or bartered their farm products for the services of local millers, weavers, and blacksmiths. Most peasants yearned to be yeomen, who were under no obligation to a landlord and owned enough land to support a family in comfort, but relatively few achieved that goal.

As among the Native Americans, many aspects of European peasant life followed a seasonal pattern. The agricultural year began in March or April, when the ground thawed and dried, allowing the villagers to begin the exhausting work of spring plowing and the planting of wheat, rye, and oats. During these busy months men sheared the thick winter wool of their sheep, which the women washed and spun into yarn. Peasants cut the first crop of hay in June and stored it as winter fodder for their livestock. In the summer life became more relaxed, and families mended their fences or repaired their barns. August and September often were marked by grief as infants and old people succumbed to epidemics of fly-borne dysentery. Fall brought the strenuous harvest time, followed by solemn feasts of thanksgiving and riotous bouts of merrymaking. As winter approached, peasants slaughtered excess livestock and salted or smoked the meat. During the cold months they completed the tasks of threshing grain and weaving textiles and had time to visit friends and relatives in nearby villages. Many rural people died in January and February, victims of viral diseases and the cold. Then, just before the agricultural cycle began again in the spring, rural residents held carnivals to celebrate with drink and dance the end of the long winter night.

For most peasants survival required unremitting labor, and the margin of existence was thin, corroding family relations. Malnourished mothers fed their babies sparingly, calling them "greedy and gluttonous," and many newborn girls were "helped to die" so that their older brothers would have enough to eat. About half of all peasant children died before the age of twenty-one. Violence—assault, murder, rape—was much more prevalent than in the modern world, and hunger and disease were constant companions. "I have seen the latest epoch of misery," a French doctor reported as famine and plague struck. "The inhabitants . . . lie down in a meadow to eat grass, and share the food of wild beasts."

Often destitute, usually exploited and dominated by landlords and aristocrats, many peasants simply accepted their condition, but others did not. It would be the deprived rural classes of Britain, Spain, and Germany, hoping for a better life for themselves and their children, who would supply the majority of white migrants to the Western Hemisphere.

HIERARCHY AND AUTHORITY

In the traditional European social order, as among the Aztec and Mayan peoples, authority came from above. Kings and princes owned vast tracts of land, conscripted men for military service, and lived in splendor off the labor of the peasantry. Yet rulers were far from supreme, given the power of the nobles, each of whom also owned large estates and controlled hundreds of peasant families. Collectively, these noblemen had the power to challenge royal authority. They had their own legislative institutions, such as the French parlements and the English House of Lords, and enjoyed special privileges, such as the right to a trial before a jury of other noblemen. But after 1450 kings began to undermine the power of the nobility and create more centralized states, laying the basis for overseas expansion.

Just as kings and nobles ruled the state, so the men in peasant families ruled their women and children. The man was the head of the house, his power justified by the teachings of the Christian Church. As one English clergyman put it, "The woman is a weak creature not embued with like strength and constancy of mind"; law and custom consequently "subjected her to the power of man." On marriage, an English woman assumed her husband's surname and was required (under the threat of legally sanctioned physical "correction") to submit to his orders. Moreover, she surrendered to her husband the legal right to all her property; on his death she received a dower, usually the use during her lifetime of one-third of the family's land and goods.

A father controlled the lives of his children with equal authority, demanding that they work for him until their middle or late twenties. Then a landowning peasant would try to provide land to sons and dowries to daughters and choose marriage partners of appropriate wealth and status for them. In many regions fathers bestowed most of the land on the eldest son, an inheritance practice known as primogeniture, forcing many younger children to join the ranks of the roaming poor. In such a society few men—and even fewer women—had much personal freedom or individual identity.

Hierarchy and authority prevailed in the traditional European social order both because of the power of established institutions and because, in a violent and unpredictable world, they offered ordinary people a measure of security. These values, which migrants carried with them to America, would shape the character of family life and the social order there well into the eighteenth century.

THE POWER OF RELIGION

The Roman Catholic Church served as one of the great unifying forces in Western European society. By A.D. 1000 virtually all of pagan Europe had adopted Christianity. The pope, as head of the Catholic Church, directed a vast hierarchy of cardinals, bishops, and priests. Latin, the language of scholarship, was preserved by Catholic priests and monks, and Christian dogma provided a common understanding of God, the world, and human history. Equally important, the Church provided another bulwark of authority and discipline in society. Every village had a church, and holy shrines dotted the byways of Europe.

Christian doctrine penetrated deeply into the everyday lives of peasants. Over the centuries the Church had devised a religious calendar that followed the

Christ's Crucifixion

This graphic portrayal of Christ's death on the cross, by the German painter Grünewald, reminded believers of the reality of death and the need for repentance.

(Isenheim Altarpiece, Colmar, Musée Unterlinden, Giraudon/Art Resource)

agricultural cycle and transformed pagan festivals into Christian holy days. Thus the winter solstice, which for pagans marked the return of the sun and the victory of light over darkness, became the feast of Christmas. This merging of the sacred and the agricultural cycle endowed all worldly events with meaning. Few Christians believed that events occurred by chance; they were the result of God's will. To avert famine and plague, peasants turned to priests for spiritual guidance and offered prayers to Christ and the saints.

The Church taught that Satan constantly challenged God by tempting people into evil. If prophets spread unusual doctrines, or "heresies," they were surely the tools of Satan. If a devout Christian fell mysteriously ill, the sickness might be the result of an evil spell cast by a witch in league with Satan. Crushing other religions and suppressing false doctrines (heresies) among Christians was an obligation of rulers and a principal task of the new orders of Christian knights. Between A.D. 1096 and 1291 successive armies of Christians, led by European kings and nobles, embarked on a series of Crusades to expel Arab Muslims—followers of the Islamic religion—from the Holy Land where Jesus had lived.

The crusaders temporarily gained control of much of Palestine, but the impact of the Crusades on Europe was more profound. Religious warfare reinforced and intensified its Christian identity, resulting in renewed persecution of Jews and their expulsion from many European countries. The Crusades also broadened the intellectual and economic horizons of the privileged classes of Western Europe, bringing them into contact with the Arab peoples of the Mediterranean region of North Africa, who controlled the trade among Europe, Asia, and Africa and led the world in scholarship.

Europe Encounters Africa and the Americas, 1450–1550

Around A.D. 1400 Europeans shook off the lethargy of their traditional agricultural society with a major revival of learning, the Renaissance (from the French word for "rebirth"). Inspired by new knowledge and a new optimism, the rulers of Portugal and Spain commissioned Italian navigators to find new trade routes to India and China. These maritime adventurers soon brought Europeans into direct contact with the peoples of Africa, Asia, and the Americas, beginning a new era in world history.

THE RENAISSANCE

Stimulated by the wealth and learning of the Arab world, first Italy and then the countries of northern Europe experienced the rebirth of learning and cultural life now known as the Renaissance. Arab traders had access to the fabulous treasures of the East, such as silks and spices, and Arab societies had acquired magnetic compasses, water-powered mills, and mechanical clocks. In great cultural centers such as Alexandria and Cairo in Egypt, Arab scholars carried on the legacy of Christian Byzantine civilization, which had preserved the great achievements of the Greeks and Romans in religion, medicine, philosophy, mathematics, astronomy, and geography. Through Arab learning, the peoples of Europe reacquainted themselves with their own classical heritage.

The Renaissance had the most profound impact on the upper classes. Merchants from the Italian city-states of Venice, Genoa, and Pisa dispatched ships to Alexandria, Beirut, and other eastern Mediterranean ports, where they purchased goods from China, India, Persia, and Arabia and sold them throughout Europe. The enormous profits from this commerce created a new class of merchants, bankers, and textile manufacturers who conducted trade, lent vast sums of money, and spurred technological innovation in silk and wool production. This moneyed elite ruled the republican city-states of Italy and created the concept of civic humanism, an ideology that celebrated public virtue and service to the state and would profoundly influence European and American conceptions of government.

Drawing inspiration from classical Greek and Roman (rather than Christian) sources, Renaissance intellectuals were optimistic in their view of human nature and celebrated individual potential. They saw themselves not as prisoners of blind fate or victims of the forces of nature but as many-sided individuals with the capacity to change the world.

This energetic view appealed to Renaissance rulers. In *The Prince* (1513), Niccolò Machiavelli provided unsentimental advice on how monarchs could increase their political power. The kings of Western Europe followed his advice, creating royal law courts and bureaucracies to reduce the power of the landed classes and seeking alliances with merchants and urban artisans. Monarchs allowed merchants to trade throughout their realms and granted privileges to artisan guilds, encouraging both domestic manufacturing and foreign trade. In return, these rulers extracted taxes from towns and loans from merchants to support their armies and officials. This alliance of monarchs, merchants, and royal bureaucrats challenged the power of the agrarian nobility, while the increasing wealth of monarchical nation-states such as Spain and Portugal propelled Europe into its first age of overseas expansion.

Under the direction of Prince Henry (1394–1460), Portugal led the great surge of maritime commercial expansion. Henry was at once a Christian warrior and a Renaissance humanist. As a general of the Crusading Order of Christ, he had fought the Muslims in North Africa, an experience that reinforced his desire to extend the bounds of Christendom—and Portuguese power. As a humanist, Henry patronized Renaissance thinkers and relied on Arab and Italian geographers for the latest knowledge about the shape and size of the continents. Imbued with the spirit of the Renaissance, he tried to fulfill the mission assigned to him by an astrologer: "to engage in great and noble conquests and to attempt the discovery of things hidden from other men."

Because Arab and Italian merchants dominated trade in the Mediterranean, Henry sought an alternate oceanic route to the wealth of Asia. In the 1420s he established a center for exploration and ocean mapping near Lisbon and sent ships to sail the African coast. His seamen soon discovered and settled the islands of Madeira and the Azores. By 1435 Portuguese sea captains were roaming the coast of West Africa, seeking ivory and gold in exchange for salt, wine, and fish. By the 1440s, they were trading in humans as well, the first Europeans to engage in the African slave trade.

WEST AFRICAN SOCIETY AND SLAVERY

Vast and diverse, West Africa stretches from present-day Senegal to Cameroon and then extends southward to Congo and Angola. In the 1400s tropical rain forest covered much of the coast, but a series of great rivers—the Senegal, Gambia, Volta, Niger, and Congo—provided relatively easy access to the woodlands, plains, and savanna of the interior (see Map 3.2, p. 76).

Most of the people of West Africa farmed small plots and lived in extended families in small villages. Normally, men cleared the land, and women planted and harvested the crops. On the plains of the savanna, millet, cotton, and livestock were the primary products, while the forest peoples grew yams and harvested oil-rich palm nuts. Forest dwellers exchanged kola nuts, a mild stimulant, for the textiles and leather goods produced by savanna dwellers. Similarly, salt produced along the seacoast was traded for iron or gold mined in the hills of the interior.

West Africans spoke many different languages and had formed hundreds of distinct cultural and political groups. A majority of the people lived in hierarchical, socially stratified societies ruled by princes. Others resided in stateless societies organized by family and lineage (much like those of the Woodland Indians of eastern North America). Both women and men had secret societies that united people from different lineages and clans and that exercised political influence by checking the powers of rulers in princely states. These societies provided sexual education for the young, conducted adult initiation ceremonies, and, by shaming individuals and officials, enforced codes of public conduct and private morality.

Spiritual beliefs varied greatly. Although some West Africans had been converted to the Muslim faith and believed in a single god, most recognized a variety of deities—ranging from a remote creator-god who seldom interfered in human affairs to numerous spirits that lived in the earth, animals, and plants. Africans treated their ancestors with great respect, for they were believed to inhabit a spiritual world from which they could intercede on behalf of their descendants. Royal families in particular paid elaborate homage to their ancestors, hoping to give themselves an aura of divinity.

At first European traders had a positive impact on life in West Africa by introducing new plants and animals. Portuguese merchants carried coconuts from East Africa, oranges and lemons from the Mediterranean, pigs from Western Europe, and (after 1500) maize, manioc, and tomatoes from the Americas. Portuguese merchants also expanded existing trade networks, stimulating the African economy.

European iron bars and metal products joined kola nuts and salt moving inland; grain, gold, ivory, and cotton textiles flowed to the coast to provision European ships. Because of disease, this inland trade remained in the hands of Africans; Europeans who lived in West Africa were quickly stricken by yellow fever, malaria, and dysentery, and their death rate was more than 50 percent a year.

However, Europeans soon joined in the long-established trade in humans. Unfree status had existed for many centuries in West Africa. Some people were held in bondage as security for debts; others were sold into servitude by their kin, often in exchange for food in times of famine; still others were war captives. Although treated as property and exploited as agricultural laborers, slaves usually were considered members of the society that had enslaved them and sometimes were treated as kin. Most retained the right to marry, and their children were often free. A small proportion of unfree West Africans were "trade slaves," sold from one kingdom to another or carried overland to the Mediterranean region, mostly by Arab traders. Thus, the first Portuguese in Senegambia found that the Wolof king

> supports himself by raids which result in many slaves from his own as well as neighboring countries. He employs these slaves in cultivating the land allotted to him; but he also sells many to the Azanaghi [Arab] merchants in return for horses and other goods, and also to the Christians, since they have begun to trade with these blacks.

Initially, Portuguese traders carried a few thousand African slaves each year to sugar plantations in Madeira and the Azore Islands and also to Lisbon, which soon had a black population of 9,000. From this small beginning the maritime slave trade expanded enormously, especially after 1550 when Europeans set up sugar plantations in Brazil and the West Indies. By 1700 slave traders were carrying hundreds of thousands of slaves to toil and die on American plantations.

EUROPE REACHES THE AMERICAS

As they traded with Africans, Portuguese adventurers continued to look for a direct ocean route to Asia. In 1488 Bartholomeu Dias rounded the Cape of Good Hope, the southern tip of Africa, and ten years later Vasco da Gama reached India (see Map 1.2). Although the Arab, Indian, and Jewish merchants who controlled the trade along India's Malabar Coast tried to exclude him, da Gama acquired a highly profitable cargo of cinnamon and pepper—spices that were especially valuable because they could be used to flavor and preserve meat. To capture the trade in spices and Indian textiles for Portugal, da Gama returned to India in 1502 with twenty-one fighting vessels, which outmaneuvered and outgunned the Arab fleets. Soon the Portuguese government set up fortified trading posts for its merchants at key points around the Indian Ocean and opened trade routes from Africa to Indonesia and up the coast of Asia to China and Japan. In a momentous transition,

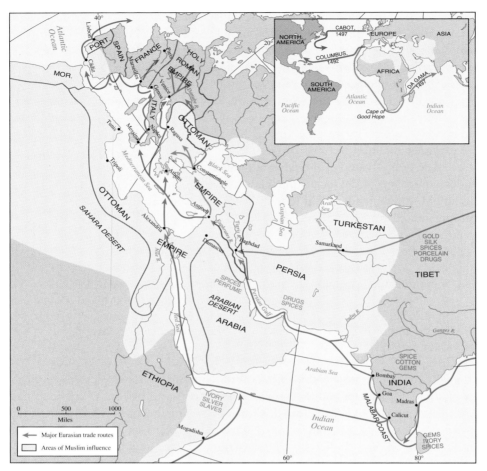

M A P 1.2
Europeans Seek Control of World Trade, 1460–1560

For centuries the Mediterranean Sea was the meeting point for the commerce of Europe, northern Africa, and southern Asia. Beginning in the 1490s, Portuguese, Spanish, and Dutch adventurers and merchants opened up new trade routes, challenging the primacy of the Muslim-dominated Mediterranean.

Portuguese replaced Arabs as the leaders in world commerce and the trade in African slaves.

Spain quickly followed Portugal's example. As Renaissance rulers, King Ferdinand of Aragon and Queen Isabella of Castile saw national unity and commerce as the keys to power and prosperity. Married in their teens in an arranged match, the young rulers (r. 1474–1516) combined their kingdoms and completed the centuries-long campaign known as the *reconquista* to oust the Muslims from their realm. In 1492 their armies reconquered Granada, the last outpost of Islam in Western Europe. Continuing their effort to use the Catholic religion to build a sense of "Spanishness," Ferdinand and Isabella launched a brutal Inquisition against suspected Christian heretics and expelled or forcibly converted thousands of Jews. Simultaneously they sought new opportunities for trade and empire.

Because Portugal controlled the southern, or African, approach to Asia, Isabella and Ferdinand listened with interest to proposals for an alternate, western route to the riches of the East. The main advocate for such a route was Christopher Columbus, a struggling Genoese sea captain who was determined to become rich and famous. Misinterpreting the findings of Italian geographers, Columbus believed that the Atlantic Ocean, long feared by Arab sailors as an endless "green sea of darkness," was little more than a narrow channel of water separating Europe from Asia. Dubious at first about Columbus's theory, Ferdinand and Isabella finally agreed to arrange financial backing from Spanish merchants. They charged Columbus with the task of discovering a new trade route to China and, in an expression of the crusading mentality of the *reconquista,* of carrying Christianity to the peoples of Asia.

Columbus set sail with three small ships on August 3, 1492. Six weeks later, after a perilous voyage of 3,000 miles, he finally found land, disembarking on one of the islands of the present-day Bahamas on October 12, 1492. Although surprised by the rude living conditions of the natives, Columbus expected them to "easily be made Christians, for it appeared to me that they had no religion." With ceremony and solemnity, he claimed the islands for Spain and for Christendom.

Believing he had reached Asia—"the Indies," in fifteenth-century parlance—Columbus called the native inhabitants Indians and the islands the West Indies. He then explored the neighboring Caribbean islands, demanding gold from the local Taino, Arawak, and Carib peoples. Buoyed by the natives' stories of rivers of gold lying "to the west," Columbus left forty men on the island of Hispaniola (present-day Haiti and Santo Domingo) and returned triumphantly to Spain, taking several Tainos to display to Isabella and Ferdinand.

Although Columbus brought back no gold, the Spanish monarchs were sufficiently impressed by his discovery to support three more voyages over the next twelve years. During those expeditions Columbus began the colonization of the West Indies, transporting more than a thousand settlers and hundreds of domestic animals. He also began the transatlantic slave trade, carrying hundreds of Indians to bondage in Europe and importing black slaves from Africa to work as artisans and farmers in the new Spanish settlements. However, Columbus failed to find either golden treasures or great kingdoms, and his death in 1506 went virtually unrecognized. Ignoring Columbus, a German geographer gave the new continents the name of a Florentine merchant, Amerigo Vespucci, who had traveled to South America around 1500 and called it a *nuevo mundo,* a New World. For its part, the Spanish crown was determined to make it a Spanish world.

THE SPANISH CONQUEST

Columbus and other Spanish adventurers ruled the peoples of the Caribbean islands with an iron hand, seizing their goods and exploiting their labor. After subduing the Arawak and Taino on Hispaniola, the Spanish probed coastal settlements on the mainland in search of booty. In 1513 Juan Ponce de León searched for gold and slaves along the coast of Florida and gave the peninsula its name. That same year Vasco Núñez de Balboa crossed the Isthmus of Darien (Panama), becoming the first European to see the Pacific Ocean basin. Although these greedy adventurers found no gold, rumors of riches to the west encouraged others to launch an invasion of the interior. These men were not explorers or merchants but hardened veterans of the wars against the Muslims who were eager to do battle and get rich. The Spanish crown offered them plunder, estates in the conquered territory, and titles of nobility in return for creating an empire.

The first great success of the Spanish conquistadors (conquerors) occurred in present-day Mexico (see Map 1.3). In 1519 Hernando Cortés landed on the Mexican

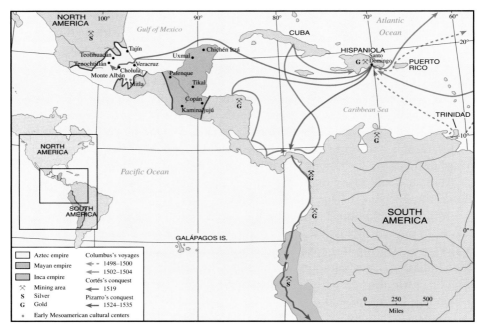

M A P 1.3
The Spanish Conquest, 1492–1535

The Spanish first invaded the islands of the Caribbean. Rumors of a magnificent golden civilization led to Cortés's invasion of the Aztec empire in 1519. By 1535, other Spanish conquistadors had conquered the Mayan temple cities and the Inca empire in Peru, completing one of the great conquests in world history.

coast with 600 men and marched toward the Aztec capital of Tenochtitlán. Fortuitously for the Spaniards, Cortés arrived in the very year in which Aztec mythology had predicted the return of the god Quetzalcoatl to his earthly kingdom. Believing that Cortés might be the returning god, Moctezuma, the Aztec ruler, acted indecisively. After the failure of an ambush against the conquistadors, he allowed Cortés to proceed without challenge to Tenochtitlán and received him with great ceremony, only to become his captive. When Moctezuma's forces finally attempted to expel the invader, they were confronted by superior European military technology. The sight of the Spaniards in full armor, with cannon that shook the heavens, made a deep impression on the Aztecs, who had learned how to purify gold and fashion it into ornate religious objects but did not produce iron tools or weapons. Moreover, the Aztecs had no wheeled carts or cavalry, and their warriors, fighting on foot with flint- or obsidian-tipped spears and arrows, were no match for mounted Spanish conquistadors, wielding steel swords and protected by heavy armor. Although heavily outnumbered and suffering great losses, Cortés and his men were able to fight their way out of the Aztec capital.

At this point, the vast population of the Aztec empire could easily have crushed the European invaders if the Indian peoples had remained united. But Cortés exploited the widespread resentment against the Aztecs, forming military alliances and raising thousands of troops from subject peoples who had seen their wealth expropriated by Aztec nobles and their people sacrificed to the Aztec sun god. The Aztec empire collapsed, the victim not of superior Spanish military technology but of a vast internal rebellion of Indian peoples (see American Voices, "Aztec Elders Describe the Spanish Conquest").

As the Spanish sought to impose their dominion over the peoples of the Aztec empire, they had a silent ally—disease. Separated from Eurasia for thousands of years, the inhabitants of the Western Hemisphere had no immunities to common European diseases. A massive smallpox epidemic lasting seventy days ravaged Tenochtitlán following the Spanish exodus, "striking everywhere in the city," according to an Aztec source, killing Moctezuma's brother and "a vast number of our people." Subsequent outbreaks of smallpox, influenza, and measles killed hundreds of thousands of the highland peoples and sapped the morale of the survivors. Exploiting this demographic weakness, Cortés quickly extended Spanish rule over the entire highland region, and his lieutenants then moved against the Mayan city-states in the Yucatan Peninsula, eventually conquering them as well.

In 1524 the Spanish conquest entered a new phase, when Francisco Pizarro led a military expedition to the mountains of Peru, home of the rich and powerful Inca empire. By the time Pizarro and his small force of 168 men and 67 horses reached Peru, half of the Inca population had died from European diseases, which had been spread by Indian traders. Weakened militarily and fighting over succession to the throne, the Inca nobility was easy prey for Pizarro's army. In little more than a decade Spain had become the master of the wealthiest and most populous regions of the Western Hemisphere.

Aztec Elders Describe the Spanish Conquest

FRIAR BERNARDINO DE SAHAGÚN

*D*uring the 1550s Friar Bernardino de Sahagún published the Florentine Codex: General History of New Spain. *According to Sahagún, the authors of the* Codex *were Aztec elders who lived through the Conquest. Here the elders describe their reaction to the invading Europeans and the devastating impact of smallpox. They speak in a repetitive style, using the conventions of Aztec oral histories.*

Moctezuma enjoyed no sleep, no food, no one spoke to him. Whatsoever he did, it was as if he were in torment. Ofttimes it was as if he sighed, became weak, felt weak. . . . Wherefore he said, "What will now befall us? Who indeed stands [in charge]? Alas, until now, I. In great torment is my heart; as if it were washed in chili water it indeed burns." . . . And when he had so heard what the messengers reported, he was terrified, he was astounded. . . . Especially did it cause him to faint away when he heard how the gun, at [the Spaniards'] command, discharged: how it resounded as if it thundered when it went off. It indeed bereft one of strength; it shut off one's ears. And when it discharged, something like a round pebble came forth from within. Fire went showering forth; sparks went blazing forth. And its smoke smelled very foul; it had a fetid odor which verily wounded the head. And when [the shot] struck a mountain, it was as if it were destroyed, dissolved . . . as if someone blew it away.

All iron was their war array. In iron they clothed themselves. With iron they covered their heads. Iron were their swords. Iron were their crossbows. Iron were their shields. Iron were their lances. And those which bore them upon their backs, their deer [horses], were as tall as roof terraces.

And their bodies were everywhere covered; only their faces appeared. They were very white; they had chalky faces; they had yellow hair, though the hair of some was black. . . . And when Moctezuma so heard, he was much terrified. It was as if he fainted away. His heart saddened; his heart failed him. . . .

[Soon] there came to be prevalent a great sickness, a plague. It was in Tepeilhuitl that it originated, that there spread over the people a great destruction of men. Some it indeed covered [with pustules]; they were spread everywhere, on one's face, on one's head, on one's breast. There was indeed perishing; many indeed died of it. No longer could they walk; they only lay in their abodes, in their beds. No longer could they move. . . . And when they bestirred themselves, much did they cry out. There was much perishing. Like a covering, covering-like, were the pustules. Indeed, many people died of them, and many just died of hunger. There was death from hunger; there was no one to take care of another; there was no one to attend to another.

SOURCE: Friar Bernardino de Sahagún, *Florentine Codex: General History of New Spain,* trans. Arthur J. O. Anderson and Charles E. Dibble (Santa Fe, NM, and Salt Lake City: The School of American Research and University of Utah Press, 1975), book 12: pp. 17–20, 26, 83.

The Spanish invasion and European diseases changed life forever throughout the Americas. Virtually the entire Indian population of Hispaniola—several million people—was wiped out by disease and warfare. Mesoamerica as a whole in 1500 had probably 40 million Indians; by 1650 that region had only 3 million Native Americans. In Peru the population plummeted from 9 million in 1530 to fewer than half a million a century later. In the present-day United States, diseases introduced by early Spanish expeditions inflicted equally catastrophic losses on the Pueblo peoples of the Southwest and the Mississippian chiefdoms of present-day Florida and the Southeast.

Once the conquistadors had triumphed, the Spanish government quickly created an elaborate bureaucratic empire, headed in Madrid by the Council of the Indies, which issued laws and decrees to viceroys and other Spanish-born officials in America. However, the conquistadors remained powerful because they had military and legal control of the native population. They ruthlessly exploited the surviving Native Americans, forcing them to work on vast plantations to raise crops for local consumption and cattle whose hides were exported to Europe. The Spaniards also altered the natural environment by introducing grains and grasses that supplanted the native flora. Horses, first brought to the mainland by Cortés, gradually spread throughout the Western Hemisphere and in the following centuries dramatically changed the way of life of many Indian peoples, especially on the Great Plains of the United States.

The Spanish invasion of the Americas had a significant impact on life in Europe and Africa as well. In a process of transfer known as the Columbian Exchange, the food products of the Western Hemisphere—maize, tomatoes, potatoes, cassava (manioc)—became available to the peoples of other continents, increasing agricultural yields and stimulating the growth of population. Similarly, the crops—and human diseases—of African and Eurasian lands became part of the lives of residents of the Americas. Nor was that all. The gold and silver that had honored Aztec gods flowed into the countinghouses of Spain and into the treasury of its monarchs, making that nation the most powerful in Europe.

By 1550 the once magnificent civilizations of Mexico and Peru lay in ruins. "Of all these wonders"—the great city of Tenochtitlán, rich orchards, overflowing markets—"all is overthrown and lost, nothing left standing," recalled Bernal Díaz, who had been a young soldier in Cortés's army. Moreover, those Native Americans who survived had lost vital parts of their cultural identity. Spanish priests had suppressed their worship of traditional gods and converted them to Catholicism; as early as 1531 an Indian convert reported a vision of a dark-skinned Virgin Mary, later known as the Virgin of Guadalupe. Soon Spanish bureaucrats imposed taxes and supervised the lives of the Indians, and no fewer than 450,000 Spanish migrants settled on their lands between 1500 and 1650. Because nearly 90 percent of the Spanish settlers were men who took Indian women as wives or mistresses, the result was a substantial mestizo (mixed-race) population. Around 1800, at the end of the colonial era, Spanish America had about 17 million people: 7.5 million Indians, 3.2 million Europeans, 1 million enslaved Africans, and 5.5 million people of mixed race and cultural heritage.

Some Indians resisted assimilation by retreating into the mountains, but they lacked the numbers or the power to oust the Spanish invaders or their descendants. Today only a single Indian tongue, Guarani in Paraguay, is a recognized national language, and no Native American state has representation in the United Nations. For the original Americans the consequences of the European intrusion in 1492 were tragic and irreversible.

The Protestant Reformation and the Rise of England, 1500–1620

Religious fervor had played an important role in the expansionary policies of Portugal and Spain, but after 1517 Christianity was no longer a unifying force in European society. New religious doctrines preached by Martin Luther and other reformers divided Christians into armed camps of Catholics and Protestants. In the 1560s a Protestant rebellion in the Spanish Netherlands drained the newfound American wealth of the Spanish crown. Meanwhile, England was undergoing a major economic transformation that would give it the resources to expand into North America—bringing about a new collision of European and Indian peoples.

THE PROTESTANT MOVEMENT

Over the centuries the Catholic Church had become a large and wealthy institution, controlling vast resources throughout Europe. Renaissance popes and cardinals were among the leading patrons of the arts, but some also misused the Church's wealth. Pope Leo X (r. 1513–1521) was the most notorious, receiving half a million ducats a year from the sale of religious offices. Ordinary priests and monks regularly used their authority to obtain economic or sexual favors. One English reformer denounced the clergy as a "gang of scoundrels" who should be "rid of their vices or stripped of their authority," but he was ignored. Other reformers, such as Jan Hus of Bohemia, were tried and executed as heretics.

In 1517 Martin Luther, a German monk and professor at the university in Wittenberg, nailed his famous Ninety-five Theses to the door of the castle church. That widely reprinted document condemned the sale of indulgences—church certificates that pardoned a sinner from punishments in the afterlife. Luther argued that redemption could come only from God through grace, not from the church for a fee. He was excommunicated by the pope and threatened with punishment by King Charles I of Spain, who in 1519 became head of the Holy Roman Empire, which embraced most of Germany. Northern German princes, who were resisting the emperor's authority for political reasons, embraced Luther's teachings and protected him from arrest.

Luther broadened his attack, articulating positions that differed from Roman Catholic doctrine in three major respects. First, Luther rejected the doctrine that Christians could win salvation through good deeds, arguing that people could be saved only by grace, which came as a gift from God. Second, he downplayed the role of clergymen and the pope as mediators between God and the people, proclaiming, "Our baptism consecrates us all without exception and makes us all priests." Third, Luther said that believers must look to the Bible (not church doctrine) as the ultimate authority in matters of faith. So that every German-speaking believer could read the Bible, he translated it from Latin into German.

Peasants as well as princes heeded Luther's attack on authority and, to his dismay, mounted protests of their own. In 1524 some German peasants rebelled against their manorial lords and were ruthlessly suppressed. Fearing social revolution, Luther urged obedience to established political institutions and condemned the teachings of new groups of religious dissidents, such as the Anabaptists (so called because they rejected infant baptism).

Embracing Luther's views, most princes in northern Germany broke from Rome, in part because they wanted the power to appoint bishops and control the Church's property. In response, Emperor Charles dispatched armies to Germany to restore his political authority and Catholicism, unleashing a generation of warfare. Eventually the Peace of Augsburg (1555) restored order by allowing princes to decide the religion of their subjects. Most southern German rulers installed Catholicism as the official religion, while those in the north made Lutheranism the state creed.

The most rigorous Protestant doctrine was established in Geneva, Switzerland, under the leadership of the French theologian John Calvin. Even more than Luther, Calvin stressed the omnipotence of God and the corruption of human nature. His *Institutes of the Christian Religion* (1536) depicted God as an awesome and absolute sovereign who governed the "wills of men so as to move precisely to that end directed by him." Calvin preached the doctrine of predestination—the idea that God had chosen certain people for salvation even before they were born, condemning the rest to eternal damnation. In Geneva he set up a model Christian community, eliminating bishops and placing spiritual power in the hands of ministers chosen by the members of each congregation. These ministers and pious laymen ruled the city, prohibiting frivolity and luxury. Despite widespread persecution, Calvinists won converts all over Europe. Calvinism was adopted by the Huguenots in France, by reformed churches in Belgium and Holland, and by Presbyterians and Puritans in Scotland and England.

In England, King Henry VIII (r. 1509–1547) initially opposed the spread of Protestantism in his kingdom. But when the pope denied his request for an annulment of his marriage to Catherine of Aragon, Henry broke with Rome in 1534 and made himself the head of a national Church of England (which promptly granted the annulment). Although Henry made few changes in church doctrine, organization, and ritual, his daughter, Queen Elizabeth I (r. 1558–1603) approved a Protestant confession of faith that incorporated both the Lutheran doctrine of salvation by grace and the Calvinist belief in predestination. To mollify tradition-alists Elizabeth retained the Catholic ritual of Holy Communion—now conducted in English rather than in Latin—as well as the hierarchy of bishops and archbishops.

Elizabeth's compromises angered radical Protestants, who condemned the power of bishops as "anti-Christian and devilish and contrary to the Scriptures" and demanded major changes in church organization. Many of these reformers took inspiration from the Presbyterian system pioneered in Calvin's Geneva and devel-oped fully by John Knox for the Church of Scotland; in Scotland local congrega-tions elected lay elders (presbyters), who assisted ministers in running the church. By 1600, 500 ministers in the Church of England wanted to eliminate bishops and install a presbyterian form of church government.

Other radical English Protestants were calling themselves "unspotted lambs of the Lord" or "Puritans." To a greater extent than most Protestants they wanted to "purify" the church of "false" teachings and practices. Following radical Calvinist principles, Puritans condemned many traditional religious rites as magical or idol-atrous. Puritan services avoided appeals to dead saints or the burning of incense and instead focused on a carefully argued sermon on ethics or dogma. Puritans also placed special emphasis on the idea of a "calling," the duty to serve God in one's work. To ensure that all men and women had access to God's commands, they encouraged everyone to read the Bible, thus promoting widespread literacy. Finally, most Puritans wanted authority over spiritual and financial matters to rest primarily with the local congregation, not with bishops or even Presbyterian synods. Even-tually thousands of Puritan migrants to America would establish churches based on these radical Protestant doctrines.

THE DUTCH AND THE ENGLISH CHALLENGE SPAIN

Luther's challenge to Catholicism in 1517 came just two years before Cortés con-quered the Aztec empire, and the two events remained linked. Gold and silver from Mexico and Peru made Spain the wealthiest nation in Europe and King Philip II (r. 1556–1598), the successor to Charles I, its most powerful ruler. In addition to Spain, Philip presided over wealthy city-states in Italy, the commercial and manu-facturing provinces of the Spanish Netherlands (present-day Holland and Belgium), and, after 1580, Portugal and all its possessions in America, Africa, and the East Indies.

Philip, an ardent Catholic, tried to root out Protestantism in the Netherlands, which had become wealthy from trade with the vast Protuguese empire and from the weaving of wool and linen. To protect their Calvinist faith and political liber-ties, the Dutch and Flemish provinces revolted in 1566, and in 1581 the seven north-ern provinces declared their independence, becoming the Dutch Republic (or Holland). When Elizabeth I of England dispatched 6,000 troops to assist the Dutch cause, Philip found a new enemy. In 1588 he sent the Spanish Armada—130 ships and 30,000 men—against England. Philip planned to reimpose Catholicism in England and then wipe out Calvinism in Holland. But the Armada failed utterly, as English ships and a fierce storm destroyed the Spanish fleet. Philip continued to spend his American gold on foreign wars, undermining the Spanish economy and prompting the migration of hundreds of thousands of Spaniards to America. By the time of his death in 1598, Spain was in serious decline.

As Spain faltered, Holland prospered, the economic miracle of the seventeenth century. Amsterdam emerged as the financial capital of northern Europe, and the Dutch Republic became the leading commercial power of Europe, replacing Portugal as the dominant trader in Asia and coastal Africa. The Dutch also looked across the Atlantic, creating the West India Company, which invested in sugar plantations in Brazil and the Caribbean and established fur-trading posts in North America.

Elizabeth I (r. 1558–1603)

Attired in richly decorated clothes to symbolize her power, Queen Elizabeth I relishes the destruction of the Spanish Armada (pictured in background) and proclaims her nation's imperial ambitions. The Queen's hand rests on a globe, asserting England's claims in the Western Hemisphere.

England also emerged as an important European state, its economy stimulated by a rise in population from 3 million in 1500 to 5 million in 1630. An equally important factor was the state-supported expansion of the merchant community. English merchants had long supplied high-quality wool to European weavers, and around 1500 they created their own system of textile production. In this *outwork* (or *putting-out*) system merchants bought wool and provided it to landless peasants, who spun and wove the wool into cloth. The merchants then sold the finished product in English and foreign markets. The government helped manufacturers to expand production by setting low rates for wages and assisted merchants to increase exports by granting special monopoly privileges to the Levant Company (Turkey) in 1581, the Guinea Company (Africa) in 1588, and the East India Company in 1600.

This system of state-supported manufacturing and trade became known as *mercantilism*. Mercantilist-minded monarchs like Elizabeth encouraged merchants to invest in domestic manufacturing, thereby increasing exports and reducing imports, in order to give England a favorable balance of trade. The queen and her advisors wanted gold and silver to flow into the country in payment for English manufactures, stimulating further economic expansion and enriching the merchant community. Increased trade also meant higher revenues from import duties, which swelled the royal treasury and enhanced the power of the national government. By 1600 the success of these merchant-oriented policies made overseas colonization possible. The English (as well as the Dutch) now had the merchant fleets and economic wealth needed to challenge Spain's monopoly in the Western Hemisphere.

THE SOCIAL CAUSES OF ENGLISH COLONIZATION

Other economic changes in England (as well as continuing religious conflict) provided a large body of willing settlers. The massive expenditure of American gold and silver by Philip II had doubled the money supply of Europe and sparked a major inflation—known today as the Price Revolution—that brought about profound social changes.

In England, the nobility were the first casualties of the Price Revolution. Aristocrats had customarily rented out their estates on long leases for fixed rents, gaining a secure income and plenty of leisure. As one English nobleman put it, "We eat and drink and rise up to play and this is to live like a gentleman." Then inflation struck. In two generations the price of goods tripled, but the nobility's income from the rents on its farmlands barely increased. As the wealth and status of the aristocracy declined, that of the gentry and the yeomen rose. The gentry (substantial landholders) kept pace with inflation by renting land on short leases at higher rates. Yeomen, described by a European traveler as "middle people of a condition between gentlemen and peasants," owned small amounts of land that they worked with family help. As wheat prices tripled, yeomen used the profits to build larger houses and provide their children with land.

Economics influenced politics. As aristocrats lost wealth, their branch of Parliament, the House of Lords, declined in influence. At the same time, members of the rising gentry entered the House of Commons, the political voice of the propertied classes. Supported by the yeomen, the gentry demanded new rights and powers for the Commons, such as control of taxation. Thus the Price Revolution encouraged the rise of governing institutions in which rich commoners and small property owners had a voice, a development with profound consequences for English—and American—political history.

Peasants and farm laborers made up three-fourths of the population of England, and their lives also were transformed by the Price Revolution. Many of these rural folk lived in open-field settlements, but the rise of domestic manufacturing increased the demand for wool, prompting profit-minded landlords and wool merchants to persuade Parliament to pass enclosure acts. These acts allowed owners to fence in open fields and put sheep to graze on them. Thus dispossessed of their land, peasant families lived on the brink of poverty, spinning and weaving wool or working as wage laborers on large estates. Wealthy men had "taken farms into their hands," an observer noted in 1600, "and rent them to those that will give most, whereby the peasantry of England is decayed and become servants to gentlemen."

These changes set the stage for a substantial migration to America. As land prices continued to rise, thousands of yeomen families looked across the Atlantic for land for their children. The enclosure movement created an even greater number of impoverished peasants, who were prepared to go to America as indentured servants. This migration of English men and women would bring about a new collision between the European and Native American worlds and, eventually, a new plantation society worked by enslaved Africans.

Before 1450 the peoples of Africa, Europe, and the Americas had lived in different worlds. But the fate of the three continents became intertwined once Spanish conquistadors vanquished the Aztec, Maya, and Inca empires and Portuguese merchants began to carry African slaves across the Atlantic. Just as the intrusion of the Spanish and Portuguese had changed forever the history of Mesoamerica and Brazil, the coming of the English—and Dutch and French—among the Indians of eastern North America after 1600 would produce a similar spectacle of disease, war, religious conversion, and cultural conflict.

TIMELINE

30,000– **10,000** **B.C.**	Settlement of the Americas	**1400–** **1550**	Renaissance invigorates European society.
3000 **2000** **B.C.**	Indians begin maize cultivation.	**1492**	Christopher Columbus's first voyage to America
		1513	Juan Ponce de León explores Florida.
A.D. **100–** **400**	Hopewell culture in the Ohio region	**1517**	Martin Luther starts the Protestant Reformation.
300– **900**	Height of Mayan and Teotihuacán civilizations in Mesoamerica	**1519**	Hernando Cortés begins the conquest of the Aztec empire.
600– **1150**	Pueblo cultures flourish in Southwest.	**1524**	Francisco Pizarro marches to the Inca empire in Peru.
700– **1100**	Spread of Arab Muslim civilization	**1534**	Henry VIII establishes Protestantism in England.
700– **1350**	Mississippian societies; great temples at Cahokia	**1536**	John Calvin publishes his doctrine of predestination.
1055– **1492**	*Reconquista* expels Muslims from Portugal and Spain.	**1550–** **1630**	Price Revolution in Europe disrupts society.
1096– **1291**	European Crusaders encounter Muslim civilization.		English mercantilism prepares the way for colonization.
			Enclosure movement creates potential American migrants.
1325	Aztecs establish a capital at Tenochtitlán.	**1560s**	English Puritan movement begins.
1440s	Portugal joins the trade in African slaves.	**1588**	The defeat of the Spanish Armada preserves Protestantism in England and Holland.

For Further Exploration

Alvin M. Josephy Jr., ed., *America in 1492: The World of the Indian Peoples Before the Arrival of Columbus* (1991), offers a panorama of the indigenous societies of the Americas in a nicely illustrated collection of essays. Recent scholarship on the prehistoric Indians of the United States is brought to life by Brian M. Fagan, *The Great Journey: The People of Ancient America* (1987). For the European background of colonization, begin with George Huppert, *After the Black Death* (2nd ed., 1998), a short and highly readable introduction of Western Europe's recovery from the devastating epidemic of the mid-fourteenth century. William D. Phillips with Carla Rahn Phillips continue the story of European expansion in *The Worlds of Christopher Columbus* (1992), an engaging biography that places Columbus's voyages in the larger context of European exploration and describes their enormous consequences.

Peter Laslett, *The World We Have Lost* (3rd ed., 1984), offers a vivid portrait of society in seventeenth-century England, while Susan Doran and Christopher Durston, *Princes, Pastors, and People: The Church and Religion in England, 1529–1689* (1991), discuss the impact of the Protestant Reformation on theology, the role of the clergy, and church services.

Two interesting Public Broadcasting Service (PBS) videos examine the ancient civilizations of MesoAmerica: *Odyssey: Maya Lords of the Jungle* (1 hour) and *Odyssey: The Incas* (1 hour). For additional information log on to "1492: An Ongoing Voyage" at <http://lcweb.loc.gov/exhibits/1492/intro.html>, which provides a survey of the native cultures of the Western Hemisphere, the impact of discovery, and full-color images of artifacts and art. Material on an early Indian civilization in the southwestern United States is available at "Sipapu: The Anasazi Emergence into the Cyber World," <http://sipapu.ucsb.edu/index.html>. "Martin Luther" at <http://www.luther.de/e/index.html> offers biographies of the leading figures of the Protestant Reformation and striking images of the era.

Chapter 2

THE INVASION AND SETTLEMENT OF NORTH AMERICA

1550–1700

Human life is reduced to real suffering, to hell, only when . . .
cultures and religions overlap.

ALBRECHT VON HALLER

Establishing colonies in the distant land of North America was not for the faint of heart. First came a long voyage in small ships over stormy, dangerous waters. Then the migrants, weakened by weeks of travel, spoiled food, and shipboard diseases, faced the challenges of life in an alien land inhabited by potentially hostile Indian peoples. "We neither fear them or trust them," Puritan Francis Higginson reported, but rely for protection on "our musketeers." Although the risks were great and the rewards uncertain, tens of thousands of Europeans crossed the Atlantic during the seventeenth century, driven by poverty and persecution at home or drawn by the lures of the New World: land, gold, and—as another Puritan settler put it—the hope of "propagating the Gospel to these poor barbarous people."

For Native Americans, the European invasion was nothing short of catastrophic. "You know our fathers had plenty of deer and skins, . . . and our coves were full of fish and fowl," the Narragansett chief Miantonomi warned the neighboring Montauk people in 1642, "but these English having gotten our land . . . their cows and horses eat the grass, and their hogs spoil our clam banks, and we shall all be starved." Whether they came as settlers or missionaries or fur traders, the white-skinned people spread havoc, bringing new diseases and religions and threatening Indian peoples with the loss of their cultures, lands, and lives. As a Narragansett warrior put it, European-style warfare "slays too many men." The first century of cultural contact foretold the course of North American history: the advance of the invaders, the dispossession of the Indian peoples, and the importation of enslaved Africans to work the lands.

36

Imperial Conflicts and Rival Colonial Models

In Mesoamerica the Spanish colonial regime forced the Indians to convert to Catholicism and to work digging gold and farming large estates. But in the sparsely populated lands north of the Rio Grande, other Europeans founded different types of colonies. In the fur-trading empires created by the French and the Dutch, the native peoples retained their lands and political autonomy, while in the quickly growing English settler-colonies, Indians were simply not welcome and were pushed ever farther to the west. Despite the differing goals of these colonial regimes—the exploitation of native labor by the Spanish, the trading of furs by the French and Dutch, the creation of farming communities by the English—nearly everywhere the Indian peoples eventually rose in revolt.

NEW SPAIN: COLONIZATION AND CONVERSION

In their ceaseless quest for gold, Spanish adventurers became the first Europeans to explore the southern and western United States. In 1540 Francisco Vásquez de Coronado searched in vain for the fabled seven golden cities of Cíbola, said to lie north of present-day Albuquerque. Continuing his search, he dispatched expeditions that discovered the Grand Canyon in Arizona, the Pueblo peoples of New Mexico, and the grasslands of central Kansas. Simultaneously, Hernando de Soto and a force of 600 adventurers cut a bloody swath across the densely populated Southeast, doing battle with the Apalachee of northern Florida and the Coosa of northern Alabama but finding no gold and few other riches.

By the 1560s few Spanish officials still dreamed of finding rich Indian empires north of Mexico. Now their main goal was to prevent other European nations from establishing settlements. Roving English "sea dogs" were already plundering Spanish possessions in the Caribbean, and French corsairs were attacking Spanish treasure ships, halving the Spanish crown's revenue. Equally ominously, French Protestants began to settle in Florida, long claimed by Spain. In response King Philip II ordered that the Frenchmen in Florida, be "cast . . . out by the best means," and Spanish troops massacred 300 members of the "evil Lutheran sect."

To safeguard Florida, in 1565 Spain established a fort at St. Augustine, the first permanent European settlement in the future United States. It also founded a dozen other military outposts and religious missions, one as far north as Chesapeake Bay, but these were soon destroyed by Indian attacks. Spain also confronted a new threat from the Atlantic. In 1586 the English sea captain Sir Francis Drake sacked the important port city of Cartagena (in present-day Colombia) and nearly wiped out St. Augustine.

These military setbacks prompted the Spanish crown to adopt a new policy toward Native Americans. The Comprehensive Orders for New Discoveries, issued in 1573, placed the "pacification" of new lands primarily in the hands of missionaries, not conquistadors. Franciscan friars promptly established missions in the Pueblo world visited by Coronado two generations before, naming the area Nuevo México (see Map 2.1). The friars built their missions and churches near existing Indian pueblos and farming villages and often learned Indian languages. Protected by Spanish soldiers, the robed and sandaled Franciscans smashed the religious idols of the native Americans and, to win their allegiance to the Christian god, dazzled them with rich vestments, gold crosses, and silver chalices.

For the Franciscans, religious conversion and cultural assimilation went hand in hand. They introduced the European practice of having men instead of women grow most of the crops and encouraged the Indians to talk, cook, dress, and walk like Spaniards. Spanish rule was hardly benevolent. Sexual sinners and spirit worshipers were whipped, and monks and settlers alike systematically ignored Spanish laws intended to protect the native peoples from coerced labor. Franciscan missions depended on Indian workers, who grew the crops and carried them to market,

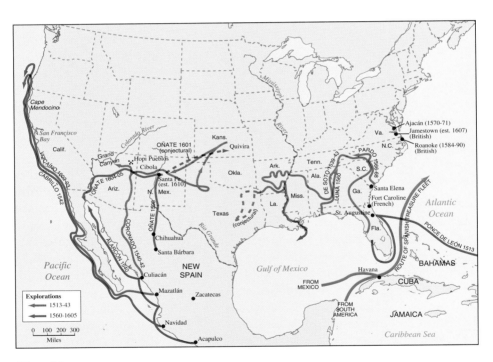

MAP 2.1
New Spain Looks North, 1513–1610

The quest for gold drew Spanish adventurers deep into North America. Cortés himself dispatched the first expeditions along the Pacific coast, and Hernando de Soto and Francisco Vásquez de Coronado led wide-ranging expeditions in the 1540s, but the first permanent settlement to the north of New Spain came only in 1565, at St. Augustine in present-day Florida. A generation later, following the explorations of Juan de Oñate, the Spanish founded Santa Fe in New Mexico.

often on their backs. Privileged Spanish landowners (*encomenderos*) collected tribute from the native population, both in goods and through forced labor. They also "ransomed" Native American women and children who had been captured by nomadic Indians and forced them to work as slaves. Most Native Americans tolerated the Franciscans out of fear of military reprisals or in hopes of learning their spiritual secrets. But when Christian prayers failed to prevent European diseases, drought, and Apache raids from devastating their communities, many Indians returned to their ancestral religions and began to question Spanish rule.

Then in 1598 Juan de Oñate led an expedition of 500 Spanish soldiers and settlers into New Mexico to establish a fort and a trading villa. Oñate's men seized corn and clothing from the Pueblo peoples and murdered or raped those who resisted. When Indians of the Acoma pueblo killed 11 soldiers, the remaining troops destroyed the pueblo, killing 500 men and 300 women and children. Faced by now-hostile Indian peoples, most of the settlers withdrew. In 1610 the Spanish returned, founding the town of Santa Fe and reestablishing the system of missions and forced labor.

By 1680 nearly a hundred years of European diseases, forced tribute, drought, and raids by Navajos and Apache threatened many pueblos in New Mexico with extinction. Their population, which had numbered 60,000 in 1600, had declined to a mere 17,000. In 1680, led by Popé, an Indian shaman (priest), the peoples of two dozen pueblos mounted a carefully coordinated rebellion, killing over 400 Spaniards and forcing the remaining 2,000 colonists to flee 300 miles down the Rio Grande to El Paso. Rejecting Christianity, the Pueblo peoples desecrated churches and tortured and killed twenty-one missionaries. Reconquered a decade later, they rebelled again in 1696, only to be subdued. Exhausted by war but now able to practice their own religion and avoid forced labor, the Pueblo peoples accepted their dependent position, joining with the Spanish to defend their lands against attacks by nomadic Indians.

With great difficulty Spain had managed to maintain its northern empire but had largely failed to achieve its goals of religious conversion and cultural assimilation. Taken aback by the costs of expansion, Spanish officials decided not to undertake the settlement of the distant region of California, delaying until 1769 the permanent European occupation of that area. For the time being, Florida and New Mexico stood as the defensive outposts of Spain's American empire.

NEW FRANCE: FURS AND SOULS

In the 1530s Jacques Cartier had claimed the lands bordered by the Gulf of St. Lawrence for France, but the first permanent settlement came only in 1608, when Samuel de Champlain founded Quebec. Even then, few French men and women migrated to America. Unlike the English peasantry, many held strong legal rights to their village lands in France and thus successfully resisted dispossession. Moreover, the government wanted an ample supply of farm laborers and military recruits in France and offered few incentives to migrants. Finally, the Catholic monarchs barred Huguenots (French Protestants) from Quebec, fearing they would not be loyal to the government. Consequently, New France did not develop as a settler-colony; in 1698 its European population was only 15,200, compared with 100,000 settlers in the English colonies.

Instead, New France became a vast fur-trading enterprise, and French explorers traveled deep into the continent to seek new suppliers. In return for French support against the Five Nations of the Iroquois, the Huron Indians (who lived just to the north of the Great Lakes) allowed Champlain, the founder of Quebec, and other fur traders into their territory. By 1673 another French explorer, Jacques Marquette, reached the Mississippi River in present-day Wisconsin and traveled as far south as Arkansas. Exploration of the majestic river was completed in 1681 by Robert de La Salle, who sought fortune as well as fame. As a French priest noted with disgust, La Salle's expedition hoped "to buy all the Furs and Skins of the remotest Savages, who, as they thought, did not know their Value; and so enrich themselves in one single voyage." To honor Louis XIV, the Sun King, La Salle named the region Louisiana; soon it included the thriving port of New Orleans on the Gulf of Mexico.

Despite their small numbers, French traders and explorers had a disastrous impact on Native Americans living near the Great Lakes. By introducing European diseases, they unwittingly triggered epidemics that killed 25 to 90 percent of the native population, including thousands of their Huron allies. Moreover, by providing a market for deerskins and beaver pelts, the French set in motion a devastating series of Indian wars. Beginning in the 1640s, the New York Iroquois seized control of the fur trade by launching aggressive wars against the Huron, forcing them to migrate to the north and west.

While French traders amassed furs, French priests sought converts among both the defeated Huron and the belligerent Iroquois. Between 1625 and 1763 hundreds of Jesuit priests lived among the Indians and, to a greater extent than the Spanish Franciscans, came to understand their values. One Jesuit reported a Huron belief that "our souls have desires which are inborn and concealed, yet are made known by means of dreams"; he then used this belief to explain the Christian doctrines of immortality and salvation to the native peoples. Indians at first welcomed the "Black Robes" as powerful spiritual beings with magical secrets, such as the ability to forge iron, but, as in New Mexico, skepticism grew when prayers to the Christian god did not protect them from disease and enemy attack. A Peoria chief charged that the priest's "fables are good only in his own country; we have our own [religious beliefs], which do not make us die as his do."

Unlike the Spanish Franciscans, the French missionaries did not use Indians for forced labor and tried to keep alcoholic beverages, which wreaked havoc among Indian peoples, from becoming a bargaining item in the French fur trade. Moreover, the French Jesuits won converts by addressing Indian needs. In the 1690s young women of the Illinois people in the Mississippi River Valley embraced the cult of the Virgin Mary, using its emphasis on chastity to assert the Algonquian belief that unmarried women were "masters of their own body." Still, the French colonial system—which brought only a few Jesuits and traders into Indian territory—allowed most Native Americans to retain their traditional beliefs, and many chose to do so.

NEW NETHERLAND: COMMERCE

Unlike the French and Spanish, the Dutch in North America had little interest in religious conversion. Their eyes were fastened on commerce, for the Dutch Republic was the trading hub of Europe. In 1609 Henry Hudson, an Englishman employed by the Dutch East India Company, found and named the Hudson River in the area of present-day New York, and a few years later the Dutch established fur-trading posts on Manhattan Island and at Fort Orange (present-day Albany). In 1621 the Dutch government chartered the West India Company, giving it a trade monopoly in West Africa and exclusive authority to establish outposts in America. Three years later the company "purchased" Manhattan Island from the Indians, founding the town of New Amsterdam as the capital of New Netherland.

These wilderness outposts attracted few Dutch settlers, and their small size made them vulnerable to invasion by rival European nations. To encourage migration, the West India Company granted huge estates along the Hudson River to wealthy Dutchmen, stipulating that each proprietor settle fifty tenants on his land within four years or lose it; by 1646 only one proprietor, Kiliaen Van Rensselaer, had succeeded. The population in Dutch North America remained small, reaching only 1,500 in 1664.

Although New Netherland failed as a settler colony, it flourished briefly as a fur-trading enterprise. In 1633 Dutch traders at Fort Orange exported 30,000 beaver and otter pelts. Subsequently, the Dutch seized prime farming land from the Algonquian-speaking peoples and took over their trading network, in which corn and wampum from Long Island were exchanged for furs from Maine. The Algonquians responded with force. By the end of a bloody two-year war more than 200 Dutch residents and 1,000 Indians had been killed, many in brutal massacres of women, children, and elderly men. After the war the Dutch traders expanded their profitable links with the Mohawk, one of the Iroquois Nations of New York, exchanging guns and other manufactures for furs. However, the West India Company now largely ignored its crippled North American settlement, concentrating instead on the profitable importation of African slaves to its sugar plantations in Brazil.

Moreover, Dutch officials in New Amsterdam ruled shortsightedly. Governor Peter Stuyvesant rejected the demands of English settlers on Long Island for a representative system of government, alienating the colony's increasingly diverse population of Dutch, English, and Swedish migrants. Consequently, in 1664, during an Anglo-Dutch war, the population of New Amsterdam offered little resistance to an English invasion and subsequently accepted English rule. For the rest of the century the renamed towns of New York and Albany remained small fur-trading centers, Dutch-English outposts in a region still dominated by Native Americans.

THE FIRST ENGLISH MODEL: TOBACCO AND SETTLERS

The first English ventures in North America, all in the 1580s, were abject failures. Sir Humphrey Gilbert's settlement in Newfoundland collapsed for lack of financing, and Sir Ferdinando Gorges's colony along the coast of Maine foundered because of inadequate supplies and the harsh climate. Sir Walter Raleigh's three expeditions to North Carolina likewise ended in disaster when the famous "lost" colony of Roanoke vanished without a trace. After these failures, merchants replaced minor gentry as the leaders of English expansion, and, initially, trade rather than settlement became the main goal. To provide adequate funding, the merchants formed joint-stock companies, which sold shares to many investors. In 1606 a group of ambitious London merchants received a charter from the new monarch, King James I (r. 1603–1625), that granted them the right to exploit North America from present-day North Carolina to southern New York. To honor the memory of Elizabeth I, the "Virgin Queen," the company's directors named the region Virginia.

The manner of their fishing

Carolina Indians, 1585

The artist John White traveled with the first English settlers to Sir Walter Raleigh's colony on Roanoke Island (in present-day North Carolina) and, before returning to England, painted a series of watercolors that provide a rich visual record of Native American life. Here the Indians of Albemarle Sound are harvesting a protein-rich diet of fish from its shallow waters.
(Trustees of the British Museum)

They promised to settle the land and "propagate the *Christian* religion" among the "infidels and Savages."

But trade for gold and other valuable goods was the main goal of the Virginia Company, and the first expedition in 1607 included no settlers, ministers, or women. The company retained ownership of all the land and appointed a governor and a small council to direct the migrants, who were its employees or "servants." They were expected to procure their own food and ship anything of value—gold, exotic crops, and Indian merchandise—to England. The traders were unprepared for the challenges they would face. Some were young gentlemen with personal ties to the shareholders of the Company but no experience in living off the land: a bunch of "unruly Sparks, packed off by their Friends to escape worse Destinies at home." The rest were cynical adventurers bent on seizing gold from the Indians or turning a quick profit from trade in English cloth and metalware. Arriving in Virginia after a hazardous four-month voyage, the newcomers settled on a swampy peninsula on a river. They named both their new home (Jamestown) and the waterway (James River) after their new sovereign.

The adventurers were immediately confronted by the Pamumkey chief Powhatan, the leader of the Algonquian-speaking tribes of the region, some 14,000 people in all. Powhatan, whom Governor John Smith described as a "grave majestical man," willingly exchanged corn for English cloth and iron hatchets and pots but treated the English as one of the dependent peoples of his chiefdom.

For their part, the English adventurers did not want to plant crops and raise food for themselves. All they wanted, as one of them said, was to "dig gold, refine gold, load gold." But there was no gold and not much food. Of the 120 Englishmen who embarked on the expedition, only 38 were alive nine months later, and death continued to take a high toll. By 1611 the Virginia Company had sent 1,200 settlers to Jamestown, but fewer than half had survived. "Our men were destroyed with cruell diseases, as Swellings, Fluxes, Burning Fevers, and by warres," one of the leaders reported, "but for the most part they died of meere famine."

Although Powhatan accused the English of coming "not to trade but to invade my people and possess my country," he eventually ceased his efforts to evict them and acquiesced in the marriage of his daughter Pocahontas to the adventurer John Rolfe in 1614. Rolfe played a leading role in the colony until his death in 1622. After importing seeds from the West Indies, he began to cultivate tobacco, which was already popular in England as a result of imports from Spanish America, and soon became the basis of economic life in Virginia.

As tobacco exports rose, the Virginia Company instituted a new and far-reaching set of policies. In 1617 it allowed individual settlers to own land, granting 100 acres to every freeman in Virginia, and established a *headright* system in which every incoming head of a household had a right to 50 acres of land and 50 additional acres for every adult family member or servant. The company also approved a system of representative government. The House of Burgesses, which first convened in Jamestown in 1619, had the authority to make laws and levy taxes, although its legislative acts could be vetoed by the governor or nullified by the company. By 1622 these incentives of land ownership and local self-government had attracted about 4,500 new English recruits. Virginia was on the verge of becoming a settler colony.

The influx of settlers sparked all-out war with the Indians. Land-hungry farmers demanded access to land that the native Americans had cleared and were using, alarming Opechancanough, Powhatan's brother and successor. Mobilizing the peoples of many Chesapeake tribes, in 1622 Opechancanough launched a surprise attack, killing nearly a third of the white population and vowing to drive the rest into the ocean. The English retaliated by harvesting the Indians' cornfields, providing food for themselves while depriving their enemies of sustenance, a strategy that gradually secured the safety of the colony.

The cost of the war was high for both sides. The Indians killed many settlers and destroyed much property, but Opechancanough's strategy had failed; rather than ending the invasion of the English, it accelerated their expansion. As one English militiaman put it, "[We now felt we could] by right of Warre, and law of Nations, invade the Country, and destroy them who sought to destroy us; whereby wee shall enjoy their cultivated places . . . possessing the fruits of others' labour." Soon the invaders excluded the Indian peoples from huge areas and sold captured warriors into slavery. By 1630 the English settlement in the region of Chesapeake Bay was well established.

The Chesapeake Experience

The English colonies in the Chesapeake brought wealth to some settlers but poverty and moral degradation to many more. Settlers forcefully dispossessed Indians of their lands, and prominent families ruthlessly pursued their dreams of wealth by exploiting the labor of English indentured servants and enslaved African laborers.

SETTLING THE TOBACCO COLONIES

Distressed by the Indian uprising of 1622, James I dissolved the Virginia Company, accusing its directors of mismanagement, and created a royal colony in 1624. Under the terms of the charter, the king and his ministers appointed the governor and a small advisory council. The House of Burgesses was retained, but any legislation it enacted required ratification by the king's Privy Council. James also legally established the Church of England in Virginia, so that all property owners had to pay taxes to support the clergy. These institutions—a royal governor, an elected assembly, and an established Anglican church—became the model for royal colonies throughout English America.

However, a second tobacco-growing settler colony, which developed in neighboring Maryland, had a different set of institutions. Maryland was owned by an aristocrat, Cecilius Calvert, who carried the title Lord Baltimore. In 1632 King Charles I (r. 1625–1649), the successor to James I, gave Baltimore a charter that made him the proprietor of the territory bordering the vast Chesapeake Bay. Baltimore could sell, lease, or give this land away as he wished. He also had the authority to appoint public officials and to found churches and appoint ministers.

Baltimore wanted Maryland to become a refuge from persecution for his fellow English Catholics. He therefore devised a policy of religious toleration intended to minimize confrontations between Catholics and Protestants, instructing the governor (his brother, Leonard Calvert) to allow "no scandall nor offence to be given to any of the Protestants" and to "cause All Acts of Romane Catholicque Religion to be done as privately as may be." In 1634, 20 gentlemen (mostly Catholics) and 200 artisans and laborers (mostly Protestants) established St. Mary's City overlooking the mouth of the Potomac River. The population grew quickly, for the Calvert family carefully planned and supervised the colony's development, hiring skilled artisans and offering ample grants of land to wealthy migrants. However, political and religious conflict threatened Maryland's stability. When Governor Leonard Calvert tried to govern without the "Advice, Assent, and Approbation" of the freemen of the colony, as the charter specified, a representative assembly elected by the freemen insisted on the right to initiate legislation, which Lord Baltimore grudgingly granted. Uprisings by Protestant settlers also threatened Maryland's religious mission. To protect his Catholic coreligionists, who remained a minority, Lord Baltimore managed to persuade the Assembly to enact a Toleration Act (1649) that granted religious freedom to all Christians.

In Maryland, as in Virginia, tobacco was the basis of the economy. Indians had long used tobacco leaves as a medicine and a stimulant. By the 1620s English men and women began to crave tobacco and the nicotine it contained, smoking, chewing, and snorting it with abandon. Initially James I condemned the use of this "vile Weed" and warned that its "black stinking fumes" were "baleful to the nose, harmful to the brain, and dangerous to the lungs." But his attitude changed as revenues from an import tax on tobacco filled the royal treasury.

European demand for tobacco set off a forty-year economic boom in the Chesapeake, attracting thousands of profit-hungry migrants. "All our riches for the present do consist in tobacco," a planter remarked in 1630. Exports rose from about 3 million pounds in 1640 to 10 million pounds in 1660. Planters moved up the river valleys, establishing large farms (plantations) that were distant from one another but easily reached by water. The scarcity of towns meant a much weaker sense of community than that existing in the open-field villages of rural England.

Unfortunately, mosquitoes as well as tobacco flourished in the mild Chesapeake climate, spreading malaria and weakening people's resistance to other diseases. Pregnant women were especially hard hit. Many died after bearing a first or second child,

The Tobacco Economy

The owners of large plantations used indentured servants and slaves to grow and process tobacco. Workers cured the tobacco by hanging it for several months in a well-ventilated shed; then they stripped the leaves off the stalks and packed them tightly into large plantation-made barrels, or "hogsheads," for shipment to Europe.

(Library of Congress)

and so settler families were small. More than 15,000 settlers arrived in Virginia between 1622 and 1640, but the population rose only from 2,000 to 8,000.

For most of the seventeenth century life in the Chesapeake colonies remained harsh and short. Most men never married because there were few women settlers. Families often were disrupted by early death; in Middlesex County in Virginia 61 percent of children lost one or both of their parents by the time they were thirteen. Orphaned children and unmarried young men constituted much of the population, making Chesapeake society very different from that in England.

MASTERS, SERVANTS, AND SLAVES

Despite the dangers, the prospect of owning land continued to lure migrants to the Chesapeake region. By 1700 over 80,000 English settlers had moved to Virginia, and another 20,000 had arrived in Maryland, the great majority not as free men and women but as indentured servants. English shipping registers provide insight into the background of these servants. Three-quarters of the 5,000 migrants from the port of Bristol were young men, many of whom had traveled hundreds of miles searching for work. Once in Bristol, these penniless wanderers were persuaded by merchants and sea captains to sign labor contracts called *indentures* and embark for the Chesapeake. The indentures bound them to work in return for room and board for a period of four or five years, after which they would be freemen, able to plant corn for sustenance and tobacco for sale.

For merchants, servants represented valuable cargo because their contracts fetched high prices from local planters in the labor-starved Chesapeake. For plantation owners, they were an incredible bargain. During the tobacco boom a male indentured servant could produce five times his purchase price in a year. Furthermore, servants were counted as household members, and so planters in Virginia received 50 acres of land for each one they imported.

Most masters ruled their servants with an iron hand, beating them for bad behavior and withholding permission to marry. If a servant ran away or became pregnant, a master went to court to increase the term of service. Female servants were especially vulnerable to abuse. As a Virginia law of 1692 stated, "dissolute masters have gotten their maids with child; and yet claim the benefit of their service." Planters got rid of uncooperative servants by selling their contracts to new masters. As an Englishman remarked in disgust, in Virginia "servants were sold up and down like horses."

For most indentured servants this ordeal did not provide the escape from poverty they had sought (see American Voices, "Hard Times in Early Virginia"). Half the men died before receiving their freedom, and another quarter remained poor. The remaining quarter benefited from their ordeal, acquiring property and respectability. If they survived, female servants generally fared better because men in the Chesapeake had grown "very sensible of the Misfortune of Wanting Wives." Many such servants married their masters or other well-established men. By migrating to the Chesapeake, these few—and very fortunate—men and women escaped a life of landless poverty in England.

The first African workers fared worse. In 1619 John Rolfe noted, "a Dutch man of warre . . . sold us twenty Negars," but for a generation the numbers of Africans remained small. About 400 Africans lived in the Chesapeake colonies in 1649, making up 2 percent of the population, and by 1670 the proportion of blacks had reached only 5 percent. Although many of these Africans served their masters for life, they were not legally enslaved. English common law acknowledged indentured servitude but not chattel slavery—the ownership of one human being by another. Consequently, a significant number of black workers escaped bondage after working for a number of years or by converting to Christianity. Some African Christian freemen even purchased slaves, bought the labor contracts of white servants, and married English women, suggesting that at this time religion and personal initiative were as important as race in determining social status. By becoming a

Hard Times in Early Virginia

RICHARD FRETHORNE

T *he lot of an indentured servant in Virginia was always hard, especially before 1630, when food was scarce and Indians were a constant danger. In 1623 Richard Frethorne begged his parents to buy out the remaining years of his labor contract so that he could return to England.*

Loving and kind father and mother . . . this is to let you understand that I your child am in a most heavy case by reason of the nature of the country . . . it causes much sickness, as the scurvy and the bloody flux [severe dysentery], and diverse other diseases, which make the body very poor and weak, and when we are sick there is nothing to comfort us. For since I came out of the ship, I never ate anything but peas and loblollie [gruel]. As for deer or venison I never saw any since I came into this land. There is indeed some fowl, but we are not allowed to go and get it, but must work hard both early and late for a mess of water gruel and a mouthful of bread and beef.

People cry out day and night, Oh that they were in England without their limbs and would not care to lose any limb to be in England again . . . we live in fear of the enemy every hour. . . . We are in great danger, for our plantation is very weak, by reason of the dearth, and sickness of our company. . . .

I have nothing to comfort me, nor there is nothing to be gotten here but sickness and death, except that one had money to lay out in some things for profit; but I have nothing at all, no not a shirt to my back, but two rags nor no clothes, but one poor suit, nor but one pair of shoes . . . my cloak is stolen by one of my own fellows, and to his dying hours would not tell me what he did with it, but some of my fellows saw him have butter and beef out of a ship, which my cloak [no] doubt paid for. . . .

SOURCE: Susan M. Kingsbury, ed., *The Records of the Virginia Company of London* (Washington, DC: Library of Congress, 1935), vol. 4: pp. 58–60.

Christian and a planter, an enterprising African could aspire to near equality with the English settlers.

Beginning in the 1660s, for reasons that are not clear, legislatures in the Chesapeake colonies enacted laws that lowered the status of Africans. Perhaps the English-born elite grew more conscious of race as the number of Africans increased. By 1671 the Virginia House of Burgesses had forbidden Africans to own guns or join the militia. It had also barred them—"tho baptized and enjoying their own Freedom"—from buying the labor contracts of white servants and specified that conversion to Christianity did not qualify Africans for eventual freedom. Being black was becoming a mark of inferior legal status, and being a slave was becoming a permanent and hereditary condition.

THE SEEDS OF SOCIAL REVOLT

By the 1660s the growing size of the Chesapeake tobacco crop triggered a collapse of the market. During the boom years of the 1620s tobacco sold for 24 pence a pound; forty years later it was fetching barely one-tenth as much. As the economic boom turned into a "bust," long-standing social conflicts flared up in political turmoil.

Political decisions in England had a lot to do with the decline of tobacco prices. In 1651, in an effort to exclude Dutch ships and merchants from England's overseas possessions, Parliament passed an Act of Trade and Navigation. Revised and extended in 1660 and 1663, the Navigation Acts permitted only English or colonial-owned ships to enter American ports. They also required the colonists to ship certain "enumerated articles," including tobacco, only to England. Thus, Chesapeake planters could no longer legally trade with Dutch merchants, who paid the highest prices. Moreover, to increase royal revenues the English monarchs continually raised the import duty on tobacco, thereby increasing the price to consumers and stifling growth of the market. As a result, by the 1670s planters got only one penny a pound for their crop.

Nonetheless, the number of planters in Virginia and Maryland grew, and tobacco exports continued to increase from 20 million pounds annually in the 1670s to 41 million pounds between 1690 and 1720. But profit margins were now thin, and the Chesapeake ceased to be a land of upward social mobility. Yeomen families grew about 10,000 tobacco plants each year but earned just enough to scrape by, and many fell into debt. Even harder hit were newly freed indentured servants. Low tobacco prices made it nearly impossible for them to pay the necessary fees to claim the 50 acres of land to which they were entitled and buy the tools and seed needed to plant it. Consequently, most former servants had to sell their labor again, signing new indentures or becoming wage workers or tenant farmers.

Gradually the Chesapeake colonies came to be dominated by an elite of planter-landlords and merchants. Landowners prospered by dividing their ample estates and leasing small plots to the growing army of former servants. They also lent money at high interest rates to hard-pressed yeomen families. Some well-to-do planters became commercial middlemen, setting up small retail stores or charging a commission for storing the tobacco of their poorer neighbors and selling it to English merchants. In Virginia this elite accumulated nearly half the land by soliciting favors from royal governors. In Maryland well-connected Catholic planters were equally dominant; by 1720 Charles Carroll owned 47,000 acres of land, farmed by scores of tenants and bound workers.

As these aggressive entrepreneurs confronted a growing number of young landless laborers, social divisions intensified, reaching a breaking point in Virginia during the corrupt regime of Governor William Berkeley. Berkeley first served as governor of Virginia between 1642 and 1652, and he won fame in 1644 by putting down the second major Indian revolt led by Opechancanough. Serving as governor again beginning in 1660, he made large land grants to himself and to members of his council, who exempted their own lands from taxation and appointed friends as county judges and local magistrates. Berkeley suppressed dissent in the House of Burgesses by assigning land grants to friendly legislators and appointing their relatives to the posts of sheriff, tax collector, and justice of the peace. Social and political unrest increased when the corrupt Burgesses changed the voting system to exclude landless freemen, who constituted half of all adult white males. Property-holding yeomen retained the vote, and—distressed by tobacco prices, rising taxes, and political corruption—some of them now rose in a rebellion against the planter elite.

BACON'S REBELLION

An Indian conflict in the summer of 1675 sparked Bacon's rebellion. By this time the Indians in Virginia were few and weak, their numbers having dwindled from 30,000 in 1607 to a mere 3,500, as compared to 38,000 Europeans and about 2,500 Africans. Most Indians lived along the frontier on lands guaranteed by treaty. Hundreds of poor freeholders and aspiring tenants who wanted cheap land insisted that the Indians be expelled or exterminated. But wealthy planters on the seacoast, who wanted a ready supply of labor, opposed expansion into Indian territory, as did the planter-merchants who traded with the Native Americans for furs.

Fighting broke out when a band of Virginia militiamen murdered thirty Indians. Defying orders from Governor Berkeley, a larger force of 1,000 militiamen then surrounded a fortified Susquehannock village and killed five chiefs who had come out to negotiate. The outraged Susquehannocks, who had recently migrated from the north, retaliated by killing 300 whites in raids on outlying plantations. Berkeley did not want war, which would disrupt the fur trade, and proposed a defensive military policy, asking the House of Burgesses in March 1676 to raise money to build a series of frontier forts. Western settlers dismissed this strategy as useless, a plot by planters and merchants to impose high taxes and, in the words of one yeoman, to take "all our tobacco into their own hands."

Nathaniel Bacon emerged as the leader of the protesters. A wealthy and bold man, he had recently arrived from England and settled on a frontier estate. Although he was only twenty-eight, Bacon commanded the respect of his neighbors because of his vigor and his high status as a member of the governor's council. When Berkeley refused to grant Bacon a military commission, Bacon marched his frontiersmen against the Indians anyway, slaughtering some of the peaceful Doeg people and triggering a political upheaval. Condemning the frontiersmen as "rebels and mutineers," Berkeley expelled Bacon from the council and placed him under arrest. Then, realizing the rebel leader's military power, the governor agreed to legislative elections and accepted the far-reaching political reforms enacted by the new House of Burgesses that curbed the powers of the governor and the council and restored voting rights to landless freemen.

These much-needed reforms did not end the rebellion. Bacon was bitter about Berkeley's arbitrary actions, and the poor farmers and indentured servants in his army were resentful of exploitation by the political elite and eager to flaunt their power. Backed by 400 armed men, Bacon seized control of the colony and issued a "Manifesto and Declaration of the People," demanding the death or removal of all Indians and an end to the rule of wealthy "parasites." "All the power and sway is got into the hands of the rich," Bacon proclaimed, as his army burned Jamestown to the ground and plundered the plantations of Berkeley's allies. When Bacon died suddenly from dysentery in October 1676, the governor took his revenge, dispersing the rebel army, seizing the estates of well-to-do rebels, and hanging twenty-three men.

Bacon's rebellion was a pivotal event in the history of Virginia. Although planter-merchants continued to dominate the colony, they limited the governor's authority and found public positions for substantial and politically ambitious property owners like Bacon. The planter-merchant elite also appeased the lower social orders by cutting their taxes and supporting the expansion of English settlement onto Indian lands. The uprising also contributed to the expansion of African slavery. To forestall another rebellion planters in Virginia and Maryland sought to limit the number of freed white servants in the colony. Instead they enacted laws explicitly legalizing slavery and imported thousands of Africans, committing their descendants to a social system based on racial exploitation.

Puritan New England

The Puritan exodus to America from 1620 to 1640 was both a worldly quest for land and a spiritual effort to preserve the "pure" Christian faith. By creating a Holy Commonwealth in the new world, these pious migrants hoped to promote reform within the established Church of England. By gaining access to land, they hoped to build a society of independent property-owning farm families. By defining their mission in spiritual terms, the Puritans gave a moral dimension to American history.

THE PURITAN MIGRATION

From the beginning New England differed from other European settlements. New Spain and Jamestown were populated initially by unruly male adventurers, and New France and New Netherland by commercial-minded fur traders. By contrast Plymouth, the first permanent community in New England, was settled by women and children as well as men, and its leaders were pious Protestants—the Pilgrims.

The Pilgrims were Puritans who had left the Church of England, thus earning the name "Separatists." When King James I embraced traditional religious doctrines in the 1610s and threatened to harry Puritans "out of the land, or else do worse," the Pilgrims left England and settled among like-minded Dutch Calvinists in Holland. Subsequently, thirty-five of them decided to migrate to America, where they hoped to maintain their English identity. Led by William Bradford and joined by sixty-seven other migrants from England, they sailed to America aboard the *Mayflower* in 1620 (see Map 2.2).

Before their departure, the Pilgrims had organized themselves into a joint-stock corporation with backing from sympathetic Puritan merchants. Arriving in America without a royal charter, they created their own covenant of government, the Mayflower Compact, to "combine ourselves together into a civill body politick." This document was the first "constitution" adopted in North America and used the Puritan model of a self-governing religious congregation as the blueprint for political society.

The first winter in America tested the Pilgrims. As in Jamestown, hunger and disease took a heavy toll; of the 102 migrants who arrived in November, only half survived until the spring. Thereafter the Plymouth colony—unlike Virginia—

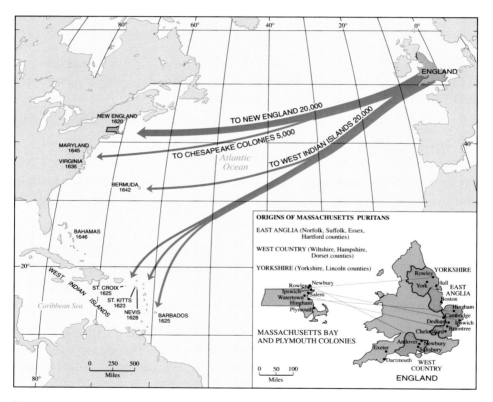

M A P 2.2
The Puritan Migration to America, 1620–1640

Nearly 50,000 Puritans left England between 1620 and 1640. In New England migrants from the three major areas of English Puritanism—Yorkshire, East Anglia, and the West Country—commonly settled among those from their own region. They named American communities after their English towns of origin and transplanted regional customs, such as the open-field agriculture practiced in Rowley in Yorkshire and Rowley in Massachusetts Bay.

became a healthy and thriving community. The cold climate inhibited the spread of mosquito-borne diseases, and the Pilgrims' religious discipline established a strong work ethic. Moreover, because a severe epidemic in 1618 had killed 90 percent of the local Wampanoag people, the migrants faced few external threats. The Pilgrims quickly built solid houses, planted ample crops, and entered the fur trade. Their numbers grew rapidly, to 3,000 by 1640, prompting the creation of ten new towns with extensive powers of self-government. A new legal code established in 1636 provided for a colonywide system of representative self-government, guaranteed various political rights, and provided for the separation of church and state by forbidding government interference in spiritual matters.

Meanwhile, England was plunging deeper into religious turmoil. King Charles I (r. 1625–1649) supported the Church of England but personally repudiated some Protestant doctrines, such as justification by faith. The Puritans, who had gained many seats in Parliament, accused the king of "popery"—holding Catholic beliefs. Charles's response was to dissolve Parliament in 1629, claiming that he ruled by "divine right," and to raise money through royal edicts, customs duties, and the sale of monopolies. The king's arbitrary rule struck at the power of the landed gentry, who expected to exercise authority through the House of Commons, and cut away at the profits of the merchant community, a stronghold of Puritanism. Then in 1633 the king chose William Laud, who loathed Puritans, to head the Church of England. Laud removed hundreds of Puritan ministers and forced Anglican rituals on their congregations, prompting thousands of Puritans to seek refuge in America.

In 1630, 900 Puritans boarded eleven ships and sailed across the Atlantic under the leadership of John Winthrop, a well-educated country squire. Winthrop believed that England was morally corrupt and "overburdened with people." He sought land and opportunity for his children and a place in history for his people. "We must consider that we shall be as a City upon a Hill," Winthrop told his fellow passengers aboard the ship *Arbella* in 1630. "The eyes of all people are upon us." Like the Pilgrims, the Puritans envisioned a reformed Christian society, a genuinely "New" England. Many Puritans saw themselves as a "saving remnant" chosen by God to preserve the true faith in America and inspire religious change in England.

Once in America, Winthrop and his associates established the Massachusetts Bay colony in the area around Boston and transformed their joint-stock business corporation, the General Court of shareholders, into a colonial legislature. Over the next decade about 10,000 Puritans migrated to the Massachusetts Bay colony, along with 10,000 others fleeing hard times in England. The Puritans created representative political institutions that were locally based, with the governor as well as the assembly and council elected by the colony's freemen. However, to ensure rule by the godly the Puritans limited the right to vote and hold office to men who were Puritan church members. Eschewing the religious toleration of the Pilgrims, they established Puritanism as the state-supported religion and barred members of other faiths from conducting services. Massachusetts Bay became a religious commonwealth with the Bible as its legal as well as spiritual guide. For example, following a biblical rule Puritans there divided inheritances among all children in a given family, with a double portion going to the oldest son. "Where there is no Law," the colony's government advised local magistrates, they should rule "as near the law of God as they can."

RELIGION AND SOCIETY, 1630–1670

In establishing their churches, the Puritans in New England tried to re-create the simplicity of the first Christians. They eliminated bishops and devised a democratic church structure controlled by the laity, or the ordinary members of the congregation—hence their name, Congregationalists. Influenced by John Calvin, Puritans embraced predestination, believing that God had decided, or "predestined," the fates of all people before they were born, choosing a few "elect" men and women (the Saints) for salvation and condemning the rest to damnation. Most congregations set extraordinarily high standards for church membership, rigorously examining those who applied. Even so, many Saints lived in great anxiety, for they could never be sure that God had predestined them for salvation.

Puritans dealt with the uncertainties of divine election in three ways. Some congregations stressed the conversion experience: when God infused a soul with grace, the person was "born again" and knew that salvation was at hand. Other Puritans stressed "preparation," the confidence in redemption that came from years of spiritual guidance and church discipline. Still others believed that God had entered into a *covenant,* or contract, with them, promising to treat them as a divinely "chosen people" as long as they lived according to His laws.

To maintain God's favor, the Puritan magistrates of Massachusetts Bay felt they must purge their society of religious dissidents. One target was Roger Williams, who in 1634 had become the minister of the Puritan church in Salem. Williams preferred the Pilgrims' separation of church and state in Plymouth Colony and condemned the legal establishment of Congregationalism in Massachusetts Bay. He taught that political magistrates should have authority over only the "bodies, goods, and outward estates of men," not their spiritual lives. Moreover, he questioned the Puritans' right to seize (rather than buy) Indian lands. In response, the Puritan magistrates banished him from Massachusetts Bay in 1635.

Williams and his followers resettled in Rhode Island in 1636, founding the town of Providence on land acquired from the Narragansett Indians. Other religious dissidents founded Portsmouth and Newport. In 1644 these towns obtained a corporate charter from the English Parliament that granted them full authority "to rule themselves." In Rhode Island as in Plymouth there was no legally established church; every congregation was autonomous, and individual men and women could worship God as they pleased.

Puritan magistrates also felt threatened by Anne Hutchinson, the wife of a merchant and a mother of seven who worked as a midwife. Hutchinson held weekly prayer meetings in her house—attended by as many as sixty women—in which she

Changing Images of Death

Death—sudden and arbitrary—was a constant presence in the preindustrial world. Pre-1700 New England gravestones often depicted death as a frightening skull, warning sinners to repent of their sins. After 1700 a smiling cherub adorned many gravestones, suggesting a more optimistic view of the afterlife.

(Peabody Essex Museum)

accused certain Boston clergymen of placing undue emphasis on church laws and good behavior. In words that recalled Martin Luther's rejection of indulgences, Hutchinson argued that salvation was not something that people could earn through good deeds; there was no "covenant of works." Instead, salvation was bestowed by God through the "covenant of grace." Hutchinson stressed the importance of revelation: the direct communication of truth by God to the individual believer. Since this doctrine diminished the role of ministers and, indeed, of all established authority, Puritan magistrates found it heretical.

The magistrates also resented Hutchinson because of her sex. Like other Christians, Puritans believed in the equality of souls: both men and women could be saved. When it came to matters concerning the governance of church and state, however, women were seen as being clearly inferior to men. As the Pilgrim minister John Robinson put it, women "are debarred by their sex from ordinary prophesying, and from any other dealing in the church wherein they take authority over the man." Puritan women could never be ministers, lay preachers, or even voting members of the congregation.

In 1637 the Massachusetts Bay magistrates put Hutchinson on trial for heresy, accusing her of believing that inward grace freed an individual from the rules of the church. Hutchinson defended her views with great skill and tenacity, and even Winthrop admitted that she was "a woman of fierce and haughty courage." But the judges found her guilty and berated her for not attending to "her household affairs, and such things as belong to women." Banished, she followed Roger Williams into exile in Rhode Island.

The coercive policies of the magistrates, along with the desire for better land, prompted some Puritans to leave Massachusetts Bay. In 1636 Thomas Hooker led a hundred settlers to the Connecticut River Valley, where they established the town of Hartford. Others followed, settling along the river at Wethersfield and Windsor. In 1639 the Connecticut Puritans adopted the Fundamental Orders, a plan of government that included a representative assembly and a popularly elected governor. Connecticut was patterned after Massachusetts Bay, with a firm union of church and state and a congregational system of church government, but voting rights were extended to most property-owning men—not just church members.

As Puritans established themselves in America, England fell into a religious war. When Archbishop Laud imposed a new Church of England prayer book on Presbyterian Scotland, a Scottish army invaded England. In 1642 thousands of English Puritans rose up in revolt, demanding greater authority for Parliament and reform of the established church. Hundreds of Puritans returned from America to join the conflict. After four years of civil war the Parliamentary forces led by Oliver Cromwell were victorious. In 1649 Parliament executed Charles I, proclaimed a republican commonwealth, and reformed the Church of England by eliminating bishops and elaborate rituals.

The Puritan triumph was short-lived. Popular support for the Commonwealth quickly ebbed, especially when Cromwell took dictatorial control of the government in 1653. After his death a repentant Parliament summoned the son of Charles I to the throne, restoring the monarch and the power of bishops in the Church of England. For many Puritans, Charles II's accession in 1660 represented the victory of the Antichrist—the false prophet described in the last book of the New Testament.

For the Puritans in Massachusetts, the restoration of the monarchy began a new phase of their "errand into the wilderness." They had come to New England to preserve the "pure" Christian church, expecting to return in triumph to a Europe ready to receive the true Gospel. Since that sacred mission had been dashed by the failure of the English Revolution, Puritan ministers articulated a new vision: they exhorted their congregations to create a permanent new society in America based on their faith and ideals.

THE PURITAN IMAGINATION AND WITCHCRAFT

Like the Native Americans they encountered in New England, the Puritans thought that the physical world was full of supernatural forces. This belief in "spirits" stemmed in part from Christian teachings, such as the Catholic belief in miracles and the Protestant faith in the powers of "grace." Devout Christians saw signs of God's (or Satan's) power in blazing stars, deformed births, and other unusual events. Noting that "more Ministers' Houses than others proportionally had been smitten with Lightning," Cotton Mather, a prominent Massachusetts minister, wondered "what the meaning of God should be in it."

The Puritans' respect for spiritual "forces" also reflected certain pagan assumptions that were held by all sections of society. When Samuel Sewall, a Puritan merchant and judge, moved into a new house, he tried to fend off evil spirits by driving a metal pin into the floor. And thousands of ordinary Puritans followed pagan astrological charts printed in farmers' almanacs to determine the best times to plant crops, marry off their children, and make other important decisions.

Zealous ministers attacked many of these beliefs and practices as a return to "superstition" and condemned "cunning" individuals who claimed to have special powers as healers or prophets. Many Christians looked on folk doctors or conjurers as "wizards" or "witches" who acted at the command of Satan. The people of Andover, Massachusetts "were much addicted to sorcery," claimed one observer, and "there were forty men in it that could raise the Devil as well as any astrologer." Between 1647 and 1662 civil authorities in Massachusetts and Connecticut hanged fourteen people for witchcraft, mostly older women who, their accusers claimed, were "double-tongued" or "had an unruly spirit."

The most dramatic episode of witch-hunting took place in Salem, Massachusetts, in 1692. The causes were complex and are still hard to fathom. Some historians stress group rivalries, pointing out that many of the accusers were the daughters and young female servants of poor farmers in a rural area of Salem, whereas many of the accused were wealthier church members or their friends. Things got out of hand when judges allowed the introduction of "spectral" evidence, visions seen only by the accusers. Soon Massachusetts authorities had arrested 175 people and executed 20 of them. Because 19 of those killed were women, other historians argue that the incident was part of a systematic attempt to intimidate women, especially those who had inherited property, and make certain they remained subordinate "helpmates" to their husbands. Other scholars have called attention to the fears raised by recent Indian attacks along the nearby frontier in Maine, attacks that took the lives of the parents of the young girls whose accusations sparked the Salem prosecutions.

The Salem episode marked a turning point for New England. Popular revulsion against the executions dealt a blow to the traditional dominance of religion in public life; there would be no more legal prosecutions for witchcraft. The European Enlightenment, a major intellectual movement that began around 1675, also promoted a more rational view of the world. Increasingly, educated people explained accidents and sudden deaths through theories about natural forces, not through religion, astrology, or witchcraft. In contrast to Cotton Mather (who died in 1728), well-read men of the next generation—such as Benjamin Franklin— would conceive of lightning as a natural phenomenon rather than a supernatural sign.

A YEOMAN SOCIETY, 1630–1700

In creating New England communities, Puritans consciously avoided the worst features of traditional Europe. They did not wish to live in a society dominated by a few wealthy landowners or under a distant government that levied oppressive taxes. Consequently, they instituted land-distribution policies that encouraged the development of self-governing communities composed primarily of property-owning families. Instead of granting thousands of acres to wealthy planters (as occurred in the Chesapeake colonies), the General Courts of Massachusetts Bay and Connecticut bestowed the title to a township on a group of settlers, or proprietors, who distributed the land among themselves. The title was given in *fee simple,* which meant that the proprietors' families held the land outright, free from manorial obligations or feudal dues; they could sell, lease, or rent it as they pleased.

Widespread ownership of land did not imply equality of wealth or status. Like most seventeenth-century Europeans, Puritans believed in a social and economic hierarchy. "God had Ordained different degrees and orders of men," proclaimed the wealthy Boston merchant John Saffin, "some to be Masters and Commanders, others to be Subjects, and to be commanded." Consequently, town proprietors normally bestowed the largest plots of land on men of high social status, who often became political leaders. However, all male heads of families received some land, laying the basis for a society of independent yeomen farmers, and all of them had a voice in the town meeting, the main institution of local government.

Local communities in New England had much more political power than did most peasant villages in Europe. Each year the town meeting chose selectmen to manage town affairs. It also levied taxes; enacted ordinances regarding fencing, lot sizes, and road building; and regulated the use of common fields for grazing livestock and cutting firewood. Beginning in 1634 each town in Massachusetts Bay elected its own representatives to the General Court. As the number of towns increased, their representatives in General Court gained authority at the expense of the governor and magistrates, further enhancing local control.

Over time the farming communities of New England became more socially divided. The larger proprietors owned enough land to divide among all their sons (usually three or four). Smallholders could provide land for only some of their sons, which forced the rest to become propertyless laborers. Newcomers who lacked the rights of proprietors were the least well off, for they had to buy land or work as tenants or laborers. By 1702 in Windsor, Connecticut, landless sons and newcomers accounted for no less than 30 percent of the male taxpayers. It would take years of saving or migration to a new town for these men and their families to become freeholders.

Despite these inequalities, nearly all New Englanders had an opportunity to acquire property, and even those at the bottom of the social scale enjoyed some economic security. When he died in the 1690s, Nathaniel Fish was one of the poorest men in Barnstable, Massachusetts, yet he owned a two-room cottage, 8 acres of land, an ox, and a cow. For him and thousands of other settlers New England had proved to be the promised land, a new world of opportunity.

The Indians' New World

Native Americans on the eastern seaboard were also living in a new world, but for them it was a bleak, dangerous, and conflict-ridden place. Some Indian peoples, like the Pequots, resisted the invaders by force. Others retreated into the Appalachian Mountains to preserve their traditional culture or to band together in new tribes.

PURITANS AND PEQUOTS

Seeing themselves as God's chosen people, the Puritans attempted to justify their intrusions on Native American lands from a moral perspective. "By what right or warrant can we enter into the land of the Savages," they asked themselves while still in England, "and take away their rightfull inheritance from them?" John Winthrop thought that a disastrous smallpox epidemic of 1633, which reduced the Indian population from 13,000 to 3,000, provided a clear answer. "If God were not pleased with our inheriting these parts," he pointed out, "why doth he still make roome for us by diminishing them as we increase?" Citing the Book of Genesis, the magistrates of Massachusetts Bay declared that the Indians had not "subdued" their land and therefore had no "just right" to it.

Imbued with moral righteousness, the Puritans often treated Native Americans with a brutality equal to that of the Spanish conquistadors and Nathaniel Bacon's frontiersmen. In 1636 when Pequot warriors attacked English farmers who had intruded onto their lands, Puritan militiamen and their Indian allies led a surprise attack on a Pequot village and massacred about 500 men, women, and children. "God laughed at the Enemies of his People," one soldier boasted, "filling the Place with Dead Bodies." Many of the survivors were ruthlessly tracked down and sold into slavery in the Caribbean.

Like most Europeans, English Puritans viewed the Indians as "savages," culturally inferior people who did not deserve civilized treatment. But the Puritans were not racist as the term is understood today. To them, Native Americans were not genetically inferior—they were white people with sun-darkened skins—and "sin," rather than race, accounted for their degenerate condition. "Probably the devil" delivered these "miserable savages" to America, wrote the Puritan minister Cotton Mather, "in hopes that the gospel of the Lord Jesus Christ would never come here to destroy or disturb his absolute empire over them."

This interpretation inspired attempts at conversion by John Eliot, who translated the Bible into Algonquian and undertook missions to Indians in eastern Massachusetts. Because Puritans demanded that Indians master Puritan theology, only a few Native Americans became full members of Puritan congregations. However, the Puritans created "praying towns" that, like the Spanish Franciscans' missions in New Mexico, sought to supervise the Indian population. Soon more than 1,000 Indians lived in fourteen special mission towns. By 1670 a combination of European diseases, military force, and Christianization had pacified most of the Algonquian-speaking peoples who lived along the seacoast of New England, guaranteeing, at least temporarily, the safety of the white settlers.

METACOM'S WAR

By the 1670s the white population of New England had reached 55,000 while the Indian population had declined from an estimated 120,000 in 1570, to 70,000 in 1620, to barely 16,000 in 1670. Like Opechancanough in Virginia and Popé in New Mexico, Metacom, leader of the Wampanoag tribe, concluded that only united resistance could stop the relentless advance of the European invaders. In 1675 Metacom forged a military alliance with the Narragansett and Nipmuck peoples and attacked white settlements throughout New England. Bitter fighting continued into 1676, ending only when Indian warriors ran short of guns and powder and Mohawks hired by the Massachusetts Bay government ambushed and killed Metacom. The war was a deadly affair. The Indians burned 20 percent of the English towns in Massachusetts and Rhode Island and killed 1,000 whites, about 5 percent of the adult population. But their own losses—from famine and disease as well as battle—were much larger: as many as 4,500, or 25 percent of an already diminished population. Many survivors were sold into slavery in the Caribbean, including Metacom's wife and nine-year-old son.

Many of the defeated New England Algonquian peoples migrated into the backcountry, where they intermarried with other tribes tied to the French. They had suffered a double tragedy, losing both their land and the integrity of their traditional cultures. Over the next century, these displaced peoples would take their revenge, allying with the French to attack their Puritan enemies (see American Voices, "The Unredeemed Captive").

THE FUR TRADE AND THE INLAND PEOPLES

Until well after 1700 the Indian peoples who lived near the Appalachian Mountains and in the great forested areas beyond remained independent, but few were able to maintain their customary way of life. The greatest threat to their cultures came from

***Metacom (King Philip),
Chief of the Wampanoag***

The Indian uprising of
1675 left an indelible
mark on the historical
memory of New England.
This painting, done on
semitransparent cloth and
lit from behind for dra-
matic effect, was used by
traveling performers dur-
ing the 1850s to tell the
story of King Philip's War.
(Shelburne Museum)

the wars and epidemics brought by the fur trade. Yet many inland tribes were eager
to control the fur trade to obtain European guns and goods. The militarily aggressive and diplomatically astute Iroquois peoples had the best chance. From their
location in central New York, Iroquois warriors could move quickly to the east and
south along the Mohawk, Hudson, Delaware, and Susquehanna Rivers to exchange
goods with (or threaten) the English and Dutch colonies. They could also travel
north via Lake Champlain and the Richelieu River to French traders in Quebec,
and west by means of the Great Lakes and the Allegheny-Ohio river system to the
rich fur-bearing lands of the Mississippi Valley. In 1600 the Iroquois in the area of
present-day New York numbered about 30,000 and lived in large towns of 500 to
2,000 inhabitants. Two decades later they had organized themselves in a great "long-
house" confederation of the Five Nations: the Senecas, Cayugas, Onondagas,
Oneidas, and Mohawks.

AMERICAN VOICES

The Unredeemed Captive

PETER SCHULYER

A decade and a half after Metacom's War, Indians mounted new attacks against Massa-chusetts frontier settlements. In 1704 Mohawk Indians devastated the town of Deerfield and took back to French Canada 112 prisoners, including seven-year-old Eunice Williams. Most of the captives were returned or ransomed, and in 1713 Peter Schulyer, an Albany fur trader, sought the return of Eunice Williams, who was now sixteen.

I arrived from Albany at Mont Reall [Montreal] on ye 15th of April. . . . Monsr. De Vau-druille [Vaudrieuil], Governor and Chief of Canada . . . gave me all the Encouragement I could immagine for her to go home. . . . Accordingly I went to the ffort of Caghenewaga [Kahnawake] being accompanied by one of the Kings officers and a ffrench Interpreter [and] likewise another of the Indian language. . . .

I thought fitt first to apply mySelf to the priests. . . . And [as I] was informed before that this infant (As I may say) was married to a young Indian, I therefore proposed to know the Reason why this poor captive should be Married to an Indian being a Christian born . . . said he they came to me to Marry them. . . . And if he would not marry them they matter'd not, for they were resolved never to leave the other. . . . He sent for her, who presently came with the Indian She was married to both together. She looking very poor in body, bashfull in the face, but proved harder than Steel in her breast. . . .

I first Spoak to her in English, Upon wch she did not Answr me; And I believe She did not understand me, she being very Young when she was taken. . . . I Imployed my Indian Languister to talk to her . . . but could not get one word from her. . . . And I could not pre-vail wth her to go home . . . that she might only go to see her father, And directly return hither again. . . .

And these two words ["Jaghte oghte, a plaine denyall"] were all we could gett from her; in allmost two hours time that we talked with her . . . and the time growing late and I be-ing very Sorrowfull, that I could not prevail upon nor get one word more from her I took her by the hand and left her in the priest's house.

[Eunice Williams remained among the Mohawk, bore two daughters, twice visited her English brothers and sisters in Massachusetts, and died in Canada in 1785, aged eighty-nine.]

SOURCE: John Demos, *The Unredeemed Captive: A Family Story from Early America* (New York: Knopf, 1994), pp. 101–08.

Although their numbers were cut by a third by a virulent smallpox epidemic in 1633, the Iroquois waged a successful series of wars against the Iroquoian-speaking Hurons (1649), Neutrals (1651), Eries (1657), and Susquehannocks. These victories gave the Iroquois control of the fur trade with the French in Quebec and the Dutch in New York and enabled them to replenish their depleted ranks by incorporating war captives. By 1667 half the population of many Mohawk towns consisted of adopted prisoners. Following these victories, the Five Nations made peace with their traditional French foes and allowed a considerable number of Jesuit missionaries in Iroquoia. Soon about 20 percent of the Five Nations were Christians, some living under French protection in separate mission-towns.

In 1680 the Iroquois renewed their struggle for control of the western fur trade to maintain their supply of guns and goods from the English in New York. Warriors of the Five Nations pushed a dozen Algonquian-speaking peoples who were allied with the French—the Ottawas, Foxes, Sauks, Kickapoos, Miamis, Illinois—out of their traditional lands north of the Ohio River and into a newly formed multitribal region (present-day Wisconsin) west of Lake Michigan. After suffering heavy losses—half of their 2,200 warriors—the Iroquois again made peace with French.

These wars and contact with European traders transformed the character of Indian society. Most tribes became smaller as European diseases devastated their peoples, and the rum and corn liquor sold by fur traders took their toll. "Strong spirits . . . Causes our men to get very sick," a Catawba leader protested, "and many of our people has Lately Died by the Effects of that Strong Drink." Many Indian peoples also lost their economic and cultural independence. As they exchanged furs for European-made iron utensils and cloth blankets, they neglected traditional artisan skills—making fewer flint hoes, clay pots, and skin garments. As a Cherokee chief complained in the 1750s, "Every necessity of life we must have from the white people." Moreover, as French missionaries won converts among the Hurons, Iroquois, and inland peoples, they divided communities into hostile religious factions.

The fur trade created other conflicts as well. The commitment to constant warfare altered tribal politics by increasing the influence of those who made war, shifting political power from cautious elders, the sachems, to headstrong young warriors. The sachems, one group of Seneca warriors said with scorn, "were a parcell of Old People who say much but who Mean or Act very little." Equally important, the position and status of women changed in complex and contradictory ways. Traditionally, the eastern Woodland women had asserted authority as the chief providers of food and hand-crafted goods, roles that were undermined because of the influx of trade goods and the disruptive impact of warfare on agricultural production. Yet the influence of women in victorious tribes increased as they assumed responsibility for assimilating captive peoples into the culture.

Finally, the sheer extent of the fur industry—the trapping and killing of hundreds of thousands of beaver, deer, otter, and other animals—profoundly altered the environment. Streams ran faster because there were fewer beaver dams, and the winter hunt for food became more arduous and less fruitful. Death from trapping and hunting had decimated the animal population of North America, just as death from disease and warfare had cut down its native peoples.

All of the European invaders—Dutch and French fur traders no less than French Jesuits, Spanish conquistadors, and English settlers—undermined traditional Native

Algonquian Beaver Bowl

Because of the impor-
tance to the fur trade, the
beaver played a significant
role in Native American
economic and cultural
life. This beaver-shaped
bowl, carved from the
root of an ash tree, was
the work of an eighteenth-
century Algonquian arti-
san in present-day Ohio
or Illinois.

(Peabody Museum, Harvard
University. Photograph by Hillel
Burger)

American societies, forcing Indians to fashion new ways of life. Among the English
migrants, Puritans tried consciously to create a different world in America, a "New"
England dedicated to the doctrines of a radical Protestant Christianity. In the Chesapeake the planters' quest for wealth likewise produced a new model of society—
one based on the naked exploitation of white indentured servants and, especially
after 1700, of enslaved African laborers. America had become a new world for all
of its peoples.

For Further Exploration

For a comprehensive and insightful narrative of the Spanish exploration and settlement of
the lands to the north of the Rio Grande, consult David Weber, *The Spanish Frontier in North
America* (1992). Bernard Bailyn, *The Peopling of British North America: An Introduction*
(1986), presents a brief, vivid history of English migration and settlement. In *American
Slavery, American Freedom* (1975) Edmund Morgan offers a compelling portrayal of white
servitude and black slavery in early Virginia, while John Demos, *The Unredeemed Captive:
A Family Story from Early America* (1994), relates the gripping tale of Eunice Williams, a
captured Puritan girl who lived her life among the Mohawks. Another fine study of Native
American life is James Merrell, *The Indians' New World: Catawbas and Their Neighbors from
European Contact Through the Era of Removal* (1989). William Cronon, *Changes in the Land:
Indians, Colonists, and the Ecology of New England* (1983), is a succinct analysis of the im-
pact of the Indians and the English on the ecology of New England. Arthur Quinn, *A New
World: An Epic of Colonial America from the Founding of Jamestown to the Fall of Quebec*
(1994), is a lively narrative filled with portraits of important political figures, macabre events,
and high hopes that end disastrously.

TIMELINE

1530s	Jacques Cartier claims Gulf of St. Lawrence lands for France.		1622	Opechancanough's uprising
1540s	Francisco Vásquez de Coronado and Hernando de Soto seek gold in the present-day United States.		1624	Virginia becomes a royal colony.
			1630	Puritans found Massachusetts Bay colony.
1565	Spain establishes St. Augustine, Florida.		1634	Maryland settled as a Catholic refuge.
1580s	Failure of Roanoke and other English settlements		1636	Roger Williams, expelled from Massachusetts Bay, founds Rhode Island.
1598	Acoma War in New Mexico		1637	Pequot War Anne Hutchinson banished
1607	Powhatan confronts the English at Jamestown in Virginia.		1640s	Five Iroquois Nations go to war over fur trade. Puritan Revolution in England
1608	Samuel de Champlain founds Quebec.			
1619	The first Africans arrive in Chesapeake. The Virginia House of Burgesses convened.		1660s–1720	Low tobacco prices spark social conflict.
1620	Pilgrims found Plymouth colony.		1664	England conquers New Netherland.
1620s–1660s	Tobacco boom in Chesapeake colonies Growth of English servitude and African slavery in Chesapeake		1675–1676	Bacon's rebellion in Virginia Metacom's (King Philip) uprising in New England
			1680	Popé's Rebellion in New Mexico
1621	Dutch West India Company settles New Netherland.		1692	Salem witchcraft trials

A PBS video, *Surviving Columbus* (2 hours), traces the experiences of the Pueblo Indians over 450 years. "First Nations Histories," at <http://www.dickshovel.com/Compacts.html>, presents short histories of many North American Indian peoples and information on their politics, language, culture, and demography. A highly acclaimed site on the Pilgrims at Plymouth is "Caleb Johnson's Mayflower Web Pages," at <http://members.aol.com/calebj/mayflower.html>. "Colonial Williamsburg," at <http://www.history.org/>, offers an extensive collection of documents, illustrations, and secondary texts about colonial life, as well as information about the archeological excavations at Williamsburg. Extensive materials on the Salem witchcraft episode can be viewed at <http://etext.lib.virginia.edu/salem/witchcraft/>.

Chapter 3

THE BRITISH EMPIRE IN AMERICA

1660–1750

The Planters in General have throve and grown Rich . . . by the help and Labour of their Slaves.

RICHARD HILL, 1743

In 1660 England was a second-class commercial power, picking up the crumbs left by Dutch merchants who dominated the Atlantic. As the Duke of Albemarle lamented, "What we want is more of the trade the Dutch now have." To achieve that goal the English government passed the Navigation Acts, which excluded Dutch merchants from its American colonies, and then went to war against the Dutch to enforce the new legislation. By the 1720s the newly unified kingdom of Great Britain (comprising England and Scotland) controlled the North Atlantic trade. "We have within ourselves and in our colonies in America," a British pamphleteer declared, "an inexhaustible fund to supply ourselves, and perhaps Europe." A generation later most British officials celebrated trade with their American possessions as a leading source of the nation's prosperity. As the ardent imperialist Malachy Postlethwayt proclaimed in 1745, the British empire "was a magnificent superstructure of American commerce and naval power on an African foundation."

The rise of the British empire in America is a central story of the period from 1660 to 1750. As Postlethwayt observed, the wealth of the empire was the direct result of the trade in African slaves and the profits generated by slave labor, primarily on the sugar plantations of the West Indies. To protect Britain's increasingly valuable sugar colonies from European rivals—the Dutch in New Netherland, the French in Quebec and the West Indies, and the Spanish in Florida—British officials expanded the navy and repeatedly went to war during these decades. The British empire was the product of calculated diplomatic and military policy, not chance.

This period also saw the beginning of a long struggle for British administrative control over its American settlements. To profit from the products and commerce of the colonies, the home government successfully imposed the economic controls of the Navigation Acts and, with less success, tried to subordinate colonial political institutions to imperial direction. These commercial, military, and administrative policies made Britain a dominant power in Europe and brought at least modest prosperity to most of the white colonists, even as they condemned hundreds of thousands of enslaved Africans to brutal work and early death.

The Politics of Empire, 1660–1713

In the first decades of settlement the Chesapeake and New England colonies were governed in a haphazard fashion. Taking advantage of the upheaval produced by religious conflict and civil war in England, local oligarchies of Puritan magistrates and tobacco-growing planters governed as they wished. However, with the restoration of the monarchy in 1660 royal bureaucrats imposed order on the unruly settlements and, with the aid of Indian allies, went to war aginst rival European powers.

THE RESTORATION COLONIES

In 1660 Charles II ascended to the English throne. A generous but extravagant man who was always in debt, Charles rewarded the aristocrats who had supported his return to power with millions of acres of American land. In 1663 he gave the Carolinas, an area long claimed by Spain and populated by thousands of Indians, to eight aristocratic friends. In 1664 he granted all the territory between the Delaware and Connecticut Rivers to his brother James, the Duke of York. In that same year James took possession of the conquered province of New Netherland, renaming it New York after himself, and passed on the ownership of the adjacent lands to two of the Carolina proprietors, who established the province of New Jersey.

In one of the great land grabs in history, a few English aristocrats had won title to vast provinces. Like Maryland, their new colonies were proprietorships; the aristocrats owned all the land and could rule as they wished as long as the laws conformed broadly to those of England. Most proprietors sought to create a traditional social order presided over by a gentry class and a legally established Church of England. Thus, the Fundamental Constitutions of Carolina (1669) prescribed a manorial system with a powerful nobility and a mass of serfs.

This aristocratic scheme was pure fantasy. The first settlers in North Carolina, poor families from Virginia, refused to work on large manors and chose to live on modest farms, raising grain and tobacco. Indeed, farmers in Albemarle County, inspired by Bacon's rebellion in Virginia and angered by taxes on tobacco exports, rebelled in 1677. They deposed the governor and forced the proprietors to abandon most of their financial claims.

The colonists of South Carolina, many of whom had come from Barbados (which became an overcrowded sugar-producing island during the 1660s), refused to accept the Fundamental Constitutions. Rather, they imposed their own design on the colony, bringing enslaved Africans from Barbados and using them to raise cattle and food crops for export to the West Indies. They also opened a lucrative trade with Native Americans, exchanging English manufactured goods for furs and Indian slaves. The growing demand for Indian slaves encouraged attacks against Indian settlements in Florida and the backcountry, raising the threat of war with Spain and in 1715 prompting a brutal war with the resident Yamasee people, which took the lives of 400 settlers. Until the 1720s South Carolina remained an ill-governed, violence-ridden frontier settlement.

In dramatic contrast to the Carolinas, the proprietary colony of Pennsylvania (which included present-day Delaware) pursued a pacifistic policy toward native Americans and quickly became prosperous. In 1681 Charles II bestowed the colony on William Penn in payment of a large debt owed to Penn's father. Born to wealth and seemingly destined for courtly pursuits, the younger Penn had converted to the Society of Friends (Quakers), a radical Protestant sect, and used his prestige to spread its influence. He designed Pennsylvania as a refuge for Quakers, who were persecuted in England because they refused to serve in the army and would not pay taxes to support the Church of England.

Like the Puritans, the Quakers wanted to restore the simplicity and spirituality of early Christianity. But Quakers were not like Puritans or other Calvinists, who restricted salvation to a small elect. Rather, Quakers followed the teachings of the English visionaries George Fox and Margaret Fell, who argued that all men and women had been imbued by God with an inner "light" of grace or understanding. In Quaker meetings for worship there were no ministers or sermons; members sat in silence until moved to speak by the inner light.

Penn's Frame of Government (1681) extended Quaker radicalism into politics. In a world dominated by established churches, it guaranteed religious freedom to Christians of all denominations, allowing all property-owning men to vote and hold office. Thousands of Quakers, primarily from the middling classes of northwestern England, settled along the Delaware River in or near the city of Philadelphia, which Penn himself planned. The proprietor sold land at low prices and, to attract other Protestant settlers, advertised the advantages of his colony in Dutch and German. In 1683 migrants from the German province of Saxony founded Germantown (just outside Philadelphia) and were soon joined by thousands of other Germans attracted by fertile land and the prospect of freedom from religious warfare and persecution. Ethnic diversity, pacifism, and freedom of conscience made Pennsylvania the most open and democratic of the Restoration colonies.

FROM MERCANTILISM TO DOMINION

In the 1650s the English government began to control the external trade of its colonies to increase England's wealth. It imposed a set of policies—known as *mercantilism*—that regulated colonial commerce and manufacturing. According to mercantilist theory, the American colonies were to produce agricultural goods and raw materials, which English merchants would carry to the home country, where they would be reexported or manufactured into finished products. Consequently, the Navigation Act of 1651 sought to oust Dutch merchants from the colonial trade and give English traders a monopoly by requiring that goods imported into England or its American settlements be carried on English-owned ships. New parliamentary acts in 1660 and 1663 strengthened the ban on foreign merchants trading with the colonies and stipulated that colonial sugar, tobacco, and indigo could be shipped only to England. To provide even more business for English merchants, the acts also required that European exports to America pass through England. To enforce these mercantilist laws and raise money, the Revenue Act of 1673 imposed a "plantation duty" on sugar and tobacco exports and created a staff of customs officials to collect it.

The English government backed its mercantilist policy with force. In three commercial wars between 1652 and 1674 the English navy drove the Dutch from New Netherland and ended Dutch supremacy in the West African slave trade. Meanwhile, English merchants expanded their fleets and dominated Atlantic commerce.

Many Americans resisted these mercantilist laws as burdensome and intrusive. Edward Randolph, an English customs official in Massachusetts, reported that the colony's Puritan-dominated government took "no notice of the laws of trade," welcoming Dutch merchants, importing goods from the French sugar islands, and claiming that its royal charter exempted it from most of the new regulations. Outraged, Randolph called for English troops to "reduce Massachusetts to obedience." Instead of using force, English officials pursued a punitive legal strategy. In 1679 they denied the claim of Massachusetts Bay to the adjoining province of New Hampshire and created a separate colony there with a royal governor. To bring the Puritans in Massachusetts Bay directly under their control, in 1684 English officials persuaded the English Court of Chancery to annul the colony's charter on the grounds that the Puritan government had virtually outlawed the Church of England and violated the Navigation Acts.

The accession to the throne of James II (r. 1685–1688), an admirer of France's authoritarian Louis XIV and of "divine-right" monarchy, prompted English officials to create a centralized imperial system in America. Backed by the king, in 1686 they revoked the corporate charters of Connecticut and Rhode Island and merged them with the Massachusetts Bay and Plymouth colonies to form a new royal province, the Dominion of New England. Two years later the home government added New York and New Jersey to the Dominion, creating a single colony that stretched from the Delaware River to Maine.

This administrative innovation went far beyond mercantilism, which had respected the political autonomy of the various colonies while regulating their trade, and extended to America the authoritarian model of colonial rule imposed on Catholic Ireland. James II appointed Sir Edmund Andros, a former military officer, as governor of the Dominion and empowered him to abolish the existing colonial legislative assemblies and rule by decree. In Massachusetts Andros advocated public worship in the Church of England, offending Puritan Congregationalists, and banned town meetings, angering villagers who prized local self-rule. Even worse, the new governor challenged all land titles granted under the original Massachusetts charter. He offered to provide new deeds but only if the colonists would agree to pay a small annual fee. The Puritans protested to the king, but James refused to restore the old charter.

THE GLORIOUS REVOLUTION OF 1688

Fortunately for the colonists, James II angered English political leaders as much as Andros alienated the Americans. The king revoked the charters of many English towns, rejected the advice of Parliament, and aroused popular opposition by openly practicing Roman Catholicism. Then in 1688 James's foreign-born Catholic wife gave birth to a son, raising the prospect of a Catholic heir to the throne. In response Protestant parliamentary leaders carried out a quick and bloodless coup known as the Glorious Revolution. Backed by popular protests and the army they forced James into exile and enthroned Mary, his Protestant daughter by his first wife, and her Protestant Dutch husband, William of Orange. Queen Mary II and King William III agreed to rule as constitutional monarchs, accepting a Bill of Rights that limited royal prerogatives and increased personal liberties and parliamentary powers.

To justify their coup parliamentary leaders relied on the political philosopher John Locke. In his *Two Treatises on Government* (1690) Locke rejected divine-right theories of monarchical rule; he argued that the legitimacy of government rests on the consent of the governed and that individuals have inalienable natural rights to life, liberty, and property. Locke's celebration of individual rights and representative government had a lasting influence in America, where many political leaders wanted to expand the powers of the colonial assemblies.

More immediately, the Glorious Revolution sparked rebellions by colonists in Massachusetts, Maryland, and New York in 1689. When the news of the coup reached Boston in April 1689, Puritan leaders seized Governor Andros and shipped him back to England. Responding to American protests the new monarchs broke up the Dominion of New England. However, they refused to restore the old Puritan-dominated government, creating instead a new royal colony of Massachusetts (which included Plymouth and Maine). According to the new charter of 1692, the king would appoint the governor (as well as naval officers who were charged with enforcing customs regulations), and members of the Church of England would enjoy religious freedom. The charter restored the Massachusetts assembly but stipulated that it be elected by all male property owners (not just Puritan church members).

The uprising in Maryland had both economic and religious causes. Since 1660 tobacco prices had been falling, threatening the livelihoods of smallholders, tenant farmers, and former indentured servants, most of whom were Protestants. They resented the rising taxes and the high fees imposed by wealthy proprietary officials, who were primarily Catholics. When Parliament ousted James II, a Protestant Association in Maryland quickly removed the Catholic officials appointed by Lord

Baltimore. The Lords of Trade suspended Baltimore's proprietorship, imposed royal government, and established the Church of England as the colony's official church. This settlement lasted until 1715, when Benedict Calvert, the fourth Lord Baltimore, converted to the Anglican faith and the crown restored the proprietorship to the Calvert family.

In New York the rebellion against the Dominion of New England was led by English settlers angered by James's prohibition of representative institutions and was strongly supported by Dutch Protestants, who welcomed the succession of Queen Mary and her Dutch husband. Dutch artisans in New York City ousted Lieutenant Governor Nicholson, an Andros appointee and an alleged Catholic sympathizer, and rallied behind a new government led by Jacob Leisler, a migrant German soldier who had married into a prominent Dutch merchant family. At first Leisler won the support of all classes and ethnic groups. But when he freed debtors from prison and championed a more democratic town-meeting form of government, most wealthy merchants (who had traditionally controlled the city

A Prosperous Dutch Farmstead

Many Dutch farmers in the Hudson River Valley prospered because they enjoyed easy access to markets and exploited the labor of African American slaves (shown here tending chickens and sheep). To record his success, Martin Van Bergen of Leeds, New York, had this mural painted over his mantelpiece.

(New-York State Historical Association, Cooperstown, NY. Photo by Richard Walker.)

government) turned against him. In 1691 a newly appointed royal governor took control of New York from Leisler, instituted a representative assembly, and supported the wealthy merchants against the Dutch artisans. He had Leisler indicted for treason, and the former governor was convicted by an English-dominated jury, hanged, and then decapitated. A new merchant-dominated Board of Aldermen passed ordinances that lowered artisans' wages, ending the social uprising.

In both America and England the Glorious Revolution of 1688 and 1689 began a new phase in imperial history. The uprisings in Boston and New York toppled the authoritarian Dominion of New England and restored internal self-government. In England, the new constitutional monarchy promoted an empire based on commerce, launching a period of "salutary neglect" that gave free rein to enterprising merchants and financiers who developed the American colonies as a source of trade. Although Parliament created a new Board of Trade (1696) to supervise the American settlements, it had little success. Settlers and proprietors resisted the Board's attempt to install royal governors in every colony, as did many English political leaders, who feared an increase in royal power. Consequently, the empire remained diverse. Colonies that were of minor economic and political importance retained their corporate governments (Connecticut and Rhode Island) or proprietary institutions (Pennsylvania, Maryland, and the Carolinas) while royal governors ruled the lucrative staple-producing settlements in the West Indies and Virginia.

IMPERIAL WARS AND NATIVE PEOPLES

Between 1689 and 1815 Britain and France vied for dominance in western Europe in a series of wars. As these wars spread to the Western Hemisphere, they involved increasing numbers of Native American warriors, who were now armed with European guns and steel knives and hatchets. Many Indian people were also familiar enough with European goals and diplomacy to turn the fighting to their own advantage.

The first significant fighting in North America occurred during the War of the Spanish Succession (1702–1713), which pitted Britain against France and Spain. The English settlers in the Carolinas tried to protect their growing settlements by launching an attack against Spanish Florida. Seeking allies, the Carolinians armed the Creeks, a 9,000-member agrarian people who lived in matrilineal clans on the fertile lands along the present-day Georgia-Alabama border. A joint English-Creek expedition burned the town of St. Augustine but failed to capture the Spanish fort. Fearing that future Carolinian-backed Indian raids would endanger its colony of Florida and pose a threat to Havana in nearby Cuba, the Spanish reinforced St. Augustine and launched unsuccessful attacks against Charleston, South Carolina.

The Creeks had their own quarrels to settle with the pro-French Choctaws to the west and the Spanish-allied Apalachees to the south, and they took this opportunity to become the dominant tribe in the region. During the 1710s a force of Creek warriors destroyed the remaining Franciscan missions in northern Florida, attacked the Spanish settlement at Pensacola, and massacred the Apalachees, selling 1,000 Apalachee prisoners to South Carolina as slaves. Subsequently, a Carolina-supplied and Creek-led army attacked the Tuscarora people of North Carolina, killing 1,400 and selling another 1,000 into slavery. The Tuscaroras who survived migrated to the north and joined the Iroquois, who now became the Six Nations.

Native Americans also played a central role in the fighting in the northeast, where French Catholics from Canada confronted English Puritans from New England. Aided by the French, Abnaki and Mohawk warriors took revenge on their Puritan enemies. They destroyed English settlements along the coast of Maine and in 1704 attacked the western Massachusetts town of Deerfield, where they killed 48 residents and carried 112 into captivity ("The Unredeemed Captive," p. 62 in Chapter 2). New England responded to these raids by launching attacks against French settlements, joining with British naval forces and troops in 1710 to seize Port Royal in Nova Scotia. However, in the following year a major British-American expedition against the French stronghold at Quebec failed miserably.

The New York frontier remained quiet because France and England did not want to disrupt the lucrative fur trade and because most of the Iroquois nations had adopted a new policy of "aggressive neutrality." In 1701 the Iroquois peoples concluded a peace with France. Simultaneously, they reinterpreted their "covenant chain" of military alliances with the English governors of New York and the Algonquin tribes of New England. For the next half century the Iroquois exploited their central geographic location by trading with the English and the French but refusing to fight for either side. The Delaware leader Teedyuscung explained this strategy by showing his people a pictorial message from the Iroquois: "You see a Square in the Middle, meaning the Lands of the Indians; and at one End, the Figure of a Man, indicating the English; and at the other End, another, meaning the French. Let us join together to defend our land against both."

Despite the military stalemate in the colonies, Britain used victories in Europe to win major territorial and commercial concessions in the Americas in the Treaty of Utrecht (1713). From France, Britain obtained Newfoundland, Acadia (Nova Scotia), the Hudson Bay region of northern Canada, and access to the western Indian trade (see Map 3.1). From Spain, Britain acquired the strategic fortress of Gibraltar at the entrance to the Mediterranean and commercial privileges in Spanish America. These gains solidified Britain's commercial supremacy and brought peace to eastern North America for a generation.

The Imperial Slave Economy

Britain's increasing administrative and military interest in American affairs reflected the growing importance of its Atlantic trade in slaves and staple crops. European merchants had created a new agricultural and commercial order—the South Atlantic system, as historians call it—that produced sugar, tobacco, rice, and other

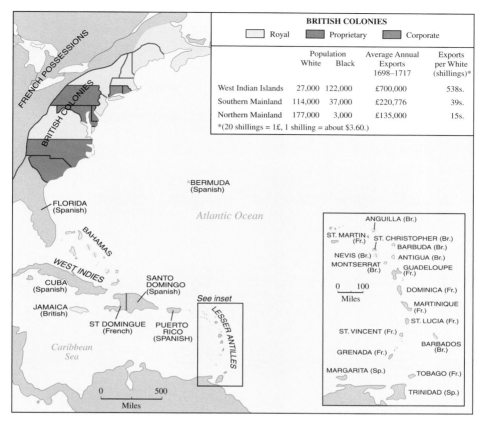

MAP 3.1
Britain's American Empire, 1713

Britain's West Indian possessions were small—mere dots on the Caribbean Sea. However, in 1713 they were by far the most valuable parts of the empire. Their sugar crops brought wealth to English merchants, trade to the northern colonies, and a brutal life (and early death) to African workers.

subtropical products. At the core of the new productive regime stood plantations staffed by enslaved labor from Africa.

THE SOUTH ATLANTIC SYSTEM

The components of the South Atlantic system were lands seized from Indians, laborers purchased from Africans, and capital invested by Europeans. Primarily in Brazil and the West Indies—but elsewhere as well—European adventurers and settlers took Indian lands to grow sugar and other valuable crops. Then European merchants and investors provided the organizational skill, ships, and money needed to

MAP 3.2
Africa in the Eighteenth Century

The tropical rain forest region of West Africa was home to scores of peoples and dozens of kingdoms. Some states, such as Dahomey, became aggressive slavers, taking tens of thousands of war captives and funneling them to the seacoast, where they were purchased by European traders. About 15 percent of the enslaved Africans died on the transatlantic voyage, the feared "Middle Passage"; most of the survivors labored on sugar plantations in Brazil and the British and French West Indies.

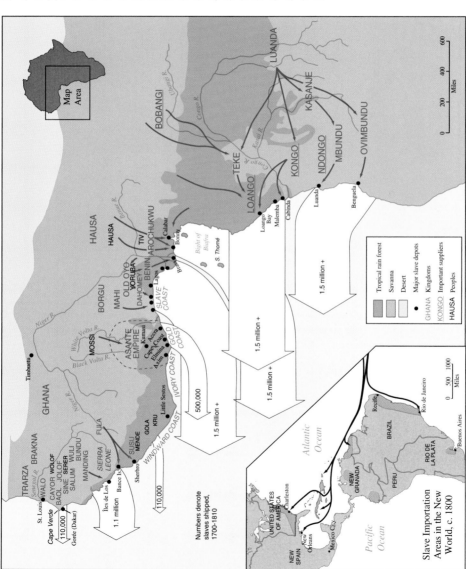

market the crops and to supply the sugar-growing plantations with European tools and equipment. To provide labor for the plantations, the merchants relied primarily on slaves from Africa. Between 1550 and 1700 Portuguese and Dutch traders annually transported about 10,000 Africans across the Atlantic. Subsequently British and French merchants took over this commerce, developing African-run slave-catching systems that extended far into the interior. Between 1700 and 1810 they carried about 7 million Africans—800,000 in the 1780s alone—to toil in the Americas (see Map 3.2).

Sugar was the cornerstone of the South Atlantic system, and its cultivation created a craving among Europeans—whose sweeteners had previously been limited to honey and fruit juices. Imitating Dutch and Portuguese planters in Brazil, English and French merchants developed sugar plantations in the West Indies, beginning with Barbados around 1650. By 1700 they were investing heavily in the Leeward Islands and Jamaica; by 1750 Jamaica, the largest island in the British West Indies, had 700 large sugar plantations worked by more than 105,000 enslaved Africans.

Sugar production required fertile land, many laborers to plant and cut the cane, and heavy equipment to process it into raw sugar and molasses. Because only wealthy merchants or landowners had the capital to outfit a plantation, a planter-merchant elite financed the sugar industry and drew annual profits of more than 10 percent on investments. As the Scottish economist Adam Smith declared in his famous treatise *The Wealth of Nations* (1776), sugar was the most profitable crop in Europe and America.

The South Atlantic system brought wealth to the entire European economy. To take England as an example, the owners of most of the plantations in the British West Indies lived as "absentees" in England, spending their profits there. Moreover, the British Navigation Acts required that American sugar be sold to English consumers or sent through England to continental markets, thus raising the level of trade. By 1750 reexports of American sugar and tobacco accounted for half of all British exports. Substantial profits also came from the slave trade, for the Royal African Company and other English traders sold male slaves in the West Indies for five times what it paid for them in Africa. Finally, the trade in American sugar and tobacco stimulated manufacturing. To transport slaves (and machinery and settlers) to America, English shipyards built hundreds of vessels. Thousands of English and Scottish men and women worked in related industries: building port facilities and warehouses, refining sugar and tobacco, distilling rum from molasses (a by-product of sugar), and manufacturing textiles and iron products for the growing markets in Africa and America. Commercial expansion also provided a supply of experienced sailors, helping to make the Royal Navy the most powerful fleet in Europe.

As the South Atlantic system enhanced prosperity in Europe, it brought economic and human tragedy to West Africa and the parts of East Africa, such as Madagascar, where slavers were also active. Between 1550 and 1870 the Atlantic slave trade uprooted about 15 million Africans, diminishing the wealth and population of the continent and provoking untold misery. Overall, the iron, tinware,

AMERICAN VOICES

The Slave Trade in Africa

VENTURE SMITH

*T*he demand for black laborers in the Americas disrupted African society, encouraging wars among peoples and forever changing millions of lives. The narrative of Venture Smith, who escaped slavery and lived out his life in London, describes the impact of African slaving on his own family and community.

I was born at Dukandarra, in Guinea, about the year 1729. My father's name was Saungm Furro, Prince of the tribe of Dukandara. My father had three wives. Polygamy was not un-common in that country, especially among the rich, as every man was allowed to keep as many wives as he could maintain. By his first wife he had three children. The eldest of them was myself, named by my father, Broteer. . . .

The first thing worthy of notice which I remember was, a contention between my father and mother, on account of my father marrying his third wife without the consent of his first and eldest, which was contrary to the custom generally observed among my countrymen. In consequence of this rupture, my mother left her husband and country, and travelled away with her three children to the eastward. I was then five years old . . . ; [a year later] the difference between my parents had been made up . . . and I was once more restored to my paternal dwelling in peace and happiness. . . .

[Shortly afterwards] my father learned that the place had been invaded by a numerous army, from a nation not far distant, . . . instigated by some white nation who equipped them [with guns] and sent them to subdue and possess the country. . . . The army of the enemy was large, I should suppose consisting of about six thousand men. Their leader was called Baukurre. After destroying the old prince [my father], they decamped and imme-diately marched towards the sea, lying to the west, taking with them myself and the women prisoners. . . .

All of us were then put into the castle, and kept for market. On a certain time I and other prisoners were . . . rowed to a vessel belonging to Rhode Island. . . . I was brought on board by one Robertson Mumford, steward of said vessel, for four gallons of rum, and a piece of calico, and called VENTURE, on account of his having purchased me with his own private venture. Thus I came by my name. All the slaves that were bought for that vessel's cargo, were two hundred and sixty.

SOURCE: John Bayles, ed., *Black Slave Narratives* (New York: Macmillan, 1970), pp. 36–44.

rum, cloth, and other European products that entered the African economy in exchange for slaves were worth from one-tenth (in the 1680s) to one-third (by the 1780s) as much as the goods those slaves subsequently produced in America.

In addition, the slave trade changed the nature of West African society by pro-moting centralized states and military conquest. In 1739 an observer noted that

"whenever the King of Barsally wants Goods or Brandy . . . the King goes and ran-
sacks some of his enemies' towns, seizing the people and selling them." War and
slaving became a way of life in Dahomey, where the royal house made the sale of
slaves a state monopoly and used the resulting access to European guns to create a
regime of military despotism. Dahomey's army, which included a contingent of
5,000 women, systematically raided the interior for captives, exporting thousands
of slaves each year (see Map 3.2 and American Voices, "The Slave Trade in Africa").
The Asante kings also used the firearms and wealth acquired through the Atlantic
trade to create a bureaucratic empire of 3 million to 5 million people. Yet slaving
remained a choice for Africans, not a necessity. The old and still powerful Kingdom
of Benin, famous for its cast bronzes and carved ivory, resolutely opposed the slave
trade, prohibiting the export of male slaves for over a century.

The trade in humans changed many aspects of African life. Class divisions
hardened as people of noble birth enslaved and sold those of lesser status. Gender
relations shifted as well. Men constituted two-thirds of the slaves sent across the
Atlantic both because European planters paid more for men and because African
traders directed women captives into local slave markets. The resulting imbalance
between the sexes allowed some African men to take several wives, changing the

An African King

This striking bronze
plaque, circa 1550–1680,
from Benin, an important
kingdom in West Central
Africa, depicts a mounted
king, his attendants, and
(probably) his children.
(The Metropolitan Museum of
Art, The Michael C. Rockefeller
Memorial Collection, Gift of
Nelson A. Rockefeller, 1965.
[1978.412.309] Photograph
© 1983 The Metropolitan
Museum of Art)

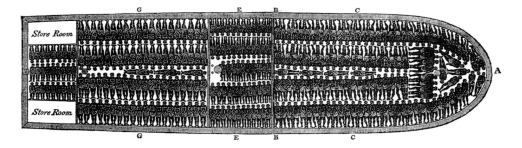

Two Views of the Middle Passage

As the slave trade boomed during the eighteenth century, ship designers packed in more and more human cargo, treating enslaved Africans with no more respect than hogsheads of sugar or tobacco. By contrast, a watercolor of 1846, painted by a ship's officer on a voyage to Brazil captures the humanity and dignity of the enslaved Africans.

(Top: Peabody Essex Museum; bottom: The Art Archive)

nature of marriage. Most important, the Atlantic trade prompted harsher forms of slavery in Africa, eroding the dignity of human life there as well as in the Western Hemisphere.

But those Africans sold into the heart of the South Atlantic system had the bleakest fate. Torn from their village homes, captives were marched in chains to coastal ports such as Elmina on the Gold Coast. From there they made the perilous Middle Passage to the New World in hideously overcrowded ships. There was little to eat and drink, and the stench of excrement was nearly unbearable. Some captives jumped overboard, choosing to drown rather than endure more suffering. Nearly a million (15 percent of the 8 million who crossed the Atlantic between 1700 and 1810) died on the journey, mostly from dysentery, smallpox, or scurvy.

For the survivors of the Middle Passage, life only got worse on arrival in northwest Brazil or the West Indies because plantation society was based on relentless exploitation and systematic violence. Planting and harvesting sugarcane required intense labor under a tropical sun, with a pace set by the overseer's whip. With sugar prices high and the cost of slaves low, many planters worked slaves to death and then imported more. Between 1708 and 1735 about 85,000 Africans were brought into Barbados, where they constituted nearly 90 percent of the inhabitants, but the black population increased only from 42,000 to 46,000 during these decades.

SLAVERY IN THE CHESAPEAKE AND SOUTH CAROLINA

As the British slave trade increased after 1700, planters in Virginia and Maryland imported thousands of Africans and created a "slave society." By 1720 Africans numbered 20 percent of the Chesapeake population, and slavery had become a defining principle of the social order, not just one of several forms of labor. Equally important, slavery was increasingly defined in racial terms. A Virginia law of 1692 prohibited sexual intercourse between English and Africans, and in 1705 another statute explicitly defined virtually all resident Africans as slaves: "All servants imported or brought into this country by sea or land who were not Christians in their native country shall be accounted and be slaves."

Living conditions in Maryland and Virginia were much less severe than in the West Indies, and slaves lived relatively long lives. In terms of labor to produce a harvest, tobacco was not as physically demanding a crop as sugar. Slaves planted the young seedlings in the spring, hoed and weeded the crop throughout the summer, and in the fall picked and hung up the leaves to cure over the winter. Epidemic diseases did not spread easily because the plantations were small and dispersed. Also, because tobacco profits were low, planters could not constantly buy new slaves and therefore treated those they had less harshly. Some tobacco planters attempted to increase their workforce through reproduction, purchasing a higher proportion of female slaves than sugar planters did and encouraging large families. In 1720 women made up about a third of the African population of Maryland, and the black population had begun to increase naturally. One absentee owner instructed his plantation agent "to be kind and indulgent to the breeding wenches, and not to force them when with child upon any service or hardship that will be injurious to them." And, he added, "the children are to be well looked after." By midcentury American-born slaves formed a majority among Chesapeake blacks.

Slaves in South Carolina labored under much more oppressive conditions. The colony had grown slowly until 1700, when Africans from rice-growing societies, who knew how to plant, harvest, and process that nutritious grain, turned it into a profitable export crop. To expand rice production, white planters imported tens of thousands of slaves. By 1720 Africans made up a majority of the population of South Carolina, with 80 percent of those living in the rice-growing areas, where many of them met an early death. Mosquito-borne epidemic diseases swept through the swampy lowlands, taking thousands of African lives. Overwork killed many more slaves because moving tons of dirt to build irrigation works was brutally hard labor. As in the West Indies, there were many deaths and few births, and the importation of new slaves constantly "re-Africanized" the black population.

South Carolina slaveowners preferred laborers from the Gold Coast and Gambia, who had a reputation as hard workers with farming experience (see Map 3.2). But as African sources of slaves shifted southward after 1730, more than 30 percent of the colony's workforce came from the Congo and Angola. As a result of such changes in the slave trade, there were no American colonies in which any African people or language group became dominant. Moreover, many white planters consciously enhanced this cultural diversity to prevent slave revolts. "The safety of the Plantations," declared a widely read English pamphlet, "depends upon having Negroes from all parts of Guiny, who do not understand each other's languages and Customs and cannot agree to Rebel."

AFRICAN AMERICAN COMMUNITY

In fact, slaves initially did not regard each other as "Africans" or "blacks" but as members of a specific people: Mende, Hausa, Ibo, Yoruba. Gradually, however, enslaved peoples found it in their interest to transcend these cultural barriers. In the West Indies and also in the lowlands of South Carolina, the largely African-born population created new languages that combined English and African words in an African grammatical structure. Thus, South Carolina blacks created the Gullah dialect. In the Chesapeake, where there were more American-born blacks (and in the northern colonies, which had small numbers of slaves), many Africans gradually gave up their native tongues for English. A European visitor to mid-eighteenth century Virginia reported with surprise that "all the blacks spoke very good English."

The acquisition of a common language, whether Gullah or English, was a prerequisite for the creation of an African American community. A more equal sex ra-

Slave Dwellings at Mulberry Plantation

Most pictures of plantations depict the imposing mansions of the slaveowners. However, this view of Mulberry plantation in South Carolina steals a look behind the big house to the meager dwellings of the slaves, whose labor produced the wealth of the plantation.
(The Gibbes Museum of Art, Carolina Art Association)

tio, which would encourage stable families, was another. In South Carolina a high death rate undermined ties of family and kinship, but after 1725 blacks in the Chesapeake colonies created strong nuclear families and extended kin relationships. These "African Americans" gradually developed a culture of their own, passing on family names, traditions, and knowledge to the next generation.

As enslaved blacks forged an identity in an alien land, their lives continued to be shaped by their African past. This heritage took tangible form in wood carvings inspired by African motifs, the large wooden mortars and pestles that slaves used to hull rice, and the design of shacks, which often had rooms arranged from front to back in a distinctive "I" pattern (not side by side, as was common in English houses). Traditional African values also persisted, as some slaves retained Muslim religious beliefs, and many more relied on the spiritual powers of conjurers, who knew the ways of African gods. Other slaves adopted Protestant Christianity but reshaped its doctrines, ethics, and rituals to fit their needs and create a spiritually rich and long-lasting religious culture of their own.

Yet there were drastic limits on African American creativity because slaves were denied education and accumulated few material goods. A well-traveled European who visited a slave hut in Virginia in the late eighteenth century found it to be

> more miserable than the most miserable of the cottages of our peasants. The husband and wife sleep on a mean pallet, the children on the ground; a very bad fireplace, some utensils for cooking. . . . They work all week, not having a single day for themselves except for holidays.

Slaves resisted the rigorous work routine at their peril. To punish slaves who disobeyed, refused to work, or ran away, planters resorted to the lash and the amputation of fingers, toes, and ears. Declaring the chronic runaway Ballazore an "incorrigeble rogue," Robert "King" Carter of Virginia ordered all his toes cut off: "nothing less than dismembering will reclaim him." Thomas Jefferson, who witnessed such cruelty on his father's plantation in mid-eighteenth-century Virginia, noted that each generation of whites was "nursed, educated, and daily exercised in tyranny," for the relationship "between master and slave is a perpetual exercise of the most unremitting despotism on the one part, and degrading submission on the other."

The extent of violence by whites depended on the size and density of the slave population. Because their numbers were so small, blacks in rural areas of New York, Pennsylvania, and other northern colonies endured low status but little violence. Conversely, assertive slaves in the predominantly African West Indian islands routinely suffered branding with hot irons. In the lowlands of South Carolina, where Africans outnumbered Europeans eight to one, black workers were forbidden to leave the plantation without special passes and risked punishment from rural patrols if they did. Slaves dealt with their plight in a variety of ways. Some newly arrived Africans fled to the frontier, where they tried to establish African villages or, more often, married into Indian tribes. Blacks familiar with white ways, especially those fluent in English, fled to towns, where they tried to pass as free blacks. But the great majority of African Americans worked out their destinies as enslaved laborers on rural plantations through a process of continual negotiation with their owners. Sometimes they agreed to do extra work in return for better food and clothes; at other times they seized a small privilege and dared the master to revoke it; or they protested their bondage silently by working slowly or stealing. Still others attacked their owners or overseers when provoked beyond endurance, even though this was punishable by mutilation or death. And despite the fact that whites were armed and, outside of coastal South Carolina, more numerous than Africans, some blacks plotted rebellion.

Predictably, South Carolina became the setting for the largest slave uprising of the eighteenth century—the Stono rebellion. The governor of Spanish Florida instigated the revolt in the late 1730s by promising freedom and land to slaves who ran away from their English owners. By February 1739 at least sixty-nine slaves had escaped to St. Augustine, and rumors circulated "that a Conspiracy was formed by Negroes in Carolina to rise and make their way out of the province." When war between England and Spain broke out later that year, seventy-five Africans—some of them Portuguese-speaking Christians from the African Kingdom of Kongo—killed a number of whites near the Stono River, stole guns and ammunition, and marched south toward Florida "with Colours displayed and two Drums beating." Unrest swept the countryside, but the white militia killed many of the Stono rebels and dispersed the rest, preventing a general uprising. Frightened whites imported fewer new slaves and tightened plantation discipline. For Africans the price of active resistance was high.

THE SOUTHERN GENTRY

As the southern colonies became full-fledged slave societies, the character of life changed for whites as well as blacks. As settlement in the Chesapeake region moved inland after 1675, away from the disease-ridden swampy lowlands, English migrants lived much longer and formed stable families and communities. Similarly, many white planters in South Carolina improved their health by transferring their residence to Charleston during the hot, mosquito-ridden summer months. As their longevity increased, men reassumed their customary control of family property. When death rates had been high, many husbands had named their wives as executors of their estates and legal guardians of their children and had given their widows large inheritances. After 1700 most wealthy planters named male kin as executors and guardians and once again gave priority to male children with respect to inheritance, limiting a widow's portion to the traditional one-third share during her lifetime.

The reappearance of strict patriarchy within the family mirrored broader social developments. The planter elite now stood at the top of a social hierarchy very much like that of Europe, exercising authority over a small yeoman class, a much larger group of white tenant farmers, and a growing host of enslaved black laborers—the American equivalent of oppressed peasants and serfs. Wealthy planters used Africans to grow food as well as tobacco; build houses, wagons, and tobacco casks; and make shoes and clothes. By increasing the self-sufficiency of their plantations, the planter elite survived the depressed tobacco market between 1660 and 1720. Small-scale planters who used family labor to grow tobacco fared less well, falling deeper into debt to their creditors among the elite.

To prevent another rebellion like Bacon's uprising, the southern gentry paid attention to the concerns of middling and poor whites. They urged smallholders to become slaveowners, and by 1770 no less than 60 percent of the English families in the Chesapeake owned at least one slave, giving them a personal stake in this exploitative labor system. In addition, the gentry gradually reduced the taxes paid by poorer whites; in Virginia the annual poll tax paid by every free man fell from 45 pounds of tobacco in 1675 to 5 pounds in 1750. And the political elite allowed poor yeomen and some tenants to vote. The strategy of the leading families—the Carters, Lees, Randolphs, Robinsons—was to curry favor with these voters at election time, bribing them with rum, money, and the promise of favorable legislation. In return, they expected yeomen and tenants to elect them to political office and defer to their authority. This "horse-trading" solidified the social authority of the planter elite, which used its control of the House of Burgesses to cut the political power of the royal governor—bargaining with him over patronage and land grants.

Even as the expansion of voting and slaveholding created new ties between rich and poor whites, wealthy Chesapeake planters set themselves apart from their less affluent neighbors. Until the 1720s the ranks of the gentry were filled with boisterous, aggressive men who enjoyed many of the amusements of common folk— from hunting, hard drinking, and gambling on horse races to sharing tales of their manly prowess in seducing female servants and slaves. As time passed, however, affluent Chesapeake planters took on the trappings of wealth, modeling themselves after the English aristocracy. Beginning in the 1720s they replaced their modest wooden houses with mansions of brick and mortar and sent their sons to London to be educated as lawyers and gentlemen. Most of the southern men who were educated in England returned to America, married, and followed in their fathers' footsteps, managing plantations, socializing with other members of the gentry class, and participating in politics.

Wealthy Chesapeake and South Carolina women also emulated the elegant and refined ways of the English gentry. They read English newspapers and fashionable magazines, wore English clothes, and dined in the English fashion, with an elaborate afternoon tea. To improve their daughters' chances of finding a desirable marriage partner, they hired English tutors to teach them etiquette. Once married, affluent gentry women deferred to their husbands' authority, reared pious children, and maintained elaborate social networks—gradually creating the new ideal of the southern genteel woman. Using the profits of the South Atlantic system, the planter elite formed an increasingly well-educated, refined, and stable ruling class.

THE NORTHERN MARITIME ECONOMY

The South Atlantic system had a broad geographic reach. As early as the 1640s, New England farmers provided bread, lumber, fish, and meat to the sugar islands. As a West Indian explained in 1647, planters in the islands "had rather buy food at very dear rates than produce it by labour, so infinite is the profit of sugar works." By 1700 the economies of the West Indies and New England were tightly interwoven. After 1720 farmers and merchants in New York, New Jersey, and Pennsylvania entered the West Indian trade, shipping wheat, corn, and bread to the sugar islands.

The South Atlantic system tied the whole British empire together economically. In return for the sugar they exported to England, West Indian planters received bills of exchange (credit slips) from London merchant houses. The planters used those bills to buy slaves from transatlantic slavers and also to reimburse North American

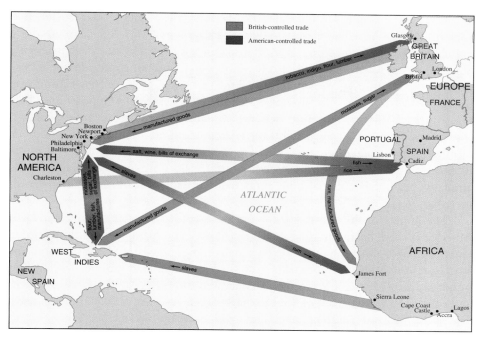

MAP 3.3
The Rise of the American Merchant, c. 1750

In accordance with mercantilist doctrine, British merchants controlled most of the transatlantic commerce in manufactures, sugar, tobacco, and slaves. However, American merchants seized control of other routes, dominating the trade between the mainland and West Indies, importing African slaves into Rhode Island, and carrying fish and rice to southern Europe.

farmers and merchants for their provisions and shipping services. Farmers and merchants then exchanged the bills for British manufactures, primarily textiles and iron goods, thus completing the cycle (see Map 3.3).

The West Indian trade created the first American merchant fortunes and the first urban industries. Merchants in Boston, Newport, Providence, Philadelphia, and New York invested their profits from the West Indian trade in new ships and in factories that refined raw sugar into finished loaves (which previously had been imported from England) and distilled West Indian molasses into rum. By the 1740s Boston distillers were exporting more than half a million gallons of rum annually. In addition, merchants in smaller ports, such as Salem and Marblehead, built a major fishing industry, providing salted mackerel and cod to feed the slaves of the sugar islands and to export to southern Europe. Southern merchants transformed Baltimore into a major port by developing a bustling trade in wheat, while Charleston traders exported deerskins, indigo, and rice to European markets.

The expansion of Atlantic commerce in the eighteenth century fueled rapid growth in American port cities and coastal towns. By 1750 Newport, Rhode Island,

and Charleston, South Carolina, had nearly 10,000 residents apiece, Boston had 15,000, and New York had almost 18,000. The largest port was Philadelphia, whose population reached 30,000 by 1776, the size of a large European provincial city. Smaller coastal towns emerged as centers of the shipbuilding and lumber industries. By the 1740s seventy sawmills dotted the Piscataqua River in New Hampshire, providing low-cost wood for homes, warehouses, and especially shipbuilding. Taking advantage of the Navigation Acts, which allowed colonists to build and own trading vessels, scores of shipwrights turned out ocean-going ships, while hundreds of other artisans made ropes, sails, and metal fittings for the new fleet. Shipyards in Boston and Philadelphia launched about 15,000 tons of ocean-going vessels annually; eventually colonial-built ships made up about one-third of the British merchant fleet.

The impact of the South Atlantic system extended into the interior of North America. A small fleet of trading vessels sailed back and forth between Philadelphia and the villages along the Delaware Bay, exchanging cargoes of European goods for barrels of flour and wheat for sale in both the West Indies and Europe. By the 1750s hundreds of professional teamsters in Maryland moved 370,000 bushels of wheat and corn and 16,000 barrels of flour to market each year—over 10,000 wagon trips. To service this traffic entrepreneurs and artisans set up taverns, horse stables, and barrel-making shops in small towns along the wagon roads, providing additional jobs. The prosperous interior town of Lancaster, Pennsylvania boasted more than 200 artisans, both German and English. The South Atlantic system thus provided not only markets for farmers (by far the largest group of northern residents) but also opportunities for merchants, artisans, and workers in country towns and seaport cities.

At the top of seaport society stood a small group of wealthy landowners and prosperous merchants. By 1750 about forty merchants controlled over 50 percent of Philadelphia's trade and had taxable assets averaging £10,000, a huge sum at the time. Like the Chesapeake gentry, these urban merchants imitated the British upper classes, importing design books from England and building Georgian-style mansions to showcase their wealth. Their wives created a genteel culture, decorating their houses with fine furniture and entertaining guests at elegant dinners.

Artisan and shopkeeper families formed the middle ranks of seaport society and numbered nearly half the population. Innkeepers, butchers, seamstresses, shoemakers, weavers, bakers, carpenters, masons, and dozens of other specialists socialized among themselves, formed mutual self-help societies, and worked to gain a "competency"—an income sufficient to maintain their families in modest comfort and dignity. Wives and husbands often worked as a team, teaching the "mysteries of the craft" to their children. Some artisans aspired to wealth and status, an entrepreneurial ethic that prompted them to hire apprentices and expand production, and the most prosperous owned their own houses and shops (sometimes run by widows continuing a family business). However, most craft workers were not well-to-do, and many of them were quite poor. In his entire lifetime a tailor was lucky to accumulate £30 worth of property—far less than the £2,000 owned by an ordinary merchant or the £300 accumulated by a successful blacksmith.

Laboring men and women formed the lowest ranks of urban society. Merchants needed hundreds of dockworkers to unload manufactured goods and molasses from inbound ships and reload the ships with barrels of wheat, fish, and rice for export. They often filled these demanding jobs with black slaves—who numbered 10 percent of the workforce in Philadelphia and New York City—or they hired unskilled men who worked for wages. Poor women—whether single, married, or widowed— could eke out a living by washing clothes, spinning wool, or working as servants or prostitutes. To make ends meet, most laboring families sent their children out to work at an early age. Indispensable to the economy yet without homes of their own, these urban laborers lived in crowded tenements in back alleys. In good times hard work brought family security or enough money to drink cheap New England rum in waterfront taverns.

Periods of stagnant commerce affected everyone, threatening merchants with bankruptcy and artisans with irregular work. For laborers and seamen, whose household budgets left no margin for sickness or unemployment, depressed trade meant hunger, dependence on charity handed out by town-appointed overseers of the poor, and—for the most desperate—a life of petty thievery. Involvement in the South Atlantic system between 1660 and 1750 brought economic uncertainty as well as jobs and opportunities to northern workers and farmers.

The New Politics of Empire, 1713–1750

The triumph of the South Atlantic system of production and trade changed the politics of empire. British ministers, pleased with the prosperous commerce in staple crops, were content to rule the colonies with a gentle hand. The colonists enjoyed a significant degree of self-government and economic autonomy, which put them in a position to challenge the rules of the mercantilist system.

THE RISE OF COLONIAL ASSEMBLIES

Before 1689 the authority of the representative assemblies in most colonies was weak. Political power rested in the hands of proprietors, royal governors, and authoritarian elites, reflecting the traditional view that "Authority should Descend from Kings and Fathers to Sons and Servants," as a royal-minded political philosopher put it. In the Glorious Revolution of 1688 the political faction known as the Whigs challenged that hierarchical outlook in England, winning the fight for a constitutional monarchy that limited the authority of the crown. English Whigs did not advocate democracy but did believe that the substantial property owners represented by the House of Commons should have some political power, especially over the levying of taxes. When Whig politicians forced William and Mary to accept a Declaration of Rights in 1689, they strengthened the powers of the Commons at the expense of the crown.

American representative assemblies also wished to limit the powers of the crown and insisted on maintaining their authority over taxes, refusing to fund military projects and other programs advocated by royal governors. Gradually the colonial legislatures won partial control of the budget and the appointment of local officials, angering imperial bureaucrats and absentee proprietors. "The people in power in America," complained the proprietor William Penn during a struggle with the Pennsylvania Assembly, "think nothing taller than themselves but the Trees." In Massachusetts during the 1720s the assembly refused repeatedly to obey the king's instructions to provide a permanent salary for the royal governor; subsequently legislatures in North Carolina, New Jersey, and Pennsylvania declined to pay their governors any salary for several years.

The rising power of the colonial assemblies created an elitist rather than a democratic political system. Although most property-owning white men had the right to vote after 1700, only men of considerable wealth and status stood for election. In Virginia in the 1750s seven members of the influential slaveowning Lee family sat in the House of Burgesses and, along with other powerful families, dominated its major committees. In New England descendants of the original Puritans had intermarried and formed a core of political leaders. "Go into every village in New England," John Adams said in 1765, "and you will find that the office of justice of the peace, and even the place of representative, have generally descended from generation to generation, in three or four families at most."

However, neither elitist assemblies nor wealthy property owners could impose unpopular edicts on the people. The crowd actions that had overthrown the Dominion of New England in 1689 were a regular part of political life in America and were used to enforce community values. In New York mobs closed houses of prostitution, while in Salem, Massachusetts, they ran people with infectious diseases out of town. In Boston in 1710 crowds prevented merchants from exporting grain during a wartime shortage, and in New Jersey in the 1730s and 1740s angry mobs obstructed proprietors who were forcing tenants from disputed lands. When officials in Boston attempted to restrict the sale of farm produce to a designated public marketplace, a crowd destroyed the building and defied the authorities to arrest them. "If you touch One you shall touch All," an anonymous letter warned the sheriff, "and we will show you a Hundred Men where you can show one" (see American Voices, "A 'Leveling' Spirit in the Colonies").

Such expressions of popular power, combined with the growing power of the assemblies, undermined the old authoritarian system. By the 1750s most colonies had representative political institutions that were broadly responsive to popular pressure and increasingly immune to British control.

AMERICAN VOICES

A "Leveling" Spirit in the Colonies

GOVERNOR JOSEPH DUDLEY AND JOHN WINCHESTER

*I*n 1705 legal authorities in Massachusetts prosecuted two woodcutters, John Winchester *and Thomas Trowbridge, for insubordination for defying Royal Governor Joseph Dudley. The following extracts from the court testimony serve to illustrate both upper-class disdain for ordinary folk and popular resistance to arbitrary authority.*

Account of Governor Joseph Dudley:

The Charet [coach] wherein the Governour was had three sitters and their Servants . . . drawn by four horses, one very unruly, & was attended only at that instant by Mr. William Dudley, the Governour's son.

When the Governour saw the two carts approaching he directed his son to bid them to give him the way. . . . Who accordingly did Ride up & told them the Govr was there, & they must give way. Immediately upon it the second Carter came up to ye first . . . & one of them says aloud he would not go out the way for the Governour whereupon the Govr came out of the Charet and told Winchester he must give way to the Charet. Winchester answered boldly . . . I am as good flesh & blood as you. I will not give way. You may go out the way, & came towards the Governour. Whereupon the Governour drew his sword to secure himself & command the Road & went forward . . . and again commanded them to give way. Winchester answered that he was a Christian & would not give way & as the Governour came toward him he advanced & at length laid hold of the Govr & broke the sword in his hands. . . . And this is averred upon the honour of the Governour. . . .

Then came up John Winchester . . . who gives the following account.

. . . I left my cart and . . . asked Mr. William Dudley why he was so rash. He replied this dog [Trowbridge] won't turn out the way for the Governor. . . . I then told his excellency, if he would have patience a minute or two I would clear that way for him. . . . The Governour followed me with his drawn sword and said run the dogs through and with his naked sword stabbed me in the back. I facing about, he struck me on the head . . . giving me there a bloody wound. . . . I caught hold of his sword and broke it.

SOURCE: David Brion Davis and Steven Mintz, *The Boisterous Sea of Liberty: A Documentary History of America from Discovery Through the Civil War* (New York: Oxford University Press, 1998), pp. 105–06.

SALUTARY NEGLECT

British colonial policy during the reigns of George I (r. 1714–1727) and George II (r. 1727–1760) contributed significantly to the rise of American self-government. Royal bureaucrats relaxed their supervision of internal colonial affairs, focusing in-

Sir Robert Walpole, the King's Minister

All eyes are on Walpole (left) as he offers advice to the Speaker of the House of Commons. A brilliant politician, Walpole used patronage to command a majority in the Commons and to win the support of George I and George II—the German-speaking monarchs from the duchy of Hanover. Walpole's personal motto, "Let sleeping dogs lie," helps to explain his colonial policy of salutary neglect. (National Trust Photographic Library/John Hammond)

stead on defense and trade. Two generations later the British political philosopher Edmund Burke would praise this strategy as "salutary [healthy] neglect."

Salutary neglect was a by-product of the political system developed by Sir Robert Walpole, the leader of the British Whigs in the House of Commons and the king's chief minister between 1720 and 1742. By strategically dispensing appointments and pensions in the name of the king, Walpole won parliamentary support for his policies. But Walpole's politically driven use of patronage weakened the imperial system by filling the Board of Trade and the royal governorships with men of little talent. When Governor Gabriel Johnson went to North Carolina in the 1730s, he vowed to curb the powers of the assembly and "make a mighty change in the face of affairs." However, Johnson was soon discouraged by the lack of support from the Board of Trade. Forsaking reform, Johnson decided "to do nothing which can be reasonably blamed, and leave the rest to time, and a new set of inhabitants."

Walpole's tactics also weakened the empire by undermining faith in the integrity of the political system. Radical-minded English Whigs were the first to raise the alarm. They argued that Walpole had betrayed the constitutional monarchy established by the Glorious Revolution by using patronage and bribery to create a strong Court (or crown) Party. A Country Party of landed gentlemen likewise warned that Walpole's policies of high taxes and a bloated royal bureaucracy threatened the liberties of the British people. Politically minded colonists adopted these arguments as their own, maintaining that royal governors likewise abused their patronage powers. To preserve American liberty, they tried to enhance the powers of the provincial representative assemblies, thus preparing the way for later demands for political equality within the British empire.

PROTECTING THE MERCANTILE SYSTEM OF TRADE

Walpole's main preoccupation was to protect British commercial interests in America from the military threats posed by the Spanish and French colonies and from the economic dangers posed by the unwillingness of the American colonists to abide by the Acts of Trade and Navigation.

One of Walpole's major initiatives was to provide a subsidy for the new colony of Georgia, chartered in 1732. In the early 1730s General James Oglethorpe and social reformers seeking a refuge for Britain's poor won King George II's support for a colony south of the Carolinas. Envisioning a society of small farms worked by independent landowners and white indentured servants, the trustees of Georgia limited most land grants to 500 acres and initially outlawed slavery.

Walpole arranged for Parliament to subsidize Georgia because he wanted to protect the valuable rice colony of South Carolina. Spain had long resented the British presence in Carolina and was outraged by the expansion into Georgia, where Spanish Franciscans had Indian missions. In addition, English merchants had steadily increased their trade in slaves and manufactured goods to Spain's colonies in Mesoamerica, eventually controlling two-thirds of that trade. To resist Britain's commercial and geographic expansion, in 1739 Spanish naval forces sparked the so-called War of Jenkins' Ear by mutilating Robert Jenkins, an English sea captain who was trading illegally with the Spanish West Indies.

Yielding to Parliamentary pressure Walpole used this provocation to launch a predatory war against Spain's American empire. In 1740 British regulars commanded by Governor Oglethorpe attacked St. Augustine without success, in part because South Carolina whites—still shaken by the Stono Revolt—refused to commit militia units to the expedition. In 1741 the governors of the other mainland colonies raised 2,500 volunteers, who joined a British naval force in an assault on the prosperous Spanish seaport of Cartagena (in present-day Colombia). The attack failed, and instead of enriching themselves with Spanish booty hundreds of colonial troops died of tropical diseases.

The War of Jenkins' Ear became part of a general European conflict, the War of the Austrian Succession, bringing a new threat from France. French naval forces roamed the West Indies, seeking without success to conquer a British sugar-producing island, but initially there was little fighting along the long frontier between the Anglo-American colonies and French Canada. Then in 1745, 3,000 New England militiamen, supported by a British naval squadron, captured the powerful French naval fortress of Louisbourg, which protected the entrance into the St. Lawrence River. The Treaty of Aix-la-Chapelle (1748) returned Louisbourg to France, but the war secured the territorial integrity of Georgia by reaffirming British military superiority over Spain.

At the same time, Walpole and other British officials confronted an unexpected American threat to British economic ascendancy. According to the mercantilist Navigation Acts, the colonies were expected to produce agricultural goods and other raw materials that British merchants would carry to England and Scotland, where they would be consumed, exported to Europe, or turned into manufactured goods. To enforce the monopoly enjoyed by British manufacturers, Parliament passed a series of acts that prohibited Americans from selling colonial-made textiles (1699), hats (1732), and iron products such as plows, axes, and skillets (1750).

However, the Navigation Acts had a major loophole because they allowed Americans to own ships and transport goods. Colonial merchants exploited those provisions, securing 95 percent of the commerce between the mainland and the West Indies and 75 percent of the trade in manufactures shipped from London and Bristol. Quite unintentionally, the Atlantic trade had created a dynamic community of colonial merchants (see Map 3.3).

Moreover, by the 1720s the British sugar islands could not use all of the flour, fish, and meat produced by the rapidly growing mainland colonies, and so colonial merchants sold them in the French West Indies. These supplies helped French planters produce low-cost sugar, enabling them to undercut British sales in Europe. When American rum distillers began to buy cheap French molasses rather than molasses from the British sugar islands, planters petitioned Parliament for help. The resulting Molasses Act of 1733 permitted the mainland colonies to export fish and farm products to the French islands but—to enhance the competitiveness of British molasses—placed a high tariff on imports of French molasses. American merchants and public officials protested that the act would cut farm exports and cripple their distilling industry, making it more difficult for colonists to purchase British goods. When Parliament ignored their petitions, American merchants turned to smuggling, importing French molasses and bribing customs officials to ignore the new tax. Luckily for the Americans, sugar prices rose sharply in the late 1730s, enriching planters in the British West Indies, so the act was not enforced.

The lack of adequate currency in the colonies led to another confrontation. American merchants sent most of the gold and silver coins and bills of exchange they earned in the West Indian trade to Britain to pay for manufactured goods, draining the domestic money supply. To remedy this problem, the assemblies of ten colonies established "land banks" that lent paper money to farmers, taking their land as collateral. Farmers used the paper money to buy tools or livestock or to pay their creditors, thereby stimulating trade. But some assemblies, such as that of Rhode Island, issued large amounts of currency, causing it to fall in value, and required merchants to accept it as legal tender. Creditors, especially English merchants, rightly complained that they were being forced to accept worthless currency. In 1751 Parliament passed a Currency Act that prevented all the New England colonies from establishing new land banks and prohibited the use of public currency to pay private debts.

These economic conflicts and the growing assertiveness of the colonial assemblies angered a new generation of British political leaders, who believed that the colonies already had too much autonomy. In 1749 Charles Townshend of the Board of Trade charged that American assemblies had assumed many of the "ancient and established prerogatives wisely preserved in the Crown." Townshend and other officials were determined to replace salutary neglect with a more rigorous system of imperial control.

The wheel of empire had come full circle. In the 1650s England set out to build a centralized colonial empire and, over the course of a century, achieved the economic part of that goal through the use of sweeping mercantilist legislation, warfare against the Dutch, French, and Spanish, and the forced labor of more than a million African slaves. However, as the result of the Glorious Revolution and the era of salutary neglect that followed, the empire unexpectedly devolved into a group of politically self-governing colonies linked together primarily by trade. And so in the 1740s British officials vowed once again to create a politically centralized colonial system.

For Further Exploration

The best short overview of England's empire is Michael Kammen, *Empire and Interest: The American Colonies and the Politics of Mercantilism* (1970), while a clearly written study of the multicultural tensions resulting from the quest for American possessions is Joyce Goodfriend, *Before the Melting Pot: Society and Culture in Colonial New York City, 1664–1730*. Two fine portrayals of imperial military and political affairs in the eighteenth century are Fred Anderson, *A People's Army: Massachusetts Soldiers and Society in the Seven Years' War* (1984), a compelling picture of army life, and Richard Bushman, *King and People in Provincial Massachusetts* (1985), a nicely crafted story of the decline of British authority in New England.

Betty Wood, *Origins of American Slavery* (1998), offers a survey of this important topic. For a lucid discussion of the diversity and evolving character of African bondage, see Ira Berlin, *Many Thousands Gone: The First Two Centuries of Slavery in North America* (1998). Peter Wood, *Black Majority: Negroes in Colonial South Carolina Through the Stono Rebellion* (1974), presents a rich analysis of the skills and culture of enslaved West Africans in South Carolina. Olaudah Equiano, *The Interesting Narrative of the Life of Olaudah Equiano* (originally published 1789; Bedford/St. Martin's, 1995), provides a powerful first-person account of a child's life in Africa, his kidnapping and sale into slavery in America, and his odyssey toward freedom and fame.

T I M E L I N E

1651	First Navigation Act creates an English monopoly of trade with American colonies.	1720– 1742	Sir Robert Walpole chief minister
1660	Restoration of Charles II	1720– 1750	Dahomey becomes a "slaving" state.
1660s	Barbados becomes a sugar-producing island. New Navigation Acts extend the English control of American trade.		Chesapeake slaves increase through reproduction. Rice exports from South Carolina soar. Africans in South Carolina create the Gullah language.
1664	New Netherland is captured and becomes New York.		Rise of planter aristocracy in southern colonies Growth of Atlantic seaport cities
1681	William Penn founds Pennsylvania.		
1686– 1689	Dominion of New England	1732	Georgia chartered
1688	The Glorious Revolution in England deposes James II.	1733	Molasses Act places a high tariff on imported French molasses.
1689	Rebellions in Massachusetts, Maryland, and New York	1739	Stono rebellion War of Jenkins' Ear
1690	John Locke's *Two Treatises on Government* rejects divine-right rule.	1750	Iron Act prohibits colonists from manufacturing iron products.
1705	Virginia legally defines resident Africans as slaves.	1751	Currency Act prevents New England colonies from creating land banks and using paper money as legal tender.
1714– 1750	British policy of "salutary neglect" Rise of colonial assemblies		

The PBS video *Africans in America, Part 1: Terrible Transformation, 1450–1750* (1.5 hours) covers the African American experience in the colonial period; the website at <http://www.pbs.org/wgbh/aia/part1/title.html> contains a wide variety of pictures, historical documents, and scholarly commentary. "Excerpts from Slave Narratives" at <http://vi.uh.edu/pages/mintz/primary.htm> presents materials selected by Steven Mintz from forty-six accounts, arranged in eleven chronological and thematic categories.

Chapter 4

GROWTH AND CRISIS IN COLONIAL SOCIETY

1720–1765

The thirst after Indian lands, is become almost universal.
SIR WILLIAM JOHNSON TO THE EARL OF SHELBURNE, 1766

In 1736 Alexander MacAllister left the Highlands of Scotland to settle in the backcountry of North Carolina, where he was soon joined by his wife and three sisters. Over the years MacAllister prospered as a landowner and mill proprietor and had only praise for his new home. Carolina was "the best poor man's country I have heard in this age," he wrote to his brother Hector, urging him to "advise all poor people . . . to take courage and come." There were no landlords to keep "the face of the poor . . . to the grinding stone," and so many Highlanders were arriving that "it will soon be a new Scotland." Here, on the margin of the British empire, people could "breathe the air of liberty, and not want the necessarys of life." Tens of thousands of European migrants—Highland Scots, English, Scots-Irish, German—heeded such advice, helping to swell the size of Britain's North American settlements from 400,000 people in 1720 to almost 2 million by 1765.

The rapid and continuous increase in the number of settlers—and slaves—transformed the character of life in every region of British America. Long-settled towns in New England became overcrowded, antagonistic ethnic and religious communities jostled uneasily with one another in the Mid-Atlantic region, and the influx of the MacAllisters and thousands of other settlers into the backcountry altered the traditional dynamics of southern politics. Moreover, in every region the impact of a European spiritual movement called Pietism changed the tone of religious life. Finally, as the new immigrants and the landless children of long-settled families moved inland, they reignited conflict with native peoples and with the other European powers contesting for dominance of North America—France and Spain. A generation of growth produced a decade of crisis.

Freehold Society in New England

In the 1630s the Puritans had migrated from a country where a handful of nobles and gentry owned 75 percent of the arable land and farmed it by using servants, leaseholding tenants, and wage laborers. In their new home they consciously created a yeoman society composed of independent farm families who owned their lands as freeholders—without feudal dues or leases. By 1750, however, the rapidly growing population outstripped the supply of easily farmed land, posing a severe challenge to the freehold ideal.

FARM FAMILIES: WOMEN'S PLACE

The Puritans' commitment to equality did not extend to the family, which by law and custom remained a patriarchy. Men claimed power in the state and authority in the family. As the Reverend Benjamin Wadsworth of Boston advised women in *The Well-Ordered Family* (1712), being richer, more intelligent, or of higher social status than their husbands mattered little: "Since he is thy Husband, God has made him the head and set him above thee." Therefore, Wadsworth concluded, it was their duty "to love and reverence him."

Throughout their lives women saw firsthand that their role was a subordinate one. Small girls watched their mothers defer to their fathers. As young adults they learned that their marriage portions would be inferior in kind and size to those of their brothers; usually daughters received not highly prized land but rather livestock or household goods. Thus Ebenezer Chittendon of Guilford, Connecticut, left all his land to his sons, decreeing that "Each Daughter have half so much as Each Son, one half in money and the other half in Cattle."

In rural New England—indeed, throughout the colonies—women were raised to be dutiful helpmeets (helpmates) to their husbands. Farmwives spun thread and yarn from flax or wool and wove it into shirts and gowns. They knitted sweaters and stockings, made candles and soap, churned milk into butter and pressed curds into cheese, fermented malt for beer, preserved meats, and mastered dozens of other household tasks. The most exemplary or "notable" practitioners of these domestic arts won praise from the community, for their labor was crucial to the rural household economy.

Bearing and rearing children were also central tasks. Most women married in their early twenties; by their early forties they had given birth to six or seven children, usually delivered with the assistance of midwives. A large family sapped a woman's physical and emotional strength, focusing her energies on domestic activities for about twenty of her most active years. A Massachusetts mother explained that she had less time than she would have liked for religious activities because "the care of my Babes takes up so large a portion of my time and attention." Yet more women than men joined the churches of New England, so "that their children may be baptized," as the revivalist Jonathan Edwards explained, and because they feared the dangers of childbirth.

A gradual reduction in farm size in long-settled communities prompted many couples to have fewer children. After 1750 women in Andover, Massachusetts, bore an average of only four children and thus gained the time and energy to pursue other tasks. Farm women made extra yarn, cloth, or cheese to exchange with neighbors or sell to shopkeepers, enhancing their families' standard of living. Or like Susan Huntington of Boston (the wife of a prosperous merchant), they spent more time in "the care & culture of children, and the perusal of necessary books, including the scriptures."

Yet women's lives remained tightly bound by a web of legal and cultural restrictions. While ministers often praised the piety of the women, they excluded them from church governance. When Hannah Heaton grew dissatisfied with her Congregationalist minister, thinking him unconverted and a "blind guide," she sought out one of the few sects (mostly Quaker or Baptist) that welcomed questioning women and allowed them to become spiritual leaders. But Heaton was an exception. Willingly or not, most New England women lived according to the conventional view that, as Timothy Dwight put it, they should be "employed only in and about the house and in the proper business of the sex."

The Character of Family Life: The Cheneys

Life in a large colonial-era family was very different from that in a small modern one. Mrs. Cheney's face shows the rigors of having borne ten children, a task that occupied her entire adult life. Her children grew up with many older (or younger) siblings, which blurred differences between the generations.

(National Gallery of Art, Washington; Gift of Edgar William and Bernice Chrysler Garbisch)

FARM PROPERTY: INHERITANCE

By contrast European men who migrated to the colonies escaped many traditional constraints, including the curse of landlessness. "The hope of having land of their own & becoming independent of Landlords is what chiefly induces people into America," an official noted in the 1730s. But acquiring a farmstead was only the first step toward family security because most migrating Europeans wanted to provide land for the next generation. Parents with small farms often indentured their sons and daughters as servants and laborers in more prosperous households, where they would have enough to eat. When the indentures ended at age eighteen or twenty-one, the more ambitious young men would begin the slow ten- to twenty-year climb up the agricultural ladder, from laborer to tenant and finally to freeholder.

Luckier sons and daughters in successful farm families received a marriage portion when they reached marriageable age—usually twenty-three to twenty-five. The marriage portion—land, livestock, or farm equipment—repaid children for their past labor and allowed parents to choose their children's partners, which they did not hesitate to do because the family's prosperity and the parents' security during old age depended on a wise choice. Normally, children had the right to refuse an unacceptable match, but they did not have the luxury of "falling in love" with whomever they pleased.

Marriage under English common law was hardly a contract between equals. A bride relinquished to her husband the legal ownership of her land and personal property. After his death, she received the right to use (but not to sell) a third of the family's estate. Her own death or remarriage canceled this use-right, and the widow's portion was divided among the children. In this way the widow's property rights were subordinated to those of the family "line," which stretched, through the children, across the generations.

It was the cultural duty of the father to provide inheritances for his children, and men who failed to do so lost status in the community. Some fathers willed the family farm to a single son, providing their other children with money, apprenticeship contracts, or uncleared land along the frontier, or requiring the inheriting son to do so. Alternatively, yeomen moved their families to the New England frontier or to other unsettled regions, where life was hard but land for the children was cheap and abundant. "The Squire's House stands on the Bank of the Susquehannah," the traveler Philip Fithian reported from the Pennsylvania backcountry in the early 1760s. "He tells me that he will be able to settle all his sons and his fair Daughter Betsy on the Fat of the Earth."

The historic accomplishment of these farmers was the creation of whole communities composed of independent property owners. A French visitor remarked on the sense of personal worth and dignity in this rural world, which contrasted sharply with European peasant life. Throughout the northern colonies, he wrote, he had found "men and women whose features are not marked by poverty, by lifelong deprivation of the necessities of life, or by a feeling that they are insignificant subjects and subservient members of society."

THE CRISIS OF FREEHOLD SOCIETY

With each generation the population of New England doubled, mostly as a result of natural increase. The Puritan colonies had about 100,000 people in 1700, 200,000 in 1725, and almost 400,000 in 1750. In long-settled areas farms had been divided and subdivided, leaving parents in a quandary. In the 1740s the Reverend Samuel Chandler of Andover, Massachusetts, was "much distressed for land for his children," seven of whom were boys. A decade later in the neighboring town of Concord, about 60 percent of farmers owned less land than their fathers had.

Because parents had less to give their children, they had less control over their children's lives. The system of arranged marriages broke down as young people engaged in premarital sex and used the urgency of pregnancy to win their fathers' permission to marry. Throughout New England the number of firstborn children conceived before marriage rose spectacularly, from about 10 percent in the 1710s to 30 percent or more in the 1740s. Given another chance, young people "would do the same again," an Anglican minister observed, "because otherwise they could not obtain their parents' consent to marry."

New England families met the threat to the freeholder ideal through a variety of strategies. Many parents chose to have smaller families by using primitive methods of birth control. Others joined with neighbors to petition the provincial government for land grants, moving inland to central Massachusetts and western Connecticut—and eventually into New Hampshire and the future Vermont—and hacking new farms out of the forest. Still other farmers learned to use their small plots more productively, replacing the traditional English crops of wheat and barley with high-yielding potatoes and Indian corn. Corn offered a hearty food for humans, and its leaves furnished feed for cattle and pigs, which in turn provided milk and meat. New England developed a livestock economy, becoming the major supplier of salted and pickled meat to the West Indies.

Finally, New England farmers made do on their smaller farms by exchanging goods and labor, developing the full potential of what one historian has called the "household mode of production." Men lent each other tools, draft animals, and grazing land. Women and children joined other families in spinning yarn, sewing quilts, and shucking corn. Farmers plowed fields owned by artisans and shopkeepers, who repaid them with shoes, furniture, or store credit. Typically, no money changed hands; instead, farmers, artisans, and shopkeepers recorded their debts and credits in personal account books and every few years "balanced" the books by transferring small amounts of cash. The system of exchange allowed households—and the entire economy—to achieve maximum output, thereby preserving the freehold ideal.

The Mid-Atlantic: Toward a New Society, 1720–1765

Unlike New England, which was settled mostly by English Puritans, the Mid-Atlantic colonies of New York, New Jersey, and Pennsylvania became home to peoples of differing origins, languages, and religions. These settlers—Scots-Irish Presbyterians, English and Welsh Quakers, German Lutherans, Dutch Reformed Protestants, and others—created ethnic and religious communities that coexisted uneasily with one another.

ECONOMIC GROWTH AND SOCIAL INEQUALITY

Ample fertile land and a long growing season attracted migrants to the Mid-Atlantic, and profits from wheat financed its settlement. Between 1720 and 1770 wheat prices doubled in Western Europe because of a population explosion, and American farmers increased their exports of wheat, corn, flour, and bread to meet the demand. This boom in exports helped the combined population of New York, New Jersey, and Pennsylvania surge from 50,000 in 1700 to 120,000 in 1720 and 350,000 in 1765.

As the population rose, so did the demand for land. Nonetheless, many migrants refused to settle in New York's Hudson River Valley, where long-established Dutch families presided over manors created by the Dutch West India Company, and wealthy British families, such as the Clarke and Livingston clans, dominated vast tracts granted by English governors between 1700 and 1714 (see Map. 4.1). Like the slaveowning planters in the Chesapeake, these landlords tried to live like European gentry by dominating a dependent peasantry, but few migrants were interested in becoming their tenants. However, as freehold land became scarce in eastern New York, manorial lords attracted tenants by granting them long leases and the right to sell any improvements they made to the next tenant. Thus, the number of tenants on the vast Rensselaer estate rose from 82 in 1714, to 345 in 1752, and nearly 700 by 1765.

Most tenant families hoped that with hard work and luck they could save enough to acquire freehold farmsteads. However, they rarely produced enough grain to do so because preindustrial technology limited their output during the crucial harvest season. As the wheat ripened, a worker with a hand sickle could reap only half an acre a day; any ripe uncut grain promptly sprouted and became useless. The cradle scythe, an agricultural tool introduced during the 1750s, doubled or tripled the amount of grain a worker could cut. Even so, a family with two adult workers could not harvest more than about 12 acres of wheat, a yield of perhaps 150 to 180 bushels of wheat and rye. After family needs were met, the remaining grain might be worth £15—enough to buy salt and sugar, tools, cloth.

Unlike New York, rural Pennsylvania and New Jersey were initially marked by relative economic equality because the original migrants arrived with approximately equal resources. They lived simply in small houses with one or two rooms, a sleeping loft, a few benches or stools, some wooden trenchers (platters), and a few

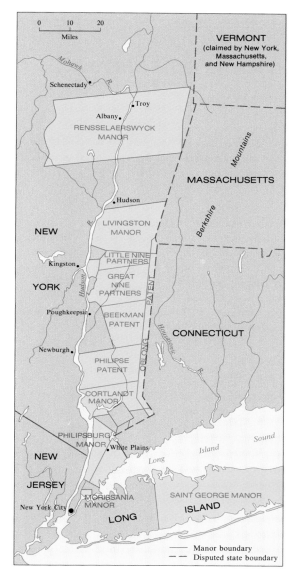

MAP 4.1
The Hudson River Manors, c. 1765

Dutch and English manorial lords dominated the fertile eastern shores of the Hudson River Valley—leasing small farms to German tenant families and refusing to sell land to migrants from overcrowded New England. This powerful landowning elite produced Patriot leaders, such as Robert Livingston and Gouverneur Morris, and leading American families, such as the Roosevelts.

wooden noggins (cups). Only the wealthiest families ate off pewter or ceramic plates imported from England or Holland. The rise of the wheat trade and an influx of poor settlers introduced marked social divisions. By the 1760s some farmers in eastern Pennsylvania had grown wealthy by buying slaves and hiring propertyless laborers to raise large quantities of wheat for market sale (see American Voices, "Runaway Servants and Slaves"). Others had become successful entrepreneurs, providing newly arrived settlers with land, equipment, goods, and services. Gradually a new class of wealthy agricultural capitalists—large-scale farmers, rural landlords,

A M E R I C A N   V O I C E S

Runaway Servants and Slaves

*B*etween 1720 and 1775 thousands of poor Europeans came to the mainland colonies as indentured servants and redemptioners and were sold to the highest bidder. "They sell the servants here as they do their horses, and advertise them as they do their beef and oat-meal," wrote an astonished British officer. Many of these servants labored side by side with enslaved Africans, and, as shown by these newspaper advertisements from the Pennsylvania Gazette, the two groups found that they shared a passion for freedom.

October 12, 1752

Run away from doctor Thomas Graeme's plantation, in Horsham township, Philadel-phia county, a Molatto slave, named Will, about 29 years of age, approaching very near the Negroe complexion, being of a Negroe father, and Indian mother, about five feet eight inches high, of an open bold countenance, somewhat pitted with the small-pox, speaks both English and Dutch, and is a very cunning sensible fellow. There went with him, a labouring man, that work'd by the day or month, called Thomas Stillwell, a tall smooth fac'd fair complexion'd fellow, with pale strait hair. . . . The said Stillwell is supposed to countenance the escape of the Molatto, by assuming the character of his master, or some such false pretence.

May 21, 1761   FIVE POUNDS Reward

Run away from the Subscribers, living at Little-Elk, Caecil County, Maryland, a Servant Woman named Margaret Sliter (but probably will change her Name) about 28 Years old, fresh colour, darkish brown Hair, born in England; had on when she ran away, two Bed-Gowns, one blue and white, the other dark Brown, both Callicoe. . . . Also a Negroe Man, named Charles, a lusty able Fellow, about 29 Years of Age, pitted with the Small-Pox, speaks good English, talks fast, is apt to get drunk, and pretends to be married to the aforesaid Margaret Sliter; had on when he ran away, a Pair of Thickset Breeches . . . a light coloured Jacket, an old brown Body-coat. . . .

Virginia, Lancaster County, Sept. 22, 1752

RUN away from the subscriber . . . on the 4th of May, A convict servant woman, named Sarah Knox (alias Howard, alias Wilson) of a middle size, brown complexion, short notes, talks broad, and said she was born in Yorkshire . . . and is a very deceitful, bold, insinuat-ing woman, and a great liar. . . . I find [in the *Gazette*] an extract of a letter from Chester, in Pennsylvania, mentioning a quack Doctor, by the name of Charles Hamilton . . . who turns out to be a woman in mens cloaths, and now assumes the name of Charlotte Hamil-ton. . . . If she talks broad, I have reason to believe that she is the very servant who belongs to me.

SOURCE: Billy G. Smith and Richard Wojtowicz, *Blacks Who Stole Themselves: Advertisements for Run-aways in the* Pennsylvania Gazette, *1728–1790* (Philadelphia: University of Pennsylvania Press, 1989), pp. 35, 50, 164.

speculators, storekeepers, and gristmill operators—accumulated estates that included mahogany tables, four-poster beds, couches, table linen, and imported Dutch dinnerware.

By 1760 there were many more people at the bottom of the Mid-Atlantic social order, for half of all white men were propertyless. Some landless men were the sons of property owners and would eventually inherit at least part of the family estate, but just as many were Scots-Irish *inmates*—single men or families "such as live in small cottages and have no taxable property, except a cow." In the predominantly German settlement of Lancaster, Pennsylvania, a merchant noted an "abundance of Poor people" who "maintain their Families with great difficulty by day Labour." Although Scots-Irish and German migrants hoped to become tenants and eventually landowners, sharply rising land prices prevented many from realizing their dreams.

Merchants and artisans took advantage of the ample supply of labor by organizing an "outwork" system. They bought wool or flax from large-scale producers and paid propertyless workers and subsistence farm families to spin it into yarn or weave it into cloth. In the 1760s an English traveler reported that hundreds of Pennsylvanians had turned "to manufacture, and live upon a small farm, as in many parts of England." Indeed, in many places the colonies had become as crowded and socially divided as rural England, and many farm families feared—with good reason—a return to the lowly status of the European peasant.

CULTURAL DIVERSITY

The middle colonies were not a melting pot in which European cultures blended into a homogeneous "American" society; rather, they were a patchwork of ethnically and religiously diverse communities. A traveler in Philadelphia in 1748 found no fewer than twelve religious denominations, including Anglicans, Quakers, Swedish and German Lutherans, Scots-Irish Presbyterians, and even Roman Catholics.

Migrants usually tried to preserve their cultural identities, marrying within their own ethnic groups or maintaining the customs of their native lands. The major exception was the Huguenots—Calvinists who were expelled from Catholic France. They settled in New York and various seacoast cities and gradually lost their French ethnic identity by intermarrying with other Protestants. More typical were the Welsh Quakers. Seventy percent of the children of the original Welsh migrants to Chester County, Pennsylvania, married other Welsh Quakers, as did 60 percent of the third generation.

Members of the Society of Friends (Quakers) became the dominant social group in Pennsylvania, at first because of their numbers and later because of their wealth and influence. Quakers controlled Pennsylvania's representative assembly until the 1750s and exercised considerable power in New Jersey as well. Because Quakers were pacifists, they dealt peaceably with Native Americans, negotiating treaties and buying land rather than seizing it by force. These conciliatory policies enabled Pennsylvania to avoid a major Indian war until the 1750s. Some Quakers extended the egalitarian values emphasized by their faith to their relations with blacks. After 1750 most Quaker meetings condemned the institution of slavery, and some expelled members who continued to keep slaves.

The Quaker vision of a "peaceable kingdom" attracted many German settlers who were fleeing war, religious persecution, and poverty. First to arrive, in 1683, was a group of religious dissenters—the Mennonites—attracted by a pamphlet promising religious freedom. In the 1720s religious upheaval and population growth in southwestern Germany and Switzerland stimulated another wave of migrants. "Wages were far better" in Pennsylvania, Heinrich Schneebeli reported to his friends in Zurich after an exploratory trip, and "one also enjoyed there a free unhindered exercise of religion." Beginning in 1749 thousands of Germans and Swiss fled their overcrowded societies; by 1756, 37,000 of these migrants had landed in Philadelphia. Some of these newcomers were redemptioners—a type of indentured servant—but many more were propertied farmers and artisans, who migrated to improve the lives of their children.

German settlements soon dominated certain areas of Pennsylvania, and thousands of Germans moved down the Shenandoah Valley into the western parts of Maryland, Virginia, and the Carolinas. They guarded their language and cultural heritage carefully, encouraging their American-born children to marry within the

A German Farm in Western Maryland

Beginning in the 1730s wheat became a major export crop in Maryland and Virginia. This engraving probably depicts a German farm because the harvesters are using oxen, not horses, and women are working in the field alongside men. (Library of Congress)

community. A minister in North Carolina admonished his congregation "not to contract any marriages with the English or Irish," explaining that "we owe it to our native country to do our part that German blood and the German language be preserved in America." Thus, these migrants and their descendants spoke German, read German-language newspapers, conducted church services in German, and preserved German agricultural practices, with women taking an active part in plowing and harvesting. English travelers remarked that German women were "always in the fields, meadows, stables, etc. and do not dislike any work whatsoever." Most German migrants felt at ease living in a British-controlled colony, for few of them came from the governing classes and many rejected political activism on religious grounds. They engaged in politics only to protect their religious liberty and property rights—insisting, for example, that as in Germany, married women should have property rights.

Emigrants from Ireland formed the largest group of incoming Europeans, some 150,000 in number. Some were Catholic but most were the descendants of the Presbyterian Scots who had been sent to Ireland between 1608 and 1650 to bolster English control of its Catholic population. In Ireland the Scots faced discrimination and economic regulation. The Irish Test Act of 1704 excluded Scottish Presbyterians as well as Irish Catholics from holding public office; English mercantilist regulations placed heavy import duties on the woolen goods produced by Scots-Irish weavers; and Scots-Irish farmers faced heavy taxes. "Read this letter, Rev. Baptist Boyd," a New York settler wrote back to his minister, "and tell all the poor folk of ye place that God has opened a door for their deliverance . . . all that a man works for is his own; there are no revenue hounds [tax collectors] to take it from us here." Lured by such reports, after 1720 thousands of Scots-Irish sailed for Philadelphia and then migrated to central Pennsylvania and southward down the Shenandoah Valley into Maryland and Virginia backcountry. Like the Germans, the Scots-Irish were determined to keep their culture. They held to their Presbyterian faith and promoted marriage within the church.

RELIGIOUS IDENTITY AND POLITICAL CONFLICT

In Western Europe government authorities condemned religious diversity, and in America many ministers remained committed to an established church and the state's enforcement of religious rules. Consequently, ministers criticized the separation of church and state in Pennsylvania. "The preachers do not have the power to punish anyone, or to force anyone to go to church," complained the minister Gottlieb Mittelberger. As a result, "Sunday is very badly kept. Many people plough, reap, thresh, hew or split wood and the like." Thus, Mittelberger concluded, "Liberty in Pennsylvania does more harm than good to many people, both in soul and body."

Mittelberger ignored the fact that religious sects in Pennsylvania enforced moral behavior among their members through communal self-discipline. For example, each Quaker family attended a weekly worship meeting and a monthly discipline meeting. Four times a year a committee met with each family to make certain the children were receiving proper religious instruction. The committee also reported on the moral behavior of adults; a Chester County meeting disciplined one of its members "to reclaim him from drinking to excess and keeping vain company." Quaker meetings gave permission to marry only to couples with sufficient land and livestock to support a family. As a result, the children of well-to-do Friends usually married within the sect; those who lacked resources remained unmarried or married without permission—in which case they were usually barred from Quaker meetings. In these various ways communal sanctions effectively sustained a self-contained and prosperous Quaker community.

In the 1750s Quaker dominance in Pennsylvania came under attack. Scots-Irish Presbyterians who migrated to frontier settlements west of the Susquehanna River challenged the pacifism of the Quaker-dominated assembly by demanding a more aggressive Indian policy. Many of the newer German migrants also opposed the Quakers; they wanted laws that respected their inheritance customs and representation in the provincial assembly in proportion to their numbers. As a European visitor noted, Scots-Irish Presbyterians, German Baptists, and German Lutherans had begun to form "a general confederacy" against the Quakers, but they found it difficult to unite because of "a mutual jealousy, for religious zeal is secretly burning." During the 1760s and again during the War for Independence, these latent religious and ethnic passions would disrupt Pennsylvania politics, but the Quaker-inspired experiment would survive the American Revolution and become a model for the future. In the centuries to come cultural pluralism, an open political order, and passionate ethnic and social conflicts would characterize much of American society.

The Enlightenment and the Great Awakening, 1740 – 1765

Two great European cultural movements reached America between the 1720s and the 1760s: the Enlightenment and Pietism. The *Enlightenment,* which emphasized the power of human reason to shape the world, appealed especially to well-educated men and women from merchant or planter families and to urban artisans. *Pietism,* an emotional, evangelical religious movement that stressed a Christian's personal relation to God, attracted many adherents, especially among farmers and urban laborers. The two movements promoted independent thinking in different ways; together they transformed American intellectual and cultural life.

THE ENLIGHTENMENT IN AMERICA

Most early Americans relied on religious teachings or folk wisdom to explain the workings of the natural world. Thus, Swedish settlers in Pennsylvania attributed medicinal powers to the great white mullein, a common wildflower, tying the leaves around their feet and arms when they had a fever. Even educated people believed that events occurred for reasons that today would be considered magical. When a measles epidemic struck Boston in the 1710s, the Puritan minister Cotton Mather thought that only God could end it. Like most Christians, Mather believed that the earth stood at the center of the universe and that God intervened directly in human affairs.

Early Americans held to these beliefs despite the scientific revolution of the sixteenth and seventeenth centuries, which had challenged both traditional Christian and folk worldviews. As early as the 1530s the astronomer Copernicus had observed that the earth traveled around the sun rather than vice versa, implying a more modest place for humans in the universe. Other scholars had conducted experiments using empirical methods—actual observed experience—to learn about the natural world. Eventually the English scientist Isaac Newton, in his *Principia Mathematica* (1687), used mathematics to explain the movement of the planets around the sun. Newton's laws of motion and concept of gravity described how the universe could operate without God's constant intervention, undermining traditional Christian explanations of the cosmos.

In the century between the publication of Newton's book and the outbreak of the French Revolution in 1789, the philosophers of the European Enlightenment applied scientific reasoning to all aspects of life, including social institutions and human behavior. Enlightenment thinkers believed that men and women could observe, analyze, understand, and improve their world. They advanced four fundamental principles: the lawlike order of the natural world, the power of human reason, the natural rights of individuals (including the right to self-government), and the progressive improvement of society.

In his *Essay Concerning Human Understanding* (1690), the English philosopher John Locke emphasized the impact of environment, experience, and reason on human behavior, proposing that the character of individuals and societies was not fixed by God's will but could be changed through education and purposeful action. Locke's *Two Treatises on Government* (1690) advanced the revolutionary theory that political authority was not given by God to monarchs (as kings such as James II had insisted) but was derived from "social compacts" that people made to preserve their "natural rights" to life, liberty, and property. In Locke's view, the people should have the right to change governmental policies—or even their form of government—through the decision of a majority.

The ideas of Locke and other Enlightenment thinkers came to America through books, travelers, and educated migrants and quickly affected the beliefs of influential colonists about religion, science, and politics. As early as the 1710s the Reverend John Wise of Ipswich, Massachusetts, used Locke's political principles to defend the decision to vest power in the ordinary members of Congregational churches. Wise argued that just as the "social compact" formed the basis of political society, the religious covenant made the congregation—not the bishops of the Church of England—the proper interpreter of religious truth. And when a smallpox epidemic threatened Boston in the 1720s, Cotton Mather sought a scientific rather than a

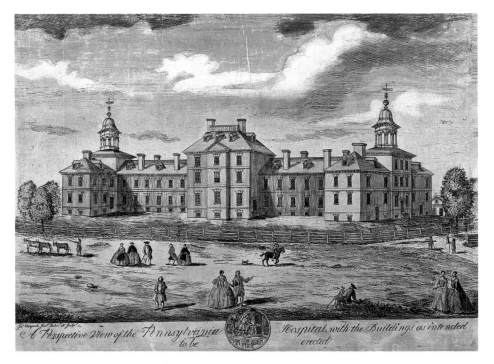

Enlightenment Philanthropy: The Philadelphia Hospital

This imposing structure, built in 1753 with public funds and private donations, embodied two Enlightenment principles—that purposeful action could improve society and that the world should express reason and order, exhibited here in the symmetrical façade. Etchings of the hospital and other important Philadelphia buildings circulated widely, bolstering the city's reputation as the center of the American Enlightenment. (Historical Society of Pennsylvania)

religious remedy, joining with a prominent Boston physician to support the new technique of inoculation.

Benjamin Franklin was the epitome of the American Enlightenment. Born in Boston in 1706 to a devout Calvinist family and apprenticed to a printer as a youth, Franklin was a self-made, self-taught man. As a tradesman, printer, and journalist in Philadelphia he formed "a club of mutual improvement" that met weekly to discuss "Morals, Politics, or Natural Philosophy." These discussions and Enlightenment literature, rather than the Bible, shaped Franklin's imagination. As Franklin explained in his *Autobiography* (1771), "from the different books I read, I began to doubt of Revelation [God-revealed truth] itself." Like many urban artisans, wealthy Virginia planters, and affluent seaport merchants, Franklin became a *deist*. Influenced by Enlightenment science, deists believed that God had created the world but allowed it to operate in accordance with the laws of nature. The deists' God was a rational being, a divine "watchmaker" who did not intervene directly in history or in people's lives. Rejecting the authority of the Bible, deists relied on people's "natural reason" to define a moral code. Adherence to the code, they believed, would be rewarded after death.

Franklin popularized the practical outlook of the Enlightenment in *Poor Richard's Almanac* (1732–1757), which was read by thousands. In 1743 he helped found the American Philosophical Society, an institution devoted to "the promotion of useful knowledge," and proceeded to invent bifocal lenses for eyeglasses, an improved stove (the Franklin stove), and the lightning rod. Franklin's book on electricity, first published in England in 1751, was praised by the English scientist Joseph Priestley as the greatest contribution to science since Newton. In Philadelphia and other American cities ambitious printers published newspapers and gentleman's magazines, the first significant nonreligious publications to appear in the colonies. Thus, the European Enlightenment added a secular dimension to colonial intellectual life, preparing the way for the great American contributions to republican political theory by John Adams, James Madison, and other Patriots during the Revolutionary era.

PIETISM IN AMERICA

As a few influential Americans—merchants and wealthy Virginia planters—and various urban artisans turned to deism, many other colonists embraced the European devotional movement known as Pietism. Pietists emphasized devout, or "pious," behavior, emotional church services, and striving for a mystical union with God—appealing to the hearts, rather than the minds, of their congregations. Their teachings came to America with German migrants in the 1720s and sparked a religious revival among many farmers, artisans, and laborers. In Pennsylvania and New Jersey the Dutch minister Theodore Jacob Frelinghuysen moved from church to church, preaching rousing, emotional sermons to German settlers. In private prayer meetings he encouraged lay members to preach a message of spiritual urgency to growing congregations. A decade later William Tennent and his son Gilbert, Presbyterian clergymen who copied Frelinghuysen's approach, led revivals among Scots-Irish migrants in the same area.

Simultaneously, a native-born pietistic movement appeared in Puritan New England. Puritanism had begun in England during the 1580s as part of an earlier pietistic upsurge, but over the decades many Puritan congregations had lost their religious zeal. In the 1730s the minister Jonathan Edwards restored spiritual enthusiasm to the Congregational churches in the Connecticut River Valley. An accomplished philosopher as well as an effective preacher, Edwards urged his hearers—especially young men and women—to commit themselves to a life of piety and prayer.

George Whitefield, a young English revivalist with what one historian has called a "flamboyant, highly sexualized style," transformed the local revivals into a "Great Awakening" that spanned the mainland settlements. Whitefield had experienced conversion after reading German pietistic tracts and had worked with John Wesley, the founder of English Methodism, who combined enthusiastic preaching with dis-ciplined "methods" of worship. In 1739 Whitefield carried Wesley's style to America and over the next two years preached to huge crowds of "enthusiasts" from Georgia to Massachusetts. "Religion is become the Subject of most Conversations," the *Pennsylvania Gazette* reported. "No books are in Request but those of Piety and Devotion." The usually skeptical and restrained Benjamin Franklin was so impressed by Whitefield's oratory that when the preacher asked for contributions, Franklin emptied his pockets "wholly into the collector's dish, gold and all." By the time the

George Whitefield, c. 1742

No painting completely captured Whitefield's magical appeal. When Whitefield spoke to a crowd near Philadelphia, an observer noted, his words were "sharper than a two-edged sword. . . . Some of the people were pale as death; others were wringing their hands . . . and most lifting their eyes to heaven and crying to God for mercy." (National Portrait Gallery, London)

The Power of a Preacher

NATHAN COLE

*G*eorge Whitefield's reputation as an inspired preacher drew thousands to his sermons, including Nathan Cole, a Connecticut farmer, and his wife. Cole recorded his impressions in a journal that relates his intense struggles with feelings of religious "unworthiness"—an internal conflict that was sparked by Whitefield and lasted for many years.

Now it please God to Send Mr. Whitefield into this land; and my hearing of his preaching at Philadelphia, like one of the old apostles . . . I felt the Spirit of God drawing me by conviction; I longed to see and hear him and wished he would come this way. . . . Then of a sudden, in the morning about 8 or 9 of the clock there came a messenger and said Mr. Whitefield . . . is to preach at Middletown this morning at ten of the clock. . . .

And when we came within about half a mile of the road that comes down . . . to Middletown, on high land I saw before me a cloud or fog rising . . . [and] a noise something like a low rumbling thunder and presently found it was the noise of horses' feet coming down the road, and this cloud was a cloud of dust made by the horses' feet . . . and as I drew nearer it seemed like a steady stream of horses and their riders. . . . And when we got to Middletown old meeting house there was a great multitude, it was said to be 3 or 4000 of people, assembled together. . . .

When I saw Mr. Whitefield come upon the scaffold, he looked almost angelical; a young slim, slender youth before some thousands of people with a bold undaunted countenance. And my hearing how God was with him everywhere as he came, it solemnized my mind and put me into a trembling fear before he began to preach; for he looked as if he was clothed with authority from the Great God, and a sweet solemnity sat upon his brow, and my hearing him preach gave me a heart wound. By God's blessing my old foundation was broken up, and I saw that my righteousness would not save me.

SOURCE: Merrill Jensen, ed., *American Colonial Documents to 1776*, vol. 9, *English Historical Documents* (New York: Oxford University Press, 1955), pp. 544–45.

evangelist reached Boston, the Reverend Benjamin Colman reported, the people were "ready to receive him as an angel of God."

Whitefield owed his appeal partly to his compelling personal presence. "He looked almost angelical; a young, slim, slender youth . . . cloathed with authority from the Great God," wrote a Connecticut farmer (see American Voices, "The Power of a Preacher"). Like most evangelical preachers, Whitefield did not read his sermons but spoke from memory as if inspired, raising his voice for dramatic effect, gesturing eloquently, making striking use of biblical metaphors, and even at times assuming a female persona—as a woman in labor struggling to deliver the word of God. The young preacher evoked a deep emotional response, telling his listeners they had all sinned and must seek salvation. Hundreds of men and women suddenly felt the "new light" of God's grace within them. Afterward, strengthened and self-confident, these New Lights were prepared to follow in Whitefield's footsteps.

RELIGIOUS UPHEAVAL IN THE NORTH

Like all cultural explosions, the Great Awakening was controversial. Conservative (or "Old Light") ministers such as Charles Chauncy of Boston condemned the "cryings out, faintings and convulsions" produced by emotional preaching. In Connecticut the Old Lights persuaded the legislative assembly to prohibit traveling preachers from speaking to established congregations without the ministers' permission. When Whitefield returned to Connecticut in 1744, he found many pulpits closed to him. But the New Lights resisted attempts by civil authorities to silence them: "I shall bring glory to God in my bonds," a dissident preacher wrote from jail. Dozens of farmers, women, and artisans roamed the countryside, condemning the Old Lights as "unconverted" sinners.

As the Awakening proceeded, it undermined support for traditional churches and challenged the authority of governments to impose taxes that supported them. In New England many New Lights left the established Congregational Church; by 1754 they had founded 125 "separatist" churches, supporting their ministers through voluntary contributions. Other religious dissidents joined Baptist congregations, which favored a greater separation of church and state. According to the Baptist preacher Isaac Backus, "God never allowed any civil state upon earth to impose religious taxes." In New York and New Jersey the Dutch Reformed Church split in two, as New Lights resisted conservative church authorities in the Netherlands.

The Awakening also challenged the authority of ministers, whose education and biblical knowledge had traditionally commanded respect. In an influential pamphlet, *The Dangers of an Unconverted Ministry* (1740), Gilbert Tennant maintained that the minister's authority came not from theological training but through the conversion experience. Reasserting Martin Luther's commitment to the priesthood of all believers, Tennent suggested that anyone who had experienced the saving grace of God could speak with ministerial authority. Not long afterward, Isaac Backus celebrated this spiritual democracy, noting that "the common people now claim as good a right to judge and act in matters of religion as civil rulers or the learned clergy."

Religious revivalism carried a social message, reaffirming the communal ethic of many farm families and questioning the growing competition and pursuit of wealth that accompanied the expansion of the American economy. "In any truly Christian society," Tennent explained, "mutual *Love* is the *Band* and *Cement*"—not the mercenary values of the marketplace. Suspicious of merchants and land speculators and dismayed by the erosion of traditional morality, Jonathan Edwards spoke for many rural Americans when he charged that a "private niggardly [miserly] spirit" was more suitable "for wolves and other beasts of prey, than for human beings."

As religious enthusiasm spread, churches founded new colleges to educate their youth and train ministers. New Light Presbyterians established the College of New Jersey (Princeton) in 1746, and New York Anglicans founded King's College (Columbia) in 1754. Baptists set up the College of Rhode Island (Brown) and the Dutch Reformed Church subsidized Queen's College (Rutgers) in New Jersey. The true intellectual legacy of the Awakening, however, was not education for the few but a new sense of religious authority among the many.

SOCIAL AND RELIGIOUS CONFLICT IN THE SOUTH

In the southern colonies religious enthusiasm also sparked social conflict. In Virginia the Church of England was the legally established religion, supported by public taxes. However, Anglican ministers generally ignored the spiritual needs of African Americans (about 40 percent of the population), and landless whites (another 20 percent) attended irregularly. Middling white freeholders, who accounted for about 35 percent of the population, formed the core of most Anglican congregations. But prominent planters and their families (a mere 5 percent of the population) held real power in the church and used their control of parish finances to discipline Anglican ministers. One clergyman complained that dismissal awaited any minister who "had the courage to preach against any Vices taken into favor by the leading Men of his Parish."

The Great Awakening challenged both the Church of England and the power of the southern planter elite. In 1743 the bricklayer Samuel Morris, inspired by his reading of George Whitefield's sermons, led a group of Virginia Anglicans out of the established church. Seeking a more vital religious experience, Morris and his followers invited New Light Presbyterian ministers from Scots-Irish settlements along the Virginia frontier to lead their prayer meetings. Soon these Presbyterian revivals spread across the backcountry and into the so-called Tidewater region along the Atlantic coast, threatening the social authority of the Virginia gentry. Planters and their well-dressed families were accustomed to arriving at Anglican services in elaborate carriages drawn by well-bred horses, and they often flaunted their power by marching in a body to their seats in the front pews. These potent reminders of the gentry's social superiority would vanish if freeholders attended New Light Presbyterian rather than Church of England services. Moreover, religious pluralism would threaten the government's ability to tax the population to support the established church.

To prevent the spread of New Light doctrines, Virginia's governor denounced them as "false teachings," and Anglican justices of the peace closed down Presbyterian meetinghouses. This harassment kept most white yeomen families and poor tenants within the Church of England, as did the fact that most Presbyterian ministers were highly educated and sought converts mainly among skilled workers and propertied farmers.

Baptists succeeded where Presbyterians failed. The evangelical Baptist preachers who came to Virginia in the 1760s drew their congregations primarily from the poor by offering them solace and hope in a troubled world. Their central ritual was adult baptism, often involving complete immersion in water. Once men and women had experienced the infusion of grace—had been "born again"—they were baptized in an emotional public ceremony that celebrated the Baptists' shared fellowship. During the 1760s thousands of yeomen and tenant farm families in Virginia were drawn to revivalist meetings by the enthusiasm and democratic ways of Baptist preachers.

Even slaves were welcome at Baptist revivals. As early as 1740 George Whitefield had openly condemned the brutality of slaveholders and urged that blacks be brought into the Christian fold. In South Carolina and Georgia a handful of New Light planters had taken up this challenge, but the hostility of the white population and the commitment of many Africans to their ancestral religions kept the number of converts low. Virginia in the 1760s witnessed the first significant conversion of slaves to Christianity, as second- and third-generation African Americans who knew the English language and English ways responded positively to the Baptist message that all people were equal in God's eyes.

The ruling planters reacted violently to the Baptists, who posed a threat to the social authority and way of life of the gentry. The Baptists emphasized equality by calling one another "brother" and "sister," and their preachers condemned the customary pleasures of Chesapeake planters—gambling, drinking, whoring, and cockfighting. To maintain the social hierarchy Anglican sheriffs and justices of the peace broke up Baptist services by force. In Caroline County, Virginia, an Anglican posse attacked a prayer meeting led by Brother Waller, who, a fellow Baptist reported, "was violently jerked off the stage; they caught him by the back part of his neck, beat his head against the ground, and a gentleman gave him twenty lashes with his horsewhip." Despite such attacks, about 20 percent of Virginia's whites and hundreds of enslaved blacks had joined Baptist churches by 1775. In the south as in the north, Protestant revivalism was on the way to becoming a powerful American religious movement.

Although the revival did not significantly undermine the political power of Anglican slaveholders in Virginia, it gave spiritual meaning to the lives of poor yeoman and tenant families and, by creating a sense of community, assisted them to assert their social values and economic interests. Moreover, as Baptist ministers spread Christianity among slaves, the cultural gulf between blacks and whites shrank, undermining one justification for slavery and giving blacks a new sense of spiritual identity. Within a generation African Americans would develop their own versions of Protestant Christianity.

The Midcentury Challenge: War, Trade, and Social Conflict, 1750–1765

Between 1750 and 1765 colonial life was transformed not only by Pietism and the Enlightenment but also by war, economic change, and frontier violence. First, Britain embarked on a war in America, the French and Indian War, which became a worldwide conflict—the Great War for Empire. Second, the expansion of transatlantic trade increased colonial prosperity but put Americans into debt to British creditors. Third, a great westward migration led to new battles with the Indians, armed conflicts between settlers and landowners, and frontier rebellions against eastern governments.

THE FRENCH AND INDIAN WAR

In 1750 the interior of North America was still controlled by Indian peoples. Most French settlers lived along the St. Lawrence River, near the fur-trading centers of Montreal and Quebec (see Map 4.2). The more numerous British inhabitants had not ventured across the Appalachian Mountains, both because there were few natural transportation routes and because of Indian resistance. For more than a generation the Iroquois and other Native Americans had used their control of the fur trade to bargain for guns and subsidies from British and French officials and had firmly resisted the intrusion of white settlers. However, this strategy of playing off the French against the British was breaking down as European governments refused to pay the rising cost of "gifts" of arms and money and as the Indian alliances crumbled. Along the upper Ohio River the Delawares and Shawnees declared that they would no longer abide by Iroquois policies.

Moreover, the escalating Anglo-American demand for Indian lands, a result of colonial population growth and European migration, was eliciting strong resistance among Indian peoples. The Mohawks rebuffed attempts by Sir William Johnson, a British Indian agent and land speculator, to settle Scottish migrants west of Albany. To the south, the Iroquois were infuriated when Governor Dinwiddie of Virginia and a group of prominent planters laid plans to settle the upper Ohio River Valley, an area that they had traditionally controlled. Supported by influential London merchants, the Virginia speculators formed the Ohio Company in 1749 and obtained a royal grant of 200,000 acres along the upper Ohio River. "We don't know what you Christians, English and French intend," the outraged Iroquois complained, "we are so hemmed in by both, that we have hardly a hunting place left."

To shore up the alliance with the Iroquois Nations, the British Board of Trade, the body charged with supervising American affairs, called for a great intercolonial meeting with the Indians at Albany, New York, in June 1754. At the meeting the American delegates assured the Iroquois that they had no designs on their lands and asked for their assistance against the French. To bolster colonial defenses, Benjamin Franklin proposed a Plan of Union among the colonies with a continental assembly that would manage all western affairs: trade, Indian policy, and defense. But neither the Albany Plan nor a similar proposal by the Board of Trade for a political "union between ye Royal, Proprietary, & Charter Governments" ever materialized because both the provincial assemblies and the imperial government feared that collaboration would undermine their authority.

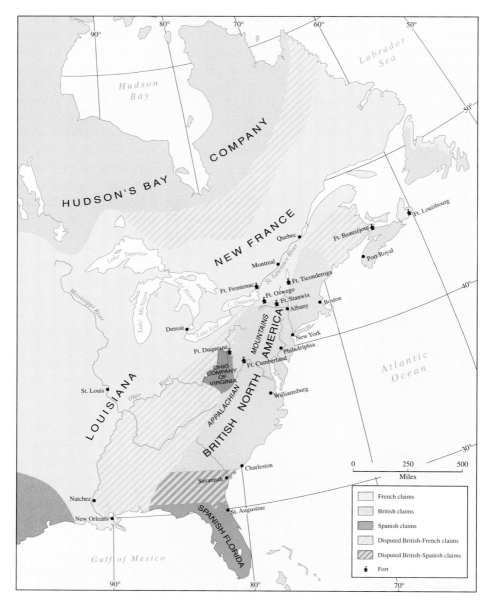

MAP 4.2
European Spheres of Influence, 1754

France and Spain laid claim to vast areas of North America and relied on Indian allies to combat the numerical superiority of British settlers. For their part, Native American peoples played off one European power against another. As a British official noted: "To preserve the Ballance between us and the French is the great ruling Principle of Modern Indian Politics." By expelling the French from North America, the Great War for Empire disrupted this system, leaving Indian peoples on their own in resisting Anglo-American settlers.

Britain's movement into the Ohio River Valley alarmed the French, who countered by constructing a series of forts, including Fort Duquesne at the point where the Monongahela and Allegheny Rivers join to form the Ohio (present-day Pittsburgh). The confrontation escalated when Governor Dinwiddie dispatched an expedition led by Colonel George Washington, a young planter and Ohio Company stockholder, to support the Company's claims. In July 1754 French troops seized Washington and his men, prompting expansionists in Virginia and Britain to demand war. But the British prime minister, Henry Pelham, urged calm: "There is such a load of debt, and such heavy taxes already laid upon the people, that nothing but an absolute necessity can justifie our engaging in a new War."

Pelham could not control the march of events. In Parliament William Pitt, a rising British statesman, and Lord Halifax, the new head of the Board of Trade, strongly advocated a policy of expansionism in the colonies. They persuaded Pelham to dispatch naval and military forces to America, where they joined with colonial militia in attacking French forts. In June 1755 British and New England troops captured Fort Beauséjour in Nova Scotia (Acadia) and deported nearly 10,000 French residents, some of whom eventually settled in Louisiana. In July as 1,400 British regulars and Virginia militiamen advanced on Fort Duquesne, they were surprised by a small force of French and a larger group of Delawares and Shawnees, who had decided to side with the French. In the ensuing battle the British commander, General Edward Braddock, lost his life and nearly two-thirds of his troops. "We have been beaten, most shamefully beaten, by a handfull of Men," Washington complained bitterly as he led the militiamen back to Virginia.

THE GREAT WAR FOR EMPIRE

By 1756 the fighting in America had spread to Europe, where the conflict aligned Britain and Prussia against France and Austria and was known as the Seven Years' War. When Britain decided to mount major offensives in India and West Africa as well as in North America and the West Indies, the conflict became a great war for empire. Britain had reaped unprecedented profits from its overseas trading empire and was determined to crush France, the main obstacle to further expansion.

William Pitt, who was appointed Secretary of State in 1757, was the grandson of the East Indies merchant "Diamond" Pitt and a committed expansionist. A haughty man, Pitt was constantly at odds with his colleagues. "I know that I can save this country and that I alone can," he declared. Indeed, Pitt was a master of strategy, both commercial and military, and planned to cripple France by attacking its colonies. In designing the critical campaign against New France, Pitt exploited a demographic advantage: on the North American mainland, Britain's 2 million subjects outnumbered the French by fourteen to one. To mobilize the colonists, Pitt agreed to pay half the cost of their troops and supply them with arms and equipment, an expenditure in America of nearly £1 million a year. He then committed a major British fleet and 30,000 British regulars to the American conflict, appointing three young officers—James Wolfe, Jeffrey Amherst, and William Howe—as the top commanders.

In 1758 the British forced the French to abandon Fort Duquesne (which they renamed Fort Pitt) and then captured Louisbourg at the mouth of the St. Lawrence River. The following year Wolfe sailed down the St. Lawrence to attack Quebec, the heart of France's American empire. After several failed attacks, 4,000 British troops scaled the high cliffs protecting the city and defeated the French. Quebec's fall was the turning point of the war. The Royal Navy prevented French reinforcements from crossing the Atlantic, and when British forces captured Montreal in 1760, the conquest of Canada was complete.

Elsewhere the British went from success to success. Fulfilling Pitt's dream, the East India Company captured French commercial outposts and took control of trade in large sections of India. British forces seized French Senegal in West Africa, the French sugar islands of Martinique and Guadeloupe, and the Spanish colonies of Cuba and the Philippine Islands. The Treaty of Paris of 1763 confirmed this triumph, granting Britain sovereignty over half the continent of North America, including French Canada, all French territory east of the Mississippi River, and Spanish Florida. Spain received

Pontiac

This portrait depicts Pontiac as both an Indian, symbolized by the necklace of bear claws, and a European-style ruler with a regal demeanor and a flowing robe. Pontiac did indeed partake of two worlds, absorbing French culture as he asserted his Indian identity. (Stock Montage, Inc.)

Louisiana west of the Mississippi, along with the restoration of Cuba and the Philippines. The French empire in North America was reduced to a handful of sugar islands in the West Indies and two rocky islands off the coast of Newfoundland.

As British armies and traders occupied French forts, Indian peoples from New York to Michigan grew increasingly concerned. Fearing an influx of Anglo-American settlers, the Ottawa chief Pontiac hoped for a return of the French, declaring, "I am French, and I want to die French." Neolin, a Delaware prophet, went further, teaching that the suffering of the Indian peoples stemmed from their dependence on the Europeans and their goods, guns, and rum. He called for the expulsion of all Europeans. Inspired by Neolin's vision and his own anti-British sentiments, in 1763 Pontiac led a group of loosely confederated tribes in a major uprising, capturing nearly every British garrison west of Fort Niagara, besieging the fort at Detroit, and killing or capturing over 2,000 frontier settlers. But the Indian alliance gradually weakened, and British military expeditions defeated the Delawares near Fort Pitt and broke the siege of Detroit. In the peace settlement that followed, Pontiac and his allies accepted the British as their new political "fathers." In return, the British addressed some of the Indians' concerns, temporarily barring Anglo-Americans from settling west of the Appalachians by establishing the Proclamation Line of 1763. Thus, the war for empire won Canada for the British crown but did not provide land for the expansion-minded American colonists.

BRITISH ECONOMIC GROWTH AND THE CONSUMER REVOLUTION

Britain owed its military and diplomatic success in large part to its unprecedented economic resources. Since 1700, when it had wrested control of many oceanic trade routes from the Dutch, Britain had been the dominant commercial power. By 1750 it was becoming the first country to undergo industrialization. Its new technology and work discipline made Britain the first—and for over a century the most powerful—industrial nation in the world.

The new machines and new business practices of the Industrial Revolution allowed Britain to produce more wool and linens, more iron tools, paper, chinaware, and glass than ever before—and to sell those goods at lower prices. British artisans had designed and built water- and steam-driven machines that powered lathes for shaping wood, jennies and looms for spinning and weaving textiles, and hammers for forging iron. The new machines produced goods far more rapidly than human hands could. Furthermore, the entrepreneurs who ran the new factories drove their employees hard, forcing them to keep pace with the machines and work long hours. To market the resulting products, English and Scottish merchants launched aggressive campaigns in the rapidly growing mainland colonies, extending a full year's credit to American traders instead of the traditional six months.

This first "consumer revolution" raised the living standard of many Americans, who soon were purchasing 20 percent of all British exports and paying for them by increasing their exports of wheat, rice, and tobacco. For example, Scottish merchants financed the settlement of the Virginia Piedmont, a region of plains and rolling hills just inland from the Tidewater counties. They granted planters and Scots-Irish migrants ample credit to purchase land, slaves, and equipment and took their tobacco crop in payment, exporting it to expanding markets in France and central Europe. In South Carolina planters supported their luxurious lifestyle by developing indigo plantations. By the 1760s they were exporting large quantities of the deep-blue dye to English textile factories as well as exporting about 65 million pounds of rice a year to Holland and southern Europe. Simultaneously, New York, Pennsylvania, Maryland, and Virginia became the breadbasket of the Atlantic world, supplying Europe's exploding population with wheat at ever-increasing profits. In Philadelphia wheat prices jumped almost 50 percent between 1740 and 1765.

This first American spending binge, like most subsequent splurges, landed many consumers in debt. Even during the boom times of the 1750s and early 1760s exports paid for only 80 percent of imported British goods. The remaining 20 percent—millions of pounds—was financed by Britain, both by the extension of credit and by Pitt's military expenditures in the colonies. As the war wound down, the loss of military supply contracts and cash subsidies made it more difficult for Americans to purchase British goods. Colonial merchants looked anxiously at their overstocked warehouses and feared bankruptcy. "I think we have a gloomy prospect before us," a Philadelphia trader noted in 1765, "as there are of late some Persons failed, who were in no way suspected." The increase in transatlantic trade had raised living standards but also had made Americans more dependent on overseas creditors and international economic conditions.

LAND CONFLICTS

In good times and bad the colonial population continued to grow, causing increased conflicts over land rights. The families who founded the town of Kent, Connecticut, in 1738 had lived in the colony for a century. Each generation their sons and daughters had moved westward to establish new farms, but now they lived at the generally accepted western boundary of the colony. To provide for the next generation, Kent families joined other Connecticut farmers in 1749 to form the Susquehanna Company to settle the Wyoming Valley in northeastern Pennsylvania, petitioning the legislature to assert jurisdiction over that region on the basis of Connecticut's "sea-to-sea" royal charter. But this land had also been granted by English kings to the Penn family, which invoked its proprietary rights and issued its own land grants. Soon settlers from Connecticut and Pennsylvania were burning down one another's houses. To avert further violence the two governments referred the dispute to the authorities in London, where it remained undecided at the time of independence.

Simultaneously, three different land disputes broke out in the Hudson River Valley. First, groups of Massachusetts settlers moved across the imprecise border with New York and claimed freehold estates on manor lands controlled by the Van Rensselaer and Livingston families. Second, the Wappinger Indians reasserted their ownership of land granted by English governors to various manorial lords. Finally, Dutch and German tenants asserted ownership rights to farms they had long held by lease and, when the landlords ignored their claims, refused to pay rent. By 1766 the tenants in Westchester, Dutchess, and Albany counties were in open rebellion against their landlords and used mob violence to close the courts. At the behest of the royal governor, General Thomas Gage and two British regiments joined local sheriffs and manorial bailiffs to suppress the tenant uprising, intimidate the Wappinger Indians, and evict the Massachusetts squatters.

Other land disputes erupted in New Jersey and the southern colonies, where resident landowners and English aristocrats successfully asserted legal claims based on long-dormant seventeenth-century charters. For example, one court decision upheld the right of Lord Granville, an heir of one of the original Carolina proprietors, to collect an annual tax on land in North Carolina; another decision awarded ownership of the entire northern neck of Virginia (along the Potomac) to Lord Fairfax.

This revival of proprietary power underscored the growing strength of the landed gentry and the increasing resemblance between rural societies in Europe and America. High-quality land east of the Appalachians was getting more expensive, and English aristocrats, manorial landlords, and wealthy speculators controlled much of it. Tenants and even yeomen farmers feared they soon might be reduced to the status of European peasants and searched for cheap freehold land in the west.

WESTERN UPRISINGS

Movement to the western frontier created new disputes over Indian policy, political representation, and debts. During the war, Delaware and Shawnee warriors had attacked farms throughout central and western Pennsylvania, destroying property and killing and capturing hundreds of residents. Subsequently, the Scots-Irish who lived along the frontier wanted to push the Indians out of the colony, but pacifistic Quakers prevented such military action. In 1763 a band of Scots-Irish farmers known as the Paxton Boys took matters into their own hands and massacred twenty members of the Conestoga tribe. When Governor John Penn tried to bring the murderers to justice, about 250 armed Scots-Irish advanced on Philadelphia. Benjamin Franklin intercepted the angry mob at Lancaster and arranged a compromise, narrowly averting a battle. Prosecution of the accused men failed for lack of witnesses. Although the Scots-Irish dropped their demand for the expulsion of the Indians, the episode left a legacy of racial hatred and political resentment.

Violence also broke out in the backcountry of South Carolina, where land-hungry whites had clashed repeatedly with Cherokees during the war with France. After the war ended in 1763, a group of landowning vigilantes, the Regulators, tried to suppress outlaw bands of whites that were roaming the countryside and stealing cattle and other property. The Regulators wanted greater political rights for their region and demanded that the eastern-controlled government provide them with more local courts, fairer taxes, and greater local representation in the provincial assembly. The government, which was dominated by lowland rice planters, wanted to suppress the Regulators but decided to compromise because it feared slave revolts if the militia were away in the backcountry. In 1767 the assembly agreed to create locally controlled courts in the west and reduce the fees for legal documents. However, it refused to reapportion the assembly or lower western taxes. Eventually a rival group, the Moderators, raised an armed force of its own and forced the Regulators to accept the authority of the colonial government. Like the Paxton Boys in Pennsylvania, the South Carolina Regulators attracted attention to western needs but ultimately failed to wrest power from the eastern elite.

In 1766 another Regulator movement arose in the newly settled backcountry of North Carolina. After the Great War for Empire tobacco prices plummeted, forcing many debt-ridden farmers into court. Eastern judges directed sheriffs to seize the property of bankrupt farmers and auction it off to pay creditors and court costs. Backcountry farmers resented merchants' lawsuits, not just because they generated high fees for lawyers and court officials but also because they violated local custom. As in rural New England farmers made loans among neighbors on trust and often allowed the loans to remain unpaid for years.

To save their farms, North Carolina debtors joined together in a Regulator movement that intimidated judges, closed down courts, and broke into jails to free their comrades. Their leader, Herman Husband, told his followers not to vote for "any Clerk, Lawyer, or Scotch merchant. We must make these men subject to the laws or they will enslave the whole community." But the North Carolina Regulators also proposed a coherent program of reforms, demanding passage of a law allowing them to pay their taxes in the "produce of the country" rather than in cash. They insisted on lower legal fees, greater legislative representation, and fairer taxes, so that each person would be taxed "in proportion to the profits arising from his estate." In 1771 the royal governor mobilized the eastern militia and defeated a large Regulator force at the Alamance River; seven insurgent leaders were summarily executed. Not since Leisler's revolt in New York in 1689 (see Chapter 3) had a domestic political conflict caused so much bloodshed in America.

In 1771 as in 1689, colonial conflicts became intertwined with imperial politics. In Connecticut the Reverend Ezra Stiles defended the Regulators. "What shall an injured & oppressed people do," he asked, when faced with "Oppression and tyranny (under the name of Government)?" Stiles's remarks reflected growing resistance to British imperial control, a result of the profound changes that had occurred in the mainland colonies between 1720 and 1765. America was still a dependent society closely tied to Britain by trade, culture, and politics, but it was also an increasingly complex society with the potential for an independent existence. British policies would determine the direction the maturing colonies would take.

TIMELINE

1700–1714	New Hudson River manors created	1743	Benjamin Franklin founds the American Philosophical Society.
1710s–1730s	Enlightenment ideas spread from Europe to America. Deists rely on "natural reason" to define a moral code.	1749	Virginia speculators create the Ohio Company. Connecticut farmers form the Susquehanna Company.
1720s	Germans and Scots-Irish settle in the Mid-Atlantic colonies. Theodore Jacob Frelinghuysen preaches Pietism to German migrants.	1750s	Industrial Revolution begins in England. "Consumer revolution" increases American imports and debt to Britain.
1730s	William and Gilbert Tennent lead Presbyterian revivals among Scots-Irish migrants. Jonathan Edwards preaches in New England.	1754	French and Indian War begins. Meeting of Iroquois and Americans at Albany; Plan of Union
1739	George Whitefield sparks the Great Awakening.	1756	Britain begins a Great War for Empire.
		1759	Britain captures Quebec.
1740s–1760s	Growing shortage of farmland in New England Religious and ethnic pluralism in the Mid-Atlantic colonies Rising grain and tobacco prices Increasing rural inequality	1760s	Land conflict along the border between New York and New England Regulator movements in the Carolinas suppress outlaw bands. Baptist revivals in Virginia
1740s	The Great Awakening sparks conflict between Old Lights and New Lights. Colleges established by religious denominations.	1763	Pontiac's uprising leads to the Proclamation of 1763. Treaty of Paris ends the Great War for Empire. Scots-Irish Paxton Boys massacre Indians in Pennsylvania.

For Further Exploration

The social history of eighteenth-century America comes alive in studies of individual lives. In *Good Wives: Image and Reality in the Lives of Women in Northern New England, 1650–1750* (1982), Laurel Thatcher Ulrich paints a vivid picture of the everyday lives of women as they assumed a variety of roles. Benjamin Franklin's *Autobiography* (available in many editions) provides an entertaining look at the bustling city of Philadelphia and demonstrates Franklin's Enlightenment sensibility and his pursuit of wealth and influence. A less successful quest for self-betterment is the subject of another autobiography, *The Infortunate: The Voyage and Adventures of William Moraley, an Indentured Servant,* edited by Susan E. Klepp and Billy G. Smith (1992). Harry S. Stout's *The Divine Dramatist: George Whitefield and the Rise of Modern Evangelicalism* (1991) shows how the charismatic preacher's flair for theatrics and self-promotion enabled him to preach effectively and fulfill his sense of duty to God.

Other well-written social histories are Rhys Isaac, *The Transformation of Virginia, 1740–1790* (1982); Patricia U. Bonomi, *A Factious People: Politics and Society in Colonial New York* (1971); and Fred Anderson, *A People's Army: Massachusetts Soldiers and Society in the Seven Years' War* (1984).

For insight into the day-to-day lives of women, see the PBS video *A Midwife's Tale* (1.5 hours), which tells the story of Martha Ballard, who lived at the end of the eighteenth century; additional materials on Ballard's experiences are available at <http://www.pbs.org/amex/midwife> and <http://www.DoHistory.org>. On day-to-day economic life, see the "Colonial Currency and Colonial Coin" site at <http://www.coins.nd.edu:8002/>, which contains detailed essays as well as pictures of colonial money. Franklin's life and times are presented at "The Electric Franklin," <http://www.ushistory.org/franklin/index/htm>. "Jonathan Edwards On-Line" at <http://www.JonathanEdwards.com/> provides access to the writings of the great philosopher and preacher, but note that this site uses Edwards's arguments to advance one side of a present-day theological debate.

Chapter 5

TOWARD INDEPENDENCE: YEARS OF DECISION
1763–1775

The said [Stamp] act is contrary to the rights of mankind, and subversive of the English Constitution.

TOWN MEETING OF LEICESTER, MASSACHUSETTS, 1765

As the Great War for Empire ended in 1763, Seth Metcalf and many other American colonists rejoiced over the triumph of British arms. A Massachusetts veteran just returned from the war, Metcalf thanked "the Great Goodness of God" for the "General Peace" that was so "perculary Advantageous to the English Nation." Two years later, God's dialogue with his chosen Puritan people seemed to carry a very different message. As Metcalf wrote in his journal: "God is angry with us of this land and is now Smiting with his Rod Especially by the hands of our [British] Rulers."

The rapid disintegration of the bonds uniting Britain and America—events that Metcalf explained in terms of Divine Providence—mystified many Americans. How had it happened, asked the president of King's College in New York in 1775, that such a "happily situated" people had armed themselves and were ready to "hazard their Fortunes, their Lives, and their Souls, in a Rebellion"? Unlike other colonial peoples of the time, the majority of Americans had enjoyed life in a prosperous and relatively free society with a strong tradition of self-government. They had little to gain and much to lose by rebelling.

Or so it seemed in 1765, before the British government attempted to reform the imperial system. The long overdue but disastrous administrative reforms prompted a violent response, beginning a downward spiral of ideological debate and political conflict that ended in civil war. Yet this course of events was far from inevitable. Careful British statecraft could have saved the empire. Instead, inflexible responses to passionate Patriot agitation brought about its demise.

The Imperial Reform Movement, 1763–1765

The Great War for Empire had a mixed legacy. By driving the French out of Canada, Britain had achieved dominance over eastern North America (see Map 5.1). But the cost of the triumph was high: a mountain of debt that prompted the British ministry to impose new taxes on its American possessions. More fundamentally, it prompted Parliament to redefine the character of the empire, moving from one based on self-government and trade to one centered on rule by imperial officials.

THE LEGACY OF WAR

The war fundamentally changed the relationship between Britain and its American colonies—and the nature of British public life. The fighting revealed basic social and administrative conflicts between the home country and the colonies. As British regiments set up quarters, Americans were shocked by the arrogance of the officers. A Massachusetts militiaman wrote in his diary that British soldiers "are but

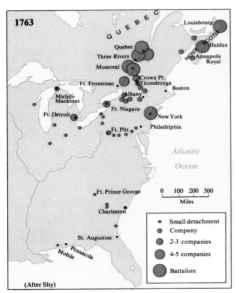

MAP 5.1
British Troop Deployments, 1763 and 1775

As the imperial crisis deepened, British military priorities changed. In 1763 most British battalions (the large circles representing 350 men) were stationed in Canada to deter French Canadian revolts and Indian attacks. Following the Stamp Act riots of 1765, the British moved more troops to the seaboard cities. By 1775 eleven battalions of British regulars occupied Boston, the center of the American Patriot movement.

little better than slaves to their officers." The disdain was mutual. General James Wolfe complained that colonial troops were drawn from the dregs of society and that "there was no depending on them in action."

The war also exposed the weak position of British royal governors and other officials, prompting immediate administrative reforms. In theory governors had extensive political powers, including command of the provincial militia, but in reality they had to share power with the colonial assemblies. Britain's Board of Trade complained that in Massachusetts "almost every act of executive and legislative power is ordered and directed by votes and resolves of the General Court." To enhance the authority of the crown in America, British officials began a strict enforcement of the Navigation Acts. Before the war colonial merchants had routinely bribed customs officials to avoid paying the duties imposed by the Molasses Act of 1733. To curb such corruption, in 1762 Parliament passed a Revenue Act that tightened the customs service. In addition, the ministry instructed the Royal Navy to seize vessels that were carrying goods between the mainland colonies and the French islands. The fact that French armies attempting "to Destroy one English province, are actually supported by Bread raised in another" was absurd, declared an outraged British politician.

The victory over France provoked a fundamental shift in imperial military policy in 1763, with the deployment of a large peacetime army of about 10,000 men in North America. The decision stemmed from a variety of motives. The ministry wanted to discourage rebellion by the 60,000 French residents of the newly captured province of Quebec and to protect Florida, which Spain wanted back. Moreover, Pontiac's rebellion had underscored the need for a substantial military garrison along the frontier both to restrain the Indians and to deter land-hungry whites from settling west of the Proclamation Line of 1763. Finally, some British politicians worried that Americans who no longer needed protection from an invasion from Canada would seek greater freedom from imperial control. As Henry Knox, a Treasury official who once had served the crown in Georgia, put it: "The main purpose of Stationing a large Body of Troops in America is to secure the Dependence of the Colonys on Great Britain." By stationing an army in America, the British ministry was indicating its willingness to use force to preserve its authority.

Yet another significant result of the war was the rapid increase in Britain's national debt, which soared from £75 million in 1754 to £133 million in 1763, and the consequent changes in government policies. To pay the rising interest charges, Lord Bute, the new prime minister, needed to raise taxes—certainly in Britain and perhaps in America as well. Treasury officials advised against increasing the British land tax, which was paid by the influential propertied classes, so Bute imposed higher import duties on tobacco and sugar, which manufacturers passed on to British consumers in the form of higher prices. The ministry also increased excise levies—essentially sales taxes—on goods such as salt, beer, and distilled spirits, once again passing on the costs of the war to the king's ordinary subjects. Left unresolved for the moment was question of imposing taxes on the colonies.

To collect these taxes and duties, the British government doubled the size of its bureaucracy and increased its powers. Customs agents and informers patrolled the coasts of southern Britain, arresting smugglers and seizing tons of goods, such as French wines and Flemish textiles, on which import duties had not been paid. Convicted smugglers faced heavy penalties, including death or "transportation" to America as indentured servants.

The price of empire abroad had turned out to be debt and a more powerful government at home. The appearance of a big and expensive government confirmed the predictions of the opposition, the Radical Whigs and Country Party landlords. They pointed out that the huge war debt had left the Treasury at the mercy of the "monied interest," the banks and financiers who were reaping millions of pounds in interest from government bonds. Moreover, the expansion of the tax bureaucracy had created thousands of patronage positions that were filled with "worthless pensioners and placemen." To reverse these developments, reformers demanded that Parliament be made more representative of the property-owning classes. The Radical Whig John Wilkes called for an end to "rotten boroughs"—tiny districts whose voters were controlled by wealthy aristocrats and merchants. In domestic affairs as in colonial policy, the war had transformed British political life, creating a more active and intrusive government.

THE SUGAR ACT AND COLONIAL RIGHTS

As the war ended, a new generation of British officials undertook a systematic reform of the imperial system. The first to act was George Grenville, who became prime minister in 1763. Grenville quickly won Parliamentary approval of a Currency Act (1764) that protected British merchants by banning the use of paper money (which was often worth less than its face value) as legal tender; colonists would have to pay their debts in gold or silver coin. Then he proposed a new Navigation Act, the Sugar Act of 1764, to replace the widely evaded Molasses Act of 1733. Treasury officials who understood the pattern of colonial trade convinced Grenville that the mainland settlers had to sell some of their wheat, fish, and lumber in the French islands. Without the molasses, sugar, and bills of exchange those sales brought, they pointed out, the colonists would lack the funds to buy British manufactured goods. Therefore, Grenville resisted demands from British sugar planters for a duty of 6 pence per gallon that would cut off colonial imports of French molasses. Instead, he settled on a smaller duty of 3 pence per gallon, arguing that it would allow British molasses to compete with the cheaper French product without destroying the trade of the North American mainland colonies or their distilling industry.

This carefully crafted policy garnered little support in America. Many New England merchants, such as John Hancock of Boston, had made their fortunes by smuggling French molasses and thus had never paid the duty. Their profits would be cut severely if the new regulations were enforced. These merchants and New

George Grenville, Architect of the Stamp Act

As prime minister from 1764 to 1766, Grenville assumed leadership of the movement for imperial reform and taxation. This portrait of 1763 suggests Grenville's energy and ambition. As events were to show, the new minister was determined to reform the imperial system and ensure that the colonists shared the cost of the empire. (The Earl of Halifax, Garrowby, Yorkshire)

England distillers, who feared a rise in the price of molasses, campaigned publicly against the Sugar Act, claiming that the new tax would wipe out trade with the French islands. Privately, they vowed to evade the duty by smuggling or by bribing officials.

More important, the merchants and their allies raised constitutional objections to the new legislation. The speaker of the Massachusetts House of Representatives argued that the duties constituted a tax, making the Sugar Act "contrary to a fundamental Principall of our Constitution: That all Taxes ought to originate with the people." The Sugar Act raised other constitutional issues as well. Merchants accused of violating the Act would be tried by vice-admiralty courts—maritime tribunals composed only of a judge—and not by a local common-law jury. For half a century colonial legislatures had vigorously opposed vice-admiralty courts, expanding the jurisdiction of colonial courts to cover customs offenses occurring in the seaports. As a result, most merchants charged with violating the Navigation Acts were tried in common-law courts and were often acquitted by local juries. By extending the jurisdiction of vice-admiralty courts to all customs offenses, the Sugar Act closed this loophole.

The new powers given to the vice-admiralty courts revived old American fears and complaints. For a century, the influential Virginia planter Richard Bland reminded his fellow settlers, the colonies had been subject to the Navigation Acts, which restricted their manufactures and commerce. But, he protested, the colonists "were not sent out to be the Slaves but to be the Equals of those that remained behind." John Adams, a young Massachusetts lawyer who was defending merchant John Hancock on a charge of smuggling, similarly condemned the new vice-admiralty courts, saying that they "degrade every American . . . below the rank of an Englishman."

While the logic of these arguments was compelling, some of the facts were wrong. The Navigation Acts certainly discriminated against the colonists, but the new vice-admiralty legislation did not—because those in Britain had long been subject to the same rules. The real issue was the new spirit of reform among British officials and the growing administrative power of the British state. Having lived for decades under a policy of salutary neglect, Americans were quick to charge that the new British policies challenged the existing constitutional structure of the empire. As a committee of the Massachusetts House put it, the Sugar Act and other British edicts "have a tendency to deprive the colonies of some of their most essential Rights as British subjects."

For their part, British officials insisted on the supremacy of Parliamentary laws and denied that the colonists were entitled to special privileges or even the traditional legal rights of Englishmen. When Royal Governor Francis Bernard of Massachusetts heard that the Massachusetts assembly had objected to the Sugar Act, claiming no taxation without representation, he asserted that Americans did not have that constitutional right. "The rule that a British subject shall not be bound by laws or liable to taxes, but what he has consented to by his representatives," Bernard argued, "must be confined to the inhabitants of Great Britain only." In the eyes of most British officials and politicians, Americans were second-class subjects of the king, their rights limited by the Navigation Acts and the national interests of the British state, as determined by Parliament.

AN OPEN CHALLENGE: THE STAMP ACT

The issue of taxation sparked the first great imperial crisis. When Grenville introduced the Sugar Act in 1764, he also intended to seek a stamp tax the following year to cover part of the cost of keeping 10,000 British troops in America—some £200,000 per year (about $20 million today). The new tax would raise revenue by requiring small embossed markings (somewhat like today's postage stamps) on all court documents, land titles, contracts, playing cards, newspapers, and other printed items. A similar tax in England was yielding an annual revenue of £290,000; Grenville hoped the American levy would raise at least £60,000 a year. The prime minister knew that some Americans would object to the tax on constitutional grounds, and so he asked explicitly whether any member of the House of Commons doubted "the power and sovereignty of Parliament over every part of the British dominions, for the purpose of raising or collecting any tax." No one rose to object.

Confident of Parliament's support, Grenville then vowed to impose a stamp tax in 1765 unless the colonists would tax themselves. This challenge threw the London representatives of the colonial legislatures into confusion because they did not see how the American assemblies could collectively raise and apportion their defense budget. Colonial officials had met together only once, at the Albany Congress of 1754, and not a single assembly had accepted that body's proposals. Benjamin Franklin, representing the Pennsylvania assembly, proposed another solution to Grenville's challenge: American representation in Parliament. "If you chuse to tax us," he suggested to an influential British friend, "give us Members in your Legislature, and let us be one People." With the exception of William Pitt, British politicians rejected Franklin's radical idea. They argued that the colonists were already "virtually" represented in the home legislature by the merchants who sat in Parliament and by other members with interests in America. Colonial leaders were equally skeptical. Americans were "situate at a great Distance from their Mother Country," the Connecticut assembly declared, and therefore "cannot participate in the general Legislature of the Nation." Influential merchants in Philadelphia, worried that a handful of colonial delegates would be powerless in Parliament, warned Franklin "to beware of any measure that might extend to us seats in the Commons."

The way was now clear for Grenville to introduce the Stamp Act. His goal was not only to raise revenue but also to assert a constitutional principle: "the Right of Parliament to lay an internal Tax upon the Colonies," as his chief assistant declared. The ministry's plan worked smoothly. The House of Commons refused to accept American petitions opposing the act and passed the new legislation by an overwhelming vote of 205 to 49. At the request of General Thomas Gage, commander of British military forces in America, Parliament also passed a Quartering Act directing colonial governments to provide barracks and food for the British troops stationed in the colonies. Finally, Parliament approved Grenville's proposal that violations of the Stamp Act be tried in vice-admiralty courts.

The design was complete. Using the doctrine of Parliamentary supremacy, Grenville had begun to fashion a genuinely imperial administrative system run by British officials without regard for the American assemblies. He thus provoked a constitutional confrontation not only on the specific issues of taxation, jury trials, and quartering of the military but also on the fundamental question of representative self-government.

The Dynamics of Rebellion, 1765–1766

Grenville had thrown down the gauntlet to the Americans. Although the colonists had often opposed unpopular laws and arbitrary governors, they had never before faced a reform-minded ministry and Parliament. But Patriots—as the defenders of

American rights came to be called—took up Grenville's challenge, organizing protest meetings, rioting in the streets, and articulating an ideology of resistance.

THE CROWD REBELS

In May 1765 the eloquent young Patrick Henry addressed the Virginia House of Burgesses and blamed the new king, George III (1760–1820) for naming—and supporting—the ministers who designed the new legislation. Comparing George to the tyrannical Charles I, Henry seemed to call for a new republican revolution. Although the Burgesses were dismayed by Henry's remarks against the king (which bordered on treason), they endorsed his attack on the Stamp Act, declaring that any attempt to tax the colonists without their consent "has a manifest Tendency to Destroy American freedom." In Massachusetts, James Otis, another republican-minded firebrand, persuaded the House of Representatives to call for a general meeting of all the colonies "to implore Relief" from the act.

Nine colonial assemblies sent delegates to the Stamp Act Congress, which met in New York City in October. The Congress issued a set of Resolves protesting against the loss of American "rights and liberties," especially trial by jury. The Resolves also challenged the constitutionality of the Stamp and Sugar Acts, declaring that only the colonists' elected representatives could impose taxes on them. However, most

The Intensity of Patrick Henry

This portrait, painted in 1795 when Henry was in his sixties, captured his lifelong seriousness and intensity. As an orator, Henry drew on evangelical Protestantism to create a new mode of political oratory. "His figures of speech . . . were often borrowed from the Scriptures," a contemporary noted, and the content of his speeches mirrored "the earnestness depicted in his own features."

(Mead Art Museum, Amherst College)

of the delegates were moderate men who sought compromise, not confrontation. They concluded by assuring Parliament that Americans "glory in being subjects of the best of Kings" and humbly petitioning for repeal of the Stamp Act. Other influential Americans advocated nonviolent resistance through a boycott of British goods.

Popular resentment was not so easily contained. When the act went into effect on November 1, disciplined mobs went into action. Led by men who called themselves the Sons of Liberty, the mobs demanded the resignation of newly appointed stamp-tax collectors, most of whom were native-born colonists. In Boston the Sons of Liberty made an effigy of the collector Andrew Oliver, which they beheaded and burned; then they destroyed a new brick building he owned. Two weeks later Bostonians attacked the house of Lieutenant Governor Thomas Hutchinson, a defender of social privilege and imperial authority, breaking the furniture, looting the wine cellar, and burning the library (see American Voices, "The Threat of Mob Rule").

In nearly every colony similar crowds of angry people—the "rabble," as their detractors called them—intimidated royal officials. Near Wethersfield, Connecticut, 500 farmers and artisans held tax collector Jared Ingersoll as a captive until he resigned his office. This was "the Cause of the People," shouted one rioter, and he would not "take Directions about it from any Body." In New York nearly 3,000 shopkeepers, artisans, laborers, and seamen marched through the streets, breaking street lamps and windows and crying "Liberty!"

Although the strength of the Liberty mobs was surprising, such plebeian crowd actions were a fact of life in both Britain and America. Every November 5 Protestant mobs burned an effigy of the pope to celebrate the failure in 1605 of a plot by Guy Fawkes and other English Catholics to blow up the Houses of Parliament. Colonial mobs regularly destroyed houses used as brothels and rioted to protest the impressment of merchant seamen by the Royal Navy.

If rioting was traditional, its political goals were new. The leaders of the Sons of Liberty in New York City were minor merchants, such as Isaac Sears and Alexander McDougall, who were Radical Whigs. They tried to direct the raw energy of the crowd against the new tax measures, but the mobs drew support from established artisans, struggling journeymen, and poor laborers and seamen who had their own agendas. Some artisans joined the crowds because imports of low-priced British shoes and other manufactured goods threatened their livelihood, and they feared the additional burden of a stamp tax. Unlike "the Common people of England," a well-traveled colonist observed, "the people of America ... never would submitt to be taxed that a few may be loaded with palaces and Pensions and riot in Luxury and Excess, while they themselves cannot support themselves and their needy offspring with Bread."

Other members of the crowd were stirred by the religious passions of the Great Awakening. As evangelical Protestants who led disciplined, hardworking lives, they resented the arrogance of British military officers and the corruption of royal bureaucrats. In New England, some protesters looked back to the English Puritan

---

AMERICAN VOICES

The Threat of Mob Rule

JOSIAH QUINCY JR.

A *lthough crowd actions were a familiar aspect of English and colonial life, they were of-*
ten condemned. To Josiah Quincy Jr., a Boston gentleman, the destruction of the house
of Chief Justice Thomas Hutchinson by the Sons of Liberty in August 1765 was an unjust at-
tack against a loyal American and an example of "lawless despotism."

There cannot, perhaps, be found in the records of time a more flagrant instance to what
a pitch of infatuation an incensed populace may arise than the last night afforded. . . . The
populace of Boston . . . assembled in King's Street; where, after having kindled a fire, they
proceeded, in two separate bodies, to attack the houses of two gentlemen of distinction
. . . and did great damage in destroying their houses, furniture, &c., and irreparable damage in destroying their papers. Both parties . . . then unitedly proceeded to the Chief-
Justice's house, who, not expecting them, was unattended by his friends who might have
assisted, or proved his innocence. . . .

　　This rage-intoxicated rabble . . . beset the house on all sides, and soon destroyed every
thing of value. . . . The destruction was really amazing. . . .

　　The distress a man must feel on such an occasion can only be conceived by those who
the next day saw his Honor the Chief-Justice come into court . . . with tears starting from
his eyes, and a countenance which strongly told the inward anguish of his soul.

> GENTLEMEN [he said]: There not being a quorum of the court without me, I
> am obliged to appear. Some apology is necessary for my dress: indeed, I had no
> other. Destitute of every thing. . . .
>
> I call my Maker to witness, that I never, in New England or Old, in Great Britain
> or America, neither directly nor indirectly, was aiding, assisting, or supporting—
> in the least promoting or encouraging—what is commonly called the Stamp Act;
> but, on the contrary, did all in my power, and strove as much as in me lay, to
> prevent it. . . .

Who, that marks the riotous tumult, confusion, and uproar of a democratic . . . state [would
not fly] . . . to that best asylum, that glorious medium, the British Constitution? . . . May
ye never lose it through a licentious abuse of your invaluable rights.

SOURCE: Jack P. Greene, ed., *Colonies to Nation: 1763–1789* (Baltimore: John Hopkins University Press,
1967), pp. 61–63.

---

revolution, reviving antimonarchial and prorepublican sentiments of their great-
grandparents. A letter sent to a Boston newspaper promising to save "all the Freeborn
Sons of America" from "tyrannical ministers" was signed "Oliver Cromwell," the English republican revolutionary of the 1640s. Finally, the mobs included apprentices,

The BOSTONIAN'S Paying the EXCISE-MAN, or TARRING & FEATHERING

Plate I.

A British View of American Mobs

This satiric attack on the Sons of Liberty questions their brutal treatment of John Malcolm, the Commissioner of the Customs in Boston, who was tarred and feathered and forced to drink huge quantities of tea. The Liberty Tree in the background raises the question: Does liberty mean anarchy?

(Courtesy of the John Carter Brown Library at Brown University)

journeymen, day laborers, and unemployed sailors—young men seeking adventure and excitement who, when fortified by drink, were ready to resort to violence.

Throughout the colonies popular resistance nullified the Stamp Act. Fearing a massive assault on Fort George on Guy Fawkes Day (November 5, 1765), New York Lieutenant Governor Cadwallader Colden called on General Gage to use his small military force to protect the stamps stored in the fort. Gage refused. "Fire from the Fort might disperse the Mob, but it would not quell them," he told Colden, and the result would be "an Insurrection, the Commencement of Civil War." Frightened collectors gave up their stamps, and angry Americans coerced officials into accepting legal documents without them. This popular insurrection gave a democratic cast to the emerging American Patriot movement, extending it far beyond the ranks of merchants, lawyers, and elected officials. "Nothing is wanting but your own Resolution," a New York Son of Liberty declared during the upheaval, "for great is the Authority and Power of the People."

Slow communication across the Atlantic meant that the ministry's response to the Stamp Act Congress and the Liberty mobs would not be known until the following spring. But it was already clear that royal officials could no longer count on the deferential political behavior that had ensured the empire's stability for three generations. As the collector of the customs in Philadelphia lamented, "What can a Governor do without the assistance of the Governed?"

IDEOLOGICAL ROOTS OF RESISTANCE

Initially the American resistance movement had no acknowledged leaders and no central organization. It had arisen spontaneously in the seaport cities because urban residents were directly affected by British policies. The Stamp Act taxed the newspapers and documents used by merchants and lawyers, the Sugar Act raised the cost of molasses to distillers, and the flood of British manufactures threatened the livelihood of urban artisans. As urban merchants and lawyers protested the new measures, they found some allies in the colonial assemblies—the traditional defenders of American interests—but the movement was slow to develop a coherent outlook and organization.

Consequently, the first protests focused narrowly on particular economic and political matters. One pamphleteer complained that colonists were being compelled to give the British "our money, as oft and in what quantity they please to demand it." Other writers alleged that the British had violated specific "liberties and privileges" embodied in colonial charters. But American Patriot publicists gradually focused the debate by defining "liberty" as an abstract ideal—a "natural right" of all people—rather than a set of historical privileges. As pamphlets of remarkable political sophistication circulated throughout the colonies, they provided the resistance movement with an intellectual rationale, a political agenda, and a visible cadre of leaders.

Patriot publicists drew on three intellectual traditions. The first was English common law—the centuries-old body of legal rules and procedures that protected the king's subjects against arbitrary acts by the government. In 1761 the Boston lawyer James Otis had cited English legal precedent in the famous Writs of Assistance case, in which he disputed the constitutionality of a general search warrant permitting customs officials to inspect the property and possessions of any and all persons. Similarly, in demanding a jury trial for John Hancock, John Adams invoked common-law tradition. "This 29th Chap. of Magna Charta," Adams argued, referring to an ancient English document that had established the right to trial by jury, "has for many Centuries been esteemed by Englishmen, as one of the ... firmest Bulwarks of their Liberties." Other lawyers protested when the terms of appointment for colonial judges were altered from "during good behavior" to "at the pleasure" of the royal governor, arguing that the change in wording compromised the independence of the judiciary.

A second major intellectual resource for educated Americans was the rationalist thought of the Enlightenment. Unlike American common-law attorneys, who used legal precedents to criticize British measures, the Virginia planter Thomas Jefferson invoked Enlightenment philosophers, such as David Hume and Francis Hutcheson, who questioned the past and relied on reason to discover and correct social ills. Jefferson and other Patriot authors also drew on the political philosopher John Locke, who argued that all individuals possessed certain "natural rights," such as life, liberty, and property, which government was responsible for protecting. And they celebrated the French theorist Montesquieu, who devised institutional curbs to prevent the arbitrary exercise of political power.

The republican and Whig strands of the English political tradition provided the third ideological basis for the American Patriot movement. In some places, particularly Puritan New England, Americans had long venerated the Commonwealth era—the brief period between 1649 and 1660 when England was a republic. After the Glorious Revolution of 1688, many colonists had welcomed the constitutional restrictions placed on the monarchy by English Whigs, such as the ban on royally imposed taxes. Later, educated Americans such as Samuel Adams of Boston absorbed the arguments of Radical Whig spokesmen who denounced political corruption. "Bribery is so common," John Dickinson of Pennsylvania had complained during a visit to London in the 1750s, "that there is not a borough in England where it is not practiced." These republican and Radical Whig sentiments made many Americans suspicious of royal officials. Joseph Warren, a physician and Patriot, reported that many Bostonians believed the Stamp Act was intended "to force the colonies into rebellion," after which the ministry would use "military power to reduce them to servitude."

These writings—swiftly disseminated thanks to the power of the printing press—provided the developing Patriot movement with a sense of identity and an ideological agenda, turning a series of impromptu riots and tax protests into a coherent political coalition.

PARLIAMENT COMPROMISES, 1766

In Britain, Parliament was in turmoil, with different political factions advocating radically different responses to the American challenge. George III had replaced Grenville with a new prime minister, Lord Rockingham, who was allied with the Old Whigs and opposed Grenville's tough policies toward the colonies. But hardliners in Parliament, outraged by the popular rebellion in America, demanded that imperial reform continue. They wanted to dispatch British soldiers to suppress the riots and force the Americans to submit to the constitutional supremacy of Parliament. "The British legislature," declared Chief Justice Sir James Mansfield, "has authority to bind every part and every subject, whether such subjects have a right to vote or not."

Three factions were willing to repeal the Stamp Act, but for different reasons. The Old Whigs advocated repeal for reasons of policy: they believed that America was more important for its "flourishing and increasing trade" than its tax revenues.

Some Old Whigs even agreed with the colonists that the new tax was unconstitutional. British merchants favored repeal out of self-interest because the American boycott of British goods had caused a drastic fall in their sales. In January 1766 the leading commercial centers of London, Liverpool, Bristol, and Glasgow deluged Parliament with petitions, pointing out the threat to their prosperity. "The Avenues of Trade are all shut up," a Bristol merchant with large inventories on hand complained. "We have no Remittances and are at our Witts End for want of Money to fulfill our Engagements with our Tradesmen." Finally, former Prime Minister William Pitt demanded that "the Stamp Act be repealed absolutely, totally, and immediately" as a failed policy. Pitt's view of the constitutional issues was confusing; he argued that Parliament could not tax the colonies but that British authority over America was "sovereign and supreme, in every circumstance of government and legislation whatsoever."

Rockingham gave each group just enough to feel satisfied. To assist British merchants and mollify colonial opinion, he repealed the Stamp Act and ruled out the use of troops against colonial crowds. He also modified the Sugar Act, reducing the duty on French molasses from 3 pence to 1 penny a gallon but extending it to British molasses as well. Thus, the revised Sugar Act regulated foreign trade, which most American officials accepted, but it also taxed a British product, which some colonists saw as unconstitutional. Finally, Rockingham pacified imperial reformers and hardliners with the Declaratory Act of 1766, which explicitly reaffirmed the British Parliament's "full power and authority to make laws and statutes . . . to bind the colonies and people of America . . . in all cases whatsoever."

Because the Stamp Act crisis ended quickly, it might have been forgotten just as quickly. As of 1766 political positions had not yet hardened. Leaders of goodwill could still hope to work out an imperial relationship that was acceptable to British officials and American colonists.

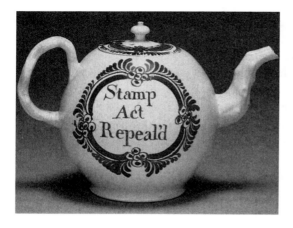

Mixing Business and Politics, 1766

Hurt by the colonists' trade boycott, British manufacturers campaigned for repeal of the Stamp Act. To celebrate the repeal—and expand the market for its teapots in America— the Cockpit Hill factory in Derby quickly produced a commemorative design.

(Courtesy of the Peabody Essex Museum, Salem, MA)

The Growing Confrontation, 1767–1770

The compromise of 1766 was short-lived. Within a year political rivalries in Britain sparked a new and more prolonged struggle with the American provinces, reviving the passions of 1765. The newfound ideological rigidity of key British ministers and American officials aggravated the conflict and dashed prospects for a quick resolution.

THE TOWNSHEND INITIATIVES

Often the course of history is changed by a small event—a leader's illness, a personal grudge, a chance remark. So it was in 1767, when Rockingham's Old Whig ministry collapsed and George III named William Pitt to head the new ministry. Pitt, the master strategist of the Great War for Empire, was chronically ill with gout and frequently missed Parliamentary debates, leaving Chancellor of the Exchequer Charles Townshend in command. Pitt was sympathetic toward America; Townshend was not. So when Grenville attacked Townshend's military budget in 1767, demanding that the colonists pay for the British troops in America, Townshend made an unplanned, fateful policy decision. Long convinced of the necessity of imperial reform and eager to reduce the English land tax, he promised that he would find a new source of revenue in America.

The new tax legislation, known as the Townshend Act of 1767, was intended to free royal officials in the colonies from financial dependence on the American legislatures, enabling them to enforce Parliamentary laws and royal directives. The tax imposed duties on paper, paint, glass, and tea imported into the colonies and was expected to raise about £40,000 a year. To pacify Grenville, part of the revenue would defray military expenses, but the major part would be used to pay the salaries of colonial governors, judges, and other imperial officials. To increase royal power, Townshend also devised the Revenue Act of 1767. The new act created a Board of American Customs Commissioners in Boston and vice-admiralty courts in Halifax, Boston, Philadelphia, and Charleston. These administrative innovations posed a greater threat to American autonomy than did the small sums raised by the import duties.

New York prompted Townshend to raise a new threat to the colonial assemblies when it refused to comply with the Quartering Act of 1765. Fearing an unlimited drain on its treasury, the New York legislature first denied General Gage's requests for barracks and supplies and then limited its assistance. In response, the British ministry instructed New York to pay the entire cost of its defense against Indian raids. If the assembly refused, some members of Parliament threatened to impose a special duty on New York's imports and exports. The earl of Shelburne, the new secretary of state, went even further, suggesting the appointment of a military governor with authority to seize funds from New York's treasury to pay for quartering the troops and "to act with Force or Gentleness as circumstances might make necessary." Townshend decided on a less provocative measure, the Restraining Act of 1767, which suspended the New York assembly until it submitted to the Quartering Act. Faced with the loss of self-government, New Yorkers appropriated the required funds.

The Restraining Act was of great significance because it threatened Americans with the loss of their representative governments. The British Privy Council had always supervised the assemblies, invalidating about 5 percent of all colonial laws (such as those establishing land banks or vesting new powers in the assemblies). Townshend's Restraining Act went much further by declaring American governmental institutions to be completely dependent on Parliamentary favor.

AMERICA AGAIN DEBATES AND RESISTS

The Townshend duties revived the constitutional debate over taxation. During the Stamp Act crisis some Americans had suggested that "external" duties on trade, which Britain had always regulated, were acceptable but that direct or "internal" taxes, which had never before been levied, were not. Townshend thought this distinction between internal and external taxes "perfect nonsense" but told Parliament that "since Americans were pleased to make that distinction, he was willing to indulge them [and] . . . to confine himself to regulations of Trade." Most colonial leaders refused to accept the legitimacy of Townshend's measures, however. They agreed with John Dickinson, author of *Letters from a Farmer in Pennsylvania* (1768), that the real issue was not whether the tax was internal or external but the intention of the legislation. Because the Townshend duties were really designed to raise revenue, they amounted to taxes imposed without consent.

Townshend's measures reinvigorated the American resistance movement. In February 1768 the Massachusetts House of Representatives sent a letter to the other assemblies condemning the Townshend Act, and by the summer Boston and New York merchants had begun a new boycott of British goods. Philadelphia merchants, sailors, and dockworkers, who were more directly involved in trade with Britain, refused to join the movement, believing they had too much to lose. Nonetheless, public support for nonimportation gradually emerged in the smaller port cities of Salem, Newport, and Baltimore and in the countryside. In Puritan New England, ministers and public officials supported the boycott by condemning the use of "foreign superfluities" and promoting the domestic manufacture of necessities such as cloth (Table 5.1).

American women, ordinarily excluded from public affairs, became crucial to the nonimportation movement through their production of "homespun" textiles. During the Stamp Act boycott of English manufactured goods, the wives and daughters of Patriot leaders had increased their output of yarn and cloth. Resistance to the Townshend duties mobilized a much broader group of women, including pious farmwives who assembled to spin yarn at the homes of their ministers. Some gatherings were openly patriotic, such as one in Berwick, Maine, where "true

TABLE 5.1
Patriot Resistance, 1762–1775

British Action	Date	Patriot Response
Revenue Act	1762	Merchants complain privately
Proclamation Line	1763	Land speculators voice discontent
Sugar Act	1764	Protests by merchants and Massachusetts House
Stamp Act	1765	Riots by Sons of Liberty Stamp Act Congress First nonimportation movement
Quartering Act	1765	New York Assembly refuses to implement until 1767
Townshend Duties	1767	Second nonimportation movement Harassment of pro-British merchants
Troops occupy Boston	1768	Boston Massacre of 1770
Gaspée affair	1772	Committees of Correspondence created
Tea Act	1773	Widespread resistance Boston Tea Party
Coercive Acts and Quebec Act	1774	First Continental Congress Third nonimportation movement
British raids on Lexington and Concord	1775	Armed resistance by Minutemen Second Continental Congress

Daughters of Liberty" celebrated American goods, "drinking rye coffee and dining on bear venison." Many more women's groups combined support for nonimportation with charitable work by spinning flax and wool to donate to the needy.

Newspapers celebrated these women as Patriots, prompting thousands to redouble their efforts at the spinning wheel and loom. One Massachusetts town proudly claimed an annual output of 30,000 yards of cloth; East Hartford, Connecticut, reported 17,000 yards. Although this surge in domestic production did not compensate for the loss of British imports, which had averaged about 10 million yards a year, it inspired support for nonimportation in hundreds of communities.

Indeed, the boycott united thousands of Americans in a common political movement. The Sons of Liberty published the names of merchants who imported British goods, broke their store windows, and harassed their employees. In March 1769 most Philadelphia merchants finally responded to public pressure and joined the nonimportation movement. Two months later the members of the Virginia House of Burgesses agreed not to buy dutied articles, luxury goods, or slaves imported by British merchants. "The whole continent from New England to Georgia seems firmly fixed," the *Massachusetts Gazette* proudly announced; "like a strong, well-constructed arch, the more weight there is laid upon it, the firmer it stands;

and thus with America, the more we are loaded, the more we are united." Reflecting colonial self-confidence, Benjamin Franklin called for a return to the pre-1763 mercantilist system and proposed a "plan of conciliation" that was really a demand for British capitulation: "repeal the laws, renounce the right, recall the troops, refund the money, and return to the old method of requisition."

But American resistance only increased British determination. When a copy of the Massachusetts House's letter opposing the Townshend duties reached London in the late spring of 1768, Lord Hillsborough, the secretary of state for American affairs, branded it as "unjustifiable opposition to the constitutional authority of Parliament." To strengthen the "Hand of Government" in Massachusetts and assist the Commissioners of the Customs, who had been forced by a mob to take refuge on a British naval vessel, Hillsborough dispatched four regiments of troops to Boston. By the end of 1768, 4,000 British regulars were encamped in Boston, and military coercion was a very real prospect. General Gage accused public leaders in Massachusetts of "Treasonable and desperate Resolves" and advised the ministry to "Quash this Spirit at a Blow." Parliament responded by threatening to appoint a special commission to hear evidence of treason, and Hillsborough tried to win support for a plan that would isolate Massachusetts from the other colonies and then use the British army to bring the rebellious New Englanders to their knees.

The stakes had risen. In 1765 American resistance to taxation had provoked a Parliamentary debate. In 1768 it produced a plan for military coercion.

LORD NORTH COMPROMISES, 1770

At this critical moment the British ministry's resolve faltered. A food shortage in Britain caused riots across the countryside; in the highly publicized "Massacre of Saint George Fields," troops killed seven demonstrators. The Radical Whig John Wilkes, supported by associations of merchants, tradesmen, and artisans, stepped up his attacks on government corruption and won election to Parliament. Overjoyed, American Patriots drank toasts in Wilkes's honor and purchased thousands of teapots and drinking mugs emblazoned with his picture. Riots in Ireland over the growing military budget there added to the ministry's difficulties.

The American trade boycott also began to hurt. Normally the colonies had an annual trade deficit of £500,000, but in 1768 they imported less from Great Britain, cutting the deficit to £230,000. In 1769 the boycott had a major impact. By continuing to export tobacco, rice, fish, and other goods to Britain while refusing to buy its manufactured goods, Americans accumulated a trade surplus of £816,000. To revive their flagging fortunes, British merchants and manufacturers petitioned Parliament for repeal of the Townshend duties. British government revenues, which were heavily dependent on excise taxes and duties on imported goods, had also suffered. By late 1769 merchants' petitions had persuaded some ministers that the Townshend duties were a mistake, and the king had withdrawn his support for Hillsborough's coercive military plans.

Early in 1770 Lord North became prime minister and arranged a new compromise. Arguing that it was foolish to tax British exports to America, raising their price and decreasing consumption, North persuaded Parliament to repeal the duties on glass, paper, paint, and other manufactured items. But he retained the tax on tea as a symbol of Parliament's supremacy. Gratified, merchants in New York and Philadelphia rejected pleas from Patriots in Boston to continue the boycott. Indeed, most Americans did not contest the symbolic levy on tea but simply avoided the tax by drinking smuggled tea.

Even violence in New York City and Boston did not rupture the compromise. During the boycott New York artisans and workers had taunted British troops, mostly with words but occasionally with stones and fists. In retaliation the soldiers tore down a Liberty Pole (a Patriot flagpole), setting off a week of street fighting. In Boston friction between the residents and British soldiers over constitutional principles and everyday issues, such as competition for part-time jobs, sparked the "Boston Massacre." In March 1770, a group of soldiers fired into a rowdy crowd, killing five men, including one of the leaders, Crispus Attucks, an escaped slave who was working as a seaman. A Radical Whig pamphlet accused the British of deliberately planning the massacre.

Although most Americans remained loyal to the empire, five years of conflict over taxes and constitutional principles had taken its toll. In 1765 American public leaders had accepted Parliament's authority; the Stamp Act Resolves had opposed only certain "unconstitutional" legislation. By 1770 the most outspoken Patriots—Benjamin Franklin in Pennsylvania, Patrick Henry in Virginia, and Samuel Adams in Massachusetts—had repudiated Parliamentary supremacy, claiming equality for the American assemblies. Franklin wanted to create a looser form of empire, with Britain and the colonies as "distinct and separate states" united under "the same Head, or Sovereign, the King." His proposal horrified Thomas Hutchinson, the American-born royal governor of Massachusetts, who rejected the idea of "two independent legislatures in one and the same state." For Hutchinson, the British empire was a single whole, its sovereignty indivisible. "I know of no line," he told the Massachusetts House of Representatives, "that can be drawn between the supreme authority of Parliament and the total independence of the colonies."

There the matter rested. The British had twice tried to impose taxes on the colonies, and American Patriots had twice forced them to retreat. If Parliament insisted on exercising its claim to sovereignty, at least some Americans would have to be subdued by force. Fearful of civil war, the ministry hesitated to take the final fateful step.

The Road to War, 1771–1775

The repeal of the Townshend duties in 1770 restored harmony to the British empire. For the next three years most disputes were resolved peacefully. Yet below the surface lay strong fears and passions and mutual distrust. Suddenly, in 1773 those undercurrents erupted, overwhelming any hope for compromise. In less than two years the Americans and the British stood on the brink of war.

THE TEA ACT: THE COMPROMISE IGNORED

Radical Boston Patriots who wanted greater rights for the colonies continued to warn Americans of the dangers of imperial domination. In November 1772 Samuel Adams persuaded the Boston town meeting to establish a Committee of Correspondence to write to Patriots in other towns and colonies in order "to state the Rights of the Colonists of this Province." Within a few months eighty Massachusetts towns had similar committees. Other colonies copied the practice when the British government set up a royal commission to investigate the burning of the *Gaspée*, a British customs vessel, in Rhode Island. The commission's powers, particularly its authority to send Americans to Britain for trial, first aroused the Virginia House of Burgesses, which created a Committee of Correspondence "to communicate with the other colonies" about the situation in Rhode Island. By July 1773 committees had sprung up in Connecticut, New Hampshire, and South Carolina.

Parliament's passage of a Tea Act in May 1773 initiated the chain of events that led directly to civil war. Lord North had designed the act to provide financial relief for the British East India Company, which was deeply in debt because of military expeditions undertaken to extend British trade in India. The Tea Act provided the company with a government loan and, more important, relieved the Company of paying tariffs on the tea it imported into Britain or exported to the colonies. Only the American consumers would pay the duty.

Lord North failed to understand how unpopular the Tea Act would be in America. Since 1768, when the Townshend Act had placed a duty of 3 pence a pound on tea, the colonies had evaded the tax by illegally importing tea from Dutch sources. However, by relieving the East India Company of English tariffs, the Tea Act was designed to make its tea cheaper than Dutch tea—and thus encourage Americans to pay the Townshend duty on tea. Consequently, radical Patriots accused the ministry of bribing Americans to give up their principled opposition to British taxation. As an anonymous woman wrote in the *Massachusetts Spy,* "the use of [British] tea is considered not as a private but as a public evil . . . a handle to introduce a variety of . . . oppressions amongst us." In addition to taxation, another such oppression was the East India Company's decision to distribute the tea directly to shopkeepers, a tactic that would exclude most colonial merchants from the profits of the trade. "The fear of an Introduction of a Monopoly in this Country," General Haldimand reported from New York, "has induced the mercantile part of the Inhabitants to be very industrious in opposing this Step and added Strength to a Spirit of Independence already too prevalent."

The newly formed Committees of Correspondence took the lead in organizing resistance to the Tea Act. They held public bonfires at which they persuaded their fellow citizens (sometimes gently, sometimes not) to consign British tea to the flames. The Sons of Liberty also prevented East India Company ships from landing new supplies. By forcing the Company's captains to return the tea to Britain or store it in public warehouses, the Patriots effectively nullified the legislation.

Governor Thomas Hutchinson of Massachusetts was determined to uphold the Tea Act and hatched a scheme to land the tea and collect the tax. When a shipment of tea arrived on the *Dartmouth,* he had the ship passed through customs immediately so that the Sons of Liberty could not prevent its landing. If necessary, he was prepared to use the British army to unload the tea and supervise its sale by auction. But Patriots foiled the governor's plan by raiding the *Dartmouth*: a group of artisans and laborers disguised as Indians boarded the ship, broke open the 342 chests of tea (valued at about £10,000, or roughly $800,000 today), and threw them into the harbor. "This destruction of the Tea is so bold and it must have so important Consequences," John Adams wrote in his diary, "that I cannot but consider it as an Epoch in History."

The British Privy Council was outraged, as was the king. "Concessions have made matters worse," George III declared. "The time has come for compulsion." Early in 1774 Parliament decisively rejected a proposal to repeal the duty on American tea; instead, it enacted four Coercive Acts to force Massachusetts into submission. A Port Bill closed Boston Harbor until the East India Company received payment for the destroyed tea. A Government Act annulled the Massachusetts charter and prohibited most local town meetings. A new Quartering Act required the colony to build barracks or accommodate soldiers in private houses. To protect royal officials from Patriot-dominated juries in Massachusetts, a Justice Act allowed the transfer of trials for capital crimes to other colonies or to Britain.

In response, Patriot leaders throughout the mainland colonies condemned these "Intolerable Acts" and rallied support for Massachusetts. In far-off Georgia, a Patriot warned the "Freemen of the Province" that "every privilege you at present claim as a birthright, may be wrested from you by the same authority that blockades the town of Boston." "The cause of Boston," George Washington declared from Virginia, "now is and ever will be considered as the cause of America." The activities of the Committees of Correspondence had created a firm sense of unity.

In 1774 Parliament passed the Quebec Act, which heightened the sense of common danger among Americans of European Protestant descent who lived in the seaboard colonies. The law extended the boundaries of Quebec into the Ohio River Valley, thus restricting the western boundaries of Virginia and other coastal colonies and angering influential land speculators and politicians with western land claims (see Map 5.2). It also gave legal recognition in Quebec to Roman Catholicism, a humane concession to the colony's predominantly French Catholics but one that aroused old religious hatreds, especially in New England, where Puritans associated Catholicism with arbitrary royal government and popish superstition. Although the ministry had not intended the Quebec Act as a coercive measure, many colonial leaders saw it as another demonstration of Parliament's power to intervene in American domestic affairs.

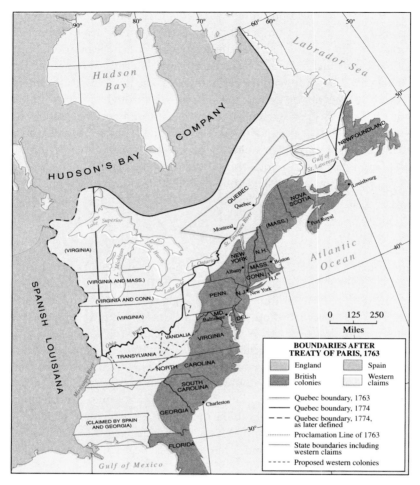

M A P 5.2
British Western Policy, 1763–1774

The Proclamation Line of 1763 prohibited white settlement west of the Appalachian Mountains. Nevertheless, colonial land speculators planned the new colonies of Vandalia and Transylvania. However, the Quebec Act of 1774 designated these western lands as Indian reserves and, by vastly increasing the boundaries of Quebec, eliminated the sea-to-sea land claims of many eastern colonies. The act angered many Americans: settlers and land speculators, New England Protestants who feared Catholicism in Quebec, and Patriots who condemned its failure to provide a representative assembly in Quebec.

THE CONTINENTAL CONGRESS RESPONDS

American leaders called for a new all-colony assembly, the Continental Congress. The newer colonies—Florida, Quebec, Nova Scotia, and Newfoundland—did not attend, nor did Georgia, whose legislature was effectively controlled by a royal gov-

Religion and Rebellion

Many American Protestants hated bishops and the ecclesiastical power they represented. This cartoon warned that the Quebec Bill of 1774, which allowed the practice of Catholicism in Canada, was part of a plot by the hierarchy of the Church of England to impose bishops on the American colonies. (Courtesy of the John Carter Brown Library at Brown University, Providence, RI)

ernor. But delegates chosen by the other twelve mainland assemblies met in Philadelphia in September 1774. New England delegates advocated political union and defensive military preparations. Southern leaders had long resented the Navigation Acts and feared a British plot "to overturn the constitution and introduce a system of arbitrary government." They favored a new economic boycott, but many delegates from the middle colonies held out for a political compromise.

Led by Joseph Galloway of Pennsylvania, these men of "loyal principles" outlined a scheme for a new imperial system that resembled the Albany Plan of Union of 1754. Under Galloway's proposal, America would have a legislative council selected by the colonial assemblies and a president-general appointed by the king. The new council would have veto power over Parliamentary legislation that affected America. Despite this feature, however, the delegates refused to endorse Galloway's plan. With British troops occupying Boston, it was thought to be too conciliatory.

Instead, the First Continental Congress passed a Declaration of Rights and Grievances that condemned the Coercive Acts and demanded their repeal. It also repudiated the Declaratory Act of 1766, which had proclaimed Parliament's supremacy over the colonies, and demanded that Britain restrict its supervision of American affairs to matters of external trade. Finally, the Congress began a program of economic retaliation, beginning with nonimportation and nonconsumption agreements that would take effect in December 1774. If Parliament did not repeal the Intolerable Acts by September 1775, virtually all colonial exports to

Britain, Ireland, and the British West Indies would be cut off. Ten years of constitutional conflict had culminated in a threat of all-out commercial warfare.

Even at this late date a few British leaders hoped for compromise. In January 1775 the earl of Chatham (William Pitt) asked that Parliament give up its claim to tax the colonies and recognize the Continental Congress as a lawful body. In return for these and other concessions, he suggested, the Congress should acknowledge Parliamentary supremacy and grant a continuing revenue to help defray the British national debt.

The British ministry rejected Chatham's plan. Twice it had backed down in the face of colonial resistance; a third retreat was impossible. The honor of the nation was at stake. Branding the Continental Congress an illegal assembly, it dismissed Lord Dartmouth's proposal to send commissioners to America to negotiate a settlement. Instead, Lord North unilaterally set stringent terms: Americans must pay for their own defense and administration and acknowledge Parliament's authority to tax them. To put teeth in these demands, North imposed a naval blockade on American trade with foreign nations and ordered General Gage to suppress dissent in Massachusetts. "Now the case seemed desperate," the prime minister told former Massachusetts Governor Thomas Hutchinson, who was living in exile in London. "Parliament would not—could not—concede. For aught he could see it must come to violence."

THE RISING OF THE COUNTRYSIDE

Ultimately, the success of the urban-led Patriot movement would depend on the actions of the large rural population. At first most farmers had little interest in imperial issues. Their lives were deeply rooted in the soil, and their prime allegiance was to family and community. But the French and Indian War intruded into their lives, taking their sons for military duty and raising their taxes. In Newtown, Long Island, farmers had paid an average of 10 shillings a year in taxes until 1754; by 1756 their wartime taxes had jumped to 30 shillings. Peace brought only slight relief, for in 1771 the British-imposed Quartering Act cost each Newtown resident 20 shillings in taxes. These levies angered rural Americans, though in fact they paid much lower taxes than did most Britons.

The urban-led nonimportation movements of 1765 and 1769 also raised the political consciousness of many rural Americans. When the Continental Congress declared a new economic boycott of British goods in 1774, it easily established a network of local Committees of Safety and Inspection to support it. Appealing to rural thriftiness, the Congress condemned those who wore expensive imported clothes to funerals, approving only "a black crape or ribbon on the arm or hat for gentlemen, and a black ribbon and necklace for ladies." In Concord, Massachusetts, 80 percent of male heads of families and a number of single women signed a Solemn League and Covenant vowing support for nonimportation.

Patriots also appealed to the yeoman tradition of agricultural independence, which was everywhere under attack. Arable land had become scarce and expensive in long-settled regions; in many new communities merchants were seizing farmsteads for delinquent debts. The new demands of the British government would further drain "this People of the Fruits of their Toil," complained the town meeting of Petersham, Massachusetts. "The duty on tea," added a Patriot pamphlet, "was only a prelude to a window-tax, hearth-tax, land-tax, and poll-tax, and these were only paving the way for reducing the country to lordships." By the 1770s many northern yeomen felt personally threatened by British imperial policy.

Despite their much higher standard of living, southern slaveowners had similar fears. Many influential Virginia Patriots—including Patrick Henry, George Washington, and Thomas Jefferson—were speculators in western lands and reacted angrily when first the Proclamation Line of 1763 and then the Quebec Act of 1774 invalidated their claims and their hopes of great fortunes. Moreover, many Chesapeake planters had fallen deeply into debt to British merchants, usually because of extravagant spending. "I must return again to a low and less expensive Prudence," planter Landon Carter vowed unsuccessfully in 1771. As Washington noted, Carter and other planters wanted to live "genteely and hospitably" and were "ashamed" to adopt frugal ways. Accustomed to being masters on their plantations, they resented their financial dependence and feared the prospect of political dependence. Once Parliament used the Coercive Acts to subdue Massachusetts, the planters feared, it might seize control of Virginia's county courts and House of Burgesses, depriving the gentry of its political power. This threat moved Patriot planters to action, closing the courts so that yeomen could bargain with Scottish merchants over tobacco prices without risking suits for debt. "The spark of liberty is not yet extinct among our people," one planter declared, "and if properly fanned by the Gentlemen of influence will, I make no doubt, burst out again into a flame."

While many wealthy planters and affluent merchants supported the Patriot cause, other prominent Americans worried that resistance to Britain would destroy respect for all political institutions, ending in mob rule. Their fears increased when the Sons of Liberty turned to violence to enforce nonimportation. As a well-to-do New Yorker complained, "No man can be in a more abject state of bondage than he whose Reputation, Property and Life are exposed to the discretionary violence . . . of the community." As the crisis continued, these men rallied to the support of the royal governors.

Other social groups also refused to support the resistance movement. In regions where many wealthy landlords became Patriots, such as the Hudson Valley of New York, tenant farmers supported the crown because they hated their landlords. Similar social divisions prompted some Regulators in the North Carolina backcountry and many farmers on the eastern shore of Chesapeake Bay in Maryland to oppose the policies advocated by the local Patriot gentry. A group of enslaved blacks in Virginia, James Madison reported in November 1774, planned to flee from their Patriot owners and had chosen "a leader who was to conduct them when the English troops should arrive." Many Quakers and Germans in Pennsylvania and New Jersey tried to remain neutral because of pacifist religious principles and fear of political change.

Beginning in 1774, prominent Americans of "loyal principles"—mostly royal officials, merchants with military contracts, clergy of the Church of England, and well-established lawyers—denounced the Patriot movement, accusing it of seeking independence. They formed an articulate pro-British party, but one that remained small and ineffective. A Tory Association started by Governor Wentworth of New Hampshire drew only fifty-nine members, fourteen of whom were the governor's relatives. At this crucial juncture Americans who favored resistance to British rule commanded the allegiance—or at least the acquiescence—of the majority of white Americans.

THE FAILURE OF COMPROMISE

When the Continental Congress met in September 1774, New England was already in open defiance of British authority. In August 150 delegates had gathered in Concord, Massachusetts, for a Middlesex County Congress. This illegal convention had advised Patriots to close the royal courts of justice and transfer their political allegiance to the popularly elected House of Representatives. Following the congress, armed crowds harassed Loyalists and ensured Patriot rule in most of New England.

General Thomas Gage, by then the military governor of Massachusetts, tried desperately to maintain imperial power. In September 1774 he ordered British troops in Boston to seize Patriot armories and storehouses at Charlestown and Cambridge. In response, 20,000 colonial militiamen mobilized to safeguard military supply depots in Concord and Worcester. The Concord town meeting voted to raise a defensive force, the famous Minutemen, to "Stand at a minutes warning in Case of alarm." Increasingly, Gage's authority was limited to Boston, where it rested primarily on the bayonets of his 3,500 troops. Meanwhile, the Massachusetts House met on its own authority, issued regulations for the collection of taxes, strengthened the militia, and assumed the responsibilities of government.

Even before the news of Massachusetts's defiance reached London, the colonial secretary, Lord Dartmouth, had proclaimed the colony to be in a state of "open rebellion." Declaring that "force should be repelled by force," he ordered Gage to march quickly against the "rude rabble." On the night of April 18, 1775, Gage dispatched 700 soldiers to capture colonial leaders and supplies at Concord. But Paul Revere and two other Bostonians warned the Patriots, and at dawn on April 19 local militiamen met the British first at Lexington and then at Concord. The skirmishes took a dozen lives. As the British retreated along the narrow roads to Boston, they were repeatedly ambushed by militiamen from neighboring towns. By the end of the day, 73 British soldiers were dead, 174 wounded, and 26 missing. British fire had killed 49 American militiamen and wounded 39 (see American Voices, "A British View of Lexington and Concord").

A British View of Lexington and Concord

LIEUTENANT-COLONEL FRANKLIN SMITH

O n April 26, 1775, the Patriot-controlled Provincial Congress issued what it called a "true, and authentic account" of the battles at Lexington and Concord, declaring that at Lexington "the regulars rushed on with great violence and first began the hostilities" and that in the retreat of the British troops "women in child-bed were driven by soldiery naked in the streets, old men peaceably in their houses were shot dead." British Lieutenant-Colonel Franklin Smith offered a very different account of those events.

At Lexington . . . [we] found on a green close to the road a body of the country people drawn up in military order, with arms and accoutrements, and, as appeared afterward, loaded. . . . Our troops advanced towards them, without any intention of injuring them . . . ; but they in confusion went off, principally to the left, only one of them fired before he went off, and three or four more jumped over a wall and fired from behind it among the soldiers; on which the troops returned it, and killed several of them. They likewise fired on the soldiers from the Meeting and dwelling-houses. . . .

While at Concord we saw vast numbers assembling in many parts; at one of the bridges they marched down, with a very considerable body, on the light infantry posted there. On their coming pretty near, one of our men fired on them, which they returned; on which an action ensued and some few were killed and wounded. In this affair, it appears that, after the bridge was quitted, they scalped and otherwise ill treated one or two of [our] men who were either killed or severely wounded. . . .

On our leaving Concord to return to Boston they began to fire on us from behind walls, ditches, trees, &c., which, as we marched, increased to a very great degree, and continued . . . for, I believe, upwards of eighteen miles; so that I can't think but it must have been a preconcerted scheme in them, to attack the King's troops the first favorable opportunity that offered; otherwise, I think they could not, in such a short a time from our marching out, have raised such a numerous body.

SOURCE: Massachusetts Historical Society, *Proceedings, 1876* (Boston, 1876), pp. 350ff.

In the aftermath of the Stamp Act and Townshend duties, political leaders had fashioned compromises that patched up the fabric of empire. By the time of the Tea Act, neither the British ministry nor the Patriot leadership was prepared to give way, and the extent of the fighting in Massachusetts settled the issue. Too much blood had now been spilled to allow another compromise. Twelve years of economic conflict and constitutional debate had ended in civil war.

T I M E L I N E

1754–1763	Seven Years (French and Indian) War	**1768**	Second nonimportation movement begins.
	British national debt doubles.		Daughters of Liberty make homespun cloth.
1760	George III becomes king.		British army occupies Boston.
1763	Proclamation Line restricts western settlement.	**1770**	North compromises: repeals most Townshend duties.
	Peacetime army in America		Boston Massacre
	Grenville becomes prime minister.	**1772**	*Gaspée* affair prompts creation of Committees of Correspondence.
1764	Sugar Act		
	Colonists oppose vice-admiralty courts.	**1773**	Tea Act leads to Boston Tea Party.
	Franklin proposes American representation in Parliament.	**1774**	Coercive Acts punish Massachusetts.
1765	Stamp Act		Quebec Act
	Stamp Act Congress and riots led by Sons of Liberty		First Continental Congress meets.
			Third nonimportation movement
1765–1766	First nonimportation movement		Loyalists organize.
1766	Parliament compromises: repeals Stamp Act and enacts Declaratory Act.	**1775**	Ministry orders Gage to suppress rebellion in Massachusetts.
			Battles of Lexington and Concord
1767	Townshend duties		
	Restraining Act in New York		

For Further Exploration

Two stimulating overviews of the prerevolutionary years are A. J. Langguth's *Patriots: The Men Who Started the American Revolution* (1988), a suspenseful story of such famous figures as George Washington, John Adams, Samuel Adams, and Patrick Henry, and Edward Countryman's *The American Revolution* (1985), which focuses on ordinary people. Edmund Morgan and Helen Morgan also use the experience of individual colonists to tell the story of *The Stamp Act Crisis* (1953). Philip Lawson's *George Grenville* (1984) offers a sympathetic biography of a reform-minded prime minister. The coming of the revolution is covered in three lucidly written and broadly conceived studies. Hiller B. Zobel's *The Boston Massacre* (1970) captures the social unrest and latent violence of these years, while Benjamin Labaree's *The Boston Tea Party* suggests how one "small" event altered the course of history. The rise of the Radical Patriots and the outbreak of the fighting in Massachusetts is captivatingly retold in David Hackett Fischer's *Paul Revere's Ride* (1994). For events in Virginia, see the exciting study by Woody Holton, *Forced Founders: Indians, Debtors, Slaves, & the Making of the American Revolution in Virginia* (1999).

Liberty! The American Revolution (6 hours), a six-part video available through PBS, provides a coherent narrative of the movement for independence. Contrasting firsthand accounts of Boston Massacre are available on the website "From Revolution to Reconstruction" at the University of Groningen, available at <http://odur.let.rug.nl/~usa/D/1751 -1775/bostonmassacre/prest.htm>, which also contains other materials on the revolutionary era. The website of the National Gallery of Art, available at <http://www.nga.gov>, has an interesting section devoted to American paintings of the colonial and revolutionary periods, including a detailed analysis of a work by Jonathan Copley. See its "Index of American Design" for a collection of eighteenth-century German-American folk art.

Part Two

THE NEW REPUBLIC
1775–1820

THEMATIC TIMELINE

	GOVERNMENT	DIPLOMACY	ECONOMY
	CREATING REPUBLICAN INSTITUTIONS	EUROPEAN ENTANGLEMENTS	EXPANDING COMMERCE AND MANUFACTURING
1775	• State constitutions devised and implemented	• Independence declared (1776) • French alliance (1778)	• Wartime expansion of manufacturing
1780	• Articles of Confederation ratified (1781) • Philadelphia convention drafts U.S. Constitution (1787).	• Treaty of Paris (1783) • British trade restrictions in West Indies • U.S. government signs treaties with Indian peoples.	• Bank of North America (1781) • Commercial recession (1783–1789) • Western land speculation
1790	• Bill of Rights (1791) • First national parties: Federalists and Republicans	• Wars of the French Revolution • Jay's and Pinckney's treaties (1795) • Undeclared war with France (1798)	• First Bank of the United States (1792–1812) • States charter business corporations. • Outwork expands.
1800	• Revolution of 1800 • Activist state legislatures • Chief Justice Marshall asserts judicial power.	• Napoleonic wars (1802–1815) • Louisiana Purchase (1803) • Embargo of 1807	• Cotton expands into Old Southwest. • Farm productivity improves. • Embargo encourages U.S. manufacturing.
1810	• Triumph of Republican Party • State constitutions democratized	• War of 1812 • Treaty of Ghent (1816) ends war.	• Second Bank of the United States (1816–1836) • Supreme Court protects business. • Emergence of a national economy

"The American war is over," the Philadelphia Patriot Benjamin Rush declared in 1787, "but this is far from being the case with the *American revolution*. On the contrary, nothing but the first act of the great drama is closed. It remains yet to establish and perfect our new forms of government." The job was even greater than Rush imagined, for the republican revolution of 1776 challenged nearly all the values and institutions of the colonial social order, forcing changes not only in politics but also in economic, religious, and cultural life.

GOVERNMENT. The first and most fundamental task was to devise a republican system of government. In 1775 no one in America knew how the new state governments should be organized and if there should be a permanent central authority along the lines of the Continental Congress. It would take time and experience to find out. It would take even longer to come to terms with a new institution, the political party. Yet by 1820 American political leaders had fashioned a successful republican system on both the state and national levels. This system of political authority had three striking characteristics: popular sovereignty—government of the people; activist legislatures that pursued the public good—government for the people; and democratic decision making by most white adult men—government by the people.

DIPLOMACY. To create and preserve their new republic, Americans of European descent had to fight two wars against Great Britain, an undeclared war against France, and many battles

SOCIETY	CULTURE
DEFINING LIBERTY AND EQUALITY	PLURALISM AND NATIONAL IDENTITY
• Emancipation of slaves begins in the North.	• Paine's *Common Sense* calls for a republic.
• Virginia Statute of Religious Freedom (1786) • Idea of republican motherhood	• Land ordinances create a national domain in the West.
• French Revolution sparks ideological debate. • Sedition Act limits freedom of the press (1798).	• Indians form Western Confederacy. • Sectional divisions emerge between South and North.
• Young choose own marriage partners. • New Jersey ends woman suffrage (1807). • Atlantic slave trade legally ended (1808)	• African Americans absorb Protestant Christianity. • Tenskwatawa and Tecumseh revive Indian identity.
• Expansion of suffrage for white men • New England abolishes established church (1820s).	• War of 1812 tests national unity. • Second Great Awakening shapes American culture.

with Indian peoples and confederations. The wars against Britain divided the country into bitter factions—Patriots versus Loyalists in 1776 and prowar Republicans against antiwar Federalists in 1812—and expended much blood and treasure. The settlement of the trans-Appalachian West by white Americans brought cultural disaster to many Indian peoples, whose lives were destroyed by European diseases and alcohol and whose lands were seized by gun-toting settlers. Yet, by 1820 the United States had emerged as a strong independent state, free from entanglement in the wars and diplomacy of Europe and prepared to exploit the riches of the continent.

ECONOMY. By this time the expansion of commerce and the market system had laid the foundations for a strong national economy. Beginning in the 1780s merchants financed commercial banks and organized a rural-based system of manufacturing, while state governments used charters and legal incentives to provide improved transportation.

Southern planters carried slavery west to Alabama and Mississippi and grew rich by exporting a new crop—cotton—to markets in Europe and the North. Simultaneously northern farm families settled new lands in the Midwest where they grew bountiful crops of wheat and corn, produced raw materials such as leather and wool for the new manufacturing enterprises, and undertook additional labor as handicraft workers. As a result of these efforts, by 1820 the new American republic was on the verge of achieving economic as well as political independence.

SOCIETY. As Americans defined the character of their new republican society, they divided along lines of gender, race, religion, and class. They also held differing views on many fundamental questions—legal equality for women, the status of slavery, the meaning of religious liberty, and the public's responsibility to address social inequality. Public sentiment and responsive political leaders resolved some of these issues, moving to end slavery in the

North and to eliminate the system of state-sponsored churches. But Americans continued to argue over southern slavery, distinctions of wealth and status, and the nature of family relations in a republican society.

CULTURE. The final task Americans faced—creating a distinct culture and identity—was complicated by the diversity of peoples and regions. Native Americans still lived in their own clans and nations, while black Americans, one-fifth of the enumerated population, were developing a new, African American culture. The white inhabitants created vigorous regional cultures and preserved parts of their ancestral heritage—English, Scottish, Scots-Irish, German, and Dutch. Nevertheless, political institutions began to unite Americans, as did their increasing participation in the market economy and in evangelical Protestant churches. By 1820 to be an American meant, for the dominant white population, being a republican, a Protestant, and an enterprising individual in a capitalist-run market system.

Chapter 6

WAR AND REVOLUTION
1775–1783

A government of our own is our natural right . . . 'TIS TIME TO PART.
—Thomas Paine, 1776

When the Patriots of Frederick County, Maryland, demanded loyalty to the American cause in 1776, Robert Gassaway would have none of it. "It was better for the poor people to lay down their arms and pay the duties and taxes laid upon them by King and Parliament," he told local Council of Safety, "than to be . . . commanded and ordered about." The story was much the same in Farmington, Connecticut, where Nathaniel Jones and seventeen other men were imprisoned for a month for "remaining neutral" and failing to join their militia unit in opposing a British raid. Everywhere, the logic of events was forcing families to choose sides. In this battle for the allegiance of ordinary men and women, the Patriots' control of local governments gave them the edge. Combining physical threats with monetary incentives, they built loyal militia units and an effective Continental army. "I admire the American troops tremendously!" exclaimed a French officer toward the end of the war. "It is incredible that soldiers composed of every age, even children of fifteen, of whites and blacks, almost naked, unpaid, and rather poorly fed, can march so well and withstand fire so steadfastly."

Military mobilization created political commitment. By forcing ordinary Americans to support the war—as soldiers, taxpayers, or loyal residents—Patriots prompted some to turn to Loyalism and many more to become active republicans. "From subjects to citizens the difference is immense," remarked the South Carolina physician and Patriot David Ramsay. "Each citizen of a free state contains . . . as much of the common sovereignty as another." By repudiating aristocratic and monarchical rule and raising a democratic army, the Patriots placed sovereignty in the people, launching the age of democratic revolutions.

Toward Independence, 1775–1776

The Battle of Concord was fought on April 19, 1775, but fourteen months would elapse before the rebels formally broke with Britain. In the meantime Patriot legislators in most of the thirteen colonies stretching from New Hampshire to

Georgia threw out their royal governors and created the two essentials for independence: a government and an army.

THE SECOND CONTINENTAL CONGRESS AND CIVIL WAR

Armed struggle in Massachusetts lent urgency to the Second Continental Congress, which met in Philadelphia in May 1775. Soon after the Congress opened, more than 3,000 British troops attacked new American fortifications on Breed's Hill and Bunker Hill overlooking Boston. After three assaults and 1,000 casualties they finally dislodged the Patriot militia. Inspired by his countrymen's valor, John Adams exhorted the Congress to rise to the "defense of American liberty" by creating a Continental army headed by George Washington of Virginia. More cautious delegates and those with Loyalist sympathies warned that these measures would commit the colonists irretrievably to rebellion. After bitter debate Congress approved the proposals—but as Adams lamented, only "by bare majorities."

Despite the blood that had been shed, a majority in Congress still hoped for reconciliation with Britain. Led by John Dickinson of Pennsylvania, these moderates passed an Olive Branch petition, expressing loyalty to George III and requesting the repeal of oppressive parliamentary legislation. But zealous Patriots such as Samuel Adams of Massachusetts and Patrick Henry of Virginia mobilized antiimperial sentiment by winning passage of a Declaration of the Causes and Necessities of Taking Up Arms. Americans dreaded the "calamities of civil war," it asserted, but were "resolved to die Freemen rather than to live [as] slaves." The king decided the issue by refusing to receive the moderates' petition and in August 1775 issuing a Proclamation for Suppressing Rebellion and Sedition.

In September the radicals in Congress won support for an invasion of Canada that they hoped would unleash a popular uprising and add a fourteenth colony to the rebellion. Patriot forces easily took Montreal, but in December they failed to capture Quebec. To aid the Patriot cause American merchants waged financial warfare, implementing the resolution of the First Continental Congress to cut off all exports to Britain and its West Indian sugar islands. By ending the tobacco trade and disrupting sugar production, they hoped to undermine the British economy. Parliament retaliated at the end of 1775 with a Prohibitory Act outlawing all trade with the rebellious colonies.

Meanwhile, skirmishes between Patriots and Loyalists broke out in Virginia. In June 1775 the Patriot-dominated House of Burgesses forced the royal governor, Lord Dunmore, to take refuge on a British warship in Chesapeake Bay. Branding the Patriots "traitors," the governor organized two military forces—one white, the Queen's Own Loyal Virginians, and one black, the Ethiopian Regiment, enlisting about 1,000 slaves who had fled from their Patriot owners. Then in November Dunmore issued a controversial proclamation, offering freedom to slaves and indentured servants who joined the Loyalist cause. White planters denounced Dunmore's "Diabolical scheme" as "pointing a dagger to their Throats, thru the hands of their slaves." Faced with black unrest and pressed by yeoman and tenant farmers demanding independence, Patriot planters called for a final break with Britain.

In North Carolina as well, military conflict increased demands for independence. Early in 1776 North Carolina's royal governor, Josiah Martin, raised a force of 1,500 Scottish Highlanders from the Carolina backcountry. In response, low-country Patriots mobilized the militia and in February defeated Martin's army at the Battle of Moore's Creek Bridge, capturing more than 800 Highlanders (see American Voices, "The Meaning of War"). By April radical Patriots had transformed the North Carolina assembly into an independent Provincial Congress, which instructed its representatives in Philadelphia "to concur with the Delegates of other Colonies in declaring Independency, and forming foreign alliances." Virginia followed suit. In May, led by James Madison, Edmund Pendleton, and Patrick Henry, Virginia Patriots met in convention and resolved unanimously to support independence.

COMMON SENSE

Resolutions favoring independence came slowly because most Americans retained a deep loyalty to the crown. Joyous crowds had toasted the health of George III following repeal of the Stamp Act, and even as the imperial crisis worsened, Benjamin Franklin had proposed that the king rule over autonomous American assemblies. The very structure of American society supported this loyalty to the crown. Americans used the same metaphors of age and family to describe both social authority and imperial rule. They often pictured the colonies as the dependent children of Britain, the "mother country." Just as the settlers respected male elders in town meetings, churches, and families, so they obeyed the king as the father of his people. Denial of the king's legitimacy might threaten all paternal authority and disrupt the hierarchical social order.

Nonetheless, by 1775 many Americans responded to escalating conflict by accusing George III of supporting oppressive legislation and ordering military retaliation against them. Surprisingly, agitation against the king became especially intense in Philadelphia, the largest but hardly the most tumultuous seaport city. Because Philadelphia merchants harbored Loyalist sympathies, the city had been slow to join the boycott against the Townshend duties. But artisans, who accounted for about half the city's population, had become a powerful force in the Patriot movement. Worried that British imports threatened their small-scale manufacturing enterprises, they organized a Mechanics Association to protect America's "just Rights and Privileges." By February 1776 forty artisans sat with forty-seven merchants on the Philadelphia Committee of Resistance, the extralegal body that enforced the latest trade boycott.

Many Scots-Irish artisans and laborers in Philadelphia became Patriots for religious reasons. They came from Presbyterian families who had fled British-controlled northern Ireland to escape economic and religious discrimination.

AMERICAN VOICES

The Meaning of War

MARY HOOKS SLOCUMB

*F*or sixteen-year-old Mary Hooks Slocumb, the outbreak of fighting in 1776 had personal significance: it threatened the safety of her husband, a member of the North Carolina Light Horse Rangers.

The men all left on Sunday morning. More than eighty went from this house with my husband. . . . I kept thinking where they had got to—how far; where and how many of the regulars and tories they would meet; [that night] . . . I had a dream. . . . I saw distinctly a body wrapped in my husband's guard cloak—bloody—dead; and others dead and wounded on the ground around him. . . . If ever I felt fear it was at that moment. . . . I went to the stable, saddled my mare—as fleet and easy a nag as ever travelled; and in one minute we were tearing down the road at full speed. . . .

When day broke I was some thirty miles from home. . . . The blind path I had been following brought me into the Wilmington road leading Moore's Creek Bridge. . . . a few yards from the road, under a cluster of trees were lying perhaps twenty men. . . . In an instant my whole soul was centered in one spot; for there, wrapped in his bloody guard-Cloak, was my husband's body! . . . I remember uncovering his head and seeing a face clothed with gore from a dreadful wound across the temple. I put my hand on the bloody face; 'twas warm; and an *unknown voice* begged for water. . . . I brought it; poured some in his mouth; washed his face; and behold—it was Frank Cogdell. He soon revived and could speak. I was washing the wound in his head. Said he, "It is not that; it is that hole in my leg that is killing me." A puddle of blood was standing on the ground around his feet. I took his knife, cut away his trousers and stocking, found the blood came from a shot-hole through and through the fleshy part of his leg. I looked about and could see nothing that looked as if it would do for dressing wounds but some heart-leaves. I gathered a handful and bound them tight to the holes; and the bleeding stopped. . . . I dressed the wounds of many a brave fellow who did good fighting long after that day! . . . Just then I looked up, and my husband, as bloody as a butcher, and as muddy as a ditcher, stood before me.

"Why Mary," he exclaimed, "What are you doing there?" . . . I would not tell my husband what brought me there. . . . In the middle of the night I again mounted my mare and started for home. . . . What a happy ride I had back! and with what joy did I embrace my child as he ran to meet me!

SOURCE: Elizabeth F. Ellet, *The Women of the American Revolution* (1850; New York: Haskell House, 1969), vol. 1: pp. 316–21.

Moreover, many of them had embraced the egalitarian message preached by Gilbert Tennent and other New Light ministers. As pastor of Philadelphia's Second Presbyterian Church, Tennent had told his congregation that all men and women were equal before God. Applying that idea to politics, New Light Presbyterians shouted in street demonstrations that they had "no king but King Jesus." Republican ideas derived from the European Enlightenment also circulated freely in Pennsylvania. Well-educated scientists and statesmen such as Benjamin Franklin and Benjamin Rush questioned not only the wisdom of George III but also the idea of monarchy itself.

At this pivotal moment with popular sentiment in flux, a single pamphlet tipped the balance. In January 1776 Thomas Paine published *Common Sense,* a call for independence and republicanism phrased in language that aroused the general public. Paine had been fired from the English Customs Service for protesting low wages. In 1774, with a letter of introduction from Benjamin Franklin, he had migrated to Philadelphia, where he met Benjamin Rush and others who shared his republican sentiments. In *Common Sense* Paine called George III "the hard hearted sullen Pharaoh of England" and blasted the British system of "mixed government," which yielded only "monarchical tyranny in the person of the King and aristocratical tyranny in the persons of the peers." Almost overnight *Common Sense* turned thousands of ordinary Americans against British rule. "There is abundance talked about independency," a Virginia conservative lamented, "it is all from Mr. Common sense." Paine's message was clear: reject the arbitrary powers of king and Parliament and create independent republican states.

INDEPENDENCE DECLARED

Throughout the colonies Patriot conventions, inspired by Paine's arguments and beset by armed Loyalists, called urgently for a break from Britain. In June 1776 Richard Henry Lee presented the Virginia Convention's resolution to the Continental Congress: "That these United Colonies are, and of right ought to be, free and independent states . . . absolved from all allegiance to the British Crown." Faced with certain defeat, staunch Loyalists and anti-independence moderates withdrew from the Congress, leaving committed Patriots to take the fateful step. On July 4, 1776, the Congress approved a Declaration of Independence.

The main author of the Declaration was Thomas Jefferson, a young Virginia planter and legislative leader who had mobilized resistance to the Coercive Acts with the pamphlet *A Summary View of the Rights of British America.* To persuade Americans and foreign observers of the need to create an independent republic, Jefferson justified the revolt by blaming the rupture on George III rather than on Parliament: "He has plundered our seas, ravaged our coasts, burned our towns, and destroyed the lives of our people. . . . A prince, whose character is thus marked by every act which may define a tyrant, is unfit to be the ruler of a free people."

Jefferson, who was steeped in the ideas and rhetoric of the European Enlightenment, preceded these accusations with a proclamation of "self-evident" truths:

"that all men are created equal"; that they possess the "unalienable rights" of "Life, Liberty, and the pursuit of Happiness"; that government derives its "just powers from the consent of the governed" and can rightly be overthrown if it "becomes destructive of these ends." By linking these doctrines of individual liberty and popular sovereignty with independence, Jefferson established revolutionary republicanism as a defining value of the new nation.

For Jefferson as for Paine the pen proved mightier than the sword. In rural hamlets and seaport cities crowds celebrated the Declaration by burning George III in effigy and toppling statues of the king. These acts of destruction broke the Patriots' psychological ties to the mother country and the father monarch. Americans were ready to create republics, state governments that would derive their authority from the people.

The Trials of War, 1776–1778

The Declaration of Independence coincided with Britain's decision to launch a full-scale military assault against the Patriots. For the next two years British forces outfought the Continental army commanded by George Washington, winning nearly every battle. A few inspiring American victories kept the rebellion alive, but in late 1776 and during the winter of 1777 to 1778 at Valley Forge the Patriot cause hung in the balance.

WAR IN THE NORTH

When the British resorted to military force to crush the American revolt, few observers gave the rebels a chance. Great Britain had 11 million people, compared with the colonies' 2.5 million, nearly 20 percent of whom were enslaved Africans. The British also had a profound economic advantage in the immense profits created by the South Atlantic system and the emerging Industrial Revolution. These financial resources paid for the most powerful navy in the world, a standing army of 48,000 men, and thousands of German mercenaries. British military officers had been tested in combat, and their soldiers were well armed. Finally, the imperial government had the support of tens of thousands of American Loyalists as well as many Indian tribes hostile to white expansion.

By contrast, the rebellious Americans were militarily weak. They had no navy, and General Washington's poorly trained army consisted of about 18,000 troops, mostly short-term militiamen hastily recruited by state governments in Virginia and New England. The Patriots could field thousands more militiamen but only for short periods and only near their own farms and towns. Although many American officers were capable veterans of the French and Indian War, even the most experienced had never commanded a large force or faced a disciplined army skilled in the intricate maneuvers of European warfare.

To exploit this military advantage Britain's prime minister, Lord North, responded quickly to the unexpected American invasion of Canada in 1775. He assembled a large invasion force and selected General William Howe, a veteran of the French and Indian War, to lead it. North ordered him to capture New York City and seize control of the Hudson River, hoping to isolate the radical Patriots in New England from the other colonies. In July 1776, as the Continental Congress was declaring independence in Philadelphia, Howe was beginning to land 32,000 troops—British regulars and German mercenaries—outside New York City.

British superiority was immediately apparent. In August 1776 Howe attacked the Americans in the Battle of Long Island and forced their retreat to Manhattan Island. There Howe outflanked Washington's troops, nearly trapping them on several occasions. Outgunned and outmaneuvered, the Continental army again retreated, first to Harlem Heights, then to White Plains, and finally across the Hudson River to New Jersey. By December the British army had pushed the rebels out of New Jersey and across the Delaware River into Pennsylvania, forcing Congress to flee from Philadelphia to Baltimore (see Map 6.1).

From the Patriots' perspective winter came just in time, for the overconfident British halted their campaign for the cold months, according to eighteenth-century military custom. The respite allowed the Americans to catch them off guard and score a few triumphs. On Christmas night in 1776 Washington crossed the Delaware River and staged a surprise attack on Trenton, New Jersey, forcing the surrender of 1,000 German mercenaries (Hessians). Then in early January 1777 the Continental army won a small engagement at nearby Princeton, raising Patriot morale and allowing the Continental Congress to return to Philadelphia. Bright stars in a dark night, these minor triumphs could not mask British military superiority. These are the times, wrote Tom Paine, that "try men's souls."

ARMIES AND STRATEGIES

Throughout 1776 Howe's strategy had been to use his superior military power to convince the Continental Congress that resistance was futile. In 1774 he had opposed the Coercive Acts, calling them too harsh, and now as British commander he hoped to negotiate a compromise with the rebels. Howe's cautious military policy also reflected the conventions of eighteenth-century warfare, which focused on winning the surrender of opposing forces rather than destroying them. The British general was also well aware that his troops were 3,000 miles from home; in case of a major defeat he could not replenish his force for six months. Although Howe's tactics were understandable, they cost the British the opportunity to nip the rebellion in the bud.

Howe's failure to win a decisive victory was paralleled by Washington's success in avoiding a major defeat. He too was cautious, challenging Howe on occasion but retreating in the face of superior strength. As Washington advised Congress, "On our Side the War should be defensive." His strategy was to draw the

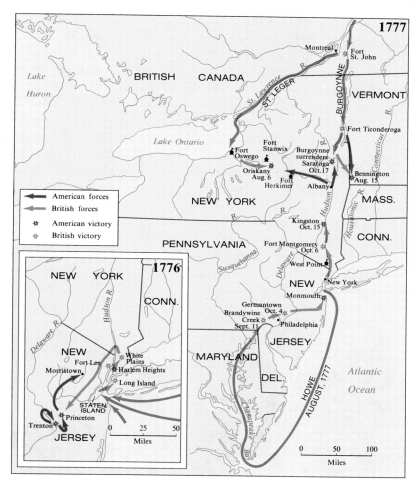

M A P 6.1
The War in the North, 1776–1777

In 1776 the British army drove Washington's forces across New Jersey into Pennsylvania. The Americans counterattacked at Trenton and Princeton, winning minor victories. In 1777 General Howe attacked Philadelphia from the south and easily captured it. Simultaneously, General Burgoyne and Colonel St. Leger launched invasions of New York from bases in Canada. Aided by thousands of New England militia Continental army forces commanded by General Horatio Gates defeated Burgoyne at Bennington (Vermont) and then at Saratoga (New York), the military turning point of the war.

British away from the seacoast, extend their lines of supply, and sap their morale while keeping the Continental army intact as a symbol and instrument of American resistance.

Congress had promised Washington a regular force of 75,000 men, but the Continental army never reached a third of that number. Yeomen preferred to serve in the local militia, and so the regular army drew most of its recruits from the lower ranks of society. General William Smallwood of Maryland commanded soldiers who were either poor American-born youths or older foreign-born men—British ex-convicts and former indentured servants. Such men enlisted not out of patriotism but for a bonus of $20 in cash (about $2,000 today) and the promise of 100 acres of land. Molding such recruits into a fighting force took time. In the face of a British artillery bombardment or flank attack many men panicked; hundreds of others deserted, unwilling to submit to the discipline and danger of military life. The soldiers who stayed resented the contemptuous way Washington and other American officers treated the women who fed and cared for the recruits.

Such personal support was crucial, for the Continental army was poorly supplied and faintly praised. Radical Whig Patriots had long viewed a peacetime standing army as a threat to liberty, and even in wartime they preferred the militia to a professional force. General Philip Schuyler of New York complained that his troops were "weak in numbers, dispirited, naked, destitute of provisions, without camp equipage, with little ammunition, and not a single piece of cannon." Given these handicaps, Washington was fortunate to have escaped an overwhelming defeat in the first year of the war.

A British Camp, circa 1778

While American troops at Valley Forge huddled from the cold in thin tents, British troops stationed just outside New York City (on upper Manhattan Island) lived in simple but well-constructed and warm log cabins. Each hut housed either a few officers or as many as ten soldiers of the 17th Regiment of Foot. This painting, based on careful archaeological fieldwork, was executed in 1915 by John Ward Dunsmore. (The New-York Historical Society)

American Militiamen

Because of the shortage of cloth the Patriot army dressed in many fabrics and fashions. This German engraving, based on a drawing by a German officer, shows two barefoot American militiamen arrayed in hunting shirts and trousers made of ticking, a strong woven linen fabric that was often used as the coverings for mattresses and pillows.

(Anne S. K. Brown Military Collection, Brown University)

VICTORY AT SARATOGA

Howe's failure to achieve a quick victory dismayed Lord North and his colonial secretary, Lord George Germain. Accepting the challenge of a long-term military commitment, the British ministry increased the land tax to finance the war and prepared to mount a major campaign in 1777.

The isolation of New England remained the primary British goal and was to be achieved by a three-pronged attack converging on Albany, New York. General John Burgoyne was to lead a large contingent of British regulars from Quebec to Albany. A second, smaller force of Iroquois warriors (who had allied themselves with the British to protect their land from American settlers) would attack from the west under Colonel Barry St. Leger. To assist Burgoyne from the south, Germain ordered Howe to dispatch a force northward from New York City (see Map 6.1).

Howe had a different scheme. He wanted to attack Philadelphia, the home of the Continental Congress, and end the rebellion with a single victory over Washington's army. With Germain's apparent approval, Howe set his plan in motion.

Rather than march overland through New Jersey, British troops sailed south from New York then up the Chesapeake Bay. Approaching Philadelphia from the south, Howe's troops easily outflanked the American positions along Brandywine Creek in Delaware and forced Washington to withdraw. On September 26 the British marched triumphantly into Philadelphia, hoping that the capture of the rebels' capital would end the uprising. But the Continental Congress fled into the interior, determined to continue the struggle.

The British paid a high price for Howe's victory in Philadelphia, for it contributed directly to Burgoyne's defeat. Initially Burgoyne's troops had sped across Lake Champlain, overwhelming the American defenses at Fort Ticonderoga and driving toward the upper reaches of the Hudson River. Then they stalled, for Burgoyne—"Gentleman Johnny," as he was called—fought with style, not speed, weighed down by comfortable tents and ample stocks of food and wine. Burgoyne's progress was further impeded by General Horatio Gates, whose troops felled trees across the crude wagon trail Burgoyne was following and raided his long supply lines to Canada.

By the end of the summer Burgoyne's army—6,000 regulars (half of them German mercenaries) and 600 Loyalists and Indians—was in trouble, bogged down in the wilderness near Saratoga, New York. In August 2,000 American militiamen left their farms to fight a bitter battle at nearby Bennington, Vermont, that cost Burgoyne 900 casualties and deprived him of much-needed supplies of food and horses. Meanwhile, Patriot forces in the Mohawk Valley forced St. Leger and the Iroquois to retreat. To make matters worse, the British commander in New York City recalled the 4,000 troops he had sent toward Albany and dispatched them to Howe in Philadelphia. While Burgoyne waited for help, thousands of Patriot militiamen from Massachusetts, New Hampshire, and New York joined Gates's forces. They "swarmed around the army like birds of prey," an alarmed English sergeant wrote in his journal, and in October 1777 forced Burgoyne to surrender.

The battle at Saratoga proved to be the turning point of the war. The Americans captured more than 5,000 British troops and their equipment. Their victory virtually ensured the success of American diplomats in Paris, who were seeking a military alliance with France. Patriots on the home front were delighted, though their joy was muted by wartime difficulties.

SOCIAL AND FINANCIAL PERILS

The war exposed tens of thousands of civilians to deprivation, displacement, and death. "An army, even a friendly one, are a dreadful scourge to any people," a Connecticut soldier wrote from Pennsylvania. "You cannot imagine what devastation and distress mark their steps." New Jersey was particularly hard hit by the fighting, as British and American armies marched back and forth across the state. Families with reputations as Patriots or Loyalists fled their homes to escape arrest—or worse. Soldiers and partisans looted farms, seeking food or political revenge. Wherever the armies went, drunk and disorderly troops harassed and raped women and girls. Families lived in fear of their approach.

Indeed, the War of Independence became a bloody partisan conflict. In New England mobs of Patriot farmers beat suspected Tories or destroyed their property. "Every Body submitted to our Sovereign Lord the Mob," a Loyalist preacher lamented. Patriots organized local Committees of Safety to collect taxes, send food and clothing to the Continental army, and impose fines or jail sentences on those who failed to support the cause.

These local initiatives reflected the weakness of the new state governments, which teetered on the brink of bankruptcy. To feed, clothe, and pay their troops, state officials borrowed gold, silver, or British currency from wealthy individuals. When those funds ran out, Patriot officials were afraid to raise taxes, knowing how unpopular that would be. Instead, individual states printed paper money, issuing a total of $260 million in currency and transferable bonds. Theoretically, the new notes could be redeemed in gold or silver, but since they were printed in huge quantities and were not backed by tax revenues or mortgages on land, many Americans refused to accept them at face value. North Carolina's paper money came to be worth so little even the state government's tax collectors refused it.

The finances of the Continental Congress collapsed too, despite the efforts of the Philadelphia merchant Robert Morris, the government's chief treasury official. The Congress lacked the authority to impose taxes and so depended on funds requisitioned from the states, which frequently paid late or not at all. Congress therefore borrowed $6 million in specie from France, using it as security to encourage wealthy Americans to purchase $27 million in Continental loan certificates. When those funds and other French and Dutch loans were exhausted, Congress followed the lead of the states and printed currency and bills of credit. Between 1775 and 1779 it issued notes with a face value of $191 million, but when funds received from the states retired only $3 million, the actual value of the bills fell dramatically.

Indeed, the excess of currency helped to spark the worst inflation in American history. The amount of goods available for purchase—both domestic foodstuffs and foreign manufactures—had shrunk significantly because of the fighting and the British naval blockade, while the money in circulation had multiplied. Because more currency was chasing fewer goods, prices rose rapidly. In Maryland a bag of salt that had cost $1 in 1776 sold for $3,900 in currency a few years later. Unwilling to accept nearly worthless currency, farmers refused to sell their crops, even to the Continental army. Instead, merchants and farmers turned to barter—trading wheat for tools or clothes—or sold goods only to those who could pay in gold or silver. The result was social upheaval. In Boston a mob of women accused merchant Thomas Boyleston of hoarding goods, "seazd him by his Neck," and forced him to sell—at the traditional prices. In rural Ulster County, New York, women surrounded the Patriot Committee of Safety, demanding steps to end the food shortages; otherwise, they said, "their husbands and sons shall fight no more." Civilian morale and social cohesion crumbled, causing some Patriot leaders to doubt that the rebellion could succeed.

Fears reached their peak during the winter of 1777 to 1778. Howe camped in Philadelphia and with his officers partook of the finest wines, foods, and entertainment the city could offer. Washington's army retreated to Valley Forge, some 20 miles to the west, where about 12,000 soldiers and hundreds of camp followers suffered horribly. "The army . . . now begins to grow sickly," a surgeon confided to his diary. "Poor food—hard lodging—cold weather—fatigue—nasty clothes—nasty cookery. . . . Why are we sent here to starve and freeze?" Nearby farmers refused to help. Some were pacifists—Quakers and German sectarians—unwilling to support either side. Others were self-interested, hoarding their grain in hopes of higher prices in the spring or willing to accept only the gold and silver offered by British quartermasters. "Such a dearth of public spirit, and want of public virtue," Washington complained—but to no effect. By spring a thousand of his hungry soldiers had vanished into the countryside, and another 3,000 had died from malnutrition and disease. One winter at Valley Forge took as many American lives as had two years of fighting against General Howe.

The Path to Victory, 1778–1783

The Patriots' prospects improved dramatically in 1778, when the United States formed a military alliance with France, the most powerful European nation. The alliance brought the Americans money, troops, and supplies and changed the conflict from a colonial rebellion to an international war.

THE FRENCH ALLIANCE

France and America were unlikely partners. France was Catholic and a monarchy; the United States, largely Protestant and a federation of republics. The two peoples had been on opposite sides in wars from 1689 to 1763. But France was intent on avenging its loss of Canada in the French and Indian War. In 1776 the Comte de Vergennes, the French foreign minister, persuaded King Louis XVI to extend a secret loan to the rebellious colonies and supply them with gunpowder. Early in 1777 Vergennes opened official commercial and military negotiations with Benjamin Franklin and two other American diplomats. When news of the American victory at Saratoga reached Paris in December 1777, Vergennes sought a formal alliance with the Continental Congress.

Franklin and his associates craftily exploited the rivalry between France and Britain, using the threat of a negotiated settlement with Britain to win an explicit French commitment to American independence. The Treaty of Alliance of February 1778 specified that once France had entered the war against Great Britain, neither partner would sign a separate peace before the "liberty, sovereignty, and independence" of the United States were ensured. The American diplomats pledged that their government would recognize any French conquests in the West Indies.

The alliance with France gave new life to the Patriots' cause. With access to military supplies and European loans, the American army soon strengthened and hopes soared. "There has been a great change in this state since the news from France," a Patriot soldier reported from Pennsylvania; farmers—"mercenary wretches," he called them—"were as eager for Continental Money now as they were a few weeks ago for British gold."

With renewed energy and purpose the Congress addressed the demands of the officer corps for pensions. Most officers came from the upper ranks of society and had used their own funds to equip themselves and sometimes their men as well. In return they demanded lifetime military pensions at half pay. John Adams condemned the petitioners for "scrambling for rank and pay like apes for nuts," but General Washington urged Congress to grant the pensions, warning the lawmakers that "the salvation of the cause depends upon it." Congress reluctantly agreed to grant the officers half pay after the war but only for seven years.

Meanwhile, the war was becoming increasingly unpopular in Britain. Radical agitators and republican-minded artisans supported American demands for greater rights and campaigned for political reform at home, including broadened voting rights and more equitable representation for cities in Parliament. The landed gentry and urban merchants protested increases in the land tax and new levies on carriages, wine, and imported goods. "It seemed we were to be taxed and stamped ourselves instead of inflicting taxes and stamps on others," a British politician complained.

But George III remained determined to crush the rebellion. If America won independence, he warned Lord North, "the West Indies must follow them. Ireland would soon follow the same plan and be a separate state, then this island would be reduced to itself, and soon would be a poor island indeed." Following the British defeat at Saratoga the king assumed a more pragmatic attitude. To head off an American alliance with France, the king authorized North to seek a negotiated settlement. In February 1778 North persuaded Parliament to repeal the Tea and Prohibitory Acts and in an amazing concession to renounce its power to tax the colonies. The prime minister then opened discussions with the Continental Congress, offering a return to the constitutional "condition of 1763," before the Sugar and Stamp Acts. But the Patriots, now allied with France, rejected the overture.

WAR IN THE SOUTH

The French alliance expanded the war but did not rapidly conclude it. When France entered the conflict in June 1778, it hoped to capture a rich sugar island and therefore concentrated its naval forces in the West Indies. Spain, which joined the war in 1779, also had its own agenda: in return for naval assistance to France, it wanted to regain Florida and Gibraltar.

The British ministry, by 1778 beset by war on many fronts, settled on a modest strategy in North America. It would use its army to recapture the rich tobacco- and rice-growing colonies of Virginia, the Carolinas, and Georgia and rely on local Loyalists to hold and administer them. The British knew that Scottish Highlanders in North Carolina retained a strong allegiance to the crown and hoped to recruit other Loyalists from the ranks of the Regulators, the enemies of the low-country Patriot planters. The ministry also hoped to take advantage of racial divisions in the South. In 1776 over 1,000 slaves had fought for Lord Dunmore under the banner "Liberty to Slaves!"; a British military offensive might prompt thousands more to flee from their Patriot owners. In fact, because African Americans formed 30 to 50 percent of the population, planters were afraid that allowing their sons or white overseers to leave the plantations and join the Continental forces would encourage slave revolts.

Implementing this southern strategy became the responsibility of Sir Henry Clinton. In June 1778 Clinton moved the main British army from Philadelphia to more secure quarters in New York. In December he launched his southern campaign, capturing Savannah, Georgia, and mobilizing hundreds of blacks to build barricades and unload supplies. Then Clinton moved inland, capturing Augusta early in 1779. By the end of the year, with the help of local Loyalists, Clinton's forces had reconquered Georgia, and 10,000 troops were poised for an assault on South Carolina. To counter this threat the Continental Congress suggested that South Carolina raise 3,000 black troops, but the state assembly overwhelmingly rejected the proposal.

During most of 1780 British forces marched from victory to victory (see Map 6.2). In May Clinton forced General Benjamin Lincoln and his 5,000 troops to surrender at Charleston, South Carolina. Shortly afterward Lord Cornwallis assumed control of the British forces and sent out expeditions to secure the countryside. In August Cornwallis routed an American force commanded by General Horatio Gates, the hero of Saratoga. Only about 1,200 Patriot militiamen joined Gates at the battle in Camden—a fifth of the number at Saratoga, and many of them panicked, handing the British control of South Carolina. Hundreds of African Americans fled to freedom in British-controlled Florida, while hundreds more found refuge with the British army, providing labor in return for their liberty.

Then the tide of battle turned. The Dutch declared war against Britain, and France finally dispatched troops to America. The French decision was partly the work of the Marquis de Lafayette, a republican-minded aristocrat who had long supported the American cause. In 1780 Lafayette persuaded Louis XVI to send General Comte de Rochambeau and 5,500 men to Newport, Rhode Island.

As the French army threatened the British in New York City, Washington called on General Nathanael Greene to recapture the Carolinas. To make use of local militiamen, who were "without discipline and addicted to plundering," Greene devised a new military strategy. He divided the militia into small groups with strong leaders and directed them to harass the less mobile British forces. In October 1780 a

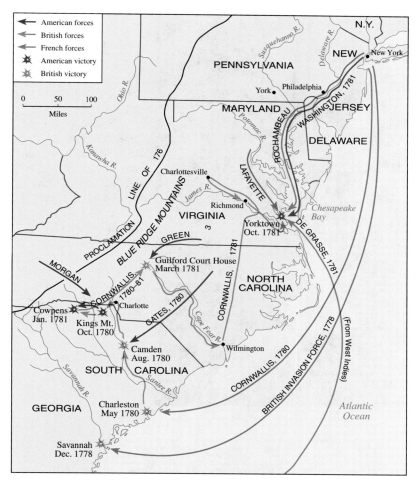

M AP 6.2
Campaigns in the South, 1778–1781

In 1778 the British ministry's southern strategy started well as its military forces captured Savannah in December 1778 and Charleston in May 1780. Over the next eighteen months brutal warfare raged in the interior, fought mostly by small bands of irregulars. When Cornwallis's army carried the battle into Virginia in late 1781, a Franco-American force led by Washington and Lafayette surrounded his troops at Yorktown, aided by the French fleet under Admiral de Grasse.

militia force of Patriot farmers defeated a regiment of Loyalists at King's Mountain, South Carolina, taking about 1,000 prisoners. Led by the "Swamp Fox," General Francis Marion, American guerrillas won a series of small but fierce battles in South Carolina, while General Daniel Morgan led another band to a bloody victory at Cowpens, South Carolina, in January 1781. But Loyalist garrisons and militia

Lafayette at Yorktown

This contemporary painting, executed by the French artist J. B. Le Paon in 1780, shows the Marquis de Lafayette and James Armistead, an enslaved African American who served as a spy for the Patriot army commanded by the French general. Receiving his freedom as a reward for exploits as a spy, James took Lafayette's surname, becoming James Lafayette. The two Lafayettes met again in 1824 when the Frenchman visited the United States.

(Lafayette College Art Collection, Easton, PA. Gift of Mrs. John Hubbard)

remained powerful, assisted by the well-organized Cherokees, who protected their lands by attacking American settlers and troops. "We fight, get beaten, and fight again," General Greene declared doggedly. In March 1781 Greene's soldiers fought Cornwallis's seasoned army to a draw at North Carolina's Guilford Court House.

Weakened by this war of attrition, Cornwallis decided to concede the southernmost states to Greene and seek a decisive victory in Virginia. Aided by reinforcements from New York, the British general invaded Virginia's Tidewater region. There Benedict Arnold, the infamous traitor to the Patriot cause, led British troops up and down the James River, where they met only slight resistance from an American force commanded by Lafayette. Then in May 1781, as the two armies sparred near the York Peninsula, France ordered its large fleet from the West Indies to North America.

Emboldened by the naval forces at his disposal, Washington launched a well-coordinated attack. Feinting an assault on New York City, he secretly marched General Rochambeau's army from Rhode Island to Virginia, where it joined his Continental army. Simultaneously, the French fleet massed off the coast, establishing control of Chesapeake Bay. By the time the British discovered Washington's audacious plan, Cornwallis was surrounded, his 9,500-man army outnumbered two to one on land and cut off from reinforcement or retreat by sea. Abandoned by the British navy, Cornwallis surrendered at Yorktown in October 1781.

The Franco-American victory at Yorktown broke the resolve of the British government. "Oh God! It is all over!" Lord North exclaimed when he heard the news. The combined French and Spanish fleet was menacing the British sugar islands, Dutch merchants were capturing European markets from British traders, and a group of European states—the League of Armed Neutrality—was demanding an end to Britain's commercial blockade of France. Isolated diplomatically in Europe, stymied militarily in America, and lacking public support at home, the British ministry gave up active prosecution of the war.

THE PATRIOT ADVANTAGE

Angry members of Parliament demanded an explanation. How could mighty Britain, victorious in the Great War for Empire, be defeated by a motley group of colonists? The ministry blamed the military leadership, pointing with some justification to a series of blunders. Why had Howe not been more ruthless in pursuing Washington's army in 1776? How could Howe and Burgoyne have failed to coordinate the movement of their armies in 1777? Why had Cornwallis marched deep into the Patriot-dominated state of Virginia in 1781?

Historians have also criticized these blunders while emphasizing the high odds against British success, given broad-based American support for the rebel cause. Although only a third of the white colonists were zealous Patriots, another third were supportive enough to pay the taxes imposed by state governments. Unlike most revolutionaries the Patriots were led by experienced politicians who commanded public support. And even though the Continental army had to be built from scratch and was never very large, it was fighting on its own territory with the assistance of thousands of militiamen. The more than 55,000 Tories and thousands of native Americans who fought for the British could not offset these advantages. Once the rebels had the financial and military support of France, they could reasonably hope for victory.

While Britain suffered mediocre generals, Americans had the inspired leadership of George Washington as commander of the Continental army. An astute politician, Washington deferred to the civil authorities, winning respect and support from the Congress and the state governments alike. Confident of his own abilities, he recruited outstanding military officers to instill discipline in the ranks of the fledgling Continental army and turn it into a respectable fighting force.

But Washington also had a greater margin for error than the British generals did because Patriots controlled local governments and at crucial moments could mobilize the militia to assist his Continental army. Thousands of militiamen had besieged General Gage in Boston in 1775, surrounded Burgoyne at Saratoga in 1777, and forced Cornwallis from the Carolinas in 1781. In the end the American people decided the outcome of the conflict. Preferring Patriot rule, they refused to support Loyalist forces or accept imperial control in British-occupied areas. Consequently, while the British won many military victories, they achieved little, and their defeats at Saratoga and Yorktown proved catastrophic.

DIPLOMATIC TRIUMPH

After Yorktown diplomats took two years to conclude the war. Peace talks began in Paris in April 1782, but the French and Spanish stalled for time, hoping for a major naval victory or territorial conquest. Their delaying tactics infuriated the American diplomats—Benjamin Franklin, John Adams, and John Jay—who feared that France might sacrifice American interests. For this reason the Americans negotiated secretly with the British, prepared if necessary to cut their ties to France and sign a separate peace. The British ministry was also eager to obtain a quick settlement, for the war had little support in Parliament and officials feared the loss of a rich West Indian sugar island.

Exploiting the rivalry between Britain and France, the American diplomats finally secured peace on very favorable terms. In the Treaty of Paris, signed in September 1783, Great Britain formally recognized the independence of its seaboard colonies and, while retaining Canada, also relinquished its claims to all the lands south of the Great Lakes between the Appalachian Mountains and the Mississippi River—the domain of undefeated, pro-British Indian peoples. Leaving the Native Americans to their fate, the British negotiators did not insist on a separate Indian territory and promised to withdraw their garrisons "with all convenient speed." "In endeavouring to assist you," a Wea Indian complained to a British general, "it seems we have wrought our own ruin." Other treaty provisions granted Americans fishing rights off Newfoundland and Nova Scotia, forbade the British from "carrying away any negroes or other property," and guaranteed freedom of navigation on the Mississippi to both British subjects and American citizens "forever." In its only concessions the American government promised to allow British merchants to recover prewar debts and to encourage the state legislatures to return confiscated property to Loyalists and grant them citizenship.

In the Treaty of Versailles, signed at the same time as the Treaty of Paris, Britain made peace with France and Spain. Neither American ally gained very much. Spain reclaimed Florida from Britain but failed in its main objective of retaking Gibraltar. France had the pleasure of reducing British power, but its only territorial gain was the Caribbean island of Tobago. Moreover, the war had quadrupled France's national debt; only six years later cries for tax relief and political liberty would spark the French Revolution. Only Americans profited handsomely from the treaties, which gave them independence from Britain and opened up the interior of the North American continent for settlement.

Republicanism Defined and Challenged

From the moment they became revolutionary republicans, Americans began to define the character of their new social order. In the Declaration of Independence Thomas Jefferson had turned to John Locke, the philosopher of private liberty, when he declared a universal human right to "Life, Liberty, and the pursuit of Happiness." But Jefferson and many other Americans also lauded "republican virtue," an enlightened quest for the public good. As the New Hampshire constitution phrased it, "Government [was] instituted for the common benefits, protection, and security of the whole community." The tension between self-interest and the public interest would shape the future of the new nation.

REPUBLICAN IDEALS UNDER WARTIME PRESSURES

Simply put, a republic is a state without a monarch and with a representative system of government. Yet for many Americans republicanism was also a social philosophy. "The word republic" in Latin, wrote Thomas Paine, "means the public good," which citizens have a duty to secure. "Every man in a republic is public property," asserted the Philadelphia Patriot Benjamin Rush, who eventually extended the notion to include women as well. "His time and talents—his youth—his manhood—his old age—nay more, life, all belong to his country." Reflecting this sense of community, members of the Continental Congress praised the militiamen who fought and fell at Lexington and Concord, Saratoga and Camden. And they applauded Henry Laurens of South Carolina, who condemned as a "total loss of virtue" the wartime demand by Continental officers for lifetime pensions. Raised as gentlemen, officers were supposed to be exemplars of virtue who gave freely to the republic.

As the war continued, military self-sacrifice declined. During the winters of 1779 and 1780 Continental troops stationed at Morristown in New Jersey mutinied, unwilling any longer to endure low pay and sparse rations. To restore military authority Washington ordered the execution of several leaders of the revolt but urged Congress to pacify the soldiers with back pay and new clothing. Later in the war unrest among officers erupted at Newburgh, New York, and Washington had to use his personal authority to thwart a dangerous challenge to the Congress's policies.

Meanwhile, economic distress tested the republican virtue of ordinary citizens. The British naval blockade had disrupted the New England fishing industry and cut the supply of European manufactures. British occupation of Boston, New York, and Philadelphia had also trimmed domestic trade and manufacturing. As unemployed shipwrights, dock laborers, masons, coopers, and bakers deserted the cities and drifted into the countryside, New York City's population declined from 21,000 residents in 1774 to less than half that number by the war's end. In the Chesapeake the British blockade deprived tobacco planters of European markets, forcing them to cultivate grain, which could be sold to the contending armies.

In those difficult times Patriot women contributed both to the war effort and the well-being of their families by increasing their production of homespun cloth. One Massachusetts town produced 30,000 yards of homespun, while women in Elizabeth, New Jersey, promised "upwards of 100,000 yards of linnen and woolen cloth." Other women assumed the burdens of farm production while their men were away at war. Some went into the fields, plowing, harvesting, and loading grain, while others supervised hired laborers or slaves, in the process acquiring a taste for decision making. "We have sow'd our oats as you desired," Sarah Cobb Paine wrote to her absent husband; "had I been master I should have planted it to Corn." Taught from childhood to value the welfare of their fathers, brothers, and husbands above their own, women were expected to act "virtuously" and often did so. Their wartime efforts not only increased farm household productivity but also boosted their self-esteem and prompted some to claim greater rights in the new republican society.

Despite the women's efforts goods were in short supply, bringing a sharp rise in prices and widespread appeals for government regulation. Hard-pressed consumers decried merchants and traders as "enemies, extortioners, and monopolizers." But in 1777, when a convention of New England states limited price increases to 75 percent, many farmers and artisans refused to sell their goods at the set prices. In the end, a government official admitted, consumers had to pay the much higher market price "or submit to starving." In civilian life as in the military, self-interest tended to triumph over republican virtue.

Spiraling inflation posed a severe challenge to American families and the notion of public virtue. By 1778 so much currency had been printed that a family needed $7 in Continental bills to buy goods worth $1 in gold or silver. The ratio steadily escalated—to 42 to 1 in 1779, 100 to 1 in 1780, and 146 to 1 in 1781, when not even the most dedicated Patriots would accept paper money. To restore the value of Continental currency, the Congress asked the states to accept tax payments in depreciated Continental bills (with $40 in paper money counting as $1 in specie). This plan redeemed $120 million in Continental bills, but at the end of the war speculators still held $71 million in currency, hoping they could eventually redeem it at face value. "Private Interest seemed to predominate over the public weal," a leading Patriot complained.

Ultimately, this currency inflation transferred most of the costs of the war to ordinary Americans. The tens of thousands of farmers and artisans who received Continental bills as payment for supplies and the soldiers who took them as pay found that the currency literally depreciated in their pockets. Every time they received a paper dollar and kept it for a week, the money lost value and could buy less, thus imposing a hidden "currency tax" on them. Each individual "tax" was small—a few pennies on each dollar they handled. But taken together—as millions of dollars changed hands multiple times—these currency taxes paid the huge cost of the war.

THE LOYALIST EXODUS

As the war turned in favor of the Patriots, more than 100,000 Loyalists, fearing for their lives, emigrated to the West Indies, Britain, and Canada. The exodus disrupted the social hierarchy in many communities because a significant minority of Loyalists came from the ranks of wealthy merchants, lawyers, and landowners of high status. Although some angry Patriots demanded that the state governments seize the property of these "traitors," most public officials argued that confiscation would be contrary to Patriot principles. In Massachusetts officials cited the state's Constitution of 1780, which declared that every citizen should be protected "in the enjoyment of his life, liberty, and property, according to the standing laws."

Thus, there was no government-led social revolution. Most states seized only a limited amount of Loyalist property and usually sold it to the highest bidder, who was often a wealthy Patriot rather than a yeoman or foot soldier. But in a few cases confiscations did produce a democratic result. In North Carolina about half the new owners of Loyalist lands were small-scale farmers. And on the former Philipse manor in New York many Patriot tenants used their hard-earned savings to buy the seized land and become fee-simple owners. When Philipse tried to reclaim his land, former tenants told him they had "purchased it with the price of their best blood" and "will never become your vassals again." But in general the revolutionary upheaval did not drastically alter the structure of rural society.

Social turmoil was greater in the cities, as Patriot merchants replaced Tories at the top of the economic ladder. In Massachusetts the Lowell, Higginson, Jackson, and Cabot families moved their trading enterprises to Boston to fill the vacuum created by the departure of the Loyalist Hutchinsons and Apthorps. In Philadelphia, small-scale traders stepped into the vacancies created by the collapse of Anglican and Quaker mercantile firms. In the countinghouses as on the battlefield, Patriots emerged triumphant. The War of Independence replaced a tradition-oriented economic elite—one that invested its profits from trade in real estate, becoming landlords—with a group of entrepreneurial-minded republican merchants who promoted new trading ventures and domestic manufacturing.

THE PROBLEM OF SLAVERY

Slavery revealed a contradiction in the Patriots' republican ideology. "How is it that we hear the loudest yelps for liberty among the drivers of Negroes?" the British author Samuel Johnson chided the rebellious white Americans, a point some Patriots took to heart. "I wish most sincerely there was not a Slave in the province," Abigail Adams wrote to her husband, John, as Massachusetts went to war. "It always appeared a most iniquitous Scheme to me—to fight ourselves for what we are daily robbing and plundering from those who have as good a right to freedom as we have."

In fact, the struggle of white Patriots for their independence from Britain raised the prospect of freedom for enslaved Africans. Many hoped for a British invasion that would free them. When the war began, a black preacher in Georgia told his fellow slaves that King George III "came up with the Book [the Bible], and was about to alter the World, and set the Negroes free." Similar rumors circulated among slaves in Virginia and the Carolinas, prompting thousands of African Americans to seek freedom by fleeing behind British lines. Two neighbors of Richard Henry Lee, the Virginia Patriot, lost "every slave they had in the world," as did many other planters. When the British army evacuated Charleston, more than 6,000 former slaves went with them; another 4,000 left from Savannah. Hundreds of these black Loyalists settled permanently in Canada. Over 1,000 others, poorly treated by British officials and settled on inferior land in Nova Scotia, sought a better life in the abolitionist settlement in Sierra Leone, West Africa.

For a variety of reasons thousands of African Americans decided to serve the Patriot cause. Knowing firsthand the meaning of slavery and anxious to raise their status in society, free blacks in New England volunteered for military service in the First Rhode Island Company and the Massachusetts "Bucks." In Maryland a large number of slaves also took up arms for the Patriot cause in return for a promise of freedom. Elsewhere in the South slaves struck informal bargains with their Patriot masters, trading loyalty in wartime for a promise of eventual liberty. In 1782 the Virginia assembly passed an act allowing manumission (liberation); within a decade planters had freed 10,000 slaves.

The Quakers, whose belief in religious and social equality had made them sharp critics of many inequities, took the lead in condemning slavery. Beginning in the 1750s the Quaker evangelist John Woolman had urged Friends to free their slaves, and during the war many did so. Other rapidly growing pietistic groups, notably

Symbols of Slavery—and Freedom

The scar on the forehead of this black woman, widely known as "Mumbet," symbolized the cruelty of slavery. Winning emancipation through a legal suit in Massachusetts, she chose a name befitting her new status: Elizabeth Freeman. This watercolor, by Susan Sedgwick, was painted in 1811.
(Massachusetts Historical Society)

the Methodists and the Baptists, also advocated emancipation and admitted both enslaved and free blacks to their congregations. In 1784 a conference of Virginia Methodists declared that slavery was "contrary to the Golden Law of God on which hang all the Law and Prophets."

Enlightenment philosophy also worked to undermine slavery and racism. John Locke had argued that ideas were not innate but stemmed from a person's experiences in the world. Accordingly, Enlightenment thinkers suggested that the oppressive conditions of slavery, not inherent inferiority, accounted for the debased situation of Africans in the Western Hemisphere. As one American put it, "A state of slavery has a mighty tendency to shrink and contract the minds of men." Anthony Benezet, a Quaker philanthropist who funded a school for blacks in Philadelphia, defied popular opinion in declaring that African Americans were "as capable of improvement as White People."

By 1784 Massachusetts had abolished slavery outright, and three other states— Pennsylvania, Connecticut, and Rhode Island—had provided for its gradual termination. Within another twenty years every state north of Delaware had enacted similar laws. Gradual emancipation laws compensated white owners by requiring more years—even decades—of servitude while promising blacks eventual freedom. Thus, the New York Emancipation Act of 1799 granted freedom only to the children of slaves and then only at age twenty-five. As late as 1810, 30,000 blacks in the northern states—nearly a fourth of their African American residents—were still enslaved. Emancipation came slowly because whites feared competition for jobs and housing and the prospect of race melding. To keep the races separate in 1786 Massachusetts reenacted an old law prohibiting whites from marrying blacks, Indians, or mulattos (see American Voices, "The Character of Northern Slavery").

The tension between the republican values of liberty and property was greatest in the South, where slaves made up 30 to 60 percent of the population and represented a huge financial investment. Some planters, moved by religious principles or oversupplied with workers on declining tobacco plantations, allowed blacks to buy their freedom through paid work as artisans or laborers. Manumission and self-purchase gradually freed about a third of the African Americans in Maryland, but in 1792 the Virginia legislature made manumission more difficult. Following the lead of Thomas Jefferson, who owned more than 100 slaves, the Chesapeake gentry argued that slavery was a "necessary evil" required to maintain white supremacy and the luxurious planter lifestyle. Resistance to freedom for blacks was even greater in North Carolina, where the legislature condemned Quaker manumissions as "highly criminal and reprehensible." And the rice-growing states of South Carolina and Georgia rejected emancipation out of hand.

The debate over emancipation among southern whites ended in 1800, when Virginia authorities thwarted an uprising planned by the enslaved artisan Gabriel Prosser and hanged him and thirty of his followers. "Liberty and equality have brought the evil upon us," a letter to the *Virginia Herald* proclaimed, for such doctrines are "dangerous and extremely wicked in this country, where every white man

The Character of Northern Slavery

ALEXANDER COVENTRY

*A*lexander Coventry migrated from Scotland to New York in 1785 and recorded his daily
experiences in a journal. The selections below provide insight into the condition of New
York's rural African Americans, most of whom were owned by farmers of Dutch descent. His
comments indicate that slavery in the rural North was very different from that on the plantations of the South.

2 February 1787 Rode through the Cocksaxie settlement. . . . The houses are substantially
built of Lime-stone, and are generally 1½ stores high; the barns are capacious. . . . Cocksaxie
farmers are supposed to be the most opulent in the state. Their fertile soil, and its convenience to market, being much in their favor. The tact [area of land] is almost exclusively
inhabited by the low Dutch . . . and each farmer has a number of Negro slaves . . . who
did all the work on the farm, and in the house. . . . Although the blacks were slaves, yet I
feel warranted in asserting that the laboring class in no country lived more easy, were better clothed and fed, or had more of life, than these slaves.

2 April 1787 [Went with] William Van Valkenburg to see his brother John, who has received a stab in his thigh about 5 inches deep. He received the wound from a negro, whom
his former master and John went to take. The negro and his wench had run away, and escaped into Boston state (Massachusetts) where negroes are free.

9–11 April 1789 Van Curen's negro Cuff came here and wanted W.C. [William Coventry,
Alexander's cousin] to buy him . . . but Van Curen and W.C. could not agree, therefore I
told him if the negro would agree to live with me, I would buy him. He asked 77 pounds.
I offered 76 pounds. We tossed up and he won. . . . I asked Cuff if he would live with me.
He said he would; he helped to drive the cows home to fodder. . . . Cuff wanted two days
next week to keep Paas [Easter Sunday]. I told him to return on Wednesday morning,
which he said he would do.

4 April 1790 While foddering, Thursday, before sunrise, a man and woman passed, the
man was black, and asked the road to Hudson. Heard since that it was a negro run off with
a white woman.

21 December 1791 Went over to Jacobus Legat's to see whether he would sell his Wench,
Cuff's wife. Legat offered her, with her youngest child for £45. I offered him £40 and so
we parted [without a sale].

3 February 1792 Cornelius Van Curen here; wants to buy Cuff back again, but Cuff
won't go to him again.

SOURCE: Coventry Manuscript Diary, New-York Historical Society.

is a master, and every black man is a slave." To preserve their privileged social position, whites would redefine republicanism so that it applied only to the master race.

A REPUBLICAN RELIGIOUS ORDER

Political revolution broadened the appeal of religious liberty, forcing Patriot lawmakers to devise a new relationship between church and state. During the colonial era only the Quaker- and Baptist-controlled governments of Pennsylvania and Rhode Island had repudiated the idea of an established church. Then in 1776 James Madison and George Mason of Virginia used Enlightenment principles to undermine the traditional commitment to a single state-supported church. They persuaded the Virginia constitutional convention to issue a Declaration of Rights that guaranteed to all Christians the "free exercise of religion." To win broad support for the war, the Virginia Anglican elite carried this doctrine into practice, accepting the legitimacy of the dissenting Presbyterian and Baptist churches that they had previously persecuted. In 1778 Virginia Anglicans launched their own religious revolution by severing their ties with the hierarchy of the Church of England in London and creating the Protestant Episcopal Church of America.

After the Revolution an established church and compulsory religious taxes were no longer the norm in the United States. Baptists in particular opposed the use of taxes to support religion. In Virginia their political influence prompted lawmakers to reject a bill supported by George Washington and Patrick Henry, which would have imposed a general tax to fund all Christian churches. Instead, in 1786 the Virginia legislature enacted Thomas Jefferson's Bill for Establishing Religious Freedom, which made all churches equal before the law and granted direct financial support to none. In New York and New Jersey the sheer number of churches—Episcopalian, Presbyterian, Dutch Reformed, Lutheran, and Quaker, among others—prevented legislative agreement on an established church or compulsory religious taxes. However, in New England Congregationalist ministers preserved an official state church until the 1830s by allowing Baptists and Methodists to pay religious taxes to their own churches.

Still, many Americans felt that firm connections between church and state were necessary to promote morality and respect for authority. "Pure religion and civil liberty are inseparable companions," a group of North Carolinians advised their minister. "It is your particular duty to enlighten mankind with the unerring principles of truth and justice, the main props of all civil government." Accepting this premise, most state governments provided churches with indirect aid by exempting their property and ministers from taxation. Thus, the separation of church and state was never complete.

Freedom of conscience proved equally difficult to achieve. In Virginia Jefferson's Bill for Establishing Religious Freedom instituted the principle of liberty of conscience by outlawing religious requirements for political and civil posts. But many other states enforced religious criteria for voting and office holding, penalizing individuals who dissented from the doctrines of Protestant Christianity. The North Carolina constitution of 1776 disqualified from public office any citizen "who shall deny the being of God, or the Truth of the Protestant Religion, or the Divine Authority of the Old or New Testament." New Hampshire's constitution contained a similar provision until 1868.

Americans influenced by the Enlightenment and by evangelical Protestantism condemned such restrictions on freedom of conscience but for different reasons. Leading American intellectuals, including Thomas Jefferson and Benjamin Franklin, argued that God had given humans the power of reason so that they could determine moral truths for themselves. To protect society from "ecclesiastical tyranny," they demanded complete freedom of expression. Many evangelical Protestants also wanted religious liberty, but their goal was to protect their churches from the government. The New England minister Isaac Backus warned Baptists not to incorporate their churches under the law or accept public funds because that might lead to state control. In Connecticut a devout Congregationalist welcomed "voluntarism" (the voluntary funding of churches by their members) for another reason: it allowed the laity to control the clergy, furthering "the principles of republicanism."

In religion as in politics, independence provided Americans with the opportunity to fashion a new institutional order. In each case they repudiated the hierarchical ways of the past—monarchy and establishment—in favor of a republican alternative. These choices reflected the outlook and increased influence of ordinary citizens, who had fought and financed the long, difficult military struggle. True to the prediction of a wealthy Virginia planter in April 1776, independence and revolution had allowed yeomen to promote "their darling Democracy."

For Further Exploration

In *Angel in the Whirlwind: The Triumph of the American Revolution* (1997), Benson Bobrick presents the break with England as a grand epic stretching from the French and Indian War to Washington's inauguration. A compelling fictional account of the life of Tom Paine is Howard Fast, *Citizen Tom Paine* (1943). Pauline Maier, *American Scripture: Making the Declaration of Independence* (1997), explains the background of the Declaration and shows how it has been redefined over the past two centuries. For some vivid firsthand accounts of the military conflict, see John C. Dann, ed., *The Revolution Remembered: Eyewitness Accounts of the War for Independence* (1980). James L. Stokesbury, *A Short History of the American Revolution* (1991), suggests parallels between the British defeat and the American failure in Vietnam. Barbara Graymont, *The Iroquois in the American Revolution* (1972), offers an assessment of the war from an Indian perspective. In *Liberty's Daughters: The Revolutionary Experience of American Women, 1750–1800* (1980), Mary Beth Norton portrays both the continuities and the changes in women's lives. Sylvia R. Frey, *Water from the Rock: Black Resistance in a Revolutionary Age* (1991), traces the impact of the revolution on African Americans and their adaptations of republican ideology and Christian beliefs.

TIMELINE

1775	Battle of Concord (April 19)	**1778**	Franco-American alliance (February 6)
	Second Continental Congress meets in Philadelphia (May).		Congress rejects negotiations with Britain.
	Battle of Bunker Hill		Britain begins a southern strategy and captures Savannah (December).
	Continental army is created and headed by George Washington.	**1779**	Spain declares war against Britain.
	Olive Branch petition is passed by moderates in Continental Congress.	**1780**	The British capture Charleston (May).
	Lord Dunmore's proclamation offers freedom to slaves and indentured servants (November).		The French army lands in Rhode Island.
	American invasion of Canada	**1781**	Cornwallis invades Virginia (April).
1776	Patriots and Loyalists battle in the south.		Cornwallis surrenders at Yorktown (October).
	Thomas Paine's *Common Sense* (January)		Large-scale Loyalist emigration
	Declaration of Independence (July 4)	**1782**	Peace talks begin in Paris (April).
	General Howe forces Washington to retreat from New York and New Jersey (December).		Virginia passes an act allowing slave manumission (reversed in 1792).
			Gradual emancipation laws in northern states
1777	Women begin to increase textile output.	**1783**	Britain signs the Treaty of Paris (September).
	Price inflation begins.		
	Howe occupies Philadelphia (September).	**1786**	Virginia Bill for Establishing Religious Freedom
	Gates defeats Burgoyne at Saratoga (October).	**1800**	Gabriel Prosser's slave rebellion is thwarted in Virginia.
	Continental army suffers at Valley Forge (December).		

Liberty! The American Revolution (PBS video; 6 hours) and the companion website at <http:/www.pbs.org/liberty> cover the war and the making of the Constitution. The "Virtual Marching Tour of the Philadelphia Campaign 1777" at <http://www.ushistory.org/brandywine/index.html> offers an interesting multimedia view of Howe's attack on Philadelphia and subsequent events. A fine, data-rich source on the black experience is "Africans in America: Revolution" at <http://www.pbs.org/wgbh/aia/part2/title.html>; other parts of this site cover the entire African American experience. To explore the political philosophy of Thomas Jefferson, log on to "Quotations from the Writings of Thomas Jefferson" at <http://etext.virginia.edu/jefferson/quotations>, a site that is conveniently arranged by topic.

Chapter 7

THE NEW POLITICAL ORDER
1776–1800

But where, say some, is the king of America? . . . in America the law is king.

—THOMAS PAINE, 1778

Like an earthquake the American Revolution shook the foundations of the traditional European political order, and its aftershocks were felt far into the nineteenth century. By "creating a new republic based on the rights of individual, the North Americans introduced a new force into the world," the great German historian Leopold von Ranke explained to the king of Bavaria in a private lecture in 1854, warning that the ideology of republicanism might cost the monarch his throne:

This was a revolution of principle. Up to this point, a king who ruled by the grace of God had been the center around which everything turned. Now the idea emerged that power should come from below [from the people]. . . . These two principles are like opposite poles, and it is the conflict between them that determines the course of the modern world.

Previous revolutions—such as that of the Puritan Commonwealth in England in the 1650s—had ended in political chaos and military rule, and many Europeans expected the new American republic to experience the same fate. But General George Washington stunned the world in 1783 when he voluntarily left public life to return to his plantation, leaving power in the hands of elected Patriot leaders. "Tis a Conduct so novel," the American painter Jonathan Trumbull reported from London, "so inconceivable to People [here], who, far from giving up powers they possess, are willing to convulse the empire to acquire more."

Fashioning republican institutions absorbed the energy and intellect of an entire generation. Between 1776 and 1800 Americans wrote new state and federal constitutions and devised a system of politics that was responsive to the popular will. When a bill was introduced into a state legislature, conservative Ezra Stiles grumbled, every elected official "instantly thinks how it will affect his constituents" rather than its impact on the welfare of the public as a whole. What Stiles criticized as an

189

excess of democracy, most ordinary Americans welcomed. For the first time the interests of ordinary citizens were represented in the halls of government, and the monarchs of Europe trembled.

Creating Republican Institutions, 1776–1787

Now that independence had been won, a Philadelphia newspaper observed, "the contest was no longer that of resistance against foreign rule but which of us shall be the rulers?" Where would power reside, in the national government or the states? Who would control the new republican institutions, traditional elites or ordinary citizens?

THE STATE CONSTITUTIONS: HOW MUCH DEMOCRACY?

In May 1776 the Continental Congress had urged Americans to suppress royal authority and establish new governing institutions. Most states quickly complied. Within six months Virginia, Maryland, North Carolina, New Jersey, Delaware, and Pennsylvania had written new constitutions, and Connecticut and Rhode Island had transformed their colonial charters into republican documents by deleting references to the king.

The Declaration of Independence had stated the principle of popular sovereignty: governments derive "their just powers from the consent of the governed." In the heat of revolution many Patriots gave this clause a democratic twist. In North Carolina the backcountry farmers of Mecklenburg County instructed their delegates to the state's constitutional convention to "oppose everything that leans to aristocracy or power in the hands of the rich and chief men exercised to the oppression of the poor." In Virginia voters elected a new assembly that, an observer remarked, "was composed of men not quite so well dressed, nor so politely educated, nor so highly born," while Delaware's constitution declared that "the Right of the People to participate in the Legislature, is the Foundation of Liberty and of all free government."

This democratic outlook received its fullest expression in Pennsylvania, thanks to a coalition of Scots-Irish farmers, Philadelphia artisans, and Enlightenment-influenced intellectuals. Pennsylvania's constitution abolished property owning as a test of citizenship and granted all men who paid taxes the right to vote and hold office. It also created a unicameral (one-house) legislature with complete power. No council or upper house was reserved for the wealthy, and no governor exercised veto power. Other constitutional provisions mandated an extensive system of elementary education, protected citizens from imprisonment for debt, and called for a society of economically independent freemen.

Pennsylvania's democratic constitution alarmed many leading Patriots, who believed that voting and especially officeholding should be restricted to "men of learning, leisure and easy circumstances." Jeremy Belknap of New Hampshire insisted that "the people be taught . . . that they are not able to govern themselves." He and other conservative Patriots feared that popular rule would lead to ordinary citizens using their numerical advantage to tax the rich.

From Boston John Adams denounced Pennsylvania's unicameral legislature as "so democratical that it must produce confusion and every evil work." To counter its appeal Adams published his *Thoughts on Government* in 1776 and sent the treatise to friends at constitutional conventions in other states. Adams adapted the British Whig theory of mixed government (in which power was shared by the king, lords, and commons) to a republican society. To preserve liberty his system dispersed authority by assigning the different functions of government—lawmaking, administering, and judging—to separate branches. Thus, legislatures would make the laws, and the executive and the judiciary would enforce them. Adams also called for a bicameral (two-house) legislature in which the upper house would be restricted to men who owned substantial property and would check the power of popular majorities in the lower house. As a further curb on democracy, he proposed an elected governor with the power to veto laws and an appointed—not elected—judiciary to review them. Adams argued that his plan was republican because the people would elect both the chief executive and the legislature.

Leading Patriots endorsed Adams's scheme because it preserved representative government while restricting popular power. Consequently, most state constitutions provided for bicameral legislatures in which membership in both houses was elective. However, only three constitutions gave the veto power to governors because many Patriots recalled the arbitrary conduct of royal governors. In line with Adams's suggestions, many states retained property qualifications for voting. In New York 90 percent of white men could vote in assembly elections, but only 40 percent could vote for the governor and the upper house. The most flagrant use of property to maintain the power of the elite occurred in South Carolina, where the 1778 constitution required candidates for governor to have a debt-free estate of £10,000 (about $600,000 today), senators to be worth £2,000, and assemblymen to own property valued at £1,000. These provisions ruled out officeholding for about 90 percent of white men.

Nonetheless, post-Revolutionary politics had a democratic tinge. The legislature emerged as the dominant branch of government, and state constitutions apportioned seats on the basis of population, giving farmers in rapidly growing western areas the representation they had long demanded. Indeed, because of backcountry pressure some legislatures moved the state capital from merchant-dominated seaports such as New York City and Philadelphia to inland cities such as Albany and Harrisburg. Even conservative South Carolina moved its seat of government inland, from Charleston to Columbia.

Most of the state legislatures were filled by new sorts of political leaders. Rather than electing their social "betters" to office, ordinary citizens increasingly chose men of "middling circumstances" who knew "the wants of the poor." By the mid-1780s middling farmers and urban artisans controlled the lower houses in most northern states and formed a sizable minority in southern assemblies. These middling men took the lead in opposing the collection of back taxes and other measures that tended "toward the oppression of the people."

The political legacy of the Revolution was complex. Only in Pennsylvania and Vermont were radical Patriots able to take power and create democratic institutions. Yet everywhere representative legislatures had more power, and the day-to-day politics of electioneering and interest-group bargaining became much more responsive to the demands of ordinary citizens.

The extraordinary excitement of the Revolutionary era also tested the dictum that only men could engage in politics. While men continued to control all public institutions—legislatures, juries, government offices—upper-class women entered into political debate, filling their letters and diaries (and undoubtedly their conversations) with opinions on public issues. "The men say we have no business [with politics]," Eliza Wilkinson of South Carolina complained in 1783. "They won't even allow us liberty of thought, and that is all I want" (see American Voices, "Women and Republicanism").

These American women did not insist on complete equality with men, but they wanted to eliminate certain restrictive customs and laws. Abigail Adams demanded equal legal rights for married women, pointing out that under existing common law they could not own most forms of property and could not enter into a contract or initiate a lawsuit without their husbands' action. "Men would be tyrants" if they continued to hold such power over women, Adams declared to her husband, criticizing him and other Patriots for "emancipating all nations" from monarchical despotism while "retaining absolute power over Wives."

Most men paid little attention to women's requests, and most husbands remained patriarchs, dominating their households. Even young men who embraced the republican ideal of "companionate" marriage did not support reform of the common law or a public role for their wives and daughters. With the partial exception of New Jersey, which until 1807 granted the vote to unmarried and widowed women of property, women remained second-class citizens, unable to participate directly in American political and economic life.

The republican quest for an educated citizenry provided the avenue for the most important advances made by American women. In her 1779 essay "On the Equality of the Sexes" (published in 1790), Judith Sargent Murray compared the intellectual faculties of men and women, arguing that women had an equal capacity for memory and superior imagination. Murray conceded that most women were inferior to men in judgment and reasoning, but only because of a lack of training: "We can only reason from what we know," she argued, and most women had been denied "the opportunity of acquiring knowledge." To remedy this situation, the attorney general in Massachusetts persuaded a jury in the 1790s that girls had an equal right to schooling under the state constitution. With greater access to public elementary schools and the creation of female academies (private high schools),

AMERICAN VOICES

Women and Republicanism

ELIZA WILKINSON

*I*n 1780 Eliza Wilkinson was a young widow managing one of her parents' plantations on the South Carolina Sea Islands, when the islands were invaded by the British. In this letter to a friend, Wilkinson casts herself as a "female patriot" and claims the right to express political opinions.

The land of Liberty! how sweet the sound! . . . O! Americans—Americans! strive to retain the glorious privilege which your virtuous ancestors left you. . . . ; and let not the blood of your brave countrymen, who have so lately (in all the States) died to defend it, be spilt in vain. Pardon this digression, my dear Mary—my pen is inspired with sympathetic ardor, and has run away with my thought before I was aware. I do not live to meddle with political matters; the men say we have no business with them, it is not in our sphere! . . . but I must beg pardon—I won't have it thought, that because we are the weaker sex as to *bodily* strength, my dear, we are capable of nothing more than minding the dairy, visiting the poultry-house, and all such domestic concerns; our thoughts can soar aloft, we can form conceptions of things of a higher nature; and have as just a sense of honor, glory, and great actions as these "lords of the Creation." . . . They won't even allow us the liberty of thought and that is all I want. I should not wish that we should meddle in what is unbecoming female delicacy, but surely we may have sense enough to give our opinions. . . .

Word was brought that a party of the enemy were at a neighboring plantation, not above two miles off, carrying provisions away. In an instant the men were under arms . . . they did not stay out long; but returned with seven [British] prisoners, four whites and three blacks. . . . Blush, O Britons, and be confounded! . . . an Almighty arm has visibly supported us; or a raw, undisciplined people, with so many disadvantages too on their side, could ever have withstood, for so long a time, an army which has repeatedly fought and conquered. . . .

SOURCE: Nancy Wolock, ed., *Early American Women: A Documentary History, 1600–1900* (Belmont, CA: Wadsworth, 1992), pp. 169–70.

---

many young women became literate and knowledgeable. By 1850 as many women as men in the northeastern states would be able to read and write, and literate women would challenge their subordinate legal and political status.

THE ARTICLES OF CONFEDERATION

As the Patriots moved toward independence in 1776, they envisioned a central government with limited powers. Carter Braxton of Virginia thought the Continental Congress should have the power to "regulate the affairs of trade, war, peace, alliances,

&c." but "should by no means have authority to interfere with the internal police [governance] or domestic concerns of any Colony."

This localistic outlook informed the Articles of Confederation, passed by Congress in November 1777. As the first national constitution, this document provided for a loose confederation in which "each state retains its sovereignty, freedom, and independence" as well as all powers and rights not "expressly delegated" to the United States. The Articles gave the confederation government the authority to declare war and peace, make treaties with foreign nations, adjudicate disputes between the states, borrow and print money, and requisition funds from the states "for the common defense or general welfare." These powers were to be exercised by a central legislature, the Congress, in which each state had one vote regardless of its wealth or population. There was no separate executive branch or judiciary. Important laws needed approval by at least nine of the thirteen states, and changes in the Articles required unanimous consent.

Because of disputes over western lands the Articles were not ratified by all the states until 1781. States with no claims to land in the West, such as Maryland and Pennsylvania, refused to accept the Articles until Virginia and other states that did have such claims (based on royal charters in which boundaries stretched to the Pacific Ocean) agreed to relinquish them to Congress to create a common national domain in the West. Threatened by Cornwallis's army in 1781, Virginia finally agreed to give up its land claims (Map 7.1 shows the dates of the actual cessions), and Maryland, the last holdout, then ratified the Articles.

Judith Sargent (Murray), Age Nineteen

The well-educated daughter of a wealthy Massachusetts merchant, Judith Sargent enjoyed a privileged childhood. But she endured a difficult seventeen-year marriage to John Stevens, a bankrupt who fled from his creditors and died in the West Indies. In 1788 she wed the Reverend John Murray, who became a leading American Universalist. Her portrait, painted around 1771 by the renowned artist John Singleton Copley, captures Murray's skeptical view of the world, an outlook that enabled her to question customary gender roles. (Private collection. Photo courtesy Frick Art Reference Library)

M A P 7.1

The Confederation and Western Land Claims

The Confederation Congress resolved the overlapping western land claims of the states by creating a "national domain" to the west of the Appalachian Mountains. Between 1781 and 1802 all the seaboard states with western land claims ceded them to the national government. The Confederation Congress established territories with representative political institutions and declared them to be open to settlement by citizens from all the states.

Formal approval of the Articles was anticlimactic. The Congress had been exercising de facto constitutional authority for four years, raising the Continental army and negotiating with foreign nations. Despite its successes the Confederation had a major weakness. Congress lacked the authority to impose taxes and therefore had to requisition funds from the state legislatures and hope they would pay, which they usually failed to do. Faced with the prospect of the Confederation's bankruptcy in 1780, General Washington called urgently for a national system of taxation, warning Patriot leaders that otherwise "our cause is lost."

In response, nationalist-minded members of Congress tried to expand the Confederation's authority. Robert Morris, who became superintendent of finance in 1781, persuaded Congress to charter the Bank of North America, a private institution in Philadelphia, hoping to use its notes to stabilize the inflated Continental currency. Morris also developed a comprehensive financial plan that apportioned some war expenses among the states while centralizing control of army expenditures and foreign debt. He hoped that the existence of a national debt would underline the Confederation's need for an import duty. But some state legislatures refused to support an increase in the Confederation's powers, which required the unanimous consent of the states. In 1781 Rhode Island rejected Morris's proposal for an import duty of 5 percent, and two years later New York refused to accept a similar plan, pointing out that it had opposed British-imposed import duties and would not accept them from Congress.

Despite its limited powers, the Congress successfully planned the settlement of the trans-Appalachian West. The Congress asserted the Confederation's title to the West in order to sell it and raise revenue for the government. Thus, in 1783 Congress began to negotiate with Indian tribes, hoping to persuade them that the Treaty of Paris had extinguished their land rights. The Congress also bargained with white squatters—"white savages," John Jay called them—allowing them to stay only if they paid for their lands. Given the natural barrier of the Appalachian Mountains, many members of Congress feared that westerners might establish separate republics and export their crops via the Mississippi River and Spanish-controlled Louisiana. The danger was real: in 1784 settlers in what is now eastern Tennessee organized the new state of Franklin. To preserve its authority over the West, Congress refused to recognize Franklin or consider its application to join the Confederation. Instead, the delegates directed the states of Virginia, North Carolina, and Georgia to administer the process of creating new states south of the Ohio River, a decision that indirectly allowed the expansion of slavery into that region.

To the north of the Ohio Congress established the Northwest Territory and issued three ordinances affecting the settlement and administration of western lands. The Ordinance of 1784, written by Thomas Jefferson, called for the admission of states carved out of the territory as soon as their populations equaled that of the smallest existing state. To deter squatters the Land Ordinance of 1785 established a grid surveying system and required that the lands be surveyed before settlement. It also specified a minimum price of $1 per acre and required that 50 percent of the townships be sold in single blocks of 23,040 acres each, which only large-scale investors and speculators could afford, and the rest in parcels of 640 acres each, which only well-to-do farmers could manage to buy (see Map 7.2).

Finally, the Northwest Ordinance of 1787 provided for the creation of three to five territories that would eventually become the states of Ohio, Indiana, Illinois, Michigan, and Wisconsin. Reflecting the Enlightenment social philosophy of Jefferson and other Patriots, the ordinance prohibited slavery in those territories and earmarked funds from the sale of some land for the support of schools. It also specified that initially Congress should appoint a governor and judges to administer a new territory. Once the number of free adult men reached 5,000, settlers could elect their own legislature. When the population grew to 60,000, residents could

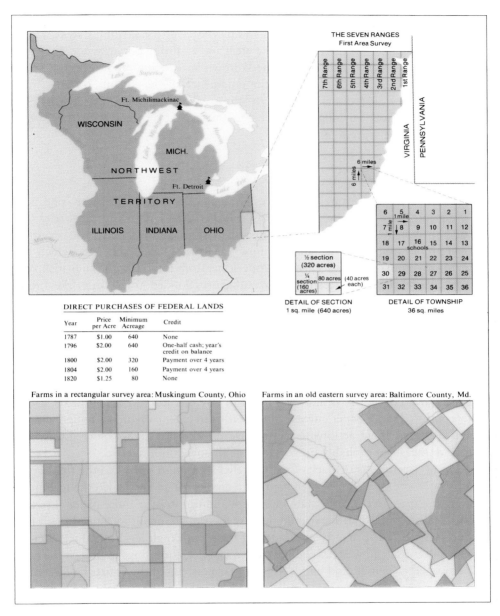

THE SEVEN RANGES
First Area Survey

DIRECT PURCHASES OF FEDERAL LANDS

Year	Price per Acre	Minimum Acreage	Credit
1787	$1.00	640	None
1796	$2.00	640	One-half cash; year's credit on balance
1800	$2.00	320	Payment over 4 years
1804	$2.00	160	Payment over 4 years
1820	$1.25	80	None

DETAIL OF SECTION
1 sq. mile (640 acres)

DETAIL OF TOWNSHIP
36 sq. miles

½ section (320 acres)
¼ section (160 acres)   80 acres   (40 acres each)

Farms in a rectangular survey area: Muskingum County, Ohio

Farms in an old eastern survey area: Baltimore County, Md.

M AP 7.2
Land Divisions in the Northwest Territory

The ordinances of 1785 and 1787 divided the Northwest Territory into uniform sections or townships. The townships were about the same size as New England communities, 36 square miles, and were divided into thirty-six sections of 1 square mile, or 640 acres, surveyed in a grid pattern. The ordinances favored speculators over yeomen by requiring that half the townships be sold in single blocks of 23,040 acres.

write a republican constitution and apply to join the Confederation. On admission a new state would enjoy all the rights and privileges of the existing states.

The ordinances of the 1780s were a great and enduring achievement. They provided for the orderly settlement of the West while reducing the prospect of secessionist movements and preventing the emergence of dependent "colonies." The ordinances also added a new "western" dimension to the national identity. The United States was no longer confined to thirteen governments on the eastern seaboard. It had space to expand.

SHAYS'S REBELLION

However bright the futures of the western states, in the East postwar conditions were grim. Peace had brought a recession rather than a return to prosperity. The war had destroyed many American merchant ships and disrupted the export of tobacco and other farm goods. And now the British Navigation Acts, which had nurtured colonial commerce, barred Americans from trading with the British West Indies. Moreover, low-priced British manufactures flooded American markets, driving many artisans and wartime textile firms out of business.

State governments emerged from the war with large debts and worthless currencies. Speculators—mostly wealthy merchants and landowners—who had purchased state debt certificates for far less than face value advocated high taxes so that the bonds could be redeemed quickly at full value. But yeomen farmers and artisans, hard hit by the postwar recession, demanded tax relief. To assist debtors many states enacted laws allowing them to pay creditors in installments. Other states printed more paper currency in an effort to extend credit. Although wealthy men deplored these actions as destructive of "the just rights of creditors," the stopgap measures probably prevented a major social upheaval.

In Massachusetts the lack of debtor-relief legislation provoked the first armed uprising in the new nation. Merchants and creditors had persuaded the legislature to impose taxes to repay the state's war debt and not to issue more paper currency. When cash-strapped farmers could not pay their debts, creditors hauled them into court, taking their property and saddling them with high legal fees. In 1786 residents of central and western counties called extralegal meetings to protest the taxes and property seizures, and bands of angry farmers closed the courts by force. The resistance gradually grew into a full-scale revolt led by Captain Daniel Shays, a former Continental army officer.

As a struggle against taxes imposed by the distant state government in Boston, Shays's Rebellion resembled colonial resistance to the British Stamp Act. "The people have turned against their teachers the doctrines which were inculcated to effect the late revolution," complained the conservative Massachusetts political leader Fisher Ames (see American Voices, "An Anti-Shaysite Interviews the Rebels"). But even the Radical Patriots of 1776 condemned the Shaysites as anti-republican. "Those Men, who . . . would lessen the Weight of Government lawfully exercised

AMERICAN VOICES

An Anti-Shaysite Interviews the Rebels

A fter Shays's Rebellion, both sides sought to justify their cause. This clever piece was published in the Massachusetts Centinel, *an anti-Shaysite newspaper. Unlike most other contributors to the* Centinel, *who explicitly condemned the rebels, this author indicates the nature of the rebels' grievances but subtly emphasizes their selfish motives, portraying them as a mob ("the mobility") intent on avoiding taxes and contesting all authority.*

What influenced them to thus rise and oppose government? What did they aim at thereby? . . . I was present with them at the late rising . . . conversed with almost every one, and penetrated to the secret recesses of their souls. . . . I inquired of an old plough jogger [plowman or farmer] the confessed aim of the people of that assembly. He said, "To get redress of grievances." I asked, "What grievances?"

He said, "We have grievances enough; I can tell you mine. I have labored hard all my days, and fared hard. I have been greatly abused, been obliged to do more than my part in the war, been loaded down with [many taxes:] class-rates, town-rates, province-rates, continental-rates, and all rates, lawsuits, and have been pulled and hauled by sheriffs, constables, and collectors, and had my cattle sold for less than they were worth. I have been obliged to pay, and nobody will pay me . . . and the great men are going to get all we have, and I think it is time for us to rise and put a stop to it, and have no more courts, nor sheriffs, nor collectors, nor lawyers. I design to pay no more. . . .

I next asked a pert lad . . . (who fancied himself a deep politician) [and he] made a long harangue upon governors, and jobbers [traders or speculators], and lawyers and judges . . . and salaries, and fees, and pensions, and such has ten times too much, and such has five times too much, and . . . the great men pocket up all the money and live easy, and we work hard, and we can't pay it, and we won't pay it. . . .

Thus I went from rank to rank, through all the mobility. . . . I got the secrets of their hearts. . . .

SOURCE: Linda R. Monk, ed., *Ordinary Americans: U.S. History Through the Eyes of Everyday People* (Alexandria, VA: Close Up, 1994), pp. 42–43.

must be Enemies to our happy Revolution and Common Liberty," charged onetime revolutionary Samuel Adams. To preserve its authority the Massachusetts legislature passed a Riot Act outlawing illegal assemblies. Governor James Bowdoin, supported by eastern merchants, equipped a strong fighting force to put down the rebellion and called for additional troops from the Continental Congress. But Shays's army dwindled during the winter of 1786–87, falling victim to freezing weather and inadequate supplies, and Bowdoin's military force easily dispersed the rebels.

"Gen. *Daniel Shays,* Col. *Job Shattuck*"

This woodcut was published in *Bickerstaff's Boston Almanack* for 1787 by "Friends of Government," who attacked the rebel leaders as upstarts and demagogues. "Liberty is still the object I have in view," a Shaysite declared in reply, but the former radical Sam Adams would have none of it: "The man who dares to rebel against the laws of a republic ought to suffer death." Shattuck was sentenced to death for treason but then pardoned; Shays fled to New York State, where he died in 1821, still a poor farmer.

(National Portrait Gallery, Smithsonian Institution/Art Resource, NY)

The collapsed rebellion provided graphic proof that the costs of war and the fruits of independence were not being shared evenly. Many ordinary families who had suffered while supporting the struggle for independence felt they had exchanged one tyranny for another. Angry Massachusetts voters turned Governor Bowdoin out of office, and debt-ridden farmers in New York, northern Pennsylvania, Connecticut, and New Hampshire closed courthouses, demanding economic relief. As British officials in Canada predicted the imminent demise of the United States, many Americans feared for the fate of their republican experiment. At this dire moment nationalists redoubled their efforts to create a central government equal to the challenges facing the new republic.

The Constitution of 1787

From the moment of its creation, the Constitution was a controversial document. Some Americans took issue with the startling ways it redefined republicanism and created a more centralized government, whereas other citizens questioned the motives of its authors.

THE RISE OF A NATIONALIST FACTION

Money questions—debts, taxes, and tariffs—dominated the postwar agenda, and men who had served the Confederation government during the war as military officers, diplomats, and officials looked at them from a "national" rather than a "state" perspective. General Washington, the financier Robert Morris, and the diplomats Benjamin Franklin, John Jay, and John Adams became advocates of a stronger central government with the power to control foreign commerce and impose tariffs. They knew that without tariff revenue Congress would be unable to pay the interest on the foreign debt and the nation's credit would collapse. However, key commercial states in the North—New York, Massachusetts, Pennsylvania—resisted national tariffs because they had devised trade policies that subsided local merchants and imposed state tariffs on imported goods. Most southern planters also opposed tariffs on cheap British textiles and ironware, which they were eager to import.

Some of the planters who opposed tariffs had other reasons for taking a nationalist stance. By 1786 many wealthy southerners were worried about the financial policies of the state governments. Legislatures in Virginia and other southern states had granted tax relief to various groups of citizens, diminishing public revenue and delaying the redemption of state debts. Taxpayers were being led to believe they would "never be compelled to pay" the public debt, lamented Charles Lee of Virginia, a wealthy bondholder. Private creditors had similar complaints. "While men are madly accumulating enormous debts, their legislators are making provisions for their nonpayment," a South Carolina creditor complained.

Nationalists took the initiative in 1786, when James Madison persuaded the Virginia legislature to call a special convention to discuss tariff and taxation policies. Twelve men representing only five states met in Annapolis, Maryland; they called for another meeting in Philadelphia to undertake an even broader review of the Confederation. Nationalists in Congress, frightened by Shays's Rebellion, secured a resolution supporting the Philadelphia convention and calling for a revision of the Articles of Confederation "adequate to the exigencies of government and the preservation of the Union." "Nothing but the adoption of some efficient plan from the Convention," a fellow nationalist wrote to James Madison, "can prevent anarchy first & civil convulsions afterwards."

THE PHILADELPHIA CONVENTION

In May 1787 fifty-five delegates arrived in Philadelphia, representing every state except Rhode Island, whose legislature opposed any increase in central authority. Some delegates, such as Benjamin Franklin of Pennsylvania, had been early leaders of the independence movement. Others, including George Washington and Robert Morris, had become prominent during the war. Several famous Patriots missed the convention. John Adams and Thomas Jefferson were in Europe, serving as the American ministers to Britain and France. The radical Samuel Adams had not been chosen as a delegate by the Massachusetts legislature, while the firebrand Patrick Henry refused to attend because he favored a strictly limited national government. Their places were taken by capable younger men such as James Madison and Alexander Hamilton; both believed that the decisions of the convention would "decide for ever the fate of Republican Government."

Most delegates to the Philadelphia convention were merchants, slaveholding planters, or "monied men." There were no artisans, backcountry settlers, or tenants and only a single yeoman farmer. Consequently, most delegates supported creditors' property rights and favored a central government that would protect the republic from "the imprudence of democracy," as Hamilton put it.

The delegates elected Washington as the presiding officer and, to forestall popular opposition, decided to deliberate behind closed doors. They agreed that each state would have one vote, as in the Confederation, and that a majority of states would decide an issue. Then the delegates exceeded their mandate to revise the Articles of Confederation and considered the Virginia Plan, a scheme for a truly national government devised by James Madison. Madison had arrived in Philadelphia determined to fashion a new political order run by men of high character. A graduate of Princeton, he had read classical and modern political theory and served in both the Confederation Congress and the Virginia assembly. His experience in Virginia had convinced him of the "narrow ambition" and lack of public virtue of many state political leaders.

Madison's Virginia Plan differed from the Articles of Confederation in three crucial respects. First, it rejected state sovereignty in favor of the "supremacy of national authority." The central government would have the power not only to "legislate in all cases to which the separate States are incompetent" but also to overturn state laws. Second, the plan called for a national republic that drew its authority directly from all the people and had direct power over them. As Madison explained, the new central government would bypass the states, operating directly "on the individuals composing them." Third, the plan created a three-tier national government with a lower house elected by voters, an upper house elected by the lower house, and an executive and judiciary chosen by the entire legislature.

From a political perspective Madison's plan had two fatal flaws. First, state politicians and citizens would strongly oppose the provision allowing the national government to veto state laws. Second, by assigning great power to the lower house, whose composition was based on population, Madison's plan increased the influence of voters who lived in the large states. Consequently, delegates from small states rejected the plan, fearing, as a Delaware delegate put it, that the states with many inhabitants would "crush the small ones whenever they stand in the way of their ambitious or interested views."

Delegates from the small states rallied behind the New Jersey Plan devised by William Paterson. This plan strengthened the Confederation by giving the central government the power to raise revenue, control commerce, and make binding requisitions on the states. But it preserved the states' control over their own laws and guaranteed their equality: each state would have one vote in a unicameral legislature, as in the Confederation. Delegates from the larger states rejected this provision and, after a month of debate, mustered a bare majority in favor of the principles of the Virginia Plan.

This decision raised the prospect of a dramatically new constitutional system. During the hot, humid summer of 1787 the delegates met six days a week, debating high principles and considering a multitude of technical details. Experienced and realistic politicians, they knew that their final plan had to be acceptable to existing political interests and powerful social groups. Pierce Butler of South Carolina invoked a classical Greek precedent: "We must follow the example of Solon, who gave the Athenians not the best government he could devise but the best they would receive."

Representation remained the central problem. To satisfy both large and small states the Connecticut delegates suggested amending the Virginia Plan so that the upper house, the Senate, would always seat two members from each state, while seats in the lower chamber, the House of Representatives, would be apportioned on the basis of population. The size of the states' delegations would be altered every ten years on the basis of a national census. This "Great Compromise" was accepted but only after bitter debate; to some it seemed less a compromise than a victory for the smaller states.

Other state-related matters were quickly settled. One delegate objected to establishing national courts within the states, warning that "the states will revolt at such encroachments." The convention therefore defined the judicial power of the United States in broad terms, vesting it "in one supreme Court" and leaving the new national legislature to decide whether to establish lower courts within the states. The convention also decided against requiring voters to own a certain amount of land. "Eight or nine states have extended the right of suffrage beyond the freeholders [landowners]," George Mason of Virginia pointed out. "What will people there say if they should be disfranchised?" The convention also placed the selection of the president in an electoral college chosen on a state-by-state basis and specified that state legislatures, not the voters at large, would elect members of the U.S. Senate. By giving state governments an important role in the new constitutional system, the delegates encouraged them to accept a reduction in their sovereignty.

Slavery was not a prominent issue at the convention, but its consideration revealed an important threefold regional division. Speaking for many northerners Gouverneur Morris of New York condemned slavery as "a nefarious institution" and hoped for its eventual demise. Reflecting the outlook of many Chesapeake planters, who wanted to retain the institution but had ample numbers of slaves, George Mason of Virginia advocated an end to Atlantic slave trade. But delegates from the rice-growing states of South Carolina and Georgia insisted that slave imports continue, warning that otherwise their states "shall not be parties to the Union."

For the sake of national unity, the delegates treated slavery as a political rather than a moral issue. To satisfy Georgia and South Carolina they denied Congress the power to regulate slave imports for twenty years, and to discourage slaves from fleeing they agreed to a "fugitive" clause that allowed masters to reclaim enslaved blacks (or white indentured servants) who took refuge in other states. To mollify the northern states the delegates did not mention slavery explicitly in the Constitution (referring instead to citizens and "all other Persons"), thus denying the institution national legal status. They also refused southern demands to count slaves and citizens equally in determining states' representation in Congress, accepting a compromise proposal in which a slave would be counted as three-fifths of a free person for purposes of representation and taxation.

Having allayed the concerns of small states and slave states, the delegates proceeded to create a powerful, procreditor national government. The finished document declared that the Constitution and all national legislation and treaties made under its authority would be the "supreme" law of the land. It gave the national government broad powers over taxation, military defense, and external commerce as well as the authority to make all laws "necessary and proper" to implement those and other provisions. To protect creditors and establish the fiscal integrity of the new government, the Constitution mandated that the United States honor the existing national debt. Finally, it restricted the ability of state governments to assist debtors by forbidding the states to issue money or enact any "Law impairing the Obligation of Contracts."

The proposed Constitution was not a "perfect production," Benjamin Franklin admitted on September 17, 1787, as he urged the forty-one delegates still present to sign it. Yet the great diplomat confessed his astonishment at finding "this system approaching so near to perfection as it does." His colleagues apparently agreed; all but three signed the document.

THE PEOPLE DEBATE RATIFICATION

The delegates hesitated to submit the Constitution to the state legislatures for their unanimous consent, as required by the Articles of Confederation, because they knew that Rhode Island (and perhaps a few other states) would reject it. So they specified that the Constitution would go into effect on ratification by special conventions in at least nine of the thirteen states. Because of its nationalist sympathies the Confederation Congress winked at this extralegal procedure.

As a great national debate began, the nationalists seized the initiative with two bold moves. First, they called themselves "Federalists," a term that suggested a loose, decentralized system of government and partially obscured their quest for a strong central authority. Second, they launched a coordinated political campaign, publishing dozens of pamphlets and newspaper articles supporting the proposed Constitution.

The opponents of the Constitution, who became known as Antifederalists, had diverse backgrounds and motives. Some, like Governor George Clinton of New York, feared losing their power at the state level. Others were rural democrats who feared that a powerful central government controlled by merchants and creditors would produce a new aristocracy. "These lawyers and men of learning and monied men expect to be managers of this Constitution," worried a Massachusetts farmer, "and get all the power and all the money into their own hands and then they will swallow up all of us little folks . . . just as the whale swallowed up Jonah." They pointed out that the Constitution, unlike most state constitutions, lacked a declaration of individual rights.

Well-educated Americans with a traditional republican outlook also opposed the new system. To keep government "close to the people," they wanted the nation to remain a collection of small sovereign republics tied together only for trade and defense—not the "United States" but the "States United." Citing the French political philosopher Montesquieu, Antifederalists argued that republican institutions were best suited to cities or small states. Thus Melancton Smith of New York warned that the large electoral districts prescribed by the Constitution would encourage the election of a few wealthy upper-class men, whereas the smaller state districts produced "a representative body, composed principally of respectable yeomanry." Patrick Henry predicted the Constitution would recreate the worst features of British rule: high taxes, an oppressive bureaucracy, a standing army, and a "great and mighty President . . . supported in extravagant munificence."

In New York, where ratification was hotly contested, James Madison, John Jay, and Alexander Hamilton countered these arguments in a series of newspaper articles published in 1787 and 1788 and collectively called *The Federalist*. They stressed the need for a strong government to conduct foreign affairs and denied that it would foster domestic tyranny. Citing Montesquieu's praise for "mixed government" (and drawing on John Adams's *Thoughts on Government*), the authors of *The Federalist* pointed out that national authority would be divided among a president, a bicameral legislature, and a judiciary. Each branch of government would "check and balance" the others, thus preserving liberty.

Indeed, in *The Federalist*, No. 10, Madison maintained that the size of the national republic would be its greatest protection against tyranny. It was "sown in the nature of man," Madison wrote, that individuals would seek power and form factions to advance their interests. Indeed, "a landed interest, a manufacturing interest, a mercantile interest, a moneyed interest, with many lesser interests, grow up of necessity in civilized nations." He argued that a free society should not suppress those groups but simply prevent any one of them from becoming dominant—an end best achieved in a large republic. "Extend the sphere," Madison concluded, "and you take in a greater variety of parties and interests; you make it less probable that a majority of the whole will have a common motive to invade the rights of other citizens."

The delegates who met at the state ratifying conventions between December 1787 and June 1788 represented a wide spectrum of Americans, from untutored farmers and middling artisans to well-educated gentlemen. Generally, delegates from the backcountry were Antifederalists, whereas those from the seacoast were Federalists. Thus, a coalition of merchants, artisans, and commercial farmers from Philadelphia and its vicinity spearheaded an easy Federalist victory in Pennsylvania. Other early Federalist successes came in the less populous states of Delaware, New Jersey, Georgia, and Connecticut, where delegates counted on a strong national government to offset the power of their larger neighbors.

The Constitution's first real test came in January 1788 in Massachusetts, one of the most populous states and a hotbed of Antifederalist sentiment (see Map 7.3). Influential Patriots, including Samuel Adams and Governor John Hancock, opposed the new constitution, as did Shaysite sympathizers in the west. But Boston artisans, who wanted tariff protection from British imports, supported ratification. Astute Federalist politicians finally persuaded wavering delegates by promising that the new government would consider a national guarantee of individual rights. By a close vote of 187 to 168, the Federalists carried the day.

Spring brought new Federalist victories in Maryland and South Carolina. When New Hampshire ratified by the narrow margin of fifty-seven to forty-seven in June, the required nine states had approved the Constitution. Still, the essential states of Virginia and New York had not yet acted. Writing in *The Federalist*, Madison, Jay, and Hamilton used their superb rhetorical skills to win support in those states. Addressing a powerful Antifederalist argument, leading Federalists reiterated their promise to amend the Constitution with a bill of rights. In the end the Federalists won narrowly in Virginia, eighty-nine to seventy-nine, and that success carried them to victory in New York by the even smaller margin of thirty to twenty-seven. Suspicious of centralized power, the yeomen of North Carolina and Rhode Island ratified only in 1789 and 1790, respectively.

Ratification of the Constitution brought an end to the Revolutionary era and the temporary ascendancy of the democratically inclined state legislatures. Working against great odds the Federalists had created a national republic that restored the political authority of established leaders. To celebrate their victory Federalists organized great processions in the seaport cities. By marching in orderly fashion (a sharp contrast to the riotous Revolutionary mobs) the citizenry affirmed its commitment to a self-governing republican community based on law. Floats carried the Constitution on an "altar of liberty," using sacred symbols to endow the new national regime with moral legitimacy and lay the foundations for a secular "civil religion."

THE FEDERALISTS IMPLEMENT THE CONSTITUTION

The Constitution expanded the dimensions of American political life, allowing voters to fill national as well as local and state offices. The Federalists swept the elec-

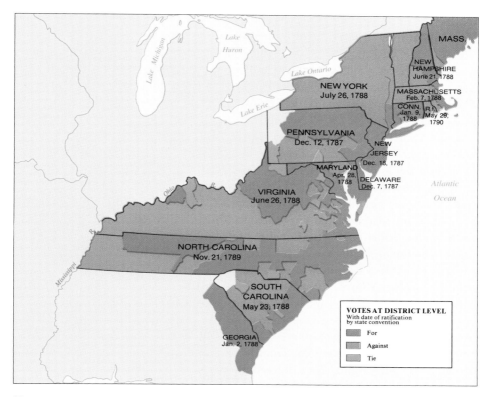

M A P 7.3
Ratifying the Constitution

In 1907 the geographer Owen Libby plotted the votes of the state ratification conventions on a map. Looking at the pattern of voting he suggested that most delegates who favored the Constitution came from commercial farming districts, while those who opposed it came primarily from subsistence regions. Subsequent research has confirmed Libby's socioeconomic interpretation in North and South Carolina and Massachusetts; however, other factors influenced delegates in some states with backcountry districts, such as Georgia, where the Constitution was ratified unanimously.

tion of 1788, placing forty-four supporters in the first Congress; only eight Antifederalists were elected. As expected, members of the Electoral College chose George Washington as president. John Adams received the second highest number of electoral votes and became vice president. The two men took up their posts in New York City, the temporary home of the national government.

Washington, the military savior of his country, became its political father as well. At fifty-seven he was a man of great personal dignity and influence. Instinctively cautious he generally followed the administrative practices of the Confederation, asking Congress to reestablish the existing executive departments: Foreign Affairs (State), Finance (Treasury), and War. The Constitution gave the president the power to appoint major officials with the consent of the Senate, but Washington insisted that only he could remove them, thus ensuring the chief executive's control over the bureaucracy. To head the Department of State Washington chose Thomas Jefferson, a fellow Virginian and an experienced diplomat. For secretary of the Treasury he turned to Alexander Hamilton, a lawyer and wartime military aide. The new president designated Jefferson, Hamilton, and Secretary of War Henry Knox as his cabinet, or advisory body.

The Constitution had created a Supreme Court but left the establishment of the court system to Congress. Because the Federalists wanted national institutions to act directly on individual citizens, they enacted the Judiciary Act of 1789, which created a hierarchical federal court system with thirteen district courts, one for each state, and three circuit courts to hear appeals. As the Constitution specified, the Supreme Court had the final say. Moreover, the Judiciary Act permitted appeals to the Supreme Court of constitutional matters that arose in the state courts, ensuring that national judges would decide contested issues.

The Federalists kept their promise to add a declaration of rights to the Constitution. Drawing on proposed lists of rights submitted by the states' ratifying conventions, James Madison, who had been elected to the House of Representatives, submitted nineteen amendments to the first Congress, and ten of them were approved by the first Congress and ratified by the states in 1791. These ten amendments, which became known as the Bill of Rights, safeguarded certain fundamental personal rights, such as freedom of speech and religion, and mandated certain legal procedures that protected the individual, such as trial by jury. The Second Amendment gave the people the right to bear arms so that they might serve in the militia and defend their liberties, while the Tenth Amendment limited the authority of the national government by reserving powers not otherwise addressed to the states or the people. In addressing Antifederalists' concerns through the Bill of Rights, Congress secured the legitimacy of the new government and ensured broad political support for the Constitution.

The Political Crisis of the 1790s

The final decade of the century brought fresh political challenges. The Federalists divided into two irreconcilable factions over financial policy, and the ideological impact of the French Revolution widened this split. In the course of these struggles Alexander Hamilton and Thomas Jefferson defined contrasting views of the American future.

HAMILTON'S FINANCIAL PROGRAM

One of George Washington's most important decisions was his choice of Alexander Hamilton as secretary of the Treasury. An ambitious self-made man of great charm and intelligence, Hamilton had served as Washington's personal aide during the war. He married the daughter of a wealthy Hudson River landowner and during the 1780s became a leading lawyer in New York City. At the Philadelphia convention Hamilton condemned the "amazing violence and turbulence of the democratic spirit," calling for an authoritarian government headed by a president with nearly monarchical powers.

As Treasury secretary Hamilton devised bold policies to enhance the authority of the national government and favor financiers and seaport merchants. He outlined his plans in three path-breaking and interrelated reports to Congress: on public credit (January 1790), a national bank (December 1790), and manufactures (December 1791).

The financial and social implications of Hamilton's "Report on the Public Credit" made it instantly controversial. It asked Congress to buy ("redeem") at face value the millions of dollars in securities issued by the Confederation, a redemption plan that would bolster the government's credit but also provide windfall profits to speculators. For example, the merchant firm of Burrell & Burrell had paid about $600 for Confederation notes with a face value of $2,500; their redemption at full value would bring the firm an enormous profit of $1,900. Equally controversial, Hamilton proposed to create a permanent national debt to pay the Burrells and other noteholders. In return for their Confederation notes they would receive new government-issued securities bearing the relatively high interest rate of 6 percent.

Hamilton's plan for a permanent national debt funded by wealthy men reawakened Radical Whig and republican fears of scheming British financiers. Speaking for the Virginia House of Burgesses Patrick Henry condemned the plan, arguing that "in an agricultural country like this, to erect, and concentrate, and perpetuate a large monied interest [must prove] . . . fatal to the existence of American liberty." Challenging the morality of Hamilton's proposal, James Madison asked Congress to assist the thousands of shopkeepers, farmers, and soliders who had accepted Confederation securities during the dark days of the war and then sold them to speculators. Madison proposed giving the present bondholders only "the highest price which has prevailed in the market" and distributing the remaining funds to the original owners. But identifying the original owners would have been difficult, and nearly half the members of the House of Representatives owned Confederation securities and would personally profit from Hamilton's plan. Melding practicality with self-interest the House rejected Madison's proposal.

Hamilton then advanced a second proposal that favored wealthy creditors, a plan by which the national government would take over ("assume") the war debts of the states. This assumption plan unleashed a flurry of speculation and some governmental corruption. Before Hamilton's announcement Assistant Secretary of the Treasury William Duer used insider knowledge to buy up the depreciated war bonds of southern states; if Congress approved the assumption plan, Duer and his speculator associates would reap an enormous profit. To win support for assumption in the House of Representatives among the delegations from Virginia and Maryland, which had already paid off part of their war debt, Hamilton agreed to repay those states and back their bid to locate the national capital along the banks of the Potomac.

In December 1790 Hamilton, bolstered by the passage of his funding and re-demption/assumption bills, asked Congress to charter a national financial institution, the Bank of the United States. The Bank would be jointly owned by private stockholders and the national government. Hamilton argued that the Bank, by making loans to merchants, handling government funds, and issuing financial notes, would provide a respected currency for the specie-starved American economy and make the new national debt easier to fund. These benefits persuaded Congress to enact Hamilton's bill and send it to the president for approval.

At this critical juncture Secretary of State Thomas Jefferson joined ranks with Madison against Hamilton. Jefferson had condemned the shady dealings in southern war bonds and the "corrupt squadron of paper dealers" who had arranged them. Now he charged that Hamilton's scheme for a national bank was unconstitutional. "The incorporation of a Bank," Jefferson told President Washington, was not a power "delegated to the United States by the Constitution." Giving a *strict* interpretation to the national charter, Jefferson maintained that the central government had only the limited powers explicitly assigned to it. In response, Hamilton articulated a *loose* interpretation, noting that Article 1, Section 8, empowered Congress to make "all Laws which shall be necessary and proper" to carry out the Constitution's provisions. Washington agreed with his Treasury secretary and signed the legislation creating the bank.

Hamilton turned now to the final element of his financial system: a national revenue that would be used to pay the annual interest on the permanent debt. At Hamilton's insistence in 1792 Congress imposed a variety of domestic excise taxes, including a duty on whiskey distilled in the United States. But the revenue from those taxes was small, and so the Treasury secretary proposed to raise tariffs on foreign imports. Although his "Report on Manufactures" (1791) called for a nation that was self-sufficient in manufactured goods, he did not ask Congress to impose high "protective" tariffs that would exclude foreign products. Such tariffs would cut trade, and so Hamilton settled for a modest increase in customs duties, a tariff for "revenue."

Hamilton's carefully designed plan worked brilliantly. As American trade increased, customs revenue rose steadily (providing about 90 percent of the U.S. government's income from 1790 to 1820), allowing the Treasury to pay for the redemption and assumption programs. In less than two years Hamilton had devised a strikingly modern fiscal system that provided the new national government with financial stability.

JEFFERSON'S AGRARIAN VISION

Hamilton paid a high price for this success. By the time Washington began his second four-year term in 1793, Hamilton's financial measures had split the Federalists who wrote and ratified the Constitution into irreconcilable factions. Most north-

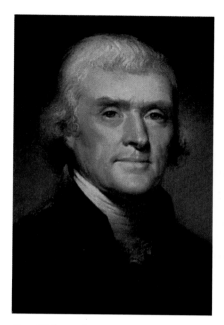

Two Visions of America

Thomas Jefferson and Alexander Hamilton confront each other in these portraits, as they did during the political battles of 1790s. Jefferson was pro-French; Hamilton, pro-British. Jefferson favored farmers and artisans; Hamilton supported merchants and financiers. Jefferson believed in democracy and rule by legislative majorities; Hamilton argued for a strong executive and judicial review. But Hamilton's timely intervention in 1800 secured the presidency for his long-time political foe.

(Jefferson by Rembrandt Peale, The White House Collection, copyright White House Historical Association; Hamilton by John Trumbull, 1792, Yale University Art Gallery, Trumbull Collection)

ern Federalists adhered to the political alliance led by Hamilton, and most southerners to a rival group headed by Madison and Jefferson. By the elections of 1794 the two factions had acquired names. Hamilton's supporters retained their original name: Federalists; Madison's and Jefferson's supporters were called Democratic-Republicans or simply Republicans.

The southern planters and western farmers who became Republicans rejected Hamilton's economic and social philosophy. Thomas Jefferson, a man of great learning, spoke for them. Well read in architecture, natural history, scientific farming, and political theory, Jefferson embraced the optimistic spirit of the Enlightenment, declaring his belief in the "improvability of the human race." But he knew that progress was not inevitable and deplored both the long-standing speculative practices of merchants and financiers and the emerging social divisions of an urban industrial economy. Having seen the masses of propertyless laborers in the manufacturing regions in Britain, Jefferson had concluded that workers who depended on wages lacked the economic independence required to sustain a republic.

Jefferson's vision of the American future was agrarian and democratic. Although he had grown up (and remained) a privileged slaveowner, he understood the needs of yeomen farmers and other ordinary white Americans. His vision took form in his *Notes on the State of Virginia* (1785): "Those who labor in the earth are the chosen people of God," he wrote. When Jefferson drafted the Ordinance of 1784, he had pictured a West settled by productive yeomen farm families. Their grain and meat would feed European nations, which "would manufacture and send us in exchange our clothes and other comforts."

During the 1790s Jefferson's vision was fulfilled as turmoil in Europe created new opportunities for American farmers. The French Revolution began in 1789, and four years later France's new republican government went to war against a British-led coalition of monarchical states. As warfare disrupted European farming, wheat prices leapt from 5 to 8 shillings a bushel and remained high for twenty years, bringing substantial profits to export-minded Chesapeake and Middle Atlantic farmers. Simultaneously, a boom in the export of raw cotton, fueled by the invention of the cotton gin and mechanization of cloth production in Britain, boosted the economy of Georgia and South Carolina. As Jefferson had hoped, European markets brought prosperity to American farmers and planters.

THE FRENCH REVOLUTION DIVIDES AMERICANS

American merchants profited even more handsomely from the European war because President Washington issued a Proclamation of Neutrality that allowed U.S. citizens to trade with both sides. As neutral carriers American ships claimed the right to pass through the British naval blockade along the French coastline and soon took over the lucrative trade between France and its West Indian sugar islands. The American merchant fleet became one of the largest in the world, increasing from 355,000 tons in 1790 to more than 1.1 million tons in 1808. Commercial earnings rose spectacularly, averaging $20 million annually in the 1790s—twice the value of cotton and tobacco exports. To keep up with demand, shipowners invested in new vessels, providing work for thousands of shipwrights, sail makers, laborers, and seamen. Hundreds of carpenters, masons, and cabinetmakers found work building warehouses and elegant Federal-style town houses for newly affluent merchants.

Even as they prospered from the European struggle, Americans argued passionately over its ideologies. Most Americans had welcomed the French Revolution of 1789 because it abolished feudalism and established a constitutional monarchy. But the creation of the democratic French republic in 1792 and the execution of King Louis XVI the following year divided public opinion. Many American artisans praised the egalitarianism of the radical French Jacobins and followed their example, addressing each other as "citizen" and founding political clubs, most of which supported Jefferson's Republican Party. But most wealthy Americans and many of those with strong Christian beliefs denounced the Terror (the executions of Louis XVI and his aristocratic supporters) and condemned the new French regime for abandoning Christianity in favor of atheism.

Federalist Gentry

A prominent New England Federalist, Oliver Ellsworth served as Chief Justice of the United States (1796–1800), while Abigail Wolcott Ellsworth was the daughter of a Connecticut governor. In 1792 the portraitist Ralph Earl captured the aspirations of the Ellsworths by giving them an aristocratic demeanor and prominently displaying their mansion (in the window). Like other Federalists who tried to reconcile their wealth and social authority with republican values, Ellsworth dressed with restraint and his manners, remarked Timothy Dwight, were "wholly destitute of haughtiness and arrogance." (Wadsworth Atheneum, Hartford)

These ideological conflicts sharpened the debate over Hamilton's economic policies and even helped foment a domestic insurrection. In 1794 farmers in western Pennsylvania mounted the Whiskey Rebellion to protest Hamilton's excise tax on spirits, which had raised the price—and thus cut the demand—for the corn whiskey they sold locally and bartered for eastern manufactures. Like the Sons of Liberty of 1765 and the Shaysites of 1786, the Whiskey rebels attacked both local tax collectors and the authority of a distant government. But these protesters also waved banners proclaiming the French revolutionary slogan "Liberty, Equality, and Fraternity!" To uphold national authority (and deter secessionist movements along the frontier) President Washington raised an army of 12,000 troops that soon suppressed the rebels.

Britain's maritime strategy also widened the growing political divisions in the United States. In November 1793 the Royal Navy began to prey on American ships bound for France from the West Indies, seizing more than 250 vessels and confiscating their sugar cargoes. To avoid war President Washington sent John Jay to Britain. Jay returned in 1795 with a treaty that required the U.S. government to make "full and complete compensation" to British merchants for all pre–Revolutionary War debts owed by American citizens. The treaty also acknowledged Britain's right to remove French property from neutral ships, overturning the American merchants' claim that "free ships make free goods." In return, the agreement allowed American merchants to submit claims of illegal seizure to arbitration and required the British to remove their military garrisons from the Northwest Territory and to end their aid to the Indians there. Jefferson and other Republicans attacked Jay's Treaty as too conciliatory, and the Senate ratified it only by the bare two-thirds majority required by the Constitution. As long as Hamilton and his Federalist allies were in power, the United States would have a pro-British foreign policy.

THE RISE OF POLITICAL PARTIES

The appearance of Federalists and Republicans marked a new stage in American politics. Although colonial legislatures had often divided into temporary factions based on family alliances, ethnicity, or region, they lacked well-organized parties. The new state and national constitutions made no provision for organized political bodies because their framers considered parties unnecessary and dangerous. Following classical republican principles, they wanted voters and legislators to act independently and in the interest of the public—not a party.

But the revolutionary ideology of popular sovereignty had drawn ordinary citizens into politics, and the financial and ideological conflicts of the 1790s created a competitive party system. Merchants and creditors favored Federalist policies, as did wheat-exporting slaveholders in the Tidewater districts of the Chesapeake. The emerging Republican coalition was more diverse and drew supporters from across the social spectrum. It included farmers in the South and the West, artisans in the seaport cities, and many Germans and Scots-Irish.

Party identity crystallized during the election of 1796. To prepare for the election Federalist and Republican leaders called legislative caucuses in Congress and conventions in the states to discuss policies and nominate candidates. To mobilize the citizenry the parties organized public festivals and processions, with the Federalists celebrating Washington's achievements and the Republicans invoking the egalitarian principles of the Declaration of Independence.

Federalist candidates triumphed in the 1796 election, winning a majority in Congress and electing John Adams as the new president. Adams continued Hamilton's pro-British foreign policy and reacted sharply when the French navy seized American merchant ships. When the French foreign minister Talleyrand solicited a loan and a bribe from American diplomats to stop the seizures, Adams urged Congress to prepare for war. He charged that Talleyrand's agents, whom he dubbed X, Y, and Z, had insulted the honor of the United States. Responding to the "XYZ Affair," the Federalist-controlled Congress cut off trade with France in 1798 and authorized American privateers to seize French ships. Party conflict, which had begun over Hamilton's financial policies, now extended to foreign affairs.

CONSTITUTIONAL CRISIS, 1798–1800

For the first time in American history (but not the last) a controversial foreign policy prompted domestic protest and governmental repression. As the United States fought an undeclared maritime war against France, pro-Republican immigrants from Ireland vehemently attacked Adams's foreign policy. Some Federalists responded in kind: "Were I president, I would hang them for otherwise they would murder me," declared a Philadelphia Federalist pamphleteer. To silence its critics, in 1798 the administration enacted a series of coercive measures. The Naturalization Act increased the residency requirement for American citizenship from five to fourteen years; the Alien Act authorized the deportation of foreigners; and the Sedition Act prohibited the publication of ungrounded or malicious attacks on the president or Congress. "He that is not for us is against us," thundered the Federalist *Gazette* of the United States. Prosecutors arrested more than twenty Republican newspaper editors and politicians, accused them of sedition, and imprisoned some of them.

The Federalists' actions created a constitutional crisis. Republicans charged that the Sedition Act violated the First Amendment's prohibition against "abridging the freedom of speech, or of the press." However, they did not appeal to the Supreme Court, both because the Court's power to review congressional legislation had not been established and because the Court was packed with Federalists. Instead, Madison and Jefferson took the fight to the state legislatures. At their urging in 1798 the Kentucky legislature declared the Alien and Sedition Acts to be "unauthoritative, void, and of no force." The Kentucky legislators justified their rejection of this national legislation by arguing that the states had created the national government and therefore had a "right to judge" the constitutionality of its laws. The Virginia legislature passed a similar resolution, also setting forth a "states' rights" interpretation of the Constitution.

The debate over the Sedition Act set the stage for the election of 1800. Jefferson, once opposed in principle to political parties, now saw them as a valuable way "to watch and relate to the people" the activities of a repressive government. Republicans strongly supported Jefferson's bid for the presidency, pointing to the wrongful imprisonment of newspaper editors and championing states' rights. President Adams responded to these attacks by reevaluating his foreign policy. Rejecting the advice of Hamilton and other Federalists to declare war against France (and benefit from an upsurge in patriotism), Adams put country ahead of party and entered into diplomatic negotiations that brought an end to the fighting.

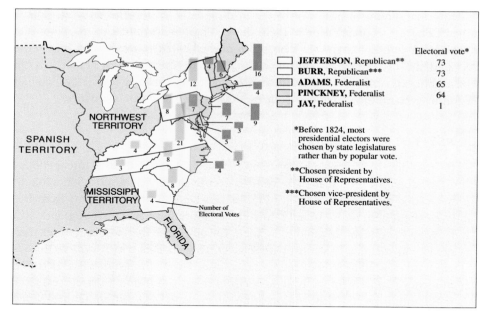

M A P 7.4
The Election of 1800

Voting in the election of 1800 followed regional lines. John Adams of Massachusetts carried every New England state and, reflecting Federalist strength in maritime and commercial areas, the eastern districts of various mid-Atlantic states. But the Republicans led by Thomas Jefferson of Virginia eked out a narrow victory by winning most of the electoral votes of the South and, thanks to the efforts of vice-presidential candidate Aaron Burr, the twelve votes of the pivotal state of New York.

Nonetheless, the election of 1800 was the first "dirty" political campaign. The Federalists attacked Jefferson's character, branding him as an irresponsible pro-French radical, "the arch-apostle of irreligion and free thought," and both parties forced changes in state election laws to favor their candidates. A low Federalist turnout in Virginia and Pennsylvania and the three-fifths rule (which boosted the voting power of white southerners) gave Jefferson a narrow seventy-three to sixty-five victory in the electoral college (see Map 7.4). But the Republican electors unexpectedly also gave seventy-three votes to Aaron Burr of New York (Jefferson's choice for vice president), throwing the presidential election into the House of Representatives. (The Twelfth Amendment, ratified in 1804, would remedy this constitutional defect by requiring electors to vote separately for president and vice president.)

Ironically, as the era of Federalism and its aristocratic outlook came to an end, Alexander Hamilton ushered in a more democratic era. For thirty-five ballots

TIMELINE

1776	Pennsylvania approves a democratic constitution.		James Madison, Alexander Hamilton, and John Jay's *The Federalist*
	John Adams's *Thoughts on Government*	1789	Judiciary Act establishes a federal court system.
	Propertied women allowed to vote in New Jersey (retracted in 1807)		
1777	Articles of Confederation (ratified 1781)	1790– 1792	Hamilton wins enactment of his financial program.
1779	Judith Sargent Murray's "On the Equality of the Sexes" (published in 1790)	1791	Bill of Rights ratified
1780s	Postwar commercial recession	1794	Madison and Jefferson found the Democratic-Republican Party.
	Creditor-debtor conflicts in the states		Whiskey Rebellion in western Pennsylvania
1781	Bank of North America chartered by Congress	1795	Jay's Treaty resolves many conflicts between United States and Britain.
1785	Thomas Jefferson's *Notes on the State of Virginia*	1798	XYZ Affair (1797) sparks undeclared war against France.
1786	Annapolis commercial convention		Alien Act, Sedition Act, and Naturalization Act
	Shays's Rebellion in Massachusetts		
1787	Northwest Ordinance		Kentucky and Virginia resolutions condemn the Alien and Sedition Acts.
	Constitutional convention in Philadelphia	1800	Jefferson elected in "Revolution of 1800"
1787– 1788	Ratification conventions in the states		

Federalists in the House of Representatives blocked Jefferson's election. Then the former Treasury secretary intervened. Calling Burr an "embryo Caesar" and the "most unfit man in the United States for the office of president," Hamilton persuaded key Federalists to permit Jefferson's selection. The Federalists' concern for political stability also played a role. As Senator James Bayard of Delaware explained, "It was admitted on all hands that we must risk the Constitution and a Civil War or take Mr. Jefferson."

Jefferson called the election the "Revolution of 1800," and so it was. The bloodless transfer of power demonstrated that governments elected by the people could be changed in an orderly way, even in times of bitter partisan conflict and foreign crisis. In his inaugural address in 1801 Jefferson praised this achievement, declaring: "We are all Republicans, we are all Federalists." Despite the predictions of European conservatives, new republican constitutional order of 1776 had survived a quarter-century of economic and political turmoil.

For Further Exploration

For a lively, drama-filled retelling of the Constitutional Convention, see Catherine Drinker Bowen's *Miracle at Philadelphia: The Story of the Constitutional Convention, May to September 1787* (1966). Jack Rakove's *Original Meanings: Politics and Ideas in the Making of the Constitution* (1996) is a more complex analysis that shows the divergent perspectives of the Framers and how they compromised their differences. Michael Kammen, *A Machine That Would Go by Itself: The Constitution in American Culture* (1986), explains the changing reputation of the founding document, while David Waldstreicher, *In the Midst of Perpetual Fetes: The Making of American Nationalism, 1776–1820* (1997), presents a fascinating analysis of the links between public celebrations and the emergence of an American national identity.

James Roger Sharp offers an engaging study of the near-disintegration of the new nation in the 1790s in *American Politics in the Early Republic: The New Nation in Crisis* (1993). A detailed study of one of the major crises of these years, Thomas P. Slaughter's *The Whiskey Rebellion* (1986), shows how this uprising reflected the localistic, antitax outlook of the Revolutionary era. Rosemarie Zagarri suggests the impact of republicanism on women and provides a concise biography of an important Patriot in *A Woman's Dilemma: Mercy Otis Warren and the American Revolution* (1995). The strong political and leadership abilities of the first president is a central theme of William Martin's fictionalized biography of *Citizen Washington* (1999); Martin also wrote the documentary *George Washington: The Man Who Wouldn't Be King* (PBS video, 1 hour). Additional material, including Washington's published correspondence, is available online at "The Papers of George Washington," <http://www.virginia.edu/gwpapers/>. For more information on Thomas Jefferson consult the PBS website "Thomas Jefferson" at <http://www.pbs.org/jefferson>, which contains information on the documentary (PBS video, 3 hours), transcripts of interviews with Jefferson scholars, and a good collection of documents relating to Jefferson's personal and public life.

Chapter 8

WESTWARD EXPANSION AND A NEW POLITICAL ECONOMY
1790–1820

It is a country in flux. That which is true today as regards its population, its establishments, its prices, its commerce will not be true six months from now.

—Duc de La Rochefoucauld-Liancourt, 1799

Many generations in the past, Shawnee diplomats told American officials in 1803, their ancestors had stood on the shores of the Atlantic Ocean and seen a strange object. "At first they took it for a great bird, but they soon found it to be a monstrous canoe filled with . . . white people." Soon the white people robbed the Shawnees of their wisdom, the diplomats explained, and then "usurped their land," purchasing it with goods that "were more the property of the Indians than the white people because the knowledge which enabled them to manufacture these goods actually belonged to the Shawnees."

Whatever the truth of this legend, the young American republic was a threat to the Shawnees and other native peoples. "The thirst after Indian lands, is become almost universal," an observer had noted as early as 1766. So when the Treaty of Paris in 1783 gave the United States access to the trans-Appalachian West, hundreds of thousands of extraordinarily self-confident Americans trekked into the interior and imposed a new system of economic production on the land.

The votes of western farmers helped to ensure the political ascendancy of the Republican Party and its western-oriented policies. To provide even more land for American farmers President Thomas Jefferson doubled the country's size through the Louisiana Purchase in 1803. Less than a decade later, western Republicans led the nation into war against Great Britain in part because of British support for the Western Indian Confederacy.

While Republican policy encouraged homesteading in the West, state legislatures in the East promoted banking, manufacturing, and commercial growth. As a result beginning around 1800 per capita income in the United States increased by more than 1 percent per year—over 30 percent in a single generation. By the 1820s this extraordinary productivity heralded a new economic order. After half a century

"The Fairview Inn" by Thomas Cole Ruckle

Scores of inns dotted the roads of the new republic, providing food, accommodations, and livery services for settlers moving west and for cattle drovers and teamsters taking western produce to eastern markets. Although executed in 1889, this painting accurately depicts the architecture of an early nineteenth-century Maryland inn and captures the character of its workforce—with free and enslaved African Americans driving cattle and tending to horses. (Maryland Historical Society)

of political independence the nation was well on its way to becoming a republic that was continental in scope and capitalist in character.

Westward Expansion

In 1790 the United States contained 3.9 million people, both white and black, but only 200,000 Americans lived west of the Appalachian Mountains. During the next thirty years the West grew much more rapidly than the rest of the nation. By 1820 there were 9.6 million white and black Americans, and 2 million of them inhabited nine new states and three new territories west of the Appalachians. The country was moving West at an astonishing pace.

NATIVE AMERICAN RESISTANCE

In the Treaty of Paris of 1783 Great Britain relinquished its claims to the trans-Appalachian region and, as one British statesman put it, left the Indian nations "to the care of their [American] neighbours." "Care" was hardly the right term, for some influential Americans advocated exterminating the natives. "Cut up every Indian Cornfield and burn every Indian town," proclaimed William Henry Drayton of South Carolina, so that their "nation be extirpated and the lands become the property of the public." Many others, including Henry Knox, President Washington's first secretary of war, favored assimilating the Indians into American society. Knox wanted commonly held tribal lands to become the private property of individual Indian families, who would become citizens of the various states, a policy that most Indians rejected out of hand.

Not surprisingly, the major struggle between Indians and whites concerned land rights. Invoking the Paris treaty and claiming that pro-British Indians were conquered peoples, the United States government asserted ownership over all Indian lands in the West. Native Americans rejected this claim, pointing out that they had not signed the treaty and had never been conquered. The Confederation Congress and the state governments brushed aside those arguments. In 1784 U.S. commissioners used military threats to force pro-British Iroquois peoples—the Mohawks, Onondagas, Cayugas, and Senecas—to sign the Treaty of Fort Stanwix and relinquish much of their land in New York and Pennsylvania. New York officials and land speculators used liquor and bribes to take title to additional millions of acres. By 1800 the once powerful Iroquois were confined to relatively small reservations.

American negotiators employed similar tactics farther to the west. In 1785 they induced the Chipewyans, Delawares, Ottawas, and Wyandots to sign away most of the future state of Ohio. The tribes quickly repudiated the agreements, claiming—justifiably—that they were made under duress. Those peoples, and the Shawnees, Miamis, and Potawatomis, formed a Western Confederacy to defend themselves against aggressive settlers. Led by Little Turtle, a Miami chief, they defeated American armies in 1790 and again in 1791.

Fearing an alliance between the Western Confederacy and the British in Canada, President Washington doubled the size of the U.S. Army and ordered General "Mad Anthony" Wayne to lead a new expedition. In August 1794 Wayne defeated the Indians in the Battle of Fallen Timbers (near present-day Toledo, Ohio). Nevertheless, the Western Confederacy remained strong, forcing a compromise peace in the Treaty of Greenville (Ohio) in 1795. American negotiators acknowledged Indian ownership rights in the trans-Appalachian West, while the Confederacy accepted American political sovereignty over the entire region and agreed to place themselves "under the protection of the United States, and no other Power whatever." In practice this agreement encouraged American officials and settlers to pressure native Americans to give up their lands, while enabling Indian peoples to demand money or goods in return. Indeed, at Greenville the Indians ceded ownership of most of

Ohio and certain strategic areas along the Great Lakes, including Detroit and the future site of Chicago (see Map 8.1). Recognizing the gains made by the United States, Britain cut some of its trading ties with the Indians and, in Jay's Treaty of 1795, reaffirmed its (still unfulfilled) obligation under the Treaty of Paris to remove its military garrisons from the region.

American westward migration increased as soon as the fighting ended. In 1805 the two-year-old state of Ohio had more than 100,000 residents. Thousands more farm families moved into the future states of Indiana and Illinois, sparking new conflicts with native peoples over land and hunting rights. As a Delaware Indian declared, "The Elks are our horses, the buffaloes are our cows, the deer are our

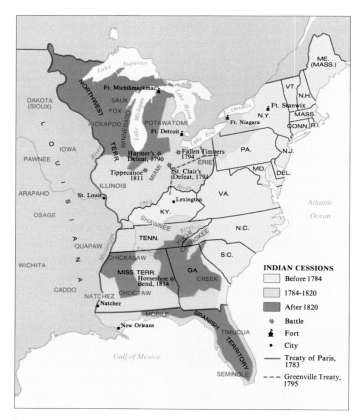

M A P 8.1
Military and Diplomatic Expansion, to 1840

The United States claimed sovereignty over the entire trans-Appalachian West by virtue of the Treaty of 1783 with Britain. When the Western Confederacy contested this claim, the American government sent armies into the West during the 1790s and again during the War of 1812. By the 1830s the continuation of this armed diplomacy had forced Native American peoples to cede by treaty most of their lands east of the Mississippi River.

sheep, & the whites shan't have them." To alleviate these tensions the U.S. government continued to encourage Native Americans to become farmers and assimilate into white society. The goal, as one Kentucky Protestant minister put it, was to make the Indian "a farmer, a citizen of the United States, and a Christian."

Most Native Americans resisted these attempts to destroy their traditional tribal cultures. Many Indian peoples drove out white missionaries and forced converts to Christianity to participate in tribal rites. As a Munsee prophet put it, "There are two ways to God, one for the whites and one for the Indians." Among the Senecas of New York the prophet Handsome Lake tried to find a middle way, from 1801 to 1807 promoting traditional ceremonies in which celebrants gave thanks to the earth, plants, animals, water, and sun and incorporating some Christian beliefs, such as heaven and hell, into his teachings. But Handsome Lake's rejection of some Indian beliefs and his support of Quaker missionaries divided the tribe into hostile religious factions. The more conservative Senecas, led by Chief Red Jacket, condemned Indians who accepted white ways and beliefs and demanded a return to ancestral customs.

Most Indian women also rejected European farming practices. Among the Iroquois, women had long been responsible for growing staple foods and, as a result, controlled the inheritance of cultivation rights and exercised considerable political power. Shawnee women had even more authority, as women "war" chiefs decided whether to dispatch a war party or to torture captives. Even those Indians who embraced Christian teachings retained many traditional values. To view themselves as individuals, as the Europeans demanded, meant repudiating the clan, the essence of Indian life.

THE CHANGING AGRICULTURAL ECONOMY

Between 1790 and 1820 more than 250,000 white and black migrants crossed the Appalachians into Kentucky and Tennessee and moved along the coastal plain of the Gulf of Mexico into the future states of Alabama and Mississippi. Most migrants who flocked through the Cumberland Gap into Kentucky and Tennessee were white tenant farmers and struggling yeomen families. They were fleeing the depleted soils and planter elite of the Chesapeake region, confident that they would prosper by growing cotton and hemp, which were in great demand.

First they had to gain title to the land. Those without ready cash based their claims for free land on "the ancient cultivation law" governing frontier tracts. Invoking the argument of the North Carolina Regulators (see Chapter 4), they argued that poor settlers had a customary right "from time out of Mind" to occupy "back waste vacant Lands" sufficient "to provide a subsistence for themselves and their posterity." The Virginia government, which administered the Kentucky Territory, had a more elitist vision. While it allowed settlers to purchase up to 1,400 acres of land at reduced prices, it also dispensed grants of 20,000 to 200,000 acres to scores of wealthy individuals and partnerships. Consequently, when Kentucky became a state in 1792, a handful of speculators owned one-fourth of the state, whereas half the adult white men owned no land and lived as squatters or tenants.

The rest of the southern frontier became a stronghold of racial slavery. Until the 1810s, wealthy planters and up-and-coming young men from the Chesapeake and the Lower South set up new slave plantations in the interior of Georgia and South Carolina and then they moved into the Old Southwest—the future states of Alabama, Mississippi, and Louisiana (see American Voices, "Settling the South-western Frontier"). They carried some slaves with them and imported more from Africa. Between 1776 and 1809, when Congress cut off the Atlantic slave trade, these planters bought about 115,000 African slaves. The black population also grew through reproduction, increasing from a half million in 1775 to 1.8 million in 1820.

Although many enslaved African Americans still toiled in tobacco and rice fields of the Chesapeake and South Carolina, it was a new crop—cotton—that financed the expansion of slavery into the Old Southwest. After 1750 technological break-throughs such as water-powered spinning jennies and weaving mules boosted European textile production and greatly increased the demand for raw wool and cotton. By the 1790s American inventors—including Connecticut-born Eli

A Slave Auction in Charleston, South Carolina, 1833

As one slave departs with his new master (far right), the auctioneer tries to interest the as-sembled planters in his next sale item, a black family. The artist, a British Canadian named Henry Byam Martin, showed his disdain for these proceedings both visually (compare the family's dignified bearing with the planters' slouching posture) and verbally, giving the sketch a sarcastic title: "The Land of the Free and the Home of the Brave."

(National Archives of Canada/C-115001)

Settling the Southwestern Frontier

REUBEN DAVIS

*B*orn around 1810, Reuben Davis grew up on the southwestern frontier, where his slave-owning father had migrated to find land and opportunities for his many children. Davis eventually became a lawyer in Mississippi and in 1890 published a memoir that describes—in a partly realistic, partly romantic fashion—the interaction among whites, Indians, and African Americans in early Alabama.

My father was one of the earliest settlers in this country. He was a man of limited means, and though of strong and vigorous intellect, had only the imperfect education of the pioneers of that day. His chief study was the Bible and a few volumes of history, which formed his only library. Although a Baptist minister of high standing, he occupied himself, during the week, with ordinary farm labor, and could never be induced to accept any compensation for his services in the church. . . .

Both my parents were born in Virginia, and remained there after marriage until ten children were added to their family. They then removed to Tennessee [and later] . . . to North Alabama. The land had been recently purchased from the Indians, and many of them yet roamed the dense forests of that section. I well remember how I hunted with these wild companions, and was taught by them to use the bow and arrow. . . . Occasional deeds of frightful atrocity were committed in the immediate neighborhood. Long before I was competent to reason on it, the problem of race-hatred was forced upon my observation. The fierce antagonism of one race for another and the frequent rising of the conquered against the conqueror were met then as practical questions,—as the fashion of the day was,—without much speculation or moralizing. . . .

At that time the country was as wild and unsettled as possible; there were no laws, no schools, and no libraries. Every man did what was right in his own eyes, but in spite of general recklessness and lawlessness, there was a rough code of honor and honesty which was rarely broken. The settlers lived a life of great toil and many privations, but they were eminently social, kindly, and friendly. . . .

Clearing land and opening a farm required constant and severe labor, and I, with my five brothers, performed our full share. . . . My brothers and myself, assisted by six colored hands, cultivated the land, and attended school only about three months in the year. In this way we learned to read and write, as well as the rudiments of arithmetic and a little Latin. . . .

There was this great advantage that, while none were very wealthy, few were poor enough to suffer actual want. . . . The simple habits of the laboring man were not shamed by the ostentation of his more prosperous neighbor; and there was none of that silent, perpetual contrast of luxury and penury, which now adds bitterness to class hatreds.

SOURCE: Reuben Davis, *Recollections of Mississippi and Mississippians* (Boston: Houghton, Mifflin, 1890), pp. 2–4.

Whitney—had developed machines (called *gins*) that efficiently extracted the seeds from the strands of cotton, and thousands of white planters in South Carolina and Georgia began growing the crop. During the 1810s planters—and their slaves—carried cotton production into Alabama and Mississippi, which entered the Union in 1817 and 1819, respectively.

As slaveowning cotton planters moved south and west, a new wave of yeoman farm families flowed out of Massachusetts and Connecticut (see Map 8.2). Previous generations had moved north and east, settling New Hampshire, Vermont, and Maine, but many towns in Massachusetts and Connecticut remained overcrowded, their lands subdivided into small, depleted farmsteads. To provide land for the four or five children who survived to adulthood, thousands of families packed their wagons with tools and household goods and migrated into New York. By 1820 nearly 800,000 New England migrants lived in a string of settlements that stretched from Albany to Buffalo. Thousands more moved on to Ohio and Indiana.

This vast migration was organized not by governments or joint-stock companies but by the settlers themselves, who often moved in large groups linked by family and religion. As a traveler reported from central New York, "The town of Herkimer is entirely populated by families come from Connecticut. We stayed at Mr. Snow's who came from New London with about ten male and female cousins." When 176 residents of Granville, Massachusetts, moved to Ohio, they transplanted their Congregational ministers and elders along with their system of freehold agriculture. Throughout the northern trans-Appalachian West many "new" communities were actually old communities that had moved inland.

In New York, as in Kentucky, well-connected speculators snapped up much of the best land. In the 1780s the financier Robert Morris acquired 1.3 million acres in the Genesee region of central New York, where the Wadsworth family also bought thousands of acres of prime land and created leasehold farms similar to those on Hudson river valley manors. To attract tenants the Wadsworths leased farms rent-free for the first seven years, after which they charged rents. Many New England yeomen preferred to sign agreements with the Dutch-owned Holland Land Company because these contracts allowed them to buy the land as they worked it. But high interest rates and the lack of markets mired thousands of these aspiring freeholders deeply in debt. As one pioneer recalled, "In the early years, there was none but a home market and that was mostly barter—it was so many bushels of wheat for a cow; so many bushels for a yoke of oxen." Fleeing declining prospects in the East these farmers found themselves at the bottom of the economic ladder in the West.

The settlement of western lands prompted changes in eastern agriculture. As low-cost western wheat began to flow to eastern markets, farmers in New England planted different crops, such as potatoes, which were nutritious and high yielding. To compensate for the lost labor of sons and daughters, Middle Atlantic farmers replaced metal-tipped wooden plows with cast-iron models that dug deeper and required a single yoke of oxen instead of two or three. These improvements allowed them to maintain production levels even with fewer laborers.

Easterners also took advantage of the progressive farming methods recently publicized by wealthy British agricultural reformers. "Improvers" rotated their crops to maintain soil fertility, planting nitrogen-rich clover to offset nutrient-hungry crops of wheat and corn. In Pennsylvania crop rotation doubled the average wheat yield per acre. Yeomen diversified production, raising sheep and selling the wool to textile manufacturers. Many farmers adopted a year-round planting cycle, sowing wheat in the winter for market and corn in the spring for animal fodder. Women and girls milked the family cows and sold butter and cheese in the growing towns and cities.

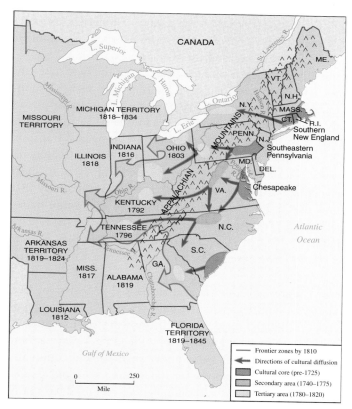

MAP 8.2
Regional Cultures Move West, 1720–1820

By 1720 four distinct "core" cultures had developed along the Atlantic seaboard. By 1775 settlers from the Middle Atlantic and Chesapeake regions had carried their customs and institutions into the southern backcountry. Between 1780 and 1820 the descendants of these migrants moved into the trans-Appalachian West, while Carolinians transplanted their slave society to the Old Southwest and New Englanders transmitted their customs to upstate New York and the Old Northwest.

In this new agricultural economy families worked harder and longer, but their efforts were rewarded with higher output and a better standard of living. Whether hacking fields out of western forests or carting manure to replenish eastern soils, farm families increased their productivity. Westward migration had boosted the entire American economy.

THE TRANSPORTATION BOTTLENECK

American geography threatened to cut short this economic advance: water transport was the quickest and cheapest way to get goods to market, but no rivers cut through the Appalachian Mountains. It had cost eighteenth-century Pennsylvania farmers as much to send crops 30 miles by road to Philadelphia as to ship them from Philadelphia to London. Without access to waterways or other cheap means of transportation, settlers west of the Appalachian Mountains would be unable to send goods to markets in the East, Europe, and the West Indies.

Improved inland trade therefore became a high priority for the new state governments, which actively encouraged transportation ventures. Between 1793 and 1812 the Pennsylvania legislature granted fifty-five corporate charters to private turnpike companies, and Massachusetts chartered over a hundred. Turnpike companies built level gravel roads that significantly reduced travel time and transport costs and charged tolls for their use. State governments and private entrepreneurs constructed even more cost-efficient inland waterways, dredging rivers to make them navigable and constructing short canals to bypass waterfalls or rapids. By 1816 the United States had about 100 miles of canals, but only three were more than 2 miles long and none breached the great Appalachian barrier. Only after 1819, when the Erie Canal began to connect the central and western counties of New York to the Hudson River, could inland farmers sell their produce in eastern markets (see Chapter 10).

For farmers further west the great streams that connected to the Mississippi River represented the great hope. Western settlers paid premium prices for land along navigable rivers, while speculators bought up property in growing towns—such as Cincinnati, Louisville, Chattanooga, and St. Louis—along the Ohio, Tennessee, and Mississippi Rivers. Western farmers and merchants built barges to float cotton and surplus grain and meat down this interconnected river system to the port of New Orleans, which by 1815 was processing about $5 million in agricultural products yearly.

But many isolated western settlers in the trans-Appalachian West had no choice but to be self-sufficient. "A noble field of Indian corn stretched away into the forest on one side," an English visitor to an Ohio farm in the 1820s noted, "and immediately before the house was a small potato garden, with a few peach and apple trees. The woman told me that they spun and wove all the cotton and woollen garments of the family, and knit all the stockings; her husband, though not a shoemaker by trade, made all the shoes. She manufactured all the soap and candles they use." Self-sufficiency meant a low standard of living. As late as 1840 per capita in-

"View of Cincinnati," by John Casper Wild, 1835

Thanks to its location on the Ohio River, Cincinnati quickly became one of the major commercial cities of the trans-Appalachian West. By the 1820s passenger steamboats as well as freight barges connected the city with Pittsburgh to the north and the ocean port of New Orleans, far to the south. (M. and M. Karolik Collection. Courtesy Museum of Fine Arts, Boston)

come in states formed out of the Northwest Territory was only 70 percent of the national average.

Despite these financial hardships and transportation bottlenecks white Americans continued to migrate westward. They knew it would take a generation to clear land, build houses, barns, and roads and plant orchards, and yet they were confident that their sacrifices and the expansion of the canal and road system would yield future security for themselves and their children. The humble achievements of thousands of yeomen and tenant families slowly transformed the landscape of the interior of the continent, turning forests into farms and crossroads into communities.

The Republicans' Political Revolution

Agricultural expansion was a central policy of the Republican Party and accounted for much of its appeal. From 1801 to 1825 three Republicans from Virginia—Thomas Jefferson, James Madison, and James Monroe—served two terms each as president. Supported by voters in the new western states and strong majorities in Congress, this "Virginia Dynasty" reversed many Federalist policies, completing what Jefferson called the Revolution of 1800. Western issues such as Indian policy and territorial disputes with Spain and Britain occupied the attention of politicians and, together with maritime disputes in the Atlantic, precipitated the War of 1812.

THE JEFFERSONIAN PRESIDENCY

Thomas Jefferson was an accomplished and versatile statesman, an insightful political philosopher, and a superb politician. On assuming the presidency in 1801 Jefferson became the first chief executive to hold office in the District of Columbia, the new national capital. However, his administration did not begin with a clean slate. After a dozen years of Federalist presidents the federal judiciary was filled with their appointees. The most important was the formidable John Marshall of Virginia, who presided over the Supreme Court. Moreover, in 1801 the outgoing Federalist-controlled Congress had passed a Judiciary Act. It created sixteen new judgeships and six additional circuit courts, which, along with a variety of existing patronage posts, President Adams had filled with "midnight appointments" just before he left office. The Federalists "have retired into the judiciary as a stronghold," Jefferson complained, "and from that battery all the works of Republicanism are to be beaten down and destroyed."

To bolster their political position Republicans in Congress repealed the Judiciary Act, and James Madison, the new secretary of state, refused to commission William Marbury, one of Adams's midnight appointees, as a justice of the peace in the District of Columbia. Marbury promptly petitioned the Supreme Court to compel delivery of his commission. However, in *Marbury v. Madison* (1803) John Marshall declared that while Marbury had a right to his commission, the Court did not have the constitutional power to enforce that right. By using this reasoning Marshall cleverly condemned Madison's action and asserted the Court's power to review laws (*judicial review*) while avoiding a direct confrontation with the Republican administration.

For his part Jefferson challenged many Federalist policies. Charging the Federalists with grossly expanding the national government's size and power, he led Republican efforts to shrink it back. When the Alien and Sedition Acts expired in 1801, the Republican Congress did not reenact them, branding the acts as politically motivated and unconstitutional. It also amended the Naturalization Act to permit resident aliens to become citizens after five years. But Jefferson governed tactfully, appointing some Federalists to government posts and allowing competent Federalist bureaucrats to remain in their jobs. During eight years as chief executive he removed only 109 of 433 Federalist officeholders, and forty of those were Adams's "midnight appointees."

In foreign affairs Jefferson faced an immediate crisis. In the 1790s the Barbary States of North Africa had systematically raided American merchant ships, and Federalist officials had paid an annual bribe ("tribute") to buy their protection. Initially Jefferson reversed this policy, declaring in 1801 that the United States would no longer pay tribute. When the Barbary "pirates" renewed their assaults, he ordered the U.S. Navy to retaliate. But Jefferson wanted to avoid all-out war, which would increase taxes and the national debt. So he accepted a diplomatic solution that granted a reduced tribute.

In domestic matters Jefferson set a clearly Republican course. He abolished all internal taxes, including the excise tax that had sparked the Whiskey Rebellion of 1794. Addressing his party's fears of a military takeover, Jefferson reduced the size of the permanent army. He tolerated the economically important Bank of the United States (which he had condemned as unconstitutional in 1791), but he chose Albert Gallatin, a fiscal conservative who believed that the national debt was "an evil of the first magnitude," as secretary of the treasury. By carefully controlling government expenditures and using customs revenues to redeem government bonds, Gallatin reduced the debt from $83 million in 1801 to $45 million in 1808. With Jefferson and Gallatin at the helm the nation was no longer run in the interests of northeastern creditors and merchants.

JEFFERSON AND THE WEST

Long before he became president Jefferson championed the settlement of the West. He celebrated the yeoman farmer in *Notes on the State of Virginia* (1785), helped compose the Confederation's western land ordinances, and strongly supported Pinckney's Treaty of 1795, which allowed settlers to ship crops down the Mississippi River for export through the Spanish-held port of New Orleans.

As president Jefferson seized the opportunity to increase the flow of settlers to the West. During the 1790s the Federalist-dominated Congresses had refused to amend the Land Ordinance of 1785 to make it easier for migrating families to buy a farm in the national domain. In fact, the Federalist Land Act of 1796 doubled the minimum price to $2 per acre. Because Jefferson wanted to see the West populated with yeomen farm families, the Republicans in Congress passed laws in 1800 and 1804 reducing the minimum allotment first to 320 and then to 160 acres. Eventually the Land Act of 1820 cut the minimum purchase to 80 acres and the price to $1.25 per acre, enabling a farmer with only $100 in cash to buy a western farm.

International events challenged Jefferson's vision for the West. In 1799 Napoleon Bonaparte seized power in France and began an ambitious campaign to establish a French empire both in Europe and America. In 1801 Napoleon coerced Spain into signing a secret treaty that returned to France its former colony of Louisiana. A year later he directed Spanish officials in Louisiana to restrict American access to New Orleans, thus violating the terms of Pinckney's Treaty of 1795. Meanwhile, Napoleon planned an invasion to restore French rule in Haiti (then called Saint-Domingue), a rich sugar island seized in 1793 by rebellious black slaves led by Toussaint L'Ouverture.

Napoleon's aggressive actions prompted Jefferson to question his party's traditionally pro-French foreign policy. Any nation that denied Americans access to the port of New Orleans, Jefferson declared, must be "our natural and habitual enemy." To avoid hostilities with France Jefferson instructed Robert R. Livingston, the American minister in Paris, to negotiate the purchase of New Orleans. Simultaneously, Jefferson sent James Monroe to Britain to seek its assistance in case of war. "The day that France takes possession of New Orleans," the president warned, "we must marry ourselves to the British fleet and nation."

Jefferson's diplomacy yielded a magnificent prize: the entire territory of Louisiana. By 1802 the French invasion of Haiti was faltering, a new war threatened in Europe, and Napoleon feared an American invasion of Louisiana. With characteristic decisiveness, in April 1803 the French ruler offered to sell not only New Orleans but also the entire territory of Louisiana. For about $15 million ($450 million today), Livingston and Monroe concluded what became known as the Louisiana Purchase (see Map 8.3). "We have lived long," Livingston remarked to Monroe, "but this is the noblest work of our lives."

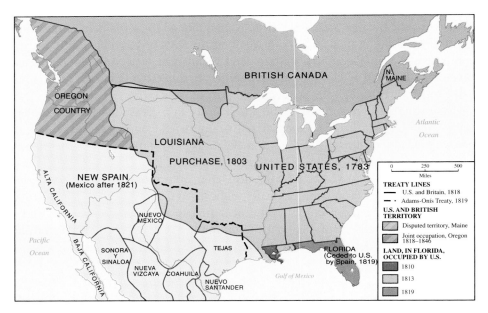

M A P 8.3
Defining the National Boundaries, to 1840

After the War of 1812 John Quincy Adams negotiated treaties with Great Britain and Spain that made Florida and northern Maine part of the United States and defined the American boundaries with Canada and New Spain (which in 1821 became the independent nation of Mexico). These treaties eliminated the threat of war until the 1840s, providing the young American nation with a much needed period of peace.

The Louisiana Purchase forced the president to reconsider his interpretation of the Constitution. Jefferson had always been a strict constructionist, maintaining that the national government possessed only the powers "expressly" delegated to it in the Constitution. There was no provision in the Constitution for adding new territory, however, so to fulfill his dreams for the West Jefferson pragmatically accepted a loose interpretation of the Constitution.

A scientist as well as a statesman, Jefferson wanted detailed information about the physical features of the new territory and its plant and animal life. In 1804 he sent his personal secretary, Meriwether Lewis, to explore the region with William Clark, an army officer. Aided by Indian guides Lewis and Clark and their group of American soldiers and frontiersmen traveled up the Missouri River, across the Rocky Mountains, and (venturing beyond the Purchase) down the Columbia River to the Pacific Ocean. After two years they returned with the first maps of the immense wilderness and vivid accounts of its natural resources and inhabitants.

The Louisiana Purchase intensified existing political conflicts. New England Federalists, fearing that western expansion would diminish their power, talked openly of leaving the Union. When Alexander Hamilton refused to support their plan for a separate Northern Confederacy, the secessionists turned to Aaron Burr, the ambitious vice president, who was seeking election as governor of New York. In July 1804 Hamilton accused Burr of participating in a conspiracy to destroy the Union, and Burr challenged him to a pistol duel. Hamilton died by gunshot in the illegal confrontation, and state courts in New York and New Jersey indicted Burr for murder.

After his vice-presidential term ended early in 1805, Burr moved West to avoid prosecution. There he conspired with General James Wilkinson, the military governor of the Louisiana Territory. Their plan remains a mystery, but it probably involved either the capture of territory in New Spain or a rebellion to establish Louisiana as a separate nation headed by Burr. Wilkinson betrayed Burr, however, and arrested him for treason as the former vice president led an armed force down the Ohio River. In a highly politicized trial presided over by Chief Justice John Marshall, the jury acquitted Burr of treason. The verdict was less important than the dangers to national unity that it revealed. The Republicans' policy of western expansion had increased sectional tension and party conflict, giving new life to states' rights sentiment and secessionist schemes.

CONFLICT WITH BRITAIN AND FRANCE

As the Napoleonic Wars ravaged Europe between 1802 and 1815, they threatened the commercial interests of the American republic. Great Britain and France, the major belligerents, refused to respect the neutrality of American merchant vessels. Napoleon imposed the "Continental System" on European ports under French control, requiring customs officials to seize neutral ships that had stopped in Britain. For its part, the British ministry set up a naval blockade, seizing ships carrying goods to Europe, including American vessels filled with sugar and molasses from the French West Indies. The British Navy also searched American ships for British deserters and impressed (or forced) them back into service. Between 1802 and 1811 British officers seized nearly 8,000 sailors, many of whom were American citizens. American resentment turned to outrage in 1807, when a British warship attacked the U.S. Navy vessel *Chesapeake,* killing or wounding twenty-one men and seizing four alleged deserters. "Never since the battle of Lexington have I seen this country in such a state of exasperation as at present," Jefferson declared.

To protect American interests while avoiding war Jefferson pursued a policy of peaceful coercion. Working closely with Secretary of State James Madison, the president devised the Embargo Act of 1807, which prohibited American ships from leaving their home ports until Britain and France repealed their restrictions on U.S. trade. Though the embargo was a creative diplomatic measure—an economic weapon similar to the nonimportation movements between 1765 and 1775—it overestimated the dependence of France and Britain on American shipping and underestimated resistance from New England merchants, who feared it would ruin them.

The embargo caused American exports to plunge from $108 million in 1806 to $22 million in 1808, hurting farmers as well as merchants and prompting Federalists to demand its repeal. When the Republican Congress passed a Force Act giving customs officials extraordinary powers to prevent smuggling into Canada, Federalists railed against government tyranny. "Would to God," exclaimed one Federalist, "that the Embargo had done as little evil to ourselves as it has done to foreign nations."

Despite discontent over the embargo voters elected James Madison, one of its authors, to the presidency in 1808. As the main architect of the Constitution, an advocate of the Bill of Rights, and a prominent congressman and party leader, Madison had served the nation well. As president Madison acknowledged the embargo's failure and replaced it with a series of new economic restrictions, none of which succeeded in persuading France and Britain to respect America's neutral rights. "The Devil himself could not tell which government, England or France, is the most wicked," an exasperated congressman declared.

Republican congressmen from the West—the future "war hawks" of 1812—thought Britain was the major offender, pointing in particular to its assistance to the Indians in the Ohio River Valley. Bolstered by British guns and supplies, in 1809 the Shawnee chief Tecumseh, assisted by his brother, the Prophet Tenskwatawa, had revived the Western Confederacy of the 1790s. Their goal was to exclude whites from all lands west of the Appalachian Mountains. Responding to this threat expansionists in Congress condemned British support of Tecumseh and threatened to invade Canada. In 1811, following a series of clashes between settlers and the Confederacy, William Henry Harrison, the governor of the Indiana Territory, led an army against Tenskwatawa's village of Prophetstown (on the Wabash River in present-day Indiana). After fending off the Confederation's warriors at the Battle of Tippecanoe, Harrison burned the village to the ground (see American Voices, "The Battle of Tippecanoe").

AMERICAN VOICES

The Battle of Tippecanoe

CHIEF SHABONEE

In this interview with a newspaper reporter, the Potawatomi chief Shabonee recalls the events surrounding the Battle of Tippecanoe in 1811 and offers a penetrating view of reality: the unfaithfulness of allies, the confidence and impulsiveness of youth, and the false promises of war leaders.

It was fully believed among the Indians that we should defeat General Harrison, and that we should hold the line of the Wabash and dictate terms to the whites. The great cause of our failure, was the Miamies, whose principal country was south of the river, and they wanted to treat with the whites so as to retain their land, and they played false to their red brethren and yet lost all. They are now surrounded and will be crushed. . . .

Our young men said: We are ten to their one. If they stay upon the other side, we will let them alone. If they cross the Wabash, we will take their scalps or drive them into the river. They cannot swim. Their powder will be wet. The fish will eat their bodies. The bones of the white men will lie upon every sand bar. Their flesh will fatten buzzards. These white soldiers are not warriors. Their hands are soft. Their faces are white. One half of them are calico peddlers. The other half can only shoot squirrels. They cannot stand before men. . . .

Such were the opinions and arguments of our warriors. They did not appreciate the great strength of the white men. I knew their great war chief, and some of his young men. He was a good man, very soft in his words to his red children, as he called us; and that made some of our men with hot heads mad. I listened to his soft words, but I looked into his eyes. They were full of fire. I knew that they would be among his men like coals of fire in the dry grass. The first wind would raise a great flame. I feared for the red men that might be sleeping in its way. . . .

Our women and children were in the town only a mile from the battle-field waiting for victory and its spoils. They wanted white prisoners. The Prophet [Tenskwatawa, the Shawnee religious leader] had promised that every squaw of any note should have one of the white warriors to use as her slave, or to treat as she pleased. Oh how these women were disappointed! Instead of slaves and spoils of the white men coming into town with the rising sun, their town was in flames and women and children were hunted like wolves and killed by hundreds or driven into the river and swamps to hide. With the smoke of that town and the loss of that battle I lost all hope of the red men being able to stop the whites.

SOURCE: Wesley Whickar, ed., "Shabonne's Account of Tippecanoe," *Indiana Magazine of History* 18 (December 1921), pp. 355–59.

Henry Clay of Kentucky, the new speaker of the House of Representatives, and John C. Calhoun, a rising young congressman from South Carolina, pushed Madison toward war with Great Britain. Southern and western Republican congressmen eyed new territory in British Canada and Spanish Florida, part of which had already been seized by American militia. They also hoped that war would discredit the Federalists, who had long pursued a pro-British foreign policy. With national elections approaching, Madison demanded British respect for American sovereignty in the West and neutral rights on the Atlantic. When the British did not respond quickly, Madison asked Congress for a declaration of war. In June 1812 a sharply divided Senate voted nineteen to thirteen for war, and the House of Representatives concurred, seventy-nine to forty-nine. To mobilize support for the war, Republicans emphasized Britain's disregard for American rights. As President Madison put it, "National honor is national property of the highest value."

The underlying causes of the War of 1812 have been much debated. Officially, the United States went to war because of violations of its neutral rights: the seizure of its ships and the impressment of its sailors. But the Federalists who represented merchants' and seamen's interests in Congress voted against the war declaration, and in the subsequent election voters in New England and the Middle Atlantic states cast their ballots (and eighty-nine electoral votes) for the Federalist candidate for president, De Witt Clinton of New York. Madison amassed most of his 128 electoral votes in the South and West, where Republican congressmen and their constituents supported the war. Because of this regional split, more than one historian has argued that the conflict was "a western war with eastern labels."

THE WAR OF 1812

The War of 1812 was a near disaster for the United States, both militarily and politically. Predictions of an easy victory over British forces in Canada ended when a first invasion resulted in a hasty American retreat back to Detroit. But Americans stayed on the offensive in the West, as Commodore Oliver Hazard Perry defeated a small British flotilla on Lake Erie. Then in October 1813 General William Henry Harrison triumphed over a combined British and Indian force at the Battle of the Thames, killing Tecumseh, who had become a general in the British army. Another American expedition burned York (present-day Toronto) but lacking sufficient men and supplies quickly withdrew.

Political divisions in the United States prevented a major invasion of Canada in the East. New Englanders opposed the war and prohibited their militias from fighting outside their states. Boston merchants and banks declined to lend money to the federal government, making the war difficult to finance. In Congress Daniel Webster, a dynamic young representative from New Hampshire, led Federalist opposition to higher taxes and tariffs and to the national conscription of state militiamen.

By 1813 the tide of battle had begun to turn in Britain's favor. Initially the British had lost scores of merchant vessels to American privateers, but the Royal Navy redeployed its forces and British commerce moved in relative safety. Now a flotilla of British warships moved up and down the American coastline, harassing American shipping and threatening seaport cities. In 1814 a British fleet sailed up

Chesapeake Bay and attacked the District of Columbia, burning government buildings. Then the troops advanced on Baltimore, where they were finally repulsed at Fort McHenry. After two years of sporadic warfare the United States had made little military progress along the Canadian frontier and was on the defensive along the Atlantic, with its new capital city in ruins. The only positive news came from the Southwest. There a rugged slaveowning planter named Andrew Jackson led an army of militiamen from Tennessee to victory over the British-supported Creek Indians in the Battle of Horseshoe Bend (1814), forcing the Indians to cede 23 million acres of land.

American military setbacks strengthened opposition to the war, especially in New England. In 1814 Federalists in the Massachusetts legislature called for a convention "to lay the foundation for a radical reform in the National Compact," and in December New England Federalists met in Hartford, Connecticut, to discuss strategy. Some delegates to the Hartford Convention proposed secession by their states, but the majority favored revising the Constitution. To end domination of the presidency by Virginians the delegates proposed a constitutional amendment that would limit the office to a single four-year term and require it to rotate among citizens from different states. Other delegates suggested amendments restricting commercial embargoes to sixty days and requiring a two-thirds' majority in Congress to declare war, prohibit trade, or admit a new state to the Union.

As a minority party in Congress and the nation, the Federalists could prevail only if the war continued to go badly—a very real prospect. In late summer of 1814 a planned British invasion of the Hudson River Valley was narrowly averted by an American naval victory at the Battle of Lake Champlain. Then while the Federalists were meeting in Hartford in December, thousands of seasoned British troops landed at New Orleans, threatening to cut off western access to the sea. The United States was under military pressure from both north and south.

Fortunately for the young American republic, Britain wanted peace. The twenty-year struggle against France had sapped its wealth and energy, and so it entered into negotiations with the United States in Ghent, Belgium. At first the American commissioners—John Quincy Adams, Albert Gallatin, and Henry Clay—demanded territory in Canada and Florida, and British diplomats insisted on an Indian buffer state between the United States and Canada. Ultimately, both sides realized that small concessions won at the bargaining table were not worth the costs of prolonged warfare. The Treaty of Ghent, signed on Christmas Eve 1814, restored the prewar borders of the United States.

This result hardly justified three years of fighting, but a final victory in combat lifted Americans' morale. Before news of the Treaty of Ghent reached the United States, newspaper headlines proclaimed an "ALMOST INCREDIBLE VICTORY!! GLORIOUS NEWS": on January 8, 1815, General Andrew Jackson's troops (including a contingent of French-speaking black Americans, the Corps d'Afrique) crushed the British forces attacking New Orleans. British losses totaled 700 dead and 2,000 wounded or taken prisoner. By contrast the Americans sustained only 13 dead and 58 wounded. The victory made Jackson a national hero and a symbol of the emerging West. It also redeemed the nation's battered pride and, together with the coming of peace, undercut the demands of the Hartford Convention.

Just as Jackson emerged as a war hero, John Quincy Adams rose to national prominence for his diplomatic efforts at Ghent and his subsequent success in resolving boundary disputes. The son of Federalist president John Adams, John Quincy had joined the Republican Party before the war, and in 1817 became secretary of state under President James Monroe (1817–1825). In 1817 Adams negotiated the Rush-Bagot Treaty with Great Britain that limited both nations' naval forces on the Great Lakes; the following year he concluded another agreement that set the border between the Louisiana Purchase and British Canada at the forty-ninth parallel. Then in 1819 Adams persuaded Spain to cede Florida to the United States in the Adams-Onís Treaty. In return the American government took responsibility for its citizens' financial claims against Spain, renounced Jefferson's earlier claim to Spanish Texas, and agreed on a compromise boundary between New Spain and the Louisiana Purchase (see Map 8.3). As a result of Adams's efforts the United States gained undisputed possession of nearly all the land south of the forty-ninth parallel and between the Mississippi River and the Rocky Mountains.

The Capitalist Commonwealth

The increasing size of the American republic was paralleled by the growth of its economic institutions and wealth. Before 1790 the United States was an agricultural society, dependent on Great Britain for markets, credit, and manufactured goods. Over the next generation the nation gradually developed a more diverse economy as some rural Americans became manufacturers, bankers supplied credit to expand industry and trade, merchants developed regional markets, and state governments actively encouraged economic development.

The emerging American economic order was capitalist in character because it was based on private property and market exchanges and because capitalists— financiers, bankers, and wealthy entrepreneurs—shaped many of its political and economic policies. But this capitalist political economy was still influenced by the political ideology of the republican commonwealth, which elevated the public good over private gain.

A MERCHANT-BASED ECONOMY: BANKS, MANUFACTURING, AND MARKETS

America was "a Nation of Merchants," a British visitor reported from Philadelphia in 1798, "always alive to their interests; and keen in the pursuit of wealth in all the various modes of acquiring it." And acquire it they did, especially during the European wars that dragged on from 1792 to 1815. Entrepreneurs such as the fur trader John Jacob Astor and the merchant Robert Oliver became the nation's first millionaires. Migrating from Germany to New York in 1784, Astor became wealthy by carrying furs from the Pacific Northwest to markets in China. He soon became the largest landowner in New York City. Oliver started in Baltimore as an agent for Irish linen merchants and then opened his own mercantile firm. Exploiting the wartime shipping boom, he reaped enormous profits in the West Indian coffee and sugar trade.

To finance such enterprises Americans needed a banking system. Before 1776 ambitious colonists found it difficult to secure loans. Farmers relied on government-sponsored land banks, while merchants arranged partnerships, borrowed funds from other merchants, or obtained credit from British suppliers. Then in 1781 Philadelphia merchants persuaded the Confederation Congress to charter the Bank of North America to provide short-term commercial loans; traders in Boston and New York founded similar banks in 1784.

In 1791, on Alexander Hamilton's initiative, Congress chartered the First Bank of the United States. The bank had the power to issue notes and make commercial loans, and although the bank's managers used their lending powers cautiously, profits still averaged a handsome 8 percent annually. By 1805, in response to the continuing demand for commercial credit, the bank had branches in eight major cities. Despite this success the First Bank of the United States did not survive. Jeffersonians accused the bank of encouraging "a consolidated, energetic government supported by public creditors, speculators, and other insidious men lacking in public spirit of any kind." When the bank's charter expired in 1811, President Madison did not seek renewal, forcing merchants, artisans, and farmers to ask their state legislatures to charter new banks. By 1816, when Madison adopted a more "national" stance with respect to economic policy and signed the congressional legislation creating the Second Bank of the United States, there were 246 state-chartered banks.

Many state banks were shady operations, issuing notes without adequate specie reserves and making ill-advised loans to insiders. Such poorly managed state banks were one cause of the Panic of 1819, a credit crisis sparked by a sharp drop in world agricultural prices. As farm income plummeted by one-third, many farmers could not pay their bills, causing bankruptcies among local storekeepers, wholesale merchants, and overextended state banks. The Panic gave Americans their first taste of the business cycle—the periodic expansion and contraction of profits and employment that is an inherent part of a market economy.

The Panic also revealed that artisans and yeomen as well as merchants now depended on regional or national markets. Before 1790 most artisans in New England and the Mid-Atlantic region sold their handicrafts locally or bartered them with neighbors. But others—shipbuilders in seacoast towns, iron smelters in Pennsylvania and Maryland, and shoemakers in Lynn, Massachusetts—sold their products in far-flung markets. Subsequently, a small group of merchant-entrepreneurs developed a rural-based manufacturing system similar to the European outwork, or putting-out, system (see Chapter 1) and sold its products in all parts of the nation.

Merchants stood at the center of this system, buying raw materials, organizing workers, and selling finished products. At the periphery were hundreds of thousands of farm families that supplied the labor. When a French traveler visited central Massachusetts in 1795, he found "almost all these houses . . . inhabited by men who are both cultivators and artisans; one is a tanner, another a shoemaker, another sells goods, but all are farmers."

By the 1820s thousands of New England farm families produced shoes, brooms, palm-leaf hats, and tinware—baking pans, cups, utensils, lanterns. Merchants shipped these products to cities and slave plantations, while New England peddlers, equipped "with a horse and a cart covered with a box or with a wagon," blanketed the South and acquired a reputation as crafty, hard-bargaining "Yankees." The success of these peddlers and merchants expanded the capitalist sector of the American domestic economy.

This economic advance stemmed initially from innovations in organization and marketing rather than in technology. Water-powered machines—the product of the Industrial Revolution in Britain—were adopted slowly in America, beginning in the textile industry. In the 1780s merchants built small mills along the waterways

The Yankee Peddler, c. 1830

Even in the 1830s most Americans lived too far from market towns to go there regularly to buy needed goods. Instead they purchased most of their tinware, clocks, textiles, and other manufactures from peddlers, often from New England, who traveled far and wide in small horse-drawn vans (such as that pictured in the doorway). (Courtesy IBM Corporation, Armonk, NY)

of New England and the Mid-Atlantic states. They installed water-powered machines and hired workers to card and comb wool—and later cotton—into long strands. For several decades the next steps in the manufacturing process were accomplished under the outwork system rather than in water-powered factories. Wage-earning farm women and children spun the strands into yarn by hand, and men in other households used foot-powered looms to weave the yarn into cloth. In his *Letter on Manufactures* (1810) Secretary of the Treasury Albert Gallatin estimated that there were 2,500 outwork weavers in New England. A decade later more than 12,000 household workers in that region wove woolen cloth, which then went to water-powered fulling mills to be pounded flat and finished smooth.

The penetration of the market economy into rural areas motivated farmers to produce more goods. Ambitious farm families switched from mixed-crop agriculture to raising dairy cows for cheese making; as a Polish traveler in central Massachusetts reported in 1798, "Along the whole road from Boston, we saw women engaged in making cheese" for sale in cities. "Straw hats and Bonnets are manufactured by many families," a Maine official commented, while another observer noted that "probably 8,000 females" in the vicinity of Foxborough, Massachusetts, braided rye straw into hats for market sale. Other farm families expanded the size of their cattle herds, selling hides to the booming shoe industry, and their sheep flocks, providing wool to textile manufacturers. Processing these raw materials brought prosperity and new businesses to many farming towns. In 1792 Concord, Massachusetts, had one slaughterhouse and five small tanneries; a decade later the town had eleven slaughterhouses and six large tanneries. Foul odors from the stockyards and tanning pits wafted over Concord, but its residents were able to acquire more goods and live more comfortably.

At first, barter transactions were a central feature of the emergent market system. When Ebenezer and Daniel Merriam of Brookfield, Massachusetts, began selling books to publishing houses in New York City, Philadelphia, and Boston in the 1810s, they received neither cash nor credit in return but other books, which they had to exchange with local storekeepers to get supplies for their business. The Merriams also paid their employees on a barter basis; a journeyman printer received a third of his "wages" in books, which he had to peddle himself. Gradually a cash economy replaced this complex barter system. As farm families joined the outwork system, they stopped making their own textiles and bought them instead, using the cash or store credit they had earned in the outwork system.

The new capitalist-run market economy had some drawbacks. Rural parents and their children now worked longer and harder, making specialized products during the winter and farming during the warmer seasons. Perhaps more important, they lost some of their economic independence. Instead of working solely for themselves as yeomen farm families, they toiled as part-time wage earners for merchants and manufacturers. The new market system decreased the self-sufficiency of families and communities even as it made them more productive. But the tide of change was unstoppable.

PUBLIC POLICY: THE COMMONWEALTH SYSTEM

Throughout the nineteenth century state governments were the most important political institutions in the United States. Beginning in the late 1810s many states decreased the property requirements for voting, reapportioned legislatures, and increased the number of elected (rather than appointed) officials. State legislatures also took the lead in regulating social life. They abolished slavery in the North but upheld it in the South, enacted laws governing criminal and civil affairs, established taxation systems, and oversaw county, city, and town officials. Consequently, state governments had a much greater impact on the day-to-day lives of Americans than did the national government.

As early as the 1790s many state legislatures devised an American plan of mercantilism, known to historians as the "commonwealth" system (because its goal was to increase the common wealth of the society). Just as the British Parliament had promoted the imperial economy through the Navigation Acts (1651–1696), state legislatures enacted measures to stimulate commerce and economic development. In particular, they granted hundreds of corporate charters to private businesses to build roads, bridges, and canals. For example, in 1794 the Pennsylvania assembly chartered the Lancaster Turnpike Company to lay a graded gravel road between Lancaster and Philadelphia, a venture that made a modest profit for the investors but greatly enhanced the regional economy by allowing a rapid movement of goods and people. "The turnpike is finished," noted a farm woman, "and we can now go to town at all times and in all weather." A boom in turnpike construction soon connected dozens of inland market centers to seaport cities.

By 1800 state governments had granted more than 300 corporate charters. Incorporation often included a grant of *limited liability* that made it easier to attract investors; in the event the business failed, the personal assets of the shareholders could not be seized to pay the corporation's debts. Most transportation charters also included the power of *eminent domain,* giving turnpike, bridge, and canal corporations the use of the judicial system to force the sale of privately owned land along proposed routes.

To some critics such uses of state power by private companies ran contrary to republicanism, "which does not admit of granting peculiar privileges to any body of men." Charters not only violated the "equal rights" of all citizens, opponents argued, but also restricted the sovereignty of the people. As a Pennsylvanian put it, "Whatever power is given to a corporation, is just so much power taken from the State" and therefore the citizenry. Nonetheless, state courts consistently upheld corporate charters and routinely approved grants of eminent domain to private corporations. "The opening of good and easy internal communications is one of the highest duties of government," a New Jersey court declared.

State mercantilism soon encompassed much more than transportation. Following the Embargo of 1807, which cut off goods and credit from Europe, New England states awarded charters to 200 iron-mining, textile-manufacturing, and banking firms, and the Pennsylvania legislature granted more than 1,100. Thus by 1820 innovative state governments had created a new political economy: the commonwealth system. The use of state incentives to encourage business and improve the general welfare would continue for another generation.

FEDERALIST LAW: JOHN MARSHALL AND THE SUPREME COURT

Both Federalists and Republicans endorsed the commonwealth idea but in different ways. Federalists looked to the national government for economic leadership and supported Hamilton's program of national mercantilism: a funded debt, tariffs, and a central bank. Jeffersonian Republicans generally opposed such policies, relying instead on state legislatures to promote economic development.

The difference between Federalist and Jeffersonian Republican conceptions of public policy emerged during John Marshall's tenure on the Supreme Court. Appointed Chief Justice of the Court by President Adams in January 1801, Marshall was a committed Federalist who upheld nationalist principles until his death in 1835. His success stemmed not from a mastery of legal principles and doctrines but from the power of his logic and the force of his personality. By winning the support of Joseph Story and other nationalist-minded Republican judges on the court, Marshall shaped constitutional interpretation on the crucial issues of judicial review, federal-state relations, and property rights.

The Marshall Court's first major decision involved judicial review. In 1798, during the dispute over the Alien and Sedition Acts, Republican-dominated legislatures in Kentucky and Virginia had asserted their authority to determine the constitutionality of national laws. However, the Constitution stated that "the judicial Power shall extend to all Cases . . . arising under this Constitution [and] the Laws of the United States," implying that the Supreme Court held the final power of judicial review over such legislation. But before 1803, when Marshall composed the decision in *Marbury v. Madison,* the Supreme Court had never overturned a national law or explicitly claimed the power of judicial review. In deciding that the Judiciary Act of 1789 violated the Constitution, the Chief Justice did both. "It is emphatically the province and duty of the judicial department to say what the law is," Marshall declared.

Thereafter, the doctrine of judicial review evolved slowly. During the first half of the nineteenth century the Supreme Court and the state courts used it sparingly and then only to overturn state laws that clearly conflicted with constitutional principles. Not until the *Dred Scott* decision of 1857 would the Supreme Court void another law passed by Congress (see Chapter 13).

The position of the Marshall Court on federal-state relations was most eloquently expressed in *McCulloch v. Maryland* (1819). In 1816 Congress created the Second Bank of the United States, giving it authority to handle the notes of

***John Marshall, by
Chester Harding, c. 1830***

Even at age seventy-five, John Marshall (1755–1835) had a commanding personal presence. On becoming
Chief Justice of the United States
Supreme Court in 1801, Marshall
elevated the court from a minor
department of the national government into a major institution in
American legal and political life. His
constitutional decisions dealing
with judicial review, contract rights,
the regulation of commerce, and
national banking permanently
shaped the character of American
law. (The Boston Athenaeum)

state-chartered banks and thus to monitor their financial reserves. To preserve the
independence and competitive position of its state banks, the Maryland legislature
passed a statute imposing an annual tax of $15,000 on notes issued by the Balti-
more branch office of the Second Bank. The Second Bank contested the constitutionality of the Maryland law, claiming that it infringed on the powers of the
national government. In response, lawyers for the state of Maryland adopted
Jefferson's argument against the First Bank of the United States, maintaining that
Congress lacked the constitutional authority to charter a national bank. Even if such
a bank could be created, the lawyers argued, Maryland had a right to tax its activities
within the state.

Marshall and the nationalist-minded Republicans on the Court firmly rejected
both arguments. The Second Bank was constitutional, said the Chief Justice, because it was "necessary and proper," given the national government's responsibility
to control currency and credit. Like Alexander Hamilton and other Federalists,
Marshall preferred a loose construction of the Constitution. If the goal of a law is

"legitimate [and] ... within the scope of the Constitution," he wrote, then "all means which are appropriate" to secure that goal are also constitutional, even if they are not explicitly mentioned in the Constitution. As for Maryland's right to tax the national bank, the Chief Justice stated that "the power to tax involves the power to destroy," suggesting that Maryland's bank tax would render the national government "dependent on the states"—an outcome that "was not intended by the American people" who ratified the Constitution.

The Marshall Court asserted the dominance of national statutes over state legislation again in *Gibbons v. Ogden* (1824), which struck down a monopoly that the New York legislature had granted to Aaron Ogden for steamboat passenger service across the Hudson River to New Jersey. Asserting that the Constitution gave the federal government the authority to regulate interstate commerce, the Chief Justice sided with Thomas Gibbons, who held a federal license to transport people and goods between the two states.

Marshall also turned to the Constitution to uphold his view of property rights. To protect individuals' property from government interference, Marshall seized on the contract clause of the Constitution (Article 1, Section 10), which prohibits the states from passing any law "impairing the obligation of contracts." Delegates at the Philadelphia convention in 1787 had included this clause primarily to allow creditors to overturn state laws that protected debtors, but Marshall expanded the scope of the contract clause by using it to defend other property rights.

To do this Marshall gave a broad definition to the term *contract,* extending it to embrace state grants and charters. The case of *Fletcher v. Peck* (1810) involved a large grant of land made by the Georgia legislature to the Yazoo Land Company. A newly elected state legislature canceled the grant, and speculators who had already purchased Yazoo lands appealed to the Supreme Court to uphold their titles. Marshall ruled that the purchasers held valid contracts that could not be later voided by the legislature. This far-reaching decision not only gave constitutional protection to those who purchased state-owned lands but also promoted the development of a national capitalist economy by protecting out-of-state investors.

The court extended its defense of property rights even further in *Dartmouth College v. Woodward* (1819). Dartmouth College was a private institution established by a charter granted by King George III. In 1816 the Republican-dominated legislature of New Hampshire tried to convert the college into a public university that would educate more of the state's citizens, thereby enhancing the commonwealth. The Dartmouth trustees resisted the legislature and engaged Daniel Webster, a great constitutional lawyer as well as a leading politician, to plead their case. Webster argued that the royal charter constituted a contract and therefore could not be tampered with by the New Hampshire legislature. Accepting Webster's argument, Marshall and Story upheld the rights of the college.

Marshall's triumph seemed complete. Many Federalist principles, such as judicial review and corporate rights, had been permanently incorporated into the American legal system. Yet when Marshall announced the *Dartmouth* and *McCulloch* decisions in 1819, the political fortunes of the Federalist Party were in severe decline. Nationalist-minded Republicans had won the allegiance of many Federalists in the East, while Jeffersonian Republicans commanded the support of most western farmers and southern planters. "No Federal character can run with success," Gouverneur Morris of New York lamented, and the election results of 1818 bore out his pessimism. Following the election Republicans outnumbered Federalists 37 to 7 in the Senate and 156 to 27 in the House of Representatives. Westward expansion and the transformation in American government begun by Jefferson's Revolution of 1800 had brought the tumultuous era of Federalist-Republican conflict to an end.

T I M E L I N E

1783	Treaty of Paris gives Americans access to the trans-Appalachian West.	1804–1806	Lewis and Clark's expedition explores Louisiana Purchase.
1790s	State mercantilism: states grant corporate charters. Entrepreneurs build turnpikes and short canals. Merchants create a rural outwork system, especially for shoes and textiles.	1807	Embargo Act cripples American shipping.
		1809	Tecumseh and Tenskwatawa mobilize Indians. Congress bans importation of slaves.
		1810	*Fletcher v. Peck* extends contract clause.
1790–1791	Little Turtle defeats American armies.	1810s	Expansion of slavery into the Old Southwest
1791	First Bank of the United States founded (dissolved in 1811)	1811	Battle of Tippecanoe
1792	Kentucky joins Union; Tennessee follows (1796).	1812–1815	War of 1812
1794	Battle of Fallen Timbers	1817	Rush-Bagot Treaty limits U.S. and British naval forces in the Great Lakes.
1795	Treaty of Greenville acknowledges Indian land rights in the trans-Appalachian West.	1817–1825	Era of Good Feeling
1801	Federalist John Marshall becomes Chief Justice.	1818	U.S. and British treaty sets the Canadian border.
1801–1808	Treasury Secretary Albert Gallatin reduces national debt. Handsome Lake leads revival among Iroquois.	1819	Adams-Onís Treaty annexes Florida and defines the Texas boundary. *McCulloch v. Maryland* enhances the power of the national government. *Dartmouth College v. Woodward* protects property rights.
1803	Louisiana Purchase asserts judicial review in *Marbury v. Madison*.		

The decline of political controversy prompted contemporary observers to dub James Monroe's two terms as president (1817–1825) the Era of Good Feeling. Actually, national political harmony was more apparent than real, for the Republican Party was now divided into a "national" faction and a Jeffersonian (or "state"-oriented) faction. The two groups fought over patronage and policy, especially the issue of federal support for internal improvement projects such as roads and canals. As the aging Jefferson himself complained about the National Republicans, "You see so many of these new republicans maintaining in Congress the rankest doctrines of the old federalists." With this division in the Republican Party, the cycle of American politics and economic debate was about to enter a new phase.

For Further Exploration

For a fine overview of the spiritual beliefs and political strategies of four Indian nations, see Gregory Evans Dowd, *A Spirited Resistance: The North American Indian Struggle for Unity, 1745–1815* (1992). Alan Taylor, *William Cooper's Town: Power and Persuasion on the Frontier of the Early American Republic* (1995), captures the feel of the European American frontier experience in New York.

Ralph Louis Ketcham's *Presidents Above Party: The First American Presidency, 1789–1829* (1984) portrays the evolving political ideology of the early republic, while Gore Vidal's *Burr: A Novel* (1973) offers an entertaining narrative of the life and times of Aaron Burr. Donald R. Hickey's *The War 1812: A Forgotten Conflict* places the war in its economic and diplomatic context. Thomas C. Cochran, *Frontiers of Change: Early Industrialism in America* (1981), is a short, engaging synthesis of industrial development from the Revolutionary era to the Civil War.

Lewis and Clark: The Journey of the Corps of Discovery (PBS video: 4 hours) tells the story of the initial European exploration of the Louisiana Purchase; the companion website at <http://www.pbs.org/lewisandclark/> contains a rich body of material on the explorers and the Indian peoples of the region. Compiled by K. M. Armstrong, the "Chickasaw Historical Research Page," at <http://home.flash.net/~kma/>, contains letters written by or about Chickasaw Indians between 1792 and 1849, the texts of more than thirty treaties, and other documents. *The Duel* (PBS Video: 1 hour) reenacts the confrontation between Alexander Hamilton and Aaron Burr, while "A Century of Lawmaking for a New Nation," at <http://memory.loc.gov/ammem/amlaw/lawhome.html>, part of the Library of Congress's American Memory project, contains congressional documents and debates, including discussions of the Northwest Ordinance, the ban on slave imports, the Embargo of 1807, and the decision for war in 1812. The site also contains information and maps of "Indian Land Cessions, 1784–1894."

Chapter 9

THE QUEST FOR A REPUBLICAN SOCIETY

1790–1820

The women in every free country, have an absolute control of manners [customs]: and . . . in a republic, manners are of equal importance with laws.

—JAMES TILTON, 1790

By the 1820s a sense of optimism pervaded white American society. "The temperate zone of North America already exhibits many signs that it is the promised land of civil liberty, and of institutions designed to liberate and exalt the human race," a Kentucky judge declared in a Fourth of July speech. Not even the deaths on July 4, 1826, of both John Adams and Thomas Jefferson shook people's optimism. Two great founding fathers had died, but the republic lived on.

There were good reasons for this enthusiasm. A half century after independence white Americans lived in a self-governing society that was free from both arbitrary taxes and a dogmatic, established church. Moreover, many citizens had come to consider themselves "republicans" not simply in their constitutional system of representative government and guaranteed individual rights but also in their political outlook, social behavior, and culture. However, Americans defined republicanism in different ways. Many white Americans in the North subscribed to "democratic republicanism," an ideology that encouraged individuals to aspire to greater equality in politics and within the family. By contrast, articulate southerners devised an "aristocratic republican" ideology that mirrored the hierarchical class and racial divisions of their society. Yet a third group of Americans—white and black, southern and northern—imbibed a "religious republicanism" that both transcended and enhanced sectional divisions. Swept up in the Second Great Awakening, they saw the United States as the republican seedbed of a new Christian civilization.

Democratic Republicanism

After independence, leading Americans developed a political system based on the principle of "ordered liberty," which in practice meant rule by the traditional elite. Gradually, white men of modest means deserted these elite political leaders and embraced the republican doctrines of political equality and social mobility. These citizens also reorganized traditional institutions such as families and schools, pursuing more egalitarian marriages and more affectionate ways of rearing and educating their children.

SOCIAL AND POLITICAL EQUALITY FOR WHITE MEN

Between 1780 and 1820 hundreds of well-educated Europeans visited the United States. Coming from countries with monarchical governments, established churches, male-dominated families, and profound divisions between social classes, they thought that the American republic represented a genuinely different and more just social order. In his famous *Letters from an American Farmer* (1782) the French-born essayist St. Jean de Crèvecoeur wrote that European society was composed "of great lords who possess everything, and of a herd of people who have nothing." America, by contrast, had "no aristocratical families, no courts, no kings, no bishops."

This absence of a hereditary aristocracy encouraged Americans to condemn inherited social privilege, and republican ideology proclaimed legal equality for all free men. "The law is the same for everyone both as it protects and as it punishes," noted one European traveler. Yet Americans accepted social divisions if they were based on personal achievement. As one letter to a newspaper put it, people should be valued not for their "wealth, titles, or connections" but for their "talents, integrity, and virtue." As individuals gained wealth, they gained a higher social standing, a result that astounded some Europeans. "In Europe to say of someone that he rose from nothing is a disgrace and a reproach," remarked an aristocratic Polish visitor. "It is the opposite here. To be the architect of your own fortune is honorable. It is the highest recommendation."

Changes in the legal profession exemplify the popular belief in the superiority of a competitive, achievement-oriented society. During the Revolutionary era American attorneys had won legislation that prevented untrained lawyers from practicing law. By 1800 most states required at least three years of formal schooling or apprenticeship, training only available to young men from well-established families. As legal rules became more central to American life, the legal profession grew in importance, and critics attacked what they called the "professional aristocracy" of lawyers. They demanded regulation of attorneys' fees, the creation of courts in which ordinary citizens could represent themselves, and easier standards for admission to the bar. By the 1820s only eleven of the twenty-six states required a fixed period of legal education. These changes probably lowered the intellectual quality of the legal profession, but they made it more democratic in composition and spirit.

Some Americans from long-distinguished families questioned the morality of a social order based on mobility and financial success. "The aristocracy of Kingston [New York] is more one of money than any village I have ever seen," complained Nathaniel Booth, whose family had once ruled Kingston but had now lost its prominence. "Man is estimated by dollars," he lamented; "what he is worth determines his character and his position at once." For most white men such a system meant the opportunity to better themselves.

By the 1810s republicanism also meant voting rights for all free white men. As early as 1776 the state constitutions of Pennsylvania and Vermont allowed all taxpayers to vote, undermining the traditional rule that political participation hinged on property ownership. By 1810 Maryland and South Carolina had extended the vote to all adult white men, and the new states of Indiana (1816), Illinois (1818), and Alabama (1819) provided for a broad male franchise in their constitutions. Within another decade fifteen states allowed all white male taxpayers to vote, and another seven had instituted universal white manhood suffrage, leaving only three states with property qualifications (see Map 9.1).

The changing tone of politics reflected the expansion of the suffrage. Increasingly, Americans rejected the deferential political views of Federalists such as Samuel Stone, who had called for "a speaking aristocracy in the face of a silent democracy." They refused to vote for politicians who flaunted their high social status, with their "top boots, breeches, and shoe buckles," their hair in "powder and queues." Instead, voters elected politicians who dressed simply, even if they still favored policies that benefited the economic elite.

As the political power of middling and poor white men grew, the rights and status of white women and free blacks declined. In 1802 Ohio disfranchised blacks, and in 1821 New York kept property-holding requirements for black voters while eliminating them for whites. The most striking case was New Jersey, where the state constitution of 1776 had granted suffrage to all property holders. As Federalists and Republicans competed for votes after 1800, they encouraged property-owning blacks and unmarried women to vote, challenging political custom. In 1807 New Jersey legislature closed this loophole, defining full citizenship (and therefore voting rights) as an attribute of males only. To justify the exclusion of women, legislators invoked both biology and tradition. As one letter to a newspaper put it, "Women, generally, are neither by nature, nor habit, nor education, nor by their necessary condition in society fitted to perform this duty with credit to themselves or advantage to the public."

REPUBLICAN MARRIAGE AND MOTHERHOOD

European and American husbands had long dominated their wives and controlled the family's property. But as John Adams had lamented in 1776, the revolutionary

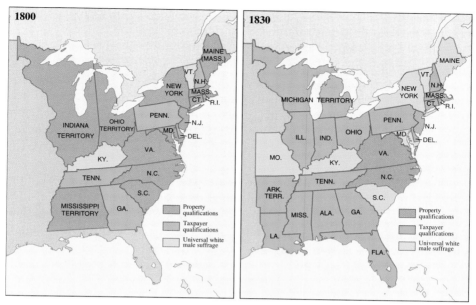

MAP 9.1

The Expansion of Voting Rights for White Men, 1800–1830

Between 1800 and 1830 the United States moved steadily toward political democracy for white men. Many existing states revised their constitutions, replacing property ownership with tax-paying or militia service as a qualification for voting, and some newly admitted western states extended the suffrage to all adult white men. As political parties competed for votes, they created an open and competitive political system that reflected the interests of ordinary people—and the patronage demands of party officials.

doctrine of political equality had "spread where it was not intended," encouraging some white women to demand the right to control their inheritances or speak out on public matters. These women argued that the subordination of women was at odds with a belief in equal natural rights. Patriarchy was not "natural" and could be justified only "for the sake of order in families," as the Patriot writer Mercy Otis Warren put it.

Economic and cultural changes also eroded customary paternal authority. Traditionally, fathers used the promise of future substantial land inheritance as a way of controlling their offspring, particularly their children's selection of a spouse. As land holdings were repeatedly divided in long-settled rural communities, parents could no longer use this incentive, and young men and women began to choose their own marriage partners. Many were influenced by European *sentimentalism*, which by 1820 had touched all classes of American society. Dripping from the pages of German and English literary works, falling from the lips of actors in popular tear-jerking melodramas, and infusing the rhetoric of revivalist preachers, sentimentalism celebrated the importance of "feeling"—that is, a physical, sensuous appreciation of God, nature, and other human beings.

As the passions of the heart overwhelmed the cool logic of the mind, a new marriage system appeared. Parents had always considered physical attraction and emotional compatibility in arranging marriages for their children, but they were more concerned with the personal character and financial resources of a prospective son- or daughter-in-law. Now magazines promoted marriages "contracted from motives of affection, rather than of interest"; this outlook encouraged a young person to seek a spouse who was, as Eliza Southgate of Maine put it, "calculated to promote my happiness."

As young people arranged their own marriages, fathers gave up the goal of patriarchal control and instead became paternalists, protecting the interests of their children. To guard against free-spending sons-in-law, wealthy fathers placed their daughters' inheritances in legal trust—out of their husbands' control. As a Virginia planter wrote to his lawyer, "I rely on you to see the property settlement properly drawn before the marriage, for I by no means consent that Polly shall be left to the Vicissitudes of Life."

Young adults who chose partners unwisely were severely disappointed when their spouses failed as providers or faithful companions, and a few sought divorces. Before 1800 most petitioners for divorce had charged their spouses with neglect,

The Wedding, 1805

The unknown artist who painted this watercolor depicts the bride and groom staring intently into each other's eyes as they exchange marriage vows, suggesting that their union stems from love rather than economic calculation. Given the plain costumes and sparse furnishings, this may be a rural Quaker wedding.

(Philadelphia Museum of Art. The Edgar and Bernice Chrysler Garbisch Collection)

abandonment, or adultery—serious offenses against the moral order of society. After 1800 emotional grounds dominated divorce petitions. One woman complained that her husband had "ceased to cherish her," and one man lamented that his wife had "almost broke his heart." Reflecting these changed cultural values, some states made divorce somewhat easier and expanded the legal grounds for divorce to include personal cruelty and drunkenness.

Theoretically the new republican ideal of "companionate" marriage gave wives "true equality, both of rank and fortune" with their husbands, as one Boston man suggested. However, husbands continued to occupy a privileged position because of deeply ingrained habits and laws that gave them control of the family's property. The new marriage system also discouraged parents from becoming involved in children's married lives, making young wives more dependent on their husbands than their mothers had been. And, as one lawyer noted, governments accepted no obligation to protect a woman who would rather "starve than submit" to the orders of her husband. The marriage contract "is so much more important in its consequences to females than to males," a young man at the Litchfield Law School in Connecticut concluded in 1820, "for besides leaving everything else to unite themselves to one man, they subject themselves to his authority. He is their all—their only relative—their only hope."

Once women were married, their main responsibilities were to run the household and to bear and raise children. However, by the 1790s the birth rate in the northern seaboard states was dropping dramatically. In the farm village of Sturbridge, Massachusetts, women who had married around 1750 had an average of eight or nine children, whereas women who married around 1810 had only about six. There was an even greater decline in urban areas, where native-born white women bore an average of only four children.

The United States was one of the first countries in the world to experience this sharp decline in the birth rate. There were several causes. Beginning in the 1790s thousands of young men migrated to the trans-Appalachian West, leaving some women without partners and delaying the marriage of many more. Women who married later had fewer children. Also, thousands of white American couples in the emerging middle class deliberately limited the size of their families. After having four or five children, they used birth control or abstained from sexual intercourse. Fathers wanted to provide each of their children with an adequate inheritance and so favored smaller families; mothers, affected by new ideas of individualism and self-achievement, were no longer willing to spend all of their active years bearing and rearing children.

As women looked for new opportunities they found support from changes in Christian thought. Traditionally, most religious writers had viewed women as morally inferior to men—as sexual temptresses or witches, but by 1800 Protestant ministers had begun to place responsibility for sexual misconduct primarily on men. In fact, Christian moralists now claimed that modesty and purity were inherent in woman's nature, making women uniquely qualified to educate the spirit.

Reflecting this sentiment, political leaders called on women to become "republican wives" and "republican mothers" who would correctly shape the characters of American men. In *Thoughts on Female Education* (1787) the Philadelphia physician Benjamin Rush argued that a young woman should receive intellectual training so that she would be "an agreeable companion for a sensible man" and ensure "his perseverance in the paths of rectitude." Rush also called for loyal "republican mothers" who would instruct "their sons in the principles of liberty and government." As the author of a list of "Maxims for Republics" commented, "Some of the first patriots of ancient times were formed by their mothers."

Christian ministers readily embraced the idea of republican motherhood. "Preserving virtue and instructing the young are not the fancied, but the real 'Rights of

Republican Motherhood

Art often reveals cultural values. In this painting executed in 1795 the artist James Peale (brother of the famous portraitist Charles Wilson Peale) depicts himself with his wife and children. The mother stands in the foreground, offering advice to her eldest daughter; the father, who was usually the center of attention in colonial era portraits (see p. 99), stands in the rear, giving pride of place to his wife and children. (Courtesy of the Pennsylvania Academy of the Fine Arts, Philadelphia. Gift of John Frederick Lewis)

Women,'" the Reverend Thomas Bernard told the Female Charitable Society of Salem, Massachusetts. He urged his audience to dismiss the public roles advocated by English women's rights advocate Mary Wollstonecraft and others. Instead, women should be content to care for their children, a responsibility that gave them "an extensive power over the fortunes of man in every generation." A few ministers went further and envisioned a public role for women based on their domestic virtues. As South Carolina minister Thomas Grimké asserted, "Give me a host of educated pious mothers and sisters and I will revolutionize a country, in moral and religious taste."

RAISING AND EDUCATING REPUBLICAN CHILDREN

Republican social thought also altered assumptions about inheritance and child rearing. Under English common law property owned by a father who died without a will passed to his eldest son, a practice known as *primogeniture*. In most American states legislators enacted statutes that required the estate of a man who died without a will to be divided among all his children (while continuing the traditional common-law dower right of his widow to use one-third of the estate during her lifetime). Most American parents supported these statutes because they had already begun to treat all of their children as equals.

Foreign visitors suggested that republicanism encouraged American parents to relax parental discipline and give their children greater freedom. Because of the "general ideas of Liberty and Equality engraved on their hearts," suggested a Polish aristocrat who traveled through the United States around 1800, American children had "scant respect" for their parents. Several decades later a British traveler was dumbfounded when an American father excused his son's "resolute disobedience" with a smile and the remark, "a sturdy republican, sir." The traveler guessed that American parents encouraged such independence to enable young people to "go their own way" in the world.

However, these childrearing habits were not universal. Foreign critics interacted primarily with well-to-do Americans, who were often members of Episcopal or Presbyterian churches. These parents followed the teachings of religious writers influenced by John Locke and the Enlightenment. In their minds children were "rational creatures" who should be encouraged to act correctly by means of praise, advice, and reasoned restraint. Training should develop the children's consciences and stress self-discipline so that young people would learn to control their own behavior and to think and act responsibly.

By contrast, many yeomen and tenant farmers influenced by the Second Great Awakening were much stricter and more authoritarian parents, especially in Calvinist-oriented families. Evangelical Baptists and Methodists believed that infants were "full of the stains and pollution of sin" and needed strict discipline. Fear was a "useful and necessary principle in family government," the minister John Abbott advised parents; a child "should submit to your authority, not to your arguments or persuasions." Abbott told parents to instill humility in children and to teach them to subordinate their personal desires to God's will.

The values transmitted within families were crucial because until the 1820s most education still took place within the household. In New England locally funded public schools provided most boys and some girls with basic instruction in reading and writing. In other regions fewer white children and virtually no African American children received schooling; about a quarter of the boys and perhaps 10 percent of the girls attended privately funded schools or had personal tutors. Even in New England only a small fraction of the men and almost no women went on to grammar (high) school. Only 1 percent of men graduated from college.

In the 1790s Bostonian Caleb Bingham, an influential textbook author, called for "an equal distribution of knowledge to make us emphatically a 'republic of letters.'" Thomas Jefferson and Benjamin Rush separately proposed ambitious schemes for a comprehensive system of primary and secondary schooling, followed by college attendance for young men. They also advocated the establishment of a university in which distinguished scholars would lecture on law, medicine, theology, and political economy.

To ordinary citizens such ideas smacked of elitism. Farmers, artisans, and laborers looked to schools for basic instruction in the "three R's": reading, 'riting, and 'rithmetic. They supported public funding for primary schools but not for secondary schools or colleges, which were of no use to their teenage children. "Let anybody show what advantage the poor man receives from colleges," an anonymous "Old Soldier" wrote to the *Maryland Gazette*. "Why should they support them, unless it is to serve those who are in affluent circumstances, whose children can be spared from labor, and receive the benefits?"

Although constitutions of many states encouraged the use of public resources to fund primary schools, there was not much progress until the 1820s. Then a new generation of reformers, primarily led by merchants and manufacturers, successfully campaigned to raise standards by certifying qualified teachers and appointing state superintendents of education. To instill self-discipline and individual enterprise in the students, the reformers chose textbooks, such as *The Life of George Washington* by "Parson" Mason Weems, that praised honesty and hard work while condemning gambling, drinking, and laziness. They also required the study of American history, believing that patriotic instruction would foster shared cultural ideals. As Thomas Low, a New Hampshire schoolboy, recalled "we were taught every day and in every way that ours was the freest, the happiest, and soon to be the greatest and most powerful country of the world."

The author Noah Webster had long championed the goal of American intellectual greatness. Asserting that "America must be as independent in literature as she is in politics," he called on his fellow citizens to detach themselves "from the dependence on foreign opinions and manners, which is fatal to the efforts of genius in this country." Webster's *Dissertation on the English Language* (1789) introduced American spelling (such as *labor* for the British *labour*) and defined words according to American usage. His "blue-backed speller," first published in 1783, sold 60 million copies over the next half-century and helped give Americans of all backgrounds a common vocabulary and grammar. "None of us was 'lowed to see a book," an enslaved African American recalled, "but we gits hold of that Webster's old blueback speller and we . . . studies [it]."

Ironically, the most accomplished and successful writer in the new republic was Washington Irving, an elitist-minded Federalist in politics and an expatriate. His essays and histories, including *Salmagundi* (1807) and *Diedrich Knickerbocker's History of New York* (1809), had substantial American sales and won fame abroad. Impatient with the slow pace of American literary development, Irving lived in Europe for seventeen years, drawn to its aristocratic manners and intense intellectual life.

Apart from Irving no American author was well known in Europe, partly because most American writers followed primary careers as planters, merchants, or lawyers. "Literature is not yet a distinct profession with us," Thomas Jefferson told an English friend. "Now and then a strong mind arises, and at its intervals from business emits a flash of light. But the first object of young societies is bread and covering." Not until the 1830s and 1840s, in the works of Ralph Waldo Emerson and novelists of the American Renaissance, would American-born authors make a real contribution to the great literature of the Western world (see Chapter 12).

Aristocratic Republicanism and African American Culture

Both in theory and in practice republicanism in the South differed significantly from that in the North. Although nearly all free white southern men had the right to vote, they had relatively little political power and few opportunities for social mobility. An elite group of white planters had grown rich by exploiting the labor of enslaved African Americans—one-third of the South's population—and used their wealth to rule over dependent white tenants and independent yeomen. For their part yeomen farmers dominated the lives of their wives and children.

THE NORTH AND THE SOUTH GROW APART

"When I was in Congress," Timothy Bloodworth of North Carolina recalled in 1789, there were distinct "Southern and Northern" differences over slavery and other issues. After 1800 these regional differences increased as the northern states ended slavery and the South expanded its slave-based agricultural economy. As the invention of the cotton gin and British demand drove up the price of cotton, farmers planted the nutrient-hungry crop year after year, quickly exhausting the soil and denuding the land. Less than a generation after they had been settled, the farms of Georgia's eastern plantation belt were described as "red old hills stripped of their native growth and virgin soil, and washed with deep gullies." Armed with British capital planters looked to the west for fertile lands.

As southern whites carried plantation agriculture into states of the lower Mississippi Valley, they tore apart hundreds of black communities in the states of the Chesapeake and the Carolinas. Between 1790 and 1820 whites relocated more than 250,000 African Americans. Some migrating slaves—perhaps as many as one-half—moved with relatives and friends when their owners sold their old plantations and began anew on the fertile plains of Alabama and Mississippi. Many other African Americans were "sold South" through a new domestic slave trade that provided tobacco and cotton planters in Maryland, Virginia, and other long-settled regions with a major source of income (see Map 9.2).

The expansion of slavery into the Southwest dashed the hope of many northerners that slavery would "die a natural death" following the demise of the Atlantic slave trade and the decline of the tobacco economy. Antislavery advocates grew increasingly concerned during the 1810s when Louisiana, Mississippi, and Alabama joined the Union with state constitutions permitting slavery. When Missouri applied for admission to the Union as a slave state in 1819, antislavery forces rose in opposition. Congressman James Tallmadge of New York proposed a ban on the importation of slaves into Missouri and the gradual emancipation of its black inhabitants. When Missouri whites rejected those conditions, the northern majority in the House of Representatives blocked the territory's admission to the Union. Southerners retaliated by using their power in the equally divided Senate

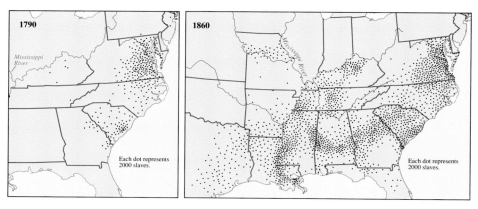

MAP 9.2
Distribution of the Slave Population, 1790–1860

The cotton boom shifted enslaved African Americans to the Mississippi Valley. In 1790 most slaves lived and worked on the tobacco plantations of the Chesapeake and in the rice and indigo areas of South Carolina. By 1860 hundreds of thousands were laboring on the cotton and sugar lands of the lower Mississippi Valley and along an arc of fertile cotton land—the "black belt"—sweeping from Mississippi through Georgia.

Arise! Arise! and weep no more
dry up your tears, we shall part
no more. Come rise we go to
Tennessee.
that happy Shore to old virginia
never — never — return.

The Internal Slave Trade

Mounted whites escort a convoy of slaves from Virginia to Tennessee in Louis Miller's *Slave Trader, Sold to Tennessee*. For white planters the trade was a lucrative one, pumping money into the declining Chesapeake economy and providing workers for the expanding plantations of the cotton belt. For blacks it was a traumatic journey, a new Middle Passage that broke up families and communities. (Abby Aldrich Rockefeller Folk Art Museum)

to withhold statehood from Maine, which was seeking to separate itself from Massachusetts.

Controversy raged for two years before Henry Clay of Kentucky and others put together a series of agreements known collectively as the Missouri Compromise. This legislation allowed Maine to enter the Union as a free state in 1820 and Missouri to be admitted as a slave state in 1821. The compromise preserved the existing balance between North and South in the Senate and set a precedent for the future admission of states in pairs—one free and one slave. To mollify antislavery sentiment in the House of Representatives southern congressmen accepted the prohibition of slavery in the rest of the Louisiana Purchase north of latitude 36°30', the southern boundary of Missouri (see Map 9.3).

Just as in the Constitutional Convention of 1787, white leaders in both the North and South had given first priority to the Union, finding complex but workable ways to reconcile regional interests. But the task had become more difficult. The Philadelphia delegates had resolved their sectional differences in two months; Congress took two years to work out the Missouri Compromise, with no guarantee that it would work. The fate of the western lands, the Union, and the black race had become inextricably intertwined and had raised the specter of civil war. As the aging

M AP 9.3
The Missouri Compromise, 1820–1821

The Missouri Compromise resolved for a generation the issue of slavery in the lands of the Louisiana Purchase. Slavery was forbidden north of the compromise line, 36°30′ north latitude, with the exception of Missouri, which entered the Union as a slave state. The compromise provided for the nearly simultaneous admission of Maine, maintaining an equal number of free and slave states in the Senate.

Thomas Jefferson exclaimed at the time of the Missouri controversy, "This momentous question, like a fire-bell in the night, awakened and filled me with terror."

THE SOUTHERN SOCIAL ORDER

After independence, white society in the South became increasingly hierarchical. During the 1770s nearly 60 percent of white families in the Chesapeake region owned at least one slave, yet within a few generations only about 25 percent of white families in the South held slaves, with the top 2 percent of southern whites owning about half of all slaves and much of the most fertile land. Wealthy, socially influential, and politically powerful, this planter elite dominated society and gave an aristocratic republican definition to politics and culture.

Members of the slaveholding elite described themselves as natural aristocrats and indulged in displays of conspicuous consumption. They married their children to one another, and their sons and daughters became commercial and cultural leaders—the men working as planters, merchants, lawyers, newspaper editors, and ministers and the women hosting plantation balls and church bazaars. John Henry Hammond, a leading South Carolina planter and politician, inhabited a Greek Revival mansion with a center hall 53 feet by 20 feet, its floor embellished with stylish Belgian tiles and expensive Brussels carpets. "Once a year, like a great feudal landlord," a guest recounted, Hammond "gave a fete or grand dinner to all the country people."

The planters justified their power by endowing it with moral purpose, a task more difficult after the Revolution when Quakers and other antislavery advocates in the North called for an end to human bondage. In the 1810s southern apologists defended slavery as a "necessary evil" to maintain white living standards and prevent racial warfare; subsequently they relied increasingly on religious justifications, pointing out that the Hebrews, God's chosen people, had owned slaves and that Christ had never condemned slavery. As Hammond told a British abolitionist in 1845: "What God ordains and Christ sanctifies should surely command the respect and toleration of man." Some defenders of slavery also depicted planters as aristocratic models of "disinterested benevolence" whose workers were adequately fed, housed, and provided for in old age. Southern writers praised planters' wives as household managers and nurses who cared for the sick and the elderly. These views helped the planter elite to see itself as a republican aristocracy, maintaining a stable, orderly society. To retain the allegiance of ambitious men from modest backgrounds, Hammond and other planters encouraged them to buy slaves and grow rich as they had.

Indeed, many proslavery apologists argued that the only genuine republic was one founded on slavery because it made all white men equal in the public sphere and preserved property rights and liberty by excluding the dangerous propertyless classes from the political process. In fact, white politics and society in the South remained deeply divided along the lines of class and region. As the system of cotton production expanded, some white yeomen became the tenants of wealthy landlords and others scraped by on small farms, growing foodstuffs for sustenance and a few bales of cotton for cash. Drawing on the patriarchal ideology of the planter class, they asserted traditional male authority over their wives and children, ruling the small world of the household with a firm hand. Other yeomen farmers retreated into the backcountry near the Appalachian Mountains, hoping to maintain economic independence and control local county governments. Owning hilly farms of 50 to 100 acres, these families grew some cotton but primarily raised corn and livestock, especially hogs. Their goal was modest: to preserve their holdings and secure enough new land or goods to set up all of their children as farmers.

These yeomen—and those who lived in the plantation belt—had to contend with the wealthy slave owners who dominated the state legislatures. By the 1830s in Alabama only 30 percent of the electorate owned slaves, but 75 percent of the legislators did; one-quarter of the legislators owned fifty or more slaves. Slaveowners used their political power to enhance their own welfare, exempting slave property from taxation. They also imposed land taxes by acreage rather than by value, thereby imposing relatively high taxes on subsistence farms in the backcountry. In addition, planters enacted laws that forced yeomen to "fence in" their livestock, sparing themselves the cost of building fences around their large properties. Finally, legislatures forced all white men—whether they owned slaves or not—to serve in patrols and militias that deterred slaves from running away or rising in rebellion. They warned tenants and yeomen that they had to support slavery or face economic competition and race warfare with freed African Americans. John Henry Hammond told his poor white neighbors, "In a slave country every freeman is an aristocrat."

Few yeomen became aristocrats or even well to do because the character of the southern economy limited their opportunities. The wealthy planters who controlled southern society wanted a compliant labor force, content with the drudgery of agricultural work. Consequently, they trained most of their slaves as field hands (allowing only a few to learn the arts of the blacksmith, carpenter, or bricklayer), and they made little or no effort to provide ordinary whites with elementary instruction in reading or arithmetic. Even as the cotton boom of the 1820s and 1830s increased the prosperity of slave owners, over one-third of white southerners could not read or write, compared to less than 1 percent of New Englanders. The illiterate signed legal documents such as wills and marriage licenses with an X or other mark.

In addition, planters discouraged the growth of manufacturing by concentrating their resources in cotton and slaves. As a result the percentage of southerners who lived in towns and worked in factories remained small. The only major cities in the South were the old seaports of Baltimore, Charleston, and New Orleans, which remained predominantly commercial centers. Lacking cities, factories, and educated workers, the South could not provide a majority of its people with a rising standard of living. Enslaved African Americans and white tenant farmers had little or no property, and landholding yeomen in the backcountry lacked access to profitable markets. Prosperity was limited primarily to the 25 percent of the white population that owned plantations and slaves. The political and social equality hoped for during the Revolutionary era was dashed by the South's aristocratic republican social order.

SLAVE SOCIETY AND CULTURE

As planters imposed their values on white society, three developments helped to create a distinct—and a more unified—culture among enslaved African Americans. First, the end of the transatlantic slave trade in 1809 gradually created an entirely American-born black population. Even in South Carolina—the destination of most of the slaves imported since independence—in 1820 only about 20 percent of the black inhabitants had been born in Africa. Second, the movement of slavery into the Mississippi Valley slowly reduced cultural differences among slaves. For example, the Gullah dialect spoken by slaves from the Carolina low country gradually died out on the cotton plantations of Alabama and Mississippi, replaced by the black English spoken by slaves from the Chesapeake. Third, in both southern and northern cities, free blacks consciously created a distinct African American community.

Even as the black population became more homogeneous, African cultural elements remained important. At least one-third of the slaves who entered the United States between 1776 and 1809 were from the Congo region of west-central Africa, and they brought their culture with them. As the traveler Isaac Holmes reported in 1821, "In Louisiana, and the state of Mississippi, the slaves . . . dance for several hours during Sunday afternoon. The general movement is in what they call the Congo dance." Similar descriptions of blacks who "danced the Congo and sang a purely African song to the accompaniment of . . . a drum" appeared as late as 1890.

Enslaved blacks in South Carolina and elsewhere continued to respect African incest taboos, shunning marriage between cousins. On the Good Hope plantation in South Carolina nearly half of the slave children born were related by blood to one another, yet only one marriage took place between cousins. (By contrast, many wealthy planter families in South Carolina and Georgia encouraged cousin marriages to keep inherited property in the family.)

However, southern state legislatures and law courts prohibited legal marriages between slaves, so that they could be sold without breaking a legal bond. African Americans therefore devised their own marriage rituals, first asking their parents' consent to marry and then seeking their owner's permission to live together. Following African custom many couples symbolized their married state by jumping over a broomstick together in a public ceremony. Christian slaves often had a religious service performed by a white or black preacher, but these rites never ended with the customary phrase "until death do you part." Everyone knew that black marriages could end with the sale of one or both of the spouses.

Separation was a common experience among many African American families. In 1790 many of the slaves on the Tayloe plantation in Virginia came from families who had lived there since the 1720s. Over the decades more slaves were born than the plantation could employ, so in 1792 John Tayloe III sold fifty slaves, separating husbands from their wives and children from their parents. Over the next two generations Tayloe and his sons moved 180 other slaves to new plantations in Alabama, where they worked "from day clean to first dark" clearing land and planting cotton. Other planters remained on their estates in Virginia, the Carolinas, and Georgia and sold their "surplus" blacks to slave traders. "I am Sold to a man by the name of Peterson a trader," lamented a Georgia slave. "My Dear wife for you and my Children my pen cannot Express the griffe I feel to be parted from you all." Some of these slaves forever lost touch with their families. "Dey sole [sold] my sister Kate," Anna Harris remembered decades later, ". . . and I ain't seed or heard of her since."

Although forced separations split many black families, the majority of slave marriages were stable. On the Good Hope plantation in South Carolina about 70 percent of the women had all their children by their husbands. On Louisiana plantations family ties were much more fragile because the dangerous disease environment and the demanding work of growing sugarcane took many black men's lives. Thirty percent of the slave women on one Louisiana plantation lived alone with their children, who were fathered by a succession of men.

To maintain their cultural identity recently imported slaves often gave their children African names. Males born on Friday were often called Cuffee—the name of that day in several west African languages. Most Chesapeake slaves chose names of British origin and named sons after fathers, uncles, or grandfathers and daughters after grandmothers. Like incest rules and marriage rituals these naming patterns solidified kinship ties, creating order in a harsh and arbitrary world.

By forming stable families and strong communities, African Americans were better able to control their own lives. In the rice-growing lowlands of South Carolina blacks won the right to labor by the task rather than work under constant supervision. Each day a worker had to complete a precisely defined task—for example, turn over a quarter acre of land, hoe half an acre, or pound seven mortars of rice. By working hard many finished their tasks "by one or two o'clock in the afternoon," a Methodist preacher reported, and had "the rest of the day for themselves, which they spend in working their own private fields . . . planting rice, corn, potatoes, tobacco &c. for their own use and profit." These private efforts provided slaves with better clothes and food, and on some large plantations planters gave decent health care to children, the sick, and the elderly. But few enslaved African Americans enjoyed a comfortable standard of living, and slaves clearly understood that planters gave them material favors not out of benevolence but to protect their investment (see American Voices, "A Child Learns the Meaning of Slavery").

In theory white masters had virtually unlimited power over their slaves. By law enslaved individuals were personal property, subject to discipline at the will of their owners and bought and sold as if they were horses. As Thomas Ruffin, a justice of the North Carolina Supreme Court, declared in a court decision in 1829, "The power of the master must be absolute to render the submission of the slave perfect." In practice both social conventions and black resistance limited the power of masters. Before 1800 the slave population was diverse and ill organized, and owners abused slaves without much fear of retribution. Although sexual assault, branding, and mutilation did not stop after 1800, they were questioned more often. Politicians and community leaders condemned rape as an aristocratic vice ill suited to a republican society, and the spread of evangelical Christianity prompted many masters to treat slaves more humanely.

But planters were never able to turn slaves into willing workers. "Should any owner increase the work beyond what is customary," a rice planter in South Carolina warned around 1800, "he subjects himself . . . to such discontent amongst his slaves as to make them of little use to him." To increase output, profit-conscious owners devised a new gang-labor system. Planters with twenty or more slaves organized disciplined teams, or "gangs," supervised by black "drivers" or white overseers and assigned them specific tasks. They instructed drivers and overseers to use the lash to work the gangs at a steady pace, clearing and plowing new land or hoeing and picking cotton. A traveler glimpsed two gangs returning from work in Mississippi:

AMERICAN VOICES

A Child Learns the Meaning of Slavery

JACOB STROYER

*J*acob Stroyer was born into slavery in South Carolina in 1849 but was emancipated and moved to Massachusetts, where he became a minister. In My Life in the South *(1885)* Stroyer relates an incident that dramatically revealed his parents' subordinate, powerless status.

Father . . . used to take care of horses and mules. I was around with him in the barnyard when but a small boy; of course that gave me an early relish for the occupation of hostler [stable boy], and soon I made known my preference to Colonel Singleton, who was a sportsman and had fine horses. . . . Hence I was allowed to be numbered among those who took care of the fine horses, and learned to ride. . . .

It was not long after I had entered my new work before they put me upon the back of a horse which threw me to the ground almost as soon as I reached his back. . . . When I got up there was a man standing near with a switch in hand, and he immediately began to beat me. . . . This was the first time I had been whipped by anyone except Mother and Father, so I cried out in a tone of voice as if I would say, this is the first and last whipping you will give me when Father gets hold of you.

When I got away from him I ran to Father with all my might, but soon my expectation was blasted, as Father very coolly said to me, "Go back to your work and be a good boy, for I cannot do anything for you." But that did not satisfy me, so I went on to Mother with my complaint and she came out to the man who whipped me. He was a groom, a white man whom master hired to train his horses . . . [and] he took a whip and started for her, and she ran from him, talking all the time. . . .

Then the idea first came to me that I, with my dear father and mother and the rest of my fellow Negroes, was doomed to cruel treatment through life and was defenseless. . . .

SOURCE: Linda R. Monk, ed., *Ordinary Americans: U.S. History Through the Eyes of Everyday People* (Alexandria, VA: Close Up Publications, 1994), pp. 71–72.

First came, led by an old driver carrying a whip, forty of the largest and strongest women I ever saw together; they were all in a simple uniform dress of a bluish check stuff, the skirts reaching little below the knee; their legs and feet were bare; they carried themselves loftily, each having a hoe over the shoulder, and walking with a free, powerful swing.

Next marched the plow hands with their mules, "the cavalry, thirty strong, mostly men, but a few of them women." Finally, "a lean and vigilant white overseer, on a brisk pony, brought up the rear."

Harvesting Sugarcane

Growing sugar was arduous work and took the lives of thousands of slaves. In both the West Indies and Louisiana sugar planters used gang labor to ditch and drain marshlands and plant cane seedlings in long ditches. Harvesting the mature cane and carrying it to the plantation's mill was equally strenuous and, as this watercolor by Franz Holzlhuber shows, was the work of women as well as men. (Collection of the Glenbow Museum, Calgary, Alberta, Canada)

To resist gang labor and other controls, slaves slowed the pace of work by feigning illness and were deliberately careless with the master's property, losing or breaking tools and setting fire to houses and barns. They also challenged the arbitrary breakup of communities, insisting that people be sold "in families" and defying their masters when they were not. One Maryland slave, faced with transport to Mississippi and separation from his wife (who was owned by another master), "neither yields consent to accompany my people, or to be exchanged or sold," his owner reported. Masters ignored such resistance at their peril because a slave's relatives might retaliate with arson, poison, or destruction of crops or equipment.

A few blacks, such as Gabriel and Martin Prosser in Virginia (1800) and Denmark Vesey in South Carolina (1822), plotted mass uprisings and murders. But in most areas blacks accounted for less than half the population, and everywhere they lacked the strong institutions—such as the communes of free peasants or serfs in Europe—needed to organize a successful rebellion. Moreover, whites were well armed, unified, and militant. Escape was equally problematic. Blacks in the lower South could seek freedom in Spanish Florida until 1819, when the United States annexed the territory. Nonetheless hundreds of blacks continued to flee to Florida, where they intermarried with the Seminole Indians. Elsewhere in the South small groups of escaped slaves eked out a living in deserted marshy areas or in mountain valleys, hoping that they would not be killed, enslaved, or returned by Indian warriors. Given these limited options most slaves had no choice but to build the best possible lives for themselves on the plantations where they lived.

THE FREE BLACK POPULATION

Meanwhile, between 1790 and 1820 the number of free blacks rose steadily from 8 percent of the total African American population to about 13 percent. About half of all free blacks lived in the North, where they performed the most menial and low-paying work and were treated as second-class citizens. In rural areas free blacks worked as farm laborers or tenant farmers; in towns and cities, as domestic servants, laundresses, or day laborers. They were usually forbidden to vote, attend public schools, or sit next to whites in churches. Of the states admitted to the Union between 1790 and 1821 only Vermont and Maine extended the vote to free blacks, and they could testify against whites in court only in Massachusetts. The federal government did not allow free African Americans to work for the postal service, claim public lands, or hold a U.S. passport.

Nonetheless, a few free blacks in the North were able to make full use of their talents, and some achieved great distinction. The mathematician and surveyor Benjamin Banneker published an almanac and helped lay out the new national capital in the District of Columbia. Joshua Johnston, a skilled painter, won praise for his portraiture, and merchant Robert Sheridan acquired a small fortune from his business enterprises. More impressive and enduring were the community institutions created by this first generation of free African Americans. In many northern communities they founded schools, mutual-benefit organizations, and fellowship societies. Discriminated against in white Protestant churches, they also formed their own congregations and an independent religious denomination—the African Methodist Episcopal (AME) Church. These institutions gave free African Americans a sense of cultural, if not political, autonomy.

Most free blacks in slave states lived in the upper South. In Maryland a quarter of the black population was free by 1820; in Delaware free blacks outnumbered slaves by three to one. Free blacks accused of crimes were often denied a jury trial, and many others had to contend with vagrancy and apprenticeship laws intended to force them back into slavery. To prove their free status blacks had to carry manumission documents and in some states needed official permission to travel across county lines. Even with valid papers free African Americans in the South had to be careful; kidnapping and sale were constant threats. Yet the shortage of skilled workers in southern cities did create opportunities for a few. Trained African American carpenters, blacksmiths, barbers, butchers, and shopkeepers in Baltimore, Richmond, Charleston, and New Orleans formed benevolent societies and churches, providing education, recreation, and social welfare programs for their communities.

As a privileged group among African Americans free blacks felt both loyalty to the welfare of their families, which often meant assimilating white culture, and loyalty to their race, which meant identification with the great mass of enslaved African Americans. Some wealthier free blacks, particularly the mulatto children of white masters and black women, drew apart from common laborers and field hands and adopted the outlook of the planter class. In New Orleans a few free African Americans even owned slaves.

Generally, however, both free and enslaved African Americans saw themselves as one people. "We's different [from whites] in color, in talk and in 'ligion and beliefs," as one put it. Knowing their own freedom was not secure as long as slavery existed, free blacks sought to win freedom for all those of African ancestry. Free southern blacks aided fugitive slaves, while free black northerners supported the antislavery movement. In the rigid caste system of American race relations free blacks stood as symbols of hope to enslaved African Americans and as omens of danger to the majority of whites.

Protestant Christianity as a Social Force

Beginning in 1790 a series of religious revivals planted the values of Protestant Christianity deep in the national character and gave a spiritual definition to American republicanism. The revivals also created new public roles for women, especially in the North, and changed African American life. Free and enslaved blacks became Christians, absorbing the faith of white Baptists and Methodists and creating a distinctive and powerful institution—the black church.

THE SECOND GREAT AWAKENING

The revivals that began around 1790 were much more complex than those of the First Great Awakening. In the 1740s most revivals had occurred in existing congregations; fifty years later they took place in frontier camp meetings as well and often involved the creation of new churches and denominations. More striking, the Second Great Awakening spawned new organizations dedicated to social and political reform.

Churches that prospered in the new nation were those that adopted a republican outlook, proclaiming doctrines of spiritual equality. Because the Roman Catholic Church was dominated by bishops and priests, it attracted few converts among Protestants, who adhered to Luther's doctrine of the priesthood of all believers, or among the unchurched, who feared clerical power. Likewise, few ordinary Americans joined the Episcopal Church (created by former members of the Church of England), which had a similar hierarchical structure and was dominated by its wealthiest members. The Presbyterian Church was more popular, in part because ordinary members elected laymen to the synods (congresses) where doctrine and practice were formulated. Methodists and Baptists attracted even more Americans because most of their preachers were fervent evangelists and promoted an egalitarian religious culture, encouraging lay preaching and communal singing.

A continuous wave of revivalism fueled the expansion of Protestant Christianity. Beginning in the 1790s Baptists and Methodists evangelized the cities and the backcountry of New England. A new sect of Universalists, who repudiated the Calvinist doctrine of predestination and preached universal salvation, attracted thousands of converts, especially in northern New England. After 1800 enthusiastic camp-meeting revivals swept the frontier regions of South Carolina, Kentucky, Tennessee, and Ohio (see American Voices, "A Camp Meeting in Indiana").

When frontier preachers got together at a revival meeting, they were electrifying. James McGready, a Scots-Irish Presbyterian preacher, "could so array hell before the wicked," an eyewitness reported, "that they would tremble and Quake, imagining a lake of fire and brimstone yawning to overwhelm them." James Finley described the Cane Ridge, Kentucky, revival of 1802:

> The noise was like the roar of Niagara. The vast sea of human beings seemed to be agitated as if by a storm. I counted seven ministers, all preaching at one time, some on stumps, others on wagons. . . . Some of the people were singing, others praying, some crying for mercy.

Because of their emotional message, revivalists were particularly successful in attracting the unchurched—the great number of Americans who had never belonged to churches. Their promise of religious fellowship also appealed to young men and women and geographically mobile families who had few social ties in their new communities.

The Second Great Awakening changed the denominational base of American religion. The leading churches of the colonial period—the Congregationalists, Episcopalians, and Quakers—declined in relative membership because they were content to maintain existing congregations or to grow slowly through natural increase. Because of their evangelism and democratic outlook Methodist and Baptist churches grew spectacularly. By the early nineteenth century they had become the largest religious denominations in the United States. In the South and West, Baptist and Methodist preachers traveled constantly. A Methodist cleric followed a circuit, "riding a hardy pony or horse . . . with his Bible, hymn-book, and Discipline." These "circuit riders" established new churches by searching out devout families, bringing them together for worship, and then appointing lay elders to lead the congregation and enforce moral discipline until the circuit rider returned.

Evangelical ministers copied the techniques of George Whitefield and other eighteenth-century revivalists, codifying their methods in manuals on "practical preaching." To attract converts preachers were cautioned to emphasize piety over theology; extemporaneous speech was deemed more powerful than a written

AMERICAN VOICES

A Camp Meeting in Indiana

FRANCES TROLLOPE

F   *rances Trollope, a successful English author, resided in the United States during the late 1820s, living for a time in Cincinnati. Her critical and at times acerbic* Domestic Manners of the Americans *(1832) achieved wide popularity in Europe and the United States. Here she provides her readers with a vivid description of a revivalist meeting in Indiana around 1830.*

We reached the ground about an hour before midnight, and the approach to it was highly picturesque. The spot chosen was the verge of an unbroken forest, where a space of about twenty acres appeared to have been partially cleared for the purpose. Tents of different sizes were pitched very near together in a circle round the cleared space. . . .

Four high frames, constructed in the form of altars, were placed at the four corners of the inclosure; on these were supported layers of earth and sod, on which burned immense fires of blazing pine-wood. On one side a rude platform was erected to accommodate the preachers, fifteen of whom attended this meeting, and with very short intervals for necessary refreshment and private devotion, preached in rotation, day and night, from Tuesday to Saturday.

When we arrived, the preachers were silent; but we heard issuing from nearly every tent mingled sounds of praying, preaching, singing, and lamentation. . . . The floor [of one of the tents] was covered with straw, [which was covered by a] close-packed circle of men and women who kneeled on the floor.

Out of about thirty persons thus placed, perhaps half a dozen were men. One of these [was] a handsome-looking youth of eighteen or twenty. . . . His arm was encircling the neck of a young girl who knelt beside him, with her hair hanging dishevelled upon her shoulders, and her features working with the most violent agitation; soon after they both fell forward on the straw, as if unable to endure in any other attitude the burning eloquence of a tall grim figure in black, who, standing erect in the center, was uttering with incredible vehemence an oration that seemed to hover between praying and preaching. . . .

At midnight, a horn sounded through the camp, which, we were told, was to call the people from private to public worship. . . . There were about two thousand persons assembled. One of the preachers began in a low nasal tone, and, like all other Methodist preachers, assured us of the enormous depravity of man. . . . Above a hundred persons, nearly all females, came forward, uttering howlings and groans so terrible that I shall never cease to shudder when I recall them. They appeared to drag each other forward, and on the word being given, "let us pray," they fell on their knees . . . and they were soon all lying on the ground in an indescribable confusion of heads and legs.

SOURCE: Frances Trollope, *Domestic Manners of the Americans* (London: Whittaker, Treacher, 1832), pp. 139–42.

sermon. "Preach without papers," advised one minister, "seem earnest & serious; & you will be listened to with Patience, & Wonder; both of your hands will be seized, & almost shook off as soon as you are out of the Church."

Beginning in the 1790s evangelical white Baptists and Methodists won the conversion of slaves and free blacks, who absorbed their teachings and adapted them to their needs. Black Christians generally preferred to envision God as a warrior who had liberated the Jews, his chosen people. Their cause was similar to the Israelites', Martin Prosser told his fellow slave conspirators as they plotted rebellion in Virginia in 1800. "I have read in my Bible where God says, if we worship him, we should have peace in all our land and five of you shall conquer a hundred and a hundred of you a hundred thousand of our enemies." Confident of their special relationship with God, the slaves prepared themselves spiritually for emancipation, which they saw as deliverance to the Promised Land.

Blacks generally ignored the doctrines of original sin and predestination as well as biblical passages that encouraged unthinking obedience to authority or portrayed the church as a lawgiver. When a white minister urged slaves in Liberty County, Georgia, to obey their masters, he noted that "one half of my audience deliberately rose up and walked off." Slaves identified with the persecuted Christ, who had suffered and died so that his followers might gain salvation. By offering eventual liberation from life's sorrows the Christian message helped many slaves endure their bondage. Amid the manifest injustice of their own lives African Americans used Christian principles to affirm their equality with whites in the eyes of God and to hope for ultimate justice in the afterlife. Black Christianity thus developed as a religion of emotional fervor and stoical endurance.

Like African Americans whites also were influenced by the times to emphasize certain Christian doctrines over others. The Calvinist preoccupation with human depravity and weakness had shaped the thinking of many earlier writers, teachers, and statesmen. By the early nineteenth century ministers (whether or not they were revivalists) had begun to place greater stress on human ability and individual free will, making the religious culture of the United States more optimistic and more compatible with republican doctrines of liberty and equality.

In New England many educated, well-off Congregationalists reacted against the emotionalism of Methodist and Baptist services by stressing the power of human reason. Rejecting the concept of the Trinity—God the Father, Son, and Holy Spirit—they worshipped an indivisible and "united" God, hence their name: Unitarians. "The ultimate reliance of a human being is, and must be, on his own mind," argued the famous Unitarian minister William Ellery Channing, "for the idea of God is the idea of our own spiritual nature, purified and enlarged to infinity." This emphasis on a believer's reason, a legacy of the Enlightenment, gave Unitarianism a humanistic and individualistic aspect.

Lyman Beecher, the preeminent New England Congregationalist clergyman, accepted the doctrine of universal salvation. Although Beecher continued to believe that humans had a natural tendency to sin, he retreated from the Calvinist doctrine of predestination, declaring that men and women had the capacity to choose God. In emphasizing choice—the free will of the believer—Beecher testified to the growing confidence in the power of human action.

For many in the years after 1800 individual salvation became linked with social reform through the concept of *religious benevolence*—the practice of disinterested virtue. According to the New York Presbyterian minister John Rodgers fortunate individuals who had received God's sanctifying grace had a duty "to dole out charity to their poorer brothers and sisters." Heeding this message pious merchants founded the New York Humane Society and other charitable organizations. By the 1820s some conservative church leaders were complaining that lay men and women were devoting themselves to secular reforms, such as the prevention of pauperism, to the neglect of spiritual goals. Their criticism underlined a key element of the new religious outlook: its emphasis on improving society. It was her belief, the social reformer Lydia Maria Child later recalled, that "the *only* true church organization [is] when heads and hearts unite in working for the welfare of the human-race."

Unlike the First Great Awakening of the 1740s, which split churches into factions, the Second Great Awakening fostered cooperation among the denominations. Five interdenominational societies were founded between 1815 and 1826: the American Education Society (1815), the American Bible Society (1816), the American Sunday School Union (1824), the American Tract Society (1824), and the American Home Missionary Society (1826). Each year these societies dispatched hundreds of missionaries to small towns and rural villages and distributed tens of thousands of religious pamphlets, organizing thousands of church members in a great collective undertaking and diminishing the importance of differences over religious doctrine. Many congregations abandoned books and pamphlets that took controversial stances on old theological debates over predestination and replaced them, a layman explained, with publications that would not give "offense to the serious Christians of any denomination."

This unity among Protestants had a galvanizing effect, as men and women scattered across the vast nation saw themselves as part of a single religious movement that could change the course of history. To do so they turned to politics. On July 4, 1827, the Reverend Ezra Stiles Ely called on the members of the Seventh Presbyterian Church in Philadelphia to begin a "Christian party in politics." In his sermon entitled "The Duty of Christian Freemen to Elect Christian Rulers," Ely set out for the American republic a new religious goal—one that the recently deceased Thomas Jefferson and John Adams would have found strange if not troubling. The two founders had believed that America's mission was to spread political republicanism. In contrast Ely urged the United States to become an evangelical Christian nation, dedicated to religious conversion at home and abroad. As Ely put it, "All our rulers ought in their official capacity to serve the Lord Jesus Christ."

WOMEN'S NEW RELIGIOUS ROLES

Pious women assumed a new leading role in many Protestant churches in the North and even founded new sects. Mother Ann Lee organized the Shaker sect in Britain and migrated in 1774 to America, where she and a handful of followers attracted numerous recruits; by the 1820s Shaker communities dotted the American countryside from New Hampshire to Kentucky and Indiana. In 1776 in Rhode Island, Jemima Wilkinson, a young Quaker woman stirred by reading the sermons of George Whitefield, had a vision that her body was infused by the "Spirit of Light." Repudiating her birth name, Wilkinson declared herself to be the Publick Universal Friend and won scores of converts to her new religion, which blended the Calvinist warning of "a lost and guilty, gossiping, dying World" with Quaker-inspired plain dress, pacifism, and abolitionism.

Far more important were the activities undertaken by women in mainstream churches. To give but a few examples, in New Hampshire women managed more than fifty local "cent" societies to raise funds for the Society for Promoting Christian Knowledge. Evangelical women in New York City founded the Society for the Relief of Poor Widows. And young Quaker women in Philadelphia ran the Society for the Free Instruction of African Females.

Women became active in religion and charitable work partly because they were excluded from other spheres of public life and partly because they formed a substantial majority in many denominations. After 1800 over 70 percent of the members of New England Congregational churches were female. Ministers acknowledged their presence by changing long-standing practices such as gender segregated seating at services and separate prayer meetings for each sex, while evangelical Methodist and Baptist preachers actively encouraged mixed seating and praying. "Our prayer meetings have been one of the greatest means of the conversion of souls," a minister in central New York reported in the 1820s, "especially those in which brothers and sisters have prayed together."

Far from promoting promiscuity as critics feared, these new practices were accompanied by greater moral self-discipline. Absorbing the principle of female virtue, many young women and the men who courted them postponed sexual intercourse until after marriage—a form of self-restraint uncommon in the eighteenth century. In Hingham, Massachusetts, and many other New England towns about 30 percent of the women who married between 1750 and 1800 had borne a child within eight months of their wedding day. By the 1820s the proportion had dropped to 15 percent.

Nevertheless, as women exercised their new social power, their religious activities and organizations were scrutinized and sometimes seen as subversive of social order. Many laymen resented the clergy's emphasis on women's moral superiority, and the religious and social activism that sprang from it. "Women have a different calling," one man argued. "They are neither required nor permitted to be exhorters or leaders in public assemblies. . . . That they be chaste, keepers at home is the Apostle's direction." Despite such criticism by the 1820s mothers throughout the United States had founded local maternal associations to encourage Christian child rearing. Newsletters such as *Mother's Magazine* were widely read in hundreds of small towns and villages, giving women a sense of shared purpose and identity as women.

Religious activism also advanced female education. Churches established scores of seminaries and academies where girls from the middling classes received sound intellectual training and moral instruction. Emma Willard, the first American to advocate higher education for women, opened the Middlebury Female Seminary in Vermont in 1814 and later founded girls' schools in Waterford and Troy, New York. Women educated in these seminaries and academies gradually displaced men as public school teachers. By the 1820s women taught the summer session in many schools; in the following decade they took on the more demanding winter term as well. Women were able to usurp these formerly male roles because women had few other opportunities and would therefore accept lower pay than men. Female schoolteachers earned from $12 to $14 per month with room and board—less than a farm laborer. However, as schoolteachers women had an acknowledged place in public life, one that had been beyond their reach in colonial and Revolutionary times. Here too, the Second Great Awakening had transformed the scope of women's lives. Just as the ideology of democratic republicanism had expanded voting rights and the political influence of ordinary men in the North, so the values of Christian repub-

T I M E L I N E

1782	St. Jean de Crèvecoeur's *Letters from an American Farmer*		Chesapeake blacks adopt Protestant beliefs.
1787	Benjamin Rush's *Thoughts on Female Education*	1807	New Jersey excludes propertied women from suffrage.
1790s	Second Great Awakening begins. Parents limit family size. "Republican motherhood" defined	1809	Washington Irving's *Diedrich Knickerbocker's History of New York*
		1810s	Expansion of suffrage for men
1800	Gabriel Prosser's rebellion in Virginia		Slavery defended as a "necessary evil"
1800s	Rise of sentimentalism and republican marriage system		Expansion of cotton South and domestic slave trade
	Women's religious activism and female academies	1819–1821	Conflict over admission of Missouri as a slave state ends with the Missouri Compromise.
	Spread of evangelical Baptists and Methodists		
	Religious benevolence linked with social reform	1820s	Reform of public education Women become schoolteachers.

licanism had encouraged women to take a more active role in the affairs of their communities.

In the South evangelical religion played a very different role. Initially revivalism was a disruptive force; by proclaiming the spiritual equality of all people—women and blacks as well as white men—it threatened the traditional authority wielded by husbands and planters and incurred their wrath. In response Methodist and Baptist preachers adapted the social content of their religious message so that it supported the rule of yeomen patriarchs and slaveowning planters. "We hold that a Christian slave must be submissive, faithful, and obedient," a Methodist Conference proclaimed, while a Baptist minister declared that a man was naturally at "the head of the woman." Ultimately Christian republicanism in the South added a sacred dimension to the ideology of aristocratic republicanism, while in the North it pushed forward the movement toward a democratic republican society.

For Further Exploration

For an intimate portrayal of family life on the Maine frontier, see Laurel Thatcher Ulrich, *A Midwife's Tale: The Life of Martha Ballard* (1990), which has also been made into a PBS dramatic documentary, *A Midwife's Tale* (1.5 hours). Additional materials on Ballard's experiences and women's lives are available on the web at <http://www.pbs.org/amex/midwife> and <http://www.DoHistory.org>. Jan Lewis's *The Pursuit of Happiness: Family and Values in Jefferson's Virginia* (1983) explores the domestic and emotional lives of the paternalistic slaveowning gentry of the late eighteenth century in the upper South, while Stephanie McCurry's *Masters of Small Worlds: Yeomen Households, Gender Relations, and the Political Culture of the Antebellum South Carolina Low Country* (1995) offers a brilliant analysis of yeomen families. In *The Ruling Race: A History of American Slaveholders* (1982) James Oakes argues that by the nineteenth century most slaveholders had become ruthless profit-seeking entrepreneurs.

Two stimulating analyses of the changing character of slavery and African American society are Ira Berlin, *Many Thousands Gone: The First Two Centuries of Slavery in North America* (1998), and Peter Kolchin, *American Slavery, 1619–1877* (1993). Douglas R. Egerton, *Gabriel's Rebellion: The Virginia Slave Conspiracies of 1800 and 1802* (1995), traces the political and economic causes of Gabriel's movement and its near success. For primary documents that illustrate the ways in which African Americans acquired and transformed the doctrines and beliefs of Protestant Christianity, log on to "Documenting the American South: The Church in the Southern Black Community," at <http://metalab.unc.edu/docsouth>.

In *The Democratization of American Christianity* (1987) Nathan Hatch traces the impact of evangelical Protestantism on the life and politics of the early republic. Bernard Weisberger, *They Gathered at the River* (1958), narrates the coming of the Second Great Awakening in engaging and witty prose, offers dramatic portraits of revivalists such as Charles Grandison Finney, and explores the many links between religious enthusiasm and social reform.

Part Three

ECONOMIC REVOLUTION AND SECTIONAL STRIFE

1820–1877

THEMATIC TIMELINE

	ECONOMY	SOCIETY	GOVERNMENT
	THE ECONOMIC REVOLUTION BEGINS	A NEW CLASS STRUCTURE EMERGES	CREATING A DEMOCRATIC POLITY
1820	• Waltham textile factory (1814) • Erie Canal completed (1825)	• Business class emerges. • Rural women and girls recruited as factory workers.	• Universal white male suffrage • Rise of Jackson and Democratic Party
1830	• Protective tariffs aid owners and workers. • Panic of 1837 • U.S. textile makers outcompete British.	• Mechanics form craft unions. • Depression shatters labor movement.	• Anti-Masonic movement • Whig Party formed (1834); Second Party System emerges
1840	• Irish join labor force. • *Commonwealth v. Hunt* (1842) legalizes unions. • Manufacturing grows.	• Working-class districts emerge in cities. • Irish immigration accelerates.	• Log Cabin campaign mobilizes voters. • Antislavery parties: Liberty and Free Soil
1850	• Growth of cotton output in South and railroads in North and Midwest • Panic of 1857	• Expansion of farm society into Midwest and Far West • Free labor ideology justifies inequality.	• Whig Party disintegrates; Republican Party founded (1854): Third Party System
1860	• Northern war industries thrive. • Republicans enact Homestead Act, aid to railroads, high tariffs.	• Emancipation Proclamation (1863) • Free blacks struggle for control of land.	• Thirteenth Amendment (1865) ends slavery; Fourteenth Amendment (1868) extends legal and political rights.
1870	• Panic of 1873	• Rise of sharecropping in the South	• Fifteenth Amendment extends vote to black men (1870).

276

Between 1820 and 1877 the United States changed from a predominantly agricultural society into one of the world's most powerful industrial economies. This profound transformation began slowly in the Northeast and then accelerated after 1830, affecting every aspect of life in the northern and midwestern states and bringing major changes to the South as well.

CULTURE	SECTIONALISM
REFORMING PEOPLE AND INSTITUTIONS	FROM COMPROMISE TO CIVIL WAR AND RECONSTRUCTION
• American Colonization Society (1817) • "Benevolent" Reform • Revivalist Charles Finney	• Missouri Compromise (1820) • David Walker's *Appeal to the Colored Race* (1829)
• Joseph Smith founds Mormonism. • Female Moral Reform Society (1834) • Temperance crusade	• Nullifications crisis (1832) • W. L. Garrison forms American Anti-Slavery Society (1833)
• Fourierist and other communal settlements founded • Seneca Falls convention (1848)	• Mexican War and Wilmot Proviso (1846) increase sectional conflict.
• Harriet Beecher Stowe's *Uncle Tom's Cabin* (1852) • Anti-immigrant nativist movement	• Compromise of 1850 • Kansas-Nebraska Act (1854) • *Dred Scott* decision (1857)
• U.S. Sanitary Commission and American Red Cross founded	• South Carolina secedes (1860). • Confederate States of America (1861–1865)
• African Americans create schools and institutions.	• Compromise of 1877 ends Reconstruction.

ECONOMY. Two interrelated economic revolutions—in manufacturing and in commerce—transformed the productive system. Factory owners used high-speed machines and new methods of labor discipline to boost production while enterprising merchants employed a newly built network of canals and railroads to create a vast national market. The share of the nation's wealth produced by the industrial sector rose from less than 5 percent in 1820 to more than 30 percent in 1877.

SOCIETY. This new economic system spurred the creation of a class-based society. A wealthy elite of merchants, manufacturers, bankers, and other entrepreneurs emerged at the top of the social order and tried to maintain social stability through a paternalistic program of religious reform. However, an urban middle class with a distinct material and religious culture grew in size and political importance. Equally striking was the growing number of propertyless workers, many of them immigrants from Germany and Ireland, who labored for wages in the new factories and built the new canals and railroads. By 1860 half the nation's free workers labored for wages, and wealth had become concentrated in the hands of relatively few families.

GOVERNMENT. The character of the emerging economic and social system affected the style and the substance of politics. The widespread ownership of property helped to spur the extension of the franchise, creating an open, democratic policy. Farmers, workers, and entrepreneurs demanded favors from politicians—improved transportation, shorter workdays, special corporate charters—and Catholic immigrants from Ireland and Germany entered the political arena to safeguard their religion and culture. Led by Andrew Jackson, the Democratic Party advanced the interests of southern planters, urban workers, and immigrants and carried through a political and constitutional revolution that cut the scope of governmental authority on both the national and state levels. To compete with the Democrats, the Whig Party (and beginning in the 1850s the Republican Party) promoted social reform and a vision of commerce as reducing class barriers and allowing a high rate of individual social mobility. The result was a two-party system that engaged the energies of the electorate and unified the fragmented social order.

CULTURE. During these years a series of reform movements, many with religious roots and goals, swept across America. Dedicated men and women preached the gospel of temperance, Sunday observance, prison reform, and dozens of other causes. A few visionaries created utopian communities in rural areas of the Midwest, but most radical activists worked within American society. Two of their major movements were for equal rights for women and the abolition of racial slavery. During the 1840s and 1850s antislavery advocates turned to political action, campaigning for "free soil" in the western territories and alleging that the "Slave Power" threatened free labor and republican values.

SECTIONALISM. These economic, political, and cultural changes combined to sharpen sectional divisions: the North and Midwest developed into diversified societies—rural and urban, farming and manufacturing—based on free labor, whereas the South remained a rural, slaveholding society dependent on the export of cotton and other staple crops. Following the conquest of vast western territories during the war with Mexico, northern and southern politicians vigorously debated whether these lands would be open to slavery. On the election of Republican Abraham Lincoln as president in 1860, the Southern states seceded from the Union, sparking a bloody four-year civil war. Because of its new industrial technology and the mass mobilization of economic resources and armies, the North emerged victorious only after each side endured unprecedented casualties and costs.

The fruits of victory were substantial. During Reconstruction the Republican Party ended slavery and imposed its economic policies and constitutional doctrines on the nation. However, the effort by Radical Republicans to extend full democratic rights to the former slaves elicited massive resistance from white southerners, and Northern leaders and voters lacked the will to undertake the fundamental transformation of a South that would have been required to provide African Americans with the full benefits of freedom.

Chapter 10

THE ECONOMIC REVOLUTION
1820–1860

[In America] all is circulation, motion, and boiling agitation . . .
enterprise follows enterprise [and] riches and poverty follow. . . .
— MICHEL CHEVALIER, FRENCH VISITOR, 1839

In 1804 life suddenly turned grim for eleven-year-old Chauncey Jerome. Following the death of his farmer-blacksmith father Jerome was hired out as an indentured servant to a farmer. Aware that few farmers "would treat a poor boy like a human being," Jerome instead bought out his indenture by finding a job making dials for clocks and eventually ended up working as a journeyman for Eli Terry. A manufacturing wizard, Terry had turned Litchfield, Connecticut, into the clockmaking center of the United States by designing an enormously popular desk-model clock with brass parts. Jerome followed in Terry's footsteps, setting up his own clock business in 1816. By organizing work more efficiently and using new machines to make interchangeable metal parts, Jerome drove down the price of a simple clock from $20 to $5 and then to less than $2. By the 1840s he was selling his clocks in England, the center of the Industrial Revolution; two decades later his workers were turning out 200,000 clocks a year, helping the United States to become a major manufacturing nation.

The French aristocrat Alexis de Tocqueville captured a key feature of Chauncy Jerome's experience and the American economic revolution in his treatise *Democracy in America* (1835). "What most astonishes me," he remarked after a two-year stay in the United States, "is not so much the marvelous grandeur of some undertakings, as the innumerable magnitude of small ones." The individual efforts of tens of thousands of artisan-inventors like Terry and Jerome had helped to propel the country into a new economic era. As the editor of *Niles Weekly Register* put it, there was an "almost universal ambition to get forward."

Not all Americans embraced the new ethic of enterprise, and many who did failed to share in the new prosperity. The Industrial Revolution and the Market Revolution created a class-divided society that challenged the founders' vision of an agricultural republic with few distinctions of wealth or power. As the philosopher Ralph Waldo Emerson warned in 1839, "The invasion of Nature by Trade with its

Money, its Credit, its Steam, [and] its Railroad threatens to . . . establish a new, universal Monarchy."

The Coming of Industry: Northeastern Manufacturing

Together, the Industrial Revolution and the Market Revolution created a new economy. Industrialization came to the United States after 1790 as American merchants and manufacturers increased the output of goods by reorganizing work and building factories. The rapid construction of turnpikes, canals, and railroads by state governments and private entrepreneurs allowed those products to be sold throughout the land. Thanks to these innovations the average per capita wealth of Americans increased by nearly 1 percent per year—30 percent over the course of a generation. Goods that once had been luxury items became part of everyday life.

DIVISION OF LABOR AND THE FACTORY

This impressive gain in output stemmed initially from changes in the organization of production. During the 1820s and 1830s merchants and manufacturers increased output in the shoe industry through a more efficient "division of labor." The employers hired journeymen and set them to work in central shops cutting leather into soles and uppers. They sent out the uppers to shoe binders, usually women who worked at home sewing in fabric linings. Finally, the manufacturers had other journeymen assemble the shoes in small shops and return them to the central shop for inspection and packing. The new system made the manufacturer into a powerful "shoe boss" and eroded the workers' control over the pace and conditions of labor. "I guess you won't catch me to do that little thing again," vowed one Massachusetts binder. Whatever the cost to workers, the division of labor dramatically increased the output of shoes while cutting their price.

For tasks that were not suited to the outwork system, entrepreneurs created an even more important new organization, the modern factory. As in the traditional artisan economy, they concentrated production under one roof but now divided the work into specialized tasks performed by different individuals. For example, in the 1830s Cincinnati merchants built slaughterhouses that rationalized the process of butchering hogs. A simple system of overhead rails moved the carcasses past workers who had specific tasks: splitting the animals, removing various organs, and trimming the carcasses before packers stuffed them in barrels and pickled them. The system was efficient and quick—sixty hogs per hour—and by the 1840s Cincinnati was butchering so many hogs that the city became known as "Porkopolis."

Some factories boasted impressive new technology. The prolific Delaware inventor Oliver Evans built a highly automated flourmill driven by waterpower. His machinery lifted the grain to the top of the mill, cleaned the grain as it fell into hoppers, ground it into flour, conveyed the flour back to the top of the mill, and

Pork Packing in Cincinnati

The only modern technology in this Cincinnati pork packing plant was the overhead pulley system that carried hog carcasses past the workers. The plant's efficiency came from organization, a division of labor so that each worker performed a specific task. Such plants pioneered the design of the moving assembly lines that Henry Ford used in his automobile factories in the early twentieth century. (Cincinnati Historical Society)

then cooled the flour during its descent into barrels. Evans's factory, remarked one observer, "was as full of machinery as the case of a watch." It needed only six men to mill 100,000 bushels of grain a year.

Subsequently, manufacturers made use of newly improved stationary steam engines to power their mills. They also extended the use of power-driven machines and assembly lines from the processing of agricultural goods—pork, leather, wool, cotton—to the manufacturing of goods and machines made of metal. Cyrus McCormick of Chicago developed power-driven conveyor belts to assemble reapers, and Samuel Colt built an assembly-line factory in Hartford, Connecticut, to produce his invention—the "six-shooter" revolver, as it became known. As a team of British observers noted with admiration, many American products were made "in large factories, with machinery applied to almost every process, the extreme subdivision of labor, and all reduced to an almost perfect system of manufacture."

THE TEXTILE INDUSTRY AND BRITISH COMPETITION

As textile manufacturers adopted new machinery and the division of labor, they achieved dramatic gains in productivity (output per worker). To protect its industrial leadership Britain prohibited the export of textile machinery and the emigration of mechanics who knew how to build it. Lured by high wages or offers of partnerships, thousands of British mechanics disguised themselves as ordinary laborers and set sail for the United States. By 1812 there were more than 300 British mechanics at work in the Philadelphia area alone.

The most important was Samuel Slater, who came to America in 1789 after working for Richard Arkwright, the inventor and operator of the most advanced machinery for spinning cotton. Having memorized the design of Arkwright's machinery, the young Slater introduced his innovations in merchant Moses Brown's cotton mill in Providence, Rhode Island. The opening of Slater's factory in 1790 marks the advent of the American Industrial Revolution.

In competing with British mills American manufacturers had one major advantage: an abundance of natural resources. America's rich agriculture produced a wealth of cotton and wool, and from Maine to Delaware its rivers provided a cheap source of energy. As rivers cascaded downhill from the Appalachian foothills to the Atlantic coastal plain, they were easily harnessed to run power machinery. All along this fall line industrial villages and towns sprang up.

Nevertheless, the British producers easily undersold their American competitors. Thanks to cheap shipping and lower interest rates in Britain, they could import raw cotton from the United States, manufacture it into cloth, and then ship the textiles back across the Atlantic. Moreover, because British companies were better established, they could engage in cutthroat competition, cutting prices briefly but sharply to drive the newer American firms out of business. The most

A New England Textile Village, 1822

Because the first textile mills used waterpower, the American Industrial Revolution began in small rural settlements, like that shown in Francis Alexander's painting of Globe Village on the Blackstone River in Massachusetts. (Jacob Edwards Library, Southbridge, MA)

important British advantage was cheap labor. Britain had a larger population—about 12.6 million in 1810 compared with 7.3 million Americans—and thousands of landless laborers who were willing to take low-paying factory jobs. Since unskilled American workers could obtain good pay for farm or construction work, American manufacturers had to pay them higher wages.

To offset these British advantages American entrepreneurs sought assistance from the federal government. In 1816 Congress passed a tariff that gave manufacturers protection from low-cost imports of cotton cloth. New protective legislation in 1824 levied a tax of 35 percent on imported iron products, higher-grade woolen and cotton textiles, and various agricultural products, and the rate rose to 50 percent in 1828. But in 1833, under pressure from southern planters, western farmers, and urban consumers—who wanted to buy inexpensive manufactures—Congress began to reduce tariffs (see Chapter 11), causing some American textile firms to go out of business.

American producers adopted two other strategies to compete with their British rivals. First they improved on British technology. In 1811 Francis Cabot Lowell, a wealthy Boston merchant, spent a holiday touring British textile mills. A well-educated and charming young man, he flattered his hosts by asking a great many questions, but his easy manner hid a serious purpose. Lowell secretly made detailed drawings of power machinery, and Paul Moody, an experienced American mechanic, then copied the machines and made improvements. In 1814 Lowell joined two other merchants, Nathan Appleton and Patrick Tracy Jackson, to form the Boston Manufacturing Company. Raising the staggering sum of $400,000, they built a textile plant in Waltham, Massachusetts, on the Charles River. The Waltham factory was the first in America to perform all the operations of cloth making under one roof. Thanks to Moody's improvements, Waltham's power looms operated at higher speeds than British looms and needed fewer workers.

The second American strategy was to find less expensive workers. In the 1820s the Boston Manufacturing Company pioneered a manufacturing system that became known as the Waltham plan. The company recruited thousands of farm girls and women, who would work at low wages, as textile operatives. To attract these workers, the company provided boardinghouses and cultural activities such as evening lectures. The mill owners reassured anxious parents by enforcing strict curfews, prohibiting alcoholic beverages, and requiring regular church attendance. At Lowell (1822), Chicopee (1823), and other sites in Massachusetts and New Hampshire, the Company built new cotton factories on the Waltham plan; other Boston-owned firms quickly followed suit.

By the early 1830s more than 40,000 young women were working in textile mills. One of them, Lucy Larcom of Lowell, Massachusetts, became an operative when she was eleven so that she would not be "a trouble or burden or expense" to her widowed mother. Many women sent their savings home to help their fathers pay off farm mortgages, defray the cost of schooling for their brothers, or accumulate a dowry for themselves. Women textile operatives often found their work

A New England Mill Worker

SARAH RICE

S arah Rice had to defy her father to take a job tending looms in a mill in Masonville, Connecticut. Her letters explain both the financial advantages of factory labor over work as a domestic servant and its toll on her health. Operatives in New England worked an average of 12 hours a day, six days a week, 309 days a year; in addition to Sundays, they had three days off: Fast Day in the spring, the Fourth of July, and Thanksgiving.

Masonville Feb 23d 1845
Dear Father
   I now take my pen in hand to let you know where I am. I have been waiting perhaps longer than I ought to without leting you know where I am yet I had a reason for so doing . . . knowing that you was dolefully prejudiced against a Cotton Factory, and being no less prejudiced myself I thought it best to wait and see how I prospered. . . .
   To be sure it is a noisy place and we are confined more than I like to be but I do not wear out my clothes and shoes as I do when I do house work. If I can make 2 dollars per week beside my board and save my clothes and shoes I think it will be better than to do housework for nine shillings [$1.12] I mean for a year or two. I should not like to spend my days in a mill . . . because I like a Farm to well for that.

Millbury [Massachusetts] Sept 14th 1845
   You surely cannot blame me for leaving the factory so long as I realised that it was killing me to work in it. Could you have seen me att the time or a week before I came away you would [have] advised me as many others did to leave immediately. I realise that if I lose my health which is all I possess on earth . . . that I shall be in a sad condition.

SOURCE: Gary Kulik, Roger Parks, Theodore Z. Penn, eds., *The New England Mill Village, 1790–1860* (Cambridge, MA: MIT Press, 1982), pp. 389–90.

oppressive and took periodic breaks before moving to another mill, but many gained a new sense of freedom and autonomy (see American Voices, "A New England Mill Worker"). "Don't I feel independent!" a mill worker wrote to her sister in the 1840s. "The thought that I am living on no one is a happy one indeed to me."
   The owners of the Boston Manufacturing Company were even happier. By combining improved technology, female labor, and tariff protection, they could sell cheap textiles for a lower price than their British rivals could. They also had an advantage over textile manufacturers in New York and Pennsylvania, where farm workers were better paid than in New England and textile wages consequently were higher. Manufacturers in those states pursued a different strategy, modifying traditional technology to produce higher-quality cloth, also with good results. In 1825

A Mill Girl, c. 1850

This fine daguerreotype (an early form of photography) shows a neatly dressed textile worker about twelve years old. Labor in the mill has taken a toll on her spirit and body: the young girl's eyes and mouth show little joy or life and her hands are rough and swollen. She probably worked either as a knotter, tying broken threads on spinning jennies, or a warper, straightening out the strands of cotton or wool as they entered the loom. (Jack Naylor Collection)

Thomas Jefferson, once a critic of industrialization, expressed his pride in the American achievement: "Our manufacturers are now very nearly on a footing with those of England."

AMERICAN MECHANICS AND TECHNOLOGICAL INNOVATION

By the 1820s American-born craftsmen had replaced British immigrants at the cutting edge of technological innovation. Although few craftsmen had a formal education and once had been viewed as "mean" or even "servile" workers, they now claimed respect as "men professing an ingenious art." In 1837 one such inventor, Richard Garsed, experimented with improvements on power looms in his father's factory and in three years nearly doubled their speed. By 1846 Garsed had patented a cam and harness device that allowed elaborately figured fabrics such as damask to be woven by machine.

In the Philadelphia region the most important inventors came from the remarkable Sellars family. Samuel Sellars Jr. invented a machine for twisting worsted woolen yarn. His son John devised more efficient ways of using waterpower to run the family's sawmills and built a machine to weave wire sieves. John's sons and grandsons built machine shops that turned out a variety of new products: riveted leather fire hoses, papermaking equipment, and eventually locomotives. In 1824 the Sellars and other mechanics founded the Franklin Institute in Philadelphia. Named after Benjamin Franklin, whom the mechanics admired for his scientific accomplishments and idealization of hard work, the institute fostered a sense of professional identity. The Franklin Institute published a journal; provided high school–level instruction in mechanics, chemistry, mathematics, and mechanical drawing; and organized annual fairs to exhibit the most advanced products. Craftsmen in Ohio and other states soon established their own mechanics institutes, which played a crucial role in diffusing technical knowledge and encouraging innovation. Around 1820 the United States Patent Office issued about 200 patents on new inventions each year, mostly to gentlemen and merchants. By 1850 it was awarding 1,000 patents annually, mostly to mechanics, and by 1860 over 4,000.

During these years American mechanics pioneered the development of machine tools—machines for making other machines—thus facilitating the rapid spread of the Industrial Revolution. Mechanics in the textile industry invented lathes, planers, and boring machines that made standardized parts, making it possible to manufacture new spinning jennies and weaving looms at a low cost and to repair broken machines. Moreover, this machinery was precise enough in design and construction to operate at higher speeds than British equipment.

Technological innovation swept through the rest of American manufacturing, with especially important advances coming in the firearms industry. To fill large-scale contracts for guns from the federal government, Eli Whitney and his coworkers in Connecticut developed machine tools that produced parts that were interchangeable and precision-crafted. After Whitney's death his partner, John H. Hall, an engineer at the federal armory at Harpers Ferry, Virginia, built a series of sixteen special-purpose lathes to make a gun stock out of sawn lumber and an array of machine tools to work metal: turret lathes, milling machines, and precision grinders. Thereafter, manufacturers could use those machine tools to produce complicated machinery with great speed, at low cost, and in large quantities.

With this expansion in the availability of machines, the American Industrial Revolution came of age. The sheer volume of output caused some products—Remington rifles, Singer sewing machines, and Yale locks—to become household names in the United States and abroad. After showing their machine-tooled goods at the Crystal Palace Exhibition in London in 1851 (the first major international display of industrial goods), these American businesses built factories in Great Britain and soon dominated many European markets.

WAGE WORKERS AND THE LABOR MOVEMENT

As the Industrial Revolution gathered momentum, it changed the nature of work and of workers' lives. Each decade, more and more white Americans ceased to be self-employed and took jobs as wage-earning workers. They had little security of employment or control over their working conditions.

Some wageworkers worked as journeymen in traditional crafts, such as the building trades. These carpenters, housepainters, stonecutters, masons, nailers, and cabinetmakers had valuable skills and a strong sense of craft identity. Consequently, they were able to form unions and bargain with the master artisans who employed them. The journeymen's main concern was the increasing length of the workday, which deprived them of time to spend with their families or improve their education. The traditional workday for artisans had averaged about twelve hours, including breaks for meals. By the 1820s masters were demanding a longer day during the summer, when it stayed light longer, while paying journeymen the old daily rate. In response, 600 carpenters in Boston went on strike in 1825, demanding a ten-hour day, 6 A.M. to 6 P.M. with an hour each for breakfast and dinner. Although the Boston protest failed, two years later journeymen carpenters in Philadelphia won a similar strike and then helped found the Mechanics' Union of Trade Associations. This citywide organization of fifty unions and 10,000 Philadelphia wage-earners set forth a broad program of reform, demanding "a just balance of power . . . between all the various classes." To secure this goal in 1828 the Philadelphia artisans founded the Working Men's Party, which campaigned for the abolition of banks, equal taxation, and a universal system of public education. By the mid-1830s skilled building-trades workers had forced many urban employers to accept a ten-hour workday and persuaded President Andrew Jackson to establish a ten-hour day at the Philadelphia navy yard.

Artisans whose occupations were threatened by industrialization were less successful. As machines changed the nature of their work, shoemakers, hatters, printers, furniture makers, and weavers faced declining incomes, unemployment, and loss of status. To avoid the regimentation of factory work some artisans moved to small towns or set up specialized shops. In New York City 800 highly skilled cabinetmakers worked in artisanlike shops that made fashionable or custom-made products. In status and income they outranked a much larger group of 3,200 semitrained workers—derogatively called "botches"—who turned out cheap, mass-produced furniture.

In many industries factory workers banded together to form craft unions to seek higher pay and better conditions. In 1830 in Lynn, Massachusetts, journeymen shoemakers founded a Mutual Benefit Society that quickly grew into a national union and formed local federations with other craft unions. In 1834 federations from Boston to Philadelphia formed the National Trades' Union, the first national union of different trades.

Union leaders mounted a critique of the new industrial order. Afraid that workers were becoming "slaves to a monied aristocracy," they condemned the new outwork and factory systems in which "capital and labor stand opposed." To restore a just society, they devised a *labor theory of value,* arguing that the price of a product should reflect the labor required to make it and should be paid primarily to the artisan or farmer who produced it, to "enable him to live as comfortably as others." Appealing to the spirit of the American Revolution, which had destroyed the aristocracy of birth, they called for a new revolution to destroy the aristocracy of capital. Armed with this artisan-republican ideology, in 1836 union men organized nearly fifty strikes for higher wages.

Agitation for workers' rights prompted strikes by women textile operatives. Competition in the industry was fierce because the output of cotton cloth increased at a rate of 5 percent a year while its price fell by more than 1 percent a year. To ward off bankruptcy employers reduced workers' wages and imposed more stringent work rules. In 1828 women mill workers in Dover, New Hampshire, struck against new rules, winning some relief; six years later more than 800 Dover women walked out to protest wage cuts. In Lowell, Massachusetts, 2,000 women operatives backed a strike by withdrawing their savings from an employer-owned bank. The *Boston Transcript* reported that "one of the leaders mounted a pump, and made a flaming . . . speech on the rights of women and the iniquities of the 'monied aristocracy.'" When conditions did not improve, young New England women refused to enter the mills, and impoverished Irish (and later French Canadian) immigrants took their places. Many of the new textile workers were men, foreshadowing the emergence of a predominately male system of factory labor (see Chapter 17).

By the 1850s workers faced yet another threat to their jobs. As machines produced more goods, the supply of available products exceeded the demand for them, prompting employers to lay off or dismiss workers. One episode of overproduction preceded the Panic of 1857—a financial crisis sparked by excess railroad investments—and resulted in a major recession. Unemployment rose to 10 percent, reminding Americans of the social costs of the new—and otherwise very successful—system of industrial production.

The Expansion of Markets

As American factories and farms turned out more goods, merchants and legislators sought faster and cheaper ways to get those products to consumers—setting in motion the Market Revolution. Beginning in the 1820s they promoted the construction of a massive system of canals and roads to link the Atlantic coast states with those in the trans-Appalachian West. By 1860 nearly one-third of the nation's people lived in the midwestern states (the five states carved out of the Northwest Territory—Ohio, Indiana, Illinois, Michigan, and Wisconsin—along with Missouri, Iowa, and Minnesota), where they created a complex society and economy that increasingly resembled that of the Northeast.

MIGRATION TO THE SOUTHWEST AND THE MIDWEST

After 1820 vast numbers of men and women migrated to the west, following in the footsteps of the thousands who had already left the seaboard states (see Map 10.1). Abandoned farms and homes dotted the countryside of the Carolinas, Vermont,

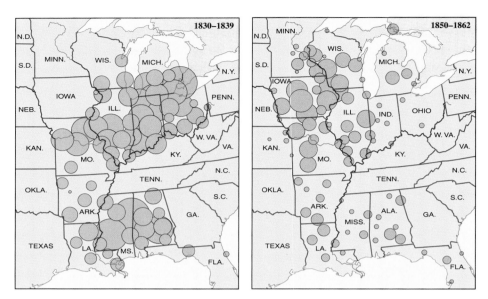

MAP 10.1
Western Land Sales, 1830s and 1850s

The federal government opened land offices along the frontier to sell farmland to settlers. Each circle centers on a land office, and the size of the circle reflects the relative amount of land sold at that office. In the 1830s land sales boomed in the Old Northwest (especially Indiana, Michigan, and Illinois) and in the Old Southwest (Alabama and Mississippi). By the 1850s the demand for land centered in the upper Mississippi River Valley (particularly Iowa and Wisconsin).

and New Hampshire. "It is useless to seek to excite patriotic emotions" for one's state of birth, complained an easterner, "when self-interest speaks so loudly." Some migrant families wanted to acquire enough land to settle their children on nearby farms, recreating traditional rural communities. Others were more entrepreneurial and hoped for greater profits from the fertile soil of the West.

As in the past the new pioneers migrated in three great streams. In the South plantation owners encouraged by the voracious demand for raw cotton moved more slaves into the Old Southwest (see Chapter 8), expanding the cotton kingdom in Louisiana, Mississippi, and Alabama, and pushing on to Missouri (1821) and Arkansas (1836). "The Alabama Feaver rages here with great violence," a North Carolina planter remarked, "and has carried off vast numbers of our Citizens."

Small-scale farmers from the upper South, especially Virginia and Kentucky, created a second stream as they crossed the Ohio River into the Northwest Territory. Some of these migrants were fleeing planter-dominated slave states. In a free community, thought Peter Cartwright, a Methodist lay preacher from southwestern Kentucky, "I would be entirely clear of the evil of slavery . . . [and] could raise my children to work where work was not thought a degradation." These southerners introduced corn and hog farming to the southern regions of Ohio, Indiana, and Illinois.

A third stream of migrants continued to flow from the overcrowded farms of New England. Thousands of settlers poured first into upstate New York and then into the fertile farmlands of the Old Northwest, establishing wheat farms throughout the Great Lakes Basin: northern Ohio, northern Illinois, Michigan (admitted in 1837), Iowa (1846), and Wisconsin (1848).

To meet the demand for cheap land, in 1820 Congress reduced the price of federal land from $2.00 an acre to $1.25—just enough to cover the cost of surveying and sale. For $100 a farmer could buy 80 acres, the minimum required under federal law. Many American families saved enough in a few years to make the minimum purchase and used money from the sale of an old farm to finance the move. By 1860 the population center of American society had shifted significantly to the west.

THE TRANSPORTATION REVOLUTION FORGES REGIONAL TIES

To enhance the "common-wealth" of their citizens the federal and state governments took measures to create a larger market. Since the 1790s they had chartered private companies to build toll-charging turnpikes in well-populated areas and subsidized road construction in the West. The most significant feat was the National Road, which started in Cumberland, Maryland, passed Wheeling (then in Virginia) in 1818, crossed the Ohio River in 1833, and reached Vandalia, Illinois, in 1839 (see Map 10.2). The National Road and other interregional highways mostly carried migrants and their heavily loaded wagons to the West and herds of livestock to the East; road travel was too slow and expensive to serve as a means of carrying manufactured goods and farm crops.

To exchange these goods Americans developed a water-borne transportation system of unprecedented size, complexity, and cost, beginning with the Erie Canal. When the New York legislature approved the building of the canal in 1817, no artificial waterway in the United States was longer than 28 miles—a reflection of their huge capital cost and the lack of American engineering expertise. The New York project had three things in its favor: the vigorous support of New York City merchants, who wanted access to western markets; the backing of New York's governor, DeWitt Clinton, who persuaded the legislature to finance the waterway from tax revenues, tolls, and bond sales to foreign investors; and the relative gentleness of the terrain west of Albany. Even so, the task was enormous. Workers—many of them Irish immigrants—had to dig out millions of cubic yards of soil, quarry thousands of tons of rock to build huge locks to raise and lower boats, and construct vast reservoirs to ensure a steady supply of water. The first great engineering project in American history, the Erie Canal altered the ecology and the economy of an entire region.

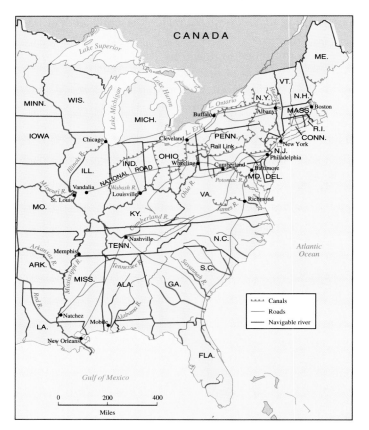

M A P 10.2
The Transportation Revolution: Roads and Canals, 1820–1850

By 1850 the United States had an efficient transportation system based on roads, natural waterways, and canals. Short canals and navigable rivers carried cotton, tobacco, and other products from the upcountry of the seaboard states into the Atlantic commercial system. Major canals—the Erie, Chesapeake and Ohio, and Pennsylvania Mainline—linked major seaport cities to the vast trans-Appalachian region, and a set of regional canals connected most of the Great Lakes region to the Ohio and Mississippi Rivers and New Orleans.

The Erie Canal was an instant success. The first section, a stretch of 75 miles opened in 1819, immediately generated enough revenue to repay its cost. When the canal was completed in 1825, a 40-foot-wide ribbon of water stretched 364 miles from the Lake Erie port of Buffalo to Albany, where it linked up with the Hudson River for a 150-mile trip to New York City. One-hundred-ton freight barges pulled by two horses moved along the canal at a steady 24 miles a day, greatly accelerating the flow of goods and cutting transportation costs. On New York's roads it took four horses to pull a 1-ton wagon 12 miles in a day.

The Erie Canal brought prosperity to central and western New York, carrying wheat and meat from farming communities in the interior to eastern cities and foreign markets. In 1818 the mills in Rochester had processed only 26,000 barrels of flour from the wheat grown by nearby farmers; ten years later the number soared to 200,000 barrels, and in 1840 to 500,000 barrels. After a trip on the canal the novelist Nathaniel Hawthorne suggested that its water "must be the most fertilizing of all fluids, for it causes towns with their masses of brick and stone, their churches and theaters, their business and hubbub, their luxury and refinement, their gay dames and polished citizens, to spring up." The canal also linked the economies of the Northeast and the Midwest. Northeastern manufacturers provided clothing, boots, and farm equipment to farm families in the Great Lakes Basin and the Ohio Valley. In payment the farmers sent grain, cattle, and hogs as well as raw materials (such as leather, wool, and hemp) to the East.

The spectacular benefits of the Erie Canal prompted a national canal boom (see Map 10.2). Civic and business leaders in Philadelphia and Baltimore proposed their own waterways to compete for the trade of the West. Copying New York's fiscal innovations they persuaded their state governments to invest directly in canal companies or force state-chartered banks to do so. They also won state guarantees for their bonds, thereby encouraging British and Dutch investors to buy them. Indeed, foreign investors provided almost three-quarters of the $400 million invested in canals by 1840. Soon these waterways connected the Midwest with the great port cities of New York (via the Erie and Pennsylvania Canals) and New Orleans (via the Ohio and Mississippi Rivers).

The steamboat, another product of the industrial age, ensured the success of this vast transportation system. The engineer-inventor Robert Fulton had built the first American steamboat, the *Clermont,* which he navigated up the Hudson in 1807. However, the first steamboats consumed huge amounts of wood or coal and could not navigate shallow western rivers. During the 1820s engineers broadened the hulls of these boats, thereby enlarging their cargo capacity and giving them a shallower draft. This improved design cut the cost of upstream river transport in half and dramatically increased the flow of goods, people, and news into the interior. In 1830 a traveler or a letter from New York could go by water to Buffalo and Pittsburgh in less than a week and to Detroit and St. Louis in two weeks. Thirty years earlier the same journeys, by road or sail, had taken twice as long.

The rapid emergence of this national system of transportation was encouraged by the Supreme Court headed by John Marshall, which struck down state controls over interstate commerce. In the crucial case of *Gibbons v. Ogden* (1824) the Court voided a New York law that created a monopoly on steamboat travel into New York City by ruling that the federal government had paramount authority over interstate commerce (see Chapter 8). This decision meant that no local or state monopolies— or tariffs—would impede the flow of goods and services across the nation.

Another product of industrial technology—the railroad—created close ties between the Northeast and the Midwest (see Map 10.3). As late as 1852 canals were

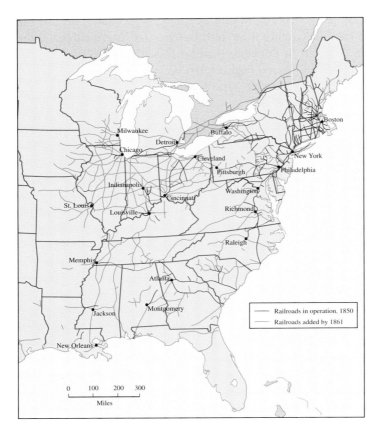

M AP 10.3
Railroads of the North and South, 1850–1860

In the decade before the Civil War the rapid construction of railroads provided the Northeast and the Midwest with extensive and dense transportation systems that stimulated economic development. The South built a much simpler system. In all regions railroad lines used different track gauges, hindering the efficient flow of goods (and, during the Civil War, of military supplies).

carrying twice the tonnage of railroads, but over the next six years track mileage increased dramatically and railroads became the main carriers of freight. The Erie Railroad, the Pennsylvania Railroad, and other trunk lines connected New York City, Philadelphia, and Boston to Cleveland and Chicago, serviced by a vast network of locomotive and freight car repair shops. Each year more and more midwestern grain moved east by rail rather than south by barge down the Ohio and Mississippi Rivers.

Tied to one another by the steel rails that ran along the route of New England migration, the Midwest and the Northeast increasingly resembled each other in ethnic composition, cultural values, and technical skills. The first migrants to the Midwest had relied on manufactured goods made in Britain or in the Northeast. They bought high-quality shovels and spades fabricated at the Delaware Iron Works, axes forged in Connecticut factories, and steel horseshoes manufactured in Troy, New York. By the 1830s midwestern entrepreneurs were producing many of these goods. As a blacksmith in Grand Detour, Illinois, John Deere made his first steel plow out of old saws in 1837; ten years later he opened a factory in Moline that used mass-production techniques. His steel plows, superior in strength to the cast-iron model developed earlier in New York by Jethro Wood, soon dominated the midwestern market. Other midwestern companies—McCormick and Hussey—mass-produced self-raking reapers that allowed a farmer to harvest twelve acres of grain a day (rather than the two or three acres he could cut by hand).

The maritime commercial links between the Northeast and the South did not produce a similar social and economic order in those regions. Southern investors concentrated their resources in cotton and slaves; by the 1840s the South was producing more than two-thirds of the world's cotton and accounted for almost two-thirds of the total value of American exports. Planters used the profits from the cotton trade to buy manufactures from the Northeast and Britain; only Richmond, Virginia, developed as an important industrial center. Lacking cities, factories, and highly trained workers, the South remained a predominantly agricultural economy and did not provide a majority of its people with a rising standard of living. In 1860 the per capita income was $141 in the North but only $103 in the South. The national system of commerce had accentuated the agricultural character of the South even as it helped to create a diversified economy in the Northeast and the Midwest.

THE GROWTH OF CITIES AND TOWNS

The expansion of industry and trade in the 1830s led to a dramatic increase in the urban population. In 1820 there were only 58 towns in the nation with more than 2,500 inhabitants; by 1840 there were 126, located mostly in the Northeast and Midwest. During those two decades the total number of urban residents grew fourfold, from 443,000 to 1,844,000.

The most rapid growth occurred in the new industrial towns that sprang up along the fall line. In 1822 the Boston Manufacturing Company built a new complex of mills in East Chelmsford, Massachusetts, quickly transforming the sleepy Merrimack River village into the bustling town of Lowell. Hartford, Connecticut, Trenton, New Jersey, and Wilmington, Delaware, also became urban centers as mill owners exploited their water power and recruited workers from the surrounding countryside.

Western commercial cities such as New Orleans, Pittsburgh, Cincinnati, and Louisville grew almost as rapidly. The initial expansion of these cities resulted from their location at points where goods were transferred from one mode of transport, such as canal boats or farmers' wagons, to another, such as steamboats or sailing vessels. As the midwestern population grew during the 1830s and 1840s, St. Louis,

Rochester, Buffalo, and Detroit emerged as dynamic centers of commerce. Merchants and bankers settled there, developing the marketing, provisioning, and financial services that were essential to farmers and small-town merchants in the hinterland.

Within a few decades these western commercial hubs—joined by Cleveland and Chicago—became manufacturing centers as well. Exploiting these cities' location as key junctions for railroad lines and steamboats, entrepreneurs established flour mills, packing plants, and docks, and provided work for hundreds of artisans and laborers. In 1846 Cyrus McCormick moved his reaper factory from western Virginia to Chicago to be closer to his midwestern customers. St. Louis and Chicago were the fastest-growing boom towns, and by 1860 had become the nation's third and fourth largest cities, respectively, after New York and Philadelphia.

Yet the old Atlantic seaports—Boston, Philadelphia, Baltimore, Charleston, and especially New York—remained important for their foreign commerce and increasingly as centers of finance and manufacturing. In 1817 New York merchants founded the New York Stock Exchange, which soon became the nation's chief market for securities. The New York metropolis grew at a phenomenal rate, diversifying into small-scale manufacturing and becoming the center of the ready-made clothing industry, which relied on the labor of thousands of low-paid seamstresses. "The wholesale clothing establishments are . . . absorbing the business of the country," a "Country Tailor" complained to the *New York Tribune*, "casting many an honest and hardworking man out of employment [and allowing] . . . the large cities to swallow up the small towns."

New York's growth stemmed primarily from its control of foreign trade. It had the best harbor in the United States, and ocean-going vessels could sail or steam up the Hudson River to Albany and the Erie Canal. The city's merchants exploited these natural advantages. In 1818 four Quaker merchants founded the Black Ball Line, a service that operated on a regular schedule and carried cargo, people, and mail between New York and the European ports of Liverpool, London, and Le Havre. New York merchants also gained an unassailable lead in commerce with the newly independent Latin American nations of Brazil, Peru, and Venezuela. New York–based traders also took over the cotton trade by offering finance, insurance, and shipping to cotton exporters in southern ports. And, by persuading the state government to build the Erie Canal, the city's merchants acquired a dominant position in the export of western grain to European markets. By 1840 the port of New York handled almost two-thirds of foreign imports and almost half of all foreign trade.

Changes in the Social Structure

The Industrial and Market Revolutions transformed the material lives of many Americans, allowing them to live in larger houses, cook on iron stoves, and wear better-made clothes. But the new economic order created distinct social classes: a wealthy industrial and commercial elite, a substantial urban middle class, and a mass of propertyless wage earners. By creating a class-divided society industrialization posed a momentous challenge to American republican ideals.

THE BUSINESS ELITE

Before industrialization white American society had been divided into various ranks, with "notables" ruling over the "lower orders." But in rural society the different ranks shared a common culture: gentlemen farmers talked easily with yeomen about crop yields, while their wives conversed about the art of quilting. In the South humble tenants and aristocratic slaveowners shared the same amusements: gambling, cockfighting, and horse racing. Rich and poor attended the same Quaker meetinghouse or Presbyterian church. "Almost everyone eats, drinks, and dresses in the same way," a European visitor to Hartford, Connecticut, reported in 1798, "and one can see the most obvious inequality only in the dwellings."

The Industrial Revolution shattered this traditional order and created a society of classes, each with its own culture. The new economic system pulled many Americans into cities and made a few of them—the business elite of merchants, manufacturers, bankers, and landlords—very rich. In 1800 the top 10 percent of the nation's families owned about 40 percent of the wealth; by 1860 the wealthiest 10 percent owned nearly 70 percent. In the cities the richest 1 percent of the population held more than 40 percent of all tangible property—such as land and buildings—and an even higher share of intangible property—such as stocks and bonds.

Government tax policies allowed this accumulation of wealth. The U.S. Treasury raised most of its revenue from tariffs—taxes on imported goods such as textiles that were purchased mostly by ordinary citizens. State and local governments also favored the wealthier classes. They usually taxed real estate and tangible personal property (such as furniture, tools, and machinery) but almost never taxed the stocks and bonds owned by the rich or the inheritances they passed on to their children.

Over time the wealthiest families consciously set themselves apart. Master artisans had labored side by side with journeymen and apprentices in small shops, but merchants and manufacturers were managers, issuing orders to hundreds of outworkers or factory operatives. Similarly, by the 1830s most employers had stopped providing their workers with housing and had moved themselves to distinct upper-class neighborhoods. Many American cities became class-segregated communities.

THE MIDDLE CLASS

Standing between wealthy owners and entrepreneurs at one end of the social spectrum and nonpropertied wage-earners at the other was a growing middle class. In the words of a Boston printer and publisher, the "middling class" was made up of "the farmers, the mechanics, the manufacturers, the traders, who carry on profes-sionally the ordinary operations of buying, selling, and exchanging merchandize." As cities and industry expanded, other professional groups—such as building con-tractors, lawyers, and surveyors—found their services in great demand and finan-cially profitable. Middle-class business owners, employees, and professionals were most numerous in the Northeast, where they numbered about 30 percent of the population in 1840, but they could be found in every American town and village, even in the agrarian South.

The size, wealth, and cultural influence of the middle class continued to grow, fueled by a dramatic rise in prosperity. Between 1830 and the Panic of 1857, the per capita income of Americans increased by about 2.5 percent a year, a remark-able rate that the United States has never since matched. This surge in income, along with the availability of inexpensive mass-produced goods, facilitated the creation of a distinct middle-class culture, especially in urban areas of the Northeast. Middle-class husbands had sufficient earnings so that their wives did not have to seek paid work. Typically these men saved about 15 percent of their income, depositing it in banks and then using it to buy a well-built house in a "respectable part of town." They purchased handsome clothes for themselves and their families and drove about town in smart carriages. Their wives and daughters were literate and accomplished, buying books and pianos as well as commodious furniture for their front parlors. And they filled their residences with the products of industrial technology: furnaces that heated water for bathing and for radiators that warmed entire rooms; stoves with ovens, including broilers and movable grates; treadle-operated sewing machines; and iceboxes, which ice-company wagons filled daily, to preserve perishable food.

If material comfort was one distinguishing mark of the middle class, moral and mental discipline was another. Seeking to pass on their status to their children, suc-cessful parents usually provided them with a high school education (in an era when most white children received only five years of schooling). Ambitious parents were equally concerned with their children's character and stressed discipline, morality, and hard work. Puritans and other American Protestants had long believed that work in an earthly "calling" was a duty people owed to God. Now the business elite and the middle class gave this idea a secular twist: they celebrated work as socially beneficial, the key to a higher standard of living for the nation and social mobility for the individual.

Benjamin Franklin gave classical expression to the secular work ethic in his *Autobiography,* which was published in full in 1818 and immediately found a huge audience. Heeding Franklin's suggestion that an industrious man would become a rich one, tens of thousands of young American men worked hard, saved their money, adopted temperate habits, and practiced honesty in their business dealings. Countless magazines, children's books, self-help manuals, and novels taught the same lessons. The ideal of the "self-made man" became a central theme of Ameri-can popular culture. Just as a rural-producer ethic had united the social ranks in

Middle-Class Family Life, 1836

The family of Azariah Caverly boasted many of the amenities of middle-class life—handsome clothes, finely decorated furniture, and a striking floor covering. Revealing the social conventions of the time, the husband and his son hold a newspaper and a square, symbolizing the worlds of commerce and industry, while the wife and her daughter are pictured next to a Bible, indicating their domestic and moral vocation. (New York State Historical Association, Cooperstown, New York)

pre-1800 America, this new goal of personal achievement and social mobility tied together the upper and middle classes of the new industrializing society.

THE NEW URBAN POOR

As thoughtful members of the business elite surveyed the emerging social landscape, they suggested that a yeomanlike society made up of independent families no longer seemed possible or even advisable. "Entire independence ought not to be wished for," Ithamar A. Beard, the paymaster of the Hamilton Manufacturing Company, told a mechanics' association in 1827. "In large manufacturing towns, many more must fill subordinate stations and must be under the immediate direction and control of a master or superintendent, than in the farming towns."

Beard had a point. By 1840 as many as half the nation's free workers were laboring for others rather than for themselves. The bottom 10 percent of this wage-earning labor force consisted of casual workers—those hired on a short-term basis for the most arduous jobs. Poor women washed clothes, while their husbands and sons carried lumber and bricks for construction projects, loaded ships and wagons, and dug out dirt and stones to build canals. Most casual laborers owned little property except the clothes they wore. During business depressions they bore the brunt of unemployment, and even in the best of times their jobs were unpredictable, seasonal, and dangerous.

Other laborers had greater security of employment, but few were prospering. In Massachusetts in 1825 the daily wage of an unskilled worker was about two-thirds that of a mechanic; two decades later it was less than half as much. The 18,000 women who made men's clothing in New York City in the 1850s were even worse off, averaging less than $80 a year. These meager wages paid for food and rent and not much more, so many wage-earners were unable to take advantage of the rapidly falling prices of manufactured goods. Only the most fortunate working families could afford to educate their children, pay the fees required for an apprenticeship, or accumulate small dowries so that their daughters could marry men with better prospects. Most families sent their children out to work, and the death of one of the parents often threw the survivors into dire poverty. As a charity worker noted, "What can a bereaved widow do, with 5 or 6 little children, destitute of every means of support but what her own hands can furnish (which in a general way does not amount to more than 25 cents a day)."

By the 1830s most urban factory workers and unskilled laborers resided in well-defined neighborhoods. Single men and women lived in large, crowded boarding-houses, while families inhabited tiny apartments carved out of the living quarters, basements, and attics of small houses. As urban populations soared, developers squeezed a number of buildings, interspersed with outhouses and connected by foul-smelling courtyards, onto a single lot.

Living in such distressing conditions, many wage-earners turned to the dubious solace of alcohol. Alcohol had long been an integral part of American life; beer and rum had lubricated ceremonies, work breaks, barn-raisings, and games. But during the 1820s urban wage-earners led Americans to new heights of alcohol consumption. Aiding them were western farmers, who distilled corn and rye into gin and whiskey as a low-cost way to get their grain to market. By 1830 the per capita consumption of liquor had risen to more than 5 gallons a year, over three times present-day levels.

Drinking patterns changed as well. Workers in many craft unions "swore off" liquor, convinced that it would undermine their skilled work as well as their health and finances. But other workers began to drink on the job—and not just during the traditional 11 A.M. and 4 P.M. "refreshers." Journeymen used apprentices to smuggle whiskey into shops, and then, as one baker recalled, "One man was stationed at the window to watch, while the rest drank." Grogshops and tippling houses appeared on almost every block in working-class districts. The saloons became focal points for crimes, including assault and vandalism, and urban disorder. Fueled by unrestrained drinking, a fistfight among young men one night could turn into a brawl the second night and a full-scale riot the third. The urban police forces, consisting of low-paid watchmen and untrained constables, were unable to contain the lawlessness.

THE BENEVOLENT EMPIRE

The disorder and lawlessness among urban wage-earners sparked concern among well-to-do Americans. Inspired by the religious ideal of benevolence—doing good for the less fortunate—they created a number of organizations that historians refer to collectively as the "Benevolent Empire." During the 1820s Congregational and Presbyterian ministers united with like-minded merchants and their wives to launch a program of social reform and regulation. Their purpose, announced Presbyterian minister Lyman Beecher of Boston, was to restore "the moral government of God." The reformers introduced new forms of moral discipline into their own lives and tried to infuse them into the lives of working people. They would regulate popular behavior—by persuasion if possible, by law if necessary.

Although the Benevolent Empire targeted age-old evils such as drunkenness, prostitution, and crime, its methods were new. Instead of relying on church sermons and moral suasion by community leaders, the reformers set out to institutionalize charity and combat evil in a systematic fashion. They established large-scale organizations—the Prison Discipline Society and the American Society for the Promotion of Temperance, among many others. Each had a managing staff, a network of volunteers and chapters, and a newspaper.

Together, these groups set out to improve society. First they encouraged people to lead well-disciplined lives, campaigning for temperance in drinking habits and an end to prostitution. Beyond that they persuaded local governments to ban carnivals of drink and dancing, such as the Negro Election Day festivities in New England, which had been enjoyed by whites as well as blacks. Second, they created new institutions to control people who were threats to society and to assist those who were unable to handle their own affairs. Reformers provided homes of refuge for the abandoned children of the poor, removed the insane from isolation in attics and cellars and placed them in newly built asylums, and campaigned for an end to corporal punishment for criminals and for their rehabilitation through moral training in penitentiaries.

Women played an increasingly active role in the Benevolent Empire. Since the 1790s upper-class women had sponsored a number of charitable organizations, such as the Society for the Relief of Poor Widows with Small Children, founded in New York by Isabella Graham, a devout Presbyterian widow. By the 1820s Graham's society was assisting hundreds of widows and their children in New York City. Her daughter, Joanna Bethune, set up other charitable institutions, including the Orphan Asylum Society and the Society for the Promotion of Industry, which found hundreds of poor women jobs as spinners and seamstresses.

Some reformers came to believe that one of the greatest threats to the "moral government of God" was the decline of the traditional sabbath. As the pace of commercial activity accelerated after 1820, merchants and shippers began to conduct business on Sunday, since they did not want their goods and equipment to lie idle one day in every seven. To restore traditional values, in 1828 Lyman Beecher and other ministers formed the General Union for Promoting the Observance of the Christian Sabbath. General Union chapters sprang up—usually with women's auxiliaries—from Maine to the Ohio Valley. Seeking a symbolic issue to rally Christians to their cause, the General Union focused on a law Congress had enacted in 1810 allowing mail to be transported—though not delivered—on Sunday. To secure its repeal the Union adopted the tactics of a political party, organizing rallies and circulating petitions. Its members also boycotted shipping companies that did business on the sabbath and campaigned for municipal laws forbidding games and festivals on the Lord's day.

Not everyone agreed with the program of the Benevolent Empire. Men who labored twelve or fourteen hours a day for six days a week refused to spend their one day of leisure in meditation and prayer. Shipping company managers demanded that the Erie Canal provide lockkeepers on Sundays and joined those Americans who argued that using boycotts and laws to enforce morality was "contrary to the free spirit of our institutions." And when the evangelical reformers proposed to teach Christianity to slaves, many white southerners were outraged. Such popular resistance or indifference limited the success of the Benevolent Empire. A different kind of message was required if religious reformers were to do more than preach to the already converted and discipline the already disciplined.

REVIVALISM AND REFORM

It was the Presbyterian minister Charles Grandison Finney who brought just such a message to Americans. Finney was not part of the traditional religious elite. Born into a poor farmer family in Connecticut, he hoped to join the new middle class as a lawyer. But in 1823 Finney underwent an intense conversion experience and decided to become a minister. Beginning in towns along the Erie Canal the young minister conducted emotional revival meetings that stressed conversion rather than instruction; what counted for Finney was the will to be saved. He maintained that God would welcome any sinner who submitted to the Holy Spirit. Finney's ministry drew on—and greatly accelerated—the Second Great Awakening, the wave of Protestant revivalism that had begun after the Revolution (see Chapter 9).

Finney's message that "God has made man a moral free agent" able to *choose* salvation was particularly attractive to members of the new middle class, who had already chosen to improve their material lives. But he became famous for converting those at the ends of the social spectrum: the haughty rich, who had placed themselves above God, and the abject poor, who seemed lost to drink, sloth, and misbehavior. His goal was to humble the pride of the rich and relieve the shame of the poor by celebrating their common fellowship in Christ and identifying them spiritually with earnest, pious middle-class respectability.

Finney's most spectacular triumph came in 1830, when he moved his revivals from small towns to Rochester, New York, a major Erie Canal city. For six months he preached every day and added a new tactic—group prayer meetings in family homes—in which women played an active role. Finney's wife, Lydia, and other pious middle-class women carried the message to the wives of the unconverted, often while their disapproving husbands were at work. Soon, one convert reported, "You could not go upon the street and hear any conversation, except upon religion."

Finney won over the influential merchants and manufacturers of Rochester, who pledged to reform their lives and those of their workers. They would attend church, join the "Cold Water" movement by giving up intoxicating beverages, and work steady hours. To encourage their employees to follow suit, wealthy businessmen founded a new Free Presbyterian Church—"free" because members did not have to pay for pew space. Other evangelical Protestants founded two similar churches to serve canal laborers, transients, and the settled poor. To reinforce the work of the churches, Rochester's business elite established a savings bank to encourage thrift, Sunday schools for poor children, and the Female Charitable Society to provide relief for the families of the unemployed.

Revivalists in cities and towns from New England to the Midwest duplicated the success of the Protestant crusade in Rochester. Dozens of younger ministers— Baptist and Methodist as well as Congregationalist and Presbyterian—adopted Finney's evangelical message and techniques. In New York City, where Finney established himself after leaving Rochester, the wealthy silk merchants Arthur and Lewis Tappan founded a magazine, *The Christian Evangelist,* that promoted his ideas across the country. The success of the revival "has been so general and thorough," concluded a General Assembly of Presbyterians, "that the whole customs of society have changed."

The temperance movement proved to be the most effective arena for national evangelical reform. In 1832 evangelicals gained control of the American Temperance Society; within a few years it had grown to 2,000 chapters with more than 200,000 members. The society adapted the methods that had worked so well in the revivals—group confession and prayer, a focus on the family and the spiritual role of women, and sudden, emotional conversion—and took them into virtually every town in the North and rural hamlet in the South. On one day in New York City in 1841, 4,000 people took the temperance "pledge" (see American Voices, "The Demon Rum"). The average annual consumption of spirits fell from about 5 gallons per person in 1830 to about 2 gallons in 1845.

Evangelical reformers reinforced the traditional moral foundations of the American work ethic. Laziness and drinking could not be cured by Benjamin Franklin's patient methods of self-discipline, they argued. Instead, people had to experience the profound change of heart achieved only in religious conversion. Then even the poorest family could look forward to a prosperous new life. Through such

AMERICAN VOICES

The Demon Rum

JOHN GOUGH

J ohn Gough (1817–1886) was twelve years old when his impoverished English parents sent him to America, where he found work as a bookbinder in New York City—and eventually turned to drink. In 1842, at age twenty-five, Gough converted to temperance. For the next four decades he used his eloquence as a lecturer to command high fees and persuade thousands to join the temperance movement.

Will it be believed that I again sought refuge in rum? Yet so it was. Scarcely had I recovered from the fright, than I sent out, procured a pint of rum, and drank it all in less than an hour. And now came upon me many terrible sensations. Cramps attacked me in my limbs, which racked me with agony; and my temples throbbed as if they would burst. . . . Then came on the drunkard's remorseless torturer—delirium tremens, in all its terrors, attacked me. For three days I endured more agony than pen could describe. . . . I was at one time surrounded by millions of monstrous spiders, that crawled slowly over every limb, whilst the beaded drops of perspiration would start to my brow, and my limbs would shiver until the bed rattled. . . . I was falling—falling swiftly as an arrow—far down into some terrible abyss. . . .

By the mercy of God, I survived this awful seizure; and when I rose, a weak, broken-down man, and surveyed my ghastly features in the glass, I thought of my mother, and asked myself how I had obeyed the instructions received from her lips. . . . Oh! how keen were my rebukes; and, in the excitement of the moment, I resolved to lead a better life, and abstain from the accursed cup.

For about a month, terrified by what I had suffered, I adhered to my resolution; then my wife came home, and, in my joy at her return, I flung my good resolutions to the wind, and, foolishly fancying that I could now restrain my appetite . . . I took a glass of brandy. That glass aroused the slumbering demon, who would not be satisfied by so tiny a libation. . . . The night of my wife's return, I went to bed intoxicated.

SOURCE: David Brion Davis, ed., *Antebellum American Culture: An Interpretive Anthology* (Lexington, MA: Heath, 1979), pp. 402–03.

means evangelical Protestantism reinforced the sense of common identity between the business elite and the middle class and implanted a commitment to individual enterprise and moral discipline among many wage-earners. Religion and the ideology of social mobility served as powerful cement, holding society together in the face of the massive changes brought by the spread of industrial enterprise and the market economy.

IMMIGRATION AND CULTURAL CONFLICT

Between 1840 and 1860 about 2 million Irish immigrants, 1.5 million Germans, and 750,000 Britons poured into the United States, placing new strains on the American social order. Most immigrants avoided the South because they opposed slavery, shunned blacks, or feared competition from enslaved workers. Many German migrants moved to states in the Midwest such as Wisconsin, Iowa, and Missouri, where they made up a majority of the settlers in many areas, while other Germans and most of the Irish settled in the Northeast, where by 1860 they accounted for nearly one-third of white adults.

The most prosperous immigrants were the British, many of whom were professionals, propertied farmers, and skilled workers. Likewise, the majority of German immigrants came from farming and artisan families and could afford to buy land in America. The poorest migrants were peasants and laborers from Ireland, who fled from a famine caused by severe overpopulation and devastating blight on the potato crop. Arriving in dire poverty Irish peasants found new homes in the cities of New England and New York, taking low-skilled, low-paying jobs as laborers in factories and on construction projects and as servants in private residences. Many Irish immigrants lived in crowded tenements with primitive sanitation systems and were the first to die when epidemics swept through American cities. In the summer of 1849 a cholera epidemic took the lives of thousands in St. Louis and New York, mostly poor immigrants.

In times of hardship and sorrow immigrants turned to their churches. Many Germans and virtually all the Irish were devout Catholics, and they fueled the growth of the Catholic Church. In the 1840s there were 16 Catholic dioceses and 700 churches in the United States, and the number increased to 45 dioceses and 3,000 churches by 1860. Under the guidance of their priests and bishops the Irish built an impressive network of institutions: charitable societies, orphanages, militia companies, parochial schools, and political organizations that helped them maintain their cultural identity.

When the first Irish immigrants arrived in the 1830s, they were greeted by a rash of anti-Catholic publications. One of the most militant critics of Catholicism was Samuel F. B. Morse (who would later make the first commercial adaptation of the telegraph). In 1834 Morse published *Foreign Conspiracy against the Liberties of the United States,* which warned of a Catholic threat to American republican institutions. Morse believed that Catholic immigrants would obey the dictates of Pope Pius IX, who had condemned republicanism as a false political ideology based on the sovereignty of the people rather than the sovereignty of God. Republican-minded Protestants of many denominations shared Morse's fears, and *Foreign Conspiracy* became their textbook.

The social tensions stemming from industrialization intensified anti-Catholic sentiment. Unemployed Protestant mechanics and factory workers joined mobs that attacked Catholics; other Protestants organized Native American Clubs, which called for limits on immigration, the restriction of public office to native-born citizens, and the exclusive use of the Protestant version of the Bible in public schools. Many reformers supported the anti-Catholic movement for reasons of public policy—to prevent the diversion of tax resources to Catholic schools and to oppose alcoholic abuse by many Irish men.

In almost every large northeastern city religious and cultural conflicts led in violence. In 1834 in Charlestown, Massachusetts, a quarrel between Catholic laborers repairing a convent owned by the Ursuline order of nuns and Protestant workers in a neighboring brickyard turned into a full-scale riot and the burning of the convent. In Philadelphia the violence peaked in 1844 when the Catholic bishop persuaded public school officials to use the Catholic as well as the Protestant ver-

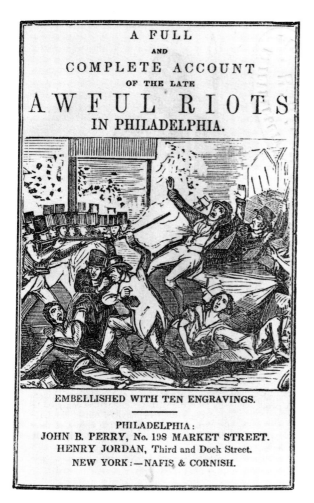

An Anti-Catholic Riot

When riots against Irish Catholics broke out in Philadelphia in 1844, the governor of Pennsylvania called out the militia to protect Catholic churches and residential neighborhoods. In the foreground two Protestant rioters, depicted by the artist as well-dressed gentlemen, attack an Irish family with sticks, while in the background the militia exchanges musket fire with other members of the mob. (Library Company of Philadelphia)

TIMELINE

1790	Samuel Slater opens a spinning mill in Providence, Rhode Island.	**1824**	*Gibbons v. Ogden* promotes interstate trade.
1807	Robert Fulton launches the *Clermont*, the first American steamboat.	**1830s**	Growth of commercial cities Labor movement gains strength
1814	Boston Manufacturing Company opens a cotton mill in Waltham, Massachusetts.		Class-segregated cities Expansion of temperance movement Charles Grandison Finney leads
1817	Erie Canal begun; completed in 1825		revivals.
1818	Benjamin Franklin's *Autobiography* published.	**1837**	John Deere invents the steel plow. Panic of 1837; seven-year recession
1820	Minimum price of federal land reduced to $1.25 per acre		begins.
1820s	New England women become textile operatives. Building workers seek a ten-hour day. Rise of the Benevolent Empire	**1840s–1850s**	Irish and German immigration Expansion of railroads Rise of machine tool industry

sion of the Bible. Anti-Irish rioting incited by the city's Native American Clubs lasted for two months and escalated into open warfare between Protestants and the Pennsylvania militia.

Thus, even as economic revolution brought prosperity to many Americans, it divided the society along the lines of class and, by encouraging the influx of immigrants, created new ethnic and religious tensions. Differences of class and culture now split the North in much the same way that race and class had long divided the South. Yet overall the majority of white Americans shared a common commitment to a dynamic economic system based on private property and a vibrant political culture of democratic republicanism.

For Further Exploration

Stuart Weems Bruchey, *Enterprise: The Dynamic Economy of a Free People* (1990), offers a panoramic history of America's economy and explains its legal and political context. Another broad study is Charles C. Sellers, *The Market Revolution: Jacksonian America, 1815–1846* (1991), which focuses on social and cultural change and underlines the tensions between market capitalism and democratic politics. David Freeman Hawke, *Nuts and Bolts of the Past: A History of American Technology, 1776–1860* (1988), offers an entertaining account of technical progress and the often eccentric inventors who made it possible.

Stephen Aron, *How the West Was Lost: The Transformation of Kentucky from Daniel Boone to Henry Clay* (1996), explores the drama of economic and political conflict in the trans-Appalachian West, while Peter Way, *Common Labor: Workers and the Digging of North American Canals, 1780–1860* (1993), describes the deprivation and anger experienced by the men who dug the western canals. The appearance of a new urban society forms the background of Stuart M. Blumin's study of *The Emergence of the Middle Class: Social Experience in the American City, 1760–1900* (1989). In *Home and Work: Housework, Wages and the Ideology of Labor in the Early Republic* (1990), Jeanne Boydston takes a critical look at the impact of the market revolution and urban life on women's lives. W. J. Rorabaugh, *The Alcoholic Republic, an American Tradition* (1979), describes a society awash in liquor and the efforts of the temperance reformers to do something about it.

For the settlement of the Great Lakes region, log on to "Pioneering the Upper Midwest: Books from Michigan, Minnesota, and Wisconsin, 1820–1910" at <http://memory.loc.gov/ammem/umhtml/umhome.html>, for the full text of first-person accounts, biographies, and promotional literature from the collections of the Library of Congress. An excellent tool for tracking social changes is the United States Historical Census Data Browser <http://fisher.lib.virginia.edu/census>, which has mined the censuses (especially the rich returns for 1850 and 1860) for information on race, slavery, immigration, religion, and other topics.

Chapter 11

A DEMOCRATIC REVOLUTION
1820–1844

A Representative Democracy Is The Ordinance Of God.
—Petition for a new Virginia Constitution, 1815

If Americans believed their political institutions were ordained by God, visiting Europeans thought them the work of the Devil. "The gentlemen spit, talk of elections and the price of produce, and spit again," Mrs. Frances Trollope reported in *The Domestic Manners of the Americans* (1832). In her view American politics was the sport of party hacks who reeked of "whiskey and onions." Other European visitors used more refined language but they found little to praise. Harriet Martineau was "deeply disgusted" by the "prostitution of moral sentiment, the claptrap of praise and pathos" uttered by a leading Massachusetts politician, while Basil Hall could only shake his head in astonishment at the shallow arguments, the "conclusions in which nothing was concluded," that were advanced by the inept "farmers, shopkeepers, and country lawyers" who sat in the New York assembly.

The verdict was unanimous and negative. As the French aristocrat Alexis de Tocqueville put it in *Democracy in America* (1835): "the most able men in the United States are very rarely placed at the head of affairs," a result he ascribed to the character of democracy itself. Ordinary citizens were jealous of their intellectual superiors and so refused to elect them to office; moreover, most voters had little time to consider important policy issues and so they "assent to the clamor of a mountebank [charlatan] who knows the secret of stimulating [their] tastes."

The Europeans were witnesses to the unfolding of a Democratic Revolution in the United States. In the early years of the nation the slogan had been *republicanism*, rule by property owning "men of TALENTS and VIRTUE." By the 1820s and 1830s the watchword was becoming *democracy*, power exercised by party politicians elected by the people as a whole. "That the majority should govern was a fundamental maxim in all free governments," declared Martin Van Buren, the most talented of the new breed of middle-class professional politicians that had taken over the halls of government. The new party politicians were often crude and usually self-interested, but by uniting ordinary Americans in "election fever," they held together an increasingly fragmented social order.

The Rise of Popular Politics, 1820–1829

Expansion of the franchise was the most dramatic expression of the democratic revolution. Beginning in the late 1810s the states revised their constitutions to eliminate property qualifications, giving the franchise to nearly every farmer and wage earner. Nowhere else in the world did ordinary men have so much political power; in England, even after passage of the Reform Bill of 1832, only 600,000 out of 6 million men—a mere 10 percent—had the right to vote.

THE DECLINE OF THE NOTABLES AND THE RISE OF PARTIES

In America's traditional agricultural society wealthy notables—northern landlords, slaveowning planters, and seaport merchants—dominated the political system. As former Supreme Court Justice John Jay put it in 1810, "Those who own the country are the most fit persons to participate in the government of it." The notables managed local elections by building up an "interest": lending money to small farmers, giving business to storekeepers and artisans, and treating their workers and tenants to rum at election time. An outlay of £5 [about $20] for refreshments, according to an experienced poll watcher, "may produce about 100 votes." As Martin Van Buren, whose father was a tavern keeper, knew from personal experience, this gentry-dominated system excluded men of modest means who lacked wealth and "the aid of powerful family connections."

The first assaults on the traditional order in which ordinary people deferred to their social "betters" came in the Midwest and Southwest. As smallholding farmers and ambitious laborers settled the trans-Appalachian region, they broke free of control by the gentry; "no white man or woman will bear being called a servant," reported a traveler in Ohio. The constitutions of the new states of Indiana (1816), Illinois (1818), and Alabama (1819) prescribed a broad male franchise. Armed with the vote ordinary citizens usually elected middling men to local and state offices. A well-to-do migrant in Illinois was surprised to find that his plowman "was a colonel of militia, and a member of the legislature." Once in public office men from modest backgrounds listened to the demands of their ordinary constituents, enacting laws that restricted imprisonment for debt and kept taxes low.

To deter migration to the western states and unrest at home the elites who ran most eastern legislatures grudgingly accepted a broader franchise. Reformers in Maryland condemned property qualifications as a "tyranny" that endowed "one class of men with privileges which are denied to another," and so in 1810 the legislature extended the vote to all adult white men. By the mid-1820s only a few states—North Carolina, Virginia, Rhode Island—required the ownership of freehold property for voting. Others, such as Ohio and Louisiana, limited suffrage to men who paid taxes or served in the militia, but a majority of the states had instituted universal white manhood suffrage. Between 1818 and 1821 the eastern states of Connecticut, Massachusetts, and New York revised their entire constitutions, reapportioning legislatures on the basis of population and instituting more democratic forms of local government, such as the election (rather than the appointment) of judges and justices of the peace.

The politics of democracy was more complex and contentious than the politics of deference. Powerful entrepreneurs and speculators—notables and self-made men alike—demanded government assistance for their business enterprises and paid bribes to legislators to get it. Bankers sought charters and opposed limits on interest rates, while land speculators demanded the eviction of squatters and the building of roads and canals to enhance the value of their holdings. Other Americans turned to politics to advance religious and cultural causes. In 1828 evangelical Presbyterians in Utica, New York, campaigned for town ordinances to restrict secular activities on Sunday; in response a member of the local Universalist church attacked this effort at coercive reform and called for "Religious Liberty."

Political parties allowed the voices of such ordinary voters and interest groups to be heard. The founders of the American republic had condemned political "factions" and "parties" as antirepublican and refused to give parties a role in the new constitutional system. But as the power of notables declined, the political party emerged as the organizing force in the American system of government. The new parties were disciplined groups run by professional politicians from middle-class backgrounds, especially lawyers and journalists. To some observers the parties resembled the mechanical innovations of the Industrial Revolution, political "machines" that, like a well-designed textile loom, wove the diverse threads of social groups and economic interests into an elaborate tapestry—a coherent legislative program.

Martin Van Buren of New York was the chief architect—and advocate—of the emerging system of party government. Between 1817 and 1821 Van Buren created the first statewide political machine, the Albany Regency; a few years later he organized the first nationwide political party, the Jacksonian Democrats. Van Buren repudiated the republican principle that political parties were dangerous to the commonwealth. Indeed, he argued, the opposite was true: "All men of sense know that political parties are inseparable from free government" because they checked the government's "disposition to abuse power . . . [and] the passions, the ambition, and the usurpations of individuals."

One key to Van Buren's success as a politician was his systematic use of the *Albany Argus* and other party newspapers to promote a platform and drum up the vote. Patronage was even more important, for the awarding of state jobs gave Van Buren a greater "interest" than any landed notable—some 6,000 appointments to the legal bureaucracy of New York (judges, justices of the peace, sheriffs, deed commissioners, and coroners) carrying salaries and fees worth $1 million. Finally, Van Buren insisted on party discipline, requiring state legislators to follow the majority decisions of a party meeting, or *caucus*. On one crucial occasion, Van Buren pleaded with seventeen legislators to "magnanimously sacrifice individual preferences for the general good" and rewarded their party loyalty with patronage and a formal banquet where, an observer wrote, they were treated with "something approaching divine honors."

THE ELECTION OF 1824

The advance of political democracy disrupted the old system of national politics managed by leading notables. The aristocratic Federalist Party virtually disappeared, and the Republican Party broke up into competing factions. As the election of 1824 approached, no fewer than five candidates, all calling themselves Republicans, campaigned for the presidency. Three were veterans of President James Monroe's cabinet: Secretary of State John Quincy Adams, the son of John Adams; Secretary of War John C. Calhoun; and Secretary of the Treasury William H. Crawford. The fourth candidate was Henry Clay of Kentucky, the dynamic speaker of the House of Representatives, and the fifth was General Andrew Jackson, now a senator from Tennessee. Although a caucus of the Republicans in Congress had selected Crawford as the "official" nominee, the other candidates refused to accept that result.

Instead they introduced democracy to national politics by seeking support among ordinary voters. Thanks to democratic reforms, eighteen of the twenty-four states used popular elections (rather than a vote of the state legislature) to choose members of the electoral college. Thus, in three-quarters of the states the contest for the presidency depended directly on the votes of ordinary men.

The battle was closely fought. Thanks to his diplomatic success as secretary of state, John Quincy Adams enjoyed national recognition. Henry Clay framed his candidacy around the American System, a national program of tariffs and internal improvements to promote economic growth. Rejecting Clay's plan for an activist central government, William Crawford of Georgia promised strong support for the rights of the states, a position that enhanced his popularity in the South. Recognizing Crawford's strength in his home region, John C. Calhoun of South Carolina switched to the vice-presidential race and endorsed Andrew Jackson for the presidency.

As the hero of the Battle of New Orleans Jackson surged to prominence on the wave of nationalistic pride that flowed from the War of 1812. Born in the Carolina backcountry, Jackson had settled in Nashville, Tennessee, where he had formed ties to influential families through his marriage and his career as an attorney, cotton planter, and slaveowner. His reputation as a man of civic virtue and "plain solid republican utility" attracted many voters, and his rise from common origins fit the tenor of the new democratic age. Nominated for the presidency by the Tennessee legislature Jackson soon commanded nationwide support.

Still, Jackson's strong showing surprised most political leaders. He received 99 electoral votes; Adams, 84 votes; Crawford (having suffered a stroke during the campaign), 41; and Clay, 37 (Map 11.1). Since no candidate had received an absolute majority, the Constitution specified that the House of Representatives would choose

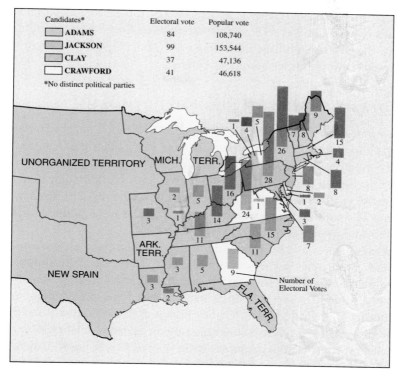

Candidates*	Electoral vote	Popular vote
ADAMS	84	108,740
JACKSON	99	153,544
CLAY	37	47,136
CRAWFORD	41	46,618

*No distinct political parties

MAP 11.1
The Election of 1824

In 1824 voting reflected regional allegiances. John Quincy Adams captured every electoral vote in New England and most of those in New York, home to many New England migrants. Henry Clay captured the western states of Ohio and Kentucky, and William Crawford garnered his votes in the South. Only Andrew Jackson claimed a national constituency, winning Pennsylvania and New Jersey in the East, Indiana and Illinois in the Midwest, and most of the South. In this last presidential election of the predemocratic era only 356,000 Americans voted, about 27 percent of the eligible electorate.

the president from among the three leading contenders. This procedure hurt Jackson, as many congressmen were horrified at the thought of a rough-hewn westerner in the White House and feared that this "military chieftain" would become a political tyrant. Personally out of the race Henry Clay used his powers as speaker to thwart Jackson's election. By the time the House met in February 1825, Clay had assembled a coalition of congressmen from New England and the Ohio Valley that voted Adams into the presidency. Adams showed his gratitude by appointing Clay secretary of state, the traditional steppingstone to the presidency.

Clay's appointment was a fatal mistake for both men. John C. Calhoun accused Adams of thwarting the popular will by using "the power and patronage of the

Executive" to select his successor. It was, he wrote, "the most dangerous stab, which the liberty of this country has yet received." Jacksonians in Congress, their numbers increased by the election results, condemned Clay for arranging this "corrupt bargain" and vowed he would never become president.

THE LAST NOTABLE PRESIDENT: JOHN QUINCY ADAMS

As president Adams called for bold national leadership. "The moral purpose of the Creator," he told Congress, was to use the president and every other public official to "improve the conditions of himself and his fellow men." To that end Adams embraced the American System of national economic development proposed by Henry Clay: (1) a protective tariff to stimulate manufacturing, (2) federally subsidized internal improvements (roads and canals) to aid commerce, and (3) a national bank to provide a uniform currency and control credit.

Adams's policies favored the business elite of the Northeast and also assisted entrepreneurs and commercial farmers in the Midwest. They won little support among southern planters, who opposed tariffs, and among smallholding farmers, who feared powerful banks. From his deathbed Thomas Jefferson condemned Adams for promoting "a single and splendid government of [a monied] aristocracy . . . riding and ruling over the plundered ploughman and beggared yeomanry." Other politicians objected on constitutional grounds. In 1817 President Madison had vetoed a Bonus Bill, proposed by Henry Clay and John C. Calhoun, that would have used the federal government's income from the Second Bank of the United States to fund internal improvement projects in the various states. Madison had argued that such projects exceeded the national government's constitutional powers, a sentiment that was widely shared. Most Americans believed that the state governments should assume the primary responsibility for economic development. A hostile Congress defeated most of Adams's ambitious proposals, approving only a few navigation improvements and a short extension of the National Road from Wheeling, Virginia, into Ohio.

The most far-reaching battle of the Adams administration came over tariffs. In 1824 a new tariff had imposed a protective tax of 35 percent on imported manufactures—iron goods and woolen and cotton cloth—and Adams and Clay wanted even higher duties to protect Pennsylvania and New England producers. When Van Buren and his Jacksonian allies took control of Congress in 1827, they also supported higher tariffs but for different reasons. By imposing tariffs on imported raw materials, such as wool and hemp, Van Buren hoped to win the support of farmers in New York, Ohio, and Kentucky for Jackson's presidential candidacy in 1828. "I fear this tariff thing," remarked Thomas Cooper of South Carolina, "by some strange mechanical contrivance . . . it will be changed into a machine for manufacturing Presidents, instead of broadcloths, and bed blankets." Disregarding southern opposition, northern Jacksonians enacted the Tariff of 1828, which raised duties on both raw materials and manufactures.

John Quincy Adams (1767–1848)

This famous daguerreotype of Adams, taken about 1843, conveys his rigid personality and high moral standards, attributes that hindered his effectiveness as president but contributed to his success as an anti-slavery congressman in the 1840s. (Metropolitan Museum of Art, Gift of I.N. Phelps Stokes, Edward S. Hawes, Alice Mary Hawes, and Marion Augusta Hawes, 1937. [37.14.34])

The new tariff enraged the South, which gained nothing from the new legislation. As the world's cheapest producer of raw cotton, the South did not need a protective tariff, and by raising the price of British manufactures, the tariff cost southern planters about $100 million a year. Now they had to buy either higher-cost American textiles and iron goods, thus enriching northeastern businesses and workers, or highly taxed British goods, thus paying the cost of the national government. This was "little less than legalized pillage" declared an Alabama legislator, a "Tariff of Abominations."

"THE DEMOCRACY" AND THE ELECTION OF 1828

Despite the Jacksonians' support for the tariff, most southerners blamed President Adams for the new act and refused to support his bid for a second term. Adams had already offended expansionist-minded southern whites by supporting the land rights of Native Americans. In 1825 U.S. commissioners had secured a treaty from one faction of Creeks that ceded the remaining Creek lands in Georgia to the United States. When the Creek National Council repudiated the treaty as fraudulent, Adams called for new negotiations. In response Governor George M. Troup vowed to take the lands by force. Troup attacked the president as a "public enemy . . . the unblushing ally of the savages" and persuaded Congress to extinguish Creek land titles, which forced most Creeks to leave the state.

Elsewhere in the nation Adams's primary weakness was political. He was the last notable to serve in the White House, and he acted the part: aloof, haughty, paternalistic. Ignoring his waning popularity, Adams failed to use patronage to reward his supporters and to oust officeholders who opposed him. In 1828 Adams "stood" for reelection, telling supporters, "If my country wants my services, she must ask for them."

Martin Van Buren and the professional politicians handling Jackson's campaign had no reservations about "running" for office. Now a U.S. senator, Van Buren created the first national campaign organization. His goal was to recreate the old Jeffersonian coalition, uniting northern farmers and artisans (the "plain Republicans of the North") with the southern slaveowners and planters who had voted Jefferson, Madison, and Monroe into the presidency. John C. Calhoun, Jackson's semiofficial running mate, brought his South Carolina allies into Van Buren's party, and Jackson's close friends in Tennessee rallied voters in the Old Southwest to the cause. Directed by Van Buren, state politicians orchestrated a massive newspaper campaign; in New York fifty newspapers declared their support for Jackson on the same day. Local Jacksonians organized mass meetings, torchlight parades, and barbecues to excite public interest. They celebrated Jackson's frontier origins and his rise to fame without the advantages of birth, education, or political intrigue. Old Hickory—the nickname came from the toughest American hardwood tree—was a "natural" aristocrat, a self-made man. "Jackson for ever!" was their cry.

Initially the Jacksonians called themselves Democratic-Republicans, but as the campaign wore on, they became Democrats or "the Democracy." The name conveyed their message. The republic, Jacksonians charged, had been corrupted by "special privilege" and corporate interests that they would root out and replace by rule of the majority—the democracy. "Equality among the people in the rights conferred by government," Jackson would declare, was the "great radical principle of freedom."

Jackson's message appealed to a variety of social groups. His hostility to special privileges for business corporations and to Clay's American System won support among urban workers and artisans in the Northeast who felt threatened by industrialization. In the Southeast and the Midwest Old Hickory's well-known animus toward Native Americans reassured white farmers who favored Indian removal. On the controversial Tariff of Abominations, Jackson benefited from the financial boost it gave to Pennsylvania ironworkers and New York farmers, but he declared his personal preference for a "judicious" tariff, thus appealing for southern votes by suggesting that the existing rates were too high.

The Democrats' strategy of seeking votes from a wide variety of social and economic groups worked like a charm. In 1824 only about a fourth of the eligible electorate had voted; in 1828 more than half went to the polls, and they voted over-whelmingly for Jackson. The senator from Tennessee received 178 of 261 electoral votes and became the first president from a western state, indeed from any state other than Virginia and Massachusetts. The massive outpouring of popular support for Jackson frightened the northern business elite. When the new president came to Washington, warned ex-Federalist Daniel Webster, he would "bring a breeze with him. Which way it will blow, I cannot tell. . . . My fear is stronger than my hope." Watching an unruly crowd clamber over the elegant furniture in the White House to shake the hand of the newly inaugurated president, Supreme Court Justice Joseph Story lamented that "the reign of King 'Mob' seemed triumphant" (see American Voices, "Republican Majesty and Mobs").

The Jacksonian Presidency, 1829–1837

Political democracy—a broad franchise, a disciplined political party, and policies tailored to specific social groups—had carried Andrew Jackson to the presidency. Jackson used his popular mandate to enhance the authority of the president, destroy the nationalistic American System of Adams and Clay, and ordain a new ideology for the Democracy. As an Ohio supporter outlined Jackson's vision: "the Sovereignty of the People, the Rights of the States, and a Light and Simple [national] Government."

JACKSON'S AGENDA: PATRONAGE AND POLICY

To decide policy, Jackson relied primarily on an informal group of advisers, his so-called Kitchen Cabinet. Its most influential members were Francis Preston Blair of Kentucky, who edited the *Washington Globe;* Amos Kendall, also from Kentucky, who helped Jackson write his public papers; Roger B. Taney of Maryland, who became attorney general and then chief justice of the United States; and, the most influential, Secretary of State Martin Van Buren.

Following Van Buren's example in New York, Jackson used patronage to create a loyal and disciplined national party. He insisted on rotation in office: when a new administration came to power, bureaucrats would have to leave government service and return "to making a living as other people do." Dismissing the argument that forced rotation would eliminate expertise, Jackson suggested that most public duties were "so plain and simple that men of intelligence may readily qualify themselves for their performance." William L. Marcy, a New York Jacksonian, put it more bluntly: government jobs were like the spoils of war, and there was "nothing wrong in the rule that to the victor belong the spoils of the enemy." Using the spoils system Jackson dispensed government jobs to aid his friends and win support for his legislative program.

AMERICAN VOICES

Republican Majesty and Mobs

MARGARET BAYARD SMITH

*A*s Andrew Jackson ascended to the presidency in 1829, he seemed to many observers to threaten the established political and social system. Writing to her son the Washington socialite Margaret Bayard Smith revealed a mixture of pride and anxiety about the coming of popular democracy.

The inauguration . . . an imposing and majestic spectacle. . . . Thousands and thousands of people, without distinction of rank, collected in an immense mass around the Capitol, silent, orderly, and tranquil, with their eyes fixed on the front of the Capitol, waiting the appearance of the president. . . . The door from the Rotunda opens, preceded by the marshall surrounded by the judges of the Supreme Court, the old man [President Jackson] with his grey hair, that crown of glory, advances, bows to the people, who greet him with a shout that rends the air.

After reading his speech, the oath was administered to him by the chief justice. The marshall presented the Bible. The president took it from his hand, pressed his lips to it, laid it reverently down, then bowed again to the people—Yes, to the people in all their majesty—and had the spectacle closed here, even Europeans must have acknowledged that a free people, collected in their might, silent and tranquil, restrained solely by a moral power, without a shadow around of military force, was majesty, rising to sublimity, and far surpassing the majesty of Kings and Princes, surrounded with armies and glittering in gold. . . .

[But at the reception that followed,] what a scene did we witness!! The *Majesty of the People* had disappeared, and a rabble, a mob . . . scrambling, fighting, romping . . . [crowded around] the President, [who,] after having literally been nearly pressed to death . . . escaped to his lodgings at Gadsby's. Cut glass and bone china to the amount of several thousand dollars had been broken in the struggle to get refreshments. . . . Ladies and gentlemen only had been expected at this [reception], not the people *en masse*. . . . The . . . rabble in the president's house brought to my mind descriptions I had read of the mobs in the Tuileries and at Versailles [during the French Revolution].

SOURCE: M. B. Smith to Mrs. Kirkpatrick, 11 March 1829, in Galliard Hunt, ed., *The First Forty Years of Washington Society . . . the Family Letters of Mrs. Samuel Harrison Smith . . .* (New York, 1906), pp. 290–97.

Jackson's main priority was to destroy Clay's American System. Maintaining that the "voice of the people" called for "economy in the expenditures of the Government," Jackson rejected federal support for transportation projects. In 1830 he vetoed four internal improvement bills, including an extension of the National Road, arguing in part that because the proposed extension would lie entirely within

President Andrew Jackson, 1830

The new president came to Washington with a well-deserved reputation as an aggressive Indian fighter and dangerous military chieftain. But in this "official" portrait of 1830 he appears "presidential"—his dress and posture (and the artist's composition) creating an image of a calm and deliberate statesman. Subsequent events would show that Jackson had not lost his hard-edged personality. (Library of Congress)

Kentucky, it amounted to "an infringement of the reserved powers of states." Then Jackson turned his attention to two complex and equally politically charged parts of the American System: protective tariffs and the national bank.

THE TARIFF AND NULLIFICATION

The Tariff of 1828 had helped Jackson win the presidency, but it saddled him with a major political crisis. The fiercest opposition to the tariff was in South Carolina, where slaveowners suffered from chronic insecurity. South Carolina was the only state with an African American majority—56 percent of the population in 1830—which made it more like Jamaica or Barbados than the rest of the South. Like white planters in the West Indies South Carolina slaveowners lived in fear of a black rebellion. They also worried about laws that would abolish slavery. The British Parliament was about to end slavery in the West Indies (and did so in August 1833), and South Carolina planters worried that the U.S. government might do the same. "If the general government shall continue to stretch their powers," a southern congressman had warned as early as 1818, antislavery societies "will undoubtedly put them to try the question of emancipation." To prevent that development South Carolina politicians tried to limit the power of the central government and chose the tariff as their target.

The crisis began in 1832, when tariff advocates in Congress ignored southern warnings that they were "endangering the Union" and refused to lower the duties imposed by the Tariff of Abominations. In November leading South Carolinians called a state convention, which boldly adopted an Ordinance of Nullification. The Ordinance declared the tariffs of 1828 and 1832 null and void, forbade the collection of those duties in the state after February 1, 1833, and threatened secession if the federal government tried to collect them.

South Carolina's act of nullification rested on the constitutional arguments developed in a tract published in 1828, *The South Carolina Exposition and Protest.* Written anonymously by Vice President John C. Calhoun, the *Exposition* denied that majority rule lay at the heart of republican government. "Constitutional government and the government of a majority are utterly incompatible," Calhoun wrote. "An unchecked majority is a despotism." To devise a mechanism to check congressional majorities Calhoun turned to the arguments advanced by Jefferson and Madison in the Kentucky and Virginia resolutions of 1798. Developing a constitutional theory that states' rights advocates would use well into the twentieth century, Calhoun maintained that the U.S. Constitution had been ratified by the people in state conventions. Consequently, he argued, a state convention could determine whether or not a congressional law was unconstitutional and declare it null and void within the state's borders.

Although Jackson wanted to limit the powers of the national government, he believed it should be done through the existing constitutional system. Confronting Calhoun at a banquet, Jackson publicly repudiated his vice president's ideas by proposing a formal toast: "Our Federal Union—it must be preserved." Two years later the president's response to South Carolina's Nullification Ordinance was equally forthright. "Disunion by armed force is treason," he declared in December 1832. Appealing to patriotism Jackson asserted that nullification violated the Constitution and was "unauthorized by its spirit, inconsistent with every principle on which it is founded, and destructive of the great object for which it was formed." At Jackson's request, Congress passed a Force Bill early in 1833 authorizing him to use the army and navy to compel obedience. Simultaneously, Jackson met South Carolina's objections to the tariff by winning new legislation for a compromise Tariff Act that provided for a gradual reduction in duties. By 1842 import taxes would revert to the modest levels set in 1816, and another part of Clay's American System would be eliminated.

The compromise worked. Having won a gradual reduction in rates, the South Carolina convention rescinded its nullification of the tariff (while defiantly nullifying the now-meaningless Force Act). Jackson was satisfied. He had upheld the principle that no state could nullify a law of the United States, a position that

Abraham Lincoln would embrace in defense of the Union during the secession crisis of 1861.

THE BANK WAR

In the middle of the tariff crisis Jackson faced a major challenge from the supporters of the Second Bank of the United States. The Second Bank stood at the center of the American financial system. A privately managed entity, it had operated since 1816 under a twenty-year charter from the federal government, which owned 20 percent of its stock. Its most important role was to stabilize the nation's money supply. Most American money consisted of notes—in effect, paper money—issued by state-chartered banks. The banks promised to redeem the notes on demand with "hard" money—that is, gold or silver coins (also known as *specie*). By collecting those notes and regularly demanding specie the Second Bank kept the state banks from issuing too many notes, preventing monetary inflation and higher prices.

During the prosperous 1820s the Second Bank had maintained monetary stability and restrained expansion-minded banks in the western states, forcing some to close. This policy was welcomed by bankers and entrepreneurs in Boston, New York, and Philadelphia, whose capital was underwriting economic development, but aroused popular hostility. Most Americans did not understand the regulatory role of the Second Bank and feared its ability to force bank closures, which left ordinary citizens holding worthless paper notes. Some wealthy Americans also opposed the Second Bank and resented the financial power wielded by its president, Nicholas Biddle. New York bankers wanted the specie owned by the federal government to be deposited in their institutions rather than in the Second Bank. Likewise, expansion-minded bankers in western cities, including friends of Jackson in Nashville, wanted to escape supervision by a central bank.

But it was a political miscalculation by the supporters of the Second Bank that brought about its downfall. In 1832 Jackson's opponents in Congress, led by Henry Clay and Daniel Webster, persuaded Biddle to request an early recharter of the Bank. They had the votes to get a rechartering bill through Congress and hoped to lure Jackson into a veto that would split the Democrats just before the 1832 elections.

Jackson turned the tables on Clay and Webster. He vetoed the bank bill and became a public hero by justifying his action in a masterful public statement. His veto message blended constitutional arguments with class rhetoric and patriotic fervor. Taking Jefferson's position he declared that Congress had no constitutional authority to charter a national bank, which was "subversive of the rights of the States." Then, using the rhetoric of the American Revolution, he attacked the Second Bank as "dangerous to the liberties of the people," a nest of special privilege and monopoly power that promoted "the advancement of the few at the expense of the many . . . the farmers, mechanics, and laborers." Finally, the president evoked patriotism by pointing out that British aristocrats owned much of the Bank's stock; any such powerful institution should be "purely American," he declared.

Jackson's attack on the Bank carried him to victory in the presidential election of 1832. He jettisoned Calhoun as a running mate because of the South Carolinian's support for nullification and his refusal to welcome Peggy Eaton, a cabinet wife accused of sexual improprieties, into Washington society. As his new vice president, Jackson chose his longtime political ally, Martin Van Buren. Together Old Hickory and "Little Van" overwhelmed Henry Clay, who headed the National Republican ticket, by 219 to 49 electoral votes. Jackson's most fervent supporters were farmers and workers whose lives had been disrupted by price fluctuations or falling wages. But many Jacksonians were promoters of economic growth. State bankers welcomed the demise of the Second Bank, and thousands of middle-class Americans—lawyers, clerks, shopkeepers, artisans—cheered his attacks on privileged corporations. They wanted equal opportunity to rise in the world.

Immediately after his reelection Jackson launched a new attack on the Second Bank, which still had four years left on its charter. He appointed Roger B. Taney, a strong opponent of corporate privilege, secretary of the Treasury and had him withdraw the government's gold and silver from the Bank and deposit it in state institutions, which critics called his "pet banks." To justify this abrupt (and probably illegal) act Jackson claimed that the recent election had given him a mandate to destroy the Second Bank. It was the first time a president had claimed that victory at the polls allowed him to act independently of Congress.

The "Bank War" escalated. In March 1834 Jackson's opponents in the Senate passed a resolution written by Henry Clay censuring the president and warning of despotism: "We are in the midst of a revolution, hitherto bloodless, but rapidly descending towards a total change of the pure republican character of the Government, and the concentration of all power in the hands of one man." But Jackson and Taney continued to oppose the Second Bank, and in 1836 it became a state-chartered bank in Pennsylvania, still a wealthy institution but one without public responsibilities.

Jackson had destroyed both national banking—the creation of Alexander Hamilton—and the American System of protective tariffs and internal improvements favored by John Quincy Adams and Henry Clay. The result was a profound change in the policies and powers of the national government. "All is gone," observed a Washington newspaper correspondent. "All is gone, which the General Government was instituted to create and preserve."

Jackson's legacy as chief executive, like that of every great president, was complex and rich. By destroying the American System, he disrupted the movement toward stronger central direction of American life and reinvigorated the Jeffersonian tradition of limited, frugal government. Having redefined the character of the Union, he firmly defended it during the nullification crisis, threatening the use of military force to uphold laws enacted by the national legislature. Finally, Jackson greatly expanded the authority of the nation's chief executive, using the rhetoric of popular sovereignty to declare that "the President is the direct representative of the American people."

INDIAN REMOVAL

The status of the Native American peoples was as difficult a political issue as the tariff and the Bank, and it also raised issues of federal versus state power. In the late 1820s white voices throughout the western states and territories called for the re-settlement of Indians to the west of the Mississippi River. Many eastern whites, including those sympathetic to the Native American peoples, also favored removal; in their view resettlement would preserve traditional cultures of the Indians and protect them from direct competition with whites.

Jackson endorsed Indian removal in his first inaugural address in 1829 and quickly began to implement it. The Old Southwest was the home of the so-called Five Civilized Tribes: the Cherokees and Creeks in Georgia, Tennessee, and Alabama; the Chickasaws and Choctaws in Mississippi and Alabama; and the Seminoles in Florida. During the War of 1812 Jackson's expeditions had forced the Creeks to relinquish millions of acres. But Indian peoples still controlled vast tracts of land, and some of them had adopted European institutions and values. By the 1820s the mixed-blood Cherokees had created a centralized political system, a thriving agricultural economy, and a wealthy slaveowning class of cotton planters. Both the mixed-blood Christians and the full-blood traditionalists were determined to retain their ancestral lands. In 1827 the Cherokee adopted a constitution and proclaimed themselves a separate nation within the United States.

The Cherokees' preferences carried no weight with the Georgia legislature, which in 1802 had given up land claims in the West in return for a federal promise to extinguish Indian land holdings in the state. It declared that the Cherokees were merely tenants on state-owned land. Nor did the Cherokees' claims impress Jackson, who had been a committed Indian fighter (and alleged Indian hater; see Chapter 8). On becoming president he threw his support to Georgia, withdrawing the federal troops that had protected Indian enclaves there and in Alabama and Mississippi; the states, he argued, were sovereign within their borders.

Jackson then pushed through Congress the Indian Removal Act of 1830, which provided territory in present-day Oklahoma and Kansas to Native Americans who would give up their ancestral holdings. To persuade Indians to move to the new lands, government officials promised them that they "can live upon it, they and all their children, as long as grass grows and water runs." When Chief Black Hawk and his Sauk and Fox followers refused to move from rich farmland along the Mississippi River in western Illinois, in 1832 Jackson sent troops to expel them (see American Voices, "A Sacred Reverence for Our Lands"). Rejecting Black Hawk's offer to surrender, the American army pursued him into the Wisconsin Territory and, in the brutal eight-hour-long Bad Axe Massacre, killed 850 of Black Hawk's 1,000 warriors. Over the next five years diplomatic pressure and military power forced

AMERICAN VOICES

A Sacred Reverence for Our Lands

BLACK HAWK

B lack Hawk (1767–1838), or Makataimeshekiakiak, was a chief of the Sauk and Fox. In 1833 he dictated his life story to a government interpreter, and a young newspaper editor published it. Here Black Hawk describes the coming of white settlers to his village, near present-day Rock Island, Illinois, and his decision to resist removal to lands west of the Mississippi River.

We had about eight hundred acres in cultivation. The land around our village . . . was covered with bluegrass, which made excellent pasture for our horses. . . . The rapids of Rock river furnished us with an abundance of excellent fish, and the land, being good, never failed to produce good crops of corn, beans, pumpkins, and squashes. We always had plenty—our children never cried with hunger, nor our people were never in want. Here our village had stood for more than a hundred years.

[In 1828] Nothing was now talked of but leaving our village. Ke-o-kuck [the principal chief] had been persuaded to consent to . . . remove to the west side of the Mississippi. . . . [I] raised the standard of opposition to Ke-o-kuck, with full determination not to leave my village. . . . I was of the opinion that the white people had plenty of land and would never take our village from us. . . .

During the [following] winter, I received information that three families of whites had arrived at our village and destroyed some of our lodges, and were making fences and dividing our corn-fields for their own use. . . . [Some weeks later] others had come, and that the greater part of our corn-fields had been enclosed. . . . The white people brought whiskey into our village, made people drunk, and cheated them out of their homes, guns, and [beaver] traps!

That fall [1829] I paid a visit to the agent, before we started to our hunting grounds. . . . He said that the land on which our village stood was now ordered to be sold to individuals; and that, when sold, *our right* to remain, by treaty, would be at an end. . . . I refused . . . to quit my village. It was here, that I was born—and here lie the bones of many friends and relatives. For this spot I felt a sacred reverence, and never could consent to leave it, without being forced therefrom.

SOURCE: David Jackson, ed., *Black Hawk, An Autobiography* (Urbana: University of Illinois Press, 1964), pp. 88–113.

seventy Indian peoples to sign treaties and move west of the Mississippi. Those agreements exchanged 100 million acres of land in the East for $68 million and 32 million acres in the West.

In the meantime the Cherokees had carried their case to the Supreme Court, claiming the status of a "foreign nation" under the U.S. Constitution. In *Cherokee*

Nation v. Georgia (1831) Chief Justice John Marshall denied their claim to national independence. Speaking for a majority of the justices Marshall declared that Indian peoples enjoyed only partial autonomy and were "domestic dependent nations." However, in *Worcester v. Georgia* (1832) Marshall sided with the Cherokees, voiding Georgia's extension of state law over them and holding that Indian nations were "distinct political communities, having territorial boundaries, within which their authority is exclusive ... [and this is] guaranteed by the United States." When Jackson heard the outcome, he reputedly responded, "John Marshall has made his decision; now let him enforce it."

Rather than protecting the Cherokees' territory, Jackson moved purposefully to take it from them. U.S. Commissioners signed a removal treaty with a minority faction and insisted that all Cherokees abide by it. By the deadline in May 1838 only 2,000 of the 17,000 Cherokees had departed. During the summer, Martin Van Buren, who had succeeded Jackson as president, ordered General Winfield Scott to enforce the treaty. Scott's army rounded up about 14,000 Cherokees and forcibly marched

Black Hawk (1767–1838)

George Catlin (1796–1872) painted many Indians, depicting them in realistic and dignified poses. His portrait of Black Hawk, rendered when the Indian leader was about sixty years old, shows a man who has endured the vicissitudes of life and was the stronger because of these experiences. To resist the Indian Removal Act Black Hawk mobilized Sauk and Fox warriors of Illinois, declaring, "It was here that I was born—and here lie the bones of many friends and relatives, I . . . could never consent to leave it." (Thomas Gilcrease Institute of American History and Art)

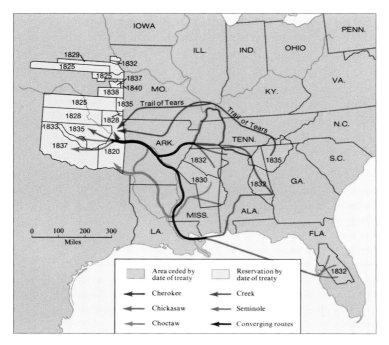

M A P 11.2
The Removal of Native Americans, 1820–1840

Between 1820 and 1840 the U.S. government concluded treaties with Native American peoples in the East, giving them designated tracts of land west of the Mississippi River. During the 1830s the Five Civilized Tribes of the Old Southwest (the Cherokee, Chickasaw, Choctaw, Creek, and Seminole) were forced to move to these reservations in the Indian Territory, the present-day state of Oklahoma; other eastern tribes were settled in Kansas.

them 1,200 miles to the new Indian Territory, an arduous journey they remembered as the Trail of Tears (Map 11.2). Along the way 3,000 Indians died of starvation and exposure. Because the Creeks, Chickasaws, and Choctaws had moved west of the Mississippi, the only remaining Indian people in the Old Southwest were the Seminoles in Florida. Aided by runaway slaves who had married into the tribe, a portion of the Seminoles fought a successful guerrilla war during the 1840s and remained in Florida. They were the exceptions. The national government had asserted its control over most eastern Indian peoples and forced their removal to the West.

THE JACKSONIAN IMPACT

Jacksonian Democrats used their political power to infuse American institutions with their principles. Following the death in 1835 of John Marshall, Jackson appointed Roger B. Taney as chief justice of the Supreme Court. During his long tenure

(1835–1864), Taney persuaded the Court to give constitutional legitimacy to Jackson's policies of antimonopoly and states' rights. Thus in the landmark case of *Charles River Bridge Co. v. Warren Bridge Co.* (1837) Taney undermined the legal position of chartered corporations by ruling that the legislative charter held by the Charles River Bridge Company did not convey a monopoly because an exclusive right was not explicitly stated in the charter. Consequently, the Massachusetts legislature retained the power to charter a competing bridge company. As Taney put it: "While the rights of private property are sacredly guarded, we must not forget that the community also has rights." This decision qualified John Marshall's interpretation of the contract clause in *Dartmouth College v. Woodward* (1819), which had emphasized the binding nature of public charters and had limited the power of states to alter or repeal them (see Chapter 8). It also encouraged competitive enterprise, opening the way for legislatures to charter railroads that would compete with existing canal and turnpike companies.

Other decisions by the Taney Court retreated from Marshall's nationalist interpretation of the commerce clause and enhanced the regulatory role of state governments. For example, in *Mayor of New York v. Miln* (1837) the Taney Court ruled that New York State could use its "police power" to inspect the health of arriving immigrants. The Taney Court also restored to the states some of the economic powers they had exercised before 1787. In *Briscoe v. Bank of Kentucky* (1837) the Court approved the issuance of currency by a bank owned and controlled by the state of Kentucky, ruling that it did not violate the provision (in Article I, Section 10, of the U.S. Constitution) that forbade states from issuing "bills of credit."

Jacksonian Democrats in the various states mounted their own constitutional revolution. Extending the democratic upsurge of the previous decades, between 1830 and 1860 twenty states called conventions to revise their basic charters. Most states extended the vote to all white men and reapportioned their legislatures on the basis of population. The new documents also brought government "near to the people" by mandating the election, rather than appointment, of most officials, including sheriffs, justices of the peace, and judges. By inserting Jacksonian ideals into the new constitutions, the delegates changed their basic character from "republican" governments that undertook public projects to "liberal" regimes that limited the power of the state. Thus most Jacksonian-era constitutions prohibited states from granting exclusive charters to corporations or extending loans or credit guarantees to private businesses. "If there is any danger to be feared in . . . government," declared a New Jersey Democrat, "it is the danger of associated wealth, with special privileges." The new state constitutions also protected taxpayers by setting strict limits on state debts and encouraging judges to enforce them. As a New York reformer put it, "We will not trust the legislature with the power of creating indefinite mortgages on the people's property." Just as Jackson had destroyed the American System's government subsidies on the national level, so his disciples in the states undermined the "commonwealth" philosophy of using chartered corporations and state funds to promote economic development. Declaring that "the world is governed too much," Jacksonians embraced a small-government, laissez-faire out-look. The first American "populists," they attacked government-granted special priv-ileges and celebrated the power of ordinary people to make decisions in the marketplace and the voting booth.

Class, Culture, and the Second Party System

The rise of the Democracy and Jackson's tumultuous presidency sparked the cre-ation in the mid-1830s of a second national party—the Whigs. For the next two decades Whigs and Democrats dominated American politics, forming what histo-rians call the Second Party System. Many evangelical Protestants became Whigs, while most Catholics and nonevangelical Protestants joined the Democrats. The two parties competed fiercely for votes, debating issues of economic policy, class power, and moral reform and offering Americans a clear choice between political programs.

THE WHIG WORLDVIEW

The Whig Party began in Congress in 1834, when opponents of Andrew Jackson banded together to protest his policies and high-handed actions. They took the name Whigs to identify themselves with the pre-Revolutionary American and British parties—also called Whigs—that had opposed the arbitrary actions of British monarchs. The congressional Whigs charged that "King Andrew I" had vi-olated the Constitution through "executive usurpation." Led by Senators Webster of Massachusetts, Clay of Kentucky, and Calhoun of South Carolina, the Whigs gradually elaborated their political vision. Beginning in the congressional elections of 1834 they sought votes especially among evangelical Protestants and upwardly mobile middle- and working-class citizens in the North. Their goal, like that of the Federalists of the 1790s, was a political world dominated by men of ability and wealth; unlike the Federalists, the Whig elite would be chosen by talent, not birth.

The Whigs celebrated the role played by enterprising entrepreneurs and activist governments in increasing the nation's wealth. Arguing that the Industrial Revolu-tion had increased social harmony, they welcomed the investments of "moneyed capitalists" as providing the poor with jobs, "bread, clothing and homes." Whig Con-gressman Edward Everett told a Fourth of July crowd in Lowell, Massachusetts, that there was a "holy alliance" among laborers, owners, and governments. Many work-ers agreed, especially those holding jobs in the New England textile factories and Pennsylvania iron mills that benefited from state subsidies and protective tariffs. To continue economic progress Everett and northern Whigs called for a return to the American System of Henry Clay and John Quincy Adams.

Southern Whigs had a different perspective. They condemned Jackson's "exec-utive usurpation" and advocated economic development, but they did not share the northern Whigs' support for high tariffs and social mobility. Indeed, Calhoun argued that the northern Whig ideal of equal opportunity was contradicted by the reality of slavery and industrial wage labor. "A conflict between labor and capital" was inevitable, Calhoun argued, urging southern slaveowners and northern factory owners to unite against their common foe: the working class of enslaved blacks and propertyless whites.

Most Whig leaders rejected Calhoun's class-conscious vision. "A clear and well-defined line between capital and labor" might fit the slave South or class-ridden Europe, Daniel Webster conceded, but in the North "this distinction grows less and less definite as commerce advances." Webster focused on the growing size and affluence of the northern middle class. Indeed, in the election of 1834 the Whigs won a majority in the House of Representatives by appealing to middling groups—the prosperous farmers, small-town merchants, and skilled industrial workers in New England, New York, and the new communities along the Great Lakes. Those voters were attracted to the Whigs' ideology of individual mobility and commitment to moral reform. Many of them had previously been Anti-Masons, members of a powerful but short-lived political movement directed against the secret Order of Freemasonry. Picking up on Anti-Masonic themes—temperance, equality of opportunity, evangelical religious values—Whigs favored legal curbs on the sale of alcohol and local bylaws that preserved Sunday as a day of worship. The Whigs also won congressional seats in the Ohio and Mississippi Valleys, where farmers, bankers, and shopkeepers favored Henry Clay's policies for governmental subsidies for roads, canals, and bridges.

Support for the Whigs in the South was fragmentary and rested on the appeal of specific policies rather than agreement with the Whigs' social vision. For example, many yeomen whites in the backcountry voted Whig to break the grip over state politics held by low-country planters, most of whom were Democrats. Yet a significant minority of wealthy planters became Whigs, especially those who had investments in railroads and banks or sold their cotton to New York merchants. Finally, some states' rights Democrats in Virginia and South Carolina condemned Andrew Jackson's crusade against nullification and, so like John C. Calhoun, joined the Whigs.

In the election of 1836 the Whigs faced Martin Van Buren, the architect of the Democratic Party and Jackson's handpicked successor. Van Buren emphasized his opposition to the American System and support for "equal rights." He also promised to preserve liberty, declaring himself an "uncompromising opponent" of those Whigs who wanted to use government power to uphold the sabbath, prohibit the sale of alcoholic beverages, or abolish slavery. "The government is best which governs least" became his motto.

To oppose Van Buren the Whigs ran four regional candidates, hoping to garner enough electoral votes to throw the contest into the House of Representatives, which they controlled. The plan failed. The Whig tally—73 electoral votes collected by William Henry Harrison of Ohio, 26 by Hugh L. White of Tennessee, 14 by Daniel

Webster of New Hampshire, and 11 by W. P. Magnum of Georgia—fell far short of Van Buren's 170 votes. Still, the size of the popular vote for the four Whig candidates—49 percent of the total—showed that the party's message of economic improvement and moral uplift appealed not only to middle-class Americans but also to farmers and workers with little or no property.

LABOR POLITICS AND THE DEPRESSION OF 1837–1843

In seeking the votes of workers, Whigs had to compete with the workingmen's parties that had sprung up in fifteen states between 1827 and 1833. Rising prices and stagnant wages had lowered the standard of living of many urban artisans and wage earners, who feared what they called "the glaring inequality of society." To redress this inequality the Working Men's Party in New York City demanded the abolition of private banks, chartered monopolies, and imprisonment for debt. The Philadelphia Working Men's Party demanded higher taxes on the wealthy and in 1834 persuaded the Pennsylvania legislature to authorize free, tax-supported schools so that workers' children could advance into the ranks of the propertied classes.

The workingmen's parties embraced the ideology of artisan republicanism. Their goal was a society in which (as the radical thinker Orestes Brownson put it) there would be no dependent wage-earners and "all men will be independent proprietors, working on their own capitals, on their own farms, or in their own shops." This vision led the Working Men's Parties, like the Democratic Party, to demand equal rights and attack legislation that created chartered corporations and monopolistic banks "for the benefit of the rich and the oppression of the poor." "The only safeguard against oppression," argued William Leggett, a leading member of the New York Loco-Foco (Equal Rights) Party, "is a system of legislation which leaves to all the free exercise of their talents and industry." At first the workingmen's parties did well in urban areas, but divisions over policy and voter apathy soon took a toll. By the mid-1830s most politically active workers had joined the Democratic Party, trying to win its support for their program of opposition to protective tariffs and the taxation of the stocks and bonds owned by wealthy capitalists.

Taking advantage of the economic boom of the early 1830s, which increased the demand for skilled labor, workers formed unions to bargain for higher wages and organized General Trade Union federations in New York City and Philadelphia. Employers responded to the workers' demands by attacking the union movement. In 1836 clothing manufacturers in New York City agreed not to hire workers belonging to the Union Trade Society of Journeymen Tailors and circulated a list—a so-called *blacklist*—of its members. The employers also brought lawsuits to overturn *closed-shop* agreements that required them to hire only union members. They argued that such contracts violated the common law and legislative statutes that prohibited "conspiracies" in restraint of trade.

Judges usually agreed. In 1835 the New York Supreme Court found that a shoemaker's union in Geneva had illegally caused "an industrious man" to be "driven out of employment." "It is important to the best interests of society that the price of labor be left to regulate itself," the court declared. When a court in New York City upheld a conspiracy verdict against a tailors' union, a crowd of 27,000 people demonstrated outside city hall, and tailors circulated handbills proclaiming that the "Freemen of the North are now on a level with the slaves of the South." In 1836 popular demonstrations prompted local juries to acquit shoemakers in Hudson, New York, carpet makers in Thompsonville, Connecticut, and plasterers in Philadelphia of similar conspiracy charges. The resistance of workers and their supporters had preserved the unions from legal attack.

At this juncture the Panic of 1837 threw the American economy into disarray. The Panic began early in the year, when the Bank of England, needing to boost the British economy, sharply curtailed the flow of money and credit to the United States. For the previous decade and a half British manufacturers and investors had stimulated the American economy, providing southern planters with credit to expand cotton production and purchasing millions of dollars of canal bonds in northern states. As the British economy faltered, textile mills cut their purchases of raw cotton from the South, causing its price to collapse from 20 cents a pound to 10 cents or less. Deprived of British funds American planters, merchants, and canal corporations had to withdraw specie from domestic banks to pay their foreign loans and commercial debts.

This drain of gold and silver set off a general financial crisis. On May 8 the Dry Dock Bank of New York City closed its doors, and panicked depositors withdrew more than $2 million in coin from other city banks, forcing them to suspend all payments in specie. Within two weeks every bank in the United States had followed suit, shocking high-flying entrepreneurs and ordinary citizens and sending the economy into a steep decline. "This sudden overthrow of the commercial credit and honor of the nation" had a "stunning effect," observed Henry Fox, the British minister in Washington. "The conquest of the land by a foreign power could hardly have produced a more general sense of humiliation and grief." The crisis engulfed state governments, as tax revenues and canal tolls fell. Nine states defaulted on bonds issued to finance canal building; others declared a moratorium on debt payments, undermining the confidence of British investors and cutting the flow of capital. Bumper crops during the late 1830s drove down cotton prices even further, bringing more bankruptcies.

The American economy fell into a deep depression. By 1843 canal construction had dropped 90 percent and prices nearly 50 percent; unemployment rose, reaching almost 20 percent of the workforce in seaports and industrial centers. From his pulpit, minister Henry Ward Beecher described a land "filled with lamentation . . . its inhabitants wandering like bereaved citizens among the ruins of an earthquake, mourning for children, for houses crushed, and property buried forever."

By creating a surplus of skilled workers the depression devastated the labor movement. In 1837, 6,000 masons, carpenters, and other building-trade workers lost their jobs in New York City, depleting the membership of unions and

The Panic of 1837

Thousands of workers, including this carpenter, lost their jobs during the panic and the subsequent depression, threatening their families with disaster. "I'm so hungry," says one child, while the landlord stands at the door, eviction notice in hand. By placing portraits of Jackson and Van Buren on the wall, the artist implicitly blames them for the family's suffering and encourages workers to turn away from the Democratic Party. (Library of Congress)

destroying their bargaining power. By 1843 most local unions and all the national labor organizations had disappeared, along with their newspapers and other publications.

However, two events during the depression years improved the long-term prospects of the labor movement. One was a major legal victory. In *Commonwealth v. Hunt* (1842) a case decided by the Massachusetts Supreme Judicial Court, Chief Justice Lemuel Shaw upheld the rights of workers to form unions and enforce a closed shop. Shaw, one of the great jurists of the nineteenth century, overturned common-law precedents by making two critical rulings: (1) a union was not an inherently illegal organization, and (2) union members could legally attempt to enforce a closed shop, even by striking. Courts in other states generally accepted Shaw's opinion, but judges (who were mostly Whigs) found other methods, such as court injunctions, to restrict strikes and boycotts. Labor's second success was political. Continuing Jackson's effort to attract workers to the Democratic Party, in 1840 President Van Buren signed an executive order establishing a ten-hour day for all federal employees. Significantly, this achievement came after the unions had been defeated in the marketplace, underlining the fact that the workers' struggle—like conflicts over tariffs, banks, and internal improvements—had moved into the political arena.

"TIPPECANOE AND TYLER TOO!"

The depression had a major impact on American politics. Few people understood the complex workings of the international economy, and so many Americans blamed the Democrats for their economic woes. In particular, they derided Jackson for destroying the Second Bank and for issuing the Specie Circular of 1836, which required western settlers to use gold and silver coins to pay for land purchases. Not realizing that shipment of specie to Britain (to pay off past debts) was the main cause of the financial panic, the Whigs blamed Jackson's policies.

The public turned its anger on Van Buren, who entered office just as the panic began. Ignoring the pleas of influential bankers, the new president refused to revoke the Specie Circular or take other actions that might reverse the downturn. Holding to his philosophy of limited government Van Buren advised Congress that "the less government interferes with private pursuits the better for the general prosperity." As the depression continued, this laissez-faire outlook commanded less and less political support. Worse, Van Buren's major piece of economic legislation, the Independent Treasury Act of 1840, actually delayed recovery. The act pulled federal specie out of Jackson's "pet banks" (which had used it to back loans) and placed it in government vaults (where it did no economic good at all). Whatever its value in placing the nation's financial reserves above politics, the Independent Treasury did little to enhance Van Buren's popularity.

Determined to exploit Van Buren's weakness, in 1840 the Whigs organized their first national convention and nominated William Henry Harrison of Ohio for president and John Tyler of Virginia for vice president. A military hero of the Battle of Tippecanoe and the War of 1812, Harrison was well advanced in age (sixty-eight) and had little political experience. But the Whig leaders in Congress, Clay and Webster, did not want a strong president; they planned to have Harrison rubber-stamp their program for protective tariffs and a national bank. Party strategists such as Thurlow Weed of New York had chosen Harrison primarily because of his military record and western background, promoting him as the Whig version of Andrew Jackson. An unpretentious, amiable man, Harrison warmed to that task, telling voters that Whig policies were "the only means, under Heaven, by which a poor industrious man may become a rich man without bowing to colossal wealth."

Panic and depression stacked the political cards against Van Buren, but the contest itself turned as much on style as on substance. It became the great "log-cabin" campaign—the first occasion on which two well-organized parties competed for the loyalties of a mass electorate. One result was a new political style of festive celebrations. Whig pamphleteering, songfests, parades, and well-orchestrated mass meetings dominated the contest, drawing new voters and new social groups into the political arena. Whig speakers assailed "Martin Van Ruin" as a manipulative politician with aristocratic tastes—a devotee of fancy wines and elegant clothes, as indeed he was. With less candor they praised Harrison, actually the son of a wealthy planter who had signed the Declaration of Independence, as a self-made soldier and statesman who lived in a simple log cabin and enjoyed hard cider, a drink of the common man.

The Whigs boosted their electoral hopes by welcoming women to their festivities. Previously women had been systematically excluded not only from voting and jury duty but also from nearly every other aspect of political life, even marching in July 4 and Washington's Birthday parades. Jacksonian Democrats celebrated politics as a "manly" affair, likening women who ventured into the political arena to the ordinary run of "public" women—the prostitutes who plied their trade in the-

The Log-Cabin Campaign, 1840

Under the Second Party System politics became more responsive to the popular will as ordinary people voted for candidates who shared their values and lifestyles. The barrels of hard cider surrounding this campaign banner depict the drink of the common man (not the wines favored by Martin Van Buren), while the picture falsely portrays William Henry Harrison as a poor frontier farmer in a log cabin. (New-York Historical Society)

aters and other public places. But the Whigs recognized that women from Yankee families, a core Whig constituency, were deeply involved in religious revivalism, the temperance movement, and other benevolent activities. And so in October 1840 Daniel Webster addressed a special meeting of 1,200 Whig women, perhaps the first mass meeting of women in American politics. Noting women's benevolent efforts, Webster praised their moral perceptions as "both quicker and juster" than those of men and identified their concerns with the Whig programs for moral reform.

"This way of making politicians of their women is something new under the sun," noted one Democrat, worried that it would bring more Whig men to the polls. More than 80 percent of the eligible voters cast ballots in 1840 (up from less than 60 percent in 1832 and 1836). Heeding the Whig slogan "Tippecanoe and Tyler Too," they voted Harrison into the White House and gave the Whigs a majority in Congress.

The Whig triumph was short-lived. One month after his inauguration Harrison died of pneumonia, and the nation got "Tyler Too." Vice President John Tyler of Virginia, who became president, had joined the Whig Party primarily because he opposed Jackson's stance against nullification. On economic issues Tyler was more like a Democrat, sharing Jackson's hostility to the Second Bank and the American System. Consequently, he vetoed bills that would have raised tariffs and created a new national bank. Also like Jackson, Tyler favored the common man and the rapid settlement of the West. He approved the Preemption Act of 1841, which helped cash-poor settlers by allowing them to stake a free claim to 160 acres of federal land. By building a house and cultivating the land, they could purchase the property later at the standard price of $1.25 an acre.

The split between Tyler and the Whigs allowed the Democrats to regroup. The party vigorously recruited supporters among subsistence farmers in the North and smallholding planters in the South. It cultivated the votes of the urban working class and was particularly successful among Irish and German Catholic immigrants—whose numbers had increased rapidly during the 1830s—supporting their demands for religious and cultural freedom. Thanks to these recruits, the Democrats remained the majority party in most parts of the nation. Their program of equal rights, states' rights, and cultural liberty was more attractive than the Whig platform of economic nationalism, moral reform, and individual mobility.

The continuing struggle between Whigs and Democrats, each claiming to speak for "the people," completed the Democratic Revolution that European visitors found so troubling. The new system perpetuated many problematic practices—denying women, Indians, and most African Americans an effective voice in political life—and introduced a few more, such as the spoils system and a coarser standard of public debate. Yet the United States now boasted universal suffrage for white men as well as a highly organized system of representative government that was responsive to ordinary citizens. In their scope and significance for American life these political innovations matched the economic advances of the industrial and market revolutions.

TIMELINE

1810s	Revised state constitutions broaden male suffrage.			South Carolina nullifies Tariff of 1832.
	Van Buren creates a disciplined party in New York.			Frances Trollope's *The Domestic Manners of the Americans*
			1833	Force Bill and compromise Tariff Act
1825	John Quincy Adams elected president by House and advocates Henry Clay's American System.		**1834**	Whig Party formed by Henry Clay, John C. Calhoun, and Daniel Webster
1827– 1833	Working Men's Parties organized		**1835**	Roger B. Taney named chief justice of U.S. Supreme Court
				Alexis de Tocqueville's *Democracy in America*
1828	Tariff of Abominations			
	Andrew Jackson elected president		**1837**	*Charles River Bridge Co. v. Warren Bridge Co.* weakens legal privileges of chartered corporations.
	The South Carolina Exposition and Protest challenges legitimacy of national legislation.			
				Panic of 1837 begins depression of 1837–1843.
1830	Jackson vetoes extension of National Road.		**1838**	Cherokee Trail of Tears
	Indian Removal Act		**1840**	Log-cabin campaign
1831	*Cherokee Nation v. Georgia* denies Cherokee claim of national independence.		**1841**	John Tyler succeeds William Henry Harrison as president.
				Preemption Act
1832	*Worcester v. Georgia* upholds political authority of Indian communities.		**1842**	*Commonwealth v. Hunt* legitimizes trade unions.
	Expulsion of Sauk and Fox; Bad Axe Massacre			
	Jackson vetoes rechartering of Second Bank.			

For Further Exploration

George Dangerfield, *The Era of Good Feelings* (1952), is the classic study of American politics between 1815 and 1828 and offers a fascinating, detailed panorama of the period and the administration of John Quincy Adams. Two concise and well-written surveys of the Jacksonian era are Harry L. Watson, *Liberty and Power: The Politics of Jacksonian America* (1990), which emphasizes the importance of republican ideology and the market revolution, and Daniel Feller, *The Jacksonian Promise: America, 1815–1840* (1995), which underlines the tremendous optimism of the period as well as conflicting views of the nation's destiny. In *The Idea of a Party System* (1969) Richard Hofstadter lucidly explains the traditional opposition to parties and their triumphant entry into America politics.

Robert V. Remini, *The Life of Andrew Jackson* (1988), highlights Jackson's triumphs without neglecting his shortcomings. The brutal impact of Jackson's Indian policy is brought to life in Robert J. Conley, *Mountain Windsong: A Novel of the Trail of Tears* (1995). Major L. Wilson, *The Presidency of Martin Van Buren* (1984), provides a shrewd assessment of the man and his policies. The political ideology and politics of the laboring population is the focus of Sean Wilentz, *Chants Democratic: New York City and the Rise of the American Working Class, 1788–1850* (1986).

Alexis de Tocqueville's classic, *Democracy in America* (1835), should be sampled for its insights into the character of American society and political institutions. The book is available on line accompanied by an excellent exhibit explaining Tocqueville's trip to the United States and a collection of essays complementing his study, at <http://xroads.virginia.edu/~hyper/detoc/home.html>. For a brief treatment of the life of Andrew Jackson and some of his important state papers, log on to the Revolution to Reconstruction site at the University of Groningen in the Netherlands at <http://odur.let.rug.nl/~usa/P/aj7/aj7.htm>. For material on the Cherokees, see the websites prepared by Ken Martin, a tribal member of the Cherokee Nation of Oklahoma, <http://pages.tca.net/martikw/default.html>, and by Golden Ink in North Georgia, <http://ngeorgia.com/history/findex.html>.

Chapter 12

RELIGION AND REFORM
1820–1860

A peaceable man can hardly venture to eat or drink, . . . to correct
his child or kiss his wife, without obtaining the permission . . . of
some moral or other reform society.

—ORESTES BROWNSON, 1838

"The spirit of reform is in every place," the children of legal reformer
David Dudley Field wrote in their handwritten monthly "Gazette" in 1842:

> the labourer with a family says "reform the common schools"; the merchant
> and the planter say, "reform the tariff"; the lawyer "reform the laws," the politi-
> cian "reform the government," the abolitionist "reform the slave laws," the
> moralist "reform intemperance," . . . the ladies wish their legal privileges
> extended, and in short, the whole country is wanting reform.

Like many Americans the young Field children sensed that a whirlwind of political change in 1830s had transformed the way people thought about themselves as
individuals and as a society. It encouraged men and women to believe that they
could improve not just their personal lives but society as a whole. Some dedicated
themselves to societal reform. Beginning as an antislavery advocate William Lloyd
Garrison went on to embrace women's rights, pacifism, and the abolition of prisons. Such individuals, the Unitarian minister Henry W. Bellows warned, were obsessed, pursuing "an object, which in its very nature is unattainable—the perpetual
improvement of the outward condition."

Many obstacles stood in the reformers' quest for a better society. The American
social order was still rigidly divided by race and gender as well as wealth and religious belief. Moreover, recent social changes imposed new burdens on some individuals even as they improved the condition of others. Thus the new industrial and
market economy imposed new forms of social control on many workers, such as
gang labor for enslaved African Americans and a strict work routine for factory
operatives. In fact the first wave of American "improvers," the benevolent reformers of the 1820s, seized on social discipline as the answer to the nation's ills, cham-

pioning regular church attendance, temperance, and the strict moral codes of the evangelical churches.

Then in the 1830s and 1840s a more powerful wave of reform spilled out of these conservative religious channels and washed over American society, threatening to submerge traditional values and institutions. Mostly middle-class northerners and midwesterners in origin, the new reformers propounded a bewildering assortment of radical ideals—extreme individualism, common ownership of property, the immediate emancipation of slaves, and sexual equality—and demanded action to satisfy their visions. The result was a far-reaching intellectual and cultural debate that challenged the premises of the American social order. As a fearful southerner saw it, the goal of the reformers was a world in which there would be "No-Marriage, No-Religion, No-Private Property, No-Law and No Government."

Individualism

In 1835 Alexis de Tocqueville coined the word *individualism* to describe Americans as a people who were "no longer attached to each other by any tie of caste, class, association, or family." Unlike Tocqueville, who feared the disintegration of society, the New England transcendentalist Ralph Waldo Emerson (1803–1882) celebrated this liberation of the individual from traditional social and institutional constraints. Emerson's vision of individual freedom balanced by personal responsibility influenced thousands of ordinary Americans and a generation of important artists and writers.

EMERSON AND TRANSCENDENTALISM

Emerson was the leading spokesman for transcendentalism, an intellectual movement rooted in the religious soil of New England. Its first advocates were spiritually inclined young men, often Unitarian ministers from well-to-do New England families, who questioned the constraints imposed by their Puritan heritage. For inspiration they turned to Europe, drawing on a new conception of self and society known as Romanticism. Romantic thinkers, such as the English poet Samuel Taylor Coleridge, rejected the ordered, rational world of the eighteenth-century Enlightenment. Instead they tried to capture the passionate character of the human spirit and sought deeper insights into the mysteries of existence. Drawing on ideas borrowed from the German philosopher Immanuel Kant, English romantics and Unitarian radicals believed that behind the concrete world of the senses was an ideal world. To reach this deeper reality people had to "transcend," or go beyond, the rational ways in which they normally comprehended the world. By tapping mysterious intuitive powers people could soar beyond the limits of ordinary experience and gain mystical knowledge of ultimate and eternal things.

Emerson had followed in the footsteps of his father and become a Unitarian minister, thus placing himself outside the religious mainstream. Unlike most Christians Unitarians held that God was a single being and not a trinity of Father, Son, and Holy Spirit. In 1832 Emerson moved still further from orthodox Christianity, resigning his Boston pulpit and rejecting organized religion in favor of individual moral insight. Moving to Concord, Massachusetts, he turned to writing essays and lecturing. His subject was what he called "the infinitude of the private man," the idea of the radically free individual.

The young philosopher saw people as being trapped in inherited customs and institutions. They wore the ideas of people from earlier times—the tenets of New England Calvinism, for example—as a kind of "faded masquerade" and needed to shed those values and practices. "What is a man born for but to be a Reformer, a Remaker of what man has made?" he asked. For Emerson an individual's remaking depended on the discovery of his or her own "original relation with Nature," an insight that would lead to a mystical private union with the "currents of Universal Being." The ideal setting for such a discovery was solitude under an open sky, among nature's rocks and trees.

Emerson's genius lay in his capacity to translate abstract ideas into examples that made sense to ordinary middle-class Americans. His essays and lectures conveyed the message that all nature was saturated with the presence of God—a pantheistic spiritual outlook that departed from traditional Christian doctrine and underlay his attack on organized religion. Emerson also criticized the new industrial society, predicting that a preoccupation with work, profits, and the consumption of factory-made goods would drain the nation's spiritual energy. "Things are in the saddle," Emerson wrote, "and ride mankind."

The transcendentalist message of inner change and self-realization reached hundreds of thousands of people, primarily through Emerson's writings and lectures. Public lectures had become a spectacularly successful new way of spreading information and fostering discussion among the middle classes. Beginning in 1826 the American Lyceum attempted to "promote the general diffusion of knowledge" by organizing lecture tours by all sorts of speakers—poets, preachers, scientists, reformers—and soon achieved great popularity, especially in the North and Midwest. In 1839, 137 local Lyceum groups in Massachusetts invited lecturers to their towns during the fall and winter to speak to more than 33,000 subscribers. Among the hundreds of lecturers on the Lyceum circuit, Emerson was the most popular. Between 1833 and 1860 he gave 1,500 lectures in more than 300 towns in twenty states.

Emerson's celebration of the individual who was liberated from traditional social restraints but self-disciplined and responsible, tapped currents that already ran deep in his middle-class audiences. The publication of Benjamin Franklin's *Autobiography* in 1818 had given Americans a down-to-earth model of an individual seeking "moral perfection" through self-discipline and self-improvement. Charles

The Founder of Transcendentalism

As this painting of Ralph Waldo Emerson reveals, the young New England philosopher was an attractive man, his face brimming with confidence and optimism. Because of his radiant personality Emerson deeply influenced dozens of influential writers, artists, and scholars and enjoyed great success as a lecturer among the emerging middle class. (Artist unknown, The Metropolitan Museum of Art, Bequest of Chester Dale, 1962. [64.97.4] © 1991 The Metropolitan Museum of Art)

Grandison Finney's account of his conversion experience in 1823 also pointed in Emersonian directions. Finney, the foremost business-class evangelist, pictured his conversion as a mystical union of an individual, alone in the woods, with God. And the great revivalist's message, like that of Emerson, affirmed the importance of individual action. As Finney put it, "God has made man a moral free agent," thus endowing individuals with the ability—and the responsibility—to determine their spiritual fate.

EMERSON'S LITERARY INFLUENCE

Emerson took as one of his tasks the remaking of American literature. In an address entitled "The American Scholar" (1837) the philosopher issued a literary declaration of independence from the "courtly muse" of old Europe. He urged American writers to celebrate democracy and individual freedom and find inspiration not in the doings and sayings of aristocratic courts but in the "familiar, the low . . . the milk in the pan; the ballad in the street; the news of the boat; the glance of the eye; the form and gait of the body."

A young New England intellectual, Henry David Thoreau (1817–1862), heeded Emerson's call by turning to the American environment for inspiration. In 1845, prompted by his beloved brother's death, Thoreau turned away from society and embraced self-reliance and the natural world, building a cabin at the edge of Walden Pond near Concord, Massachusetts, and living alone there for two years. In 1854 he published *Walden, Or Life in the Woods,* an account of his spiritual search for meaning beyond the artificiality of life in a "civilized" society:

> I went to the woods because I wished to live deliberately, to front only the essential facts of life, and see if I could not learn what it had to teach, and not, when I came to die, discover that I had not lived.

Although Thoreau's book had little impact outside transcendentalist circles during his lifetime, *Walden* has become an essential text of American literature and an inspiration to those who reject the dictates of society. Its most famous metaphor provides an enduring justification for independent thinking: "If a man does not keep pace with his companions, perhaps it is because he hears a different drummer." Beginning from this premise, Thoreau became an advocate for social nonconformity and a philosopher of civil disobedience.

As Thoreau sought independence and self-realization for men, Margaret Fuller (1810–1850) explored the possibilities of freedom for women. Born into a wealthy Boston family, Fuller learned to read the classic works of literature in six languages and educated her four siblings. After teaching in a girls' school she became interested in Emerson's ideas and in 1839 began a transcendental "conversation," or discussion group, for educated Boston women. Soon Fuller was editing the leading transcendentalist journal, the *Dial,* and in 1844 she published *Woman in the Nineteenth Century,* which proclaimed that a "new era" was coming in the relations between men and women.

Fuller's philosophy began with the transcendental belief that women, like men, had a mystical relationship with God that gave them identity and dignity. It followed that every woman deserved psychological and social independence—the ability "to grow, as an intellect to discern, as a soul to live freely and unimpeded." Thus, she declared, "We would have every arbitrary barrier thrown down" and "every path laid open to Woman as freely as to Man." Embracing that vision, Fuller became the literary critic of the *New York Tribune* and went to Italy to report on the Revolution of 1848. Her adventurous life brought an early death; returning to the United States at the age of forty, she drowned in a shipwreck. But Fuller's example and writings inspired a rising generation of women reformers.

Another writer who responded to Emerson's call was the poet Walt Whitman (1819–1892). Whitman said that when he first encountered Emerson, he had been "simmering, simmering." Then Emerson "brought me to a boil." Whitman had been a teacher, a journalist, an editor of the *Brooklyn Eagle* and other newspapers, and an active publicist for the Democratic Party. But it was poetry that was the "direction of his dreams." In *Leaves of Grass,* first published in 1855 and constantly revised and expanded for almost four decades afterward, he recorded his attempt to pass a number of "invisible boundaries": between solitude and community, between prose and poetry, and even between the living and the dead.

At the center of *Leaves of Grass* is the individual—the figure of the poet, "I, Walt." He begins alone: "I celebrate myself, and sing myself." But because he has what Emerson called an "original relation" with nature, Whitman claims not solitude but perfect communion with others: "For every atom belonging to me as good belongs to you." Whitman was celebrating democracy as well as himself, arguing that a poet could claim a profoundly intimate, mystical relationship with a mass audience. For Emerson, Thoreau, and Fuller the individual had a divine spark. For Whitman the individual had actually become divine.

The transcendentalists were not naive optimists. Whitman wrote about human suffering with passion, and Emerson's accounts of the exhilaration that could come in natural settings were tinged with anxiety. "I am glad," he said, "to the brink of fear." Thoreau's gloomy judgment of everyday life is well known: "The mass of men lead lives of quiet desperation." Still, such dark murmurings were muted in their work, woven into triumphant and expansive assertions that nothing was impossible for an individual who could break free from tradition, law, and other social restraints and discover an "original relation with Nature."

Emerson's writings also influenced two great novelists, Nathaniel Hawthorne and Herman Melville, who had more pessimistic visions. They addressed the opposition between individual transcendence and the legitimate requirements of social order, discipline, and responsibility. Both sounded powerful warnings that unfettered egoism could destroy individuals and those around them. Hawthorne's most brilliant exploration of the theme of excessive individualism appeared in his novel *The Scarlet Letter* (1850). The two main characters, Hester Prynne and Arthur Dimmesdale, challenge their seventeenth-century New England community in the most blatant way—by committing adultery and producing a child. The result of their assertion of individual freedom from social discipline is not liberation but degradation—condemnation by the community.

Melville explored the limits of individualism in even more extreme and tragic terms and emerged as a scathing critic of transcendentalism. He made his most powerful statement in *Moby Dick* (1851), the story of Captain Ahab's obsessive hunt for a mysterious white whale that brings death not only to Ahab but to all but one of his crew. Here the quest for spiritual meaning in nature brings death, not transcendence, to the liberated individual who lacks inner discipline and self-restraint.

Moby Dick was a commercial failure. The middle-class audience that was the primary target of American publishers was unwilling to follow Melville into the dark, dangerous realms of individualism gone mad. Readers also were unenthusiastic about Thoreau's advocacy of civil disobedience and Whitman's boundless claims for a mystical union between the man of genius and the democratic mass. What American readers emphatically preferred were the more modest examples of individualism offered by Emerson.

BROOK FARM

To escape the constraints of life in industrializing America transcendentalists and other radical reformers created ideal communities, or *utopias*. They hoped that these planned societies, which organized life in new ways, would allow members to realize their spiritual and moral potential. The most important communal experiment of the transcendentalists was Brook Farm, founded in 1841. Free from the tension and demands of an urban competitive society, its members hoped to develop their minds and souls and uplift society through inspiration. The Brook Farmers supported themselves by selling milk, vegetables, and hay for cash but organized their farming so that they could remain relatively independent of the market, with its competitive pressures and cycles of boom and bust.

The intellectual life at Brook Farm was electric. Hawthorne lived there for a time and later used the setting for *The Blithedale Romance* (1852). All the major transcendentalists, including Emerson, Thoreau, and Fuller, were residents or frequent visitors. A former member recalled that they "inspired the young with a passion for study, and the middle-aged with deference and admiration, while we all breathed the intellectual grace that pervaded the atmosphere." Music, dancing, games, plays, parties, picnics, and dramatic readings filled the leisure hours.

If Brook Farm offered intellectual fulfillment, it failed to achieve economic sustainability. At first most of its members were ministers, teachers, writers, and students who had few productive skills; to succeed it needed practical men and women. A reorganization in 1844 attracted more farmers and artisans but yielded only marginal economic gains. And these changes resulted in a more disciplined routine that, as one resident put it, suppressed "the joyous spirit of youth." After a devastating fire in 1846 the organizers disbanded and sold the farm.

After the failure of Brook Farm the transcendentalists abandoned their attempts to fashion a new system of social organization. Most accepted the brute reality of industrial society and tried to reform it, especially through the education of workers. However, the passion of the transcendentalists for individual freedom and social progress lived on in the movement to abolish slavery, which many of them joined.

Communalism

Even as Brook Farm faded, thousands of Americans joined other communal settlements during the 1840s, primarily in the rural areas of the Northeast and Midwest (see Map 12.1). Most communalists were ordinary farmers and artisans

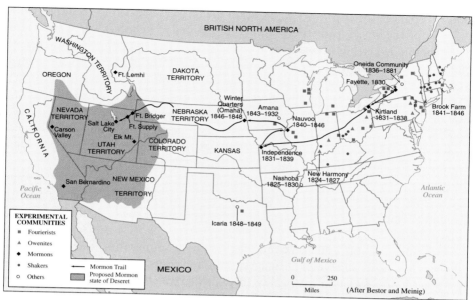

M A P 12.1
Major Communal Experiments before 1860

The United States was a vast land, so experimental communities had no difficulty finding substantial tracts of land in the East as well as the Midwest. Because of their opposition to slavery, most communalists avoided the South. Those Mormons who in the mid-1840s followed Brigham Young into the Salt Lake Basin (in what was then Mexican territory) formed the largest and most enduring communal society.

seeking refuge and security from the seven-year economic depression that had begun with the Panic of 1837. But these rural utopias were also symbols of social protest. By organizing themselves along socialist lines with common ownership of property, or by experimenting with unconventional forms of marriage and family life, they questioned acquisitive capitalist values and traditional gender roles.

THE SHAKERS

The Shakers, whose origins dated back to the Revolutionary era, were the first successful American communal movement. In 1770 Ann Lee Stanley (Mother Ann), a young cook in Manchester, England, had a vision that she was an incarnation of Christ; four years later she led a band of eight followers to America, where they established a church near Albany, New York. Because of the ecstatic dances that became part of their worship, the sect became known as "Shaking Quakers" or, more simply, "Shakers." After Mother Ann's death the Shakers decided to withdraw from the evils of the world into strictly run communities of believers. They embraced the common ownership of property, accepted strict government by the church, and pledged to abstain from alcohol, tobacco, politics, and war. Shakers also eliminated marriage and made a commitment to celibacy, in accordance with Mother Ann's testimony against "the lustful gratifications of the flesh as the source and foundation of human corruption."

The Shakers believed that God was "a dual person, male and female" and that Mother Ann represented God's female element. These doctrines provided the underpinning for their attempt to eliminate distinctions between the sexes. In practice Shakers maintained a traditional division of labor between men and women except in community governance, which in both its religious and its economic aspects, was undertaken by both women and men, the Eldresses and Elders.

Beginning in 1787 Shakers founded twenty communities, mostly in New England, New York, and Ohio. Their agriculture and crafts, especially furniture making, acquired a reputation for quality that enabled most of these communities to become self-sustaining and even comfortable. Thanks to this economic success and their ideology of sexual equality, Shaker communities attracted more than 3,000 converts during the 1830s, with women outnumbering men more than two to one. Because Shakers had no children of their own, they had to rely on converts and the adoption of young orphans to replenish their numbers. As these sources dried up in the 1840s and 1850s, the communities stopped growing and eventually began to decline. By the end of the nineteenth century most Shaker communities had virtually disappeared, leaving as their material legacy a distinctive and much-imitated furniture style.

THE FOURIERIST PHALANXES

The rise of the American Fourierist movement in the 1840s was one cause of the Shakers' decline. Charles Fourier (1777–1837) was a French utopian reformer who devised an eight-stage theory of social evolution, predicting the imminent decline of individualism and capitalism. As interpreted by his idealistic American disciple Arthur Brisbane, Fourierism would complete "our great political movement of 1776" through new social institutions that would end the "menial and slavish system of Hired Labor or Labor for Wages." In the place of capitalist waged labor there would be cooperative work in groups called *phalanxes*. The members of a phalanx would be its shareholders; they would own all its property in common, including stores and a bank as well as a school and a library. Fourier and Brisbane saw the phalanx as a practical, more humane alternative to the emerging capitalist society and one that would liberate women as well as men. "In society as it is now constituted," Brisbane wrote, "Woman is subjected to unremitting and slavish domestic

A Shaker Community

Like all Shaker communities, the settlement at Poland Hill, Maine, painted by Joshua H. Bussell around 1850, was built on a regular gridlike plan. There was a large dwelling for communal living, surrounded by various workshops and farm buildings. The design of the architecture, like that of Shaker furniture, was plain and sparse.
(Collection of the United Society of Shakers, Sabbathday Lake, Maine)

duties"; in the "new Social Order . . . based upon Associated households" women's domestic labor would be shared with men.

Brisbane skillfully promoted Fourier's ideas in his influential book *The Social Destiny of Man* (1840), a regular column in Horace Greeley's *New York Tribune,* and hundreds of lectures, many of them in towns along the Erie Canal. These ideas found a receptive audience among educated farmers and craftsmen, who yearned for economic stability and communal solidarity in the wake of the Panic of 1837. In the 1840s Brisbane and his followers started nearly 100 cooperative communities, mostly in the western New York and the midwestern states of Ohio, Michigan, and Wisconsin, but almost all were unable to support themselves and quickly collapsed. Despite its failure to establish viable communities the Fourierist movement underscored both the extent of the social dislocation caused by the economic depression and the difficulty of establishing a utopian community in the absence of charismatic leaders or a compelling religious vision.

NOYES AND THE ONEIDA COMMUNITY

The radical minister John Humphrey Noyes (1811–1886) was both charismatic and deeply religious. He believed that the Fourierists had failed because their communities lacked the strong religious ethic required for sustained altruism and cooperation and pointed to the success of the Shakers, praising them as the true "pioneers of modern Socialism." Noyes was also attracted by the Shakers' marriageless society and set about creating a community that defined sexuality and gender roles in radically new ways.

Noyes was a well-to-do graduate of Dartmouth College in New Hampshire who was inspired to join the ministry by the preaching of Charles Finney. When Noyes was expelled from his Congregational Church for unorthodox doctrines, he became a leader of "perfectionism." Perfectionism was an evangelical movement that attracted thousands of followers during the 1830s, primarily among religiously minded New Englanders who had settled in New York. Perfectionists believed that the Second Coming of Christ had already occurred and that people could therefore aspire to perfection in their earthly lives, attaining complete freedom from sin. Unlike most perfectionists (who lived conventional personal lives), Noyes believed that the major barrier to achieving this ideal state was marriage, which did not exist in heaven and should not exist on earth. "Exclusiveness, jealousy, quarreling have no place at the marriage supper of the Lamb," Noyes wrote. He wanted to reform marriage to liberate individuals from sin, as had the Shakers, but his solution was dramatically different: instead of Shaker celibacy, Noyes and his followers embraced *complex marriage*—all the members of his community were married to one another.

Complex marriage was a complex doctrine designed to attain various social goals. Noyes rejected monogamy partly because he wished to free women from being regarded (as they were by custom and by common law) as the property of their husbands. To give women even more freedom he sought to limit childbirth by urging men to have intercourse without orgasm and established community nurseries for those children they did have. By freeing women from endless childbearing and childraising Noyes hoped to help them become full and equal members of the community. To symbolize their equality with men the women cut their hair short and wore pantaloons under their calf-length skirts.

In the 1830s Noyes gathered his followers in his hometown of Putney, Vermont, but local opposition to the practice of complex marriage prompted him to move the community to Oneida, New York, in 1848. By the mid-1850s more than 200 people were living at Oneida, and it became financially self-sufficient when the inventor of a highly successful steel animal trap joined the community. With the profits from the production of traps Oneida diversified into making silverware. After Noyes fled to Canada in 1879 to avoid prosecution for adultery, the community abandoned complex marriage and founded a joint-stock silver manufacturing company, the Oneida Community, Ltd., which survived well into the twentieth century.

As with the Shakers and Fourierists, the historical significance of Noyes and his followers does not lie in their numbers, which were small, or in their fine crafts. Rather, they were important because they set up alternative communities that rejected certain social and sexual divisions of the emergent capitalist industrial society.

THE MORMON EXPERIENCE

The Shakers and the Oneidians challenged marriage and family life—two of the most deeply rooted institutions in American society—but their small communities aroused little hostility. The Mormons, or the Church of Jesus Christ of Latter-Day Saints, provoked much more animosity because of their equally controversial doctrines and their success in attracting thousands of members.

Like many social movements of the era Mormonism emerged from the religious ferment among families of Puritan descent who lived along the Erie Canal. The founder of the Mormon Church was Joseph Smith (1805–1844), a vigorous, powerful individual. Born in Vermont, he moved at the age of ten with his very religious but rather poor farming and shopkeeping family to Palmyra in central New York. In a series of religious experiences that began in 1820, Smith came to believe that God had singled him out to receive a special revelation of divine truth. In 1830 he published *The Book of Mormon,* claiming he had translated it from ancient hieroglyphics on gold plates shown to him by an angel named Moroni. Seeing himself as a prophet to a sinful, excessively individualistic society, Smith affirmed traditional patriarchal authority within the family and church control over many aspects of life. Like many Protestant ministers he encouraged his followers to work hard, save their earnings, and become entrepreneurs—practices central to success in the age of capitalist markets and factories. Unlike those ministers Smith placed equal emphasis on a communal framework that would protect the Mormon "New Jerusalem" from individualism and outside threats. His goal was a church-directed society that would inspire moral perfection.

Smith struggled for years to establish a secure home for his new religion. Facing persecution from anti-Mormons, Smith and his growing congregation trekked west, eventually settling in Nauvoo, Illinois, a town they founded on the Mississippi River. By the early 1840s Nauvoo had become the largest utopian community in the United States, with 30,000 inhabitants. The rigid discipline and secrecy of the Mormons, along with their prosperity, hostility to other sects, and bloc voting in Illinois elections, fueled resentment among their neighbors. This resentment turned to overt hostility when Smith refused to abide by any Illinois law that he did not approve, asked Congress to turn Nauvoo into a federal territory, and in 1844 declared himself a candidate for president of the United States (see American Voices, "An Illinois 'Jeffersonian' Attacks the Mormons").

An Illinois "Jeffersonian" Attacks the Mormons

*T*he solidarity of the Mormon community enraged many Illinois residents, who feared the power of the nearly independent city-state at Nauvoo and the 2,000-strong "Legion" of armed men organized as a defense force by Joseph Smith. This anonymous letter, probably written by a leading anti-Mormon editor who then published it in his own newspaper, proposes that the Mormons be forcibly expelled from the state.

Mr. Editor,
    . . . It is a low pitiable contemptable kind of electioneering, that old Tom Jefferson would have been ashamed of—when a body of men acting under the garb of religion (as the Mormons themselves say they are) shall decide our elections and act together as a body politically, we might as well bid a final farewell to our liberties and the common rights of man.
    Now Sir, under all these circumstances, it is high time that every individual should come out and clearly define the position that he occupies. I too am an Anti-Mormon both in principle and in practice. . . . Mr. Editor when I speak harshly of the Mormons . . . I do not mean every individual that advocates the Mormon cause. By no means; that there are some good, law-abiding peaceable citizens belonging to the Mormon profession I verily believe . . . but I am opposed to them because of the unprincipled manner in which the leaders of that fanatical sect, set at defiance the laws of the land . . . (as was the case in Missouri) claiming to be the chosen people of God; not subject to the laws of the state in any respect whatever, and receiving revelations direct from Heaven almost daily commanding them to take the property of the older citizens of the county and confiscate it to the use of the Mormon church. . . .
    It was for the commission of such deeds . . . that finally led to their expulsion from that state, and one of the brightest pages in the history of Missouri is that, on which is written "Governor Boggs's exterminating order" directing that the lawless rabble should be driven beyond the limits of the state, or exterminated at their own option. They chose the former, [which was] a most unfortunate thing for the state of Illinois.

SOURCE: David Brion Davis, *Antebellum America: An Interpretive Anthology* (Lexington, MA: Heath, 1979), pp. 226–27.

Moreover, Smith had received a new revelation that justified *polygamy*—a man having more than one wife at the same time. A few Mormon leaders began to practice polygamy, dividing the community from within, while Christian outrage encouraged assaults from without. In 1844 Smith was arrested and charged with treason for allegedly conspiring with foreign powers to create a Mormon colony in

Mexico. An anti-Mormon mob stormed the jail where Smith and his brother were being held in Carthage, Illinois, and murdered them.

Now led by Brigham Young the Mormon elders sought religious freedom by leaving the United States. In 1846 Young began a phased migration of more than 10,000 people across the Great Plains into Mexican territory. (Many of the migrants accepted the practice of polygamy; those who remained in the United States did not. Led by Smith's son, Joseph Smith III, they formed the Reorganized Church of Jesus Christ of Latter-Day Saints and remained in the Midwest.) Young's party eventually reached the Great Salt Lake Valley. Using communal labor and an elaborate irrigation system based on communal water rights, the Mormon pioneers transformed the region. They quickly spread planned agricultural communities along the base of the Wasatch Range in present-day Utah.

When the United States acquired the region from Mexico in 1848 (see Chapter 13), Congress rejected a Mormon petition to create a new state, Deseret, stretching all the way to Los Angeles. Instead, it set up the much smaller Utah Territory in 1850, with Young as territorial governor. In 1858 President James Buchanan removed Young from the governorship and, responding to pressure from Christian churches to eliminate polygamy, sent a small army to Salt Lake City. However, the

A Mormon Man and His Wives

Only a minority of Mormon men in Utah had more than one wife, and only a few had as many as this homesteader, who profited sexually and financially from their presence. The cabin, although cramped for such a large family, is well built, with a brick chimney and—a luxury for any pioneer home—a glass window. (Library of Congress)

"Mormon War" proved bloodless. Fearing that the forced abolition of polygamy would serve as a precedent for the ending of slavery, Buchanan withdrew the troops. The national government did not succeed in pressuring the Utah Mormons to outlaw polygamy until 1890, six years before Utah became a state.

Mormons in both Utah and the Midwest had succeeded where other social experiments and utopian communities had failed. They endorsed the private ownership of property and encouraged individualistic economic enterprise, accepting the entrepreneurial spirit of market society. But Mormon leaders resolutely used strict religious controls to create disciplined communities and patriarchal families, reaffirming values inherited from the eighteenth century. This blend of economic innovation, social conservatism, and hierarchical leadership created a prosperous church with a strong missionary impulse.

Abolitionism

In most cities and farm villages the communalists attracted far less attention than the abolitionists, whose demand for an immediate end to racial slavery led to fierce political debates, riots, and sectional conflict. Like other reform movements, abolitionism drew on the religious energy and ideas generated by the Second Great Awakening, which altered the attitude of many northern and midwestern whites toward the South's "peculiar institution." Early nineteenth-century reformers had criticized human bondage as contrary to the tenets of republicanism and liberty. Now abolitionists condemned slavery as a sin and saw it as their moral duty to end this violation of God's law.

AFRICAN COLONIZATION

By 1820 republican-minded reformers had prevented the expansion of slavery into the states of the Old Northwest and had persuaded the northern states to provide for gradual emancipation. They had also induced Congress to outlaw the importation of enslaved Africans and, in the Missouri Compromise, to prohibit slavery in most of the Louisiana Purchase. But the most difficult problem remained untouched: ending slavery in the South and the border states of Kentucky, Tennessee, and Missouri.

In 1817 the founders of the American Colonization Society, which included President James Monroe and Henry Clay, thought they had the answer. Slaveowners would gradually emancipate their slaves—some 1.5 million people in 1820—and the Society would arrange for their resettlement in Africa. The Society's leaders believed, as Clay put it, that racial bondage had placed his state of Kentucky and the other slaveholding states "in the rear of our neighbors . . . in the state of agriculture, the progress of manufactures, the advance of improvement, and the general prosperity of society."

Slavery had to go, as did the freed slaves. Emancipation without colonization, the influential Kentucky Congressman predicted, "would be followed by instantaneous collisions between the two races, which would break out into a civil war that would end in the extermination or subjugation of the one race or the other." Northerners who joined the Colonization Society had much the same outlook. They regarded the 250,000 free blacks in the northern states as "notoriously ignorant, degraded and miserable, mentally diseased, brokenspirited," as one Society report put it. Hoping to create a "white man's country," what they wanted was "African removal."

The American Colonization Society was a dismal failure. Despite appeals to wealthy individuals, churches, and state governments, it raised enough money to purchase freedom for only a few hundred slaves. Moreover, most free blacks rejected colonization, agreeing with Bishop Richard Allen of the African Methodist Episcopal Church that "this land which we have watered with our tears and our blood is now our mother country." Three thousand African Americans met in Philadelphia's Bethel Church to condemn colonization, declaring that their goal was to advance in American society using "those opportunities . . . which the Constitution and the laws allow to all." And they refused to support the only African American newspaper, *Freedom's Journal* (founded in 1827), once it endorsed colonization, causing it to collapse in 1829. Lacking significant support from either blacks or whites, the Society transported only 6,000 African Americans to Liberia, a colony it established on the west coast of Africa.

SLAVE REBELLION

Having rejected colonization, free blacks demanded an end to slavery. To build support for emancipation, African American leaders tried to "uplift" the black masses by stressing "respectability": temperance, sabbath keeping, and education. To achieve these goals they helped to create an impressive number of churches, schools, and benevolent associations. But some whites felt threatened by this quest for respectability, and in the mid-1820s led mobs against blacks in New Haven, Boston, and Pittsburgh.

Partly in response to these attacks, in 1829 David Walker published a stirring pamphlet entitled *An Appeal . . . to the Colored Citizens*. A free black from North Carolina who had moved to Boston, Walker used the pamphlet to ridicule the "colonizing trick" and the religious pretensions of bigoted whites in the North and slaveholders in the South. He justified slave rebellion, warning white Americans that the slaves would revolt if justice was delayed. "We must and shall be free. . . . And woe, woe, will be it to you if we have to obtain our freedom by fighting. . . . I do declare that one good black man can put to death six white men." Walker's *Appeal* quickly went through three printings and began to reach free blacks in the South. In 1830 Walker and other African American activists called a national convention in Philadelphia. The delegates did not adopt Walker's radical position but urged free

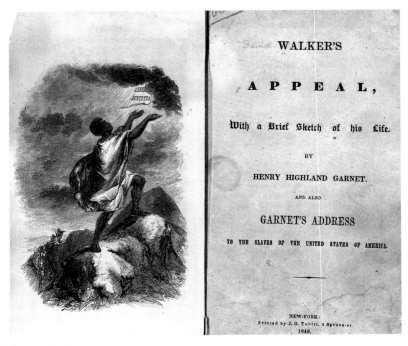

A Call for Revolution

David Walker (1785–1830) used his own savings to publish the *Appeal to the Colored Citizens of the World,* a learned and passionate attack against racial slavery. In the *Appeal,* published in 1829, Walker depicts Christ as an avenging "God of justice and of armies" and raises the banner of slave rebellion. A year later he was found in his shop, dead from unknown causes. (Library of Congress)

blacks to use every legal means to improve the condition of their race and asked for divine assistance in breaking "the shackles of slavery."

As Walker was calling for violent black rebellion from Boston, Nat Turner, a slave in Southampton County, Virginia, staged a bloody revolt—a coincidence that had far-reaching consequences. As a child Turner had taught himself to read and had hoped to be emancipated, but a new master forced him into field work and another master separated him from his wife. Turner became deeply spiritual, seeing visions and concluding that he might have been chosen to carry Christ's burden of suffering in a race war. Taking an eclipse of the sun as an omen, Turner plotted with a handful of relatives and close friends to meet the masters' terror with violence of their own. In August 1831 his men killed almost sixty whites, in many cases dismembering and decapitating them. Turner hoped that a vast army of slaves would rally to his cause, but he had mustered only sixty men by the time a white militia dispersed his poorly armed and exhausted followers. Vengeful whites now took slaves' lives at random. One company of cavalry killed forty in two days, putting the heads of fifteen on poles to warn "all those who should undertake a similar plot." Fifty slaves were prosecuted, and twenty were hanged. After hiding for nearly two months Turner was captured and hanged, still identifying his mission with Christ's.

Deeply shaken by Turner's rebellion, the Virginia legislature debated a bill providing for gradual emancipation and colonization. When the bill was rejected in 1832 by a vote of seventy-three to fifty-eight, the possibility that southern planters would legislate an end to slavery faded forever. Instead, the southern states marched down another path, toughening their slave codes, limiting the movement of slaves, and prohibiting anyone from teaching them to read. They would meet Walker's radical *Appeal* with radical measures of their own.

GARRISON AND EVANGELICAL ABOLITIONISM

Frightened by the prospect of a bloody racial revolution and inspired by the antislavery efforts of free blacks, a dedicated cadre of northern and midwestern evangelical whites launched a moral crusade to abolish slavery. Previously Quakers, along with some Methodists and Baptists, had freed their slaves and campaigned for gradual emancipation in the North. Now radical Christian abolitionists demanded that southerners free their slaves immediately. The issue was absolute: if the slaveowners did not repent and allow slaves their God-given status as free moral agents, the evangelical abolitionists believed, they faced the prospect of revolution in this world and damnation in the next.

The most uncompromising leader of the abolitionist movement was William Lloyd Garrison (1805–1879). A Massachusetts-born printer, Garrison had collaborated in Baltimore during the 1820s with a Quaker, Benjamin Lundy, who published the *Genius of Universal Emancipation,* the leading antislavery newspaper of the decade. In 1830 Garrison went to jail for seven weeks for libeling a New England merchant engaged in the domestic slave trade. Garrison went on to found his own antislavery weekly, *The Liberator,* in Boston in 1831. The next year he spearheaded the formation of the New England Anti-Slavery Society.

From the outset *The Liberator* took a radical stance. Garrison condemned the American Colonization Society, charging that its real aim was to strengthen slavery by removing troublesome African Americans who were already free. He attacked the U.S. Constitution for its implicit acceptance of racial bondage, labeling it "a covenant with death, an agreement with Hell." And he demanded the immediate abolition of slavery without reimbursement for slaveholders. As time went on, Garrison concluded that slavery was a sign of deep corruption infesting all American institutions and called for comprehensive reform of society.

Theodore Dwight Weld, who joined Garrison as a leading abolitionist, came to the movement from the religious revivals of the 1830s. The son of a Congregationalist minister and inspired by Charles Finney, Weld became an advocate of temperance and educational reform. Turning to abolitionism, he worked in northern

Presbyterian and Congregational churches, preaching the moral responsibility of all Americans for the denial of liberty to slaves. In 1834 Weld inspired a group of students at Lane Theological Seminary in Cincinnati to form an antislavery society. Weld's crusade gathered force, buttressed by the theological arguments he advanced in *The Bible against Slavery* (1837). Collaborating closely with Weld were Angelina Grimké, whom he married in 1838, and her sister, Sarah. The Grimkés had left their father's South Carolina slave plantation and converted to Quakerism and abolitionism in Philadelphia.

Weld and the Grimkés provided the abolitionist movement with a mass of evidence in *American Slavery as It Is: Testimony of a Thousand Witnesses* (1839). The book set out to answer a simple question—"What is the actual condition of the slaves in the United States?"—with evidence from southern newspapers and first-hand testimonies. In one account, Angelina Grimké told of a treadmill that slave-owners used for punishment: "One poor girl, [who was] sent there to be flogged, and who was accordingly stripped naked and whipped, showed me the deep gashes on her back—I might have laid my whole finger in them—*large pieces of flesh had actually been cut out by the torturing lash.*" The book sold over 100,000 copies in its first year alone.

In 1833 Weld, Garrison, Arthur and Lewis Tappan, and sixty other delegates, black and white, met in Philadelphia to establish the American Anti-Slavery Society. The Society received financial support from the Tappans, wealthy merchants in New York City. Women abolitionists quickly established their own organizations, such as the Philadelphia Female Anti-Slavery Society, founded by Lucretia Mott in 1833, and the Anti-Slavery Conventions of American Women, formed by a network of local societies in the late 1830s. The women's societies raised money for *The Liberator* and were a major force in the movement, especially in the farm villages and rural areas of the Midwest, distributing abolitionist literature and collecting tens of thousands of signatures on antislavery petitions.

Abolitionist leaders developed a three-pronged plan of attack, beginning with an appeal to public opinion. To foster intense public condemnation of slavery they adopted the tactics of the religious revivalists: large rallies led by stirring speakers, constant agitation by local antislavery chapters, and home visits by agents of the movement. The abolitionists also used the latest techniques of mass communication. Assisted by new steam-powered printing presses, the American Anti-Slavery Society distributed more than 100,000 pieces of literature in 1834. In 1835 the Society launched its "great postal campaign," which flooded the nation, including the South, with a million abolitionist pamphlets. In July 1835 alone abolitionists mailed more than 175,000 items at the New York City post office.

The abolitionists' second strategy was to assist the African Americans who fled from slavery. Those blacks who lived near a free state had the greatest chance of success, but fugitives from plantations deeper in the South received aid from the "underground railroad," an informal network of whites and free blacks in Richmond, Charleston, and other southern cities. In Baltimore a free African

American sailor lent his identification papers to the future abolitionist Frederick Douglass, who used them to escape to New York. Many escaped slaves, such as Harriet Tubman, returned repeatedly to the South, risking reenslavement or death to help others escape. Thanks to the "railroad" by the 1840s about 1,000 African Americans reached freedom in the North each year.

There they faced an uncertain future. Whites in the northern and midwestern states did not support civic equality for free blacks. Five New England states extended suffrage to African American men, while six northern and midwestern states changed their constitutions to deny them the franchise. Moreover, the Fugitive Slave Law (1793) allowed masters and hired slave-catchers to capture suspected fugitives and carry them back to bondage. To thwart these efforts white abolitionists in northern cities joined with crowds of free blacks to seize recaptured slaves and drive slave-catchers out of town.

Third, the abolitionists sought support from state and national legislators. In 1835 the American Anti-Slavery Society encouraged local chapters and members to bombard Congress with petitions demanding the abolition of slavery in the District of Columbia, an end to the domestic slave trade, and a ban on the admission of new slave states. By 1838 petitions with nearly 500,000 signatures had arrived in Washington.

This agitation drew thousands of middle-class men and women to abolitionism. During the 1830s the number of local abolitionist societies grew swiftly, from about 200 in 1835 to more than 500 in 1836 and nearly 2,000 by 1840—when they had nearly 200,000 members, including many leading transcendentalists. Emerson condemned American society for tolerating slavery; Thoreau was even more assertive. Seeing the Mexican War as an attempt to extend slavery, in 1846 he refused to pay his taxes and submitted to arrest. Two years later he published an anonymous essay entitled "Civil Disobedience" that outlined how individuals, by resisting governments because of loyalty to a higher moral law, could redeem themselves and the state. "A minority is powerless while it conforms to the majority," Thoreau declared, but it becomes "irresistible when it clogs by its whole weight."

OPPOSITION AND INTERNAL CONFLICT

As Thoreau recognized, the abolitionist crusade had won the wholehearted allegiance of only a small minority. Perhaps 10 percent of northerners and midwesterners strongly supported the movement; another 20 percent were sympathetic to its goals. But its opponents were much more numerous and no less aggressive. Men of wealth feared that the abolitionist attack on slave property might become a general assault on all property rights; tradition-minded clergymen condemned the public roles assumed by abolitionist women; and northern merchants and textile manufacturers rallied to the support of their white customers and suppliers in the South. Northern wage-earners feared that freed slaves would work for subsistence wages and take their jobs. Finally, whites almost universally opposed the prospect of "amalgamation"—racial mixing and intermarriage—that Garrison seemed to support.

Moved by such sentiments, northern opponents of abolitionism, often led by "gentlemen of property and standing," turned to violence. In 1833 an antiabolitionist mob of 1,500 New Yorkers stormed a church in search of Garrison and Arthur Tappan, and in 1834 a group of laborers vandalized and set fire to Lewis Tappan's house. Another white mob swept through Philadelphia's African American neighborhoods, clubbing and stoning residents, destroying homes and churches, and forcing crowds of black women and children to flee the city. In 1835 in Utica, New York, a group of lawyers, local politicians, merchants, and bankers broke up an abolitionist convention and beat several delegates. Two years later in Alton, Illinois, a mob shot and killed an abolitionist editor, Elijah P. Lovejoy. By raising the issues of emancipation and racial equality the abolitionists had shattered the possibility of a biracial middle class in the North open to "respectable" African Americans and encouraged whites—and blacks—to identify across class lines with those of their own race.

Racial solidarity was particularly strong in the South, where whites reacted to abolitionism with fury. Southern legislatures banned the movement and passed resolutions demanding that northern states follow suit. The Georgia legislature offered a $5,000 reward to anyone who would kidnap Garrison and bring him South to be tried for inciting rebellion. In Nashville vigilantes whipped a northern college student for distributing abolitionist pamphlets, and a mob in Charleston attacked the post office and destroyed sacks of abolitionist mail. After 1835 southern postmasters simply refused to deliver mail suspected to be of abolitionist origin.

Politicians joined the fray. President Andrew Jackson, though a radical on many issues, was a slaveowner and a firm supporter of the southern social order. Jackson privately approved of South Carolina's removal of abolitionist pamphlets from the U.S. mail, and in 1835 he asked Congress to restrict the use of the mails by abolitionist groups. Congress did not comply, but in 1836 the House of Representatives adopted the so-called *gag rule*. Under this rule, which remained in force until 1844, antislavery petitions were automatically tabled when they were received so that they could not become the subjects of debate in the House.

Assailed from outside abolitionists were also divided among themselves. Many antislavery clergymen denounced the public lecturing to mixed audiences by the Grimké sisters and other women as "promiscuous" and immoral. Other supporters denied any intention to promote race-mixing through marriage; others abandoned the Anti-Slavery Society because of Garrison's advocacy of further social reforms.

Indeed, Garrison had broadened his agenda and now supported pacifism and the abolition of prisons and asylums. Arguing that "our object is universal emancipation, to redeem women as well as men from a servile to an equal condition," he demanded that the American Anti-Slavery Society retain a broad platform that supported women's rights. At the convention of the American Anti-Slavery Society in 1840 Garrison precipitated a split with more conservative abolitionists by insisting on equal participation by women and helping to elect Abby Kelley to the organization's business committee. When the movement split, Kelley, Lucretia Mott, and Elizabeth Cady Stanton remained with Garrison in the American Anti-Slavery Society. They recruited new women agents, including Lucy Stone, to proclaim the common interests of enslaved blacks and free women.

Garrison's opponents founded a new organization, the American and Foreign Anti-Slavery Society, which received financial backing from Lewis Tappan. Its members worked through their churches to win public support for practical measures against slavery. Other abolitionists turned to electoral politics, establishing the Liberty Party and nominating James G. Birney for president in 1840. Birney was a former Alabama slaveowner who had been converted to abolitionism by Theodore Weld and had founded an antislavery newspaper in Cincinnati. Birney and the Liberty Party argued that the Constitution did not recognize slavery; that the Fifth Amendment, by barring any congressional deprivation of "life, liberty, or property," prevented the federal government from supporting slavery; and that slaves became automatically free when they entered areas of federal authority, such as the District of Columbia and national territories. But Birney won few votes in the election of 1840, and the future of the party and political abolitionism appeared dim.

Coming hard on the heels of popular violence and political suppression, these schisms and electoral failures stunned the abolitionist movement. It had attracted the energies and ideas of thousands of evangelical Protestants, moral reformers, and transcendentalists. But the abolitionists had aroused the hostility of a substantial majority of the white population. "When we first unfurled the banner of *The Liberator*," Garrison admitted in 1837, ". . . it did not occur to us that nearly every religious sect, and every political party would side with the oppressor."

The Women's Movement

The prominence of women among the abolitionists was the product of a broad shift in American culture. After the American Revolution women began to play a small role in public life, joining religious revivals and reform movements such as the temperance crusade. But it was the public activities of abolitionist women that created great controversy over gender issues and made some reformers into advocates for women's rights. They argued that women had rights as individuals and within marriage that were equal to those of men.

ORIGINS OF THE WOMEN'S MOVEMENT

During the American Revolution, upper-class women had raised the issue of greater legal rights for married women but won only a slightly enhanced status as "republican mothers." Subsequently the economic revolution presented young farm women with new opportunities for factory labor but imposed new constraints on middle-class married women, reinforcing their confinement to a "separate sphere." Rather than working as household producers (the traditional roles of the wives of farmers and artisans), middle-class women became full-time providers of household services, such as child care. But many of these middle-class women achieved greater authority within their families by joining religious revivals and becoming guardians of morality. Such activities bolstered their self-esteem and encouraged wives to enlarge their influence over all areas of family life, including the timing of pregnancies. Publications such as *Godey's Lady's Book* and Catharine Beecher's *Treatise on Domestic Economy* (1841) taught women how to make their homes more efficient and moral and justified a life of middle-class domesticity.

For most middle-class women a greater influence over family life was enough, but some women used their newfound religious authority to increase their involvement outside the home. Moral reform was among the first of their efforts in the public arena. In 1834 a group of middle-class women founded the New York Female Moral Reform Society and elected Lydia Finney, the wife of the evangelical minister Charles Finney, as its president. Its goals were to end prostitution, redeem "fallen" women, and protect single women from moral corruption. By 1840 it had grown into a national association, the American Female Moral Reform Society, with 555 chapters and 40,000 members throughout the North and Midwest. Employing only women as its agents, bookkeepers, and staff, the society attempted to provide moral "government" for factory girls, seamstresses, clerks, and servants who lived away from their families. Women reformers even visited brothels, where they sang hymns, offered prayers, searched for runaway girls, and noted the names of clients. They also founded homes of refuge for prostitutes and homeless women and won the passage of laws regulating men's sexual behavior—including making seduction a crime—in Massachusetts in 1846 and New York in 1848.

Women also turned their energies to the reform of social institutions, working to improve conditions in almshouses, asylums, hospitals, and jails, which grew in number in the 1830s and 1840s. The Massachusetts reformer Dorothea Dix was a leader in these efforts. Outraged that insane women were jailed alongside criminals, Dix persuaded the Massachusetts legislature to expand the state hospital to accommodate the poor and mentally ill. Dix carried her message to other states, persuading legislatures to expand their public hospitals, and nearly secured congressional legislation that would have set aside 12.5 million acres of public land to support asylums for the insane.

Both as reformers and as teachers northern women played a major role in education. From Maine to Wisconsin women vigorously supported the movement led by Horace Mann to increase the number of public elementary schools and improve their quality. As secretary of the newly created Massachusetts Board of Education from 1837 to 1848, Mann lengthened the school year; established teaching standards in reading, writing, and arithmetic; and improved instruction by recruiting well-educated women as teachers. The intellectual leader of the new corps of women educators was Catharine Beecher, who founded academies for young women in Hartford and Cincinnati. In a series of publications Beecher argued that "energetic and benevolent women" were the best qualified to impart moral and intellectual instruction to the young. By the 1850s most teachers were women both because school boards heeded Beecher's arguments and because women could be paid less than men.

ABOLITIONISM AND WOMEN

The public accomplishments of moral reformers such as Dix and Beecher inspired other women to assume public roles in the movement to end slavery. During the Revolutionary era Quaker women in Philadelphia had established schools for freed slaves, and subsequently many Baptist and Methodist women in the upper South endorsed religious arguments against slavery. When William Lloyd Garrison began his radical campaign for abolition, a few women rallied to his cause. One of the first Garrisonian abolitionists was Maria W. Stewart, an African American who spoke to mixed audiences of men and women in Boston in the early 1830s. As the abolitionist movement mushroomed, scores of white women delivered lectures condemning slavery and thousands more conducted home "visitations" to win converts.

Influenced by abolitionist ideas and their own experience of discrimination, a few women challenged the subordinate status of their sex. The most famous were Angelina and Sarah Grimké. When some Congregationalist clergymen demanded in 1836 that they cease lecturing on slavery to mixed male and female audiences, Sarah Grimké turned to the Christian Bible for justification: "The Lord Jesus defines the duties of his followers in his Sermon on the Mount . . . without any reference to sex or condition," she wrote. "Men and women are CREATED EQUAL! They are both moral and accountable beings and whatever is right for man to do is right for woman." In a debate with Catharine Beecher (who wanted women to exercise power through their domestic activities) Angelina Grimké pushed the argument beyond religion, using Enlightenment principles to claim equal civic rights for women:

> It is a woman's right to have a voice in all the laws and regulations by which she is governed, whether in Church or State. . . . The present arrangements of society, on these points are a violation of human rights, a rank usurpation of power, a violent seizure and confiscation of what is sacredly and inalienably hers.

By 1840 the Grimkés were asserting that traditional gender roles amounted to the "domestic slavery" of women.

Not all abolitionist women shared that exact view, but many soon were using the abolitionist movement as a launching point from which to address the

Sojourner Truth

Few women had as interesting a life as Sojourner Truth. Born as Isabella in Dutch-speaking rural New York about 1797, she labored as a slave until 1827. Following a religious vision, Isabella moved to New York City, learned English, and worked for deeply religious—and ultimately fanatical—Christian merchants. Seeking spiritual enlightenment in 1843 she took the name "Sojourner Truth" and left New York. After briefly joining the Millerites (who believed the world would end in 1844) Truth became famous as a forceful speaker on behalf of abolitionism and women's rights. This photograph, taken when she was in her seventies, suggests Truth's powerful personal presence. (Massachusetts Historical Society)

condition of their sex. The most prominent example was the novelist Harriet Beecher Stowe, who in the novel *Uncle Tom's Cabin* (1852) charged that among the greatest moral failings of slavery was its destruction of the slave family and the degradation of slave women. Sojourner Truth, a former slave who lectured to both antislavery and women's rights conventions, hammered home the point that women slaves were denied both basic human rights and the protected separate sphere enjoyed by free women. "I have ploughed and planted and gathered into barns, and no man could head me—and ain't I a woman?" she asked. Drawn into public life

A Farm Woman Defends the Grimké Sisters

KEZIAH KENDALL

*T*he New England lecture tour of the Grimké sisters sparked a huge outcry, including a lecture on "The Legal Rights of Women," by Simon Greenleaf, Royall Professor of Law at Harvard College. Replying to Greenleaf's advocacy of a restricted role for women, Keziah Kendall—possibly the fictional creation of a contemporary women's rights advocate—penned the following letter.

My name is Keziah Kendall. I live not many miles from Cambridge, on a farm with two sisters, one older, one younger than myself. I am thirty two. Our parents and only brother are dead—we have a good estate—comfortable house—nice barn, garden, orchard &c and money in the bank besides. . . . Under these circumstances the whole responsibility of our property, not less than twenty five thousand dollars rest upon me.

Well—our milkman brought word when he came from market that you were a going to lecture on the legal rights of women, and so I thought I would go and learn. Now I hope you wont think me bold when I say, I did not like that lecture much . . . [because] there was nothing in it but what every body knows. . . .

What I wanted to know, was good reasons for some of those laws that I cant account for. . . . One Lyceum lecture that I heard in C[ambridge] stated that the Americans went to war with the British, because they were taxed without being represented in Parliament. Now we [women] are taxed every year to the full amount of every dollar we possess—town, county, state taxes—taxes for land, for movable, for money and all. Now I don't want to [become a legislative] representative . . . any more than I do to be a "constable or a sheriff," but I have no voice about public improvements, and I don't see the justice of being taxed any more than the "revolutionary heroes" did.

Nor do I think we are treated as Christian women ought to be, according to the Bible rule of doing to others as you would others should do unto you. . . . Another thing . . . women have joined the Antislavery societies, and why? Women are kept for slaves as well as men—it is a common cause, deny the justice of it, who can! To be sure I do not wish to go about lecturing like the Misses Grimkie, but I have not the knowledge they have, and I verily believe that if I had been brought up among slaves as they were . . . I should run the venture of your displeasure, and that of a good many others like you.

SOURCE: Dianne Avery and Alfred S. Konefsky, "The Daughters of Job: Property Rights and Women's Lives in Mid-Nineteenth-Century Massachusetts," *Law and History Review*, 10 (Fall 1992), pp. 323–56.

by abolitionism, thousands of northern and midwestern women had become firm advocates of greater rights not only for African Americans but also for white women (see American Voices, "A Farm Woman Defends the Grimké Sisters").

THE PROGRAM OF SENECA FALLS

The commitment to full civil equality for women emerged during the 1840s as activists devised a pragmatic program of reform. While championing the rights of women, they did not challenge the institution of marriage or even the conventional division of labor within the family. Instead, harking back to the efforts of Abigail Adams and other Revolutionary era women, they tried to strengthen the legal rights of married women, especially with respect to property. In 1848 New York adopted legislation giving married women greater control over their own property, and similar laws were enacted in fourteen other states. Affluent men provided crucial support for this legislation. They wanted to protect their wives' assets in case their own businesses went into bankruptcy and to guard against dissolute sons-in-law who might waste their daughters' inheritances.

To advance the nascent women's movement Elizabeth Cady Stanton and Lucretia Mott, who had become friends at the World Anti-Slavery Convention in London in 1840, organized a gathering in Seneca Falls in central New York in 1848. The group, composed mostly of men and women from the immediate area, outlined for the first time a coherent program for women's equality. Taking the republican ideology of the Declaration of Independence as a starting point, the group declared that "all men and women are created equal" but that "the history of mankind is a history of repeated injuries and usurpations on the part of man toward woman, having in direct object the establishment of an absolute tyranny over her." To persuade Americans to right this long-standing wrong, they resolved to "use every instrumentality within our power. . . . We shall employ agents, circulate tracts, petition the State and national legislatures, and endeavor to enlist the pulpit and the press on our behalf." By staking out claims for equality for women in public life, the Seneca Falls activists repudiated the idea that the assignment of separate spheres for men and women was the natural order of society.

Although most men dismissed the Seneca Falls Declaration as nonsense, it drew women—and a few radical men—into the movement. In 1850 the first national women's rights convention in Worcester, Massachusetts, began to hammer out a reform program. Local and state conventions of women called on churches to revise concepts of female inferiority in their theology and worked for legal changes that would allow married women to control their property and earnings, guarantee the custody rights of mothers in the event of divorce or the father's death, and ensure women's right to sue and testify in court. Finally, and above all else, they began a concerted campaign to win the vote for women. In 1851 the national convention of women declared that suffrage was "the corner-stone of this enterprise, since we do not seek to protect woman, but rather to place her in a position to protect herself."

The struggle for legislation required leaders who had talents as organizers and lobbyists. The most prominent political operative was Susan B. Anthony (1820–1906). Anthony came from a Quaker family and as a young woman had been ac-

Susan B. Anthony, circa 1850

As a child, Susan B. Anthony worked on the Rochester, New York, farm of her father, a failed textile manufacturer. During the Civil War she showed her organizational skills as the founder (with Elizabeth Cady Stanton) of the National Women's Loyal League, which promoted the cause of women's suffrage and gathered 400,000 signatures in favor of a constitutional amendment prohibiting slavery. (Courtesy Meserve-Kunhardt Collection, Mt. Kisco, NY)

tive in temperance and antislavery efforts. Her experience in the temperance movement, Anthony explained, had taught her "the great evil of woman's utter dependence on man." In 1851 she joined the movement for women's rights and forged an enduring friendship with Elizabeth Cady Stanton. Anthony created a network of political "captains," all women, who relentlessly lobbied the legislature in New York and other states. In 1860 her efforts culminated in a New York law granting women the right to collect and spend their own wages (which fathers or husbands previously could insist on controlling), bring suit in court, and, if widowed, acquire full control of the property they had brought to the marriage. Such successes would provide the basis for more aggressive reform attempts after the Civil War.

The attack by women's rights activists against the traditional legal and social prerogatives of husbands, like the abolitionists' assault on the power and property of southern slaveholders, prompted many Americans to fear that social reform might not perfect their society but destroy it. The various movements for reform, begun with such confidence and religious zeal, had raised legal and political issues that threatened the fabric of society and the unity of the nation.

TIMELINE

1817	American Colonization Society founded	1841	Transcendentalists found Brook Farm. Dorothea Dix promotes hospitals for the insane.
1829	David Walker's *Appeal . . . to the Colored Citizens* advocates slave rebellion.		
1830	Joseph Smith's *The Book of Mormon*	1844	Margaret Fuller's *Woman in the Nineteenth Century*
1831	William Lloyd Garrison begins publishing *The Liberator.* Nat Turner's rebellion	1845	Henry David Thoreau withdraws to Walden Pond.
1832	Ralph Waldo Emerson rejects organized religion and embraces transcendentalism.	1846	Mormons begin trek to Salt Lake.
		1848	John Humphrey Noyes founds Oneida Community. Seneca Falls meeting on women's rights
1833	American Anti-Slavery Society founded		
1834	New York Female Moral Reform Society established	1850	Nathaniel Hawthorne's *The Scarlet Letter*
1835	Abolitionist mail campaign; antiabolitionist riots	1851	Herman Melville's *Moby Dick* Susan B. Anthony joins movement for women's rights.
1836	House of Representatives adopts a gag rule against antislavery petitions. Grimké sisters defend public roles for women.	1852	Harriet Beecher Stowe's *Uncle Tom's Cabin*
		1855	Walt Whitman's *Leaves of Grass*
1840	Liberty Party runs James G. Birney for president.	1858	The "Mormon War"
1840s	Creation of Fourierist communities		

For Further Exploration

Ronald Walters, *American Reformers, 1815–1860* (1978), offers a succinct discussion of the major antebellum reform movements. Robert H. Abzug, *Cosmos Crumbling: American Reform and the Religious Imagination* (1994), demonstrates the religious roots of the reform impulse and provides profiles of leading activists. David S. Reynolds, *Walt Whitman's America: A Cultural Biography* (1995), is a comprehensive study of the poet and nineteenth-century society. Charles Capper, *Margaret Fuller: An American Romantic Life* (1992), provides an illuminating analysis of Fuller's intellectual milieu. Fuller was the inspiration for the character of Zenobia in Nathaniel Hawthorne's *The Blithedale Romance* (1852), which reflects his life at Brook Farm and touches on many issues (and fads) of the day, including communalism and mesmerism. For a study of religious utopianism gone mad, see Paul E. Johnson and Sean Wilentz, *The Kingdom of Matthias: A Story of Sex and Salvation in Nineteenth-Century America* (1995).

James B. Stewart, *Holy Warriors: The Abolitionists and American Slavery* (1976), places the Garrisonian movement in a broader social and economic context. Stephen B. Oates, *The Fires of Jubilee: Nat Turner's Fierce Rebellion* (1975), is a short and imaginative narrative of the life of the insurrectionist, while the *Narrative of the Life of Frederick Douglass, An American Slave, Written by Himself,* is a literary and social masterpiece. For antiabolitionism, see the probing studies by Leonard L. Richards, *"Gentlemen of Property and Standing": Anti-Abolition Mobs in Jacksonian America* (1970), and David Roetiger, *The Wages of Whiteness* (1995).

Mary Ryan, *Women in Public: Between Banners and Ballots, 1825–1880* (1990), explores the limits on women's civic activities, and Eleanor Flexner, *Century of Struggle* (1959), narrates the history of the women's movement. The PBS video directed by Ken Burns, *Not for Ourselves Alone: The Story of Elizabeth Cady Stanton and Susan B. Anthony* (3 hours), presents a comprehensive view of the first generation of activists.

"Women and Social Movements in the United States, 1830–1930," at <http://womhist.binghamton.edu./>, prepared by Kathryn Kish Sklar and Thomas Dublin, provides a fine introductory essay and an extensive selection of primary documents. Additional source materials (newspapers and periodicals, with an index to articles and contributors) for the period 1830 to 1877 are available through Cornell University's "Making of America" project at <http://moa.cit.cornell.edu/> and its companion site at the University of Michigan at <http://moa.umdl.umich.edu/>.

Chapter 13

THE CRISIS OF THE UNION
1844–1860

This government was made by our fathers, by white men for the
benefit of white men and their posterity forever.

—STEPHEN DOUGLAS, 1858

During the 1850s the crusaders in the temperance and antislavery movements faced off against the defenders of traditional rights. The resulting struggle was nowhere more intense than in South Carolina. When local temperance activists demanded a law like that in Maine to prohibit the sale of intoxicants, Randolph Turner was outraged: any such "legislation upon Liquor would cast a shade on my character which as a Caucassian (sic) and a white man, I am not willing to bear." A candidate for the South Carolina assembly, Turner vowed to shoulder his musket and, along with "hundreds of men in this district, . . . fight for individual rights, as well as State Rights." In Washington Congressman Preston Brooks and other South Carolinians battled against abolitionists to defend "Southern Rights." In an inflammatory speech in 1856, Senator Charles Sumner of Massachusetts denounced the South and accused Senator Andrew P. Butler of South Carolina of having taken "the harlot slavery" as his mistress. Outraged by Sumner's verbal attack on his uncle, Brooks accosted the Massachusetts senator at his desk and beat him unconscious with a walking cane. As Brooks struck down Sumner in Washington, Axalla Hoole of South Carolina and other proslavery migrants leveled their guns at an armed force of abolitionist settlers in the Kansas Territory. Passion and violence had replaced political compromise as the hallmark of American public life.

The pivotal events that sparked much of the political violence of the 1850s were the admission of Texas to the Union in 1845 and the war with Mexico that followed. But the ultimate causes lay deep in the process of economic and cultural change that had widened the long-standing differences between North and South—sectional differences that were increasingly *felt*, especially in the South. As John C. Calhoun warned in 1850, white southerners feared the North's wealth, political power, and moral righteousness, especially its "long-continued agitation of the slavery question." A massive surge of westward migration accentuated the importance of those divisions. Many Americans believed that the nation's "Manifest Destiny" was to extend republican institutions to the Pacific Ocean. But whose republican institutions: those of the slaveholding South or those of the reform-minded North and Midwest? The answer would determine the future of the nation.

Manifest Destiny

For nearly a generation after the Missouri Compromise of 1820 the two major political parties prevented another confrontation over slavery by devising programs that were national in appeal. But the compromise worked only so long as the territory of the United States remained unchanged, and by the 1840s the nation was on the move.

THE INDEPENDENCE OF TEXAS

During the 1830s, as northeastern farmers and European migrants were settling the Midwest, migrants from the Ohio Valley and the South were claiming the best lands in Arkansas and southern Missouri, pushing just beyond their western boundaries to the ninety-fifth meridian of longitude. Beyond this north-south line stretched the semiarid Great Plains. In 1820 an army explorer, Major Stephen H. Long, had described the area between the Missouri River and the Rocky Mountains as a Great American Desert, "almost wholly unfit for cultivation." Sharing this assumption, land-hungry American planters looked southward toward the Mexican province of Texas.

Texas had long been a zone of conflict between European nations. During the eighteenth century the Spanish had used Texas as a buffer against the French. After the Louisiana Purchase in 1803 Texas became Spain's buffer against Americans. Although adventurers from the United States did arrive, the Adams-Onís treaty of 1819 guaranteed Spanish sovereignty over Texas.

After winning independence from Spain in 1821 the Mexican government encouraged settlement by its own citizens and migrants from the United States. To win the allegiance of the Americans officials granted them some of the best land (see Map 13.1). One early grantee was Moses Austin, whose son Stephen F. Austin later acquired about 180,000 acres, which he sold to new migrants. The Americans did not assimilate Mexican culture and in 1829 won special exemption from a law ending slavery in Mexico. By 1835, 27,000 white Americans and their 3,000 African American slaves were raising cotton and cattle in eastern and central Texas; they far outnumbered the 3,000 Mexican residents, most of whom lived in the southwestern towns of Goliad and San Antonio.

When the Mexican government began to assert control over Texas in the mid-1830s, the Americans split into two groups. The "peace party," led by Stephen Austin and other longtime settlers, worked to win more self-government for the province, while the "war party," led by recent smallholder migrants from Georgia, demanded independence. Austin won significant concessions from Mexican authorities, but

M A P 13.1
American Settlement in Texas,
1821–1850

In 1821 Stephen F. Austin established the first organized Anglo-
American settlement in Texas on
land granted to his father by the
Mexican authorities. By 1835 he
had issued land titles to more than
1,000 families, who grew cotton
and exported it from Corpus
Christi Bay and Galveston Bay. At
the time of rebellion in 1836 there
were nearly 30,000 Americans in
Texas; anticipating a flood of settlers, the new Texas republic
claimed all Mexican lands east of
the Rio Grande.

these were nullified by the new president, General Antonio López de Santa Anna.
A strong nationalist, Santa Anna appointed a military commandant for Texas,
prompting the American war party to provoke a rebellion that most of the American settlers ultimately supported. On March 2, 1836, the rebels proclaimed the independence of Texas and adopted a constitution legalizing slavery.

Santa Anna vowed to put down the rebellion. On March 6 his army wiped out
the rebel garrison defending the Alamo in San Antonio and soon thereafter captured the settlement of Goliad (see American Voices, "A Mexican View of the
Battle of the Alamo"). With these victories Santa Anna thought he had crushed the
rebellion, but the battle of the Alamo had captured the attention of New Orleans
and New York newspapers. Their correspondents romanticized the heroism of the
Texans at the Alamo and the deaths of the folk heroes Davy Crockett and Jim Bowie.
Using strong anti-Catholic rhetoric the newspapers described the Mexicans as tyrannical butchers in the service of the pope. Thousands of American adventurers, lured
by Texan offers of land bounties, flocked in from neighboring states. Reinforced by
the new arrivals and led by General Sam Houston, in April 1836 the rebels routed
the Mexicans in the Battle of San Jacinto, establishing de facto independence. The
Mexican government refused to recognize the new republic but abandoned efforts
to reconquer it.

The Texans immediately voted by plebiscite for annexation by the United States,
but Presidents Andrew Jackson and Martin Van Buren refused to act. They knew
that adding Texas as a slave state would divide the Democratic Party and the nation and almost certainly lead to war with Mexico.

SIEGE OF THE ALAMO.

Assault on the Alamo

After a thirteen-day siege, a Mexican army of 4,000 stormed the small mission on March 6, 1836. "The first to climb were thrown down by bayonets . . . or by pistol fire," reported a Mexican officer, and it took the attackers a half hour of continuous assaults to gain control of the wall. The battle took the lives of all 250 American defenders; the Mexicans suffered 1,500 dead or wounded. (Texas State Library and Archives Commission)

THE PUSH TO THE PACIFIC: OREGON AND CALIFORNIA

The annexation of Texas became a more pressing issue in the 1840s, as American expansionists developed continental ambitions. Those dreams were captured by the term *Manifest Destiny,* coined in 1845 by John L. O'Sullivan, the editor of the *Democratic Review.* As O'Sullivan put it, "Our manifest destiny is to overspread the continent allotted by Providence for the free development of our yearly multiplying millions." Behind the rhetoric of Manifest Destiny was a sense of cultural and even racial superiority; "inferior" peoples—such as Native Americans and Mexicans—were to be brought under American dominion, taught about republican forms of government, and converted to Protestantism.

Already many residents of the Ohio River Valley were casting their eyes westward to the fertile valleys of the Oregon Country. This region stretched along the Pacific Coast from the forty-second parallel in the south (the border with Mexican California) to the fifty-fourth in the north (54° 40′, the border with Russian Alaska) and was claimed by both Great Britain and the United States. Since 1818

AMERICAN VOICES

A Mexican View of the Battle of the Alamo

Colonel José Enrique de la Peña

In February 1836 a Mexican army led by General Antonio López de Santa Anna laid siege to the Alamo, an old San Antonio mission held by about 250 Americans commanded by William B. Travis. Colonel Peña, a Mexican officer, recorded a dramatic and critical-minded account of the ensuing events.

Our commander [president-general Santa Anna] became more furious when he saw that the enemy resisted the idea of surrender. He believed as others did that the fame and honor of the army were compromised the longer the enemy lived. . . . But prudent men . . . were of the opinion that victory over a handful of men concentrated in the Alamo did not call for a great sacrifice. In fact, it was necessary only to await the artillery's arrival . . . for these to surrender. . . .

Travis's resistance was on the verge of being overcome, for several days his followers had been urging him to surrender, giving the lack of food and the scarcity of munitions as reasons . . . on the 5th he promised them if no help arrived on that day they would surrender the next day or would try to escape under the cover of darkness. . . . It was said as a fact . . . that the president-general knew of Travis's decision, and it was for this reason that he precipitated the assault, because he wanted to create a sensation and would have regretted taking the Alamo without clamor and without bloodshed, for some believed that without these there is no glory.

The columns, bravely storming the fort in the midst of a terrible shower of bullets and cannon-fire, had reached the base of the walls. . . . A lively rifle fire coming from the roof . . . caused painful havoc. . . . [Finally] our soldiers, some stimulated by courage and others by fury, burst into the quarters. . . . Our losses were grievous . . . [but] a horrible carnage [of the Americans] took place. . . . This scene of extermination went on for an hour before the curtain of death covered and ended it. . . . The taking of the Alamo was not considered a happy event, but rather a defeat that saddened us all.

SOURCE: José Enrique de la Peña, *With Santa Anna in Texas: A Personal Narrative of the Revolution*, trans. Carmen Perry (College Station: Texas A&M University Press, 1975), pp. 40–57.

a British-American convention had allowed both Britons and Americans to settle anywhere in the disputed region. The British-run Hudson's Bay Company developed a lucrative fur trade north of the Columbia River, while several hundred Americans settled to the south, mostly in the Willamette Valley. On the basis of this settlement the United States established a claim to the zone between the forty-second parallel and the Columbia River (see Map 13.2).

In 1842 American interest in Oregon increased dramatically. Navy lieutenant Charles Wilkes published glowing reports of the potential harbors he had found in the area of Puget Sound, news of great interest to New England merchants plying the China trade. In the same year a party of a hundred settlers journeyed along the Oregon Trail that fur traders and explorers had blazed through the Great Plains and the Rocky Mountains (see Map 13.3). Their reports told of a mild climate and fertile soil.

"Oregon fever" suddenly raged. In May 1843 over a thousand men, women, and children gathered in Independence, Missouri, for the trek to Oregon. The migrants were mostly farming and trading families from Missouri, Kentucky, and Tennessee. They had more than 100 wagons and 5,000 oxen and cattle. With military-style organization, the pioneers overcame flooding streams, dust storms, dying livestock, and encounters with Indians. After a journey of six months they reached the Willamette Valley, more than 2,000 miles across the continent. During the next two seasons another 5,000 people reached Oregon.

By 1860 about 350,000 Americans had braved the Oregon Trail. Over 34,000 of them died in the effort, mostly from disease and exposure; 400 deaths came from

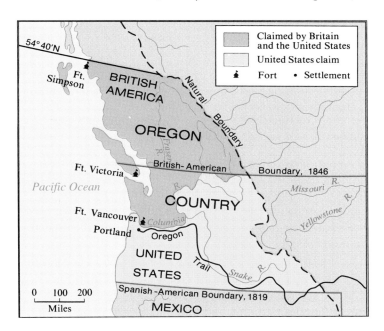

M A P 13.2
Territorial Conflict in Oregon, 1819–1846

As thousands of American settlers poured into the so-called Oregon Country in the early 1840s, British authorities tried to confine them south of the Columbia River. But the migrants—and fervent midwestern expansionists—asserted that American (and British) citizens could settle anywhere in the territory. In 1846 British and American diplomats resolved the dispute by drawing the boundary at the forty-ninth parallel.

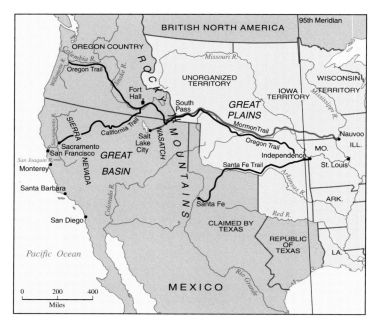

M A P 13.3
Settlement of the Trans-Missouri West

In the 1840s tens of thousands of Americans crossed the Great Plains in huge wagon trains. The Mormons settled in the Salt Lake Basin; other pioneers pressed on to Mexican California and the Oregon Country. There was remarkably little crime on these treks because most migrants were deeply religious or were committed to the rule of Anglo-American law, which they enforced through political compacts and self-created institutions.

Indian attacks. The walking migrants wore 3-foot-deep paths, and their wagons carved 5-foot-deep ruts, across sandstone formations in southern Wyoming—tracks that are visible today. Women found the trail especially difficult, for it exaggerated the authority of their husbands and added to their traditional chores the labor of driving wagons and animals.

Some pioneers ended up in the Mexican province of California. They left the Oregon Trail at the Snake River and struggled southward down the California Trail, settling in the interior valley along the Sacramento River. California had been the remotest corner of Spain's American empire, and Spain had established a significant foothold there only in the 1770s, when it built a chain of coastal missions and presidios along the coast (see Chapter 8). New England merchants soon struck up trade with the settlers in California, buying sea otter pelts that they carried to China. Commerce increased after Mexico won independence. To promote California's development the new Mexican government took over the California missions, liberating more than 20,000 Indians who worked on them, and promoted large-scale cattle ranching.

The rise of cattle ranching had created a new society and economy. While some mission Indians joined native American peoples in the interior, many remained in the coastal region. They intermarried with the local *mestizos* (Mexicans of mixed Spanish and Indian ancestry) and worked as laborers and cowboys. New England merchants carried the leather and tallow produced on the large California ranches to the booming Massachusetts boot and shoe industry. To handle the increased business New England firms dispatched dozens of resident agents to California. Unlike the American settlers in Texas many of those New Englanders assimilated Mexican culture. They married into the families of the elite Mexicans—the *Californios*—and adopted their dress, manners, outlook, and Catholic religion. A crucial exception was Thomas Oliver Larkin, the most successful merchant in Monterey. Larkin established a close working relationship with Mexican authorities, but he remained an American citizen and plotted for the peaceful annexation of California to the United States.

Like Larkin, American settlers in the Sacramento Valley had no desire to assimilate into Mexican society. Their legal standing was uncertain because they had received dubious land grants or had squatted without any title. They hoped to emulate the Americans in Texas by colonizing the country, overwhelming what they regarded as an inferior culture, and seeking annexation by the United States. However, these settlers numbered only about 700 in the early 1840s, compared to the coastal population of 7,000 Mexicans and 300 American traders.

A Californio *Patriarch*

Mariano Guadalupe Vallejo was descended from a Spanish family that had lived—and prospered—in Mexico since the Spanish Conquest. He served in California as a military officer and in the 1820s acquired 270,000 acres of land in the Sonoma Valley north of San Francisco. The father of nine children, Vallejo presents himself in this photograph as a proud patriarch, surrounded by two daughters and three granddaughters. During the American takeover in 1846 he was imprisoned for a short period but then lived out his life in California, gradually losing most of his vast holdings.

(Courtesy of the Bancroft Library, University of California, Berkeley)

THE FATEFUL ELECTION OF 1844

The election of 1844 determined the course of the American government's policy toward California, Oregon, and Texas. Since 1836, when Texas requested annexation, some southern leaders had favored territorial expansion to extend the slave system. They had been opposed not only by cautious party politicians and northern abolitionists but also, southerners came to think, by British antislavery advocates. In 1839 Britain and France had intervened in Mexico to force it to pay its foreign debts, and there were rumors that Britain wanted California as payment. Southern leaders also believed that Britain was encouraging Texas to remain independent and had designs on Spanish Cuba, which some southerners wanted to annex. To thwart any such British schemes southern expansionists demanded the immediate annexation of Texas.

At this moment "Oregon fever" and Manifest Destiny altered the political and diplomatic landscape in the North. In 1843 Americans throughout the Ohio Valley and the Great Lakes states called on the federal government to renounce the joint occupation of Oregon. Democrats and Whigs jointly organized "Oregon conventions," and in July a bipartisan national convention demanded that the United States seize Oregon all the way to 54° 40′ north latitude, the southern limit of Russian Alaska.

Now that northerners were demanding expansion southern Democrats could champion the annexation of Texas without threatening party unity. President John Tyler, disowned by the Whigs because of his opposition to Henry Clay's nationalist economic program, hoped to win reelection in 1844 as a Democrat. To curry favor among expansionists Tyler proposed both the annexation of Texas and the seizure of Oregon to the 54° 40′ line. In April 1844 Tyler and John C. Calhoun, his new secretary of state, submitted to the Senate a treaty to annex Texas. The treaty was opposed by two other leaders with presidential ambitions: the Democrat Martin Van Buren and the Whig Henry Clay, who knew annexation would alienate many northern voters. At their urging Whigs and northern Democrats united to defeat the treaty.

Texas became the central issue in the election. The Democrats passed over Tyler, whom they did not trust, and Van Buren, whom southern Democrats despised for his opposition to annexation. They selected former Governor James K. Polk of Tennessee, a slaveowner who was Andrew Jackson's personal favorite and who carried the nickname "Young Hickory." Unimpressive in appearance, Polk was a man of iron will and boundless ambition for the nation. He called for the annexation of Texas and taking all of Oregon. "Fifty-four forty or fight!" became the patriotic cry of his campaign.

The Whigs nominated Henry Clay, who once again championed his American System of internal improvements, high tariffs, and national banking. Initially Clay dodged the issue of Texas, finally suggesting that he might support annexation. His position disappointed thousands of northern Whigs and Democrats who opposed any expansion of slavery. Rather than vote for Clay, some antislavery advocates supported the Liberty Party's candidate, James G. Birney of Kentucky. Birney won less than 3 percent of the popular vote but probably took enough votes from Clay in New York to cause him to lose that state by 5,000 votes. By taking New York's 36 electoral votes, Polk won by a margin of 170 to 105 in the electoral college.

After Polk's victory congressional Democrats closed ranks and moved immediately to bring Texas into the Union. Unable to secure a two-thirds majority in the Senate for a treaty with the Texas Republic, they approved annexation by a joint resolution of Congress, which required only a majority vote in each house. Polk's strategy of linking Texas and Oregon had been successful.

War, Expansion, and Slavery, 1846–1850

James K. Polk and the Democrats had swept to victory in 1844 by promising the immediate annexation of Texas and laying claim to all of Oregon. But Polk had even greater territorial ambitions: he wanted all of Mexico between Texas and the Pacific Ocean and was prepared to go to war to get it. What he was not prepared for, though he should have been, was the major crisis over slavery unleashed by the success of his expansionist dreams.

THE WAR WITH MEXICO, 1846–1848

Mexico had not prospered in the twenty-five years since it won independence from Spain in 1821. Its population remained small at 7 million people, and its stagnant economy yielded only modest tax revenue, which was eaten up by interest payments on foreign debt and a bloated government bureaucracy. Consequently, the Mexican republic lacked the money and people to settle its distant northern provinces. The Spanish-speaking population of California and New Mexico remained small—about 75,000 in 1840—and contributed little to the national economy. Still, the Mexican government was determined to retain all its historical territories, and when the breakaway Texas Republic accepted American statehood on July 4, 1845, Mexico broke off diplomatic relations with the United States.

President James Polk viewed that action as a great opportunity and had already devised a secret plan to acquire Mexico's far northern provinces. To intimidate the Mexican government he ordered General Zachary Taylor and an American army of 2,000 soldiers to occupy the disputed lands between the Nueces River (the historical boundary of the Mexican province of Texas) and the Rio Grande, which the expansionist-minded Texas Republic had claimed as its southern and western border (see Map 13.1). Then Polk launched a diplomatic initiative, dispatching John Slidell on a secret mission to Mexico City. Slidell was instructed to secure Mexico's acceptance of the Rio Grande boundary and buy the Mexican provinces of New Mexico and California, paying as much as $30 million. When Slidell arrived in December 1845, Mexican officials refused to see him, declaring that the American annexation of Texas was illegal.

Anticipating the failure of Slidell's mission, Polk had already embarked on an alternative plan to take California. The president's strategy was to foment a revolution that, as in Texas, would lead to the creation of an independent republic and a request for annexation. In October 1845 he had Secretary of State James Buchanan advise Thomas O. Larkin, who had become the U.S. consul in the port of Monterey, to encourage leading Mexican residents to declare independence and support peaceful annexation. To add military muscle to any uprising Polk sent orders to American naval commanders in the Pacific to seize San Francisco Bay and California's coastal towns in the event of war. The president also had the War Department dispatch Captain John C. Frémont and an "exploring" party of heavily armed soldiers deep into Mexican territory. By December 1845 Frémont had reached California's Sacramento Valley.

Events now moved quickly toward war. When Polk learned of the failure of Slidell's mission, he ordered General Taylor to build a fort near the Rio Grande, hoping to incite an armed response by Mexico. As Ulysses S. Grant, a young officer serving with Taylor, said much later, "We were sent to provoke a fight, but it was essential that Mexico should commence it." When Mexican and American forces clashed near the Rio Grande in May 1846, Polk delivered the war message he had drafted long before, saying that Mexico "has passed the boundary of the United States, has invaded our territory, and shed American blood upon the American soil." Ignoring Whig pleas for a peaceful resolution of the dispute the Democratic majority in Congress voted for war with Mexico, unleashing large and almost hysterical demonstrations of popular support. To avoid a simultaneous war with Britain over Oregon the president retreated from his campaign pledge of "fifty-four forty or fight" and accepted a British proposal to divide the Oregon region at the forty-ninth parallel.

As the Senate ratified the Oregon Treaty with Great Britain in June 1846, fighting broke out in California between American naval forces and Mexican authorities. Naval commander John Sloat landed 250 marines and seamen in Monterey and declared that California "henceforward will be a portion of the United States." American settlers in the interior staged a revolt and, supported by Frémont's forces, captured the town of Sonoma. To ensure American control of California Polk ordered army units to capture Santa Fe in New Mexico and march to the Pacific Ocean. Despite stiff resistance from the Mexicans American forces secured control of all of California early in 1847.

Zachary Taylor's army in Texas had been equally successful. In May 1846 the American forces had crossed the Rio Grande, occupied Matamoros, and after a fierce six-day battle in September took the interior town of Monterrey. Two months later a U.S. naval squadron in the Gulf of Mexico seized Tampico, Mexico's second most important port. By the end of 1846 the United States controlled much of north-eastern Mexico.

Polk expected that these American victories in Texas, New Mexico, California, and northern Mexico would prompt the Mexicans to sue for peace, but he had underrated their national pride and the determination of President Santa Anna. Santa Anna went on the offensive, attacking the depleted units of Zachary Taylor at Buena Vista in February 1847. Only superior artillery enabled Taylor to eke out a victory and hold the American line in northeastern Mexico.

To bring Santa Anna to terms Polk accepted the plan devised by General Winfield Scott to strike deep into the heart of Mexico. In March 1847 Scott captured the port of Veracruz and began the 260-mile march to Mexico City. Leading Scott's 14,000 troops was a cadre of talented West Point officers who would become famous in the Civil War: Robert E. Lee, George Meade, and P.G.T. Beauregard. Scott's troops crushed Santa Anna's attempt to block their march at Cerro Gordo and after inflicting heavy losses on the Mexican army at the Battle of Churubusco seized Mexico City in September 1847. Santa Anna was overthrown, and the new Mexican government agreed to make peace. The war was finally over.

A DIVISIVE VICTORY

Initially many Americans viewed the war with Mexico as a noble struggle to extend American republican institutions, but the conflict quickly became politically divisive. A few Whigs, such as Charles Francis Adams of Massachusetts and Joshua Giddings of Ohio, had opposed the war from the beginning on moral grounds (and became known as "conscience Whigs"), viewing it as a conspiracy to add new slave states in the West. They argued that the expansion of slavery would jeopardize the Jeffersonian ideal of a yeoman freeholder society and ensure control of the federal government by slaveholding Democrats. These antislavery Whigs grew bolder after the elections of 1846, which gave their party control of Congress.

Polk's expansionist policy split the Democrats into sectional factions. In August 1846 David Wilmot, a Democratic representative from Pennsylvania, proposed a simple amendment to a military appropriations bill to prohibit slavery in any new territories acquired from Mexico. This amendment, known as the Wilmot Proviso, quickly became a rallying point for antislavery northerners. In the House the Democratic supporters of Martin Van Buren joined forces with antislavery Whigs to pass the Proviso. The Senate, dominated by southerners and proslavery northern Democrats, killed it.

In this heated atmosphere the most fervent Democrat expansionists became even more aggressive. Polk, Secretary of State Buchanan, and Senators Stephen A. Douglas of Illinois and Jefferson Davis of Mississippi wanted the United States to take at least part of Mexico south of the Rio Grande. But some southerners worried that the United States could not absorb the Mexicans and feared that a longer war would augment the power of the federal government. John C. Calhoun supported taking only California and New Mexico, the most sparsely populated areas of Mexico.

To reunify the Democratic Party before the next election Polk and Buchanan abandoned their expansionist dreams in Mexico and accepted Calhoun's policy. In February 1848 Polk signed the Treaty of Guadalupe Hidalgo, in which the United States agreed to pay Mexico $15 million in return for more than one-third of its territory: Texas north of the Rio Grande, New Mexico, and California (see Map 13.4). The United States also agreed to assume all the claims of its citizens, totaling $3.2 million, against the Mexican government. The Senate ratified the treaty in March 1848.

The passions aroused by the war dominated the election of 1848. The Wilmot Proviso had energized abolitionists who had been seeking a legislative solution to the problem of slavery, and the Senate's refusal to pass it alarmed them. Antislavery advocates now claimed that southern planters and their northern business allies had entered into a massive "Slave Power" conspiracy to expand the bounds of

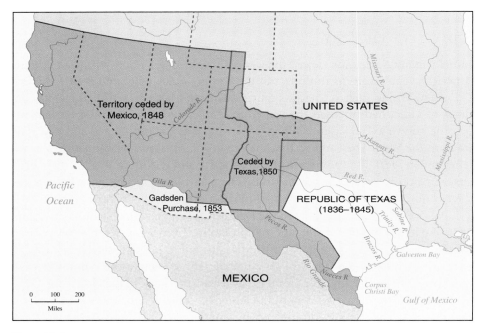

M A P 13.4
The Mexican Cession, 1848–1853

In the Treaty of Guadalupe Hidalgo (1848) and the Gadsden Purchase (1853) Mexico ceded to the United States its vast northern territories—the present-day states of California, Nevada, Utah, Arizona, New Mexico, and half of Colorado and Texas. These new territories, President Polk boasted to Congress, "constitute of themselves a country large enough for a great empire, and the acquisition is second in importance only to that of Louisiana in 1803."

slavery. To defeat this alleged plan a significant number of northerners joined a new "free-soil" movement. The free-soilers abandoned the Liberty Party's focus on the sinfulness of slavery and the natural rights of African Americans. Instead they depicted slavery as a threat to republican institutions and yeoman farming. This shift in emphasis—toward keeping the West open for settlement by white families and away from freeing slaves—led the radical abolitionist William Lloyd Garrison to denounce free-soil doctrine as racist "whitemanism."

Despite Garrison's hostility the new political approach worked. The Wilmot Proviso's call for free soil was the first antislavery proposal to attract broad popular support. Hundreds of women in the Great Lakes states joined female free-soil organizations formed by the American and Foreign Anti-Slavery Society. Frederick Douglass, the foremost black abolitionist, also endorsed free soil, seeing it as the best way to provoke a political struggle between the North and the South that would overthrow slavery.

The conflict over slavery took a toll on Polk and the Democratic Party. Opposed by free-soilers and exhausted by his rigorous dawn-to-midnight work regime, Polk declined to run for a second term and died three months after leaving office. The Democrats nominated Senator Lewis Cass of Michigan, an avid expansionist who had advocated buying Cuba, annexing Mexico's Yucatan Peninsula, and taking all of Oregon. To maintain party unity Cass was deliberately vague on the question of slavery in the West. He promoted a new idea—squatter sovereignty—that would give settlers in each territory the power to determine its status as free or slave.

Cass's political ingenuity failed to hold the party together. Demanding unambiguous opposition to the expansion of slavery, some northern Democrats joined the newly formed Free Soil Party, which nominated Martin Van Buren for president. Van Buren's conversion to free soil was genuine, but he also wanted to punish southern Democrats for having denied him the presidential nomination in 1844. To attract Whig votes the Free Soil Party chose conscience Whig Charles Francis Adams as its candidate for vice president.

To avoid similar divisions the Whigs nominated General Zachary Taylor. Taylor was a southerner and a Louisiana slaveowner, but he had not taken a position on the politically charged issue of slavery in the territories. Equally important the general's exploits during the War with Mexico had made him a popular hero. Known as "Old Rough and Ready," Taylor possessed a common touch that had won him the affection of his troops. "Our Commander on the Rio Grande," wrote Walt Whitman, "emulates the Great Commander of our revolution"—George Washington.

In 1848, as in 1840, running a military hero worked for the Whigs but only barely. Taylor and his vice-presidential running mate Millard Fillmore took 47 percent of the popular vote against 42 percent for Cass, but the margin in the electoral college was thin: 163 to 127. The Free Soil ticket of Van Buren and Adams made the difference in the election, winning 10 percent of the popular vote and depriving the Democrats of enough votes in New York to cost Cass that state and the presidency. The popularity of the Wilmot Proviso had changed the dynamics of American politics.

1850: CRISIS AND COMPROMISE

Even before President Taylor took office, events in California sparked a major political crisis that threatened the Union. In January 1848 workmen building a mill for John A. Sutter discovered flakes of gold in the Sierra Nevada foothills in northern California. Sutter was a Swiss immigrant who arrived in California in 1839, became a Mexican citizen, and established an estate in the Sacramento Valley. He tried to keep the discovery a secret, but by May Americans from San Francisco were pouring into the foothills. When President Polk confirmed the discovery in December, the gold rush was on. By January 1849 sixty-one crowded ships had departed from northeastern ports to sail around Cape Horn for San Francisco, and by May, 12,000 wagons had crossed the Missouri River, also bound for the gold fields. In 1849 alone more than 80,000 migrants—the "forty-niners"—arrived in California.

California Prospectors

Beginning in 1849 thousands of fortune seekers from all parts of the world converged on the California gold fields. By 1852 the state had 200,000 residents, including 25,000 Chinese, many of whom worked as wage laborers in the gold fields, and thousands of African Americans, both enslaved and free. These 1852 prospectors at Head of Auburn Ravine are using a primitive technique—panning—to separate gold from sand and gravel.

(Courtesy of the California History Room, California State Library, Sacramento, CA)

The rapid influx of settlers revived the national debate over free soil. The forty-niners, who lived in crowded, chaotic towns and mining camps, demanded the formation of a territorial government to protect their lives and property. To avoid an extended debate over slavery President Taylor advised the Californians to apply for statehood immediately, and in November 1849 they ratified a state constitution that prohibited slavery. Few of the many southerners who flocked to the gold fields or to San Francisco owned slaves or wanted to. For his part Taylor wanted to attract Free Soilers and northern Democrats into the Whig Party and urged Congress to admit California as a free state.

Southern politicians were alarmed by the swift victory of the antislavery forces in California. Not only had a valuable area been lost to free soil, but the admission of California would threaten the carefully maintained balance in the Senate. In 1845 the entry of Texas and Florida had raised the total of slave states to fifteen, against thirteen free states. However, the entry of Iowa in 1846 and Wisconsin in 1848 had reestablished the balance. Now southern leaders feared that admitting California as a free state would place their section at a political disadvantage from which it would never recover. They decided to block its entry unless the federal government guaranteed the future of slavery.

The resulting impasse produced long and passionate debates in Congress. As usual John C. Calhoun took the most extreme states'-rights position, warning of possible secession by the slave states and civil war. To avoid that outcome he proposed that slavery be guaranteed in all the territories and that a constitutional amendment be adopted to create a permanent balance of power between the sections. In making these proposals Calhoun advanced the radically new constitutional doctrine that Congress had no constitutional authority to regulate slavery in the territories. This argument ran counter to a half century of practice. Congress had prohibited slavery in the Northwest Territory in 1787 and in most of the Louisiana Purchase in the Missouri Compromise in 1821.

While Calhoun's new doctrine won support in the Deep South, many southerners were prepared to accept a more moderate position: an extension of the Missouri Compromise line to the Pacific Ocean. This extension would guarantee slaveowners access to some western territory, including a separate state in southern California. Some northern Democrats, including former Secretary of State James Buchanan, also favored this plan as a way to resolve the crisis.

A third alternative was squatter sovereignty, the plan advanced by Lewis Cass in 1848 and now championed by Democratic Senator Stephen Douglas of Illinois. Douglas called his plan "popular sovereignty" to emphasize its roots in republican ideology, and it had considerable appeal. Popular sovereignty would place decisions about slavery in the hands of local settlers and their territorial governments, removing the explosive issue from national politics. However, popular sovereignty was a vague and slippery concept: could slavery be accepted or banned when the territory was first organized or only when it framed a constitution and applied for statehood?

Antislavery advocates were unwilling to accept any plan that involved the expansion of slavery. In 1850 Senator Salmon P. Chase of Ohio, elected by a Democratic–Free Soil coalition, and Senator William H. Seward, a New York Whig, urged federal authorities to contain slavery and then extinguish it completely. Condemning slavery as "morally unjust, politically unwise, and socially pernicious" and invoking "a higher law than the Constitution," Seward demanded bold action to protect freedom, "the common heritage of mankind."

Standing on the brink of disaster, senior Whigs and Democrats desperately sought a compromise to preserve the Union. Through a long, complex legislative process the Whig leaders Henry Clay and Daniel Webster and the Democrat Stephen A. Douglas organized a complex package of six laws known collectively as the Compromise of 1850. To mollify the South the Compromise included a new Fugitive Slave Act allowing slaveowners to use federal magistrates to return runaway slaves. To satisfy the North the Compromise admitted California as a free state, resolved a boundary dispute between New Mexico and Texas in favor of New Mexico, and abolished the slave trade (but not slavery) in the District of Columbia. Finally, the Compromise organized the rest of the lands acquired from Mexico into the territories of New Mexico and Utah on the basis of popular sovereignty (see Map 13.5).

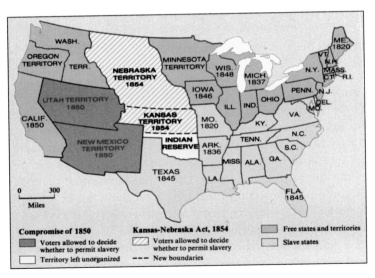

M AP 13.5
The Compromise of 1850 and the Kansas-Nebraska Act of 1854

Vast territories were at stake in the contest over the extension of slavery. The Compromise of 1850 resolved the status of lands in the Far West: California would be a free state, and the settlers of the Utah and New Mexico territories would decide their own fate. In 1854 the implementation of popular sovereignty in Kansas sparked a bitter local war between the advocates of free soil and slavery, revealing a fatal flaw in the concept.

The Compromise averted a secession crisis in 1850—but only barely. In the midst of the struggle the governor of South Carolina declared that there was not "the slightest doubt" that his state would secede. He and other "fire-eaters" in Georgia, Mississippi, and Alabama organized special conventions to protect "Southern Rights" and demand secession. To persuade the convention delegates to support the Compromise moderate southern politicians agreed to support secession in the future if Congress abolished slavery anywhere or refused to grant statehood to a territory with a proslavery constitution. Lacking sufficient support, the "fire-eaters" drew back from secession, averting a constitutional crisis. The fact that the Compromise of 1850 elicited such a passionately negative response throughout the Deep South—and among many northern Whigs and Free Soilers as well—did not augur well for its success.

The End of the Second Party System, 1850–1858

The architects of the Compromise of 1850 hoped that their agreement would resolve the issue of slavery for a generation. Their hopes were quickly dashed. Demanding freedom for fugitive slaves and free soil in the West, some northerners undermined the Compromise, while some southerners plotted to expand slavery in the West and the Caribbean. These disputes destroyed the Second Party System, deepening the crisis of the Union.

RESISTANCE TO THE FUGITIVE SLAVE ACT

The most controversial element of the Compromise proved to be the Fugitive Slave Act. Under its terms federal judges or special commissioners in the northern states determined the status of blacks who were accused of being runaway slaves. The accused blacks were denied jury trials and even the right to testify. Because federal marshals were legally required to support slave-catchers, the new legislation was effective, and about 200 fugitives (as well as some free blacks) were sent to the South and enslaved.

The plight of runaways and the appearance of slave-catchers aroused popular hostility in the North and Midwest, and free blacks and abolitionists defied the new law. In October 1850 Boston abolitionists helped two slaves escape to freedom and drove a Georgia slave-catcher out of town. A year later rioters in Syracuse, New York, broke into a courthouse to free a fugitive slave. Abandoning pacifism, Frederick Douglass declared that "the only way to make a Fugitive Slave Law a dead letter is to make half a dozen or more dead kidnappers." As if in response, in September 1851 a deadly confrontation took place in the Quaker village of Christiana, Pennsylvania. About twenty African Americans exchanged gunfire with a group of slave-catchers from Maryland, killing two of them. Federal marshals arrested thirty-six

Uncle Tom's Cabin, 1852

The cover of this "Young Folks Edition" of *Uncle Tom's Cabin* shows Tom as a well-dressed and kindly older man, reading the Bible to Little Eva, whom he has saved from drowning. Like the book's text, this image offered whites a sympathetic view of African Americans, challenging generations of negative stereotypes.

(The Charles L. Blockson Afro-American Collection, Temple University)

blacks and four whites and had them indicted for treason for defying the law. But a jury acquitted one defendant, and northern public opinion forced the government to drop its charges against the rest.

Harriet Beecher Stowe's abolitionist novel, *Uncle Tom's Cabin* (1852), increased northern opposition to the Fugitive Slave Act. By translating the moral principles of abolitionism into heartrending personal situations, Beecher's novel evoked empathy and outrage throughout the North. Responding to popular sentiment, northern legislatures challenged federal authority by enacting personal-liberty laws that extended legal rights to accused fugitives. In 1857 the Wisconsin Supreme Court went even further, ruling in *Ableman v. Booth* that the Fugitive Slave Act could not be enforced in Wisconsin because it violated the Constitution and contesting the power of the federal courts to review their decision. When the case was considered by the U.S. Supreme Court in 1859, Chief Justice Taney led a unanimous court in affirming the supremacy of federal over state courts—a position that has stood the test of time—and upheld the constitutionality of the Fugitive Slave Act. By that time popular opposition had made it impossible to catch fugitive blacks. As Douglass had hoped, the act had become a "dead letter."

THE WHIGS' DECLINE AND THE DEMOCRATS' DIPLOMACY

The conflict over fugitive slaves split the Whig Party, which went into the election of 1852 weakened by the death of Henry Clay, one of its greatest leaders. Rejecting Millard Fillmore, who had become president on the death of Zachary Taylor, the Whigs nominated General Winfield Scott, another hero of the war with Mexico. But about a third of southern Whigs refused to support Scott because northern members of the party refused to support slavery; they threw their support to the Democrats.

The Democrats too were divided. Southerners wanted a candidate who would support Calhoun's position that all territories should be open to slavery. But northern and midwestern Democrats advocated the principle of popular sovereignty, as did the three leading candidates—Lewis Cass of Michigan, Stephen Douglas of Illinois, and James Buchanan of Pennsylvania. At the national convention no candidate could secure the necessary two-thirds majority. Exhausted after forty-eight ballots, the convention settled on a compromise nominee, Franklin Pierce of New Hampshire, a congenial man reputed to be sympathetic to the South.

The Democrats' cautious strategy paid off, and they swept the election. Pleased by the admission of California as a free state, Martin Van Buren and many other Free Soilers voted for Pierce, reuniting the Democratic Party. Conversely, the election fragmented the Whig Party into sectional wings; it would never again wage a national campaign.

As president, Pierce pursued an expansionist foreign policy. To assist northern merchants he sent a mission to Japan to negotiate a commercial treaty. Pierce was even more solicitous of southern interests. To resolve a dispute over the southern boundary of New Mexico the president revived Polk's plan to annex a large amount of territory south of the Rio Grande and named James Gadsden as his negotiator. Mexican officials rejected Pierce's annexation bid but agreed to sell a small amount of land that Gadsden, a railroad promoter, wanted to construct a southern-based transcontinental railroad to the Pacific (see Map 13.4).

Pierce's most dramatic foreign policy initiative came in the Caribbean. Southern expansionists had already funded three clandestine military expeditions to Spanish Cuba, where they hoped to prod the slaveowning elite into declaring independence and then joining the Union. In 1853 Pierce covertly supported a new Cuban expedition led by John A. Quitman, a former governor of Mississippi. While Quitman was building up his forces, the Pierce administration threatened war with Spain over the seizure of an American ship, demanding an apology and a large indemnity. But when northern Democrats in Congress refused to support this aggressive diplomacy, Pierce and Secretary of State William L. Marcy had to back down. Still determined to seize Cuba, Marcy tried to buy the island from Spain and then prompted American diplomats in Europe to pressure Pierce to seize it. In the Ostend Manifesto (1854), the diplomats declared that the United States would be justified in seizing Cuba "by every law, human and Divine." Quickly leaked to the press by antiexpansionists, the Ostend Manifesto triggered a new wave of northern resentment against the South and forced Pierce to halt his efforts. But his expansionist policy had already revived northern fears of a "Slave Power" conspiracy.

THE KANSAS-NEBRASKA ACT AND THE RISE OF NEW PARTIES

In the wake of the Ostend Manifesto a new struggle over westward expansion enflamed sectional divisions. Because the Missouri Compromise prohibited slavery in the Louisiana Purchase north of 36° 30′, southern senators had delayed the political organization of that area. But westward-looking residents of the Ohio River Valley and the upper South demanded its settlement, and Senator Stephen A. Douglas of Illinois became their spokesman, in part because he supported a northern transcontinental railroad from Chicago to California. In 1854 Douglas introduced a bill to extinguish Native American rights on the central Plains and organize a large territory to be called Nebraska. Because Nebraska was north of 36° 30′, it would be a free territory.

Douglas's bill conflicted with the plans of southern senators, who wanted to extend slavery throughout the Louisiana Purchase and, like James Gadsden, hoped that a southern city—New Orleans, Memphis, or St. Louis—would become the eastern terminus of a transcontinental railroad. To win southern support for the organization of Nebraska Douglas made two major concessions. First, he amended his bill so that it explicitly repealed the Missouri Compromise and organized the region on the basis of popular sovereignty. Second Douglas agreed to the formation of two new territories, Nebraska and Kansas, giving slaveholders a chance to dominate the settlement of Kansas, the more southern territory (see Map 13.5). To win northern and midwestern support for this scheme Douglas argued that Kansas would be settled primarily by nonslaveholders because its climate and terrain were not suited to plantation agriculture. Supported primarily by southern representatives, the Kansas-Nebraska Act passed in May 1854.

The Kansas-Nebraska Act proved to be the last nail in the coffin of the Second Party System. Abolitionists and free-soilers denounced the act, calling it "part of a great scheme for extending and perpetuating supremacy of the slave power." Antislavery northern Whigs and "Anti-Nebraska" Democrats abandoned their respective parties to create a new party, taking the Jeffersonian name Republican. Emphasizing uncompromising opposition to the expansion of slavery, the Republicans ran a slate of candidates, primarily in the Midwest, in the congressional election of 1854.

Like most American parties, the Republican Party was a coalition of diverse groups—Free Soilers, antislavery Democrats, conscience Whigs—but its founders shared a distinct vision. They opposed slavery because it degraded manual labor, creating poor black and white workers who were subservient to wealthy landlords. In contrast, Republicans such as Senator Thaddeus Stevens of Pennsylvania celebrated the moral virtues of a society based on "the middling classes who own the soil and work it with their own hands." Abraham Lincoln, an Illinois Whig who became a Republican, articulated the party's vision of social mobility. "There is no permanent class of hired laborers among us," he argued, and every man had a chance to become a property owner. In the face of increasing class divisions in the industrializing North and Midwest, Lincoln and his fellow Republicans asserted the values of republican freedom and individual enterprise.

Competing for Whig and Democratic votes was another new party, the American, or "Know-Nothing," Party. The American Party had its origins in the anti-immigrant and anti-Catholic organizations of the 1840s (see Chapter 10). In 1850 these secret societies banded together as the Order of the Star-Spangled Banner; a year later they formed the American Party. The secrecy-conscious members sometimes answered outsiders' questions by saying "I know nothing," giving the party its nickname, but its program was far from secret. Know-Nothings hoped to unite native-born Protestants against the "alien menace" of Irish and German Catholics, banning further immigration and instituting literacy tests for voting. In 1854 the Know-Nothings gained control of the state governments of Massachusetts and Pennsylvania and, allied with the Whigs, commanded a majority in the U.S. House of Representatives. The emergence of a new major party led by nativists suddenly became a real possibility.

At the same time, the results of the Kansas-Nebraska Act were creating a new political crisis. In 1854 thousands of settlers rushed into the Kansas Territory, putting Douglas's theory of popular sovereignty to the test. On the side of slavery Senator David R. Atchison of Missouri organized residents of his state to cross into Kansas and vote in crucial elections. Opposing him were agents of the abolitionist New England Emigrant Aid Society, which colonized Kansas with free-soilers. In March 1855 the Pierce administration recognized the territorial legislature in Lecompton, Kansas, which had been elected largely by border-crossing Missourians and had adopted proslavery legislation, but free-soilers rejected the legitimacy of the territorial government.

In May 1856 both sides turned to violence (see American Voices, "'Bleeding Kansas': A Southern View"). A proslavery gang, 700 strong, sacked the free-soil town of Lawrence, destroying two newspaper offices, looting stores, and burning down buildings. The attack enraged John Brown, an abolitionist from New York and Ohio, whose free-state militia force arrived too late to save the town. Brown was a complex man with a checkered past. Born in 1800, he had started more than twenty businesses in six states and had often been sued by his creditors. Nonetheless, he had an intelligence and a moral intensity that won the trust of influential people, including leading abolitionists. Taking vengeance for the sack of Lawrence, he and a few followers murdered and mutilated five proslavery settlers. We must "fight fire with fire" and "strike terror in the hearts of the proslavery people," Brown declared. The sack of Lawrence and the "Pottawatomie massacre," as the killings became known, initiated a guerrilla war in Kansas that cost about 200 lives.

"Bleeding Kansas": A Southern View

AXALLA JOHN HOOLE

*E*arly in 1856 Axalla John Hoole and his bride left South Carolina to support the Southern cause while building a new life in Kansas. These letters show that things went badly
from the start and only got worse; after eighteen months the Hooles returned to South Carolina. A Confederate militia captain, Axalla Hoole died in the Battle of Chickamauga in September 1863.

Kansas City, Missouri, Apl. 3d., 1856

My Dear Brother . . .
    The Missourians . . . are very sanguine about Kansas being a slave state & I have heard
some of them say it shall be . . . but generally speaking, I have not met with the reception
which I expected. Everyone seems bent on the Almighty Dollar, and as a general thing that
seems to be their only thought. . . .

Lecompton, K.T., Sept. 12, 1856

My Dear Mother . . .
    I have been unwell ever since the 9th of July. . . . I thought of going to work in a few
days, when the Abolitionists broke out and I have had to stand guard of nights when I
ought to have been in bed, took cold which . . . caused diarrhea. . . . Betsie is well—
    You perceive from the heading of this that I am now in Lecompton, almost all of the
Proslavery party between this place and Lawrence are here. We brought our families here,
as we thought that we would be better able to defend ourselves. . . . Lane [and a Free State
army] came against us last Friday (a week ago to-day). As it happened we had about 400
men with two cannon . . . but we were acting on the defensive, and did not think it prudent to commence the engagement.

Douglas, K.T., July the 5th., 1857

Dear Sister . . .
    I fear, Sister, that [our] coming here will do no good at last, as I begin to think that this
will be made a Free State at last. 'Tis true we have elected Proslavery men to draft a state
constitution, but I feel pretty certain, if it is put to a vote of the people, it will be rejected,
as I feel pretty confident that they have a majority here at this time. The South has ceased
all efforts, while the North is redoubling her exertions. . . .

SOURCE: William Stanley Hoole, ed., "A Southerner's Viewpoint of the Kansas Situation, 1856–1857,"
Kansas Historical Quarterly (1934), vol. 3: pp. 43–68, 145–71, passim.

BUCHANAN'S FAILED PRESIDENCY

The violence in Kansas dominated the presidential election of 1856. The Democrats reaffirmed their support for popular sovereignty and the Kansas-Nebraska Act and nominated James Buchanan of Pennsylvania. A tall, dignified figure of sixty-four, Buchanan was an experienced but unimaginative and timid politician.

The two-year-old Republican Party counted on anger over "Bleeding Kansas" to boost its fortunes. The party's platform denounced the Kansas-Nebraska Act and, alleging a "Slave Power" conspiracy, insisted that the federal government prohibit slavery in all the territories. The platform also called for federal subsidies to transcontinental railroads, reviving the element of the Whig economic program that was most popular among midwestern Democrats. For president the Republicans nominated Colonel John C. Frémont, a free-soiler famous for his role in the conquest of California.

The American Party entered the election with high hopes, but it quickly split into sectional factions over Kansas. The Republicans cleverly maneuvered the northern faction into endorsing Frémont and won the support of many Know-Nothing workingmen by adding anti-Catholic nativism to its program of high tariffs on foreign manufactures. As a Pennsylvania congressman declared, "Let our motto be, protection to everything American, against everything foreign," while in New York Republicans worked "to cement into a harmonious mass . . . all of the Anti-Slavery, Anti-Popery and Anti-Whiskey" voters. The southern faction of the American Party nominated former president Millard Fillmore, who won 21 percent of the national vote but only 8 electoral votes.

James Buchanan, the Democrat, won the three-way race. He drew 1.8 million votes (45 percent) to 1.3 million (33 percent) for Frémont. Frémont demonstrated the appeal of the new Republican Party in the North by carrying eleven free states with 114 electoral votes. Buchanan took only five free states, and a small shift of the popular vote to Frémont in Illinois and Pennsylvania would have cost Buchanan the presidency.

The dramatic restructuring of parties was now apparent. With the collapse of the Know-Nothings, the Republicans had replaced the Whigs as the second major party. Because the Republicans had no support in the South, a victory for the new party in the next presidential election might mean the end of the Union. The fate of the republic hinged on the ability of President Buchanan to defuse the passions of the past decade and achieve a new compromise that would protect free soil in the West and slavery in the South.

Events—and his own values and weaknesses—conspired against Buchanan. Although Congress had long regulated slavery in the territories, its constitutional authority to do so had never been tested in the courts. In 1856 the case of Dred Scott reached the Supreme Court. Scott was an enslaved African American who had lived for a time with his master, an army surgeon, in the free state of Illinois and at Fort Snelling, then in the Wisconsin Territory, where the Northwest Ordinance (1787) prohibited slavery. In his suit Scott claimed that his residence in a free state and a free territory had made him free. In March 1857, after Buchanan had pressured several justices, the Court announced its decision in *Dred Scott v. Sandford*.

Seven members of the Court concurred on one critical point: Scott remained a slave. But they could not agree on the legal issues, and each justice wrote a separate opinion. In the most influential opinion, Chief Justice Roger B. Taney of Maryland declared that African Americans, slave or free, could not be citizens of the United States and that Scott therefore had no right to sue in federal court. That argument was controversial enough, since free African Americans could be citizens of a state. But Taney went on to make two even more controversial points. First, he repeated John C. Calhoun's argument that because the Fifth Amendment prohibited the taking of property without due process of law, Congress could not prevent southern citizens from taking their slave "property" into the territories or owning it there. Therefore, the chief justice concluded, the Northwest Ordinance and the Missouri Compromise—which prohibited slavery in the territories—had never been constitutional. Second, Taney declared that Congress could not give to territorial governments any powers that Congress itself did not possess. Since Congress had no authority to prohibit slavery in a territory, neither did a territorial government. Thus Taney endorsed Calhoun's interpretation of popular sovereignty: only when settlers wrote a constitution and requested statehood could they prohibit slavery. In a single stroke a Democrat-dominated Supreme Court had declared the Republicans' antislavery platform unconstitutional, a decision the Republicans could never accept. Led by Senator William H. Seward of New York, they accused the Supreme Court and President Buchanan of participating in the "Slave Power" conspiracy.

Buchanan then made things worse. In early 1858 he recommended the admission of Kansas as a slave state under the Lecompton constitution. Many observers—including the Democrat Stephen Douglas—believed that the constitution had been enacted by fraudulent means. Angered that Buchanan would not permit a referendum in Kansas on the constitution, Douglas broke with the president and his southern allies and persuaded Congress to deny statehood to Kansas. (Kansas would enter the Union as a free state in 1861.) By pursuing a proslavery agenda—first in the *Dred Scott* decision and then in Kansas—Buchanan had split his party and the nation.

Abraham Lincoln and the Republican Triumph, 1858–1860

The crisis of the Union intensified as the national Democratic Party fragmented into sectional factions and the Republicans gained the support of a majority of northern voters. During this transition Abraham Lincoln emerged as the pivotal figure in American politics, the only Republican leader whose policies and temperament might have saved the Union. But few southerners trusted Lincoln, and his election threatened to unleash the secessionist movement that had menaced the nation since 1850.

LINCOLN'S EARLY CAREER

The rise of the middle class in the small towns of the Ohio River Valley shaped Lincoln's early career. He came from an illiterate farming family of modest means that had moved from Kentucky, where Lincoln was born in 1809, to Indiana and then Illinois. In 1831 Lincoln rejected the farmer's life of his father and became a store clerk in New Salem, Illinois. Socially ambitious, Lincoln sought entry into the middle class, joining the New Salem Debating Society and reading Shakespeare and other literary works.

Lincoln's ambition was "a little engine that knew no rest," as a close associate later remarked. Admitted to the bar in 1837, Lincoln moved to Springfield, the small country town that had become the new state capital. There he met Mary Todd, the cultured daughter of a Kentucky banker; they married in 1842. The couple were a picture in contrasts. Her tastes were aristocratic; his were humble. She was volatile; he was easygoing. Bouts of depression, which plagued Lincoln throughout his life, tried her patience and tested his character. Entering political life, Lincoln served four terms as a Whig in the Illinois assembly, where he promoted education, state banking, and internal improvements such as canals and railroads. In 1846 Lincoln won election to Congress.

As a member of Congress during the war with Mexico, Lincoln had to take a stand on the contentious issue of slavery. He had long felt that slavery was unjust but had little sympathy for abolitionism and did not believe that the federal government had the constitutional authority to tamper with slavery in the South. Lincoln took the middle ground. He supported military appropriations for Polk's war in Mexico but voted for the Wilmot Proviso. He also proposed the gradual compensated emancipation of slaves in the District of Columbia. Lincoln argued that such measures—firm opposition to the expansion of slavery, gradual emancipation, and the colonization of freed slaves in Africa and elsewhere—represented the only practical way to address the issue. But his ideas were derided by both abolitionists and proslavery activists. Dismayed, Lincoln withdrew from politics and devoted his energies to a lucrative legal practice representing railroads and manufacturers.

Lincoln returned to the political fray after the passage of Stephen Douglas's Kansas-Nebraska Act. Attacking Douglas's doctrine of popular sovereignty, Lincoln articulated a clear position on slavery. He would not threaten the institution in areas where it existed but would use the authority of the national government to exclude it from the territories. Beyond that, Lincoln expressed his conviction that the nation must eventually cut out slavery like a "cancer."

Abandoning the Whig Party in favor of the Republicans, Lincoln soon emerged as their leader in Illinois. Campaigning for the U.S. Senate against Stephen Douglas in 1858, Lincoln alerted his audiences to the dangers of the "Slave Power" conspiracy. He warned that the proslavery Supreme Court might soon declare that the Constitution "does not permit a state to exclude slavery from its limits," just as it had decided (in *Dred Scott*) that "neither Congress nor the territorial legislature can do it." In that event, he continued, "we shall awake to the reality . . . that the Supreme Court has made Illinois a slave state." This fear informed Lincoln's famous "House Divided" speech. Quoting from the Bible, "A house divided against itself cannot stand," he predicted a constitutional crisis: "I believe this government cannot endure permanently half slave and half free. . . . It will become all one thing, or all the other."

THE REPUBLICAN POLITICIAN

Lincoln's 1858 duel with Stephen Douglas for the U.S. Senate attracted national interest because of Douglas's prominence and Lincoln's reputation as a formidable speaker. During a series of seven debates Douglas declared his support for white supremacy and attacked Lincoln for his alleged belief in "negro equality." Put on the defensive by Douglas's racist tactics, Lincoln advocated economic opportunity for blacks (but not equal political rights) and asked Douglas how he could accept the *Dred Scott* decision (which protected slaveowners' property in the territories) and at the same time advocate popular sovereignty. Douglas responded with the so-called Freeport Doctrine, asserting that settlers could exclude slavery simply by not adopting local legislation to protect it. Douglas's statement upset both proslavery advocates, who feared they would be denied the victory won in the *Dred Scott* decision, and abolitionists, who were not convinced that local regulations would halt the expansion of slavery. Nonetheless, the Democrats carried Illinois, and the state legislature reelected Douglas to the U.S. Senate. Yet Lincoln had established himself as a national leader, and the Republican Party, by winning control of the House of Representatives in the election of 1858, had moved a step closer to national power.

In the wake of Republican gains southern Democrats divided into two groups. Moderates such as Senator Jefferson Davis of Mississippi, who were known as Southern Rights Democrats, pursued the traditional policy of seeking ironclad commitments to protect slavery in the territories. Radicals such as Robert Barnwell Rhett of South Carolina and William Lowndes Yancey of Alabama actively promoted secession.

Radical northerners played into their hands. In 1858 Senator William Seward declared that freedom and slavery were locked in "an irrepressible conflict." In October 1859 the militant abolitionist John Brown led eighteen heavily armed black and white men in a raid that temporarily seized the federal arsenal at Harpers Ferry, Virginia. Brown's explicit purpose was to provide arms for a slave rebellion that

Abraham Lincoln and Stephen Douglas, 1860

When Douglas and Lincoln squared off in the presidential election of 1860, they distributed thousands of silk campaign-ribbons bearing their portraits and signatures. The well-known photographer Matthew Brady took pictures and retouched the images to make them more flattering—smoothing out Lincoln's gaunt and well-lined face and slimming down Douglas's ample cheeks.

(Collection of Janice L. and David J. Frent)

would establish an African American state in the South. Republican leaders disavowed Brown's raid, but Democrats called his plot "a natural, logical, inevitable result of the doctrines and teachings of the Republican party." Fueling the Democratic charges were letters that linked six leading abolitionists to the financing of Brown's raid. Brown was charged with treason, sentenced to death, and hanged—only to be praised by reformer Henry David Thoreau as "an angel of light." Slaveholders were horrified by northern admiration of Brown and looked toward the future with fear. "The aim of the present black republican organization is the destruction of the social system of the Southern States, without regard to consequences," warned one newspaper.

Nor could the South count on the Democratic Party to protect its interests. At the April 1860 party convention northern Democrats rejected Jefferson Davis's program to protect slavery in the territories, prompting the delegates from eight southern states to leave the hall. At a second Democratic convention in Baltimore northern and western delegates nominated Douglas; southern Democrats met separately and nominated Buchanan's vice president, John C. Breckinridge of Kentucky. The Democratic Party had broken into two sectional factions.

The Republicans sensed victory. They courted white voters by opposing both slavery and racial equality: "Missouri for white men and white men for Missouri," declared that state's Republican platform. On the national level the Republican convention chose Lincoln as its presidential candidate. Lincoln's position on slavery was more moderate than that of the best-known Republicans, Senator William H. Seward of New York and Salmon P. Chase of Ohio, who demanded its abolition. Lincoln also conveyed a compelling egalitarian image that appealed to smallholding farmers and wage earners. And Lincoln's home territory—the rapidly growing Midwest—was crucial in the competition between Democrats and Republicans. The Republican platform followed Lincoln's views and struck a moderate tone, upholding free soil in the West and denying the right of states to secede but ruling out direct interference with slavery in the South. In addition, the platform endorsed the old Whig program of economic development, which had gained increasing support in the Midwest, especially after the Panic of 1857.

The Republican strategy was successful. Lincoln received only 40 percent of the popular vote but won every northern and western state except New Jersey and garnered a majority in the electoral college. Douglas took 30 percent of the total vote, drawing support from all regions except the South, but won electoral votes only in Missouri and New Jersey. Breckinridge captured every state in the Deep South as well as Delaware, Maryland, and North Carolina, while John Bell, a former Tennessee Whig who became the nominee of the compromise-seeking Constitutional Union Party, carried the upper South states where the Whigs had been strongest: Kentucky, Tennessee, and Virginia.

The Republicans had united the Northeast, the Midwest, and the Far West behind free soil and had seized national power. To many southerners it now seemed time to think carefully about the meaning of Lincoln's words of 1858 that the Union must "become all one thing, or all the other."

For Further Exploration

Patricia Nelson Limerick, *The Legacy of Conquest: The Unbroken Past of the American West* (1989), provides a sharply written interpretation of the struggle among individuals, groups, and nations for control of the resources of the vast region. David Potter, *The Impending Crisis, 1848–1861* (1976), presents a lucid and detailed account of the political history of the years leading up to the Civil War, while the classic study by Avery Craven, *The Growth of Southern Nationalism* (1953), traces the emergence of sectional feeling and stresses the importance of John Brown's raid in the southern movement toward secession. For an eloquent discussion of the ideology and politics of the Republican Party, see Eric Foner, *Free Soil, Free Labor, Free Men* (1970). Michael Holt's *The Crisis of the 1850s* (1978) shows how the loss of morale among voters and the collapse of the Second-Party System allowed sectional rivalries to engulf the nation in war. For an incisive treatment of Lincoln's personal and political life, see Stephen Oates, *With Malice Toward None: A Life of Abraham Lincoln* (1977).

A fine video documentary, *The West* (6 hours), by Ken Burns and Stephen Ives has a useful website—"New Perspectives on the West" at <http://www.pbs.org/thewest>—that

TIMELINE

1820s	Growth of cattle ranching in Mexican California		Fugitive Slave Act antagonizes northern abolitionists.
1821	Mexico wins independence from Spain.	1851	American (Know-Nothing) Party formed
1836	Texas proclaims independence from Mexico.	1852	Harriet Beecher Stowe's *Uncle Tom's Cabin*
1842	Overland migration to Oregon begins.	1854	Ostend Manifesto
1845	John O'Sullivan coins term *Manifest Destiny*.		Kansas-Nebraska Act
	Texas Republic admitted to Union as slave state		Republican Party formed
1846	War with Mexico begins.	1856	"Bleeding Kansas" devastated by guerrilla war, showing problems in Douglas's scheme of popular sovereignty
	Treaty with Britain divides Oregon Country at 49th parallel.		
	Wilmot Proviso to prohibit slavery in annexed Mexican territories dies in Congress.	1857	*Dred Scott v. Sandford* allows slavery in territories.
1848	Gold discovered in California	1858	James Buchanan backs Lecompton constitution.
	In Treaty of Guadalupe Hidalgo Mexico cedes Texas, New Mexico, and California to U.S.		Lincoln-Douglas debates
	Free Soil Party organized	1859	John Brown's raid on Harpers Ferry
1850	Compromise of 1850 seeks to preserve Union.	1860	Abraham Lincoln elected president in four-way contest

includes a good collection of maps, biographical essays, original documents, and images. The PBS documentary *The U.S.-Mexican War* (4 hours) and its website at <http://www.pbs.org/usmexicanwar> view the war both from the American and the Mexican perspectives, drawing on the expertise of historians from each country. *"Uncle Tom's Cabin* and American Culture: A Multi-Media Archive" at <http://jefferson.village.virginia.edu/utc/> is an extremely rich website that explores the literary and cultural context of the time through essays, original documents, and recordings of minstrel music.

Chapter 14

TWO SOCIETIES AT WAR
1861–1865

Our fathers made this country, we their children are to save it.
— Enlistee, 12th Ohio Regiment, Union Army, 1861

"What a scene it was," the Union soldier Elisha Hunt Rhodes wrote in his diary as the battle of Gettysburg ended in 1863. "Oh the dead and the dying on this bloody field." The passions kindled by Southern Rights and American nationalism had inspired thousands of men to die in battle, and the slaughter would continue for two more years. "What is this all about?" asked Confederate lieutenant R. M. Collins at the end of another gruesome battle. "Why is it that 200,000 men of one blood and tongue . . . [should be] seeking one another's lives? We could settle our differences by compromising and all be at home in ten days." But there was no compromise—not in 1861 or even in 1865.

To explain why the war was fought—and fought to the bitter end—is not simple, but racial slavery is an important part of the answer. For political leaders in the South the Republican victory in 1860 presented a clear and immediate danger to their way of life. They knew that Lincoln regarded slavery as morally wrong and that the Republicans would prevent the extension of slavery into the territories and might well attack the institution in the South. Soon, a southern senator warned, "cohorts of Federal office-holders, Abolitionists, may be sent into [our] midst" to mobilize the African American population. The result, he and many others predicted, would be waves of bloody slave revolts and the prospect of racial intermixture. "Better, far better! [to] endure all horrors of civil war," declared a Confederate recruit from Virginia, "than to see the dusky sons of Ham leading the fair daughters of the South to the altar." To save slavery and white supremacy radical southern leaders embarked on the dangerous journey of secession.

But Lincoln and the North would not let them go in peace. In a world still ruled by kings and princes they believed that the dissolution of the American Union would endanger forever the principle of a republican government based on majority rule, constitutional procedures, and democratic elections. "We cannot escape history," the new president declared. "We shall nobly save, or meanly loose, the last best, hope of earth." As a young Union army recruit from Ohio put the issue, "If our institutions prove a failure . . . of what value will be house, family, or friends?"

And so came the Civil War. Called the "War Between the States" by southerners and the "War of the Rebellion" by northerners, the struggle went on until the great issues of the Union and of slavery had been resolved once and for all. The cost was incredibly high: more lives lost than in all the nation's subsequent wars put together and a century-long legacy of bitterness between the triumphant North and the vanquished South.

Secession and Military Stalemate, 1861–1862

After Lincoln's election in November 1860 secessionist fervor swept through the Deep South. In the four months before Lincoln's inauguration in March 1861 political leaders in Washington struggled to forge a new compromise that (like those of 1787, 1821, and 1850) would preserve the Union.

CHOOSING SIDES

The movement toward secession was most rapid in South Carolina—the home of Calhoun, nullification, and the Southern Radical movement. Robert Barnwell Rhett and other South Carolina fire-eaters had been planning for secession since 1850 and now called a convention to achieve their goal. On December 20 the convention voted unanimously to dissolve "the union now subsisting between South Carolina and other States."

Moving quickly, fire-eaters elsewhere in the Deep South called similar conventions and organized vigilante groups and militia. In early January, amid an atmosphere of public celebration, Mississippi enacted a secession ordinance. Within a month Florida, Alabama, Georgia, Louisiana, and Texas had also left the Union (see Map 14.1). In early February the jubilant secessionists met in Montgomery, Alabama, to proclaim a new nation—the Confederate States of America. They adopted a provisional constitution and named Jefferson Davis, a former U.S. senator and secretary of war, as provisional president.

Secessionist fervor was less intense in the eight slave states of the upper South (Virginia, Delaware, Maryland, North Carolina, Kentucky, Tennessee, Missouri, and Arkansas), where there were fewer slaves and yeomen farmers had greater political power. In January 1861 the legislatures of Virginia and Tennessee voted to resist any federal invasion but went no further. Seeking a compromise that would restore the Union, upper South leaders proposed federal guarantees for slavery in the states where it existed.

Meanwhile, the Union government floundered. In his last message to Congress in December 1860 President Buchanan declared secession illegal but said that the federal government lacked the authority to restore the Union by force. South Carolina immediately claimed that Buchanan's message implicitly recognized its independence and demanded the surrender of Fort Sumter, a federal garrison in

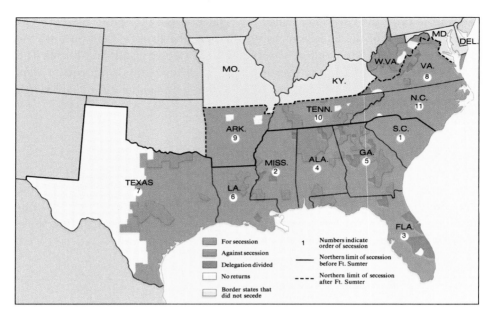

MAP 14.1
The Process of Secession, 1860–1861

The states with the highest concentration of slaves (see Map 9.2) led the secessionist movement. After the attack on Fort Sumter they were joined by the states of the upper South.
Yeomen farmers in Tennessee and the backcountry of Alabama, Georgia, and Virginia opposed
secession but, except in the future state of West Virginia, generally rallied to the Confederate
cause and until 1864 supported the war effort.

Charleston harbor. Reluctant to turn over federal property, Buchanan tested the secessionists' resolve by ordering an unarmed merchant ship to resupply the fort.
When the South Carolinians fired on the ship, Buchanan backed down, refusing to
order the navy to escort it into the harbor.

As the crisis continued, Buchanan urged Congress to find a compromise. The
proposal that received the most support was submitted by Senator John J. Crittenden of Kentucky, who hoped to follow in the footsteps of his mentor, Henry Clay,
and devise a compromise similar to that of 1850. Crittenden advanced a two-part
plan. First he proposed—and won congressional approval for—a constitutional
amendment that would permanently protect slavery from federal interference in
any state where it presently existed. Second, to deal with the territories, he called
for the westward extension of the Missouri Compromise line (36° 30' north) to the
California border, with slavery barred north of the line and protected to the south—
including any territories "hereafter acquired." After consulting with President-elect
Lincoln, congressional Republicans rejected this part of Crittenden's plan. Lincoln
was determined to uphold the doctrine of free soil and feared that extending the

Missouri Compromise line would encourage the South to embark on new imp…
alist adventures in Mexico, the Caribbean, and Latin America.

In his inaugural address on March 4, 1861, Lincoln carefully balanced a call for reconciliation with a firm commitment to the Union. He promised to permit slavery in states where it existed but stood firm for free soil in the territories. Most important, he stated that secession was illegal and that acts of violence against the Union constituted insurrection. He announced his intention to enforce federal law throughout the United States and—of particular relevance to Fort Sumter—to hold federal property in the seceded states. The choice was the South's: return to the Union or face war.

The decision came quickly. Within a month of Lincoln's inauguration the garrison at Fort Sumter urgently needed supplies. To maintain his credibility the new president dispatched a relief expedition, promising that it would not land troops or arms unless the rebels disrupted the delivery of food and medicine. Jefferson Davis and his government welcomed Lincoln's decision, believing that a confrontation would turn the wavering upper South against the North and win foreign support for the Confederate cause. Resolving to take the fort immediately, Davis demanded its surrender. When Major Robert Anderson refused to comply, the Confederate forces opened fire on April 12, forcing the surrender of the Fort two days later. The next day Lincoln called 75,000 state militiamen into federal service for ninety days to put down an insurrection "too powerful to be suppressed by the ordinary course of judicial proceedings." All talk of compromise was past.

Northerners responded to Lincoln's call to arms with enthusiasm. Asked to provide thirteen regiments of volunteers, Republican Governor William Dennison of Ohio sent twenty. "The lion in us is thoroughly roused," he explained. Many northern Democrats were equally committed to the Union cause. As Stephen Douglas declared six weeks before his death: "Every man must be for the United States or against it. There can be no neutrals in this war, only patriots—or traitors."

The white residents of the upper South now had to choose between the Union and the Confederacy, and their decision was crucial. Those eight states accounted for two-thirds of the South's white population, more than three-fourths of its industrial production, and well over half its food and fuel. They were home to many of the nation's best military leaders, including Colonel Robert E. Lee of Virginia, a career officer whom General-in-Chief Winfield Scott recommended to Lincoln as field commander of the new Union army. And they were geographically strategic. Kentucky, with its 500-mile border on the Ohio River, was essential to the movement of troops and supplies. Maryland was vital to the Union's security because it surrounded the nation's capital on the north.

The weight of history decided the outcome in Virginia, the original home of American slavery. Three days after the fall of Fort Sumter a Virginia convention passed an ordinance of secession by a vote of eighty-eight to fifty-five. The dissenting votes came mainly from the yeoman-dominated northwestern counties (see Map 14.1); elsewhere in Virginia whites rallied to the Confederate cause. Refusing

...ott's offer to command the Union troops, Robert E. Lee resigned from the army. "Save in defense of my native state," Lee told Scott, "I never desire again to draw my sword." Arkansas, Tennessee, and North Carolina quickly joined Virginia in the Confederacy.

Lincoln moved aggressively to hold the rest of the upper South. In May he ordered General George B. McClellan to take control of northwestern Virginia, thus securing the railway line between Washington and the Ohio Valley. In October voters there overwhelmingly approved the creation of a new state, West Virginia, which was admitted to the Union in 1863. The Union cause also triumphed in Delaware but it was much less popular in Maryland, where slavery was well entrenched. A pro-Confederate mob attacked Massachusetts troops marching between railroad stations in Baltimore, causing the war's first combat deaths: four soldiers and twelve civilians. When other Maryland secessionists destroyed railroad bridges and telegraph lines, Lincoln ordered military occupation of the state and imprisoned suspected secessionists, including members of the state legislature. He released them only in November 1861, after Unionists had gained control of the Maryland legislature.

In Missouri the key to communications and trade on the Missouri and upper Mississippi Rivers, Lincoln mobilized support among the large German American community. In July a force of German American militia defeated Confederate sympathizers commanded by the governor. Despite continuing raids by Confederate guerrilla bands led by William Quantrill and Jesse and Frank James, the Union retained control of Missouri.

In Kentucky secessionist and Unionist sentiment was evenly balanced, so Lincoln moved cautiously. He waited until August, when Unionists took control of the state government, before ordering federal troops to cut Kentucky's thriving export trade in horses, mules, whiskey, and foodstuffs. When the Confederacy responded to this cut-off by moving troops into Kentucky, the Unionist legislature asked for federal protection. In September Illinois volunteers under the command of the relatively unknown brigadier general Ulysses S. Grant crossed the Ohio River and drove out the Confederates. Of the eight states of the upper South, Lincoln had kept four (Delaware, Maryland, Kentucky, and Missouri) and a portion of a fifth (western Virginia) in the Union.

SETTING OBJECTIVES AND DEVISING STRATEGIES

After secession Confederate leaders called on their people to defend the independence of the new nation. At his inauguration in February 1861 Jefferson Davis identified the Confederate cause with that of the American Revolution; like their grandfathers, white southerners were fighting against tyranny and for the "sacred right of self-government." As Davis put it, the Confederacy sought "no conquest, no aggrandizement, no concession of any kind from the states with which we were lately confederated; all we ask is to be let alone." The decision to focus on the defense of the Confederacy (and not to conquer western territories) gave southern leaders a strong advantage: they needed only a military stalemate to guarantee independence.

Lincoln made his first major statement on Union goals and strategy in a speech to Congress on July 4, 1861. He portrayed secession as an attack on popular government, America's great contribution to world history, telling his audience that the issue was simple: "Whether a constitutional republic, or a democracy—a government of the people, by the same people—can or cannot maintain its territorial integrity against its domestic foes." Only by crushing the rebellion could the nation preserve its principles. Lincoln therefore rejected General Winfield Scott's plan to use economic sanctions and a naval blockade to persuade the Confederates to return to the Union. Instead, the president called for an aggressive military strategy and insisted on a policy of unconditional surrender.

The president knew that the northern public wanted a strike toward Richmond, the Confederate capital, and he hoped an early victory would end the rebellion. He therefore dispatched General Irwin McDowell and an army of 30,000 men to attack P.G.T. Beauregard's force of 20,000 troops at Manassas, a major rail junction in Virginia 30 miles southwest of Washington. McDowell attacked strongly on July 21 near Manassas Creek (also called Bull Run), but panic swept through his troops during a Confederate counterattack. For the first time Union soldiers heard the hair-raising rebel yell. "The peculiar corkscrew sensation that it sends down your backbone under these circumstances can never be told," one Union veteran wrote. "You have to feel it." McDowell's troops retreated in disarray to Washington, along with the many civilians who had come to observe the battle. The victorious Confederate troops also dispersed, confused and without the wagons and supplies they needed to pursue McDowell's army.

It was now clear that the rebellion would not be easily crushed. To bolster northern morale, shattered by the rout at Bull Run, Lincoln replaced McDowell with General George B. McClellan and signed bills for the enlistment of an additional million men, who would serve for three years in the newly created Army of the Potomac. A cautious military engineer, McClellan spent the winter of 1861 to 1862 training raw recruits, and in 1862 he launched the first major offensive of the war, a thrust toward Richmond. In a maneuver that required skillful logistics, the Union general transported about 100,000 troops by boat down the Potomac River and Chesapeake Bay and then up the peninsula between the York and James Rivers toward the South's capital. But McClellan moved slowly, despite Lincoln's advice to "strike a blow" quickly, allowing the Confederates to mount a counterstroke. In May a Confederate army under Thomas J. ("Stonewall") Jackson marched rapidly north up the Shenandoah Valley in western Virginia, threatening Washington. To head off the danger Lincoln diverted 30,000 troops from McClellan's army, but Jackson, a brilliant general, defeated three Union armies in the valley. Then Jackson joined the Confederates' formidable commanding general, Robert E. Lee, who had confronted McClellan outside Richmond. Lee launched a ferocious attack that lasted for seven days (June 25 to July 1), suffering heavy casualties (20,000 to the Union's 10,000). But McClellan failed to exploit his advantage, refusing to renew the offensive unless he received fresh troops. Lincoln ordered the withdrawal of the Army of the Potomac, and Richmond remained secure.

Lee promptly went on the offensive, hoping for victories that would humiliate Lincoln's government. Joining with Jackson in northern Virginia, Lee routed a Union army in the Second Battle of Bull Run (August 1862) and then struck north through western Maryland, where he met with near disaster. When Lee divided his force—sending Jackson to capture Harpers Ferry in West Virginia—a copy of his orders fell into McClellan's hands. But the Union general again failed to pursue his advantage, delaying his attack until Lee's depleted army had occupied a strong defensive position behind Antietam Creek, near Sharpsburg, Maryland. Outnumbered 87,000 to 50,000, Lee desperately fought off McClellan's attacks. Just as Union regiments were about to overwhelm his right flank, Jackson's troops arrived, saving the Confederates from a major defeat. Appalled by Union casualties, McClellan let Lee retreat to Virginia.

The fighting at Antietam was savage. A Wisconsin officer described his men as "loading and firing with demoniacal fury and shouting and laughing hysterically." At a critical point in the battle a sunken road, nicknamed Bloody Lane, was filled with Confederate bodies two and three deep, and the attacking Union troops knelt on "this ghastly flooring" to shoot at the retreating Confederates. The battle at Antietam on September 17, 1862, remains the bloodiest single day in U.S. military history. Together the Confederate and Union dead numbered 4,800 and the wounded 18,500, of whom 3,000 soon died. (In comparison, 6,000 Americans were wounded or killed on D-Day, which began the invasion of Nazi-occupied France, in World War II.)

In public Lincoln declared Antietam a victory, but privately he declared that McClellan should have fought Lee to the finish. A masterful organizer of men and supplies, McClellan lacked the stomach for an all-out attack. Dismissing McClellan, Lincoln began a long search for an effective replacement. His first choice was Ambrose E. Burnside, who proved to be more daring but less competent. In December, after heavy losses in futile attacks against well-entrenched Confederate forces at Fredericksburg, Virginia, Burnside resigned his command and Lincoln replaced him with Joseph ("Fighting Joe") Hooker. As 1862 ended, the Confederates had some reason to be content: the war in the East was a stalemate.

In the West Union forces had been more successful (see Map 14.2). Their goal was to control the Ohio, Mississippi, and Missouri Rivers, dividing the Confederacy and reducing the mobility of its armies. The decision of Kentucky not to join the rebellion had already given the Union dominance in the Ohio River Valley. In 1862 the Union army launched a series of highly innovative land and water operations to gain control of the Tennessee and Mississippi Rivers as well. In the north, General Ulysses S. Grant used riverboats clad with iron plates to take Fort Henry on the Tennessee River and Fort Donelson on the Cumberland. Grant then moved south

M AP 14.2
The Western Campaigns, 1861–1862

As the Civil War intensified during the course of 1861, Union and Confederate military and naval forces fought to control the great valleys of the Ohio, Tennessee, and Mississippi Rivers. By the end of 1862 Union forces had achieved dominance over most of these crucial transportation routes, allowing them to keep Missouri in the Union, drive Confederate armies out of Kentucky and half of Tennessee, and capture New Orleans. With their victory at Shiloh (along the Tennessee River), northern forces carried the war to the borders of the states of the Deep South.

along the Tennessee to seize critical railroad lines. A Confederate army under Albert Sidney Johnston and P.G.T. Beauregard caught Grant by surprise on April 6 near a small log church named Shiloh. Grant relentlessly threw troops into the battle, forcing a Confederate withdrawal the following day but taking huge casualties. Grant described a large field "so covered with dead that it would have been possible to walk over the clearing in any direction, stepping on dead bodies, without a foot touching the ground." The cost in lives was high, but Lincoln was pleased. "What I want . . . is generals who will fight battles and win victories." Grant had done that, creating military momentum for the Union in the West.

Three weeks later Union naval forces commanded by David G. Farragut struck from the south, moving through the Mississippi Delta from the Gulf of Mexico to capture New Orleans. The Union now held the South's financial center and largest city as well as a major base for future naval operations. Union victories in the West had thus significantly undermined Confederate strength in the Mississippi Valley.

Toward Total War

The carnage at Antietam and Shiloh had made it clear that the war would be long and costly. After Shiloh, Grant later noted, he "gave up all idea of saving the Union except by complete conquest." The conflict became a total war—arraying the entire resources of the two societies against each other and eventually resulting in warfare against enemy civilians. Aided by a strong party and a talented cabinet, Lincoln skillfully mobilized the North for all-out war, organizing an effective central government. Jefferson Davis was less successful in harnessing the resources of the South because the eleven states of the Confederacy remained deeply suspicious of centralized rule.

MOBILIZING ARMIES AND CIVILIANS

Initially, patriotic fervor filled both armies with eager volunteers. The call for soldiers was especially successful in the South, which had a strong military tradition and an ample supply of trained officers. But the initial surge of enlistments fell off as the people saw the realities of war: heavy losses to disease and dreadful battlefield carnage. Soon both governments faced the necessity of forced enlistment (see American Voices, "A Doctor on the Health and Patriotism of Union Recruits").

The Confederacy was the first to act. In April 1862, after the defeat at Shiloh, the Confederate Congress imposed the first legally binding draft in American history. One law extended all existing enlistments for the duration of the war; another required three years of military service from all able-bodied men between the ages of eighteen and thirty-five. In September, after the heavy casualties at Antietam, the age limit was raised to forty-five. The Confederate draft had two loopholes. First, it exempted one white man—either the planter or an overseer—for each twenty slaves, allowing men on large plantations to avoid military service. Second, drafted men could hire substitutes. Before this provision was repealed in 1864, the price for a substitute had risen to $300 in gold, about three times the annual wages of a skilled worker. Laborers and yeomen farmers angrily complained that it was "a rich man's war and a poor man's fight."

Consequently, some southerners refused to serve, and the Confederate government lacked the power to compel them. Because the Confederate constitution vested sovereignty in the individual states, strong governors such as Joseph Brown of Georgia and Zebulon Vance of North Carolina simply ignored Davis's first draft call in early 1862. Elsewhere state judges issued writs of habeas corpus (a legal process designed to protect people from arbitrary arrest) and ordered the Confederate army to release protesting draftees. Reluctantly the Confederate Congress overrode the judges' authority to free conscripted men, enabling the Confederacy to keep substantial armies in the field well into 1864.

A Doctor on the Health and Patriotism of Union Recruits

HORACE O. CRANE

D r. Horace O. Crane was an army medical examiner for the Union army in Wisconsin. *In the following report to his superiors, he dissected the various reasons that men tried to avoid service in the Union army. Nonetheless, Wisconsin provided more Union soldiers (in relation to population) than almost any other state, in part because many of its people were native-born American Protestants who strongly opposed slavery.*

While on duty [in Wisconsin] . . . I examined fourteen thousand one hundred and sixty-five men, mostly enrolled or drafted men, nearly all of whom claimed severe indisposition of some kind. . . .

A large preponderance of this [examined] population is foreign, representing every state and duchy in Europe. They subsist by the cultivation of small farms and the manufacture of lumber and shingles from their pine-forests. Necessity compels them to be industrious, but they are usually very poor and ignorant, mostly Roman Catholics, and as such generally *hostile to the conscription act.* . . . Demagogues, interested in preserving their [Democratic] party ascendancy, have educated this people to believe that the war was not only useless and cruel, but that its effect would be to finally subvert their civil and political privileges.

The frauds practiced by enrolled and drafted men are so numerous and varied as to require the utmost vigilance on the part of the surgeon. . . . [For example:] Alleged blindness of the right eye is very common; the pupil often appearing fully and apparently permanently dilated. . . . Some of these men had *belladonna* [a poison plant that causes dilation] upon their persons at the time of the examination, which they had been using freely. . . .

Occupation, in this district, is of far greater importance in the selection of recruits than locality. . . . The lumbermen (unless they have hernia) are universally good recruits, having abundance of vitality, with muscles well developed; they are a brave, cheerful, and hardy class. In one sub-district is a large tannery, and a boot and shoe manufactory . . . ; of these mechanics, nearly sixty-five percent, were discharged from enrollment, *before the draft,* for physical disability [because of] . . . organic disease of heart or lungs. . . . From four years' experience . . . I am decidedly of opinion that the . . . descendants of the early settlers of New England, New York, Pennsylvania, and Ohio, where physical development and courage are combined with intelligence and patriotism, make the best soldiers the world has ever seen.

SOURCE: Peter T. Harstad, ed., "A Civil War Examiner: The Report of Dr. Horace O. Crane," *Wisconsin Magazine of History* 48 (Spring 1965), pp. 226–31.

The Union government took a more authoritarian stance toward potential foes and ordinary citizens. To prevent opposition to the war Lincoln suspended habeas corpus and over the course of the war imprisoned about 15,000 Confederate sympathizers without trial. The president also extended martial law to civilians who discouraged enlistment or resisted the draft, making them subject to military courts rather than local juries. This firm policy had the desired effect. The Militia Act of 1862 set a quota of volunteers for each state, which was increased by the Enrollment Act of 1863. States and towns enticed volunteers with cash bounties, prompting the enlistment or reenlistment of almost a million men. As in the South wealthy men could avoid the draft by providing a substitute or paying a $300 commutation, or exemption, fee.

The Enrollment Act sparked significant opposition, as thousands of recent immigrants refused to serve in the Union army, saying it was not their fight. Northern Democrats exploited this resentment by charging that Lincoln was drafting poor whites to free the slaves and flood the cities with black laborers. Some Democrats opposed the war, believing that the South should be allowed to secede; others simply wanted to protect the interests of immigrants, most of whom were Democratic voters. In July 1863 hostility to the draft and to African Americans spilled onto the streets of New York City. For five days immigrant Irish and German workers ran rampant, burning draft offices, sacking the homes of important Republicans, and attacking the police. The rioters lynched and mutilated a dozen African Americans, drove hundreds of black families from their homes, and burned down the Colored Orphan Asylum. Lincoln rushed in Union troops, who killed more than a hundred rioters and suppressed the insurrection.

The Union government's determination to wage total war won greater support among native-born citizens. In 1861 prominent New Yorkers established the United States Sanitary Commission. Its task was to provide medical services and prevent deaths from disease, which accounted for three-fourths of the casualties in the recently concluded Crimean War between Britain and Russia. Through its network of 7,000 local auxiliaries, the Sanitary Commission gathered supplies; distributed clothing, food, and medicine to the army; improved the sanitary standards of camp life; and recruited battlefield nurses and doctors for the Union Army Medical Bureau. These efforts were not consistently successful. Diseases—dysentery, typhoid, and malaria as well as childhood viruses such as mumps and measles, to which many rural men had not developed an immunity—killed about 250,000 Union soldiers, about twice the number who died in combat. Still, because of better sanitation and high-quality food the mortality rate among Union troops from disease and wounds was substantially lower than that in other major nineteenth-century wars. Confederate soldiers were less fortunate. Although thousands of white women volunteered as nurses, the Confederate health system was poorly organized. Thousands of southern soldiers contracted scurvy because of the lack of vitamin C in their diets, and they died from camp diseases at higher rates than did Union soldiers.

Draft Riots in New York City

The Enrollment Act of 1863 enraged many workers who opposed the war, especially recent Irish and German immigrants. In July in New York City they took out their anger on free blacks in a week-long riot. As the club-waving mob hangs an African American, three other blacks escape by climbing over a fence. The violence against African Americans received wide publicity (this engraving appeared in the *Illustrated London News* on August 8, 1863) and prompted many northerners to increase their support for the war effort.
(Culver Pictures)

Women took a leading role in the Sanitary Commission and other wartime agencies. As superintendent of female nurses, Dorothea Dix became the first woman to receive a major federal appointment. Dix used her influence to combat the prejudice against women treating men, opening a new occupation to women. Thousands of educated Union women also joined the war effort as clerks in the expanding governmental bureaucracy, while in the South women staffed the efficient Confederate postal service. Indeed, in both sections millions of women assumed new economic responsibilities and worked with far greater intensity. They took over many farm tasks previously done by men and went to work in schools and textile, clothing, and shoe factories. A number of women even took on military duties as spies, scouts, and (disguised as men) soldiers. As the nurse Clara Barton, who later founded the American Red Cross, recalled, "At the war's end, woman was at least fifty years in advance of the normal position which continued peace would have assigned her."

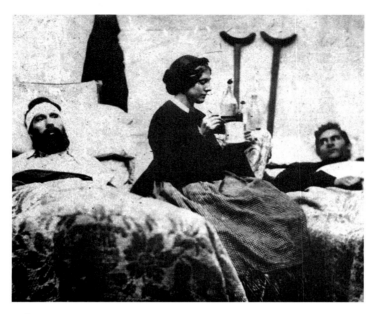

Hospital Nursing

Working as nurses in chaotic battlefront hospitals, thousands of Union and Confederate women gained firsthand experience of the horrors of war. But a sense of calm prevails in this behind-the-lines Union hospital in Nashville, Tennessee, as nurse Anne Belle tends to the needs of those recovering from their wounds. Most nurses were unpaid volunteers, cooking and cleaning for their patients as well as tending to their injuries.
(Massachusetts Commandery Military Order of the Loyal Legion and the U.S. Army Military History Institute)

MOBILIZING RESOURCES

Wars are usually won by the side with superior resources and economic organization, and in this regard the Union entered the war with a distinct advantage. With nearly two-thirds of the American people, about two-thirds of the nation's railroad mileage, and nearly 90 percent of American industrial output, the North's economy was far superior to the South's. The North had an especially great advantage in the manufacture of cannon and rifles because many of its arms factories were equipped for mass production.

But the Confederate position was far from weak. Virginia, North Carolina, and Tennessee had substantial industrial capacity. Richmond, with its Tredegar Iron Works, was an important industrial center, and in 1861 the Confederacy transported to Richmond the gun-making machinery from the U.S. armory at Harpers Ferry. The production of the Richmond armory, the purchase of Enfield rifles from Britain, and the capture of 100,000 Union guns enabled the Confederacy to provide every infantryman with a modern rifle-musket by 1863.

Moreover, with 3 million slaves, the Confederacy commanded an enormous workforce. Kept in the fields by their masters, slaves produced food for the army and cotton for export. Confederate leaders counted on "King Cotton" to provide revenue to purchase clothes, boots, blankets, and weapons from abroad. They also counted on cotton as a diplomatic weapon, hoping that the British, who depended on the South to supply their textile factories, would grant diplomatic recognition and provide military aid. Although the British government never recognized the Confederacy as an independent nation, it regarded the conflict as a war (rather than a domestic insurrection), thereby giving the rebels the status of a belligerent power with the right under international law to borrow money and purchase weapons. Thus the odds did not necessarily favor the Union, despite its superior resources.

The outcome depended on the success of the rival governments in mobilizing their societies. To build political support for their party and boost industrial output, Lincoln and the Republicans enacted the program of national mercantilism previously advocated by Henry Clay and the Whig Party. First the Republicans raised tariffs, winning praise from northeastern manufacturers and laborers who feared competition from cheap foreign goods. Then Secretary of the Treasury Salmon P. Chase created a national banking system—an important element of every modern centralized government—by linking thousands of local banks. This integrated system was far more effective in raising capital and controlling inflation than earlier efforts by the First and Second Banks of the United States had been. Finally, the Lincoln administration devised a far-reaching system of internal improvements. In 1862 the Republican Congress began to build transcontinental railroads, chartering the Union Pacific and Central Pacific railways and subsidizing them lavishly. It gave them 20 square miles of federal land for every mile of track they put down and in 1864 provided a similar subsidy to the Northern Pacific. In addition, the Republicans moved aggressively to provide northern farmers with "free land" in the West. The Homestead Act of 1862 gave heads of families or individuals age twenty-one or older the title to 160 acres of public land after five years of residence and improvement. This economic program sustained the allegiance of many northerners to the Republican Party while bolstering the Union's ability to fight the war.

In contrast, the Confederate government had a much less coherent economic policy. True to its states'-rights philosophy the Confederacy left most economic matters in the hands of the state governments. But as the realities of total war became clear, the Davis administration took some extraordinary measures: it built and operated shipyards, armories, foundries, and textile mills; commandeered food and scarce raw materials such as coal, iron, copper, and lead; requisitioned slaves to work on fortifications; and exercised direct control over foreign trade. As the war wore on, ordinary southern citizens resented these measures, especially in areas where Confederate leaders failed to manage wartime shortages. To sustain the war effort they increasingly counted on racial solidarity: Jefferson Davis warned whites that a

Union victory would destroy slavery "and reduce the whites to the degraded position of the African race."

For both the North and the South the cost of fighting a total war was enormous. In the Union government spending shot up from less than 2 percent of gross national product to about 15 percent. To meet those expenses the Republicans established a powerful modern state that raised money in three ways. First the government increased revenue by increasing tariffs on consumer goods and imposing direct taxes on business corporations, large inheritances, and incomes. These levies paid for about 20 percent of the cost of the war. The sale of Treasury bonds financed another 65 percent of the northern war effort. Led by Jay Cooke, a Philadelphia banker, the Treasury used newspaper advertisements and 2,500 subagents to persuade nearly a million northern families to buy war bonds. In addition, the National Banking Acts of 1863 and 1864 essentially forced state banks to accept a national charter and to purchase Treasury bonds.

The Union financed the remaining cost of the war by printing paper money beginning in 1862 and requiring the public to accept it as legal tender. By the end of the war there were nearly $450 million of these "greenbacks" in circulation. Unlike the "Continentals" issued during the War for Independence, the greenbacks depreciated only moderately, primarily because they funded only about 15 percent of wartime expenses (as opposed to 80 percent in the Revolutionary War). By imposing broad-based taxes, borrowing from the middle classes, and creating a national monetary system, the Union government had created the financial foundations of a modern nation-state.

The financial demands on the South were just as great, but it lacked a powerful central government that could tax and borrow. The Confederate Congress fiercely opposed taxes on cotton exports and slaves, the most valuable property of wealthy planters. Taxes fell primarily on urban middle-class and nonslaveholding yeomen farm families, who often refused to pay. Consequently, the Confederacy covered less than 5 percent of its expenditures through taxation. The government paid for another 35 percent by borrowing, although many wealthy planters refused to buy large quantities of Confederate bonds, and foreign bankers were equally wary.

Thus the Confederacy was forced to finance about 60 percent of its expenses with unbacked paper money. The flood of currency created a spectacular inflation, which was compounded by the widespread circulation of counterfeit Confederate notes. As the huge supply of money (and shortages of goods) caused food prices to soar, riots broke out in more than a dozen southern cities and towns. In Richmond several hundred women broke into bakeries, crying, "Our children are starving while the rich roll in wealth." By the spring of 1865 prices had risen to ninety-two times their 1861 levels. Inflation not only undermined civilian morale but also prompted farmers to refuse Confederate money. Supply officers had to seize what they needed, offering payment in worthless IOUs. Fearful of a strong government and taxation, the Confederacy was forced to violate the property rights of its citizens to sustain the war.

The Turning Point: 1863

By 1863 the Lincoln administration had mobilized northern society, creating a complex war machine and a coherent financial system. "Little by little," the young diplomat Henry Adams noted at his post in London, "one began to feel that, behind the chaos in Washington power was taking shape; that it was massed and guided as it had not been before." Slowly but surely the tide of battle shifted toward the Union.

EMANCIPATION

From the beginning of the conflict antislavery Republicans had tried to persuade their party to make abolition a Union war aim. They based their argument not just on morality but on "military necessity," pointing out that slave-grown crops sustained the Confederate war effort. As Frederick Douglass put it, "the very stomach of this rebellion is the Negro in the form of a slave. Arrest that hoe in the hands of the Negro, and you smite the rebellion in the very seat of its life." As war casualties mounted in 1862, Lincoln and some Republican leaders accepted Douglass's argument and began to redefine the war as a struggle against slavery—the cornerstone of southern society.

But it was enslaved African Americans who forced the issue by seizing freedom for themselves. Exploiting the disorder of wartime tens of thousands of slaves escaped and sought refuge behind Union lines. The first Union official to confront this issue was General Benjamin Butler. When three slaves reached his camp on the Virginia coast in May 1861, he labeled them "contraband of war" and refused to return them to their owner. His term stuck, and for the rest of the war slaves behind Union lines were known as *contrabands*. Within a few months a thousand contrabands were camping with Butler's army. To define their status and undermine the Confederate war effort, in August 1861 Congress passed the First Confiscation Act, which authorized the seizure of all property—including slaves—used to support the rebellion.

Radical Republicans, who had long condemned slavery, now saw a way to use the war to end it. By the spring of 1862 leading Radicals—Treasury secretary Chase; Charles Sumner, chair of the Senate Committee on Foreign Relations; and Thaddeus Stevens, chair of the House Ways and Means Committee—had pushed moderate Republicans toward abolition. In April Congress enacted legislation ending slavery in the District of Columbia, with compensation for owners. In June it outlawed slavery in the federal territories, finally enacting the Wilmot Proviso and the Republicans' free-soil policy. And in July Congress passed the radical Second Confiscation Act, which, overriding the property rights of Confederate slaveowners, declared "forever free" all fugitive slaves and all slaves captured by the Union army.

Lincoln now seized the initiative from the radicals. In July 1862 he prepared a general proclamation of emancipation and, viewing the battle of Antietam as "an indication of the Divine Will," issued it on September 22, 1862. Based on the president's war powers the proclamation declared Lincoln's intention to free the slaves in all states still in rebellion on January 1, 1863. The seceding states had a hundred days to preserve slavery by returning to the Union. None chose to do so.

The proclamation was politically astute. Because Lincoln needed to keep the loyalty of the border states still in the Union, he left slavery intact there. He also wanted to win the allegiance of the areas occupied by Union armies—western and central Tennessee, western Virginia, and southern Louisiana, including New Orleans—so he left slavery untouched there. Consequently, because Lincoln's order of course would not be followed within the Confederacy, the Emancipation Proclamation did not free a single slave. Yet it dramatically changed the nature of the conflict. Union troops became agents of liberation, transforming the struggle to preserve the Union into (as Lincoln put it) a war of "subjugation" in which "the old South is to be destroyed and replaced by new propositions and ideas."

As a war aim emancipation was extremely controversial. During the congressional election of 1862 the Democrats denounced emancipation as unconstitutional, warned of slave uprisings and massive bloodshed in the South, and claimed that a "black flood" would wash away the jobs of northern workers. Democrat Horatio Seymour won the governorship of New York by declaring that if abolition was the purpose of the war, the South should not be conquered. Other Democrats swept to victory in New York, Pennsylvania, Ohio, and Illinois, and the party gained thirty-four seats in Congress. However, the Republicans still held a twenty-five-seat majority in the House and had gained five seats in the Senate. Lincoln refused to retreat. On New Year's Day 1863 he signed the Emancipation Proclamation. To reassure northerners who sympathized with the South or feared race warfare, Lincoln urged slaves to "abstain from all violence." But he now justified emancipation as an "act of justice." "If my name ever goes into history," he said, "it was for this act."

VICKSBURG AND GETTYSBURG

The fate of the proclamation would depend on the success of Union armies and the Republicans' ability to win support for their program. The outlook was not encouraging. Not only had Democrats registered gains in the election of 1862; there was increased popular support for Democrats who favored a negotiated peace. Two brilliant victories by Lee, whose army defeated Hooker's forces at Fredericksburg (December 1862) and Chancellorsville, Virginia (May 1863), caused further erosion of northern support for the war, as did rumors of a new draft.

At this crucial juncture General Grant mounted a major offensive in the West designed to split the Confederacy in two. Grant drove south along the west bank of the Mississippi and then moved his troops across the river near Vicksburg, Mississippi, where he defeated two Confederate armies and laid siege to the city. After repelling Union assaults for six weeks the exhausted and starving Vicksburg garrison surrendered on July 4, 1863. Five days later Union forces took Port Hudson, Louisiana, establishing Union control of the Mississippi. Grant had taken 31,000 prisoners, cut off Louisiana, Arkansas, and Texas from the rest of the Confederacy, and prompted hundreds of slaves to desert their plantations.

Grant's initial advance down the Mississippi had created an argument over strategy within the Confederate leadership. Davis and other civilian leaders wanted to throw in reinforcements to defend Vicksburg and send troops to Tennessee to draw Grant out of Mississippi. But Lee, buoyed by his recent victories over Hooker, favored a new invasion of the North. He argued that a military thrust into the free states would relieve the pressure on Vicksburg by drawing the Union armies east. Beyond that Lee hoped for a major victory that would undermine northern support for the war.

Lee won out. In June 1863 he maneuvered his army north through Maryland into Pennsylvania. The Union's Army of the Potomac moved along with him, positioning itself between Lee and Washington. The two great armies met in an accidental but decisive confrontation at Gettysburg, Pennsylvania (see Map 14.3). On the first day of battle, July 1, Lee drove the Union's advance guard to the south of town. There General George G. Meade, who had just taken over command of the Union forces from Hooker, placed his troops in well-defended hilltop positions and

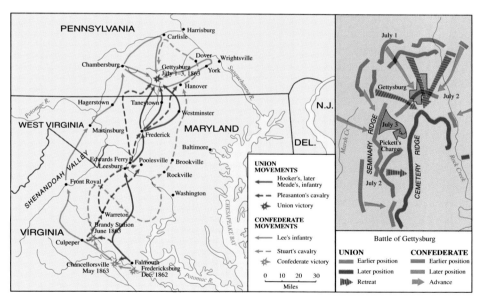

MAP 14.3
The Battle of Gettysburg, 1863

After Lee's victory at Chancellorsville, Virginia, in May the two armies jockeyed for position as the Confederate forces moved northward. At Gettysburg the Union army commanded by General George Meade emerged victorious primarily because it was much larger than the Confederate force and held well-fortified positions along Cemetery Ridge, which gave its units a major tactical advantage.

called up reinforcements. By the morning of the second day Meade had 90,000 troops to Lee's 75,000. Aware that he was outnumbered but bent on victory, Lee attacked both of Meade's flanks but failed to turn them. General Richard B. Ewell, assigned to attack the Union right, was unwilling to risk his men in an all-out assault, and General Longstreet, on the Union left, was unable to dislodge Meade's forces from Little Round Top.

On July 3 Lee decided to attempt a frontal assault on the center of the Union lines. He felt this might be his last chance to inflict a crushing defeat on the North, and he had enormous confidence in his troops. After the heaviest artillery barrage of the war Lee ordered 14,000 men under General George E. Pickett to take Cemetery Ridge. But Meade had reinforced the center of his line with artillery and his best troops. When Pickett's men charged across a mile of open terrain, they were met by massive fire; thousands were killed, wounded, or captured. By the end of the battle Lee had suffered 28,000 casualties, one-third of the Army of Northern Virginia, and Meade had 23,000 killed or wounded, making Gettysburg the most lethal battle of the Civil War.

Gettysburg was a great Union victory; never again would a southern army invade the North. Shocked by the bloodletting, Meade allowed the remaining Confederate soldiers to escape, thus losing an opportunity to end the war. "As it is," Lincoln brooded, "the war will be prolonged indefinitely." Nonetheless, the victories at Gettysburg and at Vicksburg were a major turning point in the conflict. In the fall of 1863 Republicans reaped political gains from those victories by sweeping state and local elections in Pennsylvania, Ohio, and New York. In the South the military setbacks accentuated war weariness. The Confederate elections of 1863 went sharply against the politicians who supported Jefferson Davis, and a large minority in the new Confederate Congress was outspokenly hostile to his policies. A few advocated peace negotiations, and many more criticized the ineffectiveness of the war effort.

Vicksburg and Gettysburg also represented a great diplomatic victory for the North, ending the Confederacy's prospect of winning foreign recognition and acquiring advanced weapons. In 1862 British shipbuilders had begun to supply armed cruisers to the Confederacy, and one of them, the *Alabama*, had sunk or captured more than a hundred Union merchant ships. Union diplomats in London despaired of preventing the scheduled delivery of two more ironclad cruisers in mid-1863. But news of the Union victories changed everything, and the American minister persuaded the British government to impound the ships.

Moreover, cotton had not become a diplomatic weapon, as the South had hoped. British manufacturers had stockpiled raw cotton before the war, and when those stocks were depleted, they found new sources in Egypt and India. Equally important, the dependence of British consumers on cheap wheat from the North deterred the government from supporting the Confederacy. Finally, British workers and reformers were enthusiastic champions of abolition, which the Emancipation Proclamation had established as a Union war aim. The results at Vicksburg and

Gettysburg confirmed British neutrality by demonstrating the military might of the Union. The British did not want to risk Canada or their merchant marine by provoking a strong, well-armed United States.

The Union Victorious, 1864–1865

The Union victories of 1863 made it clear that the South could not win the war on the battlefield, but the Confederacy still hoped for a stalemate and a negotiated peace. Lincoln and his generals faced the daunting task of winning a quick and decisive military victory; otherwise a majority of northern voters might well desert the Republican Party and its policies.

SOLDIERS AND STRATEGY

Free African Americans and fugitive slaves had tried to enlist in the Union army as early as 1861, and the black abolitionist Frederick Douglass had embraced their cause: "Once let the black man get upon his person the brass letters, 'U.S.' . . . a musket on his shoulder and bullets in his pockets, and there is no power on earth which can deny that he has earned the right to citizenship in the United States." Such an outcome frightened many northern whites, who were determined to keep blacks subjugated. Moreover, most Union generals doubted that former slaves would make good soldiers, and so the Lincoln administration initially refused to consider blacks for military service.

The Emancipation Proclamation changed popular thinking and military policy. If blacks were to benefit from a Union victory, some northern whites argued, they should share in the fighting and dying. The valor exhibited by the first African American regiments also influenced northern opinion. In January 1863 Thomas Wentworth Higginson, the white abolitionist commander of the First South Carolina (Black) Volunteers, wrote a glowing newspaper account of their military prowess: "No officer in this regiment now doubts that the key to the successful prosecution of the war lies in the unlimited employment of black troops." The War Department authorized the enlistment of free blacks and contraband slaves, and as white resistance to conscription increased, the Lincoln administration recruited as many African Americans as it could. Without black soldiers, the president suggested in the autumn of 1864, "we would be compelled to abandon the war in three weeks." By the spring of 1865 there were nearly 200,000 African American soldiers and sailors.

Military service did not end racial discrimination. Black soldiers served under white officers in segregated regiments and were used primarily to build fortifications, garrison forts, and guard supply lines. At first they were paid less than white soldiers ($7 versus $13 per month), and only a few were promoted to higher ranks. Despite such treatment African Americans volunteered for military service in

Black Soldiers in the Union Army

Tens of thousands of African Americans volunteered for military service and a chance to fight for the freedom of their people. These proud soldiers were members of the 107th Colored Infantry, stationed at Fort Corcoran near Washington, D.C. In January 1865 their regiment participated in the daring capture of Fort Fisher, which protected Wilmington, North Carolina, the last Confederate port open to blockade runners. (Library of Congress)

disproportionate numbers and diligently served the Union cause. They knew they were fighting for freedom and the possibility of a new social order. "Hello, Massa," said one black soldier to his former master, who had been taken prisoner. "Bottom rail on top dis time." The worst fears of the secessionists had come true: through the agency of the Union army blacks had enlisted in a great rebellion against slavery.

As African Americans joined the ranks, Lincoln finally found a commanding general in whom he had confidence. In March 1864 he put General Ulysses S. Grant in charge of all the Union armies and wholeheartedly approved Grant's plan to advance simultaneously against all the major Confederate forces—a strategy he had long favored. Both the general and the president wanted a decisive victory before the election of 1864.

As the successful western campaigns of 1863 showed, Grant understood how to fight a modern war—a war relying on industrial technology and directed at an entire society. At Vicksburg he had besieged an entire city and forced its surrender. A few months later, in November 1863, he had used the North's superior technology, utilizing railroad transport to charge to the rescue of a Union army near Chattanooga, Tennessee, and drive an invading Confederate army back into Georgia. Moreover, Grant was willing to accept heavy casualties in assaults on strongly defended positions, abandoning the caution of earlier Union commanders. Their attempts "to conserve life" had in fact prolonged the war, Grant argued. But Grant's aggressive tactics earned him a reputation as a butcher both of his own men and of enemy armies, which he pursued relentlessly. Finally, to crush the South's will to resist, the new Union commander was willing to terrorize the civilian population.

In May 1864 Grant ordered major new offensives on two fronts. Personally taking charge of the 115,000-strong Army of the Potomac, he set out to destroy Lee's force of 75,000 troops in Virginia. Simultaneously he instructed General William Tecumseh Sherman, who shared his views on warfare, to invade Georgia and take Atlanta. As Sherman prepared for battle, he wrote that "all that has gone before is mere skirmish. The war now begins."

Grant advanced toward Richmond, hoping to force Lee to fight in open fields, where the Union's superior manpower and artillery could prevail. Lee, remembering Gettysburg, maintained strong defensive positions, attacking only when he held a tactical advantage. He seized such opportunities twice, winning narrow victories in the battles of the Wilderness on May 5–7 and Spotsylvania Court House on May 8–12. Nevertheless Grant drove on toward Richmond (see Map 14.4). In early June he attacked Lee at Cold Harbor but withdrew after losing 7,000 men in a frontal assault. Grant had severely eroded Lee's forces, which had suffered 31,000 casualties, but Union losses were even higher at 55,000 men.

William Tecumseh Sherman

Sherman was a nervous man who smoked cigars and talked continuously, a journalist noted, his fingers constantly "twitching his red whiskers—his coat buttons—playing a tattoo on the table—or running through his hair." But he was a decisive general who commanded the loyalty of his troops and dealt a devastating blow to the Confederacy. (Library of Congress)

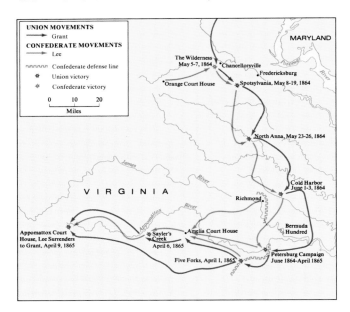

M A P 14.4
The Closing Virginia Campaigns, 1864–1865

During the last eight months of 1864 the armies of Grant and Lee were locked in a deadly dance across the Virginia countryside. By threatening Lee's lines of communication, Grant attempted to lure him into open battle. But Lee avoided a major test of strength, falling back and taking defensive positions that forced the Union army to undertake protracted sieges. As the number of casualties mounted, northern support for the war declined dramatically.

The fighting took a heavy psychological toll. "Many a man has gone crazy since this campaign began from the terrible pressure on mind and body," complained a Union officer. Previous battles had lasted only a few days and had been separated by long intervals. But in this campaign Grant's relentless advance and Lee's defensive tactics produced sustained fighting and grueling attrition. In June Grant pulled some of his troops away from Richmond to lay siege to Petersburg, an important railroad center. Protracted trench warfare, which foreshadowed that of World War I, made the spade as important as the sword. Union and Confederate soldiers built complex networks of trenches, tunnels, and artillery emplacements for almost 50 miles around Richmond and Petersburg. An officer described the continuous artillery firing and sniping as "living night and day within the 'valley of the shadow of death.'" The stress was especially great for the outnumbered Confederate troops, who spent months in the muddy, sickening trenches without rotation to the rear. As time passed, Lincoln and Grant felt pressures of their own; the enormous casualties and continued military stalemate threatened Lincoln with defeat in the November election.

The outlook for the Republicans worsened in July 1864, when a raid by Jubal Early's cavalry near Washington forced Grant to divert his best troops from the

Petersburg campaign. To punish farmers in the Shenandoah Valley, who provided a base for Early and food for Lee's army, Grant ordered General Philip H. Sheridan to turn the region into "a barren waste." Through the fall Sheridan's troops conducted a scorched-earth campaign, destroying grain supplies, barns, farming implements, and gristmills. This terrorism went beyond the military norms of the day, for most officers regarded civilians as noncombatants and feared that punishing them would erode military discipline. But Grant's decision to carry the war to Confederate civilians had changed the definition of conventional warfare.

THE ELECTION OF 1864 AND SHERMAN'S MARCH TO THE SEA

As the siege at Petersburg dragged on, Lincoln's reelection hopes came to rest on General William Sherman in Georgia. Sherman had gradually penetrated to within about 30 miles of Atlanta, a great railway hub that lay at the heart of the Confederacy. Although his army outnumbered that of General Joseph E. Johnston 90,000 to 60,000, he avoided a direct attack and slowly pried the Confederates out of one defensive position after another. Finally, on June 27 at Kennesaw Mountain Sherman engaged Johnston in a set battle, in which Sherman suffered 3,000 casualties while inflicting only about 600. By late July the Union general had laid siege to Atlanta on the north, but the next month brought little gain. Like Grant, Sherman seemed bogged down in a hopeless campaign.

Meanwhile, the presidential campaign of 1864 was well under way. In June the Republican convention endorsed Lincoln's war measures, demanded the unconditional surrender of the Confederacy, and called for a constitutional amendment to abolish slavery. To attract Democratic support the party temporarily renamed itself the National Union Party and nominated Andrew Johnson, a Unionist Tennessee Democrat, for vice president. The Democratic convention met in late August and nominated General George B. McClellan. The delegates declared their opposition to emancipation and divided over continuing the war. By threatening to bolt the convention the "Peace Democrats" forced through a platform calling for "a cessation of hostilities" and a convention to restore peace "on the basis of the Federal Union." Although personally a "War Democrat" McClellan promised if elected to recommend an immediate armistice and a peace convention. Rejoicing in "the first ray of real light I have seen since the war began," Confederate Vice President Alexander Stephens declared that if Atlanta and Richmond held out, Lincoln could be defeated and then northern Democrats could be persuaded to accept an independent Confederacy.

But on September 2 Atlanta fell. In a stunning move Sherman pulled his troops from the trenches and swept around the city to destroy its roads and rail links to the rest of the Confederacy, forcing its surrender. In her diary Mary Chestnut, a slaveowning plantation mistress, despaired of victory: "We are going to be wiped off the earth." Amid the 100-gun salutes in northern cities that greeted the news of

Atlanta in Ruins

As the Confederate army retreated from Atlanta, it blew up manufacturing facilities and munitions factories to keep them out of Union hands. Sherman's forces destroyed the remaining industries, including the roundhouse and car repair sheds of the Georgia Central Railroad. The devastation of Atlanta and southern Georgia during Sherman's "march to the sea" was a severe blow to Confederate morale. (Library of Congress)

Sherman's victory, McClellan repudiated the Democratic peace platform. But Republicans charged that he was still a peace candidate and attacked Peace Democrats as "copperheads" (a poisonous snake) who were hatching treasonous plots.

Sherman's success in Georgia gave Lincoln a clear-cut victory in November. He took 212 of 233 electoral votes, winning 55 percent of the popular vote in the free and border states and carrying all states except Delaware, Kentucky, and New Jersey. Republicans won 145 of the 185 seats in the House of Representatives and increased their Senate majority to 42 of 52 seats. Many of those victories came from the votes of Union troops, most of whom wanted the war to continue until the Confederacy met every Union demand, including emancipation.

Already the pace of legal emancipation had accelerated. In 1864 Maryland and Missouri amended their constitutions to free their slaves, and the three occupied states of Tennessee, Arkansas, and Louisiana followed suit. Abolitionists still worried that the Emancipation Proclamation, based on the president's wartime powers, would lose its force at the end of the war and that southern states would reestablish slavery. Urged on by Lincoln the Republican-dominated Congress took a major step to guarantee black freedom. On January 31, 1865, it approved the Thirteenth Amendment, which prohibited slavery throughout the United States, and sent it to the states for ratification. Slavery was nearly dead.

And so was the Confederacy. After the capture of Atlanta Sherman declined to follow the retreating Confederate army into Tennessee and decided on a bold strategy. Rather than spread his troops dangerously thin by protecting supply lines to the rear, he would "cut a swath through to the sea," living off the land. To persuade Lincoln and Grant to approve this unconventional plan Sherman pointed out that such a march would devastate Georgia and score a major psychological victory. It would be "a demonstration to the world, foreign and domestic, that we have a power [Jefferson] Davis cannot resist."

Sherman carried out the concept of total war he and Sheridan had pioneered: destruction of the enemy's economic resources and will to resist. "We are not only fighting hostile armies," Sherman wrote, "but a hostile people, and must make old and young, rich and poor, feel the hard hand of war." He left Atlanta in flames and during his 300-mile march to the sea destroyed railroads, property, and supplies (see Map 14.5). A Union veteran wrote that "[we] destroyed all we could not eat,

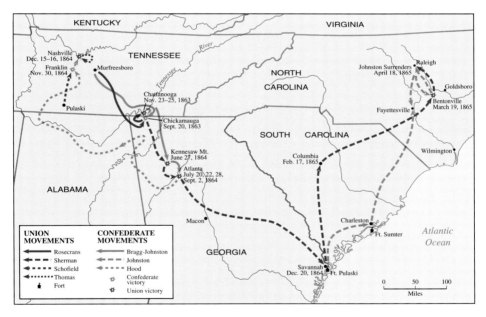

M A P 14.5
Sherman's March through the Confederacy, 1864–1865

The Union victory in November 1863 at Chattanooga, Tennessee (on that state's border with Georgia), was almost as critical as those in July at Gettysburg and Vicksburg. Having already split the Confederacy along the Mississippi, the Union was now in position to divide it again by driving through Georgia to the sea. After capturing Atlanta in September 1864, Sherman relied on other Union armies to repulse General John B. Hood's invasion of Tennessee, and swept to the Atlantic.

Sherman's March through Georgia

DOLLY SUMNER LUNT

"We must make old and young, rich and poor, feel the hand of war," General William Tecumseh Sherman wrote to General Grant late in 1864. A few weeks later Dolly Sumner Lunt of Covington, Georgia, found out what he meant. Born in Maine in 1817, Dolly Sumner came south to teach school, married a slaveowner, and, following his death, ran the family's plantation. Her Wartime Journal describes its destruction by Sherman's army.*

November 19, 1864

Slept in my clothes last night, as I heard that the Yankees went to neighbor Montgomery's on Thursday night at one o'clock, searched his house, drank his wine, and took his money and valuables. As we were not disturbed, I walked after breakfast . . . up to Mr. Joe Perry's, my nearest neighbor, where the Yankees were yesterday. Saw Mrs. Laura [Perry] in the road surrounded by her children . . . looking for her husband. . . . Before we were done talking, up came Joe and Jim Perry from their hiding-place. Jim was very much excited. Happening to turn and look behind, as we stood there, I saw some blue-coats coming down the hill. Jim immediately raised his gun, swearing he should kill them anyhow.

"No, don't" said I, and ran home as fast as I could.

I could hear them cry "Halt! Halt!" and their guns went off in quick succession. Oh God, the time of trial has come. . . .

I hastened back to my frightened servants [slaves] and told them they had better hide, and then went back to the gate to claim protection and a guard. But like demons they [Sherman's troops] rushed in! . . . The thousand pounds of meat in my smokehouse is gone in a twinkling, my flour, my meat, my lard, butter, eggs . . . all gone. My eighteen fat turkeys, hens, chickens . . . are shot down in my yard and hunted as if they were rebels themselves. Utterly powerless I ran out and appealed to the guard.

"I cannot help you, Madam; it is orders." . . .

Sherman himself and a greater portion of his army passed my house that day . . . ; they tore down my garden palings, made a road through my back-yard and lot field . . . desolating my home—wantonly doing it when there was no necessity for it.

Such a day, if I live to the age of Methuselah, may God spare me from ever seeing again!

As night drew its sable curtains around us, the heavens from every point were lit up with flames from burning buildings.

SOURCE: *Eyewitnesses and Others: Readings in American History* (New York: Holt, Rinehart and Winston, 1995), vol. 1: pp. 413–17.

stole their niggers, burned their cotton & gins, spilled their sorghum, burned & twisted their R.Roads and raised Hell generally" (see American Voices, "Sherman's March through Georgia"). The havoc so demoralized Confederate soldiers that many deserted and fled home to protect their farms and families. When Sherman reached Savannah, Georgia, in mid-December, the 10,000 Confederate defenders left without a fight.

In February 1865 Sherman invaded South Carolina. He planned to link up with Grant at Petersburg and along the way punish the state where secession had begun. "The truth is," Sherman wrote, "the whole army is burning with an insatiable desire to wreak vengeance upon South Carolina." His troops cut a comparatively narrow swath across the state but ravaged the countryside even more thoroughly than they had in Georgia. By March Sherman had reached North Carolina and was on the verge of linking up with Grant and crushing Lee's army.

Sherman's march exposed an internal Confederate weakness: rising class resentment on the part of poor whites. Long angered by the "twenty-negro" exemption from military service given to slaveowners and fearing that the Confederacy was doomed, ordinary southern farmers resisted military service. "It is no longer a reproach to be known as a deserter," a Confederate officer in South Carolina complained in late 1863. By early 1865 the Confederacy was experiencing such a severe manpower crisis that its leaders decided to take an extreme measure: arming the slaves. Urged on by Lee the Confederate Congress voted to enlist black soldiers; Davis issued an executive order granting freedom to all blacks who served in the Confederate army. But the war ended too soon to reveal whether any slaves would have fought for the Confederacy.

The symbolic end of the war took place in Virginia. In April 1865 Grant finally forced Lee into a showdown by gaining control of the crucial railroad junction at Petersburg and cutting off his supplies. Lee abandoned the defense of Richmond and turned west, hoping to join up with Confederate forces in North Carolina. While Lincoln visited the ruins of the Confederate capital, mobbed by joyful former slaves, Grant cut off Lee's escape route. On April 9, almost precisely four years after the attack on Fort Sumter, Lee surrendered to Grant at Appomattox Court House, Virginia. In accepting the surrender of the Confederate general Grant set a tone of generosity, allowing Lee's men to take their horses home for spring planting. By May 26 all the Confederate generals had ceased to fight, and the Confederate army and government simply dissolved (see Map 14.6).

The armies of the Union had destroyed the Confederacy and much of the South's economy. Its factories, warehouses, and railroads were in ruins, as were many of its farms and some of its most important cities. Almost 260,000 Confederate soldiers had paid for secession with their lives. Most significant, the Union had been preserved and slavery destroyed. But the cost of victory was enormous in money, resources, and lives. Over 360,000 Union soldiers were dead, and hundreds of thousands were maimed and crippled. The hard and bitter war was over, and a reunited nation turned to the tasks of peace. These were to be equally hard and bitter.

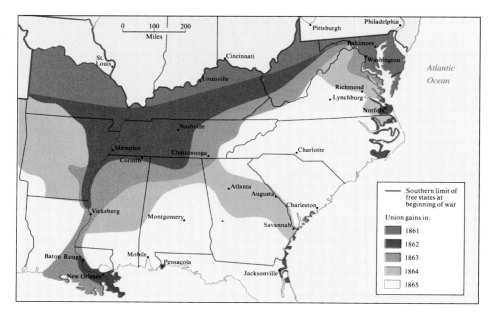

M A P 14.6
The Conquest of the South, 1861–1865

It took four years for the Union army to occupy the territory of the Confederacy, and much of the South remained under Confederate control until the last year of the war. Most of the Union's victories came on the western front, where its domination of strategic lines of communication—the Ohio and Mississippi Rivers and important railroad lines—allowed it to mount large-scale attacks against Confederate armies.

For Further Exploration

Charles P. Roland, *An American Iliad: The Story of the Civil War* (1991), is an excellent brief survey, while James M. McPherson, *The Battle Cry of Freedom* (1988), offers a fine synthesis of the coming of the conflict and the wartime years. For a lucid description of the complex mixture of goals, personalities, and accident that precipitated the conflict, read Richard Current, *Lincoln and the First Shot* (1963). John Hope Franklin, *The Emancipation Proclamation* (1963), explains the background of Lincoln's edict and its impact in the United States and other nations.

Nancy Scott Anderson and Dwight Anderson, *The Generals: Ulysses S. Grant and Robert E. Lee* (1988), is a vivid popular account of their personal histories and military exploits. James M. McPherson, *For Cause and Comrades: Why Men Fought in the Civil War* (1997), draws on the letters of ordinary soldiers to explain their extraordinary commitment to the cause of the Union and Confederacy. For experiences of black soldiers told in their own words, see Ira Berlin et al., eds., *Freedom's Soldiers: The Black Military Experience in the Civil War* (1998). Earl J. Hess, *The Union Soldier in Battle: Enduring the Ordeal of Combat* (1997),

TIMELINE

1861	Confederate States of America formed (February 4)
	Abraham Lincoln inaugurated (March 4)
	Confederates fire on Fort Sumter (April 12).
	Virginia secession (April 17) leads upper South out of Union.
	General Benjamin Butler declares runaway slaves "contraband of war" (May).
	Union forces routed at first Battle of Bull Run (July 21)
1862	Congress begins to print "greenbacks."
	Homestead Act
	Federal aid to transcontinental railroads
	Battle of Shiloh (April 6–7) advances Union cause in West.
	Confederacy introduces conscription.
	Battle of Antietam (September 17) halts Confederate offensive.
	Lincoln issues preliminary Emancipation Proclamation (September 22).
1863	Lincoln signs Emancipation Proclamation (January 1).
	Enrollment Act begins conscription in North; riots in New York City (July).
	Union victories at Battles of Gettysburg (July 1–3) and Vicksburg (July 4)
1864	General Ulysses S. Grant given charge of all Union armies (March)
	Grant advances on Richmond (May).
	General William Tecumseh Sherman invades Georgia (May).
	Sherman takes Atlanta (September 2).
	Lincoln reelected (November)
	Sherman marches through Georgia (November and December).
1865	Congress approves Thirteenth Amendment, which outlaws slavery (January).
	Robert E. Lee surrenders at Appomattox Court House, Virginia (April 9).

presents a vivid and convincing account of the heat, smell, sounds, and feel of battle, as does Michael Sharra's *Killer Angels* (1974), a masterful novel of the battle of Gettysburg.

Peter Quinn's novel, *Banished Children of Eve* (1994), recounts the New York City draft riots from an Irish American perspective. *Mary Chesnut's Civil War,* edited by C. Vann Woodward (1981), is the diary of a planter's wife that provides a witty and incisive view of southern society.

Two award-winning websites treat the events of these years. "The Valley of the Shadow" at <http://jefferson.village.virginia.edu/vshadow2/> traces the experiences of two communities—one northern, one southern—during the prewar era using a multitude of hyperlinked sources, including newspaper, letters, diaries, photographs, and maps. "The Freedmen and Southern Society Project" at <http://www.inform.umd.edu/ARHU/Depts/History/Freedman/home.html> captures the drama of war and emancipation in the words of the participants: liberated slaves and defeated masters, soldiers and civilians, common folk and leaders.

Chapter 15

RECONSTRUCTION
1865–1877

I felt like a bird out of a cage. Amen. Amen. Amen. I could hardly
ask to feel any better than I did that day.

—HOUSTON H. HOLLOWAY, A FORMER SLAVE
RECALLING HIS EMANCIPATION IN 1865

In his second inaugural address, President Lincoln spoke of the need
to "bind up the nation's wounds." No one knew better than Lincoln how daunting
a task that would be. Foremost, of course, were the terms on which the rebellious
states would be restored to the Union. But America's Civil War had opened more
fundamental questions. Slavery was finished. That much was certain. But what system of labor should replace plantation slavery? What rights should the freedmen
be accorded beyond emancipation itself? How far should the federal government
go to settle these questions? And who should decide—the president or Congress?

While the war was still on, the North began to grope for answers. Taking the
initiative, Lincoln in December 1863 offered a general amnesty to all but high-
ranking Confederates willing to pledge loyalty to the Union and abolish slavery.
When 10 percent of a state's 1860 voters had taken this oath, they could organize
a new government and be restored to the Union. Only states under military occupation—Louisiana, Arkansas, and Tennessee—took advantage of Lincoln's generous offer. Although it reflected Lincoln's conciliatory bent, his Ten Percent Plan was
really aimed at subverting the southern war effort.

What it also did, however, was to reveal the rocky road that lay ahead for Reconstruction. Thus, in Louisiana sugar planters used the restored government to
regain control over the freed slaves, employing curfew laws to restrict their movements and vagrancy regulations to force them back to work. But the Louisiana
freedmen fought back. Led by the well-established free-black community of New
Orleans, they began to agitate for political rights. No less than their former masters, former slaves intended to be actors in the savage drama of Reconstruction.

With the struggle in Louisiana in mind, congressional Republicans proposed a
stricter substitute for Lincoln's Ten Percent Plan. The initiative came from the Radical wing—those bent on a stern peace and full rights for the freedmen—but with
broad support among congressional Republicans generally. The Wade-Davis Bill,
passed on July 2, 1864, laid down, as conditions for the restoration of the rebellious

states to the Union, an oath of allegiance by a majority of each state's adult white men, new state governments formed and operated only by those who had never carried arms against the Union, and permanent loss of voting rights by Confederate leaders. The Wade-Davis Bill served notice that the congressional Republicans were not about to hand reconstruction policy over to the president.

Lincoln was not perturbed. Rather than openly challenging Congress, he executed a "pocket" veto of the Wade-Davis Bill by not signing it before Congress adjourned. At the same time he initiated informal talks with congressional leaders aimed at finding a common ground. The last speech he ever delivered, on April 11, 1865, demonstrated Lincoln's cautious realism. Reconstruction, he pleaded, had to be regarded as a practical, not a theoretical, problem. It could be solved only if Republicans remained united, even if that meant compromising, and only if the defeated South gave its consent, even if that meant forgiveness. What the speech showed, above all, was Lincoln's sense of the fluidity of events, of policy toward the South as an evolving, not a fixed, position.

What course Reconstruction might have taken had Lincoln lived is one of the unanswerable questions of American history. On April 14, 1865—five days after Lee's surrender at Appomattox—Lincoln was shot in the head at Ford's Theater in Washington by a wild-eyed actor named John Wilkes Booth. Ironically, Lincoln might have been spared if the war had dragged on longer, for Booth and his Confederate associates had originally plotted to kidnap the president to force a negotiated settlement. Without regaining consciousness, Lincoln died on April 15.

With one stroke John Wilkes Booth had sent Lincoln to martyrdom, hardened many northerners against the South, and handed the presidency to a man utterly lacking in Lincoln's moral sense and political judgment, Vice President Andrew Johnson.

Presidential Reconstruction

At the end of the Civil War, a big constitutional question remained in dispute— whether, on seceding, the Confederate states had legally left the Union. If so, then they became conquered territory whose fate could be decided only by Congress. If not, if even in rebellion they remained states of the Union, then the terms for their restoration might appropriately be left to the president. This was Andrew Johnson's view, and by an accident of timing he was free to act on it: under leisurely rules that went back to the early republic, the 39th Congress elected in November 1864 was not scheduled to convene until December 1865.

JOHNSON'S INITIATIVE

Andrew Johnson was a self-made man from the hills of eastern Tennessee. A Jacksonian Democrat, he saw himself as the champion of the common man. He hated what he called the "bloated, corrupt aristocracy" of the Northeast, and he was

Andrew Johnson

The president was not an easy man. This photograph of Andrew Johnson (1808–1875) conveys some of the personal qualities that contributed so centrally to his failure to reach an agreement with Republicans on a program of moderate reconstruction. (Library of Congress)

equally disdainful of the wealthy planters, whom he blamed for the poverty of the South's small farmers. It was poor whites he championed; Johnson, a slaveholder himself, had little sympathy for the enslaved blacks. His political career had taken him to the U.S. Senate, where he remained when the war broke out, loyal to the Union. After federal forces captured Nashville, he became Tennessee's military governor. The Republicans nominated him in 1864 for vice president in an effort to promote wartime political unity and to court southern Unionists.

In May 1865, just a month after Lincoln's death, Johnson executed his own plan for restoration. He offered amnesty to all southerners who took an oath of allegiance to the Constitution, except for high-ranking Confederate officials and wealthy property owners, whom he held responsible for secession. Such persons could be pardoned only by the president. Johnson appointed provisional governors for the southern states and, as conditions for their restoration, required only that they revoke their ordinances of secession, repudiate their Confederate debt, and ratify the Thirteenth Amendment, which abolished slavery. Within months all the former Confederate states had met Johnson's requirements for rejoining the Union and had functioning, elected governments.

At first Republicans responded favorably. The moderates among them were sympathetic to Johnson's states-rights argument that it was for the states, not the federal government, to decide what civil and political rights the freedmen should have. Even the Radicals held their fire. They liked the stern treatment of Confederate leaders, and they hoped that the restored governments would show good faith by generous treatment of the freed slaves.

Nothing of the sort happened. The South lay in ruins. But white southerners held fast to the old order. The newly seated legislatures moved to restore slavery in all but name. They enacted laws—known as Black Codes—designed to drive the former slaves back to the plantations and deny them elementary civil rights. The new governments had been formed mostly by southern Unionists, but when it came to racial attitudes, not a lot distinguished these loyalists from the Confederates. The latter, moreover, soon filtered back into the corridors of power. Despite his hard words against them, Johnson forgave ex-Confederate leaders easily so long as he got the satisfaction of making them submit to his personal authority.

His perceived indulgence of their efforts to restore white supremacy emboldened the former Confederates. They packed the delegations to the new Congress with old comrades—nine members of the Confederate Congress, seven former officials of Confederate state governments, four generals and four colonels, and even the vice president of the Confederacy, Alexander Stephens. For Republicans, this was the last straw.

Under the Constitution, Congress is "the judge of the elections, returns and qualifications of its members" (Article 1, Section 5). With this power, the Republican majorities in both houses refused to admit the southern delegations when Congress convened in early December 1865. Although relations with the president had already cooled, the Republicans assumed he would cooperate with them in formulating the new terms on which the South would be readmitted to Congress. To that end, a House-Senate committee—the Joint Committee on Reconstruction—was formed and began public hearings on conditions in the South.

In response, the southern states backed away from the most flagrant of the Black Codes, replacing them with nonracial ordinances whose effect was the same: in practice, they applied to blacks, not to whites. On top of that, a wave of violence erupted across the South against the freedmen. Listening to the graphic testimony of officials, observers and victims, Republicans concluded that the South had embarked on a concerted effort to circumvent the Thirteenth Amendment. The only possible response was for the federal government to intervene.

Back in March 1865, before adjourning, the 38th Congress had established the Freedmen's Bureau to provide emergency aid to former slaves during the chaotic period between war and peace. Now in early 1866, under the leadership of the moderate Republican senator Lyman Trumbull, chairman of the Judiciary Committee, Congress voted to extend the Bureau's life, gave it federal funding for the first time, and authorized its agents to investigate cases of discrimination against blacks.

More extraordinary was Trumbull's proposal for a Civil Rights bill, declaring all persons born in the United States to be citizens and guaranteeing them—without regard to race—equal rights of contract, of access to the courts, and of protection of persons and property. Trumbull's bill nullified all state laws depriving citizens of these rights, authorized U.S. attorneys to bring enforcement suits in the federal courts, and provided for fines and imprisonment for violators, including public officials. Provoked by an unrepentant South, Republicans of the most moderate persuasion demanded that the federal government accept responsibility for securing the basic civil rights of the freedmen.

ACTING ON FREEDOM

While Congress debated, African Americans acted on their own idea of freedom. News of emancipation left them exultant and hopeful. Freedom meant many things—the reuniting of separated families, the end of punishment by the lash, the ability to move around, the opportunity to begin schools and churches, and, not least, the chance to engage in politics. Across the South, freed slaves held mass meetings, paraded, and formed organizations. Topmost among their demands were equality before the law and the right to vote—"an essential and inseparable element of self-government."

First of all, however, came economic independence, which emancipated blacks believed was the basis for true freedom. During the Civil War they had acted on this assumption whenever Union armies drew near. In the chaotic final months of the war, as plantation owners fled Union forces, freedmen seized control of land where they could. Most famously, General William T. Sherman reserved vast tracts of coastal lands in Georgia and South Carolina—the Sea Islands and the abandoned plantations within 30 miles of the coast—for liberated blacks and settled them on 40-acre tracts. Sherman wanted only to shift the responsibility for the refugees from his army as it marched across the lower South. But the freedmen assumed that Sherman's order meant that the land would be theirs. When the war ended, resettlement became the responsibility of the Freedmen's Bureau, which was charged with distributing confiscated land to "loyal refugees and freedmen." Many black families stayed expectantly on their old plantations. When the South Carolina

Schoolhouse, Port Hudson, Louisiana

This was probably the first schoolhouse built for freedmen by Union forces. In front, African American soldiers from the Port Hudson "Corps d'Afrique" pose with their textbooks. It stood to reason that former slaves who had taken up arms should be first to receive the education so coveted by all freedmen. (Chicago Historical Society)

planter Thomas Pinckney returned, his freed slaves told him, "We ain't going nowhere. We are going to work right here on the land where we were born and what belongs to us."

Johnson's amnesty plan, entitling pardoned Confederates to recover confiscated property, shattered these hopes. In October 1865 President Johnson ordered General Oliver O. Howard, head of the Freedmen's Bureau, to tell Sea Island blacks that they would have to surrender the land they occupied. When Howard reluctantly obeyed, the dispossessed farmers protested: "Why do you take away our lands? You take them from us who have always been true, always true to the Government! You give them to our all-time enemies! That is not right!" (see American Voices, "A Plea for Land"). In the Sea Islands and elsewhere, former slaves resisted efforts to remove them. Led by black veterans of the Union army, they fought pitched battles with plantation owners and bands of former Confederate soldiers. Generally, the local whites prevailed in this land war.

As planters prepared for a new growing season, a great struggle took shape over the labor system that would replace slavery. Convinced that blacks needed supervision, planters insisted on retaining the gang labor of the past, only now with wages replacing the food, clothing, and shelter that their slaves had previously received. The Freedmen's Bureau, although watchful against too exploitative labor contracts, sided with the planters. The Bureau, anxious that former slaves be weaned from the habits of dependency, saw the planters' offer of wage work as a halfstep to independence. But the blacks knew better. It was not only their unequal bargaining power they worried about or even that their former masters' real desire was to reenslave them under the guise of "free" contracts. In their eyes, the condition of wage labor was itself debasing. The rural South was not like the North, where working for wages was the norm and qualified a man as independent. In the South, selling one's labor to another—and in particular, selling one's labor to work another's land—implied not freedom but dependency. To be a "freeman"—a fully empowered citizen—meant heading a household, owning some property, conducting one's own affairs.

So the issue of wage labor cut to the very core of the former slaves' struggle for freedom. Nothing had been more horrifying than the fact that as slaves their persons had been the property of others. In a famous oration celebrating emancipation, the Reverend Henry M. Turner spoke bitterly of the time when his people had "no security of domestic happiness," when "our wives were sold and husbands bought, children were begotten and enslaved by their fathers." That was why formalizing marriage was so urgent a matter after emancipation and why, when hard-pressed planters demanded that freedwomen go back into the fields, they resisted so resolutely. "I seen on some plantations," one former slave recounted, "where the white men would . . . tell colored men that their wives and children could not live on their places unless they worked in the fields. The colored men [answered that] whenever they wanted their wives to work they would tell them themselves; and if he could not rule his own domestic affairs on that place he would leave it and go someplace else."

AMERICAN VOICES

A Plea for Land

F ollowing is a painfully written letter by the freed slaves of Edisto Island to President Andrew Johnson, pleading for a reversal of his order that the lands they now worked be returned to the plantation owners.

Edisto Island S.C. Oct 28th, 1865.

To the President of these United States. We the freedmen Of Edisto Island South Carolina have learned . . . with deep sorrow and Painful hearts of the possibility of government restoring These lands to the former owners. . . . Here is where secession was born and Nurtured Here is where we have toiled nearly all Our lives as slaves and were treated like dumb Driven cattle. This is our home, we have made These lands what they are. . . . Shall not we who Are freedmen and have always been true to this Union have the same rights as are enjoyed by Others? Have we broken any Law of these United States? have we forfeited our rights of property In Land?—If not then! are not our rights as A free people and good citizens of these United States To be considered before the rights of those who were Found in rebellion against this good and just Government. . . . And we who have been abused and oppressed For many long years But be subject To the will of these large Land owners? God forbid.

. . . We the freedmen of this Island and the State of South Carolina—Do hereby petition to you as the President of these United States, that some provisions be made by which Every colored man can purchase land. and Hold as his own. We wish to have A home if It be but A few acres. . . . May God bless you in the Administration of your duties as the President Of these United States is the humble prayer Of us all.—

In behalf of the Freedmen

Henry Bram

Committee   Ishmael. Moultrie

yates. Sampson

SOURCE: Eileen Boris and Nelson Lichtenstein, eds., *Major Problems in the History of American Workers: Documents and Essays* (Lexington, MA: Heath, 1990), pp. 137–39.

The reader will see the irony in this definition of freedom: it assumed the wife's subordinate role and designated her labor as the husband's property. But if that was the price of freedom, freedwomen were prepared to pay it. Far better to take a chance with their own men than with their former masters.

Many freedpeople voted with their feet, abandoning their old plantations and seeking better lives and more freedom in the towns and cities of the South. Those who remained in the countryside refused to work the cotton fields under the hated gang labor or negotiated tenaciously over the terms of their labor contracts. Whatever system of labor finally might emerge, it was clear that the freedmen and their families would never settle for anything resembling the old plantation system.

The efforts of former slaves to control their own lives ran counter to deeply entrenched white attitudes. "The destiny of the black race," asserted one Texan, could be summarized "in one sentence—subordination to the white race." Southern whites, a Freedmen's Bureau official observed, could not "conceive of the negro having any rights at all." And when freedmen resisted, white retribution was swift and often terrible. The toll of murdered and beaten blacks mounted into untold thousands. The governments established under Johnson's plan put the stamp of legality on the pervasive efforts to enforce white supremacy. Blacks "would be *just as well* off with no law at all or no Government," concluded a Freedmen's Bureau agent, as with the justice they got under the restored white rule.

In this unequal struggle, blacks turned to Washington. "We stood by the government when it wanted help," a black Mississippian wrote President Johnson. "Now . . . will it stand by us?"

CONGRESS VERSUS PRESIDENT

Andrew Johnson was not, alas, the man to ask. In February 1866 he vetoed the Freedmen's Bureau Bill, declaring it unconstitutional because Congress lacked authority to provide a "system for the support of indigent people" and because the states most directly affected by its provisions were not yet represented in Congress. The Bureau was an "immense patronage," showering benefits on blacks never granted to "our own people." Republicans could not muster enough votes to override his veto. A month later, in a further rebuff to his critics, Johnson vetoed Trumbull's Civil Rights bill, again arguing that federal protection of black civil rights constituted "a stride toward centralization." His racism, hitherto muted, now blazed forth. In his view, granting blacks the privileges of citizenship was discriminatory, operating "in favor of the colored and against the white race" and fraught with evil consequences, including racial mixing.

Galvanized by Johnson's attack on the Civil Rights bill, the Republicans went into action. In early April they got the necessary two-thirds majorities in both Houses and enacted the Civil Rights Act of 1866. This was a truly historic event, the first time Congress had prevailed over a presidential veto on a major piece of legislation. The Republican resolve was reinforced by news of mounting violence in the South, culminating in three days of bloody rioting in Memphis. In July an angry Congress renewed the Freedmen's Bureau over a second Johnson veto.

Anxious to consolidate their gains, Republicans moved to enshrine black civil rights in an amendment to the Constitution. The heart of the Fourteenth Amendment was Section 1, which declared that "all persons born or naturalized in the United States" were citizens. No state could abridge "the privileges or immunities of citizens of the United States," deprive "any person of life, liberty, or property, without due process of law," or deny anyone "the equal protection of the laws." These phrases were vague, intentionally so, but they established the constitutionality of the Civil Rights Act and, more important, the basis on which the courts and

Congress could over time erect an enforceable standard of equality before the law in the states.

For the moment, however, the Fourteenth Amendment was most important for its impact on national politics. With the 1866 congressional elections approaching, Johnson somehow figured he had a winning issue in the Fourteenth Amendment. He urged the states not to ratify it. Months earlier, Johnson had begun to maneuver politically against the Republicans, aiming to build a coalition of white southerners, northern Democrats, and conservative Republicans under the banner of National Union. Any hope of creating a new national party, however, was shattered by Johnson's intemperate behavior and by escalating violence in the South. A dissension-ridden National Union convention in July ended inconclusively, and Johnson's campaign against the Fourteenth Amendment became, effectively, a campaign for the Democratic Party.

Republicans responded furiously, unveiling an attack that would become known as "waving the bloody shirt." The Democrats were traitors, charged Indiana governor Oliver Morton; their party was "a common sewer and loathesome receptacle into which is emptied every element of treason." In late August Johnson embarked on a disastrous "swing around the circle"—a railroad tour from Washington to Chicago and St. Louis and back. It was unprecedented for a president to campaign personally for his party, and Johnson made matters worse by engaging in shouting matches with hecklers and insulting the hostile crowds.

The 1866 congressional elections inflicted a humiliating defeat on Johnson. The Republicans won a three-to-one majority in Congress, so that, to begin with, the Republicans considered themselves "masters of the situation," free to proceed "entirely regardless of [Johnson's] opinions or wishes." As a referendum on the Fourteenth Amendment, moreover, the election registered overwhelming popular support for securing the civil rights of the former slaves. The Republican Party emerged with a new sense of unity—a unity coalescing not at the center but on the left, around the unbending program of the Radical minority.

The Radicals represented the abolitionist strain within the Republican Party. Most of them hailed from New England or from the area of the upper Midwest settled by New Englanders. In the Senate they were led by Charles Sumner of Massachusetts; in the House, by Thaddeus Stevens from Pennsylvania. For them, Reconstruction was never primarily about restoring the Union but about remaking southern society. "The foundations of their institutions . . . must be broken up and relaid," declared Stevens, "or all our blood and treasure will have been spent in vain."

Only a handful went as far as Stevens in demanding that the plantations be treated as "forfeited estates of the enemy" and broken up into small farms for the former slaves. About protecting the civil rights of the freedmen and granting them the suffrage, however, there was agreement. In this endeavor Radicals had no qualms about using the powers of the federal government. Nor were there qualms about being aggressively partisan. The Radicals regarded the Republican Party as the instrument of the Lord and black votes as the means by which the party would bring about the regeneration of the South.

At first, in the months after Appomattox, few but the Radicals imagined that so extreme a program had any chance of enactment. Black suffrage especially seemed beyond reach, since the northern states themselves (except in New England) denied blacks the vote at this time. And yet, as fury mounted against the intransigent South, Republicans became ever more radicalized until, in the wake of the smashing victory of 1866, they embraced the Radicals' vision of a reconstructed South.

Radical Reconstruction

Afterward thoughtful southerners admitted that the South had brought radical Reconstruction on itself. "We had, in 1865, a white man's government in Alabama," remarked the man who had been Johnson's provisional governor, "but we lost it." The state's "great blunder" was not to "have at once taken the negro right under the protection of the laws." Remarkably, the South remained defiant even after the 1866 congressional elections. Every state legislature (excepting Tennessee) rejected the Fourteenth Amendment, mostly by virtual acclamation. It was as if they could not imagine that governments installed under the presidential imprimatur and fully functioning might be swept away. But that, in fact, is just what the Republicans intended to do.

CONGRESS TAKES COMMAND

The Reconstruction Act of 1867, enacted in March, organized the South as a conquered land, dividing it (with the exception of Tennessee) into five military districts, each under the command of a Union general (see Map 15.1). The price for reentering the Union was granting the vote to the freedmen and disenfranchising the South's prewar political class. Each military commander was ordered to register all eligible adult men (black as well as white), supervise the election of state conventions, and make certain that the new constitutions guaranteed black suffrage. Congress would readmit a state to the Union if its voters ratified the state constitution, if that document proved acceptable to Congress, and if the new state legislature approved the Fourteenth Amendment (thereby ensuring the three-fourths of the states need for ratification). Johnson vetoed the act, but Congress overrode the veto.

Republicans also restricted President Johnson's room for maneuver. The Tenure of Office Act, companion legislation to the Reconstruction Act, ordered the president not to remove without Senate consent any official whose appointment had required Senate confirmation. Congress chiefly wanted to protect Secretary of War Edwin M. Stanton, a Lincoln hold-over and the only member of Johnson's cabinet who favored radical Reconstruction. In his position Stanton could do much

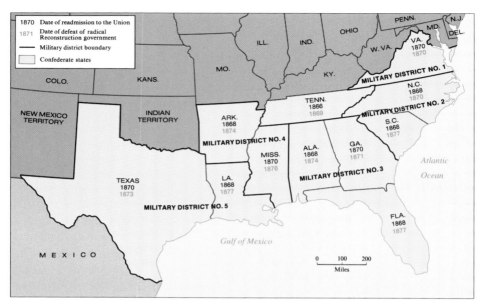

M A P 15.1
Reconstruction

The federal government organized the Confederate states into five military districts during radical Reconstruction. For each state the first date indicates when that state was readmitted to the Union; the second date shows when radical Republicans lost control of the state government. All the ex-Confederate states rejoined the Union from 1868 to 1870, but the periods of radical rule varied widely. Radicals lasted only a few months in Virginia; they held on until the end of Reconstruction in Louisiana, Florida, and South Carolina.

to prevent Johnson from frustrating the goals of Reconstruction. The law also required the president to issue all orders to the army through its commanding general, Ulysses S. Grant. In effect, Congress was attempting to reconstruct the presidency as well as the South.

Seemingly defeated, Johnson appointed generals recommended by Stanton to command the five military districts in the South. But he was just biding his time. In August 1867, after Congress had adjourned, he "suspended" Stanton and replaced him with Grant, believing that the general would be a good soldier and follow orders. Next Johnson replaced four of the commanding generals, including Philip H. Sheridan, Grant's favorite cavalry general. Johnson, however, had misjudged Grant, who publicly registered his opposition to the president's machinations. When the Senate reconvened in the fall, it overruled Stanton's suspension. Grant, now an open enemy of Johnson's, resigned so that Stanton could resume his office.

On February 21, 1868, Johnson dismissed Stanton. The feisty secretary of war barricaded his office and refused to admit the replacement Johnson had appointed.

Resistance in the South

This engraving, entitled *If He Is a Union Man or Freedman: Verdict, Hang the D—Yankee and Nigger,* appeared in *Harper's Weekly* on March 23, 1867, just as the Reconstruction Act was being adopted. Thomas Nast's cartoon encapsulated the outrage at the South's murderous intransigence that led even moderate Republicans to support radical Reconstruction.

(Library of Congress)

Three days later, House Republicans introduced articles of impeachment against President Johnson, employing the power of the Congress under the Constitution to remove high federal officers guilty of "Treason, Bribery, or other high Crimes and Misdemeanors." The House overwhelmingly approved eleven counts of presidential misconduct, nine of which dealt with violations of the Tenure of Office Act.

The case went to the Senate, which acts as the court in impeachment cases, with Chief Justice Salmon P. Chase presiding. After an eleven-week trial, thirty-five senators on May 15 voted for conviction, one vote short of the two-thirds majority required. Seven moderate Republicans broke ranks, voting for acquittal along with twelve Democrats. Congress had removed federal judges from office but never a president. The reluctant Republicans were overwhelmed by the drastic nature of the attack on Johnson. They felt the Tenure of Office Act that Johnson had violated was of dubious validity (in fact, it was subsequently declared unconstitutional by the Supreme Court). The real issue was a political dispute, and removing a president for disagreeing with Congress seemed too extreme, too threatening to the constitutional system of checks and balances, even for the sake of punishing Johnson.

Even without being convicted, however, Johnson had been defanged. For the remainder of his term he was helpless to alter the course of Reconstruction.

The impeachment controversy made Grant, already the North's most popular war hero, a Republican hero as well, and he easily won the party's presidential nomination in 1868. In the fall campaign he supported radical Reconstruction, but he also urged reconciliation between the sections. His Democratic opponent was Horatio Seymour, a former governor of New York and a Peace Democrat who almost declined the nomination, certain that the Democrats could not overcome the stigma of being the party of the disloyal South.

As Seymour feared, the Republicans waved the bloody shirt, stirring up old wartime emotions against the Democrats to great effect. Grant won about the same share of the northern vote (55 percent) that Lincoln had won in 1864 and received 214 of 294 electoral votes. The Republicans also retained two-thirds majorities in both houses of Congress.

In the wake of their smashing victory, the Republicans quickly produced the last major piece of Reconstruction legislation—the Fifteenth Amendment, which forbade either the federal government or the states from denying citizens the right to vote on the basis of race, color, or "previous condition of servitude." The amendment left room for poll taxes and property or literacy tests that could be used to discourage blacks from voting. But its authors did not want to alienate northern states that already relied on such qualifications to keep immigrants and the "unworthy" poor from the polls. A California senator warned that in his state, with its rabidly anti-Chinese sentiment (see Chapter 16), any restriction on that power would "kill our party as dead as a stone."

Despite grumbling by Radical Republicans, the amendment passed without modification in February 1869. Congress required the states still under federal control—Virginia, Mississippi, Texas, and Georgia—to ratify it as a condition of being readmitted to the Union. A year later the Fifteenth Amendment became part of the Constitution.

WOMAN SUFFRAGE DENIED

If the Fifteenth Amendment troubled some proponents of black suffrage, this was nothing as compared to the outrage felt by women's rights advocates. They had fought the good fight for the abolition of slavery for so many years, only to be abandoned by their male allies when their chance finally came; all it would have taken was one more word in the Fifteenth Amendment, so that the protected categories for voting would have read "race, color, *sex,* or previous condition of servitude." Leading suffragists such as Susan B. Anthony and Elizabeth Cady Stanton did not want to hear from Radical Republicans that this was "the Negro's hour" and that women would have to wait for another day. How could the suffrage be granted to former slaves, Elizabeth Cady Stanton demanded, but not to them?

In her despair, Stanton lashed out in ugly terms against "Patrick and Sambo and Hans and Ung Tung," men ignorant of the Declaration of Independence and yet entitled to vote, while the best and most accomplished of American women remained voteless. In 1869 the annual meeting of the Equal Rights Association, the lead organization in the struggle for the rights of blacks and women, broke up in acrimony, and Stanton and Anthony came out against the Fifteenth Amendment.

At this searing moment, a schism opened in the ranks of the women's movement. The majority, led by Lucy Stone and Julia Ward Howe, reconciled themselves to disappointment and accepted the priority of black suffrage. Organized into the American Woman Suffrage Association, these moderates remained allied to the Republican Party in the forlorn hope that once Reconstruction had been settled, it would be time for the woman's vote. The Stanton-Anthony group, however, struck out in a new direction. Stanton declared that woman "must not put her trust in man" in fighting for her rights. The new organization she headed, the New York–based National Women Suffrage Association, accepted only women, focused exclusively on women's rights, and resolutely took up the battle for a federal woman suffrage amendment.

The fracturing of the women's movement obscured the common ground the two sides shared. Both now realized that a broader popular constituency had to be built beyond the small elite of evangelical reformers who had founded the movement. Both elevated suffrage into the preeminent women's issue. And both were energized by a shared anger not evident in earlier times. "If I were to give vent to all my pent-up wrath concerning the subordination of woman," Lydia Maria Child wrote to the Republican warhorse Charles Sumner in 1872, "I might frighten *you*. . . . Suffice it, therefore, to say, either the theory of our government is *false,* or women have the right to vote." If radical Reconstruction seemed a barren time for women's rights, in fact it had planted the seeds of the modern feminist movement.

THE SOUTH UNDER RADICAL RECONSTRUCTION

Between 1868 and 1871 all the southern states met the congressional stipulations and rejoined the Union. Protected by federal troops and encouraged by northern party leaders, Republican organizations took hold across the South and won control of the newly established Reconstruction governments. These Republican administrations remained in power for periods ranging from a few months in Virginia to nine years in South Carolina, Louisiana, and Florida. Their core support came from African Americans, who constituted a majority of registered voters in Alabama, Florida, South Carolina, Mississippi, and Louisiana and nearly a majority in Georgia, Virginia, and North Carolina.

The southern whites who became Republicans faced the scorn of Democratic former Confederates, who mocked them as *scalawags*—an ancient Scots-Irish term for runty, worthless animals. Whites who had come from the North they denounced as *carpetbaggers*—self-seeking interlopers who carried all their property in cheap cloth suitcases called carpetbags. Such labels glossed over the actual diversity of these groups.

Some carpetbaggers, while motivated by personal gain, also brought capital and skills. Others were Union army veterans taken with the South—its climate, people, and economic opportunities. And interspersed with the self-seekers were many idealists anxious to advance the cause of emancipation.

The scalawags were even more diverse. Some were former slaveowners, ex-Whigs and even ex-Democrats, drawn to Republicanism as the best way to attract northern capital to southern railroads, mines, and factories. In southwest Texas, the large population of Germans was strongly Republican. They sent to Congress Edward Degener, an immigrant and a San Antonio grocer whom Confederate authorities had imprisoned and whose sons had been executed for treason. But most numerous among the scalawags were yeomen farmers from the backcountry who wanted to rid the South of its slaveholding aristocracy. Scalawags had generally fought against (or at least refused to support) the Confederacy; they believed that slavery had victimized whites as well as blacks. "Now is the time," a Georgia scalawag wrote, "for every man to come out and speak his principles publickly and vote for liberty as we have been in bondage long enough."

The Democrats' scorn for black political leaders as ignorant and impressionable field hands was just as ill-founded. The first African American leaders in the South came from an elite of blacks free before the Civil War. They were joined by northern blacks who moved south when radical Reconstruction offered the prospect of meaningful freedom. Some had fought in the antislavery crusade or were Union army veterans; a number were employed by the Freedmen's Bureau or northern missionary societies. Others had escaped from slavery and were returning home, like Blanche K. Bruce, who first taught school in Missouri and then in 1874 became Mississippi's second black U.S. senator.

With the formation of the reconstructed Republican governments, this diverse group of ministers, artisans, shopkeepers, and former soldiers reached out to the freedmen. African American speakers, some financed by the Republican Party, fanned out into the old plantation districts and recruited freed slaves for leadership roles. Still, few among these former slaves had been field hands; most had been preachers or artisans. The literacy of one freedman, Thomas Allen, who was a Baptist minister and shoemaker, helped him win election to the Georgia legislature. "In my county," he recalled, "the colored people came to me for instructions, and I gave them the best instructions I could. I took the *New York Tribune* and other papers, and in that way I found out a great deal, and I told them whatever I thought was right."

Although never proportionate to their size in the population, black office holders held positions of importance throughout the South. In South Carolina African Americans occupied a majority of the seats in one house of the state legislature in 1868. They were heavily represented in states' executive offices, elected three members of Congress, and won a place on the state supreme court. Over the entire course

THE FIRST COLORED SENATOR AND REPRESENTATIVES.
In the 41st and 42nd Congress of the United States.

African American Congressional Delegation, 1872

This Currier and Ives lithograph celebrates one of the notable achievements of radical Reconstruction—the representation that former slaves won, however briefly, in the U.S. Congress. Hiram Revels of Mississippi, the Senate's first African American member, is seated at the extreme left. (Granger Collection)

of Reconstruction twenty African Americans served in the executive branch as governor, lieutenant governor, secretary of state, treasurer, or superintendent of education, more than 600 served as state legislators, and sixteen as Congressmen.

The Republicans who took office had ambitious plans for a reconstructed South. They wanted to end its dependence on cotton agriculture and build instead an industrial economy like the North's. They fell short of achieving this vision but accomplished more than their critics gave them credit for.

The Republicans modernized state constitutions, eliminated property qualifications for the vote, and made more offices elective. They attended especially to the personal freedom of the former slaves, sweeping out the shadow Black Codes that imposed labor discipline on them and limited their mobility. Women also benefited from the Republican defense of personal liberty. Nearly all the new constitutions expanded the rights of married women, enabling them to hold property and personal earnings independent of their husbands. Republican social programs called for hospitals, more humane penitentiaries, and asylums for orphans and the insane.

Reconstruction governments built roads in areas where roads had never existed. They poured money into reviving the region's railroad network. And they did all this without federal financing.

To pay for their ambitious programs, the Republicans copied taxes that Jacksonian reformers had earlier introduced in the North—in particular, general property taxes applying not only to real estate but to personal wealth. The goal was to force planters to pay their fair share of taxes and to force uncultivated land onto the market. In many plantation counties, especially in South Carolina, Louisiana, and Mississippi, former slaves served as tax assessors and collectors, administering the taxation of their onetime owners.

Increasing tax revenues never managed to offset the burgeoning obligations undertaken by the Reconstruction governments. State debts mounted rapidly, and as interest payments on bonds fell into arrears, public credit collapsed. On top of that, much of the spending was wasted or ended in the pockets of state officials. Corruption was endemic to American politics, present in the southern states before the Republicans came on the scene and rampant everywhere in this era, not least in the Grant administration itself. Still, in the free-spending atmosphere of the early Republican regimes, corruption was especially widespread and damaging to the cause of radical Reconstruction.

Nothing, however, could dim the achievement in public education. Here the South had lagged woefully; only Tennessee had a system of public schooling before the Civil War. Republican state governments vowed to make up for lost time, viewing education as the foundation for a democratic order. African Americans of all ages rushed to attend the newly established schools, even when they had to pay tuition. An elderly man in Mississippi explained his desire to go to school: "Ole missus used to read the good book [the Bible] to us . . . on Sunday evenin's, but she mostly read dem places where it says, 'Servants obey your masters.' . . . Now we is free, there's heaps of tings in that old book we is just suffering to learn." By 1875 about half of all the children in Florida, Mississippi, and South Carolina were in classrooms.

The building of schools was part of a larger effort by African Americans to fortify the institutions that had sustained their spirit during the days of slavery. Religious belief had struck deep roots in nineteenth-century slave society. Now, in freedom, the African Americans left the white-dominated congregations, where they had been relegated to segregated balconies and denied any voice in church governance, and built churches of their own. These churches joined together to form African American versions of the Southern Methodist and Southern Baptist denominations, including, most prominently, the National Baptist Convention and the African Methodist Episcopal Church. Everywhere, the robust new churches served not only as places of worship but as schools, social centers, and political meeting halls.

Black ministers were community leaders and often political officeholders. As Charles H. Pearce, a Methodist minister in Florida, declared, "A man in this State cannot do his whole duty as a minister except he looks out for the political interests of his people." Calling for the brotherhood of man and the special destiny of the former slaves as the "Children of Israel," black ministers provided a powerful religious underpinning for the Republican politics of their congregations.

SHARECROPPING

In the meantime, the freedmen were locked in a great economic struggle with their former owners. In 1869 South Carolina established a land commission empowered to buy property and resell it on easy terms to the landless. In this way about 14,000 black families acquired farms. South Carolina's land distribution plan showed what was possible, but it was the exception, not the rule. Despite a lot of rhetoric, Republican regimes elsewhere did little to help the freedmen fulfill their dreams of becoming independent farmers. Federal efforts proved equally feeble. The Southern Homestead Act of 1866 offered 80-acre grants to settlers, limited for the first year to freedmen and southern Unionists. The advantage was mostly symbolic, however, since the public land made available to homesteaders was off the beaten track in swampy, infertile parts of the lower South and since homesteaders lacked the resources to get started. Only about 1,000 homesteading families finally succeeded.

There was no reversing President Johnson's order restoring confiscated lands to the former Confederates. Property rights, it seemed, trumped everything else, even for most radical Republicans. The Freedmen's Bureau, which had earlier championed the land claims of former slaves, now devoted itself to teaching them how to be good agricultural laborers.

So while they yearned for farms of their own, most freedmen started out landless and with no option but to labor for their former owners. But not, they vowed, under the conditions of slavery—no gang work, no overseers, no fines or punishments, no regulation of their private lives or personal freedom. In certain parts of the agricultural South—for example, on the great sugar plantations of Louisiana taken over after the war by northern investors—wage work became the norm. The problem was that cotton planters lacked the money to pay wages, at least not until the crop came in, and sometimes, in lieu of a straight wage, they offered a share of the crop. As a *wage,* this was a bad deal for the freedmen, but if they could be paid in shares for their work, why could they not pay in shares to rent the land they worked?

This form of share tenantry, already familiar in parts of the white South, freedmen now seized on for the independence it offered them. Planters resisted, believing, as one wrote, that "wages are the only successful system of controlling hands." But in a battle of wills that broke out across the cotton South, the planters yielded to "the inveterate prejudices of the freedmen, who desire to be masters of their own time."

Thus there sprang up the distinctive laboring system for cotton agriculture— *sharecropping,* in which the freedmen worked as tenant farmers, exchanging their labor for the use of land, house, implements, sometimes seed and fertilizer, typically turning over half to two-thirds of their harvested crops to the landlord (see Map 15.2). The sharecropping system joined laborers and the owners of land and capital in a common sharing of risks and returns. But it was a very unequal relationship, given the force of southern law and custom on the white landowner's side and given the sharecroppers' dire economic circumstances. Starting out in poverty, they had no way of making it through the first growing season without borrowing for food and supplies.

Country storekeepers stepped in. Bankrolled by their northern suppliers, they "furnished" the sharecropper and took as collateral a *lien* on the crop, effectively assuming ownership of the cropper's share. Under lien laws passed after radical Reconstruction collapsed, sharecroppers received only the proceeds that remained after their debts had been paid. Once indebted at one store, the sharecropper was no longer free to shop around and became an easy target for exorbitant prices, unfair interest rates, and crooked bookkeeping. As cotton prices declined during the 1870s, more and more sharecroppers failed to settle accounts and fell into permanent debt.

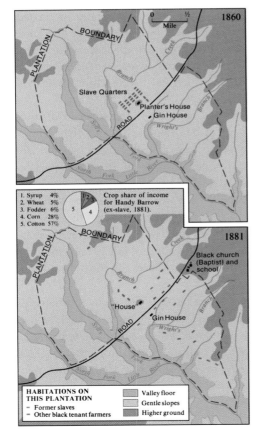

M AP 15.2
The Barrow Plantation, 1860 and 1881

Comparing the 1860 map of this central Georgia plantation with the 1881 map reveals the changing patterns of black residence and farming. In 1860 the slave quarters were clustered near the planter's house, which sat on a small hilltop. The sharecroppers of 1881 built cabins along the spurs or ridges of land between the streams, scattering their community over the plantation. A black church and school were built by this date. A typical sharecropper on the plantation earned most of his income from growing cotton.

Sharecropping

This sharecropping family seems proud of its new cabin and crop of cotton, which it planted in every available bit of ground. But the presence of the white landlord in the background suggests that sharecropping was only a limited kind of economic freedom. (Brown Brothers)

And if the merchant was also the landowner or conspired with the landowner, the debt became a pretext for forced labor, or *peonage,* although evidence now suggests that sharecroppers generally managed to pull up stakes and move on once things became hopeless. Sharecroppers always thought twice about moving, however, because part of their "capital" was being known and well-reputed in their communities. Freedmen who lacked that local standing generally found sharecropping hard going and ended up in the ranks of agricultural laborers.

In the face of all this adversity, the freedpeople struggled to better themselves. The fact that it enabled *family* struggle was, in truth, the saving advantage of sharecropping because it mobilized husbands and wives in common enterprise while shielding both from personal subordination to whites. The trouble with sharecropping, grumbled one planter, was that "it makes the laborer too independent; he becomes a partner, and has to be consulted." By the end of Reconstruction, about one-quarter of sharecropping families had managed to save enough to rent with cash payments, and eventually black farmers owned about a third of the land they cultivated—but rarely the best land and usually at a cost greater than its fertility warranted.

For the freedmen, sharecropping was not the worst choice; it certainly beat wage work for their former owners. But for southern agriculture, the costs were devastating. Sharecropping committed the South inflexibly to cotton, despite soil depletion and unprofitable prices. Crop diversification declined, costing the South its self-sufficiency in grains and livestock. And with farms leased year to year, the tenant had little incentive to improve the property. The crop-lien system lined merchants' pockets with unearned profits that might otherwise have gone into agricultural improvement. The result was a stagnant farm economy, blighting the South's future and condemning it to economic backwardness—a kind of retribution, in fact, for the fresh injustices visited on the people it had once enslaved.

The Undoing of Reconstruction

Former Confederates were blind to the benefits of radical Reconstruction. Indeed, no amount of achievement could have persuaded them that it was anything but an abomination, undertaken without their consent and intended to deny them their rightful place in southern society. Led by the planters, former Confederates staged a massive counterrevolution—one designed to "redeem" the South and restore them to political power under the banner of the Democratic Party. But the Redeemers could not have succeeded on their own. They needed the complicity of the North. The undoing of Reconstruction is as much about northern acquiescence as it is about southern resistance.

COUNTERREVOLUTION

Insofar as they could win at the ballot box, the Democrats took that route. They worked hard to get former Confederates restored to the rolls of registered voters, they appealed to racial solidarity and southern patriotism, and they campaigned against black rule as a threat to white supremacy. But force was equally acceptable. Throughout the Deep South, especially where black voters were heavily concentrated, former Confederate planters and their supporters organized secret societies and waged campaigns of terror against blacks and their white allies.

The most widespread of these groups, the Ku Klux Klan, first appeared in 1866 as a Tennessee social club but quickly became a paramilitary force under Nathan Bedford Forrest, the Confederacy's most decorated cavalry general. Forrest was notorious for a wartime incident at Fort Pillow, Tennessee, when his troops massacred African American soldiers after they had surrendered.

By 1870 the Klan was operating almost everywhere in the South as an armed force serving the Democratic Party. The Klan murdered and whipped Republican politicians, burned black schools and churches, and attacked party gatherings (see American Voices, "The Intimidation of Black Voters"). In October 1870 a group of Klansmen assaulted a Republican rally in Eutaw, Alabama, killing four African Americans and wounding fifty-four. Such terrorist tactics enabled the Democrats to seize power in Georgia and North Carolina in 1870 and make substantial gains

Klan Portrait, 1868

Two armed Klansmen from Alabama pose proudly in their disguises. Northern audiences saw a lithograph based on this photograph in *Harper's Weekly* in December 1868.

(Rutherford B. Hayes Presidential Center, Spiegel Grove, Fremont, Ohio)

elsewhere. An African American politician in North Carolina wrote, "Our former masters are fast taking the reins of government."

Congress responded by passing enforcement legislation, including the Ku Klux Klan Act of 1871, authorizing President Grant to use federal prosecutions, military force, and martial law to suppress conspiracies to deprive citizens of the right to vote, hold office, serve on juries, and enjoy equal protection of the law. Federal agents penetrated the Klan and gathered evidence that provided the basis for widespread arrests; federal grand juries indicted more than 3,000 Klansmen. In South Carolina, where the Klan was most deeply entrenched, federal troops occupied nine counties, driving as many as 2,000 Klansmen from the state.

The Grant administration's assault on the Klan raised the spirits of southern Republicans, but it also emphasized how dependent they were on the federal government. The potency of the Ku Klux Klan Act, a Mississippi Republican wrote, "derived alone from its source" in the federal government. "No such law could be enforced by state authority, the local power being too weak." If Republicans were to prevail over former Confederate terrorists, they needed what one carpetbagger described as "steady, unswerving power from without."

The Intimidation of Black Voters

Harriet Hernandes

*T*he following testimony was given in 1871 by Harriet Hernandes, a black resident of
Spartanburg, South Carolina, to the Joint Congressional Select Committee investigating
conditions in the South. The terrorizing of black women through rape and other forms of
physical violence was among the means of oppression used by the Ku Klux Klan.

Question: How old are you?
Answer: Going on thirty-four years. . . .
Q: Are you married or single?
A: Married.
Q: Did the Ku-Klux come to your house at any time?
A: Yes, sir; twice. . . .
Q: Go on to the second time. . . .
A: They came in; I was lying in bed. Says he, "Come out here, sir; come out here, sir!" They
took me out of bed; they would not let me get out, but they took me up in their arms and
toted me out—me and my daughter Lucy. He struck me on the forehead with a pistol,
and here is the scar above my eye now. Says he, "Damn you, fall." I fell. Says he, "Damn
you, get up." I got up. Says he, "Damn you, get over this fence!" and he kicked me over
when I went to get over; and then he went on to a brush pile, and they laid us right down
there, both together. They laid us down twenty yards apart, I reckon. They had dragged
and beat us along. They struck me right on top of my head, and I thought they had killed
me; and I said, "Lord o'mercy, don't, don't kill my child!" He gave me a lick on the head,
and it liked to have killed me; I saw stars. He threw my arm over my head so I could not
do anything with it for three weeks, and there are great knots on my wrist now.
Q: What did they say this was for?
A: They said, "You can tell your husband that when we see him we are going to kill
him. . . ."
Q: Did they say why they wanted to kill him?
A: They said, "He voted the radical ticket [slate of candidates], didn't he?" I said, "Yes," that
very way. . . .
Q: When did [your husband] get back home after this whipping? He was not at home, was
he?
A: He was lying out; he couldn't stay at home, bless your soul! . . .
Q: Has he been afraid for any length of time?
A: He has been afraid ever since last October. He has been lying out. He has not laid in
the house ten nights since October.
Q: Is that the situation of the colored people down there to any extent?
A: That is the way they all have to do—men and women both.
Q: What are they afraid of?
A: Of being killed or whipped to death.
Q: What has made them afraid?

A: Because men that voted radical tickets they took the spite out on the women when they could get at them.

Q: How many colored people have been whipped in that neighborhood?

A: It is all of them, mighty near.

SOURCE: *Report of the Joint Congressional Select Committee to Inquire into the Condition of Affairs in the Late Insurrectionary States, House Reports,* 42d Cong., 2d sess. (Washington, DC: U.S. Government Printing Office, 1972), vol. 5, South Carolina, December 19, 1871.

But northern Republicans were growing weary of Reconstruction and the bloodshed it seemed to produce. Although reelected handily in 1872, Grant did not see his victory as a mandate for an endless war against the white South. Prosecuting Klansmen under the enforcement acts was an uphill battle. U.S. attorneys usually faced all-white juries, and the Justice Department lacked the resources to prosecute effectively. After 1872, prosecutions dropped off, and many Klansmen received hasty pardons; only a small fraction served significant prison terms.

The faltering zeal for Reconstruction stemmed from more than discouragement about prosecuting the Klan, however. The worst depression in the nation's history struck in 1873, and the North became preoccupied with its own economic problems. Northern business interests complained that the turmoil of Reconstruction retarded the South's economic recovery and harmed their investment opportunities. Sympathy for the freedmen also began to wane. The North was flooded with one-sided, often racist reports, such as James M. Pike's *The Prostrate State* (1873), describing extravagant, corrupt Republican rule and a South in the grip of "a mass of black barbarism." In the 1874 elections, the Republicans suffered a crushing defeat, losing control of the House of Representatives for the first time since secession and also losing seven normally Republican states to the Democrats. For party strategists, the political costs in a disillusioned North began to outweigh their hopes for a Republican-dominated South.

In a kind of self-fulfilling prophesy, the unwillingness of the Grant administration to shore up Reconstruction guaranteed that it would fail. Republican governments that were denied federal help found themselves overwhelmed by massive resistance from former Confederates. Democrats overthrew Republican governments in Texas in 1873, in Alabama and Arkansas in 1874, and in Mississippi in 1875.

The Mississippi campaign showed all too clearly what the Republicans were up against. As elections neared in 1875, paramilitary groups such as the Rifle Clubs and Red Shirts operated openly. Often local Democrats paraded armed, as if they were militia companies. They identified black leaders in assassination lists called "dead-books," broke up Republican meetings, provoked rioting that left hundreds of African Americans dead, and threatened voters, who still lacked the protection of the secret ballot. Mississippi's Republican governor, Adelbert Ames, a Congressional Medal of Honor winner from Maine, appealed to President Grant for federal troops, but Grant refused. Ames then contemplated organizing a state militia but ultimately decided against it, believing that only blacks would join and that the state would be plunged into racial war. Brandishing their guns and stuffing the ballot boxs, the Redeemers swept the 1875 elections and took command of Mississippi. Facing impeachment by the new Democratic legislature, Governor Ames resigned his office and returned to the North.

THE POLITICAL CRISIS OF 1877

Northerners were not much troubled by the South's counterrevolution. National politics had moved on, and other concerns absorbed voters. Foremost was the stench of scandal that hung over the White House. In 1875 Grant's secretary of the treasury, Benjamin Bristow, exposed the so-called Whiskey Ring, a network of distillers and government agents who had defrauded the U.S. Treasury of millions of dollars of excise taxes on liquor. The ringleader was a Grant appointee, and Grant's own private secretary, Orville Babcock, had a hand in the thievery. The others went to prison, but Grant stood by Babcock, possibly perjuring himself to save his secretary. On top of this, the economic depression deepened. Grant's administration responded ineffectually, rebuffing the pleas of debtors for relief by increasing the money supply (see Chapter 18).

Among the casualties of the bad economy was the Freedman's Savings and Trust Company, which had been sponsored by the Freedmen's Bureau and held the small deposits of thousands of former slaves. When the bank failed in 1874, Congress refused to compensate the depositors, and many lost their life savings. In denying the depositors' pleas, Congress was signaling that Reconstruction had lost its moral claim on the country.

Abandoning Grant, the Republicans in 1876 nominated Rutherford B. Hayes, governor of Ohio, a colorless figure but untainted by corruption, or by strong convictions—in a word, a safe man. His Democratic opponent was Samuel J. Tilden, governor of New York, a wealthy lawyer with ties to Wall Street and a reform reputation for helping to break the hold of the thieving Tweed Ring over New York City politics. The Democrat Tilden favored "home rule" for the South, but so, more discretely, did the Republican Hayes. Reconstruction actually did not figure prominently in the campaign and was mostly subsumed under broader Democratic charges of "corrupt centralism" and "incapacity, waste, and fraud." By now, Republicans had written off the South and scarcely campaigned there. They paid little attention to the states still ruled by Reconstruction governments—Florida, South Carolina, and Louisiana.

Once the returns started coming in on election night, however, those three states began to loom very large indeed. Tilden led in the popular vote, and with victories in key northern states, he seemed headed for the White House. But sleepless politicians at Republican headquarters realized that if they kept Florida, South Carolina, and Louisiana, Hayes would win by a single electoral vote. The campaigns in those states had been bitterly fought, with the same kinds of Democratic assaults on blacks that had overturned Republican regimes everywhere else in the South. But Republicans still controlled the election machinery in those states, and citing Democratic fraud and intimidation they could certify Republican victories. Late on election night the audacious announcement came forth from Republican headquarters: Hayes had carried the three southern states and won the election. But newly elected Democratic officials in the three states also sent in electoral votes for Tilden. When Congress met in early 1877, it faced two sets of electoral votes from those states.

The Constitution did not provide for this contingency. All it said was that the President of the Senate (in 1877, a Republican) opens the electoral certificates before the House (Democratic) and the Senate (Republican) and that "The votes shall then be counted." An air of crisis gripped the country. There was talk of inside deals, of a new election, even of a violent coup and civil war. Just in case, the commander of the army, General William T. Sherman, deployed four artillery companies in Washington. Finally, Congress decided to appoint an electoral commission to settle the question. The commission included seven Republicans, seven Democrats, and, as the deciding member, David Davis, a Supreme Court justice not known to have fixed party loyalties. But Davis disqualified himself by accepting an Illinois seat in the Senate. He was replaced by Republican Justice Joseph P. Bradley, and by a vote of 8 to 7, the commission awarded the disputed votes to Hayes.

Outraged Democrats had one more trick up their sleeves. They controlled the House, and they set about stalling a final count of the electoral votes so as to prevent Hayes's inauguration on March 4, 1877. But a week earlier, secret talks had begun between southern Democrats and Ohio Republicans representing Hayes. Other issues may have been on the table, but the main thing was the situation in South Carolina and Louisiana, where rival governments were encamped at the state capitols, with federal soldiers holding the Democrats at bay. Exactly what deal was struck or how involved Hayes himself was will probably never be known, but on March 1 the House Democrats suddenly ended their filibuster, the ceremonial counting of votes went forward, and Hayes was inaugurated on schedule. He soon ordered the Union troops back to their barracks, and the Republican regimes in South Carolina and Louisiana fell. Reconstruction had ended.

In 1877 political leaders on all sides seemed ready to say that what Lincoln had called "the work" was complete. But for the freedmen, the work had only begun. Reconstruction turned out to have been a magnificent aberration, a magnum jump beyond what most white Americans actually felt was due their black fellow citizens. Redemption represented a sad falling back to the norm. Still, something real had been achieved—three rights-defining amendments to the Constitution, some elbow room to advance economically, and, not least, a stubborn confidence among

TIMELINE

1863	Lincoln's Ten Percent Plan	**1870**	Ku Klux Klan at peak of power	
1864	Wade-Davis Bill "pocket"-vetoed by Lincoln.		Congress responds with Enforcement Acts.	
			Fifteenth Amendment ratified	
1865	Freedmen's Bureau established	**1872**	Grant reelected president.	
	Lincoln assassinated	**1873**	Panic of 1873 ushers in depression of 1873–77.	
	Andrew Johnson becomes President and implements his restoration plan.			
1866	Civil Rights Act passes over Johnson's veto.	**1874**	Democrats gain majority in House of Representatives.	
	Johnson makes disastrous "swing around the circle."	**1875**	Whiskey Ring scandal undermines Grant administration.	
	Congressional elections repudiate Johnson.	**1876**	Disputed presidential election	
1867	Reconstruction Acts	**1877**	Congressional compromise makes Rutherford B. Hayes president.	
1868	Impeachment crisis		Reconstruction ends.	
	Fourteenth Amendment ratified			
	Ulysses S. Grant elected president			

blacks that by their own efforts they could lift themselves up. Things would, in fact, get worse before they got better, but the work of Reconstruction was imperishable and could never be erased.

For Further Exploration

The best current book on Reconstruction is Eric Foner's major synthesis, *Reconstruction: America's Unfinished Revolution, 1863–1877* (1988), available also in a shorter version. *Black Reconstruction in America* (1935), by the African American activist and scholar W. E. B. Du Bois, deserves attention as the first book to challenge traditional racist interpretations of Reconstruction and stress the role of blacks in their own emancipation. For the presidential phase of Reconstruction, see Dan T. Carter, *When the War Was Over: The Failure of Self-Reconstruction in the South, 1865–1867* (1985). On the freedmen, Leon F. Litwack, *Been in the Storm So Long: The Aftermath of Slavery* (1979), provides a stirring account. More recent emancipation studies emphasize slavery as a labor system: Julie Saville, *The Work of Reconstruction; From Slave to Wage Laborer in South Carolina, 1860–1870* (1994), and Amy Dru Stanley, *From Bondage to Contract* (1999), which expands the discussion to show what the onset of wage labor meant for freedwomen. Eric Foner, *Nothing But Freedom: Emancipation and Its Legacy* (1983), helpfully places emancipation in a comparative context. William S. McFeely, *Grant: A Biography* (1981), deftly explains the politics of Reconstruction. The emergence of the sharecropping system is explored in Gavin Wright, *Old South, New South* (1986), and Edward Royce *The Origins of Southern Sharecropping* (1993). On the Compromise of 1877, see C. Vann Woodward's classic *Reunion and Reaction* (1956). Two informative websites are <http://womhis .binghampton.edu/intro.htm>, which deals with northern women who assisted the freedpeople, and <1cweb2.loc.gov/ammen/aaohtml/aollist.html>, which provides Library of Congress documents and illustrations on African Americans during Reconstruction.

Part Four

A MATURING INDUSTRIAL SOCIETY
1877–1914

THEMATIC TIMELINE

	ECONOMY	SOCIETY	CULTURE
	THE TRIUMPH OF INDUSTRIALIZATION	RACIAL, ETHNIC, AND GENDER DIVISIONS	THE RISE OF THE CITY
1877	• Andrew Carnegie launches modern steel industry. • Knights of Labor becomes national movement (1878).	• Struggle for black equality defeated • Nomadic Indian life ends.	• National League founded (1876) • Dwight L. Moody pioneers urban revivalism.
1880	• Gustavus Swift pioneers vertically integrated firm. • American Federation of Labor (1886)	• Chinese Exclusion Act (1882) • Dawes Severalty Act divides tribal lands (1887).	• Electrification transforms city life. • First *Social Register* defines high society (1888).
1890	• United States surpasses Britain in iron and steel output. • Economic depression (1893–1897) • Era of farm prosperity begins.	• Black disfranchisement and segregation in the South • Immigration from southeastern Europe rises sharply.	• Settlement houses spread progressive ideas to cities. • William Randolph Hearst's *New York Journal* pioneers yellow journalism.
1900	• Great industrial merger movement • Immigrants dominate factory work. • Industrial Workers of the World (1905)	• Women lead social reform. • Struggle for civil rights revived • Movement to restrict immigration	• Muckraking journalism • Movies begin to overtake vaudeville.
1910	• Henry Ford builds first automobile assembly line.	• NAACP (1910) • Women vote in western states. • World War I ends European migration.	• Urban liberalism

While the nation was absorbed by the political drama of Reconstruction, few people noticed an equally momentous watershed in American economic life. For the first time, as the decade of the 1870s passed, farmers no longer constituted a majority of working Americans. Henceforth, America's future would be linked to its development as an industrial society.

ECONOMY. The effects of accelerating industrialization were felt, first of all, in the manufacturing sector itself. Production became increasingly mechanized and increasingly directed at making the capital goods that undergirded economic growth. As the railroad system was completed, modern organizational and management techniques began to dominate American enterprise. The labor movement became firmly established, and as immigration surged, the foreign-born and their children became America's workers. What had been partial and limited now became general and widespread as America turned into a land of factories, corporate enterprise, and industrial workers.

SOCIETY. The final surge of western settlement across the Great Plains was largely driven by the pressures of this industrializing economy. Cities demanded new sources of food; factories, the Far West's mineral resources. Defending their way of life, western Indians were ultimately defeated not so much by army rifles as by the unceasing encroachment of railroads, mines, ranches, and proliferating farms. These same forces disrupted the old established Hispanic communities of the Southwest but spurred Asian, Mexican, and European migrations that made for a multiethnic western society.

GOVERNMENT	DIPLOMACY
FROM INACTION TO PROGRESSIVE REFORM	AN EMERGING WORLD POWER
• Election of Rutherford B. Hayes ends Reconstruction.	• United States becomes a net exporter.
• Ethnocultural issues dominate state and local politics. • Civil service reform (1883)	• Diplomacy of inaction • Naval buildup begins.
• Populist Party founded (1892) • William McKinley wins presidency; defeats Bryan's free silver crusade (1896).	• Social Darwinism and Anglo-Saxonism promote expansion. • Spanish-American War (1898–1899); conquest of the Philippines.
• Progressivism in national politics • Theodore Roosevelt attacks the trusts. • Hepburn Act regulates railroads (1906).	• Panama cedes Canal Zone to United States (1903). • Roosevelt Corollary to Monroe Doctrine (1904)
• Woodrow Wilson elected (1912) • New Freedom legislation creates Federal Reserve, FTC.	• Taft's diplomacy promotes U.S. business. • Wilson proclaims U.S. neutrality in World War I.

CULTURE. Industrialization also transformed the nation's urban life. By 1900 one in five Americans lived in cities. That was where the jobs were—as workers in the factories; as clerks and salespeople; as members of a new salaried middle class of managers, engineers, and professionals; and at the apex as a wealthy elite of investors and entrepreneurs. The city was more than just a place to make a living, however. It provided a setting for an urban lifestyle unlike anything seen before in America.

GOVERNMENT. The unfettered, booming economy of the Gilded Age tended at first to marginalize political life. The major parties remained robust not because they stood for much programmatically but because they exploited a culture of popular participation and embraced the ethnocultural interests of their constituencies. The depression of the 1890s triggered a major challenge to the political status quo by the agrarian Populist Party, with its demand for free silver. The election of 1896 turned back that challenge and established the Re-publicans as the dominant national party.

Still unresolved, however, was the threat that corporate power posed to the marketplace and democratic politics. How to curb the trusts dominated national debate during the Progressive Era. In those years, too, the country took a critical look at its institutions and began to address its social ills. From different angles political reformers, women progressives, and urban liberals went about the business of cleaning up machine politics and making life better for America's urban masses. African Americans, disfranchised and segregated, found allies among white progressives and launched a new drive for racial equality.

DIPLOMACY. Finally, the dynamism of America's economic development decisively altered the country's foreign relations. In the decades after the Civil War, America had been inward-looking, neglectful of its navy and inactive diplomatically. The business crisis of the 1890s, however, brought home the need for a more aggressive foreign policy that would advance the nation's overseas economic interests. In short order the United States went to war with Spain, acquired an overseas empire, and became actively engaged in Latin America and Asia. There was no mistaking America's standing as a Great Power and as World War I approached no evading the responsibilities and entanglements that came with that status.

Chapter 16

THE AMERICAN WEST

Who are to go there? The territory consists of mountains almost inaccessible, and low lands . . . where rain never falls, except during spring. . . . Why, sir, sir, of what use will this be for agricultural purposes? I would not, for that purpose, give a pinch of snuff for the whole territory.

—SENATOR GEORGE MCDUFFIE SPEAKING IN CONGRESS
ABOUT ACQUIRING CALIFORNIA FROM MEXICO, 1843

During the last decades of the nineteenth century American society seemed at odds with itself. From one angle the nation looked like an advanced industrial power, with humming factories and enormous, crowded cities. But from another angle America remained a frontier country, with pioneers streaming onto the Great Plains, repeating the old dramas of "settlement" they had been performing ever since Europeans had first set foot on the continent. Not until the census of 1890 did the federal government declare that a "frontier of settlement" no longer existed: the country's "unsettled area has been so broken into . . . that there can hardly be said to be a frontier line."

That same year, 1890, the country surpassed Great Britain in the production of iron and steel. Newspapers reported Indian wars and labor strikes in the same edition. The last tragic episode in the suppression of the plains Indians, the Sioux massacre at Wounded Knee, South Dakota, occurred only eighteen months before the great Homestead steel strike of 1892. This alignment of events from the distant worlds of factory and frontier was not accidental. The final surge of settlement across the Great Plains and the Far West was driven primarily by the dynamism of American industrialism.

The Great Plains

During the 1860s agricultural settlement reached the western margins of the high-grass prairie country, roughly at the ninety-eighth meridian. Beyond stretched vast, arid plains. It seemed no place for farmers accustomed to forested land and ample rainfall (see Map 16.1).

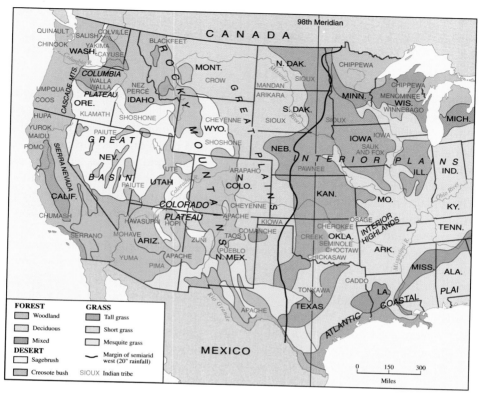

MAP 16.1

The Natural Environment of the West

As settlers pushed into the Great Plains beyond the line of semiaridity, they sensed the overwhelming power of the natural environment. In a landscape without trees for fences and barns and without adequate rainfall, ranchers and farmers had to relearn their business. The Native Americans peopling the plains and mountains had in time learned to live in this environment, but this knowledge counted for little against the ruthless pressure of the settlers to domesticate the West.

The geologic event that created the Great Plains had occurred 60 million years earlier when the Rocky Mountains had been thrust up out of the ocean covering western North America. With no outlet the shallow inland sea to the east dried up, forming a hard pan on which sediment washing down from the mountains built up a loose, featureless surface layer. The mountain barrier also made for a dry climate because the moisture-laden winds from the Pacific spent themselves on the western slopes. Only vegetation capable of withstanding drought and bitter winters could take hold on the plains. Short Gramma grass, the linchpin of this fragile ecosystem, matted the easily blown soil into place and sustained a rich wildlife dominated by the grazing antelope and buffalo. What the dry short-grass country had not sustained, until Indians began migrating there three centuries earlier, was human settlement.

INDIANS OF THE GREAT PLAINS

Probably 100,000 Native Americans lived on the Great Plains at mid-nineteenth century. They were a diverse people, divided into six linguistic families and at least thirty tribal groupings. On the eastern margins and along the Missouri River, the Mandans, Arikaras, and Pawnees planted corn and beans and lived in permanent villages. Smallpox and measles brought by Europeans ravaged these settled tribes. Less vulnerable to epidemics were the nomadic tribes that had first arrived on the Great Plains in the seventeenth century: Kiowas and Comanches in the southwest; Arapahos and Cheyennes on the central plains; and to the north Blackfeet, Crows, Cheyennes, and the great Sioux nation.

Originally the Sioux had been eastern prairie people, occupying settlements in the lake country of northern Minnesota. With fish and game dwindling, some Sioux tribes drifted westward and around 1760 began to cross the Missouri River. These Sioux became a nomadic people, living in portable skin tepees and following the buffalo. From tribes to the southwest, they acquired horses. Once mounted, the Sioux became splendid hunters and formidable fighters, claiming the entire Great Plains north of the Arkansas River as their hunting grounds.

The westernmost Sioux—they called themselves the Teton people, or Lakotas (meaning "allies")—made up a loose confederation of seven tribes. In the winter months the tribes broke up into small bands, but each spring they assembled and prepared for the summer hunt and for battle. Raiding parties rode forth intent on capturing ponies and taking scalps, but occasionally long columns of warriors mounted territorial campaigns against rival tribes. The Sioux, it must be remembered, were an invading people who dominated the northern Great Plains by driving out or subjugating longer-settled tribes.

A society that celebrates the warrior virtues is likely to define gender roles sharply. But before the Sioux acquired horses, chasing down the buffalo demanded the cooperation of the entire community, so that hunting could not be an exclusively male enterprise. It took the efforts of both women and men to construct the "pounds" into which, beating the brush side by side, they endeavored to stampede the herds. Once they had horses, the men rode out on the chase while the women remained in the encampment, laboring on the mounting piles of buffalo skins the hunters brought back. This was hard and painstaking work. Fanny Kelly, once a Sioux captive, considered the women's lives "a servitude," but she also noticed their high temper and independence. Subordination to men was not how Sioux women understood their unrelenting labor; it was their allotted share in a partnership on which the proud, nomadic life of the Sioux depended.

Living so close to nature, depending on its bounty for survival, the Sioux saw sacred meaning in every manifestation of the natural world. Unlike Europeans they conceived of a god who was not a supreme being but, in the words of the ethnologist Clark Wissler, was "a controlling power or series of powers pervading the universe"—Wi, the sun; Skan, the sky; Maka, the earth; Inyan, the rock. Below these came the moon, the wind, the buffalo, down through a hierarchy embodying the entire natural order.

By prayer and fasting Sioux prepared themselves to commune with these mysterious powers. Medicine men provided instruction, but the religious experience was personal and open to both sexes. The vision, when a supplicant achieved it, attached itself to some object—a feather, the skin of an animal, or a shell—that was tied into a sacred bundle that became the person's lifelong talisman. In the Sun Dance the entire tribe celebrated the rites of coming of age, fertility, the hunt, and combat, followed by four days of fasting and dancing in supplication to Wi, the sun.

The world of the Teton Sioux was not self-contained. All along they had exchanged pelts and buffalo robes for the produce of agriculturalist Mandans and Pawnees. When white traders appeared on the upper Missouri River during the eighteenth century, the Sioux began to trade with them as well. Although the buffalo remained their staff of life, the Sioux came to rely on manufactured pots, kettles, blankets, knives, and firearms. The trade system they entered was linked to the Euro-American market economy, yet it was also integrated into the Sioux way of life. Everything depended on the survival of the Great Plains as the Sioux had found it—wild grassland on which the antelope and buffalo ranged free.

WAGON TRAINS, RAILROADS, AND RANCHERS

On first encountering the Great Plains, Euro-Americans themselves thought the place best left to the Indians. After exploring a drought-stricken stretch in 1820, Major Stephen H. Long declared it "almost wholly unfit for cultivation, and of course uninhabitable by a people depending upon agriculture for their subsistence."

For years thereafter maps marked the plains region as the Great American Desert. With that notion in mind Congress formally designated the Great Plains in 1834 as permanent Indian country. Trade with the Indians would continue but now closely supervised and licensed by the federal government, with the Indian country otherwise off limits to whites.

Events swiftly overtook the nation's solemn commitment to the Native Americans. During the 1840s settlers began moving westward to Oregon and California. Instead of serving as a buffer against the British and Mexicans, the Indian country became a bridge to the Pacific. The first wagon train headed west for Oregon from Missouri in 1842. Soon thousands of emigrants traveled the Oregon Trail to the Willamette Valley or cutting south beyond Fort Hall down into California. Approaching that juncture in 1859, it seemed to Horace Greeley as if "the white coverings of the many emigrant and transport wagons dott[ing] the landscape" gave "the trail the appearance of a river running through great meadows, with many ships sailing on its bosom." Only these "ships" left behind not a trailing wake of foam but a rutted landscape devoid of game and littered with abandoned wagons and rotting garbage.

Talk about the need for a railroad to the Pacific soon began to be heard in Washington. How else could the distant territories formally acquired from Mexico and Britain in 1848 be firmly linked to the Union or the ordeal of overland travel be alleviated? The project languished while North and South argued over the terminus for the route to the Pacific. Meanwhile, the Indian country was crisscrossed by overland freight lines, and pony express riders delivered mail between Missouri and California. In 1861 telegraph lines brought San Francisco into instant communication with the East. The next year, with the South in rebellion and no longer a factor, the federal government finally went forward with the transcontinental project.

No private company could be expected to foot the bill by itself. The construction costs were staggering, and in the short run not much traffic could be expected on the thinly populated route. So the federal government awarded generous land grants along the right of way plus millions of dollars in loans to the two companies that undertook the transcontinental project.

The Union Pacific, building westward from Omaha, made little headway until the Civil War ended but then advanced rapidly across Indian country, reaching Cheyenne, Wyoming, in November 1867. It took the Central Pacific nearly that long, moving eastward from Sacramento, to cross the crest of the Sierra Nevada. Both then worked furiously—since the government subsidy was based on miles of track laid—until, to great fanfare, the tracks met at Promontory Point, Utah, in 1869. No other land-grant railroads made it as far as the Rockies before the Panic of 1873 hit, throwing them into bankruptcy and bringing work to an abrupt halt.

By then, however, railroad tycoons had changed their minds about the Great Plains. No longer did they see it through the eyes of the Oregon-bound settlers— as a place to be gotten through en route to the Pacific. Rail transportation, they realized, was laying the basis for the economic exploitation of the Great Plains. This calculation spurred the railroad boom that followed economic recovery in 1877. Construction soared. During the 1880s, 40,000 miles of track were laid west of the Mississippi, linking southern California via the Southern Pacific Railroad to New Orleans and via the Santa Fe Railroad to Kansas City and linking the Northwest via the Northern Pacific Railroad to St. Paul, Minnesota.

Of all the beckoning opportunities, most obvious was cattle raising. The grazing buffalo made it easy to imagine the Great Plains as cow country. But first the buffalo had to go. A small market for buffalo robes had existed for years. Then in the early 1870s eastern tanneries discovered how to cure the hides, sparking a huge demand from shoe and harness manufacturers. The systematic slaughter of the buffalo began. Already diminished by disease and shrinking pasturage, the great herds almost vanished within ten years. Many people spoke out against this mass killing, but no way existed to stop hunters bent on making a quick dollar. Besides, as General Philip H. Sheridan pointed out, exterminating the buffalo would starve the Indians into submission.

Killing the Buffalo

This woodcut shows passengers shooting buffalo from a Kansas Pacific Railroad train—a small thrill added to the modern convenience of traveling west by rail.
(North Wind Picture Archives)

In south Texas about 5 million head of longhorn cattle grazed on Anglo ranches, hardly worth bothering about because they could not be profitably marketed. In 1865, however, the Missouri Pacific Railroad reached Sedalia, Missouri, far enough west to be accessible across open land to the Texas herds. At the Sedalia railhead, which connected to eastern markets, a longhorn worth $3 in Texas might command $40. With this incentive, Texas ranchers inaugurated the famous Long Drive, hiring cowboys to herd cattle hundreds of miles north to the railroads that were pushing west across Kansas.

At Abilene, Ellsworth, and Dodge City ranchers sold their cattle, and trail-weary cowboys went on a binge. These cattle towns captured the nation's imagination as symbols of the Wild West. The reality was much more ordinary. The cowboys, many of them African Americans and Hispanics, were in fact farm hands on horseback, working long hours under harsh conditions for small pay. Colorful though it seemed, the Long Drive was actually a makeshift means of bridging a gap in the developing transportation system. As soon as railroads reached the Texas range country during the 1870s, ranchers abandoned the Long Drive.

The Texas ranchers owned or leased the land they used, sometimes in huge tracts. North of Texas, where the land was in the public domain, cattlemen simply helped themselves, treating the land as a free commodity for anyone able to put it to use. Hopeful ranchers would spot a likely area along a creek and claim as much land as they could qualify for as settlers under federal homesteading laws, plus what might be added by fraudulent claims taken out by one or two ranch hands. By a custom that quickly became established, ranchers had a "range right" to all the adjacent land rising up to the divide—the point where the land sloped down to the next creek.

The Cowboy at Work

The cowboy, celebrated in dime novels, was really a farm hand on horseback, with the skills to work on the range, including the ability to stay glued to his saddle while lassoing a steer. He earned $25 a month, plus meals and a bed in the bunkhouse, in return for long hours of lonesome, grueling work. But one can see in Charles Russell's vivid painting, *Jerked Down* (1907), why the cowhand could so readily be converted into a western hero.

(Thomas Gilcrease Institute of American History and Art)

News of easy money traveled fast. Calves cost only $5 a head, while steers sold for maybe $60 on the Chicago market. Rail connections were in place or coming in. And the grass was free. Profits of 40 percent per annum seemed sure. The rush was on, attracting from as far away as Europe both shrewd investors and romantics (like the recent Harvard graduate Teddy Roosevelt) eager for a taste of the Wild West. By the early 1880s the plains overflowed with cattle, decimating the grass and trampling the water holes.

A cycle of good weather only postponed the inevitable disaster. When it came— a hard winter in 1885, a severe drought the following summer, then record blizzards and bitter cold—cattle died by the hundreds of thousands. An awful scene of rotting carcasses greeted the cowhands riding out onto the range the following spring. Beef prices plunged when hard-pressed ranchers dumped the surviving cattle on the market. The boom collapsed, and investors fled, leaving behind a more enduring ecological disaster: the native grasses never recovered from the relentless overgrazing in the drought cycle.

Open-range ranching came to an end. Ranchers fenced their land and planted hay for the winter. No longer would cattle be left to fend for themselves on the open range. Hispanic grazers from New Mexico brought sheep in to feed on the mesquite and prickly pear that had replaced the native grasses. Sheep raising, previously scorned by ranchers as unmanly and resisted as a threat to cattle, became a major enterprise in the sparser high country. Some ranchers even sold out to the despised "nesters"—those who wanted to try farming the Great Plains.

HOMESTEADERS

Potential settlers, of course, needed first of all to be persuaded that crops would grow in that dry country. Powerful interests devoted themselves to overcoming the notion of a Great American Desert. Foremost were the railroads, eager to sell off the public land they had been granted—180 million acres of it—and develop traffic for their routes. They advertised aggressively, offered cut-rate tickets, and sold off their land holdings at bargain prices. Land speculators, steamship lines, and the western states and territories did all they could to encourage settlement of the Great Plains. So did the federal government, with its offer under the Homestead Act (1862) of 160 acres of public land to settlers.

"Why emigrate to Kansas?" asked a testimonial in *Western Trail*, the Rock Island Railroad's gazette. "Because it is the garden spot of the world. Because it will grow anything that any other country will grow, and with less work. Because it rains here more than any other place, and at just the right time."

As if to confirm the optimists, an exceptionally wet cycle occurred between 1878 and 1886. "As the plains are settled up we hear less and less of drouth, hot winds, alkali and other bugbears that used to hold back the adventurous," remarked one Nebraska man. Some settlers attributed the increased rainfall to soil cultivation and tree planting. Others credited God. As one settler remarked, "The Lord just knowed we needed more land an' He's gone and changed the climate."

No amount of optimism, however, could dispel the pain of migration. "That last separating word *Farewell!* sinks deeply into the heart," one pioneer woman recorded in her diary, thinking of family and friends left behind. But then came the treeless plains. "Such an air of desolation," wrote a Nebraska-bound woman; and from another woman in Texas, "Such a lonely country." To a Swedish emigrant like Ida Lindgren (see American Voices, "Swedish Emigrant in Frontier Kansas"), no place could have seemed farther from home or offered less hope of seeing family and friends again.

For some women this hard experience had a liberating side. Prescribed gender roles broke down as women shouldered men's work and became self-reliant in the face of danger and hardship. When husbands died or gave up, wives operated farms on their own. Under the Homestead Act, which accorded widows and single women the same rights as men, women filed 10 percent of the claims. "People afraid of coyotes and work and loneliness had better leave ranching alone," advised one woman homesteader. "At the same time, any woman who can stand her own company . . . will certainly succeed; will have independence, plenty to eat all the time, and a home of her own in the end."

Even with a man around, however, women contributed crucially to the farm enterprise. Farming might be thought of as a dual economy, in which men's labor

AMERICAN VOICES

Swedish Emigrant in Frontier Kansas

IDA LINDGREN

L ike many emigrants, Ida Lindgren did not find it easy to adjust to the harsh new life on the frontier. Her diary entries and letters home show that the adjustment for the first generation was never complete.

May 15, 1870 [Lake Sibley, Nebraska]

What shall I say? Why has the lord brought us here? Oh, I feel so oppressed, so unhappy! . . . We drove across endless, endless prairies, on narrow roads; no, no, not roads, tracks like those in the fields at home when they harvested grain. No forest but only a few trees which grow along the rivers and creeks. And then here and there you see a homestead and pass a little settlement. . . .

No date [probably written July 1870]

Claus and his wife lost their youngest child at Lake Sibley and it was very sad in many ways. There was no real cemetery but out on the prairie stood a large, solitary tree, and around it they bury their dead, without tolling of bells, without a pastor, and sometimes without any coffin. A coffin was made here for their child, it was not painted black, but we lined it with flowers and one of the men read the funeral service, and then there was a hymn, and that was all.

August 25, 1874 [Manhattan, Kansas]

It has been a long time since I have written, hasn't it? . . . When one never has anything fun to write about, it is no fun to write. . . . We have not had rain since the beginning of June, and then with this heat and often strong winds as well, you can imagine how everything has dried out. . . . Then one fine day there came millions, trillions of grasshoppers in great clouds, hiding the sun, and coming down into the fields, eating up everything that was still there, the leaves on the trees, peaches, grapes, cucumbers, onions, cabbage, everything, everything. Only the peach stones still hung on the trees, showing what had once been there.

July 1, 1877 [Manhattan, Kansas]

. . . It seems so strange to me when I think that more than seven years have passed since I have seen you all. . . . I can see so clearly that last glimpse I had of Mamma, standing alone amid all the tracks of Eslov station. Oliva I last saw sitting on her sofa in her red and black dress, holding little Brita, one month old, on her lap. And Wilhelm I last saw in Lund at the station, as he rolled away with the train, waving his last farewell to me. . . .

SOURCE: H. Arnold Barton, ed., *Letters from the Promised Land* (Minneapolis: University of Minnesota Press, 1975), pp. 143–45, 150–56.

brought in the big wage at harvest time while women's labor provisioned the family day by day and produced a steady bit of money for groceries. And if the crop failed, it was women's labor that carried the family through. No wonder farming communities placed a high premium on marriage: a mere 2.4 percent of Nebraska women in 1900 had never married.

Male or female, the vision of new land beckoned people onto the plains. By the 1870s the older agricultural states had filled up, and farmers looked hungrily westward. The same excitement took hold in northern Europe. Germans came and also, for the first time, Russians, Norwegians, and Swedes. At the peak of the "American fever" in 1882 over 105,000 Scandinavians emigrated to the United States. Swedish and Norwegian became the primary languages in parts of Minnesota and the Dakotas. Roughly a third of the farmers on the northern plains were foreign-born.

The motivation for most settlers, American or European, was to better themselves economically. But for some southern blacks Kansas briefly represented something more precious—a new promised land of Canaan. In the spring of 1879, with Reconstruction over and federal protection withdrawn, black communities fearful of white vengeance were swept by religious enthusiasm for Kansas. Within a month or so some 6,000 blacks from Mississippi and Louisiana had arrived via St. Louis, most of them with nothing more than the clothes on their backs and faith in the Lord. How many of these Exodusters remained is hard to say, but the 1880 census reported 40,000 blacks in Kansas—by far the largest African American concentration in the West aside from Texas, whose expanding cotton frontier attracted hundreds of thousands of black migrants during the 1870s and 1880s.

No matter where they came from, homesteaders found the plains an alien land. A cloud of grasshoppers might descend and destroy a crop in a day; a brushfire or hailstorm could do the job in an hour. What forested land had always provided—springs for water, lumber for cabins and fencing, ample firewood—was absent. For shelter settlers often cut dugouts into hillsides and, after a season or two, erected sod houses made of turf.

The absence of trees, on the other hand, meant an easier time clearing the land. New technology overcame obstacles once thought insurmountable: steel plows enabled homesteaders to break the tightly matted ground, barbed wire provided cheap fencing against roaming cattle. Strains of hard-kernel wheat tolerant of the extreme temperatures of the plains came from Europe. Homesteaders harvested good crops while the wet cycle held and began to anticipate the wood-frame house, deep well, and full coal bin that might make life tolerable on the plains.

Then in the latter 1880s the dry years came and shattered those hopeful calculations. "From day to day," reported the budding novelist Stephen Crane from Nebraska, "a wind hot as an oven's fury . . . raged like a pestilence," destroying the crops and leaving farmers "helpless, with no weapon against this terrible and inscrutable wrath of nature." Land only recently settled emptied out as homesteaders fled in defeat. The Dakotas lost 50,000 settlers between 1885 and 1890, and comparable departures occurred up and down the drought-stricken plains.

Buffalo Chips

With no trees around for firewood, settlers on the plains had to make do with dried cow and buffalo droppings. Gathering the "buffalo chips" must have been a regular chore for Ada McColl on her homestead near Lakin, Kansas (1893).

(The Kansas State Historical Society, Topeka)

Other settlers held on grimly. Stripped of the illusion that rain followed the plow, the survivors came to terms with the semiarid climate prevailing west of the ninety-eighth meridian. Mormons in the area near the Great Salt Lake (see Chapter 12) had demonstrated how irrigation could turn a wasteland into a garden. But the Great Plains generally lacked the surface water needed for irrigation. The answer lay in dry-farming methods, which involved deep planting to bring subsoil moisture to the roots and quick harrowing after rainfalls to turn over a dry mulch that slowed evaporation. Dry farming developed most fully on the corporate farms that covered up to 100,000 acres in the Red River Valley in North Dakota. But in semiarid country even family farms were not viable with less than 300 acres of cereal crops and machinery for plowing, planting, and harvesting. Dry farming was not for the unequipped homesteader.

By the turn of the century the Great Plains had fully submitted to agricultural development. About half the nation's cattle and sheep, a third of its cereal crops, and nearly three-fifths of its wheat came from the newly settled lands. In this process there was little of the "pioneering" that Americans associated with the westward movement. The railroads came before the settlers, eastern capital financed the ranching bonanza, and agriculture depended on sophisticated dry-farming techniques and modern machinery.

And where was the economic capital of the Great Plains? Far off in Chicago. There, at the hub of the nation's rail system, the wheat pit traded western grain and consigned it to world markets; the great packing houses slaughtered western cattle and supplied the nation with sausage, bacon, and sides of beef. In return western farmers and ranchers got lumber, barbed wire, McCormick reapers, and Sears Roebuck catalogues. Chicago was truly "nature's metropolis."

THE FATE OF THE INDIANS

What of the Native Americans who had inhabited the Great Plains? Basically, their history has been told in the foregoing account of western settlement. "The white children have surrounded me and have left me nothing but an island," lamented the great Sioux chief Red Cloud in 1870, the year after the completion of the transcontinental railroad. "When we first had all this land we were strong; now we are all melting like snow on a hillside, while you are grown like spring grass."

Settlement occurred despite the provisions for a permanent Indian country that had been written into federal law and ratified by treaties with various tribes. As incursions into their lands increased from the late 1850s onward, the Indians resisted as best they could, striking back all along the frontier: the Apaches in the Southwest, the Cheyennes and Arapahos in Colorado, the Sioux in the Wyoming and Dakota territories. Indians hoped that if they resisted stubbornly enough and exacted a high enough price, whites would tire of the struggle and leave them in peace. This reasoning seemed not altogether fanciful, given the country's exhaustion after the Civil War. But the federal government did not give up; instead, it formulated a new reservation policy for dealing with the western Indians.

Few whites questioned the necessity of moving the Native Americans out of the path of settlement and into reservations. That, indeed, had been the fate of the eastern and southern tribes. Now, however, Indian removal included something new: a planned approach for weaning the Indians from their tribal way of life. To this end a peace commission was appointed in 1867 to end the fighting and negotiate treaties by which the western Indians would cede their lands and move to reservations. There, under the guidance of the Office of Indian Affairs, they would be wards of the government until they learned "to walk on the white man's road."

The government set aside two extensive areas. It allocated the southwestern quarter of the Dakota Territory—present-day South Dakota west of the Missouri River—to the Teton Sioux tribes. And it assigned what is now Oklahoma to the southern plains Indians as well as to the Five Civilized Tribes—the Choctaws, Cherokees, Chickasaws, Creeks, and Seminoles—who had been forceably removed there thirty years before (see Chapter 11). Scattered reservations went to the Apaches, Navahos, and Utes in the Southwest and to the mountain Indians in the Rockies and beyond.

That the Indians would resist was inevitable. "You might as well expect the rivers to run backward as that any man who was born a free man should be contented when penned up and denied liberty to go where he pleases," said Chief Joseph of the Nez Percé, who led his people in 1877 on a remarkable 1,500-mile march from eastern Oregon almost to Canada trying to escape confinement on a small reservation.

The U.S. Army was thinly spread, having been cut after the Civil War to a total force of 27,000. But these were seasoned troops, including 2,000 black cavalrymen of the Ninth and Tenth regiments, whom Indians called, with grim respect, "buffalo soldiers." Technology also favored the army. Telegraph communications and railroads enabled the troopers to concentrate quickly; repeating rifles and Gatling machine guns increased their firepower. As fighting intensified in the mid-1870s, a reluctant Congress appropriated funds for more western troopers. Because of tribal rivalries, the army could always find Indian allies. Worst of all for the Indians, however, beyond the formidable U.S. Army or their own disunity, was the overwhelming impact of white settlement.

Resisting the reservations, the Indians fought on for years—in Kansas in 1868 and 1869, in the Red River Valley of Texas in 1874, and sporadically in New Mexico among the Apaches until the capture of Geronimo in 1886. On the northern plains the crisis came in 1875, when the Indian Office, despite an 1868 treaty guarantee, ordered the Sioux to vacate their Powder River hunting grounds and withdraw to the reservation.

Led by Sitting Bull, Sioux and Cheyenne warriors gathered on the Little Big Horn River to the west of the Powder River country. In a typical concentrating maneuver, army columns from widely separated forts converged on the Little Big Horn from three sides. The Seventh Cavalry, commanded by George A. Custer, came upon the main Sioux encampment on June 25, 1876. Disregarding orders the reckless Custer sought out battle on his own. He attacked from three sides, hoping to capitalize on the element of surprise. But his forces were stretched too thin. Two groups fell back to defensive positions, but Custer's force of 256 men was surrounded and annihilated by Crazy Horse's warriors. It was a great Indian victory but not a decisive one. The day of reckoning was merely postponed.

Pursued by the military and physically exhausted, the Sioux bands one by one gave up and moved onto the reservation. Last to give up were Sitting Bull's followers. They had retreated to Canada, but in 1881 after five hard years they recrossed the border and surrendered at Fort Buford, Montana.

Not Indian resistance but white land hunger wrecked the reservation solution. In the mid-1870s prospectors began to dig gold in the Black Hills—sacred ground to the Sioux and entirely inside their reservation. Unable to hold back the prospectors or to buy out the Sioux, the government opened up the Black Hills to gold seekers at their own risk. In 1877 after Sioux resistance had crumbled, federal agents forced the tribes to cede the western third of their Dakota reservation.

The Indian Territory of Oklahoma met the same fate. Two million acres in the heart of the territory had not been assigned to any tribe, and white homesteaders coveted that fertile land. The "Boomer" movement, stirred up initially by railroads operating in the Indian Territory, agitated tirelessly to open this so-called Oklahoma District. In 1889 the government gave in and placed the Oklahoma District under the Homestead Act. On April 22, 1889, a horde of claimants rushed in and staked out the entire district within a few hours. Two tent cities—Guthrie with 15,000 people and Oklahoma City with 10,000—were in full swing by nightfall.

The completion of the land-grabbing process was hastened, ironically, by the avowed friends of the Native Americans. The Indians had never lacked sympathizers, especially in the East. After the Civil War reformers created the Indian Rights Association. The movement got a boost from Helen Hunt Jackson's powerful book *A Century of Dishonor* (1881), which told the story of the unjust treatment of the Indians. The reformers, however, had little sympathy for the tribal way of life. They could imagine no other future for the Indian than assimilation into white society (see American Voices, "Becoming White"). And this in turn required that Native Americans enjoy the same rights and have the same benefit of private property as did all American citizens.

The resulting policy called for the division of reservation lands into individually owned parcels. With the blessing of reformers the Dawes Act of 1887 authorized the allotment of tribal lands, with 160 acres for each family head and smaller parcels for individuals. The land would be held in trust by the government for twenty-five years, and the Indians would become U.S. citizens. Remaining reservation lands would be sold off, with the proceeds placed in an Indian education fund.

The Sioux were among the first to bear the brunt of the Dawes Act. The federal government, announcing that it had gained tribal approval, opened their "surplus" land to white settlement on February 10, 1887. But no surveys had been made nor any provision for the Indians living in the ceded areas. On top of these signs of bad faith drought wiped out the Indians' crops. It seemed beyond endurance: they had lost their ancestral lands, they faced a future as farmers that was alien to all their traditions, and immediately confronting them was a winter of starvation.

But news of salvation had also come. An Indian messiah, a holy man who called himself Wovoka, was preaching a new religion on a Paiute reservation in Nevada. In a vision Wovoka had gone to heaven and received God's word that the world would be regenerated. The whites would disappear, all the Indians of past generations would return to earth, and life on the Great Plains would be as it was before the white man appeared. All this would come to pass in the spring of 1891. Awaiting that great day the Indians should follow Wovoka's commandments and practice the Ghost Dance, a daylong ritual that sent the spirits of the dancers rising to heaven. As the frenzy of the Ghost Dance swept through the Sioux encampments in the fall of 1890, resident whites became alarmed and called for army intervention.

Wovoka had an especially fervent following in the Minneconjou tribe, where the medicine man Yellow Bird held sway. But their chief Big Foot had fallen desperately ill with pneumonia, and the Minneconjous agreed to come in under military escort to an encampment at Wounded Knee Creek on December 28. The next morning when the soldiers attempted to disarm the Indians, a battle exploded in the camp. Among the U.S. troopers, 25 died; among the Indians, 146 men, women, and children perished, many of them shot down as they fled.

AMERICAN VOICES

Becoming White

ZITKALA-SA (GERTRUDE SIMMONS BONNIN)

Zitkala-Sa, afterward the author Gertrude Simmons Bonnin, recalled in 1900 her painful transformation from Sioux child to pupil at a mission school.

The first day . . . a paleface woman, with white hair, came up after us. We were placed in a line of girls who were marching into the dining room. These were Indian girls, in stiff shoes and closely clinging dresses. The small girls wore sleeved aprons and shingled hair. As I walked noiselessly in my soft mocassins, I felt like sinking into the floor, for my blanket had been stripped from my shoulders. . . . Late in the morning, my friend Judewin gave me a terrible warning. Judewin knew a few words of English; and she had overheard the paleface woman talk about cutting our long, heavy hair. Our mothers had taught us that only unskilled warriors who were captured had their hair shingled by the enemy. Among our people, short hair was worn by mourners, and shingled hair by cowards! . . . In spite of myself, I was carried downstairs and tied fast in a chair. I cried aloud, shaking my head all the while until I felt the cold blades of the scissors against my neck, and heard them gnaw off one of my thick black braids. Then I lost my spirit. . . .

Now, as I look back upon the recent past, I see it from a distance, as a whole. I remember how, from morning till evening, many specimens of civilized peoples visited the Indian school. The city folks with canes and eyeglass, the countrymen with sunburned cheeks and clumsy feet . . . alike astounded at seeing the children of savage warriors so docile and industrious. . . .

In this fashion many have passed through the Indian schools during the last decade, afterward to boast of their charity to the North American Indian. But few there are who have paused to question whether real life or long lasting death lies beneath this semblance of civilization.

SOURCE: Linda K. Kerber and Jane De-Hart Mathews, eds., *Women's America: Refocusing the Past*, 2d ed. (New York: Oxford University Press, 1987), pp. 254–57.

Wounded Knee was the final episode in the long war of suppression of the plains Indians. The division of communal lands now proceeded without hindrance. In the Dakota Territory the Teton Sioux fared relatively well, and many of the younger generation settled down as small farmers and stock raisers. Ironically, the more fortunate tribes were probably those occupying poor land that did not attract white settlement and thus were spared the allotment process. The flood of whites into South Dakota and Oklahoma, on the other hand, left the Indians as small minorities in lands once wholly theirs—20,000 Sioux in a South Dakotan population of 400,000 in 1900, 70,000 of various tribes in a population of a million when Oklahoma became a state in 1907.

The Far West

On the western edge of the Great Plains, the Rocky Mountains rise up to form a great barrier between the mostly flat eastern two-thirds of the country and the Far West. Beyond the Rockies lie two vast plateaus, the Columbian plateau extending into eastern Oregon and Washington and, flanking the southern Rockies, the Colorado plateau. Where they break off, the plateaus carve out the desertlike Great Basin that covers western Utah and all of Nevada. Separating this arid interior from the Pacific Ocean are two great mountain ranges—the Sierra Nevada and, to the north, the Cascades—beyond which lies a coastal region that is cool and rainy to the north but increasingly dry southward, until in southern California rainfall becomes almost as sparse as in the interior.

What most impressed Americans about this far western country was its sheer inhospitability. The transmountain West could not be occupied in standard American fashion—that is, by a multitude of settlers moving westward along a broad front, blanketing the land and, homestead by homestead, bringing it under cultivation. The wagon trains moving to Oregon's Willamette River Valley adopted an entirely different method of occupation—the planting of scattered settlements in a vast, mostly barren landscape.

New Spain had pioneered this strategy when in 1598 it had sent the first contingents of soldiers and settlers 700 miles northward from Mexico into the upper Rio Grande Valley. When the United States seized the Southwest 250 years later, major Hispanic settlements existed in New Mexico and California, with lesser settlements scattered along the borderlands into south Texas. At that time, aside from Oregon, the only significant Anglo settlement was around the Salt Lake in Utah, where Mormons had moved to escape persecution and plant a New Zion. Fewer than 100,000 Euro-Americans—roughly 25,000 of them Anglo, the rest Hispanic—lived in the entire Far West when it became U.S. territory in 1848.

THE MINING FRONTIER

More emigrants would be coming certainly, but the Far West seemed unlikely to be much of a magnet. California was "hilly and mountainous," noted a U.S. naval officer in 1849, too dry for farming and surely not "susceptible of supporting a very large population." He had not taken account of the recent discovery of gold in the Sierra foothills, however. California would indeed support a very large population, drawn not by the lure of arable land but by dreams of gold.

Extraction of mineral wealth became the basis for the Far West's development (see Map 16.2). This meant, first of all, explosive growth. By 1860, when the Great Plains was still Indian country, California was a booming state with 300,000 residents. There was also a burst of city building. Overnight San Francisco became a bustling metropolis—it had 57,000 residents by 1860—and was the hub of a mining empire that stretched to the Rockies. The distinctive pattern of geographically

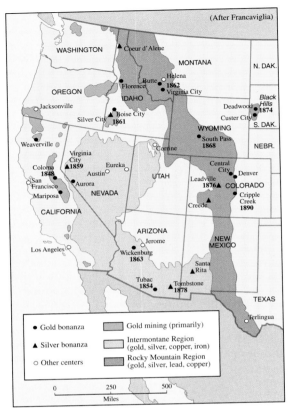

(After Francaviglia)

M A P 16.2
The Mining Frontier, 1848–1890

The Far West was America's gold country because of its geological history. Veins of gold and silver form when molten material from the earth's core is forced up into fissures caused by the tectonic movements that create mountain ranges, such as the ones that dominate the far western landscape. It was these veins, the product of mountain-forming activity many thousands of years earlier, that prospectors began to discover after 1848 and furiously exploit. Although widely dispersed across the Far West, the lodes that they found followed the mountain ranges, bisecting the region and bypassing the great plateaus not shaped by the ancient tectonic activity.

dispersed settlement persisted, driven now, however, by a proliferation of mining sites and by people moving not east to west but west to east, coming mainly from California.

By the mid-1850s as easy pickings in the California gold country diminished, prospectors began to pull out and spread across the West in hopes of striking it rich elsewhere. Gold was discovered on the Nevada side of the Sierras, in the Colorado Rockies, and along the Fraser River in British Columbia. New strikes occurred in Montana and Wyoming during the 1860s, a decade later in the Black Hills of South Dakota, and in the Coeur d'Alene region of Idaho during the 1880s.

As the news of each gold strike spread, a wild, remote area turned almost overnight into a mob scene of prospectors, traders, gamblers, prostitutes, and saloon keepers. At least 100,000 fortune seekers flocked to the Pike's Peak area of Colorado in the spring of 1859. Trespassers on government or Indian land, the prospectors made their own law. The mining codes devised at community meetings limited the size of a mining claim to what a person could reasonably work. This kind of informal lawmaking also became an instrument for excluding or discriminating against Mexicans, Chinese, and African Americans in the gold fields. And it turned into hangman's justice for the many outlaws who infested the mining camps.

The heyday of the prospectors at each site was always brief. They were equipped only to skim gold from stream beds and surface outcroppings. Extracting the metal locked in underground lodes required mine shafts and crushing mills—and hence capital, technology, and business organization. The original claim holders quickly sold out when a generous bidder came along, as gold-rush prospecting gave way to entrepreneurial development and large-scale mining. Rough camps turned into big towns.

Nevada's Virginia City, for example, started out as a bawdy, ramshackle mining camp, but with the opening of the Comstock silver lode in 1859 it soon boasted a stock exchange, ostentatious mansions for the mining kings, fancy hotels, and even Shakespearean theater. Virginia City remained a boomtown nevertheless. It was a magnet for job seekers of both sexes: men laboring as miners at $4 a day; the wage-earning women, many of them, becoming dance-hall entertainers and prostitutes because that was the best they could do in Virginia City. In 1870 a hundred saloons operated day and night, brothels lined D Street, and men outnumbered women two to one.

In its final stage the mining frontier entered the industrial economy. At some sites gold and silver proved less profitable than the commoner metals—copper, lead, zinc—for which there was a huge demand in manufacturing industries. Copper mining thrived in the Butte district of Montana. In the 1890s the Coeur d'Alene silver district became the nation's main source of lead and zinc. Entrepreneurs raised capital, built rail connections, devised new extraction methods for the lower-grade copper deposits, constructed smelting facilities, and recruited a labor force.

Western miners were industrial workers, and like other workers they organized trade unions. But relations with management, once they soured during the depressed 1890s, became unusually violent. In 1892 at Coeur d'Alene, Idaho, striking miners fought gun battles with company guards, sent a car of explosive powder careening into the Frisco mine, and threatened to blow up the smelters. Martial law was declared, strikers were crowded into "bullpens" (enclosed stockades), and the strike was broken. Similarly violent strikes took place in 1894 at Cripple Creek, Colorado, in 1896 at Leadville, Colorado, and again at Coeur d'Alene in 1899.

But for its mineral wealth the Far West's history would certainly have been very different. Before the discovery of gold at Sutter's mill Oregon's Willamette River Valley, not dry California, attracted most westward-bound settlers. And without the gold rush California would likely have remained like the Willamette Valley—an economic backwater with no markets for its products and a slow-growing population. In 1860, although already a state, Oregon had scarcely 25,000 inhabitants, and its principal city, Portland, was little more than a village. Booming California and its tributary mining country pulled Oregon from the doldrums by creating a market for the state's produce and timber. During the 1880s Oregon and Washington (which became a state in 1889) grew prodigiously. Where scarcely 100,000 settlers had lived twenty years earlier, there were by 1890 nearly three-quarters of a million. Portland and, even more dramatically, Seattle blossomed into important commercial centers, both prospering from a robust mixed economy of farming, ranching, logging, and fishing.

At a certain point, especially as railroads opened up eastern markets, this diversified growth became self-sustaining. But what had triggered it, what had provided the first markets and underwritten the economic infrastructure, was the bonanza mining economy, at the hub of which stood San Francisco, metropolis for the entire Far West.

HISPANICS, CHINESE, ANGLOS

The first Europeans to enter the Far West—two centuries before the earliest Anglos—were Hispanics moving northward out of Mexico. There, along a 1,500-mile southwestern borderland, outposts had been planted over many years by the viceroys of New Spain. Most populous and best established were the settlements along New Mexico's upper Rio Grande Valley; the main town, Santa Fe, was over 200 years old and contained 4,635 residents in 1860. Farther down the Rio Grande was El Paso, nearly as old but much smaller, and to the west in present-day Arizona, Tucson, an old presidio, or garrison, town. At the western end of this Hispanic crescent, in California, a Spanish-speaking population was spread thinly in presidio towns along the coast and on a patchwork of great ranches.

The economy of the Hispanic Southwest was pastoral, consisting primarily of cattle and sheep ranching. In south Texas there were family-run ranches. Everywhere else the social order was highly stratified. At the top stood an elite, beneficiaries of royal land grants, proudly Spanish, devoted to the traditional life of a landed aristocracy. Below them, with little in between, was a laboring population of servants, artisans, vaqueros (cowboys), and farm hands. New Mexico also contained a large mestizo population—people of mixed Hispanic and Indian blood. They were a Spanish-speaking and Catholic peasantry but still faithful in their village life and farming methods to their Pueblo heritage.

Pueblo Indians, although their dominance of the Rio Grande Valley had long passed, still occupied much of the region, living in the old ways in abobe villages and making the New Mexico countryside a patchwork of Hispanic and Pueblo settlements. To the north a vibrant new people, the Navajos, had appeared, warriors like the Apaches from whom they had sprung but also skilled at crafts and sheep raising.

New Mexico was one place where European and native American cultures managed a successful, if uneasy, coexistence and where the Indian inhabitants were equipped to hold their own against the Anglo challenge. In California, by contrast, the Hispanic occupation was harder on the indigenous hunter-gatherer peoples, undermining their tribal structure, reducing them to coerced labor, and making them easy prey for the aggressive Anglo miners and settlers, who, in short order, nearly wiped out California's once numerous Indian population.

The fate of the Hispanic Southwest after its incorporation into the United States depended on the rate of Anglo immigration. In New Mexico, which remained off the beaten track even after the arrival of railroads in the 1880s, the Santa Fe elite more than held its own, incorporating the Anglo newcomers into Hispanic society through intermarriage and business partnerships. In California, on the other hand, the expropriation of the great ranches was relentless, even though the 1848 peace treaty with Mexico had recognized the property rights of the *californios* and had made them U.S. citizens. Around San Francisco the ranch system disappeared almost in a puff of smoke. Farther south, where Anglos were slow to arrive, the dons held on longer, but by the 1880s just a handful of the original families still retained their Mexican land grants.

The New Mexico peasants found themselves equally embattled. Crucial to their livelihood were grazing rights on communal lands. But these were customary rights that could not withstand legal challenge when Anglo ranchers established title and began putting up fences. The peasants responded resiliently. Their subsistence economy relied on a division of labor that gave women a central productive role in the village economy. Women tended the small gardens, engaged in village bartering, and maintained the households. With the loss of the communal lands the men began migrating seasonally to railway work or the Colorado mines and sugar-beet fields, earning crucial dollars while leaving the village economy in their wives' hands.

Elsewhere, hard-pressed Hispanic inhabitants struck back for what they considered rightfully theirs. When Anglo ranchers began to fence in communal lands in San Miguel County, the New Mexicans long settled there, *los pobres* (the poor ones), organized themselves as masked raiders and in 1889 and 1890 mounted an effective campaign of harassment against the interlopers. After 1900 when Anglo farmers swarmed into south Texas bent on exploiting new irrigation methods, the displaced *Tejanos* responded with sporadic but persistent night-riding attacks. Much of the raiding by Mexican "bandits" from across the border in the years before World War I was really more in the nature of a civil war by embittered *Tejanos* who had lived north of Rio Grande for generations.

But they, like the New Mexico villagers who became seasonal wage laborers, could not avoid being driven into the ranks of a Mexican American working class as the Anglo economy developed. This same development also began to attract increasing numbers of immigrants from Old Mexico.

All along the Southwest borderlands economic activity was picking up in the late nineteenth century. Railroads were being built, copper mines opening in Arizona, cotton and vegetable agriculture developing in south Texas, and fruit growing in southern California. In Texas the Hispanic population increased from about 20,000 in 1850 to 165,000 in 1900. Some came as contract workers for railway gangs and harvest crews; virtually all were relegated to the lowest-paying and most backbreaking work; and everywhere they were discriminated against and reviled by higher-status Anglo workers.

What stimulated the Mexican migration, of course, was the enormous demand for workers by a region undergoing explosive development, which also accounted for the high numbers of European immigrants in the West. In California where they were most heavily concentrated, roughly one-third of the population was foreign-

Mexican Miners

When large-scale mining began to develop in Arizona and New Mexico in the late nineteenth century, Mexicans crossed the border to earn Yankee dollars. In this unidentified photograph from the 1890s the men are wearing traditional clothing, indicating perhaps that they are recent arrivals at the mine. (Wyoming State Archives, Department of State Parks and Cultural Resources)

born, more than twice the level for the country as a whole. Many came from Europe. Most numerous were the Irish, followed by the Germans and British. But there was also another immigrant group unique to the West—the Chinese.

Attracted first by the California gold rush of 1849, 200,000 Chinese came to the United States over the next three decades. In those years they constituted a considerable minority of California's population—around 9 percent—and because virtually all were actively employed, they represented a much larger proportion of the state's labor force, probably a quarter. Elsewhere in the West, at the crest of mining activity, their presence could surge spectacularly—for example, to over 25 percent of Idaho's population in 1870.

The arrival of the Chinese in North America was part of a worldwide Asian migration that began in the mid-nineteenth century. Driven by poverty Chinese went to Australia, Hawaii, and Latin America; Indians went to Fiji and South Africa; and Javanese to Dutch colonies in the Caribbean. Most of these Asians migrated as indentured servants, which in effect made them the property of others. In America, however, indentured servitude was no longer lawful—by the 1820s state courts were ruling that it constituted involuntary servitude—so the Chinese came as free workers. Their passage was financed by a *credit-ticket system,* by which they borrowed passage money from a broker while retaining their personal freedom and right to choose their employers.

Once in America, however, Chinese immigrants normally entered the orbit of the Six Companies—a powerful confederation of Chinese merchants in San Francisco's Chinatown. Most of the arrivals were unattached males eager to earn a stake and return to their native Cantonese villages. The Six Companies acted not only as an employment agency but provided new arrivals with the social and commercial services they needed to survive in an alien world. The few Chinese women— the male to female ratio was thirteen to one—worked mostly as servants and prostitutes, sad victims of the desperate poverty that drove the Chinese to America. Some were sold by impoverished parents; others were tricked by procurers and transported to America.

Until the early 1860s when surface mining played out, Chinese men labored mainly in the California gold fields—as prospectors where the white miners permitted it, as laborers and cooks where they did not. Then, when construction began on the transcontinental railroad, the Central Pacific hired Chinese workers. Eventually they constituted four-fifths of the railroad's labor force, doing most of the pick-and-shovel labor laying the railroad track across the Sierras. Many were recruited directly from around Canton by labor agents to work in gangs run by "China bosses," who not only supervised but fed, housed, paid, and often cheated them.

When the transcontinental railroad was completed in 1869, the Chinese scattered. Some stayed in railway construction gangs, while others labored on swamp-drainage projects in the Central Valley, worked as agricultural workers, and, if they were lucky, became small farmers and orchardists. The mining districts of Idaho, Montana, and Colorado also attracted large numbers of Chinese, but according to the 1880 census nearly three-quarters remained in California. "Wherever we put them, we found them good," remarked Charles Crocker, one of the promoters of the Central Pacific. "Their orderly and industrious habits make them a very desirable class of immigrants."

White workers, however, did not share the employers' enthusiasm for the Chinese. In other parts of the country racism was directed against African Americans; in California, where there were few blacks, it found a target in the Chinese. "They practice all the unnameable vices of the East," wrote the young journalist Henry George. "They are utter heathens, treacherous, sensual, cowardly and cruel." Sadly, this vicious racism was intertwined with labor's republican ideals. The Chinese, argued George, would drive out free labor, "make nabobs and princes of our capitalists, and crush our working classes into the dust . . . substitut[ing] . . . a population of serfs and their masters for that population of intelligent freemen who are our glory and our strength."

The anti-Chinese frenzy climaxed in San Francisco in the late 1870s when mobs ruled the streets. The fiercest agitator, an Irish teamster named Denis Kearney, quickly became a dominant figure in the California labor movement. Under the slogan "The Chinese Must Go!" Kearney led a Workingmen's Party against the state's major parties. Democrats and Republicans, however, jumped on the bandwagon, joining together in 1879 to write a new state constitution replete with anti-Chinese provisions and pressuring Washington to take up the issue. In 1882 Congress finally passed the Chinese Exclusion Act, which barred the further entry of Chinese laborers into the country.

The injustice of this law—no other nationality was similarly targeted—rankled the Chinese. Why us, protested one woman to a federal agent, and not the Irish, "who [are] always drunk and fighting?" Middle-class and American-born Chinese, who were free to come and go, routinely registered a newly born son after each trip to China, enabling many an unrelated "paper son" to enter the country. Even so, resourceful as the Chinese were at evading the exclusion law, the flow of immigrants slowed to a trickle.

But the job opportunities that had attracted the Chinese to America did not subside. If anything, the West's agricultural development intensified the demand for cheap labor, especially in California, which was shifting from wheat, the state's first great cash crop, to fruits and vegetables. Such intensive agriculture required lots of workers—stoop labor, meagerly paid, and mostly seasonal. This was not, as one San Francisco journalist put it, "white men's work." That ugly phrase serves as a touchstone for California agricultural labor as it would thereafter develop—a kind of caste labor system, always drawing some downtrodden, footloose whites, yet basically defined along color lines.

But if not the Chinese, then who? First, Japanese immigrants, who came in increasing numbers and by the early twentieth century constituted half the state's agricultural labor force. Then, when anti-Japanese agitation closed off that population flow in 1908, Mexico became the next, essentially permanent, source of migratory workers for California's booming commercial agriculture.

The irony of the West's social evolution is painful to behold. Here was a land of limitless opportunity, boastful of its democratic egalitarianism, and yet simultaneously, and from its very birth, a racially torn society, at once exploiting and despising the Hispanic and Asian minorities whose hard labor helped make the Far West the enviable land it was.

GOLDEN CALIFORNIA

Life in California contained all that the modern world of 1890 had to offer—cosmopolitan San Francisco, comfortable travel, a high living standard, colleges and universities, even resident painters and writers. Yet California was still remote from the rest of America, still a long journey away, and, of course, differently and spectacularly endowed by nature. Location, environment, and history all conspired to set California somewhat apart from the American nation. And so, in certain ways, did the Californians.

What Californians yearned for was a cultural tradition of their own. Closest to hand was the bonanza era of the forty-niners, captured on paper by one Samuel Clemens. Clemens did a bit of prospecting, became a reporter, and adopted the pen name Mark Twain. Listening to the old miners of Angel's Camp in 1865, Twain jotted one tale down in his notebook, as follows:

> Coleman with his jumping frog—bet stranger $50—stranger had no frog, and C. got him one:—in the meantime stranger filled C's frog full of shot and he couldn't jump. The stranger's frog won.

In Twain's hands, this fragment was transformed in 1875 into a tall tale that caught the imagination of the country and made his reputation as a humorist. "The Celebrated Jumping Frog of Calaveras County" somehow encapsulated the entire world of make-or-break optimism in the mining camps.

In short stories such as "The Luck of Roaring Camp" and "The Outcasts of Poker Flat," Twain's fellow San Franciscan Bret Harte developed this theme in a more literary fashion and firmly implanted it in California's memory. But this past was too raw, too suggestive of the tattered beginnings of so many of the state's leading citizens—in short, too disreputable—for an up-and-coming society.

Then in 1884 Helen Hunt Jackson published her novel *Ramona*. In this story of a half-Indian girl caught between two cultures, Jackson intended to advance the cause of the Native Americans, but she placed her tale in the evocative context of Old California, and that rang a bell. By then the chain of missions planted by the Catholic Church had been long abandoned. The padres were wholly forgotten, their Indian converts scattered and in dire poverty. Now that lost world of "sun, silence and adobe" became all the rage. Sentimental novels and histories appeared in abundance. There was a movement to restore the missions. Many communities began to stage Spanish fiestas, and the mission style of architecture enjoyed a great vogue among developers.

In its Spanish past California found the cultural traditions it needed. The same kind of discovery was taking place elsewhere in the Southwest, although in the case of Santa Fe and Taos there were live Hispanic cultures to celebrate.

All this enthusiasm was, of course, strongly tinged with commercialism. And so was a second distinctive feature of California's development—the exploitation of its climate. While northern California boomed, the southern part of the state was neglected and thinly populated, too dry for anything but grazing and some chancy wheat growing. What it did have, however, was an abundance of sunshine. At the beginning of the 1880s there burst on the country amazing news of the charms of southern California, where "there is not any malaria, hay fever, loss of appetite, or languor in the air; nor any thunder, lightning, mad dogs . . . or cold snaps." This publicity was mostly the work of the Southern Pacific Railroad, which

***Kitty Tatch and Friend on Glacier
Point, Yosemite***

From the time the Yosemite Valley
was set aside in 1864 as a place for
"public pleasuring, resort, and recreation," it attracted a stream of
tourists eager to experience the
grandeur of the American West. As is
suggested by this photograph taken
sometime in the 1890s, the magic of
Yosemite was enough to set even
staid young ladies dancing.
(Yosemite National Park Research Library,
Yosemite National Park, CA)

had reached Los Angeles in 1876 and was eager for business. When the Santa Fe arrived in 1885, a furious rate war broke out, and it became possible to travel by train
from Chicago or St. Louis to Los Angeles for $25 or less. Thousands of people,
mostly midwesterners, poured in. Los Angeles County, with fewer than 3 percent
of the state's population in 1870, had 12 percent by 1900. By then southern
California had firmly established itself as the land of sunshine and orange groves.
It had found a way to translate climate into riches.

That California was specially favored by nature some Californians knew even
as the great stands of redwoods and sugar pine were being hacked down, the streams
polluted, and the hills torn apart by reckless mining techniques. Back in 1864 influential Americans who had seen the Sierras prevailed on Congress to grant to the
state of California "the Cleft, or Gorge in the granite peak of the Sierra Nevada
Mountain, known as Yosemite Valley," which would be reserved "for public pleasuring, resort, and recreation." When the young naturalist John Muir arrived in California four years later, he headed straight for Yosemite. Its "grandeur . . . comes as

an endless revelation," he wrote. Muir and others like him became devoted to protecting the High Sierras from "despoiling gain-seekers . . . eagerly trying to make everything immediately and selfishly commercial." One result was the creation of California's national parks in 1890—Yosemite, Sequoia, King's Canyon. Another was the formation in 1892 of the Sierra Club, which became a powerful voice for the defenders of California's wilderness.

They won some and lost some. Advocates of water-resource development insisted that California's irrigated agriculture and thirsty cities could not grow without tapping the abundant snowpack of the Sierras. By the turn of the century Los Angeles faced a water crisis that threatened its growth. The answer was a 238-mile aqueduct to the Owens River in the southern Sierras. A bitter controversy blew up over this immense project, driven by the resistance of local residents to the flooding of the beautiful Owens Valley. More painful for John Muir and his preservationist allies was their failure to save the Hetch Hetchy gorge, north of Yosemite National Park. After years of controversy the federal government in 1913 approved the damming of Hetch Hetchy Valley to serve the water needs of San Francisco.

When the stakes became high enough, nature lovers like John Muir generally came out on the short end. Even so, something original and distinctive had been added to California's heritage—the linking of a society's well-being with the preservation of its natural environment. This realization, in turn, said something important about the nation's relationship to the West. If the urge to conquer and exploit persisted, at least it was now tempered by a sense that nature's bounty was not limitless. And this, more than any announcement by the census that a "frontier line" no longer existed, registered the country's acceptance that the era of heedless westward expansion had ended.

For Further Exploration

The starting point for western history is Frederick Jackson Turner's famous essay, "The Significance of the Frontier in American History" (1893). In recent years there has been a reaction against Turnerian scholarship for being Eurocentric—for seeing western history only through the eyes of frontiersmen and settlers—and for masking the rapacious and environmentally destructive underside of western settlement. Patricia N. Limerick's skillfully argued *The Legacy of Conquest* (1987) opened the debate. Richard White, *"It's Your Misfortune and None of My Own": A New History of the American West* (1991), provides the fullest synthesis. On women's experiences—another primary concern of the new scholarship—a useful introduction is Susan Armitage and Elizabeth Jameson, eds., *The Women's West* (1987). On the plains Indians a lively account is Robert M. Utley, *The Indian Frontier of the American West* (1984). The ecological impact of plains settlement is subtly probed in Frieda Knobloch, *The Culture of Wilderness: Agriculture as Colonization in the American West* (1996). On the integration of the plains economy with the wider world an especially rich book is William Cronon, *Nature's Metropolis: Chicago and the Great West* (1991). Sarah Deutsch, *No Separate*

T I M E L I N E

1848	California is formally acquired from Mexico.	**1875**	Sioux ordered to vacate Powder River hunting grounds; war breaks out.
1849	California Gold Rush Chinese migration begins.	**1876**	Battle of Little Big Horn
		1877	San Francisco anti-Chinese riots
1861	Telegraph lines connect San Francisco with the East.	**1879**	Exoduster migration to Kansas
1862	Homestead Act offers public land to settlers.	**1882**	Chinese Exclusion Act bars further immigration of Chinese laborers.
1864	Yosemite Valley reserved as public park.	**1884**	Helen Hunt Jackson's *Ramona*
1865	Long Drive of Texas longhorns begins.	**1886**	Dry cycle begins on the Great Plains.
1867	Reservation policy for plains Indians	**1887**	Dawes Act divides tribal land into individual holdings.
1868	Sioux treaty rights to their Powder River hunting grounds confirmed	**1889**	Oklahoma opened to white settlers.
1869	Union Pacific and Central Pacific transcontinental railroad tracks meet at Promontory Point, Utah.	**1890**	Indian massacre at Wounded Knee, South Dakota U.S. census declares end of the frontier.
1874	Barbed wire invented.		

Refuge (1987), offers an imaginative treatment of the New Mexican peasantry. On the Asian migration to America the best introduction is Ron Takaki, *Strangers from a Different Shore* (1989). Kevin Starr, *California and the American Dream, 1850–1915* (1973), provides a full account of the emergence of a distinctive California culture. A comprehensive website with many links is <http://americanwest.com/>.

Chapter 17

CAPITAL AND LABOR IN THE AGE OF ENTERPRISE

1877–1900

An almost total revolution has taken place, and is yet in progress, in every branch and in every relation of the world's industrial and commercial system.

—David A. Wells, *Recent Economic Changes*, 1899

The year that Reconstruction ended, 1877, also marked the end of the first great crisis of America's industrializing economy. Four years earlier the Panic of 1873 had led to a severe depression that bankrupted 47,000 firms and drove down prices by about 30 percent. Hundreds of thousands of workers lost their jobs, and suffering was widespread. Before long the foundations of the social order began to shake.

On July 16, 1877, disgruntled railroad employees spontaneously stopped work across the Baltimore and Ohio system. After four years of economic depression and relentless wage cuts, they had had enough. In towns along the B&O tracks crowds cheered as the strikers attacked company property and prevented trains from running. The strike spread like wildfire across the entire national rail system. In Pittsburgh the Pennsylvania Railroad's roundhouse went up in flames on July 21. At many rail centers rioters and looters roamed freely. Only the arrival of federal troops restored order. On August 15 President Rutherford B. Hayes wrote in his diary: "The strikers have been put down *by force*." The Great Strike of 1877 had been crushed but only after raising the specter of social revolution.

And then recovery came. Within months the economy was booming again. In the next fifteen years the output of manufactured goods increased more than 150 percent. The nation's confidence in its industrial future rebounded. "Upon [material progress] is founded all other progress," asserted a railroad president in 1888. "Can there be any doubt that cheapening the cost of necessaries and conveniences of life is the most powerful agent of civilization and progress?" How that happened—how scarcity gave way to abundance—is the core event of America's industrial revolution.

Industrial Capitalism Triumphant

Economic historians speak of the late nineteenth century as the age of the Great Deflation. Prices fell steadily, not only in the United States but worldwide. Normally, falling prices signal economic stagnation: there is not enough demand for the available goods and services. For England, a mature industrial power, the Great Deflation did indeed signal economic decline. But not in the United States. Industrial expansion went into high gear (see Figure 17.1) because increasing manufacturing efficiencies enabled American firms to cut prices and yet earn profits for financing still better equipment.

GROWTH OF THE INDUSTRIAL BASE

By the 1870s factories were a familiar sight in America. But the early industries had really been appendages of the agricultural economy. They produced *consumer* goods—textiles, shoes, paper, and furniture—that replaced articles made at home or by individual artisans. Gradually, however, a different kind of demand developed, driven by the country's surging economic growth. Railroads needed locomotives; new factories needed machinery; cities needed trolley lines, sanitation systems, and commercial buildings. Railroad equipment, machinery, and construction materials were *capital* goods—that is, goods that themselves added to the productive capacity of the economy. Although consumer goods remained very important, it was capital goods that now drove America's industrial economy.

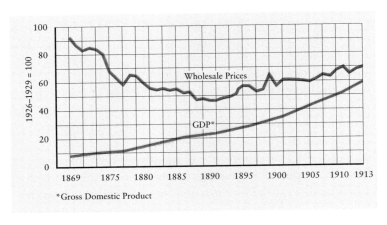

FIGURE 17.1
Business Activity and Wholesale Prices, 1869–1913

This graph shows the key feature of the performance of the late nineteenth-century economy: while output was booming, the price of goods was falling.

Central to this development was a new technology for manufacturing steel. The country already produced large quantities of wrought iron, a malleable metal easily worked by country blacksmiths and farmers. But wrought iron was expensive—it was produced in small batches by skilled puddlers—and not suited for heavy use as railway track. In 1856 the British inventor Henry Bessemer designed a furnace—the Bessemer converter—that refined raw pig iron into an essentially new product, steel, a metal harder and more durable than wrought iron. Bessemer's invention quickly attracted many users, but Andrew Carnegie was the one who fully exploited its revolutionary potential.

An ironmaker and former railroad manager, Carnegie in 1872 erected a massive steel mill outside Pittsburgh, with the Bessemer converter as its centerpiece. The converter broke a bottleneck at the refining stage and enabled Carnegie's engineers to design a mill that functioned on the basis of continuous operation. Iron ore entered the blast furnaces at one end and emerged without interruption at the other end as finished steel rails. Named after Carnegie's admired boss at the Pennsylvania Railroad, the Edgar Thompson Works became a model for the modern steel industry. Large integrated steel plants swiftly replaced the puddling mills that had once dotted western Pennsylvania.

The technological breakthrough in steel spurred the intensive exploitation of the country's rich mineral resources. Once iron ore began to be shipped down the Great Lakes from the rich Mesabi range in northern Minnesota, the industry was assured of an ample supply of its primary raw material. The other key ingredient, coal, came in great abundance from the Appalachian field that stretched from Pennsylvania to Alabama. Of minor importance before the Civil War, coal production doubled every decade after 1870, exceeding 400 million tons a year by 1910.

As steam engines became the nation's energy workhorse, prodigious amounts of coal began to be consumed by railroads and factories. Industries previously dependent on water power rapidly converted to steam. The turbine, utilizing continuous rotation rather than the steam engine's back-and-forth motion, marked another major advance during the 1880s. With the coupling of the steam turbine to the electric generator, the nation's energy revolution was completed, and after 1900 America's factories began a massive conversion to electric power.

THE RAILROAD BOOM

Before the Civil War most goods moved by water, a mode of transportation quite adequate for the country's economic needs at that time. But it was love at first sight when locomotives arrived from Britain in the 1830s. Americans were impatient for the year-round, on-time service that canal barges and riverboats could not provide. By 1860, with a network of tracks already crisscrossing the country east of the Mississippi, the railroad clearly was on the way to being industrial America's preferred mode of transportation (see Map 17.1).

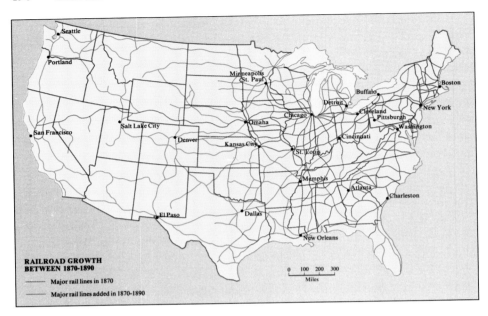

MAP 17.1
The Expansion of the Railroad System, 1870–1890

In 1870 the nation had 53,000 miles of rail track; in 1890, 167,000 miles. That burst of construction essentially completed the nation's rail network, although there would be additional expansion for the next two decades. The main areas of growth were in the South and west of the Mississippi. The Great Plains and the Far West accounted for over 40 percent of all railroad construction in this period.

The question was: Who would pay for it? Railroads could be state enterprises, like the canals, or they could be financed by private investors. Unlike most European countries the United States chose free enterprise. Even so, government played a big role. Anxious for the economic benefits, many states and localities lured railroads with offers of financial aid. The federal government, mainly interested in encouraging interregional development, provided financial credit and land grants; huge tracts went to the transcontinental railroads tying the Far West to the rest of the country.

The most important boost that government gave the railroads, however, was not money or land but a legal form of organization—the corporation—that enabled them to raise private capital in prodigious amounts. Investors who bought stock in the railroads enjoyed *limited liability:* they risked only the money they had invested and were not personally liable for the railroad's debts. Corporations were also empowered to borrow money by issuing interest-bearing bonds, which was how the railroads actually raised most of the money they needed.

Railroad building itself generally was handed over to construction companies, which, despite the name, were primarily another arm of the complex financing system. Hiring contractors and suppliers often involved persuading them to accept the railroad's bonds as payment and, when that failed, wheeling and dealing to raise cash by selling or borrowing on the bonds. Since the railroad promoters actually ran the construction companies, the opportunities for plunder were enormous. The most notorious, the Union Pacific's Credit Mobilier, disbursed probably half its funds into the pockets of the promoters.

The railroad business was not for the faint of heart. Most successful were promoters with the best access to capital, such as John Murray Forbes, a great Boston merchant in the China trade, who developed the Chicago, Burlington, and Quincy Railroad in the Midwest; or Cornelius Vanderbilt, who started with the fortune he had made in the steamboat business. Vanderbilt was primarily a consolidator, linking previously independent lines crossing New York State and ultimately developing the New York Central into a trunk line to Chicago. James J. Hill, who without federal subsidy made the Great Northern into the best of the transcontinental railroads, was certainly the nation's champion railroad builder. In contrast, Jay Gould, at various times owner of the Erie, Wabash, Union Pacific, and Missouri Pacific systems, always remained a stock-market speculator at heart.

Railroad development was often sordid, fiercely competitive, and subject to boom and bust. Yet vast sums of capital were raised, and a network was built exceeding that of the rest of the world combined. By 1900 virtually no corner of the country lacked rail service.

Along with this prodigious growth came increasing efficiency. The early railroads, built by competing local companies, had been a jumble of discontinuous segments. Gauges of track—the width between the rails—varied widely, and at terminal points railroads were not connected. As late as 1880 goods could not be shipped through from Massachusetts to South Carolina. Eight times along the way freight cars had to be emptied, and their contents transferred to other cars across a river or at a different terminal.

In 1883 the railroads rebelled against the jumble of local times that made scheduling a nightmare and, acting on their own, divided the country into the four standard time zones still in use. By the end of the 1880s a standard track gauge (4 feet, 8 1/2 inches) had been adopted everywhere. Fast-freight firms and standard accounting procedures enabled shippers to use the railroad network as if it was a single unit, moving their goods without breaks in transit, transfers between cars, or the other delays that had once bedeviled them.

At the same time, railroad technology was advancing. Durable steel rails permitted heavier traffic. Locomotives became more powerful and capable of pulling more freight cars. To control the greater mass being hauled the inventor George Westinghouse perfected the automatic coupler, the air brake, and the friction gear for starting and stopping a long line of cars. Costs per ton-mile fell by 50 percent between 1870 and 1890, resulting in a steady drop in freight rates for shippers.

The railroads more than met the transportation needs of the maturing industrial economy. For the investors, however, the costs of freewheeling competition and unrestrained growth were painfully high. On the many routes served by too many railroads, competitors fought for the available traffic by cutting rates to the bone. Many were saddled with huge bonded debt from the extravagant construction years; about a fifth of these bonds failed to pay interest, even in a pretty good year like 1889. When the economy turned bad, as it did in the Panic of 1893, a third of the industry went into receivership.

Out of the rubble came a major railroad reorganization. This was primarily the handiwork of Wall Street investment banks such as J. P. Morgan & Co. and Kuhn Loeb & Co., whose main role had been to market railroad stock and bond issues. When railroads failed, the investment bankers stepped in to pick up the pieces. They persuaded investors to accept lower interest rates or put up more money. And they eased competitive pressures by consolidating rivals. By the early twentieth century, a half dozen great regional systems had emerged, and the nerve center of American railroading had shifted to Wall Street.

MASS MARKETS AND LARGE-SCALE ENTERPRISE

Until well into the industrial age, all but a few manufacturers operated on a small scale and mainly for nearby markets. They left distribution to wholesale merchants and commission agents. After the Civil War the scale of economic activity began to change. "Combinations of capital on a scale hitherto wholly unprecedented constitute one of the remarkable features of modern business methods," the economist David A. Wells wrote in 1889. He could see "no other way in which the work of production and distribution can be prosecuted." What was there about the nation's economy that led to Wells's sense that large-scale enterprise was inevitable?

Most of all, the American market. Unlike Europe the United States was not carved up into many national markets; no political frontiers impeded the flow of goods across the continent. The population, swelled by immigration and a high birth rate, jumped from 40 million in 1870 to over 60 million in 1890. People flocked to the cities. The railroads brought these tightly packed markets within the reach of distant producers. The telegraph, fully operational by the Civil War, speeded communications. Nowhere else did manufacturers have so vast and accessible a home market for their products.

How they seized that opportunity is perhaps best revealed in the meat-packing industry. With the opening of the Union Stock Yards in 1865, Chicago became the cattle market for the country. Livestock came in by rail from the Great Plains, was auctioned off at the Chicago stockyards, and then was shipped to eastern cities, where, as before, the cattle were slaughtered in local "butchertowns." Such an arrangement—national distribution but local processing—adequately met the needs of an exploding urban population and could have done so indefinitely. In Europe no further development ever did occur.

But Gustavus F. Swift, a shrewd Chicago cattle dealer from Massachusetts, saw the future differently. He recognized that livestock deteriorated en route to the East and that local slaughterhouses lacked the scale to utilize waste by-products or cut labor costs. If dressed beef could be kept fresh in transit, however, it could be produced in bulk at the Chicago stockyards. Once his engineers developed an effective cooling system, Swift invested in a fleet of refrigerator cars and constructed a central beef-processing plant in Chicago.

This was only the beginning of Swift's innovations. No refrigerated warehouses existed in the cities that received his chilled beef, so Swift built his own network of branch houses. Next, he acquired a fleet of wagons to distribute his products to retail butcher shops. Swift constructed additional facilities to process the fertilizer, chemicals, and other usable by-products from his slaughtering operations. He also began to handle other perishable commodities so that he could fully utilize his refrigerated cars and branch houses. As demand grew, Swift built more packing houses in other stockyard centers, including Kansas City, Fort Worth, and Omaha.

Step by step Swift created a new kind of enterprise—a national company capable of handling within its own structure all the functions of an industry. Swift & Co. was a *vertically integrated* firm, absorbing the functions of many small, specialized enterprises within a single national structure. Swift's lead was followed by several big Chicago packers already operating plants that preserved pork products. By 1900 five firms, all of them nationally organized and vertically integrated, produced nearly 90 percent of the meat shipped in interstate commerce.

In most fields, no single innovation was as decisive as Swift's refrigerator car. But others did share Swift's insight that the essential step was to identify a mass market and then develop a national enterprise capable of serving it. In the petroleum industry John D. Rockefeller built the Standard Oil Company partly by taking over rival firms, but he also built a national distribution system to reach the enormous market for kerosene for lighting and heating homes. The Singer Sewing Machine Company formed its own sales organization, using both retail stores and door-to-door salesmen. Through such distribution systems manufacturers were able also to provide technical information, credit, and repair facilities.

Americans were ready consumers of standardized, mass-marketed goods. Because they were geographically mobile, they lost the local loyalties that were so strong in Europe. Social class in America, though by no means absent, was blurred at the edges and did not, for example, call for class-specific ways of dressing. Foreign visitors often noted that ready-made clothing made it difficult to tell salesgirls from debutantes on city streets.

The American consumer's receptivity to standardized goods should not be exaggerated. Gustavus Swift, for example, encountered great resistance to his Chicago beef. How could it be wholesome weeks later in Boston or Philadelphia? Cheap prices helped, but advertising mattered more. Modern advertising was born in the late nineteenth century, bringing brand names and a billboard-cluttered urban landscape. By 1900 companies spent over $90 million a year for space in newspapers and magazines. Advertisements urged readers to bathe with Pears' soap, eat Uneeda biscuits, sew on a Singer machine, and snap pictures with a Kodak camera. The active molding of demand for brand names became a major function of American business.

Quaker Oats

Like crackers, sugar, and other nonperishable foods, cereal had traditionally been marketed to consumers in bulk from barrels. In 1882 the grain merchant Henry P. Cowell completed the first continuous-process mill for oatmeal, cutting production costs and greatly increasing output. He also hit on the idea of selling cereal in boxes of standard size and weight to a national market. Broadsides showing the Quaker Oats man soon appeared in every American town, advertising a product of reliable quality and uniform price.

(Division of Political History, Smithsonian Institution)

THE NEW SOUTH

"Shall we dethrone our idols?" Southerners had to ask themselves as they observed the burst of economic activity in the North. For many the answer was a resounding yes. Nostalgia for the Old South had to be put aside, advocates of economic development argued. Led by Henry W. Grady, editor of the Atlanta *Constitution*, they made "the practical wisdom of businessmen" the credo of a "New South."

The plantation economy of the Old South had impeded industrial development. The slave states had few cities, a primitive distribution system, and not much manufacturing. This modest infrastructure, wrecked by the Civil War, was quickly restored. After Reconstruction a railroad boom developed. Track mileage doubled in the next decade, and at least by that measure the South became nearly competitive with the rest of the country (see Map 17.2).

But the South remained overwhelmingly agricultural. Farming and poverty are not necessarily linked, but in the South they were. Tenant systems required a cash crop (see Chapter 15), committing the South to cotton despite soil depletion, low productivity, and unprofitable prices. Wages for southern farm labor fell steadily, down to roughly 75 cents a day by the 1890s.

From this low agricultural wage, surprisingly, sprang the South's hopes for industrialization. Consider, for example, how southern textile mills got started in the Piedmont uplands in the mid-1870s. The mills recruited workers from the surrounding hill farms, where people struggled to make ends meet. To attract them mill wages had to exceed farm earnings but not by much. Paying rock-bottom wages, the new mills had a competitive advantage over the long-established New England industry—as much as 40 percent lower labor costs in 1897.

The labor system that evolved was based on hiring whole families. "Papa decided he would come because he didn't have nothing much but girls and they had to get out and work like men," recalled one woman. It was not Papa, in fact, but his

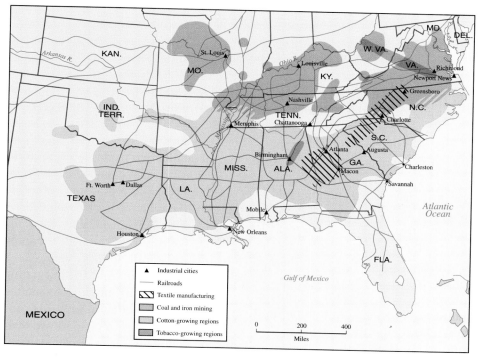

M A P 17.2
The New South, 1900

The economy of the Old South focused on raising staple crops, especially cotton and tobacco. In the New South staple agriculture continued to dominate, but there was marked industrial development as well. Industrial regions emerged, producing textiles, coal and iron, and wood products. By 1900 the South's industrial pattern was well defined.

girls whom the mills wanted, to work as spinners and loom tenders. Only they could not be recruited individually: no right-thinking parent would have permitted that. Hiring by families, on the other hand, was already familiar; after all, everyone had been expected to work on the farm. And so the family system of mill labor developed, with a labor force that was half female and very young. In the 1880s a quarter of all southern textile workers were under fifteen years of age.

The hours were long—twelve hours a day—but life in the mill villages was, in the words of one historian, "like a family." Employers tended to be paternalistic, providing company housing and a variety of services. The mill workers themselves built close-knit, supportive communities, but for whites only. Although blacks sometimes worked as day laborers and janitors, they hardly ever got jobs as operatives in the cotton mills.

Cheap, abundant labor might have been termed the South's most valuable natural resource. But the region was blessed with other resources as well. From its rich soil came tobacco, the South's second cash crop. When cigarettes became fashionable in the 1880s, the young North Carolina entrepreneur James B. Duke seized the new market by taking advantage of a southern invention—James A. Bonsack's machine for producing cigarettes automatically. Blacks stemmed and stripped the leaf as they always had, but Duke followed the textile example and restricted machine tending to white women.

Lumbering, by contrast, was racially integrated, with a labor force evenly divided between black and white men. Cutting down the South's pine forests was a growth business in these years. Alabama's coal and iron ore deposits also attracted investors; by 1890 the Birmingham district was producing nearly a million tons of iron and steel annually.

Despite the South's high hopes, this burst of industrial development did not lift the region out of poverty. In 1900 two-thirds of all southerners made their living from the soil, just as they had in 1870. Moreover, the industries that did develop produced raw materials (forestry and mining) or engaged in the low-tech processing of coarse products. Industry by industry the key statistic—the value added by manufacturing—showed the South consistently lagging behind the North (see Table 17.1).

Southerners tended to blame the North: the South was a "colonial" economy controlled by New York and Chicago. There was some truth to this charge. Much of the capital—by no means all—did come from the North. And the integrating processes of the economy did subordinate regional to national interests. When the railway network moved to a uniform gauge in 1886, the southern railroads converted to the northern standard. Nor did northern interests hesitate to use their muscle to maintain the interregional status quo. Railroads, for example, manipulated freight rates so that it was cheap for southern cotton and timber to flow out and for northern manufactured goods to flow in.

Yet in the end the South's economic backwardness was mostly of its own making. The crowning irony was that the great advantage of the South—its cheap labor—also kept it from becoming a more technologically advanced economy. First, low wages discouraged employers from replacing workers with machinery. Second,

TABLE 17.1

Comparison of Annual Value Added per Worker, South and Non-South, 1910

Type of Industry	South	Non-South
Lumber and timber products	$ 820	$1020
Cotton goods	544	764
Cars and general shop construction by steam railroad companies	657	746
Turpentine and resin	516	—
Tobacco manufactures	1615	1394
Foundry and machine-shop products	1075	1307
Printing and publishing	1760	2100
Cottonseed oil	1715	—
Hosiery and knit goods	461	724
Furniture and refrigerators	732	1052
Iron and steel	1182[a]	1433
Fertilizer	1833	1947

Source: Gavin Wright, *Old South, New South: Revolutions in the Southern Economy Since the Civil War* (New York: Basic Books, 1986), p. 163.
[a]Partially estimated.
Note: This table reveals the consistency with which northern industries (except tobacco manufactures) controlled the more skilled—and hence more value-creating—processes of production.

low wages attracted labor-intensive industry, such as textiles. Third, a cheap labor market inhibited investment in education because of the likelihood that better-educated workers would flee to higher-wage markets.

What distinguished the southern labor market was that it was *insulated* from the rest of the country. Northern workers and European immigrants steered clear of the South because wages were too low and attractive jobs too scarce. Harder to explain is why so few southerners, black or white, left for the higher-wage North prior to World War I. At its core, the explanation is that the South was a place apart, with social and racial mores that discouraged all but the most resourceful from seeking opportunities elsewhere. The result was that a normal flow of workers back and forth did not occur, and wage differentials did not narrow. So long as this isolation persisted, the South would remain a tributary economy, a supplier on unequal terms to the advanced industrial heartland of the North.

The World of Work

In a free-enterprise system, profit drives the entrepreneur. But the industrial order is populated not only by profit makers. It includes—in vastly larger numbers—wage earners. Economic change always affects those who work for wages, but never so drastically as it did in the late nineteenth century.

LABOR RECRUITS

Industrialism invariably set people in motion. Farm folk migrated to cities. Artisans entered factories. An industrial labor force emerged. This happened in the United States just as it did in Europe, but with a difference: the United States did not rely primarily on its own population for a supply of workers.

The demand for labor was ravenous, tripling between 1870 and 1900. Rural Americans were highly mobile in the late nineteenth century, and of those who moved, half ended up in cities. But except in the South native-born whites mostly rejected factory work. They had a basic education, they could read and calculate, and they understood American institutions and ways of doing things. City-bound white Americans found their opportunities in the multiplying white-collar jobs in offices and retail stores.

Modest numbers of blacks began to migrate out of the South—roughly 80,000 between 1870 and 1890, another 200,000 between 1890 and 1910. Most of them settled in cities, but they were restricted to casual labor, janitorial work, and for the women domestic service. Employers turned black applicants away from the factory gates—and away from their one best chance for a fair shake at American opportunity—because immigrant workers already supplied them with as much cheap labor as they needed.

The great migration from the Old World had started in the 1840s, when over a million Irish peasants fled the potato famine. In the following years, as European agriculture became increasingly commercialized, peasant populations lost their hold on the land. The peasant economy failed first in Germany and Scandinavia and then later in the nineteenth century across Austria-Hungary, Russia, Italy, and the Balkans. In Europe's industrial districts new technologies also cut loose many workers in obsolete artisan trades such as hand-loom weaving.

Ethnic origin largely determined the kind of work that the immigrants took in America. Seeking the jobs they had held in the Old World, the Welsh labored as tin-plate workers, the English as miners, the Germans as machinists and traditional artisans (for example, bakers and carpenters), the Belgians as glass workers, and the Scandinavians as seamen on Great Lakes boats. For common labor employers had long counted on the brawn of Irish rural immigrants, although all emigrating groups contributed to the pool of unskilled workers.

As technology advanced, American employers needed fewer European craftsmen, while the demand for ordinary labor skyrocketed. The sources of immigration began to shift, and by 1895 arrivals from southern and eastern Europe far outstripped immigration from western Europe (see Figure 17.2). Italian and Slavic immigrants without industrial skills flooded into American factories. Heavy, low-paid labor became the domain of the recent immigrants. Blast-furnace jobs, a job-seeking investigator heard, were "Hunky work," not suitable for him or any other American.

Not only skill determined where immigrants ended up in American industry. The newcomers, although generally traveling on their own, moved within well-defined net-

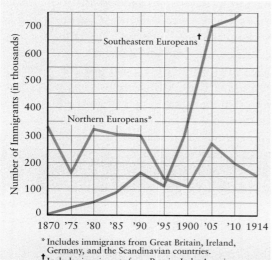

700
600
500
400
300
200
100
0

Number of Immigrants (in thousands)

Southeastern Europeans†

Northern Europeans*

1870 '75 '80 '85 '90 '95 1900 '05 '10 1914

* Includes immigrants from Great Britain, Ireland, Germany, and the Scandinavian countries.
† Includes immigrants from Russia, Italy, Austria-Hungary, and other eastern European countries.

Figure 17.2
American Immigration, 1870–1914

This graph shows the surge of European immigration in the late nineteenth century. While northern Europe continued to send substantial numbers, it was overshadowed after 1895 by south-eastern Europeans pouring into America to work in mines and factories.

works, following relatives or fellow villagers already in America and relying on them to land a job. A high degree of ethnic clustering resulted, even within a single factory. At the Jones and Laughlin steel works in Pittsburgh, for example, the carpentry shop was German, the hammer shop Polish, and the blooming mill Serbian. Immigrants also had different job preferences. Men from Italy, for example, preferred outdoor work, often laboring in gangs under a *padrone* (boss), much as they had in Italy.

Immigrants entered a modern industrial order, but it was not a world they wanted. They were peasants, displaced by the breakdown of the traditional rural economies of eastern and southern Europe. Many had lost their land and fallen into the class of dependent, propertyless servants. They could avoid that bitter fate only if they had money to buy property, and it was that purpose that drove the peasant immigrants who came to America. They never intended to stay permanently. About half did return, departing in great numbers during depression years. No one knows how many left because they had saved enough and how many left for lack of work. For their American employers it scarcely mattered. What mattered was that the immigrants took the worst jobs and were always available when they were wanted. For the new industrial order they made an ideal labor supply.

WORKING WOMEN

Over 4 million women worked for wages in 1900. They made up a quarter of the nonfarm labor force and were increasingly important in the industrial economy. The opportunities they found were shaped by gender. Contemporary beliefs about womanhood largely determined which women took jobs and how they were treated once they became wage earners (see American Voices, "Getting Organized").

Wives were not supposed to work outside the home, and in fact fewer than 5 percent did so in 1890. Only among African Americans did many married women—above 30 percent—work for wages. Among whites the typical working woman at that time was under twenty-four and unmarried. When older women worked, remarked one observer, it "was usually a sign that something had gone wrong": their husbands had died, deserted, or lost their jobs.

Since women were held to be inherently different from men, it followed that they not be permitted to do "men's work." Nor, regardless of their skills, could they be paid a man's wage. The dominant view was that a woman did not require a "living wage" because, as one investigator reported, "it is expected that she has men to support her." The occupation that served as the baseline for all women's jobs was domestic service, which was always very poorly paid or, in a woman's own home, not paid at all.

At the turn of the century women's work fell into three categories. One third of women worked as maids or other types of domestic servants. Another third held "female" white-collar jobs in teaching, nursing, sales, and office work. The remaining third worked in industry, heavily concentrated in the garment trades and textile mills but present also in many other industries as inspectors, packers, assemblers, and other "light" occupations. Few worked as supervisors, fewer in the crafts, and nearly none as day laborers.

Just how jobs came to be defined as male or female—in sociological terms, the *sex-typing* of occupations—is not easy to explain. Jobs as telephone operator and store clerk, originally male, had by the 1890s become female. Wherever an occupation became female-dominated, people came to think of it as having feminine attributes, even though very similar or even identical work elsewhere was done by men. Jobs identified as women's work became unsuitable for men. There were no male telephone operators by 1900.

As with male workers, ethnicity and race played a big part in the distribution of women's jobs. Exclusion from all but the most menial jobs applied as rigidly to black women as it did to black men. White-collar jobs were reserved for native-born women, which in the cities increasingly included the second-generation daughters of immigrants. And as with men ethnicity created clustering patterns in women's jobs or, in the case of Italians, restricted them to sewing or other subcontracted tasks that could be done within the family.

Disapproval of wives who took paying jobs, though expressed in sentimental and moral terms, was based on solid necessity. Cooking, cleaning, and tending the children were not income-producing or reckoned in terms of money. But everyone knew that the family household could not function without the wife's contribution. Therefore, her place was in the home.

Working-class families, however, found the going hard on a single income. Only among highly skilled workers, wrote one investigator, "was it possible for the hus-

AMERICAN VOICES

Getting Organized

ROSE SCHNEIDERMAN

*R*ose Schneiderman (1882–1972) typified the young Jewish garment workers who became the firebrands of their industry. Schneiderman went on to an illustrious career as a unionist and reformer.

We had no idea that there was a union in our industry and that women could join it. Nor did we have a full realization of the hardships we were needlessly undergoing. There was the necessity of owning a sewing machine before you could work. Then you had to buy your own thread. But the worst of it was the incredibly inefficient way in which work was distributed. Because we were all pieceworkers, any time lost during the season was a real hardship. . . .

We formed a committee composed of my friend Bessie Mannis, who worked with me, myself, and a third girl. Bravely we ventured into the office of the United Cloth Hat and Cap Makers Union. . . . We were told that we would have to have at least twenty-five women. . . . We waited at the doors of factories and, as the girls were leaving for the day, we would approach them and speak our piece. . . . Within days we had the necessary number, and in January 1903 we were chartered as Local 23, and I was elected secretary. . . .

The only cloud in the picture was mother's attitude toward my becoming a trade unionist. She kept saying I'd never get married because I was so busy—a prophecy which came true. . . .

That June we decided to put our strength to the test. . . . On Saturdays . . . we women had to hang around until three or four o'clock before getting our pay. I headed a committee which informed Mr. Fox that we wanted to be paid at the same time as the men. . . . He didn't say outright that he agreed; he wouldn't give us that much satisfaction. But on the first Saturday in July, when we went for our pay at twelve noon, there it was ready for us.

SOURCE: Rose Schneiderman, *All for One* (1967), reprinted in Irving Howe and Kenneth Libo, eds., *How We Lived* (New York: New American Library, 1979), pp. 139–41.

band unaided to support his family." The rockiest period came during the child-bearing years, when there were many mouths to feed and only the earnings of the father to provide the food. Thereafter, as the children grew old enough to work, the family income began to increase. Not only unmarried sons and daughters but also the younger children contributed their share. In 1900 one of every five children under sixteen worked. "When the people own houses," remarked a printer from Fall River, Massachusetts, "you will generally find that it is a large family all working together."

Switchboard Operators

When the first telephone exchange was set up in Boston in 1878, it was operated by teenage boys, which followed the practice set in the telegraph industry. During the 1880s, however, young women increasingly replaced the boys, and by 1900 switchboard operation was defined strictly as women's work. In this photograph of a telephone exchange in Columbus, Ohio, in 1907, the older woman at left has risen to the position of supervisor, but it is the two men in the picture who are clearly in charge. (Corbis-Bettmann)

By the 1890s all the northern industrial states had passed laws prohibiting child labor and regulating work hours for teenagers. Most of these states also required children under fourteen to attend school for a certain number of weeks each year. Working-class families continued to need more than one income, but this money came increasingly from the wives. After 1890 the proportion of working married women crept steadily upward. About a fifth of the wives of unskilled and semi-skilled men in Chicago held jobs in 1920. Wage-earning wives and mothers were on their way to becoming a primary part of America's labor force.

AUTONOMOUS LABOR

No one supervised the nineteenth-century coal miner (see American Voices, "A Miner's Son"). He was a tonnage worker who was paid for the amount of coal he produced. He provided his own tools, worked at his own pace, and knocked off early when he chose. Such autonomous craft workers—almost all of them men— flourished in many branches of nineteenth-century industry. They were mule spin-

A Miner's Son

JOHN BROPHY

J ohn Brophy (1883–1963), an important mine union official in the twentieth century, recalls what mining was like in his boyhood.

I got a thrill at the thought of having an opportunity to go and work in the mine, to go and work along side my father. . . . It was a great satisfaction to me that my father was a skilled, clean workman with everything kept in shape, and the timbering done well. . . . It's plain that the individual miner in those early days had considerable freedom of judgment. I think that was one of the great satisfactions that a miner had—that he was his own boss within his workplace. . . .

The miner is always aware of danger, that he lived under dangerous conditions in the workplace. . . . Then there is the further fact that the miner by and large lived in purely mining communities which were often isolated. They developed a group loyalty under all these circumstances. They were both individualists and they were group conscious. . . . You find time and again miners, in an effort to rescue their fellow workers, taking chances which quite often meant death for themselves. . . .

Along with that is a sense of justice. There was the very fact the miner was a tonnage worker and that he could be short weighed and cheated in various ways, and that the only safeguard against it was organization. . . . The miner in my day in the United States was aware that all knowledge didn't start with his generation. . . . At least on one side of my family there are at least four generations of [British] miners, and I say this with a sense of pride; very much so. I'm very proud of the fact that there is this long tradition of miners who have struggled with the elements.

SOURCE: Jerold S. Auerbach, ed., *American Labor: The Twentieth Century* (Indianapolis: Bobbs-Merrill, 1969), pp. 44–48.

ners in cotton mills; puddlers and rollers in iron works; molders in stove making; and machinists, glass blowers, and skilled workers in many other industries.

In the shop they abided by the *stint,* a self-imposed limit on how much they would produce each day. This informal system of restricting output infuriated efficiency-minded engineers. But to the worker it signified personal dignity and "unselfish brotherhood" with fellow employees. The male craft worker took pride in a "manly" bearing, toward both his fellows and the boss. One day a shop in Lowell, Massachusetts, posted regulations requiring all employees to be at their posts in work clothes at the opening bell and to remain, with the shop door locked, until the dismissal bell. A machinist promptly packed his tools, declaring that he had not "been brought up under such a system of slavery."

The Ironworkers' Noontime

The qualities of the nineteenth-century craft worker—dignity, "unselfish brotherhood," a "manly" bearing—shine through in this painting by Thomas Anshutz. *The Ironworkers' Noontime* became a popular painting when it was reproduced as an engraving in *Harper's Weekly* in 1884. (Fine Arts Museum of San Francisco. Gift of Mr. and Mrs. John D. Rockefeller 3rd, 1979.7.4)

Underlying this ethical code was a keen sense of the craft, each with its own history and customs. Hat finishers—masters of the art of applying fur felting to top hats and bowlers—had a language of their own. When a hatter was hired, he was "shopped"; if fired, he was "bagged"; when he quit work, he "cried off"; and when he took an apprentice, the boy was "under teach." The hatters, most of whom worked in Danbury, Connecticut, or Orange, New Jersey, formed a distinctive, self-contained community.

Women workers found much the same kind of social meaning in their jobs. Department store clerks, for example, developed a work culture and language just as robust as that of any male craft group. The most important fact about wage-earning women was their youth. For many the first job was a chance to be independent, to form friendships with other young women, and to experience, however briefly, a fun-loving time of nice clothes, dancing, and other "cheap amusements."

To some degree, their youthful preoccupations made it easier for working women to accept the miserable terms under which they labored. But this did not mean that they lacked a sense of solidarity or self-respect. A pretty dress might appear frivolous to the casual observer, but it also conveyed the message that the working girl considered herself as good as anyone. Rebellious youth culture sometimes united with job grievances to produce astonishing strike movements, as, for example, by Jewish garment workers in New York and Irish American telephone operators in Boston.

Rarely, however, did women workers wield the kind of craft power that the skilled male worker commonly enjoyed. He hired his own helpers, supervised their work, and paid them from his earnings. In the late nineteenth century, when increasingly sophisticated production called for closer shop-floor supervision, many factory managers deliberately shifted this responsibility to craft workers. In metal-fabricating firms that did precise machining and complex assembling, a system of inside contracting developed, in which skilled employees bid for a production run, taking full responsibility for the operation, paying their crew and pocketing the profits.

Dispersal of authority was characteristic of nineteenth-century industry. The aristocracy of the workers—the craftsmen, inside contractors, and foremen—enjoyed a high degree of autonomy. However, their subordinates often paid dearly for that independence. Any worker who paid his helpers from his own pocket might be tempted to exploit them. In the Pittsburgh area foremen were known as "pushers," notorious for driving their gangs mercilessly. On the other hand, industrial labor in the nineteenth century remained on a human scale. People dealt with each other face to face and often developed cohesive ties within the shop. Striking craft workers commonly received the support of helpers and laborers, and labor gangs sometimes walked out on behalf of a popular foreman.

SYSTEMS OF CONTROL

As technology advanced, workers increasingly lost the proud independence characteristic of nineteenth-century craft work. One cause of this deskilling process was a new system of production—Henry Ford called it *mass production*—that lent itself to mechanization. Agricultural implements, typewriters, bicycles, and after 1900 automobiles were assembled from standardized parts. The machine tools that cut, drilled, and ground these metal parts were originally operated by skilled machinists. But because they produced long runs of a single item, machine tools became more specialized; they became *dedicated* machines—machines set up to do the same job over and over—and the need for skilled operatives disappeared. In the manufacture of sewing machines, one machinist complained in 1883, "the trade is so subdivided that a man is not considered a machinist at all. One man may make just a particular part of a machine and may not know anything whatever about another part of the same machine." Such a worker, noted an observer, "cannot be master of a craft, but only master of a fragment."

Employers were attracted to dedicated machinery because it increased output; the impact on workers was not uppermost in their minds. They recognized that mechanization made it easier to control workers, but that was only an incidental benefit. Gradually, however, the idea took hold that managing workers might itself be a way to reduce the cost of production.

The pioneer in this field was Frederick W. Taylor. An expert on metal-cutting methods, Taylor believed that the engineer's approach might be applied to managing workers, hence the name for his method: *scientific management*. To get the maximum work from the individual worker, Taylor suggested two basic reforms. The first would eliminate the brain work from manual labor. Managers would assume "the burden of gathering together all of the traditional knowledge which in the past has been possessed by the workmen and then of classifying, tabulating, and reducing this knowledge to rules, laws, and formulae." The second reform, a logical consequence of the first, would deprive workers of the authority they had exercised on the shop floor. Workers would "do what they are told promptly and without asking questions or making suggestions. . . . The duty of enforcing . . . rests with the management alone."

Once managers had the knowledge and the power, they would put labor on a "scientific" basis. This meant subjecting each task to *time-and-motion study* by an engineer who would analyze and time each job with a stopwatch. Workers would be paid at a differential rate—that is, a certain amount if they met the stopwatch standard and a higher rate for additional output. Taylor claimed that his techniques would guarantee optimum worker efficiency. His assumption was that only money mattered to workers and that they would automatically respond to the lure of higher earnings.

Scientific management was not, in practice, a roaring success. Implementing it proved very expensive, and workers stubbornly resisted the job-analysis method. "It looks to me like slavery to have a man stand over you with a stopwatch," complained one iron molder. A union leader insisted that "this system is wrong, because we want our heads left on us." Far from solving the labor problem, as Taylor claimed it would, scientific management embittered relations on the shop floor.

Yet Taylor achieved something of fundamental importance. He was a brilliant publicist, and his teachings spread throughout American industry. Taylor's disciples moved beyond his simplistic economic psychology, creating the new fields of personnel work and industrial psychology, whose practitioners purported to know how to extract more and better labor from workers. A threshold had been crossed into the modern era of labor management.

So the circle closed on American workers. With each advance the quest for efficiency cut deeper into their cherished autonomy. The process occurred unevenly. For textile workers the loss had come early. Miners and iron workers felt it much more slowly. Others, such as construction workers, escaped almost entirely. But increasing numbers of workers found themselves in an environment that crushed any sense of mastery or even understanding.

The Labor Movement

Wherever industrialization took hold, workers organized and formed labor unions. However, the movements they built varied from one industrial society to another. In the United States workers were especially uncertain about the path they wanted to take. Only in the 1880s did the American labor movement settle into a steady course.

REFORMERS AND UNIONISTS

Thomas B. McGuire, a New York wagon driver, was ambitious. He had saved $300 from his wages "so that I might become something of a capitalist eventually." But his venture as a cab driver in the early 1880s soon failed:

> Corporations usually take that business themselves. They can manage to get men, at starvation wages, and put them on a hack, and put a livery on them with a gold band and brass buttons, to show that they are slaves—I beg pardon; I did not intend to use the word slaves; there are no slaves in this country now—to show that they are merely servants.

Slave or liveried servant, the symbolic meaning was the same to McGuire. He was speaking of the crushed aspirations of the independent American worker.

What would satisfy the Thomas McGuires of the nineteenth century? Only the establishment of an egalitarian society, one in which every citizen might hope to become economically independent. This republican goal did not mean returning to the agrarian past but rather moving beyond the existing wage system to a more just order that did not distinguish between capitalists and workers. All would be "producers" laboring together in what was commonly called the "cooperative commonwealth." This was the ideal that inspired the Noble and Holy Order of the Knights of Labor.

Founded in 1869 as a secret society of garment workers in Philadelphia, the Knights of Labor spread to other cities and by 1878 emerged as a national movement. The Knights boasted an elaborate ritual and ceremony calculated to appeal to the fraternal spirit of nineteenth-century workers. They enjoyed a sense of comradeship very much like that offered by the Masons or Odd Fellows. For the Knights, however, fraternalism was harnessed to labor reform. The goal was to "give voice to that grand undercurrent of mighty thought, which is today [1880] crystallizing in the hearts of men, and urging them on to perfect organization through which to gain the power to make labor emancipation possible."

But how was "emancipation" to be achieved? Through cooperation, the Knights argued. They intended to set up factories and shops that would be owned and run by the employees. As these cooperatives flourished, American society would be transformed into a cooperative commonwealth. But little was actually done. Instead, the Knights devoted themselves to "education." Their leader, Grand Master Workman Terence V. Powderly, regarded the organization as a vast labor lyceum open to all but lawyers and saloonkeepers. The cooperative commonwealth would arrive in some mysterious way as more and more "producers" became members and learned the group's message from lectures, discussions, and publications. Social evil would not end in a day but "must await the gradual development of educational enlightenment."

The labor reformers expressed the higher aspirations of American workers. Another kind of organization—the trade union—tended to their day-to-day needs. Unions had long been at the center of the lives of craft workers. Apprenticeship rules regulated entry into a trade, and the closed shop—by reserving all jobs for union members—kept out lower-wage and incompetent workers. Union rules specified the terms of work, sometimes in minute detail. The trade union also expressed the social identity of the craft. A Birmingham iron puddler claimed that his union's "main object was to educate mechanics up to a standard of morality and temperance, and good workmanship." Some unions emphasized mutual aid. Because operating trains was a high-risk occupation, the railroad brotherhoods provided accident and death benefits and encouraged members to assist one another.

The earliest unions were local organizations of workers in the same craft and sometimes, more narowly, those in a single ethnic group, such as German bakers or Bohemian cigar makers. As expanding markets intruded, breaking down their ability to control local conditions, unions began to form national organizations. The first was the International Typographical Union in 1852. By the 1870s molders, ironworkers, bricklayers, and about thirty other trades had done likewise. The national union was becoming the dominant organizational form for American trade unionism.

The practical job interests that trade unions espoused might have seemed a far cry from the idealism of the Knights of Labor. But both kinds of motives arose from a single workers' culture. Seeing no conflict, many workers carried membership cards in both the Knights of Labor and a trade union. For many years little separated a trade assembly of the Knights from a local trade union; both engaged in fraternal and job-oriented activities. And because the Knights, once established in a town or city, tended to become politically active and field independent slates of candidates, that too became a magnet attracting trade unionists.

Trade unions generally barred women, and so did the Knights until in 1881 women shoe workers in Philadelphia struck in support of their male coworkers and won the right to form their own local assembly. By 1886 probably 50,000 women belonged to the Knights of Labor. Their courage on the picket line prompted Powderly's rueful remark that women "are the best men in the Order." For a handful, such as the hosiery worker Leonora M. Barry, the Knights provided a rare chance to take up leadership roles as organizers and officials.

Similarly, the Knights of Labor grudgingly expanded the opportunity for black workers to join out of the need for solidarity and, just as important, in deference to the Order's egalitarian principles. The Knights could rightly boast that their "great work has been to organize labor which was previously unorganized."

THE TRIUMPH OF "PURE AND SIMPLE" UNIONISM

In the early 1880s the Knights began to act more and more like trade unions. Boycott campaigns against the products of "unfair" employers achieved impressive results. With the economy booming and workers in short supply, the Knights began to win strikes, including a major victory against Jay Gould's Southwestern railway system in 1885. Workers flocked into the organization, and its membership jumped from 100,000 to perhaps 700,000. For a brief time the Knights stood poised as a potential industrial-union movement capable of bringing all workers into its fold.

The rapid growth of the Knights of Labor frightened the national trade unions. They began to insist on a clear separation of roles, with the Knights confined to labor reform. This was partly a battle over turf, but it reflected also a deepening divergence of labor philosophies.

Samuel Gompers, a cigar maker from New York City, led the ideological assault on the Knights. Gompers hammered out the philosophical position that would become known as "pure and simple" unionism. His starting point was that grand theories and schemes like those that excited the labor reformers should be strictly avoided. Unions, Gompers thought, should focus instead on concrete, achievable gains, and they should organize workers not as an undifferentiated mass of "producers" but by craft and occupation. The battleground should be at the workplace, where workers could best mobilize their power, and not in the quicksands of politics. "No matter how just," Gompers pronounced, "unless the cause is backed up with power to enforce it, it is going to be crushed and annihilated."

Samuel Gompers

This is a photograph of the labor leader in his forties taken when he was visiting striking miners in West Virginia, an area where mine operators resisted unions with special fierceness. The photograph was taken by a company detective.

(The George Meany Memorial Archives Negative #91)

The struggle for the eight-hour day crystallized the conflict between the rival movements. Both, of course, favored a shorter workday, but for different reasons. For the Knights, it was desirable because workers had duties "to perform as American citizens and members of society." Trade unionists took a more hard-boiled view of the eight-hour day: it would spread the available jobs among more workers, protect them against overwork, and give them a better life. When the trade unions set May 1, 1886, as the deadline for achieving the eight-hour day, the leadership of Knights objected. But workers everywhere responded enthusiastically, and as the deadline approached, a wave of strikes and demonstrations broke out.

At one such eight-hour strike, at the McCormick agricultural-implement works in Chicago, a battle erupted on May 3, leaving four strikers dead. Chicago was a hotbed of *anarchism*—the revolutionary advocacy of a stateless society—and local anarchists, most of them German immigrants, called a protest meeting the next evening at Haymarket Square. When police moved in to break it up, someone threw a bomb that killed and wounded several of the police. Despite no proof of their involvement, the anarchists were tried and found guilty of murder and criminal conspiracy. Four were executed, one committed suicide, and the others received long prison sentences. They were victims of one of the great miscarriages of American justice.

Seizing on the antiunion hysteria set off by the Haymarket affair, employers took the offensive. They broke strikes violently, compiled blacklists of strikers, and forced others to sign *yellow-dog contracts* guaranteeing that, as a condition of employment, they would not join a labor organization. If trade unionists needed any further confirmation of the tough world in which they lived, they found it in Haymarket and its aftermath.

In December 1886, having failed to persuade the Knights of Labor to desist from union activity, the national trade unions formed the American Federation of Labor (AFL), with Samuel Gompers as president. The AFL in effect locked into place the trade-union structure as it had evolved by the 1880s. Underlying this structure was the conviction that workers had to take the world as it was, not as they dreamed it might be. At this point, the American movement definitely diverged from the European model, for fundamental to Gompers' AFL was opposition to a political party for workers.

The Knights of Labor never recovered from their defeats after the Haymarket affair. Powderly retreated to the rhetoric of labor reform, but wage earners had lost interest, and he was unable to formulate a viable new strategy. By the mid-1890s, the Knights of Labor had faded away.

INDUSTRIAL WAR

American trade unions were conservative. They accepted the economic order. All they wanted was a larger share for working people. But it was precisely that claim against company profits that made American employers so opposed to collective bargaining. In the 1890s they unleashed a fierce counterattack on the trade-union movement.

In Homestead, Pennsylvania, site of one of Carnegie's great steel mills, the skilled men thought themselves safe from that threat. Mostly homeowners, they elected fellow workers to public office and considered the town very much their community. And they had faith in Andrew Carnegie, who had announced in a famous magazine article that workers had the right to organize and a right to their jobs that employers should honor during labor disputes: it was wrong to bring in strikebreakers.

Espousing high-toned principles made Carnegie feel good, but a healthy bottom line made him feel even better. He decided that collective bargaining had become too expensive, and he was confident that his skilled workers could be replaced by the advanced machinery he was installing. Lacking the stomach for the hard battle, Carnegie fled to a remote estate in Scotland, leaving behind a second-in-command well qualified to do the dirty work. This was Henry Clay Frick, a former coal baron and a veteran of labor wars in the coal fields.

After a brief pretense at bargaining Frick announced that effective July 1, 1892, the company would no longer deal with the Amalgamated Association of Iron and Steel Workers. The plant had already been fortified so that strikebreakers could be brought in to resume operations. At stake for Carnegie's employees now was not just wage cuts but the defense of a way of life. The town mayor, a union man, turned away the county sheriff when he tried to take possession of the plant. The entire community mobilized in defense of the union.

At dawn on July 6 two barges were seen approaching Homestead up the Monogahela River. On board were armed guards hired by the Pinkerton Detective Agency to take control of the steel works on behalf of the company. Behind hastily erected barricades the strikers opened fire and a bloody battle ensued. When the Pinkertons surrendered, they were mercilessly pummeled by the enraged women of Homestead as they retreated to the railway station. Frick appealed to the governor of Pennsylvania, who called out the state militia and placed Homestead under martial law. The great steel works was taken over and opened to strikebreakers, while union leaders and town officials were arrested on charges of riot, murder, and treason.

The Homestead strike ushered in a decade of strife that pitted working people against the formidable power of corporate industry and the even more formidable power of their own government. That hard reality was driven home to workers at a place that seemed an even less likely site for class warfare than Homestead. Pullman, Illinois, was a model factory town built by George M. Pullman, inventor of the sleeping car that brought comfort and luxury to railway travel. When the Panic of 1893 struck, business fell off, and Pullman cut wages but not the rents for company housing. When a workers' committee complained in May 1894, Pullman answered that there was no connection between his roles as employer and landlord. And he fired the workers' committee.

The Pullman Strike

Chicago was the hub of the railway network and the strategic center of the battle between the Pullman boycotters and the trunk line railroads. For the strikers, the crucial thing was to prevent those trains with Pullman cars attached from running; for the railroads, it was to get the trains through at any cost. To help in that endeavor, President Cleveland sent in the federal troops. (*Harper's Weekly*, July 21, 1894)

The strike that ensued would have warranted only a footnote in American labor history but for the fact that the Pullman workers belonged to the American Railway Union (ARU), a rapidly growing industrial union of railroad workers. Its leader, Eugene V. Debs, directed ARU members not to handle Pullman sleeping cars, which, although operated by the railroads, were owned and serviced by the Pullman Company. This was a *secondary labor boycott:* force was applied on a second party (the railroads) to bring pressure on the primary target (Pullman). Since the railroads insisted on running the Pullman cars, a far-flung strike soon spread across the country, threatening the entire economy.

Quite deliberately, the railroads maneuvered to bring the federal government into the dispute. Their hook was the U.S. mail cars, which they attached to every train hauling Pullman cars. When strikers stopped these trains, the railroads appealed to President Cleveland to protect the U.S. mail and halt the growing violence. Richard Olney, Cleveland's attorney general, was a former railroad lawyer who unabashedly sided with his former employers. When federal troops failed to get the trains running again, Olney obtained court injunctions prohibiting the ARU leaders from conducting the strike. Debs and his associates, refusing to obey, were charged with contempt of court and jailed. Now leaderless and uncoordinated, the strike quickly disintegrated.

No one could doubt why the great Pullman boycott had failed: it had been crushed by the naked use of government power on behalf of the railroad companies.

AMERICAN RADICALISM IN THE MAKING

Very little in Eugene Debs's background would have suggested that he would one day become the nation's leading socialist. A native of Terre Haute, Indiana, a prosperous railroad town, Debs grew up believing in the essential goodness of American society. A popular young man-about-town, Debs considered a career in politics or business but instead got involved in the local labor movement. In 1880 at the age of twenty-five he was elected national secretary-treasurer of the Brotherhood of Locomotive Firemen, one of the craft unions that represented the skilled operating trades on the railroads.

Troubled by his union's indifference to the low-paid track and yard laborers, Debs unexpectedly resigned from his comfortable post to devote himself to a new organization, the American Railway Union, that would organize all railroad workers irrespective of skill—that is, an *industrial union*.

The Pullman strike visibly changed Debs. Sentenced to six months in the federal penitentiary, Debs emerged an avowed radical, committed to a lifelong struggle against a system that enabled employers to enlist the powers of government to beat down working people. Initially Debs identified himself as a Populist (see Chapter 18), but he quickly gravitated to the socialist camp.

German refugees had brought the ideas of Karl Marx, the radical German philosopher, to America after the failed revolution of 1848 in Europe. Marx postulated a class struggle between capitalists and workers, ending in a revolution that would abolish private ownership of the means of production and bring about a classless society. Little noticed by most Americans, Marxist socialism struck deep roots in the German American communities of Chicago and New York. With the formation of the Socialist Labor Party in 1877, Marxist socialism established itself as a permanent, if narrowly based, presence in American politics.

When Eugene Debs appeared in their midst in 1897, the socialists were in disarray. American capitalism had just gone through its worst crisis, yet they had failed to make much headway. Many blamed the party head, Daniel De Leon, an ideological purist not greatly interested in attracting voters. Debs joined in the revolt against the dogmatic De Leon and helped launch the rival Socialist Party of America in 1901.

A spellbinding campaigner, Debs talked socialism in an American idiom, making Marxism understandable and persuasive to many ordinary Americans. Under him the new party began to break out of its immigrant base and attract American-born voters. In Texas, Oklahoma, and Minnesota socialism exerted a powerful appeal among distressed farmers radicalized by Populism. The party was also highly successful at attracting women activists. Inside of a decade, with a national network of branches and state organizations, the Socialist Party had become a force to be reckoned with in American politics.

For some radical unionists, especially veterans of the fierce labor wars in the West (see Chapter 16), electoral politics seemed too tame. Led by Ed Boyce and "Big Bill" Haywood, the Western Federation of Miners joined with left-wing socialists in 1905 to create a new movement, the Industrial Workers of the World (IWW). The Wobblies, as IWW members were called, fervently supported the Marxist class struggle—but at the workplace rather than in politics. By resistance at the point of production and ultimately by means of a general strike, they believed that the workers would bring about a revolution. A new society would emerge, run directly by the workers through their industrial unions. The term *syndicalism* describes this brand of workers' radicalism.

T I M E L I N E

1869	Knights of Labor founded in Philadelphia First transcontinental railroad completed	1892	Homestead steel strike crushed
1872	Andrew Carnegie starts construction of the Edgar Thompson steel works near Pittsburgh.	1893	The Panic of 1893 starts the depression of the 1890s. Wave of railroad bankruptcies; reorganization by investment bankers
1873	The Panic of 1873 ushers in economic depression.	1894	President Cleveland sends troops to break Pullman boycott.
1877	Baltimore and Ohio workers initiate a nationwide railroad strike.	1895	Frederick W. Taylor launches scientific management. Immigration from southern and eastern Europe exceeds immigration from western Europe for the first time.
1878	Gustavus Swift introduces the refrigerator train car.	1901	Eugene V. Debs helps found the Socialist Party of America.
1883	Railroads establish national time zones.	1905	Industrial Workers of the World (IWW) launched
1886	Haymarket Square anarchist bombing in Chicago American Federation of Labor (AFL) founded		

In both its major forms—politically oriented socialism and the syndicalist IWW—American radicalism flourished after the crisis of the 1890s, but only on a limited basis and never with the possibility of seizing power. Nevertheless, socialists and Wobblies served a larger purpose. The new industrial economy—a wealth-creating machine beyond the world's imagining—was also brutally indifferent to the many who fell by the wayside. American radicalism, by its sheer vitality, bore witness to what was exploitative and unjust in the new industrial order.

For Further Exploration

For students new to economic history, biography offers an accessible entry point into what can be a dauntingly technical subject. The biographical literature is especially rich in American history because of this country's fascination with its great magnates and because of a long-standing debate among historians over what contribution (if any) the business moguls made to America's industrializing economy. The initiating book was Matthew Josephson's classic *The Robber Barons* (1934), which, as the title implies, argued that America's great fortunes were built on the wealth that others had created. The contrary view was taken by the financial historian Julius Grodinsky, whose *Jay Gould: His Business Career, 1867–1892* (1957) explained masterfully how this railroad buccaneer helped shape the transportation system. Since then, there have been superb, mostly sympathetic, business biographies, including Joseph F. Wall, *Andrew Carnegie* (1970); Ron Chernow, *Titan: The Life of John D. Rockefeller* (1998); and Jean Strause, *Morgan: American Financier* (1999). The founder of scientific management has also recently been the subject of a robust biography: Robert Kanigel, *The One Best Way: Frederick W. Taylor and the Enigma of Efficiency* (1997). On labor's side, the biographical literature is nearly as rich. The founder of the AFL is the subject of a lively brief biography by Harold Livesay, *Samuel Gompers and Organized Labor in America* (1978); Gompers's autobiography, *Seventy Years of Life and Labor* (2 vols., 1925), also makes rewarding reading. His main critic is treated with great insight in Nick Salvatore, *Eugene V. Debs: Citizen and Socialist* (1982). The IWW leader William D. Haywood left a colorful autobiography, *Bill Haywood's Book* (1929), and Haywood is also the subject of Peter Carlson's biography, *Roughneck* (1982). Biography, of course, tends to overlook the foot soldiers of history, but social historians have striven mightily in recent years to tell their story. An excellent example is Paul Krause, *The Battle for Homestead, 1880–1892* (1992), which rescues from obscurity the working people who led that decisive steel strike. There is an excellent website on Andrew Carnegie at <pbs.org/wgbh/amex/pandeoi.html> and a site on the Bessemer converter that established his dominance in steel at <anglia.co.uk/angmulti/indrev/steel5.html>.

Chapter 18

THE POLITICS OF LATE NINETEENTH-CENTURY AMERICA

Politics has now become a gainful profession, like advocacy,
stockbroking, [or] the dry goods trade. . . . People go into it to make
a living by it.

—JAMES BRYCE, *AMERICAN COMMONWEALTH*, 1888

Ever since the founding of the Republic, foreign visitors had been coming to America to study its political system. Most famous of the early observers was the French aristocrat Alexis de Tocqueville, the author of *Democracy in America* (1835). When an equally brilliant visitor, the Englishman James Bryce, sat down to write his own account fifty years later, he decided that Tocqueville's great book could not serve as his model. For Tocqueville, Bryce noted, "America was primarily a democracy, the ideal democracy, fraught with lessons for Europe." In his own book, *The American Commonwealth* (1888), Bryce was much less rhapsodic. Tocqueville's robust democracy had devolved a half century later into the dreary machine politics of post–Civil War America.

Bryce was anxious, however, that his European readers not misunderstand him. Europeans would find in his book "much that is sordid, much that will provoke unfavourable comment." But they needed to be aware of "a reserve of force and patriotism more than sufficient to sweep away all the evils now tolerated, and to make a politics of the country worthy of its material grandeur and of the private virtues of its inhabitants." Bryce was ultimately an optimist: "A hundred times in writing this book have I been disheartened by the facts I was stating; a hundred times has the recollection of the abounding strength and vitality of the nation chased away these tremours."

Just what Bryce found so disheartening in the practice of American politics is this chapter's first subject. The second is the underlying vitality that Bryce sensed and how it reemerged and began to reinvigorate the nation's politics by the century's end.

516

The Politics of the Status Quo, 1877–1893

In times of national ferment public life becomes magnified. Leaders emerge. Great issues are debated. The powers of government expand. All this had been true of the Civil War era, when the crises of Union and Reconstruction had severely tested the nation's political structure, not least by the contested presidential election of 1876. In 1877, with Rutherford B. Hayes safely settled in the White House, the era of sectional strife finally ended.

Political life went on, but drained of its earlier drama. In the 1880s there were no Lincolns, no great national debates. An irreducible core of public functions remained and even, as on the question of railroad regulation, grudging acceptance of new federal responsibilities. But the dominant rhetoric celebrated government that governed least, and compared to the Civil War era, American government did govern less.

THE NATIONAL SCENE

There were five presidents from 1877 to 1893: Rutherford B. Hayes (Republican, 1877–1881), James A. Garfield (Republican, 1881), Chester A. Arthur (Republican, 1881–1885), Grover Cleveland (Democrat, 1885–1889), and Benjamin Harrison (Republican, 1889–1893). All were estimable men. Hayes had served effectively as governor of Ohio for three terms, and Garfield had done well as a congressional leader. Arthur, despite his reputation as a hack politician, had shown fine administrative skills as head of the New York customs house. Cleveland had an enviable reputation as reform mayor of Buffalo and governor of New York. None was a charismatic leader, but circumstances, more than personal qualities, explain why these presidents did not make a larger mark on history.

The president's biggest job was to dispense political patronage. Under the spoils system government appointments were treated as rewards for those who had served the victorious party. Reform of this system became urgent after President Garfield was shot in 1881 by Charles Guiteau, a deranged religious fanatic. Although Guiteau's motives were murky, advocates of civil-service reform blamed the poisonous atmosphere of a spoils system that left many disappointed in the scramble for office. The resulting Pendleton Act of 1883 created a list of jobs to be filled on the basis of examinations administered by the new Civil Service Commission. The list originally covered only 10 percent of all federal jobs, however, and patronage remained a preoccupation in the White House. Though standards of public administration did rise, there was no American counterpart to the elite civil services taking shape in Britain and Germany in these years.

The functions of the executive branch were, in any event, very modest. Its biggest job was delivering the mail; of 100,000 federal employees in 1880, 56 percent worked for the Post Office. Even the important cabinet offices—Treasury, State,

"Where Is He?"

This *Puck* cartoon, which appeared two weeks after Benjamin Harrison's defeat for reelection at Grover Cleveland's hands in 1892, is a commentary on Harrison's insignificance as president. The hat in Uncle Sam's hands belonged to Benjamin Harrison's grandfather, President William Henry Harrison. *Puck* started using the hat as a trademark for Benjamin Harrison after he had been elected in 1888. As his term progressed, the hat grew progressively larger, and the president progressively smaller. By the time of his defeat, just the hat is left and Harrison has disappeared altogether.

(Courtesy of the Bancroft Library, University of California at Berkeley. *Puck*, November 16, 1892)

War, Navy, Interior—were sleepy places carrying on largely routine duties. Virtually all federal funding came from customs duties and excise taxes on liquor and tobacco. These sources produced more money than the government spent. How to reduce the federal surplus ranked as one of the most troublesome issues of the 1880s.

On matters of national policy the presidents took a back seat to Congress. But Congress functioned badly. Procedural rules frequently stymied legislative business. Nor were the two parties especially anxious to get things done. Historically, they represented somewhat different traditions. The Democrats favored states' rights, while the Republicans were heirs to the Whig enthusiasm for federally assisted economic development. After Reconstruction, however, the Republicans backed away from that interventionist position, and, in truth, party differences became muddy. On most leading issues of the day—civil-service reform, the currency, and regulation of the railroads—the divisions occurred within the parties, not between them.

Only the tariff remained a fighting issue. From Lincoln's administration onward high duties had protected American industry from imported goods. The

Democrats, free traders by tradition, regularly attacked Republican protectionism. But in practice even the tariff was a negotiable issue, like any other. Congressmen voted their constituents' interests, regardless of party rhetoric. As a result, every tariff bill was a patchwork of bargains among special interests.

Issues were treated gingerly partly because the parties were so equally balanced. The Democrats, in retreat immediately after the Civil War, quickly regrouped and by the end of Reconstruction stood on virtually equal terms with the Republicans. Every presidential election from 1876 to 1892 was decided by a thin margin, and neither party gained permanent command of Congress. Political caution seemed wise; any false move on national issues might tip the scales to the other side.

The weakening of principled politics was evident in the Republicans' retreat from their Civil War legacy. The major unfinished business after 1877 involved the plight of the former slaves. The Republican agenda called for federal funding to combat illiteracy and, even more contentious, federal protection for black voters in southern congressional elections. Neither measure managed to make it through Congress. With little mileage left in Reconstruction politics, Republicans backpedaled on the race issue and abandoned African Americans to their fate.

That did not stop Republican orators from "waving the bloody shirt" against the Democrats. Service in the Union army gave candidates a strong claim to public office, and veterans' benefits always stood high on the Republican agenda. The Democrats played the same patriotic card in the South as defenders of the Lost Cause.

Alternatively, campaigns could descend into comedy. In the hard-fought election of 1884, for example, the Democrat Cleveland burst on the scene as a reformer, fresh from his victories over corrupt machine politics in New York State. But years earlier Cleveland, a bachelor, had fathered an illegitimate child, and throughout the campaign he was dogged by the ditty, "Maw, Maw, where's my Paw?" (After election day, Cleveland's supporters gleefully responded, "He's in the White House, haw-haw-haw.") Cleveland's opponent, James G. Blaine, already on the defensive for taking favors from the railroads, was weakened by the unthinking charge of a too ardent Republican supporter that the Democrats were the party of "Rum, Romanism and Rebellion." In a twinkling, he had insulted Catholic voters and possibly lost the election for Blaine. In the midst of all the mudslinging, the issues got lost.

THE IDEOLOGY OF INDIVIDUALISM

The characteristics of public life in the 1880s—the inactivity of the federal government, the evasiveness of the political parties, the absorption in politics for its own sake—derived ultimately from the conviction that little was at stake in public affairs. In 1887 Cleveland vetoed a small appropriation for drought-stricken Texas farmers with the remark that "though the people support the Government, the Government should not support the people." Governmental activity was itself considered a bad thing. All that the state could do, said Republican Senator Roscoe

Facing the World

The cover of this Horatio Alger novel (1893) captures the myth of opportunity. Our hero, Harry Vane, is a poor but earnest lad, ready to make his way in the world and, despite the many obstacles thrown in his path, sure to succeed. In some 135 books Horatio Alger repeated this story, with minor variations, for an eager reading public that numbered in the millions.

(Frank and Marie-Therese Wood Print Collections, Alexandria, Virginia)

Conkling, was "to clear the way of impediments and dangers, and leave every class and every individual free and safe in the exertions and pursuits of life." Conkling was expressing the political corollary to the economic doctrine of *laissez-faire*—the belief that the less government did, the better.

A flood of popular writings trumpeted the creed of individualism, from the rags-to-riches tales of Horatio Alger to innumerable success manuals with such titles as *Thoughts for the Young Men of America, or a Few Practical Words of Advice to Those Born in Poverty and Destined to Be Reared in Orphanages* (1871). Self-made men like Andrew Carnegie became cultural heroes. A best seller was Carnegie's *Triumphant Democracy* (1886), which paid homage to a country that enabled a penniless Scottish child to rise from bobbin boy to steel magnate.

From the pulpit came the assurances of the Episcopal bishop William Lawrence of Massachusetts that "Godliness is in league with riches." Bishop Lawrence was voicing a familar theme of American Protestantism: success in one's earthly calling revealed the promise of eternal salvation. It was all too easy for a conservative ministry to make morally reassuring the furious acquisitiveness of industrial America. "To secure wealth is an honorable ambition," intoned the Baptist minister Russell H. Conwell in his lecture "Acres of Diamonds."

The celebration of American acquisitiveness drew strong intellectual support from science. In *The Origin of Species* (1859) the British naturalist Charles Darwin had developed a bold hypothesis to explain the evolution of plants and animals. In nature, Darwin wrote, all living things struggle to survive. Individual members of a species are born with genetic mutations that enable them to compete better in their particular environment—camouflage coloring for a bird, for example, or resistance to thirst in a camel. These survival characteristics, since they are genetically transmissible, become dominant in future generations, and the species evolves. This process of evolution, which Darwin called *natural selection,* created a revolution in biology.

Drawing on Darwin, the British philosopher Herbert Spencer spun out an elaborate analysis of how human society had evolved through competition and "survival of the fittest." Social Darwinism, as Spencer's ideas became known, was championed in America by William Graham Sumner, a sociology professor at Yale. Competition, said Sumner, is a law of nature that "can no more be done away with than gravitation." And who are the fittest? "The millionaires. . . . They may fairly be regarded as the naturally selected agents of society. They get high wages and live in luxury, but the bargain is a good one for society."

Social Darwinists regarded with horror any interference with social processes. "The great stream of time and earthly things will sweep on just the same in spite of us," Sumner wrote in a famous essay, "The Absurd Attempt to Make the World Over" (1894). As for the government, it had "at bottom . . . two chief things . . . with which to deal. They are the property of men and the honor of women. These it has to defend against crime."

THE SUPREMACY OF THE COURTS

Suspicion of government not only paralyzed political initiative; it also shifted power away from the executive and legislative branches. "The task of constitutional government," declared Sumner, "is to devise institutions which shall come into play at critical periods to prevent the abusive control of the powers of a state by the controlling classes in it." Sumner meant the judiciary. From the 1870s onward the courts increasingly accepted the role that he assigned to them, becoming the guardians of the rights of private property against the grasping tentacles of government.

The main target of the courts was the states rather than the national government. This was because, under the federal system as it was understood in the late nineteenth century, the residual powers—those not delegated by the Constitution to the federal government—left to the states primary responsibility for social welfare and economic regulation. They exercised their *police powers* to ensure the health, safety, and morals of their citizens. The leading question in American law was how to strike a balance between state responsibility for the general welfare and the liberty of individuals to pursue their private interests. Most states, caught up in the conservative ethos of the day, were cutting back on expenditures and public services. Even so, there were more than enough state initiatives to alarm vigilant judges. Thus, in the landmark case *In Re Jacobs* (1885), the New York Supreme Court struck down a state law prohibiting cigar manufacturing in tenements on the grounds that such regulation exceeded the police powers of the state.

Increasingly, however, federal judges took up the battle against state activism. The Supreme Court's crucial weapon in this campaign was the Fourteenth Amendment (1868), which prohibited the states from depriving "any person of life, liberty, or property, without due process of law." The due-process clause had been adopted during Reconstruction to protect the civil rights of the former slaves. But due process protected the property rights and contractual liberty of any "person," and legally corporations counted as persons. So interpreted, the Fourteenth Amendment became by the turn of the century a powerful restraint on the states in the use of their police powers to regulate private business.

The Supreme Court similarly hamstrung the federal government. In 1895 the Court ruled that the federal power to regulate interstate commerce did not cover manufacturing and struck down a federal income tax law. And in areas where federal power was undeniable—such as the regulation of railroads—the Supreme Court watched like a hawk for undue interference with the rights of property.

Power conferred status. The law, not politics, attracted the ablest people and held the public's esteem. A Wisconsin judge boasted: "The bench symbolizes on earth the throne of divine justice. . . . Law in its highest sense is the will of God." Judicial supremacy reflected how dominant the ideology of individualism had become in industrial America and also how low American politicians had fallen in the esteem of their countrymen.

Politics and the People

For all the criticism leveled against it, politics figured centrally in the nation's life. Proportionately more voters turned out in presidential elections from 1876 to 1892 than at any other time in American history. People voted Democratic or Republican loyally for a lifetime. National conventions attracted huge crowds. "The excitement, the mental and physical strains," remarked an Indiana Republican after the 1888 convention, "are surpassed only by prolonged battle in actual warfare, as I have been told by officers of the Civil War who later engaged in convention struggles." The convention he described had nominated the colorless Benjamin Harrison on a routine platform. What was all the excitement about?

CULTURAL POLITICS: PARTY, RELIGION, AND ETHNICITY

In the late nineteenth century politics was a vibrant part of the nation's culture. During the election season the party faithful marched in impressive torchlight parades. Party paraphernalia flooded the country—handkerchiefs, mugs, posters, and buttons emblazoned with the Democratic donkey or the Republican elephant, symbols that had been adopted in the 1870s. In the 1888 campaign the candidates were featured on cards, like baseball players, packed into Honest Long Cut tobacco. In an age before movies and radio, politics ranked as one of the great American forms of entertainment.

Party loyalty was a deadly serious matter, however. Long after the killing ended, Civil War emotions ran high. Among family friends in Cleveland, recalled the urban reformer Brand Whitlock, the Republican Party was "a synonym for patriotism, another name for the nation. It was inconceivable that any self-respecting person should be a Democrat"—or, among former Confederates in the South, that any self-respecting person could be a Republican.

Beyond these sectional differences, the most important determinants of party loyalty were religion and ethnicity (see Figure 18.1). Statistically, northern Democrats tended to be foreign-born and Catholic, while Republicans tended to be native-born and Protestant. Among Protestants, the more *pietistic* a person's faith—that is, the more personal and direct the believer's relationship to God—the more likely he or she was to be a Republican and to favor using the powers of the state to uphold social values.

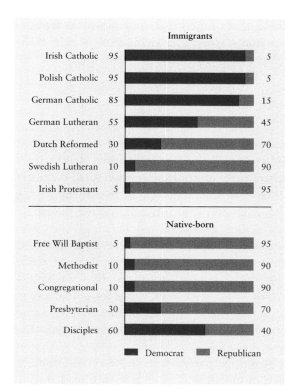

FIGURE 18.1
Ethnocultural Voting Patterns in the Midwest, 1870–1892

These figures demonstrate how voting patterns among midwesterners reflected ethnicity and religion in the late nineteenth century. Especially striking is the overwhelming preference by immigrant Catholics for the Democratic Party. Among Protestants there was an equally strong preference for the Republican Party by certain groups of immigrants (Swedish Lutherans and Irish Protestants) and native-born (Free Will Baptists, Methodists, and Congregationalists), but other Protestant groups were more evenly divided in their party preferences.

During the 1880s, as ethnic tensions built up in many cities, education became an arena of bitter conflict. One issue was whether instruction would be in English. Immigrant groups often wanted their children taught in their own languages. In St. Louis, a heavily German city, the long-standing policy of teaching German to all students was overturned after a heated campaign. Religion was an even more explosive educational issue. Catholics fought a losing battle over public aid for parochial schools, which by 1900 was prohibited by twenty-three states. In Boston a furious controversy broke out in 1888 over the use of an anti-Catholic history textbook. When the school board withdrew the offending book, angry Protestants threw the moderates off the board and returned the text to the curriculum.

Then there was the regulation of public morals. In many states so-called blue laws restricted activity on Sundays. When Nebraska banned Sunday baseball, the state supreme court approved the law as a blow struck in "the contest between Christianity and wrong." But German and Irish Catholics, who saw nothing evil in a bit of fun on Sunday, considered blue laws a violation of their personal freedom. Ethnocultural conflict also flared over the liquor question. Many states adopted strict licensing and local-option laws governing the sale of alcoholic beverages. Indiana permitted drinking, but only joylessly in rooms containing "no devices for amusement or music . . . of any kind."

Because the hottest social issues of the day—education, the liquor question, and observance of the sabbath—were also party issues, they lent deep significance to party affiliation. And because these issues were fought out mostly at the state and local levels, they hit very close to home. Crusading Methodists thought of Republicans as the party of morality. For embattled Irish and German Catholics the Democratic Party was the defender of their freedoms.

ORGANIZATIONAL POLITICS

Political life was also important because of the organizational activity it generated. By the 1870s both major parties had evolved formal, well-organized structures. At the base lay the precinct or ward, where party meetings were open to all members. County, state, and national committees ran the ongoing business of the parties. Conventions determined party rules, adopted platforms, and selected the party's candidates.

Party administration seemed, on its face, highly democratic, since in theory all power derived from the party members in the precincts and wards. In practice, however, the parties were run by unofficial internal organizations—*machines*—which consisted of insiders willing to do party work in exchange for public jobs or the sundry advantages of being connected. The machines tended toward one-man rule, although the "boss" ruled more by the consent of the secondary leaders than by his own absolute power.

Absorbed in the tasks of power brokerage, party bosses treated public issues as somewhat irrelevant. The high stakes of money, jobs, and influence made for intense factionalism. After Ulysses S. Grant left the White House in 1877, the Republican Party divided into two warring factions—the Stalwarts, who followed Senator Roscoe Conkling of New York, and the Halfbreeds, led by James G. Blaine of Maine. The split was sparked by a personal feud between Conkling and Blaine, but it persisted because of a furious struggle over patronage. The Halfbreeds represented a newer Republican generation that was more favorably disposed than the Stalwarts to political reform and was less committed to shopworn Civil War issues. But issues were secondary in the strife between Stalwarts and Halfbreeds. They were really fighting over the spoils of party politics.

And yet the record of machine politics was not wholly negative. In certain ways the standards of governance got better. Disciplined professionals, veterans of machine politics, proved effective as state legislators and congressmen because they were more experienced in the give-and-take of politics. More important, party machines filled a void in the nation's public life. They did informally much of what the governmental system left undone, especially in the cities (see Chapter 19).

But machine politics never managed to win public approval. Many of the nation's social elite—intellectuals, well-to-do businessmen, and old-line families—resented a politics that excluded people like themselves, the "best men." There was, too, a genuine clash of values. Political reformers called for "disinterestedness" and "independence"—the opposite of the self-serving careerism and party regularity fostered by the machine system. Many of these critics had earned their spurs as Liberal Republicans who had broken from the party and fought President Grant's reelection in 1872.

In 1884 Carl Schurz, Edwin L. Godkin, and Charles Francis Adams Jr. again left the Republican Party because they could not stomach its presidential candidate, James G. Blaine, whom they associated with corrupt politics. Mainly from New York and Massachusetts, these Republicans became known as Mugwumps—a derisive bit of contemporary slang, supposedly of Indian origin, referring to pompous or self-important persons. The Mugwumps threw their support to the Democrat Grover Cleveland and may have ensured his victory by giving him the winning margin in New York State.

After the 1884 election the enthusiasm for reform spilled over into local politics, spawning good-government campaigns across the country. Although they won some municipal victories, the Mugwumps were more adept at molding public opinion than reforming government. Controlling the newspapers and journals read by the educated middle class, the Mugwumps defined the terms of political debate and denied the machine system public legitimacy.

The Mugwumps were reformers, but not on behalf of social justice. The problems of working people did not evoke their sympathy, nor did they favor using the the state to help the poor. As far as the Mugwumps were concerned, that government was best that governed least. Theirs was the brand of "reform" perfectly in keeping with a politics of the status quo.

WOMEN'S POLITICAL CULTURE

The young Theodore Roosevelt, an up-and-coming Republican state politician in 1884, referred to the Mugwumps contemptuously as "man-milliners." The sexual slur was not accidental. In attacking organizational politics the Mugwumps were challenging one of the bastions of male society. At party meetings and conventions men carried on not only the business of politics but also the rituals of male sociability amid cigar smoke and whiskey. Politics was identified with manliness. It was competitive. It dealt in the commerce of power. Party politics, in short, was no place for a woman.

So, naturally, the woman suffrage movement met fierce opposition. Blocked in their efforts to get a constitutional amendment, suffragists concentrated on state campaigns. But except in Wyoming, Idaho, Colorado, and Utah the most they could win was the right to vote for school boards or on tax issues. "Men are ordained to govern in all forceful and material things, because they are men," asserted an anti-suffrage resolution, "while women, by the same decree of God and nature, are equally fitted to bear rule in a higher and more spiritual realm"—that is to say, not in politics.

Yet this invocation of the doctrine of "separate spheres" did open a channel for women to enter public life. "Women's place is Home," acknowledged the journalist Retha Childe Dorr. "But Home is not contained within the four walls of an individual house. Home is the community. The city full of people is the Family. . . . And badly do the Home and Family need their mother." So believing, women had since the early nineteenth century engaged in charitable activities. Women's organizations fought prostitution, assisted the poor, agitated for prison reform, and tried to expand educational and job opportunities for women. Since many of these goals required state intervention, women's organizations of necessity became politically active. Partisan politics, they stressed, was not their game. Quite the contrary: women were bent on creating their own political sphere.

No issue joined home and politics more poignantly than did the liquor question. Just before Christmas in 1873 the women of Hillsboro, Ohio, began to hold vigils in front of the town's saloons, pleading with the owners to close and end the suffering of families of hard-drinking fathers. Thus began a spontaneous uprising of women that spread across the country and closed an estimated 3,000 saloons. From this agitation came the Women's Christian Temperance Union (WCTU), which after its formation in 1874 rapidly blossomed into the largest women's organization in the country.

Because it excluded men, the WCTU was the spawning ground for women leaders. Under the guidance of Frances Willard, who became president in 1879, the WCTU moved beyond temperance and adopted a "Do-Everything" policy. Alcoholism, women recognized, was not simply a personal failing; it stemmed from larger social problems in American society. Willard also wanted to attract women

Wanted, Sober Men

This drawing appeared in a magazine in 1899, twenty-five years after the women of Hillsboro, Ohio, rose in revolt against the town's saloonkeepers and launched the Woman's Christian Temperance Union (WCTU). But the emotion it expresses had not changed—that the saloon was the enemy of the family.
(Culver Pictures)

who had no particular interest in the liquor question. By 1889 the WCTU had thirty-nine departments concerned with labor, prostitution, health, and international peace as well as temperance.

Most important, the WCTU was drawn to woman suffrage. This was necessary, Willard argued, "because the liquor traffic is entrenched in law, and law grows out of the will of majorities, and majorities of women are against the liquor traffic." The WCTU began by stressing moral suasion and personal discipline—hence the word "temperance" in its name—but expanded its attack on liquor to include prohibition by law. Women needed the vote, said Willard, to fulfill their social responsibilities *as women* (see American Voices, "The Case for Women's Political Rights"). This was very different from the claim made by the suffragists—that the ballot was an inherent right of all citizens *as individuals*—and was less threatening to masculine pride.

Not much changed in the short run. But by linking women's social concerns to women's political participation, the WCTU helped lay the groundwork for a fresh attack on male electoral politics in the early twentieth century. And in the meantime, even without the vote, the WCTU demonstrated how potent a voice women could find in the public arena and how vibrant a political culture they could build.

The Case for Women's Political Rights

HELEN POTTER

*I*n 1883 Helen Potter, a New York educator, testified before the Senate Committee on Education and Labor. She meant to speak about the sanitary conditions of the poor in New York City, but in the course of her testimony she delivered a powerful indictment of the unequal treatment of women that spoke volumes about the evolving women's political culture of the late nineteenth century.

The Witness. It is really an important question—this of the condition of women in our community. When I was a young girl I had some ambition, and when I heard a good speaker, or when I read something written by a good writer, I had an ambition to do something of that kind myself. I was exceedingly anxious to preach, but the churches would not have me; why, they said that a woman must not be heard. . . .

Q. What would be the effect of conferring suffrage upon women? Would not the effect be injurious to the moral character and high influence of woman, if she should devote herself to the tricks of the politician's trade, which you very properly criticize so severely?

A. . . . I certainly think it would clean our streets, and I think it would purify politics, at least for the next two hundred years. It would take about that time to get women to understand the tricks of politicians as at present practiced. I do not think that women would be injured by it. . . . This Government is based upon the will of the people—women are "people," yet we have not a word to say about the laws. You will hear women in the course of your acquaintance say they wish they were men; I never heard a man say he wished he was a woman. . . .

Q. What effect do you think the extension of the suffrage to women would have upon their material condition, their wage-earning power and the like?

A. They would get equal pay for equal work of equal value. I do not think a woman ought to be paid the price of an expert, when she is not herself an expert, but I believe there would be a stimulus for a woman to fit herself for the very best work. What stimulus is there for woman to fit herself properly, if she never can attain the highest pay, no matter what sort of work she does? If women had a vote I think larger avenues of livelihood would be opened for them and they would be more respected by the governmental powers.

SOURCE: U.S. Senate, Committee on Education and Labor, *Report upon Relations Between Labor and Capital* (1885), II: 627, 629–32.

Race and Politics in the South

When Reconstruction ended in 1877, so did the promise of racial equality for the South's African Americans. Schooling was strictly segregated. Access to jobs, the courts, and social welfare was racially determined and unequal. But public accommodations were not yet legally segregated, and practices varied a good deal across the South. Only on the railroads, as rail travel became more common, did whites demand that blacks be excluded from first-class cars, with the result that southern railroads became after 1887 the first public accommodation subject to segregation laws.

In politics the situation was still more fluid. Blacks had not been driven from politics. On the contrary, their turnout at elections was not far behind whites. But blacks did not participate on equal terms with whites. In the Black Belt areas where African Americans sometimes outnumbered whites, voting districts were gerry-mandered to ensure that while blacks got some offices, political control remained in white hands. Blacks, moreover, were routinely intimidated during political cam-paigns. Even so, an impressive majority remained staunchly Republican, refusing, as the last black congressman from Mississippi told his House colleagues in 1882, "to surrender their honest convictions, even upon the altar of their personal ne-cessities."

Whatever hopes blacks entertained for better days, however, faded during the 1880s and then, in the next decade, expired in a terrible burst of racial terrorism.

BIRACIAL POLITICS

No democratic society can survive if it does not enable competing economic and social interests to be heard. In the United States the two-party system performs that role. The Civil War crisis severely tested the two-party system because, both North and South, political opposition came to be seen as treasonable. In the North, de-spite the best efforts of the Republicans, the Democrats shed their disgrace after the war and reclaimed their status as a major party. In the defeated South, however, the scars of war cut deep, and Reconstruction cut even deeper. The struggle for "home rule" empowered southern Democrats. They had "redeemed" the South from Re-publican domination; hence the name they adopted: Redeemers. Cloaked in the mantle of the Lost Cause, the Redeemers claimed a monopoly on political legiti-macy.

The Republican Party in the South did not fold up, however. On the contrary, it soldiered on, sustained by tenacious black loyalty, a hard core of white support, patronage from Republican national administrations, and a key Democrat vulner-ability. This was the gap between the universality the Democrats claimed as the party of Redemption and its actual domination by a single interest, the South's eco-nomic elite.

Class antagonism, though masked by sectional patriotism, was never absent from southern society. The Civil War had brought out long-smoldering differences between planters and hill-country farmers, who were called on to shed blood for a slaveholding system in which they had no interest. Afterward class tensions were exacerbated by the spread of farm tenantry and by the emergence of the low-wage factory system. Unable to make their grievances heard, economically distressed

southerners broke with the Democratic Party in the early 1880s and mounted insurgent movements across the region. Most notable were the Readjusters, who
briefly gained power in Virginia over the issue of speculation in Reconstruction
debt: they opposed repayment that would have rewarded bond-holding speculators while leaving the state destitute. After subsiding briefly, this agrarian discontent revived with a vengeance in the late 1880s as tenant farmers now sought
political power through farmers' alliances and the newly evolving Populist Party
(see p. 537).

As this insurgency against the Democrats accelerated, the question of black participation became critical. Racism cut through southern society and, so some
thought, most infected the lowest rungs. "The white laboring classes here," wrote
an Alabaman in 1886, "are separated from the Negroes, working all day side by side
with them, by an innate consciousness of race superiority." Yet when times got bad
enough, hard-pressed whites could also see blacks as fellow victims. "They are in
the ditch just like we are," asserted one white Texan. Southern Populists never fully
reconciled these contradictory impulses. They did not question the conventions of
social inequality. Nor were the interests of white farmers and black tenants and laborers always in concert. But once agrarian protest turned political, the logic of interracial solidarity became hard to deny.

Black farmers had developed a political structure of their own. The Colored
Farmers' Alliance operated much less openly than its white counterparts—it could
be worth a black man's life to make too open a show of his independence—but
nevertheless made black voters a factor in the political calculations of southern Populists. The demands of partisan politics, once the break with the Democrats came,
clinched the argument for interracial unity. Where the Populists fused with the Republican Party, as in North Carolina and Tennessee, they automatically became allies of black leaders. Where the Populists fielded separate third-party tickets, they
needed to appeal directly to black voters. "The accident of color can make no difference in the interest of farmers, croppers, and laborers," argued the Georgian Tom
Watson. "You are kept apart that you may be separately fleeced of your earnings."
By making this interracial appeal, even if not always wholeheartedly, the Populists
put at risk the foundations of conservative southern politics.

ONE-PARTY RULE TRIUMPHANT

The conservative Democrats struck back with all their might. They played the race
card to the hilt, parading as the "white man's party" while denouncing the Populists
for promoting "Negro rule." Yet they shamelessly competed for the black vote. In
this they had many advantages: money, control of the local power structures, and
a paternalistic relationship to the black community. When all else failed, mischief
at the polls enabled the Democrats to beat back the Populists. Across the South in
the 1892 elections the Democrats snatched victory from defeat by a miraculous vote
count of blacks—including many long dead or gone. Thus the Mississippian Frank

Burkitt's bitter attack on the conservatives: they were "a class of corrupt office-seekers" who had "hypocritically raised the howl of white supremacy while they debauched the ballot boxes . . . disregarded the rights of the blacks . . . and actually dominated the will of the white people through the instrumentality of the stolen negro vote."

In the midst of these deadly struggles the Democrats decided to settle matters once and for all. Disfranchising the blacks, hitherto suggested hesitantly, now became a potent regionwide movement (Map 18.1). In 1890 Mississippi adopted a literacy test that effectively drove the state's blacks out of politics. The motives behind it were cynical, but the literacy test could be dressed up as a reform for white Mississippians tired of electoral fraud and violence. Their children and grandchildren, argued one influential figure, should not be left "with shotguns in their hands, a lie in their mouths and perjury on their lips in order to defeat the negroes." This logic persuaded even some weary Populists: Frank Burkitt, for example, was arguing *for* the Mississippi literacy test in the words quoted in the previous paragraph.

The race issue had helped bring down the Populists; now it helped reconcile them to defeat. Embittered poor whites, deeply ambivalent all along about interracial cooperation, turned their fury on blacks. Insofar as disfranchising measures

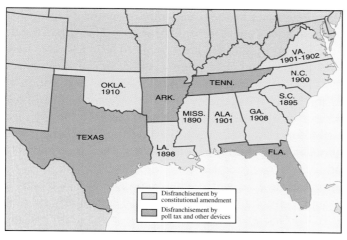

M AP 18.1
Disfranchisement in the South

In the midst of the Populist challenge to Democratic one-party rule in the South, a movement to deprive blacks of the right to vote spread from Mississippi across the South. By 1910 every state in the region except Tennessee, Arkansas, Texas, and Florida had made constitutional changes designed to prevent blacks from voting, and these four states accomplished much the same result through poll taxes and other exclusionary methods. For the next half century the political process in the South would be for whites only.

asserted militant white supremacy, poor whites approved. It was important, of course, that their own vulnerability—their own lack of education—be partially off-set by lenient enforcement of the literacy test. Thus, to take a blatant instance, Louisiana's grandfather clause exempted from the test those entitled to vote on January 1, 1867 (before the Fifteenth Amendment gave freedmen that right), together with their sons and grandsons. But poor whites were not protected from property and poll-tax requirements, and many stopped voting. Poor whites might have objected more had their spokesmen not been conceded a voice within the Democratic Party. A new brand of demagogic politician came forward to speak for them, appealing not to their class interests but to their racial prejudices. Tom Watson, the fiery Georgia Populist, rebuilt his political career as a brilliant practitioner of race baiting.

The color line, hitherto incomplete, became rigid and comprehensive. Segregated seating in trains, widely adopted in the late 1880s, provided a precedent for the legal separation of the races. The enforcing legislation, known as Jim Crow laws, soon applied to every type of public facility—restaurants, hotels, streetcars, even cemeteries. In the 1890s the South became for the first time a society fully segregated by law.

The U.S. Supreme Court soon ratified the South's decision. In the case of *Plessy v. Ferguson* (1896) the Court ruled that segregation was not discriminatory—that is, it did not violate black civil rights under the Fourteenth Amendment—provided that blacks received accommodations equal to those of whites. The "separate but equal" doctrine ignored the realities of southern life: segregated facilities were rarely if ever "equal" in any material sense, and segregation was itself intended to underscore the inferiority of blacks (see American Voices, "A Black Man on Segregation"). With a similar disregard for reality the Supreme Court in *Williams v. Mississippi* (1898) validated the disfranchising devices of the southern states: so long as race was not a specified criterion for disfranchisement, the Fifteenth Amendment was not being violated even though the practical effect was the virtual exclusion of blacks from politics in the South.

Race hatred manifested itself in a wave of lynchings and race riots, and public vilification of blacks became commonplace. Benjamin R. Tillman, governor of South Carolina and after 1895 a U.S. senator, vilified blacks as "an ignorant and debased and debauched race." This ugly racism stemmed from several sources, including job competition between whites and blacks during the depressed 1890s and white anger against a less submissive black generation born after slavery.

But what had triggered the antiblack impulse was the Populist challenge to one-party rule. From then on white supremacy propped up the one-party system that the Redeemers had been fighting for ever since Reconstruction. If power had to be shared with demagogic poor-white politicians, it would be on terms agreeable to the conservative elite—the exclusion from politics of any serious challenge to the economic status quo.

A Black Man on Segregation

C. H. JOHNSON

W hen C. H. Johnson, a porter at an auction house, spoke up before a visiting Senate committee in 1883, the movement for a segregated South was just gathering steam. But even then, Johnson makes clear, southern blacks were not deceived about the fraudulence of "separate but equal."

Columbus, Ga., November 20, 1883

Question. Do you feel as though your people have had a fair chance to be heard by the committee?

Answer. I do. . . .

Q. And you think they have said all they want to say?

A. Well, I won't say that they did that. . . . It is just like as it was in the time of slavery . . . and they have got the same feelings now, a great many of them, and they want to say things, but they are afraid of the white people. . . .

Q. What do you mean by social equality?

A. . . . If I get on the cars to ride from here to Montgomery, or to Atlanta, although I pay the same fare that you pay—they make me do that—I do not have the same accommodations.

Q. Suppose you have a car just as good as the one white folks have, but are not allowed to go into their car, will that be satisfactory?

A. But that is not going to be done. They are not going to make a law of that kind. . . .

Q. That would be a different case. I am supposing a case where the accommodations provided for the two races are just the same.

A. . . . I would be satisfied. But don't allow a man to come in over my wife, or any other lady that respects herself as a lady, swearing and spitting and cursing around. . . . I do not want to kick up a fuss with any one, or with white people about getting in amongst them . . . but if a colored man comes along and pays the same fare that the white man pays, he has the same rights as the white man. . . .

SOURCE: U.S. Senate, Committee on the Relations Between Capital and Labor, *Report* (1885), IV: 635–38, reprinted in Stanley I. Kutler, ed., *Looking for America* (2nd ed., New York: Norton, 1979), II: 234–38.

RESISTING WHITE SUPREMACY

Southern blacks resisted as best they could. When Georgia adopted the first Jim Crow law applying to streetcars in 1891, Atlanta blacks declared a boycott, and over the next fifteen years blacks boycotted segregated streetcars in at least twenty-five

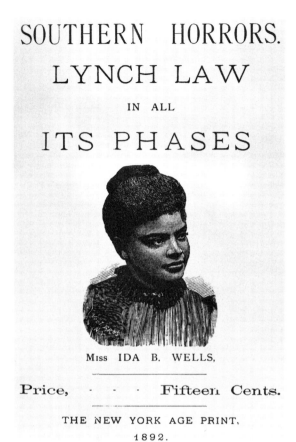

SOUTHERN HORRORS.
LYNCH LAW
IN ALL
ITS PHASES

Miss IDA B. WELLS,

Price, · · · Fifteen Cents.

THE NEW YORK AGE PRINT,
1892.

Ida B. Wells

In 1887 Ida B. Wells (Wells-Barnett after she married in 1895) was thrown bodily from a train in Tennessee for refusing to vacate her seat in a section reserved for whites, launching her into a lifetime crusade for racial justice. Her mission was to expose the evil of lynching in the South. This portrait is from the title page of a pamphlet she published in 1892 entitled, "Southern Horrors. Lynch Law in All Its Phases."

(Photographs and Prints Division, Schomburg Center for Research in Black Culture, The New York Public Library, Astor, Lenox and Tilden Foundations)

cities. "Do not trample on our pride by being 'jim crowed,'" the Savannah *Tribune* urged its readers: "Walk!" Ida Wells-Barnett emerged as the most outspoken black crusader against lynching, so enraging the Memphis white community by the editorials in her newspaper *Free Speech* that she was forced in 1892 to leave the city.

Some blacks were drawn to the Back-to-Africa movement, abandoning all hope that they would ever find justice in America. But emigration was not a real choice, and African Americans everywhere had to bend to the raging forces of racism and find a way to survive.

Booker T. Washington, the foremost black leader of his day, marked out the path in a famous speech in Atlanta in 1895. Washington retreated from the defiant stand of an older generation of black abolitionists exemplified by Frederick Douglass, who died the same year that the Atlanta speech launched Washington into national prominence. Conciliatory toward the South, Washington considered "the agitation of the question of social equality the extremest folly." He accepted segregation, provided that blacks had equal facilities. He accepted literacy tests and property qualifications for the vote, provided that they applied equally to blacks and whites.

Washington's doctrine came to be known as the Atlanta Compromise. His approach was "accommodationist," in the sense that it avoided a direct assault on white supremacy. Despite the humble face he put on before white audiences, however, Washington did not concede the struggle. Behind the scenes he lobbied hard against Jim Crow laws and disfranchisement. More important, his Atlanta Compromise, while abandoning the field of political protest, opened up a second front of economic struggle.

Booker T. Washington sought to capitalize on a southern dilemma about the economic role of the black population. Racist dogma dictated that blacks be kept down and conform to their image as lazy, shiftless workers. But for the South to prosper it needed an efficient labor force. Washington made this need the target of his efforts. As founder of the Tuskegee Institute in Alabama in 1881, Washington advocated *industrial education*—manual and agricultural training. He preached the virtues of thrift, hard work, and property ownership. Washington's industrial education program won generous support from northern philanthropists and businessmen and, following his Atlanta speech, applause from local proponents of the New South.

Washington assumed that black economic progress would be the key to winning political and civil rights. He regarded members of the white southern elite as crucial allies because only they had the power to change the South. More important, they could see "the close connection between labor, industry, education, and political institutions." When it was in their economic interest, when they had grown dependent on black labor and black enterprise, white men of business and property would recognize the justice of black rights. As Washington put it, "There is little race prejudice in the American dollar."

To what extent black self-help—hard work, industrial education, the husbanding of small resources—might counterbalance race prejudice was the nub of Booker T. Washington's problem. Where the almighty dollar reigned, there was some hope of progress. Elsewhere, as Washington saw it, there was none.

For twenty years after his Atlanta address Washington dominated the organized African American community. In an age of severe racial oppression no black dealt more skillfully with the elite of white America or wielded greater political influence. Black leaders knew Washington as a hard taskmaster. Intensely jealous of his authority, he did not regard opposition kindly. Black politicians, educators, and editors stood up to him at their peril.

Even so, opposition surfaced, especially among younger, educated blacks. They thought Washington was conceding too much. He instilled black pride but of a narrowly middle-class and utilitarian kind. What about the special genius of blacks that W.E.B. DuBois celebrated in his collection of essays, *The Souls of Black Folk* (1903)? And what of the "talented tenth" of the black population, whose promise could only be stifled by manual education? Blacks also became increasingly impatient with

Washington's silence on segregation and lynching. By the time of his death in 1915 Washington's approach had been superseded by a more militant strategy that relied on the courts and political protest, not on black self-help and accommodation.

The Crisis of American Politics: The 1890s

Populism was a catalyst for political crisis not only in the South but across the entire nation. But while in the South the result was preservation of one-party rule, in national politics the effect was the two-party system revitalized.

Ever since Reconstruction national politics had been stalemated by too evenly balanced parties. In the late 1880s this equilibrium began to break down. Benjamin Harrison's election to the presidency in 1888 was the last of the cliff-hanger victories (the Democrat, Grover Cleveland, actually got a larger popular vote). Thereafter, the tide turned against the Republicans. In 1890 Democrats took the House of Representatives decisively and won a number of governorships in normally Republican states. In 1892 Cleveland regained the presidency by the largest margin in twenty years.

Had everything else remained equal, the events of 1890 and 1892 might have inaugurated a long period of Democratic supremacy. But everything else did not remain equal. By the time of Cleveland's inauguration, farm foreclosures and railroad bankruptcies signaled economic trouble. On May 3, 1893, the stock market crashed. In Chicago 100,000 jobless workers walked the streets; nationwide the unemployment rate soared to over 20 percent.

As economic depression set in, which party would prevail—and on what platform—became an open question. The first challenge arrived from the West and South in the form of the Populist Party.

THE POPULIST REVOLT

Farmers were of necessity joiners. They needed organization to overcome their social isolation and provide economic services—hence the appeal of the Granger movement, which had spread across the Midwest after 1867, and, after the Grange's decline, the appeal of farmers' alliances in many rural districts. From these diffuse organizational beginnings two dominant organizations emerged. One was the Farmers' Alliance of the Northwest, confined mainly to the midwestern states. More dynamic was the National (or Southern) Farmers' Alliance, which in the mid-1880s spread rapidly from Texas onto the Great Plains and eastward into the cotton South, as "travelling lecturers" extolled the virtues of cooperative activity and reminded farmers of "their obligation to stand as a great conservative body against the encroachments of monopolies and . . . the growing corruption of wealth and power."

The Texas branch established a massive cooperative, the Texas Exchange, that marketed the crops of cotton farmers and provided them with cheap credit. When cotton prices fell sharply in 1891, the Texas Exchange failed. The Texas Alliance then proposed a new scheme: a subtreasury system that would enable farmers to borrow against their unsold crops from a public fund until their cotton could be profitably marketed. The credit and marketing functions would be as in the defunct Texas Exchange but with a crucial difference: the federal government would play the key role. When the subtreasury plan was rejected by the Democratic Party as too radical, the Texas Alliance decided to strike out in politics independently.

These events in Texas revealed, with special clarity, a process of politicization that engulfed the Alliance movement. Across the South and West, as state alliances grew stronger and more impatient, they began to field independent slates. The confidence gained at the state level led to the formation of the national People's (Populist) Party in 1892. In the elections that year, with the veteran antimonopoly campaigner James B. Weaver as their presidential candidate, the Populists captured a million votes and carried four western states (see Map 18.2). For the first time agrarian protest truly challenged the national two-party system.

Populism was distinguished by the many women in the movement. In the established parties the grassroots political clubs were for men only. Populism, on the other hand, arose from a network of alliances that had formed for largely social purposes and that welcomed women. Although they participated actively and served prominently as speakers and lecturers, few women achieved high office in the alliances, and their role diminished with the shift into politics. In deference to the southern wing the Populist platform was silent on woman suffrage. Still, neither Democrats nor Republicans would have countenanced a spokeswoman such as the fiery Mary Elizabeth Lease, who became famous for calling on farmers "to raise less corn and more hell." Lease insisted just as strenuously on Populism's "grand and

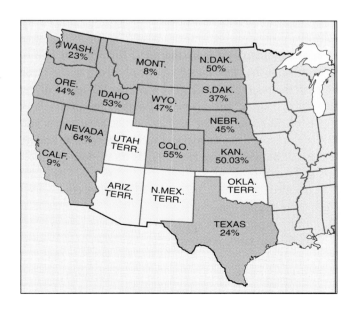

MAP 18.2
The Heyday of Western Populism, 1892

This map shows the percentage of the popular vote won by James B. Weaver, the People's Party candidate, in the presidential election of 1892. Except in California and Montana, the Populists won broad support across the West and genuinely threatened the established parties in that region.

En Route to a Populist Rally, Dickinson County, Kansas

Farm people traveled miles to rallies and meetings for the chance to voice their grievances and socialize with like-minded folks. This tradition infused Populism with a special fervor. Gatherings such as the one these Kansans were heading for were a visible sign of what Populism meant—a movement of the "people." (The Kansas State Historical Society, Topeka)

holy mission . . . to place the mothers of this nation on an equality with the fathers."

Populism was driven as much by ideology as by the quest for political power. The problems afflicting farmers, Populists felt, could stem only from some basic evil. They identified this evil with the business interests controlling the levers of the economic system. "There are but two sides," proclaimed a Populist manifesto. "On the one side are the allied hosts of monopolies, the money power, great trusts and railroad corporations. . . . On the other are the farmers, laborers, merchants and all the people who produce wealth. . . . Between these two there is no middle ground."

By this reasoning farmers and workers formed a single producer class. The claim was not merely rhetorical. Texas railroad workers and Colorado miners cooperated with the farmers' alliances, got their support in strikes, and actively participated in forming state Populist parties. In its explicit class appeal—in recognizing that "the irrepressible conflict between capital and labor is upon us"—Populism parted company from the two mainstream parties.

In an age dominated by laissez-faire doctrine what most distinguished Populism from the major parties was its positive attitude toward the state. Spokesmen such as Lorenzo Dow Lewelling, Populist governor of Kansas, considered it to be "the business of the government to make it possible to live and sustain the life of my family."

The Omaha Platform, adopted at the founding convention in 1892, called for nationalization of the railroads and communications; protection of the land, including natural resources, from monopoly and foreign ownership; a graduated income tax; the Texas Alliance's subtreasury plan; and the free and unlimited coinage of silver. From this array of issues free coinage of silver emerged as the overriding demand of the Populist Party.

In the early 1890s, reeling from rock-bottom prices, embattled farmers gravitated to free silver because they hoped that an increase in the money supply would raise farm prices and give them some relief. In addition the party's slim resources would be fattened by hefty contributions from silver-mining interests who, scornful though they might be of Populist radicalism, yearned for the day when the government would buy at a premium all the silver they could produce.

Free silver triggered a debate for the soul of the Populist Party. Social democrats such as Henry Demarest Lloyd of Chicago and agrarian radicals such as Georgia's Tom Watson argued that free coinage of silver, if it became the defining party issue, would undercut the broader Populist program and alienate wage earners, who had no enthusiasm for inflationary measures. Any chance of a farmer-labor alliance that might transform Populism into an American version of the social-democratic parties of Europe would be doomed. The practical appeal of free silver, however, was simply too great.

But once Populists made that choice, they had fatally compromised their party's capacity to maintain an independent existence. For free silver was not an issue over which the Populists held a monopoly. Free silver was, on the contrary, a question at the very center of mainstream politics in the 1890s.

MONEY AND POLITICS

In a rapidly developing economy the money supply is bound to be a big political issue. Money has to increase rapidly enough to meet the economy's needs or growth will be stifled. How fast the money supply should grow, however, is a question that creates sharp divisions. Debtors and commodity producers want a larger money supply: more money in circulation inflates prices and reduces the real cost of borrowing. The "sound-money" people—creditors, individuals on fixed incomes, those in the slower-growing sectors of the economy—have an opposite interest.

Before the Civil War the main source of the nation's money supply had been state-chartered banks, several thousand of them, all issuing banknotes to borrowers that then circulated as money. This free-wheeling activity was sharply curtailed by the U.S. Banking Act of 1863. Because the Lincoln administration itself was printing paper money—greenbacks, so-called—to finance the Civil War, the economic impact of the Banking Act was not immediately felt. Afterward the sound-money interests lobbied for a return to the traditional national policy, which was to base the federal currency on the amount of specie—gold and silver—held by the U.S. Treasury. The issue was hotly contested for a decade, but in 1875 the inflationists were defeated, and the circulation of greenbacks as legal tender—that is, backed by nothing more than the good faith of the federal government—came to an end. With state banknotes also in short supply, the country entered an era of chronic deflation and tight credit.

This was the context out of which the silver question emerged. The country had always operated on a bimetallic standard, but the supply of silver had gradually tightened, and, as silver coins became more valuable as metal than as money, they disappeared from circulation. In 1873 silver was officially dropped as a medium of exchange. Soon afterward western mines began producing silver in abundance; silver prices plummeted. Inflationists began to agitate for a resumption of the bimetallic policy: if the government resumed buying at the fixed ratio prevailing before 1873—16 ounces of silver equaling 1 ounce of gold—silver would flow into the Treasury and greatly expand the money in circulation.

With so much at stake for so many people, the currency question became one of the staples of post-Reconstruction politics. Twice the prosilver coalition in Congress won modest victories. First, the Bland-Allison Act of 1878 required the U.S. Treasury to purchase and coin between $2 million and $4 million worth of silver each month. Then in the more sweeping Sherman Silver Purchase Act of 1890 an additional 4.5 million ounces of silver bullion was to be purchased monthly to serve as the basis for new issues of U.S. Treasury notes.

These legislative battles, although hard-fought, cut across the parties in the familiar fashion of post-Reconstruction politics. But when the Panic of 1893 hit, silver suddenly became a burning issue that divided politics along party lines.

As the party in power the Democrats bore the brunt of responsibility for handling the economic crisis. The demands for relief by their own constituencies in agriculture and labor magnified the party's problems. Any Democratic president would have been hard pressed, but the man who actually had the job, Grover Cleveland, could hardly have made a bigger hash of it. When jobless marchers—the so-called Coxey's Army—arrived in Washington in 1894 to appeal for federal relief, Cleveland's response was to disperse them forcibly and arrest their leader, Jacob S. Coxey, for trespassing on the Capitol grounds. Cleveland's brutal handling of the Pullman strike further alienated the labor vote. Nor did he live up to his reputation as a tariff reformer. He lost control of the battle for repeal of the unpopular McKinley Tariff of 1890, allowing weak revisions to be passed into law without his signature.

Most disastrous, however, was Cleveland's rigidity on the silver question. Cleveland was a committed sound-money man. Nothing that happened after the depression set in—not collapsing prices, not the suffering of farmers, not the groundswell of support for free silver within his own party—budged Cleveland. With the government's gold reserves dwindling Cleveland persuaded Congress in

1893 to repeal the Sherman Silver Purchase Act, in effect sacrificing the country's painfully crafted program for maintaining a limited bimetallic standard. Then as his administration's problems deepened, Cleveland turned in 1895 to a syndicate of private bankers led by J. P. Morgan to arrange the gold purchases needed to replenish the Treasury's depleted reserves. The administration's secret negotiations with Wall Street, once discovered, enraged Democrats and completed Cleveland's isolation from his party.

At their Chicago convention in 1896 the Democrats repudiated Cleveland and turned left. The leader of the triumphant silver Democrats was William Jennings Bryan of Nebraska. Bryan was a political phenomenon. Only thirty-six years old, he had already served two terms in Congress and become a passionate advocate of free silver. He was a consummate politician and an inspiring public speaker. Bryan, remarked the journalist Frederic Howe, was "pre-eminently an evangelist," whose zeal sprang from "the Western self-righteous missionary mind." With biblical fervor Bryan swept up his audiences when he joined the debate on free silver at the Democratic convention. He locked up the presidential nomination with a stirring attack on the gold standard: "You shall not press down upon the brow of labor this crown of thorns, you shall not crucify mankind on a cross of gold."

Bryan's nomination meant that the Democrats had become the party of free silver; his "cross of gold" speech meant that he would turn the money question into a national crusade. No one could be neutral on this defining issue. Silver Republicans bolted their party; gold Democrats went for a splinter Democratic ticket or supported the Republican Party. The Populists, meeting after the Democratic convention, accepted Bryan as their candidate. The free-silver issue had become so vital that they could not do otherwise. Although they nominated their own vice-presidential candidate, the Georgian Tom Watson, the Populists found themselves for all practical purposes absorbed into the Democratic silver campaign.

The Republicans took up the challenge. Their party leader was the wealthy Cleveland ironmaker Mark Hanna, a brilliant political manager and an exponent of the new industrial capitalism. Hanna orchestrated an unprecedented money-raising campaign among America's corporate interests. His candidate, William McKinley of Ohio, personified the virtues of Republicanism, standing solidly for high tariffs, honest money, and prosperity. While Bryan broke with tradition and crisscrossed the country in a furious whistle-stop campaign, the dignified McKinley received delegations at his home in Canton, Ohio. Bryan orated with moral fervor; McKinley talked of industrial progress and a full dinner pail.

Not since 1860 had the United States witnessed so hard-fought an election over such high stakes. For the middle class sound money stood symbolically for the soundness of the social order. With jobless workers tramping the streets and bankrupt farmers up in arms, Bryan's fervent assault on the gold standard struck fear in many hearts. Republicans denounced the Democratic platform as "revolutionary and anarchistic" and Bryan's supporters as "social misfits who have almost nothing in common but opposition to the existing order and institutions."

McKinley won handily, with 271 electoral votes to Bryan's 176 (Map 18.3). He kept the ground Republicans had regained in the 1894 midterm elections and pushed into Democratic strongholds, especially in the cities. Boston, New York, Chicago, and Minneapolis, all taken by Cleveland in 1892, went for McKinley in 1896. Bryan ran strongly only in the South, in silver-mining states, and in the Populist West. But the gains his evangelical style brought him in some Republican rural areas did not compensate for his losses in traditionally Democratic urban districts.

The paralyzing equilibrium in American politics ended in 1896. The Republicans had skillfully handled both the economic and the cultural challenges. They persuaded the nation that they were the party of prosperity and convinced many traditionally Democratic urban voters of their sympathy for ethnic diversity. The Republicans had become the nation's majority party. In 1896, too, electoral politics regained its place as an arena for national debate, setting the stage for the reform politics of the Progressive era.

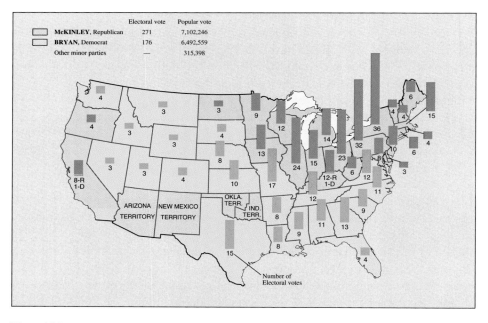

M A P 18.3
The Election of 1896

The 1896 election was one of the truly decisive elections in American history. The Republican Party won by its largest margin since 1872. More important, the Republicans established a firm grip on the key midwestern and Middle Atlantic states—especially New York, Indiana, Ohio, and Illinois—that had been the decisive states in every national election since Reconstruction. The 1896 election broke a party stalemate of twenty years' duration and began a period of Republican domination that would last until 1932.

T I M E L I N E

1874	Women's Christian Temperance Union founded		Mississippi becomes the first state to adopt a literacy test to disfranchise blacks.
1877	Rutherford B. Hayes inaugurated president; end of Reconstruction	1892	Populist Party founded
1881	President James A. Garfield assassinated; succeeded by Chester A. Arthur	1893	The Panic of 1893 leads to national depression.
1883	Pendleton Act creates a civil-service system.	1894	Coxey's Army
1884	Grover Cleveland the first Democrat elected president since 1856	1895	Booker T. Washington sets out the Atlanta Compromise.
1886	Andrew Carnegie's *Triumphant Democracy*	1896	Election of William McKinley; free-silver campaign crushed; era of Republican dominance begins
1887	Florida adopts the first law segregating railroads.		*Plessy v. Ferguson* upholds the constitutionality of "separate-but-equal" segregation.
1888	Benjamin Harrison elected president	1903	W.E.B. DuBois's *The Souls of Black Folk*
1890	Democrats sweep congressional elections, inaugurating a brief era of Democratic Party dominance.		

For Further Exploration

The literature on late nineteenth-century politics offers an embarrassment of riches. On the ideological underpinnings, an older book by Robert G. McCloskey, *American Conservatism in the Age of Enterprise* (1951), still retains its freshness. The mass appeal of Gilded Age politics is incisively explored in Michael E. McGerr, *The Decline of Popular Politics: The American North, 1865–1928* (1986). John G. Sproat, *The "Best Men": Liberal Reformers in the Gilded Age* (1965), is excellent on the Mugwumps. Kathryn Kish Sklar, *Florence Kelley and the Nation's Work* (1995), traces the emergence of women's political culture through the life of a leading reformer. On southern politics the seminal book is C. Vann Woodward, *Origins of the New South, 1877–1913* (1951), which still defines the terms of discussion among historians. The most far-reaching revision is Edward L. Ayers, *The Promise of the New South* (1992). A powerful analysis of southern racism, stressing its psychosocial roots, is Joel Williamson, *A Rage for Order* (1986). The preeminent African American accommodationist is the subject of a superb two-volume biography by Louis B. Harlan, *Booker T. Washington: The Making of a Black Leader* (1973) and *Wizard of Tuskegee* (1983), and equally fine on Washington's main critic is David Levering Lewis, *W.E.B. Du Bois: Biography of a Race 1868–1919* (1993). Richard D. Hofstadter, *The Age of Reform* (1955), stresses the darker side of Populism, in which intolerance and paranoia figure heavily. Hofstadter's thesis, which once dominated debate among historians, has given way to a much more positive assessment. The key book here is Lawrence Goodwyn, *Democratic Promise: The Populist Moment* (1976), which argues that Populism was a broadly based response to industrial capitalism. The most recent synthesis is Robert C. McMath, *American Populism* (1993). Michael Kazin, *The Populist Persuasion* (1995), describes how the language of Populism entered the discourse of mainstream American politics. Much information on the Gilded Age presidents can be found at the website <americanpresident.org/presidentialresources.htm>.

Chapter 19

THE RISE OF THE CITY

These vast aggregations of humanity, where he who seeks isolation
may find it more truly than in the desert; where wealth and poverty
touch and jostle; where one revels and another starves within a few
feet of each other—they are centers and types of our civilization.

—HENRY GEORGE, 1883

Visiting his fiancée's Missouri homestead in 1894, Theodore Dreiser
was struck by "the spirit of rural America, its idealism, its dreams." But this was an
"American tradition in which I, alas!, could not share." Said Dreiser, "I had seen
Pittsburgh. I had seen Lithuanians and Hungarians in their [alleys] and hovels. I
had seen the girls of the city—walking the streets at night." Dreiser would go on to
write one of the great American urban novels—*Sister Carrie* (1900)—about one
young woman in the army of small-town Americans flocking to the Big City. But
the young Dreiser, part of that army, already knew that between rural America and
Pittsburgh an unbridgeable chasm had opened up.

In 1820, after 200 years of settlement, fewer than one in twenty Americans lived
in urban places of more than 10,000 people. After that, decade by decade, the urban
population swelled until by 1900 one of every five Americans lived in cities. Nearly
6.5 million inhabited just three great cities: New York, Chicago, and Philadelphia.

The city was the arena of the nation's vibrant economic life. Here the factories
went up, and here the new immigrants settled, constituting in 1900 a third of the
residents of the major American cities. Here, too, lived the millionaires and a growing white-collar middle class. For all these people the city was more than a place to
make a living. It provided the setting for an urban culture unlike anything seen before in the United States. City people, although differing vastly among themselves,
became distinctively and recognizably urban.

Urbanization

The march to the cities seemed inevitable to nineteenth-century Americans. "The
greater part of our population must live in cities," declared the Congregational minister Josiah Strong. "In due time we shall be a nation of cities." Urbanization became
inevitable because of another inevitability of American life—industrialism.

545

INDUSTRIAL SOURCES OF CITY GROWTH

Until the Civil War cities were centers of commerce, not industry. They were the places where merchants bought and sold goods for distribution into the interior or out to world markets. Early industry, on the other hand, was largely rural because factories needed water power from streams, access to fuel and raw materials, and workers recruited from the countryside.

But once steam engines came along, mill operators no longer depended on water-driven power. In the iron industry coal replaced charcoal as the primary fuel, so it was not necessary to be near forests. Improved transportation, especially the railroads, allowed entrepreneurs to locate in places most convenient to suppliers and markets. The result was a geographic concentration of industry. Iron makers gravitated to Pittsburgh because of its superior access both to coal and iron ore fields and also to markets for their products. Chicago, ideally situated between live-stock suppliers and consuming markets, became a great meat-packing center.

As factories became bigger, that expansion in itself contributed to urban growth. A plant that employed thousands of workers instantly created a small city in its vicinity. Sometimes this took the form of a company town like Aliquippa, Pennsylvania, which became body and soul the property of the Jones and Laughlin Steel Company. Many firms set up their plants near a large city so they could draw on its labor supply and transportation facilities. Older commercial cities also became more industrial. Warehouse districts could readily be converted to small-scale manufacturing; a distribution network was right at hand. Boston, Philadelphia, Baltimore, and San Francisco became hives of small-scale, labor-intensive industrial activity. New York's enormous pool of immigrant workers made that city a magnet for the garment trades, cigar making, and diversified light industry. New York was, in fact, the nation's largest producer of manufactured goods.

CITY BUILDING

The commercial cities of the early nineteenth century had been compact places, densely settled around harbors or river fronts. As late as 1850, when it had 565,000 people, greater Philadelphia covered only 10 square miles. From the foot of Chestnut Street on the Delaware River a person could walk almost anywhere in the city within forty-five minutes. Thereafter, as it developed, Philadelphia spilled out and, like American cities everywhere, engulfed the surrounding countryside.

A downtown area emerged, usually in what had been the original commercial city. Downtown in turn broke up into shopping, financial, warehousing, manufacturing, hotel and entertainment, and red-light districts. Moving out from the center, industrial development tended to follow the arteries of transportation—railroads, canals, and rivers—and, at the city's outskirts, to create concentrations of heavy industry.

While highly congested at the center, American cities actually had lower population densities than European cities: 22 persons per acre for fifteen American cities in the 1890s, for example, versus 157.6 for a comparable group of German cities. Given their dispersed populations, American cities pressed harder to develop an efficient transport system.

The first innovation, dating back to the 1820s, was the omnibus, an elongated version of the horse-drawn carriage. Much better was the horsecar. The key advantage was that it ran on iron tracks, so that the horses could pull more passengers and move them at a faster clip through congested city streets and out into residential areas. From the 1840s onward horsecars were the mainstay of urban transit across America.

Then came the electric trolley car. Its development was the work primarily of Frank J. Sprague, an engineer once employed by the great inventor Thomas A. Edison. In 1887 Sprague designed an electric-driven system for Richmond, Virginia: a "trolley" carriage running along an overhead power line was attached by cable to streetcars equipped with an electric motor—hence the name trolley car. After Sprague's success the trolley swiftly displaced the horsecar and became the primary mode of transportation in most American cities.

In the great metropolitan centers, however, mounting congestion led to demands that public transit be moved off the streets. In 1879 the first elevated lines went into operation on Sixth and Ninth Avenues in New York City. Powered at first by steam engines, the "els" converted to electricity following Sprague's success with the trolley. Chicago developed elevated transit most fully. New York, meanwhile, turned to the subway. Boston opened a short underground line in 1897, but it was the completion in 1904 of a subway running the length of Manhattan that demonstrated the full potential of the high-speed underground train. Mass transit had become *rapid* transit.

Equally remarkable was the architectural revolution sweeping metropolitan business districts. With steel girders, durable plate glass, and the passenger elevator available by the 1880s, a wholly new way of construction opened up. A steel skeleton supported the building, while the walls, previously weight-bearing, served as curtains enclosing the structure. The sky, so to speak, became the limit.

The first "skyscraper" to be built on this principle was William Jenney's ten-story Home Insurance Building (1885) in Chicago. Although this pioneering effort appeared unremarkable—it looked just like the other downtown buildings—the steel-girdered technology it contained liberated the aesthetic perceptions of American architects. A Chicago school sprang up, dedicated to the design of buildings whose form expressed, rather than masked, their structure and function. Chicago pioneered skyscraper construction, but New York, with its unrelenting need for prime downtown space, took the lead after the mid-1890s. Completed in 1913, the fifty-five story Woolworth Building marked the beginning of the modern Manhattan skyline.

The Chicago Elevated, 1900

This is Wabash Avenue, looking north from Adams Street. For Americans from farms and small towns, this photograph by William Henry Jackson captured something of the peculiarity of the urban scene. What could be stranger than a railroad suspended above the streets in the midst of people's lives? (KEA Publishing Services Ltd.)

For ordinary citizens the electric lights that dispelled the gloom of the city at night offered the most dramatic evidence that times had changed. Gaslight—illuminating gas produced from coal—had been in use since the early nineteenth century, but its 12 candlepower lamps lighted the city's public spaces only dimly. The first use of electricity, once generating technology made it commercially feasible in the 1870s, was for better city lighting. Charles F. Brush's electric arc lamps, installed in Wanamaker's department store in Philadelphia in 1878, threw a brilliant light and soon replaced gaslight on city streets and public buildings across the country. Electric lighting then entered the American home, thanks to Thomas Edison's invention of a serviceable incandescent bulb in 1879. Edison's motto—"Let there be light!"—truly described the experience of the modern city.

Before it had any significant effect on industry, electricity gave the city its modern tempo, lifting elevators, powering streetcars and subway trains, turning night into day. Meanwhile, Alexander Graham Bell's telephone (1876) sped communication beyond anything imagined previously. By 1900, 1.5 million telephones were in use, linking urban people in a network of instant communication.

THE CITY AS PRIVATE ENTERPRISE

City building was very much an exercise in private enterprise. The lure of profit spurred the great innovations—the trolley car, electric lighting, the skyscraper, the elevator, the telephone—and drove urban real-estate development. The investment opportunities looked so tempting that new cities sprang up almost overnight from the ruins of the Chicago fire of 1871 and the San Francisco earthquake of 1906. Real-estate interests, eager to develop subdivisions, often were instrumental in pushing streetcar lines outward from the central districts of cities.

America gave birth to what the urban historian Sam Bass Warner has called the "private city"—shaped primarily by the actions of many individuals, all pursuing their own goals and bent on making money. The prevailing belief was that the sum of such private activity would far exceed what the community could accomplish through public effort. This meant that the city itself handled only functions that could not be undertaken efficiently or profitably by private enterprise.

Even so, American cities compiled an impressive record in the late nineteenth century. Though by no means free of the corruption and wastefulness of earlier days, municipal government became more centralized, better administered, and above all, more expansive in the functions undertaken. Nowhere in the world were there more massive public projects: water aqueducts, sewage systems, street paving, bridge building, extensive park systems.

Yet streets were often filthy and badly maintained. "Three or four days of warm spring weather," remarked a New York journalist, would turn Manhattan's garbage-strewn, snow-clogged streets into "veritable mud rivers." The environment likewise suffered. A visitor to Pittsburgh noted "the heavy pall of smoke which constantly overhangs her . . . until the very sun looks coppery through the sooty haze." As for the lovely hills rising from the rivers, "they have been leveled down, cut into, sliced off, and ruthlessly marred and mutilated." Pittsburgh presented "all that is unsightly and forbidding in appearance, the original beauties of nature having been ruthlessly sacrificed to utility."

Hardest hit by urban growth were the poor. In earlier times they had mainly lived in makeshift wooden structures in alleys and back streets and then, as more prosperous families moved away, in the subdivided homes left behind. As land values climbed after the Civil War, speculators tore down these houses and began to erect buildings specifically designed for the urban masses. In New York City the dreadful result was five- or six-story tenements housing twenty or more families in cramped, airless apartments. In New York's Eleventh Ward an average of 986 persons occupied each acre, a density matched only in Bombay, India.

Reformers recognized the problem but seemed unable to solve it. Some favored model tenements financed by public-spirited citizens willing to accept a limited return on their investment. When private philanthropy failed to make much of a dent, cities turned to housing codes. The most advanced of these was New York's Tenement House Law of 1901, which required interior courts, indoor toilets, and fire safeguards for new structures but did little for existing housing stock. Commercial development had pushed up land values in downtown areas. Only high-density, cheaply built housing could earn a sufficient profit for the landlords of the poor. This economic fact defied nineteenth-century solutions.

It was not that America lacked an urban vision. On the contrary, an abiding rural ideal had influenced American cities for many years. Frederick Law Olmsted, who designed New York's Central Park, wanted cities that exposed people to the beauties of nature. One of Olmsted's projects, the Chicago Columbian Exposition of 1893, gave rise to the influential "City Beautiful" movement. The results included larger park systems, broad boulevards and parkways, and after the turn of the century zoning laws and planned suburbs.

But cities usually heeded urban planners too little and far too late. "Fifteen or twenty years ago a plan might have been adopted that would have made this one of the most beautiful cities in the world," Kansas City's park commissioners reported in 1893. At that time, "such a policy could not be fully appreciated." Nor, even if Kansas City had foreseen its future, would it have shouldered the "heavy burden" of trying to shape its development. The American city had placed its faith in the dynamics of the marketplace, not the restraints of a planned future. The pluses and minuses are perhaps best revealed by comparing a German city and an American city.

A BALANCE SHEET: CHICAGO AND BERLIN

Chicago and Berlin had virtually equal populations in 1900. But they had very different histories. Seventy years earlier, when Chicago had been a muddy frontier outpost, Berlin was already a city of 250,000 and the royal seat of the Hohenzollerns of Prussia.

With German unification in 1871 the imperial authorities rebuilt Berlin on a grander scale. "A capital city is essential for the state, to act as a pivot for its culture," proclaimed the Prussian historian Heinrich von Treitschke. Berlin served that national purpose—"a center where Germany's political, intellectual, and material life is concentrated, and its people can feel united." Chicago had no such pretensions. It was strictly a place of business, made great by virtue of its strategic grip on the commerce of America's industrial heartland. Nothing in Chicago evoked the grandeur of Berlin's boulevards or its monumental palaces and public buildings, nor were Chicagoans ever witness to the pomp and ceremony of the imperial parades up broad, tree-lined Unter den Linden to the national cathedral.

Yet as a functioning city Chicago was in many ways superior to Berlin. Chicago's waterworks pumped 500 million gallons of water a day, or 139 gallons of water per person, while Berliners had to make do with 18 gallons. Flush toilets, a rarity in Berlin in 1900, could be found in 60 percent of Chicago's homes. Chicago's streets were lit by electricity, while Berlin still relied mostly on gaslight. Chicago had a much bigger streetcar system, twice as much acreage devoted to parks, and a public library containing many more volumes. And Chicago had just completed an amazing sanitation project, reversing the course of the Chicago River so that its waters—and the city's sewage—would flow away from Lake Michigan and southward down into the Illinois and Mississippi Rivers.

Giant sanitation projects were one thing; an inspiring urban environment was something else. For well-traveled Americans admiring of things European, the sense of inferiority was palpable. "We are enormously rich," admitted the journalist Edwin L. Godkin, "but . . . what have we got to show? Almost nothing. Ugliness from an artistic point of view is the mark of all our cities." Thus the urban balance sheet: a utilitarian infrastructure that was superb by nineteenth-century standards but "no municipal splendors of any description, nothing but population and hotels."

Upper Class/Middle Class

In the compact city of the early republic class distinctions had been expressed by the way men and women dressed, how they behaved, and the deference they demanded from or granted to others. As the industrial city grew, these interpersonal marks of class began to lose their force. In the anonymity of a large city recognition and deference no longer served as mechanisms for conferring status. Instead people began to rely on external signs: conspicuous display of wealth, membership in exclusive clubs and organizations, and above all choice of neighborhood.

For the poor, place of residence depended, as it always had, on being close to their jobs. But for higher-income urbanites where to live became a matter of personal means and social preference.

THE URBAN ELITE

As early as the 1840s Boston merchants had taken advantage of the new railways to escape the congested city. Fine rural estates appeared in Milton, Newton, and other outlying towns. By 1848 roughly 20 percent of Boston's businessmen were making the trip by train to their downtown offices. Ferries that plied the harbor between Manhattan and Brooklyn or New Jersey served the same purpose for New Yorkers.

As commercial development engulfed downtown residential areas, the exodus by the well-to-do spread across America. In Cincinnati wealthy families settled on the scenic hills rimming the crowded, humid tableland that ran down to the Ohio River. On those hillsides, a traveler noted in 1883, "the homes of Cincinnati's merchant princes and millionaires are found . . . elegant cottages, tasteful villas, and substantial mansions, surrounded by a paradise of grass, gardens, lawns, and tree-shaded roads."

Despite the attractions of country life many of the very richest people preferred the heart of the city. Chicago boasted its Gold Coast; San Francisco, Nob Hill;

Denver, Quality Hill; and Manhattan, Fifth Avenue. The New York novelist Edith Wharton recalled how the comfortable midcentury brownstones gave way to the "'new' millionaire houses," which spread northward on Fifth Avenue along Central Park. Great mansions, emulating the aristocratic houses of Europe, lined Fifth Avenue at the turn of the century.

But great wealth did not automatically confer social standing. An established elite dominated the social heights, even in such relatively raw cities as San Francisco and Denver. It had taken only a generation—and sometimes less—for money made in commerce or real estate to shed its tarnish and become "old" and genteel. In the oldest cities such as Boston, wealth passed intact through several generations, creating a closely knit tribe of Brahmin families that kept moneyed newcomers at bay. Elsewhere urban elites tended to be more open, but only to the socially ambitious who were prepared to make visible and energetic use of their money.

New York City became the home of a national elite as the most ambitious gravitated to this preeminent capital of American financial and cultural life. Manhattan's extraordinary vitality in turn kept the city's high society fluid and relatively open. In Theodore Dreiser's novel *The Titan* (1914) the tycoon Frank Cowperwood reassures his unhappy wife that if Chicago society will not accept them, "there are other cities. Money will arrange matters in New York—that I know. We can build a real place there, and go in on equal terms, if we have money enough." New York thus came to be a magnet for millionaires. The city attracted them not only because of its importance as a financial center but for the opportunities it offered for display and social recognition.

This infusion of wealth shattered the older elite society of New York. Seeking to be assimilated into the upper class, the flood of moneyed newcomers simply overwhelmed it. There followed a curious process of reconstruction, a deliberate effort to define the rules of conduct and identify those who properly "belonged" in New York society.

The key figure was Ward McAllister, a southern-born lawyer who had made a quick fortune in gold-rush San Francisco and then devoted himself to a second career as the arbiter of New York society. In 1888 McAllister compiled the first *Social Register,* which announced that it would serve as a "record of society, comprising an accurate and careful list" of all those deemed eligible for New York society. McAllister instructed the socially ambitious on how to select guests, set a proper table, arrange a party, and launch a young lady into society. He presided over a round of assemblies, balls, and dinners that defined the boundaries of an elite society. At the apex stood "The Four Hundred"—the true cream of New York society. McAllister's list corresponded to those invited to Mrs. William Astor's gala ball of February 1, 1892.

Americans were adept at making money, remarked the journalist Edwin L. Godkin in 1896, but they lacked the aristocratic traditions of Europe for spending it. "Great wealth has not yet entered our manners," Godkin remarked. In their struggle to find the rules and establish the manners, the moneyed elite made an indelible mark on urban life. If there was magnificence in the American city, that was mainly their handiwork. And if there was conspicuous waste and display, that too was their doing.

THE SUBURBAN WORLD

The middle class left a smaller imprint on the public face of urban society. Its members, unlike the rich, preferred privacy and retreated into the domesticity of suburban comfort and family life.

Since colonial times the American economy had spawned a robust middle class of mostly self-employed lawyers, doctors, merchants, and proprietors. This older middle class remained important, but it was joined by a new salaried middle class brought forth by industrialism. Corporate organizations required managers, accountants, and clerks. The new technology called for engineers, chemists, and designers, while the distribution system needed salesmen, advertising executives, and buyers. These salaried ranks increased sevenfold between 1870 and 1910—much faster than any other occupational group. Nearly 9 million people held white-collar jobs in 1910, more than a fourth of all employed Americans.

Some members of this salaried class lived in the row houses of Baltimore and Boston or the comfortable apartment buildings of New York City. But more preferred to escape the clamor and congestion of the city. They were attracted by a persisting "rural ideal," agreeing with the landscape architect Andrew Jackson Downing that "nature and domestic life are better than the society and manners of town." As trolley service expanded out from the central city, middle-class Americans followed the wealthy into the countryside. All sought what one Chicago developer promised for his North Shore subdivision in 1875—"qualities of which the city is in a large degree bereft, namely, its pure air, peacefulness, quietude, and natural scenery."

No major American city escaped suburbanization during the late nineteenth century. City limits everywhere expanded rapidly, but even so, much of the suburban growth took place beyond city limits. By 1900 more than half of Boston's people lived in "streetcar suburbs" outside Boston proper; and nationwide, according to the 1910 census, about 25 percent of the urban population lived in such autonomous suburbs.

The geography of the suburbs was truly a map of class structure because where a family lived told where it ranked. The farther out from the city center, the finer the houses and the larger the lots. Affluent businessmen and professionals had the time and flexibility to travel a long distance into town. People closer in wanted transit lines that went straight into the city center and carried them quickly between home and office. Lower-income commuters were more likely to have more than one wage-earner in the family, less secure employment, and jobs requiring movement around the city. It was better for them to be closer to the city center because they then had access to cross-town lines that afforded the mobility they needed for their work.

Middle-Class Domesticity

For middle-class Americans the home was a place of nurture, a refuge from the world of competitive commerce. Perhaps that explains why their residences were so heavily draped and cluttered with bric-a-brac, every space filled with overstuffed furniture. All of it emphasized privacy and pride of possession. The young woman shown playing the piano symbolizes another theme of American domesticity—wives and daughters as ornaments and as bearers of culture and refinement. (Museum of the City of New York, Byron Collection)

Suburban boundaries were ever shifting, as working-class city residents who wanted to better their lives moved to the cheapest suburbs, prompting an exodus of older residents, who in turn pushed the next higher group farther out in search of space and greenery. Suburbanization was the sum of countless individual decisions. Each family's move represented an advance in living standards—not only more light, air, and quiet but better accommodation than the city afforded. Suburban houses were typically larger for the same money and came equipped with flush toilets, hot water, central heating, and by the turn of the century electricity.

The suburbs also restored an opportunity that rural Americans thought they had lost when they moved to the city. In the suburbs home ownership again became the norm. "A man is not really a true man until he owns his home," propounded the Reverend Russell H. Conwell in his famous sermon on the virtues of making money, "Acres of Diamonds."

The small towns of rural America had fostered community life. Not so the suburbs. The grid street pattern, while efficient for laying out lots, offered no natural focus for group life. Nor did the stores and services that lay scattered along the trolley-car streets. Suburban development conformed to the economics of real estate and transportation, and so did the thinking of middle-class home seekers entering the suburbs. They wanted a house that gave them good value and convenience to the trolley line.

The need for community had lost some of its force for middle-class Americans. Two other attachments assumed greater importance: one was work; the other, family.

MIDDLE-CLASS FAMILIES

In the preindustrial economy farmers, merchants, and artisans generally worked at home. The family included not only blood relatives but everyone living and working in the household. As industrialism progressed, economic activity moved out of the home. For the middle class in particular the family became dissociated from employment. The father left every morning to earn a living, and children spent more years in school. Clothing was bought ready-made; food came increasingly in cans and packages. Middle-class families became smaller, excluding all but nuclear members and consisting typically by 1900 of husband, wife, and three children.

Within this family circle relationships became intense and affectionate. "Home was the most expressive experience in life," recalled the literary critic Henry Seidel Canby of his growing up in the 1890s. "Though the family might quarrel and nag, the home held them all, protecting them against the outside world." In a sense, the family served as a refuge from the competitive, impersonal business world. The quiet, tree-lined streets created a domestic place insulated from the hurly-burly of commerce and enterprise.

The burdens of this domesticity fell heavily on the wife. It was nearly unheard of for her to seek an outside career; that was her husband's role. Her job was to manage the household. "The woman who could not make a home, like the man who could not support one, was condemned," Canby remembered. But with fewer children, the wife's workload declined. Moreover, servants still played an important part in middle-class households. In 1910 there were about 2 million domestic servants, the largest job category for women.

As the physical burdens of household work eased, higher-quality homemaking became the new ideal. This was the message of Catharine Beecher's best-selling book *The American Woman's Home* (1869) and of such magazines as the *Ladies' Home Journal* and *Good Housekeeping*, which first appeared during the 1880s. This advice literature told wives that, in addition to their domestic duties, they were responsible for bringing sensibility, beauty, and love to the household. "We owe to women the charm and beauty of life," wrote one educator. "For the love that rests, strengthens and inspires, we look to women." In this idealized view the wife made the home a refuge for her husband and a place of nurture for their children.

Womanly virtue, even if much glorified, by no means put wives on equal terms with their husbands. Although the legal status of married women—their right to own property, control separate earnings, make contracts, and get a divorce—improved markedly during the nineteenth century, custom still dictated a wife's submission to her husband. She relied on his ability as the family breadwinner, and despite her superior virtues and graces she ranked below him in vigor and intellect. Her mind could be employed "but little and in trivial matters," wrote one prominent physician, and her proper place was as "the companion or ornamental appendage to man" (see American Voices, "We Did Not Know . . . Whether Women's Health Could Stand the Strain of Higher Education").

No wonder that bright, independent-minded women rebelled against marriage. By the late nineteenth century more than 10 percent of women of marriageable age remained single, and the rate was much higher among college graduates and professionals. Married life, remarked the writer Vida Scudder, "looks to me often as I watch it terribly impoverished, for women."

Around 1890 a change set in. Although the birth rate continued to decline, more young people married and at an earlier age. These developments reflected the beginnings of a sexual revolution in the American middle-class family. Experts began to abandon the notion, put forth by one popular medical text, that "the majority of women (happily for society) are not very much troubled by sexual feeling of any kind." In succeeding editions of his book *Plain Home Talk on Love, Marriage, and Parentage* the physician Edward Bliss Foote began to favor a healthy sexuality that gave pleasure to women as well as men.

During the 1890s the artist Charles Dana Gibson created the image of the "new woman" in his drawings for *Life* magazine. The Gibson girl was tall, spirited, athletic, and chastely sexual. She eshewed bustles, hoop skirts, and hourglass corsets, preferring shirtwaists and other natural styles that did not hide or disguise her female form. In the city, women's sphere began to take on a more public character. Among the new urban institutions catering to women, the most important was the department store, which became a temple for their emerging role as consumers.

The children of the middle class experienced their own revolution. In the past American children had been regarded as an economic asset—added hands for the family farm, shop, or countinghouse. Especially for the urban middle class, that no longer held true. Parents stopped expecting their children to be working members of the family. There was such a thing as "the juvenile mind," lectured Jacob Abbott in his book *Gentle Measures in the Management and Training of the Young* (1871). The family was responsible for providing a nurturing environment in which the young personality could grow and mature.

Preparation for adulthood became increasingly linked to formal education. School enrollment went up 150 percent between 1870 and 1900. High school attendance, while still encompassing only a small percentage of teenagers, increased

---

AMERICAN VOICES

"We Did Not Know . . . Whether Women's Health Could Stand the Strain of Higher Education"

M. CAREY THOMAS

M. *Carey Thomas (1857–1935), president of Bryn Mawr College for many years, recalls her dreams of college as a girl growing up in Baltimore in the 1870s.*

The passionate desire of women of my generation for higher education was accompanied thruout its course by the awful doubt, felt by women themselves as well as by men, as to whether women as a sex were physically and mentally fit for it. . . . I often remember praying about it, and begging God that if it were true that because I was a girl I could not successfully master Greek and go to college and understand things to kill me at once, as I could not bear to live in such an unjust world. . . .

We did not know when we began whether women's health could stand the strain of college education. We were haunted in those early days by the clanging chains of that gloomy little specter, Dr. Edward H. Clarke's *Sex in Education*. With trepidation of spirit I made my mother read it, and was much cheered by her remark that, as neither she, nor any of the women she knew, had ever seen girls or women of the kind described in Dr. Clarke's book, we might as well act as if they did not exist. . . .

When . . . I went to Leipzig to study after graduating from Cornell, my mother used to write me that my name was never mentioned to her by the women of her acquaintance. I was thought by them to be as much disgrace to my family as if I had eloped with the coachman. . . .

We are now [1908] living in the midst of great and, I believe on the whole beneficent, social changes which are preparing the way for the coming economic independence of women. . . . The passionate desire of the women of my generation for a college education seems, as we study it now in the light of coming events, to have been part of this greater movement.

SOURCE: Linda K. Kerber and Jane De Hart-Mathews, eds., *Women's America: Refocusing the Past,* 2nd ed. (New York: Oxford University Press, 1987), pp. 263–65.

---

at the fastest rate. As the years between childhood and adulthood began to stretch out, a new stage of life—adolescence—emerged. While rooted in longer years of family dependency, adolescence shifted much of the socializing role from parents to peer group. A youth culture—one of the hallmarks of American life in the twentieth century—was starting to take shape.

The New Woman

John Singer Sargent's painting *Mr. and Mrs. Isaac Newton Phelps Stokes* (1897) captures on canvas the essence of the "new woman" of the 1890s. Nothing about Mrs. Phelps Stokes, neither how she is dressed nor how she presents herself, suggests physical weakness or demure passivity. She confidently occupies center stage, a fit partner for her husband, who is relegated to the shadows of the picture.

(The Metropolitan Museum of Art, Bequest of Edith Minturn Phelps Stokes (Mrs. I.N.), 1938. [38.104] Photograph © 1992 The Metropolitan Museum of Art)

City Life

When the budding writer Hamlin Garland and his brother arrived in Chicago from Iowa in 1881, they knew immediately that they had entered a new world: "Everything interested us. . . . Nothing was commonplace, nothing was ugly to us." In one way or another every city-bound migrant, whether from the American countryside or from a foreign land, experienced something of this sense of wonder.

But with the boundless variety came disorder and uncertainty. The city was utterly unlike the rural world the newcomers had left. In the countryside every person had been known to his or her neighbors. Mark Twain found New York "a splendid desert, where a stranger is lonely in the midst of a million of his race. . . . Every man rushes, rushes, rushes, and never has time to be companionable [or] to fool away on matters which do not involve dollars and duty and business." If rural roles and obligations had been well understood, in the city the only predictable relationships were those dictated by the marketplace.

Rural people could never recreate in the city the communities they had left behind. But they found ways to gain a sense of belonging, they built a multitude of new institutions, and they learned how to function in an impersonal, heterogeneous environment. An urban culture emerged, and through it there developed a new breed of American who was entirely at home in the modern city.

NEWCOMERS

At the turn of the century upwards of 30 percent of the residents of New York, Chicago, Boston, Cleveland, Minneapolis, and San Francisco were foreign-born. The biggest ethnic group in Boston was Irish; in Minneapolis, Swedish; in most other northern cities, German. But by 1910 the influx from southern and Eastern Europe had changed the ethnic complexion of many of these cities. In Chicago Poles took the lead; in New York, Eastern European Jews; in San Francisco, Italians.

As the older "walking cities" disappeared, so did the opportunities for intermingling with the older populations. The later arrivals from southern and eastern Europe had little choice about where they lived; they needed to find cheap housing near their jobs. Some gravitated to the outlying factory districts; others settled in the congested downtown ghettos. The immigrants tended to settle by ethnic group. In New York Italians crowded into the Irish neighborhoods west of Broadway, and Russian and Polish Jews pushed the Germans out of the Lower East Side. A colony of Hungarians lived around Houston Street, and Bohemians occupied the Upper East Side between Fiftieth and Seventy-sixth Streets.

Capitalizing on fellow-feeling within ethnic groups, institutions of many kinds sprang up to meet the immigrants' needs. Wherever substantial numbers lived, newspapers appeared. In 1911 the 20,000 Poles in Buffalo, New York, supported two Polish-langage daily papers. Immigrants throughout the country avidly read *Il Progresso Italo-Americano* and the Yiddish-language *Jewish Daily Forward,* both published in New York City (see American Voices, "Bintel Brief"). Companionship could always be found on street corners, in barbershops and club rooms, and in saloons. Italians marched in saint's day parades, Bohemians gathered in singing societies, and New York Jews patronized a lively Yiddish theater. To provide help in times of sickness and death the immigrants organized mutual-aid societies. The Italians of

Mulberry Street, New York City, c. 1900

The influx of southern and eastern Europeans created teeming ghettos in the heart of New York City and other major American cities. The view is of Mulberry Street, with its pushcarts, street peddlers, and bustling traffic. The inhabitants are mostly Italians, and some of them, noticing the photographer preparing his camera, have gathered to be in the picture.
(Library of Congress)

Chicago had sixty-six of these organizations in 1903, each mostly composed of people from a particular province or district. Immigrants built a rich and functional institutional life in urban America to an extent unimagined in their native villages.

The great African American migration from the rural South to northern cities was just beginning at the turn of the century. The black population of New York increased by 30,000 between 1900 and 1910, making New York second only to Washington, D.C., as a black urban center, but the 91,000 African Americans in New York in 1910 represented fewer than 2 percent of the population, and that was true of Chicago and Cleveland as well.

Despite their relatively small numbers urban blacks could not escape discrimination. They retreated from the scattered black neighborhoods of older times

Bintel Brief

*T*he Yiddish phrase bintel brief *means "bundle of letters." That was the name of the fa- mous column of the* Jewish Daily Forward *devoted to letters from immigrant readers about their trials and tribulations in America.*

I was born in a small town in Russia, and until I was sixteen I studied in *Talmud Torahs* and *yeshivas,* but when I came to America I developed spiritually and became a freethinker. Yet every year when the time of *Rosh Hashana* and *Yom Kippur* comes around I become very gloomy. . . . So strong are my feelings that I enter the synagogue, not in order to pray to God but to heal and refresh my aching soul by sitting among *landsleit* [countrymen] and listening to the cantor's sweet melodies. The members of my Progressive Society don't understand. They say I am a hypocrite. . . . What do you think? *Answer:* No one can tell another what to do with himself on *Yom Kippur.*

I am a Russian revolutionist and a freethinker. Here in America I became acquainted with a girl who is also a freethinker. We decided to marry, but the problem is that she has Orthodox parents, and if we refuse a religious ceremony we will be cut off from them for- ever. I don't know what to do. Therefore, I ask you to advise me how to act. *Answer:* There are times when it is better to be kind in order not to grieve old parents.

I am a young man of twenty-five, and I recently met a fine girl. She has a flaw, how- ever—a dimple in her chin. It is said that people who have this lose their first husband or wife. I love her very much. But I'm afraid to marry her lest I die because of the dimple. *Answer:* The tragedy is not that the girl has a dimple in her chin but that some people have a screw loose in their heads.

SOURCE: Irving Howe and Kenneth Libo, eds., *How We Lived* (New York: New American Library, 1979), pp. 88–90.

into concentrated ghettos—Chicago's Black Belt on the South Side, for example, or the early outlines of New York's Harlem. Race prejudice likewise cut down job opportunities. Twenty-six percent of Cleveland's blacks had been skilled workers in 1870, but only 12 percent were by 1890, and entire occupations such as bar- bering (except for those shops that served a black clientele) became exclusively white. Two-thirds of Cleveland's blacks in 1910 worked as domestics and day la- borers, with little hope of moving up the job ladder.

In the face of pervasive discrimination urban blacks built their own commu- nities. They created a flourishing press, fraternal orders, a vast array of women's or- ganizations, and a middle class of doctors, lawyers, and small entrepreneurs. Above all there were the black churches—twenty-five in Chicago in 1905, mainly Methodist and Baptist. More than any other institution, remarked one scholar in 1913, it was the church "which the Negro may call his own. . . . A new church may be built . . .

and . . . all the machinery set in motion without ever consulting any white person.
. . . [It] more than anything else represents the real life of the race." As in the southern countryside the church was the central institution for city blacks, and the
preacher the most important local citizen. Manhattan's Union Baptist Church,
housed like many others in a storefront, attracted the "very recent residents of this
new, disturbing city" and, ringing with spirituals and fervent prayer, made Christianity come "alive Sunday mornings."

WARD POLITICS

Race and ethnicity tended to divide newcomers and turn them in on themselves.
Politics, by contrast, integrated them into urban society. Every migrant to an American city automatically became a ward resident and immediately acquired a
spokesman at city hall in the form of his local alderman. Immigrants learned very
quickly that if they needed anything from city hall, this was the man to see. That
was how streets got paved, water mains extended, or variances granted—so that,
for example, in 1888 Vito Fortounescere could "place and keep a stand for the sale
of fruit, inside the stoop-line, in front of the northeast corner of Twenty-eight Street
and Fourth Avenue" in Manhattan, or the parishioners of Saint Maria of Mount
Carmel could set off fireworks at their Fourth of July picnic.

Machine control of political parties, although present at every level, flourished
most luxuriantly in the big cities. Urban machines depended on a loyal grassroots
constituency, so each ward was divided into election districts of a few blocks. The
district captain reported to the ward boss, who was likely also to be the alderman.
The main job of these functionaries was to be accessible and, as best they could,
serve the needs of the party faithful.

The machine acted as a rough-and-ready social service agency, providing jobs
for the jobless, a helping hand for a bereaved family, and intercession against an
unfeeling city bureaucracy. The Tammany ward boss George Washington Plunkitt
had a "regular system" when fires broke out in his district. He arranged for housing for burned-out families, "fix[ing] them up till they get things runnin' again. It's
philanthropy, but it's politics, too—mighty good politics."

The business community was similarly served. Contractors sought city business; gas companies and streetcar lines wanted licenses and privileges; manufacturers needed services and not-too-nosy inspectors; and the liquor trade and
numbers racket relied on a tolerant police force. All of them turned to the machine
boss and his lieutenants.

Of course, the machine exacted a price for these services. The tenement dweller
gave his vote. The businessman wrote a check. Naturally, some of the money that
changed hands leaked into the pockets of machine politicians. This "boodle" could
be blatantly corrupt—kickbacks by contractors; protection money from gamblers,
saloonkeepers, and prostitutes; payoffs from gas and trolley companies. Tammany
ward boss Plunkitt, however, insisted that he had no need for kickbacks and bribes.

He favored what he called "honest graft"—the easy profits that came to savvy insiders. Plunkitt made most of his money building wharves on Manhattan's waterfront. One way or another, legally or otherwise, machine politics rewarded its supporters.

For the young and ambitious, this was reason enough to favor the machine system. In the mid-1870s over half of Chicago's forty aldermen were foreign-born, sixteen of them Irish immigrants. The first Italian was elected in 1885, the first Pole in 1888. Blacks did not manage to get on Chicago's board of aldermen until after 1900, but Baltimore's Eleventh Ward elected an African American in 1890, and Philadelphia had three black aldermen by 1899. As a ladder for social mobility machine politics was the most democratic of American institutions.

Ward boss Plunkitt was an Irishman, and so were most of the machine politicians controlling Tammany Hall. But by the 1890s Plunkitt's Fifteenth District was filling up with Italians and Eastern European Jews. In general the New York Irish had no love for these newer immigrants, but Plunkitt played no favorites. On any given day (as recorded in a diary) he might attend an Italian funeral in the afternoon and a Jewish wedding in the evening, and at each he probably paid his respects with a few Italian words or a bit of Yiddish.

In an era when so many forces acted to isolate ghetto communities, politics served an *integrating* function, cutting across ethnic lines and giving immigrants and blacks a stake in the larger urban order.

RELIGION IN THE CITY

For African Americans, as we have seen, the church was a central institution of urban life. So it was for many other city dwellers. But they found the city difficult ground for religious practice. All the major American faiths present at the time—Judaism, Catholicism, Protestantism—had to scramble to reconcile religious belief with the secular demands of the urban world.

About 250,000 Jews, mostly of German origin, were living in America when the Eastern European Jews began arriving in the 1880s. Well-established and prosperous, the German Jews had embraced Reform Judaism, abandoning religious practices—from keeping a kosher kitchen to conducting services in Hebrew—"not adapted to the views and habits of modern civilization." Anxious to preserve their traditional piety, Yiddish-speaking immigrants from Eastern Europe founded their own Orthodox synagogues, often in vacant stores and ramshackle buildings, and practiced Judaism in the old way.

In the villages of Eastern Europe, however, Judaism had involved not only worship and belief but an entire way of life. Insular though it might be, ghetto life in the American city could not recreate the communal environment on which strict religious observance depended. "The very clothes I wore and the very food I ate had a fatal effect on my religious habits," confessed the hero of Abraham Cahan's novel *The Rise of David Levinsky* (1917). "If you . . . attempt to bend your religion to the spirit of your surroundings, it breaks. It falls to pieces." Levinsky shaved off his beard and plunged into the Manhattan clothing business. Orthodox Judaism survived this shattering of faith only by reducing its claims on the lives of the faithful.

Catholics faced much the same problem. The issue, defined within the Roman Catholic Church as "Americanism," turned on the extent to which Catholicism should adapt to American society. Should Catholic children attend parochial or public schools? Should they intermarry with non-Catholics? Should the traditional education for the clergy be changed? Bishop John Ireland of St. Paul, Minnesota, felt that "the principles of the Church are in harmony with the interests of the Republic." But traditionalists, led by Archbishop Michael A. Corrigan of New York, denied the possibility of such harmony and argued in effect for insulating the Church from the pluralistic American environment.

Immigrant Catholics generally supported the Church's conservative wing because of their felt need to preserve what they had known in Europe. But that meant also a desire that church life express their ethnic identities. Settling in ethnically distinct neighborhoods, newly arrived Catholics wanted their own parishes where they could celebrate their customs, speak their languages, and establish their own parochial schools. When they became numerous enough, they also demanded their own bishops. The Catholic hierarchy, which was dominated by Irish Catholics, felt that the integrity of the Church itself was at stake. The demand for ethnic parishes implied local control of church property. And if there were bishops for specific ethnic groups, this would mean disrupting the diocesan structure that unified the Church. Indeed, fifty parishes in 1907 broke away and formed the Polish National Catholic Church of America, which adhered to Catholic ritual without recognizing the pope's authority.

On the whole, however, the Church managed to satisfy the immigrant faithful. It met the demand for representation in the hierarchy by appointing immigrant priests as auxiliary bishops within existing dioceses. Ethnic parishes also flourished. Before World War I American Catholics worshipped in more than 2,000 foreign-language churches, and many others were bilingual. Not without strain, the Catholic Church made itself a central institution for the expression of ethnic identity in urban America.

For the Protestant churches the city posed different but not easier challenges. Every major city retained great downtown churches where wealthy Protestants worshipped. Some of these churches, richly endowed, took pride in nationally prominent pastors, such as Henry Ward Beecher of Plymouth Congregational Church in Brooklyn and Phillips Brooks of Trinity Episcopal Church in Boston. But the eminence of these churches, with their fashionable congregations and imposing edifices, could not disguise the growing remoteness of Protestantism from much of its urban constituency. "Where is the city in which the Sabbath day is not losing ground?" lamented a minister in 1887. The families of businessmen, lawyers, and doctors could be seen in any church on Sunday morning, he noted, "but the workingmen and their families are not there."

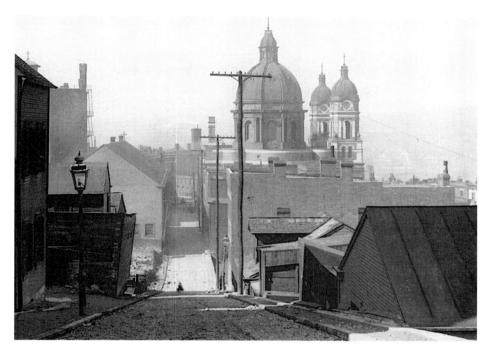

Immaculate Heart of Mary Church, 1908

In crowded immigrant neighborhoods the church rose from undistinguished surroundings to assert the centrality of religious belief in the life of the community. This photograph is a view of Immaculate Heart of Mary Church taken from Polish Hill in Pittsburgh in 1908.

(Archives of Industrial Society, University Library System, University of Pittsburgh)

To counter this decline the Protestant churches responded in two ways. They evangelized among the unchurched and indifferent, for example, through the Sunday-school movement. Protestants also made their churches instruments of social uplift. Starting in the 1880s many city churches provided reading rooms, day nurseries, clubhouses, and vocational classes. Some churches linked evangelism and social improvement. The Salvation Army, which arrived from Great Britain in 1879, spread the gospel of repentance among the urban poor and built an assistance program that ranged from soup kitchens to shelters for former prostitutes. When all else failed, the down-and-outers of American cities knew they could count on the Salvation Army.

The social meaning that people sought in religion explained the enormous popularity of a book called *In His Steps* (1896). The author, the Congregational minister Charles M. Sheldon, told the story of a congregation that resolved to live by Christ's precepts for one year. "If the church members were all doing as Jesus would do," Sheldon asked, "could it remain true that armies of men would walk the streets for jobs, and hundreds of them curse the church, and thousands of them find in the saloon their best friend?"

The most potent form of urban evangelism—revivalism—said little about social uplift. From their origins in the eighteenth century revival movements had steadfastly focused on individual redemption. The resolution of earthly problems, revivalists believed, would follow the conversion of the people to Christ. Beginning in the mid-1870s revival meetings swept through the cities.

The pioneering figure was Dwight L. Moody, a former Chicago shoe salesman and YMCA official. After preaching in Britain for two years Moody returned to America in 1875. With his talented chorister and hymn writer, Ira D. Sankey, Moody staged revival meetings that drew thousands. He preached an optimistic, uncomplicated, nondenominational message. Eternal life could be had for the asking, Moody shouted as he held up his Bible. His listeners needed only "to come forward and take, TAKE!"

Many other preachers followed in Moody's path. The most colorful was Billy Sunday, a hard-drinking former outfielder for the Chicago White Stockings who mended his ways and found religion. Like Moody and other city revivalists Sunday was a farm boy. His rip-snorting attacks on fashionable ministers and the "booze traffic" carried the ring of rustic America. By realizing that many people remained villagers at heart, revivalists found a key to bringing city dwellers back into the church.

CITY AMUSEMENTS

City people compartmentalized life's activities, setting workplace apart from home and working time apart from free time. "Going out" became a necessity, demanded not only as solace for a hard day's work but also as proof that life was better in the New World than in the Old. "He who can enjoy and does not enjoy commits a sin," a Yiddish-language paper told its readers. And enjoyment now meant buying a ticket and being entertained.

Amusement parks went up on the outskirts of cities across the country. Most glittering was Luna Park at New York's Coney Island—"an enchanted, storybook land of trellises, columns, domes, minarets, lagoons, and lofty aerial flights. . . . It was a world removed—shut away from the sordid clatter and turmoil of the streets." In fact, escape from everyday urban life explains the appeal of amusement parks. The creators of Luna Park intended it to be "a different world—a dream world . . . where all is bizarre and fantastic . . . gayer and more different from the every-day world."

The theater likewise attracted huge audiences. Chicago had six vaudeville houses in 1896 and twenty-two in 1910. Evolving from tawdry variety and minstrel shows, vaudeville cleaned up its routines, making them suitable for the entire family, and turned into thoroughly professional entertainment handled by national booking agencies. With its standard program of nine singing, dancing, and com-

Amusement Park, Long Beach, California

The origins of the roller coaster go back to LaMarcus Thompson's Switchback Railway, installed at Coney Island in 1884 and featuring gentle dips and curves. By 1900, when Long Beach's Jack Rabbit Race was constructed, the goal was to create the biggest possible thrill. Angelenos journeyed out by trolley to Long Beach not only to take a dip in the ocean but to ride the new roller coaster. The Airplane Ride in the foreground is a further wrinkle on the peculiarly modern notion that the way to have fun is to be scared to death.
(Curt Teich Postcard Archives)

edy acts, vaudeville attained enormous popularity just as the movies arrived. The first primitive films, a minute or so of humor or glimpses of famous people, appeared in 1896 in penny arcades and as filler in vaudeville shows. Within a decade millions of city people were watching films of increasing length and artistry at nickelodeons (named after the five-cent admission charge) across the country.

For young unmarried workers the cheap amusements of the city created a new social space. "I want a good time," a New York clothing operator told an investigator. "And there is no . . . way a girl can get it on $8 a week. I guess if anyone wants to take me to a dance he won't have to ask me twice." Hence the widespread ritual among the urban working class of "treating." The girls spent what money they had dressing up; their beaus were expected to pay for the fun. Parental control over courtship broke down, and amid the bright lights and lively music of the dance hall and amusement park working-class youth forged a more easygoing culture of sexual interaction and pleasure seeking.

The geography of the big city carved out ample space for commercialized sex. Prostitution was not new to urban life, but in the late nineteenth century it became less closeted and more intermingled with other forms of public entertainment. In New York the red-light district was the Tenderloin, running northward from Twenty-third Street between Fifth and Eighth Avenues.

The Tenderloin and the Bowery farther downtown were also the sites of a robust gay subculture. The long-held notion that homosexual life was covert—"in the closet"—in Victorian America appears not to be true, at least not in the country's premier city. Homosexuality was illegal, but as with prostitution the law was mostly a dead letter. In certain corners of the city a gay world flourished, with a full array of saloons, meeting places, and drag balls, which were widely known and patronized by uptown "slummers."

Of all forms of (mostly) male diversion none was more specific to the city or so spectacularly successful as professional baseball. The game's promoters decreed that baseball had been created in 1839 by Abner Doubleday in the village of Cooperstown, New York. Actually, baseball was neither of American origin—it developed from the British game of rounders—nor a product of rural life. The game first appeared in the early 1840s in New York City, where a group of gentlemen enthusiasts competed on an empty lot. Over the next twenty years the aristocratic tone of baseball disappeared. Clubs sprang up across the country, and intercity competition developed on a scheduled basis. In 1868 baseball became openly professional, following the lead of the Cincinnati Red Stockings in signing players to contracts for the season.

Big-time commercial baseball came into its own with the launching of the National League in 1876. The team owners were profit-minded businessmen who shaped the sport to please the fans. Wooden grandstands gave way to the concrete and steel stadiums of the early twentieth century, such as Fenway Park in Boston, Forbes Field in Pittsburgh, and Shibe Park in Philadelphia.

For the urban multitudes baseball grew into something more than an afternoon at the ballpark. By rooting for the home team fans found a way of identifying with the city they lived in. Amid the diversity and anonymity of urban life, the common experience and language of baseball acted as a bridge among strangers.

Most efficient at this task, however, was the newspaper. James Gordon Bennett, founder of the *New York Herald* in 1835, wanted "to record the facts . . . for the great masses of the community." The news was whatever interested city readers, starting with crime, scandal, and sensational events. After the Civil War Charles A. Dana of the *New York Sun* added the human-interest story, which made news of ordinary happenings. Newspapers also targeted specific audiences. A women's page offered recipes and fashion news, separate sections covered sports and high society, and the Sunday supplement helped fill the weekend hours.

The competition for readers became fierce when Joseph Pulitzer, the owner of the *St. Louis Post-Dispatch*, invaded New York in 1883 by buying the *World*. Pulitzer was in turn challenged by William Randolph Hearst, who arrived from San Francisco in 1895 prepared to beat the *New York World* at its own game. Hearst's sensation-alist style of newspaper reporting became known as *yellow journalism*. The term, linked to the first comic strip to appear in color, "The Yellow Kid" (1895), meant a type of reporting in which accuracy was second to eliciting a "Gee Whiz!" feeling in the reader.

"He who is without a newspaper," said the great showman P. T. Barnum, "is cut off from his species." Barnum was speaking of city people and their hunger for in-formation. By meeting this need newspapers revealed their sensitivity to the pub-lic they served.

THE HIGHER CULTURE

In the midst of this popular ferment new institutions of higher culture were tak-ing shape in America's cities. A desire for the cultivated life was not, of course, specifically urban. Before the Civil War the lyceum movement had sent lecturers to the remotest towns, bearing messages of culture and learning. The Chautauqua movement, founded in northern New York in 1874, carried on this work of cul-tural dissemination. However, great institutions such as museums, public libraries, opera companies, and symphony orchestras could flourish only in metropolitan centers.

The nation's first major art museum, the Corcoran Gallery of Art, opened in Washington, D.C., in 1869. New York's Metropolitan Museum of Art started in rented quarters two years later, moved in 1880 to its permanent site in Central Park, and launched an ambitious program of art acquisition. When J. P. Morgan became chairman of the board in 1905, the Metropolitan's preeminence was assured. The Boston Museum of Fine Arts was founded in 1876, and Chicago's Art Institute in 1879.

Symphony orchestras also appeared, first in New York under the conductors Theodore Thomas and Leopold Damrosch in the 1870s and then in Boston and Chicago during the next decade. National tours by these leading orchestras planted the seeds for orchestral societies in many other cities. Public libraries grew from modest collections (in 1870 only seven had as many as 50,000 books) into major urban institutions. The greatest library benefactor was Andrew Carnegie, who announced in 1881 that he would build a library in any town or city that was prepared to maintain it. By 1907 Carnegie had spent more than $32.7 million to establish about a thousand libraries throughout the country.

The late nineteenth century was the great age not only of moneymaking but of money *giving*. Generous with their surplus wealth, new millionaires patronized the arts partly as a civic duty, partly to help establish themselves in society, and also partly out of a sense of national pride.

"In America there is no culture," pronounced the English critic G. Lowes Dickinson in 1909. Science and the practical arts, yes, "every possible application of life to purposes and ends," but "no life for life's sake." Such condescending remarks received a respectful American hearing because of a sense of cultural inferiority to the Old World. In 1873 Mark Twain and Charles Dudley Warner published a novel, *The Gilded Age*, satirizing America as a land of money grubbers and speculators. This enormously popular book touched a nerve in the American psyche. Its title has in fact been appropriated by historians to characterize the late nineteenth century—America's Gilded Age—as an era of materialism and cultural shallowness.

Some members of the upper class, like the novelist Henry James, despaired of the country and moved to Europe. But the more common response was to try to raise the nation's cultural level. The newly rich had a hard time of it. They did not have much opportunity to cultivate a taste for art, and a great deal of what they collected was mediocre and garish. On the other hand, George W. Vanderbilt, grandson of the rough-hewn Cornelius Vanderbilt, was an early champion of French Impressionism, and the coal and steel baron Henry Clay Frick built a brilliant art collection that is still housed, as a public museum, in his mansion in New York City. The enthusiasm of moneyed Americans largely fueled the great cultural institutions that sprang up during the Gilded Age.

A deeply conservative idea of culture sustained this generous patronage. The aim was to embellish life, not to probe or reveal its meaning. "Art," says the hero of the Reverend Henry Ward Beecher's sentimental novel *Norwood* (1867), "attempts to work out its end solely by the use of the beautiful, and the artist is to select out only such things as are beautiful." The idea of culture also took on an elitist cast: Shakespeare, once a staple of popular entertainment (in various bowdlerized versions), was appropriated into the domain of "serious" theater. And simultaneously, the world of culture became feminized. "Husbands or sons rarely share those interests," noted one observer. In American life, remarked the clergyman Horace Bushnell, men represented the "force principle," women the "beauty principle."

The depiction of life, the eminent editor and novelist William Deans Howells wrote, "must be tinged with sufficient idealism to make it all of a truly uplifting character. We cannot admit stories which deal with false or immoral relations. . . . The finer side of things—the idealistic—is the answer for us." The *genteel tradition*, as this literary school came to be known, dominated the nation's elite cultural institutions—its universities and publishers—from the 1860s onward.

But the urban world could not finally be kept at bay. Howells himself resigned in 1881 as editor of the *Atlantic Monthly,* a stronghold of the genteel tradition, and called for a literature that seeks "to picture the daily life in the most exact terms possible." In a series of realistic novels—*A Modern Instance* (1882), *The Rise of Silas Lapham* (1885), and *A Hazard of New Fortunes* (1890)—Howells captured the urban middle class. Stephen Crane's *Maggie: Girl of the Streets* (1893), privately printed because no publisher would touch it, unflinchingly described the destruction of a slum girl. In another urban novel, *The Cliff-Dwellers* (1893), Henry Blake Fuller followed the fortunes of the occupants—"cliff-dwellers"—of a giant Chicago office building.

The city had entered the American imagination and become, by the early 1900s, a main theme of American art and literature. And because it challenged so many assumptions of an older, republican America, the city also became an overriding concern of reformers and a main theater in the drama of the Progressive Era.

For Further Exploration

The starting point for modern urban historiography is Sam Bass Warner's pioneering book on Boston, *Streetcar Suburbs, 1870–1900* (1962). In a subsequent work, *The Private City: Philadelphia in Three Periods* (1968), Warner broadened his analysis to show how private decision making shaped the character of the American city. Innovations in urban construction are treated in Carl Condit, *Rise of the New York Skyscraper, 1865–1913* (1996); Alan

TIMELINE

1871	Metropolitan Museum of Art opens in New York City.	1885	William Jenney builds first steel-frame structure, Chicago's Home Insurance Building.
1873	Mark Twain and Charles Dudley Warner's *The Gilded Age*	1887	First electric trolley line constructed in Richmond, Virginia
1875	Evangelist Dwight L. Moody launches urban revival movement.	1888	Ward McAllister compiles the *Social Register*.
1876	Alexander Graham Bell patents the telephone. National Baseball League founded	1893	Chicago Columbian Exposition "City Beautiful" movement begins.
1878	Electric arc-light system installed in Philadelphia	1895	William Randolph Hearst enters New York journalism. The comic strip "The Yellow Kid" appears.
1879	Thomas Edison creates a practical incandescent light bulb. First elevated train lines open in New York City. Salvation Army arrives from Britain.	1897	Boston builds first American subway.
		1904	New York subway system opens.
1881	Andrew Carnegie offers to build a library for every American city.	1913	Woolworth Building completed in New York City
1883	Joseph Pulitzer purchases the New York *World*.		

Trachtenberg, *The Brooklyn Bridge* (1965); and Harold L. Platt, *The Electric City: Energy and the Growth of the Chicago Area, 1880–1930* (1991).

On the social elite, see Frederic C. Jaher, *The Urban Establishment* (1982). Aspects of middle-class life are revealed in Margaret Marsh, *Suburban Lives* (1990); Michael A. Ebner, *Creating Chicago's North Shore: A Suburban History* (1988); Susan Strasser, *Never Done: A History of American Housework* (1983); John F. Kasson, *Rudeness and Civility: Manners in Nineteenth-Century America* (1990); and, on the entry of immigrants into the middle class, Andrew R. Heinze, *Adapting to Abundance* (1990).

On urban life, see especially Gunther Barth, *City People: The Rise of Modern City Culture* (1982); *John F. Kasson, Amusing the Million: Coney Island at the Turn of the Century* (1978); Timothy J. Gilfoyle, *City of Eros: New York City, Prostitution and the Commercialization of Sex, 1790–1920* (1991); Kathy Peiss, *Cheap Amusements: Working Women and Leisure in Turn-of-the-Century New York* (1986). The best introduction to Gilded Age intellectual currents is Alan Trachtenberg, *The Incorporation of America: Culture and Society, 1865–1893* (1983).

On the Columbian Exposition of 1893, an excellent website is "The World's Columbian Exposition: Idea, Experience, Aftermath" at <http://xroads.virginia.edu/~ma96/wce/title>, including detailed guides to every site at the fair and analysis of its lasting impact. "On the Lower East Side" at <http://acad.smumn.edu/history/contents.html> offers a collection of first-rate articles and documents written at the turn of the century about life on New York's Lower East Side, from housing and child labor to ethnic communities and pushcarts.

Chapter 20

THE PROGRESSIVE ERA
1900–1914

Society is looking itself over, in our day, from top to bottom. . . . We are in a temper to reconstruct economic society.

—Woodrow Wilson, 1913

On the face of it, the political ferment of the 1890s ended with the election of 1896. After the bitter struggle over free silver the victorious Republicans had no stomach for political crusades. The McKinley administration devoted itself to maintaining business confidence: sound money and high tariffs were the order of the day. The main thing, as party chief Mark Hanna said, was to "stand pat and continue Republican prosperity."

Yet beneath the surface a deep uneasiness had set in. The depression of the 1890s had unveiled truths not acknowledged in better days—that a frightening chasm, for example, had opened between America's social classes. In Richard Olney's view the great Pullman strike of 1894 had brought the country "to the ragged edge of anarchy." As Cleveland's attorney-general, it had been Olney's job to crush the strike, which he had done with ruthless efficiency (see Chapter 17). But Olney took little satisfaction from his success. He asked himself what might be done to avoid such repressive government actions in the future. His answer was federal regulation of labor relations on the railroads so that crippling rail strikes would not happen. As a first step toward Olney's goal Congress adopted the Erdman Mediation Act in 1898. In such ways did the crisis of the 1890s turn the nation's thinking to reform.

The problems themselves, however, were of much older origin. For more than half a century Americans had been absorbed in building the world's most advanced industrial economy. At the beginning of the twentieth century they paused, looked around, and began to add up the costs—a frightening concentration of corporate power, a restless working class, misery in the cities, the corruption of machine politics. It was as if social awareness reached a critical mass around 1900 and set reform activity in motion as a major, self-sustaining phenomenon. For this reason the years from 1900 to World War I have come to be known as the Progressive Era.

The Course of Reform

Historians have sometimes spoken of a progressive "movement." But progressivism was not a movement in any meaningful sense. There was no single progressive constituency, no agreed-upon agenda, no unifying organization. At different times and places different social groups became active. People who were reformers on one issue might be conservative on another. The term *progressivism* embraces a widespread, many-sided effort after 1900 to build a better society. Progressive reformers shared only this objective, plus an intellectual style that can be called "progressive."

THE PROGRESSIVE MIND

If the facts could be known, everything else was possible. That was the starting point for progressive thinking. Hence the burst of enthusiasm for scientific investigation—statistical studies by the federal government of immigration, child labor, and economic practices; social research by privately funded foundations into industrial conditions; vice commissions in many cities looking into prostitution, gambling, and other moral ills of an urban society. Progressives likewise placed great faith in academic expertise. In Wisconsin the state university became a key resource for Governor Robert La Follette's reform administration—the reason, one supporter boasted, for "the democracy, the thoroughness, and the accuracy of the state in its legislation."

The main thing, in the progressive view, was to resist ways of thinking that discouraged purposeful action. Social Darwinists who had so dominated Gilded Age thought (see Chapter 18) were wrong in their belief that society developed according to fixed and unchanging laws. "It is folly," protested the Harvard philosopher William James, "to speak of the 'laws of history,' as of something inevitable, which science only has to discover, and which anyone can then foretell and observe, but do nothing to alter or avert." Man could "shape environmental forces to his own advantage," argued the sociologist Lester F. Ward.

Nowhere were the battle lines more sharply drawn than in economics, where the classical school had long proceeded on the assumption that markets were perfectly competitive and perfectly responsive to supply and demand. Such an imagined world left no room for reform because any interference with the market could only disrupt what was already working perfectly. Critics of classical economics—they called themselves "institutional economists"—turned to statistics and history to reveal how the economy really functioned and why, without trade unions and public regulation, the strong would devour the weak.

Progressives similarly argued against treating questions of law as if they could be answered by eternal and self-evident ideas. An example of this legal reasoning was reliance on the principle of liberty of contract in the *Lochner v. New York* decision (1905): the Supreme Court struck down a state law limiting the working hours of bakers on the grounds that such a restriction violated the liberty of contract of the bakers (as well as their employers). Nonsense, responded the dissenting Justice Oliver Wendell Holmes. If the choice was between working and starving, could it really be said that bakers freely accepted jobs requiring them to labor fourteen hours a day or that a law reducing their working hours violated their liberty of contract?

Legal realism, as Justice Holmes's reasoning came to be known, rested on his conviction that "the life of the law has not been logic; it has been experience. The felt necessities of the time, even the prejudices which judges share with their fellowmen, have had a good deal more to do than logic in determining the rules by which men shall be governed." The law, moreover, should not claim a false neutrality; on the contrary, as Holmes's student Felix Frankfurter argued, law should be "a vital agency for human betterment."

The philosophical underpinnings for legal realism came from William James, who denied the existence of absolute truths and offered instead a philosophy of *pragmatism,* which judged ideas by their consequences. Philosophy should be concerned with solving problems, James insisted, not with contemplating ultimate ends.

Progressives prided themselves on being tough-minded. They had confidence in people's capacity to take purposeful action. But there was another side to the progressive mind. It was infused with idealism. Progressives framed their intentions in terms of high principle. Their cause, proclaimed Theodore Roosevelt, "is based on the eternal principles of righteousness."

Much of this idealism was rooted in American radical traditions. Many progressives traced their awakening to Henry George's *Progress and Poverty* (1879), which asked why, in the midst of fabulous wealth, so many Americans should be condemned to poverty. His answer was that private control of land siphoned the community's wealth into the hands of landlords. George's single-tax movement—advocating a confiscatory tax on the unearned value of land—served as a school for many budding progressives. Others credited Edward Bellamy's utopian novel *Looking Backward* (1888), with its technocratic vision of an orderly, affluent American socialism, or Henry Demarest Lloyd's *Wealth Against Commonwealth* (1894), with its searing indictment of the Standard Oil trust. In later years this radical tradition was transmitted mainly through the Socialist Party, which flourished after 1900 under the leadership of Eugene V. Debs. Many young reformers passed through socialism on the way to progressivism, although there were some, like Charlotte Perkins Gilman, who remained faithful to the socialist cause.

The most important source of progressive idealism, however, was religion. Protestant churches had long been troubled by the plight of the urban poor (see Chapter 19). Now that concern blossomed into a major doctrine—the Social Gospel. The Baptist cleric Walter Rauschenbush, its most influential exponent, had been driven by his ministry in the squalid Hell's Kitchen section of New York City to become an activist on behalf of his poor parishioners and their neighbors. The churches had to uphold the "social aims of Jesus," he believed. The Kingdom of God on Earth would be achieved not by striving for personal salvation but in the cause of social justice.

Progressive leaders characteristically grew up in families imbued with evangelical piety. Many went through a religious crisis, seeking and failing to experience a conversion, and ultimately settling on a career in social work, education, or politics, where religious striving might be translated into secular action. Jane Addams, for example, took up settlement-house work believing that by uplifting the poor she would herself be uplifted: she would experience "the joy of finding Christ" by acting "in fellowship" with the needy.

The progressive mode of thought—idealistic in intent and tough-minded in practice—nurtured a new kind of reform journalism. During the 1890s bright new magazines like *Collier's* and *McClure's* began to find an urban audience for lively, fact-filled reporting. At the turn of the century, almost by accident, editors discovered that what most interested readers was the exposure of mischief in American life.

Lincoln Steffens's article "Tweed Days in St. Louis" in the October 1902 issue of *McClure's* is credited with starting the trend. In a powerful series Steffens wrote about "the shame of the cities"—the corrupt ties between business and political machines. Ida M. Tarbell attacked Standard Oil, and David Graham Phillips told how money controlled the Senate. William Hard exposed industrial accidents in "Making Steel and Killing Men" (1907) and child labor in "De Kid Wot Works at Night" (1908). Hardly a sordid corner of American life escaped the scrutiny of these tireless reporters. They were moralists as well, infusing their factual accounts with personal indignation. "The sights I saw," wrote the pioneering slum investigator Jacob Riis, "gripped my heart until I felt I must tell of them, or burst, or turn anarchist."

Theodore Roosevelt, among many others, thought these journalists went too far. In a 1906 speech he compared them to the man with a muckrake in *Pilgrim's Progress* (by the seventeenth-century English preacher John Bunyan) who was too absorbed with raking the filth on the floor to look up and accept a celestial crown. Thus the term *muckraker* became attached to journalists who exposed the underside of American life. Their efforts were in fact health-giving. More than any other group, the muckrakers called the people to arms (see American Voices, "Muckraking").

WOMEN PROGRESSIVES

Among the first to respond were middle-class women who, in their well-established role as "social housekeepers," had long carried the burden of humanitarian work in American cities. They had been the foot soldiers for the charity organization societies that coordinated private relief after the 1870s, visiting needy families, assessing their problems, and referring them to relief agencies.

After many years of such dedicated labors Josephine Shaw Lowell of New York City concluded that giving assistance to the poor was not enough. "If the working

Ida Tarbell Takes on Rockefeller

A popular biographer of Napoleon and Lincoln in the 1890s, Ida Tarbell turned her journalistic talents to muckraking. Her first installment of "The History of the Standard Oil Company" appeared in *Mc-Clure's* in November 1902. John D. Rockefeller, she wrote, "was willing to strain every nerve to obtain for himself special and illegal privileges from the railroads which were bound to ruin every man in the oil business not sharing them with him." As Tarbell built her case, criticism rained down on Rockefeller. A more sympathetic cartoon in the magazine *Judge* pleads with Rockefeller's critics: "Boys, don't you think you have bothered the old man just about enough?"

(Ida M. Tarbell Collection, Pelletier Library, Allegheny College, Meadville, Pennsylvania; Culver Pictures)

people had all they ought to have, we should not have the paupers and criminals," she declared. "It is better to save them before they go under, than to spend your life fishing them out afterward." Lowell founded the New York Consumers' League in 1890. Her goal was to improve the wages and working conditions of female clerks in the city's stores.

AMERICAN VOICES

Muckraking

CHARLES EDWARD RUSSELL

I n this autobiographical account Charles Edward Russell, a newspaperman, describes how he got into muckraking journalism and what he thought it was all about. He never did, by the way, get back to writing music.

All America had been accustomed to laud and bepraise the makers of great fortunes. . . . Now, of a sudden, men began to discover that these great and adored fortunes had been gathered in ways that not only grazed the prison gate but imposed burdens and disadvantages upon the rest of the community. . . . In the shock of this discovery, a literature of exposition arose. . . .

Pure accident cast me, without the least desire, into the pursuit of this fashion. I had finally withdrawn from the newspaper business, and having enough money to live modestly I was bent upon carrying out a purpose long cherished [to compose music]. Upon this task I was intent when the whole business was upset with a single telegram.

One day, Mr. J. W. Midgley, who was a famous expert on railroad rates and conditions . . . let loose a flood of startling facts about the impositions practised by the owners and operators of refrigerator cars. My friend, Mr. Erman J. Ridgway . . . of *Everybody's Magazine* wired asking me to see Mr. Midgley [who] positively refused all offers to become an exposé writer. [So] Ridgway wire[d] asking me to furnish the article *Everybody's* wanted. I had not the least disposition to do so, except only that Ridgway was my friend. . . . The next thing I knew a muckrake was put into my hand and I was plunged into the midst of the game. . . .

I wrote two or three articles on the refrigerator car scandal and then went on to write a series on the methods of the Beef Trust. . . . We were all up and away, full of the pleasures of the chase . . . and all that business about poetry and music sheets forgotten. It was exhilarating sport, hunting the money octopus.

SOURCE: Charles Edward Russell, *Bare Hands and Stone Walls* (New York, Charles Scribner's Sons, 1933), pp. 135–39.

From these modest beginnings the league spread to other cities and blossomed into the National Consumers' League in 1899. By then the women at its head had lost faith in voluntary action; only the state had the resources to rescue poor urban families. Under the crusading leadership of Florence Kelley, formerly a chief factory inspector in Illinois, the Consumers' League became a powerful lobby for protective legislation for women and children.

Among its achievements none was more important than the *Muller v. Oregon* decision (1908), which upheld an Oregon law limiting the workday for women to ten hours. The Consumers' League recruited the brilliant Boston lawyer Louis D.

Brandeis to defend the Oregon law before the Supreme Court. In his brief Brandeis devoted a scant two pages to the narrow constitutional issue—whether, under its police powers, Oregon had the right to regulate women's working hours. Instead Brandeis rested his case on data gathered by the Consumers' League showing the damage long hours did to women's health and family roles. The *Muller* decision, resting on Brandeis's social brief, cleared the way for a wave of protective laws across the country.

Women's organizations became a mighty lobby on behalf of women and children. Their victories included the first law providing public assistance for mothers with dependent children, in Illinois in 1911; the first minimum wage law for women, in Massachusetts in 1912; more effective child labor laws, in many states; and at the federal level, the Children's and Women's bureaus in the Labor Department, in 1912 and 1920, respectively. The welfare state, insofar as it arrived in America in these years, was what women progressives had made of it; they erected a "maternalist" welfare system.

A parallel path for women's reform came via the settlement-house movement. The seed in America was Hull House, which Jane Addams and Ellen Gates Starr established in 1889 on Chicago's West Side after visiting Toynbee Hall in the London slums. During the progressive years scores of settlement houses sprang up in the poor neighborhoods of the nation's cities. Hull House had meeting rooms, an art gallery, clubs for children and adults, and a kindergarten. Addams herself led battles for garbage removal, playgrounds, better street lighting, and police protection.

Besides the modest good they did in the slum neighborhoods, the settlement houses also satisfied the needs of the middle-class residents for meaningful lives. In a famous essay Jane Addams spoke of the "subjective necessity" of the settlement house. She meant that it was as much for educated young men and women eager to serve as it was a response to the needs of slum dwellers. Addams herself was a case in point. Born in 1860 in Cedarville, Illinois, she grew up in comfortable circumstances and graduated from Rockford College. Then Addams faced an empty future—an ornamental wife if she married, a sheltered spinster if she did not. Hull House became her salvation, enabling her to "begin with however small a group to accomplish and to live."

Almost imperceptibly women activists like Jane Addams and Florence Kelley breathed new life into the suffrage movement. Why, they asked, should a woman who was capable of running a settlement house or lobbying a bill be denied the right to vote? If women had the right to vote, they would demand more enlightened legislation and better government. And by encouraging working-class women to help themselves, women progressives got a whole new class interested in fighting for suffrage.

In 1903 social reformers founded the National Women's Trade Union League. Financed and led by wealthy supporters, the league organized women workers, played a considerable role in their strikes, and trained working-class leaders. One such was Rose Schneiderman, who became a union organizer among New York's garment workers; another was Agnes Nestor, who led Illinois glove workers. Although they often resented the patronizing ways of their well-to-do patrons, such trade-union women identified their cause with the broader struggle for women's rights.

Around 1910 suffrage activity began to quicken, and tactics shifted. In Britain suffragists had begun to picket Parliament, assault politicians, and stage hunger strikes while in jail. Inspired by their example, Alice Paul, a young Quaker once resident in Britain, applied similar confrontational tactics to the American struggle. Although women suffrage had been won in six western states since 1910, Paul rejected the state-by-state route as too slow (see Map 20.1). She advocated a constitutional amendment that in one stroke would grant women everywhere the right to vote. In 1916 Paul organized the militant National Woman's Party.

The National American Woman Suffrage Association (NAWSA), from which Paul had split off, was also rejuvenated. Carrie Chapman Catt, a skilled organizer from the New York movement, took over as national leader in 1915. Under her guidance NAWSA brought a broad-based organization to the campaign for a federal amendment.

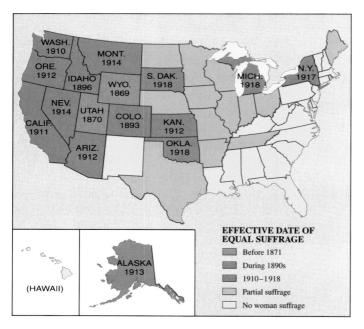

M A P 20.1
Woman Suffrage, 1869–1918

By 1909, after more than sixty years of agitation, only four lightly populated western states had granted women full voting rights. A number of other states offered partial suffrage, limited mostly to voting for school boards and such issues as taxes. Between 1910 and 1918, as the effort shifted to the struggle for a constitutional amendment, eleven states (and Alaska) joined the list granting full suffrage. The most stubborn resistance was in the South.

In the midst of this suffrage struggle something new and more fundamental began to happen. A younger generation of college-educated, self-supporting women refused to be hemmed in by the social constraints of women's "separate sphere." "Breaking into the Human Race" was the intention they proclaimed at a mass meeting in New York in 1914. "We intend simply to be ourselves," declared the chair Marie Jenny Howe, "not just our little female selves, but our whole big human selves."

The women at this meeting called themselves *feminists,* a term that was just coming into use. In this, its first incarnation, feminism meant freedom for full personal development. Thus did Charlotte Perkins Gilman, famous for her advocacy of communal kitchens as a means of liberating women from homemaking, imagine the new woman: "Here she comes, running, out of prison and off the pedestal; chains off, crown off, halo off, just a live woman."

Feminists were militantly prosuffrage, but unlike their more traditional suffragist sisters they had no interest in arguing that women would have an uplifting effect on American politics. Rather they demanded the right to vote because they considered themselves fully equal to men. At the moment the suffrage movement was about to triumph, it was overtaken by a larger revolution that redefined the struggle for women's rights as a battle against all the constraints that prevented women from achieving their potential as human beings.

Feminism brought forth a more radical type of woman social progressive—most notably, Margaret Sanger. As a public health nurse in New York City, Sanger had been repeatedly asked by immigrant women the "secret" of how to avoid having more babies. When one of her patients died of a botched abortion, Sanger decided to devote herself to the cause of birth control. This activity was illegal; nineteenth-century laws treated birth-control literature and contraceptive devices as obscene materials. While the educated middle class had little trouble evading these laws, birth control could reach the poor only by an open campaign of education. Undeterred by police raids or public disapproval, Sanger gave speeches, published pamphlets, and in 1916 opened the first birth-control clinic in the United States. If her ends were the same as Jane Addams's—both wanted to uplift the downtrodden—the means Sanger chose laid down a sharper challenge to the status quo.

REFORMING POLITICS

Like the Mugwumps of the Gilded Age, progressive reformers attacked the boss rule of the party system, but more adeptly and more aggressively. Indeed, because politics was about power, in this realm the motives of progressives were always mixed, with the ideals of civic betterment elbowing uneasily with the drive for self-aggrandizement.

Robert M. La Follette of Wisconsin led the way. Born in 1855, La Follette started as a conventional politician, rising from the Republican ranks to service in Congress for three terms. He was a party regular, never doubting that he was in honorable company until, by his own account, a Republican boss offered him a bribe

Robert M. La Follette

La Follette was transformed into a political reformer when a Wisconsin Republican boss attempted to bribe him in 1891. As he described it in his *Autobiography,* "Out of this awful ordeal came understanding; and out of understanding came resolution. I determined that the power of this corrupt influence . . . should be broken." This photograph captures La Follette at the top of his form, taking his case in 1897 to the people of Cumberland, Wisconsin.
(State Historical Society of Wisconsin, Madison, WI)

to fix a judge in a railroad case. Awakened by this "awful ordeal" La Follette broke with the Wisconsin machine in 1891 and became a tireless exponent of political reform, which for him meant restoring America's democratic ideals. "Go back to the first principles of democracy; go back to the people," he told his audience when he launched his campaign against the state Republican machine. In 1900, after battling for a decade, La Follette won the governorship on a platform of higher taxes for corporations, stricter utility and railroad regulation, and political reform.

The key to party reform, La Follette felt, was to deny the bosses the power to choose the party's candidates. This could be achieved by requiring that nominations be decided not in party conventions but by popular vote. Enacted in 1903, Wisconsin's direct primary expressed La Follette's democratic idealism, but it also suited his particular political talents. The party regulars opposing him were insiders, more comfortable in the caucus room than out on the stump. But that was where La Follette, a superb campaigner, excelled. The direct primary gave La Follette an iron grip on Republican politics in Wisconsin that he did not relinquish until his death twenty-five years later.

What was true of La Follette was more or less true of all successful progressive politicians. They typically described their work as political restoration, frequently confessing that they had converted to reform after discovering how far party politics had drifted from the ideals of representative government. Like La Follette, Albert B. Cummins of Iowa, William U'Ren of Oregon, and Hiram Johnson of California all espoused democratic ideals, and all skillfully used the direct primary as the stepping stone to political power. They practiced a new kind of popular politics, which in a reform age could be a more effective way to power than the backroom techniques of the old-fashioned machine politicians.

Even the most democratizing of reforms espoused by the progressives—the initiative and recall—were really exercises in power politics. The *initiative* enabled citizens to have burning issues placed on the ballot; *recall* empowered them to remove officeholders who had lost the public's confidence. It soon became clear, however, that direct democracy did not supplant organized politics. Initiative and recall campaigns required organization, money, and expertise, and these were attributes not of the people at large but of well-financed interests. Like the direct primary, the initiative and recall had as much to do with power relations as with democratic idealism.

URBAN LIBERALISM

When the Republican Hiram Johnson ran for California governor in 1910, he was the reform candidate of the state's middle class. Famous as prosecutor of the corrupt San Francisco boss Abe Ruef, Johnson pledged to purify California politics and curb the Southern Pacific Railroad—the dominating economic power in the state. By his second term Johnson was championing social and labor legislation. His original base in the middle class had eroded, and he had become the champion of California's immigrant working class.

Johnson's career reflected a shift in the center of gravity of progressivism, which had begun as a movement of the middle class but then took on board America's working people. A new strain of progressive reform emerged that historians have labeled *urban liberalism*. To understand this phenomenon we have to begin with city machine politics.

Thirty minutes before quitting time on Saturday afternoon, March 25, 1911, fire broke out at the Triangle Shirtwaist Company in downtown New York. The flames trapped the workers, mostly young immigrant women. Forty-seven leapt to their deaths; another ninety-nine never reached the windows (see American Voices, "Working for the Triangle Shirtwaist Company"). In the wake of the tragedy, the New York State Factory Commission developed over a four-year period a remarkable program of labor reform: fifty-six laws dealing with fire hazards, unsafe machines, industrial homework, and wages and hours for women and children. The chairman of the commission was Robert F. Wagner; the vice chairman, Alfred E. Smith. Both were Tammany Hall politicians, serving at the time as leaders in the

AMERICAN VOICES

Working for the Triangle Shirtwaist Company

PAULINE NEWMAN

*P*auline Newman was an organizer and educational director for the International Ladies Garment Workers Union until her death in 1986. As a child she had worked at the notorious Triangle Shirtwaist factory in New York.

A cousin of mine worked for the Triangle Shirtwaist Company and she got me on there in October of 1901. . . .

Well, of course, there were [child labor] laws on the books, but no one bothered to enforce them. The employers were always tipped off if there was going to be an inspection. "Quick," they'd say, "into the boxes!" And we children would climb into the big boxes the finished shirts were stored in. Then some shirts were piled on top of us, and when the inspector came—no children. The factory always got an okay from the inspector, and I suppose someone at City Hall got a little something, too.

The employers didn't recognize anyone working for them as a human being. . . . If you went to the toilet and you were there longer than the floor lady thought you should be, you would be laid off for half a day and sent home. And, of course, that meant no pay. You were not allowed to have your lunch on the fire escape in the summertime. The door was locked to keep us in, That's why so many people were trapped when the fire broke out. . . .

I stopped working at the Triangle Factory during the strike in 1909 and I didn't go back. The union sent me out to raise money for the strikers. I apparently was able to articulate my feelings and opinions about the criminal conditions, and they didn't have anyone else who could do better so they assigned me. . . .

After the 1909 strike I worked with the union, organizing in Philadelphia and Cleveland and other places, so I wasn't at the Triangle Shirtwaist Factory when the fire broke out, but a lot of my friends were. . . .

Conditions were dreadful in those days. But . . . even when things were terrible, I always had that faith. . . . Only now, I'm a little discouraged sometimes when I see the workers spending their free hours watching television—trash. We fought so hard for those hours and they waste them. We used to read Tolstoy, Dickens, Shelley, by candlelight, and they watch the *Hollywood Squares*. Well, they're free to do what they want. That's what we fought for.

SOURCE: Joan Morrison and Charlotte Fox Zabusky, eds., *American Mosaic: The Immigrant Experience in the Words of Those Who Lived It* (New York: Dutton, 1980), pp. 9–14. Copyright © 1980 by Joan Morrison and Charlotte Fox Zabusky. Reprinted by permission.

state legislature. They established the commission, participated fully in its work, and marshaled the party regulars to pass the proposals into law—all with the approval of the Tammany machine.

In thus responding to the Triangle fire, Tammany was conceding that social problems had grown too big to be handled informally by party machines. Only the state could prohibit industrial firetraps or cope with the evils of factory work and slum life. And if that meant a weakening of the traditional bonds of rank-and-file loyalty to Tammany, so be it. Al Smith and Robert Wagner absorbed the lessons of the Triangle investigation. They formed durable ties with such middle-class progressives as the social worker Frances Perkins, who sat on the commission as the representative of the New York Consumers' League, and became urban liberals—advocates of active intervention by the state in uplifting the laboring masses of America's cities.

It was not only altruism that converted seasoned politicians like Smith and Wagner. The city machines faced strong competition from a new breed of middle-class progressive, skilled urban reformers like Mayor Brand Whitlock of Toledo, Ohio, whose administration not only attacked city hall corruption but also provided better schools, cleaner streets, and more social services for Toledo's needy. Combining campaign magic and popular programs, progressive mayors in Cleveland, Jersey City, and elsewhere won over the urban masses and challenged the rule of the machines. Also confronting the bosses was a challenge from the left. The Socialist Party was making headway in the cities, electing Milwaukee's Victor Berger as the nation's first socialist congressman in 1910 and winning municipal elections across the country. The political universe of the urban machines had changed, and they had to pay closer attention to opinion in the precincts.

City machines, always pragmatic, adopted urban liberalism without much ideological struggle. The same could not be said of the trade unions, the other institution that represented American working people. In its early years the American Federation of Labor (AFL) had strongly opposed state interference in labor's affairs. Samuel Gompers preached that workers should not seek from government what they could accomplish by their own economic power and self-help. *Voluntarism,* as trade unionists called this doctrine, did not die out, but it weakened substantially during the progressive years.

One reason was that the labor movement came under severe attack by the courts. In the *Danbury Hatters* case (1908) the Supreme Court declared a boycott by the Hatters' Union against the antiunion D. E. Loewe & Company to be a conspiracy in restraint of trade under the Sherman Act, awarding triple damages that threatened the homes and life savings of hundreds of union members and rendering trade unions vulnerable to antitrust suits. Even worse was the willingness of judges to grant injunctions—court orders—prohibiting unions from carrying on strikes or boycotts. The justification was to prevent "irreparable damage" to an employer while the court was considering the legality of the union's actions. But the effect of this "temporary" measure was invariably to immobilize and defeat the union.

Only a political response could blunt these assaults on labor's economic weapons. In its "Bill of Grievances" of 1906, the AFL demanded that Congress grant unions immunity from antitrust suits and injunctions. Rebuffed, the unions became more politically active, entering campaigns and giving nonpartisan support to candidates who favored their program.

Once into politics the labor movement had difficulty denying the case for social legislation. The AFL, after all, claimed to speak for the entire working class. When muckrakers exposed exploitation of workers and middle-class progressives came forward with solutions, how could the labor movement fail to respond? In state after state organized labor joined the battle for progressive legislation and increasingly became its strongest advocate, including most particularly workers' compensation for industrial accidents.

Accidents took an awful toll at the workplace. Two thousand coal miners were killed every year, dying from cave-ins and explosions at a rate 50 percent higher than in German mines. Liability laws, based on common law, so heavily favored employers that victims of industrial accidents rarely got more than token compensation. The tide turned quickly once the labor movement pushed the issue; between 1910 and 1917 all the industrial states enacted insurance laws covering on-the-job injuries.

Maimed Factory Worker

Lewis Hine, a great photographer of immigrant life, took this undated picture of a disabled factory worker. Two of his four children are in the background. How was he to support them? If his accident occurred before the passage of workers' compensation laws in 1910, they were probably out of luck. (George Eastman House)

The United States hesitated, however, to broaden the attack on the hazards of modern industrial life. Health insurance and unemployment compensation, although popular in Europe, scarcely made it onto the American political agenda. Old-age pensions, which Britain adopted in 1908, got a serious hearing, only to come up against an odd barrier: the United States already had a pension system of a kind, for Civil War veterans, providing benefits to as many as half of all native-born men over sixty-four or their survivors in the early twentieth century.

Not until the Great Depression would the country be ready for social insurance. A secure old age, unemployment payments, health benefits—these human needs of a modern industrial order were beyond the reach of urban liberals in the Progressive Era.

RACISM AND REFORM

The direct primary was the flagship of progressive politics—the crucial reform, as La Follette said, for defeating the party bosses and returning politics to "the people." The primary originated not in Wisconsin, however, but in the South, and by the time La Follette got his primary law in 1903, primaries were already operating in seven southern states. In the South, however, the primary was a *white* primary. Since the Democratic nomination was tantamount to election, excluding African Americans from the nominating process effectively disfranchised them. The southern primary was dressed up as an attack on back-room party rule, but it also served to deprive blacks of their political rights.

Democratic reform and white supremacy thus were wedded together by the racism of the age. In a 1902 book on Reconstruction Professor John W. Burgess of Columbia University denounced the Fifteenth Amendment: granting blacks the vote after the Civil War had been a "monstrous thing." Burgess was southern-born, but he was confident that his northern audience saw the "vast differences in political capacity" between blacks and whites and approved of black disfranchisement. Even the Republican Party offered no rebuttal. Indeed, as president-elect in 1908 William Howard Taft applauded the southern laws as necessary to "prevent entirely the possibility of domination by. . . an ignorant electorate." Taft assured southerners that "the federal government has nothing to do with social equality."

In the North racial tensions were on the rise. Over 200,000 blacks migrated from the South between 1900 and 1910. Their arrival in northern cities invariably sparked white resentment. Attacks on blacks became widespread, capped by a bloody race riot in Springfield, Illinois, in 1908. Equally reflective of racist sentiment was the huge success of D. W. Griffith's epic film *Birth of a Nation* (1915), which depicted Reconstruction as a moral struggle between rampaging blacks and a chivalrous Ku Klux Klan. Woodrow Wilson found the film's history "all so terribly true." His Democratic administration marked a low point for the federal government as the ultimate guarantor of equal rights: during Wilson's tenure segregation of the U.S. civil service would have gone into effect but for an outcry among black leaders and influential white allies.

In these bleak years a core of young black professionals, mostly northern-born, began to fight back. The key figure was William Monroe Trotter, the pugnacious editor of the *Boston Guardian* and an outspoken critic of Booker T. Washington. "The policy of compromise has failed," Trotter argued. "The policy of resistance and aggression deserves a trial." In this endeavor Trotter was joined by W.E.B. Du Bois, a Harvard-trained sociologist and author of *Souls of Black Folk*. In 1906, after breaking with Washington, they called a meeting of twenty-nine supporters at Niagara Falls—but in Canada because no hotel on the U.S. side would admit blacks. The Niagara Movement that resulted from that meeting had an impact far beyond the scattering of members and local bodies it organized. The principles it affirmed would define the struggle for the rights of African Americans: first, encouragement of black pride by all possible means; second, an uncompromising demand for full political and civil equality; and above all the resolute denial "that the Negro-American assents to inferiority, is submissive under oppression and apologetic before insults."

Going against the grain, a handful of white reformers rallied to the African American cause. Among the most devoted was Mary White Ovington, who grew up in an abolitionist family. Like Jane Addams, Ovington became a settlement-house worker but among urban blacks in New York rather than immigrants in a Chicago neighborhood. News of the Springfield race riot of 1908 changed her life. Convinced that her duty was to fight racism, Ovington called a meeting of sympathetic white progressives, which led to the formation of the National Association for the Advancement of Colored People (NAACP) in 1909.

Torn by internal disagreements, the Niagara Movement was breaking up; most of the black activists joined the NAACP. The organization's national leadership was dominated by whites, with one crucial exception. Du Bois became the editor of the NAACP's journal, *The Crisis*. With a passion that only a black voice could provide, Du Bois used that platform to proclaim the demand for equal rights.

In social welfare the National Urban League became the lead organization, uniting in 1911 the many agencies serving black migrants arriving in northern cities. Like the NAACP the Urban League was interracial, including both white reformers such as Ovington and black welfare activists such as William Lewis Bulkley, a New York school principal who was the League's main architect. In the South social welfare was very much the province of black women, mostly working in the churches and schools but also as members of the southern branches of the National Association of Colored Women's Clubs, which had started in 1896. And because their activities seemed unthreatening to white supremacy, black women were able to reach across the color line and find allies and supporters among white women in the South.

Progressivism was a house of many chambers. Most were infected by the racism of the age, but not all. A saving remnant of white progressives rallied to the cause of racial justice. National institutions—the NAACP, the Urban League, and such black organizations as the National Association of Colored Women's Clubs—took shape that would lead the black struggle for a better life over the next half century.

Progressivism and National Politics

The gathering forces of progressivism reached the national scene slowly. Reformers had been spurred by immediate and visible problems, far from Washington. But in 1906 Robert La Follette left Wisconsin for the U.S. Senate. Other seasoned progressives, also ambitious for a wider stage, followed. By 1910 a vocal progressive bloc was making itself heard in both houses of Congress.

Progressivism came to national politics not via Congress, however, but by way of the presidency. This was partly because the White House provided a "bully pulpit"—to use Theodore Roosevelt's phrase. But just as important was the twist of fate that brought Roosevelt to the White House on September 14, 1901.

THE MAKING OF A PROGRESSIVE PRESIDENT

Except for his upper-class background Theodore Roosevelt was cut from much the same cloth as other progressive politicians. Born in 1858 he came from a wealthy old-line New York family, attended Harvard, and contemplated the life of a leisured man of letters. Instead, scarcely out of college, he plunged into Republican politics and entered the New York state legislature. Like many other budding progressives, Roosevelt was motivated by a high-minded, Christian upbringing. He always identified himself—loudly—with the cause of righteousness. But Roosevelt did not scorn power and its uses. Contemptuous of the Mugwump reformers (see Chapter 18), he much preferred the professionalism of party politics. Roosevelt rose in the New York party because he skillfully developed broad popular support and thus forced himself on reluctant state Republican bosses.

Safely back from the Spanish-American War as the hero of San Juan Hill (see Chapter 21), Roosevelt won the New York governorship in 1898. During his single term he clearly signaled his progressivism by pushing through civil-service reform and a tax on corporate franchises. He discharged the corrupt superintendent of insurance over the Republican Party's objections and asserted his confidence in the government's capacity to improve the life of the people.

Hoping to neutralize him the party chieftains promoted Roosevelt in 1900 to what seemed a dead-end job, as William McKinley's vice president. Roosevelt accepted reluctantly. But on September 6, 1901, an anarchist named Leon F. Czolgosz shot the president. When McKinley died eight days later, Roosevelt became president. It was a sure bet, groaned Republican boss Mark Hanna, that "that damn cowboy" would make trouble in the White House.

Roosevelt in fact moved cautiously, attending first of all to politics. He adroitly used the patronage powers of the presidency to gain control of the Republican Party. But he was also uncertain about what reform role the federal government ought to play. At first the new president might have been described as a progressive without a cause.

Even so, Roosevelt displayed his activist bent. An ardent outdoorsman, he emphasized conservation in his first annual message to Congress. Unlike John Muir (see Chapter 16) Roosevelt was not a preservationist wholly opposed to the exploitation of the nation's wilderness. Rather he wanted to conserve the country's resources and make certain that commercial development was mindful of the public interest. In 1902 he backed the Newlands Reclamation Act, which designated the proceeds from public land sales for irrigation in arid regions. His administration expanded the national forests, upgraded land management, and to the chagrin of some Republicans energetically prosecuted violators of federal land laws. In the cause of conservation Roosevelt demonstrated his disdain for those who sought profit "by betraying the public."

That same energetic bent prompted Roosevelt's intervention in the miners' strike of 1902. Hard coal (anthracite) was the main fuel for home heating in those days. As cold weather approached, it became urgent to settle the strike. The United Mine Workers, led by John Mitchell, was willing to submit to arbitration, but the coal operators would have nothing to do with the union. Although lacking any legal grounds for intervening, the president called both sides to a White House conference on October 1, 1902. When the operators balked, Roosevelt threatened a government takeover of the mines. He also persuaded the financier J. P. Morgan to

Theodore Roosevelt at Yellowstone National Park, 1903

President Roosevelt, a devoted conservationist is pictured here about to enter Yellowstone, the first of America's national parks and a favorite of his. The photograph of him on horseback must have delighted Roosevelt. It showed him as he liked to be seen—as a great outdoorsman.
(Picture Research Consultants & Archives)

use his considerable influence. At that point the coal operators caved in. The strike ended with the appointment by Roosevelt of an arbitration commission, another unprecedented step. While not especially sympathetic to organized labor, Roosevelt blamed the crisis on the "arrogant stupidity" of the mine owners.

"Of all the forms of tyranny the least attractive and the most vulgar is the tyranny of mere wealth," Roosevelt wrote in his autobiography. He was prepared to deploy all his presidential authority against the "tyranny" of irresponsible business.

REGULATING THE MARKETPLACE

The economic issue that most troubled Roosevelt was the threat posed by big business to competitive markets. The drift toward large-scale enterprise was itself not new; for many years efficiency-minded entrepreneurs had been building vertically integrated national firms (see Chapter 17). But bigger business, they knew, also meant power to control markets. And when, in the aftermath of the depression of the 1890s, promoters scrambled to merge rival firms, the primary motive was not efficiency but the elimination of competition. These mergers—*trusts,* as they were called— greatly increased business concentration in the economy. By 1910, 1 percent of the nation's manufacturers accounted for 44 percent of the nation's industrial output.

As early as his first annual message, Roosevelt acknowledged the nation's uneasiness with the "real and grave evils" of economic concentration. But what weapons could the president use in response?

The legal principles upholding free competition were already firmly established under common law: anyone injured by monopoly or illegal restraint of trade could sue for damages. With the passage of the Sherman Antitrust Act of 1890, these common-law rights entered the U.S. statute books and could be enforced by the federal government where offenses involved interstate commerce. Neither Cleveland nor McKinley showed much interest, but the Sherman Act was there waiting to be used. Its potential consisted above all in the fact that it incorporated common-law principles of unimpeachable validity. In the right hands the Sherman Act could be a mighty weapon against the abuse of economic power.

Roosevelt made his opening move in 1903 by establishing a Bureau of Corporations empowered to investigate business practices and bolster the Justice Department's capacity to mount antitrust suits. The department had already filed such a suit in 1902 against the Northern Securities Company, a combination of the railroad systems of the Northwest. In a landmark decision the Supreme Court ordered Northern Securities dissolved in 1904.

In the presidential election that year Roosevelt handily defeated a weak conservative Democratic candidate, Judge Alton B. Parker. Now president in his own right, Roosevelt stepped up the attack on the trusts. He took on forty-five of the nation's giant firms, including Standard Oil, American Tobacco, and DuPont. His rhetoric rising, Roosevelt became the nation's trust-buster, a crusader against "predatory wealth."

Jack and the Wall Street Giants

In this vivid cartoon from the humor magazine *Puck* Jack (Theodore Roosevelt) has come to slay the giants of Wall Street. To ordinary Americans trust-busting took on the mythic qualities of the fairy tale—with about the same amount of awe for the fearsome Wall Street giants and hope in the prowess of the intrepid Roosevelt. J. P. Morgan is the giant leering at front right.

(Library of Congress)

But Roosevelt was not antibusiness. He regarded large-scale enterprise as a natural tendency of modern industrialism. Only firms that abused their power deserved punishment. But how would those companies be identified? Under the Sherman Act, following common-law practice, the courts decided whether an act in restraint of trade was "unreasonable"—that is, actually harmed the public interest. In the *Trans-Missouri* decision of 1897, however, the Supreme Court abandoned this discretionary "rule of reason," holding now that actions that restrained or monopolized trade, regardless of the public impact, automatically violated the Sherman Act.

Little noticed at first, *Trans-Missouri* placed Roosevelt in a quandary. He had no desire to hamstring legitimate business activity, but he could not rely on the courts to distinguish between "good" and "bad" trusts. The only solution was for Roosevelt to do so himself, a power he had because as president he decided whether to initiate antitrust prosecutions in the first place. It was his negative power that counted here: he could choose not to prosecute a trust.

In November 1904, with an antitrust suit looming, the United States Steel Corporation's chairman Elbert H. Gary approached Roosevelt with a deal: cooperation in exchange for preferential treatment. The company would open its books to the Bureau of Corporations; if it found evidence of wrongdoing, the company would be warned privately and given a chance to set matters right. Roosevelt accepted this "gentlemen's agreement" because it met his interest in accommodating the realities of the modern industrial order while maintaining his public image as slayer of the trusts.

The railroads posed a different kind of problem. As quasi-public enterprises, they had always been subject to state regulation; after 1887 they came under federal regulation by the Interstate Commerce Commission (ICC). As with the Sherman Act this assertion of federal authority was essentially symbolic at first. Convinced that the railroads needed firmer oversight, Roosevelt pushed through the Elkins Act of 1903, which prohibited discriminatory rates that gave an unfair advantage to preferred or powerful customers; and then, with the 1904 election behind him, he launched a drive for real railroad regulation. In 1906, after nearly two years of wrangling, Congress passed the Hepburn Railway Act, which empowered the ICC to set maximum shipping rates and prescribe uniform methods of bookkeeping. As a concession to the conservative Republican bloc, however, the courts retained broad powers to review the ICC's rate decisions.

The Hepburn Act was a triumph of Roosevelt's skills as a political operator. He had maneuvered brilliantly against determined opposition and come away with the essentials of what he wanted. Despite grumbling by Senate progressives, Roosevelt was satisfied. He had achieved a landmark expansion of the government's regulatory powers over business.

The protection of consumers, another signature issue for progressives, was very much the handiwork of muckraking journalism. What sparked the issue was riveting articles in *Collier's* by Samuel Hopkins Adams exposing the patent-medicine business. For a time industry lobbies stymied legislative action. Then in 1906 Upton Sinclair's novel *The Jungle* appeared. Sinclair thought he was writing about the exploitation of workers in Chicago meat-packing plants, but what caught the nation's attention were his descriptions of rotten meat and filthy conditions. President Roosevelt, weighing into the legislative battle, authorized a federal investigation of the stockyards. Within months the Pure Food and Drug and the Meat Inspection acts passed, and another administrative agency joined the expanding federal bureaucracy: the Food and Drug Administration.

During the 1904 presidential campaign Roosevelt had taken to calling his program the Square Deal. This kind of labeling was new to American politics, emblematic of a political style that dramatized issues, mobilized public opinion, and asserted leadership. After many years of passivity and weakness the federal government was reclaiming the role it had abandoned after the Civil War. Now, however, the target was the new economic order. When companies abused their corporate power, the government would intercede to assure ordinary Americans a "square deal."

THE FRACTURING OF REPUBLICAN PROGRESSIVISM

During his presidency Theodore Roosevelt had struggled to bring a modern corporate economy under public control. He was well aware, however, that his Square Deal was built on nineteenth-century foundations; in particular, antitrust doctrine, which aimed at enforcing competition, seemed inadequate when the economy's tendency was toward industrial concentration. Better for the government to regulate big business than try to break it up. Roosevelt's final presidential speeches dwelt on the need for a reform agenda for the twentieth century. This was the task he bequeathed to his chosen successor, William Howard Taft.

Taft was an estimable man in many ways. An able jurist and superb administrator, he had served Roosevelt loyally as governor-general of the Philippines and as secretary of war. He was an avowed Square Dealer. But he was not by nature a progressive politician. He disliked the give-and-take of politics, he distrusted power, and he revered the processes of law. He could not, for example, have imagined intruding into the 1902 anthracite strike, as Roosevelt had done, or taken so flexible a view of the Sherman Act. He was, in fundamental ways, a conservative.

Taft's Democratic opponent in the 1908 campaign was William Jennings Bryan. This was Bryan's last hurrah, his third attempt at the presidency, and he made the most of it. Eloquent as ever, Bryan attacked the Republicans as the party of the "plutocrats" and outdid them in urging tougher antitrust legislation, lower tariffs, stricter railway regulation, and advanced labor legislation. Bryan's campaign moved the Democratic Party into the mainstream of national progressive politics, but it was not enough to offset Taft's advantages as Roosevelt's candidate.

Taft won comfortably, and he entered the White House with a mandate to pick up where Roosevelt had left off. That was not to be.

By 1909 the ferment of reform had unsettled the Republican Party. On the right the conservatives were girding themselves against further losses. Led by the formidable Senator Nelson W. Aldrich of Rhode Island, they were still a force to be reckoned with. On the left progressive Republicans were rebellious. They had broad popular support—especially in the Midwest—and Robert La Follette, a fiery leader. The progressives felt that Roosevelt had been too easy on business, and with him gone from the White House they intended to make up for lost time. Reconciling these conflicting forces within the Republican Party would have been a daunting task for the most accomplished politician. For Taft it spelled disaster.

First there was the tariff. Progressives considered protective tariffs a major reason that competition had declined and the trusts had taken hold. Although Taft had campaigned for tariff reform, he was won over by the conservative Republican bloc and ended up approving the protectionist Payne-Aldrich Tariff Act of 1909.

Next came the Pinchot-Ballinger affair. U.S. Chief Forester Gifford Pinchot, an ardent conservationist and a chum of Roosevelt's, accused Secretary of the Interior Richard A. Ballinger of conspiring to transfer Alaskan public land—rich in natural resources—to a private syndicate. When Pinchot aired these charges in January

1910, Taft fired him for insubordination. Despite Taft's strong conservationist credentials, in the eyes of the progressives the Pinchot-Ballinger affair marked him for life as a friend of the "interests" bent on plundering the nation's resources.

Taft found himself propelled into the conservative Republican camp, an ally of "Uncle Joe" Cannon, the dictatorial speaker of the House of Representatives. When a House revolt finally broke Cannon's power in 1910, it was regarded as a defeat for the president as well. Galvanized by Taft's defection the reformers in the Republican Party became a dissident faction, calling themselves "Progressives" or in more belligerent moments "Insurgents." Taft answered by backing their conservative foes in the Republican primaries that year.

The Progressives emerged from the 1910 elections stronger and angrier. In January 1911 they formed the National Progressive Republican League and began a drive to take over the Republican Party. Though La Follette was their leader, the Progressives knew that their best chance to topple Taft lay with Theodore Roosevelt.

Home from a year-long safari in Africa, Roosevelt yearned to reenter the political fray. Taft's dispute with the Progressives gave Roosevelt the cause he needed. But Roosevelt was a loyal party man and too astute a politician not to recognize that a party split would benefit the Democrats. He could be spurred into rebellion only by a true clash of principles. On the question of the trusts just such a clash materialized.

By distinguishing between good and bad trusts Roosevelt had managed to reconcile public policy (the Sherman Act) and economic reality (the tendency toward corporate concentration). But this was a makeshift solution that depended on a president who was willing to stretch his powers to the limit. Taft had no such inclination. His legalistic mind rebelled at the notion that he as president should decide which trusts should be prosecuted. The Sherman Act was on the books. "We are going to enforce that law or die in the attempt," Taft promised grimly.

In the *Standard Oil* decision (1911) the Supreme Court eased Taft's problem by reasserting the rule of reason, which meant that, once again, the courts themselves would distinguish between good and bad trusts. With that burden lifted from the executive branch Attorney General George W. Wickersham stepped up the pace of antitrust actions.

United States Steel became an immediate target. Among the charges against the Steel Trust was that it had violated the antimonopoly provision of the Sherman Act by acquiring the Tennessee Coal and Iron Company in 1907. Roosevelt had personally approved the acquisition, believing this was necessary—so U.S. Steel representatives had told him—to prevent a financial collapse on Wall Street. Taft's suit against U.S. Steel thus amounted to an attack on Roosevelt that he could not, without dishonor, ignore.

Ever since leaving the White House Roosevelt had been pondering the trust problem. There was, he concluded, a third way between breaking up big business and submitting to corporate rule. The federal government could be empowered to oversee the nation's industrial corporations to make sure they acted in the public interest. They would be regulated by a federal trade commission as if they were natural monopolies or public utilities.

In a speech in Osawatomie, Kansas, in August 1910 Roosevelt made the case for what he called the New Nationalism. The central issue, he argued, was human welfare versus property rights. In modern society property had to be controlled "to whatever degree the public welfare may require it." The government would become "the steward of the public welfare."

This formulation clarified Roosevelt's thinking about reform. He took up the cause of social justice, adding to his program a federal child labor law, regulation of labor relations, and a national minimum wage for women. Most radical, perhaps, was Roosevelt's attack on the legal system. Insisting that the courts stood in the way of reform, Roosevelt proposed sharp curbs on their powers, even raising the possibility of popular recall of court decisions.

Early in 1912 Roosevelt announced his candidacy for the presidency and immediately swept the Progressive Republicans into his camp. A bitter party battle ensued. Roosevelt won the states that held primary elections, but Taft controlled the party machinery elsewhere. Dominated by the party regulars, the Republican convention chose Taft. Considering himself cheated out of the nomination, Roosevelt led his followers into a new Progressive Party, soon nicknamed the "Bull Moose" Party. In a crusading campaign Roosevelt offered the New Nationalism to the people.

WOODROW WILSON AND THE NEW FREEDOM

While the Republicans battled among themselves, the Democrats were on the move. The scars caused by the free-silver campaign of 1896 had faded, and in the 1908 campaign William Jennings Bryan had established the rejuvenated party's progressive credentials. The Democrats made dramatic gains in 1910, taking over the House of Representatives for the first time since 1892 and capturing a number of traditionally Republican governorships. After fourteen years as the party's standard-bearer, Bryan made way for a new generation of leaders.

The ablest was Woodrow Wilson of New Jersey, a noted political scientist who, as university president, had brought Princeton into the front rank of American universities. In 1910, with no political experience, he accepted the Democratic nomination for governor of New Jersey and won. Wilson compiled a sterling reform record, including the direct primary, workers' compensation, and stringent utility regulation. He went on to win the Democratic presidential nomination in 1912 in a bruising battle.

Wilson possessed, to a fault, the moral certainty that characterized the progressive politician. A brilliant speaker, he instinctively assumed the mantle of righteousness. Only gradually, however, did he hammer out, in reaction to Roosevelt's New Nationalism, a coherent reform program, which he called the New Freedom.

Wilson cast his differences with Roosevelt in fundamental terms of slavery and freedom. "This is a struggle for emancipation," he proclaimed in October 1912. "If

America is not to have free enterprise, then she can have freedom of no sort whatever." Wilson also scorned Roosevelt's social program. Welfare might be benevolent, he declared, but it also would be paternalistic and contrary to the traditions of a free people. The New Nationalism represented a future of collectivism, Wilson warned, whereas the New Freedom would preserve political and economic liberty.

Wilson actually had much in common with Roosevelt. "The old time of individual competition is probably gone by," Wilson admitted. Like Roosevelt he opposed not bigness but the abuse of economic power. Nor did Wilson think that the abuse of power could be prevented without a strong federal government. He parted company from Roosevelt over *how* government should restrain private power.

Despite all the rhetoric the 1912 election fell short of being a referendum on the New Nationalism versus the New Freedom. The outcome turned on a more humdrum reality: Wilson was elected because he kept the traditional Democratic vote, while the Republicans split between Roosevelt and Taft. Despite a landslide in the electoral college, Wilson received only 42 percent of the popular vote. At best the 1912 election signified that the American public was in the mood for reform. Only 23 percent, after all, had voted for the one candidate who stood for the status quo, President Taft. Wilson's own program, however, had received no mandate from the people.

Yet the 1912 election proved decisive in the history of economic reform. The debate between Roosevelt and Wilson had brought forth in the New Freedom a program capable of finally resolving the crisis over corporate power that had gripped the nation for a decade. Just as important the election created a rare legislative opportunity in Washington. With Congress in Democratic hands the time was ripe to act on the New Freedom.

Long out of power the Democrats were hungry for tariff reform. From the prevailing average of 40 percent, the Underwood Tariff Act of 1913 pared rates down to 25 percent. Targeting especially the trust-dominated industries, Democrats confidently expected the Underwood Tariff to spur competition and reduce prices for consumers.

Wilson's administration then turned to the nation's banking system, whose key weakness was the absence of a central bank, or federal reserve. The main function of central banks at that time was to regulate commercial banks and back them up in case they could not meet their obligations to depositors. In the past this backup role had been assumed by the great New York banks that handled the accounts of outlying banks. If the New York banks weakened, the entire system could collapse. This had nearly happened in 1907, when the Knickerbocker Trust Company failed and panic swept through the nation's financial markets.

While the need for a central bank was clear, the form it should take was hotly disputed. Wall Street wanted a unified system run by the bankers. Rural Democrats and their spokesman, Senator Carter Glass of Virginia, preferred a decentralized network of reserve banks. Progressives in both parties agreed that the essential feature should be strong public control. The bankers, whose practices were already under scrutiny by Congress, were on the defensive.

President Wilson, initially no expert, learned quickly and reconciled the reformers and bankers. The monumental Federal Reserve Act of 1913 gave the nation a banking system that was resistant to financial panic. The act delegated financial functions to twelve district reserve banks, which would be controlled by their member banks. The Federal Reserve Board imposed public regulation on this regional structure. In one stroke the act strengthened the banking system and placed a measure of restraint on the "money trust."

Having dealt with tariff and banking reform, Wilson turned to the big question of how to curb the trusts. In this effort Wilson relied heavily on a new adviser, Louis D. Brandeis, famous as the "people's lawyer" for his public service in many progressive causes (including the landmark *Muller* case). Brandeis denied that bigness meant efficiency. On the contrary, he argued, trusts were wasteful compared with firms that vigorously competed in a free market. The main thing was to prevent the trusts from unfairly using their power to curb competition.

This could be done by strengthening the Sherman Act, but the obvious course—defining with precision what constituted anticompetitive practices—proved hard to implement. Was it feasible to say exactly when interlocking directorates, discriminatory pricing, or exclusive contracts became illegal? Brandeis decided that it was not, and Wilson assented. In the Clayton Antitrust Act of 1914, amending the Sherman Act, the definition of illegal practices was left flexible, subject to the test of whether an action "substantially lessen[ed] competition or tend[ed] to create a monopoly."

This retreat from a definitive antitrust prescription meant that a federal trade commission would be needed to back up the Sherman and Clayton Acts. Wilson was understandably hesitant, given his principled opposition to Roosevelt's powerful trade commission in the campaign. At first Wilson favored an advisory, information-gathering agency. But ultimately, under the 1914 law establishing it, the Federal Trade Commission (FTC) received broad powers to investigate companies and issue "cease and desist" orders against unfair trade practices that violated antitrust law.

Despite a good deal of commotion this arduous legislative process was actually an exercise in consensus building. Wilson himself had opened the debate in a conciliatory way. "The antagonism between business and government is over," he said, and the time ripe for a program representing the "best business judgment in America." Afterward, Wilson felt he had brought the long controversy over corporate power to a successful conclusion, and in fact he had. Steering a course between Taft's conservatism and Roosevelt's radicalism, Wilson had carved out a middle way that brought to bear the powers of government without threatening the constitutional order and curbed abuse of corporate power without threatening the capitalist system.

On social policy, too, Wilson charted a middle way. Having denounced Roosevelt's social program as paternalistic, he was at first unreceptive to what he saw as special-interest demands by labor and farm organizations. On the leading issue—that they be exempt from antitrust prosecution—the most Wilson was willing to accept was cosmetic language in the Clayton Act that did not grant them the immunity they sought.

As his second presidential campaign drew near, Wilson lost some of his scruples about prolabor legislation. In 1915 and 1916 he championed a host of bills beneficial to American workers: a federal child labor law, the Adamson eight-hour law for railroad workers, and the landmark Seamen's Act, which eliminated age-old abuses of sailors aboard ship. Likewise, after earlier resistance, Wilson approved in 1916 the Federal Farm Loan Act, which provided the low-interest rural credit system long demanded by farmers.

Wilson encountered the same dilemma that confronted all successful progressives: the claims of moral principle versus the unyielding realities of political life. Progressives were high-minded but not radical. They saw evils in the system, but they did not consider the system itself to be evil. They also prided themselves on being realists as well as moralists. So it stood to reason that Wilson, like other progressives who achieved power, would find his place at the center. But it would be wrong to underestimate their achievement. Progressives made presidential leadership important again, they brought government back into the nation's life, and they laid the foundation for twentieth-century social and economic policy.

For Further Exploration

The historical literature on the Progressive Era offers an embarrassment of riches. A good entry point is John Milton Cooper, *Pivotal Decades: 1900–1920* (1990). Richard Hofstadter, *Age of Reform* (1955), is an elegantly written interpretation that remains worth reading despite its disputed central arguments. The following books are a sampling of the best that has been written about Progressivism: Robert M. Crunden, *Ministers of Reform, 1889–1920* (1982), on the religious underpinnings; Charles Forcey, *The Crossroads of Liberalism* (1961), on the reform intellectuals; Nancy S. Dye, *As Equals and Sisters* (1980), on working women in the movement; David P. Thelen, *The New Citizenship* (1972), on La Follette and Wisconsin progressivism; John D. Buenker, *Urban Liberalism and Progressive Reform* (1973), on the politics of urban liberalism; Nancy F. Cott, *The Grounding of Modern Feminism* (1987); Naomi Lamoreaux, *The Great Merger Movement in American Business, 1895–1904* (1985); Martin J. Sklar, *The Corporate Reconstruction of American Capitalism, 1890–1916* (1988), on the progressive struggle to fashion a regulatory policy for big business.

Among the stimulating recent books, see Linda Gordon, *Pitied but Not Entitled: Single Mothers and the History of Welfare, 1890–1935* (1994), which uses the current debate over welfare reform as a lens for probing the tangled origins of the American welfare system; Sara Hunter Graham, *Woman Suffrage and the New Democracy* (1996), which treats the battle for the vote as a precocious exercise in modern single-issue politics; Elizabeth Lasch-Quinn, *Black Neighbors* (1993), on the racial conservatism of settlement-house progressives; Glenda Elizabeth Gilmore, *Gender and Jim Crow: Women and the Politics of White Supremacy in*

T I M E L I N E

1890	Sherman Antitrust Act	**1908**	*Muller v. Oregon* upholds regulation of working hours for women.
1899	National Consumers' League founded		William Howard Taft elected president
1900	Robert M. La Follette elected Wisconsin governor	**1909**	National Association for the Advancement of Colored People (NAACP) formed
1901	President McKinley assassinated; Theodore Roosevelt succeeds. United States Steel Corporation formed	**1910**	Roosevelt announces the New Nationalism. Woman suffrage movement revives; victories in western states begin.
1902	President Roosevelt settles national anthracite strike.	**1911**	*Standard Oil* decision restores "rule of reason." Triangle Shirtwaist fire
1903	National Women's Trade Union League founded	**1912**	Progressive Party formed Woodrow Wilson elected president
1904	Supreme Court dissolves the Northern Securities Company.	**1913**	Underwood Tariff Act Federal Reserve Act
1905	*Lochner v. New York* overturns state law restricting workhours for bakers.	**1914**	Clayton Antitrust Act Federal Trade Commission established
1906	Hepburn Railway Act Niagara Movement begins the struggle for black equality. AFL adopts Bill of Grievances. Upton Sinclair's *The Jungle*	**1915**	D. W. Griffith's *Birth of a Nation*

North Carolina, 1869–1920 (1996), on black women's political activity in the Progressive Era. The following biographies offer another rewarding avenue into Progressivism: John Milton Cooper, *The Warrior and the Priest* (1983), a joint biography of Roosevelt and Wilson; Allen F. Davis, *American Heroine: Jane Addams* (1973); Kathryn Kish Sklar, *Florence Kelley and the Nation's Work* (1995); Ellen Chesler, *Woman of Valor: Margaret Sanger and the Birth Control Movement* (1992); David Levering Lewis, *W.E.B. DuBois: Biography of a Race, 1868–1919* (1993).

"Votes for Women: NAWSA, 1848–1921" at <http://lcweb2.loc.gov/ammem/naw/nawshome.html> is a searchable archive of over 160 documents from the NAWSA collection. "Theodore Roosevelt: Icon of the American Century" at <http://www.npg.si.edu/exh/roosevelt.htm> presents pictures from the National Portrait Gallery, a biographical narrative, and information on Roosevelt's family and friends. "The Evolution of the Conservation Movement" at <http://memory.loc.gov/ammem/amrvhtml/conshome.html> offers a timeline and archive of materials on the development of the conservation movement from 1850 to 1920.

Chapter 21

AN EMERGING WORLD POWER
1877–1914

God has marked the American people as His chosen nation to
finally lead in the generation of the world. This is the divine mission
of America, and it holds for us all the profit, all the glory, all the
happiness possible to man.

—Senator Albert J. Beveridge, arguing for U.S. acquisition
of the Philippines, 1900

In 1881 Great Britain sent a new envoy to Washington. He was Sir
Lionel Sackville-West, son of an earl, brother-in-law of the Tory leader Lord Denby,
but otherwise distinguished only as the lover of a celebrated Spanish dancer. His
well-connected friends wanted to park Sir Lionel somewhere comfortable but out
of harm's way. So they made him minister to the United States.

Twenty years later such an appointment would have been unthinkable. All the
European powers had by then elevated their missions in Washington to embassies
and staffed them with top-of-the-line ambassadors. And they treated the United
States, without question, as a fellow Great Power.

In Sir Lionel's day the United States scarcely cast a shadow on world affairs.
America's army in 1881 was smaller than Bulgaria's; its navy ranked thirteenth in
the world and was a threat mainly to the crews manning its unseaworthy ships. By
1900, however, the United States was flexing its muscles. It had just made short
work of Spain in a brief but decisive war and acquired for itself an empire that
stretched from Puerto Rico to the Philippines. America's standing as a rising naval
power was manifest, and so was its muscular assertion of national interest in the
Caribbean and the Pacific.

The European powers could not be sure what America's role would be, since
the United States retained its traditional policy of nonalignment in European affairs. But in foreign offices across the Continent the importance of the United States
was universally acknowledged, and its likely response to every event carefully
assessed.

The Roots of Expansion

In 1880 the United States had a population of 50 million and by that measure ranked with the great European powers. In industrial production the nation stood second only to Britain and was rapidly closing the gap. Anyone who doubted the military prowess of the Americans needed only to recall the ferocity with which they had fought one another in the Civil War. The great campaigns of Lee, Sherman, and Grant had entered the military textbooks and were closely studied by army strategists everywhere.

And when its vital interests were at stake, the United States had not shown itself lacking in diplomatic vigor. The Civil War had put the United States at odds with both France and Britain. The dispute with France involved the establishment in Mexico of a French-sponsored regime under Archduke Maximilian, a move regarded by the United States as a threat to its security in the Southwest. When American troops under General Philip Sheridan began to mass on the Mexican border in 1867, the French military withdrew, abandoning Maximilian to a Mexican firing squad.

With Britain the thorny issue involved damages to Union shipping by the *Alabama* and other Confederate sea raiders operating from English ports. American hopes of taking Canada as compensation were dashed by Britain's grant of dominion status to Canada in 1867. But four years later, after lengthy negotiations, Britain expressed regret for its unneutral acts and agreed to the arbitration of the *Alabama* claims, settling to America's satisfaction the last outstanding diplomatic issue of the Civil War.

DIPLOMACY IN THE GILDED AGE

In the years that followed the United States lapsed into diplomatic inactivity, not out of weakness but for lack of any clear national purpose in world affairs. The business of building the nation's industrial economy absorbed Americans and turned their attention inward. And though the new international telegraphic cables provided the country with swift overseas communication after the 1860s, wide oceans still kept the world at a distance and gave Americans a sense of isolation and security.

In these circumstances, with no external threat to be seen, what was the point of maintaining a big navy? After the Civil War the fleet gradually deteriorated. Of the 125 ships on the navy's active list, only about twenty-five were seaworthy at any one time. No effort was made to keep up with European advances in weaponry or battleship design; the American fleet consisted mainly of sailing ships and obsolete ironclads modeled on the *Monitor* of Civil War fame.

During the administration of Chester A. Arthur (1881–1885) the navy began a modest upgrading program, commissioning new ships, raising the standards for the officer corps, and founding the Naval War College. But the fleet remained small, without a unified naval command and with little more to do than maintain coastal defenses.

The conduct of diplomacy was likewise of little account. Appointment to the foreign service was mostly through the spoils system. American envoys and consular officers were a mixed lot, with many idlers and drunkards among the hard-working and competent. Domestic politics, moreover, made it difficult to develop a coherent foreign policy. Although diplomacy was a presidential responsibility, the U.S. Senate jealously guarded its constitutional right to give "advice and consent" on treaties and diplomatic appointments. For its part the State Department tended to be inactive, exerting little control over either policy or its missions abroad. In distant places the American presence was likely to be Christian missionaries proselytizing among the native populations of Asia, Africa, and the Pacific Islands.

In the Caribbean the expansionist enthusiasms of the Civil War era subsided. Nothing came of the grandiose imperial plans of William H. Seward, Andrew Johnson's secretary of state, or of President Grant's efforts to purchase Santo Domingo (the future Dominican Republic) in 1870, and the Senate regularly blocked later moves to acquire bases in Haiti, Cuba, and Venezuela. The long-cherished interest in an interoceanic canal across Central America also faded. Despite its claims of exclusive rights the United States stood by when a French company headed by the builder of the Suez Canal, Ferdinand de Lesseps, started to dig across the Isthmus of Panama in 1880. That project failed after a decade, but the reason was bankruptcy, not American opposition.

Diplomatic activity quickened when the energetic James G. Blaine became secretary of state in 1881. He got involved in a border dispute between Mexico and Guatemala, tried to settle a war Chile was waging against Peru and Bolivia, and called the first Pan-American conference. Blaine's interventions in Latin American disputes went badly, however, and his successor cancelled the Pan-American conference after Blaine left office in late 1881.

Pan-Americanism—the notion of a community of American states—took root, however, and Blaine, returning in 1889 for a second stint at the State Department, took up the plans of the outgoing Cleveland administration for a new Pan-American conference. But little came of it except for provisions for an agency in Washington that became the Pan-American Union. Any Latin American goodwill won by Blaine's efforts was soon blasted by the humiliation the United States visited on Chile because of a riot against American sailors in the port of Valparaiso in 1891. Threatened with war, Chile was forced to apologize to the United States and pay an indemnity of $75,000.

In the Pacific American interest centered on Hawaii. With a climate ideal for raising sugarcane the islands had become a magnet for American planters and investors. Nominally an independent nation, Hawaii fell increasingly under American control. Under an 1875 treaty Hawaiian sugar gained duty-free entry to the American market, and the islands were declared off limits to other powers. A second treaty in 1887 granted the United States naval rights at Pearl Harbor.

When Hawaii's favored access to the American market was abruptly cancelled by the McKinley Tariff of 1890, sugar planters began to plot an American takeover of Hawaii. They organized a revolt in January 1893 against Queen Liliuokalani and quickly negotiated a treaty of annexation with the Harrison administration. Before the Senate could approve, however, Grover Cleveland returned to the presidency and withdrew the treaty. To annex Hawaii, he declared, would violate both America's "honor and morality" and an "unbroken tradition" against acquiring territory far from the nation's shores.

Meanwhile, the American presence elsewhere in the Pacific was growing. The purchase of Alaska from imperial Russia in 1867 gave the United States not only a huge territory with vast natural resources but an unlooked-for presence stretching across the northern Pacific. And far to the south, in the Samoan Islands, the United States secured rights in 1878 to a coaling station at Pago Pago harbor—a key link on the route to Australia—and established an informal protectorate there. In 1889, after some jostling with Germany and Britain, the rivalry over Samoa ended in a tripartite protectorate, with America retaining its rights in Pago Pago.

American diplomacy in these years has been characterized as a series of incidents, not the pursuit of a foreign policy. Many things happened, but intermittently and without any well-founded conception of national objectives. This was possible because, as the Englishman James Bryce remarked in 1888, America still sailed "upon a summer sea." In the stormier waters that lay ahead a different kind of diplomacy would be required.

THE ECONOMY OF EXPANSIONISM

"A policy of isolation did well enough when we were an embryo nation," remarked Senator Orville Platt of Connecticut in 1893. "But today things are different. . . . We are 65 million people, the most advanced and powerful on earth, and regard to our future welfare demands an abandonment of the doctrines of isolation." What especially demanded that Americans look outward was their prodigious economy.

America's gross domestic product—the total value of goods and service—quadrupled between 1870 and 1900. But were there markets big enough to absorb the output of America's farms and factories? Over 90 percent of American goods in the late nineteenth century was consumed at home. Even so, foreign markets mattered. Roughly a fifth of the nation's agricultural output was exported, and as the industrial economy expanded, so did factory exports. Between 1880 and 1900 the industrial share of total exports jumped from 15 percent to over 30 percent.

American firms began to establish themselves overseas. As early as 1868 the Singer Sewing Machine Company established its first foreign factory in Glasgow, Scotland. The giant among American firms doing business abroad was Rockefeller's Standard Oil, with European branches operating tankers and marketing kerosene across the continent. In Asia, Standard Oil cans, converted into utensils and roofing tin, became a visible sign of American market penetration.

The Singer Sewing Machine

The sewing machine was an American invention that swiftly found markets abroad. The Singer Company, the dominant firm, not only exported large quantities but produced 200,000 machines annually at a Scottish plant that employed 6,000 workers. Singer's advertising rightly boasted of its prowess as an international company and of a product that was "The Universal Machine." (New-York Historical Society)

Foreign trade was important partly for reasons of international finance. As a developing economy, the United States attracted a lot of foreign capital. The result was a heavy outflow of dollars to pay interest and dividends to foreign investors. To balance this account the United States needed to export more goods than it imported. In fact, a favorable import-export balance was achieved in 1876 (Figure 21.1). But because of its dependence on foreign capital America had to be constantly vigilant about its export trade.

Even more important, however, was the relationship that many Americans perceived between foreign markets and the nation's social stability. Hard times always sparked agrarian unrest and labor trouble. The problem, many thought, was that the nation's capacity to produce was outrunning its capacity to consume. When the economy slowed, cutbacks in domestic demand drove down farm prices and caused layoffs across the country. The answer was to make sure there would always be enough buyers for America's surplus products, and this meant, more than anything else, buyers in foreign markets.

How did these concerns about overseas trade relate to America's foreign policy? The bulk of American exports in the late nineteenth century—over 80 percent—went to Europe and Canada. In these countries the normal instruments of diplomacy sufficed to protect the nation's economic interests. But in Asia, Latin America, and other regions that Americans considered "backward" a tougher brand

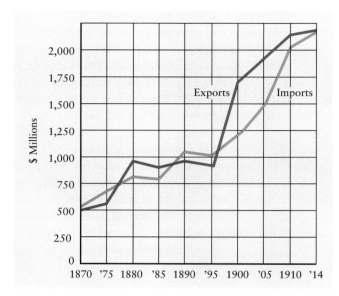

FIGURE 21.1
Balance of U.S. Imports, 1870–1914

By 1876 the United States had become a net exporting nation. The brief reversal after 1888 aroused fears that the United States was losing its foreign markets and helped fuel the expansionist drive of the 1890s.

of intervention seemed necessary because there the United States was competing with other industrial powers.

Asia and Latin America represented only a modest part of America's export trade—roughly an eighth of the total in the late nineteenth century. Still, this trade was growing—it was worth $200 million in 1900—and parts of it mattered a great deal to specific industries (for example, the Chinese market for American textiles). The real importance of these non-Western markets, however, was not so much their current value as their future promise. China especially exerted a powerful hold on the American mercantile imagination. Many felt that the China trade, although quite small at the time, would one day be the key to American prosperity. Therefore, China and other beckoning markets must not be closed to the United States.

In the mid-1880s the pace of European imperialism picked up. After the Berlin Conference of 1884 Africa was rapidly carved up by the European powers. In a burst of modernizing energy Japan transformed itself into a major power and began to challenge China's dominance in Korea. In the Sino-Japanese War of 1894–1895, Japan won an easy victory and started a scramble among the great powers, including Russia, to divide China into spheres of influence. In Latin America U.S. interests began to be challenged more aggressively by Britain, France, and Germany.

On top of all this came the Panic of 1893, setting in motion industrial strikes and agrarian protests that Cleveland's secretary of state, Walter Q. Gresham, like many other Americans, took to be "symptoms of revolution." With the nation's stability seemingly at risk, securing the markets of Latin America and Asia became an urgent necessity, inspiring the expansionist diplomacy of the 1890s.

THE MAKING OF AN EXPANSIONIST FOREIGN POLICY

"Whether they will or no, Americans must now begin to look outward. The grow-ing production of the country requires it." So wrote Captain Alfred T. Mahan, America's leading naval strategist, in his book *The Influence of Seapower upon History* (1890), which argued that the key to imperial power was control of the seas. From this insight Mahan developed a naval analysis that became the cornerstone of American strategic thinking.

The United States should regard the oceans not as barriers, Mahan argued, but as "a great highway . . . over which men pass in all directions." Traversing that high-way required a robust merchant marine (America's had fallen on hard times since its heyday in the 1850s), a powerful navy to protect American commerce, and strate-gic overseas bases. Having converted from sails to steam, navies required coaling stations far from home. Without such stations, Mahan warned, warships were "like land birds, unable to fly far from their own shores."

Mahan called for a canal across Central America to connect the Atlantic and Pacific oceans. Such a canal would enable the eastern United States to "compete with Europe, on equal terms as to distance, for the markets of East Asia." The canal's approaches would need to be guarded by bases in the Caribbean Sea. And Hawaii would have to be annexed to extend American power into the Pacific. What Mahan envisioned was a form of colonialism different from Europe's—not rule over ter-ritories and populations but control over strategic points in defense of America's trading interests.

Other exponents of a powerful America flocked to Mahan, including such up-and-coming politicians as Theodore Roosevelt and Henry Cabot Lodge. The influ-ence of these men, few in number but well connected, increased during the 1890s. They pushed steadily for what Lodge called a "large policy." But mainstream politi-cians also accepted Mahan's underlying logic, and from the inauguration of Benjamin Harrison in 1889 onward a surprising consistency began to emerge in the conduct of American foreign policy.

The next year Congress appropriated funds for three battleships as the first in-stallment on a two-ocean navy. Battleships might be expensive, said Benjamin F. Tracy, Harrison's ambitious secretary of the navy, but they were "the premium paid by the United States for the insurance of its acquired wealth and its growing industries." The battleship took on a special aura for those—like the young Roosevelt—who had grand dreams for the United States. "Oh, Lord! if only the people who are ignorant about our Navy could see those great warships in all their majesty and beauty, and could realize how [well fitted they are] to uphold the honor of America!"

The incoming Cleveland administration was less spread-eagled and by cancel-ing Harrison's scheme for annexing Hawaii established its antiexpansionist cre-dentials. But after hesitating briefly, Cleveland picked up the naval program of his Republican predecessor, pressing Congress just as forcefully for more battleships (five were authorized) and making the same basic argument. The nation's commercial vitality—"free access to all markets," in the words of Cleveland's second secretary of state, Richard Olney—depended on its naval power.

While rejecting the territorial aspects of Mahan's thinking, Cleveland absorbed the underlying strategic arguments about where America's vital interests lay. This explains the remarkable crisis that suddenly blew up in 1895 over Venezuela.

For years a border dispute had simmered between Venezuela and British Guiana. Now the United States demanded that it be resolved. The European powers were carving up Africa and Asia. How could the United States be sure that Europe did not have similar designs on Latin America? Secretary of State, Olney made that point in a bristling note to London on July 25, 1895, insisting that Britain accept arbitration or face the consequences. Invoking the Monroe Doctrine, Olney warned that the United States would brook no challenge to its vital interests in the Caribbean. These vital interests were America's, not Venezuela's; Venezuela was not consulted during the entire dispute.

Despite its suddenness, the pugnacious stand of the Cleveland administration was no aberration but a logical step in the new American foreign policy. Once the British realized that Cleveland meant business, they agreed to arbitration of the boundary dispute. Afterward Olney remarked with satisfaction that as a great industrial nation the United States needed "to accept [a] commanding position" and take its place "among the Powers of the earth." Other countries would have to accommodate America's need for access to "more markets and larger markets for the consumption and products of the industry and inventive genius of the American people."

THE IDEOLOGY OF EXPANSIONISM

As policymakers hammered out a new foreign policy, a sustaining ideology took shape. One source of expansionist dogma was the Social Darwinist theory that dominated the political thought of this era (see Chapter 17). If, as Charles Darwin had shown, animals and plants evolved through the survival of the fittest, so did nations. "Nothing under the sun is stationary," warned the American social theorist Brooks Adams in *The Law of Civilization and Decay* (1895). "Not to advance is to recede." By this criterion the United States had no choice; if it wanted to survive, it had to expand.

Linked to Social Darwinism was a spreading belief in the inherent superiority of the Anglo-Saxon "race." In the late nineteenth century Great Britain basked in the glory of its representative institutions, industrial prosperity, and far-flung empire—all ascribed to the supposed racial superiority of its people and, by extension, of their American cousins as well. On both sides of the Atlantic Anglo-Saxonism was in vogue. Thus did John Fiske, an American philosopher and historian, lecture the nation on its future responsibilities: "The work which the English race began when it colonized North America is destined to go on until every land on the earth's surface that is not already the seat of an old civilization shall become English in its language, in its religion, in its political habits, and to a predominant extent in the blood of its people."

Fiske titled his lecture "Manifest Destiny." A half century earlier this term had expressed the sense of national mission—America's "manifest destiny"—to sweep aside the Native American peoples and occupy the continent. In his widely read book *The Winning of the West* (1896) Theodore Roosevelt drew a parallel between the expansionism of his own time and the suppression of the Indians. To Roosevelt what happened to "backward peoples" mattered little because their conquest was "for the benefit of civilization and in the interests of mankind." More than historical parallels, however, linked the Manifest Destiny of the past and present.

In 1890 the U.S. Census reported the end of the westward movement on the North American continent: there was no longer a frontier beyond which land remained to be conquered. The psychological impact of that news on Americans was profound, spawning among other things a new historical interpretation that stressed the importance of the frontier in shaping the nation's character. In a landmark essay setting out this thesis—"The Significance of the Frontier in American History" (1893)—the young historian Frederick Jackson Turner suggested a link between the closing of the frontier and overseas expansion. "He would be a rash prophet who should assert that the expansive character of American life has now entirely ceased," Turner wrote. "Movement has been its dominant fact, and, unless this training has no effect upon a people, the American energy will continually demand a wider field for its exercise." As Turner predicted, Manifest Destiny did turn outward.

Thus a strong current of ideas, deeply rooted in American experience and traditions, justified the new diplomacy of expansionism. The United States was eager to step onto the world stage. All it needed was the right occasion.

An American Empire

Ever since Spain had lost its South American empire in the early nineteenth century, still-subjugated Cubans yearned to join their mainland brothers and sisters in freedom. In February 1895 Cuban patriots rebelled and began a guerrilla war. A standoff developed; the Spaniards controlled the towns, the insurgents much of the countryside. In early 1896 the newly appointed Spanish commander, Valeriano Weyler, adopted a harsh policy of *reconcentration,* forcing entire populations into guarded camps. Because no aggressive pursuit followed, reconcentration only inconvenienced the guerrilla fighters. The toll on civilians, however, was devastating. Out of a population of 1,600,000 as many as 200,000 died of starvation, exposure, or dysentery.

THE CUBAN CRISIS

Rebel leaders recognized that their best hope was not military but political: they had to draw the United States into their struggle. A key group of exiles, the *junta*, set up shop in New York to make the case for *Cuba Libre*. Their timing was lucky. William Randolph Hearst had just purchased the *New York Journal*, and he was in a hurry to build readership. Cuba was ideal for Hearst's purposes. Locked in a furious circulation war with Joseph Pulitzer's *New York World*, Hearst elevated Cuba's agony into flaming front-page headlines.

Across the country powerful sentiments stirred: humanitarian concern for the suffering Cubans, sympathy with their aspirations for freedom, and, as anger against Spain rose, a superheated patriotism that became known as *jingoism*. Congress began calling for Cuban independence.

Grover Cleveland, still in office when the rebellion broke out, took a cooler view of the situation. His concern was with America's vital interests, which, he told Congress, were "by no means of a wholly sentimental or philanthropic character." The Cuban civil war was disrupting the sizable trade between the two countries and harming American property interests, especially in Cuban sugar plantations. Cleveland was also worried that Spain's troubles might draw other European powers into the situation. A chronically unstable Cuba was incompatible with America's strategic interests, in particular a planned interoceanic canal whose Caribbean approaches would have to be safeguarded. If Spain could put down the rebellion, that was fine with Cleveland. But there was a limit, he felt, to how long the United States could tolerate Spain's impotence.

The McKinley administration, on taking office in March 1897, adopted much the same pragmatic line. Like Cleveland, McKinley was motivated by a conception of the United States as the dominant Caribbean power, with vital interests that had to be defended. McKinley, however, was inclined to be tougher on the Spaniards. He was appalled by their "uncivilized and inhumane conduct" in Cuba. And he had to contend with rising jingoism in the Senate. But the notion, long held by historians, that McKinley was swept along against his better judgment by popular opinion and by a Republican war faction led by Henry Cabot Lodge, Alfred J. Beveridge, and other aggressive advocates of a "large policy" was not true. McKinley was very much his own man. He was a skilled politician and a canny, if undramatic, president. In particular, McKinley was sensitive to business fears of any rash action that might disrupt an economy just recovering from depression.

On September 18, 1897, the American minister in Madrid informed the Spanish government that it was time to "put a stop to this destructive war." If Spain could not ensure an "early and certain peace," the United States would take whatever steps it "should deem necessary to procure this result." At first America's hard line seemed to work. The conservative regime fell, and a liberal government, on taking office in October 1897, moderated its Cuban policy. Spain recalled General Weyler, backed away from reconcentration, and offered Cuba a degree of self-rule but not inde-

"*Remember the* Maine!"

In late January 1898 the *Maine* entered Havana harbor on a courtesy call. On the evening of
February 15 a mysterious blast sent the U.S. battlecruiser to the bottom. This dramatic lithograph conveys something of the impact of that event on American public opinion. Although
no evidence ever linked the Spanish authorities to the explosion, the sinking of the *Maine*
fed the emotional fires that prepared the nation for war with Spain. (Granger Collection)

pendence. Madrid's incapacity soon became clear, however. In January 1898 Spanish loyalists in Havana rioted against the offer of autonomy. The Cuban rebels, encouraged by the prospect of American intervention, demanded full independence.

On February 9, 1898, Hearst's *New York Journal* published a private letter of
Dupuy de Lôme, the Spanish minister to the United States. In it de Lôme called
President McKinley "weak" and "a bidder for the admiration of the crowd." Worse,
his letter suggested that the Spanish government was not taking the American demands seriously. De Lôme immediately resigned, but the damage had been done.

A week later the U.S. battlecruiser *Maine* blew up and sank in Havana harbor,
with the loss of 260 seamen. "Whole Country Thrills with the War Fever," proclaimed the *New York Journal.* From that moment onward popular passions against
Spain became a major factor in the march toward war.

McKinley kept his head. He assumed that the sinking had been accidental. A
naval board of inquiry, however, issued a damaging report. Disagreeing with a
Spanish inquiry, the American board concluded improbably that the sinking
had been caused by a mine. (A 1976 naval inquiry faulted the ship's design,
which located the explosive magazines too close to coal bunkers that were prone to
spontaneous fires.) No evidence linked the Spanish to the purported mine. But if

a mine did sink the ship, then the Spanish were responsible for not protecting a peaceful American vessel within their jurisdiction.

President McKinley had no stomach for the martial spirit engulfing the country. He was not swept along by the calls for blood to avenge the *Maine*. But he did have to attend to an aroused public opinion. Hesitant business leaders now also became impatient for the dispute with Spain to end. War was preferable to the unresolved Cuban crisis. On March 27 McKinley cabled to Madrid what was in effect an ultimatum: an immediate armistice for six months, abandonment of the practice of reconcentration, and, with the United States as mediator, peace negotiations with the rebels. A telegram the next day added that only Cuban independence would be regarded as a satisfactory outcome to the negotiations. Spain categorically rejected these humiliating demands.

On April 11 McKinley asked Congress for authority to intervene to end the fighting in Cuba. His motives were as he described them: "In the name of humanity, in the name of civilization, in behalf of endangered American interests which give us the right and the duty to speak and to act, the war in Cuba must stop." The War Hawks in Congress—a mixture of Republicans and western Democrats—chafed under McKinley's cautious progress. But the president did not lose control, and he defeated the War Hawks on the crucial issue of recognizing the rebel republican government, which would have greatly reduced the administration's freedom of action in dealing with Spain.

The resolutions authorizing intervention in Cuba contained an amendment by Senator Henry M. Teller of Colorado disclaiming any intention by the United States of taking possession of Cuba. No European government should say that "when we go out to make battle for the liberty and freedom of Cuban patriots, that we are doing it for the purpose of aggrandizement." This had to be made clear with regard to Cuba, "whatever," Senator Teller added, "we may do as to some other islands."

Did McKinley contemplate "some other islands"? Was this really a war of aggression, secretly motivated by a desire to seize strategic territory from Spain? In a strict sense, almost certainly no. It was not *because* of expansionist ambitions that McKinley forced Spain into a corner. But once war came, McKinley saw it as an opportunity. As he wrote privately after hostilities began: "While we are conducting war and until its conclusion, we must keep all we get; when the war is over we must keep what we want." Precisely what would be forthcoming, of course, depended on the fortunes of battle.

THE SPOILS OF WAR

Hostilities formally began when Spain declared war on April 24, 1898. Across the country regiments began to form up. Theodore Roosevelt immediately resigned as assistant secretary of the navy, ordered a fancy uniform, and was commissioned lieutenant colonel in a volunteer cavalry regiment that would become famous as the Rough Riders. Raw recruits poured into makeshift bases around Tampa, Florida. Confusion reigned. Tropical uniforms did not arrive; the food was bad, the sanitation worse; and rifles were in short supply. No provision had been made for getting the troops to Cuba; the government hastily began to collect a miscellaneous fleet of yachts, lake steamers, and commercial boats. Fortunately, the small regular army was a disciplined, highly professional force, and its 28,000 seasoned troops provided a nucleus for the 200,000 civilians who had to be turned into soldiers inside of a few weeks.

The navy was in better shape. Spain had nothing to match America's seven battleships and armored cruisers, and the ships it did have were undermanned and ill-prepared for battle. The Spanish admiral, Pascual Cervera, gloomily expected that his fleet would "like Don Quixote go out to fight windmills and come back with a broken head."

On April 23, acting on plans already drawn up, Commodore George Dewey's small Pacific fleet set sail from Hong Kong for the Philippines. Here, at this Spanish possession in the far Pacific, not in Cuba, the decisive engagement of the war took place. On May 1 American ships cornered the Spanish fleet in Manila Bay and destroyed it (Map 21.1). The victory produced euphoria in the United States. Immediately, part of the army being trained for the Cuban campaign was diverted to the Philippines. Manila, the Philippine capital, fell on August 13, 1898.

With Dewey's naval victory American strategic thinking clicked into place. "We hold the other side of the Pacific and the value to this country is almost beyond imagination," declared Senator Lodge. "We must on no account let the [Philippine] Islands go." President McKinley agreed, and so did his key advisers. Naval strategists had long coveted an anchor in the western Pacific. At this time, too, the Great Powers were carving up China into spheres of influence. If American merchants wanted a crack at that glittering market, the United States would have to project its power into Asia.

Once the decision for a Philippine base had been made, other decisions followed almost automatically. The question of Hawaii was quickly resolved. After stalling the previous year, Hawaiian annexation went through Congress by joint resolution in July 1898. Hawaii had suddenly acquired a crucial strategic value: it was a halfway station on the way to the Philippines. The navy pressed for a coaling base in the central Pacific; that meant Guam, a Spanish island in the Marianas. There was need also for a strategically located base in the Caribbean; that meant Puerto Rico. By July, before the assault on Cuba, the full scope of McKinley's war aims had crystallized.

The campaign in Cuba was something of an anticlimax. Santiago, where the Spanish fleet was anchored, became the key to the military campaign. Half trained and ill equipped, the American forces moving on the city might have been checked by a determined opponent.

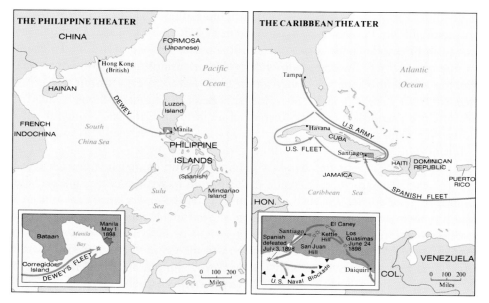

M A P 21.1
The Spanish-American War of 1898

The swift American victory in the Spanish-American War resulted from overwhelming naval superiority. Dewey's destruction of the Spanish fleet in Manila harbor doomed the Spaniards in the Philippines. In Cuba, American ground forces won a hard victory on San Juan Hill, for they were ill equipped and poorly supplied. With the United States in control of the seas, the Spaniards saw no choice but to give up the battle for Cuba.

The main battle, on July 1, occurred near Santiago on the heights commanded by San Juan Hill. Roosevelt's dismounted Rough Riders (there had been no room for horses on the transports) seized Kettle Hill. Then the frontal assault against the San Juan heights began. Four black regiments took the brunt of the fighting. White observers grudgingly credited much of the victory to the "superb gallantry" of the black soldiers (see American Voices, "Black Soldiers in a White Man's War"). In fact, it was not quite a victory. The Spaniards, driven from their forward positions, retreated to a well-fortified second line. The exhausted Americans had suffered heavy casualties; whether they could have mounted a second assault was questionable. They were spared this test, however, by the Spanish. On July 3 Cervera's fleet in Santiago harbor made a daylight attempt to run the American blockade and was destroyed. A few days later, convinced that Santiago could not be saved, the Spanish forces surrendered.

The two nations signed an armistice in which Spain agreed to liberate Cuba and cede Puerto Rico and Guam to the United States. American forces occupied Manila pending a peace treaty.

The Battle of San Juan Hill

On July 1, 1898, the key battle for Cuba took place on heights overlooking Santiago. African American troops bore the brunt of the fighting. Although generally overlooked, the black role in the San Juan battle is done justice in this contemporary lithograph, without the demeaning stereotypes by which blacks were normally depicted in an age of intensifying racism. Even so, the racial hierarchy is maintained. The blacks are the foot soldiers; their officers are white. (Library of Congress)

THE IMPERIAL EXPERIMENT

The big question was the Philippines, an archipelago of over 7,000 islands populated—as William R. Day, McKinley's secretary of state, put it in the racist language of that era—by "eight or nine millions of absolutely ignorant and many degraded people." Not even the most avid American expansionists had advocated colonial rule over subject peoples—that was European-style imperialism, not the strategic bases that Mahan and his followers had in mind. Both Mahan and Lodge initially advocated keeping only Manila. It gradually became clear, however, that Manila was not defensible without the whole of Luzon, the large island on which the city was located.

McKinley and his advisers surveyed the options. One possibility was to return most of the islands to Spain, but the reputed evils of Spanish rule made that a "cowardly and dishonorable" solution. Another possibility was to partition the Philippines with one or more of the Great Powers. But as McKinley observed, to turn

AMERICAN VOICES

Black Soldiers in a White Man's War

GEORGE W. PRIOLEAU

George W. Prioleau, the chaplain of the Ninth Cavalry regiment, expresses his bitterness against the racism experienced by black troopers in the South on their way to battle in Cuba.

Hon. H. C. Smith
Editor, *Gazette*

Dear Sir:

All the way from northwest Nebraska this regiment was greeted with cheers and hurrahs. At places where we stopped the people assembled by the thousands. While the Ninth Cavalry band would play some national air the people would raise their hats, men, women, and children would wave their handkerchiefs, and the heavens would resound with their hearty cheers. . . . These demonstrations, so enthusiastically given, greeted us all the way until we reached Nashville. . . . From there until we reached Chattanooga there was not a cheer given us. . . .

The prejudice against the Negro soldier and the Negro was great, but it was of heavenly origin to what it is in this part of Florida. . . . The southerners have made their laws and the Negroes know and obey them. They never stop to ask a white man a question. He (Negro) never thinks of disobeying. . . . Talk about fighting and freeing poor Cuba and of Spain's brutality; of Cuba's murdered thousands, and starving reconcentradoes. Is America any better than Spain? Has she not subjects in her very midst who are murdered daily without a trial of judge or jury? Has she not subjects in her own borders whose children are half-fed and half-clothed, because their father's skin is black. . . . Yet the Negro is loyal to his country's flag. . . .

The four Negro regiments are going to help free Cuba, and they will return to their homes, some then mustered out and begin again to fight the battle of American prejudice. . . .

Yours truly,
Geo. W. Prioleau, Chaplain, Ninth Cavalry

SOURCE: *Cleveland Gazette* (May 13, 1898), reprinted in Willard B. Gatewood, *"Smoked Yankees" and the Struggle for Empire, 1898–1902* (Urbana: University of Illinois Press, 1971), pp. 27–29.

over valuable territory to "our commercial rivals in the Orient—that would have been bad business and discreditable."

Most plausible was the option of granting the Philippines independence. As in Cuba, Spanish rule had already stirred up a rebellion, led by the fiery patriot Emilio Aguinaldo. An arrangement might have been possible like the one being negotiated with the Cubans over Guantanamo Bay: the lease of a naval base to the Americans as the price of freedom. But after some hesitation McKinley was persuaded that "we could not leave [the Filipinos] to themselves—they were unfit for self-rule—and they would soon have anarchy and misrule over there worse than Spain's was."

As for the Spaniards, they had little choice against what they considered "the immoderate demands of a conqueror." In the Treaty of Paris they ceded the Philippines to the United States for a payment of $20 million. The treaty encountered harder going at home and was ratified by the Senate (requiring a two-thirds majority) on February 6, 1899, with only a single vote to spare.

The administration's narrow margin signaled the revival of an antiexpansionist tradition that had been briefly silenced by the patriotic passions of a nation at war. In the Senate opponents of the treaty invoked the country's republican principles. Under the Constitution, argued the conservative Republican George F. Hoar, "no power is given to the Federal Government to acquire territory to be held and governed permanently as colonies" or "to conquer alien people and hold them in subjugation." The alternative—making 8 million Filipinos American citizens—was equally unpalatable to the antiimperialists, who were no more champions of "these savage people" than were the expansionists who denigrated the self-governing capacity of the Filipinos.

Emilio Aguinaldo

At the start of the war with Spain, U.S. military leaders brought the Filipino patriot Aguinaldo back from Singapore because they thought he would stir up a popular uprising that would help defeat the Spaniards. Aguinaldo came because he thought the Americans favored an independent Philippines. These differing intentions—it has remained a matter of dispute what assurances Aguinaldo received— were the root cause of the Filipino insurrection that proved far costlier in American and Filipino lives than the war with Spain that preceded it. (Corbis-Bettmann)

Leading citizens enlisted in the anti-imperialist cause, including the steelmaker Andrew Carnegie, who offered a check for $20 million to purchase the independence of the Philippines; the labor leader Samuel Gompers, who feared the competition of cheap Filipino labor; and Jane Addams, who believed that women should stand for peace. The key group, however, was a social elite of old-line Mugwump reformers such as Carl Schurz, Charles Eliot Norton, and Charles Francis Adams. In November 1898 a Boston group formed the first of the Anti-Imperialist leagues that began to spring up around the country.

Although skillful at publicizing their cause, the anti-imperialists never developed a popular movement. They shared little but their anti-imperialism and, within the Mugwump core, lacked the common touch. Nor was anti-imperialism easily translated into a viable political cause because the Democrats, once the treaty had been adopted, waffled on the issue. Although an outspoken anti-imperialist, William Jennings Bryan, the Democratic standard-bearer, confounded his friends by favoring ratification of the treaty and afterward hesitated to stake his party's future on a crusade against a national policy he privately believed to be irreversible. Still, if it was an accomplished fact, Philippine annexation lost the moral high ground because of the grim events that began to unfold in the Philippines.

On February 4, 1899, two days before the Senate ratified the treaty, fighting broke out between American and Filipino patrols on the edge of Manila. Confronted by American annexation, Aguinaldo asserted his nation's independence and turned his guns on the occupying American forces.

The ensuing conflict far exceeded in ferocity the war just concluded with Spain. Fighting tenacious guerrillas, the U.S. Army resorted to the reconcentration tactic the Spaniards had employed in Cuba, moving people into towns, carrying out indiscriminate attacks beyond the perimeters, and burning crops and villages (see American Voices, "The Water Cure"). Atrocities became commonplace on both sides. In three years of warfare 4,200 Americans and many thousands of Filipinos died. The fighting ended in 1902, and William Howard Taft, who had been appointed governor-general, set up a civilian administration. He intended to make the Philippines a model of American road building and sanitary engineering.

McKinley's convincing victory over William Jennings Bryan in the 1900 election, though by no means a referendum on American expansionism, suggested popular satisfaction with America's overseas adventure. Yet a strong undercurrent of misgivings was evident. Americans had not anticipated the brutal methods needed to subdue the Filipino guerrillas. "We are destroying these islanders by the thousands, their villages and cities," protested the philosopher William James. "No life shall you have, we say, except as a gift from our philanthropy after your unconditional surrender to our will. . . . Could there be any more damning indictment of that whole bloated ideal termed 'modern civilization'?"

There were, moreover, disturbing constitutional issues to be resolved. Did the Constitution extend to the acquired territories? Did their inhabitants automatically become U.S. citizens? In 1901 the Supreme Court ruled negatively on both ques-

AMERICAN VOICES

The Water Cure

CORPORAL DANIEL J. EVANS

*I*n *1902, after the fighting had ceased, the U.S. Senate held hearings on the conduct of the war in the Philippines. This is the testimony of Corporal Daniel J. Evans, Twelfth Infantry, about his service on the island of Luzon.*

Question: The committee would like to hear . . . whether you were the witness to any cruelties inflicted upon the natives of the Philippine Islands; and if so, under what circumstances.—*Answer:* The case I had reference to was where they gave the water cure to a native in the Ilicano Province at Ilocos Norte . . . about the month of August 1900. There were two native scouts with the American forces. They went out and brought in a couple of insurgents. . . . They tried to get from this insurgent . . . where the rest of the insurgents were at that time. . . . The first thing one of the Americans—I mean one of the scouts for the Americans—grabbed one of the men by the head and jerked his head back, and then they took a tomato can and poured water down his throat until he could hold no more. . . . Then they forced a gag into his mouth; they stood him up . . . against a post and fastened him so that he could not move. Then one man, an American soldier, who was over six feet tall, and who was very strong, too, struck this native in the pit of the stomach as hard as he could. . . . They kept that operation up for quite a time, and finally I thought the fellow was about to die, but I don't believe he was as bad as that, because finally he told them he would tell, and from that time on he was taken away, and I saw no more of him. . . .

    Question: What is your observation as to the treatment of the people engaged in peaceable pursuits, as to kindness and consideration, or the reverse, from the American officers and the men?—*Answer:* They were never molested if they seemed to be peaceable natives. They would not be molested unless they showed some signs of hostility. . . . If we struck a part of the island where the natives were hostile and they would fire on our soldiers or even cut the telegraph lines, the result would be that their barrios would probably be burned.

SOURCE: Henry F. Graff, ed., *American Imperialism and the Philippine Insurrection* (Boston: Little, Brown, 1969), pp. 80–84.

tions; these were matters for Congress to decide. A special commission appointed by McKinley recommended independence for the islands after an indefinite period of U.S. rule, during which the Filipinos would be prepared for self-government. In 1916 the Jones Act formally committed the United States to granting Philippine independence but set no date.

    The ugly business in the Philippines rubbed off some of the moralizing gloss but left undeflected America's global aspirations. In a few years the United States had acquired the makings of an overseas empire: Hawaii, Puerto Rico, Guam, the

Philippines, and finally, in 1900, several of the Samoan Islands that had been jointly administered with Germany and Britain. The United States, remarked the legal scholar John Bassett Moore in 1899, had moved "from a position of comparative freedom from entanglements into a position of what is commonly called a world power."

Onto the World Stage

In Europe the flexing of America's muscles against Spain caused a certain amount of consternation. At the instigation of Kaiser Wilhelm II of Germany, the major powers had tried before war broke out to intercede on Spain's behalf—but tentatively because no one was looking for trouble with the Americans. President McKinley had listened politely to their envoys and had then proceeded with his war.

The decisive outcome confirmed what the Europeans already suspected. After Dewey's naval victory the semiofficial French paper *Le Temps* observed that "what passes before our eyes is the appearance of a new power of the first order." And the London *Times* concluded: "This war must . . . effect a profound change in the whole attitude and policy of the United States. In the future America will play a part in the general affairs of the world such as she has never played before."

A POWER AMONG POWERS

The politician most ardently agreeing with the London *Times*'s vision of America's future was the man who, with the assassination of William McKinley, became president on September 14, 1901. Theodore Roosevelt was an avid student of world affairs, widely traveled and acquainted with many of the European leaders. He had no doubt about America's role in the world.

It was important, first of all, to uphold the country's honor in the community of nations. Nor should the country shrink from righteous battle. "All the great masterful races have been fighting races," Roosevelt declared. But when he spoke of war, Roosevelt had in mind actions by the "civilized" nations against "backward peoples." Roosevelt felt "it incumbent on all the civilized and orderly powers to insist on the proper policing of the world." That was why Roosevelt sympathized with European imperialism and how he justified American dominance in the Caribbean.

As for the "civilized and orderly" policemen of the world, the worst thing that could happen was for them to fall to fighting among themselves. Roosevelt had an acute sense of the fragility of world peace, and he was farsighted about the likelihood—in this he was truly exceptional among Americans—of a catastrophic world war. He believed in American responsibility for helping to maintain the balance of power.

The cornerstone of Roosevelt's thinking was Anglo-American amity. The British, increasingly isolated in world affairs, eagerly reciprocated. In the Hay-Pauncefote Agreement (1901) they gave up their treaty rights to participate in any Central American canal project, clearing the way for a canal under exclusive U.S.

The Panama Canal

The Canal Zone was acquired through devious means from which Americans could take little
pride (and which led in 1978 to the Senate's decision to restore the property to Panama). But
the building of the Panama Canal itself was a triumph of American ingenuity and drive.
Dr. William C. Gorgas cleaned out the malarial mosquitoes that had earlier stymied the
French. Under Colonel George W. Goethals the U.S. Army overcame formidable obstacles in a
mighty feat of engineering. This photograph shows the massive effort underway in December
1904 to excavate the Culebra Cut so that oceangoing ships would be able to pass through.
(Corbis-Bettmann)

control. And two years later the last of the vexing U.S.-Canadian border disputes—
this one involving British Columbia and Alaska—was settled, again to American
satisfaction. No formal alliance was forthcoming, but Anglo-American friendship
had been placed on such a firm basis that after 1901 the British admiralty designed
its war plans on the assumption that America was "a kindred state with whom we
shall never have a parricidal war."

Among nations, however, what counted was strength, not merely goodwill.
Roosevelt wanted "to make all foreign powers understand that when we have adopted
a line of policy we have adopted it definitely, and with the intention of backing it up
with deeds as well as words." As Roosevelt famously said: "Speak softly and carry a big
stick." By a "big stick" he meant above all naval power. Under Roosevelt the battleship
program went on apace. By 1904 the U.S. Navy stood fifth in the world; by 1907 it was
third. At the top of Roosevelt's agenda was a canal across Central America.

Having secured Britain's surrender of its joint canal rights in 1901, Roosevelt proceeded to the more troublesome task of leasing from Colombia the needed strip of land across Panama, a Colombian province. Furious when the Colombian legislature voted down the proposed treaty, Roosevelt contemplated outright seizure of Panama but settled on a more devious solution. With an independence movement brewing in Panama, the United States lent covert assistance that ensured the success of a bloodless revolution against Colombia. On November 7, 1901, the United States recognized Panama and received two weeks later a perpetually renewable lease on a canal zone. Roosevelt never regretted the victimization of Colombia, although the United States, as a kind of conscience money, paid Colombia $25 million in 1922.

Building the canal, one of the heroic engineering feats of the century, involved a swamp-clearing project to rid the area of malaria and yellow fever, the construction of a series of great locks, and the excavation of 240 million cubic yards of earth. It took the U.S. Army Corps of Engineers eight years to finish the huge project. When the Panama Canal opened in 1914, it gave the United States a commanding commercial and strategic position in the Western Hemisphere (Map 21.2).

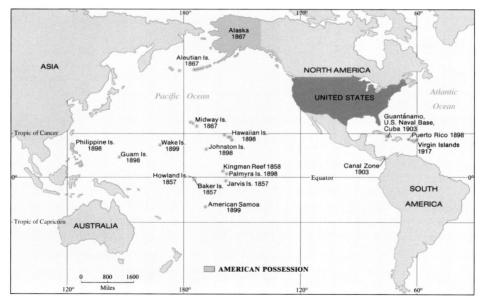

M A P 21.2
The American Empire

In 1890 Alfred T. Mahan wrote that the United States should regard the oceans as "a great highway" across which America would carry on world trade. That was precisely what resulted from the empire the United States acquired after the Spanish-American War. The Caribbean possessions, the strategically located Pacific Islands, and in 1903 the Panama Canal Zone gave the United States commercial and naval access to a wider world.

Next came the task of making the Caribbean basin secure. The countries there, said Secretary of State Elihu Root, had been placed "in the front yard of the United States" by the Panama Canal. Therefore, as Roosevelt put it, they had to "behave themselves." Believing that instability in the Caribbean invited the intervention of European powers, Roosevelt announced in 1904 that the United States would act as "policeman" of the region, stepping in, "however reluctantly, in flagrant cases . . . of wrong doing or impotence." This policy became known as the Roosevelt Corollary to the Monroe Doctrine. It transformed what had been a broad principle of opposition against European expansionist ambitions in Latin America into an unrestricted American right to regulate Caribbean affairs. The Roosevelt Corollary was not a treaty with other states; it was a unilateral declaration sanctioned only by American power and national interest.

Citing the Roosevelt Corollary, the United States intervened regularly in the internal affairs of Caribbean states. In the case of Cuba a condition for its independence had been a 1902 proviso in its constitution called the Platt amendment, which gave the United States the right to intervene if Cuba's independence or internal order was threatened. Elsewhere there was not even this semblance of legality. American authorities took over the customs and debt management of the Dominican Republic in 1905, of Nicaragua in 1911, and of Haiti in 1916. When domestic order broke down, the U.S. Marines occupied Cuba in 1906, Nicaragua in 1909, and Haiti and the Dominican Republic in later years (Map 21.3).

THE OPEN DOOR IN ASIA

In China the occupying powers quickly instituted discriminatory trade regulations in their zones of control. Fearful of being frozen out, U.S. Secretary of State John Hay in 1899 sent them an "open-door" note claiming the right of equal trade access—an open door—for all nations that wanted to do business in China. Despite its Philippine bases the United States lacked real leverage in East Asia and elicited only noncommittal responses from the occupying powers. But Hay chose to interpret them as accepting the American open-door position.

When a secret society of Chinese nationalists, the Boxers, rebelled against the foreigners in 1900, the United States joined the multinational campaign to break the Boxers' siege of the diplomatic missions in Peking (Beijing). America took this opportunity to assert a second principle of the open door: that China would be preserved as a "territorial and administrative entity." As long as the legal fiction of an independent China survived, so would American claims to equal access to the China market.

The European powers had acceded to American preeminence in the Caribbean. But Britain, Germany, France, and Russia were strongly entrenched in East Asia and not inclined to defer to American interests. The United States also confronted a powerful Asian nation—Japan—that had its own vital interests. Although the open-door policy was important to him, Roosevelt perceived in the Pacific a deadlier game calling for American involvement.

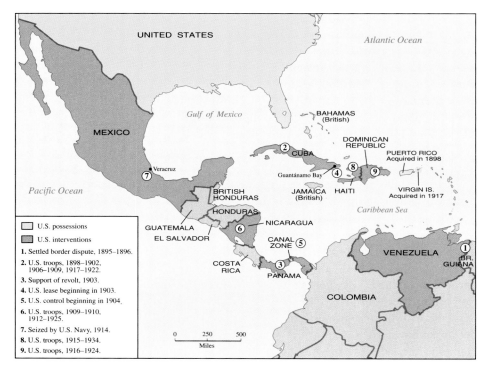

M A P 21.3
Policeman of the Caribbean

After the Spanish-American War the United States vigorously asserted its interest in the affairs of its neighbors to the south. As the record of interventions shows, the United States truly became the "policeman" of the Caribbean.

Japan had unveiled its military strength in the Sino-Japanese War of 1894–1895. A decade later, provoked by Russian rivalry in Manchuria and Korea, Japan suddenly attacked the tsar's fleet at Port Arthur, Russia's leased port in China. In a series of brilliant victories the Japanese smashed the Russian forces in Asia. Anxious to restore some semblance of a balance of power, Roosevelt mediated a settlement of the Russo-Japanese War at Portsmouth, New Hampshire, in 1905. Japan emerged as the predominant power in East Asia.

Contemptuous of other Asian nations, Roosevelt admired the Japanese—"a wonderful and civilized people . . . entitled to stand in absolute equality with all the other peoples of the civilized world." He conceded that Japan had "a paramount interest in what surrounds the Yellow Sea, just as the United States has a paramount interest in what surrounds the Caribbean." But American strategic and commercial interests in the Pacific had to be accommodated. The United States approved of Japan's protectorate over Korea in 1905 and then of its declaration of full sovereignty six years later. However, a surge of anti-Asian feeling in California complicated Roosevelt's efforts. In 1906 San Francisco's school board placed all Asian students in a segregated school, infuriating Japan. The "gentlemen's agreement" of 1907, in which Japan agreed to restrict immigration to the United States, smoothed matters over, but periodic racist slights by Americans made for continuing tensions with the Japanese.

Roosevelt meanwhile moved to balance Japan's military power by increasing American naval strength in the Pacific. American battleships visited Japan in 1908 on a global tour that impressively displayed U.S. sea power. Late that year, near the end of his administration, Roosevelt achieved a formal accommodation with Japan. The Root-Takahira Agreement confirmed the status quo in the Pacific, as well as the principles of free oceanic commerce and equal trade opportunity in China.

William Howard Taft, however, entered the White House in 1909 convinced that the United States had been shortchanged. He pressed for a larger role for American investors, especially in the railroad construction going on in China. An exponent of *dollar diplomacy*—the aggressive coupling of American political and economic interests abroad—Taft hoped that American capital would counterbalance Japanese power and pave the way for increased commercial opportunities. When the Chinese Revolution of 1911 toppled the ruling Manchu dynasty, Taft supported the victorious Chinese Nationalists, who wanted to modernize their country and liberate it from Japanese domination. The United States thus entered a long-term rivalry with Japan that would end in war thirty years later.

The United States had become embroiled in a distant struggle that promised many future liabilities but few of the fabulous profits that had lured Americans to Asia.

WILSON AND MEXICO

When Woodrow Wilson became president in 1913, he was bent on reforming American foreign policy no less than domestic politics. Wilson did not really differ with his predecessors on the importance of economic development overseas. He applauded the "tides of commerce" that would arise from the Panama Canal. But he opposed dollar diplomacy, which he believed bullied weaker countries financially and gave undue advantage to American business. It seemed to Wilson "a very perilous thing to determine the foreign policy of a nation in terms of material interest."

The United States, Wilson insisted, should conduct its foreign policy in conformity with its democratic principles. He intended to foster the "development of constitutional liberty in the world" and above all in the nation's neighbors in Latin America. Wilson vowed that the United States would "never again seek one additional foot of territory by conquest." He was committed to advancing "human rights, national integrity, and opportunity" in Latin America. To do otherwise would make "ourselves untrue to our own traditions."

Mexico became the primary object of Wilson's ministrations. A cycle of revolutions had begun there in 1911. The dictator Porfirio Diaz was overthrown by Francisco Madero, who spoke much as Wilson did about liberty and constitutionalism. But before Madero got very far with his reforms, he was deposed and murdered in February 1913 by one of his generals, Victoriano Huerta. Other powers quickly recognized Huerta's provisional government but not the United States. Wilson abhorred Huerta; he called him a murderer and pledged "to force him out."

By intervening in this way, "we act in the interest of Mexico alone. . . . We are seeking to counsel Mexico for its own good." Wilson meant that he intended to put the Mexican revolution back on the constitutional path started by Madero. Wilson was not deterred by the fact that American business interests, with big investments in Mexico, favored Huerta.

The emergence of armed opposition in northern Mexico under Venustiano Carranza strengthened Wilson's hand. But Carranza's Constitutionalist movement, ardently nationalist, had no desire for American intervention in Mexican affairs. Carranza angrily rebuffed Wilson's efforts to bring about elections by means of a compromise with the Huerta government. He also vowed to fight any intrusion of U.S. troops in his country. All he wanted from Wilson, Carranza asserted, was recognition of the Constitutionalists' belligerent status, so they could purchase arms in the United States. In exchange for vague promises to respect property rights and "fair" foreign concessions, Carranza finally got his way in 1914. American weapons began to flow to his troops.

When it became clear that Huerta was not about to fall, the United States threw its own forces into the conflict. On the pretext of a minor insult to the U.S. Navy at Tampico, Wilson ordered the occupation of the port of Veracruz on April 21, 1914, at the cost of 19 American and 126 Mexican lives. At that point the Huerta regime began to crumble. Carranza nevertheless condemned the United States, and his forces came close to engaging the Americans. When he entered Mexico City in triumph in August 1914, Carranza had some cause to thank the Yankees. But if any sense of gratitude existed, it was overshadowed by the anti-Americanism inspired by Wilson's insensitivity to Mexican pride and revolutionary zeal.

THE GATHERING STORM IN EUROPE

In the meantime Europe had begun to drift toward world war. There were two main sources of tension. One was the rivalry between Germany, the new military and economic superpower of Europe, and the European states threatened by its might— above all France, which had been humiliated in the Franco-Prussian War of 1870. The second danger zone was the Balkans, where the Ottoman empire was disintegrating and where, in the midst of explosive ethnic rivalries, Austria-Hungary and Russia were maneuvering for dominance. Out of these conflicts an alliance system had emerged, with Germany, Austria-Hungary, and Italy (the Triple Alliance) on one side and France and Russia (the Dual Alliance) on the other.

The tensions in Europe were partially released by European imperial adventures, especially by France in Africa and by Russia in Asia. These activities placed France and Russia in opposition to imperial Britain, effectively excluding Britain from the European alliance system. Fearful of Germany, however, Britain in 1904 resolved her differences with France, and the two countries reached a friendly understanding, or *entente*. When Britain came to a similar understanding with Russia in 1907, the basis was laid for the Triple Entente. A deadly confrontation between two great European power blocs became possible.

In these European quarrels Americans had no obvious stake nor any inclination, in the words of a cautionary Senate resolution, "to depart from the traditional American foreign policy which forbids participation . . . [in] political questions which are entirely European in scope." But on becoming president Theodore Roosevelt took a lively interest in European affairs and was eager, as the head of a Great Power, to make a contribution to the cause of peace there. In 1905 he got his chance.

The Anglo-French entente of the previous year was based partly on an agreement over spheres of influence in North Africa: the Sudan went to Britain, Morocco to France. Then Germany suddenly challenged France over Morocco—a disastrous move, conflicting with Germany's self-interest in keeping France's attention diverted from Europe. The German ruler, Kaiser Wilhelm, turned to Roosevelt for help. Roosevelt arranged an international conference, which was held in January 1906 at Algeciras, Spain. With U.S. diplomats playing a key role, the crisis was defused. Germany got a few token concessions, but France's dominance over Morocco was sustained.

Algeciras marked an ominous turning point—the first time the power blocs that would become locked in battle in 1914 first squared off against one another. But in 1906 the outcome of the conference seemed a diplomatic triumph. Roosevelt's secretary of state, Elihu Root, boasted of America's success in "preserv[ing] world peace because of the power of our detachment."

Root's words prefigured how the United States would define its role among the Great Powers: it would be the apostle of peace, distinguished by its lack of selfish interest in European affairs. Opposing this internationalist impulse, however, was America's traditional isolationism.

Americans had applauded the international peace movement launched by the Hague Peace Conference of 1899. The Permanent Court of Arbitration that resulted offered new hope for the peaceful settlement of international disputes. Both the Roosevelt and the Taft administrations negotiated arbitration treaties with other countries, pledging to submit their disputes to the Hague Court, only to have the treaties emasculated by a Senate unwilling to permit any erosion of the nation's sovereignty. Nor was there any sequel to Roosevelt's initiative at Algeciras. It was coolly received in the Senate and by the nation's press.

When Wilson became president, he chose William Jennings Bryan to be secretary of state. An apostle of world peace, Bryan devoted himself to negotiating a series of "cooling off" treaties with other countries—so called because the parties agreed to wait one year while disputed issues were submitted to a conciliation process. Although admirable these bilateral agreements had no bearing on the explosive power politics of Europe. As tensions there reached the breaking point in 1914, the United States remained effectively on the sidelines.

Yet at Algeciras Roosevelt had correctly anticipated what the future would demand of America. So did the French journalist Andre Tardieu, who remarked in 1908:

> The United States is . . . a world power. . . . Its power creates for it . . . a duty— to pronounce upon all those questions that hitherto have been arranged by agreement only among European powers. . . . The United States intervenes thus in the affairs of the universe. . . . It is seated at the table where the great game is played, and it cannot leave it.

T I M E L I N E

1875	Treaty brings Hawaii within U.S. orbit.	**1901**	Theodore Roosevelt becomes president; "big stick" diplomacy.
1881	Secretary of State James G. Blaine inaugurates Pan-Americanism.		Hay-Pauncefote Agreement
			United States recognizes Panama and receives grant of Canal Zone.
1889	Germany, Britain, and United States share protectorate in Samoa.	**1902**	Platt amendment gives United States right of intervention in Cuba.
1890	Alfred Thayer Mahan's *The Influence of Seapower upon History*	**1904**	Roosevelt Corollary
1893	Annexation of Hawaii fails.	**1905– 1906**	United States mediates Franco-German crisis over Morocco at Algeciras.
	Frederick Jackson Turner's "The Significance of the Frontier in American History"	**1907**	Gentlemen's Agreement restricts Japanese immigration.
	Panic of 1893 ushers in economic depression.	**1908**	Root-Takahira Agreement
1894	Sino-Japanese war begins breakup of China into spheres of influence.	**1909**	William Howard Taft becomes president; dollar diplomacy.
1895	Venezuela crisis	**1913**	Wilson asserts new principles for American diplomacy.
1898	Outbreak of Spanish-American War in Cuba and Philippines		Intervention in the Mexican Revolution
	Hawaii annexed	**1914**	Panama Canal opens.
	Anti-imperialist movement launched		World War I begins.
1899	Hague Peace Conference		
	Guerrilla war in the Philippines		
	Open-door policy in China		

For Further Exploration

Walter LaFeber, *The American Search for Opportunity, 1865–1913* (1993), is an excellent, up-to-date synthesis. LaFeber emphasizes economic interest—the need for overseas markets—as the source of American expansionism. His immensely influential *The New Empire, 1860–1898* (1963) initiated the scholarly debate on this issue. A robust counterpoint is Fareed Zakaria's recent *From Wealth to Power* (1998), which asks why the United States was so slow (compared to other imperial nations) to translate its economic power into international muscle. The debate can be explored at greater depth in Thomas J. McCormick, *China Market: America's Quest for Informal Empire, 1893–1901* (1967); Michael Hunt, *Ideology and U.S. Foreign Policy* (1987); and Mark R. Shulman, *Navalism and the Emergence of American Sea Power, 1882–1893* (1995). On the war with Spain the liveliest narrative is still Frank Freidel, *A Splendid Little War* (1958). For fuller treatments see David S. Trask, *The War with Spain in 1898* (1981); Ivan Musicant, *Empire by Default* (1998); and Lewis Gould, *The Spanish-American War and President McKinley* (1982), which emphasizes McKinley's strong leadership. Ernest R. May, *Imperial Democracy: The Emergence of America as a Great Power* (1961), exemplifies the earlier view that McKinley was a weak figure driven to war by jingoistic pressures. On the Mexican involvement see John S. D. Eisenhower, *Intervention! The United States and the Mexican Revolution* (1993). The revolution as experienced by the Mexicans is brilliantly depicted in John Womack, *Zapata and the Mexican Revolution* (1968).

The Library of Congress maintains an excellent website, "The Spanish-American War," at <lcweb.loc.gov/rr/hispanic/1898/> with separate sections on the war in Cuba, the Philippines, Puerto Rico, and Spain. "American Imperialism" at <http://boondocksnet.com> includes an extensive collection of stereoscopic images, political cartoons, maps, photographs, and documents from the period.

Part 5

THE MODERN STATE AND SOCIETY
1914–1945

THEMATIC TIMELINE

	GOVERNMENT	DIPLOMACY	ECONOMY
	THE RISE OF THE STATE	FROM ISOLATION TO WORLD LEADERSHIP	PROSPERITY, DEPRESSION, AND WAR
1914	• Wartime agencies expand power of the federal government.	• United States enters World War I (1917). • Wilson's Fourteen Points (1918)	• Shift from debtor to creditor nation • Agricultural glut
1920	• Republican ascendancy • Prohibition (1920–1933) • Business-government partnership • Nineteenth Amendment gives women the vote.	• Treaty of Versailles rejected by U.S. Senate (1920) • Washington Conference sets naval limits (1922).	• Economic recession (1920–1921) • Booming prosperity (1922–1929) • Rise in welfare capitalism
1930	• Franklin D. Roosevelt becomes president (1933). • The New Deal: unprecedented government intervention in economy, social welfare, arts	• Roosevelt's Good Neighbor Policy toward Latin America (1933) • Abraham Lincoln Brigade fights in Spanish Civil War. • U.S. neutrality proclaimed (1939)	• Great Depression (1929–1941) • Rise of labor movement • Married women increasingly participate in the workforce.
1940	• Government mobilizes industry for war production and rationing.	• United States enters World War II (1941). • Allies defeat Axis powers; bombing of Hiroshima (1945).	• War mobilization ends depression.

By 1914 industrialization, economic expansion abroad, massive immigration, and the growth of a vibrant urban culture had set the foundations for a distinctly modern American society. In all facets of politics, the economy, and daily life, American society was becoming more organized, more bureaucratic, and more complex. By 1945, after Americans had fought in two world wars and weathered a dozen years of economic depression, the edifice of the new society was largely complete.

GOVERNMENT. A strong national state, an essential building block of modern society, came late and haltingly to America compared to industrialized countries of Western Europe. American participation in World War I called forth an unprecedented mobilization of the domestic economy, but policymakers quickly dismantled the centralized wartime bureaucracies in 1919. During the 1920s the Harding and Coolidge administrations embraced a philosophy of business-government partnership, believing that unrestricted corporate capitalism would best serve the American people. The Great Depression, with its uncounted business failures and unprecedented levels of unemployment, overthrew that long-cherished idea. Franklin D. Roosevelt's New Deal dramatically expanded federal responsibility for the economy and the welfare of ordinary citizens. The national state further expanded with the massive mobilization necessitated by America's entry into World War II. Unlike after World War I, the new state apparatus remained in place when the war ended.

SOCIETY	CULTURE
NATIVISM, MIGRATION, AND SOCIAL CHANGE	A MASS NATIONAL CULTURE EMERGES
• Southern blacks begin migration to northern cities.	• Silent screen; Hollywood becomes movie capital of the world.
• Rise of nativism • National Origins Act (1924) • Mexican American immigration increases.	• Consumer culture—advertising, radio, magazines, movies—flourishes. • Consumer culture promotes image of emancipated womanhood, the Flapper.
• Farming families migrate from Dust Bowl states to California and the West. • Indian New Deal • Increased use of birth control leads to smaller families.	• Documentary impulse • Federal patronage of the arts
• Rural whites and blacks migrate to war jobs in cities. • Cival rights movement revitalized	• Film industry enlisted to aid war effort

DIPLOMACY. America was slowly and somewhat reluctantly drawn into a position of world leadership. World War I provided the major impetus: before 1914 the world had been dominated by Europe, but from that point on the United States increasingly dominated the world. In 1918 American troops provided the margin of victory for the Allies, and President Wilson helped shape the treaties that ended the war. The United States, however, refused to join the League of Nations created by those treaties. America's dominant economic position guaranteed an active role in world affairs in the 1920s and 1930s nonetheless. The globalization of America accelerated in 1941, when the nation joined a second world war that had its roots in the imperfect settlement of the first one. Of all the powers that participated in this most devastating of global conflagrations, only America emerged physically unscathed. And only America possessed a dangerous new weapon—the atomic bomb. Within wartime decisions lay the roots of the cold war that followed.

ECONOMY. In this period the American economy took on its modern contours. Between 1914 and 1945 the nation's industrial economy was the most productive in the world. The Great Depression, which slashed the nation's gross national product and left millions unemployed and destitute, hit the United States harder than any other industrialized nation. Yet although it had a powerful effect on the country's politics and culture, it did not permanently affect its global economic standing. Indeed, American businesses still successfully competed in world markets, and American financial institutions played the leading role in international economic affairs. Large-scale corporate organizations replaced smaller family-run businesses. White-collar jobs, ranging from managerial to clerical, expanded dramatically and contributed to the growing presence of women in the workforce. The automobile industry symbolized the ascendancy of mass-production techniques. Many workers shared in the general prosperity but also bore the brunt of economic downturns.

These uncertainties fueled the dramatic growth of the labor movement in the 1930s.

SOCIETY. American society was transformed by the great wave of European immigration and the movement from farms to cities. The growth of metropolitan areas gave the nation an increasingly urban tone, and geographical mobility broke down regional differences. Many old-stock white Americans viewed these processes with alarm; in 1924 nativists succeeded in all but eliminating immigration from everywhere but other Western Hemisphere nations, as migration across the border from Mexico continued to shape the West and Southwest. Internal migration also changed the face of America, as African Americans moved north and west to take factory jobs and Dust Bowl farmers in the 1930s moved to the Far West to find better livelihoods. World War II accelerated these migration patterns even more.

CULTURE. Finally, modern America saw the emergence of a mass national culture. By the 1920s Americans were increasingly drawn into a web of interlocking cultural experiences. Advertising and the new entertainment media—movies, radio, and magazines—disseminated the new values of consumerism; the movies exported this vision of the American experience worldwide. Not even the Great Depression could divert Americans from their desire for leisure, self-fulfillment, and consumer goods. The emphasis on consumption and a quest for a rising standard of living would define the American experience for the rest of the twentieth century.

Chapter 22

WAR AND THE AMERICAN STATE
1914–1920

It is not an army we must shape and train for war, it is a nation.

WOODROW WILSON, 1917

"It's Up to You—Protect the Nation's Honor—Enlist Now." "Turn Your Silver into Bullets at the Post Office." "Rivets Are Bayonets—Drive Them Home!" "Women! Help America's Sons Win the War: Buy U.S. Government Bonds." "Food Is Ammunition—Don't Waste It." At every turn during the eighteen months of U.S. participation in the Great War—at the movies, in schools and libraries, in shop windows and post offices, at train stations and factories—Americans encountered dramatic posters urging them to do their bit. More than colorful reminders of a bygone era, these propaganda tools were meant to unify the American people in voluntary, self-sacrificing service to the nation. They suggest not only that the federal government had increased its presence in the lives of Americans but also that in modern war victory demanded more than armies. On the home front, businessmen, workers, farmers, housewives, and even children had important roles to play. The story of the United States' involvement in World War I, then, is a story of battles and diplomacy abroad and mobilization at home, all of which would have lasting impact on the nation's future.

The American decision to enter the conflict in 1917 confirmed one of the most important shifts of power in the twentieth century. Before the outbreak of the Great War in 1914, the world had been dominated by Europe; the postwar world was increasingly dominated by the United States. The historian Akira Iriye calls this broad transformation the "globalization" of America. Increasingly, the United States became "involved in security, economic, and cultural affairs in all parts of the world." This development, which is usually thought to begin with World War II and its aftermath, actually started in 1917.

Related changes that shaped the country for the rest of the twentieth century also emerged at home. New federal bureaucracies had to be created to coordinate the efforts of business, labor, and agriculture—a process that hastened the emergence of a national administrative state. War meant new opportunities, albeit

America and the War Effort

Popular magazines like *Leslie's Illustrated Weekly Newspaper* teamed up with the federal government to promote food conservation. If a patriotic reader affixed a 1 cent stamp to the cover's top right corner, the magazine would be sent to soldiers or sailors at the front.

(*Leslie's*, September 29, 1917/Picture Research Consultants & Archives)

temporary, for white women and for members of ethnic minorities. It also meant new divisions among Americans and new hatreds, first of Germans and Austrians and then of "Bolshevik" Reds. When the war ended, the United States was forced to confront the deep class, racial, and ethnic divisions that had surfaced during wartime mobilization.

The Great War, 1914–1918

When war erupted in August 1914, most Americans saw no reason to involve themselves in the struggle among Europe's imperialistic powers. No vital U.S. interests were at stake. Indeed, the United States had a good relationship with both sides, and its industries benefited from providing war material for the combatants. Many Americans placed their faith in what historians call "U.S. exceptionalism"—the belief that their superior democratic values and institutions made their country immune from the corruption and chaos of other nations. Horrified by the carnage and sympathetic to the suffering, Americans nevertheless expected that they would be able to follow their president's dictum "to be neutral in fact as well as in name."

WAR IN EUROPE

Almost from the moment France, Russia, and Britain formed the Triple Entente in 1907 to counter the Triple Alliance of Germany, Austria-Hungary, and Italy (see Chapter 21), European leaders began to prepare for what they saw as an inevitable conflict. The spark that ignited the war came in Europe's perennial tinderbox, the Balkans, where Austria-Hungary and Russia competed for power and influence. Austria's seizure of the provinces of Bosnia and Herzegovina in 1908 had enraged Russia and its client, the independent state of Serbia. Serbian terrorists responded by recruiting Bosnians to agitate against Austrian rule. On June 28, 1914, a nineteen-year-old Bosnian student, Gavrilo Princip, assassinated Franz Ferdinand, the heir to the Austro-Hungarian throne, and his wife, the Duchess of Hohenberg, in the town of Sarajevo.

After the assassination the complex European alliance system, which had for years maintained a fragile peace, drew all the major powers into war. Austria-Hungary, blaming Serbia for the assassination, declared war on Serbia on July 28. Russia, which had a secret treaty with Serbia, mobilized its armies; Germany responded by declaring war on Russia and its ally, France, and by invading neutral Belgium. The brutality of the invasion, and Britain's commitment to Belgian neutrality, prompted Great Britain to declare war on Germany on August 4. Within a few days all the major European powers had formally entered the conflict.

The combatants were divided into two rival blocs. The Allied Powers—Great Britain, France, Japan, Russia, and, in 1915, Italy—were pitted against the Central Powers—Germany, Austria-Hungary, Turkey, and, in 1915, Bulgaria (see Map 22.1).

MAP 22.1
Europe at the Start of World War I

In early August 1914 a complex set of interlocking alliances drew the major European powers into war. At first the United States avoided the conflict. Not until April 1917 did America enter the war on the Allied side.

Because the alliance system encompassed competing imperial powers, the conflict spread to parts of the world far beyond Europe, including the Middle East, Africa, and China. Its worldwide scope gave it the name the Great War, or later, World War I.

The term "Great War" also suggested the terrible devastation the conflict produced. It was the first modern war in which extensive harm was done to civilian populations. New military technology, much of it from the United States, made armies more deadly than ever before. Soldiers carried long-range, high-velocity rifles that could hit a target at 1,000 yards—a vast improvement over the 300-yard range of the rifle-musket used in the American Civil War. Another innovation was the machine gun, whose American-born inventor, Hiram Maxim, moved to Great Britain in the 1880s to follow a friend's advice: "If you want to make your fortune, invent something which will allow those fool Europeans to kill each other more quickly."

The concentrated firepower of rifles and machine guns gave troops in defensive positions a tremendous advantage. For four bloody years, between 1914 and 1918, the Allies and the Central Powers faced each other on the Western Front, a

The Landscape of War

World War I devastated the countryside: this was the battleground at Ypres in 1915. The carnage of trench warfare also scarred the soldiers who served in these surreal settings, causing the "gas neurosis," "burial-alive neurosis," and "soldiers' heart"—all symptoms of shell shock. (Imperial War Museum, London)

narrow swath of territory in Belgium and northern France crisscrossed by 25,000 miles of heavily fortified trenches, protected by deadly barbed wire. Trench warfare produced unprecedented numbers of casualties. If one side tried to break the stalemate by venturing into the "no man's land" between the trenches, its soldiers, caught in the sea of barbed wire, were mowed down by artillery fire or poison gas, first used by the Germans at Ypres in April 1915. Between February and December 1916, the French suffered 550,000 casualties and the Germans 450,000, as Germany tried to break through the French lines at Verdun. The front did not move.

THE PERILS OF NEUTRALITY

As the bloody stalemate continued, the United States grappled with its role in the international conflagration. Two weeks after the outbreak of war in Europe, President Woodrow Wilson had made the American position clear. In a message widely printed in the newspapers, the president called on Americans to be "neutral in fact as well as in name, impartial in thought as well as in action." Wilson wanted to keep the nation out of the war partly because he believed that if America kept aloof from the quarrel, he could arbitrate—and influence—its ultimate settlement.

The nation's divided loyalties also influenced Wilson's policy. Many Americans, including Wilson, felt deep cultural ties to the Allies, especially Britain and France. Yet most Irish Americans resented Britain's centuries-long occupation of their homeland and the cancellation of Home Rule in 1914. Pro-German sentiments drew strength from America's 10 million immigrants from Germany and Austria-Hungary. Indeed, German Americans made up one of the largest and best-established ethnic groups in the United States, and many aspects of German culture, including classical music and the German university system, were widely admired. Wilson could not easily have rallied the nation to the Allied side in 1914.

Many Americans had no strong sympathy for either side. Some progressive leaders—both Republicans and Democrats—vehemently opposed American participation in the European conflict. Newly formed pacifist groups, among them the American Union against Militarism and the Women's Peace Party, both founded in 1915, also mobilized popular opposition. Virtually the entire political left, led principally by Eugene Debs and the Socialist Party, condemned the war as imperialistic. African American leaders such as A. Philip Randolph viewed it as a conflict of the white race only. And some prominent industrialists bankrolled antiwar activities. In December 1915 Henry Ford spent almost half a million dollars to send more than a hundred men and women to Europe on a "peace ship" in an attempt to negotiate an end to the war.

All these factors might have kept the nation neutral if the conflict had not spread to the high seas. Here the United States wished to assert its neutrality rights—freedom to trade with nations on both sides of a conflict. But the warring nations would not long let America trade in peace. By the end of August 1914 the British had imposed a naval blockade on the Central Powers, hoping to cut off military supplies and starve the German people into submission. But their actions also prevented neutral nations like the United States from trading with Germany and its allies. The United States chafed at the infringement of its neutral rights but chose to do little besides complain, largely because the war had produced a spectacular increase in trade with the Allies that more than made up for the lost commerce with the Central Powers. American trade with Britain and France grew from $824 million in 1914 to $3.2 billion in 1916. By 1917 U.S. banks had lent the Allies $2.5 billion. In contrast, American trade with and loans to Germany totaled only $29 million and $27 million, respectively, by 1917. This trade imbalance translated into closer U.S. ties with the Allies, despite the nation's official posture of neutrality.

To challenge British control of the seas, the German navy launched a devastating new weapon, the U-boat. In April 1915 the German embassy in the United States had issued a warning to civilians that all ships flying the flags of Britain or its allies were liable to destruction. A few weeks later, on May 7, a German U-boat off the coast of Ireland torpedoed the British luxury liner *Lusitania*, killing 1,198 people, 128 of them Americans. The attack on the unarmed passenger vessel (which was later revealed to have been carrying munitions) incensed Americans—news-papers branded it a "mass murder"—and prompted President Wilson to send a se-ries of strongly worded protests to Germany. Mounting tension between the two nations temporarily subsided in September 1915, when Germany announced its submarines would no longer attack passenger ships without warning.

The *Lusitania* crisis was one factor that prompted Wilson to rethink his op-position to preparedness. He was further discouraged by the failure of his repeated attempts in 1915 and 1916 to mediate an end to the European conflict through his aide, Colonel Edward House. With neither side apparently interested in seri-ous peace negotiations, Wilson worried that the potential for the United States to be drawn into the conflict was deepening. In the fall of 1915 he endorsed a $1 billion buildup of the army and the navy, and by 1916 armament was well under way.

Nevertheless, public opinion still ran against entering the war, a factor that pro-foundly shaped the election of 1916. The Republican Party passed over the bel-ligerently prowar Theodore Roosevelt in favor of Supreme Court Justice Charles Evans Hughes, a former governor of New York. The Democrats renominated Wil-son, whose campaign emphasized his progressive reform record (see Chapter 20) but whose telling campaign slogan was, "He kept us out of war." Wilson won re-election by only 600,000 popular votes and by 23 votes in the electoral college, a slim margin that limited his options in mobilizing the nation for war.

The events of early 1917 diminished Wilson's lingering hopes of staying out of the conflict. On January 31 Germany announced the resumption of unre-stricted submarine warfare, a decision dictated by the impasse in the land war. In response, Wilson broke off diplomatic relations with Germany on February 3. A few weeks later, newspapers published an intercepted communication from Germany's foreign secretary, Arthur Zimmermann, to the German minister in Mexico City, in which Zimmermann urged Mexico to join the Central Powers in the war. In return, Germany promised to help Mexico recover "the lost territory of Texas, New Mexico, and Arizona." This threat to the territorial integrity of the United States jolted both congressional and public opinion, especially in the West, where opposition to entering the war was strong. Combined with the resump-tion of unrestricted submarine warfare, the Zimmermann telegram inflamed anti-German sentiment. Although the likelihood of Mexico's reconquering the border states was small, the continued instability there in the final phases of the Mexican Revolution (see Chapter 21) had led to border raids that killed sixteen U.S. citizens in January 1916 and made American policymakers take the German threat seriously.

Throughout March, U-boats attacked American ships without warning, sink-ing three on March 18 alone. On April 2, 1917, after consulting his cabinet, Wilson appeared before a special session of Congress to ask for a declaration of war. The rights of the nation had been trampled, and its trade and citizens' lives imperiled, he charged. But while U.S. self-interest shaped the decision to go to war, Americans' long-standing sense of their exceptionalism, coupled with Progressive Era zeal to right social injustices, also played a part. Believing that the United States, in sharp contrast to other nations, was uniquely high minded in the conduct of its international affairs, many Americans accepted Wilson's claim that America had no selfish aims: "We desire no conquest, no dominion. We seek no indemnities for ourselves, no material compensation for the sacrifices we shall freely make. We are but one of the champions of the rights of mankind." In a memorable phrase intended to ennoble the nation's role, Wilson proposed that U.S. participation in the war would make the world "safe for democracy."

Four days after Wilson's speech, on April 6, 1917, the United States declared war on Germany. Reflecting the divided feelings of the country as a whole, the vote was far from unanimous. Six senators and fifty members of the House voted against the action, including Representative Jeannette Rankin of Montana, the first woman elected to Congress. "I want to stand by my country," she declared, "but I cannot vote for war."

"OVER THERE"

To native-born Americans, Europe seemed a great distance away—literally "over there," as the lyrics of George M. Cohan's popular song described it. After the declaration of war many citizens were surprised to learn that the United States planned to send troops to Europe, optimistically having assumed that the nation's participation could be limited to military and economic aid.

In May 1917 General John J. Pershing traveled to London and Paris to determine how the United States could best support the war effort. The answer, as Marshal Joseph Joffre of France put it, was clear: "Men, men, and more men." The problem was that the United States had never maintained a large standing army in peacetime. To field a fighting force strong enough to enter a global war, the government turned to conscription. The passage of the Selective Service Act in May 1917 demonstrated the increasing impact of the state on ordinary citizens. Though draft resistance had been common during the Civil War, no major riots occurred in 1917. The Selective Service System worked in part because it combined central direction from Washington with local administration and civilian control and thus did not tread on the nation's tradition of individual freedom and local autonomy. Draft registration also demonstrated the potential bureaucratic capacity of the American state. On a single day, June 5, 1917, more than 9.5 million men between the ages of twenty-one and thirty were processed for military service in their local voting precincts. By the end of the war almost 4 million men, plus a few thousand female navy clerks and army nurses, were in uniform. Another 300,000 men, called "slackers," evaded the draft, and 4,000 were classified as conscientious objectors.

Wilson chose Pershing to head the American Expeditionary Force (AEF). But the newly raised army did not have an immediate impact on the fighting. The fresh recruits had to be trained and outfitted and then wait for transport across the submarine-infested Atlantic. The nation's first main contribution was to secure the safety of the seas. Aiming for safety in numbers in the face of mounting German submarine activity, the government began sending armed convoys across the Atlantic. The plan worked: no American soldiers were killed on the way to Europe, and Allied shipping losses were cut dramatically.

Meanwhile, trench warfare on the Western Front continued its deadly grind. Allied commanders pleaded for American reinforcements, but Pershing was reluctant to put his soldiers under foreign commanders, preferring to delay introducing American troops until the AEF could be brought up to strength and ready to fight. Thus, until May 1918 the brunt of the fighting continued to fall on the French and British. Their burden increased when the Eastern Front collapsed after the Russian Revolution in November 1917. Under the Treaty of Brest-Litovsk, the new Bolshevik regime under Vladimir Ilych Lenin surrendered about one-third of Russia's territories, including Russian Poland, Ukraine, and the Baltic provinces, in return for an end to hostilities.

Once hostilities with Russia had ended, the Germans launched a major offensive against the Allies on the Western Front on March 21, 1918. By May the German army had advanced to the Marne River, within 50 miles of Paris, and was attempting to subdue the city by bombardment. When Allied leaders intensified their calls for American troops, Pershing committed about 60,000 Americans to help the French repel the Germans in the battles of Château-Thierry and Belleau Wood (see Map 22.2).

American reinforcements now began to arrive in large numbers. Slowly they worked their way to the front through the clogged French transportation system. Augmented by American troops, the Allied forces brought the German offensive to a halt in mid-July. The counteroffensive began with a successful campaign to drive the Germans back from the Marne. In mid-September 1918, American and French troops led by General Pershing forced the Germans to retreat at St. Mihiel (see American Voices, "Trench Warfare"). The last major assault of the war began on September 26, when Pershing pitted over a million American soldiers against vastly outnumbered and exhausted German troops. The Meuse-Argonne campaign pushed the enemy back across the Selle River near Verdun and broke the German defenses, at a cost of over 26,000 American lives.

World War I ended on November 11, 1918, when German and Allied representatives signed an armistice in the railway car of Marshal Ferdinand Foch of France. The flood of American troops and supplies during the last six months of the war had helped secure the Allied victory. The nation's decisive contribution signaled a shift in international power as European diplomatic and economic dominance declined and the United States emerged as a world leader.

About 2 million American soldiers were in France at the war's end. Two-thirds of them had seen action at least briefly on the Western Front, but most had escaped the horrors of sustained trench warfare that sapped the morale of Allied and German

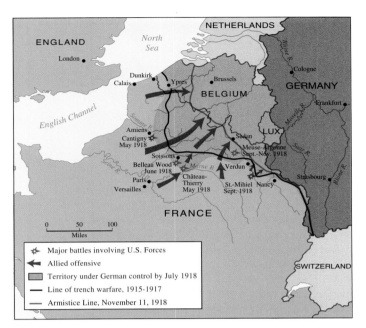

MAP 22.2
U.S. Participation on the Western Front, 1918

When American troops reached the European front in significant
numbers in 1918, the Allied and Central Powers had been grinding
each other down in a war of attrition for almost four years. The influx
of American troops and supplies broke the stalemate. Successful
offensive maneuvers by the American Expeditionary Force included
those at Belleau Wood and Château-Thierry, and the Meuse-
Argonne campaign.

troops. During the eighteen months in which the United States fought, 48,000 American servicemen were killed in action or died from wounds. Another 27,000 died
from other causes, mainly the influenza epidemic that swept the world in 1918 and
1919. But the nation's casualties were minimal compared with the 8 million soldiers lost by the Allies and Central Powers. The French lost far more soldiers in the
siege of Verdun than the United States did in the entire war.

After the armistice the war lived on in the minds of the men and women who
had gone "over there." Many members of the AEF, especially those who had been
spared the horror of sustained battle, experienced the war more as tourists than as
soldiers. Before joining the army, most had barely traveled beyond their hometowns;
for them the journey across the ocean was a monumental, once-in-a-lifetime event.
Their letters described "old cathedrals, chateaux and ancient towns . . . quite wonderful . . . to eyes so accustomed to the look of the New World." In 1919 a group
of former AEF officers formed the American Legion, "to preserve the memories and
incidents of our association in the great war." The word *legion* captured the

AMERICAN VOICES
Trench Warfare
WILLIAM L. LANGER

Sergeant William L. Langer, of Battery E, 1st Gas Regiment, describes the effort to work through the trenches to get to the front lines to set up devices for launching bombs at the Germans at the battle of St. Mihiel in September 1918.

There was not much activity in the trenches, certainly not enough to give reason to suppose that a large scale attack was about to start. The enemy, to be sure, kept up his Vérey lights and fired at intervals. Still, most of us were quite startled and surprised when, about 1:00 in the morning, the sky lit up behind us and the American barrage began. . . .

After depositing our loads at the position we started back for another. . . . And going back was quite a different proposition than going, for, as if by magic, the trenches had filled with men, most of them Marines . . . and troops of the 9th Infantry . . . who were to go over the top with the first wave. Those rows of cold, shivering men, equipped with grenades and with bayonets fixed, crouching in the mud of the trenches and waiting for the crucial moment, is another sight we shall never forget. . . .

We were just about to start back for the trenches [with a second load of bombs] when the Boche suddenly opened up with a concentrated bombardment of the town. Everywhere the shells were bursting. For a moment we were undecided, but then we set out on a run. . . . We reached the trenches without mishap. The first wave was just about to go over, and our machine guns had just opened a rolling barrage to precede it. For green men it was a novel experience—this stuttering breathless chatter of the machine guns behind one. The trenches were in places so congested that to get through would have been impossible had we not struck on a rather clever idea. "Heads up, men, high explosives, watch these sacks";—shouting words to that effect worked like magic and we secured an easy passage.

SOURCE: Frank Freidel, *Over There: The Story of America's First Great Overseas Crusade* (McGraw-Hill, rev. ed. 1990), 127–28.

---

romantic, almost chivalric memories many veterans held of their wartime service. Only later did disillusionment over the contested legacy of World War I set in.

For African Americans, the war experience had never been very romantic. Encouraged by black leaders to enlist as a means of proving their loyalty and achieving first-class citizenship, black soldiers instead suffered continued discrimination. Placed in segregated units under white officers, they served in the most menial positions as laborers, stevedores, and messboys. Many African Americans emerged from the war determined to stand up for their rights and contributed to a spirit of black militancy that characterized the early 1920s.

Portrait of a Corporal

Black soldiers such as this corporal in the 15th New York Infantry received segregated and unequal treatment at every level of military service. Yet their pride in serving their country remained strong, as this 1918 painting by Raymond Desvarraus suggests.

(West Point Museum, United States Military Academy, West Point, NY)

War on the Home Front

Fighting World War I required extraordinary economic mobilization on the home front in which corporations, workers, and the general public all cooperated. Although the federal government did expand its power and presence during the emergency, the watchword was voluntarism. The government avoided compulsion as much as possible. Ambivalence about expanding state power, coupled with the pressures of wartime mobilization, severely damaged the impetus for progressive reforms that had characterized the prewar era. Yet even in the context of international crisis, some reformers expected that the war could serve the cause of improving American society.

MOBILIZATION

The continuing impact of the prewar progressive reform movement was evident in the financing of the war, the cost of which would eventually mount to $33 billion. The government paid for the war in part by using the Federal Reserve System established in 1913 (see Chapter 20) to expand the money supply, making it easier to borrow money. Two-thirds of the funds came from loans, especially the popular liberty bonds. Treasury Secretary William McAdoo encouraged the small, heavily advertised bond sales as a way of widening support for the war and demonstrating the voluntary self-sacrifice of the nation's citizenry. To augment the funds raised by bonds, McAdoo increased the federal income tax. Income taxes had been instituted by Congress after the passage of the Sixteenth Amendment to the Constitution in 1913. Now the War Revenue Bills of 1917 and 1918 transformed the tax into the foremost method of federal fund raising. The Wilson administration took a progressive approach, rejecting a tax on all wages and salaries in favor of a tax on corporations and wealthy individuals. The excess-profits tax signaled a direct and unprecedented intrusion of the state into the workings of corporate capitalism. By 1918 U.S. corporations were paying over $2.5 billion in excess-profits taxes per year—more than half of all federal taxes.

The revenue bills should not mask the fact that the federal government for the most part took a collaborative rather than a coercive approach to big business during the war. To the dismay of many progressives who had hoped that the war emergency would increase federal regulation of business, the government suspended antitrust laws to encourage cooperation and promote efficiency. For economic expertise the administration turned to those who knew the capacities of the economy best—the nation's business leaders. Executives flocked to Washington, where they served with federal officials on a series of boards and agencies that sought a middle ground between total state control of the economy and total freedom for business.

The central agency for mobilizing wartime industry was the War Industries Board (WIB), established in July 1917. In March 1918, after a fumbling start that showed the limits of voluntarism in a national emergency, the Wilson administration reorganized the board under the direction of Bernard Baruch, a Wall Street financier. The WIB produced an unparalleled expansion of the federal government's economic powers: it allocated scarce resources, gathered economic data and statistics, controlled the flow of raw materials, ordered the conversion from peacetime to war production, set prices, imposed efficiency and standardization procedures, and coordinated purchasing. Though the board had the authority to compel compliance, Baruch preferred to win voluntary cooperation by industry, often through personal intervention. Business generally supported this governmental oversight because it coincided with its own interests in improving efficiency and productivity. Despite higher taxes, corporate profits soared, aided by the suspension of antitrust laws and the institution of price guarantees for war work. War profits produced an economic boom that continued without interruption until 1920.

The reliance on voluntarism was best exemplified in the Food Administration, created in August 1917 and led by Stanford-trained engineer Herbert Hoover, who proposed to "mobilize the spirit of self-denial and self-sacrifice in this country." Using the slogan "Food will win the war," Hoover encouraged farmers to expand production of wheat and other grains from 45 million acres in 1917 to 75 million in 1919. Although the Food Administration issued reams of rules and regulations for producers and retailers, at no time did the government contemplate domestic food rationing. Rather, Hoover sent women volunteers from door to door to secure housewives' cooperation in observing "wheatless" Mondays, "meatless" Tuesdays, and "porkless" Thursdays and Saturdays—a campaign that resulted in substantial voluntary conservation of food resources.

In some instances, new federal agencies took dramatic, decisive action. In the face of the severe winter of 1917 to 1918, which led to coal shortages in northeastern cities and industries, the Fuel Administration ordered all factories east of the Mississippi River to shut down for four days. An even more striking example of the temporary use of federal power came in December 1917. When a massive railroad traffic snarl interfered with the transport of troops, the Railroad War Board, which coordinated the nation's sprawling transportation system, took over the railroads. Guaranteeing railroad owners a "standard return" equal to their average earnings between 1915 and 1917, the board promised that the carriers would be returned to private control no later than twenty-one months after the end of the war. Although reformers hoped to continue this experiment in government control on behalf of labor and consumers, the government fulfilled its pledge.

With the signing of the armistice in November 1918, the United States scrambled to dismantle wartime controls. Wilson, determined to "take the harness off," disbanded the WIB on January 1, 1919, resisting suggestions that the board would help stabilize the economy during demobilization. Like most Americans, Wilson could tolerate government planning power during an emergency but not as a permanent feature of the economy.

Although the nation's participation in the war lasted just eighteen months, it left an enduring legacy, the modern bureaucratic state. Entire industries had been organized as never before, linked to a maze of government agencies and executive departments. A modern system of income taxation had been established, with the potential for vastly increasing federal reserves. Finally, the collaboration between business and government had been mutually beneficial, teaching both partners a lesson they would put to use in state building in the 1920s and afterward.

Besides mobilizing armies and businesses to wage war, the federal government also needed to ensure a reliable workforce, especially in war industries. Acute labor shortages, caused by the demands of the draft, the abrupt decline in European immigration, and the urgency of war production, had enhanced workers' bargaining power. The National War Labor Board (NWLB), formed in April 1918, also helped to improve labor's position. Composed of representatives of labor, management, and the public, the NWLB established an eight-hour day for war workers, with time and a half for overtime, and endorsed equal pay for women workers. Workers were not allowed to disrupt war production through strikes or other disturbances. In return, the NWLB supported the workers' right to organize unions, required employers to deal with shop committees, and arbitrated labor disputes.

Wartime Opportunities

Women took on new jobs during the war, working as mail carriers, police officers, drill-press operators, and farm laborers attached to the Women's Land Army. These three women clearly enjoyed the camaraderie of working in a railroad yard in 1918. When the war ended, women usually lost such employment. (National Archives, photo by M. Rudolph Vetter)

A Southern Migrant

T he Great Migration of southern African Americans to the cities of the North disrupted communities and families, but the migrants kept in touch with friends and kin through letters and visits. While cities like Chicago offered new opportunities and experiences, as this letter indicates, migrants often found churches that provided important continuity with their southern past.

My dear Sister: I was agreeably surprised to hear from you and to hear from home. . . . I got here in time to attend one of the greatest revivals in the history of my life—over 500 people joined the church. . . . It was snowing some nights and if you didnt hurry you could not get standing room. Please remember me kindly to any who ask of me. The people are rushing here by the thousands and I know if you come and rent a big house you can get all the roomers you want. You write me exactly when you are coming. I am not keeping house yet I am living with my brother and his wife. . . . I can get a nice place for you to stop until you can look around and see what you want. I am quite busy. I work in Swifts packing Co. in the sausage department. My daughter and I work for the same company— We get $1.50 a day and we pack so many sausages we don't have much time to play but it is a matter of a dollar with me and I feel that god made the path and I am walking therein.

Tell your husband work is plentiful here and he wont have to loaf if he want to work. . . . Well goodbye from your sister in Christ.

SOURCE: *Journal of Negro History,* vol. 4, no. 4, 1919, p. 457.

After years of federal hostility toward labor, the NWLB's actions brought a welcome change in labor's status and power. From 1916 to 1919 AFL membership grew by almost 1 million workers, reaching over 3 million at the end of the war. Few of the wartime gains lasted, however. Like other agencies, the NWLB was quickly disbanded. Wartime inflation ate up most of the wage hikes, and a virulent postwar antiunion movement caused a rapid decline in union membership that lasted into the 1930s.

While the war emergency benefited labor, it had a special effect on workers who were traditionally excluded from many industrial jobs. For the first time, northern factories actively recruited African Americans, spawning the "Great Migration" from the South. The lure of decent jobs was potent. As one Mississippi man said in anticipation of working in northern meat-packing houses: "You could not rest in your bed at night for thoughts of Chicago." Over 400,000 African Americans moved northward to cities such as St. Louis, Chicago, New York, and Detroit during the war. Though they encountered discrimination there as well, they found new opportunities and an escape from the repressive southern agricultural system (see American Voices, "A Southern Migrant").

Mexican Americans in California, Texas, New Mexico, and Arizona also found new opportunities. Wartime labor shortages prompted many Mexican Americans to leave farm labor for industrial jobs in rapidly growing southwestern cities. Continuing political instability in Mexico following the revolution encouraged many Mexicans to relocate, temporarily or permanently, across the border, a process facilitated by newly opened railroad lines. At least 100,000 Mexicans entered the United States between 1917 and 1920, often settling in segregated neighborhoods (barrios) in urban areas, meeting discrimination similar to that faced by African Americans.

Women were the largest group to take advantage of new wartime opportunities. White women and, to a lesser degree, black and Mexican American women found that factory jobs usually reserved for men had been opened to them. About 1 million women joined the labor force for the first time, while many of the 8 million women who already held jobs switched from low-paying fields like domestic service to higher-paying industrial work. Americans soon got used to the sight of female streetcar conductors, train engineers, and defense workers. But everyone—including most working women—believed that those jobs would return to men after the war.

PROGRESSIVE REFORM IN WARTIME

Supporters of woman suffrage hoped that the war would reinvigorate reform. The National American Woman Suffrage Association (NAWSA) continued to lobby for the proposed woman suffrage amendment to the Constitution. It also threw the support of its 2 million members behind the Wilson administration, encouraging women to do their part to win the war. Women in communities all over the country labored exhaustively to promote food conservation, to protect children and women workers, and to distribute emergency relief through organizations like the Red Cross. Many agreed with Carrie Chapman Catt, president of NAWSA, that women's patriotic service could advance the cause of woman's suffrage.

Alice Paul and the National Woman's Party (NWP) took a more militant tack. To the dismay of NAWSA leaders, NWP militants began picketing the White House in July 1917 to protest their lack of the vote. Arrested and sentenced to seven months in jail, Paul and other women prisoners went on a hunger strike, which prison authorities met with forced feeding. Public shock at the women's treatment made them martyrs, drawing attention to the issue of woman's suffrage.

The combination of NWP's and NAWSA's policy of patient persuasion finally brought results. In January 1918 Woodrow Wilson withdrew his opposition to a federal woman suffrage amendment. The constitutional amendment quickly passed the House but took eighteen months to get through the Senate. Then came another year of hard work for ratification by the states. Finally, on August 26, 1920, Tennessee gave the Nineteenth Amendment the last vote it needed. The goal that had first been declared publicly at the Seneca Falls convention in 1848 was finally achieved seventy-two years later, in large part because of women's contributions to the war effort. The suffragists had posed a simple but effective moral challenge: how could the United States fight to make the world safe for democracy while denying half its citizens the right to vote?

Throughout the mobilization period, reformers pushed for a wide range of social reforms. In the name of army efficiency, or "keeping fit to fight," the federal government launched an ambitious campaign against sexually transmitted diseases, forcing the shutdown of "red-light" districts in cities with military training camps. With the cooperation of the YMCA and the YWCA, the government undertook a far-reaching sex education program, designed to enlighten both men and women about the dangers of sexual activity and the value of "social purity." Other reformers addressed the welfare of children, whom they characterized as the nation's most valuable resource. The Women's Council of National Defense, a voluntary organization with federal backing, proclaimed 1918 the year of the child, conducted a nationwide growth-monitoring program, and disseminated information about child health and nutrition. All of these idealistic crusaders described the war as just the start of a continuing battle for social welfare.

Especially active were temperance advocates, who viewed alcoholic beverages as the key social evil. In the early twentieth century, many Americans viewed the legal prohibition of alcohol as a progressive reform, not a denial of individual freedom. Urban reformers, concerned about good government, poverty, and public morality, supported a nationwide ban on drinking. The drive for Prohibition also had substantial backing in rural communities. Many people equated liquor with all the sins of the city: prostitution, crime, immigration, machine politics, and public disorder. The churches with the greatest strength in rural areas, including the Methodists, the Baptists, and the Mormons, also strongly condemned drinking. Protestants from rural areas dominated the membership of the Anti-Saloon League, which supplanted the Women's Christian Temperance Union as the leading proponent of Prohibition early in the century.

Temperance advocates were right in identifying cities as the sites of resistance to Prohibition. Alcoholic beverages, especially beer and whiskey, played an important role in the social life of certain ethnic cultures in the nation's heavily urbanized areas, especially those of German Americans and Irish Americans. Most saloons were in working-class neighborhoods and served as gathering places for workers. Machine politicians indeed conducted much of their business in bars. Thus many immigrants and working-class people opposed Prohibition, not only as an attack on drinking but as an attempt to impose middle-class cultural values on them.

Numerous states—mostly southern and midwestern states without a significant immigrant presence—already had prohibition laws, but World War I offered the impetus for national action. Because several major breweries had German names (Pabst and Busch, for example), beer drinking became unpatriotic in many people's minds. To conserve food, Congress prohibited the use of foodstuffs such as hops and barley in breweries and distilleries. Finally, in December 1917, Congress passed the Eighteenth Amendment, which would prohibit the "manufacture, sale, or transportation of intoxicating liquors." Ratified in 1919 and effective on January 16, 1920, the Eighteenth Amendment demonstrated the widening influence of the state in matters of personal behavior.

The Eighteenth Amendment was an example of how "progressive" reform efforts could benefit from the climate of war. But despite the stimulus the Great War gave to some types of reform, for the most part it blocked rather than furthered reforms. Though many Progressives had anticipated that the stronger federal presence in wartime would lead to stronger economic controls and corporate regulation, federal agencies were quickly disbanded once the war was over, reflecting the unease most Americans felt about a strong bureaucratic state. The wartime collaboration between government and business gave corporate leaders more influence in shaping the economy and government policy, not less.

PROMOTING NATIONAL UNITY

For the liberal reformers convinced that the war for democracy could promote a more just society at home, perhaps the most discouraging development was the campaign to promote "One Hundred Percent Americanism," which meant an insistence on conformity and an intolerance of dissent. It was Woodrow Wilson who had predicted what came to pass: "Once lead this people into war, and they'll forget there ever was such a thing as tolerance." But the president also recognized the need to manufacture support for the war. Ironically, his efforts to drum up support for the war themselves encouraged a repressive spirit hostile to reform.

In April 1917 Wilson formed the Committee on Public Information (CPI) to promote public support for the war. This government propaganda agency, headed by the journalist George Creel, quickly attracted progressive reformers and muckraking journalists. Professing lofty-sounding goals such as educating citizens about democracy, promoting national unity, assimilating immigrants, and breaking down the isolation of rural life, the committee also acted as a nationalizing force by promoting the development of a common ideology.

During the war the CPI touched the lives of practically every American. It distributed 75 million pieces of patriotic literature and sponsored speeches at local movie theaters, reaching cumulative audiences estimated at more than 300 million—three times the population of the United States at the time. In its zeal, the committee often ventured into hatemongering. In early 1918, for example, it encouraged speakers to use inflammatory stories of alleged German atrocities to build support for the war effort.

As a spirit of conformity pervaded the home front, many Americans found themselves targets of suspicion. Local businesses paid for newspaper and magazine ads that asked citizens to report to the Justice Department "the man who spreads pessimistic stories, cries for peace, or belittles our efforts to win the war." Posters encouraged Americans to be on the lookout for German spies. And quasi-vigilante groups such as the American Protective League mobilized about 250,000 self-appointed agents, furnished with badges issued by the Justice Department, to spy on neighbors and coworkers.

The CPI also urged ethnic groups to give up their Old World customs in the spirit of One Hundred Percent Americanism. German Americans bore the brunt of this campaign. In an orgy of hostility generated by propaganda about German militarism and atrocities, everything associated with Germany became suspect. German music, especially opera, was banished from the concert halls. Publishers removed pro-German references from textbooks, and many communities banned the teaching of the German language. Sauerkraut was renamed "liberty cabbage," and hamburgers were transformed into "liberty sandwiches." Though anti-German hysteria dissipated when the war ended, hostility toward the "hyphenated" American survived into the 1920s.

In law enforcement, officials tolerated little criticism of established values and institutions, as the suffragists picketing the White House during wartime had discovered. The main legal tools for curbing dissent were the Espionage Act of 1917 and the Sedition Act of 1918. The Espionage Act imposed stiff penalties for antiwar activities and allowed the federal government to ban treasonous materials from the mails. The postmaster general revoked the mailing privileges of groups considered to be radical, virtually shutting down their publications.

Individuals suffered as well. Because these acts defined treason and sedition loosely, they led to the conviction of more than a thousand people. The Justice Department focused particularly on socialists, who criticized the war and the draft, and on radicals like the Industrial Workers of the World (see Chapter 17), whose attacks on militarism threatened to disrupt war production in the western lumber and copper industries. Socialist party leader Eugene Debs was sentenced to ten years in jail for stating that the master classes declared war while the subject classes fought the battles. (Debs was pardoned by President Warren G. Harding in 1921.) Victor Berger, a Milwaukee socialist who had been jailed under the Espionage Act, was twice prevented from taking the seat to which he had been elected in the U.S. House of Representatives.

The courts rarely resisted these wartime excesses. In *Schenck v. United States* (1919), the Supreme Court upheld the conviction of the general secretary of the Socialist Party, Charles T. Schenck, who had been convicted of mailing pamphlets urging draftees to resist induction. In a unanimous decision, Justice Oliver Wendell Holmes ruled that an act of speech uttered under circumstances that would "create a clear and present danger to the safety of the country" could be constitutionally restricted. Because of the national war emergency, then, the Court upheld limits on freedom of speech that would not have been acceptable in peacetime. In wartime, the drive for conformity reigned, dashing reformers' optimistic hopes that war could be what philosopher John Dewey had called a "plastic juncture," in which the country would be more open to reason and progressive ideas.

An Unsettled Peace, 1919–1920

The war's end did not bring the tranquillity Americans had hoped for. Demobilization proceeded with little planning, in part because Wilson was so preoccupied with the peacemaking process. Spending only ten days in the United States between December 1918 and June 1919, for more than six months he was virtually an absentee president. Unfortunately, many urgent domestic issues demanded strong leadership that never emerged. In particular, racial, ethnic, and class tensions racked the nation as it attempted to adjust to a postwar order.

THE TREATY OF VERSAILLES

In January 1917 Woodrow Wilson had proposed a "peace without victory," since only a "peace among equals" could last. His goal was "not a balance of power, but a community of power; not organized rivalries, but an organized common peace." The keystone of Wilson's postwar plans was a permanent league of nations. But he would first have to win over a Senate that was Republican controlled and openly hostile to the treaty he had brought home.

President Wilson brought to the 1919 peace negotiations in France an almost missionary zeal. Confident in his own vision for a new world order, he believed that if necessary, "I can reach the peoples of Europe over the heads of their rulers." He scored an early victory when the Allies accepted his Fourteen Points as the basis for the peace negotiations that began in January 1919. In this blueprint for the postwar world, the president called for open diplomacy, "absolute freedom of navigation upon the seas," arms reduction, the removal of trade barriers, and an international commitment to national self-determination. Essential to Wilson's vision was the creation of a multinational organization "for the purpose of affording mutual guarantees of political independence and territorial integrity to great and small States alike." The League of Nations became Wilson's obsession.

The Fourteen Points were imbued with the spirit of progressivism. Widely distributed as propaganda during the final months of the war, Wilson's plan proposed to extend the ideals of America—democracy, freedom, and peaceful economic expansion—to the rest of the world. The League of Nations, acting as a kind of international Federal Trade Commission, would supervise disarmament and—according to the crucial Article X of its covenant—curb aggressor nations through collective military action. More grandiosely, Wilson anticipated that the League would mediate disputes between nations, preventing future wars, and thus ensuring that the Great War would be "the war to end all wars." By emphasizing these lofty goals, Wilson guaranteed disappointment: his ideals for world reformation were too far-reaching to be practical or attainable.

Twenty-seven countries sent representatives to the peace conference in Versailles, near Paris. Distrustful of the new Bolshevik regime in Russia and its call for proletarian revolution against capitalism and imperialism, the allies deliberately excluded its representatives. Nor was Germany invited. The Big Four—Wilson, Prime Minister David Lloyd George of Great Britain, Premier Georges Clemenceau of France, and Prime Minister Vittorio Orlando of Italy—did most of the negotiating. The three European leaders sought a peace that differed radically from Wilson's plan. They wanted to punish Germany and treat themselves to the spoils of war by demanding heavy reparations. In fact, before the war ended, Britain, France, and Italy had already made secret agreements to divide up the German colonies.

It is a tribute to Wilson that he managed to influence the peace settlement as much as he did. He was able to soften some of the harshest demands for reprisal against Germany. National self-determination, a fundamental principle of Wilson's Fourteen Points, bore fruit in the creation of the independent states of Austria, Hungary, Poland, Yugoslavia, and Czechoslovakia from the defeated empires of the Central Powers. The establishment of the new nations of Finland, Estonia, Lithuania, and Latvia not only upheld the principle of self-determination but also served Wilson's (and the Allies') desire to isolate Soviet Russia from the rest of Europe.

Wilson had less success in achieving other goals. He won only limited concessions regarding the colonial empires of the defeated powers. The old Central and Eastern European colonial empires were dismantled, but instead of becoming independent countries the colonies were assigned to victorious Allied nations to administer as trustees, a far cry from Wilson's ideal of national self-determination. Certain topics, such as freedom of the seas and free trade, never even appeared on the agenda because of Allied resistance. Finally, Wilson had only partial success in scaling back French and British demands for reparations from Germany, which eventually were set at $33 billion.

In the face of these disappointments, Wilson consoled himself with the negotiators' commitment to his proposed League of Nations. He acknowledged that the peace treaty had defects but expressed confidence that they could be resolved by a permanent international organization dedicated to the peaceful resolution of disputes.

On June 28, 1919, representatives gathered in the Hall of Mirrors at the Palace of Versailles to sign the peace treaty. Wilson sailed home to a public enthusiastic about a league of nations in principle. Major newspapers and the Federal Council of Churches of Christ of America supported the treaty, and even an enemy of the proposed League, Henry Cabot Lodge, acknowledged that "[T]he people of the country are very naturally fascinated by the idea of eternal preservations of the world's peace."

But by the time Wilson presented the treaty to the Senate on July 10, it was clear that the treaty was in trouble, with support in the Senate being far short of the two-thirds vote necessary for ratification. Wilson had not paid much attention to the political realities of building support for the League of Nations and the treaty in the Senate. He had failed to include a prominent Republican in the American commission that represented the United States at Versailles. Stubbornly convinced of his own rectitude and ability, he had kept the negotiations firmly in his own hands. When the Senate balked at the treaty, Wilson adamantly refused to compromise. "I shall consent to nothing," he told the French ambassador. "The Senate must take its medicine."

The Senate, however, did not oblige. And despite the president's attempt to make the 1918 congressional elections a referendum for his peace plans, Americans returned a Republican majority to Congress. Wilson and the League faced stiff opposition in the Senate. Some progressive senators, who endorsed the idea of American internationalism, felt that the peace agreement was too conservative, that it served to "validate existing empires" of the victorious Allies. The "irreconcilables," including progressive senators William E. Borah of Idaho, Hiram W. Johnson of California, and Robert M. La Follette of Wisconsin, disagreed fundamentally with the premise of permanent U.S. participation in European affairs. More influential was a group of Republicans led by Senator Henry Cabot Lodge of Massachusetts. They proposed a list of amendments that focused on Article X, the section of the League covenant that called for collective security measures when a member nation was attacked. This provision, they argued, would restrict Congress's constitutional authority to declare war and would limit the freedom of the United States to pursue a unilateral foreign policy.

Wilson refused to budge, especially not to placate Lodge, his hated political rival. Hoping to mobilize support for the treaty, in September 1919 the president launched an extensive speaking tour during which he brought large audiences to tears with his impassioned defense of the treaty. But the tour had to be cut short when the ailing sixty-two-year-old president collapsed in Pueblo, Colorado, late in September. One week later, in Washington, Wilson suffered a severe stroke that paralyzed one side of his body. While his wife, Edith Bolling Galt Wilson, his physician, and the various cabinet heads oversaw the routine business of government, Wilson slowly recovered, but he was never the same again.

From his sickbed, Wilson remained inflexible in his refusal to compromise, ordering Democratic senators to vote against all Republican amendments. The treaty came up for a vote in November 1919 but was not ratified. When another attempt in March 1920 fell seven votes short, the issue was dead. Wilson died in 1924, "as much a victim of the war," David Lloyd George noted, "as any soldier who died in the trenches."

The United States never ratified the Versailles treaty or joined the League of Nations. Many wartime issues were only partially resolved, notably Germany's future, the fate of the colonial empires, and rising nationalist demands for self-determination. These unsolved problems played a major role in the coming of World War II; some, like the competing ethnic nationalisms in the Balkans, remain unresolved today.

RACIAL STRIFE AND LABOR UNREST

Shortly after the end of the war, an author in the popular periodical *World's Work* observed that "the World War has accentuated all our differences. It has not created those differences, but it has revealed and emphasized them." Nowhere was this more evident than in race relations. Many African Americans emerged from the war determined to stand up for their rights and they contributed to a spirit of black militancy that characterized the early 1920s. The volatile mix of black migration and blacks' raised expectations as a result of service in World War I combined to exacerbate white racism. In the South the number of lynchings rose from forty-eight in 1917 to seventy-eight in 1919. Several African American men were lynched while wearing military uniforms. In the North, race riots broke out in more than twenty-five cities, with one of the first and most deadly occurring in 1917 in East St. Louis, Illinois, where nine whites and more than forty blacks died in a conflict sparked by competition over jobs at a defense plant.

By the summer of 1919, the death toll from racial violence had reached 120. One of the worst race riots in American history took place in Chicago in July, where five days of rioting left twenty-three blacks and fifteen whites dead. A variety of tensions were at work in cities where violence erupted. Black voters often determined the winners of close elections, thereby enraging white racists who resented black political influence. Blacks also competed with whites for jobs and scarce housing. Even before the July riot, blacks in Chicago had suffered the bombing of their homes and other forms of harassment. They did not sit meekly by as whites destroyed their neighborhoods: they fought back in self-defense and for their rights as citizens. Wilson's rhetoric about democracy and self-determination had raised their expectations, too.

Workers of all races harbored similar hopes for a better life after the war. The war years had brought them higher pay, shorter hours, and better working conditions. Yet many native-born Americans continued to identify unions with radicalism and foreigners, and soon after the armistice many employers resumed their attacks on union activity. In addition, rapidly rising inflation—in 1919 the cost of living was 77 percent higher than its prewar level—threatened to wipe out workers' wage increases. Nevertheless, workers hoped to hold onto and perhaps even expand their wartime gains.

The result of workers' determination—and employers' resistance—was a dramatic wave of strikes. More than 4 million workers—one in every five—went on strike in 1919, a proportion never since equaled. The year began with a walkout by shipyard workers in Seattle, a strong union town. Their action spread into a general strike that crippled the city. Another hard-fought strike disrupted the steel industry when 350,000 steel workers demanded union recognition and an end to twelve-hour shifts and the seven-day workweek. And in the fall the Boston police force shocked many Americans by going on strike. Governor Calvin Coolidge of

Massachusetts propelled himself into the political spotlight by declaring, "There is no right to strike against the public safety by anybody, anywhere, any time." Coolidge fired the entire police force, and the strike failed. The public supported this harsh reprisal, and Coolidge was rewarded with the Republican vice presidential nomination in 1920.

THE RED SCARE

A crucial factor in organized labor's failure to win many of its strikes in the postwar period was the pervasive fear of radicalism. This concern coincided with mainstream Americans' long-standing anxiety about unassimilated immigrants—an anxiety that the war had made worse. The Russian Revolution of 1917 so alarmed the Allies that Wilson sent several thousand troops to Russia in the summer of 1918 in hopes of weakening the Bolshevik regime. When the Bolsheviks founded the Third International (or Comintern) in 1919 to export communist doctrine throughout the world, American fears deepened. As domestic labor unrest increased, Americans began to see radicals everywhere. Hatred of the German Hun was quickly replaced by hostility toward the Bolshevik Reds.

Ironically, as public concern about domestic Bolshevism increased, radicals were rapidly losing members and political power. No more than 70,000 Americans belonged to either the fledgling U.S. Communist Party or the Communist Labor Party in 1919. Both the IWW and the Socialist Party had been weakened by wartime repression and internal dissent. Yet the public and the press continued to blame almost every disturbance, especially labor conflicts, on alien radicals. "REDS DIRECTING SEATTLE STRIKE—TO TEST CHANCE FOR REVOLUTION," warned a typical newspaper headline.

Tensions mounted with a series of bombings in the early spring. "The word 'radical' in 1919," the historian Robert Murray observed, "automatically carried with it the implication of dynamite." In June a bomb detonated outside the Washington townhouse of the recently appointed attorney general, A. Mitchell Palmer. His family escaped unharmed, but the bomber was blown to bits. Angling for the presidential nomination, Palmer capitalized on the event, fanning fears of domestic radicalism.

In November 1919, on the second anniversary of the Russian Revolution, the attorney general staged the first of what became known as "Palmer raids." Federal agents stormed the headquarters of radical organizations, capturing supposedly revolutionary booty such as a set of blueprints for a phonograph (at first thought to be sketches for a bomb). The dragnet pulled in thousands of aliens who had committed no crime but were suspect because of their anarchist or revolutionary beliefs or their immigrant backgrounds. Lacking the protection of U.S. citizenship, they faced deportation without formal trial or indictment. In December 1919 the U.S.S. *Buford*, nicknamed the "Soviet Ark," embarked for Finland and the Soviet state with a cargo of 294 deported radicals.

The peak of Palmer's power came with his New Year's raids in January 1920. In one night, with the greatest possible publicity, federal agents rounded up 6,000 radicals, invading private homes, union headquarters, and meeting halls and arresting citizens and aliens alike. Palmer was riding high in his ambitions for the presidency, but then he overstepped himself. He predicted that on May Day 1920 an unnamed conspiracy would attempt to overthrow the U.S. government. State militia units and police went on twenty-four-hour alert to guard the nation against the threat of revolutionary violence, but not a single incident occurred. As the summer of 1920 passed without major labor strikes or renewed bombings, the hysteria of the Red Scare began to abate.

The wartime legacy of antiradicalism and anti-immigrant sentiment, however, persisted well into the next decade. In May 1920, at the height of the Red Scare, Nicola Sacco, a shoemaker, and Bartolomeo Vanzetti, a fish peddler, were arrested for the robbery and murder of a shoe company's paymaster in South Braintree, Massachusetts. The two men, self-proclaimed anarchists and alien draft evaders, were both armed at the time of their arrest.

Convicted in 1921, Sacco and Vanzetti sat on death row for six years while supporters appealed their verdicts. Although new evidence suggesting their innocence surfaced, Judge Webster Thayer denied a motion for a new trial. Scholars still debate the question of their guilt, but most agree that the two anarchists did not receive a fair trial, that both the evidence and procedures were tainted. The verdict stemmed as much from their status as radicals and immigrants as it did from evidence. As future Supreme Court jurist Felix Frankfurter said at the time, "The District Attorney invoked against them a riot of political passion and patriotic sentiment." Nevertheless, shortly before his execution in the electric chair on August 23, 1927, Vanzetti claimed triumph:

> If it had not been for these thing, I might have live out my life among scorning men. I might have die, unmarked, unknown, a failure. . . . Never in our full life can we hope to do such work for tolerance, for justice, for man's understanding of man, as now we do by an accident.

This oft-quoted elegy captures the eloquence and tolerance of a man caught in the last spasm of antiradicalism and fear that capped America's participation in the Great War.

That participation left other legacies as well. World War I did not have the catastrophic effect on the United States that it did on European countries. With relatively few casualties and no physical destruction at home, America emerged from the conflict stronger than ever before. Consolidating developments that had begun with the Spanish-American War, the United States became a major international power, both economically and politically. Increased efficiency and technological advancements fostered exceptional industrial productivity, making the United States the envy of the rest of the world in the postwar decade. And though mobilization

T I M E L I N E

1914	Outbreak of war in Europe		Armistice ends war.
	United States declares neutrality.		U.S. troops intervene in Russia.
1915	German submarine sinks *Lusitania*.	1919	Treaty of Versailles
			Chicago race riot
1916	Woodrow Wilson reelected president		Steel strike
1917	U.S. enters World War I.		Red Scare and Palmer raids
	Selective Service Act passed		*Schenck v. United States*
	War Industries Board established		American Legion founded
	Suffrage militancy		League of Nations defeated in Senate
	East St. Louis race riot		Eighteenth Amendment (Prohibition) ratified
	Espionage Act passed		War Industries Board disbanded
	Bolshevik Revolution		
	Committee on Public Information established	1920	Nineteenth Amendment (woman suffrage)
1918	Wilson proposes Fourteen Point peace plan.		Sacco and Vanzetti arrested
	Meuse-Argonne campaign	1924	Woodrow Wilson dies.
	Eugene Debs imprisoned under Sedition Act		

was accompanied by an insistence on as much voluntarism as possible, the war emergency did leave a legacy of a stronger federal government and an enlarged bureaucracy. Finally, the war—especially the nationalism that accompanied it—contributed to a climate that was inhospitable to liberal social reforms, a climate that would persist until the crisis of the Great Depression.

For Further Exploration

Meirion Harries and Susie Harries, *The Last Days of Innocence: America at War, 1917–1918* (1997), is a recent overview that admirably captures America's war experience at home and abroad. Frank Freidel, *Over There: The Story of America's First Great Overseas Crusade* (1990), offers soldiers' vivid firsthand accounts of the war. William M. Tuttle Jr., *Race Riot: Chicago in the Red Summer of 1919* (1970), provides a moving and thoughtful analysis of that devastating riot, as well as a good summary of the "Great Migration" of African Americans. For the war in fiction begin with William March, *Company K* (1993), and Ernest Hemingway's *In Our Time* (1925) and *A Farewell to Arms* (1929). *Pale Horse, Pale Rider* (1939) by Katherine Anne Porter offers insight to the war on the homefront.

The Library of Congress website, "American Leaders Speak: Recordings from World War I and the 1920 Election," available at <http://memory.loc.gov/ammem/nfhome.html>, offers voice recordings of John J. Pershing and other key figures of the World War I era. "The

Diary of Bugler Benjamin Edgar Cruzan," Battery F, 341st Field Artillery, 89th Division, 3rd Army, in which an ordinary soldier poignantly discusses his battle experiences, friendships, and the peace negotiations, is provided at <http://www2.mo-net.com/~mcruzan/diary.htm>. "World War I Documents Archive" at <http://www.lib.byu.edu/~rdh/wwi> provides extensive primary documents as well as a series of World War I links. The Public Broadcasting Service's "The Great War and the Shaping of the Twentieth Century" at <http://www.pbs.org/greatwar/index.html> is a companion to the documentary series. Its rich offerings, which emphasize the European context of the war, include bibliographies and maps.

Chapter 23

MODERN TIMES
The 1920s

> Modern life is everywhere complicated, but especially so in the
> United States. . . . The tendency to seize upon new types of
> machines, rich natural resources and vast driving power, have
> hurried us dizzily away from the days of the frontier into a whirl of
> modernisms which almost passes belief.
>
> —REPORT OF THE PRESIDENT'S COMMISSION
> ON RECENT SOCIAL TRENDS, 1933

In 1924 the sociologists Robert Lynd and Helen Merrell Lynd arrived in Muncie, Indiana, to study the life of a small American city. They observed how the citizens of Middletown (the fictional name they gave the city) made a living, maintained a home, educated their young, practiced their religion, organized community activities, and spent their leisure time. As the Lynds' fieldwork proceeded, they were struck by how much had changed over the past thirty-five years—the lifetime of a middle-aged Middletown resident—and decided to contrast the Muncie of the 1890s with the Muncie of the 1920s. When *Middletown* was published in 1929, this "study in modern American culture" became an unexpected best seller. Its success spoke to Americans' desire to understand the forces that were transforming their society.

This transformation had begun with World War I. The United States emerged from the war as a powerful modern state and a major player in the world economy. The 1920s, however, rather than World War I were the watershed in the development of a mass national culture. Only then did the Protestant work ethic and the old values of self-denial and frugality begin to give way to the fascination with consumption, leisure, and self-realization that is the essence of modern American culture. In economic organization, political outlook, and cultural values, the 1920s had more in common with the United States today than with the industrializing America of the late nineteenth century.

Business-Government Partnership of the 1920s

The business-government partnership fostered by World War I continued on an informal basis throughout the 1920s. As the *Wall Street Journal* enthusiastically proclaimed, "Never before, here or anywhere else, has a government been so completely fused with business." From 1922 to 1929 the nation's prosperity seemed to confirm the economy's ability to regulate itself with minimal government intervention. Gone or at least submerged was the reform impulse of the Progressive Era. Business leaders were no longer villains but respected public figures. President Warren G. Harding captured the prevailing political mood when he offered the American public "not heroics but healing, not nostrums but normalcy."

POLITICS IN THE REPUBLICAN "NEW ERA"

Except for Woodrow Wilson's two terms, the Republican Party had controlled the presidency since 1896. When Wilson's progressive coalition floundered in 1918, the Republicans had a chance to regain the White House. With the ailing Wilson out of the picture, in the 1920 election the Democrats nominated Governor James M. Cox of Ohio for president and Assistant Secretary of the Navy Franklin D. Roosevelt as vice president. The Democratic platform called for U.S. participation in the League of Nations and a continuation of Wilson's progressivism. The Republicans, led by Warren G. Harding and Calvin Coolidge, promised a return to "normalcy," which meant a strong probusiness stance and conservative cultural values. Harding and Coolidge won in a landslide, marking the beginning of a Republican dominance that would last until 1932.

Central to what Republicans termed the "New Era" was business-government cooperation. Although Republican administrations generally opposed expanding state power to promote progressive reforms, they had no qualms about using federal policy and power to assist corporations. Thus, Harding's secretary of the treasury, financier Andrew W. Mellon, engineered a tax cut that undercut the wartime Revenue Acts, benefiting wealthy individuals and corporations. The Republican-dominated Federal Trade Commission (FTC) for the most part ignored the antitrust laws rather than using federal power to police industry. In this the Commission followed the lead of the Supreme Court, which in 1920 had dismissed the long-pending antitrust case against U.S. Steel, ruling that largeness in business was not against the law as long as some competition remained.

Perhaps the best example of government-business cooperation emerged in the Department of Commerce, headed by Herbert Hoover, who was a believer in what historian Ellis Hawley has called the "associative state." Hoover thought that with the offer of government assistance, businessmen would voluntarily work in behalf of the public interest, thereby benefiting the entire country. Under Hoover the Commerce Department expanded dramatically, offering new services like the compilation and distribution of trade and production statistics to American business. It also assisted private trade associations in their efforts to rationalize and make more efficient major sectors of industry and commerce by cooperating in such areas as product standardization and wage and price controls.

Unfortunately, not all government-business cooperation was as high-minded as Hoover had anticipated. President Harding was basically an honest man, but some of his political associates were not. When Harding died suddenly of a heart attack in San Francisco in August 1923, evidence of widespread fraud and corruption in his administration had just come to light. In 1924 a particularly damaging scandal concerned the secret leasing of government oil reserves in Teapot Dome, Wyoming, and in Elk Hills, California, without competitive bidding. Secretary of the Interior Albert Fall was eventually convicted of taking $300,000 in bribes; he became the first cabinet officer in American history to serve a prison sentence.

After Harding's death the taciturn vice president, Calvin Coolidge, moved into the White House. In contrast to his predecessor's political cronyism and outgoing style, Coolidge personified an austere rectitude. As vice president "Silent Cal" often sat through official functions without uttering a word. A dinner partner once challenged him by saying, "Mr. Coolidge, I've made a rather sizable bet with my friends that I can get you to speak three words this evening." Responded Coolidge icily, "You lose." Although Coolidge was quiet and unimaginative, his image of unimpeachable integrity reassured voters, and he soon announced his candidacy for the presidency in 1924.

When the Democrats gathered that July in the sweltering heat of New York City, they faced a divided party that drew its support mainly from the South and from northern urban political machines like Tammany Hall in New York. These two constituencies often collided. They disagreed mightily over Prohibition, immigration restriction, and most seriously the mounting power of the racist and anti-immigrant Ku Klux Klan. The resolutions committee remained deadlocked for days over whether the party should condemn the Klan, eventually reaching a weak compromise that affirmed its general opposition to "any effort to arouse religious or racial dissension."

With this contentious background, the convention took 103 ballots to nominate John W. Davis, a Wall Street lawyer, for the presidency. To attract rural voters, the Democrats chose as their vice presidential candidate Governor Charles W. Bryan of Nebraska, William Jennings Bryan's brother. But the Democrats could not mount an effective challenge to their more popular and better-financed Republican rivals, whose strength came chiefly from the native-born Protestant middle class, augmented by small-business people, skilled workers, farmers, northern blacks, and wealthy industrialists. Until the Democrats could overcome their sectional and cultural divisions and build an effective national organization to rival that of the Republicans, they would remain a minority party.

The 1924 campaign also featured a third-party challenge by Senator Robert M. La Follette of Wisconsin, who ran on the Progressive Party ticket. La Follette's candidacy mobilized reformers and labor leaders as well as disgruntled farmers in an effort to reinvigorate the reform movement both major parties had abandoned. Their platform called for nationalization of railroads, public ownership of utilities, and the right of Congress to overrule Supreme Court decisions. It also favored the direct election of the president by the voters rather than by indirect election through the electoral college.

In an impressive Republican victory Coolidge received 15.7 million popular votes to Davis's 8.4 million and won a decisive margin in the electoral college. La Follette chalked up almost 5 million popular votes, but he carried only Wisconsin in the electoral college. Perhaps the most significant aspect of the election was the low voter turnout. Only 52 percent of the electorate cast their ballots in 1924, compared to more than 70 percent in presidential elections of the late nineteenth century. Newly enfranchised women voters were not to blame, however; a long-term drop in voting by men, rather than apathy among women, caused the decline.

Instead of resting after their suffrage victory, women increased their political activism in the 1920s. African American women struggled for voting rights in the Jim Crow South and pushed unsuccessfully for a federal antilynching law. Many women tried to break into party politics, but Democrats and Republicans granted them only token positions on party committees. Women were more influential as lobbyists. The Women's Joint Congressional Committee, a Washington-based coalition of ten major white women's organizations, including the newly formed League of Women Voters, lobbied actively for reform legislation (see American Voices, "Women Get the Vote"). Its major accomplishment was the passage in 1921 of the Sheppard-Towner Federal Maternity and Infancy Act, which appropriated $1.25 million for well-baby clinics, educational programs, and visiting-nurse projects. Such major reform legislation was rare in the 1920s, however, and its success short-lived. Once politicians realized that women did not vote as a bloc, they stopped listening to the women's lobby, and in 1929 Congress cut off the act's funding.

The roadblocks women activists faced were part of a broader public antipathy to ambitious reforms. Although some states—such as New York, where an urban liberalism was coalescing under leaders like Al Smith—did enact a flurry of legislation that promoted workmen's compensation, public health programs, and conservation measures, on the national level reforms that would strengthen federal power made little headway. After years of progressive reforms and an expanded federal presence in World War I, Americans were unenthusiastic about increased taxation or more governmental bureaucracy. The Red Scare had given ammunition to opponents of reform by making it easy to claim that legislation calling for governmental activism was the first step toward Bolshevism. The general prosperity of the 1920s further hampered the reform spirit. With a strong economy, the Republican policy of an informal partnership between business and government seemed to work and made reforms regulating corporations and the economy seem unnecessary and even harmful.

THE HEYDAY OF BIG BUSINESS

Although prosperity and the 1920s seem almost synonymous, the decade got off to a bumpy start in the transition from a wartime to a peacetime economy. In the immediate postwar years the nation suffered rampant inflation: prices jumped by a third in 1919, accompanied by feverish business activity. Federal efforts to halt

AMERICAN VOICES

Women Get the Vote

DAISY HARRIMAN AND EMILY NEWELL BLAIR

*I*n her autobiography, Daisy Harriman recounted the comments of another activist woman, *Emily Newell Blair, about the difficulties of encouraging newly enfranchised women to vote. Both Blair and Harriman hoped to harness these potential new voters to promote a broad agenda of social reform and women's rights. Of particular concern, as this passage indicates, was the plight of working women.*

Men and women are just alike, human beings with the same hopes and instincts, [yet] still we have to go on talking about "the woman vote" as though it were something separate, because we are all so interested in going after women who never have taken the slightest interest in politics, and in introducing them for the first time to the political sphere. And to do this, since most women work and live in "the home," one has to have a special organization to reach "women" as they bend over cradles and roll out the biscuits on the breadboard, as they darn Pa's socks or wash up the family dishes. Women are still separate, not only biologically, which doesn't count for so much in politics, but economically. They are the vast body of homeworkers, sometimes sweated and sometimes petted. The American wife is supposed to be a member of the great leisure-class and I suppose it is true that more American wives have more time to waste or to pursue culture than any other people in the world. . . . [But] of all statistics the ones that have impressed and shocked me the most are those that Margaret Hinchey, the laundry worker, once gave me,—that in New York alone more than 14,000 old women over sixty-five years of age are dependent upon their own labors for support. I suppose most of those 14,000 old women spent the best part of their lives doing domestic service for some man. I look forward to a time when women, even if they keep on at the old business of having for their main job the making of man comfortable, and themselves too,—sometimes, of course,—will use the vote in order to make the world a more pleasant place to be thrown on, and to work in, when their heads are gray and their joints stiff.

SOURCE: Mrs. J. Borden Harriman, *From Pinafores to Politics* (London: Allen & Unwin, [1923?]), p. 353.

inflation—through spending cuts and a contraction of the supply of credit—produced the recession of 1920 and 1921, the sharpest short-term downturn the United States had ever faced. Unemployment reached 10 percent. Foreign trade dropped by almost half as European nations resumed production after the disruptions of war. Prices fell dramatically—more than 20 percent—and reversed much of the wartime inflation.

The recession was short. In 1922, stimulated by an abundance of consumer products, particularly automobiles, the economy began a recovery that continued with only brief interruptions through 1929. Between 1922 and 1929 the gross national product (GNP) grew from $74.1 billion to $103.1 billion, approximately 40 percent. Per capita income rose from $641 in 1921 to $847 in 1929. Soon the federal government was recording a budget surplus. This economic expansion provided the backdrop for the partnership between business and government.

As industries churned out an abundance of new consumer products—cars, appliances, chemicals, electricity, radios, aircraft, and movies—manufacturing output expanded 64 percent. Behind the growth lay new techniques of management and mass production, which brought a 40 percent increase in workers' productivity. The demand for goods and services kept unemployment low in most industries throughout the decade. High employment rates, combined with low inflation, enhanced the spending power of many Americans, especially skilled workers and the middle class.

The economy, however, had some weaknesses. Income distribution reflected significant disparity: 5 percent of the nation's families received one-third of all income. In addition, a number of industries were unhealthy. Agriculture never fully recovered from the 1920 and 1921 recession. During the inflationary period of 1914 to 1920 farmers had borrowed heavily to finance mortgages and equipment in response to government incentives, increased demand, and rising prices. When the war ended, European countries resumed agricultural production, glutting the world market. The price of wheat dropped 40 percent as the government withdrew wartime price supports. Corn prices fell 32 percent, and hog prices 50 percent. Farmers were not the only ones whose incomes plunged. Certain "sick industries," such as coal and textiles, had also expanded in response to wartime demand, which dropped sharply at war's end. Their troubles foreshadowed the Great Depression of the 1930s.

But for the most part, despite these ominous signs, the nation was in a confident mood about the economy and the corporations that shaped it. Throughout the decade business leaders enjoyed enormous popularity and respect; their reputations often surpassed those of the era's lackluster politicians. The most revered businessman of the decade was Henry Ford, whose rise from poor farm boy to corporate giant embodied both the traditional value of individualism and the triumph of mass production. Success stories like Ford's prompted President Calvin Coolidge to declare solemnly, "The man who builds a factory builds a temple. The man who works there worships there."

In this apotheosis of big business the 1920s saw the triumph of the managerial revolution that had been reshaping American business since the late nineteenth century (see Chapter 17), as large-scale corporate organizations with bureaucratic structures of authority replaced family-run enterprises. There were more mergers in the 1920s than at any time since the flourishing of business combinations in the 1880s and 1890s, with the largest number occurring in rapidly growing industries like chemicals, electrical appliances, and automobiles. By 1930 the 200 largest corporations controlled almost half the nonbanking corporate wealth in the United States. Rarely did any single corporation monopolize an entire industry; instead, oligopolies, in which a few large producers controlled an industry, became the norm, as in auto manufacturing, oil, and steel. The nation's financial institutions expanded and consolidated along with its corporations. Total bank assets rose dramatically as mergers between Wall Street banks enhanced New York's role as the financial center of the world. In 1929 almost half the nation's banking resources were controlled by 1 percent of American banks (250 banks).

Most Americans benefited from corporate success in the 1920s. Although unskilled African Americans and immigrants participated far less fully in the prosperity of the decade, many members of the working class enjoyed higher wages and a better standard of living. A shorter workweek (five full days and a half day on Saturday) and paid vacations gave many more leisure time. But despite those benefits labor had less power in the workplace. Scientific management techniques, first introduced in 1895 by Frederick W. Taylor but widely implemented only in the 1920s, reduced workers' control over their labor.

The 1920s were also the heyday of "welfare capitalism," a system of labor relations that stressed management's responsibility for employees' well-being. At a time when unemployment compensation and government-sponsored pensions did not exist, large corporations offered workers stock plans, health insurance, and old-age pension plans. Employee security was not, however, the primary aim of the programs, which were established mainly to deter the formation of unions. The approach reflected the conservative values of the 1920s, which placed the responsibility for economic welfare in the private sector to avoid government interference on the side of labor. Coupled with an aggressive drive for what corporate leaders called the American Plan (or an open, nonunion shop) and with Supreme Court decisions that limited workers' ability to strike, welfare capitalism helped to erode the unions' strength. Membership dropped from 5.1 million in 1920 to 3.6 million in 1929—about 10 percent of the nonagricultural workforce—and the number of strikes also fell dramatically from the level in 1919. Technology and management had combined to undermine workers' power.

ECONOMIC POWER ABROAD

The power of American corporations emerged also in the international arena. During the 1920s the United States was the most productive country in the world, with an enormous capacity to compete in foreign markets that eagerly desired American consumer products such as radios, telephones, automobiles, and sewing machines. The demand for U.S. capital was just as great. American investment abroad more than doubled between 1919 and 1930: by the end of the 1920s American corporations had invested $15.2 billion in foreign countries. Soon the United States became the world's largest creditor nation, reversing its pre–World War I status as a debtor and causing a dramatic shift of power in the world's capital markets.

A wide variety of American companies aggressively sought investment opportunities abroad. General Electric built plants in Latin America, China, Japan, and Australia; Ford had major facilities throughout the British empire. The United Fruit Company developed plantations in Costa Rica, Honduras, and Guatemala. American capital ran sugar plantations in Cuba and rubber plantations in the Philippines, Sumatra, and Malaya. Standard Oil of New Jersey led American oil companies in acquiring oil reserves in Mexico and Venezuela.

American power abroad was also evident in the country's new role as a creditor nation. European countries, particularly Germany, needed American capital to

Bananas
... a good mixer
with every fruit that grows

Oranges, apples, grapefruit, pineapples, pears, melons, grapes—all these and many others—blend perfectly with bananas. The distinctive flavor of the banana, when added to a fruit cup, a fruit salad, or any fruit combination, brings out the flavor of the other fruits and makes them taste better.

"Ripe bananas are good for little children."

"EAT plenty of fresh fruits" is now an accepted principle of diet—and the mere sight of mellow, luscious bananas is an invitation to serve many delicious and nourishing fruit combinations.

All year round from the tropics ... Easter, Fourth of July, Thanksgiving, Christmas—every season, every day—bananas are available. Thanks to the nearness and all-year-round productiveness of the tropics, they always can be had at your grocery or fruit store.

Children crave the temptingly flavored banana instinctively. And it is well that they do, for bananas are one of the most important energy-producing foods. Doctors and dietitians consider the banana not only one of the most *valuable* foods, but also one of the most *easily digested* ... as beneficial for grown-ups as for children.

Serve bananas with other fruits, with cereals, with milk or cream ... or serve them plain. But always be sure they are fully ripe (generously flecked with brown spots). If they are not at the proper stage of ripeness when you buy them, let them ripen at room temperature. Never place them in the ice-box.

UNIFRUIT BANANAS
Reg. U. S. Pat. Off.
A United Fruit Company Product
Imported and Distributed by Fruit Dispatch Company
17 Battery Place, New York, N. Y.

American Companies Abroad

United Fruit was one of the many American companies that found opportunities for investment in South America in the 1920s. Bananas were such a new and exotic fruit that advertisements had to tell consumers such facts as how to tell when bananas are ripe and how to store them (never refrigerate). (Duke University Library, Special Collections)

finance their economic recovery following World War I. Germany had to rebuild its economy and pay reparations to the Allies; Britain and France had to repay wartime loans. As late as 1930 the Allies still owed the United States $4.3 billion. American political leaders, responding to voters' disenchantment with the cost of the war, rigidly demanded payment. "They hired the money, didn't they?" President Coolidge scoffed.

European countries had difficulty repaying their debts because the United States was maintaining high protective tariffs against foreign-made goods. The Fordney-McCumber Tariff of 1922 and the Hawley-Smoot Tariff of 1930 advanced the long-standing Republican policy of protectionism and economic nationalism. Most American manufacturers favored high tariffs because they feared foreign competition would reduce their profits. But the difficulty of selling goods in the United States hindered European nations' efforts to pay off their debts in dollars.

In 1924, at the prodding of the United States, the nations of France, Great Britain, and Germany joined with the United States in a plan to promote European financial stability. The Dawes Plan (named for Charles G. Dawes, the Chicago banker who negotiated the agreement) offered Germany substantial loans from American banks and a reduction in the amount of reparations owed to the Allies. But the Dawes Plan did not provide a permanent solution because the international economic system was inherently unstable. It depended on the flow of American capital to Germany, reparations payments from Germany to the Allies, and the repayment of the Allies' debts to the United States. If the outflow of capital from the United States were to slow or stop, the international financial structure could collapse.

American efforts to shore up the international economy belie the common view of U.S. foreign affairs as isolationist in the interwar period—as representing a time when the United States, disillusioned after World War I, willfully retreated from involvement in the rest of the world. In fact, the United States played an active role in world affairs during this period. Expansion into new markets was fundamental to the prosperity of the 1920s. U.S. officials ardently sought a stable international order to facilitate American investments in Latin American, European, and Asian markets.

They continued the quest for peaceful ways to dominate the Western Hemisphere both economically and diplomatically but retreated slightly from military intervention in Latin America. U.S. troops withdrew from the Dominican Republic in 1924 but remained in Nicaragua almost continuously from 1912 to 1933 and in Haiti from 1915 to 1934. Relations with Mexico remained tense, a legacy of U.S. intervention during the Mexican Revolution and of U.S. resentment over the Mexican government's efforts to wrest control of its oil and mineral deposits away from foreign owners, a policy that particularly alarmed American oil companies.

There was little popular or political support, however, for entangling diplomatic commitments to allies, European or otherwise. The United States never joined the League of Nations or the Court of International Justice (the World Court). International cooperation had to come through other forums, such as the 1921 Washington Naval Arms Conference. At that meeting, the leading naval powers—Britain, the United States, Japan, Italy, and France—agreed to halt construction of large battleships for ten years and to limit their future shipbuilding to a set ratio between the five nations of 5 to 5 to 3 to 1.75 to 1.75, respectively. By placing limits on naval expansion, policymakers hoped to encourage stability in areas like the Far East and to protect the fragile postwar economy from an expensive arms race. A thinly veiled agenda was to contain Japan, whose expansionist tendencies in Asia were alarming other nations.

Seven years later, in a similar spirit of international cooperation the United States joined other nations in condemning militarism through the Kellogg-Briand Peace Pact. Fifteen nations signed the pact in Paris in 1928; forty-eight more approved it later. The signatories agreed to "condemn recourse to war for the solution of international controversies, and renounce it as an instrument of national policy." U.S. peace groups such as the Women's International League for Peace and Freedom enthusiastically supported the pact, and the U.S. Senate ratified it eighty-five to one. Yet critics complained that it lacked mechanisms for enforcement, calling it nothing more than an "international kiss."

In the end, fervent hopes and pious declarations were no cure for the massive economic, political, and territorial problems created by World War I. U.S. policymakers vacillated, as they would in the 1930s, between wanting to play a larger role in world events and fearing that treaties and responsibilities would limit their ability to act unilaterally. Their diplomatic efforts ultimately proved inadequate to the mounting crises that followed in the wake of the war.

A New National Culture

The 1920s represented an important watershed in the development of a mass national culture. A new emphasis on leisure, consumption, and amusement characterized the era, although their benefits were more accessible to the middle class than to disadvantaged groups. Automobiles, paved roads, the parcel post service, movies, radios, telephones, mass-circulation magazines, brand names, chain stores—all linked mill towns in the southern Piedmont, rural outposts on the Oklahoma plains, and ethnic enclaves on the coasts in an expanding web of national experience. In fact, with the exportation of automobiles, radios, and movies to consumers throughout the world, the American experience became a global model.

A CONSUMER CULTURE

In homes across the country Americans sat down to a breakfast of Kellogg's corn flakes and toast from a General Electric toaster. Then they got into a Ford Model T to go about their business, perhaps shopping at one of the chain stores that had sprung up across the country, such as Safeway or A&P. In the evening the family gathered to listen to radio programs like *Great Moments in History* or to read the latest issue of the *Saturday Evening Post;* on weekends they might go to see the newest Charlie Chaplin film at the local theater. Millions of Americans, in other words, now shared similar daily experiences.

Yet participation in commercial mass culture was not universal, nor did it necessarily mean total conversion to mainstream values, as is often assumed. The historian Lizabeth Cohen concluded that "Chicago's ethnic workers were not transformed into more Americanized, middle-class people by the objects they consumed. Buying an electric vacuum cleaner did not turn Josef Dobrowolski into *True Story's* Jim Smith." What is more, the unequal distribution of income limited many consumers' ability to buy the enticing new products. At the height of the nation's prosperity in the 1920s about 65 percent of families had incomes of less than $2,000 a year, which barely supported a decent standard of living. Poor minority families in particular were isolated from the new consumerism. Many Americans stretched their incomes by buying on the newly devised installment plan: in 1927 two-thirds of the cars in the United States had been bought "on time." Once consumers saw how easily they could finance a car, they bought radios, refrigerators, and sewing machines on credit. "A dollar down and a dollar forever," one cynic remarked.

Many of the new products were household appliances made feasible by the rapid electrification of American homes. Such technological advances had a dramatic impact on women's lives, for despite enfranchisement and participation in the workforce the primary role for most women continued to be that of housewife. Electric appliances made housewives' chores less arduous. Plugging in an electric iron was far easier than heating an iron on the stove; using a vacuum cleaner was quicker and easier than wielding a broom and a rug beater. Paradoxically, however, the new products did not dramatically increase women's leisure time. Instead, more middle-class housewives began to do their own housework and laundry, replacing human servants with electric ones. The new gadgets also raised standards of cleanliness, encouraging women to spend more time doing household chores.

Few of the new consumer products could be considered necessities. But the advertising industry, which became big business in this period, spent billions of dollars annually to entice consumers into buying automobiles, cigarettes, radios, and refrigerators. Advertisers appealed to people's social aspirations by projecting images of successful and elegant sophisticates who smoked a certain brand of cigarette or drove a recognizable make of car. Ad writers also sold products by preying on people's insecurities, coming up with a variety of socially unacceptable "diseases," from "office hips" and "ashtray breath" to the dreaded "B.O." (body odor).

Yet consumers were not merely passive victims. Advertisers recognized that the buying public made choices and struggled to offer messages that appealed to their targeted audiences. In the process they made consumption a cultural ideal for most of the middle class. Character, religion, and social standing, once the main criteria for judging self-worth, became less important than the gratification of personal needs through the acquisition of more and better possessions.

No possession typified the new consumer culture better than the automobile. "Why on earth do you need to study what's changing this country?" a Muncie, Indiana, resident asked the sociologists Robert and Helen Lynd. "I can tell you what's happening in just four letters: A-U-T-O!" The showpiece of modern capitalism, the automobile revolutionized the way Americans spent their money and leisure time. In the wake of the automobile the isolation of rural life broke down. Cars touched so many aspects of American life that the word *automobility* was coined to describe their impact on production methods, the landscape, and American values.

Mass production of cars stimulated the prosperity of the 1920s. Before the introduction of the moving assembly line in 1913, Ford workers took twelve and a half hours to put together an auto; on an assembly line they took only ninety-three minutes. By 1927 Ford was producing a car every twenty-four seconds. Auto sales climbed from 1.5 million in 1921 to 5 million in 1929, a year in which Americans spent $2.58

All in a Day's Work

Parked in the testing ground at Ford's huge River Rouge plant in Dearborn, Michigan, sit 1,000 assembled chassis, a single day's production.

(From the Collections of the Henry Ford Museum and Greenfield Village)

billion on new and used cars. By the end of the decade Americans owned about 80 percent of the world's automobiles—an average of one car for every five people.

The success of the auto industry had a ripple effect on the American economy. In 1929, 3.7 million workers owed their jobs to the automobile, either directly or indirectly. Auto production stimulated the steel, petroleum, chemical, rubber, and glass industries. Highway construction became a billion-dollar-a-year enterprise, financed by federal subsidies and state gasoline taxes. Car ownership also spurred the growth of suburbs, contributed to real-estate speculation, and in 1924 spawned the first shopping center, Country Club Plaza in Kansas City. Not even the death of 25,000 people a year in traffic accidents—70 percent of them pedestrians—could dampen America's passion for the automobile.

The auto also changed the way Americans spent their leisure time. They took to the roads, becoming a nation of tourists. The American Automobile Association, founded in 1902, reported that in 1929 about 45 million people—almost a third of the population—took vacations by automobile, patronizing the "autocamps" and tourist cabins that were the forerunners of motels. And like movies and other products of the new mass culture, cars changed the dating patterns of young Americans. Contrary to many parents' views, premarital sex was not invented in the backseat of a Ford, but a Model T offered more privacy and comfort than did the family living room or the front porch and contributed to increased sexual experimentation among the young.

MASS MEDIA AND NEW PATTERNS OF LEISURE

Equal in importance to the automobile in transforming American culture were the increasingly significant mass media. The movie industry probably did more than anything else to disseminate common values and attitudes. In contrast to Europe where cinema developed as an avant-garde, highbrow art form, in America movies were part of popular culture almost from the start. They began around the turn of the century in nickelodeons, where for a nickel the mostly working-class audience could see a one-reel silent film like the spectacularly successful *The Great Train Robbery* (1903). Because the films, mostly comedies and melodramas, were silent, they could be understood by immigrants who did not speak English. Both democratic and highly lucrative, the new medium quickly became popular.

By 1910 the movie-making industry had concentrated in southern California, which had cheap land, plenty of sunshine, and varied scenery—mountains, deserts, cities, and the Pacific Ocean—within easy reach. Another attraction was Los Angeles's reputation as an antiunion town. By war's end the United States was producing 90 percent of the world's films. Foreign distribution of Hollywood films stimulated the market for the material culture so lavishly displayed on the screen.

As directors turned to feature films and began exhibiting them in large, ornate theaters, movies quickly outgrew their working-class audiences and began to appeal to the middle class. Early movie stars—the comedians Buster Keaton, Charlie

Chaplin, and Harold Lloyd; Mary Pickford ("America's Sweetheart," though born in Canada); and dashing leading men Douglas Fairbanks, Wallace Reid, and John Gilbert—became national idols who helped to set national trends in clothing and hairstyles. Then a new cultural icon, the flapper, burst on the scene to represent emancipated womanhood. Clara Bow, the It Girl (*It* represented "sex appeal"), was Hollywood's favorite flapper, a bobbed-haired "jazz baby" who rose to stardom almost overnight. Decked out in short skirt and rolled-down silk stockings, the flapper wore makeup (once assumed to be a sign of sexual availability in lower-class women), smoked, and danced to jazz, flaunting her liberated lifestyle. Like so many cultural icons, the flapper represented only a tiny minority of women. Yet the movies, along with advertising, mass-marketed this symbol of women's emancipation, suggesting it was the norm.

Movies became even more powerful cultural influences with the advent of the "talkies." Warner Brothers' *The Jazz Singer* (1927), starring Al Jolson, was the first feature-length film to offer sound. Two years later all the major studios had made

The Flapper

The flapper phenomenon was not limited to Anglos. This 1921 photograph of a young Mexican American woman shows how mainstream fads and fashions reached into Latino communities across the country.

(Arizona Historical Society)

the transition to talkies. By the end of the 1920s the nation had almost 23,000 movie theaters, including elaborate picture palaces built by the studios in major cities. Movie attendance rose from 60 million in 1927 to 90 million in 1930. In two short decades movies had become thoroughly entrenched as the most popular—and probably the most influential—form of urban-based mass media.

That the first talkie was *The Jazz Singer* was perhaps no coincidence. Jazz was such an important part of the new mass culture that the 1920s are often referred to as the Jazz Age. An improvisational style whose notes were (and are) rarely written down, jazz originated in the dance halls and bordellos of New Orleans around the turn of the century. A synthesis of African American music forms, such as ragtime and the blues, it also drew on African and European styles. Most of the early jazz musicians were blacks who brought to Chicago, New York, and other northern cities music that had originated in the South. Some of the best-known performers were the composer-pianist Ferdinand "Jelly Roll" Morton; the trumpeter Louis Armstrong; the singer Bessie Smith, the "Empress of the Blues"; and composer-bandleader Edward "Duke" Ellington. Phonograph records increased the appeal of jazz by capturing its spontaneity and distributing it to a wide audience; jazz, in turn, boosted the infant recording industry. Soon this uniquely American art form had caught on in Europe, especially in France. That jazz, which expressed black dissent in the face of mainstream white values, also appealed to white audiences signifies the role that African Americans played in shaping the contours of American popular culture.

Other forms of mass media also helped to establish national standards of taste and behavior. In 1922 ten magazines claimed a circulation of at least 2.5 million, including the *Saturday Evening Post,* the *Ladies' Home Journal, Collier's Weekly,* and *Good Housekeeping. Reader's Digest, Time,* and the *New Yorker,* still found today in homes throughout the country, all started publication in the 1920s. Tabloid newspapers also became part of the national scene. Thanks to syndicated newspaper columns and features people across the United States could read the same articles. They could also read the same books, preselected by a board of expert judges for the Book-of-the-Month Club, founded in 1926.

The newest instrument of mass culture, professional radio broadcasting, began in 1920. By 1929 about 40 percent of the nation's households owned a radio. More than 800 stations, most affiliated with the Columbia Broadcasting Service (CBS) or the National Broadcasting Company (NBC), were on the air. Unlike European networks, which were government monopolies, American radio stations operated for profit. Though the federal government licensed the stations, their revenue came primarily from advertisers and corporate sponsors.

Americans loved radio. They listened avidly to the World Series and other sports events and to variety shows sponsored by advertisers. One of the most popular radio shows of all time, *Amos 'n' Andy,* premiered on NBC in 1928, featuring two white actors playing stereotypical black characters. Soon fractured phrases from *Amos 'n' Andy,* such as "Check and double check," became part of everyday speech. So many

CRAZY BLUES

By PERRY BRADFORD

Get this number for your phonograph on Okeh Record No. 4169

PUBLISHED BY
PERRY BRADFORD
MUSIC PUB. CO.
1547 BROADWAY, N. Y. C.

All That Jazz

The phonograph dramatically expanded the popularity and market for jazz recordings like this one by Mamie Smith and her Jazz Hounds. The success of "Crazy Blues" convinced record companies that there was a market to be tapped in black communities for what were called "race records," and Mamie Smith skyrocketed to fame with this 1920 recording.

(Division of Political History, Smithsonian Institution, Washington, DC)

people "tuned in" (another new phrase of the 1920s) that the country seemed to come to a halt during popular programs—a striking example of the pervasiveness of mass media.

The automobile and new forms of entertainment like movies and radio pointed to a new emphasis on leisure. As the workweek shrank and some workers won the right to paid vacations, Americans had more time and energy to spend on recreation. Like so much else in the 1920s leisure became increasingly tied to consumption and mass culture. Public recreation flourished as cities and suburbs built baseball diamonds, tennis courts, swimming pools, and golf courses. Americans not only played sports but had the time and money to watch professional athletes perform in increasingly commercialized enterprises. They could see a game in a comfortable stadium, or they could listen to it on the radio or catch highlights in the newsreel at the local movie theater.

Americans reveled vicariously in the accomplishments of the superb athletes of the 1920s. Baseball continued to be the national pastime, drawing as many as 10 million fans a year. Tarnished in 1919 by the "Black Sox" scandal, in which some Chicago White Sox players took bribes to throw the World Series, baseball bounced back with the rise of stars like Babe Ruth of the New York Yankees. African Americans, however, had different heroes. Excluded from the white teams, black athletes like Satchel Paige played in Negro leagues formed in the 1920s.

Thanks to the media's attention, the popularity of sports figures rivaled that of movie stars. In football Red Grange of the University of Illinois was a major star, while Jack Dempsey and Gene Tunney attracted a loyal following in boxing and Bobby Jones helped to popularize golf. Bill Tilden dominated men's tennis, while Helen Wills and Suzanne Lenglen reigned in the women's game. The decade's best-known swimmer was Gertrude Ederle, who crossed the English Channel in 1926 in just over fourteen hours.

The decade's most popular hero, however, was neither an athlete nor a movie star. On May 20, 1927, aviator Charles Lindbergh, flying the small plane *The Spirit of St. Louis,* made the first successful nonstop solo flight between New York and Paris, a distance of 3,610 miles, in 33^1/$_2$ hours. Returning home to tickertape parades and effusive celebrations, he became *Time* magazine's first Man of the Year in 1928. Lindbergh captivated the nation by combining his mastery of the new technology (the airplane) with the pioneer virtues of individualism, self-reliance, and hard work. He symbolized Americans' desire to enjoy the benefits of modern industrialism without renouncing their traditional values.

Dissenting Values and Cultural Conflict

As movies, radio, advertising, and mass-production industries helped to transform the country into a modern, cosmopolitan nation, many Americans welcomed them as exciting evidence of progress. But others were uneasy. Flappers dancing to jazz, youthful sexual experimentation in the back of Ford Model Ts, hints of a decline in religious values: these harbingers of a new era worried more tradition-minded folk. In the nation's cities the powerful presence of immigrants and African Americans suggested the waning of white Protestant cultural dominance. Beneath the clichés of the Roaring Twenties were deeply felt tensions that surfaced in conflicts over immigration, religion, Prohibition, and race relations.

THE RISE OF NATIVISM

Tensions between the fast-paced city and the traditional, small-town values of the country partially explain the decade's conflicts. As farmers struggled with severe economic problems, rural communities lost residents to the cities at an alarming rate. The 1920 census revealed that for the first time in the nation's history city people outnumbered rural people: 52 percent of the population lived in urban areas, compared with just 28 percent in 1870. Though the census exaggerated the extent of urbanization—its guidelines classified towns with only 2,500 people as cities— there was no mistaking the trend (see Map 23.1). By 1929 ninety-three cities had populations over 100,000. The mass media generally reflected the cosmopolitan values of these urban centers, and many old-stock Americans worried that the cities and the immigrants who clustered there would soon dominate the culture.

Yet the polarities between city and country should not be overstated. Rural and small-town people were affected by the same forces that influenced urban residents. Much of the new technology—especially automobiles—enhanced rural life. Country people, like their urban counterparts, were tempted by the materialistic new

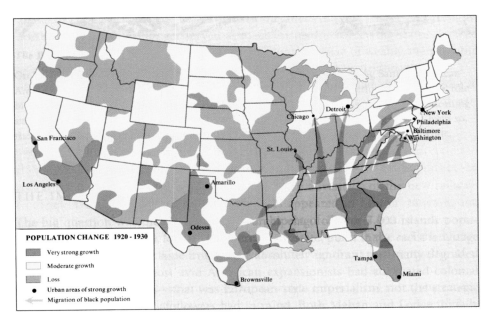

M A P 23.1
The Shift from Rural to Urban Population, 1920–1930

Despite the increasingly urban tone of modern America after 1920, regional patterns of population growth and decline were far from uniform. Cities in the South and West grew most dramatically as southern farmers moved to more promising areas with familiar climates. An important factor in the growth of northern cities, such as New York and Chicago, was the migration of southern blacks set in motion by World War I.

values proclaimed on the radio, in magazines, and in movies. Moreover, many urban residents—immigrant Catholics, for example—were just as alarmed about declining moral standards as rural Protestants were. A simplified urban-rural dichotomy misrepresents the complexity of the decade's cultural conflicts.

These conflicts often centered on the question of growing racial and ethnic pluralism. When native-born white Protestants—both rural and city dwellers—looked at their communities in 1920, they saw a nation that had changed dramatically in only forty years. During that time more than 23 million immigrants had come to America, many of them Jews or Catholics, most of peasant stock. Senator William Bruce of Maryland branded them "indigestible lumps" in the "national stomach," implying that mainstream society could not absorb their large numbers and foreign customs. This sentiment, termed *nativism,* was widely shared.

Nativist animosity fueled a new drive against immigration. The Chinese had been excluded in 1882, and Theodore Roosevelt had negotiated a "gentleman's agreement" to limit Japanese immigration in 1908 (see American Voices, "A Foreigner in America"). Yet efforts to restrict European immigration did not meet with much success until after World War I, which had heightened suspicion of "hyphenated" Americans. During the Red Scare, nativists had played up the supposed association of the immigrants with radicalism and labor unrest, charging that Southern and Eastern European Catholics and Jews were incapable of becoming true Americans.

In response Congress passed an emergency bill in 1921, limiting the number of immigrants to 3 percent of each national group as represented in the 1910 census. President Woodrow Wilson refused to sign it, but the bill was reintroduced and passed under Warren Harding. In 1924 a more restrictive measure, the National Origins Act, reduced immigration until 1927 to 2 percent of each nationality's representation in the 1890 census—which had included relatively small numbers of people from Southeastern Europe and Russia. After 1927 the law set a cap of 150,000 immigrants per year and continued to tie admission into the United States to a quota system that intentionally limited immigration from those regions. Japanese immigrants were excluded entirely.

One remaining loophole in immigration law permitted unrestricted immigration from countries in the Western Hemisphere. This source became increasingly significant over the years (see Figure 23.1), as Mexicans and Central and South Americans crossed the border to fill jobs made available by the cutoff of immigration from Europe and Asia. Over 1 million Mexicans entered the United States between 1900 and 1930. Nativists and representatives of organized labor, who viewed Mexican immigrants as unwanted competition, lobbied Congress to close the loophole but were unsuccessful until the 1930s when the economic devastation of the Great Depression minimized the need for immigrant labor.

Another expression of nativism in the 1920s was the revival of the Ku Klux Klan. Shortly after the premiere of *Birth of a Nation* in 1915, a popular film glorifying the Reconstruction-era Ku Klux Klan, a group of southerners had gathered on

AMERICAN VOICES

A Foreigner in America

KAZUO KAWAI

*A*sian immigrants' experience of prejudice was much sharper than that of Europeans, but nonetheless Japanese immigrant Kazuo Kawai's experience echoes the problems that many young ethnic Americans in the 1920s had as they recognized that they did not belong in the old country, nor were they accepted as "One Hundred Percent Americans."

But it hurt because I couldn't say: "This is my own, my native land." What was my native land? Japan? True, I was born there. But it had seemed a queer, foreign land to me when I visited it. America? I had, until now, thought so. I had even told my father once that even in case of war between Japan and America, I would consider America as my country. In language, in thought, in ideals, in custom, in everything, I was American. But America wouldn't have me. She wouldn't recognize me in high school. She put the pictures of those of my race at the tail end of the year book. (I was a commencement speaker, so they had to put my picture near the front.) She won't let me play tennis on the courts in the city parks of Los Angeles, by city ordinance. She won't give me service when I go to a barber's shop. She won't let me own a house to live in. She won't give me a job, unless it is a menial one that no American wants. I thought I was American, but America wouldn't have me. Once I was American, but America made a foreigner out of me—Not a Japanese, but a foreigner—a foreigner to any country, for I am just as much a foreigner to Japan as to America.

SOURCE: *Stanford Survey of Race Relations* (Stanford University, 1924), Hoover Institute Archives.

Stone Mountain outside Atlanta to revive the racist organization. Taking as its motto "Native, white, Protestant supremacy," the modern Klan appealed to both urban and rural folk, though its largest "klaverns" were in urban areas. Spreading out from its southern base, the group found significant support in the Far West, the Southwest, and the Midwest, especially Oregon, Indiana, and Oklahoma. Unlike the Klan that was founded after the Civil War, the Klan of the 1920s did not limit its harassment to blacks; Catholics and Jews were just as likely to be its targets. Many of its tactics, however, were the same: arson, physical intimidation, and economic boycotts. The new Klan also turned to politics, succeeding in electing hundreds of Klansmen to public office. At the height of its power in 1925 the Klan had over 3 million members—including a strong contingent of women who pursued a political agenda that combined racism, nativism, and equal rights for white Protestant women.

After 1925 the Klan declined rapidly. Internal rivalries and the disclosure of rampant corruption hurt the group's image. Especially damaging was the revelation that Grand Dragon David Stephenson, the Klan's national leader, had kidnapped

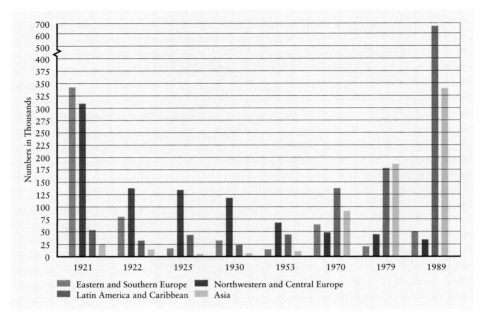

F IGURE 23.1
American Immigration after World War I

Legislation reflecting nativism slowed the influx of immigrants after 1920, as did the dislocations brought on by depression and war in the 1930s and 1940s. Note the higher rate of non-
European immigration since the 1970s.

and sexually assaulted his former secretary, driving her to suicide. And the passage
of the National Origins Act in 1924 reduced the nativist fervor, robbing the Klan
of its most potent issue.

LEGISLATING VALUES: THE SCOPES
TRIAL AND PROHIBITION

Other cultural tensions erupted over religion. The debate between modernist and
fundamentalist Protestants, which had been simmering since the 1890s (see Chapter 19), came to a boil in the 1920s. Modernists, or liberal Protestants, tried to reconcile religion with Charles Darwin's theory of evolution and recent technological
and scientific discoveries. Fundamentalists clung to a literal interpretation of the
Bible. At the same time most major Protestant denominations, especially the Baptists and the Presbyterians, experienced heated internal conflicts. However, the most
conspicuous evangelical figures came from outside mainstream denominations.
Popular preachers like Billy Sunday and Aimee Semple McPherson used revivals,
storefront churches, and open-air preaching to popularize their own blends of
charismatic fundamentalism and traditional values.

Religious controversy soon entered the political arena when fundamentalists, worried about increasing secularism and declining morality, turned to the law to shore up their vision of a righteous Protestant nation. Some states enacted legislation to block the teaching of evolution in the schools. In 1925, for instance, Tennessee passed a law declaring that "it shall be unlawful . . . to teach any theory that denies the story of the Divine creation of man as taught in the Bible, and to teach instead that man has descended from a lower order of animals." In a test case involving John T. Scopes, a high school biology teacher in Dayton, Tennessee, the fledgling American Civil Liberties Union (ACLU) challenged the constitutionality of that law. Clarence Darrow, the famous criminal lawyer, defended Scopes; the spellbinding orator William Jennings Bryan, three-time presidential candidate and ardent fundamentalist, was the most prominent member of the prosecution's team.

The Scopes trial was quickly dubbed the "monkey trial," referring both to Darwin's theory that human beings and primates share a common ancestor and to the circus atmosphere in the courtroom. In July 1925 more than 100 journalists crowded the sweltering courthouse in Dayton, Tennessee, giving massive publicity to the knotty questions of faith and scientific theory that the trial addressed. The jury took only eight minutes to deliver its verdict: guilty. Though the Tennessee Supreme Court later overturned the conviction on a technicality, the reversal prevented further appeals of the case, and the controversial law remained on the books more than thirty years. Historically, the trial symbolizes the conflict between the two competing value systems, cosmopolitan and traditional, that clashed in the 1920s. It suggests that despite the period's image as a frivolous and decadent time, religion continued to matter deeply to many Americans.

Like the dispute over evolution, Prohibition involved the power of the state to enforce social values. Americans did drink less overall after passage of the Eighteenth Amendment, which took effect in January of 1920 (see Chapter 22). Yet more than any other issue, Prohibition gave the decade its reputation as the Roaring Twenties. In major cities, whose ethnic populations had always opposed Prohibition, noncompliance was widespread. People imitated rural moonshiners by distilling "bathtub gin." Illegal saloons called "speakeasies" sprang up everywhere—more than 30,000 of them in New York City alone. Liquor smugglers operated with ease along borders and coastlines. Organized crime, already a presence in major cities, supplied a ready-made distribution network for the bootleg liquor, using the "noble experiment," as Prohibition was called, to entrench itself more deeply in city politics. Said the decade's most notorious gangster, Al Capone, "Everybody calls me a racketeer. I call myself a businessman. When I sell liquor, it's bootlegging. When my patrons serve it on a silver tray on Lake Shore Drive, it's hospitality."

By the middle of the decade, Prohibition was clearly failing. Government appropriations for its enforcement were woefully inadequate; the few highly publicized raids hardly made a dent in the liquor trade. Forces for repeal—the "wets," as opposed to the "drys," who continued to support the Eighteenth Amendment—began the long process to obtain the necessary votes in Congress and state

Scopes Trial

As this picture of a stall selling antievolution material in Dayton, Tennessee, suggests, the Scopes trial in 1925 became a focus of the antievolution movement. Pitting the old-time religion of rural America against modern values, the trial symbolized much of the cultural conflict of the 1920s and demonstrated the continued importance of religion to many Americans. (Corbis-Bettmann)

legislatures to amend the Constitution once more. The wets argued that Prohibition had undermined respect for the law and had seriously impinged on individuals' liberty. The onset of the Great Depression hastened the repeal process, as politicians began to see alcohol production as a way to create jobs and prop up the faltering economy. On December 5, 1933, the Eighteenth Amendment was repealed. Ironically, drinking became more socially acceptable, though not necessarily more widespread, than it had been before the experiment began.

INTELLECTUAL CROSSCURRENTS

The most articulate and embittered dissenters of the 1920s were writers and intellectuals disillusioned by the horrors of World War I and the crass materialism of the new consumer culture. Some artists were so repelled by what they saw as the complacent, moralistic, and anti-intellectual tone of American life that they settled in Europe—some temporarily, like the novelists Ernest Hemingway and F. Scott Fitzgerald, others permanently, like writer Gertrude Stein. Prominent African American artists, such as dancer Josephine Baker and writer Langston Hughes, sought temporary escape from racism in France. The poet T. S. Eliot, who left the United States before the war, ultimately became a British citizen. His despairing poem *The Waste Land* (1922), with its images of a fragmented civilization in ruins after the war, influenced a generation of writers. Other writers too made powerful antiwar statements, including John Dos Passos, whose first novel, *The Three Soldiers* (1921), was inspired by the war, and whose *1919* (1932), the second volume of his magnificent *USA* trilogy, railed against the obscenity of "Mr. Wilson's war." Ernest Hemingway's novels *In Our Time* (1924), *The Sun Also Rises* (1926), and *A Farewell to Arms* (1929) also powerfully described the dehumanizing consequences and the futility of war.

But the artists and writers who migrated to Europe, particularly Paris, were not simply a "lost generation" fleeing America. They were also drawn to Paris as the cultural and artistic capital of the world and a beacon of modernism. Paris, as Gertrude Stein put it, was "where the twentieth century was happening." Indeed, the modernist movement, which was marked by skepticism and technical experimentation in literature, art, and music, invigorated American writing both abroad and at home. Many American writers, whether they settled in Paris or remained in their home country, joined the movement, which had begun before the war as intellectuals reacted with excitement to the cultural and social changes that science, industrialization, and urbanization had brought. In the 1920s the business culture and political corruption of the Harding years caused intellectuals to cast a more critical eye on American society. One of the sharpest critics, the Baltimore journalist H. L. Mencken, directed his mordant wit against mass culture, small-town America with its guardians of public morals, and the "booboisie," his contemptuous term for the middle class. In the *American Mercury,* the journal he founded in 1922, Mencken championed writers like Sherwood Anderson, Sinclair Lewis, and Theodore Dreiser, who satirized the provincialism of American society.

The literature of the 1920s was rich and varied. Poetry enjoyed a renaissance in the works of Robert Frost, Wallace Stevens, Marianne Moore, and William Carlos Williams. Edith Wharton won a Pulitzer Prize—the first woman so honored—for *The Age of Innocence* (1920). Influenced by Freudian psychology, William Faulkner achieved his first critical success with *The Sound and the Fury* (1929), set in the fictional Mississippi county of Yoknapatawpha, where inhabitants clung to the values of the old agrarian South as they struggled to adjust to modern industrial capitalism. Playwright Eugene O'Neill also showed the influence of Freudian psychology in his experimental plays, including *The Hairy Ape* (1922) and *Desire Under the Elms* (1924). Although both Faulkner and O'Neill went on to produce additional major works in the 1930s, on the whole the creative energy of the literary renaissance of the 1920s did not survive into the 1930s. The Great Depression, social and ideological unrest, and the rise of totalitarianism would reshape the intellectual landscape.

A different kind of cultural affirmation took place in the African American community of Harlem in the 1920s. In the words of the Reverend Adam Clayton Powell Sr., pastor of the influential Abyssinian Baptist Church, Harlem loomed as "the symbol of liberty and the Promised Land to Negroes everywhere." One aspect of this hope was the Harlem Renaissance, a movement of young writers and artists who broke with older genteel traditions of black literature to reclaim a cultural identity with African roots. Alain Locke, editor of the anthology *The New Negro* (1926), summed up the movement when he stated that, through art, "Negro life is seizing its first chances for group expression and self-determination." Authors like Claude McKay, Jean Toomer, Jessie Fauset, and Zora Neale Hurston explored the black experience and represented the "New Negro" in fiction. Countee Cullen and Langston Hughes turned to poetry, and Augusta Savage to sculpture. Their outpouring of artistic expression gave voice to the African American struggle to find a way, as W. E. B. Du Bois put it, "to be both a Negro and an American."

The vitality of the Harlem Renaissance was short-lived. Although the NAACP's magazine *The Crisis* provided a forum for the Harlem writers, the black middle class and Harlem's intellectual elite were relatively small and could not adequately support its efforts. The movement had depended on white patronage for financial backing and access to publication. During the Jazz Age, when Harlem was in vogue, publishing houses courted Harlem writers, but when the stock market crashed in 1929, their interest in funding black writers withered, and the movement waned as the Depression deepened. But the works of the Harlem Renaissance would influence a new generation of black writers when black intellectuals rediscovered them during the civil rights movement of the 1960s.

Although the Harlem Renaissance had little impact on the masses of African Americans, other movements built racial pride and challenged white political and cultural hegemony. The most successful was the Universal Negro Improvement Association (UNIA), which championed black separatism under the leadership of the Jamaican-born Marcus Garvey. Based in Harlem, the UNIA was the black working class's first mass movement. At its height it claimed 4 million followers, many of whom were recent migrants to northern cities. Like several nineteenth-century reformers, Marcus Garvey urged blacks to return to Africa because, he reasoned, blacks would never be treated justly in countries ruled by whites. Although he did not anticipate a massive migration, he did envision a strong black Africa that could use its power to protect blacks everywhere. Garvey's wife, Amy Jacques Garvey, appealed to black women by combining black nationalism with an emphasis on women's contributions to culture and politics.

The UNIA grew rapidly in the early 1920s. It published a newspaper called *Negro World* and undertook extensive business ventures to support black enterprise. The most ambitious project, the Black Star Line steamship company, was supposed to ferry cargo between the West Indies and the United States and take African Americans back to Africa. Irregularities in fund raising for the project, however, led to Garvey's conviction for mail fraud in 1925, and he was sentenced to five years in prison. President Coolidge commuted his sentence in 1927, but Garvey was deported to Jamaica. Without his charismatic leadership, the movement collapsed.

CULTURAL CLASH IN THE ELECTION OF 1928

The works of the lost generation and the Harlem Renaissance touched only a small minority of Americans in the 1920s, but emotionally charged issues like Prohibition, fundamentalism, and nativism eventually spilled over into national politics. The Democratic Party, which attracted both rural Protestants in the South and the West and ethnic minorities in northern cities, was especially vulnerable to the cultural conflicts of the time. The 1924 Democratic National Convention had revealed an intensely polarized party, split between the urban machines and its rural wing.

In 1928 the urban wing held sway and succeeded in nominating New York's Governor Alfred E. Smith, a descendant of Irish immigrants and a product of Tammany Hall. Proud of his background, Smith adopted "The Sidewalks of New York" as his campaign song. His candidacy troubled many voters, however. His heavy New York accent, his brown derby, and his colorful style highlighted his urban working-class origins, and his early career in Tammany Hall suggested—incorrectly—that he was little more than a cog in the machine. Smith's stand on Prohibition—although he promised to enforce it, he wanted it repealed—alienated even more voters.

An additional handicap, however, was his religion. In 1928 most Protestants were not ready for a Catholic president. Although Smith insisted that his religion would not interfere with his duties as president, his perceived allegiance to Rome cost him the support of Democrats and Republicans alike. Protestant clergymen, who already opposed Smith because he supported the repeal of Prohibition, led the drive against him. "No Governor can kiss the papal ring and get within gunshot of the White House," declared one Methodist bishop.

Smith's candidacy met with much opposition, but for his supporters he embodied a new America. Throughout the decade, attacks on immigrants, Catholics, and Jews had repeatedly labeled them as unwelcome outsiders. Ethnic and religious leaders and communities had vehemently countered these criticisms by offering a more inclusive vision of citizenship. One Catholic bishop summed it up neatly in 1921, stating that "National aspirations constitute Americanism. We are the blend of all the peoples of the world, and I think we are much the better for that. Americanism is not a matter of birth, Americanism is a matter of faith, of consecration to the ideals of America." That Al Smith, a man of Catholic immigrant stock, could be the Democratic Party's nominee for president suggested to many in 1928 that the country might yet embrace a more pluralistic conception of American identity.

Just as Smith was a new kind of presidential candidate for the Democrats, so was Herbert Hoover for the Republicans. As a professional administrator and engineer who had never before been elected to political office, Hoover embodied the new managerial and technological elite that was restructuring the nation's economic order. During his campaign, in which he gave only seven speeches, Hoover asserted that his vision of individualism and cooperative endeavor would banish poverty from the United States. That rhetoric, as well as his reputation for organizing a drive for humanitarian relief during the war, caused many voters to see him as more progressive than Smith.

Hoover won a stunning victory, receiving 58 percent of the popular vote to Smith's 41 percent and 444 electoral votes to Smith's 87. The election reflected important underlying political changes. Despite the overwhelming loss, the Democrats' turnout increased substantially in urban areas. Smith won the industrialized states of Massachusetts and Rhode Island and carried the nation's twelve largest cities. The Democrats were on their way to fashioning a new identity as the party of the urban masses, a reorientation the New Deal completed in the 1930s.

It is unlikely that any Democratic candidate, let alone a Catholic, could have won the presidency in 1928. With a seemingly prosperous economy, national consensus on foreign policy, and strong support from the business community, the Republicans were unbeatable. Ironically, Herbert Hoover's victory would put him in the unenviable position of leading the United States when the Great Depression struck in 1929. Having claimed credit for the prosperity of the 1920s, the Republicans could not escape blame for the depression; twenty-four years would pass before a Republican won the presidency again.

But as Hoover began his presidency in early 1929, most Americans expected progress and prosperity to continue. The New Era the Republicans had touted meant more than Republican ascendancy in politics, more than business-government cooperation, and more than a decline in the progressive reform movement. To most Americans, the New Era embodied the industrial productivity and technological advances that made consumer goods widely available and the movies and the radio an exciting part of American life. At home and abroad the nation seemed unprecedentedly vigorous and powerful. Despite disruptive cultural conflicts and a changing workplace that undermined workers' power, despite inequities in the racial order and in the distribution of income, the general tone was one of optimism, of faith in the modern society the country had become. That faith made the harsh realities of the Great Depression that would follow all the more shocking.

T I M E L I N E

1920	Eighteenth Amendment takes effect (January) and outlaws alcohol (repealed in 1933).		U.S. troops withdraw from the Dominican Republic.
	First commercial radio broadcast		Teapot Dome scandal
	Republican Warren G. Harding elected president		National Origins Act further limits immigration.
	Census reveals a population shift from farms to cities.	**1925**	Height of power for the Ku Klux Klan
			Scopes trial
	Edith Wharton's *The Age of Innocence*	**1926**	Alain Locke's *The New Negro*
1920–1921	National economic recession		The Book-of-the-Month Club is founded.
1921	Sheppard-Towner Act appropriates money for women's and infants' health.	**1927**	*The Jazz Singer* becomes the first "talkie."
	Immigration Act limits immigration.		Charles Lindbergh flies solo across the Atlantic.
	Washington Conference supports naval disarmament.	**1928**	Herbert Hoover defeats Al Smith for the presidency.
1922	T. S. Eliot's *The Waste Land*		Kellogg-Briand Peace Pact condemns the use of war.
1922–1929	Record economic expansion		*Amos 'n' Andy* premieres on NBC radio.
1923	Harding dies in office and is succeeded by Calvin Coolidge as president.	**1929**	*Middletown* is published.
			Ernest Hemingway's *A Farewell to Arms*
1924	Dawes Plan reduces German reparations payments.		William Faulkner's *The Sound and the Fury*

For Further Exploration

A recent overview of the decade that pays extensive attention to racial, religious, and ethnic pluralism is Lynn Dumenil, *The Modern Temper: American Culture and Society in the 1920s*. Invaluable collections of primary documents include Alain Locke, ed., *The New Negro* (1925), which features authors of the Harlem Renaissance; Loren Baritz, ed., *The Culture of the Twenties* (1970), which covers such diverse topics as the Lost Generation and Ku Klux Klan; and Freda Kirchwey, ed., *Our Changing Morality: A Symposium* (1924), which brings together a series of 1920s essays on women. For fiction, in addition to the titles offered in the text, see Sinclair Lewis's two classic midwestern novels, *Babbitt* (1922) and *Mainstreet* (1920); Sherwood Anderson's dark stories in *Winesburg, Ohio* (1919); and Nella Larsen's novel *Quicksand* (1928) about an African American woman's conflicted identity.

The State University of New York at Binghamton's page on "Women and Social Movements in the United States, 1830–1930" at <http://womhist.binghamton.edu/> is especially rich on the 1920s, with material on conflicts between African American and white women activists, women in the peace movement, and women's participation in partisan politics. The Library of Congress's American Memory Collection, *Prosperity and Thrift: The Coolidge Era and the Consumer Economy, 1921–1929,* at <http://memory.loc.gov/ammem/coolhtml/coolhome.html> is an extensive site with original documents, film footage, and scholarly insights on a variety of topics dealing with the 1920s. Douglas O. Linder of University of Missouri–Kansas City, maintains a "Famous Trials" website at <http://www.law.umkc.edu/faculty/projects/ftrials/scopes/scopes.htm> that offers photos, cartoons, biographies of the participants, and firsthand accounts of the Scopes trial. "Greatest Films of the 1920s" at <http://www.filmsite.org/20sintro.html> is an informative site that provides summaries and reviews of such significant movies as *King of Kings* (1927) and *The Sheik* (1921).

Chapter 24

THE GREAT DEPRESSION

Mass unemployment is both a statistic and an empty feeling in the stomach. To fully comprehend it, you have to both see the figures and feel the emptiness.

—CABELL PHILLIPS

Our images of the 1920s and the decade that followed are polar opposites. Flappers and movie stars, admen and stockbrokers, caught up in what F. Scott Fitzgerald called the "world's most expensive orgy"—these are our conceptions of the Jazz Age. The 1930s we remember in terms of bread lines and hobos, dust bowl devastation and hapless migrants piled into dilapidated jalopies. Almost all our impressions of that decade are black and white, in part because widely distributed photographs taken by Farm Security Administration photographers etched this dark visual image of depression America on the popular consciousness.

But this contrast between the flush times of the 1920s and the hard times of the 1930s is too stark. The vaunted prosperity of the 1920s was never as widespread or as deeply rooted as many believed. Though America's mass-consumption economy was the envy of the world, many people lived on its margins. Nor was every American devastated by the depression. Those with a secure job or a fixed income survived the economic downturn in relatively good shape. Yet few could escape the depression's wide-ranging social, political, and cultural effects. Whatever their personal situation was, Americans understood that the nation was deeply scarred by the pervasive struggle to survive and overcome "hard times."

The Coming of the Great Depression

Booms and busts are a permanent feature of the business cycle in capitalist economies. Since the beginning of the Industrial Revolution early in the nineteenth century, the United States had experienced recessions or panics at least once every twenty years. But none was as severe as the Great Depression of the 1930s. The country would not recover from the depression until World War II put American factories and people back to work.

CAUSES OF THE DEPRESSION

The downturn began slowly and almost imperceptibly. After 1927 consumer spending declined, and housing construction slowed. Soon inventories piled up; in 1928 manufacturers began to cut back production and lay off workers, reducing incomes and buying power and reinforcing the slowdown. By the summer of 1929 the economy was clearly in recession.

Yet stock-market activity continued unabated. By 1929 the stock market had become the symbol of the nation's prosperity, an icon of American business culture. In a *Ladies' Home Journal* article titled "Everyone Ought to Be Rich," the financier John J. Raskob advised that $15 a month invested in sound common stocks would grow to $80,000 in twenty years. Not everyone was playing the market, however. Only about 4 million Americans, or roughly 10 percent of the nation's households, owned stock in 1929.

Stock prices had been rising steadily since 1921, but in 1928 and 1929 they surged forward, rising on average over 40 percent. At the time market activity was essentially unregulated. Margin buying in particular proceeded at a feverish pace, as customers were encouraged to buy stocks with a small down payment and finance the rest with a broker loan. But then on "Black Thursday," October 24, 1929, and again on "Black Tuesday," October 29, the bubble burst. On those two bleak days, more than 28 million shares changed hands in frantic trading. Overextended investors, suddenly finding themselves heavily in debt, began to sell their portfolios. Waves of panic selling ensued. Practically overnight stock values fell from a peak of $87 billion (at least on paper) to $55 billion.

The impact of what became known as the Great Crash was felt far beyond the trading floors of Wall Street. Commercial banks had invested heavily in corporate stock. Speculators who had borrowed from banks to buy their stocks could not repay their loans because they could not sell their shares. Throughout the nation bank failures multiplied. Since bank deposits were uninsured, a bank collapse meant that depositors lost all their money. The sudden loss of their life savings was a tremendous shock to members of the middle class, many of whom had no other resources to cope with the crisis. More symbolically the crash destroyed the faith of those who viewed the stock market as the crowning symbol of American prosperity, precipitating a crisis of confidence that prolonged the depression.

Although the stock-market crash precipitated the Great Depression, long-standing weaknesses in the economy accounted for its length and severity. Agriculture, in particular, had never recovered from the recession of 1920 and 1921. Farmers faced high fixed costs for equipment and mortgages, which they had incurred during the inflationary war years. When prices fell because of over-production, many farmers defaulted on their mortgage payments, risking foreclosure. Because farmers accounted for about a fourth of the nation's gainfully employed workers in 1929, their difficulties weakened the general economic structure.

Certain basic industries also had economic setbacks during the prosperous 1920s. Textiles, facing a steady decline after the war, abandoned New England for cheaper labor in the South but suffered still from decreased demand and overproduction. Mining and lumbering, which had expanded in response to wartime demand, confronted the same problems. And the railroad industry, damaged by stiff competition from trucks, faced shrinking passenger revenues and stagnant freight levels, worsened by inefficient management. While these older sectors of the economy faltered, newer and more successful consumer-based industries, such as appliances and food processing, proved not yet strong enough to lead the way to recovery.

The unequal distribution of the nation's wealth was another underlying weakness of the economy. During the 1920s the share of national income going to families in the upper- and middle-income brackets increased. The tax policies of Secretary of the Treasury Andrew Mellon contributed to a concentration of wealth by lowering personal income tax rates, eliminating the wartime excess-profits tax, and increasing deductions that favored corporations and the affluent. In 1929 the lowest 40 percent of the population received only 12.5 percent of aggregate family income, while the top 5 percent of the population received 30 percent. Once the depression began, this skewed income distribution left the majority of people unable to spend the amount of money that was needed to revive the economy.

The Great Depression became self-perpetuating. The more the economy contracted, the longer people expected the depression to last. The longer they expected it to last, the more afraid they became to spend or invest their money, if they had any. The economy showed some improvement in the summer of 1931, when low prices encouraged consumption, but plunged again late that fall.

The nation's banks, already weakened by the stock-market crash, contributed to the worsening contraction. When agricultural prices and income fell more steeply than usual in 1930, many farmers went bankrupt, causing rural banks to fail. By December 1930 so many rural banks had defaulted on their obligations that urban banks too began to collapse. The wave of bank failures frightened depositors, who withdrew their savings, deepening the crisis.

In 1931 a change in the nation's monetary policy compounded the banks' problems. In the first phase of the depression, the Federal Reserve System had reacted cautiously. But in October 1931 the Federal Reserve Bank of New York significantly increased the discount rate—the interest rate charged on loans to member banks—and reduced the amount of money placed in circulation through the purchase of government securities. This miscalculation squeezed the money supply, forcing prices down and depriving businesses of funds for investment. In the face of the money shortage, the American people could have pulled the country out of the depression only by spending faster. But because of falling prices, rising unemployment, and a troubled banking system, Americans preferred to keep their dollars, stashing them under the mattress rather than depositing them in the bank, further limiting the amount of money in circulation. Economic stagnation solidified.

THE WORLDWIDE DEPRESSION

President Hoover later blamed the severity of the depression on the international economic situation. Although domestic factors far outweighed international causes of America's protracted decline, Hoover was correct in surmising that economic problems in the rest of the world affected the United States, and vice versa. Indeed, the international economic system had been out of kilter since World War I. It functioned only as long as American banks exported enough capital to allow European countries to repay their debts and to buy U.S. manufactured goods and foodstuffs. By the late 1920s European economies were staggering under the weight of huge debts and trade imbalances with the United States, which effectively undercut their recovery from the war. By 1931 most European economies had collapsed.

In an interdependent world, the economic downturn in America had enormous repercussions. When U.S. companies cut back production, they also cut their purchases of raw materials and supplies abroad, devastating many foreign economies. When American financiers sharply reduced their foreign investment and consumers bought fewer European goods, debt repayment became even more difficult, straining the gold standard, the foundation of international commerce in the interwar period. As European economic conditions worsened, demand for American exports fell drastically. Finally, when the Hawley-Smoot Tariff of 1930 went into effect, raising rates to all-time highs, foreign governments retaliated by imposing their own trade restrictions, further limiting the market for American goods and intensifying the worldwide depression.

No other nation was as hard hit as the United States. From the height of its prosperity before the stock-market crash in 1929 to the depths of the depression in 1932 and 1933, the U.S. gross national product (GNP) was cut almost in half, declining from $103.1 billion to $58 billion in 1932. Consumption expenditures dropped by 18 percent, construction by 78 percent; private investment plummeted 88 percent, and farm income, already low, was more than halved. In this period 9,000 banks went bankrupt or closed their doors, and 100,000 businesses failed. The consumer price index (CPI) declined by 25 percent, and corporate profits fell from $10 billion to $1 billion.

Most tellingly, unemployment rose from 3.2 percent to 24.9 percent, affecting approximately 12 million workers. Statistical measures at the time were fairly crude, so the figures were probably understated. At least one in four workers was out of a job, and even those who had jobs faced wage cuts, work for which they were overqualified, or layoffs. Their stories put a human face on the almost incomprehensible dimensions of the economic downturn.

Hard Times

"We didn't go hungry, but we lived lean." That statement sums up the experiences of many families during the Great Depression. The vast majority of Americans were neither very rich nor very poor. For most the depression did not mean losing thousands of dollars in the stock market or pulling children out of boarding school; nor did it mean going on relief or living in a shantytown. In a typical family in the 1930s the husband still had a job, and the wife was still a homemaker. Families usually managed to "make do." But life was far from easy, and most Americans worried about an uncertain future that might bring even harder times into their lives.

THE INVISIBLE SCAR

"You could feel the depression deepen," recalled the writer Caroline Bird, "but you could not look out the window and see it." Many people never saw a bread line or a man selling apples on the corner. The depression caused a private kind of despair that often simmered behind closed doors. "I've lived in cities for many months broke, without help, too timid to get in bread lines," the writer Meridel LeSueur remembered. "A woman will shut herself up in a room until it is taken away from her, and eat a cracker a day and be as quiet as a mouse."

Many variables—race, ethnicity, age, class, and gender—influenced how Americans experienced the depression. Blacks, Mexican Americans, and others already on the economic margins saw their opportunities shrink further. Hard times weighed heavily on the nation's senior citizens of all races, many of whom faced total destitution. Many white middle-class Americans now experienced downward mobility for the first time. An unemployed man in Pittsburgh told the journalist Lorena Hickok, "Lady, you just can't know what it's like to have to move your family out of the nice house you had in the suburbs, part paid for, down into an apartment, down into another apartment, smaller and in a worse neighborhood, down, down, down, until finally you end up in the slums." People like this, who strongly believed in the Horatio Alger ethic of upward mobility through hard work, suddenly found themselves floundering in a society that no longer had a place for them. Thus, the depression challenged basic American tenets of individualism and success. Yet even in the midst of pervasive unemployment, many people blamed themselves for their misfortune. This sense of damaged pride pervaded letters written to President Franklin D. Roosevelt and his wife Eleanor, summed up succinctly in one woman's plea for assistance: "Please don't think me unworthy."

After exhausting their savings and credit, many families faced the humiliation of going on relief. Seeking aid from state or local government hurt their pride and disrupted the traditional custom of turning to relatives, neighbors, church, and mutual-aid society in time of need. Even if families endured the demeaning process of certification for state or local relief, the amount they received was a pittance. In New York State, where benefits were among the highest in the nation, a family on relief received only $2.39 a week. Such hardships left a deep wound: Caroline Bird described it as the "invisible scar." For the majority of Americans, even those who were not forced onto the relief rolls, the fear of losing control over their lives was the crux of the Great Depression.

The Bread Line

Some of the most vivid images from the depression were bread lines and men selling apples on street corners. Note that all the people in this bread line are men. Women rarely appeared in bread lines, often preferring to endure private deprivation rather than violate standards of respectable behavior.

(Franklin D. Roosevelt Library, Hyde Park, NY)

FAMILIES FACE THE DEPRESSION

Sociologists who studied family life during the 1930s found that the depression usually intensified existing behavior. If a family had been stable and cohesive before the depression, then members pulled together to overcome the new obstacles. But if a family had shown signs of disintegration, the depression made the situation worse. On the whole, far more families hung together than broke apart.

Men and women experienced the Great Depression differently, partly because of the gender roles that governed male and female behavior in the 1930s. From childhood men had been trained to be breadwinners; they considered themselves failures if they could no longer support their families (see American Voices, "A Working-Class Family Encounters the Great Depression"). But while millions of men lost their jobs, few of the nation's 28 million homemakers lost their positions in the home. In contrast to men, women's sense of self-importance increased as they struggled to keep their families afloat. The sociologists Robert and Helen Lynd noticed this phenomenon in their follow-up study of *Middletown* (Muncie, Indiana), published in 1937:

> The men, cut adrift from their usual routine, lost much of their sense of time and dawdled helplessly and dully about the streets; while in the homes the women's world remained largely intact and the round of cooking, housecleaning, and mending became if anything more absorbing.

Even if a wife took a job when her husband lost his, she retained almost total responsibility for housework and child care. To economize women sewed their own clothes and canned fruits and vegetables. They bought day-old bread and heated several dishes in the oven at once to save fuel. Women who had once employed servants did their own housework. Eleanor Roosevelt described the stressful effects of the depression on these women's lives: "It means endless little economies and constant anxiety for fear of some catastrophe such as accident or illness which may completely swamp the family budget." Housewives' ability to watch every penny often made the difference in a family's survival.

Despite hard times Americans as a whole maintained a fairly high level of consumption. As in the 1920s households in the middle-income range—in 1935 the 50.2 percent of American families with an income of $500 to $1,500—did much of the buying. Several trends allowed those families to maintain their former standard of living despite pay cuts and unemployment. Between 1929 and 1935 deflation lowered the cost of living almost 20 percent. And buying on the installment plan increased in the 1930s, permitting many families to stretch their reduced incomes.

Americans spent their money differently in the depression, though. Telephone use and clothing sales dropped sharply, but cigarettes, movies, radios, and newspapers, once considered luxuries, became necessities. The automobile proved one of

AMERICAN VOICES

A Working-Class Family Encounters the Great Depression

Larry Van Dusen

Although many families endured the privations of the Great Depression with equanimity, others, like Larry Van Dusen's family, experienced tremendous strains. In this passage from his oral history account to journalist Studs Terkel, he describes the pressures on male wage earners and their children.

My father led a rough life: he drank. During the Depression, he drank more. There was more conflict in the home. A lot of fathers—mine among them—had a habit of taking off. They'd go to Chicago to look for work. To Topeka. This left the family at home, waiting and hoping that the old man would find something. And there was always the Saturday night ordeal as to whether or not the old man would get home with his paycheck. Everything was sharpened and hurt more by the Depression.

Heaven would break out once in a while, and the old man would get a week's work. I remember he'd come home at night, and he'd come down the path through the trees. He always rode a bicycle. He'd stop and sometimes say hello, or give me a hug. And that smell of fresh sawdust on those carpenter overalls, and the fact that Dad was home, and there was a week's wages. . . . That's the good you remember.

And then there was always the bad part. That's when you'd see your father coming home with the toolbox on his shoulder. Or carrying it. That meant the job was over. The tools were home now, and we were back on the treadmill again.

I remember coming back home, many years afterwards. Things were better. It was after the Depression, after the war. To me, it was hardly the same house. My father turned into an angel. They weren't wealthy, but they were making it. They didn't have the acid and the recriminations and the bitterness that I had felt as a child.

SOURCE: Studs Terkel, *Hard Times* (New York: Pantheon Books, 1986), pp. 107–08.

---

the most depression-proof items in the family budget. Though sales of new cars dropped, gasoline sales held stable, suggesting that families bought used cars or kept their old models running longer.

Another measure of the impact of the depression on family life was the change in demographic trends. The marriage rate fell from 10.14 per thousand persons in 1929 to 7.87 per thousand in 1932. The divorce rate decreased as well because couples could not afford the legal expense of dissolving failed unions. And between 1930 and 1933 the birth rate, which had fallen steadily since 1800, dropped from 21.3 live births per thousand to 18.4, a dramatic 14 percent decrease. The new level would have produced a decline in population if maintained. Though it rose slightly after 1934, by the end of the decade it was still only 18.8. (In contrast, at the height of the baby boom following World War II, the birth rate was 25 per thousand.)

The drop in the birth rate during the Great Depression could not have happened without increased access to effective contraception. In 1936, in *United States v. One Package of Japanese Pessaries,* a federal court struck down all federal restrictions on the dissemination of contraceptive information. The decision gave doctors wide discretion in prescribing birth control for married couples, making it legal everywhere except the heavily Catholic states of Massachusetts and Connecticut. While abortion remained illegal, the number of women who underwent the procedure increased. Because many abortionists operated under unsafe or unsanitary conditions, between 8,000 and 10,000 women died each year from the illegal operations.

Margaret Sanger played a major role in encouraging the availability and popular acceptance of birth control. Sanger began her career as a public health nurse

Women Face the Depression

Most information for the 1930 census, conducted just as the depression gripped the nation, was gathered in personal interviews. This well-dressed census taker, Marie Cioffi, was probably lucky to get the job. The woman she is interviewing on East 112th Street in New York City, Margaret Napolitana, was likely a homemaker and, from her attire and expression, a struggling one. Meanwhile her daughter is not quite sure what to make of the two women's conversation.

(Corbis-Bettmann)

in the 1910s in the slums of New York City. At first she joined forces with social-ists trying to help working-class families to control their fertility. In the 1920s and 1930s, however, she appealed to the middle class for support, identifying those fam-ilies as the key to the movement's success. Sanger also courted the medical profes-sion, pioneering the establishment of professionally staffed birth control clinics and winning the American Medical Association's endorsement of contraception in 1937. As a result of Sanger's efforts, birth control became less a feminist issue and more a medical question. And in the context of the depression it became an economic issue as well, as financially pressed couples sought to delay or limit their child-bearing while they weathered hard times.

One way for families to make ends meet was to send an additional member of the household to work. At the turn of the century that additional member was of-ten a child or a young, unmarried adult. The married working woman was most likely to be an African American, employed in domestic service. In the 1930s the most striking changes were that married white women expanded their presence in the labor market and the total number of married women employed outside the home rose 50 percent. The 1940 census reported almost 11 million women in the workforce—approximately a fourth of the nation's workers—and a small increase over 1930.

Working women, especially white married women, encountered sharp re-sentment and outright discrimination in the workplace. After calculating that the number of employed women roughly equaled total unemployment in 1939, the editor Norman Cousins suggested this tongue-in-cheek remedy: "Simply fire the women, who shouldn't be working anyway, and hire the men. Presto! No un-employment. No relief rolls. No depression." Many people agreed with the idea. When asked in a 1936 Gallup poll whether wives should work when their hus-bands had jobs, 82 percent of those interviewed said no. Such public disapproval encouraged restrictions on women's right to work. From 1932 to 1937 the fed-eral government would not allow a husband and a wife to hold government jobs at the same time. Many states adopted laws that prohibited married women from working.

Married or not, most women worked because they had to. A sizable minority were the sole support of their families because their husbands had left home or lost their jobs. Single, divorced, deserted, or widowed women had no husbands to sup-port them. This was especially true of poor black women. A survey of Chicago re-vealed that two-fifths of adult black women in the city were single. These working women rarely took jobs away from men. "Few of the people who oppose married women's employment," observed one feminist in 1940, "seem to realize that a coal miner or steel worker cannot very well fill the jobs of nursemaids, cleaning women, or the factory and clerical jobs now filled by women." Custom made crossovers from one field to another rare.

The division of the workforce by gender gave white women a small edge dur-ing the depression. Many fields where they had concentrated—including clerical, sales, and service and trade occupations—reinforced the traditional stereotypes of female work but suffered less from economic contraction than heavy industry, which employed men almost exclusively. As a result unemployment rates for white women, although extremely high, were somewhat lower than those for their male counterparts. This small bonus came at a high price, however. When the depression ended, women were even more concentrated in low-paying, dead-end jobs than when it began. White women also benefited at the expense of minority women. To make ends meet white women willingly sought jobs usually held by blacks or other minority workers—domestic service jobs, for example—and employers were quick to act on their preference for white workers.

White men also took jobs once held by minority males. Contemporary observers' concerns about the crisis of the male breadwinner or married women in the workforce rarely extended to blacks. Most commentators paid scant attention to the impact of the depression on the black family, for example, focusing instead on the perceived threats to the stability of white households. As historian Jacqueline Jones explains it, few leaders worried "over the baneful effects of economic independence on the male ego when the ego in question was that of a black husband."

During the Great Depression there were few feminist demands for equal rights, at home or on the job. On an individual basis, women's self-esteem probably rose because of the importance of their work to family survival. Most men and women, however, continued to believe that the two sexes should have fundamentally different roles and responsibilities and that a woman's life cycle should be shaped by marriage and her husband's career.

The depression hit another segment of the family—the nation's 21 million young people—especially hard. Though small children often escaped the sense of bitterness and failure that gripped their elders, hard times made children grow up fast. About 250,000 young people became so demoralized that they took to the road as hobos and "sisters of the road," as female tramps were called. Others chose to stay in school longer: public schools were free, and they were warm in the winter. In 1930 less than half the nation's youth attended high school, compared with three-fourths in 1940, at the end of the depression. College, however, remained the privilege of a distinct minority. About 1.2 million young people, or 7.5 percent of the population between eighteen and twenty-four, attended college in the 1930s. Forty percent of them were women. After 1935 college became slightly more affordable when the National Youth Administration (NYA) gave part-time employment to more than 2 million college and high school students. The government agency also provided work for 2.6 million out-of-school youths.

College students worked hard in the 1930s; financial sacrifice encouraged seriousness of purpose. Interest in fraternities and sororities declined as many students became involved in political movements. Fueled by disillusionment with World War I, thousands of youth took the "Oxford Pledge" never to support United States involvement in a war. In 1936 the Student Strike Against War drew support from several hundred thousand students across the country.

Although many youths enjoyed more education in the 1930s, the depression damaged their future prospects. Studies of social mobility confirm that young men who entered their twenties during the depression era had less successful careers than those who came before or after. After extensive interviews with these youths all over the nation, the writer Maxine Davis described them as "runners, delayed at the gun," adding, "The depression years have left us with a generation robbed of time and opportunity just as the Great War left the world its heritage of a lost generation."

POPULAR CULTURE VIEWS THE DEPRESSION

Americans turned to popular culture to alleviate some of the trauma of the Great Depression. In June 1935 a Chicago radio listener wrote station WLS, "I feel your music and songs are what pulled me through this winter." She explained that "Half the time we were blue and broke. One year during the depression and no work. Kept from going on relief but lost everything we possessed doing so. So thanks for the songs, for they make life seem more like living." Mass culture flourished in the 1930s, offering not just entertainment but commentary on the problems that beset the nation. Movies and radio served as a forum for criticizing the system— especially politicians and bankers—as well as vehicles for reaffirming traditional ideals.

Despite the closing of one-third of the country's theaters by 1933, the movie industry and its studio system flourished. Sixty percent of Americans—some 60 to 75 million people—flocked to the cinema each week, seeking solace from the pain of the depression. In the early thirties moviegoers might be titillated or scandalized by Mae West, who was noted for her sexual innuendos: "I used to be Snow White, but I drifted." But in response to public outcry against immorality in the movies, especially from the Protestant and Catholic churches, the industry established a means of self-censorship, the Production Code Administration. After 1934 somewhat racy films were supplanted by sophisticated, fast-paced, screwball comedies like *It Happened One Night,* which swept the Oscars in 1934. The musical comedies of Fred Astaire and Ginger Rogers, including *Top Hat* (1935) and *The Gay Divorcee* (1934), in which the two dancers seemed to glide effortlessly through opulent sets, provided a stark contrast with most moviegoers' own lives.

But Hollywood, which produced 5,000 films during the decade, offered much more than what on the surface might seem to be escapist entertainment. Many of its movies contained complex messages that reflected a real sense of the societal crisis that engulfed the nation. The cultural historian Lawrence W. Levine has argued that depression-era films were "deeply grounded in the realities and intricacies of the Depression" and thus offer "a rich array of insights" into the period. Even if they did not deal specifically with the economic or political crisis, many films reaffirmed traditional values like democracy, individualism, and egalitarianism. They

THEY'RE DANCING CHEEK-TO-CHEEK AGAIN!

FRED ASTAIRE   **GINGER ROGERS**

TOP HAT

MUSIC AND LYRICS BY **IRVING BERLIN**

WITH
EDWARD EVERETT HORTON
HELEN BRODERICK
ERIK RHODES · ERIC BLORE
Directed by MARK SANDRICH
A PANDRO S. BERMAN Production

Dancing Cheek to Cheek

During the Great Depression, Americans turned to inexpensive recreational activities such as listening to the radio and going to the movies. One of the most popular attractions in Hollywood movies was the dance team of Fred Astaire and Ginger Rogers, who starred together in ten movies.
(Steve Schapiro)

also contained criticisms—suggestions that the system was not working or that law and order had broken down. Thus, popular gangster movies, such as *Public Enemy* (1931), with James Cagney, or *Little Caesar* (1930), starring Edward G. Robinson, could be seen as perverse Horatio Alger tales, in which the main character struggled to succeed in a harsh environment. Often these movies suggested that incompetent or corrupt politicians, police, and businessmen were as much to blame for organized crime as the gangsters themselves.

Depression-era films repeatedly portrayed politicians as cynical and corrupt. In *Washington Merry-Go-Round* (1932), lobbyists manipulated weak congressmen to undermine democratic rule. The Marx Brothers' irreverent comedies more humorously criticized authority—and most everything else. In *Duck Soup* (1933) Groucho Marx played Rufus T. Firefly, president of the mythical Freedonia, who sings gleefully:

> The last man nearly ruined this place,
> He didn't know what to do with it.
> If you think this country's bad off now,
> Just wait till I get through with it.

Few filmmakers left more of a mark on the decade than Frank Capra. An Italian immigrant who personified the possibilities for success the United States offered, Capra made films that spoke to Americans' idealism. In movies like *Mr. Deeds Goes to Town* (1936) and *Mr. Smith Goes to Washington* (1939), he pitted the virtuous small-town hero against corrupt urban shysters—businessmen, politicians, lobbyists, and newspaper publishers—whose machinations subverted the nation's ideals. Though the hero usually prevailed, Capra was realistic enough to suggest that the victory was not necessarily permanent and that the problems the nation faced were serious.

Radio occupied an increasingly important place in popular culture during the 1930s. At the beginning of the decade about 13 million households had radios; by the end 27.5 million owned them. Listeners tuned in to daytime serials like *Ma Perkins*, picked up useful household hints on the *The Betty Crocker Hour*, or enjoyed the Big Band "swing" of Benny Goodman, Duke Ellington, and Tommy Dorsey. Weekly variety shows featured Jack Benny; George Burns and Gracie Allen, and the ventriloquist Edgar Bergen and his impudent dummy, Charlie McCarthy. And millions of listeners followed the adventures of the Lone Ranger (with his cry "Heigh-ho, Silver"), Superman, and Dick Tracy.

Like movies, radio offered Americans more than escape. A running gag in comedian Jack Benny's show was his stinginess; audiences could identify with an unwillingness—or inability—to spend money. Even more relevant was Benny's distrust of banks. He kept his money in an underground vault guarded by a pet polar bear named Carmichael—presumably a more reliable place than the nation's financial institutions. *Amos 'n' Andy* (see Chapter 23) is remembered primarily for its racial stereotyping. But the exceptionally popular show also dealt with hard times, often referring explicitly to the depression. A central theme was the contrast between Amos's hard work and Andy's more carefree approach to life. Amos, tending to believe that the nation's economic crisis had been brought about by the extravagant spending of the 1920s, criticized his friend's fiscal irresponsibility. As the historian Arthur Frank Wertheim notes, "The way that the characters' hopes for monetary success were turned into business failures mirrored the lives of many Americans." Though *Amos 'n' Andy* reinforced racial stereotypes, it also reaffirmed the traditional values of "diligence, saving, and generosity."

Mr. Smith Goes to Washington

In director Frank Capra's classic 1939 film, *Mr. Smith Goes to Washington*, actor Jimmy Stewart plays an idealistic young senator who exposes the unscrupulous political machine that dominates his home state. In response, the machine frames Senator Smith for corruption. Although he is eventually vindicated, in this scene the despairing Smith encounters the avalanche of hostile mail generated against him by his crooked opponents. (MOMA-Film Stills Archive)

Americans did not spend all their leisure time in commercial entertainment. In a resurgence of traditionalism, attendance at religious services rose, and the home again became a center for pleasurable pastimes. Amateur photography and stamp collecting enjoyed tremendous vogues, as did the board game Monopoly. Reading aloud from books borrowed from the public library was another affordable diversion. But Americans bought books, too. Taking advantage of new manufacturing processes that made books cheaper, they made best sellers of Margaret Mitchell's *Gone with the Wind* (1936), James Hilton's *Lost Horizon* (1933), and Pearl Buck's *The Good Earth* (1932). Finally, "talking was the Great Depression pastime," recalled the columnist Russell Baker. "Unlike the movies, talk was free."

Harder Times

Much writing about the 1930s has focused on white working-class or middle-class families caught suddenly in a downward spiral. For African Americans, farmers, and Mexican Americans, times had always been hard; during the 1930s they got much harder. As the poet Langston Hughes noted, "The depression brought everybody down a peg or two. And the Negroes had but few pegs to fall."

AFRICAN AMERICANS IN THE DEPRESSION

The African American worker had always known discrimination and limited opportunities and thus viewed the depression differently from most whites. "It didn't mean too much to him, the Great American Depression, as you call it," one man remarked. "There was no such thing. The best he could be is a janitor or a porter or shoeshine boy. It only became official when it hit the white man." The novelist and poet Maya Angelou, who grew up in Stamps, Arkansas, recalled, "The country had been in the throes of the Depression for two years before the Negroes in Stamps knew it. I think that everyone thought the Depression, like everything else, was for the white folks."

Despite the black migration to northern cities, which had begun before World War I, as late as 1940 more than 75 percent of African Americans still lived in the South. Nearly all black farmers lived in the South, their condition scarcely better than it had been at the end of Reconstruction. Only 20 percent of black farmers owned their own land; the rest toiled at the bottom of the South's exploitative agricultural system as tenant farmers, farm hands, and sharecroppers. African Americans rarely earned more than $200 a year, less than a quarter of the annual average wages of a factory worker. In one Louisiana parish black women averaged only $41.67 a year picking cotton.

Throughout the 1920s southern agriculture had suffered from falling prices and overproduction. The depression made an already desperate situation worse. Some black farmers tried to protect themselves by joining the Southern Tenant Farmers Union (STFU), which was founded in 1934. The STFU was one of the few southern groups that welcomed both blacks and whites. Landowners, however, had a stake in keeping sharecroppers from organizing, and they countered the union's efforts with repression and harassment. In the end the STFU could do little to reform an agricultural system that depended on a single crop—cotton.

All blacks faced harsh social and political discrimination throughout the South. In a celebrated 1931 case in Scottsboro, Alabama, two white women who had been riding a freight train claimed to have been raped by nine black youths, all under twenty years old. The two women's stories contained many inconsistencies, and one woman later recanted. But in the South when a white woman claimed to have been raped by a black, she was taken at her word. Two weeks later juries composed entirely of white men found all nine defendants guilty of rape; eight were sentenced to death. (One defendant escaped the death penalty because he was a minor.) Though the U.S. Supreme Court overturned the sentences in 1932 and ordered new trials on grounds that the defendants had been denied adequate legal counsel, five of the men eventually were reconvicted and sentenced to long prison terms.

The hasty trials and the harsh sentences, especially given the defendants' young age, stirred public protest, prompting the International Labor Defense (ILD), a labor organization tied closely to the Communist Party, to take over the defense. Though the Communist Party had targeted the struggle against racism as a priority in the early 1930s, it was making little headway recruiting African Americans. "It's bad enough being black, why be red?" was a common reaction. White southerners resented radical groups' interference, noting that almost all those involved in the Scottsboro defense were northerners and Jews. Declared a local solicitor, "Alabama justice cannot be bought and sold with Jew money from New York."

The Scottsboro case received wide coverage in black communities across the country. Along with an increase in lynching in the early 1930s (twenty blacks were lynched in 1930, twenty-four in 1933), it gave black Americans a strong incentive to head for the North and the Midwest. Harlem, one of their main destinations, was already strained by the enormous influx of African Americans in the 1920s. The depression only aggravated the housing shortage. Residential segregation kept blacks from moving elsewhere, so they paid excessive rents to live in deteriorating buildings where crowded living conditions fostered disease and premature death. As whites clamored for jobs traditionally held by blacks—as waiters, domestic servants, elevator operators, and garbage collectors—unemployment in Harlem rose to 50 percent, twice the national rate. At the height of the depression, shelters and soup kitchens staffed by the Divine Peace Mission, under the leadership of the charismatic black religious leader Father Divine, provided 3,000 meals a day for Harlem's destitute.

In March 1935 Harlem exploded in the only major race riot of the decade. Anger about the lack of jobs, a slowdown in relief services, and economic exploitation of the black community had been building for years. Although white-owned stores were entirely dependent on black trade, store owners would not employ blacks. The arrest of a black shoplifter, followed by rumors that he had been severely beaten by white police, triggered the riot. Four blacks were killed, and $2 million worth of property was damaged.

There were some signs of hope for African Americans in the 1930s. Partly in response to the 1935 riot but mainly in return for growing black allegiance to the

Lynching

The threat of lynching remained a terrifying part of life for African Americans in the 1930s, and not just in the South. Artist Joe Jones set this canvas in 1933, perhaps influenced by the fact that twenty-four blacks were lynched that year. He gave it the ironic title of *American Justice, 1933 (White Justice)*. (Collection of Philip J. and Suzanne Schiller)

Democratic Party (see Chapter 25), the New Deal would channel significant amounts of relief money toward blacks outside the south. And the National Association for the Advancement of Colored People (NAACP) continued to challenge the status quo of race relations. Though calls for racial justice went largely unheeded during the depression, World War II and its aftermath would further the struggle for black equality.

DUST BOWL MIGRATIONS

A distressed agricultural sector had been one of the causes of the Great Depression. In the 1930s conditions only got worse, especially for farmers on the Great Plains. In the semiarid states of Oklahoma, Texas, New Mexico, Colorado, Arkansas, and

Kansas, farmers had always risked the ravages of drought (see Chapter 16), but the years 1930 to 1941 witnessed the worst drought in the country's history. Low rainfall alone did not create the Dust Bowl, however. National and international market forces, like the rising demand for wheat during World War I, had caused farmers to push the farming frontier beyond its natural limits. To capture a profit they had stripped the land of its natural vegetation, destroying the delicate ecological balance of the plains. When the rains dried up and the winds came, nothing remained to hold the soil. Huge clouds of dust rolled over the plains, causing streetlights to blink on as if night had fallen. Dust seeped into houses and "blackened the pillow around one's head, the dinner plates on the table, the bread dough on the back of the stove."

The ecological disaster prompted a mass exodus from the plains. Their crops ruined, their lands barren and dry, their homes foreclosed for debts they could not pay, at least 350,000 Okies (so-called whether or not they were from Oklahoma) loaded their belongings into beat-up Fords and headed west, encouraged by handbills distributed by growers that promised good jobs in California. Some went to metropolitan areas, but about half settled in rural areas where they worked for low wages as migratory farm laborers. John Steinbeck's novel *The Grapes of Wrath* (1939) immortalized them and their journey. In the novel the Joads abandon their land not only because of drought but also as a result of the economic transformation of American agriculture that had begun during World War I. By the 1930s large-scale commercialized farming had spread to the plains, where family farmers still used draft animals. In Steinbeck's novel, after the bank forecloses on the Joads' farm, a gasoline-engine tractor, the symbol of mechanized farming, plows under their crops and demolishes their home. Though it was a powerful novel, *The Grapes of Wrath* did not convey the diversity of the westward migration. Not all Okies were destitute dirt farmers; perhaps one in six was a professional, a business proprietor, or a white-collar worker. For most the drive west was fairly easy. Route 66 was a paved two-lane road; in a decent car, the journey from Oklahoma or Texas to California took only three to four days.

Before the 1930s Californians had developed a different type of agriculture from that practiced in the Southwest and Midwest. Basically industrial in nature, California agriculture was large-scale, intensive, and diversified, ironically requiring a massive irrigation system that would lay the groundwork for serious future environmental problems. The key crops were specialty foods—citruses, grapes, potatoes—whose staggered harvests required a great deal of transient labor during short picking seasons. A steady supply of cheap migrant labor provided by Chinese, Mexicans, Okies, Filipinos, and, briefly, East Indians made this type of farming economically feasible.

The migrants had a lasting impact on California culture. At first they met outright hostility from old-time Californians—a demoralizing experience for white native-born Protestants, who were ashamed of the Okie stereotype. But they stayed, filling important roles in California's expanding economy. Soon some communities in the San Joaquin Valley—Bakersfield, Fresno, Merced, Modesto, and Stockton—took on a distinctly Okie cast, identifiable by southern-influenced evangelical religion and the growing popularity of country music.

MEXICAN AMERICAN COMMUNITIES

As Okies arrived in California, many Mexican Americans were leaving. In the depths of the depression, with fear of competition from foreign workers at a peak, perhaps a third of the Mexican American population, most of them immigrants, returned to Mexico. The federal government's deportation policy—fostered by racism and made feasible by the proximity of Mexico—was partly responsible for the exodus, but many more Mexicans left voluntarily when work ran out and local relief agencies refused to assist them. Los Angeles lost approximately one-third of its Mexican community of 150,000—the largest concentration of Mexicans outside Mexico—during the deportations, which separated families, disrupted children's education, and caused extreme financial hardship during the worst years of the depression. Although forced repatriation slowed after 1932, for those who remained in America deportation was still a constant threat, an unmistakable reminder of their fragile status in the United States.

Discrimination and exploitation were omnipresent in the Mexican community. The harsh experiences of migrant workers influenced a young Mexican American named César Chávez, who would become one of the twentieth century's most influential labor organizers. In the mid-1930s, Chávez's father became involved in several bitter labor struggles in California's Imperial Valley. Thirty-seven major agricultural strikes occurred in California in 1933 alone, including one in the San Joaquin Valley that mobilized 18,000 cotton pickers—the largest agricultural strike to date. All these strikes failed, but they gave the young Chávez a background in labor organizing, which he would use to found a national farm workers' union in 1962.

Not all Mexican Americans were migrant farm workers. Many worked as miners; others held industrial jobs, especially in steel mills, meat-packing plants, and refineries, where they established a vibrant tradition of labor activism. In California, Mexican Americans also found employment in fruit- and vegetable-processing plants. Young single women especially preferred the higher-paying cannery work to domestic service, needlework, and farm labor. In plants owned by corporate giants like Del Monte, McNeill, and Libby, Mexican American women earned around $2.50 a day, while their male counterparts received $3.50 to $4.50. Labor unions came to the canneries in 1939 with the formation of the United Cannery, Agricultural, Packing, and Allied Workers of America, an unusually democratic union in which women, the majority of the rank-and-file workers, played a leading role.

Activism in the fields and factories demonstrated how a second generation of Mexican Americans, born in the United States, had turned increasingly to the struggle for political and economic justice in the United States rather than retaining primary allegiance to Mexico. According to the historian George Sánchez, they were creating "their own version of Americanism without abandoning Mexican culture." Joining American labor unions and becoming more involved in American politics (see Chapter 25) were important steps in the creation of a distinct Mexican American ethnic identity.

Herbert Hoover and the Great Depression

Had Herbert Hoover been elected in 1920 instead of 1928, he probably would have been a popular president. As the director of successful food conservation programs at home and charitable food relief abroad during World War I, he was respected as an intelligent and able administrator. Although Hoover's name frequently emerged as a possible candidate in 1920, he did not run for president until the end of the decade. Timing was against him. Although his optimistic predictions in the 1928 campaign—that "the poorhouse is vanishing from among us" and that America was "nearer to the final triumph over poverty than ever before in the history of any land"—reflected beliefs that many Americans shared, that prosperity and Hoover's reputation were soon to be dramatically undermined. When the stock market crashed in 1929, he stubbornly insisted that the downturn was only temporary. In June 1930 he greeted a business delegation with the words "Gentlemen, you have come sixty days too late. The Depression is over." As the country hit rock bottom in 1931 and 1932, the president finally acted, but by then it was too little, too late.

HOOVER RESPONDS

Hoover's approach to the Great Depression was shaped by his priorities as secretary of commerce. Hoping to avoid coercive measures on the part of the federal government, he turned to the business community for leadership in overcoming the economic downturn. Hoover asked business executives to maintain wages and production levels voluntarily and to work with the government to build people's confidence in the economic system.

Hoover did not rely solely on public pronouncements, however; he also used public funds and federal action to encourage recovery. Soon after the stock-market crash he cut federal taxes and called on state and local governments to increase their expenditures on public construction projects. He signed the 1929 Agricultural Marketing Act, which gave the federal government an unprecedented role in stabilizing agriculture. In 1930 and the first half of 1931 Hoover raised the federal budget for public works to $423 million, a dramatic increase in expenditures not traditionally considered to be the federal government's responsibility. Hoover also eased the international crisis by declaring a moratorium on the payment of Allied debts and reparations early in the summer of 1931. The depression continued, however. When

AMERICAN VOICES

Public Assistance Fails a Southern Farm Family

W *hen times were bad, even public assistance could be bad for a family in dire straits. Here a young mother living in the farming community of Commerce, Georgia, relates how relief efforts ironically proved to be a burden to her family of eight.*

I've just met with a problem I cannot solve alone. I am a Mother of six children the oldest is only 11 years old the youngest 18 months and I'm expecting another in March. We couldn't get any crop for 1936 because we could neither furnish ourselves or had any stock. So here we are having made out on a little work once in a while all summer. And then in Aug I had to have a serious operation and now I'm not able to feed & clothe our six children as my husband couldnt find anything at all to do was compelled to get on relief job at $1.28 a day 16 days a month. Well you take 8 meals 3 times a day out of $1.28 and what will you have left is 24 meals and what kind of meals do you have? We have to buy everything we eat. We have nothing except what we buy. Our bedclothes are threadbare our clothes the same. No shoes and no money to buy yet the relief say that cant help us as he is working. Can he work naked. Can he sleep cold. I don't know of any one at all that can help me and I know we cant go on like this. . . .

I hate to be like this but can a person that is willing to work for a living and that honest and disable to help themselves sit idle and see their small children suffer day after day without enough food or clothes to keep their bodies warm when there are thousands of people with plenty to give if they knew your need.

How it hurts to know that you are almost starving in the land of plenty.

SOURCE: Julia Kirk Blackwelder, "Letters from the Great Depression," in *Southern Exposure* 6, no. 3 (Fall 1978), p. 77.

the president asked Congress for a 33 percent tax increase to balance the budget, the ill-advised move choked investment and, to a lesser extent, consumption, contributing significantly to the continuation of the depression.

Hoover's most innovative program—one the New Deal would later draw on— was the Reconstruction Finance Corporation (RFC), approved by Congress in January 1932. Modeled on the War Finance Corporation of World War I and developed in collaboration with the business and banking communities, the RFC was the first federal institution created to intervene directly in the economy during peacetime. To alleviate the credit crunch for business, the RFC would provide federal loans to railroads, financial institutions, banks, and insurance companies in a strategy that has been called *pump priming*. In theory, money lent at the top of the economic structure would stimulate production, creating new jobs and increasing consumer spending. These benefits would eventually "trickle down" to the rest of the economy.

Unfortunately, the RFC lent its funds too cautiously to make a significant difference. Nonetheless, it represents a watershed in American political history and the growth of the federal government. When voluntary cooperation failed, the president had turned to federal action to stimulate the economy. Yet Hoover's break with the past had clear limits. In many ways, his support of the RFC was just another attempt to encourage business confidence. Compared with previous chief executives—and in contrast to his popular image as a "do-nothing" president—Hoover responded to the national emergency on an unprecedented scale. But the nation's needs were also unprecedented, and Hoover's programs failed to meet them (see American Voices, "Public Assistance Fails a Southern Farm Family").

In particular, federal programs fell short of helping the growing ranks of the unemployed. Hoover remained adamant in his refusal to consider any plan for direct federal relief to those out of work. Throughout his career he had believed that privately organized charities were sufficient to meet the nation's social welfare needs. During World War I he had headed the Commission for Relief of Belgium, a private group that distributed 5 million tons of food to Europe's suffering civilian population. And in 1927 he had coordinated a rescue and cleanup operation after a devastating flood of the Mississippi River left 16.5 million acres of land under water in seven states. The success of these and other predominantly voluntary responses to public emergencies had confirmed Hoover's belief that private charity, not federal aid, was the "American way" of solving social problems. He would not undermine the country's hallowed faith in individualism, even in the face of evidence that charities and state and local relief agencies could not meet the needs of a growing unemployed population.

RISING DISCONTENT

As the depression deepened, many citizens came to hate Herbert Hoover. Once the symbol of business prosperity, he became the scapegoat for the depression. "In Hoover we trusted, now we are busted," declared the hand-lettered signs carried by the down and out. New terms entered the vocabulary: Hoovervilles (shantytowns where people lived in packing crates and other makeshift shelters), Hoover flags (empty pockets turned inside out), Hoover blankets (newspapers). Hoover's declarations that nobody was starving, that hobos were better fed than ever before, seemed cruel and insensitive. His apparent willingness to bail out businesses and banks while leaving individuals to fend for themselves added to his reputation for cold-heartedness.

As the country entered the fourth year of depression, signs of rising discontent and rebellion emerged. Farmers were among the most vocal protestors, banding together to harass the bank agents and government officers who enforced evictions and foreclosures and to protest the low prices they received for their

Hoovervilles

By 1930 shantytowns had sprung up in most of the nation's cities. In New York City squatters camped out along the Hudson River railroad tracks, built makeshift homes in Central Park, or lived in the city dump. This scene from the old reservoir in Central Park looks east toward the fancy apartment buildings of Fifth Avenue and the Metropolitan Museum of Art, at left.
(Grant Smith/Corbis)

crops. Midwestern farmers had watched the price of wheat fall from $3 a bushel in 1920 to barely 30 cents in 1932. Now they formed the Farm Holiday Association, barricaded local roads, and dumped milk, vegetables, and other farm produce in the dirt rather than accept prices that would not cover their costs. Nothing better captured the cruel irony of maldistribution than farmers destroying food at a time when thousands were going hungry.

Protest was not confined to rural America, however. Bitter labor strikes occurred in the depths of the depression, despite the threat that strikers would lose their jobs. In Harlan County, Kentucky, in 1931 miners struck over a 10 percent wage cut. Their union was crushed by mine owners and the National Guard. In 1932 at Ford's River Rouge factory outside Detroit a demonstration provoked violence from police and Ford security forces; three demonstrators were killed, and fifty more seriously injured. Later some 40,000 people viewed the coffins under a banner charging that "Ford Gave Bullets for Bread."

In 1931 and 1932 violence broke out in the nation's cities. Groups of the unemployed battled local authorities over inadequate relief, staging rent riots and hunger marches. Some of these actions were organized by the Communist Party—still a tiny organization with only 12,000 members—as a challenge to the capitalist system, such as "unemployment councils" that agitated for jobs and food and a hunger march on Washington, D.C., in 1931. Though the marches were well attended and often got results from local and federal authorities, they did not necessarily win converts to communism.

Not radicals but veterans staged the most publicized—and most tragic—protest. In the summer of 1932 the "Bonus Army," a ragtag group of about 15,000 unemployed World War I veterans, hitchhiked to Washington to demand immediate payment of their bonuses, originally scheduled for distribution in 1945. While their leaders lobbied Congress, the Bonus Army camped out in the capital. "We were heroes in 1917, but we're bums now," one veteran complained bitterly. When the marchers refused to leave their Anacostia Flats camp, Hoover called out riot troops to clear the area. Led by General Douglas MacArthur, assisted by Major Dwight D. Eisenhower and Major George S. Patton, the troops burned the encampment to the ground. In the fight that followed, more than a hundred marchers were injured. Newsreel footage captured the deeply disturbing spectacle of the U.S. Army moving against its own veterans, and Hoover's popularity plunged even lower.

THE 1932 ELECTION: A NEW ORDER

Despite the evidence of discontent, the nation overall was not in a revolutionary mood as it approached the 1932 election. Having internalized Horatio Alger's ideal of the self-made man, many Americans initially blamed themselves rather than the system for their hardship. Despair and apathy, not anger, was their mood. The Republicans, who could find no credible way to dump an incumbent president, unenthusiastically renominated Hoover. The Democrats turned to Governor Franklin Delano Roosevelt of New York, who won the nomination by capitalizing on that state's reputation for innovative relief and unemployment programs.

Roosevelt, born into a wealthy New York family in 1882, had attended Harvard College and Columbia Law School. He had served in the New York State legislature and as assistant secretary of the navy in the Wilson administration, a post that had earned him the vice-presidential nomination on the Democratic ticket in 1920. Roosevelt's rise to the presidency was interrupted in 1921 by an attack of polio that left both his legs paralyzed for life. But he fought back from illness, emerging from the ordeal a stronger, more resilient man. "If you had spent two years in bed trying to wiggle your toe, after that anything would seem easy," he explained. His wife, Eleanor Roosevelt, strongly supported his return to public life and helped to mastermind his successful campaign for the governorship of New York in 1928.

The 1932 campaign for the presidency foreshadowed little of the New Deal. Roosevelt hinted only vaguely at new approaches to alleviating the depression: "The country needs and, unless I mistake its temper, the country demands bold, persistent experimentation." He won easily, receiving 22.8 million votes to Hoover's 15.7

million. Despite the nation's economic collapse, Americans remained firmly committed to the two-party system. The Socialist Party candidate, Norman Thomas, got fewer than a million votes, and the Communist Party candidate, party leader William Z. Foster, drew only 100,000 votes.

The 1932 election marked a turning point in American politics, the emergence of a Democratic coalition that would help to shape national politics for the next four decades. Roosevelt won the support of the Solid South, which returned to the Democratic fold after defecting in 1928 because of Al Smith's Catholicism and his views on Prohibition. Roosevelt drew substantial support in the West and in the cities, continuing a trend first noticed in 1928, when the Democrats appealed successfully to recent immigrants and urban ethnic groups. However, Roosevelt's election was hardly a mandate to reshape American political and economic institutions. Many people voted as much against Hoover as for Roosevelt.

Having spoken, the voters had to wait until Roosevelt's inauguration in March 1933 to see him put his ideas into action. (The four-month interval between the election and the inauguration was shortened by the Twentieth Amendment in 1933.) In the worst winter of the depression, Americans could do little but hope that things would get better. According to the most conservative estimates, unemployment stood at 20 to 25 percent nationwide. The rate was 50 percent in Cleveland, 60 percent in Akron, and 80 percent in Toledo—cities dependent on manufacturing jobs in industries that had essentially shut down. The nation's banking system was so close to collapse that many state governors closed banks temporarily to avoid further panic.

By the winter of 1932 to 1933 the depression had totally overwhelmed public welfare institutions. Private charity and public relief, both of whose expenditures had risen dramatically, still reached only a fraction of the needy. Hunger haunted cities and rural areas alike. When a teacher tried to send a coal miner's daughter home from school because she was weak from hunger, the girl replied, "It won't do any good . . . because this is sister's day to eat." In New York City hospitals reported ninety-five deaths from starvation. This was the America that Roosevelt inherited when he took the oath of office on March 4, 1933.

For Further Exploration

The 1930s are particularly rich in document collections of oral histories and other primary sources. Robert S. McElvaine's *Down and Out in the Great Depression* (1983) offers poignant letters written by ordinary people to the Roosevelts, Herbert Hoover, and other government officials. Studs Terkel's *Hard Times: An Oral History of the Great Depression* (1970) is an invaluable collection, as is Ann Banks, ed., *First-Person America*. See also Russell Baker's memoir about his depression-era childhood, *Growing Up* (1982). Similarly, there is much to choose from in the literature of the decade. The most familiar novel is John Steinbeck's *The Grapes of Wrath* (1939), but see also the radical novel *Pity Is Not Enough* (1933) by Josephine

TIMELINE

1929	Stock market crash
1930	Midwestern drought (through 1941)
	Hawley-Smoot Tariff slashes demand for U.S. imports.
1931	Scottsboro case
	Hoover declares a moratorium on Allied war debts.
	Miners strike in Harlan County, Kentucky.
	Communist-led hunger marches
1932	Reconstruction Finance Corporation created
	Bonus Army war veterans dispersed by U.S. Army troops
	Height of deportation of Mexican migrant workers
	Pearl S. Buck's *The Good Earth*
	Farm Holiday Association founded
	Violent strike at Ford's River Rouge plant in Michigan

	Franklin Delano Roosevelt is elected president.
1933	Unemployment rises to its highest level.
	Birth rate drops to its lowest level.
	Marx Brothers' *Duck Soup*
1934	Southern Tenant Farmers Union founded
	It Happened One Night sweeps the Oscars.
1935	National Youth Administration created
	Harlem race riot
1936	Margaret Mitchell's *Gone with the Wind*
	Birth control legalized
1939	John Steinbeck's *The Grapes of Wrath*
	Frank Capra's *Mr. Smith Goes to Washington*

Herbst and Richard Wright's *Native Son* (1940), his classic novel about Bigger Thomas, a young African American man in Chicago mired in a life of poverty and violence. A haunting account of southern poverty is *Let Us Now Praise Famous Men* (1940) by James Agee, with photographs by Walker Evans. For a collection of poetry, fiction, and nonfiction writing, see Harvey Swados, *The American Writer and the Great Depression* (1966).

The University of Virginia's "America in the 1930s" is a comprehensive site. See especially "On the Air," which offers audio clips of *Amos 'n' Andy* and other series at <http://xroads.virginia.edu/~1930s/home_1.html>. Much valuable material can be found on the University of Utrecht's "American Culture in the 1930s" site at <http://www.let.ruu.nl/ams/xroads/1930proj.htm>, which in turn points to other sites dealing with literature, film, and other aspects of American culture during the depression. The Library of Congress's American Memory collection has extensive material on the Depression, including a multimedia presentation, "Voices from the Dust Bowl: The Charles L. Todd and Robert Sonkin Migrant Worker Collection, 1940–41," at <http://lcweb2.loc.gov/ammem/afctshtml/tshome.html>.

Chapter 25

THE NEW DEAL
1933–1939

> I have been seeing people who, according to almost any standard, have practically nothing to look forward to or hope for. But there is hope; confidence, something intangible and real: the president won't forget us.
>
> —MARTHA GELHORN, GASTON COUNTY, NORTH CAROLINA, 1934

In his bold inaugural address on March 4, 1933, President Franklin Delano Roosevelt told a despondent, impoverished nation, "The only thing we have to fear is fear itself." That memorable phrase rallied a nation that had already endured almost four years of the worst economic contraction in its history—with no end in sight. His demeanor grim and purposeful, Roosevelt preached his first inaugural address like a sermon. Issuing ringing declarations of his vision of governmental activism—"This Nation asks for action, and action now"—he repeatedly compared combating the Great Depression to fighting a war. The new president was willing to ask Congress for "broad Executive power to wage a war against the emergency, as great as the power that would be given to me if we were in fact invaded by a foreign foe." He promised to "assume unhesitatingly the leadership of this great army of our people dedicated to a disciplined attack upon our common problems."

To wage this war, Roosevelt proposed the New Deal—a term that he first used in his acceptance speech at the Democratic National Convention in 1932 and that eventually came to stand for his administration's complex set of responses to the nation's economic collapse. The New Deal was never a definitive plan of action but rather evolved and expanded over the course of Roosevelt's presidency. In a time of major crisis it was meant to relieve suffering and conserve the nation's political and economic institutions through unprecedented activity on the part of the national government. Its legacy would be an expanded federal presence in the economy and in the lives of ordinary citizens.

The New Deal Takes Over, 1933–1935

The Great Depression destroyed Herbert Hoover's political reputation and helped to make Roosevelt's. Although some Americans—especially wealthy conservatives—hated FDR, he was immensely popular and beloved by many. Ironically, the ideological differences between Hoover and Roosevelt were not that vast. Both were committed to maintaining the nation's basic institutional structure. Both believed in the basic morality of a balanced budget and extolled the values of hard work, cooperation, and sacrifice. But Roosevelt's personal charisma, his political savvy, and his willingness to experiment made all the difference. Above all, his New Deal programs put people to work, instilling hope and restoring the nation's confidence.

ROOSEVELT'S STYLE OF LEADERSHIP

While the New Deal represented many things to many people, one unifying factor was the personality of Franklin Roosevelt. A superb and pragmatic politician, Roosevelt crafted his administration's program in response to shifting political and economic conditions rather than according to a set ideology or plan. He experimented with an idea; if it did not work, he tried another. "I have no expectation of making a hit every time I come to bat," Roosevelt told his critics. "What I seek is the highest possible batting average."

Roosevelt established an unusually close rapport with the American people. "Mr. Roosevelt is the only man we ever had in the White House who would understand that my boss is a son of a bitch," remarked one worker. Many ordinary citizens credited Roosevelt with the positive changes in their lives, saying. "He gave me a job" or "He saved my home." Roosevelt's masterful use of the new medium of radio, typified by the "fireside chats" he broadcast during his first two terms, fostered this personal identification. In the week after the inauguration more than 450,000 letters, many of which addressed Roosevelt as a friend or a member of the family, poured into the White House. An average of 5,000 to 8,000 arrived weekly for the rest of the decade. Whereas one person had handled public correspondence during the Hoover administration, a staff of fifty was required under Roosevelt.

Roosevelt's personal charisma allowed him to continue the expansion of presidential power begun in the administrations of Theodore Roosevelt and Woodrow Wilson. From the beginning he dramatically expanded the role of the executive branch in initiating policy, thereby helping to create the modern presidency. For policy formulation he turned to his talented cabinet, which included Secretary of the Interior Harold Ickes, Frances Perkins at Labor, Henry A. Wallace at Agriculture, and an old friend, Henry Morgenthau Jr., at Treasury. During the interregnum (the period between election and inauguration) Roosevelt relied so heavily on the advice of the Columbia University professors Raymond Moley, Rexford Tugwell, and Adolph A. Berle Jr. that the press dubbed them the "Brain Trust."

FDR

President Franklin Delano Roosevelt was a consummate politician who loved the adulation of a crowd, such as this one greeting him in Warm Springs, Georgia, in 1933. He consciously adopted a cheerful mien to keep people from feeling sorry for him because of his infirmity, knowing that he could not be a successful politician if the public pitied him.

(Corbis-Bettmann)

THE HUNDRED DAYS

The first problem the new president confronted was the banking crisis. Since the stock-market crash about 9 million people had lost their savings. On the eve of the inauguration thirty-eight states had closed their banks, and the remaining ten had restricted their hours of operation. On March 5, the day after the inauguration, the president declared a national "bank holiday"—a euphemism for closing all the banks—and called Congress into special session. Four days later Congress, which responded enthusiastically to most early New Deal legislative proposals, passed Roosevelt's proposed emergency banking bill, which permitted banks to reopen beginning on March 13—but only if a Treasury Department inspection showed they had sufficient cash reserves. The House approved the plan after only thirty-eight minutes of debate.

The Emergency Banking Act, which Roosevelt developed in consultation with banking leaders, was a conservative document that mirrored Herbert Hoover's proposals. The difference was the public's reaction. On the Sunday evening before the banks reopened, Roosevelt broadcast his first fireside chat to a radio audience estimated at 60 million. In simple terms he reassured citizens that the banks were safe, and Americans believed him. When the banks reopened on Monday morning, deposits exceeded withdrawals. "Capitalism was saved in eight days," observed Raymond Moley, who had served as Roosevelt's speechwriter in the 1932 campaign. By using the federal government to investigate the nation's banks and restore confidence in the system, the banking act did its job. Though more than 4,000 banks failed in 1933—the vast majority in the months before the law took effect—only 61 closed their doors in 1934.

The Banking Act was the first of fifteen pieces of major legislation enacted by Congress in the opening months of the Roosevelt administration. This legislative session, known as the "Hundred Days," remains one of the most productive ever. Congress created the Home Owners Loan Corporation to refinance home mortgages threatened by foreclosure. A second banking law, the Glass-Steagall Act, curbed speculation by separating investment banking from commercial banking and created the Federal Deposit Insurance Corporation (FDIC), which insured deposits up to $2,500. Another act established the Civilian Conservation Corps (CCC), which sent 250,000 young men to do reforestation and conservation work. The Tennessee Valley Authority (TVA) received legislative approval for its innovative plan of government-sponsored regional development and public energy. And in a move that lifted public spirits immeasurably, Roosevelt legalized beer in April. Full repeal of Prohibition came eight months later in December 1933.

To speed economic recovery the Roosevelt administration targeted three pressing problems—agricultural overproduction, business failures, and unemployment relief. Roosevelt considered a healthy farming sector crucial to the nation's economic well-being. As he put it in 1929, "If farmers starve today, we will all starve tomorrow." Thus, he viewed the Agricultural Adjustment Act (AAA) as a key step toward the nation's recovery. The AAA established a system for seven major commodities (wheat, cotton, corn, hogs, rice, tobacco, and dairy products) that provided cash subsidies to farmers who cut production—a tradition that continues to the present day. These benefits were financed by a tax on processing (such as the milling of wheat), which was passed on to consumers. New Deal planners hoped prices would rise in response to the federally subsidized scarcity, spurring a general recovery.

Though the AAA stabilized the agricultural sector, its benefits were distributed unevenly. Subsidies for reducing production went primarily to the owners of large and medium-size farms, who often cut production by reducing their renters' and sharecroppers' acreage rather than their own. In the South, where many sharecroppers were black and the landowners and government administrators white, that strategy had racial overtones. As many as 200,000 black tenant farmers were displaced from their land by the AAA. Thus, New Deal agricultural policies fostered the migration of marginal farmers in the South and Midwest to northern cities and California, while they consolidated the economic and political clout of larger land-holders.

The New Deal's major response to the problem of economic recovery, the National Industrial Recovery Act, launched the National Recovery Administration (NRA). The NRA established a system of industrial self-government to handle the problems of overproduction, cutthroat competition, and price instability that had caused business failures. For each industry a code of prices and production quotas, similar to those for farm products, was hammered out. In effect, these legally enforceable agreements suspended the antitrust laws. The codes also established minimum wages and maximum hours and outlawed child labor. One of the most far-reaching provisions, Section 7(a), guaranteed workers the right to organize and bargain collectively, "through representatives of their own choosing." These union rights dramatically spurred the growth of the labor movement in the 1930s.

General Hugh Johnson, a colorful if erratic administrator, headed the NRA. Johnson supervised negotiations for more than 600 NRA codes, ranging from large industries such as coal, cotton, and steel to small ones such as dog food, costume jewelry, and even burlesque theaters. Trade associations, controlled by large companies, tended to dominate the code-drafting process, thus solidifying the power of large businesses at the expense of smaller enterprises. Labor had little input, and consumer interests almost none.

The early New Deal also addressed the critical problem of unemployment. In the fourth year of the depression the total exhaustion of private and local sources of charity made some form of federal relief essential. Reluctantly, Roosevelt moved toward federal assumption of responsibility for the unemployed. The Federal Emergency Relief Administration (FERA), set up in May 1933 under the direction of Harry Hopkins, a social worker from New York, offered federal money to the states for relief programs. FERA was designed to keep people from starving until other recovery measures took hold. In his first two hours in office Hopkins distributed $5 million. Over the program's two-year existence FERA spent $1 billion.

Roosevelt and his advisers maintained a strong distaste for the dole. As Hopkins worried, "I don't think anybody can go year after year, month after month, accepting relief without affecting his character in some ways unfavorably. It is probably going to undermine the independence of hundreds of thousands of families." Whenever possible New Deal administrators promoted work relief over cash subsidies, and they consistently favored jobs that would not compete directly with the private sector. When the Public Works Administration (PWA), under Secretary of the Interior Harold L. Ickes, received a $3.3 billion appropriation in 1933, Ickes's cautiousness in initiating public works projects limited the agency's effectiveness. But in November 1933 Roosevelt established the Civil Works Administration (CWA) and named Harry Hopkins its head. Within thirty days the CWA had put 2.6 million men and women to work; at its peak in January 1934 it employed 4 million in jobs such as repairing bridges, building highways, constructing public buildings, and setting up community projects. The CWA, regarded as a stopgap measure to get the country through the winter of 1933 to 1934, lapsed the next spring after spending all its funds.

Many of these early emergency measures were deliberately inflationary. They were designed to trigger price increases, which were thought necessary to stimulate recovery and halt the steep deflation. Another element of this strategy was Roosevelt's executive order of April 18, 1933, to abandon the international gold standard and allow gold to rise in value like any other commodity. As the price of gold rose, administrators hoped, so too would the prices of manufactured and agricultural goods. Though removing the country from the gold standard did not have much impact on the American economy, it did provide the Federal Reserve System freedom to pursue domestic goals such as stable prices and full employment without being tied to the value of gold on the international market. Now it could manipulate the value of the dollar in response to fluctuating economic conditions.

When an exhausted Congress recessed in June 1933, much had been accomplished. Rarely had a president so dominated a legislative session. A mass of "alphabet soup agencies," as the New Deal programs came to be known, had been created. But though they gave the impression of action and initiated a slight economic upturn, they did not turn the economy around.

After the Hundred Days, with no end to the depression in sight, Roosevelt and Congress continued to pass legislation to promote recovery and restore confidence. Much of it focused on reforming business practices to prevent future depressions. In 1934 Congress established the Securities and Exchange Commission (SEC) to regulate the stock market and prevent insider trading, fraud, and other abuses. The Banking Act of 1935 authorized the president to appoint a new Board of Governors of the Federal Reserve System, placing control of interest rates and other money-market policies at the federal level rather than with regional banks. By requiring all large state banks to join the Federal Reserve System by 1942 to take advantage of the federal deposit insurance system, the law further encouraged centralization of the nation's banking system.

THE NEW DEAL UNDER ATTACK

As Congress and the president consolidated the New Deal, their work came under attack from several quarters. Although Roosevelt billed himself as the savior of capitalism, noting that "to preserve we had to reform," his actions provoked strong hostility from many Americans. To the wealthy Roosevelt became simply "that man," a traitor to his class. Business leaders and conservative Democrats formed the Liberty League in 1934 to lobby against the New Deal and its "reckless spending" and "socialist" reforms.

The conservative majority on the Supreme Court also disagreed with the direction of the New Deal. On "Black Monday," May 27, 1935, the Supreme Court struck down the NRA in *Schechter v. United States,* ruling unanimously that the National Industrial Recovery Act represented an unconstitutional delegation of legislative power to the executive. The so-called sick-chicken case concerned a Brooklyn, New York, firm convicted of violating NRA codes by selling diseased poultry. In its decision the court also ruled that the NRA regulated commerce within states, while the Constitution limited federal regulation to interstate commerce. Roosevelt protested that the Court's narrow interpretation would return the Constitution "to the horse-and-buggy definition of interstate commerce" and worried privately that the Court might invalidate the entire New Deal.

Other citizens thought the New Deal had not gone far enough. Francis Townsend, a Long Beach, California, doctor, spoke for the nation's elderly. Many Americans feared poverty in old age because few had pension plans and many had lost their life savings in bank failures. In 1933 Townsend proposed the Old Age Revolving Pension Plan, which would have given $200 a month—a considerable sum at the time—to citizens over the age of sixty. To receive payments the elderly would have had to retire from their jobs, thus opening their positions to others, and would also have had to agree to spend the money within a month. Townsend Clubs soon sprang up across the country, particularly in the Far West.

Father Charles Coughlin also challenged Roosevelt's leadership, attracting a large following, especially in the Midwest. A parish priest in the Detroit suburb of Royal Oak, Coughlin had turned to the radio in the mid-1920s to enlarge his pastorate. In 1933 about 40 million Americans listened regularly to the Radio Priest's broadcasts. At first Coughlin supported the New Deal, but he soon broke with Roosevelt over the president's refusal to support the nationalization of the banking system and expansion of the money supply. In 1935 Coughlin organized the National Union for Social Justice to promote his views, billing them as an alternative to those of "Franklin Double-Crossing Roosevelt." Because he was Canadian-born and a priest, Coughlin was not likely to make a run for president, but his rapidly growing constituency threatened to complicate the 1936 election.

The most direct threat to Roosevelt came from Senator Huey Long. In a single term as governor of Louisiana the flamboyant Long had achieved stunning popularity. He had increased the share of state taxes paid by corporations and had embarked on a program of public works that included construction of new highways, bridges, hospitals, and schools. But Long's accomplishments came at a price: to push through his reforms he had seized almost dictatorial control of the state government. He maintained control over Louisiana's political machine even after his election to the U.S. Senate in 1930. Though he supported Roosevelt in 1932, he made no secret of his own presidential ambitions.

In 1934 Senator Long broke with the New Deal, arguing that its programs did not go far enough. Like Coughlin he established his own national movement, the Share Our Wealth Society, which boasted over 4 million followers by 1935. Arguing that the unequal distribution of wealth in the United States was the fundamental cause of the depression, Long advocated taxing 100 percent of all incomes over $1

The Kingfish

Huey Long, the Louisiana governor and senator, was one of the most controversial figures in American political history. He took his nickname "Kingfish" from a character in the popular radio show *Amos 'n' Andy*. Long inspired one of the most powerful political novels of all time, Robert Penn Warren's *All the King's Men,* which won a Pulitzer Prize in 1946. (UPI/Corbis-Bettmann)

million and all inheritances over $5 million, distributing the money to the rest of the population. He knew his plan was unworkable but confided privately, "When they figure that out, I'll have something new for them."

Like Coughlin, Long offered simple solutions to the nation's economic ills. Their extreme proposals alarmed liberals. Coughlin's rhetoric, furthermore, often had anti-Semitic overtones, and both men showed little regard for the niceties of representative government. Coughlin had actually promised to dictate if necessary to preserve democracy. And the demagogic Long had dismissed complaints about his unconstitutional interference with the Louisiana legislative process by announcing, "I'm the Constitution around here." Long's and Coughlin's ideas and their rapid rise in popularity suggested strong currents of public dissatisfaction with the Roosevelt administration. The president's strategists feared that Long might join forces with Coughlin and Townsend to form a third party, enabling the Republicans to win the 1936 election.

The Second New Deal, 1935–1938

As the depression continued and attacks on the New Deal mounted, Roosevelt and his advisers embarked on a new course, which historians have labeled the Second New Deal. By 1935, frustrated by his inability to win the support of big business, Roosevelt began to openly criticize the "money classes," proudly stating that "We have earned the hatred of entrenched greed." Pushed to the left by the popularity of movements like Long's as well as by signs of militancy among workers, Roosevelt, his eye fixed firmly on the 1936 election, began to construct a new coalition and broaden the scope of his response to the depression. Unlike the First New Deal, which focused on recovery, the Second New Deal emphasized reform and promoted legislation to increase the role of the federal government in providing for the welfare of citizens.

LEGISLATIVE ACCOMPLISHMENTS

The first beneficiary of Roosevelt's change in direction was the labor movement. The rising number of strikes in 1934—about 1,800 involving a total of 1.5 million workers—reflected the dramatic growth of rank-and-file militancy. After the Supreme Court declared the NRA unconstitutional in 1935, invalidating Section 7(a), labor representatives demanded effective legislation. The Wagner Act (1935), named for its sponsor, Senator Robert F. Wagner of New York, offered a degree of protection to labor. It upheld the right of industrial workers to join a union (farm workers were not covered) and outlawed many unfair labor practices used to squelch unions, such as firing workers for union activities. The act also established the nonpartisan National Labor Relations Board (NLRB) to protect workers from employer coercion, supervise elections for union representation, and guarantee the process of collective bargaining.

The Social Security Act signed by Roosevelt on August 14, 1935, was partly a response to the political mobilization of the nation's elderly through the Townsend and Long movements. But it also reflected prodding from social reformers like Grace Abbott, head of the Children's Bureau, and Secretary of Labor Frances Perkins. The Social Security Act provided pensions for most workers in the private sector, although originally agricultural workers and domestics were not covered. Pensions were to be paid out of a federal-state fund to which both employers and employees would contribute. The act also established a joint federal-state system of unemployment compensation, funded by an unemployment tax on employers.

The Social Security Act was a milestone in the creation of the modern welfare state. Now the United States joined industrialized countries like Great Britain and Germany in providing old-age pensions and unemployment compensation to citizens. (The Roosevelt administration chose not to push for national health insurance, even though most other industrialized nations offered such protection.) The act also mandated categorical assistance to the blind, deaf, and disabled and to dependent children—the so-called deserving poor, who clearly could not support themselves. Categorical assistance programs, only a small part of the New Deal, gradually expanded over the years until they became an integral part of the American welfare system.

Roosevelt was never enthusiastic about large expenditures for social welfare programs. But in the sixth year of the depression 10 million Americans were still out of work, creating a pressing moral and political issue for FDR and the Democrats. Un-

"Gulliver's Travels"

So many new agencies flooded out of Washington in the 1930s that one almost needed a score-card to keep them straight. Here a July 1935 *Vanity Fair* cartoon by William Gropper substitutes Uncle Sam for Captain Lemuel Gulliver, tied to the ground by Lilliputians, in a parody of Jonathan Swift's *Gulliver's Travels.*

(Courtesy Vanity Fair. © 1935 [renewed 1963] by The Conde Nast Publications, Inc.)

der Harry Hopkins the Works Progress Administration (WPA) became the main fed-eral relief agency for the rest of the depression. While FERA had supplied grants to state relief programs, the WPA put relief workers directly onto the federal payroll. Between 1935 and 1943 the WPA employed 8.5 million Americans, spending $10.5 billion. The agency's employees constructed 651,087 miles of roads, 125,110 public buildings, 8,192 parks, and 853 airports and built or repaired 124,087 bridges.

Though the WPA was an extravagant operation by the standards of the 1930s (it inspired nicknames such as "We Putter Around" and "We Poke Along"), it never reached more than a third of the nation's unemployed. The average wage of $55 a month—well below the government-defined subsistence level of $100 a month—barely enabled workers to eke out a living. In 1941 the government cut the pro-gram severely. It ended in 1943 when the economy returned to full employment during World War II.

The Revenue Act of 1935, a tax reform bill that increased estate and corporate taxes and instituted higher personal income tax rates in the top brackets, showed Roosevelt's willingness to push for reforms that were considered too controversial earlier in his presidency. Much of the business community had already turned violently against Roosevelt in reaction to the NRA, the Social Security Act, and the Wagner Act. Wealthy conservatives quickly labeled the measure an attempt to "soak the rich." Roosevelt, seeking to defuse the popularity of Huey Long's Share Our Wealth plan, was just as interested in the political mileage of the tax bill as its actual results, which increased federal revenue by only $250 million a year.

As the 1936 election approached, the broad range of New Deal programs (Table 25.1) brought new voters into the Democratic coalition. Many had been personally helped by federal programs; others benefited because their interests had found new support in the federal expansion. Roosevelt could count on a potent coalition of urban-based workers, organized labor, northern blacks, farmers, white ethnic groups, Catholics, Jews, liberals, intellectuals, progressive Republicans, and middle-class families concerned about unemployment and old-age dependence. The Democrats also held on, though with some difficulty, to their traditional constituency of white southerners.

The Republicans realized that they could not directly oppose Roosevelt and the New Deal. To run against the president they chose the progressive governor of Kansas, Alfred M. Landon, who accepted the general precepts of the New Deal. Landon and the Republicans concentrated on criticizing the inefficiency and expense of many New Deal programs, stridently accusing FDR of harboring dictatorial ambitions.

Roosevelt's victory in 1936 was one of the biggest landslides in American history. The assassination of Huey Long in September 1935 had deflated the threat of a serious third-party challenge; the candidate of the combined Long-Townsend-Coughlin camp, Congressman William Lemke of North Dakota, garnered fewer than 900,000 votes (1.9 percent) for the Union Party ticket. Roosevelt received 60.8 percent of the popular vote and carried every state except Maine and Vermont. The New Deal was at high tide.

STALEMATE

From this high point the New Deal soon slid into retrenchment, controversy, and stalemate. The first setback came when Roosevelt attempted to make fundamental changes in the structure of the Supreme Court. Shortly after finding the NRA unconstitutional in *Schechter v. United States,* the Court had struck down the Agricultural Adjustment Act, a coal conservation act, and New York State's minimum wage law. With the Wagner Act, the TVA, and Social Security coming up on appeal, the future of New Deal reform measures seemed in doubt.

Roosevelt's response, two weeks after his second inauguration, was to propose the addition of one new justice for each sitting justice over the age of seventy—a

TABLE 25.1
Major New Deal Legislation

Agriculture

1933	Agricultural Adjustment Act (AAA)
1935	Resettlement Administration (RA)
	Rural Electrification Administration
1937	Farm Security Administration (FSA)
1938	Agricultural Adjustment Act of 1938

Business and Industry

1933	Emergency Banking Act
	Glass-Steagall Act (FDIC)
	National Industrial Recovery Act (NIRA)
1934	Securities and Exchange Commission (SEC)
1935	Banking Act of 1935
	Revenue Act (wealth tax)

Conservation and the Environment

1933	Tennessee Valley Authority (TVA)
	Civilian Conservation Corps (CCC)
1936	Soil Conservation and Domestic Allotment Act

Labor and Social Welfare

1933	Section 7(a) of NIRA
1935	National Labor Relations Act (Wagner Act)
	National Labor Relations Board (NLRB)
	Social Security Act
1937	National Housing Act
1938	Fair Labor Standards Act (FLSA)

Relief

1933	Federal Emergency Relief Administration (FERA)
	Civil Works Administration (CWA)
	Public Works Administration (PWA)
1935	Works Progress Administration (WPA)
	National Youth Administration (NYA)

scheme that would have increased the number of justices from nine to fifteen. Roosevelt's opponents quickly protested that he was trying to "pack" the Court with justices who favored the New Deal. The president's proposal was also regarded as an assault on the principle of the separation of powers. But the issue became a moot one when the Supreme Court upheld several key pieces of New Deal legislation and a series of resignations created vacancies on the Court. Within four years Roosevelt managed to reshape the Supreme Court to suit his liberal philosophy through seven new appointments, including Hugo Black, Felix Frankfurter, and William O. Douglas.

Yet his handling of the court issue was a costly blunder at a time when his second-term administration was vulnerable to the lame-duck syndrome. No one yet suspected that FDR would break with tradition by seeking a third term.

Congressional conservatives had long opposed the direction of the New Deal, but the court-packing episode galvanized them by demonstrating that Roosevelt was no longer politically invincible. Throughout Roosevelt's second term a conservative coalition composed mainly of southern Democrats and Republicans from rural areas blocked or impeded social legislation. Two pieces of reform legislation that did win passage were the National Housing Act of 1937, which mandated the construction of low-cost public housing, and the Fair Labor Standards Act of 1938, which made permanent the minimum wage, maximum hours, and anti–child labor provisions in the NRA codes.

The "Roosevelt recession" of 1937 to 1938 dealt the most devastating blow to the president's political standing in the second term. Until that point the economy had made steady progress. From 1933 to 1937 the gross national product had grown at a yearly rate of about 10 percent, and by 1937 industrial output and real income had finally returned to 1929 levels. Unemployment had declined from 25 percent to 14 percent. Many Americans agreed with Senator James F. Byrnes of South Carolina that "the emergency has passed."

The steady improvement of the economy cheered Roosevelt, who had never been comfortable with large federal expenditures. Accordingly, Roosevelt slashed the federal budget in 1937. Between January and August Congress cut the WPA's funding in half, causing layoffs of about 1.5 million workers. The Federal Reserve, fearing inflation, tightened credit, creating a sharp drop in the stock market. Unemployment soared to 19 percent. Roosevelt soon found himself in the same situation that had confounded Hoover. Having taken credit for the recovery between 1933 and 1937, he had to take the blame for the recession.

Shifting gears, Roosevelt spent his way out of the downturn. Large WPA appropriations and a resumption of public works projects poured enough money into the economy to lift it out of the recession by early 1938. Roosevelt and his economic advisers were groping their way toward the general theory advanced by John Maynard Keynes, a British economist who proposed that governments use deficit spending to stimulate the economy when private spending proves insufficient. But Keynes's theory would not be widely accepted until a dramatic increase in defense spending for World War II finally ended the Great Depression.

Still struggling with attacks on the New Deal, Roosevelt decided to "purge" the Democratic Party of some of his most conservative opponents as the 1938 election approached. In the spring primaries he campaigned against members of his own party who had been hostile or unsympathetic to New Deal initiatives. The purge failed abysmally and widened the liberal-conservative rift in the party. In the general election of 1938 Republicans capitalized on the "Roosevelt recession" and the backlash against the court-packing attempt to pick up eight seats in the Senate and eighty-one in the House. The Republicans also gained thirteen governorships.

Even without these political reversals the reform impetus of the New Deal probably would not have continued. Roosevelt had always set clear limits on how far he was willing to go. His instincts were basically conservative, not revolutionary; he had wanted only to save the capitalist economic system by reforming it. The new activism of the Second New Deal was a major step beyond the informal, one-sided business-government partnership of the preceding decade—a step Roosevelt took only because the emergency of the depression had pushed him in that direction.

The New Deal's Impact on Society

Despite the limits of the New Deal, it had a tremendous impact on the nation and fundamentally altered Americans' relationship to their government. With an optimistic faith in using government for social purposes, New Dealers sponsored programs in the arts. They created vast projects to conserve the country's natural beauty and resources and to make them more accessible to its citizens. The "broker state" that emerged in the New Deal also brought the voices of more citizens—women, blacks, labor, Mexican Americans—into the public arena, helping to promote the view that Roosevelt and his party represented and mediated for the common people.

NEW DEAL CONSTITUENCIES

The New Deal accelerated the expansion of the federal bureaucracy that had been under way since the turn of the century. In a decade the number of civilian government employees increased 80 percent, exceeding a million by 1940. The number of federal employees who worked in Washington grew at an even faster rate, doubling between 1929 and 1940. Power was increasingly centered in the nation's capital, not in the states (see American Voices, "A New Deal Activist").

The growth of the federal government increased the potential impact of its decisions (and spending) on various constituencies. During the 1930s the federal government operated as a broker state—mediating between contending pressure groups seeking power and benefits. Democrats recognized the importance of satisfying certain blocs of voters to cement their allegiance to the party. Even before the depression they had begun to build a coalition based on urban political machines and white ethnic voters. In the 1930s organized labor, women, African Americans, and other groups joined that coalition, receiving increased attention from the Democrats and the federal government they controlled.

During the 1930s labor relations became a legitimate arena for federal action and intervention, and organized labor claimed a place in national political life. Labor's dramatic growth in the 1930s represented one of the most important social and economic changes of the decade—an enormous contrast to its demoralized state at the end of the 1920s. Several factors encouraged the growth of the labor movement—the inadequacy of welfare capitalism in the face of the depression, New

AMERICAN VOICES

A New Deal Activist

JOE MARCUS

*A*s an economist working for Harry Hopkins, Joe Marcus was one of thousands who formed the growing New Deal bureaucracy. Marcus's account, as told to Studs Terkel, captures some of the excitement that the New Deal generated. Marcus also suggests the way in which Roosevelt's administration expanded opportunities for Jews and other "outsiders."

I graduated college in '35. I went down to Washington and started to work in the spring of '36. The New Deal was a young man's world. Young people, if they showed any ability, got an opportunity. . . . In a few months I was made head of the department. We had a meeting with hot shots: What's to be done? I pointed out some problems: let's define what we're looking for. They immediately had me take over. . . .

The climate was exciting. You were part of a society that was on the move. You were involved in something that could make a difference. Laws could be changed. So could the conditions of people.

The idea of being involved close to the center of political life was unthinkable, just two or three years before all this happened. Unthinkable for someone like me, of lower middle-class, close to ghetto, Jewish life. Suddenly you were a significant member of society. It was not the kind of closed society you had lived in before. . . .

You were really part of something, changes could be made. Bringing *immediate* results to people who were starving. You could do something about it: that was the most important thing. . . .

We weren't thinking of remaking society. That wasn't it. I didn't buy this dream stuff. What was happening was a complete change in social attitudes at the central government level. The question was: How can you do it within this system? . . . The basic feeling—and I don't think this is just nostalgia—was one of excitement, of achievement, of happiness. Life was important, life was significant.

SOURCE: Studs Terkel, *Hard Times* (New York: Pantheon, 1986), pp. 265–66.

Deal legislation like the Wagner Act, the rise of the Congress of Industrial Organizations (CIO), and the growing militancy of rank-and-file workers. By the end of the decade the number of unionized workers had tripled to almost 9 million, or 23 percent of the nonfarm workforce. Organized labor won the battle not only for union recognition but for higher wages, seniority systems, and grievance procedures.

The CIO served as the cutting edge of the union movement by promoting industrial unionism—that is, organizing all the workers in an industry, both skilled and unskilled, into one union. John L. Lewis, leader of the United Mine Workers (UMW) and a founder of the CIO in 1935, was the foremost exponent of industrial unionism. Lewis began to detach himself from the American Federation of Labor (AFL), which favored organizing workers on a craft-by-craft basis, in 1935; by 1938 the break was complete.

The CIO achieved some of its momentum through the presence in its ranks of members of the Communist Party. The rise of fascism in Europe had prompted the Soviet Union to mobilize support in democratic countries. In Europe and the United States communist parties called for a "popular front," welcoming the cooperation of any group concerned about the threat of fascism to civil rights, organized labor, and world peace. Under the popular front communists softened their revolutionary rhetoric and concentrated on becoming active leaders in many CIO unions. While few workers actually joined the Communist Party, its influence in labor organizing in the thirties was far greater than its numbers, which in 1936 reached 40,000.

The CIO's success also stemmed from the recognition that to succeed unions must be more inclusive. The CIO worked deliberately to attract new groups to the labor movement. Mexican Americans and African Americans found the CIO's commitment to racial justice a strong contrast to the AFL's long-established patterns of

Organize

The Steel Workers Organizing Committee was one of the most vital labor organizations contributing to the rise of the CIO. Though steelworkers were all male, women workers in other sectors of the economy also joined the CIO in large numbers.

(Library of Congress)

exclusion and segregation. And about 800,000 women workers also found a limited welcome in the CIO. Few blacks, Mexican Americans, or women held leadership positions, however.

The CIO scored its first major victory in the automobile industry. On December 31, 1936, General Motors workers in Flint, Michigan, staged a sit-down strike, vowing to stay at their machines until management agreed to collective bargaining. The workers lived in the factories and machine shops for forty-four days before General Motors recognized their union, United Automobile Workers (UAW). Shortly thereafter the CIO won another major victory, at the U.S. Steel Corporation. Despite a long history of bitter opposition to unionization (as demonstrated in the 1919 steel strike—see Chapter 22), Big Steel executives capitulated without a fight and recognized the Steel Workers Organizing Committee (SWOC) on March 2, 1937.

Labor's new vitality spilled over into political action. The AFL generally had stood aloof from partisan politics, but the CIO quickly allied itself with the Democratic Party, hoping to use its influence to elect candidates sympathetic to labor and social justice. Through Labor's Nonpartisan League, the CIO gave $770,000 to Democratic campaigns in 1936. Labor also provided solid support for Roosevelt's plan to reorganize the Supreme Court.

Despite the breakthroughs of the New Deal the labor movement never developed into a dominant force in American life. Roosevelt never made the growth of the labor movement a high priority, and many workers remained indifferent or even hostile to unionization. And although the Wagner Act guaranteed unions a permanent place in American industrial relations, it did not revolutionize working conditions. The right to collective bargaining, rather than redistributing power in American industry, merely granted labor a measure of legitimacy. Management even found that unions could be used as a buffer against rank-and-file militancy. New Deal social welfare programs also tended to diffuse some of the pre-1937 radical spirit by channeling economic benefits to workers whether or not they belonged to unions. The road to union power, even with New Deal protection, continued to be a rocky and uncertain one.

Like organized workers white women achieved new influence in the experimental climate of the New Deal, as unprecedented numbers of them were offered positions in the Roosevelt administration. Frances Perkins, the first woman named to a cabinet post, served as secretary of labor throughout Roosevelt's presidency. Molly Dewson, a social reformer turned politician, headed the Women's Division of the Democratic National Committee, where she pushed an issue-oriented program that supported New Deal reforms. Roosevelt's appointments of women included the first female director of the mint, the head of a major WPA division, and a judge on a circuit court of appeals. Many of those women were close friends as well as professional colleagues and cooperated in an informal network to advance feminist and reform causes.

Eleanor Roosevelt exemplified the growing prominence of women in public life. In the 1920s she had worked closely with other reformers to increase women's power in political parties, labor unions, and education. The experience proved an invaluable apprenticeship for her White House years, when her marriage to FDR developed into one of the most successful political partnerships of all time. He was the pragmatic politician, always aware of what could be done; she was the idealist, the gadfly, always pushing him—and the New Deal—to do more. Eleanor Roosevelt served as the conscience of the New Deal.

Despite the advocacy of a female political network for equal opportunity for women, grave flaws still marred New Deal programs. A fourth of the NRA codes set a lower minimum wage for women than for men performing the same jobs. New Deal agencies like the Civil Works Administration and the Public Works Administration gave jobs almost exclusively to men: only 7 percent of CWA workers were female. And the CCC excluded women entirely, prompting critics to ask, "Where is the 'she-she-she'?"

When they did hire women, New Deal programs tended to reinforce the broader society's gender and racial attitudes. Thus program administrators resisted placing women in nontraditional jobs. Under the WPA sewing rooms became a sort of dumping ground for unemployed women. African American and Mexican American women, if they had access to work relief at all, often found themselves shunted into training as domestics, whose work was not covered by the Social Security and Fair Labor Standards Acts.

Just as the New Deal did not seriously challenge gender inequities, it did little to battle racial discrimination. In the 1930s the vast majority of the American people did not regard civil rights as a legitimate area for federal intervention. Indeed, many New Deal programs reflected prevailing racist attitudes. CCC camps segregated blacks and whites, and many NRA codes did not protect black workers. Most tellingly, Franklin Roosevelt repeatedly refused to support legislation to make

Eleanor Roosevelt and Civil Rights

One of Eleanor Roosevelt's greatest legacies was her commitment to civil rights. For example, she publicly resigned from the Daughters of the American Revolution (DAR) in 1939 when the group refused to let the black opera singer Marian Anderson perform at Constitution Hall. Roosevelt developed an especially close working relationship with Mary McLeod Bethune of the National Youth Administration, shown here at a conference on black youth in 1939. (AP/Wide World Photos)

lynching a federal crime, claiming it would antagonize southern members of Congress whose support he needed to pass New Deal measures.

Nevertheless, blacks did receive significant benefits from those New Deal relief programs that were directed toward the poor regardless of their race or ethnic background. Blacks made up about 18 percent of the WPA's recipients, although they constituted only 10 percent of the population. The Resettlement Administration, established in 1935 to help small farmers buy land and to resettle sharecroppers and tenant farmers on more productive land, fought for the rights of black tenant farmers in the South—until angry southerners in Congress drastically cut its appropriations. Still, many blacks reasoned that the tangible aid from Washington outweighed the discrimination that marred many federal programs.

African Americans were also pleased to see blacks appointed to federal office. Mary McLeod Bethune, an educator who ran the Office of Minority Affairs of the National Youth Administration, headed the "black cabinet." This informal network worked for fairer treatment of blacks by New Deal agencies, in the same way the women's network advocated feminist causes. Both groups benefited greatly from the support of Eleanor Roosevelt. The first lady's promotion of equal treatment for blacks ranks as one of her greatest legacies.

Help from the WPA and other New Deal programs and a belief that the White House—or at least Eleanor Roosevelt—cared about their plight, caused a dramatic change in African Americans' voting behavior. Since the Civil War blacks had voted Republican, a loyalty based on Abraham Lincoln's freeing of the slaves. As late as 1932 black voters in northern cities overwhelmingly supported Republican candidates. But in 1936 black Americans outside the South (where blacks were still largely prevented from voting) gave Roosevelt 71 percent of their votes. In Harlem, where relief dollars increased dramatically in the wake of the 1935 riot (see Chapter 24), their support was an extraordinary 81.3 percent. Black voters have remained overwhelmingly Democratic ever since.

The election of Franklin Roosevelt also had an immediate effect on Mexican American communities, demoralized by the depression and the deportations of the Hoover years. In cities like Los Angeles and El Paso Mexican Americans qualified for relief more easily under New Deal guidelines, and there was more relief to go around (see American Voices, "A Chicana Youth Gets New Deal Work"). Even though New Deal guidelines prohibited discrimination based on an immigrant's legal status, the new climate encouraged a marked rise in requests for naturalization papers. Mexican Americans also benefited from New Deal labor policies; for many, joining the CIO was an important stage in becoming an American. Inspired by New Deal rhetoric about economic recovery and social progress through cooperation, Mexican Americans increasingly identified with the United States rather than with Mexico. This shift was especially evident among American-born children of Mexican immigrants (see Chapter 24). Participating in the political system increasingly became part of Mexican American life. Los Angeles activist Beatrice Griffith noted, "Franklin D. Roosevelt's name was the spark that started thousands of Spanish-speaking persons

AMERICAN VOICES

A Chicana Youth Gets New Deal Work

Susana Archuleta

*A*lthough African Americans and Chicanos often experienced discrimination in New Deal programs, many did find opportunities in New Deal agencies like the Civilian Conservation Corps, the National Youth Administration, or the Works Progress Administration. And they attributed the help they received directly to Franklin Delano Roosevelt's election, as Susana Archuleta's reminiscence of life in Wyoming suggests.

I was born in New Mexico, on a farm up North in Mora County. I was the fifth of eight children. When I was very little, my dad moved us all to Wyoming. You see, he heard that they had free textbooks in Wyoming, while here in New Mexico the parents had to pay for the books. Daddy didn't have much money, and he felt that we all needed an opportunity for education. We left the farm—the animals, the machinery, everything—and he went to work in the mines up in Rock Springs, Wyoming. . . .

During the Depression, things got bad. My dad passed away when I was about twelve, leaving my mother with eight children and no means of support. There wasn't any welfare. My mother took in washings to make a living, and our job was to pick up the washings on the way home from school. We'd pick up clothes from the schoolteachers, the attorney, and what-have-you. Then, at night, we'd help iron them and fold them. . . .

When I was a teenager, the Depression began to take a turn. Franklin Roosevelt was elected, and the works projects started. The boys and young men who'd been laid off at the mines went to the CCC camps, and the girls joined the NYA. When school was over, we'd go and work right there in the school building. We'd help out in the office, do filing and other things. Actually, we didn't do much work—it was our first job. But we learned a lot. It was good experience.

They paid us about twenty-one dollars a month. Out of that we got five and the other sixteen was directly issued to our parents. The same was true of the boys working in the camps. They got about thirty dollars a month. They were allowed to keep five of it. The rest was sent to their families. All of us were hired according to our family income. If a man with a lot of children was unemployed, he was given preference over someone who had less children. They also had projects for women who were widows. They made quilts and mattresses. Those programs were great. Everybody got a chance to work. I think there should be more training programs like that, instead of giveaway programs like welfare. . . .

SOURCE: Nan Elsasser, "Susana Archuleta," in Nan Elsasser et al., *Las Mujeres: Conversations from a Hispanic Community* (New York: Feminist Press, 1980), pp. 36–37.

to the polls." The Democrats made it clear that they welcomed Mexican American voters and considered them an important part of the New Deal coalition.

But what about groups that did not mobilize politically or were not recognized as key participants in the New Deal coalition? Native Americans were one of the nation's most disadvantaged and powerless minorities. The average annual income of a Native American in 1934 was only $48; the unemployment rate among Native Americans was three times the national average. Concerned New Deal administrators like Secretary of the Interior Harold Ickes and Commissioner of the Bureau of Indian Affairs John Collier tried to correct some of those inequities. The Indian Section of the Civilian Conservation Corps brought needed money and projects to reservations throughout the West. Indians also received benefits from FERA and CWA work relief projects.

More ambitious was the Indian Reorganization Act of 1934, sometimes called the "Indian New Deal." That law reversed the Dawes Severalty Act of 1887 by promoting more extensive self-government through tribal councils and constitutions. The government also abandoned the attempt to force Native Americans to assimilate into mainstream society in favor of promoting cultural pluralism. The New Deal pledged to help preserve Indian languages, arts, and traditions and to restore some lands lost in the allotment program (see Chapter 16).

Despite the intention to redress some of the ills produced by earlier government policies, the Indian New Deal was profoundly flawed. Reflecting Collier's paternalistic approach, it tended to treat all tribes as identical, with the same needs and structures. Its imposition of American-style democracy did not always mesh with Native Americans' consensus style of decision making. The Seneca, for example, argued that the Indian Reorganization Act violated their treaty rights and the system of self-government they had adopted in 1848. Only 174 nations accepted the reorganization policy, while 78 refused to participate. While some native groups may have benefited from the Indian New Deal, the problems of Native Americans were so severe that these changes in federal policy did little to improve their lives or reinvigorate tribal communities.

THE NEW DEAL AND THE LAND

Concern for the land was one of the dominant motifs of the New Deal, and the shaping of the public landscape was among its most visible legacies. The expansion of federal responsibilities in the 1930s created a climate conducive to conservation efforts, as did public concern heightened by the dramatic images of drought and devastation in the Dust Bowl. Although the long-term success of New Deal resources policy was mixed, it innovatively stressed scientific management of the land, conservation instead of commercial development, and the aggressive use of public authority to safeguard both private and public holdings.

The most extensive New Deal environmental undertaking was the Tennessee Valley Authority. The need for dams to control flooding and erosion in the Tennessee River Basin, a seven-state area with some of the country's heaviest rainfall, had been recognized since World War I. But not until 1933 was the Tennessee Valley Authority established to develop the region's resources under public control. The TVA was the ultimate watershed demonstration area, integrating flood control, reforestation, and agricultural and industrial development, including the production of chemical fertilizers. A hydroelectric grid provided cheap electric power for the valley's residents.

The Dust Bowl helped to focus attention on land management and ecological balance. Agents from the Soil Conservation Service in the Department of Agriculture taught farmers the proper technique for tilling hillsides. Government agronomists also tried to remove marginal land from cultivation and to prevent soil erosion through better agricultural practices. One of their most widely publicized programs was the creation of the Shelterbelts, which involved the planting of 220 million trees running along roughly the ninety-ninth meridian from Abilene, Texas, to the Canadian border. Planted as a windbreak, the trees also prevented soil erosion. Another priority of the Roosevelt administration was helping rural Americans to stay on the land. The Rural Electrification Administration, established in 1935, brought power to farms in an attempt to improve the quality of rural life.

Today New Deal projects affecting the environment can be seen throughout the country. CCC and WPA workers built the Blue Ridge Parkway, which connects the Shenandoah National Park in Virginia with the Great Smoky Mountain National Park in North Carolina. In the West government workers built the San Francisco Zoo, Berkeley's Tilden Park, and the canals of San Antonio. The CCC helped to complete the East Coast's Appalachian Trail and the West Coast's Pacific Crest Trail through the Sierras. In state parks across the country cabins, shelters, picnic areas, lodges, and observation towers, built in a style that has been called *government rustic,* are witness to the New Deal ethos of recreation coexisting with conservation.

Although the New Deal was ahead of its time in its attention to conservation, its legacy to later environmental movements in mixed. Many of the tactics used in New Deal projects—damming rivers, blasting fire roads, altering the natural landscape through the construction of buildings and shelters—are now considered intrusive. In the 1970s the TVA came under attack for its longstanding practice of strip mining and the pollution caused by its power plants and chemical factories. Because of environmental concerns a project as massive as the TVA probably could not be built today—an ironic comment on what was once hailed as an enlightened use of government power.

THE NEW DEAL AND THE ARTS

In the arts, the depression dried up traditional sources of patronage. Like most Americans creative artists had nowhere to turn but Washington. A WPA project known as "Federal One" put unemployed artists, actors, and writers to work, but its spirit and purpose extended far beyond relief. New Deal administrators wanted to redefine the relationship between artists and the community so that art would no longer be the exclusive province of the elite. "Art for the millions" became a popular New Deal slogan.

The Federal Art Project (FAP) gave work to many of the twentieth century's leading painters, muralists, and sculptors at a point in their careers when the lack of private patronage might have prevented them from continuing their artistic production. Under the direction of Holger Cahill, an expert on American folk art, the FAP commissioned murals for public buildings and post offices across the country. Jackson Pollock, Alice Neel, Willem de Kooning, and Louise Nevelson all received support from the FAP.

The Federal Music Project employed 15,000 musicians under the direction of Nicholas Sokoloff, the conductor of the Cleveland Symphony Orchestra. Government-sponsored orchestras toured the country, presenting free concerts of both classical and popular music. Like many New Deal programs the Music Project emphasized American themes. The composer Aaron Copland wrote his ballets *Billy the Kid* (1938) and *Rodeo* (1942) for the WPA, basing the compositions on western folk motifs. The distinctive "American" sound and athletic dance style of these works made them immensely appealing to audiences. The federal government also employed the musicologist Charles Seeger and his wife, the composer Ruth Crawford Seeger, to catalog hundreds of American folk songs.

The former journalist Henry Alsberg headed the Federal Writers' Project (FWP), which at its height employed about 5,000 writers. Young FWP employees who later achieved fame included Saul Bellow, Ralph Ellison, Tillie Olsen, and John Cheever. The black folklorist and novelist Zora Neale Hurston finished three novels while on the Florida FWP, among them *Their Eyes Were Watching God* (1937). And Richard Wright won the 1938 *Story* magazine prize for the best tale by a WPA writer. Wright used his spare time to complete his novel *Native Son* (1940).

Of all the New Deal arts programs the Federal Theatre Project (FTP) was the most ambitious. American drama thrived in the 1930s, the only time at which the United States had a federally supported national theater. Under the gifted direction of Hallie Flanagan, former head of Vassar College's Experimental Theater, the Theatre Project reached an audience of 25 to 30 million people in the four years of its existence. Talented directors, actors, and playwrights, including Orson Welles, John Huston, and Arthur Miller, offered their services.

The WPA arts projects were influenced by a broad artistic trend called the *documentary impulse*. Combining social relevance with distinctively American themes, this approach—which presented actual facts and events in a way that aroused the interest and emotions of the audience—characterized the artistic expression of the 1930s. The documentary, probably the decade's most distinctive genre, influenced practically every aspect of American culture—literature, photography, art, music, film, dance, theater, and radio. It is evident in John Steinbeck's fiction (see Chapter 24) and in John Dos Passos's *USA* trilogy, which used actual newspaper clippings, dispatches, and headlines in its fictional story. *The March of Time* newsreels, which movie audiences saw before feature films, presented the news of the world for the pretelevision age. The filmmaker Pare Lorentz commissioned the composer Virgil Thompson to create music that set the mood for documentary movies such as *The Plow That Broke the Plains* (1936) and *The River* (1936). The new photo-journalism magazines, including *Life* and *Look,* also reflected this documentary approach. And the New Deal institutionalized the trend by sending investigators like the journalist Lorena Hickok and the writer Martha Gellhorn into the field to report on the conditions of people on relief.

Finally, the federal government played a leading role in compiling the photographic record of the 1930s. The Historical Section of the Resettlement Administration had a mandate to document and photograph the American scene for the government. Through their haunting images of sharecroppers, Dust Bowl migrants, and the urban homeless, the photographers Dorothea Lange, Walker Evans, Ben Shahn, and Margaret Bourke-White permanently shaped the image of the Great Depression. The government hired photographers solely for their professional skills, not to provide them relief, as in Federal One projects. Their photographs, collected by the Historical Section, which in 1937 became part of the newly created Farm Security Administration (FSA), rank as the best visual representation of life in the United States during the depression years.

THE LEGACIES OF THE NEW DEAL

The New Deal set in motion far-reaching changes, notably the growth of a modern state of significant size. For the first time people experienced the federal government as a concrete part of everyday life. During the 1930s more than a third of the population received direct government assistance from new federal programs, including Social Security payments, farm loans, relief work, and mortgage guarantees. Furthermore, the government had made a commitment to intervene in the economy when the private sector could not guarantee economic stability. New legislation regulated the stock market, reformed the Federal Reserve system by placing more power in the hands of Washington policymakers, and brought many practices of modern corporate life under federal regulation. Thus, the New Deal accelerated the pattern begun during the Progressive Era of using federal regulation to bring order and regularity to economic life, a pattern that would persist for the rest of the twentieth century, despite recurring criticism about the increased presence of the state in American life.

One particularly important arena of expansion was the development of America's welfare state—that is, the federal government's acceptance of primary responsibility for the individual and collective welfare of the people. But although the New Deal offered more benefits to American citizens than they had ever received before, its safety net had many holes, especially in comparison with the far more extensive welfare systems of Western Europe. The Social Security Act did not include national health care. Another serious defect of the emerging welfare system was its failure to reach a significant minority of American workers, including do-mestics and farm workers, for many years. And since state governments adminis-tered the programs, benefits varied widely, with southern states consistently providing the lowest amounts.

To its credit the New Deal recognized that poverty was an economic problem, not a matter of personal failure. Reformers assumed that once the depression was over, full employment and an active economy would take care of the nation's wel-fare needs and poverty would wither away. It did not. When later administrations confronted the persistence of inequality and unemployment, they grafted welfare programs onto the jerrybuilt system left over from the New Deal. Thus the Amer-ican welfare system would always be marked by its birth during the crisis atmo-sphere of the Great Depression.

Even if the depression-era welfare system had some serious flaws, it was brilliant politics. The Democratic Party courted the allegiance of citizens who benefited from New Deal programs. Organized labor aligned itself with the administration that had made it a legitimate force in modern industrial life. Blacks voted Democratic in direct relation to the economic benefits that poured into their communities. At the grassroots level, the Women's Division of the Democratic National Committee mobilized 80,000 women who recognized what the New Deal had done for their communities. The unemployed also looked kindly on the Roosevelt administration. According to one of the earliest Gallup polls, 84 percent of those on relief voted the Democratic ticket in 1936.

But the Democratic Party did not attract only the down-and-out. Roosevelt's magnetic personality and the dispersal of New Deal benefits to families through-out the social structure brought middle-class voters, many of them first- or second-generation immigrants, into the Democratic fold. Thus the New Deal completed the transformation of the Democratic Party that had begun in the 1920s toward a coalition of ethnic groups, city dwellers, organized labor, blacks, and a broad cross-section of the middle class. Those voters would form the backbone of the Demo-cratic coalition for decades to come and would provide support for liberal reforms that extended the promise of the New Deal.

The New Deal coalition contained potentially fatal contradictions, involving mainly the issue of race. Because Roosevelt depended on the support of southern white Democrats to pass New Deal legislation, he was unwilling to challenge the economic and political marginalization of blacks in the South. At the same time New Deal programs were changing the face of southern agriculture by undermin-ing the sharecropping system and encouraging the migration of southern blacks to northern and western cities. Outside the South blacks were not prevented from vot-ing, guaranteeing that civil rights would enter the national agenda. The resulting fissures would eventually weaken the coalition that seemed so invincible at the height of Roosevelt's power.

With all its shortcomings the New Deal nonetheless had a profound impact on the nation, all the more remarkable in light of its short duration. After 1936 the only

TIMELINE

1933	FDR's inaugural address and first fireside chat			Works Progress Administration (WPA)
	The Emergency Banking Act begins the Hundred Days.			Huey Long assassinated
	Glass-Steagall Act establishes FDIC.			Congress of Industrial Organizations (CIO) is formed.
	Civilian Conservation Corps (CCC)	1935–1939		Communist Party at height of influence
	Agricultural Adjustment Act (AAA)			Supreme Court finds the Agricultural Adjustment Act unconstitutional.
	National Industrial Recovery Act (NIRA)			Rural Electrification Administration (REA)
	Tennessee Valley Authority (TVA)			
	United States abandons the gold standard.			*The Plow That Broke the Plains* and *The River*
	Townsend Clubs participate in an Old Age Revolving Pension Plan.			
	Prohibition is repealed.	1936		General Motors sit-down strike
1934	Securities and Exchange Commission	1937		FDR's attempted Supreme Court reorganization fails.
	Indian Reorganization Act			
	Share Our Wealth Society established by Senator Huey Long	1937–1938		"Roosevelt recession"
1935	Supreme Court finds the NRA unconstitutional in *Schechter v. United States*.	1938		Aaron Copland's *Billy the Kid*
				Fair Labor Standards Act (FLSA)
	National Union for Social Justice (Father Charles Coughlin)	1939		The Federal Theatre Project is terminated.
	National Labor Relations (Wagner) Act			
	Social Security Act			

major pieces of reform legislation passed were the National Housing Act of 1937 and the Fair Labor Standards Act of 1938. While the Supreme Court–packing scheme, the "Roosevelt recession," and the political successes of Republicans in 1938 helped to bring an end to the New Deal, the darkening international scene also played a part. As Europe moved toward war and Japan flexed its muscles in the Far East, Roosevelt became increasingly preoccupied with international relations and placed domestic reform further and further into the background. After the United States entered the war in 1941, Roosevelt made the end of his depression program official when he announced in 1943 that it was time for "Dr. Win the War" to take the place of "Dr. New Deal." But in reality the New Deal had long ceased to propel the nation toward social reform.

For Further Exploration

A valuable synthesis of the New Deal is Robert S. McElvaine, *The Great Depression* (1984). An older but still engaging account of FDR is James MacGregor Burns, *Roosevelt* (1956). Insights into Eleanor Roosevelt's life are compellingly offered in Blanche Wiesen Cook's two-volume biography, *Eleanor Roosevelt* (vol. 1, 1992; vol. 2, 1999). For other New Dealers, see Katie Loucheim, ed., *The Making of the New Deal: The Insiders Speak* (1983). For contemporary material from the Federal Writers' Project, see *These Are Our Lives* (1939). Photography of the New Deal era is presented and analyzed in Carl Fleischhauer, ed., *Documenting America 1935–1943* (1988).

"The New Deal Network," sponsored by the Franklin and Eleanor Roosevelt Institute and the Institute for Learning Technologies, has an impressive site at <http://www.newdeal.feri.org/> with extensive images, features such as "Work-Study-Live: The Resident Youth Centers of the NYA," and links to other New Deal sites. The Library of Congress page on the "Federal Theater 1933–1939" at <http://memory.loc.gov/ammem/fedtp/fthome.html> offers scripts, still photographs, costumes, and production materials for several plays put on by the Federal Theater Project. See also the library's excellent posting of over 55,000 photographs from the Farm Security Administration and Office of War Information Collection at <http://www.nara.gov/exhall/newdeal/newdeal.html>. The National Archives' site at <http://memory.loc.gov/ammem/fsowhome.html> contains "A New Deal for the Arts," which covers folklore, music, writing, photography, film, and painting sponsored by New Deal agencies.

A number of sites offer resources for local and state history. An excellent example is the Michigan State History Museum's "The Great Depression," with material on the Flint sit-down strike and New Deal relief programs at <http://www.sos.state.mi.us/history/museum/explore/museums/hismus/hismus.html>.

Chapter 26

THE WORLD AT WAR
1939–1945

The great majority of the American people understand very well
that this war is not a war only, but an end and a beginning—an end
to things known and a beginning of things unknown.
— ARCHIBALD MACLEISH, *ATLANTIC*, 1943

Times Square, New York City, on August 15, 1945, was awash with
people celebrating V-J (Victory over Japan) Day. World War II was over. Civilians
and soldiers "jived in the streets and the crowd was so large that traffic was halted
and sprinkler trucks were used to disperse pedestrians." The spontaneous street
party seemed a fitting end to what had been the country's most popular war. For
many Americans World War II had been what one man described to journalist Studs
Terkel as "an unreal period for us here at home. Those who lost nobody at the front
had a pretty good time."

Americans had many reasons to view World War II as the "good war." Shocked
by the Japanese attack on Pearl Harbor on December 7, 1941, they united in their
determination to fight German and Japanese totalitarianism in defense of their way
of life. When evidence of the grim reality of the Jewish Holocaust came to light,
U.S. participation in the war seemed even more just. And despite their sacrifices,
many people found the war a positive experience because it ended the devastating
Great Depression, bringing full employment and prosperity. The unambiguous nature of the victory and the subsequent emergence of the United States as an unprecedentedly powerful nation further contributed to the sense of the war as one
worth fighting.

But the good war had other sides. The period brought significant social disruption, accompanied by widespread anxiety about women's presence in the workforce and a rise in juvenile delinquency. In a massive violation of civil liberties over
100,000 people of Japanese ancestry were incarcerated in internment camps, victims of racially based hysteria. African Americans served in a segregated military
and, with Chicanos, faced discrimination and violence at home. World War II also
fostered the rise of a military industrial complex and unleashed the terrible potential of the atomic bomb. Finally, another enduring legacy developed out of the

unresolved issues of the wartime alliance: the debilitating cold war, which would dominate American foreign policy for decades.

The Road to War

The rise of fascism in Europe and Asia in the 1930s threatened the fragile peace that had prevailed since the end of World War I. When the League of Nations proved too weak to deal with the emerging crises, President Roosevelt foresaw the possibility of America's participation in another war. An internationalist at heart, he wanted the United States to play a prominent role in world affairs to foster the long-term prosperity necessary for a lasting peace. Hampered at first by the pervasive isolationist sentiment in the country, by 1939 he was leading the nation toward war.

DEPRESSION DIPLOMACY

During the early years of the New Deal America's involvement in international affairs, especially those in Europe, remained limited. One of Roosevelt's few diplomatic initiatives had been the formal recognition of the Soviet Union in November 1933. A second significant development was the Good Neighbor Policy, under which the United States voluntarily renounced the use of military force and armed intervention in the Western Hemisphere. This policy was predicated on the recognition that the friendship of Latin American countries was essential to the security of the United States. One practical outcome came in 1934 when Congress repealed the Platt Amendment, a relic of the Spanish-American War, which asserted the United States' right to intervene in Cuba's affairs. Indicating the limits to the Good Neighbor Policy, the U.S. Navy kept (and still maintains) a major base at Cuba's Guantanamo Bay and continued to meddle in Cuban politics. And in numerous Latin American countries U.S. diplomats frequently resorted to economic pressure to solidify the influence of the United States and benefit its international corporations.

Roosevelt and his secretary of state, Cordell Hull, might have hoped to pursue more far-reaching diplomatic initiatives. But isolationism had been building in both Congress and the nation throughout the 1920s, a product in part of disillusionment with American participation in World War I. In 1934 Gerald P. Nye, a Republican senator from North Dakota, began a congressional investigation into the profits of munitions makers during World War I and then widened the investigation to determine the influence of economic interests on America's decision to declare war. Nye's committee concluded that war profiteers, whom it called "merchants of death," had maneuvered the nation into World War I for financial gain.

Though most of the committee's charges were dubious or simplistic, they gave momentum to the isolationist movement, contributing to the passage of the Neutrality Act of 1935. Designed explicitly to prevent a recurrence of the events that had pulled the United States into World War I, the act imposed an embargo on arms trading with countries at war and declared that American citizens traveled on the ships of belligerent nations at their own risk. In 1936 Congress expanded the Neutrality Act to ban loans to belligerents, and in 1937 it adopted a "cash-and-carry" provision: if a country at war wanted to purchase nonmilitary goods from the United States, it had to pay for them in cash and pick them up in its own ships.

The same year Congress explicitly reinforced earlier bans on sales of arms to Spain, where a bloody civil war had erupted in 1936. There Francisco Franco, strongly supported by the fascist regimes in Germany and Italy, was leading a rebellion against the democratically elected republican government. Backed officially only by the Soviet Union and Mexico, the republicans, or Loyalists, relied heavily on individual volunteers from other countries, including the American Lincoln Brigade, which fought courageously and sustained heavy losses throughout the war. The governments of the United States, Great Britain, and France, despite their Loyalist sympathies, remained neutral, a policy that dismayed many American intellectuals and activists and virtually ensured a fascist victory.

AGGRESSION AND APPEASEMENT

The nation's neutrality was soon challenged by the aggressive actions of Germany, Italy, and Japan, all determined to expand their borders and their influence. The first crisis was precipitated by Japan, a country whose militaristic regime was intent on dominating the Pacific basin. In 1931 Japan occupied Manchuria, the northernmost province of China; then in 1937 it launched a full-scale invasion of China. In both instances the League of Nations condemned Japan's action but was helpless to stop the aggression. Japan simply served the required one-year notice of withdrawal from the League.

Japan's defiance of the League encouraged a fascist dictator half a world away. Italy's Benito Mussolini had long been unhappy with the Versailles treaty, which had not awarded Italy any formerly German or Turkish colonies. In 1935 Italy invaded Ethiopia, one of the few independent countries left in Africa. The Ethiopian emperor, Haile Selassie, appealed to the League of Nations, which condemned the invasion and imposed sanctions but to little effect. By 1936 the Italian subjugation of Ethiopia was complete.

Not Italy but Germany presented the gravest threat to the world order in the 1930s. There huge reparations payments, runaway inflation, fear of communism, labor unrest, and rising unemployment fueled the rise of Adolf Hitler and his National Socialist (Nazi) Party. In 1933 Hitler became chancellor of Germany and assumed dictatorial powers. Aiming at nothing short of world domination, as he made clear in his book *Mein Kampf* (My Struggle), Hitler sought to overturn the territorial settlements of the Versailles treaty, to "restore" all the Germans of Central and Eastern Europe to a single greater German fatherland, and to annex large areas of Eastern Europe. In his warped vision "inferior races" such as Jews, Gypsies, and Slavs as well as "undesirables" such as homosexuals and the mentally impaired

This is the Enemy

WINNER R. HOE & CO., INC. AWARD — NATIONAL WAR POSTER COMPETITION
HELD UNDER AUSPICES OF ARTISTS FOR VICTORY, INC. – COUNCIL FOR DEMOCRACY–MUSEUM OF MODERN ART

Why We Fight

This 1942 award-winning lithograph by Karl Koehler and Victor
Ancona painted a sinister, menacing portrait of a Nazi officer, leaving little room for doubt as to why
it was necessary to end Nazism.
(National Museum of American Art,
Smithsonian Institution, Washington, DC)

would have to make way for the "master race." In 1933 Hitler established the first concentration camp at Dachau and opened a campaign of persecution against Jews, which expanded to a campaign of extermination once the war began.

Hitler's strategy for gaining territory through the use of troops and intimidation provoked a series of crises that gave Britain and France no alternative but to let him have his way or risk war. British Prime Minister Neville Chamberlain was a particularly insistent proponent of what became known as "appeasement." Germany withdrew from the League of Nations in 1933; two years later Hitler announced that he planned to rearm the nation in violation of the Versailles treaty. Not willing to risk war, no one stopped him. In 1936 Germany reoccupied the Rhineland, a region that had been declared a demilitarized zone under the treaty. Once again France and Britain took no action. Later that year Hitler and Mussolini joined forces in the Rome-Berlin Axis, a political and military alliance. When the Spanish Civil War broke out, Germany and Italy armed the Spanish fascists. The same year Germany and Japan signed the Anti-Comintern Pact, a precursor to the military alliance between Japan and the Axis that was formalized in 1940.

In 1938 Hitler's ambitions expanded: he sent troops to annex Austria, while simultaneously scheming to seize part of Czechoslovakia. Because Czechoslovakia had an alliance with France, war seemed imminent. But at the Munich Conference in September 1938 Britain and France capitulated, agreeing to let Germany annex the Sudetenland—the German-speaking border areas of Czechoslovakia—in return for Hitler's pledge to seek no more territory.

Within six months, however, Hitler's forces had overrun the rest of Czechoslovakia and were threatening to march into Poland. Britain and France realized that their policy of appeasement had been disastrous and prepared to take a stand. Then in August 1939 Hitler shocked the world by signing the Nonaggression Pact with the Soviet Union, which assured Germany it would not have to wage war on two fronts at once. On September 1, 1939, German troops attacked Poland; two days later Britain and France declared war on Germany. World War II had begun.

AMERICA AND THE WAR

Because the United States had become a major world power, its response would affect the course of the European conflict. Two days after the war started the United States officially declared its neutrality. Roosevelt made no secret of his sympathies, however. He pointedly rephrased Woodrow Wilson's declaration of 1914: "This nation will remain a neutral nation, but I cannot ask that every American remain neutral in thought as well." The overwhelming majority of Americans supported the Allies (Britain and France) over the Nazis, but most Americans did not want to be drawn into another world war.

At first the need for American intervention seemed remote. After the German conquest of Poland in September 1939, a false calm settled over Europe. But then on April 9, 1940, Nazi tanks overran Denmark. Norway fell to the Nazi Blitzkrieg ("lightning war") next, then the Netherlands, Belgium, and Luxembourg. Finally, on June 22, 1940, France fell. Britain stood alone against Hitler's plans for world domination.

In America the developments in Europe stirred debate over neutrality. The journalist William Allen White and his Committee to Defend America by Aiding the Allies led the interventionists. Isolationists, including the aviator Charles Lindbergh, formed the America First Committee to keep the nation out of the war. They attracted the support of the *Chicago Tribune,* the Hearst newspapers, and other conservative publications.

Despite the isolationist pressure in 1940 the United States moved closer to involvement in the war. In May Roosevelt began putting the economy and the government on a defense footing by creating the National Defense Advisory Commission and the Council of National Defense. During the summer he traded fifty World War I destroyers to Great Britain in exchange for the right to build military bases on British possessions in the Atlantic, thus circumventing the nation's neutrality law by executive order. In October Congress approved a large increase in defense spending and instituted the first peacetime draft registration and conscription in American history.

While the war expanded in Europe, Asia, North Africa, and the Middle East, the United States was preparing for the 1940 presidential election. The conflict had convinced Roosevelt that he should seek an unprecedented third term. Despite some conservative opposition Roosevelt chose the liberal secretary of agriculture Henry A. Wallace as his running mate. The Republicans nominated Wendell Willkie of Indiana, a former Democrat who supported many New Deal policies. The two parties' platforms differed only slightly. Both pledged aid to the Allies but stopped short of calling for American participation in the war. Though Willkie's spirited campaign resulted in a closer election than those of 1932 or 1936, Roosevelt and the Democrats won 55 percent of the popular vote and a lopsided total in the electoral college.

With the election behind him Roosevelt concentrated on persuading the American people to increase aid to Britain, whose survival he viewed as the key to American security. In November 1939 FDR had won a bitter battle in Congress to amend the Neutrality Act of 1935 to allow the Allies to buy weapons from the United States—but only on the cash-and-carry basis established for nonmilitary goods in 1937. In March 1941, with German submarines sinking British ships faster than they could be replaced and Britain no longer able to afford to pay cash for arms, Roosevelt convinced Congress to pass the Lend-Lease Act. The legislation authorized the president to "lease, lend, or otherwise dispose of" arms and other equipment to any country whose defense was considered vital to the security of the United States. After Germany invaded the Soviet Union in June 1941 (abandoning the Nazi-Soviet pact of two years earlier), the United States extended lend-lease to the Soviet Union, which became part of the Allied coalition.

In his State of the Union address to Congress in January 1941 Roosevelt had connected lend-lease to the defense of democracy at home as well as in Europe. He spoke about what he called "four essential human freedoms everywhere in the world"—freedom of speech and expression, freedom of worship, freedom from want, and freedom from fear. Although Roosevelt avoided stating explicitly that America had to enter the war to protect those freedoms, he intended to justify exactly that, for he regarded the United States' entry in the war as inevitable. And indeed the implementation of lend-lease marked the unofficial entrance of the United States into the European war.

The United States became even more involved in August 1941, when Roosevelt and the British prime minister, Winston Churchill, conferred secretly to discuss goals and military strategy. Their joint press release, which became known as the Atlantic Charter, provided the ideological foundation of the Western cause and of the peace to follow. Like Wilson's Fourteen Points the Charter called for economic collaboration and guarantees of political stability after the war ended to ensure that "all men in all the lands may live out their lives in freedom from fear and want." The Charter also supported free trade, national self-determination, and the principle of collective security.

As in World War I, when Americans started supplying the Allies, Germany attacked American and Allied ships. By September 1941 Nazi submarines and American vessels were fighting an undeclared naval war in the Atlantic, unknown to the American public. Without a dramatic enemy attack, however, and with the public reluctant to enter the war, Roosevelt hesitated to ask Congress for a declaration of war.

The final provocation came not from Germany but from Japan. Throughout the 1930s Japanese military advances in China had upset the balance of political and economic power in the Pacific, where the United States had long enjoyed the economic benefits of the open-door policy. After the Japanese invasion of China in 1937 Roosevelt had denounced "the present reign of terror and international lawlessness," suggesting that aggressors such as Japan be "quarantined" by peace-loving nations. Despite such rhetoric, however, the United States avoided taking a stand. During the brutal sack of Nanking in 1937 the Japanese had sunk an American gunboat, the *Panay,* in the Yangtze River. The crisis was smoothed over, however, when the United States accepted Japan's apology and more than $2 million in damages.

Japan soon became more expansionist in its intentions, signing the Tri-Partite Pact with Germany and Italy in 1940. In the fall of 1940 Japanese troops occupied the northern part of French Indochina. The United States retaliated by restricting trade with Japan and placing an embargo on aviation fuel and scrap metal. Despite mounting tensions Roosevelt hoped to avoid war with Japan. But in July 1941 Japanese troops occupied the rest of Indochina. Roosevelt responded by freezing Japanese assets in the United States and instituting an embargo on trade with Japan, including vital oil shipments that accounted for almost 80 percent of Japanese consumption.

In September 1941 the government of Prime Minister Hideki Tojo began secret preparations for war against the United States. By November American military intelligence knew that Japan was planning an attack but did not know where it would come. Early on Sunday morning, December 7, 1941, Japanese bombers attacked Pearl Harbor in Hawaii, killing more than 2,400 Americans. Eight battleships, three cruisers, three destroyers, and almost two hundred airplanes were destroyed or heavily damaged.

Although the attack was devastating, it infused the American people with a determination to fight. Pearl Harbor Day is still etched in the memories of millions of Americans who remember precisely what they were doing when they heard about the attack. The next day Roosevelt went before Congress. Calling December 7 "a date which will live in infamy," he asked for a declaration of war against Japan. The Senate voted unanimously for war, and the House concurred by a vote of 388 to 1. The lone dissenter was Jeannette Rankin of Montana, who had also opposed American entry into World War I. Three days later Germany and Italy declared war on the United States, and the United States in turn declared war on those nations.

Organizing for Victory

The task of fighting a global war accelerated the growing influence of the state on all aspects of American life. A dramatic expansion of power occurred at the presidential level when Congress passed the War Powers Act of December 18, 1941, giving Roosevelt unprecedented authority over all aspects of the conduct of the war. Coordinating the changeover from civilian to war production, raising an army, and assembling the necessary workforce taxed government agencies to the limit. Mobilization on such a scale demanded cooperation between business executives and political leaders in Washington, solidifying a partnership that had been growing since World War I.

DEFENSE MOBILIZATION

Defense mobilization had a powerful impact on the federal government's role in the economy. During the war the federal budget expanded by a factor of ten, and the national debt grew sixfold, peaking at $258.6 billion in 1945. At the same time the national government became more closely tied to its citizens' pocketbooks. The Revenue Act of 1942 continued the income tax reform that had begun during World War I by taxing not just wealthy individuals and corporations but average citizens as well. Tax collections rose from $2.2 billion to $35.1 billion, facilitated by payroll deductions and tax withholding, instituted in 1943. This system of mass taxation, a revolutionary change in the financing of the modern state, was sold to the taxpayers as a way to express their patriotism.

The war also brought significant changes in the federal bureaucracy. The number of civilians employed by the government increased almost fourfold, to 3.8 million—a far more dramatic growth than the New Deal period had witnessed. Leadership of federal agencies also changed as the Roosevelt administration turned to business executives to replace the reformers who had staffed New Deal relief agencies in the 1930s. The executives became known as "dollar-a-year men" because they volunteered for government service while remaining on the corporate payroll.

Many wartime agencies extended the power of the federal government. One of the most important was the War Production Board (WPB), which awarded defense contracts, evaluated military and civilian requests for scarce resources, and oversaw the conversion of industry to military production. The WPB used the carrot more often than the stick. To encourage businesses to convert to war production, the board granted generous tax write-offs for plant construction and approved contracts with cost-plus provisions that guaranteed a profit and promised that businesses could keep the new factories after the war. As Secretary of War Henry Stimson put it, in capitalist countries at war "you had better let business make money out of the process or business won't work."

In the interest of efficiency and maximum production the WPB preferred to deal with major corporations rather than with small businesses. The fifty-six largest corporations got three-fourths of the war contracts; the top ten a third. This system of allocating contracts, along with the suspension of antitrust prosecution during the war, hastened the trend toward large corporate structures. In 1940 the hundred largest companies manufactured 30 percent of the nation's industrial output; by 1945 their share was 70 percent. These very large businesses would form the core of the military-industrial complex of the postwar years, which linked the federal government, corporations, and the military in an interdependent partnership (see Chapter 27).

Together business and government turned out an astonishing amount of military goods. By 1945 the United States had turned out 86,000 tanks, 296,000 airplanes, 15 million rifles and machine guns, 64,000 landing craft, and 6,500 ships. Mobilization on this gigantic scale gave a tremendous boost to the economy, causing it to more than double, rising from a gross national product in 1940 of $99.7 billion to $211 billion by the end of the war. After years of depression Americans' faith in the capitalist system was restored. But it was a transformed system that relied heavily on the federal government's participation in the economy.

An expanded state presence was also evident in the government's mobilization of a fighting force. By the end of World War II the armed forces of the United States numbered more than 15 million men and women. Draft boards had registered about 31 million men between the ages of eighteen and forty-four. More than half the men failed to meet the physical standards: many were rejected because of defective teeth or poor vision. The military also tried to screen out homosexuals, but its attempts were ineffectual. Once in service homosexuals found opportunities to participate in a gay subculture more extensive than that in civilian life.

Racial discrimination prevailed in the armed forces, directed mainly against the approximately 700,000 blacks who fought in all branches of the armed forces in segregated units. Though the National Association for the Advancement of Colored People (NAACP) and other civil rights groups chided the government with reminders such as "A Jim Crow army cannot fight for a free world," the military continued to segregate African Americans and to assign them the most menial duties. In contrast, Mexican Americans were never officially segregated. Unlike blacks they were welcomed into combat units, and seventeen Mexican Americans won the Congressional Medal of Honor. Native Americans also served in nonsegregrated combat, and some, like the Navajo Code Talkers, played a unique role in circumventing Japanese codebreaking efforts by using their native language to send military messages.

About 350,000 American women enlisted in the armed services and achieved a permanent status in the military, serving in agencies such as the WACS (Women's Army Corps) and the WAVES (Women Appointed for Volunteer Emergency Service). The armed forces limited the types of duty assigned to women, as it did with black men. Women were barred from combat, although nurses and medical personnel sometimes served close to the front lines, risking capture or death. Most of the jobs women did—clerical work, communications, and health care—reflected stereotypes of women's roles in civilian life.

WORKERS AND THE WAR EFFORT

When millions of citizens entered military service, the United States faced a critical labor shortage, which the War Manpower Commission sought to remedy. Well-organized government propaganda urged women into the workforce. "Longing won't bring him back sooner . . . GET A WAR JOB!" one poster beckoned, and the artist Norman Rockwell's famous "Rosie the Riveter" appealed to women from the cover of the *Saturday Evening Post*. Although the government directed its propaganda at housewives, women who were already employed gladly abandoned low-paying "women's" jobs as domestic servants or file clerks for higher-paying jobs in the defense industry. Suddenly the nation's factories were full of women working as riveters, welders, and drill press operators. Women made up 36 percent of the labor force in 1945, compared with 24 percent at the beginning of the war. Despite their new opportunities, women war workers faced much discrimination on the job. In shipyards women with the most seniority and responsibility earned $6.95 a day, while the top men made as much as $22.

When the men came home from war and the nation's plants returned to peacetime operations, Rosie the Riveter was out of a job. But many women refused to put on aprons and stay home. Though women's participation in the labor force dropped temporarily when the war ended, it rebounded steadily for the rest of the 1940s, especially among married women (see Chapter 27).

Wartime Workers

The photographer Dorothea Lange captured these shipyard construction workers coming off their shift at a factory in Richmond, California, in 1942. Note the large number of women workers and the presence of minority workers. Several of the workers prominently display their union buttons.

(Copyright by the Dorothea Lange Collection, Oakland Museum of California, City of Oakland. Gift of Paul S. Taylor)

Wartime mobilization also opened up opportunities to advance the labor movement. Organized labor responded to the war with an initial burst of patriotic unity. On December 23, 1941, representatives of the major unions made a "no-strike" pledge—though it was nonbinding—for the duration of the war. In January 1942 Roosevelt set up the National War Labor Board (NWLB), composed of representatives of labor, management, and the public. The NWLB established wages, hours, and working conditions and had the authority to order government seizure of plants that did not comply. Forty plants were seized during the war.

During its tenure the NWLB handled 17,650 disputes affecting 12 million workers. It resolved the controversial issue of union membership through a compromise. New hires did not have to join a union, but those who already belonged had to maintain their membership over the life of a contract. Agitation for wage increases caused a more serious disagreement. Because managers wanted to keep production running smoothly and profitably, they were willing to pay higher wages. However, pay raises would conflict with the government's efforts to combat inflation, which drove prices up dramatically in the early war years. Incomes rose as much as 70 percent during the war because workers earned overtime pay, which was not covered by wage ceilings.

Although incomes were higher than anyone could have dreamed during the depression, many union members felt cheated as they watched corporate profits soar in relation to wages. Dissatisfaction peaked in 1943. That year a nationwide railroad strike was narrowly averted, and John L. Lewis led more than half a million United Mine Workers out on strike, demanding an increase in wages over that recommended by the NWLB. Though Lewis won concessions, he alienated Congress; and because he had defied the government, he became one of the most disliked public figures of the 1940s.

Congress countered Lewis's action by overriding Roosevelt's veto of the Smith-Connally Labor Act of 1943, which required a thirty-day cooling-off period before a strike and prohibited entirely strikes in defense industries. Nevertheless, about 15,000 walkouts occurred during the war. Though less than one-tenth of 1 percent of working hours were lost to labor disputes, the public perceived the disruptions to be far more extensive. Thus although union membership increased dramatically during the war, from 9 million to almost 15 million workers—a third of the nonagricultural workforce—the labor movement also evoked significant public and congressional hostility that would hamper it in the postwar years.

Just as labor sought to benefit from the war, African Americans manifested a new mood of militancy. "A wind is rising throughout the world of free men everywhere," Eleanor Roosevelt wrote during the war, "and they will not be kept in bondage." Black leaders pointed out parallels between anti-Semitism in Germany and racial discrimination in America and pledged themselves to a "Double V" campaign: victory over Nazism abroad and victory over racism and inequality at home.

Even before Pearl Harbor black activism was on the rise. In 1940 only 240 of the nation's 100,000 aircraft workers were black, and most of them were janitors.

Black leaders demanded that the government require defense contractors to integrate their workforces. When the government took no action, A. Philip Randolph, head of the Brotherhood of Sleeping Car Porters, a black union, announced plans for a "March on Washington" in the summer of 1941. Though Roosevelt was not a strong supporter of civil rights, he feared the embarrassment of a massive public protest. Even more, he worried about a disruption of the nation's war preparations.

In June 1941, in exchange for Randolph's cancellation of the march, Roosevelt issued Executive Order 8802, declaring "that there shall be no discrimination in the employment of workers in defense industries or government because of race, creed, color, or national origin," and established the Fair Employment Practices Commission (FEPC). Though this federal commitment to minority employment rights was unprecedented, it was limited in scope; for instance, it did not affect segregation in the armed forces. Moreover, the FEPC could not require compliance with its orders and often found that the needs of defense production took precedence over fair employment practices. The committee resolved only about a third of the more than 8,000 complaints it received.

Encouraged by the ideological climate of the war years, civil rights organizations increased their pressure for reform. The League of United Latin American Citizens (LULAC) built on their community's patriotic contributions to national defense and the armed services to challenge long-standing patterns of discrimination and exclusion. In Texas, where it was still common to see signs reading, "No Dogs or Mexicans Allowed," the organization protested segregation in schools and public facilities. African American groups also flourished. The NAACP grew ninefold to 450,000 by 1945. Although the NAACP generally favored lobbying and legal strategies, a student chapter of the NAACP at Howard University used direct tactics. In 1944 it forced several restaurants in Washington, D.C., to serve blacks after picketing them with signs that read "Are You for Hitler's Way or the American Way? Make Up Your Mind." In Chicago James Farmer helped to found the Congress of Racial Equality (CORE), a group that became known nationwide for its use of direct action like demonstrations and sit-ins. These wartime developments—both federal intervention and resurgent African American militancy—laid the groundwork for the civil rights revolution of the 1950s and 1960s.

POLITICS IN WARTIME

Although the federal government expanded dramatically during the war years, there was little attempt to use the state to promote social reform on the home front, as in World War I. An enlarged federal presence was justified only insofar as it assisted war aims. During the early years of the war Roosevelt rarely pressed for social and economic change, in part because he was preoccupied with the war but also because he wanted to counteract Republican political gains. Republicans had picked up ten seats in the Senate and forty-seven seats in the House in the 1940 elections, thus bolstering conservatives in Congress who sought to roll back New

Deal measures. With little protest Roosevelt agreed to drop several popular New Deal programs, including the Civilian Conservation Corps and the National Youth Administration, which were less necessary once war mobilization brought full employment.

Later in the war Roosevelt began to promise new social welfare measures. In his State of the Union address in 1944, he called for a second bill of rights, which would serve as "a new basis of security and prosperity." This extension of the New Deal identified jobs, adequate food and clothing, decent homes, medical care, and education as basic rights. But the president's commitment to them remained largely rhetorical; congressional support for this vast extension of the welfare state did not exist in 1944. Some of those rights did become realities for veterans, however. The Servicemen's Readjustment Act (1944), known as the GI Bill of Rights, provided education, job training, medical care, pensions, and mortgage loans for men and women who had served in the armed forces during the war.

Roosevelt's call for more social legislation was part of a plan to woo Democratic voters. In the 1942 election Republicans gained seats in both houses of Congress and increased their share of state governorships. The Democrats realized they would have to work hard to maintain their strong coalition in 1944. Once again Roosevelt headed the ticket, reasoning that the continuation of the war made a fourth term necessary. Democrats, concerned about Roosevelt's health and the need for a successor, dropped Vice President Henry Wallace, whose outspoken support for labor, civil rights, and domestic reform was too extreme for many party leaders. In his place they chose Senator Harry S Truman of Missouri.

The Republicans nominated Governor Thomas E. Dewey of New York. Only forty-two years old, Dewey had won fame fighting organized crime as a U.S. attorney. He accepted the broad outlines of the welfare state and was among those Republicans who rejected isolationism in favor of an internationalist stance. The 1944 election was the closest since 1916: Roosevelt received only 53.5 percent of the popular vote. The Democrats lost ground among farmers, but most ethnic minorities remained solidly Democratic. The party's margin of victory came from the cities: in urban areas of more than 100,000 people the president drew 60 percent of the vote. A significant segment of this urban support came from organized labor. The CIO's Political Action Committee made substantial contributions to the party, canvassed door to door, and conducted voter registration campaigns—a role organized labor would continue to play after the war.

Life on the Home Front

Although the United States did not suffer the physical devastation that ravaged much of Europe and the Pacific, the war affected the lives of those who stayed behind. Every time relatives of a loved one overseas saw the Western Union boy on his bicycle, they feared a telegram from the War Department saying that their son, husband, or father would not be coming home. All Americans tolerated small deprivations daily. "Don't you know there's a war on?" became the standard reply to any request that could not be fulfilled. People accepted the fact that their lives would be different "for the duration." They also accepted, however grudgingly, the increased role of the federal government in shaping their daily lives.

CIVILIAN WAR EFFORTS

Just like the soldiers in uniform people on the home front had a job to do. They worked on civilian defense committees, collected old newspapers and scrap material, and served on local rationing and draft boards. About 20 million home "Victory gardens" produced 40 percent of the nation's vegetables. All these endeavors were encouraged by various federal agencies, especially the Office of War Information (OWI), which strove to disseminate information and promote patriotism. Working closely with advertising agencies, the OWI urged them to link their clients' products to the "four freedoms," explaining that patriotic ads would not only sell goods but would "invigorate, instruct and inspire [the citizen] as a functioning unit in his country's greatest effort."

Popular culture, especially the movies, reinforced the connections between the home front and troops serving overseas. Average weekly movie attendance soared to over 100 million during the war. Demand was so high that many theaters operated around the clock to accommodate defense workers on the swing and night shifts. Many movies, encouraged in part by the OWI, had patriotic themes; stars such as John Wayne, Anthony Quinn, and Spencer Tracy portrayed the heroism of American fighting men in films like *Back to Bataan* (1945), *Guadalcanal Diary* (1943), and *Thirty Seconds over Tokyo* (1945). Other movies, such as *Watch on the Rhine* (1943), warned of the danger of fascism at home and abroad, while the Academy Award–winning *Casablanca* (1943) demonstrated the heroism and patriotism of ordinary citizens. *Since You Went Away* (1943), starring Claudette Colbert as a wife who took a war job after her husband left for war, was one of many films that portrayed struggles on the home front. Newsreels accompanying the feature films kept the public up to date on the war, as did on-the-spot radio broadcasts by commentators such as Edward R. Murrow. Thus popular culture reflected America's new international involvement at the same time that it built morale on the home front.

Perhaps the major source of Americans' high morale was wartime prosperity. Federal defense spending had solved the depression; unemployment had disappeared, and per capita income had risen from $691 in 1939 to $1,515 in 1945. Despite geographical dislocations and shortages of many items, about 70 percent of Americans admitted midway through the war that they had personally experienced "no real sacrifices." A Red Cross worker put it bluntly: "The war was fun for America. I'm not talking about the poor souls who lost sons and daughters. But for the rest of us, the war was a hell of a good time."

For many Americans the major inconveniences of the war were the limitations placed on their consumption. In contrast to the largely voluntaristic approach used during World War I, federal agencies such as the Office of Price Administration subjected almost everything Americans ate, wore, or used during World War II to rationing or regulation. In response to depleted domestic gasoline supplies and a shortage of rubber the government restricted the sale of tires, rationed gas, and imposed a nationwide speed limit of 35 miles per hour. By 1943 the amount of meat, butter, sugar, and other foods Americans could buy was also regulated. Most people cooperated with the complicated system of restrictions, but almost a fourth occasionally bought items on the black market, especially meat, gasoline, and cigarettes.

The war and the government affected not only what people ate, drank, and wore, but where they lived. When men entered the armed services, their families often followed them to training bases or points of debarkation. The lure of high-paying defense jobs encouraged others—Native Americans on reservations, white southerners in the hills of Appalachia, African Americans in the rural South—to move. About 15 million Americans changed residence during the war years, half of them moving to another state.

As a center of defense production California was affected by wartime migration more than any other state. The western mecca welcomed nearly 3 million new residents during the war, a 53 percent growth in population. "The Second Gold Rush Hits the West," headlined the *San Francisco Chronicle* in 1943. During the war one-tenth of all federal dollars went to California, and the state turned out one-sixth of the total war production. People went where the defense jobs were—to Los Angeles, San Diego, and the San Francisco Bay area. Some towns grew practically overnight: just two years after the Kaiser Corporation opened a shipyard in Richmond, the population quadrupled.

Migration and relocation often caused strains. In many towns with defense industries housing was scarce, and public transportation inadequate. Conflicts over public space and recreation erupted between old-timers and newcomers. Of special concern were the young people the war had set adrift from traditional community safeguards. Newspapers were filled with stories of "latchkey" children who stayed home alone while their mothers worked in defense plants. Adolescents were even more of a problem. Teenage girls who hung around army bases looking for a good time became known as "victory girls." In 1942 and 1943 juvenile delinquency seemed to be reaching epidemic proportions.

Another significant result of the growth of war industries was the migration of more than a million African Americans to defense centers in California, Illinois, Michigan, Ohio, and Pennsylvania. The migrants' need for jobs and housing led to racial conflict in several cities. Early in 1942 black families encountered resistance and intimidation when they tried to move into the Sojourner Truth housing project, in the Polish community of Hamtramck near Detroit—the new home of a large number of southern migrants, both black and white. In June 1943 similar tensions erupted in Detroit itself, where a major race riot left thirty-four people dead. Racial conflicts broke out in forty-seven cities across the country during 1943.

Other Americans also experienced racial violence. In Los Angeles male Latinos who belonged to *pachuco* (youth) gangs dressed in "zoot suits"—broad-brimmed felt hats, pegged trousers, and clunky shoes—wore their long hair slicked down and carried pocket knives on gold chains. The young women they hung out with favored long coats, huarache sandals, and pompadour hairdos. Blacks and some working-class white teenagers in Los Angeles, Detroit, New York, and Philadelphia also wore zoot suits as a symbol of alienation and self-assertion. To adults and to many Anglos, however, the zoot suit symbolized wartime juvenile delinquency.

In Los Angeles white hostility toward Mexican Americans had been smoldering for some time, and zoot-suiters soon became the targets. In July 1943 rumors that a *pachuco* gang had beaten a white sailor set off a four-day riot, during which white servicemen entered Mexican American neighborhoods and attacked zoot-suiters, taking special pleasure in slashing their pegged pants. The attacks occurred in full view of white police officers, who did nothing to stop the violence.

Although racial confrontations and zoot-suit riots recalled the widespread racial tensions of World War I, the mood on the home front was generally calm in the

Zoot Suits

Zoot suits gained wide popularity among American youth during the war. In 1943 this well-dressed teenager greased his hair in a duck-tail and wore a loosely cut coat with padded shoulders ("finger-tips") that reached midthigh, baggy pleated pants cut tight ("pegged") around the ankles, and a long gold watch chain. (Corbis-Bettmann)

1940s. German Americans generally did not experience the intense prejudice of World War I nor did Italian Americans, though some aliens in both groups were interned. Leftists and communists faced little repression, mainly because after Pearl Harbor the Soviet Union became an ally of the United States.

JAPANESE INTERNMENT

The internment of Japanese Americans on the West Coast was a glaring exception to this record of tolerance, a reminder of the fragility of civil liberties in wartime. California had a long history of antagonism toward both Japanese and Chinese immigrants (see Chapters 16 and 21). The Japanese Americans, who clustered together in highly visible communities, were a small, politically impotent minority, numbering only about 112,000 in the three coastal states. Unlike German and Italian Americans the Japanese stood out. "A Jap's a Jap," snapped General John DeWitt. "It makes no difference whether he is an American citizen or not." This sort of sentiment, coupled with fears of the West Coast's vulnerability to attack and the inflammatory rhetoric of newspapers and local politicians, fueled mounting demands that the region be rid of supposed Japanese spies.

In early 1942, in Executive Order 9066, Roosevelt approved a War Department plan to intern Japanese Americans in relocation camps for the rest of the war. Despite the lack of any evidence of their disloyalty or sedition—no Japanese American was ever charged with espionage—few public leaders opposed the plan. The announcement shocked Japanese Americans, more than two-thirds of whom were native-born American citizens. (They were *Nisei,* children of the foreign-born *Issei.*) Most had to sell their property and possessions at cut-rate prices and were then rounded up in temporary assembly centers and sent by the War Relocation Authority to internment camps in California, Arizona, Utah, Colorado, Wyoming, Idaho, and Arkansas—places "where nobody had lived before and no one has lived since," a historian commented (see American Voices, "Japanese Relocation").

Almost every Japanese American in California, Oregon, and Washington was involuntarily detained for some period during World War II. Ironically, the Japanese Americans who made up one-third of the population of Hawaii, and presumably posed a greater threat because of their numbers and proximity to Japan, were not interned. Less vulnerable to suspicion because of the islands' multiracial heritage, the Japanese also provided much of the unskilled labor on the islands. The Hawaiian economy simply could not function without them.

Cracks soon appeared in the relocation policy. A labor shortage in farming led the government to furlough seasonal agricultural workers from the camps as early as 1942. About 4,300 young people who had been in college when they were interned were allowed to return to school if they would transfer out of the West Coast military zone. Another route out of the camps was enlistment in the armed ser-

AMERICAN VOICES

Japanese Relocation

MONICA SONE

M onica (Itoi) Sone's autobiography, Nisei Daughter *(1953) tells the story of Japanese relocation from the perspective of a young woman in Seattle, Washington. Here she describes the Itoi family's forced evacuation to a temporary encampment called Camp Harmony; later they were moved to a settlement in Idaho. Although her parents spent the entire war in the camp, Monica Sone was allowed to leave in 1943 to attend college in Indiana.*

All through the night I heard people getting up, dragging cots around. I stared at our little window, unable to sleep. I was glad Mother had put up a makeshift curtain on the window for I noticed a powerful beam of light sweeping across it every few seconds. The lights came from high towers placed around the camp where guards with Tommy guns kept a twenty-four hour vigil. I remembered the wire fence encircling us, and a knot of anger tightened in my breast. What was I doing behind a fence like a criminal? If there were accusations to be made, why hadn't I been given a fair trial? Maybe I wasn't considered an American anymore. My citizenship wasn't real, after all. Then what was I? I was certainly not a citizen of Japan as my parents were. On second thought, even Father and Mother were more alien residents of the United States than Japanese nationals for they had little tie with their mother country. In their twenty-five years in America, they had worked and paid their taxes to their adopted government as any other citizen.

Of one thing I was sure. The wire fence was real. I no longer had the right to walk out of it. It was because I had Japanese ancestors. It was also because some people had little faith in the ideas and ideals of democracy. They said that after all these were but words and could not possibly insure loyalty. New laws and camps were surer devices. I finally buried my face in my pillow to wipe out burning thoughts and snatch what sleep I could.

SOURCE: Monica Sone, *Nisei Daughter* (Boston: Little, Brown, 1953), pp. 176–78.

vices. The 442d Regimental Combat Team, a segregated unit composed almost entirely of Nisei volunteers, served in Europe and became one of the most decorated units in the armed forces.

The Supreme Court upheld the constitutionality of internment as a legitimate exercise of power during wartime in *Hirabayashi v. United States* (1943) and in *Korematsu v. United States* (1944). It was not until 1988 that Congress decided to issue a public apology and to give $20,000 in cash to each of the 80,000 surviving internees—small restitution indeed. Though with each generation the memory of internment grows dimmer, this shameful episode has been burned into the national conscience.

Behind Barbed Wire

As part of the forced relocation of 120,000 Japanese Americans, Los Angeles photographer Toyo Miyatake and his family were sent to Manzanar, a camp in the California desert east of the Sierra Nevada. Miyatake secretly began shooting photographs of the camp, although he eventually received permission from the authorities to document life in the camp. This photograph of three young boys behind barbed wire with a watchtower in the distance must have been shot with official sanction because the photographer is on the other side of the barbed wire. It gives new meaning to the phrase "prisoners of war." (Toyo Miyatake)

Fighting and Winning the War

World War II, noted the military historian John Keegan, was "the largest single event in human history." Fought on six continents at a cost of 50 million lives, it was far more global than World War I. At least 405,000 Americans were killed and 671,000 wounded in the global fighting—less than half of 1 percent of the U.S. population. In contrast the Soviets lost as many as 21 million soldiers and civilians during the war, or about 8 percent of their population.

WARTIME AIMS AND STRATEGIES

The Allied coalition was composed mainly of Great Britain, the United States, and the Soviet Union; other nations, notably China and France, played lesser roles. President Franklin Roosevelt, Britain's Prime Minister Winston Churchill, and Premier Joseph Stalin of the Soviet Union took the lead in setting overall strategy. The Atlantic Charter, which Churchill and Roosevelt had drafted in August 1941, formed the basis of the Allies' vision of the postwar international order. But Stalin had not been part of that agreement, a fact that would later cause disagreements over its goals.

One way to wear down the Germans would have been to open a second front on the European continent, preferably in France. The Russians argued strongly for this strategy because it would draw German troops away from Russian soil. The issue came up so many times that the Soviet foreign minister, Vyacheslav Molotov, was said to know only four English words: yes, no, and second front. Though Roosevelt assured Stalin informally that a second front would be opened in 1942, British opposition and the need to raise American war production to full capacity stalled the effort. At a conference in Teheran, Iran, in late November 1943 Churchill and Roosevelt agreed to open a second front within six months in return for Stalin's promise to join the fight against Japan after the war in Europe ended. Both sides kept their promises. However, the long delay in creating a second front meant that for most of the war the Soviet Union bore the brunt of the land battle against Germany. Roosevelt and Churchill's foot-dragging angered Stalin, who was suspicious about American and British intentions. His mistrust and bitterness carried over into the cold war that followed the Allied victory.

During the first six months of 1942 the military news was so bad it threatened to swamp the Grand Alliance. The Allies suffered severe defeats on land and sea in both Europe and Asia. German armies pushed deeper into Soviet territory, reaching the outskirts of Moscow and Leningrad. Simultaneously, they began an offensive in North Africa aimed at seizing the Suez Canal. At sea German submarines were crippling American convoys carrying vital supplies to Europe.

The major turning point of the war in Europe occurred in the winter of 1942 to 1943, when the Soviets halted the German advance in the Battle of Stalingrad. By 1944 Stalin's forces had driven the German army out of the Soviet Union. Meanwhile, the Allies launched a major offensive in North Africa, Churchill's substitute for a second front in France. Between November 1942 and May 1943 Allied troops under the leadership of General Dwight D. Eisenhower and General George S. Patton defeated Germany's crack *Afrika Korps,* led by General Erwin Rommel.

From Africa the Allied command moved to attack the Axis through what Churchill called its "soft underbelly": Sicily and the Italian peninsula. In July 1943 Benito Mussolini's fascist regime fell, and Italy's new government joined the Allies. The Allied forces fought bitter battles against the German army during the Italian campaign, finally entering Rome in June 1944 (see Map 26.1). The last German forces in Italy did not surrender until May 1945, however.

The long-promised invasion of France came on D-Day, June 6, 1944. That morning, after an agonizing delay caused by bad weather, the largest armada ever assembled moved across the English Channel. Over the next few days, under the command of General Dwight Eisenhower, more than 1.5 million American, British, and Canadian soldiers crossed the Channel. In August Allied troops helped to liberate Paris; by September they had driven the Germans out of most of France and Belgium.

The Germans were not yet ready to give up, however. In December 1944 their forces in Belgium mounted an attack that began the Battle of the Bulge, so called because their advance made a large balloon in the Allied line on war maps. After ten days of heavy fighting in what was to be the final German offensive of the war, the Allies regained their momentum and pushed the Germans back across the Rhine River. American and British troops led the drive from the west toward Berlin, while Soviet troops advanced from the east through Poland, arriving there first. On April 30, with much of Berlin in rubble from intense Allied bombing, Hitler committed suicide in his bunker. Germany surrendered on May 8, 1945, the date that became known as V-E (Victory in Europe) Day.

When Allied troops advanced into Germany in the spring of 1945, they came face to face with Hitler's "final solution of the Jewish question": the extermination camps where 6 million Jews had been put to death, along with another 6 million Poles, Slavs, Gypsies, homosexuals, and other "undesirables." Photographs of the Nazi death camps at Buchenwald, Dachau, and Auschwitz, showing bodies stacked like cordwood and survivors so emaciated they were barely alive, horrified the American public. But government officials could not claim that no one knew about the camps before the German surrender. The Roosevelt administration had had reliable information about the death camps as early as November 1942.

The lack of response by the U.S. government to the systematic near annihilation of European Jewry ranks as one of the gravest failures of the Roosevelt administration. So few Jews escaped the Holocaust because the United States and the rest of the world would not take them in. State Department policies allowed only 21,000 refugees to enter the United States during the war. The War Refugee Board, established in 1944 with little support from the Roosevelt administration, eventually helped to save about 200,000 Jews, who were placed in refugee camps in countries such as Morocco and Switzerland.

Several factors combined to inhibit U.S. action: anti-Semitism; fears of economic competition from a flood of refugees to a country just recovering from the depression; the failure of the media to grasp the magnitude of the story and to publicize it accordingly; and the failure of religious leaders, Jews and non-Jews alike, to speak out. In justifying the American course of action Roosevelt claimed that winning the war would be the strongest contribution America could make to liberating the camps. But one cannot escape the conclusion that the United States could have done much more to lessen the Holocaust's terrible human toll.

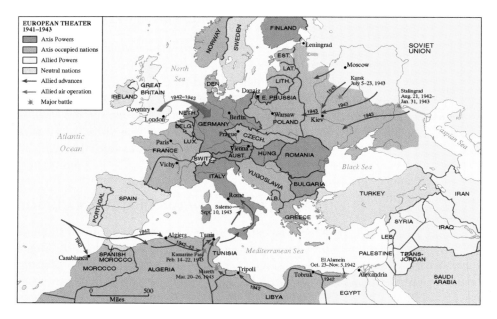

M A P 26.1
World War II in Europe

1941–1943 Hitler's Germany reached its greatest extent in 1942, when Nazi forces stalled at Leningrad and Stalingrad. The tide of battle turned in the fall, when the Soviet army launched a massive counterattack at Stalingrad and Allied forces began to drive the Germans from North Africa. In 1943 the Allies invaded Sicily and the Italian mainland. **1944–1945** On June 6, 1944 (D-Day), the Allies finally invaded France. It took almost a year for the Allied forces to close in on Berlin—the Soviets from the east and the Americans, British, and French from the west. Germany surrendered on May 8, 1945.

Hitting the Beach at Normandy

These American soldiers, part of almost 150,000 Allied troops, stormed the beaches of Normandy, France, on D-Day, June 6, 1944. More than a million Allied troops came ashore during the next month. Filmmaker Stephen Spielberg recreated the carnage and confusion of the landing in the opening scene of *Saving Private Ryan* (1998). (Library of Congress)

After the victory in Europe the Allies still had to defeat Japan. American forces bore the brunt of the fighting in the Pacific, just as the Russians had done in the land war in Europe. In early 1942 the news from the Pacific was uniformly grim. In the wake of Pearl Harbor Japan had scored quickly with seaborne invasions of Hong Kong, Wake Island, and Guam. Japanese forces soon conquered much of Burma, Malaya, the Philippines, and the Solomon Islands and began to threaten Australia and India (see American Voices, "An Army Nurse in Bataan"). But on May 7 and 8, 1942, in the Battle of the Coral Sea near southern New Guinea, American naval forces halted the Japanese offensive against Australia. In June at the island of Midway the Americans inflicted crucial damage on the Japanese fleet. With that success the American military command, led by General Douglas MacArthur and Admiral Chester W. Nimitz, took the offensive in the Pacific. For the next eighteen months American forces advanced arduously from one island to the next. In October 1944 the reconquest of the Philippines began with a victory in the Battle of Leyte Gulf, a massive naval encounter in which the Japanese lost practically their entire fleet, while the Americans suffered only minimal losses (see Map 26.2).

By early 1945 victory over Japan was in sight. The campaign in the Pacific moved slowly toward what military leaders anticipated would be a massive and

An Army Nurse in Bataan

JUANITA REDMOND

B *ataan in the Philippines is infamous for a demoralizing American defeat and its sequel, a horrific "death march" in which between 5,000 and 11,000 prisoners of war perished. Army Nurse Juanita Redmond recounts her experiences as one of the last nurses to remain as the Japanese advanced. She was evacuated shortly before the Americans surrendered on May 6, 1942. Her description reveals both the horror of warfare and the extraordinary service performed by military nurses.*

[The bomb] landed at the hospital entrance and blew up an ammunition truck that was passing. The concussion threw me to the floor. There was a spattering of shrapnel and pebbles and earth on the tin roof. Then silence for a few minutes.

I heard the corpsmen rushing out with litters, and I pulled myself to my feet. . . .

The first casualties came in. The boys in the ammunition truck had been killed, but the two guards at the hospital gate had jumped into their foxholes. By the time they were extricated from the debris that filled up the holes they were both shell-shock cases.

There were plenty of others. . . .

Only one small section of my ward remained standing. Part of the roof had been blown into the jungle. There were mangled bodies under the ruins; a blood-stained hand stuck up through a pile of scrap; arms and legs had been ripped off and flung among the rubbish. Some of the mangled torsos were almost impossible to identify. One of the few corpsmen who had survived unhurt climbed a tree to bring down a body blown into the top branches. Blankets, mattresses, pajama tops hung in the shattered trees.

We worked wildly to get to the men who might be buried, still alive, under the mass of wreckage, tearing apart the smashed beds to reach the wounded and the dead. These men were our patients, our responsibility; I think we were all tortured by an instinctive, irrational feeling that we had failed them.

SOURCE: Judy Barrett Litoff and David C. Smith, eds., *American Women in a World at War: Contemporary Accounts from World War II* (Wilmington, DE: Scholarly Resource Books, 1997), pp. 85–86. Reprinted from Juanita Redmond, *I Served on Bataan* (Philadelphia: Lippincott, 1943), pp. 106–22.

costly invasion of Japan. In some of the fiercest fighting of the war, American marines won the battles for Iwo Jima and Okinawa, where they sustained more than 52,000 casualties, including 13,600 dead. The closer U.S. forces got to the Japanese home islands, the more fiercely the Japanese fought. On Iwo Jima almost all the 21,000 Japanese died.

By mid-1945 Japan's army, navy, and air force had suffered devastating losses. American bombing of the mainland had killed about 330,000 civilians and crippled the Japanese economy. In a last-ditch effort to stem the tide, Japanese

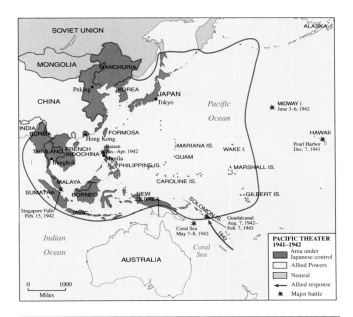

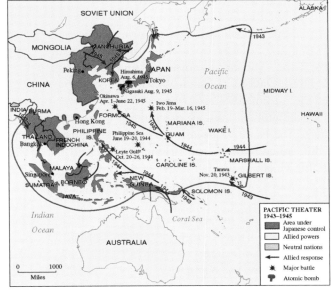

M A P 26.2
World War II in the Pacific

1941–1942 After the attack on Pearl Harbor in December 1941 the Japanese rapidly extended their domination in the Pacific. The Japanese flag soon flew as far east as the Marshall and Gilbert Islands and as far south as the Solomon Islands and parts of New Guinea. Japan also controlled the Philippines, much of Southeast Asia, and parts of China, including Hong Kong. American naval victories at the Coral Sea and Midway stopped further Japanese expansion.
1943–1945 Allied forces retook the islands in the Central Pacific in 1943 and 1944 and the Philippines early in 1945. The capture of Iwo Jima and Okinawa put U.S. bombers in position to attack Japan itself. The Japanese offered to surrender on August 10, after the United States dropped atomic bombs on Hiroshima and Nagasaki.

pilots began flying suicidal kamikaze missions, crashing their planes and boats into American ships. This desperate action, combined with the Japanese military leadership's refusal to surrender, suggested to military strategists that Japan would continue to fight despite overwhelming losses. American commanders grimly predicted millions of casualties in the upcoming invasion.

PLANNING THE POSTWAR WORLD

When Roosevelt, Churchill, and Stalin met in February 1945 at Yalta, a resort on the Black Sea, victory in Europe and the Pacific was in sight, but no agreement had been reached on the peace to come. Roosevelt focused on maintaining Allied unity, the key to postwar peace and stability. The fate of British colonies such as India, where an independence movement had already begun, caused friction between Roosevelt and Churchill. Some of the tensions with the Russians were resolved when, in return for additional possessions in the Pacific, Stalin agreed to enter the war against Japan within three months of the German surrender.

A more serious source of conflict was Stalin's desire for a band of Soviet-controlled satellite states to protect the Soviet Union's western border. With Soviet armies in control of much of Eastern Europe Stalin had become increasingly inflexible on the issue of Eastern Europe, insisting that he needed friendly (that is, Soviet-dominated) governments there to provide a buffer zone that would guarantee the Soviet Union's national security. Roosevelt acknowledged the legitimacy of that demand but, with the Atlantic Charter's principle of self-determination in mind, hoped for democratically elected governments in Poland and the neighboring countries. Unfortunately, the two goals proved mutually exclusive.

At Yalta Roosevelt and Churchill agreed in principle on the idea of a Soviet sphere of influence in Eastern Europe but deliberately left its dimensions vague. Stalin in return pledged to hold "free and unfettered elections" at an unspecified time. (Those elections never took place.) The compromise the three leaders reached at Yalta was open to multiple interpretations. Admiral William D. Leahy, Roosevelt's chief military aide, described the agreement as "so elastic that the Russians can stretch it all the way from Yalta to Washington without ever technically breaking it."

At Yalta the three leaders proceeded with plans to divide Germany into four zones to be controlled by the United States, Great Britain, France, and the Soviet Union. The capital city, Berlin, which lay in the middle of the Soviet zone, would also be partitioned among the four powers. The issue of German reparations remained unsettled.

The Big Three made further progress toward the establishment of an international organization in the form of the United Nations. They agreed that the Security Council of the United Nations would include the five major Allied powers—the United States, Britain, France, China, and the Soviet Union—plus six other nations elected on a rotating basis. They also decided that the permanent members of the Security Council should have veto power over decisions of the General Assembly, in which all nations would be represented. Roosevelt, Churchill, and Stalin announced that the United Nations would convene in San Francisco on April 25, 1945.

Roosevelt returned to the United States in February, visibly exhausted by his 14,000-mile trip. He neglected to inform the American public of the concessions he had made to maintain the increasingly fragile wartime alliance. When he reported to Congress on the Yalta agreements, he made an unusual acknowledgment of his physical infirmity. Referring to the heavy steel braces he wore on his legs, he asked Congress to excuse him for giving his speech while sitting down. The sixty-three-year-old president was a sick man, suffering from heart failure and high blood pressure. On April 12, 1945, during a short visit to his vacation home in Warm Springs, Georgia, Roosevelt suffered a cerebral hemorrhage and died.

When Harry S Truman took over the office, he learned about the top-secret Manhattan Project, charged with developing an atomic bomb. The project, which cost $2 billion and employed 120,000 people, culminated in Los Alamos, New Mexico, where the country's top physicists assembled the first bomb. Not until the first test—at Alamogordo, New Mexico, on July 16, 1945—did scientists know that the bomb would work. A month later Truman ordered the dropping of atomic bombs on two Japanese cities, Hiroshima on August 6 and Nagasaki on August 9.

Many later questioned why the United States did not warn Japan about the attack or choose a noncivilian target; the rationale for dropping the second bomb was even less clear. Some historians have argued that American policymakers, already worried about potential conflicts with the Soviets over the postwar order, used the bomb to intimidate the Soviets. Others have suggested that the fact that the Japanese were a nonwhite race facilitated the momentous decision to use the new, alarming weapon. At the time, however, the belief that Japan's military leaders would never surrender unless their country was utterly devastated convinced policymakers that they had to deploy the atom bomb. One hundred thousand people died at Hiroshima, 60,000 at Nagasaki; tens of thousands more died slowly of radiation poisoning. Japan offered to surrender on August 10 and signed a formal treaty of surrender on September 2, 1945.

Franklin Roosevelt's death and the dropping of the atomic bomb came at a critical juncture in world affairs. Many issues had been left deliberately unresolved, in hopes of keeping the wartime alliance intact through the transition to peace. But as the war ended, issues such as the fates of Poland and Germany demanded action. The resulting compromises, not all of which were fully reported to the American people, tended to promote spheres of influence, rather than the ideals of national self-determination and economic cooperation laid out in the Atlantic Charter, as the new basis of international power.

Once the common enemies had been defeated, the wartime alliance became strained and then began to split apart in ways so fundamental that Roosevelt could not likely have kept it together had he lived. Perhaps the greatest legacy of World War II, then, was the cold war that followed.

For Further Exploration

An engaging overview of war on the homefront that emphasizes social and cultural conflicts embodied in the war effort is John Morton Blum, *V Was for Victory* (1976). An anthology that focuses on popular culture—including an analysis of glamorous movie icons

T I M E L I N E

1935	Italy invades Ethiopia.			Atlantic Charter
				Japanese attack Pearl Harbor.
1935–1937	U.S. Neutrality Acts		**1942**	Battles of Coral Sea and Midway halt Japanese advance.
1936	Germany reoccupies Rhineland demilitarized zone.			Women recruited for war industries
	Rome-Berlin Axis established			Internment of Japanese Americans
	Japan and Germany sign Anti-Comintern Pact.		**1942–1945**	Rationing
1937	Japan invades China.		**1943**	Race riots in Detroit and Los Angeles
				Fascism falls in Italy.
1938	Munich agreement		**1944**	D-Day
1939	Nazi-Soviet Nonaggression Pact			GI Bill of Rights
	Germany invades Poland.		**1945**	Yalta Conference
	Britain and France declare war on Germany.			Battles of Iwo Jima and Okinawa
1940	Conscription reinstated			Germany surrenders.
	Tri-Partite Pact signed by Germany, Italy, and Japan			Harry S Truman becomes president after Roosevelt's death.
1941	Roosevelt promulgates Four Freedoms.			United Nations convenes.
	Germany invades Soviet Union.			Atomic bombs dropped on Hiroshima and Nagasaki
	Lend-Lease Act passed			Japan offers to surrender.
	Fair Employment Practices Commission			

like Betty Grable—as a means to understanding the wartime experience is Lewis A. Erenberg and Susan E. Hirsch, eds., *The War in American Culture* (1996). Stephen J. Ambrose offers insight into military life from the ordinary man's point of view with *Citizen Soldiers* (1997). Two oral history collections are indispensable. Studs Terkel, *The Good War* (1984), examines the notion that in contrast to America's more recent war in Vietnam World War II is largely remembered in positive terms. Sherna B. Gluck, *Rosie the Riveter Revisited* (1988), offers compelling accounts by women war workers. Powerful novels inspired by the war include James Jones, *From Here to Eternity* (1951), Norman Mailer, *The Naked and the Dead* (1948), and John Hersey, *Bell for Adano* (1944).

The National Archives Administration at <http://www.nara.gov/exhall/exhibits.html> has two World War II sites. "A People at War" offers a number of documents, including a letter about the Navajo Code Talkers. "Powers of Persuasion: Poster Art from World War II" contains thirty-three color posters and a sound file of the song "Any Bonds Today." The Library of Congress at <http://lcweb.loc.gov/exhibits/wcf/wcf0001.html> has an online exhibit, "Women Come to the Front: Journalists, Photographers, and Broadcasters During World War II," that features articles, biographies, and photographs of eight women who covered the war. See also "Rosie Pictures: Select Images Relating to American Women Workers

During World War II" at <http://lcweb.loc.gov/rr/print/126_rosi.html>. There are many sites on Japanese internment. The University of Washington provides a particularly interesting one at <http://www.lib.washington.edu/exhibits/harmony/default.htm> on the experiences of the Seattle Japanese American community's incarceration at the Puyallup Assembly Center; it includes letters, photographs, and other documents. The Rutgers Oral History Archive of World War II at <http://history.rutgers.edu/oralhistory/orlhom.htm> offers over 100 oral histories that cover not just the interviewees' war experiences but their life histories as well, providing valuable insights into community life in depression and wartime New Jersey.

Part Six

AMERICA AND THE WORLD
1945 to the Present

	DIPLOMACY	GOVERNMENT	ECONOMY
	THE COLD WAR ERA—AND AFTER	REDEFINING THE ROLE OF THE STATE	UPS AND DOWNS OF U. S. ECONOMIC DOMINANCE
1945	• Truman Doctrine (1947) • Marshall Plan (1948) • NATO (1949)	• Harry Truman's Fair Deal liberalism • Taft-Hartley Act (1947)	• Bretton Woods system established: World Bank, IMF, GATT
1950	• Permanent mobilization: NSC-68 (1950) • Korean War (1950–1953)	• Eisenhower's modern Republicanism • Warren Court activism	• Rise of military-industrial complex • Service sector expands.
1960	• Cuban missile crisis (1962) • Nuclear test ban treaty (1963) • Vietnam War escalates (1965).	• Great Society, War on Poverty • Richard Nixon ushers in conservative era.	• Kennedy-Johnson tax cut, military expenditures fuel economic growth.
1970	• Nixon visits China (1972). • SALT initiates détente (1972). • Paris Peace Accords (1973)	• Watergate scandal; Nixon resigns (1974). • Deregulation begins under Gerald Ford and Jimmy Carter.	• Arab oil embargo (1973–1974); inflation surges. • Unemployment in "Rustbelt." • Income stagnation
1980	• Ronald Reagan begins arms buildup. • Berlin Wall falls (1989).	• Reagan Revolution • Supreme Court conservatism	• Reaganomics • Deficits soar. • Savings and loan bailout
1990–2000	• War in the Persian Gulf (1990) • Cold war ends. • U.S. peacekeeping forces in Bosnia	• Republican Congress shifts federal government tasks to states. • George W. Bush narrowly elected President	• Corporate down-sizing • NAFTA (1993) • Recovery from recession

In 1945 the United States entered an era of unprecedented international power and influence. Unlike the period after World War I, American leaders did not avoid international commitments: instead, they aggressively pursued U.S. interests abroad, vowing to contain communism around the globe. The consequences of that struggle profoundly influenced the nation's domestic economy, political affairs, and social and cultural trends for the next half-century.

SOCIETY	CULTURE
SOCIAL MOVEMENTS AND DEMOGRAPHIC DIVERSITY	CONSUMER CULTURE AND THE INFORMATION REVOLUTION
• Urban migration • Armed forces desegregated (1948)	• End of wartime rationing • Rise of television
• *Brown v. Board of Education* (1954) • Montgomery bus boycott (1955)	• Growth of suburbia • Baby boom
• Student activism • Civil Rights Act (1964) • Voting Rights Act (1965) • Revival of feminism	• Shopping malls spread. • Youth counterculture
• *Roe v. Wade* (1973) • New Right urges conservative agenda.	• Gasoline shortages • Apple introduces first personal computer (1977).
• New Hispanic and Asian immigration	• MTV debuts. • AIDS epidemic
• Affirmative action challenged • Welfare reform	• Health-care crisis • Information superhighway

DIPLOMACY. First and most important, the United States took a leading, or hegemonic, role in global diplomatic and military affairs. When the Soviet Union challenged America's vision of postwar Europe, the Truman administration responded by crafting the policies and alliances that came to define the cold war. That bipolar struggle lasted for more than forty years, spawned two "hot" wars in Korea and Vietnam, and fueled a terrifying and debilitating nuclear arms race. Although the moderate policy of détente pursued by Richard Nixon and later presidents helped ease tensions, the cold-war mentality prevailed until the collapse of the Soviet Union in 1991.

GOVERNMENT. America's global commitments had dramatic consequences for American government and politics. Until the national consensus fractured over the Vietnam War, liberals and conservatives agreed on keeping the country in a state of permanent mobilization and maintaining a large and well-equipped military establishment. The end of the cold war brought modest cutbacks in defense spending, but an explosion of ethnic and religious conflicts in the former Yugoslavia, Africa, and other areas required U.S. military participation in several international peacekeeping missions in the 1990s. In the area of economic policy all administrations, Republican and Democratic, were willing to intervene in the economy when private initiatives could not maintain steady growth. But liberals also pushed for a larger role for the federal government in the areas of social welfare and environmental protection. Under Harry S Truman, John F. Kennedy, and especially Lyndon B. Johnson, the government went beyond the New Deal by erecting an extensive federal and state apparatus to provide for the social well-being of the people. In subsequent years, particularly under the presidency of Ronald Reagan in the 1980s and Republican control of Congress in the mid-1990s, conservatives cut back on many of the major programs and tried to delegate federal powers to the states. By the turn of the century the long-term significance of the efforts to end the "era of big government" were not yet clear.

ECONOMY. Thanks to the growth of a military industrial complex of enormous size and the expansion of consumer culture, the quarter-century after 1945 represented the heyday of American capitalism. Economic dominance abroad translated into unparalleled affluence at home. A heady sense of unlimited progress and affluence lasted until the early 1970s, when slow growth, environmental problems, and foreign competition undermined America's economic supremacy. For the next two decades many American workers experienced high unemployment, declining real wages, stagnant incomes, and a standard of living that could not match that of their parents. Following this period of global economic restructuring, the U.S. economy rebounded in the mid-1990s, reclaiming its position of undisputed dominance. Underlying the optimism about this extraordinary national prosperity, however, were fears that it was too dependent on consumer confidence and a potentially volatile stockmarket and concerns that disparities in wealth and opportunity were growing.

SOCIETY. The victory over fascism in World War II led to renewed calls for America to make good on its promise of liberty and equality for all. In great waves of protests in the 1950s and 1960s African Americans—and then women, Latinos, and other groups—challenged the political status quo. The resulting hard-won reforms brought concrete gains for many Americans, but in the 1980s and 1990s conservatives challenged many of these initiatives. And as immigration from Latin America and Asia swelled, new tensions arose over cultural and ethnic pluralism. As the new century began, the promise of social justice and equality remained unfulfilled.

CULTURE. American economic power in the postwar era accelerated the development of a consumer society based on suburbanization and technology. As millions of Americans migrated to new suburban developments after World War II, growing baby-boom families provided an expanded market for household products of all types. Among the most significant were new technological devices—television, video recorders, personal computers—that helped break down the isolation of suburban and rural living. In the 1990s the popularization of the Internet initiated an "information revolution," which both expanded and challenged the power of corporate-sponsored consumer culture.

Today, more than half a century after the end of World War II, Americans are living in an increasingly interwoven network of national and international forces. Outside events shape ordinary lives in ways that were inconceivable a century ago. As the cold war era fades into history, the United States remains the sole military superpower, but it shares economic leadership in the new interdependent global system.

Chapter 27

COLD WAR AMERICA
1945–1960

We have been in the process of fighting monsters without stop for a generation and half, looking all that time into the nuclear abyss. And the abyss has looked back into us.

— Daniel Ellsberg, 1971

When Harry Truman arrived at the White House on April 12, 1945, after Franklin Roosevelt died, he asked the president's widow, "Is there anything I can do for you?" Eleanor Roosevelt responded, "Is there anything we can do for you? For you are the one in trouble now." Truman inherited the presidency at one of the most perilous times in modern history. Unscathed by bombs and battles on the home front, U.S. industry and agriculture had grown rapidly during World War II. The nation wielded enormous military power as the sole possessor of the atomic bomb. The most powerful country in the world, the United States had become a preeminent force in the international arena. Only the Soviet Union represented an obstacle to American *hegemony,* or dominance, in global affairs. Soon the two superpowers were locked in a cold war of economic, political, and military rivalry but no direct engagement on the battlefield.

Soviet-American confrontations during the postwar years had important domestic repercussions. The cold war boosted military expenditures, fueling a growing arms race. It fostered a climate of fear and suspicion of "subversives" in government, education, and the media who might undermine American democratic institutions. But the economic benefits of internationalism also gave rise to a period of unprecedented affluence and prosperity during which the United States enjoyed the highest standard of living in the world (see Chapter 28). That prosperity helped to continue and in some cases to expand federal power, perpetuating the New Deal state in the postwar era.

The Early Cold War

The defeat of Germany and Japan did not bring stability to the world. Six years of devastating warfare had destroyed prewar governments and geographical bound-

Postwar Devastation, 1945

Cologne, Germany, was one of many European cities reduced to rubble during World War II. Here one of the 120,000 remaining inhabitants of Cologne (from a prewar population of 780,000) sits homeless with all of her belongings amid the ruins of this once beautiful and prosperous city. U.S. policymakers worried that physical devastation and economic disorder would make many areas of Europe vulnerable to communist influence.

(Johnny Florea, LIFE Magazine, © 1945 Time, Inc.)

aries, creating new power relationships that helped to dissolve colonial empires. Even before the war ended, the United States and the Soviet Union were struggling for advantage in those unstable areas; after the war they engaged in a protracted global conflict. Hailed as a battle between communism and capitalism, the cold war was in reality a more complex power struggle covering a range of economic, strategic, and ideological issues. As each side tried to protect its own national security and way of life, its actions aroused fear in the other, contributing to a cycle of distrust and animosity that would shape U.S.-Soviet relations for decades to come.

DESCENT INTO COLD WAR, 1945–1946

During the war Franklin Roosevelt had worked effectively with Soviet leader Joseph Stalin and had determined to continue good relations with the Soviet Union in peacetime. In particular, he hoped that the United Nations would provide a forum for resolving postwar conflicts. Avoiding the disagreements that had doomed American membership in the League of Nations after World War I, the Senate approved America's participation in the United Nations in December 1945. Coming eight months after Roosevelt's death, the vote was in part a memorial to the late president's hopes for peace.

Shortly before his death, however, Roosevelt had been disturbed by Soviet actions in Eastern Europe. As the Soviet army drove the Germans out of Russia and back through Eastern Europe, the USSR sponsored provisional governments in the occupied countries. Since the Soviet Union had been a victim of German aggression in both world wars, Stalin was determined to prevent the rebuilding and rearming of its traditional foe, and he insisted on a security zone of friendly governments in Eastern Europe for further protection. At the Yalta Conference in February both America and Britain had agreed to recognize this Soviet "sphere of influence," with the proviso that "free and unfettered elections" would be held as soon as possible. But in succeeding months the Soviets made no move to hold elections and rebuffed western attempts to reorganize the Soviet-installed governments.

When Truman assumed the presidency after Roosevelt's death, he took a belligerent stance toward the Soviet Union. Recalling Britain's disastrous appeasement of Hitler in 1938, he had decided that the United States had to take a hard line against Soviet expansion. "There isn't any difference in totalitarian states," he said. "Nazi, Communist, or Fascist." At a meeting held shortly after he took office, the new president berated the Soviet foreign minister, V. M. Molotov, over the Soviets' failure to honor their Yalta agreement (see Chapter 26) to support free elections in Poland. Truman used what he called "tough methods" that July at the Potsdam Conference, which brought together the United States, Britain, and the Soviet Union. After learning of the successful test of America's atomic bomb, Truman "told the Russians just where they got off and generally bossed the whole meeting," recalled British Prime Minister Winston Churchill. Negotiations on critical postwar issues deadlocked, revealing serious cracks in the Grand Alliance.

One issue tentatively resolved at Potsdam was the fate of occupied Germany. At Yalta the defeated German state had been divided into four zones of occupation, controlled by the United States, France, Britain, and the Soviet Union. At Potsdam the Allies agreed to disarm the country, dismantle its military production facilities, and permit the occupying powers to extract reparations from the zones they controlled. Plans for future reunification stalled, however, as the United States and the Soviet Union each worried that a united Germany would fall into the other's sphere. The foundation was thus laid for what would become the political division into East and West Germany four years later.

As tensions over Europe divided the former allies, hopes of international co-operation in the control of atomic weapons faded as well. In the Baruch Plan, sub-mitted to the United Nations in 1946, the United States proposed a system of international control that relied on mandatory inspection and supervision but pre-served American nuclear monopoly. The Soviets rejected the plan categorically and worked assiduously to complete their own bomb. Meanwhile, the Truman admin-istration pursued plans to develop nuclear energy and weapons further. Thus the failure of the Baruch Plan signaled the beginning of a frenzied nuclear arms race between the two superpowers.

A POLICY OF CONTAINMENT

As tensions mounted between the superpowers, the United States increasingly per-ceived Soviet expansionism as a threat to its own interests, and a new American policy, called *containment,* began to take shape. The most influential expression of the policy came in February 1946 from George F. Kennan in an 8,000-word cable, dubbed the "long telegram," from his post at the U.S. Embassy in Moscow to his superiors in Washington. Kennan, who was identified only as "X," warned that the USSR was moving "inexorably along the prescribed path, like a persistent toy au-tomobile wound up and headed in a given direction, stopping only when it meets unanswerable force." To stop Soviet expansionism, Kennan argued, the United States should pursue a policy of "firm containment . . . at every point where [the Russians] show signs of encroaching upon the interests of a peaceful and stable world."

The emerging policy of containment crystallized in 1947 over a crisis in Greece. In the spring of 1946, several thousand local communist guerrillas, whom Ameri-can advisers mistakenly believed were taking orders from Moscow, launched a full-scale civil war against the government and the British occupation authorities. In February 1947 the British informed Truman that they could no longer afford to assist anticommunists in Greece. American policymakers worried that Soviet in-fluence in Greece threatened American and European interests in the eastern Mediterranean and the Middle East, especially in strategically located Turkey and the oil-rich state of Iran.

In response the president announced what would be known as the Truman Doctrine. In a speech to the Republican-controlled Congress on March 12, he re-quested large-scale military and economic assistance to Greece and Turkey. If Greece fell to communism, Truman warned, the effects would be serious not only for Turkey but for the entire Middle East. This notion of an escalating communist contagion was an early version of what Dwight Eisenhower would later call the "domino the-ory." Not just Greece but freedom itself was at issue, Truman declared: "If we fal-ter in our leadership, we may endanger the peace of the world," and "we shall surely endanger the welfare of our own nation." Despite the open-endedness of this mil-itary commitment, Congress quickly approved Truman's request for $300 million in aid to Greece and $100 million for Turkey. The appropriation reversed the post-war trend toward sharp cuts in foreign spending and marked a new level of commitment to the emerging cold war.

During this period Secretary of State George Marshall proposed a plan to provide economic as well as military aid to Europe. In June 1947 Marshall urged the nations of Europe to construct a comprehensive recovery program and then ask the United States for aid. In Truman's words the Marshall Plan was "the other half of the walnut" (the first half being the aggressive containment of communism). By bolstering European economies devastated by war, Marshall and Truman believed, the United States could forestall severe economic dislocation, which might give rise to communism. American economic self-interest was also a contributing factor; the legislation required that foreign-aid dollars be spent on U.S. goods and services. A revitalized Europe centered on a strong West German economy would provide a better market for U.S. goods.

Truman's pledge of economic aid to European economies, however, met with significant opposition in Congress. Republicans castigated the Marshall Plan as a huge "international W.P.A." But in the midst of the congressional stalemate, on February 25, 1948, came a communist coup in Czechoslovakia. A stark reminder of the menace of Soviet expansion in Europe, the coup rallied congressional support for the Marshall Plan. In March 1948 Congress voted overwhelmingly to approve funds for the program. Like most other foreign-policy initiatives of the 1940s and 1950s, the Marshall Plan won bipartisan support despite the opposition of an isolationist wing of the Republican Party.

Over the next four years the United States contributed nearly $13 billion to a highly successful recovery effort. Western European economies revived, and industrial production increased 64 percent, opening new opportunities for international trade. The Marshall Plan did not specifically exclude Eastern Europe or the Soviet Union, but it required that all participating nations exchange economic information and work toward the elimination of tariffs and other trade barriers. Denouncing those conditions as attempts to draw Eastern Europe into the American orbit, Soviet leaders forbade the satellite states of Czechoslovakia, Poland, and Hungary to participate.

The Marshall Plan accelerated American and European efforts to rebuild and unify the West German economy. In June 1948, after agreeing to fuse their zones of occupation, the United States, France, and Britain initiated a program of currency reform in West Berlin. The economic revitalization of Berlin, located deep within the Soviet zone of occupation, alarmed the Soviets, who feared a resurgent Germany aligned with the West. As a response, they imposed a blockade on all highway, rail, and river traffic to West Berlin. Truman countered with an airlift: for nearly a year American and British pilots, who had been dropping bombs on Berlin only four years earlier, flew in 2.5 million tons of food and fuel—nearly a ton for each resident. On May 12, 1949, Stalin lifted the blockade, which had made West Berlin a symbol of resistance to communism.

The coup in Czechoslovakia and the crisis in Berlin convinced U.S. policy-makers of the need for a collective security pact. In April 1949, for the first time since the end of the American Revolution, the United States entered into a peace-time military alliance, the North Atlantic Treaty Organization (NATO). Truman asked Congress for $1.3 billion in military assistance to NATO and authorized the basing of four U.S. army divisions in Western Europe. Under the NATO pact, twelve nations—the United States, Canada, Britain, France, Italy, Belgium, the Netherlands, Luxembourg, Denmark, Norway, Portugal, and Iceland—agreed that "an armed attack against one or more of them in Europe or North America shall be considered an attack against them all." In May 1949 those nations also agreed to the creation of the Federal Republic of Germany (West Germany), which joined NATO in 1955 (Map 27.1).

In October 1949, in response to the creation of NATO, the Soviet Union tightened its grip on Eastern Europe by creating a separate government for East Germany, which became the German Democratic Republic. The Soviets also organized an economic association, the Council for Mutual Economic Assistance (COMECON) in 1949, and a military alliance for Eastern Europe, the Warsaw Pact, in 1955. The postwar division of Europe was nearly complete.

New impetus for the policy of containment came in September 1949, when American military intelligence detected a rise in radioactivity in the atmosphere—proof that the Soviet Union had detonated an atomic bomb. The American atomic monopoly, which some military and political advisers had argued would last for decades, had ended in just four years, forcing a major reassessment of the nation's foreign policy.

M A P 27.1
Cold War Europe, 1955

In 1949 the United States sponsored the creation of the North Atlantic Treaty Organization—an alliance of ten European nations, the United States, and Canada. West Germany was formally admitted to NATO in May 1955. A few days later the Soviet Union and seven other communist nations established a rival alliance, the Warsaw Pact.

To devise a new diplomatic and military blueprint Truman turned to the National Security Council (NSC), an advisory body established in 1947 to set defense and military priorities. In April 1950 the NSC delivered its report, known as NSC-68, to the president. Filled with alarmist rhetoric and exaggerated assessments of Soviet capabilities, the document made several specific recommendations, including the development of a hydrogen bomb, an advanced weapon a thousand times more destructive than the atomic bombs that had destroyed Hiroshima and Nagasaki. (The United States would explode its first hydrogen bomb in November 1952; the Soviet Union its first in 1953.) NSC-68 also supported increases in U.S. conventional forces and the establishment of a strong system of alliances. Most important, it called for increased taxes to finance "a bold and massive program of rebuilding the West's defensive potential to surpass that of the Soviet world."

Though Truman was an aggressive anticommunist, he was reluctant to commit to a major defense buildup, fearing that it would overburden the budget. But the Korean War, which began just two months after NSC-68 was completed, helped to transform the report's recommendations into reality, as the cold war spawned a hot war.

CONTAINMENT IN ASIA

As mutual suspicion deepened between the United States and the Soviet Union, cold-war doctrines began to influence the American position in Asia as well. American policy there was based on Asia's importance to the world economy as much as on the desire to contain communism. At first American plans for the region centered on a revitalized China, but political instability there prompted the Truman administration to focus on developing the Japanese economy instead. After dismantling Japan's military forces and weaponry, American occupation forces under General Douglas MacArthur began the job of transforming the country into a bulwark of Asian capitalism. MacArthur drafted a democratic constitution and oversaw the rebuilding of the economy, paving the way for the restoration of Japanese sovereignty in 1951.

In China the situation was more precarious. Since the 1930s a civil war had been raging, as communist forces led by Mao Zedong (Mao Tse-tung) and Zhou Enlai (Chou En-lai) contended for power with conservative Nationalist forces under Jiang Jieshi (Chiang Kai-shek). Although dissatisfied with the corrupt and inefficient Jiang regime, officials for the Truman administration did not see Mao as a good alternative, and they resigned themselves to working with the Nationalists. Between 1945 and 1949 the United States provided more than $2 billion to Jiang's forces but to no avail. In 1947 General Albert Wedemeyer, who had tried to work with Jiang, reported to President Truman that, until the "corrupt, reactionary, and inefficient Chinese National government" undertook "drastic political and economic reforms," the United States could not accomplish its purpose. In August 1949, when those reforms did not occur, the Truman administration cut off aid to the

Nationalists, sealing their fate. The People's Republic of China was formally established under Mao on October 1, 1949, and what was left of Jiang's government fled to Taiwan.

Many Americans viewed Mao's success as a defeat for the United States. A pro-Nationalist "China lobby," supported by the powerful publisher Henry R. Luce and by Republican senators Karl Mundt of South Dakota and William S. Knowland of California, protested that under Truman's newly appointed secretary of state, Dean Acheson, the State Department was responsible for the "loss of China." The China lobby's influence led to the United States' refusal to recognize what it called "Red China"; instead, the nation recognized the exiled Nationalist government in Taiwan. The United States also used its influence to block China's admission to the United Nations. For almost twenty years U.S. administrations treated mainland China, the world's most populous country, as a diplomatic nonentity.

In Korea as in China cold-war confrontation grew out of World War II roots. Both the United States and the Soviet Union had troops in Korea at the end of the war. As a result Korea was divided at the thirty-eighth parallel into competing spheres of influence. The Soviets supported a communist government, led by Kim Il Sung, in North Korea; the United States backed a longtime Korean nationalist, Syngman Rhee, in South Korea. Soon sporadic fighting broke out along the thirty-eighth parallel, and a civil war began.

On June 25, 1950, the North Koreans launched a surprise attack across the thirty-eighth parallel (Map 27.2). The initiative for Korean reunification came from Kim Il Sung, but Stalin supported the mission (although the extent of Soviet involvement was unknown at the time). Soviet and North Korean leaders may have expected Truman to ignore this armed challenge, but the president felt that the United States must take a firm stance against the spread of communism. "There's no telling what they'll do if we don't put up a fight now," he said. Truman immediately asked the U.N. Security Council to authorize a "police action" against the invaders. Because the Soviet Union was temporarily boycotting the Security Council to protest the exclusion of the People's Republic of China from the United Nations, it could not veto Truman's request. Three days after the Security Council voted to send what was called a "peacekeeping force," Truman ordered U.S. troops to Korea.

Though fourteen other noncommunist nations sent troops, the rapidly assembled United Nations army in Korea was overwhelmingly American. At the request of the Security Council President Truman named General Douglas MacArthur to head the U.N. forces. At first the North Koreans held an overwhelming advantage, controlling practically the entire peninsula except for the area around Pusan. But on September 15, 1950, MacArthur launched a surprise amphibious attack at Inchon, far behind the North Korean front line, while U.N. forces staged a breakout from Pusan. Within two weeks the U.N. forces controlled Seoul, the South Korean capital, and almost all the territory up to the thirty-eighth parallel.

Encouraged by this success MacArthur sought the authority to lead his forces across the thirty-eighth parallel and into North Korea. Truman's initial plan had

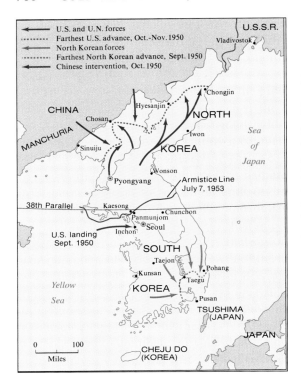

MAP 27.2
The Korean War, 1950–1953

The first months of the Korean War featured dramatic shifts in control up and down the 600-mile peninsula. From June to September 1950 North Korean troops overran most of the territory south of the thirty-eighth parallel. On September 15, U.N. forces under General Douglas MacArthur counterattacked behind enemy lines at Inchon and pushed north almost to the Chinese border. Massive Chinese intervention forced the U.N. troops to retreat to the thirty-eighth parallel in January 1951, and the war was a stalemate for the next two years.

been to restore the 1945 border, but he managed to win U.N. support for the broader goal of creating "a unified, independent and democratic Korea." Though the Chinese government in Beijing warned repeatedly that such a move would provoke retaliation, American officials ignored the warnings. MacArthur's troops crossed the thirty-eighth parallel on October 9, reaching the Chinese border at the Yalu River by the end of the month. Just after Thanksgiving a massive Chinese counterattack of almost 300,000 troops forced MacArthur to retreat to the thirty-eighth parallel. Then on January 4, 1951, communist troops reoccupied Seoul.

Two months later American forces and their allies counterattacked, regained Seoul, and pushed back to the thirty-eighth parallel. Then stalemate set in. Public support in the United States had dropped after Chinese intervention increased the likelihood of a long war. A poll revealed in early January 1951 that 66 percent of Americans thought the United States should withdraw; 49 percent felt intervening in the war had been a mistake. Given domestic opinions and the stalemate in Korea, Truman and his advisers decided to work for a negotiated peace. They did not want to tie down large numbers of U.S. troops in Asia, far from what were considered more strategically important trouble spots in Europe and the Middle East.

MacArthur disagreed. Headstrong, arrogant, and brilliant, the general fervently believed that the nation's future lay in Asia, not Europe. Disregarding Truman's

The Korean War

These men of the Second Infantry battalion, shown here in Korea in 1950, helped pave the way for the formal integration of all U.S. Army units by 1954. The Korean War marked the first time in the nation's history that all troops served in racially integrated combat units. (National Archives)

instructions MacArthur traveled to Taiwan and urged the Nationalists to join in an attack on mainland China. He pleaded for permission to use the atomic bomb against China. In an inflammatory letter to the House minority leader, Republican Joseph J. Martin of Massachusetts, he denounced the Korean stalemate. "We must win," MacArthur declared. "There is no substitute for victory."

Martin released MacArthur's letter on April 6, 1951, as part of a concerted Republican campaign to challenge Truman's conduct of the war. The strategy backfired. On April 11 Truman relieved MacArthur of his command in Korea and Japan, accusing him of insubordination—a decision the Joint Chiefs of Staff supported. Truman's decision was nonetheless highly unpopular. The allure of decisive victory under a charismatic military leader temporarily overshadowed the public's doubts about the war. Returning to tumultuous receptions in San Francisco, Chicago, and New York, the general delivered an impassioned address to a joint session of Congress. But when the shouting subsided, Truman had the last word. After failing to win the Republican presidential nomination in 1952, MacArthur faded from public view.

The war dragged on for more than two years after MacArthur's dismissal. Truce talks began in Korea in July 1951, but a final armistice was not signed until July

1953. Approximately 45 percent of American casualties were sustained during this period. The final settlement left Korea divided very near the original border at the thirty-eighth parallel, with a demilitarized zone between the two countries. North Korea remained firmly allied with the Soviet Union; South Korea signed a mutual defense treaty with the United States in 1954.

The Korean War had a lasting impact on the conduct of American foreign policy. Calling it a "police action" rather than a war, Truman had committed troops to Korea without congressional approval, arguing that he had the power to do so as commander in chief of the armed forces and as executor of the treaty binding the United States to the United Nations. His act expanded executive power and set a precedent for other undeclared wars. The Korean War also widened American involvement in Asia, transforming containment into a truly global policy. During and after the war the United States stationed large numbers of troops in South Korea and increased military aid to the Nationalist Chinese forces in Taiwan and to French forces fighting communist insurgents in Indochina (see Chapter 29). American foreign policy had become more global, more militarized, and more costly. Even in times of peace the United States functioned in a state of permanent mobilization.

Harry Truman and the Cold War at Home

Harry S Truman brought a complex personality to the presidency. Alternately humble and cocky, he had none of Roosevelt's patrician ease and was a distinctly unpopular president. Yet he handled affairs with an assurance and a crisp dispatch that have endeared him to later generations. "If you can't stand the heat, stay out of the kitchen," he liked to say of presidential responsibility. The major domestic issues he faced were reconversion to a peacetime economy and fears of communist infiltration and subversion—fears his administration played a part in perpetuating.

POSTWAR DOMESTIC CHALLENGES

The public's main fear in 1945—that the depression would return once war production had ended—proved unfounded. Despite a drop in government spending after the war, consumer spending increased; workers had amassed substantial wartime savings and were eager to spend them. The Servicemen's Readjustment Act of 1944, popularly known as the GI Bill, also put money into the economy by providing educational and economic assistance to returning veterans. Despite some temporary dislocations as war production shifted back to civilian production and veterans entered the workforce, unemployment did not soar.

But the transition was hardly trouble free. The main domestic problem was inflation. Consumers wanted to end wartime restrictions and price rationing, but Truman feared economic chaos if he lifted all controls immediately. In the summer of 1945 he eased industrial controls but retained the wartime Office of Price

Administration (OPA). When he disbanded the OPA and lifted almost all the remaining controls in the following year, prices soared, producing an annual inflation rate of 18.2 percent. Rising prices and persistent shortages of food and household goods irritated consumers.

The rapidly rising cost of living prompted workers' demands for higher wages. Under government-sanctioned agreements the labor movement had held the line on salary increases during the war. But after the war ended, union leaders expressed frustration. Corporate profits had doubled while real wages had declined as a result of inflation and the loss of overtime pay. Determined to make up for their war-induced sacrifices, workers mounted crippling strikes in the automobile, steel, and coal industries. General strikes effectively closed down business in more than a half dozen cities in 1946. By the end of that year 5 million workers had idled factories and mines for a total of 107,476,000 workdays.

Truman responded dramatically. In the face of a devastating railway strike he used his executive authority to place the nation's railroad system under federal control and asked Congress for the power to draft striking workers into the army—a move that infuriated labor leaders but pressured strikers to go back to work. Three days later he seized control of the nation's coal mines to end a strike by the United Mine Workers. Such actions won Truman support from many Americans but outraged organized labor, an important partner in the Democratic coalition.

These domestic upheavals did not bode well for the Democrats at the polls. In 1946 the Republicans gained control of both houses of Congress and set about undoing New Deal social welfare measures, especially targeting labor legislation. In 1947 Congress passed the Taft-Hartley Act, a rollback of several provisions of the 1935 National Labor Relations Act. Unions especially disliked Section 14b of Taft-Hartley, which outlawed the closed shop and allowed states to pass "right-to-work" laws that further limited unions' operations. The act also restricted unions' political power by prohibiting use of their dues for political activity and allowed the president to declare an eighty-day cooling-off period in strikes that had a national impact. Truman issued a ringing veto of the Taft-Hartley bill in June 1947, calling it "bad for labor, bad for management, and bad for the country." Congress easily overrode the veto, but Truman's actions countered some of workers' hostility to his earlier antistrike activity and kept labor in the Democratic fold.

Most observers believed that Truman faced an impossible task in the presidential campaign of 1948. The Republicans were united, and with Thomas E. Dewey, the politically moderate governor of New York, as their candidate once again, they had a good chance of attracting traditional Democratic voters. To increase their appeal in the West the Republicans nominated Earl Warren, governor of California, for vice president. In their platform they promised to continue most New Deal reforms and to support a bipartisan foreign policy.

Truman, in contrast, led a party in disarray. Both the left and the right wings of the Democratic Party split off and nominated their own candidates. Henry A. Wallace, a former New Deal liberal whom Truman had fired as secretary of commerce in 1946 because he was perceived as too "soft" on communism, ran as the candidate of the new Progressive Party. Wallace advocated increased government intervention in the economy, more power for labor unions, and cooperation with the Soviet Union. The right-wing challenge came from the South. At the Democratic national convention, northern liberals such as Mayor Hubert H. Humphrey of Minneapolis had pushed through a platform calling for the repeal of the Taft-Hartley Act and increased federal commitment to civil rights. Southern Democrats, unwilling to tolerate federal interference in race relations, bolted the convention and created the States' Rights Party, popularly known as the Dixiecrats. They nominated Governor J. Strom Thurmond of South Carolina for president.

Truman responded to these challenges with one of the most effective presidential campaigns ever waged. He launched a strenuous cross-country speaking tour in which he hammered away at the Republicans' support for the antilabor Taft-Hartley Act. He also criticized Republicans for opposing legislation for housing, medical insurance, and civil rights. By combining these issues with attacks on the Soviet menace abroad, Truman began to salvage his troubled campaign. At his rallies enthusiastic listeners shouted, "Give 'em hell, Harry!"

Truman won a remarkable victory, receiving 49.6 percent of the vote to Dewey's 45.1 percent. The Democrats also regained control of both houses of Congress. Strom Thurmond carried only four southern states, and Henry Wallace failed to win any electoral votes. Truman retained the support of organized labor. Jewish and Catholic voters in the big cities and black voters in the North offset his losses to the Dixiecrats. Most important, Truman appealed effectively to people like himself from the farms, towns, and small cities in the nation's heartland.

FAIR DEAL LIBERALISM

Shortly after becoming president, Truman had proposed to Congress a twenty-one-point plan for expanded federal programs based on individual "rights," including the right to a "useful and remunerative" job, controls over monopolies, good housing, "adequate medical care," "protection from the economic fears of old age," and a "good education." Later, Truman added support for civil rights and in his 1949 State of the Union address christened his program the Fair Deal. Although to some extent the Fair Deal represented an extension of the New Deal's liberalism—with faith in the positive influence of government and the use of federal power to ensure public welfare—it also took some new directions. Its attention to civil rights reflected the growing importance of African Americans to the Democratic Party's coalition of urban voters. And the desire to extend a high standard of living and other benefits of capitalism to an ever-greater number of citizens reflected a new liberal vision of the role of the state. Economically, the liberals of Truman's era were more moderate than the Progressive Era and New Deal reformers who had proposed extensive federal regulation of corporations and intrusive planning of the economy. They believed that the essential role of the federal government was to manage the economy indirectly through fiscal policy. Drawing on the Keynesian notion of using government spending to spur economic growth, they expected that welfare programs not only would provide a safety net for disadvantaged citizens but also would maintain consumer purchasing power, keeping the economy healthy.

Truman's agenda met with a generally hostile Congress, despite the Democratic majority. The same conservative coalition that had blocked Roosevelt's initiatives in his second term and dismantled or cut popular New Deal programs during wartime continued to fight against Truman's proposals. Only parts of the Fair Deal won adoption: the minimum wage was raised; the Social Security program was extended to cover 10 million new workers; and Social Security benefits were increased by 75 percent. The National Housing Act of 1949 called for the construction of 810,000 units of low-income housing, but only half that number were actually built.

Interest groups successfully opposed other key items in the Fair Deal. The American Medical Association (AMA) quashed a labor-backed movement for national health insurance by denouncing it as the first step toward "socialized medicine." Catholics successfully opposed aid to education because it did not include subsidies for parochial schools. Trade associations, the National Association of Manufacturers, and other business groups also actively opposed what they called "creeping socialism." Though most corporate leaders recognized that some state involvement in the economy was necessary and even beneficial to business interests, they felt the Fair Deal went too far. As a lobbyist for the National Association of Real Estate Boards explained, "In our country we prefer that government activity shall take the form of assisting and aiding private business rather than undertake great public projects of a governmental character." Through extensive lobbying and public relations campaigns, business groups agitated not only to defeat specific pieces of Fair Deal legislation but also to forestall increased taxes, antitrust activity, and other unwanted federal interference in corporate affairs. Their activities helped to block support for enlarged federal responsibilities for economic and social welfare.

Truman's record on civil rights illustrates still other obstacles that faced the Fair Deal. Black demands for justice, which had accelerated during World War II, continued into the postwar years, spurred by symbolic victories such as Jackie Robinson's breaking through the color line in major league baseball by joining the Brooklyn Dodgers in 1947. Truman offered some support for modest civil rights measures, in part because of his desire to solidify the Democrats' hold on African American voters as they migrated from the South, where they were effectively disfranchised, to northern and western cities. Truman was also concerned about America's image abroad, especially since the Soviet Union often compared the segregation of southern blacks with the Nazis' treatment of the Jews. The desire to gain the allegiance of emerging African nations and of India provided further incentive for the United States to address the problem of racial discrimination.

Lacking a popular mandate on civil rights Truman turned to executive action. In 1946 he appointed a National Civil Rights Commission, which in its 1947 report called for an expanded federal role in civil rights that foreshadowed much of the civil rights legislation of the 1960s. He ordered the Justice Department to prepare an *amicus curiae* ("friend of the court") brief in the Supreme Court case of *Shelley v. Kraemer* (1948), which struck down as unconstitutional restrictive covenants that enforced residential segregation by barring home buyers of a certain race or religion. In the same year Truman signed an executive order to desegregate the armed forces. His administration also proposed a federal antilynching law, federal protection of voting rights (such as an end to poll taxes), and a permanent federal agency to guarantee equal employment opportunity, but a filibuster by southern conservatives blocked the legislation.

The outbreak of the Korean War in 1950 also limited the chances of the Fair Deal being passed by diverting national attention and federal funds from domestic affairs. So did the nation's growing paranoia concerning internal subversion, the most dramatic manifestation of the cold war's effect on American life.

THE GREAT FEAR

As American relations with the Soviet Union deteriorated, fear of communism at home fueled a widespread campaign of domestic repression. Americans often call this phenomenon "McCarthyism," after Senator Joseph R. McCarthy of Wisconsin, the decade's most vocal anticommunist, but more was involved than the work of just one man. The Great Fear built on the longstanding distrust of radicals and foreigners that had exploded in the Red Scare after World War I. Worsening cold-war tensions intersected with both those deep-seated anxieties and partisan politics to spawn an obsessive concern with internal subversion. Ultimately, few Communists were found in positions of power; far more Americans became innocent victims of false accusations and innuendos.

The roots of postwar anticommunism dated back to 1938, when Congressman Martin Dies of Texas and other conservatives launched the House Committee on Un-American Activities (HUAC) to investigate alleged fascist and communist influence in labor unions and New Deal agencies. HUAC gained heightened visibility after the war, especially after revelations in 1946 of a Soviet spy ring operating in Canada and the United States accentuated fears of Soviet subversion.

In 1947 HUAC helped launch the Great Fear by holding widely publicized hearings on alleged communist infiltration in the film industry. A group of writers and directors, soon dubbed the Hollywood Ten, went to jail for contempt of Congress when they cited the First Amendment in refusing to testify about their past associations. Hundreds of other actors, directors, and writers whose names had been mentioned in the HUAC investigation or whose associates and friends the committee had labeled as "reds" were unable to get work, victims of an unacknowledged but very real blacklist honored by industry executives. HUAC also investigated playwrights, authors, university professors, labor activists, organizations, and government officials thought to be "left wing."

Although HUAC bore much of the responsibility for spawning the witch hunt, its effects spread far beyond the congressional committee. In March 1947 President Truman issued an executive order initiating a comprehensive investigation into the loyalty of federal employees. Following Washington's lead, many state and local governments, universities, political organizations, churches, and businesses undertook their own antisubversion campaigns, including the requirement that employees take loyalty oaths. In the labor movement, which Communists had been active in organizing in the 1930s, charges that Soviet-led Communists were taking over American unions led to a purge of Communist members. Civil rights organizations such as the NAACP and the National Urban League also expelled Communists or "fellow travelers." Thus the Great Fear was particularly devastating to the political left; accusations of guilt by association affected progressives of all stripes.

The anticommunist crusade intensified in 1948 when HUAC began an investigation of Alger Hiss, a former New Dealer and a State Department official who had accompanied Franklin Roosevelt to Yalta. A former Communist, Whittaker Chambers, claimed that Hiss was a member of a secret Communist cell operating within the government and had passed him classified documents in the 1930s. Hiss categorically denied the allegations and denied even knowing Chambers. HUAC's investigation was orchestrated by Republican Congressman Richard M. Nixon of California. Because the statute of limitations on the crime Hiss was accused of had expired, he was charged instead with perjury for lying about his communist affiliations and acquaintance with Chambers. In early 1950 Hiss was found guilty and sentenced to five years in federal prison. Although recently released evidence from Soviet archives has helped to harden the case against Hiss, the question of his guilt continues to be a contentious one among historians and journalists.

Hiss's conviction fueled the paranoia about a Communist conspiracy in the federal government, contributing to the meteoric rise of Senator Joseph McCarthy of Wisconsin. In February 1950 McCarthy delivered a bombshell during a speech in Wheeling, West Virginia: "I have here in my hand a list of the names of 205 men that were known to the Secretary of State as being members of the Communist Party and who nevertheless are still working and shaping the policy of the State Department." McCarthy later reduced his numbers, first to fifty-seven, then to one "policy risk," and he never released any names or proof, but he had gained the attention he sought. For the next four years he was the central figure in a virulent campaign of anticommunism. Like other Republicans in the late 1940s McCarthy leveled accusations of Communist subversion in the government to embarrass President Truman and the Democratic Party. Critics who disagreed with him exposed themselves to charges of being "soft" on communism. Because McCarthy charged that his critics were themselves part of "this conspiracy so immense," few political leaders challenged him. Truman called McCarthy's charges "slander, lies, character assassination" but could do nothing to curb them. When the Republican Dwight D. Eisenhower was elected president in 1952, he refrained from publicly challenging his party's most outspoken senator.

Despite McCarthy's failure to identify a single Communist in government, a series of national and international events allowed him to retain credibility. Besides the Hiss case, the sensational 1951 espionage trial of Julius and Ethel Rosenberg fueled McCarthy's allegations. Convicted of passing atomic secrets to the Soviet Union in a highly controversial trial, the Rosenbergs were executed in 1953. (As in the case of Hiss their convictions continue to be debated; the recent release of declassified documents from a top-secret intelligence mission has provided some new evidence of Julius Rosenberg's guilt.) The Korean War, which embroiled the United States in a frustrating fight against communism in a faraway land, also made Americans susceptible to McCarthy's claims. Blaming disloyal individuals rather than complex international factors for the problems of the cold war undoubtedly helped many Americans make sense of a disordered world of nuclear

McCarthy's Assault on Civil Liberties

Senator Joseph McCarthy's reckless attacks on alleged Communists in the U.S. government stirred widespread public fears of Soviet subversion in the 1950s. His critics, such as cartoonist Al Hirschfeld, expressed alarm at what they saw as McCarthy's assault on American liberty.

(© Al Hirschfeld. Drawing reproduced by special arrangement with The Margo Feiden Galleries, NY)

bombs, "police actions," and other world crises that seemed to come with alarming regularity.

In early 1954 McCarthy overreached himself by launching an investigation into possible subversion in the U.S. Army. When the lengthy televised hearings brought McCarthy's smear tactics and leering innuendos into the nation's living rooms, support for him declined. The end of the Korean War and the death of Stalin in 1953 also undercut public interest in McCarthy's red-baiting campaign. In December 1954 the Senate voted sixty-seven to twenty-two to censure McCarthy for unbecoming conduct. He died an alcoholic three years later at the age of forty-eight, his name forever attached to a period of political repression of which he was only the most flagrant manifestation (see American Voices, "Resisting the Tactics of McCarthyism").

"Modern Republicanism"

In 1952, in the middle of the Korean stalemate and at the height of the Great Fear, a newly elected president, Dwight D. Eisenhower, succeeded Harry Truman, ousting the Democrats from the White House. Eisenhower set the tone for what historians have called "modern Republicanism," an updated party philosophy that emphasized a slowdown, rather than a dismantling, of federal responsibilities. Compared with their predecessors in the 1920s and their successors in the 1980s and 1990s, modern Republicans were more tolerant of government intervention in social and economic affairs, though they did seek to limit the scope of federal action. More important to the average voter than Eisenhower's political philosophy, however, was his proven leadership in trying times; he seemed the right man to guide the nation through the perils of the cold war.

"I LIKE IKE"

Eisenhower's status as a war hero was his greatest political asset. Born in 1890 and raised in Abilene, Kansas, he had graduated from the U.S. Military Academy at West Point in 1915. Rising quickly through the ranks, during World War II he became Supreme Commander of Allied Forces in Europe. To hundreds of thousands of soldiers and to the millions of civilians who followed the war on newsreels, he was simply "Ike," the best known and best liked of the nation's military leaders.

As a professional military man Eisenhower claimed to stand "above politics." While in the army he had never voted, insisting that such political activity represented an intrusion of the military into civilian affairs. Many Democrats had hoped to make him their candidate for president in 1948 and again in 1952. Eisenhower did want the office but as a Republican. After winning several primaries, he secured the Republican nomination and asked Senator Richard M. Nixon of California to be his running mate. Nixon, young, tirelessly partisan, and with a strong

Resisting the Tactics of McCarthyism

MELVIN RADER

I *n addition to Congress's House Un-American Activities Committee, many states had their*
own committees investigating alleged Communists. In Washington State the Canwell com-
mittee scrutinized the loyalty of faculty at the University of Washington. In 1948 a witness be-
fore the committee identified Professor Melvin Rader as having attended a secret communist
school in New York during the 1930s. Rader took the unusual course of filing perjury charges
against his accuser, George Hewitt, and eventually not only cleared his name but helped to
discredit the Canwell committee's methods and accusations. Despite his vindication the anti-
communist crusade extracted a heavy toll on Rader and his family, as this account of the re-
sponse to Hewitt's charges suggests.

The number of anonymous telephone calls we received [during this time] was upsetting.
I could never know, when I answered the phone, whether I was about to be denounced by
some unidentified person as "a Communist rat." . . . Even when we talked to friends, we
felt constrained for fear that our line was being tapped.

The newspapers and radio had spread the news of the hearing far and wide. Wherever
we went, to the drugstore or the grocery, to the university or the theater, people knew about
Hewitt's charges. Many were friendly, but some were hostile. . . .

[My wife] Virginia and I spent many hours racking our memories. She or I would wake
up excitedly in the middle of the night with the sudden recollection of something we had
done in those distant summers. But it is difficult to remember and even harder to prove
what you were doing eight, nine, or ten years ago. For weeks and even months we investigated every lead that occurred to us. We interrogated every storekeeper who might have
kept invoices of our purchases; checked with the gas and electric and telephone companies to see if they had kept records; . . . went to the County-City Building to look up
voting registrations; interviewed innumerable friends and acquaintances who might remember my presence in the Seattle area during the three summers in question. Many kindly
persons and even total strangers cooperated in our search. A heroic librarian, Dolly Cooper,
searched thousands of books in the University of Washington Library to find in the back
pocket of the books withdrawal cards, dated by a librarian, that I had signed, and was successful in discovering several crucial signatures and dates. . . . Virginia and I were disappointed to discover that most memories are short and most records are not kept for longer
than five or six years, but we were heartened by the fact that so many cooperated in our
search.

SOURCE: Melvin Rader, *False Witness* (Seattle: University of Washington Press, 1969), pp. 91–93.

anticommunist record from his crusade against Alger Hiss, brought an aggressive campaign style as well as regional balance to the Republican ticket.

The Democrats never seriously considered renominating Harry Truman, who by 1952 was a thoroughly discredited leader. Lack of popular enthusiasm for the Korean War had dealt the most severe blow to Truman's support, but a series of scandals involving federal officials in bribery, kickback, and influence-peddling schemes had caused a public outcry about the "mess in Washington." With a certain relief the Democrats turned to Governor Adlai E. Stevenson of Illinois, who enjoyed the support of respected liberals such as Eleanor Roosevelt and of organized labor. To appease southern voters who feared Stevenson's liberal agenda, the Democrats nominated Senator John A. Sparkman of Alabama for vice president.

Throughout the 1952 campaign Stevenson advocated New Deal and Fair Deal policies with an almost literary eloquence. But Eisenhower's artfully unpretentious speeches and "I Like Ike" slogan were more effective with voters. Eager to win the support of the broadest electorate possible, Eisenhower played down specific questions of policy. Instead, he attacked the Democrats with the "K_1C_2" formula—"Korea, Communism, and Corruption." In a campaign pledge that ultimately clinched the election, he vowed to go to Korea, with the implication that he would end the stalemated war if elected.

The Republican campaign was temporarily set back by the revelation that wealthy Californians had set up a secret "slush fund" for Richard Nixon. Eisenhower contemplated dropping Nixon from the ticket, but Nixon adroitly used a televised speech to convince voters that he had not misused campaign funds. Nixon did admit to accepting one gift—a puppy his young daughters had named Checkers. That gift he would not give back, he declared earnestly. Nixon's televised speech turned an embarrassing incident into an advantage, as sympathetic viewers flooded Republican headquarters with supportive telegrams and phone calls. Outmaneuvered, Republican leaders had no choice but to keep Nixon on the ticket. The "Checkers speech" showed how the powerful new medium of television could be used to a politician's advantage.

That November Eisenhower won 55 percent of the popular vote, carrying all the northern and western states and four southern states. Republican candidates for Congress did not fare quite as well. They regained the Senate from the Democrats but took the House of Representatives by a slender margin of only four seats. In 1954 they would lose control of both houses to the Democrats. Even though the enormously popular Eisenhower would easily win reelection over Adlai Stevenson in 1956, the Republicans would remain in the minority in Congress.

The political scientist Fred Greenstein has characterized Eisenhower's style of leadership as the "hidden-hand presidency," pointing out that the president maneuvered deftly behind the scenes while seeming not to concern himself in public with partisan questions. Seeking a middle ground between liberalism and conservatism, Eisenhower did his best to set a quieter national mood, hoping to decrease the need for federal intervention in social and economic issues, while avoiding conservative demands for a complete roll back of the New Deal.

Eisenhower nonetheless presided over new increases in federal activity. When the Soviet Union launched the first satellite, *Sputnik,* in 1957, Eisenhower supported a U.S. space program to catch up in this new cold-war competition. The National Aeronautics and Space Administration (NASA) was founded the following year. Alarmed that the United States was falling behind the Soviets in technological expertise, the president also persuaded Congress to appropriate additional money for college scholarships and for research and development at universities and in industry. After 1954, when the Democrats took over control over Congress, the Eisenhower administration also acceded to legislation promoting social welfare. Federal outlays for veterans' benefits, unemployment compensation, housing, and Social Security were increased, and the minimum wage was raised from 75 cents an hour to $1. The creation of the new Department of Health, Education, and Welfare (HEW) in 1953 consolidated government control of social welfare programs, confirming federal commitments in that area. Congress also passed the Interstate Highway Act of 1956, which authorized $26 billion over a ten-year period for the construction of a nationally integrated highway system. This enormous public works program surpassed anything undertaken during the New Deal.

The Sputnik Crisis

The Soviet launching of the *Sputnik* space satellite in 1957 precipitated a crisis of confidence in American science and education. That sense of crisis was reflected in a 1950s "Space Race" card game, in which those dealt the *Sputnik* card would lose two turns.

(The Michael Barson Collection/Past Perfect)

Thus Republicans, though they resisted the unchecked expansion of the state, did not generally cut back federal power. In social welfare programs and defense expenditures modern Republicanism signaled an abandonment of the traditional Republican commitment to limited government. When Eisenhower retired from public life in 1961, the federal government had become an even greater presence in everyday life than it had been when he took office. Some of the most controversial federal initiatives occurred in the area of civil rights.

EMERGENCE OF CIVIL RIGHTS AS A NATIONAL ISSUE

The civil rights movement was arguably the most important force for change in postwar America, and its accelerating momentum had profound implications for the federal government. Legal segregation of the races still governed southern society in the early 1950s. In most southern states in the 1950s whites and blacks could not eat in the same rooms at restaurants and luncheonettes or use the same waiting rooms and toilets at bus and train stations. All forms of public transportation were rigidly segregated by custom or by law. Even drinking fountains were labeled "White" and "Colored."

Beginning with World War II the National Association for the Advancement of Colored People (NAACP) had redoubled its efforts to combat segregation in housing, transportation, and other areas. The first significant victory came in 1954, when the Supreme Court handed down its most far-reaching decision in *Brown v. Board of Education of Topeka*. The NAACP's chief legal counsel, Thurgood Marshall, had argued that the segregated schools mandated by the Board of Education in Topeka, Kansas, were inherently unconstitutional because they stigmatized an entire race, denying black children the "equal protection of the laws" guaranteed by the Fourteenth Amendment. In a unanimous decision announced on May 17, 1954, the Supreme Court, following the lead of Chief Justice Earl Warren (see Chapter 30), agreed with Marshall and overturned the longstanding "separate but equal" doctrine of *Plessy v. Ferguson* (see Chapter 19).

Over the next several years, in response to NAACP suits, the Supreme Court used the *Brown* precedent to overturn segregation in city parks, public beaches, and golf courses; in interstate and intrastate transportation; and in public housing. In the face of these Court decisions white resistance to integration solidified. In 1956, 101 members of Congress signed the Southern Manifesto, denouncing the *Brown* decision as "a clear abuse of judicial power" and encouraging their constituents to defy it. That same year, 500,000 southerners joined White Citizens' Councils dedicated to blocking school integration and other civil rights measures. Some whites revived old tactics of violence and intimidation, swelling the ranks of the Ku Klux Klan to levels not seen since the 1920s.

Unlike Harry Truman, Eisenhower showed little interest in civil rights. Though he proved extremely reluctant to intervene in what was widely seen as a state issue, entrenched southern resistance to federal authority eventually forced his hand. In

1957 the governor of Arkansas, Orval Faubus, defied a federal court order to de-segregate Little Rock's Central High School. Faubus called out the National Guard to bar nine black students who were attempting to enroll in the all-white school. After scenes of vicious mobs harassing the determined students aired on televi-sion, President Eisenhower reluctantly intervened, sending 1,000 federal troops and 10,000 nationalized members of the Arkansas National Guard to protect the students. Eisenhower thus became the first president since Reconstruction to use federal troops to enforce the rights of blacks.

White resistance to the *Brown* decision, as well as Eisenhower's hesitancy to act in Little Rock, showed that court victories were not enough to overturn segrega-tion. In 1955 one tiny but monumental act of defiance gave black leaders an opportunity to implement a new strategy, nonviolent protest. On December 1 Rosa Parks, a seamstress and a member of the NAACP in Montgomery, Alabama, refused to give up her seat on a city bus to a white man. "I felt it was just something I had to do," Parks stated. She was promptly arrested and charged with violating a local segregation ordinance. When the black community in Montgomery met to discuss

Integration at Little Rock, Arkansas

With chants such as "Two-four-six-eight, we ain't gonna integrate," angry crowds taunted Elizabeth Eckford (shown here walking past white students and National Guardsmen) and eight other black students who tried to register at the previously all-white Central High School in Little Rock, Arkansas, on September 4, 1957. The court-ordered integration proceeded only after President Eisenhower reluctantly nationalized the Arkansas National Guard to protect the students. (Francis Miller, LIFE Magazine, © Time, Inc.)

the proper response, they turned to the Reverend Martin Luther King Jr., who had become the pastor at a local church the year before. King endorsed a plan by a Montgomery black women's organization to boycott the city's bus system until it was integrated. For the next 381 days members of a united black community formed carpools or walked to work. The bus company neared bankruptcy, and downtown stores saw their business decline. But not until the Supreme Court ruled in November 1956 that bus segregation was unconstitutional did the city of Montgomery finally relent, prompting one woman boycotter to proclaim, "My feets is tired, but my soul is rested."

The Montgomery bus boycott catapulted King to national prominence. In 1957, with the Reverend Ralph Abernathy and other southern black clergy, he founded the Southern Christian Leadership Conference (SCLC), based in Atlanta. The black church had long been the center of African American social and cultural life. Through the SCLC the church lent its moral and organizational strength, as well as the voices of its most inspirational preachers, to the civil rights movement. Black churchwomen flocked to the movement, transferring the skills they had honed through years of church work to the fight for racial change. Soon the SCLC had joined the NAACP as one of the major advocates for racial justice. While the two groups achieved only limited victories in the 1950s, they laid the organizational groundwork for the dynamic civil rights movement that would emerge in the 1960s.

THE "NEW LOOK" OF FOREIGN POLICY

Eisenhower felt far more comfortable exercising leadership in military and diplomatic affairs than in civil rights. One of his first acts as president was to put that skill to use in negotiating an end to the Korean War. As he had pledged in the campaign, he visited Korea in December 1952. The final settlement was signed in July 1953, after the parties reached a compromise on the tricky issue of prisoner exchange.

Once the Korean War was settled, Eisenhower turned his attention to Europe. Stalin's death in March 1953 precipitated an intraparty struggle in the Soviet Union, which lasted until 1956, when Nikita S. Khrushchev emerged as Stalin's successor. Although Khrushchev surprised westerners by calling for "peaceful coexistence" between communist and capitalist societies, he made certain that the USSR's Eastern European satellites did not deviate too far from the Soviet path. When nationalists revolted in Hungary in 1956 and moved to take the country out of the Warsaw Pact, Soviet tanks moved rapidly into Budapest—an action the United States could condemn but could not realistically resist. Soviet repression of the Hungarian revolt showed that American policymakers had few, if any, options for rolling back Soviet power in Eastern Europe, short of going to war with the USSR.

Although Eisenhower strongly opposed communism, he hoped to keep the cost of containment at a manageable level. Under his "New Look" defense policy,

Eisenhower and Secretary of State John Foster Dulles decided to economize by developing a massive nuclear arsenal as an alternative to more expensive conventional forces. Nuclear weapons delivered "more bang for the buck," explained Defense Secretary Charles E. Wilson. To that end the Eisenhower administration expanded its commitment to the hydrogen bomb, approving extensive atmospheric testing in the South Pacific and in western states such as Nevada, Colorado, and Utah. To improve the nation's defenses against an air attack from the Soviet Union the administration made a commitment to develop the long-range bombing capabilities of the Strategic Air Command and installed the Distant Early Warning line of radar stations in Alaska and Canada in 1958.

Those measures did little to improve the nation's security, however, as the Soviets matched the United States weapon for weapon in an escalating arms race. The Soviet Union carried out atmospheric tests of its own of hydrogen bombs between 1953 and 1958 and developed a fleet of long-range bombers. By 1958 both nations had intercontinental ballistic missiles (ICBMs). When an American nuclear submarine launched an atomic-tipped Polaris missile in 1960, Soviet engineers raced to produce an equivalent weapon. While the arms race boosted the military-industrial sectors of both nations, it debilitated their social welfare programs by funneling immense resources into soon-to-be-obsolete weapons systems.

The New Look policy also extended collective security agreements between the United States and its allies. To complement the NATO alliance in Europe, for example, Secretary of State Dulles orchestrated the creation of the Southeast Asia Treaty Organization (SEATO), which in 1954 linked America and its major European allies with Australia, Pakistan, Thailand, New Zealand, and the Philippines. This extensive system of defense tied the United States to more than forty other countries.

U.S. policymakers tended to support stable governments, no matter how repressive, as long as they were overtly anticommunist. Some of America's staunchest allies—the Philippines, Iran, Cuba, South Vietnam, and Nicaragua—were governed by dictatorships or repressive right-wing regimes that lacked broad-based popular support. In fact, Dulles often resorted to covert interventions against governments that were, in his opinion, too closely aligned with communism.

For such tasks he used the newly formed Central Intelligence Agency (CIA), which had moved beyond its original mandate of intelligence gathering into active, albeit covert, involvement in the internal affairs of foreign countries, even to the extent of overthrowing several governments. When Iran's nationalist premier, Muhammad Mossadegh, seized British oil properties in 1953, CIA agents helped the young shah of Iran, Muhammad Reza Pahlavi, depose him. In 1954 the CIA supported a coup in Guatemala against the popularly elected Jacobo Arbenz Guzman, who had expropriated 250,000 uncultivated acres held by the American-owned United Fruit Company and accepted arms from the communist government of Czechoslovakia. Eisenhower specifically approved those efforts. "Our traditional ideas of international sportsmanship," he wrote privately in 1955, "are scarcely applicable in the morass in which the world now flounders."

THE COLD WAR IN THE MIDDLE EAST

American leaders had devised the policy of containment in response to Soviet expansion in Eastern Europe, but they soon extended it to new nations emerging in
the developing world. Before World War II nationalism, socialism, and religion had
inspired powerful anticolonial movements; in the 1940s and 1950s those forces intensified and spread, especially in the Middle East, Africa, and the Far East. Between
1947 and 1962 the British, French, Dutch, and Belgian empires all but disintegrated.
Seeking to draw the new countries into an American-led world system, U.S. policymakers encouraged the development of stable market economies in those areas. They
also sought to further the ideal of national self-determination that had shaped American participation in both world wars. But influenced by their polarized perspective
of the cold war both the Truman and the Eisenhower administrations often failed
to recognize that indigenous nationalist or socialist movements in emerging nations
had their own goals and were not, as they assumed, necessarily under the control of
either local communists or the Soviet Union. Their failure to appreciate the complexity of local conditions limited the effectiveness of American policies and often
had devastating effects on the very people they were intended to help.

The Middle East, an oil-rich area that was playing an increasingly central role
in strategic planning, presented one of the most complicated challenges. After World
War II many Jewish survivors of Nazi extermination camps had resettled in Palestine,
where with U.N. assistance and despite Arab resistance, they established the nation
of Israel in 1948. President Truman quickly recognized the new state, alienating the
Arabs but winning crucial support from Jewish Americans in the 1948 election.

Egypt was another site of conflict with the Arab nations, one that reflected the
way in which developing countries became embroiled in the cold war. When Gamal
Abdel Nasser came to power in Egypt in 1954, two years after his nation won independence from Britain, he pledged to lead not just Egypt but the entire Middle
East out of its dependent colonial relationship with the West through a form of
pan-Arab socialism. From the Soviet Union Nasser obtained arms and promises of
economic assistance, including help in building the Aswan Dam on the Nile. Secretary of State Dulles countered with an offer of American assistance, but Nasser
refused to distance himself from the Soviets, declaring Egypt's neutrality in the cold
war. Unwilling to accept this stance of nonalignment, Dulles abruptly withdrew his
offer in July 1956.

A week later Nasser retaliated against the withdrawal of Western financial aid
by seizing control of the Suez Canal, over which Britain had retained administrative authority and through which three-quarters of Western Europe's oil passed.
After several months of fruitless negotiation, Britain and France, in alliance with
Israel, attacked Egypt and retook the canal. Their attack occurred at the same time
as the Soviet repression of the Hungarian revolt, placing the United States in the
potentially awkward position of denouncing Soviet aggression while tolerating a
similar action by its own allies. President Eisenhower and the United Nations

Testing an Atomic Bomb

Throughout the 1950s the Atomic Energy Commission conducted above-ground tests of atomic and hydrogen bombs. Thousands of soldiers were exposed to fallout during the tests, such as this one at Yucca Flats, Nevada, in April 1952. The AEC, ignoring or suppressing medical evidence to the contrary, mounted an extensive public relations campaign to convince local residents that the tests did not endanger their health. (Archive Photo/Getty)

condemned the European actions in Egypt, forcing France and Britain to pull back. Egypt retook the canal and proceeded to build the Aswan Dam with Soviet support. In the end the Suez crisis increased Soviet influence in the developing world, intensified antiwestern sentiment in Arab countries, and produced dissension among leading members of the NATO alliance.

In early 1957, in the aftermath of the Suez crisis, the president persuaded Congress to approve the Eisenhower Doctrine. Addressing concerns over declining British influence in the Middle East, the joint policy stated that American forces would assist any nation in the region "requiring such aid, against overt armed aggression from any nation controlled by International Communism." Later that year Eisenhower invoked the doctrine when he sent the U.S. Sixth Fleet to the Mediterranean to aid King Hussein of Jordan. A year later he landed 8,000 troops to back a pro–United States government in Lebanon.

The attention the Eisenhower administration paid to developments in the Middle East in the 1950s reflected the nation's growing desire for access to steady supplies of oil—a desire that increasingly affected foreign policy. Indeed, by the late 1950s the Middle East contained about 65 percent of the world's known reserves. But more broadly, attention to the Middle East confirmed the global scope of American interests. Just as the Korean War had stretched the application of the containment policy from Europe to Asia, the Eisenhower Doctrine revealed the U.S. intention to bring the Middle East into its sphere as well.

DOMESTIC IMPACT OF THE COLD WAR

While the cold war extended to the most distant corners of the globe, it also had a devastating impact on the health of American citizens at home, some of whom became unwitting guinea pigs in the nation's nuclear weapons program. In the late 1950s a small but growing number of citizens became concerned about the effects of radioactive fallout from above-ground bomb tests. In later years federal investigators documented a host of illnesses, deaths, and birth defects among families of veterans who had worked on weapons tests and among "downwinders"—people who lived near nuclear test sites and weapons facilities. The most shocking revelations, however, came to light in 1993, when the Department of Energy released millions of previously classified documents on human radiation experiments conducted in the late 1940s and 1950s under the auspices of the Atomic Energy Commission (AEC) and other federal agencies. Many of the subjects were irradiated without their consent or understanding.

The nuclear arms race affected all Americans by fostering a climate of fear and uncertainty. Bomb shelters, civil defense drills, and other survival measures provided a daily reminder of the threat of nuclear war (see American Voices, "Memories of a Cold War Childhood"). Eisenhower himself had second thoughts about a nuclear policy based on the premise of annihilating the enemy, even if one's own country was destroyed—the aptly named acronym MAD (Mutual Assured Destruction) policy. He also found spiraling arms expenditures a serious hindrance to balancing the federal budget, one of his chief fiscal goals. Consequently, Eisenhower tried to negotiate an arms-limitation agreement with the Soviet Union. Progress along those lines was cut short, however, when on May 5, 1960, the Soviets shot down an American U-2 spy plane over their territory and captured and imprisoned its pilot, Francis Gary Powers. Eisenhower at first denied that the plane was engaged in espionage but later admitted that he had authorized the mission and other secret flights over the USSR. In the midst of the dispute a proposed summit meeting was canceled, and Eisenhower's last chance to negotiate an arms agreement evaporated.

When Eisenhower left office in January 1961, he used his final address to warn against the growing power of what he termed the "military-industrial complex," which by then employed 3.5 million Americans. Its pervasive influence, he noted,

AMERICAN VOICES

Memories of a Cold War Childhood

RON KOVIC

T he menacing threat of the atom bomb, the looming presence of the Soviet Union, and the fear of internal subversion were part of everyday life in the 1950s. In his autobiography, Born on the Fourth of July, *Ron Kovic conveys the anxiety Americans felt when the Soviets launched the satellite* Sputnik, *revealing that Americans were behind in the race to conquer outer space.*

We joined the cub scouts and marched in parades on Memorial Day. We made contingency plans for the cold war and built fallout shelters out of milk cartons. We wore spacesuits and space helmets. We made rocket ships out of cardboard boxes. And one Saturday afternoon in the basement Castiglia [a friend] and I went to Mars on the couch we had turned into a rocket ship. . . . And the whole block watched a thing called the space race begin. On a cold October night Dad and I watched the first satellite, called *Sputnik,* moving across the sky above our house like a tiny bright star. I still remember standing out there with Dad looking up in amazement at that thing moving in the sky above Massapequa. It was hard to believe that this thing, this *Sputnik,* was so high up and moving so fast around the world, again and again. Dad put his hand on my shoulder that night and without saying anything I quietly walked back inside and went to my room thinking that the Russians had beaten America into space and wondering why we couldn't even get a rocket off the pad. . . .

The Communists were all over the place back then. And if they weren't trying to beat us into outer space, Castiglia and I were certain they were infiltrating our schools, trying to take over our classes and control our minds. We were both certain that one of our teachers was a secret Communist agent and in our next secret club meeting we promised to report anything new he said during our next history class. We watched him very carefully that year.

SOURCE: Ron Kovic, *Born on the Fourth of July* (New York: Pocket Books, 1976), pp. 56–57.

was "felt in every city, every statehouse, every office of the Federal Government." Even though his administration had fostered the growth of the defense establishment, Eisenhower was gravely concerned about its implications for a democratic people. "We must guard against the acquisition of unwarranted influence, whether sought or unsought, by the military-industrial complex," he warned. "We must never let the weight of this combination endanger our liberties or democratic processes." With those words Dwight Eisenhower showed how well he understood the major transformations that the cold war had wrought in the nation. The conflict between the Soviet Union and the United States not only had far-reaching international implications; it had powerful effects on domestic politics, the economy, and cultural values, and it permanently altered the contours of the modern state.

T I M E L I N E

1945	Yalta and Potsdam conferences	**1950**	Alger Hiss convicted of perjury
	Harry S Truman succeeds Roosevelt as president.		Joseph McCarthy's "list" of Communists in government
	End of World War II		NSC-68 calls for permanent mobilization.
	Senate approves U.S. participation in United Nations.	**1952**	Dwight D. Eisenhower elected president
1946	Kennan sends "long telegram" outlining containment policy.		United States detonates hydrogen bomb.
	Baruch Plan for international control of atomic weapons fails.	**1953**	Soviet Union explodes hydrogen bomb.
1947	Taft-Hartley Act limits union power.	**1954**	Army-McCarthy hearings on army subversion
	Jackie Robinson joins Brooklyn Dodgers.		*Brown v. Board of Education of Topeka*
	House Un-American Activities Committee (HUAC) investigates film industry.	**1955**	Montgomery bus boycott begins.
	Truman Doctrine		Warsaw Pact
	Marshall Plan	**1956**	Crises in Hungary and Suez
1948	Communist coup in Czechoslovakia		Southern Manifesto defies *Brown*.
	Executive order desegregating armed forces		Interstate Highway Act
	State of Israel created	**1957**	Eisenhower Doctrine commits aid to Middle East.
	Stalin blockades West Berlin; Berlin airlift begins.		Eisenhower sends U.S. troops to enforce integration of Little Rock Central High School.
1949	North Atlantic Treaty Organization (NATO) founded		Southern Christian Leadership Conference founded
	Berlin airlift ends.		Soviet Union launches *Sputnik*.
	National Housing Act	**1958**	National Aeronautics and Space Administration (NASA) established
	Soviet Union detonates atomic bomb.		
	Mao Zedong establishes People's Republic of China.	**1960**	U-2 spy plane shot down over Soviet Union
1950– 1953	Korean War		

For Further Exploration

An excellent overview of the diplomatic history of the cold war is Stephen Ambrose and Douglas Brinkley, *Rise to Globalism* (8th ed., 1997). A good introduction to the Great Fear is the collection of documents in Ellen Schrecker, ed., *The Age of McCarthyism* (1994), which offers primary sources covering court cases, Hollywood, spy scandals, the Rosenbergs, and other topics. Another valuable set of sources that help to explain the early stages of the cold war is Ernest R. May, ed., *American Cold War Strategy: Interpreting NSC 68* (1993), which includes essays by both American and foreign scholars. David Halberstam's *The Fifties* (1993) offers a brief but searing account of CIA covert activities in Iran and Guatemala. For a powerful fictional account of growing up with the bomb see Tim O'Brien, *The Nuclear Age* (1996). Taylor Branch's biography of Martin Luther King Jr., *Parting the Waters: American in the King Years, 1954–1963* (1988), while focusing on King's leadership, provides an engaging account of the early civil rights movement.

The Woodrow Wilson International Center for Scholars has established the "Cold War International History Project" at <http://cwihp.si.edu/default.htm>, an exceptionally rich website offering documents on the cold war, including materials from former communist-bloc countries. The Center for the Study of the Pacific Northwest's site, "The Cold War and Red Scare in Washington State" at <http://www.washington.edu/uwired/outreach/cspn/curcan/main.html> provides detailed information on how the Great Fear operated in one state. Its bibliography includes books, documents, and videos. "Project Whistlestop: Harry Truman" at <http://whistlestop.org>, a program sponsored by the U.S. Department of Education, is a searchable collection of images and documents from the Harry S Truman Presidential Library. The site is organized into categories such as the origins of the Truman Doctrine, the Berlin airlift, the desegregation of the armed forces, and the 1948 presidential campaign. Users can also browse through the president's correspondence.

Chapter 28

THE AFFLUENT SOCIETY AND THE LIBERAL CONSENSUS
1945–1965

> The nation of the well-off must be able to see through the wall of affluence and recognize the alien citizens on the other side. And there must be vision in the sense of purpose, of aspiration. . . . there must be a passion to end poverty, for nothing less than that will do.
>
> —MICHAEL HARRINGTON, *THE OTHER AMERICA* (1962)

In 1959 Vice President Richard Nixon traveled to Moscow to open the American National Exhibit, one of several efforts to reduce cold-war tensions in the period. While touring the kitchen of a model American home, Nixon and Soviet Premier Nikita Khrushchev got into a heated debate about the relative merits of Soviet and American societies. Instead of discussing rockets, submarines, and missiles, however, they talked dishwashers, toasters, and televisions. In what was quickly dubbed the "kitchen debate," Nixon used the exhibit and its representation of American affluence and mass consumption to assert the superiority of capitalism over communism and inevitable American victory in the cold war.

During the postwar era millions of Americans, enjoying the highest standard of living in the nation's history, pursued the promise of consumer society in the burgeoning suburbs. But affluence was never as widespread as the Moscow exhibit implied. The middle-class suburban lifestyle was beyond the reach of many poor and nonwhite Americans, particularly those in the decaying central cities. Hoping to spread the abundance of a flourishing economy to greater numbers of Americans, the Democratic administrations of the early 1960s pressed for the expansion of New Deal social welfare programs. The administrations of John F. Kennedy and—to a much greater extent—Lyndon B. Johnson tried to use federal power to ensure the public welfare in areas such as health care, education, and civil rights. In the Great Society program—a burst of social legislation in 1964 and 1965 that marked the high tide of postwar liberalism—the Johnson administration attempted to use the fiscal powers of the state to redress the imbalances of the economy without directly challenging capitalism.

Liberal politicians also pursued an activist stance abroad. Continuing and in some cases expanding the cold-war policies of Truman and Eisenhower, the Kennedy and Johnson administrations took aggressive action against communist influence in Europe, the Caribbean, Vietnam (see Chapter 29), and other areas. The growing financial and political costs of that ambitious agenda, however, hampered further progress on the domestic front and revealed ominous cracks in the postwar liberal coalition.

The Affluent Society

By the end of 1945 war-induced prosperity had made the United States the richest country in the world, a preeminence that would continue unchallenged for twenty years. U.S. corporations and banking institutions so dominated the world economy that the period has been called the *Pax Americana* (American peace). U.S. military policy and foreign aid, as well as the absence of major economic competitors, were vital factors in extending the global reach of American corporate capitalism, which enjoyed remarkable growth in productivity and profits. American economic leadership abroad translated into affluence at home. As many Americans, especially whites, moved to home ownership in new suburban communities, it was clear that domestic prosperity was benefiting a wider segment of society than anyone would have dreamed possible in the dark days of the Great Depression.

THE ECONOMIC RECORD

These years witnessed the heyday of modern American capitalism, characterized by the consolidation of economic and financial resources by *oligopolies*—a few large producers that controlled the national and, increasingly, the world market. In 1970, for example, the top four American firms produced 91 percent of the motor vehicles sold in the domestic market. Large firms maintained their dominance by diversifying. Combining companies in unrelated industries, these *conglomerates* ensured for themselves protection from instability in any single market, making them more effective international competitors. International Telephone and Telegraph became a diversified conglomerate by acquiring companies in unrelated industries, including Continental Baking, Sheraton Hotels, Avis Rent-a-Car, Levitt and Sons home builders, and Hartford Fire Insurance. This pattern of corporate acquisition developed into a great wave of mergers that peaked in the 1960s.

The development of giant corporations also depended on the penetration of foreign markets. Unlike the Soviet Union, Western Europe, and Japan, America emerged physically unscathed from the war, with its defense industries eager to convert to consumer production. The weakness of the competition enabled American business to enter foreign regions when domestic markets became saturated or when

American recessions cut into sales. Soon American companies provided products and services for war-torn European and Asian markets, giving the nation a trade surplus close to $5 billion in 1960.

America's global economic supremacy stemmed in part from institutions created at a monetary conference of twenty-eight nations at Bretton Woods, New Hampshire, in 1944. The International Bank for Reconstruction and Development (known commonly as the World Bank) provided private loans for the reconstruction of war-torn Europe as well as for the development of Third World countries. The International Monetary Fund (IMF), designed to stabilize the value of currencies, helped to guide the world economy after the war. Backed by the United States' money and influence, these international organizations tended to favor American-style internationalism over the economic nationalism traditional in most other countries.

U.S. economic supremacy abroad helped boost the domestic economy, creating millions of new jobs. One of the fastest-growing groups was salaried office workers, whose numbers increased by 61 percent between 1947 and 1957. Growing corporate bureaucracies and increased access to a college education through the GI Bill helped expand the male white-collar ranks. These "organization men," as sociologist William Whyte called them, were joined by millions of women who moved into clerical work and other lower-paying service-sector occupations. Although the percentage of blue-collar manufacturing jobs declined slightly during this period, the power of organized labor reached an all-time high. In 1955 the Congress of Industrial Organizations made a formal alliance with its old adversary, the American Federation of Labor. That merger created a single organization—the AFL-CIO—which represented more than 90 percent of the nation's 17.5 million union members. In exchange for labor peace and stability—that is, fewer strikes—corporate managers often cooperated with unions, agreeing to contracts that gave many workers secure, predictable, and steadily rising incomes, guaranteeing them a share in the new prosperity.

As the income of many American workers grew, consumer spending soared. That spending, combined with federal outlays for defense and domestic programs, seemed to promise a continuously rising standard of living. The gross national product (GNP) grew from $213 billion in 1945 to more than $500 billion in 1960. With the inflation rate under 3 percent in the 1950s this steady economic growth meant a 25 percent rise in real income between 1946 and 1959. American homeownership rates reflected the rising standard of living: in 1940, 43 percent of American families owned their homes; by 1960, 62 percent did. The postwar boom was marred, however, by periodic bouts of recession and unemployment that particularly hurt low-income and nonwhite workers. Moreover, the rising standard of living was not accompanied by a redistribution of income: the top 10 percent of Americans still earned more than the bottom 50 percent. Nevertheless, most Americans had more money to spend than ever before.

THE SUBURBAN EXPLOSION

Although Americans had been gravitating toward urban areas throughout the twentieth century, the postwar period was characterized by two new patterns: one was a shift away from older cities in the Northeast and Midwest and toward newer urban centers in the South and West; the other, a mass defection from the cities to the suburbs. Both processes were stimulated by the dramatic growth of a car culture and the federal government's support of housing and highway initiatives.

At the end of World War II many cities were surrounded by pastures and working farms, but just five to ten years later those cities were surrounded by tract housing, factories, and shopping centers. By 1960 more Americans—particularly whites—lived in suburbs than in cities. People flocked to the suburbs in part because they followed the available housing. Few new dwellings had been built during the depression or war years, and the returning veterans and their families faced a critical housing shortage. The difficulty was partly resolved by an innovative Long Island building contractor. Arthur Levitt revolutionized the suburban housing market by applying mass-production techniques to home construction. Levitt's company could build 150 homes per week. In Levittown a basic four-room house, complete with kitchen appliances and an attic that a handy homeowner could convert into two additional bedrooms, was priced at less than $10,000 in 1947. Other developers soon followed suit in subdivisions all over the country, hastening the exodus from the farm and central city.

Many families financed their homes with mortgages from the Federal Housing Administration (FHA) and the Veterans Administration at rates dramatically lower than those offered by private lenders. In 1955 those two agencies wrote 41 percent of all nonfarm mortgages. Such lending demonstrated the quiet yet revolutionary way in which the federal government was entering and influencing daily life.

The new suburban homes—and much of the FHA and Veterans Administration loan funds—were reserved almost exclusively for whites. Levittown homeowners had to sign a covenant prohibiting occupation "by members of other than the Caucasian Race"; Levitt did not sell houses directly to blacks until 1960. Other communities adopted similar covenants to exclude Jews or Asians. Although the Supreme Court had ruled in *Shelley v. Kraemer* (1948) that restrictive covenants were illegal, the custom continued informally until the civil rights laws of the 1960s banned private discrimination.

The new patterns of growth and development were most striking in the South and West, where open space allowed for sprawling suburban-style expansion. Fueled by World War II defense spending, the postwar development of the southern and western cities accelerated as industry took advantage of inexpensive land, unorganized labor, low taxes, and warm climates (now made more bearable through the new technology of air conditioning). Some of the most explosive growth occurred in Florida, Texas, and California—states that would become the industrial leaders of the emerging Sun Belt economy (Map 28.1). Spurred by massive defense spend-

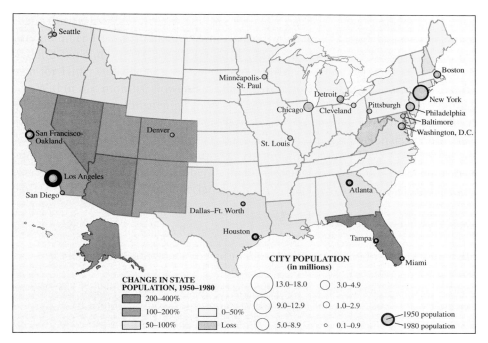

M A P 28.1
Metropolitan Growth, 1950–1980

A metropolitan area is generally defined as a central city that in combination with its surrounding territory forms an integrated economic and social unit. The U.S. Census Bureau introduced the Standard Metropolitan Statistical Area (SMSA) in 1950, but later changes in the definition of SMSA make it difficult to generalize from the 1950 figures. This map compares the population of central cities in 1950 with population figures for the more broadly defined metropolitan areas in 1980 to illustrate the extent and geographical distribution of metropolitan growth in the postwar period.

ing, California grew the most rapidly, adding 2.6 million people in the 1940s and 3.1 million more in the 1950s.

Automobiles were essential both to suburban growth and to the development of the Sun Belt states of the South and the West. Suburbanites throughout the country needed cars to get to work and to take their children to school and piano lessons. In 1945 Americans owned 25 million cars; by 1965 the number had tripled to 75 million. As the car culture that first emerged in the 1920s expanded dramatically in the 1950s, cars—extravagant gas guzzlers with elaborate tail fins and ostentatious chrome detail—became symbols of status and success.

More cars required more highways, which were funded largely by the federal government. In 1947 Congress authorized the construction of 37,000 miles of highways; the National Interstate and Defense Highway Act of 1956 increased this commitment by another 42,500 miles. One of the largest civil engineering projects in world history, the new interstate system would link the entire country with roads at least four lanes wide. The interstate system changed both the cities and the countryside. It rerouted traffic away from small towns and through rural areas, creating isolated pockets of gas stations, fast-food outlets, and motels along highway exits. In urban areas new highways cut wide swaths through old neighborhoods and caused air pollution and traffic jams; critics complained about "autosclerosis," a hardening of the urban arteries.

Highway construction had far-reaching effects on patterns of consumption and shopping. Instead of taking a train into the city or walking to a corner grocery store, people drove to suburban shopping malls and supermarkets. The first mall had appeared in Kansas City in the 1920s, and there were still only eight in 1945; by 1960 the number had mushroomed to almost 4,000. When a 110-store complex at Roosevelt Field on suburban Long Island opened in 1956, it was conveniently situated at an expressway exit and had parking for 11,000 cars. Downtown department stores and other retail outlets soon declined, helping to precipitate the decay of American central cities.

At the time few Americans understood that tradeoffs were involved in the postwar economic boom. With a strong economic position internationally and government spending to help fuel expansion at home, Americans expected an unending trajectory of progress. Their faith led to complacency—an unwillingness to look beneath the surface for the hidden implications of the forces that were transforming America.

American Life during the Baby Boom

Hula Hoops and poodle skirts, sock hops and rock 'n' roll, shiny cars and gleaming appliances—all signify the "fifties," a period that really stretched from 1945 through the early 1960s. The postwar years are remembered as a time of affluence and stability, a time when Americans enjoyed an optimistic faith in progress and technology and a serene family-centered culture, reflected in a booming birth rate known as the baby boom and enshrined in television sitcoms such as *Father Knows Best*. This powerful myth, like many myths, has some truth to it, but there were other sides to the story. Focusing solely on affluence, popular culture, and consumption does not do justice to this complex period of economic and social transformation, which included challenges to the status quo as well as conformity.

CONSUMER CULTURE

The new prosperity of the 1950s was aided by a dramatic increase in consumer credit, which enabled families to stretch their incomes. Between 1946 and 1958 short-term consumer credit rose from $8.4 billion to almost $45 billion. The Diners Club introduced the first credit card in 1950, followed by the American Express card and Bank Americard in 1959. By the 1970s the omnipresent plastic credit card had revolutionized personal and family finances.

Aggressive advertising contributed to the massive increase in consumer spending. In 1951 businesses spent more on advertising ($6.5 billion) than taxpayers did on primary and secondary education ($5 billion). The 1950s gave Americans the Marlboro man; M&Ms that "melt in your mouth, not in your hand"; Wonder Bread to "build strong bodies in twelve ways"; and the "Does she or doesn't she?" Clairol woman.

Consumers had more free time in which to spend their money than ever before. In 1960 the average worker put in a five-day week, with eight paid holidays a year (double the 1946 standard) plus a two-week paid vacation. Americans took to the interstate highway system by the millions, encouraging dramatic growth in motel chains, roadside restaurants, and fast-food eateries. (The first McDonald's restaurant opened in 1954 in San Bernardino, California; the Holiday Inn motel chain started in Memphis in 1952.) Among the most popular destinations were state and national parks and Disneyland, which opened in Anaheim, California, in 1955.

Perhaps the most significant hallmark of postwar consumer culture was television. TV's leap to cultural prominence was swift and overpowering. There were only ten broadcasting stations in the country and a meager 7,000 sets in American homes in 1947. By 1960, 87 percent of American families had at least one television set. Soon television supplanted radio as the chief diffuser of popular culture, its national programming promoting shared interests and tastes and reducing regional and ethnic differences.

What Americans saw on television, besides the omnipresent commercials, was an overwhelmingly white, middle-class world of nuclear families living in suburban homes. *Leave It to Beaver, Ozzie and Harriet,* and similar sitcoms featured characters who adhered to clear-cut gender roles and plots based on minor family crises that were always happily resolved by the end of the show. Programs such as *The Honeymooners,* starring Jackie Gleason as a Brooklyn bus driver, and *Life of Reilly,* a situation comedy featuring a California aircraft worker, were rare in their treatment of working-class lives. Nonwhite characters appeared mainly as servants, such as comedian Jack Benny's black "houseboy" Rochester or the Latino gardener with the anglicized name "Frank Smith" on *Father Knows Best.* Although the new medium did offer some serious programming, notably live theater and documentaries, Federal Communications Commissioner Newton Minow concluded in 1963 that television was "a vast wasteland." Its reassuring images of family life and postwar society, however, dovetailed with the social expectations of many Americans.

THE SEARCH FOR SECURITY: RELIGION AND THE FAMILY

The dislocations of the depression and war years made Americans yearn for security and a reaffirmation of traditional values. Some of this sentiment was expressed in a renewed emphasis on religion. Church membership rose from 49 percent of the population in 1940 to 69 percent in 1960. All the major denominations shared in the growth, which was accompanied by an ecumenical movement to bring Catholics, Protestants, and Jews together. The stress on religion meshed with cold-war Americans' view of themselves as a righteous people opposed to "godless communism." In 1954 the phrase "under God" was inserted into the Pledge of Allegiance, and in 1956 Congress added "In God We Trust" to all U.S. coins.

Beyond patriotism religion also served more deeply felt needs. In his popular television program Bishop Fulton Sheen asked, "Is life worth living?" He and countless others optimistically answered in the affirmative. None was more positive than Norman Vincent Peale, whose best-selling book *The Power of Positive Thinking* (1952) embodied the trend toward the therapeutic use of religion to assist men and women in coping with the stresses of modern life. Evangelical religion also experienced a resurgence, most evident in the dramatic rise to popularity of the Reverend Billy Graham, who used television, radio, advertising, and print media to spread the gospel. Although critics suggested that middle-class interest in religion stemmed not so much from a renewed spirituality as from a surging impulse toward conformity, the revival nonetheless spoke to Americans' search for spiritual meaning in uncertain times.

Even more dramatic testimony to the desire for stability in the postwar era was the emphasis Americans placed on the family and children. As one popular advice book put it, "The family is the center of your living. If it isn't, you've gone far astray." Family demographics between 1940 and 1960 moved notably away from depression and war trends. Marriages were remarkably stable; not until the mid-1960s did the divorce rate begin to rise sharply. But the average age at marriage fell during the period, to twenty-two for men and twenty for women. In 1951 a third of all women were married by age nineteen. More important, the drop in the average age at marriage resulted in a surge of young married couples who produced a bumper crop of children. After a century and a half of declining family size, the birth rate shot up and peaked in 1957: more babies were born between 1948 and 1953 than had been born in the previous thirty years. As a result of this trend and a lengthened life expectancy because of improvements in diet, public health, and medicine, the American population rose dramatically from 140 million in 1945 to 179 million in 1960, and to 203 million in 1970.

The baby boom had a broad and immediate impact on American society. It prompted a major expansion of the nation's educational system: by 1970 school expenditures were double those of the 1950 level. In addition, babies' consumer needs fueled the economy as families bought food, diapers, toys, and clothing for their expanding broods. Together with federal expenditures on national security, family spending on consumer goods fueled the unparalleled prosperity and economic growth of the 1950s and 1960s.

CONTRADICTIONS IN WOMEN'S LIVES

The parents of baby boomers experienced multiple economic and social pressures. In addition to providing for their children materially and emotionally, they were expected to adhere to rigid gender roles as a way of maintaining the family and undergirding the social order. The mass media, educators, and experts urged men to conform to a masculine ideal that emphasized their role as responsible bread-winners. Women's proper place, they advised, was in the home. Endorsing what Betty Friedan has called the "feminine mystique" of the 1950s—the ideal that "the highest value and the only commitment for women is the fulfillment of their own femininity"—many psychologists pronounced motherhood the only "normal" fe-male gender role and berated mothers who worked outside the home, charging that they damaged their children's development.

Though the power of these ideas stunted the lives of many women, not all housewives were unhappy or neurotic, as Friedan would later charge in her 1963 best seller, *The Feminine Mystique*. Many working-class women embraced their new roles as housewives; unlike their mothers and unmarried sisters, they were not com-pelled to take low-paid employment outside the home. But not all Americans could or did live by the norms of suburban domesticity, ideals that were out of reach of or irrelevant to many racial minorities, inner-city residents, recent immigrants, rural Americans, and homosexuals. At the height of the postwar period, more than one-third of American women held jobs outside the home (see American Voices, "A Woman Encounters the Feminine Mystique"). The increase in the number of work-ing women coincided with another change of equal significance—a dramatic rise in the number of older, married middle-class women who took jobs.

How could the society of the 1950s cling so steadfastly to the domestic ideal while an increasing number of wives and mothers worked? Often women justified their jobs as an extension of their family responsibilities, enabling their families to enjoy more of the fruits of the consumer culture. Working women also still bore full responsibility for child care and household management, allowing families and society to avoid facing the implications of their new roles. Thus the reality of women's lives departed significantly from the cultural stereotypes glorified in advertising, sitcoms, and women's magazines.

CULTURAL DISSENTERS

Beneath the surface of family togetherness lay other tensions—those between par-ents and children. Dating back to the 1920s the emergence of a mass youth culture had its roots in the democratization of education, the growth of peer culture, and the increasing purchasing power of teenagers in an age of affluence. Youth, eager to escape the climate of suburban conformity of their parents, had become a dis-tinct new market that advertisers eagerly exploited. In 1956 advertisers projected an adolescent market of $9 billion for items such as transistor radios (introduced in 1952), clothing, and fads such as Hula Hoops (1958).

What really defined this generation's youth culture, however, was its music. Rejecting the rigid boundaries of traditional popular music, teenagers in the 1950s discovered rock 'n' roll, an amalgam of white country and western music and the black urban music known as rhythm and blues. The Cleveland disc jockey Alan

AMERICAN VOICES

A Woman Encounters the Feminine Mystique

T *he power of the feminine mystique in the 1950s made it difficult for middle-class women who challenged the view that women's proper place was in the home. In this oral history account, "Sylvia" describes her struggle to pursue a career as an ophthalmologist.*

We sat on a bench in the middle of the lobby there—I remember it looked like a train station—and he [her professor] said, "Do you plan to get pregnant or married?" I promised him I wouldn't do either. I felt like I was about ten years old. They gave me a year's trial in the research department and after that I could get a residency. Most people there, the men, had a three-year residency. I was only the second woman they'd ever accepted, and I was the only woman out of twenty men.

I had a fellowship, so when I finished with my work I'd have to go over to see how my research projects were coming along. I never, never, goofed off. These guys were watching me all the time and complaining that I wasn't doing my work. It was hard enough to be a first-year resident, where you're the bottom person who gets kicked by everybody. I had no friends. My fellow physicians were constantly telling me I should switch to obstetrics or pediatrics, I should be home having babies, that a man could earn a wonderful living for his family in my place. Finally I was at my wits' end and I called my old ophthalmology professor and told him I didn't know if I could psychologically take this for another two and a half years. He said, "You know, if you give up now I'll never be able to get another woman in there." So I went on.

SOURCE: Brett Harvey, *The Fifties: A Women's Oral History* (New York: Harper, 1993), pp. 154–55.

Freed played a major role in introducing white America to the new African American sound by playing rhythm and blues records on white radio stations beginning in 1954. Young white performers such as Bill Haley, Buddy Holly, and especially Elvis Presley incorporated the new mixture into their own music and capitalized on the new youth market. Between 1953 and 1959 record sales increased from $213 million to $603 million, with 45-rpm rock-'n'-roll records as the driving force. The new teen music shocked many white adults, who saw rock 'n' roll as an invitation to race-mixing, sexual promiscuity, and juvenile delinquency.

The youth rebellion was only one aspect of a broader undercurrent of discontent with the conformist culture of the 1950s. In major cities across the nation, gay men and women, many of whom had served in the military during World War II, fought back against homophobic laws and personal attacks. In Los Angeles homosexual men founded the Mattachine Society, a gay-rights organization, in 1951, and in 1954 lesbians established the Daughters of Bilitis. While for the most part the gay subculture remained closeted, this did not stop gay baiting or local police raids on gay bars. And because homosexuals were viewed as emotionally unstable or vulnerable to blackmail, they were assumed to be security risks. As a result of publicity attached to raids, as well as government investigations, many gays lost their jobs, a testament to the perceived threat they represented to mainstream sexual and cultural norms.

Postwar artists, musicians, and writers expressed their alienation from mainstream society through intensely personal, introspective art forms. In New York Jackson Pollock and other painters rejected the social realism of the 1930s for an unconventional style that became known as abstract expressionism. Swirling and splattering paint onto giant canvases, Pollock emphasized self-expression in the act of painting, capturing the chaotic atmosphere of the nuclear age.

A similar trend developed in jazz, as black musicians originated a hard-driving improvisational style known as bebop. Black jazz musicians found eager fans not only in the African American community but among young white Beats in New York and San Francisco. Disdaining middle-class conformity, corporate capitalism, and suburban materialism, the Beats were a group of writers and poets who were

A Woman's Dilemma in Postwar America

This 1959 cover of the *Saturday Evening Post* depicts some of the difficult choices facing women in the postwar era. Women's consignment to low-paid, dead-end jobs in the service sector encouraged many to become full-time homemakers. Once back in their suburban homes, however, many middle-class women felt isolated and trapped amid endless rounds of cooking, cleaning, and diaper changing. (© The Curtis Publishing Company)

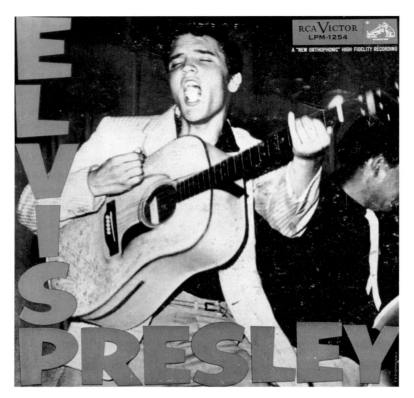

Elvis Presley

The young Elvis Presley shown here on the cover of his first album in 1956, embodied cultural rebellion against the conservatism and triviality of adult life in the 1950s. (© 1956 BGM Music)

both literary innovators and outspoken social critics. In his poem "Howl" (1956), which became a manifesto of the Beat generation, Allen Ginsberg lamented: "I saw the best minds of my generation destroyed by madness, starving hysterical naked, dragging themselves through the angry streets at dawn looking for an angry fix." In works such as Jack Kerouac's novel *On the Road* (1957) the Beats glorified spontaneity, sexual adventurism, drug use, and spirituality. Although they were most often apolitical—their rebellion was strictly cultural—in the 1960s they inspired a new generation of rebels who would champion both political and cultural change.

The Other America

As middle-class whites flocked to the suburbs, a diverse group of poor and working-class migrants, many of them nonwhite, moved into the central cities. With jobs and financial resources flowing to the suburbs, urban newcomers inherited a declining economy and a decaying environment. To those enjoying new prosperity, *The Other America*—as the social critic Michael Harrington called it in 1962—remained largely invisible.

URBAN MIGRATION

Newly arrived immigrants were one of several groups moving into the nation's cities in the postwar era. Although until 1965 U.S. immigration policy followed the restrictive national origins quota system set up in 1924 (see Chapter 23), Congress modified the law during and after World War II. The War Brides Act of 1945, permitting the entry and naturalization of the wives and children of Americans living abroad (mainly servicemen), brought thousands of new immigrants between 1950 and 1965, including some 17,000 Koreans. Three years later the Displaced Persons Act admitted approximately 415,000 European refugees. The repeal of the Chinese Exclusion Act in 1943, in deference to America's wartime alliance with China, and the passage of the McCarran-Walter Act in 1952 ended the exclusion of Chinese, Japanese, Korean, and Southeast Asian immigrants. Finally, in recognition of the freeing of the Philippines from American control in 1946, Filipinos received their own quota.

One of the largest groups of postwar migrants came from Mexico. Nearly 275,000 Mexicans came in the 1950s, and almost 444,000 in the 1960s. They moved primarily to western and southwestern cities such as Los Angeles, El Paso, and Phoenix, where they found jobs as migrant workers or in the expanding service sector. Before World War II most Mexican Americans had lived in rural areas and engaged in agricultural work; by 1960 a majority were living in urban areas where they joined more settled communities of service and manufacturing workers.

Part of the stimulus for Mexican immigration was the reinstitution of the *bracero* program from 1951 to 1964. Originally devised as a means of importing temporary labor during World War II, the program brought 450,000 Mexican workers to the United States at its peak in 1959. But even as the federal government welcomed braceros, it deported those who stayed on illegally. In response to the recession of 1953 to 1954 and the resulting high rate of unemployment throughout the nation, federal authorities deported nearly 4 million Mexicans in a program called "Operation Wetback." The deportations discouraged illegal immigration for a few years, but the level increased again after the bracero program ended.

Another group of Spanish-speaking migrants came from the American-controlled territory of Puerto Rico. Residents of that island had been American citizens since 1917, so their migration was not subject to immigration laws. The inflow from the territory increased dramatically after World War II, when mechanization of the island's sugarcane industry pushed many rural Puerto Ricans off the land. When airlines began to offer cheap direct flights between San Juan and New York City (in the 1940s the fare was about $50, or two weeks' wages), Puerto

Ricans—most of whom settled in New York—became this country's first group to immigrate by air.

Cuban refugees constituted the third large group of Spanish-speaking immigrants. In the six years after communist Fidel Castro's overthrow of the Batista dictatorship in 1959, an estimated 180,000 people fled Cuba for the United States. The Cuban refugee community grew so quickly that it turned Miami into a cosmopolitan, bilingual city almost overnight. Unlike most new immigrants Miami's Cubans prospered, in large part because they had arrived with more resources.

Internal migration from rural areas also brought large numbers of people to the cities, especially African Americans, continuing a trend that had begun during World War I (see Chapter 22). Although both whites and blacks left the land, the starkest decline was among black farmers. Their migration was hastened by the transformation of southern agriculture, especially by the introduction of innovations like the mechanical cotton-picker, which significantly reduced the demand for farm labor.

Some of the migrants settled in southern cities, where they found industrial jobs. White southerners from Appalachia moved north to "hillbilly" ghettos such as Cincinnati's Over the Rhine neighborhood and Chicago's Uptown. As many as 3 million blacks headed to Chicago, New York, Washington, Detroit, Los Angeles, and other cities between 1940 and 1960. So pervasive were the migrants that certain sections of Chicago seemed like the Mississippi Delta transplanted. By 1960 about half of the nation's black population was living outside the South, compared with only 23 percent before World War II.

In western cities an influx of Native Americans also contributed to the rise in the nonwhite urban population. Seeking to end federal responsibility for Indian affairs, Congress in 1953 authorized a "Termination" program aimed at liquidating the reservation system and integrating Native Americans into mainstream society. The program, which reflected a cold-war preoccupation with conformity and assimilation, enjoyed strong support from mining, timber, and agricultural interests that wanted to open reservation lands for private development. The Bureau of Indian Affairs encouraged voluntary relocation to urban areas with a program subsidizing moving costs and establishing relocation centers in San Francisco, Denver, Chicago, and other cities. The relocation program proved problematic, however, as many Indians found it difficult to adjust to an urban environment and culture. Although forced termination was halted in 1958, by 1960 some 60,000 Indians had moved to the cities. Despite the program's stated goal of assimilation, most Native American migrants settled together in poor urban neighborhoods alongside other nonwhite groups.

THE URBAN CRISIS

American cities thus saw their nonwhite populations swell at the same time that whites were flocking to the suburbs. From 1950 to 1960 the nation's twelve largest cities lost 3.6 million whites and gained 4.5 million nonwhites. As affluent whites left the cities, urban tax revenues shrank, leading to the decay of services and infrastructure, which, coupled with growing racial fears, accelerated white suburban flight in the 1960s.

By the time that blacks, Latinos, and Native Americans moved into the inner cities, urban America was in poor shape. Housing continued to be a crucial problem. City planners, politicians, and real-estate developers responded with urban renewal programs, razing blighted city neighborhoods to make way for modern construction projects. Local residents were rarely consulted about whether they wanted their neighborhoods "renewed," and redevelopment programs often produced grim high-rise housing projects that destroyed community bonds and created anonymous open areas that were vulnerable to crime. Between 1949 and 1967 urban renewal demolished almost 400,000 buildings and displaced 1.4 million people.

Postwar urban areas were increasingly becoming places of last resort for the nation's poor. Lured to the cities by the promise of plentiful jobs, migrants found that many of those opportunities had relocated to the suburban fringe, putting steady employment out of reach for those who needed it most. Migrants to the city, especially blacks, also faced racial hostility and institutional barriers to mobility—biased school funding, hiring and promotion decisions, and credit practices. Two separate Americas were emerging: a largely white society in suburbs and peripheral areas and an inner city populated by blacks, Latinos, and other disadvantaged groups.

The stereotypes of boundless affluence and contentment in the 1950s—of "Happy Days"—are thus misleading, for they hide those persons who did not share equally in the American dream—displaced factory workers, destitute old people, female heads of households, blacks and other racial minority groups. In the turbulent decade to come the contrast between suburban affluence and the "other America," between the lure of the city for the poor and minorities and its grim, segregated reality, and between a heightened emphasis on domesticity and the widening opportunities for women would spawn growing demands for social change that the nation's leaders in the 1960s could not ignore.

John F. Kennedy and the Politics of Expectation

In his 1961 inaugural address President John Fitzgerald Kennedy challenged a "new generation of Americans" to take responsibility for the future: "Ask not what your country can do for you, ask what you can do for your country." Few presidents came to Washington more primed for action than John F. Kennedy. His New Frontier program promised to "get America moving again" through vigorous governmental activism at home and abroad. But the legislative achievements of Kennedy's New Frontier, particularly in domestic affairs, were modest.

THE NEW POLITICS

The Republicans would have been happy to renominate Dwight D. Eisenhower for president, but the Twenty-second Amendment prevented them from doing so. Passed in 1951 by a Republican-controlled Congress to prevent a repetition of Franklin Roosevelt's four-term presidency, the amendment limited future presidents to two full terms. So in 1960 the Republicans turned to Vice President Richard M. Nixon, who campaigned for an updated version of Eisenhower's policies but was hampered by lukewarm support from the popular president.

The Democrats chose Senator John F. Kennedy of Massachusetts, with the Senate majority leader, Lyndon B. Johnson of Texas, as the vice-presidential nominee. First elected to Congress in 1946, John Kennedy moved to the Senate in 1952. Ambitious and hard-driven, Kennedy launched his campaign in 1960 with a platform calling

The Kennedy Magnetism

John Kennedy, the Democratic candidate for president in 1960, used his youth and personality to attract voters. Here the Massachusetts senator draws an enthusiastic crowd on a campaign stop in Elgin, Illinois. (AP/Wide World Photos)

for civil rights legislation, health care for the elderly, aid to education, urban renewal, expanded military and space programs, and containment of communism abroad.

At forty-three Kennedy was poised to become the youngest man ever elected to the presidency and the nation's first Catholic chief executive. Turning his age into a powerful campaign asset, Kennedy practiced what came to be called the "new politics," an approach that emphasized youthful charisma, style, and personality more than issues and platforms. Using the power of the media—particularly television—to reach voters directly, practitioners of the new politics relied on professional media consultants, political pollsters, and mass fund raising.

A series of four televised debates between the two principal candidates, a major innovation of the 1960 campaign, showed how important television was becoming to political life. Nixon, far less photogenic than Kennedy, looked sallow and unshaven under the intense studio lights. Kennedy, in contrast, looked vigorous, cool, and self-confident on screen. Polls showed that television did sway political perceptions: voters who listened to the first debate on the radio concluded that Nixon had won, but those who viewed it on TV judged in Kennedy's favor.

Despite the edge Kennedy enjoyed in the debates, he won only the narrowest of electoral victories, receiving 49.7 percent of the popular vote to Nixon's 49.5 percent. Kennedy successfully appealed to the diverse elements of the Democratic coalition, attracting large numbers of Catholic and black voters and a significant sector of the middle class; the vice-presidential nominee, Lyndon Johnson, brought in southern white Democrats. Yet only 120,000 votes separated the two candidates, and the shift of a few thousand votes in key states such as Illinois (where there were confirmed cases of voting fraud) would have reversed the outcome.

ACTIVISM ABROAD AND AT HOME

Kennedy's greatest priority as president was foreign affairs. A resolute cold warrior, Kennedy took a hard line against communist expansionism. In contrast to Eisenhower, whose cost-saving New Look program had built up the American nuclear arsenal at the expense of conventional weapons, Kennedy proposed a new policy of "flexible response," stating that the nation must be prepared "to deter all wars, general or limited, nuclear or conventional, large or small." Congress quickly granted Kennedy's military requests, and by 1963 the defense budget reached its highest level as a percentage of total federal expenditures in the cold-war era, greatly expanding the military-industrial complex.

Flexible response measures were designed to deter direct attacks by the Soviet Union. To prepare for a new kind of warfare, evident in the wars of national liberation that had broken out in many developing countries, Kennedy adopted a new military doctrine of *counterinsurgency*. Soon U.S. Army Special Forces, called Green Berets for their distinctive headgear, were receiving intensive training in repelling the random, small-scale attacks typical of guerrilla warfare. Vietnam would soon provide a testing ground for counterinsurgency techniques (see Chapter 29).

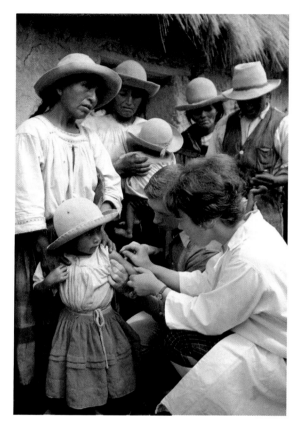

The Peace Corps

The Peace Corps, a New Frontier program initiated in 1961, attracted thousands of idealistic young Americans to volunteer in development projects overseas. Volunteers Rita Helmkamp and Ed Dennison worked in a vaccination program in Bolivia.

(David S. Boyer/National Geographic Society Image Collection)

Another of Kennedy's projects, the Peace Corps, established in 1961, embodied the commitment to public service that the president had called for in his inaugural address. Thousands of men and women agreed to devote two or more years to programs that had them teaching English to Filipino schoolchildren or helping African villagers obtain adequate supplies of water. Embodying the idealism of the early 1960s, the Peace Corps was also a cold-war weapon intended to bring developing countries into the American orbit and away from communist influence.

For the same reason Kennedy pushed for economic aid to developing countries. The State Department's Agency for International Development coordinated foreign aid for the Third World, including surplus agricultural products distributed to developing nations through its Food for Peace program. In Latin America the Alliance for Progress provided funds for food, education, medicine, and other services, although it did little to enhance economic growth or improve social conditions there.

Latin America was the site of Kennedy's first major foreign policy initiative and one of his biggest failures—an effort to overthrow the new Soviet-supported regime in Cuba. The United States had long exercised nearly total economic and political dominance of the island. But on New Year's Day in 1959 the revolutionary Fidel Castro overthrew the corrupt and unpopular dictator Fulgencio Batista. When Castro began agrarian reforms and nationalized American-owned banks and industries, relations with Washington deteriorated. By early 1961 the United States had declared an embargo on all exports to Cuba, cut back on imports of Cuban sugar, and broken off diplomatic relations with Castro's regime.

Isolated by the United States, Cuba turned increasingly toward the Soviet Union for economic and military support. Concerned about Castro's growing friendliness with the Soviets, in early 1961 Kennedy used plans originally drawn up by the Eisenhower administration to dispatch Cuban exiles living in Nicaragua to foment an anti-Castro uprising. Although the invaders had been trained by the Central Intelligence Agency (CIA), they were ill prepared for their task and had little popular support. After landing at Cuba's Bay of Pigs on April 17, the tiny force of 1,400 men was crushed by Castro's troops (Map 28.2).

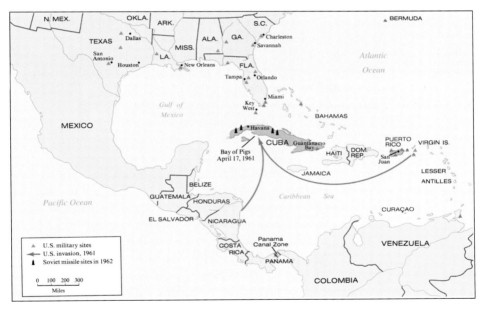

M A P 28.2
The United States and Cuba, 1961–1962

Fidel Castro's takeover in Cuba in 1959 brought cold-war tensions to the Caribbean. In 1961 the United States tried unsuccessfully to overthrow Castro's regime by supporting the Bay of Pigs invasion of Cuban exiles launched from Nicaragua and other points in the Caribbean. In 1962 a major confrontation with the Soviet Union occurred over Soviet missile sites in Cuba. The Soviets removed the missiles after President Kennedy ordered a naval blockade of the island, which lies just 90 miles south of Florida.

Already weakened by the Bay of Pigs invasion, U.S.-Soviet relations deteriorated further in June 1961 when Soviet Premier Khrushchev deployed soldiers to isolate communist-controlled East Berlin from the western sector of the city controlled by West Germany. With congressional approval Kennedy responded by adding 300,000 troops to the armed forces and promptly dispatching 40,000 of them to Europe. In mid-August, to stop the exodus of East Germans to the West, the Soviets ordered construction of the Berlin Wall, and East German guards began policing the border. Until it was dismantled in 1989 the Berlin Wall remained the supreme symbol of the cold war.

The climactic confrontation of the cold war came in October 1962. After the failed Bay of Pigs invasion the Kennedy administration increased economic pressure against Cuba and resumed covert efforts to overthrow the Castro regime. In response the Soviets stepped up military aid to Cuba, including the installation of nuclear missiles. In early October American reconnaissance planes photographed Soviet-built bases for intermediate-range ballistic missiles (IRBMs), which could reach U.S. targets as far as 2,200 miles away. Some of those weapons had already been installed, and more were on the way.

In a somber televised address on Monday, October 22, Kennedy confronted the Soviet Union, and announced that the United States would impose a "quarantine on all offensive military equipment" intended for Cuba. As the two superpowers went on full military alert, people around the world feared that the confrontation would end in nuclear war. Americans living within range of the missiles restocked their bomb shelters or calculated the fastest route out of town. When Khrushchev denounced the quarantine, tension mounted. But as the world held its breath, ships carrying the Soviet-made missiles turned back. After a week of tense negotiations, both Kennedy and Khrushchev made concessions: Kennedy pledged not to invade Cuba, and Khrushchev promised to dismantle the missile bases.

Although the risk of nuclear war was greater during the Cuban missile crisis than it was at any other time in the postwar period, it led to a slight thaw in U.S.-Soviet relations. In the words of national security advisor McGeorge Bundy, "having come so close to the edge, the leaders of the two governments have since taken care to keep away from the cliff." Kennedy softened his cold-war rhetoric and began to strive for peaceful coexistence. Soviet leaders, similarly chastened, were willing to talk. In August 1963 the three nuclear powers—the United States, the Soviet Union, and Great Britain—agreed to ban the testing of nuclear weapons in the atmosphere, in space, and underwater. Underground testing, however, was allowed to continue. The new emphasis on peaceful coexistence also led to the establishment of a Washington-Moscow telecommunications "hot line" in 1963 so that leaders could contact each other quickly during potential crises.

But no matter how often American leaders talked about opening channels of communication with the Soviets, the preoccupation with the Soviet military threat to American security remained a cornerstone of U.S. policy. Nor did Soviet leaders moderate their concern over the threat that they believed the United States posed to the survival of the USSR. The cold war, and the escalating arms race that accompanied it, would continue for another twenty-five years.

The expansive vision of presidential leadership that Kennedy and his advisors brought to the White House worked less well at home than it did abroad. Hampered by the lack of a popular mandate in the 1960 election, Kennedy could not mobilize public support for the domestic agenda of the New Frontier. A conservative coalition of southern Democrats and western and midwestern Republicans effectively stalled most liberal initiatives. More important, Kennedy was not nearly as impassioned about domestic reform as he was about foreign policy.

One program that did win both popular and congressional support was increased funding for the National Aeronautics and Space Administration (NASA), whose Mercury space program had begun in 1958. On May 5, 1961, just three months after Kennedy took office, Alan Shepard became the first American in space. (The Soviet cosmonaut Yuri Gagarin became the first person in space when he made a 108-hour flight in April 1961.) The following year, American astronaut John Glenn manned the first space mission to orbit the earth. At the height of American fascination with space flight Kennedy proposed that the nation commit itself to landing a man on the moon within the decade. To support this mission (accomplished in 1969), Kennedy persuaded Congress to greatly increase NASA's budget.

Kennedy's most striking domestic achievement was his use of modern economic theory to shape government fiscal policy. New Dealers had gradually moved away from the ideal of a balanced budget, turning instead to deliberate deficit spending to stimulate economic growth. In addition to relying on federal spending to create the desired deficit, Kennedy and his advisors proposed a reduction in income taxes. A tax cut, they argued, would put more money in the hands of taxpayers, who would spend it, thereby creating more jobs. For a time federal expenditures would exceed federal income, but after a year or two the expanding economy would raise American incomes and generate higher tax revenues.

Congress balked at this unorthodox proposal, and the measure failed to pass. But Lyndon Johnson pressed for it after Kennedy's assassination, signing it into law in February 1964. The Kennedy-Johnson tax cut—the Tax Reduction Act (1964)— marked a milestone in the use of fiscal policy to encourage economic growth, an approach that Republicans and other fiscal conservatives would later embrace.

Kennedy's interest in stimulating economic growth did not include a commitment to spending for domestic social needs, although he did not entirely ignore the liberal legislative agenda of Franklin Roosevelt and Harry Truman. Kennedy managed to push through legislation raising the minimum wage and expanding Social Security benefits. But on other issues—federal aid to education, wilderness preservation, federal investment in mass transportation, and medical insurance for the elderly—he ran into determined congressional opposition from both Republicans and dissenters in his own party.

JFK AND CIVIL RIGHTS

Perhaps the gravest failure of the Kennedy administration was its reluctance to act on civil rights—the most important domestic issue of the 1960s. Building on the strategy of nonviolent direct action pioneered by Martin Luther King Jr. and the Montgomery bus boycotters in the 1950s, a younger generation of activists in the 1960s initiated new, more assertive tactics such as sit-ins, freedom rides, and voter registration campaigns.

This new phase of the civil rights movement began in Greensboro, North Carolina, on February 1, 1960, when four black college students took seats at the "whites-only" lunch counter of a local Woolworth's, determined to "sit in" until they were served. Although the protesters were arrested, the sit-in tactic worked and quickly spread to other southern cities. A few months later Ella Baker, an administrator with the Southern Christian Leadership Conference (SCLC) and a lifelong activist, helped to organize the Student Non-Violent Coordinating Committee (SNCC, known as "Snick") to facilitate student sit-ins. By the end of the year about 50,000 people had participated in sit-ins or other demonstrations, and 3,600 of them had been jailed. But lunch counters had been desegregated in 126 cities throughout the South (see American Voices, "A Badge of Honor").

The success of SNCC's unorthodox tactics encouraged the Congress of Racial Equality (CORE), an interracial group founded in 1942, to organize a series of *freedom rides* in 1961 on interstate bus lines throughout the South to call attention to the continuing segregation of public transportation. The activists who rode the buses, mostly young and both black and white, were brutally attacked by white mobs in Anniston, Montgomery, and Birmingham, Alabama. Governor John Patterson refused to intervene, claiming, "I cannot guarantee protection for this bunch of rabble rousers."

Although the Kennedy administration generally opposed the freedom riders' activities, films of their beatings and the bus burning shown on the nightly news prompted Attorney General Robert Kennedy to send federal marshals to Alabama to restore order. Faced with Department of Justice intervention against those who defied the Interstate Commerce Commission's prohibition of segregation in interstate vehicles and facilities, most southern communities quietly acceded to the changes. And civil rights activists learned that nonviolent protest could succeed if it provoked vicious white resistance and generated publicity. Only when forced to, it appeared, would the federal authorities act.

This lesson was confirmed in Birmingham, Alabama, when Martin Luther King Jr. and the Reverend Fred Shuttlesworth called for a protest against conditions in what King called "the most segregated city in the United States." In April 1963 thousands of black demonstrators marched downtown to picket Birmingham's department stores. They were met by Eugene ("Bull") Connor, the city's commissioner of public safety, who used snarling dogs, electric cattle prods, and high-pressure fire hoses to break up the crowd. Television cameras captured the scene for the evening news.

A Badge of Honor

JOHN LEWIS

T *wenty-year-old John Lewis, a student at American Baptist Theological Seminary in
      Nashville, was one of 500 students to participate in the 1960 sit-ins at the city's lunch
counters. His oral account reveals the tactical planning that went into the students' efforts, the
virulence of the resistance they encountered, and the spirit of commitment and courage that
sustained civil rights activists. Lewis went onto join the Student Non-Violent Coordinating
Committee (SNCC) and to participate in the Freedom Rides, Freedom Summer, and the March
on Washington.*

The first day nothing in terms of violence or disorder happened. This continued for a few
more days and it continued day in and day out. Finally, on Saturday, February twenty-
seventh, when we had about a hundred students prepared to go down—it was a very beautiful day in Nashville—we got a call from a local white minister who had been a real
supporter of the movement. He said that if we go down on this particular day, he understood that the police would stand to the side and let a group of white hoodlums and thugs
come in and beat people up, and then we would be arrested. We made a decision to go,
and we all went to the same store. It was a Woolworth in the heart of the downtown area,
and we occupied every seat at the lunch counter, every seat in the restaurant, and it did
happen. A group of young white men came in and they started pulling and beating primarily the young women. They put lighted cigarettes down their backs, in their hair, and
they were really beating people. In a short time police officials came in and placed all of
us under arrest, and not a single member of the white group, the people that were opposing our sit-in, was arrested.

   That was the first time that I was arrested. Growing up in the rural South, you learned
it was not the thing to do. To go to jail was to bring shame and disgrace on the family. But
for me it was like being involved in a holy crusade. It became a badge of honor. I think it
was in keeping with what we had been taught in the workshops, so I felt very good, in the
sense of righteous indignation, about being arrested, but at the same time I felt the commitment and dedication on the part of the students.

SOURCE: Henry Hampton and Steve Fayer, *Voices of Freedom: An Oral History of the Civil Rights
Movement from the 1950s Through the 1980s* (New York: Bantam Books, 1991), p. 58.

   President Kennedy, realizing that he could no longer postpone decisive action,
decided to step up the federal government's role in civil rights. On June 11, 1963,
Kennedy went on television to promise major legislation banning discrimination
in public accommodations and empowering the Justice Department to enforce desegregation. Black leaders hailed the speech as the "Second Emancipation Proclamation," but for one person Kennedy's speech came too late. That night, Medgar

Racial Violence in Birmingham

When thousands of blacks marched through downtown Birmingham, Alabama, to protest racial segregation in April 1963, they were met with fire hoses and attack dogs unleashed by Police Chief "Bull" Connor. The violence, which was televised on the national evening news, shocked many Americans and helped build sympathy for the civil rights movement among northern whites. (Bill Hudson/Wide World Photos, Inc.)

Evers, president of the Mississippi chapter of the NAACP, was shot in the back and killed in his driveway in Jackson. The martyrdom of Evers became a spur to further action.

To rouse the conscience of the nation and to marshal support for Kennedy's bill, civil rights leaders adopted a tactic A. Philip Randolph had first suggested in 1941 (see Chapter 26): a massive march on Washington. Martin Luther King Jr. of the SCLC, Roy Wilkins of the NAACP, Whitney Young of the National Urban League, and the black socialist Bayard Rustin were the principal organizers. On August 28, 1963, about 250,000 black and white demonstrators—the largest crowd at any demonstration up to that time—gathered at the Lincoln Memorial. The march culminated in a memorable speech delivered, indeed preached, by King, in the evangelical style of the black church. He ended with an exclamation from an old Negro spiritual: "Free at last! Free at last! Thank God almighty, we are free at last!"

King's eloquence and the sight of blacks and whites marching solemnly together did more than any other event to make the civil rights movement acceptable to white Americans. The March on Washington marked the climax of the nonviolent phase of the civil rights movement and confirmed King's position, especially among white liberals, as the leading speaker for the black cause. In 1964 King won the Nobel Peace Prize for his leadership.

Despite the impact of the march on public opinion, it changed few congressional votes. Southern senators continued to block Kennedy's legislation by threatening a filibuster. Even more troubling was a new outbreak of violence by white extremists determined to oppose equality for blacks at all costs. In September a Baptist church in Birmingham was bombed, and four black Sunday school students were killed. The violence shocked the nation and stiffened the resolve of civil rights activists to escalate their demands for change. Two months later, President Kennedy was assassinated.

THE KENNEDY ASSASSINATION

Although the first two years of Kennedy's presidency had been plagued by foreign-policy crises and domestic inaction, many political observers believed that by 1963 Kennedy was maturing as a national leader. On November 22, 1963, Kennedy went to Texas. As he and his wife, Jacqueline, rode in an open car past the Texas School Book Depository in Dallas, he was shot through the head and neck by a sniper. Kennedy died a half hour later. (Whether accused killer Lee Harvey Oswald, a twenty-four-year-old loner who had spent three years in the Soviet Union, was the sole gunman is still a matter of controversy.) Before Air Force One left Dallas to take the president's body back to Washington, a grim-faced Lyndon Johnson was sworn in as president. Kennedy's stunned widow, still wearing her bloodstained pink suit, looked on.

Kennedy's youthful image, the trauma of his assassination, and the collective sense that Americans had been robbed of a promising leader contributed to a powerful mystique. This romantic aura has overshadowed what most historians agree was at best a mixed record. Kennedy exercised bold presidential leadership in foreign affairs, but his initiatives in Cuba and Berlin marked the height of superpower confrontation during the cold war. Moreover, his enthusiasm for fighting communism abroad had no domestic equivalent. Kennedy's proposals for educational aid, medical insurance, and other liberal reforms stalled, and his tax-cut bill languished in Congress until after his death. Perhaps his greatest domestic failure was his reluctance to act boldly on civil rights.

Lyndon B. Johnson and the Great Society

Lyndon Baines Johnson, a seasoned politician who was best at negotiating in the backrooms of power, was no match for the Kennedy style, but less than a year after assuming office Johnson won the 1964 presidential election in a landslide that far surpassed Kennedy's meager mandate in 1960. Johnson then used his astonishing energy and genius for compromise to bring to fruition many of Kennedy's stalled programs and more than a few of his own. Those legislative accomplishments—Johnson's "Great Society"—fulfilled and in many cases surpassed the New Deal liberal agenda of the 1930s.

THE MOMENTUM FOR CIVIL RIGHTS

On assuming the presidency Lyndon Johnson promptly turned the passage of civil rights legislation into a memorial to his slain predecessor—an ironic twist in light of Kennedy's lukewarm support for the cause. The Civil Rights Act, passed finally in June 1964, was a landmark in the history of American race relations. Its keystone, Title VII, outlawed discrimination in employment on the basis of race, religion, national origin, or sex. Another section barred discrimination in public accommodations. But while the act forced the desegregation of public facilities throughout the South, including many public schools, obstacles to black voting rights remained.

In 1964, with the Civil Rights Act on the brink of passage, black organizations and churches mounted a major civil rights campaign in Mississippi. Known as Freedom Summer, the effort drew several thousand volunteers from across the country, including many idealistic white college students. Freedom Summer workers established freedom schools, which taught black children traditional subjects as well as their own history, conducted a major voter registration drive, and organized the Mississippi Freedom Democratic Party, a political alternative to the all-white Democratic organization in Mississippi. White southerners reacted swiftly and violently to their efforts. Fifteen civil rights workers were murdered; only about 1,200 black voters were registered that summer.

The need for federal action to support voting rights became even clearer in March 1965, when Martin Luther King Jr. and other black leaders called for a massive march from Selma, Alabama, to the state capital in Montgomery to protest the murder of a voting-rights activist. As soon as the marchers left Selma, mounted state troopers attacked them with tear gas and clubs. The scene was shown on national television that night.

Calling the episode "an American tragedy," President Johnson redoubled his efforts to persuade Congress to pass the pending voting-rights legislation. In a televised speech to a joint session of Congress on March 15, quoting the best-known slogan of the civil rights movement, "We shall overcome," he proclaimed voting rights a moral imperative.

On August 6 Congress passed the Voting Rights Act of 1965, which suspended the literacy tests and other measures most southern states used to prevent blacks from registering to vote. The act authorized the attorney general to send federal examiners to register voters in any county where less than 50 percent of the voting-age population was registered. Together with the adoption in 1964 of the

Twenty-fourth Amendment to the Constitution, which outlawed the federal poll tax, and successful legal challenges to state and local poll taxes, the Voting Rights Act allowed millions of blacks to register and vote for the first time. Congress reauthorized the Voting Rights Act in 1970, 1975, and 1982.

In the South the results were stunning. In 1960 only 20 percent of blacks of voting age had been registered to vote; by 1964 the figure had risen to 39 percent, and by 1971 it was 62 percent. As Hartman Turnbow, a Mississippi farmer who risked his life to register in 1964, later declared, "It won't never go back where it was."

ENACTING THE LIBERAL AGENDA

Johnson's success in pushing through the 1965 Voting Rights Act stemmed in part from the 1964 election, in which he won the presidency in his own right by defeating the conservative Republican senator Barry Goldwater of Arizona. With his running mate, Senator Hubert H. Humphrey of Minnesota, Johnson achieved one of the largest margins in history, 61.1 percent of the popular vote. And Johnson's coattails were long—his sweeping victory brought democratic gains in both Congress and the state legislatures. Thus strengthened politically, he used this mandate not only to promote a civil rights agenda but also to bring to fruition what he called the "Great Society."

Like most New Deal liberals, Johnson took an expansive view of presidential leadership and the role of the federal government. Johnson's first major success came in education. The Elementary and Secondary Education Act, passed in 1965, authorized $1 billion in federal funds to benefit impoverished children. The same year the Higher Education Act provided the first federal scholarships for college students. The Eighty-ninth Congress also gave Johnson enough votes to enact the federal health insurance legislation first proposed by Truman. The result was two new programs: Medicare, a health plan for the elderly funded by a surcharge on Social Security payroll taxes, and Medicaid, a health plan for the poor paid for by general tax revenues.

Although the Great Society is usually associated with programs for the disadvantaged, many Johnson administration initiatives actually benefited a wide spectrum of Americans. Federal urban renewal and home mortgage assistance helped those who could afford to live in single-family homes or modern apartments. Medicare covered every elderly person eligible for Social Security, regardless of need. Much of the federal aid to education benefited the children of the middle class. Finally, the creation of the National Endowment for the Arts and the National Endowment for the Humanities in 1965 supported artists and historians in their efforts to understand and interpret the nation's cultural and historical heritage.

Another aspect of public welfare addressed by the Great Society was the environment. President Johnson pressed for expansion of the national park system, improvement of the nation's air and water, and increased land-use planning. At the insistence of his wife, Lady Bird Johnson, he promoted the Highway Beautification Act of 1965. His approach marked a significant break with past conservation efforts, which had tended to concentrate on maintaining natural resources and national wealth. Under Secretary of the Interior Stewart Udall, Great Society programs emphasized quality of life, battling the problem "of vanishing beauty, of increasing ugliness, of shrinking open space, and of an overall environment that is diminished daily by pollution and noise and blight."

Taking advantage of the Great Society's reform climate, liberal Democrats also brought about significant changes in immigration policy. The Immigration Act of 1965 abandoned the quota system of the 1920s that had discriminated against Asians and southern and Eastern Europeans, replacing it with more equitable numerical limits on immigration from Europe, Africa, Asia, and countries in the Western Hemisphere. Since close relatives of individuals who were already legal residents of the United States could be admitted over and above the numerical limits, the legislation led to an immigrant influx far greater than anticipated, with the heaviest volume coming from Asia and Latin America.

Perhaps the most ambitious part of Johnson's liberal agenda was the War on Poverty, based on his expectation that the Great Society could put "an end to poverty in our time." During Johnson's presidency, poor people made up about a fourth of the American population; three-fourths of the poor were white. The poor included isolated farmers and miners in Appalachia, blacks and Puerto Ricans in urban ghettos, Mexican Americans in migrant labor camps and urban barrios, Native Americans on reservations, women raising families on their own, and the abandoned and destitute elderly.

To reduce poverty the Johnson administration expanded long-established social insurance, welfare, and public works programs. It broadened the Social Security program to include more workers. Social welfare expenditures increased rapidly, especially for Aid to Families with Dependent Children (AFDC), public housing, rent subsidies, and food stamps. As during the New Deal these social welfare programs developed in piecemeal fashion, without central coordination.

The Great Society's showcase in the War on Poverty was the Office of Economic Opportunity (OEO), established by the omnibus Economic Opportunity Act of 1964. OEO programs produced some of the most innovative measures of the Johnson administration. Head Start provided free nursery schools to prepare disadvantaged preschoolers for kindergarten. The Job Corps, Upward Bound, and Volunteers in Service to America (VISTA), modeled on the Peace Corps, provided poor youths with training and jobs. And the Community Action Program encouraged the poor to demand "maximum feasible participation" in decisions that affected them.

By the end of 1965 the Johnson administration had compiled the most impressive legislative record of liberal reforms since the New Deal. It had put issues of poverty, justice, and access at the center of national political life, and it had expanded the federal government's role in protecting citizens' welfare. Yet the Great

Society never quite measured up to the extravagant promises made for it, and by the end of the decade many of its programs were under attack.

In part, the political necessity of bowing to pressure from various interest groups hampered Great Society programs. For example, the American Medical Association (AMA) used its influence to shape the Medicare and Medicaid programs, to ensure that Congress did not impose a cap on medical expenses. Its intervention produced escalating federal expenditures and contributed to skyrocketing medical costs. And Democratic-controlled urban political machines criticized VISTA and Community Action Program agents who encouraged poor people to demand the public services long withheld by unresponsive local governments. In response to such political pressure the Johnson administration gradually phased out the Community Action Program and instead channeled spending for housing, social services, and other urban poverty programs through local municipal governments.

Another inherent problem was the limited funding of Great Society programs. The annual budget for the War on Poverty was less than $2 billion. Despite the limited nature of the program, the statistical decline in poverty during the 1960s suggests that the Great Society was successful on some levels. From 1963 to 1968 the proportion of Americans living below the poverty line dropped from 20 percent to 13 percent. Among African Americans economic advancement was even more marked. In the 1960s the black poverty rate was cut in half, and millions of blacks moved into the middle class, some through federal jobs in antipoverty programs. But critics charged that the reduction in the poverty rate was due to the decade's booming economy, not to the War on Poverty. Another criticism was that while the nation's overall standard of living increased during this period, distribution of wealth was still uneven. The poor were better off in an absolute sense, but they remained far behind the middle class in a relative sense.

Other factors also hampered the success of the Great Society. Following in the steps of Roosevelt's New Deal coalition, Kennedy and Johnson had gathered an extraordinarily diverse set of groups—middle-class and poor; white and nonwhite; Protestant, Jewish, and Catholic; urban and rural—in support of an unprecedented level of federal activism. For a brief period between 1964 and 1966 the coalition held together. But inevitably the demands of certain groups—such as blacks' demands for civil rights and the urban poor's demands for increased political power—conflicted with the interests of other Democrats, such as white southerners and northern political bosses. In the end the Democratic coalition could not sustain a consensus on the purposes of governmental activism powerful enough to resist a growing backlash of conservatives who increasingly resisted expanded civil rights and social welfare legislation.

At the same time Democrats were plagued by disillusionment over the shortcomings of their reforms. In the early 1960s the lofty rhetoric of the New Frontier and the Great Society had raised unprecedented expectations for social change. But competition for federal largesse was keen, and the shortage of funds for the War on

Poverty left many promises unfulfilled, especially after 1965 when the escalation of the Vietnam War siphoned funding away from domestic programs. In 1966 the government spent $22 billion on the Vietnam War and only $1.2 billion on the War on Poverty. Ultimately, as Martin Luther King Jr. put it, the Great Society was "shot down on the battlefields of Vietnam."

T I M E L I N E

1944	Bretton Woods economic conference World Bank and International Monetary Fund (IMF) founded	**1962**	Michael Harrington's *The Other America* Cuban missile crisis
1947	Levittown, New York, built	**1963**	Betty Friedan's *The Feminine Mystique* Civil rights protest in Birmingham, Alabama
1952	Norman Vincent Peale's *The Power of Positive Thinking*		March on Washington Test-ban treaty prohibits U.S., Soviet, and British nuclear tests in air, space, or water.
1953– 1958	Operation Wetback and Indian termination programs		John F. Kennedy assassinated; Lyndon B. Johnson assumes presidency.
1954	First McDonald's opens.		
1955	AFL and CIO merge. Disneyland opens.	**1964**	Civil Rights Act Freedom Summer
1956	National Interstate and Defense Highway Act Congress adds "In God We Trust" to coins. Allen Ginsberg's "Howl"		Economic Opportunity Act inaugurates War on Poverty. Johnson elected president in his own right and begins the Great Society program.
1957	Postwar baby boom peaks. Jack Kerouac's *On the Road*	**1965**	Immigration Act abolishes national quota system. Civil rights march from Selma to Montgomery
1959	"Kitchen debate" Fidel Castro leads Cuban revolution.		Voting Rights Act Medicare and Medicaid established
1960	Sit-ins in Greensboro, North Carolina John F. Kennedy elected president and begins New Frontier.		National Endowment for the Arts and National Endowment for the Humanities created
1961	Peace Corps established Freedom rides Bay of Pigs invasion crushed by Cuban army. Berlin Wall erected		

For Further Exploration

Two engaging introductions to postwar society are Paul Boyer, *Promises to Keep* (1995), and James T. Patterson, *Grand Expectations* (1996). Elaine Tyler May, *Homeward Bound* (1988), is the classic introduction to postwar family life. For youth culture see William Graebner, *Coming of Age in Buffalo* (1990). For insightful essays on the impact of television see Karal Ann Marling, *As Seen on TV* (1996). Powerful literary works of the period include Jack Kerouac, *On the Road* (1957); Allen Ginsberg, *Howl and Other Poems* (1996), and Arthur Miller, *Death of a Salesman* (1949). An excellent award-winning memoir of the Beat generation is Joyce Johnson, *Minor Characters* (1983). Good starting points for understanding Kennedy's presidency are Richard Reeves, *President Kennedy: Profile of Power* (1993), and David Halberstam, *The Best and the Brightest* (1972). For Lyndon Johnson see Robert Dallek, *Flawed Giant* (1998), and Doris Kearns, *Lyndon Johnson and the American Dream* (1976). There are many engaging accounts of the civil rights movement, including Henry Hampton and Steve Fayer's oral history, *Voices of Freedom* (1991), and Harvard Sitkoff, *The Struggle for Black Equality* (2nd ed., 1993).

The John F. Kennedy Library and Museum's site at <http://www.cs.umb.edu/~rwhealan/jfk/main.html> provides a large collection of records from Kennedy's presidency. The Reference Desk area contains frequently requested information, including transcripts and recordings of JFK's speeches, a database of his executive orders, and a number of other resources. The Avalon Project at the Yale Law School's site, "Foreign Relations of the United States: 1961–1963 Cuban Missile Crisis and Aftermath," at <http://www.yale.edu/lawweb/avalon/diplomacy/forrel/cuba/cubamenu.htm> contains almost 300 official documents related to the crisis, including State Department memoranda, records of telephone conversations, transcripts of conversations in the White House, and CIA reports. "Literary Kicks: The Beat Generation," at <http://www.charm.net/~brooklyn/LitKicks.html>, is an independent site created by New York writer Levi Asher devoted to the literature of the Beat generation. The site includes writings by Jack Kerouac, Allen Ginsberg, Neil Cassidy, and others; material on Beats, music, religion, and film; an extensive bibliography; biographical information; and photographs.

Chapter 29

WAR ABROAD AND AT HOME: THE VIETNAM ERA

1961–1975

In our excessive involvement in the affairs of other countries, we are not only living off our assets and denying our own people the proper enjoyment of their resources; we are also denying the world the example of a free society enjoying its freedom to the fullest. This is regrettable indeed for a nation that aspires to teach democracy to other nations.

—J. WILLIAM FULBRIGHT, 1966

On June 16, 1972, three hundred mourners assembled at Arlington National Cemetery for the funeral of John Paul Vann, a well-known Army lieutenant colonel who had died in a helicopter crash in Vietnam the week before. Though he supported the United States' commitment to the war, Vann had nonetheless publicly criticized the way it was being fought. Politicians and military leaders closely associated with the war effort—General William Westmoreland, Secretary of State William Rogers—were very much in evidence, but so were Daniel Ellsberg, a former Pentagon official who had publicly turned against the war, and Senator Edward Kennedy, another war opponent. Vann's family also showed the rifts over Vietnam. His wife, Mary Jane, requested her husband's favorite piece of music: the upbeat "Colonel Bogie March" from the film *The Bridge on the River Kwai* but added the haunting antiwar ballad "Where Have All the Flowers Gone?" to voice her own opposition to the war. One of his sons expressed his hatred of the war by tearing his draft card in two at the funeral, placing half of it on his father's casket. Although unusually public the Vann funeral provides a dramatic example of the ruptures the Vietnam War brought to families, institutions, and the American social fabric.

Vietnam spawned a vibrant antiwar protest movement, which intersected with a broader youth movement that questioned traditional American political and cultural values. The challenges posed by youth, together with the revival of feminism, the rise of the black and Chicano power movements, and explosive riots in the cities, produced a profound sense of social disorder at home. Vietnam split the Democratic Party and shattered the liberal consensus. The high monetary cost of the war diverted resources from domestic uses, spelling an end to the Great Society. Beyond its domestic impact the war wreaked extraordinary damage on the country of Vietnam and undermined U.S. credibility abroad. For the first time average Americans began to question their assumptions about the nation's cold-war objectives and the beneficence of American foreign policy.

Into the Quagmire, 1945–1968

Like many new nations that emerged from the dissolution of European empires after World War II, Vietnam was characterized by a volatile mix of nationalist sentiment, religious and cultural conflict, economic need, and political turmoil. The rise of communism there was just one phase of the nation's larger struggle, which would eventually climax in a bloody civil war. But American policymakers viewed these events through the lens of the cold war, interpreting them as part of an international communist movement toward global domination. Their failure to understand the complexity of Vietnam's internal conflicts led to a long and ultimately disastrous attempt to influence the course of the war.

AMERICA IN VIETNAM: FROM TRUMAN TO KENNEDY

Vietnam had been part of the French colony of Indochina since the late nineteenth century but had been occupied by Japan during World War II. When the Japanese surrendered in 1945, Ho Chi Minh and the Vietminh, the communist nationalist group that had led Vietnamese resistance to the Japanese, took advantage of the resulting power vacuum. With words drawn from the American Declaration of Independence, Ho proclaimed the establishment of the independent republic of Vietnam that September. The next year, when France rejected his claim and reasserted control over the country, an eight-year struggle that the Vietminh called the Anti-French War of Resistance ensued. Appealing to American anticolonial sentiment Ho called on President Truman to support the struggle for Vietnamese independence. But Truman ignored his pleas and instead offered covert financial support to the French, in hopes of stabilizing the politically chaotic region and rebuilding the French economy.

By the end of the decade cold-war developments had prompted the United States to step up its assistance to the French. After the Chinese revolution of 1949 the United States became concerned that China—along with the Soviet Union—might actively support anticolonial struggles in Asia and that newly independent countries might align themselves with the communists. At the same time Republican charges that the Democrats had "lost" China influenced Truman to take a firmer stand against perceived communist aggression in both Korea and Vietnam. Truman also wanted to maintain good relations with France, whose support was crucial to the success of the new NATO alliance. Finally, Indochina played a strategic role in

Secretary of State Dean Acheson's plans for an integrated Pacific Rim economy centered on a reindustrialized Japan.

For all these reasons, when the Soviet Union and the new Chinese leaders recognized Ho's republic early in 1950, the United States—along with Great Britain—recognized the French-installed puppet government of Bao Dai. Subsequently, both the Truman and the Eisenhower administrations provided substantial military support to the French in Vietnam. President Eisenhower argued that such aid was essential to prevent the collapse of all noncommunist governments in the area, in a chain reaction he called the *domino effect:* "You have a row of dominoes set up, you knock over the first one, and what will happen to the last one is the certainty that it will go over very quickly."

Despite joint French-American efforts the Vietminh forces gained strength in northern Vietnam. In the spring of 1954 they seized the isolated administrative fortress of Dienbienphu after a fifty-six-day siege. The spectacular victory gave the Vietminh negotiating leverage in the 1954 Geneva Accords, which partitioned Vietnam temporarily at the seventeenth parallel (see Map 29.1) and committed France to withdraw its forces from the area north of that line. The Accords also provided that within two years, in free elections, the voters in the two sectors would choose a unified government for the entire nation. The United States refused to sign the agreements and instead issued a separate protocol acknowledging the Accords and promising to "refrain from the threat or use of force to disturb them."

Eisenhower had no intention of allowing a communist victory in Vietnam's upcoming election. With the help of the CIA he made sure that a pro-American government took power in South Vietnam in June 1954, just before the accords were signed. Ngo Dinh Diem, an anticommunist Catholic who had spent eight years in the United States, returned to Vietnam as the premier of the French-backed South Vietnamese government. The next year, in a rigged election, Diem became president of an independent South Vietnam. Realizing that the popular Ho Chi Minh would easily win in both north and south, Diem then called off the reunification elections that were scheduled for 1956, a move the United States supported.

In March 1956 the last French soldiers left Saigon, the capital of South Vietnam, and the United States replaced France as the dominant foreign power in the region. American policymakers quickly asserted that a noncommunist South Vietnam was vital to U.S. security interests. In reality, Vietnam was too small a country to upset the international balance of power, and its communist movement was regional and intensely nationalistic rather than expansionist. Nevertheless, Eisenhower and subsequent U.S. presidents persisted in viewing Vietnam as part of the cold-war struggle to contain the communist threat to the free world. Between 1955 and 1961 the Eisenhower administration sent Diem an average of $200 million a year in aid and stationed approximately 675 American military advisers in Saigon. Having stepped up U.S. involvement there considerably, Eisenhower left office, passing the Vietnam situation to his successor, John F. Kennedy.

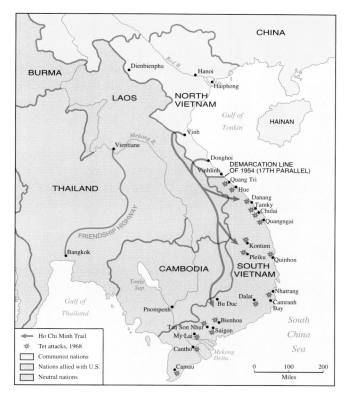

MAP 29.1
The Vietnam War, 1954–1975

The Vietnam War was a guerrilla war, fought in skirmishes and inconclusive encounters rather than decisive battles. Supporters of the National Liberation Front filtered into South Vietnam along the Ho Chi Minh Trail, which wound through Laos and Cambodia. In January 1968 Vietcong forces launched the Tet offensive, a surprise attack on several South Vietnamese cities and provincial centers. American vulnerability to these attacks served to undermine U.S. credibility and fueled opposition to the war.

President Kennedy saw Vietnam as an ideal testing ground for the counterinsurgency techniques that formed the centerpiece of his military policy (see Chapter 28). But he first had to prop up Diem's unpopular regime, which faced a growing military threat. In December 1960 the Communist Party in North Vietnam organized most of Diem's opponents in South Vietnam into a revolutionary movement known as the National Liberation Front (NLF). In response, Kennedy increased the number of American military "advisers" (an elastic term that included helicopter units and special forces), raising it to more than 16,000 by November 1963. To win the "hearts and minds" of Vietnamese peasants away from the insurgents and to increase agricultural production, he also sent economic development specialists. But

Kennedy refused to send combat troops to assist the South Vietnamese in what had become a guerrilla-style civil war with the north.

American aid did little good in South Vietnam. Diem's political inexperience and corruption, combined with his Catholicism in a predominantly Buddhist country, prevented him from creating a stable popular government. The NLF's guerrilla forces—called the Viet Cong by their opponents—made considerable headway against Diem's regime, using the revolutionary tactics of the Chinese leader Mao Zedong to blend into South Vietnam's civilian population "like fish in the water." They found a receptive audience among peasants who had been alienated by Diem's "strategic hamlet" program, which uprooted families and whole villages and moved them into barbed-wire compounds in a vain attempt to separate them from Ho Chi Minh's sympathizers.

Anti-Diem sentiment also flourished among Buddhists, who charged the government with religious persecution. Starting in May 1963 militant Buddhists staged a dramatic series of demonstrations against Diem, including several self-immolations that were recorded by American television crews. Diem's regime retaliated with raids on temples and mass arrests of Buddhist priests in August, prompting more antigovernment demonstrations.

As opposition to Diem deepened, Kennedy decided that he would have to be removed. Ambassador Henry Cabot Lodge Jr. let it be known in Saigon that the United States would support a military coup that had "a good chance of succeeding." On November 1, 1963, Diem was driven from office and assassinated by officers in the South Vietnamese army. America's role in the coup reinforced the links between the United States and the new regime in South Vietnam, making the prospect of withdrawal from the region less acceptable to U.S. policymakers.

Less than a month later Kennedy himself was assassinated. Although historians continue to debate whether Kennedy would have withdrawn American forces from Vietnam had he lived, his administration's actions clearly accelerated U.S. involvement. When Lyndon Johnson became president, he retained many of Kennedy's foreign policy advisers. Asserting that "I am not going to be the President who saw Southeast Asia go the way China went," he quickly declared he would maintain U.S. support for South Vietnam.

ESCALATION: THE JOHNSON YEARS

Diem's removal did not improve the efficiency or the popularity of the government in Saigon. Secretary of Defense Robert McNamara and other top advisers argued that only a rapid, full-scale deployment of U.S. forces could prevent the imminent defeat of the South Vietnamese. But Johnson would need at least tacit congressional support, perhaps even a declaration of war, to commit U.S. forces to an offensive strategy. During the summer of 1964 the president saw his opportunity. American naval forces were conducting surveillance missions off the North Vietnamese coast to aid South Vietnamese amphibious attacks. When the North Vietnamese resisted the attacks, President Johnson told the nation that on two separate occasions North Vietnamese torpedo boats had fired on American destroyers in international waters in the Gulf of Tonkin. At Johnson's request Congress authorized him to "take all necessary measures to repel any armed attack against the forces of the United States and to prevent further aggression." On August 7 the Gulf of Tonkin resolution passed in the Senate eighty-eight to two and in the House 416 to 0. Johnson's deceptive characterization of the unverified attack got him what he wanted—a sweeping mandate to conduct operations in Vietnam as he saw fit. The only formal approval of American intervention in Vietnam that Congress ever granted, the Tonkin resolution represented a significant expansion of presidential power.

Once congressional support was ensured and the 1964 elections had passed (see Chapter 28), the Johnson administration moved toward the Americanization of the war with Operation Rolling Thunder, a protracted bombing campaign. Begun in March 1965, by 1968 it had dropped a million tons of bombs on North Vietnam. Each B-52 sortie cost $30,000: by early 1966 the direct costs of the air war had exceeded $1.7 billion. From 1965 to 1973 the United States dropped three times as many bombs on North Vietnam, a country roughly the size of Texas, as had fallen on all of Europe, Asia, and Africa during World War II. The several hundred captured U.S. pilots downed in the raids then became pawns in prisoner-of-war negotiations with the North Vietnamese.

To the amazement of American advisers the bombings did not appear to impede the North's ability to wage war. The flow of troops and supplies to the South continued unabated as the North Vietnamese quickly rebuilt roads and bridges, moved munitions plants underground, and constructed networks of tunnels and shelters. Instead of destroying enemy morale and bringing the North Vietnamese to the bargaining table, Operation Rolling Thunder intensified their nationalism and will to fight.

A week after the launch of Operation Rolling Thunder the United States sent its first official ground troops into combat duty. Soon U.S. Marines were skirmishing with the enemy. Over the next three years the number of American troops in Vietnam grew dramatically. Although U.S. troops were accompanied by military forces from Australia, New Zealand, and South Korea, the war increasingly became an American war, fought for American aims. By 1966 more than 380,000 American soldiers were stationed in Vietnam; by 1967, 485,000; by 1968, 536,000.

The massive commitment of troops and air power threatened to destroy Vietnam's countryside. Besides the bombardment a defoliation campaign had seriously damaged agricultural production, undercutting the economic and cultural base of Vietnamese society. After one devastating but not unusual engagement a commanding officer reported, using the logic of the time, "It became necessary to destroy the town in order to save it." Graffiti on a plane that dropped defoliants read "Only you can prevent forests." (In later years defoliants such as Agent Orange were found to have highly toxic effects on both humans and the environment.) The destruction was not limited to North Vietnam; South Vietnam, America's ally, absorbed more than twice the bomb tonnage dropped on the North. In Saigon and other South Vietnamese cities the influx of American soldiers and dollars distorted local economies, spread corruption and prostitution, and triggered uncontrollable inflation and black-market activity.

Why did the dramatically increased American presence in Vietnam fail to turn the tide of the war? Some advisors argued that military intervention would accomplish little unless it was accompanied by reform in Saigon and increased popular support in the countryside. Other critics claimed that the United States never fully committed itself to a total victory—although what that term meant was never settled. Military strategy was inextricably tied to political considerations. For domestic reasons policymakers often searched for an elusive "middle ground" between all-out invasion (and the possibility of sparking a nuclear exchange between the two superpowers) and the politically unacceptable alternative of disengagement. Hoping to win a war of attrition, the Johnson administration assumed that American superiority in personnel and weaponry would ultimately triumph. But that limited commitment was never enough to ensure victory—however it was defined.

AMERICAN SOLDIERS' PERSPECTIVES ON THE WAR

Approximately 2.8 million Americans served in Vietnam. At an average age of only nineteen most of those servicemen and women were too young to vote or drink (the voting age was twenty-one until passage of the Twenty-sixth Amendment in 1971), but they were old enough to fight and die. Some were volunteers, including 7,000 women enlistees. Many others served because they were drafted. Until the nation shifted to an all-volunteer force in 1973, the draft stood as a concrete reminder of the government's impact on the lives of ordinary Americans. Blacks were drafted and died roughly in the same proportion as their share of the draft-age population (about 12 to 13 percent), although early in the war black casualty rates were significantly higher than average. Even more than in other recent wars, sons of the poor and the working class shouldered a disproportionate amount of the fighting, forming an estimated 80 percent of the enlisted ranks. Young men from more affluent backgrounds were more likely to avoid combat through student deferments, medical exemptions, and appointments to National Guard and reserve units— alternatives that made Johnson's Vietnam policy more acceptable to the middle class.

At first many draftees and enlistees shared common cold-war assumptions about the need to fight communism and the superiority of the American military. However, their experience in Vietnam quickly challenged simple notions of patriotism and the inevitability of victory. In "Nam" long days of boring menial work were punctuated by brief flashes of intense fighting. "Most of the time, nothing happened," a soldier recalled, "but when something did, it happened instantaneously and without warning." Rarely were there large-scale battles, only skirmishes; rather than front lines and conquered territory, there were only daytime operations in areas the Vietcong controlled at night.

Racism was a fact of everyday life. Because differentiating between friendly South Vietnamese and Vietcong sympathizers was difficult, many soldiers lumped

A Vietnam Vet Remembers

DAVE CLINE

*B*orn in 1947, Dave Cline grew up in a working-class family outside Buffalo, New York. Drafted by the army in 1967, Cline was eager to help fight communist aggression in Vietnam. But after his arrival in Danang seven months later, his attitude toward the war quickly changed. Cline described this transformation in an interview conducted in 1992.

I went to basic training at Fort Dix. . . . Down there, they used to give you basically two raps on why you were going to Vietnam. One was that rap about we're going to help the heroic South Vietnamese people. We're going to go fight for freedom [and repel] communist aggression. They'd show you the maps and stuff, the domino theory, the Red Chinese are trying to engulf all of southeast Asia. The other rap was: killing communists was your duty. . . .

First thing you do when you get in-country is, they give you these indoctrination classes and they say, "Forget all that shit they told; you can't trust any of these people. They're not really people anyway; they're gooks." . . . In other words: You see anyone with slant eyes, that's your potential enemy—don't trust them. That sort of blows away any "help the people" thing. . . .

I got wounded the last time out near the Cambodian border. This happened on December 20, 1967. . . . The north Vietnamese launched a massive human wave attack. . . .

A guy came running up to my foxhole. We saw him coming from the next hole over and we didn't know if it was an American retreating over to us or a Vietnamese, because it was two in the morning. . . . I was sitting there with my rifle waiting to see, and all of a sudden he stuck his rifle in. I saw the front side of an AK-47 and a muzzle flash, and then I pulled my trigger. I shot him through the chest. I blacked out initially, but then I came to and found a round went right through my knee. . . .

They carried me over to this guy I had shot. . . . He was dead. The sergeant started giving me this pep talk, "Here's the gook you killed!" . . .

The kid looked about the same age as me. The first thing I started thinking was, Why is he dead and I'm alive? . . .

Then after going into the hospital, I started thinking about that guy. I wonder if his mother knows he's dead? I wonder if he had a girlfriend? Looking back, I think I was retaining the sense that he was a human being.

SOURCE: Richard Stacewicz, *Winter Soldiers: An Oral History of the Vietnam Veterans Against the War* (New York: Twayne, 1997), pp. 135–36, 140–41.

them together as "gooks." As a draftee noted of his indoctrination, "The only thing they told us about the Vietcong was they were gooks. They were to be killed. Nobody sits around and gives you their historical and cultural background. They're the enemy. Kill, kill, kill" (see American Voices, "A Vietnam Vet Remembers").

Fighting and surviving under such conditions took its toll. One veteran explained that "The hardest thing to come to grips with was the fact that making it through Vietnam—surviving—is probably the only worthwhile part of the experience. It wasn't going over there and saving the world from communism or defending the country." Cynicism and bitterness were common. The pressure of waging war under such conditions drove many soldiers to seek escape in alcohol or drugs, which were cheap and readily available.

The women who served in Vietnam shared many of these experiences. As Women's Army Corp members (WACs), nurses, and civilians serving with organizations such as the United Service Organizations (USO), women volunteers witnessed death and mutilation on a massive scale. Though they tried to maintain a professional distance, as a navy nurse recalled, "It's pretty damn hard not getting involved when you see a nineteen- or twenty-year-old blond kid from the Midwest or California or the East Coast screaming and dying. A piece of my heart would go with each."

The Cold-War Consensus Unravels

In the twenty years following World War II, despite widespread affluence and confidence in the nation's cold-war leadership, there emerged a variety of challenges to the status quo. From the nonconforming Beats came a critical assault on corporate capitalism. Teenagers' embracing of rock 'n' roll defied the cultural norms of their elders. African Americans' boycotts, sit-ins, and freedom rides signaled a rising wind of protest about racial injustice. By 1965 such angry expressions of disaffection from mainstream America had multiplied dramatically. Criticism of the war in Vietnam mounted, as youthful protesters rebelled against traditional respect for the "system." The civil rights movement took on a more militant thrust and expanded beyond African Americans to other minority groups, while the feminist movement revived to challenge social values and the family structure itself. Together the various movements forced Americans to reassess basic assumptions about the nature of their society.

PUBLIC OPINION ON VIETNAM

President Kennedy and at first President Johnson enjoyed broad support for their conduct of foreign affairs. Both Democrats and Republicans approved Johnson's escalation of the war, and public opinion polls in 1965 and 1966 showed strong popular support for his policies. But in the late 1960s public opinion began to turn against the war. In July 1967 a Gallup poll revealed that for the first time a majority of Americans disapproved of Johnson's Vietnam policy and believed the war had reached a stalemate.

A Televised War

This harrowing scene from Saigon during the Tet offensive in 1968 depicts the head of the South Vietnamese National Police preparing to shoot a captured member of the Viet Cong. Telecast on U.S. network news, it was one of scores of disturbing images that flooded American living rooms during the Vietnam era and helped to sway public opinion against continued participation in what commentator Walter Cronkite called a "bloody experience" that would end in "stalemate." (AP/Wide World Photos)

Television had much to do with these attitudes. Vietnam was the first war in which television brought films of the fighting directly into the nation's living rooms. At the beginning of the conflict Americans watched footage of U.S. soldiers apparently advancing steadily through the countryside and heard reports of staggering Viet Cong losses and minimal U.S. casualties. Despite the glowing reports filed by the media and the administration on the progress of the war, by 1967 many administration officials had privately reached a more pessimistic conclusion. In November Secretary of Defense Robert McNamara sent a memo to the president arguing that continued escalation "would be dangerous, costly in lives, and unsatisfactory to the American people," but President Johnson continued to insist that victory in Vietnam was vital to U.S. national security and prestige. Journalists, especially those who had spent time in Vietnam, soon began to warn that the Johnson administration suffered from a "credibility gap." The administration, they charged, was concealing important and discouraging information about the war's progress. In February 1966 television coverage of hearings by the Senate Foreign Relations Committee (chaired by J. William Fulbright, an outspoken critic of the war) raised further questions about the administration's policy.

Economic developments put Johnson and his advisers even more on the defensive. In 1966 the federal deficit was $9.8 billion; in 1967 the Vietnam War cost the taxpayers $27 billion and the deficit jumped to $23 billion. Although the war consumed just 3 percent of the gross national product, its costs became more evident as the growing federal deficit nudged the inflation rate upward. Only in the summer of 1967 did Johnson ask for a 10 percent surcharge on individual and corporate income taxes, an increase that Congress did not approve until 1968. By then the inflationary spiral that would plague the U.S. economy throughout the 1970s was well under way.

Another major problem facing the Johnson administration was the growing strength and visibility of the antiwar movement. Between 1963 and 1965 peace activists in a variety of organizations staged periodic protests, vigils, and petition- and letter-writing campaigns against U.S. involvement in the war. After the escalation of combat in the spring of 1965 various antiwar coalitions, swelled by growing numbers of students, clergy, housewives, politicians, artists, and others opposed to the war, organized several mass demonstrations in Washington, bringing out 20,000 to 30,000 people at a time. A diverse lot, participants in these rallies shared a common skepticism about the means and aims of U.S. policy. The war was morally wrong, they argued, and antithetical to American ideals; the goal of an independent, anticommunist South Vietnam was unattainable; and American military involvement in Vietnam would not help the Vietnamese people.

STUDENT ACTIVISM AND THE COUNTERCULTURE

Although some of the most potent images of the 1960s show civil rights demonstrators, youthful protesters rebelling against the war in Vietnam, or "hippies" high on drugs and psychedelic music, American youth were not monolithic. Many young people, especially those in the working class, were critical of the more extreme expressions of rebellion. It was primarily college students—many of whom had been raised in a privileged environment, showered with consumer goods, and inculcated with faith in American institutions and leaders—who began to question U.S. foreign policy, racial injustice, and middle-class morals and conformity. Not all youth challenged authority in the 1960s, but those who did had a powerful impact.

In June 1962 forty students from Big Ten and Ivy League universities, disturbed by the gap they perceived between the ideals they had been taught to revere and the realities in American life, met in Port Huron, Michigan, to found Students for a Democratic Society (SDS). Tom Hayden wrote their manifesto, the Port Huron Statement, which expressed their disillusionment with the consumer culture and the gulf between the prosperous and the poor. These students rejected cold-war ideology and foreign policy, including but not limited to the Vietnam conflict. The founders of SDS referred to their movement as the "New Left" to distinguish themselves from the "Old Left"—communists and socialists of the 1930s and 1940s. Consciously adopting the activist tactics pioneered by members of the civil rights movement, they turned to grassroots organizing in cities and on college campuses.

The first major student protests erupted in the fall of 1964 at the University of California at Berkeley after administrators banned political activity near the Telegraph Avenue entrance, where student groups had traditionally distributed leaflets and recruited volunteers. In protest the major student organizations formed a coalition called the Free Speech Movement (FSM) and organized a sit-in at the administration building. The FSM owed a strong debt to the civil rights movement. Some students had just returned from Freedom Summer in Mississippi, radicalized by their experience. Mario Savio spoke for many of them:

> Last summer I went to Mississippi to join the struggle there for civil rights. This fall I am engaged in another phase of the same struggle, this time in Berkeley. The two battlefields may seem quite different to some observers, but this is not the case. The same rights are at stake in both places—the right to participate as citizens in a democratic society and to struggle against the same enemy. In Mississippi an autocratic and powerful minority rules, through organized violence, to suppress the vast, virtually powerless majority. In California, the privileged minority manipulates the university bureaucracy to suppress the students' political expression.

On a deeper level Berkeley students were challenging a university that in their view had grown too big and was too far removed from the major social issues of the day. Emboldened by the Berkeley movement students across the nation were soon protesting their universities' academic policies and then more passionately the Vietnam War.

The highly politicized activists of the New Left, who had developed a wide-ranging critique of American society, increasingly focused on the war, and they were joined by thousands of other students in protesting American participation in the Vietnam conflict. When President Johnson escalated the war in March 1965, faculty and students at the University of Michigan organized a teach-in against the war. Abandoning their classes, they debated the political, diplomatic, and moral aspects of the nation's involvement in Vietnam. Teach-ins quickly spread to other universities as students turned from their studies to protest the war.

Many protests centered on the draft, especially after the selective service system abolished student deferments in January 1966. To avoid the draft some young men enlisted in the National Guard or the reserves; others declared themselves conscientious objectors. Several thousand young men ignored their induction notices, risking prosecution for draft evasion. Others left the country, most often for Canada or Sweden. In public demonstrations of civil disobedience opponents of the war burned their draft cards, closed down induction centers, and on a few occasions broke into selective service offices.

As antiwar and draft protests multiplied students realized that their universities were deeply implicated in the war effort. In some cases as much as 60 percent

Columbia University Protests, 1968

At the height of the Vietnam War in 1968 Columbia University students launched a series of protests against military research contracts, university governance, and the construction of a gymnasium in a nearby Harlem neighborhood. (Steve Schapiro/Black Star)

of a university's research budget came from government contracts, especially those of the Defense Department. Protesters blocked recruiters from the Dow Chemical Company, the producer of napalm and Agent Orange. Arguing that universities should not train students for war, they demanded that the Reserve Officer Training Corps (ROTC) be removed from college campuses.

In the late 1960s student protesters joined the much larger antiwar movement of peace activists, housewives, religious leaders, and a few elective officials. After 1967 nationwide student strikes, mass demonstrations, and other organized protests became commonplace. In October 1967 more than 100,000 antiwar demonstrators marched on Washington, D.C., as part of "Stop the Draft Week." The event culminated in a "siege of the Pentagon," in which protesters clashed with police and federal marshals. Hundreds of people were arrested and several demonstrators beaten. Lyndon Johnson, who had once dismissed antiwar protesters as "nervous Nellies," rebellious children, or communist dupes, now had to face the reality of large-scale public opposition to his policies.

While the New Left took to the streets in protest, a growing number of young Americans embarked on a general revolution against authority and middle-class respectability. The "hippie"—attired in ragged blue jeans, tie-dyed T-shirt, beads, and army fatigues, with long, unkempt hair—symbolized the new counterculture, a youthful movement that glorified liberation from traditional social strictures.

Not surprisingly, given the importance of rock 'n' roll to 1950s' youth culture, popular music formed an important part of the counterculture. The folksinger Pete Seeger set the tone for the era's political idealism with songs such as the antiwar ballad "Where Have All the Flowers Gone?" Another folksinger, Joan Baez, gained national prominence for her rendition of the African American protest song "We Shall Overcome" and other folk and political anthems she performed at protest rallies in the mid-1960s. In 1963, the year of the Birmingham demonstrations and President Kennedy's assassination, Bob Dylan's "Blowin' in the Wind" reflected the impatience of people whose faith in "the system" was wearing thin.

Other winds of change in popular music came from the Beatles, four English working-class youths, who burst onto the American scene early in 1964. The Beatles' music, by turns lyrical and driving, was phenomenally successful, spawning a commercial and cultural phenomenon called Beatlemania. American youth's eager embrace of the Beatles deepened the generational divide between teenagers and their elders already set in motion by the popularity of rock 'n' roll in the 1950s. The Beatles also helped to pave the way for the more rebellious, angrier music of other British groups, notably the Rolling Stones, whose raunchy 1965 "(I Can't Get No) Satisfaction" not only signaled a new openness about sexuality but also made fun of the consumer culture ("He can't be a man 'cause he doesn't smoke the same cigarettes as me").

Drugs intertwined with music as a crucial element of the youth culture. The recreational use of drugs—especially marijuana and the hallucinogen lysergic acid diethylamide, popularly known as LSD, or "acid"—was celebrated in popular music. San Francisco bands, such as the Grateful Dead and the Jefferson Airplane, and musicians like the Seattle-born guitarist Jimi Hendrix developed a musical style known as "acid rock," which was characterized by long, heavily amplified guitar solos accompanied by psychedelic lighting effects. In August 1969, 400,000 young people journeyed to Bethel, New York, to "get high" on music, drugs, and sex at the three-day Woodstock Music and Art Fair. Despite torrential rain and numerous drug overdoses, most enjoyed the festival, which was heralded as the birth of the "Woodstock nation."

For a brief time adherents of the counterculture believed a new age was dawning. They experimented in communal living and glorified uninhibited sexuality. In 1967 the "world's first Human Be-In" drew 20,000 people to Golden Gate Park in San Francisco. The Beat poet Allen Ginsberg "purified" the site with a Buddhist ritual, and the LSD advocate Timothy Leary, a former Harvard psychology instructor, urged the gathering to "turn on to the scene, tune in to what is happening, and drop out." That summer—dubbed the "Summer of Love"—San Francisco's Haight-Ashbury, New York's East Village, and Chicago's Uptown neighborhoods swelled with young dropouts, drifters, and teenage runaways dubbed "flower children" by observers. Their faith in instant love and peace quickly turned sour, however, as they suffered bad drug trips, venereal disease, loneliness, and violence. Although many young people kept their distance from both the counterculture and the antiwar movement, to many adult observers it seemed that all of American youth were rejecting political, social, and cultural norms.

THE WIDENING STRUGGLE FOR CIVIL RIGHTS

The counterculture and the antiwar movement were not the only social movements to challenge the status quo in the 1960s. The frustration and anger of blacks boiled over in a new racial militance as the struggle moved outside the South and took on the more stubborn problems of entrenched poverty and racism. The rhetoric and tactics of the emerging black-power movement shattered the existing civil rights coalition and galvanized white opposition.

Once the system of legal, or *de jure,* segregation had fallen, the civil rights movement turned to the more difficult task of eliminating the *de facto* segregation, enforced by custom, that made blacks second-class citizens throughout the nation. Outside the South racial discrimination was less flagrant, but it was pervasive, especially in education, housing, and employment. Although the *Brown* decision outlawed separate schools, it did nothing to change the educational system in areas where schools were all-black or all-white because of residential segregation. Not until 1973 did federal judges begin to extend the desegregation of schools, which had begun in the South two decades earlier, to the rest of the country.

As civil rights leaders took on northern racism, the movement fractured along generational lines. Some younger activists, eager for confrontation and rapid social change, questioned the very goal of integration into white society. Black separatism, espoused by earlier black leaders such as Marcus Garvey in the 1920s (see Chapter 23), was revived in the 1960s by the Nation of Islam, a religious group with more than 10,000 members and many more sympathizers. Popularly known as the Black Muslims, the organization was hostile to whites and stressed black pride, unity, and self-help.

The Black Muslims' most charismatic figure was Malcolm X. A brilliant debater and spellbinding speaker, Malcolm X preached a philosophy quite different from Martin Luther King's. He advocated militant protest and separatism, though he condoned the use of violence only for self-defense. Hostile to the traditional civil rights organizations, he caustically referred to the 1963 March on Washington as the "Farce on Washington." In 1964, after a power struggle with the founder of the Black Muslims, Elijah Muhammed, Malcolm X broke with the Nation of Islam. Following a pilgrimage to Mecca and a tour of Africa, he embraced the liberation struggles of all colonized peoples. But before he could fully pursue his new agenda, he was assassinated while delivering a speech at the Audubon Ballroom in Harlem on February 21, 1965. Three Black Muslims were later convicted of his murder.

A more secular black nationalist movement emerged in 1966 when young black SNCC and CORE activists, following the lead of Stokely Carmichael, began to call for black self-reliance and racial pride under the banner of "Black Power." Amid growing distrust of white domination, SNCC effectively ejected its white members.

In the same year Huey Newton and Bobby Seale, two college students in Oakland, California, founded the Black Panthers, a militant self-defense organization dedicated to protecting local blacks from police violence. The Panthers' organization quickly spread to other cities, where members undertook a wide range of community organizing projects, including interracial efforts, but their affinity for Third World revolutionary movements and armed struggle became their most publicized attribute.

Among the most significant legacies of black power was the assertion of racial pride. Many young blacks insisted on using the term *Afro-American* rather than *Negro,* a term they found demeaning because of its historical association with slavery and racism. Rejecting white tastes and standards, blacks wore African clothing and hairstyles and helped to awaken interest in black history, art, and literature. By the 1970s many colleges and universities were offering programs in black studies.

The new black assertiveness alarmed many white Americans. They had been willing to go along with the moderate reforms of the 1950s and early 1960s but became wary when blacks began demanding immediate access to higher-paying jobs, housing in white neighborhoods, education in integrated schools, and increased political power. Another major reason for the erosion of white support was a wave of riots that struck the nation's cities. Lacking education and skills, successive generations of blacks had moved out of the rural South in search of work that paid an adequate wage. In the North many remained unemployed. Resentful of white landlords who owned the substandard housing they were forced to live in and white shopkeepers who denied them jobs in their neighborhoods, many blacks also hated police, whose violent presence in black neighborhoods seemed that of "an occupying army." Stimulated by the successes of southern blacks who had challenged whites and gotten results, young urban blacks expressed their grievances through their own brand of direct action.

The first "long hot summer" began in July 1964 in New York City, when police shot a young black criminal suspect in Harlem. Angry youths looted and rioted there for a week. Over the next four years the volatile issue of police brutality set off riots in dozens of cities. In August 1965 the arrest of a young black motorist in the Watts section of Los Angeles sparked six days of rioting that left thirty-four blacks dead. The riots of 1967 were the most serious (see Map 29.2), engulfing twenty-two cities in July and August. The most devastating outbreaks occurred in Newark and Detroit. Forty-three people were killed in Detroit alone, nearly all of them black, and $50 million worth of property destroyed. As in most of the riots, the arson and looting in Detroit targeted white-owned stores and property, but there was little physical violence against white people.

On July 29, 1967, President Johnson appointed a special commission to investigate the riots. The final report of the National Advisory Commission on Civil Disorders, released in March 1968, detailed the continuing inequality and racism of urban life. It also issued a warning: "Our nation is moving toward two societies, one black, one white—separate and unequal. . . . What white Americans have never

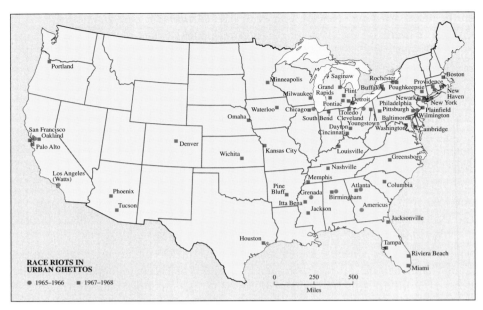

M A P 29.2
Racial Unrest in America's Cities, 1965–1968

American cities suffered through four "long hot summers" of rioting in the mid-1960s. In 1967, the worst year, riots broke out across the United States, including the South and West. Major riots did not usually occur in the same city two years in a row.

fully understood—but what the Negro can never forget—is that white society is deeply implicated in the ghetto. White institutions created it, white institutions maintain it, and white society condones it."

On April 4, 1968, barely a month after the Commission on Civil Disorders released its report, Martin Luther King Jr. was assassinated in Memphis, Tennessee, by James Earl Ray, a white ex-convict whose motive was unknown. King's death set off an explosion of urban rioting. Violence broke out in more than a hundred cities. With King's assassination the civil rights movement lost the one leader best able to stir the conscience of white America.

THE LEGACY OF THE CIVIL RIGHTS MOVEMENT

The 1960s brought permanent, indeed revolutionary, changes in American race relations. Jim Crow segregation was overturned, and federal legislation passed to ensure protection of black Americans' most basic civil rights. The enfranchisement of blacks in the southern states ended political control by all-white state Democratic Parties and allowed black candidates to enter the political arena. White candidates who had once been ardent segregationists began to court the black vote. In time Martin Luther King's greatness was recognized even among whites in the South; in 1986 his birthday became a national holiday.

Yet much remained undone. The more entrenched forms of segregation and discrimination persisted. African Americans, particularly those in the central cities, continued to make up a disproportionate number of the poor, the unemployed, and the undereducated. As the civil rights movement gradually splintered, its agenda remained unfinished.

Despite its limitations, the black civil rights movement provided a fresh and innovative model for social change. Although Mexican Americans had been working actively for civil rights since the 1930s (see Chapter 24), poverty, an uncertain legal status, and language barriers made their political mobilization difficult. That situation began to change when the Mexican American Political Association (MAPA) mobilized support for John F. Kennedy and in return Kennedy appointed several Mexican American leaders to posts in Washington. Over the next four years MAPA and other political organizations worked successfully to elect Mexican American candidates to Congress: in the House Edward Roybal of California and

Mourning Martin Luther King Jr.

Thousands of African Americans mourned the death of the country's foremost civil rights leader, Martin Luther King Jr., who had been assassinated in Memphis, Tennessee, on April 4, 1968. Among those who marched alongside King's casket, borne by a simple farm wagon pulled by mules, were future presidential candidate Jesse Jackson (in green) and future U.N. ambassador Andrew Young (at the left corner of the casket). During that week racial uprisings broke out in more than a hundred cities. (Wide World Photos, Inc.)

Henry González and Elizo de la Garza of Texas; in the Senate Joseph Montoya of New Mexico.

Younger Mexican Americans quickly grew impatient with MAPA, however. The barrios of Los Angeles and other western cities produced the militant Brown Berets, modeled on the Black Panthers (who wore black berets). Rejecting the assimilationist approach of their elders, 1,500 Mexican American students met in Denver in 1969 to hammer out a new nationalist political and cultural agenda. They proclaimed a new term, *Chicano,* to replace *Mexican American,* and later organized a new political party, La Raza Unida (The United Race), to promote Chicano interests and candidates. In California and other southwestern states students staged demonstrations and boycotts to press for bilingual education, the hiring of more Chicano teachers, and the creation of Chicano studies programs. By the 1970s dozens of such programs were offered at universities throughout the region.

Chicano strategists also pursued economic objectives. Working in the fields around Delano, California, the labor leader Cesar Chavez organized the United Farm Workers (UFW), the first union to represent migrant workers successfully. A 1965 grape pickers' strike and a nationwide boycott of table grapes brought Chavez and his union national publicity and won support from the AFL-CIO and from Senator Robert F. Kennedy of New York. Victory came in 1970 when California grape growers signed contracts recognizing the UFW.

North American Indians also found a model in the civil rights movement. Numbering nearly 800,000 in the 1960s, Indians were an exceedingly diverse group, divided by language, tribal history, region, and degree of integration into the mainstream of American life. But they shared an unemployment rate ten times the national average, as well as the worst poverty, the most inadequate housing, the highest disease rates, and the least access to education of any group in the United States.

As early as World War II the National Council of American Indians had lobbied for improvement of those conditions. In the 1960s some Indian groups became more assertive. Like the young militants in the black civil rights movement, they challenged the accommodationist approach of their elders. Proposing a new name for themselves—*Native Americans*—they organized protests and demonstrations to build support for their cause (see American Voices, "The Trail of Broken Treaties"). In 1968 several Chippewas from Minnesota organized the militant American Indian Movement (AIM), which drew its strength from the third of the Native American population who lived in "red ghettos" in cities throughout the West.

In February 1973, 200 Sioux organized by AIM leaders began an occupation of the tiny village of Wounded Knee, South Dakota, the site of an army massacre of the Sioux in 1890 (see Chapter 16). They were protesting the light sentences given to a group of white men convicted of killing a Sioux in 1972. To dramatize their cause the protesters took eleven hostages and occupied several buildings. But when a gun battle with the FBI left one protester dead and another wounded, the seventy-one-day siege collapsed. Although the new Native American activism helped to

The Trail of Broken Treaties

MARY CROW DOG

I n November 1972, nineteen-year-old Mary Crow Dog traveled to Washington, D.C., with several hundred other Sioux from the Rosebud and Pine Ridge reservations in South Dakota. As she explains in her autobiography, their group was one of several caravans participating in a protest known as the Trail of Broken Treaties, which ended in a six-day occupation of the Bureau of Indian Affairs (BIA) headquarters. Their demands included restoration of native lands and resources, reinstitution of the treaty-making rights of the Indian Nations, and replacement of the BIA with an agency more attuned to their rights and cultures.

We had been promised food and accommodation, but due to government pressure many church groups which had offered to put us up and feed us got scared and backed off. . . .

Somebody suggested, "Let's all go to the BIA." It seemed the natural thing to do, to go to the Bureau of Indian Affairs building on Constitution Avenue. . . . It was "our" building after all. Besides, that was what we had come for, to complain about the treatment the bureau was dishing out to us. . . . Next thing I knew we were in it. We spilled into the building like a great avalanche. Some people put up a tipi on the front lawn. . . . The building finally belonged to us and we lost no time turning it into a tribal village. . . .

We pushed the police and guards out of the building. . . . We had formulated twenty Indian demands. These were all rejected by the few bureaucrats sent to negotiate with us. . . . Soon we listened to other voices as the Occupation turned into a siege. I heard somebody yelling, "The pigs are here." . . . A fight broke out between the police and our security. Some of our young men got hit over the head with police clubs and we saw the blood streaming down their faces. . . .

From then on, every morning we were given a court order to get out by six P.M. Come six o'clock and we would be standing there ready to join battle. I think many brothers and sisters were prepared to die right on the steps of the BIA building. . . .

In the end a compromise was reached. The government said . . . they would appoint two high administration officials to seriously consider our twenty demands. . . . Of course, our twenty points were never gone into afterward. . . . But morally it had been a great victory. We had faced White America collectively, not as individual tribes. We had stood up to the government and gone through our baptism of fire.

SOURCE: Mary Crow Dog, *Lakota Woman* (New York: Grove Weidenfeld, 1990), pp. 84–85, 88–91.

alienate many white onlookers, it did spur government action on tribal issues (see Chapter 31).

Civil rights also sparked a new awareness among some predominantly white groups. Homosexual men and women banded together to protest legal and social oppression based on their sexual orientation. In 1969 the gay liberation movement

Wounded Knee Revisited

In 1973 members of the American Indian Movement staged a seventy-one-day protest at Wounded Knee, South Dakota, the site of the 1890 massacre of 200 Sioux by U.S. soldiers. The takeover was sparked by the murder of a local Sioux by a group of whites but quickly expanded to include demands for basic reforms in federal Indian policy and tribal governance. (UPI/Corbis-Bettmann)

was born in the "Stonewall riot" in New York City, when patrons of a gay bar fought back against police harassment. The assertion of gay pride that followed the incident drew heavily on the language and tactics of the civil rights movement. Activists took the new name of *gay* rather than *homosexual;* founded advocacy groups, newspapers, and political organizations to challenge discrimination and prejudice; and offered emotional support to those who "came out" and publicly affirmed their homosexuality. For gays as well as members of various ethnic and cultural groups, political activism based on heightened group identity represented one of the most significant legacies of the African American struggle.

THE REVIVAL OF FEMINISM

The black civil rights movement also helped to reactivate feminism, a movement that had been languishing since the 1920s. Just as the abolition movement had been the training ground for women's rights advocates in the nineteenth century, the black struggle became an inspiration for young feminists in the 1960s. But the revival of feminism also sprang from social and demographic changes that affected women young and old. By 1970, 42.6 percent of women were working, and four out of ten working women were married. Especially significant was the growth in the number of working women with preschool children—up from 12 percent in 1950 to 30 percent in 1970.

Another significant change was increased access to education for women. Immediately after World War II the percentage of college students who were women declined. The GI Bill gave men a temporary advantage in access to higher education. At the height of the baby boom many college women dropped out of school to marry and raise families. By 1960, however, the percentage of college students who were women had risen to 35 percent; in 1970 it reached 41 percent.

The meaning of marriage was changing, too. The baby boom turned out to be only a temporary interruption of a century-long decline in the birth rate. The introduction of the birth control pill, first marketed in 1960, and the intrauterine device (IUD) helped women control their fertility. Women had fewer children, and because of an increased life expectancy (seventy-five years in 1970—up from fifty-four years in 1920), they devoted proportionally fewer years to raising children. At the same time the divorce rate, which had risen slowly throughout the twentieth century, rose markedly as the states liberalized divorce laws. As a result of these changes traditional gender expectations were dramatically undermined. American women's lives now usually included work and marriage, often child rearing and a career, and possibly bringing up children alone after a divorce. Those changing social realities created a major constituency for the emerging women's movement of the 1960s.

Older, politically active professional women sought change by working through the political system. This group was galvanized in part by a report by the Presidential Commission on the Status of Women (1963), which documented the employment and educational discrimination women faced. More important than the report's rather conservative recommendations was the rudimentary nationwide network of women in public life that formed in the course of the commission's work.

Another spark that ignited the revival of feminism was Betty Friedan's pointed indictment of suburban domesticity, *The Feminine Mystique,* published in 1963. Women responded enthusiastically to Friedan's book—especially white, college-educated, middle-class women. The book sold 3 million copies and was excerpted in many women's magazines. *The Feminine Mystique* gave women a vocabulary with which to express their dissatisfaction and promoted women's self-realization through employment, continuing education, and other activities outside the home.

Like so many other constituencies in postwar America, women's rights activists looked to the federal government for help. Especially important was the Civil Rights Act of 1964, which had as great an impact on women as it did on blacks and other minorities. Title VII, which barred discrimination in employment on the basis of race, religion, national origin, or sex, eventually became a powerful tool in the fight against sex discrimination. At first, however, the Equal Employment Opportunity Commission (EEOC) avoided implementing it.

Dissatisfied with the Commission's reluctance to defend women's rights, Friedan and others founded the National Organization for Women (NOW) in 1966. Modeling itself on groups such as the NAACP, NOW aimed to be a civil rights organization for women. "The purpose of NOW," an early statement declared, "is to take action to bring women into full participation in the mainstream of American society now, exercising all the privileges and responsibilities thereof in truly equal partnership with men." Under Friedan, who served as NOW's first president, membership grew from 1,000 in 1967 to 15,000 in 1971. Men made up a fourth of NOW's early membership. The group is still the largest feminist organization in the United States.

Another group of new feminists, the women's liberationists, came to the women's movement through their civil rights work. White women had made up about half the students who went south with SNCC in the Freedom Summer project of 1964. These college women developed self-confidence and organizational skills working in the South, and they found role models in older southern women like Ella Baker, Anne Braden, and Virginia Foster Durr, who were prominent in the civil rights movement. Yet women volunteers also found they were expected to do all the cleaning and cooking at the Freedom Houses where SNCC volunteers lived.

After 1965 black militants made white women unwelcome in the civil rights movement. But when these women transferred their energies to the antiwar groups that were emerging in that period, they found the New Left equally male-dominated. When the antiwar movement adopted draft resistance as a central strategy, women found themselves marginalized. Those women who tried to raise feminist issues at conventions were shouted off the platform with jeers such as "Move on, little girl, we have more important issues to talk about here than women's liberation."

Around 1967 the contradiction between the New Left's lip service to egalitarianism and women's treatment by male leaders caused women radicals to realize that they needed their own movement. In contrast to groups such as NOW, which had traditional organizational structures and dues-paying members, these women formed loose collectives whose shifting membership often lacked any formal structure. They organized independently in five or six different cities, including Chicago, San Francisco, and New York.

Members of the women's liberation movement (or "women's lib," as it was dubbed by the somewhat hostile media) went public in 1968 in a protest at the Miss America Pageant. Their demonstration featured a "freedom trash can" into which they encouraged women to throw false eyelashes, hair curlers, brassieres, and girdles—all of which they branded as symbols of female oppression. An activity with a more lasting impact was consciousness raising—group sessions in which women shared their experiences of being female. Swapping stories about being passed over for a promotion, needing a husband's signature on a credit-card application, or enduring the whistles and leers of men while walking down the street helped participants to realize that their individual problems were part of a wider pattern of oppression. The slogan "The personal is political" became a rallying cry of the movement.

By 1970 a growing convergence of interests began to blur the distinction between women's rights and women's liberation. Radical women realized that key feminist goals—child care, equal pay, and abortion rights—could best be achieved in the political arena. At the same time more traditional activists developed a broader view of the women's movement, tentatively including divisive issues such as abortion and lesbian rights. Although the movement remained largely white and

Women's Liberation

Arguing that beauty contests were degrading to women, members of the National Women's Liberation Party staged a protest against the Miss America pageant held in Atlantic City, New Jersey, in September 1968. (Wide World Photos, Inc.)

middle class, feminists were beginning to think of themselves as part of a broad, growing, and increasingly influential social crusade that would continue to grow.

The Long Road Home, 1968–1975

In 1968, as Lyndon Johnson planned his reelection campaign, antiwar protests and rising battlefield casualties had begun to erode public support for a war that seemed to have no end. Moreover, since Diem's assassination in 1963 South Vietnam had undergone a confusing series of military coups and countercoups. In the spring of 1966 the Johnson administration pressured the unpopular South Vietnamese government to adopt democratic reforms, including a new constitution and popular elections. In September 1967 U.S. officials helped to elect General Nguyen Van Thieu president of South Vietnam. Thieu's regime, the administration hoped, would stabilize politics in South Vietnam, advance the military struggle against the communists, and legitimize the South Vietnamese government in the eyes of the American public.

1968: A YEAR OF SHOCKS

The administration's hopes evaporated on January 30, 1968, when the Viet Cong unleashed a massive, well-coordinated assault on major urban areas in South Vietnam. Known as the Tet offensive, the assault was timed to coincide with the lunar new year, a festive Vietnamese holiday. Viet Cong forces struck thirty-six of the forty-four provincial capitals and five of the six major cities, including Saigon, where they raided the supposedly impregnable U.S. embassy (see Map 29.1). In strict military terms the Tet offensive was a failure for the Viet Cong since it did not provoke the intended collapse of the South Vietnamese government. But its long-term effect was quite different. The daring attack made a mockery of official pronouncements that the United States was winning the war and swung American public opinion more strongly against the war. Just before the offensive a Gallup poll found that 56 percent of Americans considered themselves "hawks" (supporters of the war), while only 28 percent identified with the "doves" (opponents). Three months after Tet the doves outnumbered the hawks 42 to 41 percent. This turnaround in public opinion did not mean that a majority of Americans supported the peace movement, however. Many who called themselves doves had simply concluded that the war was unwinnable and were therefore opposed to it on pragmatic rather than moral grounds. As a housewife told a pollster, "I want to get out, but I don't want to give up."

The growing opposition to the war spilled over into the 1968 presidential campaign. Even before Tet, Senator Eugene J. McCarthy of Minnesota had entered the Democratic primaries as an antiwar candidate. President Johnson won the early New Hampshire primary, but McCarthy received a stunning 42.2 percent of the vote. His strong showing against the president reflected profound public dissatisfaction with the course of the war—even among those who were hawks.

Johnson realized that his political support was evaporating. On March 31 and at the end of an otherwise mundane televised address, he stunned the nation by announcing that he would not seek reelection. Johnson had already reversed his policy of incremental escalation of the war. Now he called a partial bombing halt and vowed to devote his remaining months in office to the search for peace. On May 10, 1968, preliminary peace talks between the United States and North Vietnam opened in Paris.

Just four days after Johnson's withdrawal from the presidential race, Martin Luther King Jr. was assassinated in Memphis. The ensuing riots in cities across the country left forty-three people dead. Soon afterward, students protesting Columbia University's plans for expanding into a neighboring ghetto and displacing its residents occupied several campus buildings. The brutal response of the New York City police helped to radicalize even more students. The next month a massive strike by students and labor unions toppled the French government. Student unrest seemed likely to become a worldwide phenomenon.

Then came the final painful tragedy of the year. Senator Robert Kennedy, who had entered the Democratic presidential primaries in March, had quickly become a front runner. On June 5, 1968, as he celebrated his victory in the California primary, he was shot dead by a young Palestinian who was thought to oppose Kennedy's pro-Israeli stance. Robert Kennedy's assassination shattered the dreams of many who had hoped that social change could be achieved by working through the political system. His death also weakened the Democratic Party. In his brief but dramatic campaign Kennedy had excited and energized the traditional members of the New Deal coalition, including blue-collar workers and black voters, in a way that the more cerebral Eugene McCarthy, who appealed mostly to the antiwar movement, never did.

The Democratic Party never fully recovered from Johnson's withdrawal and Kennedy's assassination. McCarthy's campaign limped along, while Senator George S. McGovern of South Dakota entered the Democratic race in an effort to keep the Kennedy forces together. Meanwhile, Vice President Hubert H. Humphrey lined up pledges from traditional Democratic constituencies—unions, urban machines, and state political organizations. Democrats found themselves on the verge of nominating not an antiwar candidate but a public figure closely associated with Johnson's war policies.

At the August Democratic nominating convention the political divisions generated by the war consumed the party. Most of the drama occurred not in the convention hall but outside on the streets of Chicago. Led by Jerry Rubin and Abbie Hoffman around 10,000 protesters descended on the city, calling for an end to the war, the legalization of marijuana, and the abolition of money. To mock those inside the convention hall, these "Yippies," as the group called themselves, nominated a pig for president. Their stunts, geared toward maximizing their media exposure, diverted attention from the more serious and far more numerous antiwar activists who had come to Chicago as convention delegates or volunteers.

Richard J. Daley, the Democratic mayor of Chicago, who had grown increasingly angry as protesters disrupted his convention, called out the police to break up the demonstrations. Several nights of skirmishes between protesters and police culminated on the evening of the nominations. In what an official report later described as a "police riot," patrolmen attacked protesters with Mace, tear gas, and clubs as demonstrators chanted, "The whole world is watching!" Television networks broadcast a film of the riot as the nominating speeches were being made, cementing a popular impression of the Democrats as the party of disorder. Inside the hall the Democrats dispiritedly nominated Hubert H. Humphrey, who chose Senator Edmund S. Muskie of Maine as his running mate. The delegates approved a middle-of-the-road platform that endorsed continued fighting in Vietnam while the administration explored diplomatic means of ending the conflict.

The disruptive Democratic convention unleashed a backlash against antiwar protesters. The general public did not differentiate between the disruptive antics of the Yippies and the more responsible behavior of those activists who were trying to work within the system. Polls showed overwhelming support for Mayor Daley and the police.

The turmoil surrounding the New Left and the antiwar movement strengthened support for proponents of "law and order," which became a conservative catch phrase for the next several years. Indeed, many Americans, though opposed to the war, were fed up with protest and dissent. Governor George C. Wallace of Alabama, a third-party candidate, skillfully exploited their growing disapproval of the antiwar movement by making student protests and urban riots his chief campaign issues. But Wallace, who in 1963 had promised to enforce "segregation now . . . segregation tomorrow . . . and segregation forever," also exploited the mounting backlash against the civil rights movement. Articulating the resentments of many working-class whites, he combined attacks on liberal intellectuals and government elites with strident denunciations of school desegregation and forced busing.

Even more than George Wallace, Richard Nixon tapped the increasingly conservative mood of the electorate. After his unsuccessful presidential campaign in 1960 and his loss in the California gubernatorial race in 1962, Nixon engineered an amazing political comeback and in 1968 won the Republican presidential nomination. He chose Spiro Agnew, the conservative governor of Maryland, as his running mate to attract southern voters, especially Wallace supporters, who opposed Democratic civil rights legislation. Nixon pledged to represent the "quiet voice" of the "great majority of Americans, the forgotten Americans, the nonshouters, the nondemonstrators."

Despite the Democratic debacle in Chicago the election was a close one. In the last weeks of the campaign Humphrey rallied by gingerly disassociating himself from Johnson's war policies. Then in a televised address on October 31 President Johnson announced a complete halt to the bombing of North Vietnam. Nixon countered by intimating that he had his own plan to end the war—although in reality no such plan existed. On election day Nixon received 43.4 percent of the vote to Humphrey's 42.7 percent, defeating him by a scant 510,000 votes out of the 73 million that were cast. Wallace finished with 13.5 percent of the popular vote. Though Nixon owed his election largely to the split in the Democratic coalition, the success of his southern strategy presaged the emergence of a new Republican majority. In the meantime, however, the Democrats retained a majority in both houses of Congress.

The closeness of the 1968 election suggested how polarized American society had become. Nixon appealed to a segment of society that came to be known as the *silent majority*—the hard-working, nonprotesting, generally white American. Although his victory suggested a growing consensus among voters who were "unblack, unpoor, and unyoung," heated protest and controversy would persist until the war ended.

NIXON'S WAR

Vietnam, long Lyndon Johnson's war, now became Richard Nixon's. At first Nixon sought to end the war by expanding its scope, as a means of pressuring the North Vietnamese to negotiate. But Nixon and his national security adviser, Henry

Kissinger, soon realized that the public would not support such an approach. Thus, shortly after Nixon took office, he sent a letter to the North Vietnamese leaders proposing mutual troop withdrawals. In March 1969, to convince North Vietnam that the United States meant business, Nixon ordered clandestine bombing raids on neutral Cambodia, through which the North Vietnamese had been transporting supplies and reinforcements.

When the intensified bombing failed to end the war, Nixon and Kissinger adopted a policy of Vietnamization. On June 8, 1969, Nixon announced that 25,000 American troops would be withdrawn by August and replaced by South Vietnamese forces. As the U.S. ambassador to Vietnam, Ellsworth Bunker, noted cynically, Vietnamization was just a matter of changing "the color of the bodies." Antiwar demonstrators denounced the new policy, which protected American lives at the expense of the Vietnamese but would not end the war. On October 15, 1969, in cities across the country, millions of Americans joined a one-day "moratorium" against the war. A month later more than a quarter of a million people mobilized in Washington in the largest antiwar demonstration to date.

To discredit his critics Nixon denounced student demonstrators as "bums" and stated that "North Vietnam cannot defeat or humiliate the United States. Only Americans can do that." Vice President Spiro Agnew attacked dissenters as "ideological eunuchs" and "nattering nabobs of negativism." Nixon staunchly insisted that he would not be swayed by the mounting protests against the war. During the November 1969 march on Washington the president barricaded himself in the White House and watched football on television.

On April 30, 1970, the bombing of Cambodia, which Nixon had kept secret from both the public and from Congress, culminated in an "incursion" into Cambodia by American ground forces to destroy enemy havens there. The invasion proved only a short-term setback for the North Vietnamese. More critically, the American action in Cambodia—along with the ongoing North Vietnamese intervention there—destabilized the country, exposing it to a takeover by the ruthless Khmer Rouge later in the 1970s.

When the *New York Times* uncovered the secret invasion of Cambodia, outrage led antiwar leaders to organize a national student strike. On May 4 at Kent State University outside Cleveland, panicky National Guardsmen fired into a crowd of students at an antiwar rally. Four people were killed and eleven more wounded. Only two of those who were killed had been attending the demonstration; the other two were just passing by on their way to class. Soon afterward National Guardsmen stormed a dormitory at Jackson State College in Mississippi, killing two black students. More than 450 colleges closed in protest, and 80 percent of all campuses experienced some kind of disturbance. In June 1970, immediately after the Kent State slayings, a Gallup poll identified campus unrest as the issue that most troubled Americans.

At the same time, however, dissatisfaction with the war continued to spread. Congressional opposition to the war, which had been growing since the Fulbright hearings in 1966, intensified with the invasion of Cambodia. In June 1970 the Senate expressed its disapproval by voting to repeal the Gulf of Tonkin resolution and by cutting off funding for operations in Cambodia. Even the soldiers in Vietnam were showing mounting opposition to their mission. The number of troops who refused to follow combat orders increased steadily, and thousands of U.S. soldiers deserted. Among the majority who fought on, many sewed peace symbols on their uniforms. In the heat of battle a number of overbearing junior officers were sometimes "fragged"—killed or wounded in grenade attacks by their own soldiers. At home members of a group called Vietnam Veterans Against the War turned in their combat medals at demonstrations outside the U.S. Capitol.

In 1971 Americans were appalled by revelations of the sheer brutality of the war when Lieutenant William L. Calley was court-martialed for atrocities committed in the village of My Lai. In March 1968 Calley and the platoon under his command had apparently murdered 350 Vietnamese villagers in retaliation for casualties sustained in an earlier engagement. The military court sentenced Calley to life in prison for his part in the massacre. Yet George Wallace and some congressional conservatives called him a hero. President Nixon had Calley's sentence reduced; he was paroled in 1974.

After a final outbreak of protest and violence following the incident at Kent State, antiwar activism began to ebb. The antiwar movement was weakened in part by internal divisions within the New Left. In the late 1960s SDS and other antiwar groups fell victim to police harassment, and Federal Bureau of Investigation (FBI) and Central Intelligence Agency (CIA) agents infiltrated and disrupted radical organizations. After 1968 the New Left splintered into factions, its energy spent. One radical faction broke off from SDS and formed the Weathermen, a tiny band of self-styled revolutionaries who embraced terrorist tactics that alienated more moderate activists.

Nixon's Vietnamization policy also played a role in the decline of antiwar protest by dramatically reducing the number of soldiers in combat. When Nixon took office, more than 543,000 American soldiers were serving in Vietnam; by the end of 1970 there were 334,000, and two years later there were 24,200. Nixon's promise to continue troop withdrawals, end the draft, and institute an all-volunteer army by 1973 further deprived the antiwar movement of important organizing issues, particularly on college campuses. Student commitment to social causes, however, did not disappear altogether. In the early 1970s many student activists refocused their energies on issues such as feminism and environmentalism.

DÉTENTE AND THE END OF THE WAR

At the same time Nixon had been prosecuting the war in Vietnam, ostensibly to halt the spread of communism, he had been formulating a new policy toward the Soviet Union and China. Known as *détente* (the French word for a relaxation of tensions), Nixon's policy was to seek peaceful coexistence with the two communist powers and to link his overtures of friendship with a plan to end the Vietnam War.

In his talks with Chinese and Soviet leaders Nixon urged them to reduce their military aid to the North Vietnamese as a means of pressuring the North Vietnamese to the negotiating table.

A lifelong anticommunist crusader, Nixon was better able to reach out to the two communist superpowers without arousing American mistrust than a Democratic president would have been. Since the Chinese revolution of 1949 the United States had refused to recognize the government of the People's Republic of China. Instead, the State Department had recognized the Nationalist Chinese government in Taiwan. Nixon moved away from that policy, reasoning that the United States could exploit the growing rift between the People's Republic of China and the Soviet Union. In February 1972 Nixon journeyed to China in a symbolic visit that set the stage for the establishment of formal diplomatic relations in 1979.

In a similar spirit Nixon journeyed to Moscow in May 1972 to sign the first Strategic Arms Limitations Treaty (SALT I) between the United States and the Soviet Union. Although SALT I fell far short of ending the arms race, it did limit the production and deployment of intercontinental ballistic missiles (ICBMs) and antiballistic missile systems (ABMs). The treaty also signified that the United States could no longer afford the massive military spending that would have been necessary to regain the nuclear and military superiority it had enjoyed immediately following World War II. By the early 1970s inflation, domestic dissent, and the decline in American hegemony had limited and reshaped American aims and options in international relations. Most of all Nixon hoped that a rapprochement with the Soviets would help to resolve the prolonged crisis in Vietnam.

The Paris peace talks had been in stalemate since 1968. Though the war had been "Vietnamized," and American casualties had decreased, the South Vietnamese military proved unable to hold its own. In late 1971, as American troops withdrew from the region, communist forces stepped up their attacks on Laos, Cambodia, and South Vietnam. The next spring North Vietnamese forces launched a major new offensive against South Vietnam. In April, as the fighting intensified, Nixon ordered B-52 bombing raids against North Vietnam, and a month later he approved the mining of North Vietnamese ports.

That spring the increased combat activity and growing political pressure at home helped revive the Paris peace negotiations. Nixon hoped to undercut antiwar critics by making concessions to the North Vietnamese in the peace talks. In October Henry Kissinger and the North Vietnamese negotiator Le Duc Tho reached a cease-fire agreement calling for the withdrawal of the remaining U.S. troops; the return of all American prisoners of war; and the continued presence of North Vietnamese troops in South Vietnam. Nixon and Kissinger also promised the North Vietnamese substantial aid for postwar reconstruction. On the eve of the 1972 presidential election Kissinger announced "peace is at hand," and Nixon returned to the White House with a resounding electoral victory (see Chapter 30).

The peace initiative, however, soon stalled when the South Vietnamese rejected the provision concerning North Vietnamese troop positions, and the North declined

Hanoi Devastated

The North Vietnamese capital of Hanoi sustained heavy damage from bombing raids by American B-52 jets. The most devastating raids occurred during the "Christmas bombings" in December 1972, just weeks before the Paris Peace Accords were signed.

(Marc Riboud/Magnum Photos, Inc.)

to compromise further. With negotiations deadlocked, Nixon stepped up military action once more. From December 17 to December 30, 1972, American planes subjected civilian and military targets in Hanoi and Haiphong to the most devastating bombing of the war, referred to in the press as the "Christmas bombings." Finally, on January 27, 1973, representatives of the United States, North and South Vietnam, and the Viet Cong signed a cease-fire in Paris. But the Paris Peace Accords, which differed little from the proposal that had been rejected in October, did not fulfill Nixon's promise of "peace with honor." Basically, they mandated the unilateral withdrawal of American troops in exchange for the return of American prisoners of war from North Vietnam. For most Americans that was enough.

Without massive U.S. military and economic aid and with North Vietnamese guerrillas operating freely throughout the countryside, the South Vietnamese government of General Nguyen Van Thieu soon fell to the more disciplined and popular communist forces. In March 1975 North Vietnamese forces launched a final offensive. Horrified American television viewers watched as South Vietnamese officials and soldiers struggled with American embassy personnel to board the last helicopters that would fly out of Saigon before North Vietnamese troops entered the city. On April 29, 1975, Vietnam was reunited, and Saigon was renamed Ho Chi Minh City in honor of the communist leader, who had died in 1969.

THE LEGACY OF VIETNAM

Spanning nearly thirty years, the Vietnam War occupied American administrations from Truman to Nixon's successor Gerald Ford. U.S. troops fought in Vietnam for more than eleven years, from 1961 to 1973. In human terms the nation's longest war exacted an enormous cost. Some 58,000 U.S. troops died, and another 300,000 were wounded. Even those who returned unharmed encountered a sometimes hostile or indifferent reception. Arriving home alone without the fanfare that had greeted soldiers of America's victorious wars, most Vietnam veterans found the transition to civilian life abrupt and disorienting. The psychological tensions of serving in Vietnam and the difficulty of reentry sowed the seeds of what is now recognized as *post-traumatic stress disorder*—recurring physical and psychological problems that often lead to divorce, unemployment, and suicide. Only in the 1980s did America begin to make its peace with those who had served in the nation's most unpopular war.

In Southeast Asia the damage was far greater. The war claimed an estimated 1.5 million Vietnamese lives and devastated the country's physical and economic infrastructure. Neighboring Laos and Cambodia also suffered, particularly Cambodia, where between 1975 and 1979 the Khmer Rouge killed an estimated 2 million Cambodians—a quarter of the population—in a brutal relocation campaign. All told, the war produced nearly 10 million refugees, many of whom immigrated to the United States. Among them were thousands of Amerasians, the offspring of American soldiers and Vietnamese women. Spurned by their fathers and by most Vietnamese, more than 30,000 Amerasians arrived in the 1990s.

The defeat in Vietnam prompted Americans to think differently about foreign affairs and to acknowledge the limits of U.S. power abroad. The United States became less willing to plunge into overseas military commitments, a controversial change that conservatives dubbed the "Vietnam syndrome." In 1973 Congress declared its hostility to undeclared wars like those in Vietnam and Korea by passing the War Powers Act, which required the president to report any use of military force within forty-eight hours and directed that without a declaration of war by Congress hostilities must cease within sixty days. On those occasions when Congress did agree to foreign intervention, as in the Persian Gulf War of 1990 to 1991, American leaders would insist on obtainable military objectives and carefully channeled information to the news media. In the future any foreign entanglement would be evaluated in terms of its potential to become "another Vietnam."

The Vietnam War also distorted American economic and social affairs. At a total price of over $150 billion, the war siphoned resources from domestic needs, added to the deficit, and fueled inflation (see Chapter 32). Lyndon Johnson's Great Society programs had been pared down, and domestic reform efforts slowed thereafter. Moreover, the war shattered the liberal consensus that had supported the Democratic coalition. Even more seriously, the conduct of the war—the lies about American successes on the battlefield, the questionable representation of events in the Gulf of Tonkin, the secret war in Cambodia—spawned a deep distrust of government among American citizens. The discrediting of liberalism, the increased

T I M E L I N E

1946–1954	France and Vietminh struggle for Vietnam.	1967	Hippie counterculture's Summer of Love
			Antiwar protest in Washington, D.C.
1950	United States begins sending military aid to French in Vietnam.	1968	Tet offensive
			Lyndon Johnson withdraws from presidential race.
1954	Vietminh defeat French at Dienbienphu.		Martin Luther King Jr. assassinated
	Geneva Accords temporarily partition Vietnam at seventeenth parallel.		Robert F. Kennedy assassinated
			Riot at Democratic National Convention in Chicago
1960	Ngo Dinh Diem president of pro-American Vietnamese government		Women's liberation movement emerges
	Birth control pill first marketed		American Indian Movement (AIM) organized
1962	Students for a Democratic Society (SDS) founded	1969	Stonewall riot leads to gay liberation movement.
			Woodstock Music and Art Fair
1963	Militant Buddhists protest Diem.		Richard Nixon begins troop withdrawal.
	Diem assassinated	1970	Nixon orders invasion of Cambodia.
	Bob Dylan's "Blowin' in the Wind"		Killings at Kent State and Jackson State
	Presidential Commission on the Status of Women		Lieutenant William L. Calley court-martialed for My Lai atrocities
1964	Free Speech Movement at Berkeley	1972	Nixon visits People's Republic of China.
	Gulf of Tonkin resolution approves U.S. intervention in Vietnam.		SALT I Treaty with Soviet Union
			Christmas bombing of North Vietnam
1965	Malcolm X assassinated	1973	Paris Peace Accords
	Operation Rolling Thunder mass bombings		War Powers Act
	First U.S. combat troops arrive in Vietnam.		AIM occupies village of Wounded Knee, South Dakota.
	Six-day riot in Watts district of Los Angeles	1975	Fall of Saigon
1966	National Organization for Women (NOW) founded		

cynicism toward government, and the growing social turmoil that accompanied the war would continue into the next decade, paving the way for a resurgence of the Republican Party and a new mood of conservatism.

For Further Exploration

Two insightful overviews of the 1960s are David Farber, *The Age of Great Dreams* (1994), and Maurice Isserman and Michael Kazin, *America Divided: The Civil War of the 1960's* (1999). The period is unusually rich in compelling primary accounts. *Takin' It to the Streets,* edited by Alexander Bloom and Wini Breines (1995), offers an impressive array of documents that encompass the war, counterculture, civil rights, feminism, gay liberation, and other issues. Henry Hampton and Steve Fayer's oral history, *Voices of Freedom* (1991), and *The Autobiography of Malcolm X* (1995), cowritten with Alex Haley, provide insight into black power movements. Mary Crow Dog recounts her experiences as a Native American activist in *Lakota Woman* (1990). Memoirs of Vietnam are numerous. Secretary of Defense Robert McNamara offers an insider's view and belated apologia in *In Retrospect* (1995); in *An American Requiem: God, My Father, and the War That Came Between Us* (1996), the antiwar former priest James Carroll writes eloquently of the fissures Vietnam created in his family and the culture more generally; and Ron Kovic's *Born on the Fourth of July* (1976) is one soldier's powerful account of the war experience and its aftermath. Documents concerning the My Lai Massacre may be found in James S. Olson and Randy Roberts, eds., *My Lai* (1999).

"The Sixties Project," which is hosted by the University of Virginia at Charlottesville, offers personal narratives, special exhibits, and a bibliography of articles published in "Vietnam Generation," at <http://lists.village.virginia.edu/sixties/>. A useful Vietnam site is edited by Professor Vincent Ferraro of Mount Holyoke College and includes state papers and official correspondence from 1941 to the fall of Saigon, <http://www.mtholyoke .edu/acad/intrel/vietnam.htm>. The University of California Library's site, "Free Speech Movement: Student Protest–U.C. Berkeley, 1964–65," at <http://www.lib.berkeley.edu/ BANC/FSM/>, offers newsletters, oral histories, student newspaper accounts, legal defense material, and audio recordings, as well as good links to related sites. Historians at the University of Michigan maintain "A Study and Timeline of the Lakota Nation," at <http://www-personal.umich.edu/~jamarcus/>, which includes material on the American Indian Movement, the occupation of Wounded Knee in 1973, and the confrontation at the Bureau of Indian Affairs Office in 1972.

Chapter 30

THE LEAN YEARS
1969–1980

We've always believed in something called progress. We've always
had a faith that the days of our children would be better than our
own. Our people are losing that faith, not only in government itself
but in their ability as citizens to serve as the ultimate rulers and
shapers of our democracy.

—Jimmy Carter, 1979

"The United States Steel Corporation announced yesterday that it
was closing 14 plants and mills in eight states. About 13,000 production and white-
collar workers will lose their jobs." "Weyerhaeuser Co. may trim about 1,000 salaried
employees from its 11,000 member workforce over the next year." "Philadelphia:
Food Fair Inc. plans to close 89 supermarkets in New York and Connecticut." Newspaper articles in the 1970s told the story of the widespread downsizing that cost
millions of workers their jobs when rising oil prices, runaway inflation, declining
productivity, and stagnating incomes caused the biggest economic downturn in
three decades. Beyond the individual hard-luck stories of demeaning low-paid jobs,
lost homes, forced relocations, broken marriages, and alcoholism, the economic uncertainties facing working- and middle-class Americans in this period created a
sense of disillusionment about the nation's future. Already reeling from the nation's
withdrawal from Vietnam and its implications for the United States' international
power, many people also grew disenchanted with their political leadership in the
1970s, as one public official after another, including President Richard Nixon, resigned for misconduct. In the wake of Nixon's resignation, the lackluster administrations of Presidents Gerald Ford and Jimmy Carter failed to provide the leadership
necessary to cope with the nation's economic and international insecurities—a failure that fed Americans' growing skepticism about government and its capacity to
improve people's lives.

Paradoxically, in the midst of this growing disaffection and skepticism, a commitment to social change persisted. Some of the social movements born in the
1960s, such as feminism and environmentalism, had their greatest impact in the
1970s. As former student radicals moved into the political mainstream, they took

their struggles with them, from streets and campuses into courts, schools, workplaces, and community organizations. But like the civil rights and antiwar movements of the 1960s, the social activism of the 1970s stirred fears and uncertainties among many Americans. Furthermore, the darkening economic climate of the new decade undercut the sense of social generosity that had characterized the 1960s, fueling a new conservatism that would become a potent political force by the decade's end.

The Nixon Years

Richard Nixon set the stage for the conservative political resurgence. His election gave impetus to a long-standing Republican effort to trim back the Great Society and shift some federal responsibilities back to the states. At the same time Nixon embraced the use of federal power—within limits—to uphold governmental responsibility for social welfare, environmental protection, and economic stability. The president's domestic accomplishments, however, as well as his international initiatives, were ultimately overshadowed by the Watergate scandal, which swept him from office in disgrace and undermined Americans' confidence in their political leaders.

THE REPUBLICAN DOMESTIC AGENDA

In a 1968 campaign pledge to "the average American," Nixon had vowed to "reverse the flow of power and resources from the states and communities to Washington and start power and resources flowing back . . . to the people." One hallmark of this approach was the 1972 revenue-sharing program, which distributed a portion of federal tax revenues to the states as block grants, to be spent as state officials saw fit. In later years revenue sharing would become a key Republican strategy for reducing federal social programs and federal bureaucracy.

Nixon also worked to scale down certain federal government programs that had grown dramatically during the two preceding administrations. He reduced funding for many War on Poverty programs and dismantled the Office of Economic Opportunity altogether in 1971. Urban renewal, pollution control, and other environmental initiatives suffered when Nixon *impounded* (refused to spend) billions of dollars appropriated for them by Congress. Nixon's lack of interest in extending the gains of the civil rights movement, as well as his effort, albeit unsuccessful, to reform the social welfare system further exemplified the Republicans' desire to roll back the consolidation of federal power that had characterized American political life since the New Deal.

Still, with Democratic majorities in both houses of Congress, Nixon needed to be flexible in legislative matters. He agreed to the growth of major entitlement programs, including Medicare, Medicaid, and Social Security. In 1970 he signed a bill establishing the Environmental Protection Agency (EPA), and in 1972 he approved legislation creating the Occupational Safety and Health Administration (OSHA) and the Consumer Products Safety Commission. Thus, his administration witnessed the expansion of federal power in numerous areas.

Nixon demonstrated his conservative social values most clearly in his appointments to the Supreme Court. The liberal thrust of the Court under the direction of Chief Justice Earl Warren (1953–1969) had disturbed many conservatives. Its *Brown v. Board of Education* decision in 1954 requiring the desegregation of public schools (see Chapter 27) was followed by other landmark decisions in the 1960s. The *Miranda v. Arizona* (1966) decision reinforced defendants' rights by requiring arresting officers to notify suspects of their legal rights. In *Baker v. Carr* (1962) and *Reynolds v. Sims* (1964) the Court put forth the doctrine of "one person, one vote," meaning that all citizens' votes should have equal weight, no matter where they lived. The ruling substantially increased the representation in state legislatures and Congress of both suburban and urban areas (with their concentrations of African American and Spanish-speaking residents) at the expense of rural regions. One of the most controversial decisions was *Engel v. Vitale* (1962), which banned organized prayer in public schools as a violation of the First Amendment. When Earl Warren retired in 1969, President Nixon took the opportunity to begin reshaping the court and nominated conservative Warren Burger to become chief justice. After some difficulties in getting nominees confirmed by the Senate, Nixon eventually named three other justices: Harry Blackmun (who proved more liberal than expected), Lewis F. Powell Jr., and William Rehnquist.

Nixon's appointees did not always hand down decisions the president approved, however. Despite attempts by the Justice Department to halt further desegregation in the face of determined white opposition, the Court ordered busing to achieve racial balance. In 1972 it issued restrictions on the implementation of capital punishment, though it did not rule the death penalty unconstitutional. And in the controversial 1973 case *Roe v. Wade* Justice Harry Blackmun wrote the decision that struck down laws prohibiting abortion in Texas and Georgia.

THE 1972 ELECTION

Nixon's reelection in 1972 was never much in doubt. In May the threat of a conservative third-party challenge from Alabama governor George Wallace ended abruptly when an assailant shot Wallace, paralyzing him from the waist down. With Wallace out of the picture Nixon's strategy of wooing southern white voters away from the Democrats got a boost. Nixon also benefited from the disarray of the Democratic Party. Divided over Vietnam and civil rights the Democrats were plagued by tensions between their newer, more liberal constituencies—women, minorities, and young adults—and the old-line officeholders and labor union leaders who had always dominated the party. Recent changes in the party's system of selecting delegates and candidates benefited the newer groups, and they helped to nominate Senator George McGovern of South Dakota, a noted liberal and an out-spoken opponent of the Vietnam War.

McGovern's campaign quickly ran into trouble. On learning that his running mate, Senator Thomas F. Eagleton of Missouri, had undergone electroshock ther-apy for depression some years earlier, McGovern first supported him and then abruptly insisted that he quit the ticket. But McGovern's waffling on the matter made him appear weak and indecisive. Moreover, he was far too liberal for many traditional Democrats, who rejected his ill-defined proposals for welfare reform and his call for unilateral withdrawal from Vietnam.

Nixon's campaign took full advantage of McGovern's weaknesses. Although the president had failed to end the war, his Vietnamization policy had virtually elimi-nated American combat deaths by 1972. Henry Kissinger's premature declaration that "peace is at hand" raised voters' hopes for a negotiated settlement (see Chap-ter 29). Not only did those initiatives rob the Democrats of their greatest appeal—their antiwar stance—but a short-term upturn in the economy further favored the Republicans. Nixon won handily, receiving nearly 61 percent of the popular vote and carrying every state except Massachusetts and the District of Columbia. Yet the president failed to kindle strong loyalty in the electorate. Only 55.7 percent of eli-gible voters bothered to go to the polls, and the Democrats maintained control of both houses of Congress. A far graver threat to Nixon's leadership would emerge shortly after the election, when the news broke that the White House was impli-cated in the 1972 break-in at the Democratic National Committee's headquarters at the Watergate apartment complex in Washington, D.C.

WATERGATE

Though the Watergate scandal, one of the great constitutional crises of the twen-tieth century, began in 1972, its roots lay in the early years of Nixon's first adminis-tration. Obsessed with the antiwar movement, the White House had repeatedly authorized illegal surveillance—opening mail, tapping phones, arranging break-ins—of citizens such as Daniel Ellsberg, a former Defense Department analyst who had become disillusioned with the war. In 1971 Ellsberg had leaked the so-called Penta-gon Papers to the *New York Times.* This secret study, commissioned by Secretary of Defense McNamara in 1967, detailed so many American blunders in Vietnam that, after reading it, McNamara had commented, "You know, they could hang people for what is in there." To discredit Ellsberg, White House underlings broke into his psy-chiatrist's office in an unsuccessful search for damaging personal information. When their break-in was revealed, the court dismissed the government's case against Ellsberg.

In another abuse of presidential power the White House had established a clan-destine intelligence group known as the "plumbers" that was supposed to plug leaks of government information. The plumbers relied on tactics such as using the In-ternal Revenue Service to harass the administration's opponents, who were named on an "enemies list" drawn up by presidential counsel John Dean. One of the plumbers' major targets was the Democratic Party, whose front-running primary candidate in 1972, Senator Edmund Muskie of Maine, became the object of several of their "dirty tricks," including the distribution of phony campaign posters reading "Help Muskie in Busing More Children Now."

These secret and highly questionable activities were financed by massive illegal fund-raising efforts by Nixon's Committee to Re-Elect the President (known as CREEP). To obtain contributions from major corporations, Nixon's fund-raisers had used high-pressure tactics that included implied threats of federal tax audits if companies failed to cooperate. CREEP raised over $20 million, a portion of which was used to finance the plumbers' dirty tricks, including the Watergate break-in.

Early in the morning of June 17, 1972, police arrested five men carrying cameras, wiretapping equipment, and a large amount of cash and charged them with breaking into the Democratic National Committee's headquarters at the Watergate apartment complex in Washington, D.C. Two accomplices were apprehended soon afterward. Three of the men had worked in the White House or for CREEP, and four had CIA connections. Nixon later claimed that White House counsel John Dean had conducted a full investigation of the incident (no such investigation ever took place) and that "no one on the White House staff, no one in this administration, presently employed, was involved in this very bizarre incident."

Subsequent investigations revealed that shortly after the break-in the president had ordered his chief of staff, H. R. Haldeman, to instruct the CIA to tell the FBI not to probe too deeply into connections between the White House and the burglars. When the burglars were convicted in January 1973, John Dean, with Nixon's approval, tried to buy their continued silence with $400,000 in hush money and hints of presidential pardons.

The cover-up of the White House's involvement began to unravel when one of the convicted burglars began to talk. Two tenacious investigative reporters at the *Washington Post*, Carl Bernstein and Bob Woodward, exposed the attempt to hide the truth and traced it back to the White House. Reports of CREEP's "dirty tricks" and illegal fund-raising soon compounded the public's suspicions about the president. In February the Senate voted seventy-seven to zero to establish an investigative committee. Two months later Nixon accepted the resignations of Haldeman, Assistant Secretary of Commerce Jeb Stuart Magruder, and chief domestic advisor John Ehrlichman, all of whom had been implicated in the cover-up. He fired Dean, who had agreed to testify in the case in exchange for immunity from prosecution. In May the Senate Watergate committee began holding nationally televised hearings. In June Magruder testified before the committee, confessing his guilt and implicating former Attorney General John Mitchell, Dean, and others. Dean, in turn, implicated Nixon in the plot. Even more startling testimony from a Nixon aide revealed that Nixon had installed a secret taping system in the Oval Office.

The president steadfastly "stonewalled" the committee's demand that he surrender the tapes, citing executive privilege and national security. But Archibald Cox, a special prosecutor whom Nixon had appointed to investigate the case, successfully petitioned a federal court to order the president to hand the tapes over. Still Nixon refused to comply. After receiving additional federal subpoenas the following spring, Nixon finally released a heavily edited transcript of the tapes, peppered with the words "expletive deleted." Senate Republican leader Hugh Scott called the transcripts "deplorable, disgusting, shabby, immoral." Most suspicious was an eighteen-minute gap in the tape covering a crucial meeting between Nixon, Haldeman, and Ehrlichman on June 20, 1972—three days after the break-in.

The Watergate affair moved into its final phase when on June 30 the House of Representatives voted three articles of impeachment against Richard Nixon: obstruction of justice, abuse of power, and acting to subvert the Constitution. Two days later the Supreme Court ruled unanimously that Nixon could not claim executive privilege as a justification for refusing to turn over additional tapes. Under duress, on August 5 Nixon released the unexpurgated tapes, which contained evidence that he had ordered the cover-up as early as six days after the break-in. Facing certain conviction in a Senate trial, on August 9, 1974, Nixon became the first U.S. president to resign.

The next day Vice President Gerald Ford was sworn in as president. Ford, a former Michigan congressman and house minority leader, had replaced Vice President Spiro Agnew in 1973 after Agnew resigned under indictment for accepting

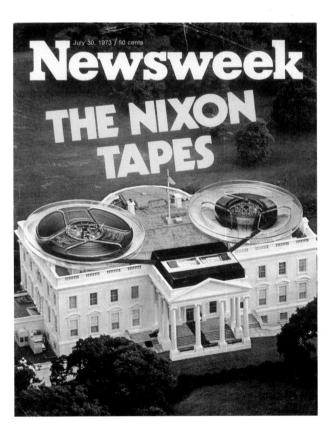

July 30, 1973 / 50 cents

Newsweek

THE NIXON TAPES

Watergate

In July 1973 White House aide Alexander Butterfield testified before the Senate Watergate Committee that all Oval Office telephone communications had been recorded on a secret taping system. Although Nixon tried in vain to suppress the tapes by claiming executive privilege, their eventual release— including statements directly implicating the president in the Watergate cover-up—led to Nixon's resignation in August of 1974.

kickbacks on construction contracts. The transfer of power proceeded smoothly. A month later, however, Ford stunned the nation by granting Nixon a "full, free, and absolute" pardon "for all offenses he had committed or might have committed during his presidency." Ford took that action, he said, to spare the country the agony of rehashing Watergate in a criminal prosecution. Twenty-five members of Nixon's administration went to prison, but he refused to admit guilt for what had happened, conceding only that he had made an error in judgment.

In response to the abuses of the Nixon administration and to contain the power of what the historian Arthur M. Schlesinger Jr. called "the imperial presidency," Congress adopted several reforms. In 1974 a strengthened Freedom of Information Act gave citizens greater access to files federal agencies had amassed on them. The Fair Campaign Practices Act of 1974 limited campaign contributions and provided for stricter accountability and public financing of presidential campaigns. Ironically, because the act allowed an unlimited number of political action committees (PACs) to donate up to $5,000 per candidate, corporations and lobbying groups found they could actually increase their influence by making multiple donations. By the end of the decade close to 3,000 PACs were playing an increasingly pivotal— and some would argue unethical—role in national elections.

Perhaps the most significant legacy of Watergate, however, was the wave of cynicism that swept the country in its wake. Beginning with Lyndon Johnson's "credibility gap" during the Vietnam War, public distrust of government had risen steadily with the disclosure of the secret bombing of Cambodia and the illegal surveillance and harassment of antiwar protesters and other political opponents. The saga of Watergate confirmed what many Americans had long suspected: that politicians were hopelessly corrupt and that the federal government was out of control (see American Voices, "Watergate Diary").

An Economy of Diminished Expectations

Economic difficulties compounded Americans' political disillusionment. Growing international demand for natural resources, particularly oil, coupled with unstable access to foreign oil supplies wreaked havoc with the American economy. At the same time foreign competitors successfully expanded their share of the world market, edging out American-made products. The resulting sharp downturn in the domestic economy marked the end of America's twenty-five-year dominance of the world economy.

ENERGY CRISIS

Until the mid-twentieth century the United States was the world's leading producer and consumer of oil. During World War II the nation had produced two-thirds of the world's oil, but by 1972 its share had fallen to only 22 percent, even though

AMERICAN VOICES

Watergate Diary

ELIZABETH DREW

*J*ournalist Elizabeth Drew kept a diary during the Watergate crisis. This passage, written
on August 5, 1974, shortly after President Nixon was forced to release some exceptionally
damaging tape transcripts, explores the implications of the revelations for Americans' faith in
the presidency.

For those who believed that the President was aware of, and even directed, the cover-up,
it must still be a shock to *read his conversation* about it. . . .

There is an inexplicable difference between the experiences of suspecting a lie and being whacked in the face with the evidence of one. Many Americans had become accustomed to thinking of the President as a liar, and had alternately suspended belief in, scoffed
at, or become enraged at his statements. But I wonder whether the enormity of his lying
has sunk in yet—whether we have, or can, come to terms with the thought that so much
of what he said to us was just noise, words, and that we can no longer begin by accepting
any of it as the truth. This is a total reversal of the way we were brought up to think about
Presidents, a departure from deeply ingrained habits. One's mind resists the thought of
our President as a faithless man, capable of looking at us in utter sincerity from the other
side of the television camera and telling us multiple, explicit, barefaced lies. One is torn
between the idea that people must be able to have some confidence in their leaders and
the idea that in this day of image manipulation a certain skepticism may serve them well.
I do not think there is much comfort to be taken from the fact that eventually Nixon's
lies—like Johnson's—caught up with him. It took a long time, and a great deal of damage
was done meanwhile.

SOURCE: Elizabeth Drew, *Washington Journal: The Events of 1973–1974* (New York: Random House,
1974), pp. 391–92.

domestic production had continued to rise. By the late 1960s the United States was
buying more and more of its oil on the world market to keep up with shrinking
domestic reserves and growing demand.

The imported oil came primarily from the Middle East, where production had
increased a stupendous 1,500 percent in the twenty-five years following World War
II. The rise of nationalism and the corresponding decline of colonialism in the postwar era had encouraged the Persian Gulf nations to wrest control from the European
and American oil companies that once dominated petroleum exploration and production in that region. In 1960, joining with other oil-producing developing countries, they had formed the Organization of Petroleum Exporting Countries (OPEC).
Just five of the founding countries—the Middle Eastern states of Saudi Arabia,

Kuwait, Iran, and Iraq, plus Venezuela—were the source of more than 80 percent of the world's crude oil exports. During the early 1970s when world demand climbed and oil reserves fell, they took advantage of market forces to maximize their profits. Between 1973 and 1975 OPEC raised the price of a barrel of oil from $3 to $12. By the end of the decade the price had peaked at $34 a barrel, setting off a round of furious inflation in the oil-dependent United States.

OPEC members also found that oil could be used as a weapon in global politics. In 1973 OPEC instituted an oil embargo against the United States, Western Europe, and Japan in retaliation for their aid to Israel during the Yom Kippur War, which had begun when Egypt and Syria invaded Israel. The embargo, which lasted until 1974, forced Americans to curtail their driving or spend long hours in line at the pumps; in a matter of months, gas prices climbed 40 percent. Since the U.S. automobile industry had little to offer except "gas-guzzlers" built to run on cheap fuel, Americans turned to cheaper, more fuel-efficient foreign cars manufactured in Japan and West Germany. Soon the auto industry was in a slump, weakening the American economy.

No Gas

During the energy crisis of 1973 and 1974 American motorists faced widespread gasoline shortages for the first time since World War II. Although gas was not rationed, gas stations were closed on Sundays, air travel was cut by 10 percent, and a national speed limit of 55 miles per hour was imposed.

(Tony Korody/Sygma)

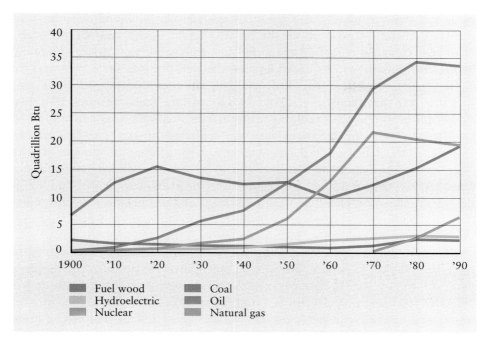

FIGURE 30.1
U.S. Energy Consumption, 1900–1990

Coal was the nation's primary source of energy until the 1950s, when oil and natural gas became the dominant fuels. The use of nuclear and hydroelectric power also rose substantially in the postwar era. Since the late 1970s fuel-efficient automobiles and conservation measures have reduced total energy use.

The energy crisis was an enormous shock to the American psyche. Suddenly Americans felt like hostages to economic forces that were beyond their control. As OPEC's leaders pushed prices higher and higher, they seemed to be able to determine whether Western economies would grow or stagnate. Despite an extensive public conservation campaign and a second gas shortage in 1979 caused by the Iranian revolution, Americans could not wean themselves from foreign oil. In fact, they used even more foreign oil after the energy crisis than they had before—a testimony to the enormous thirst of modern industrial and consumer societies for petroleum (see Figure 30.1).

ECONOMIC WOES

While the energy crisis dealt a swift blow to the U.S. economy, other developments had equally damaging results. The high cost of the Vietnam War and the Great Society had contributed to a steadily growing federal deficit and spiraling inflation. A

business downturn in 1970 had led to rising unemployment and declining productivity. In the industrial sector the reviving economies of West Germany and
Japan over time had reduced demand for American goods worldwide. As a result,
in 1971 the dollar fell to its lowest level on the world market since 1949, and the
United States posted its first trade deficit in almost a century.

That year Nixon took several bold steps to turn the economy around. To stem
the decline in currency and trade, he suspended the Bretton Woods system that had
been set up at the United Nations monetary conference in 1944 (see Chapter 28).
Once again, the dollar would fluctuate in relation to the price of an ounce of gold.
The change, which effectively devalued the dollar in hopes of encouraging foreign
trade, represented a frank acknowledgment that America's currency was no longer
the world's strongest. Nixon also instituted wage and price controls to curb inflation, and to boost the sluggish economy he offered a "full employment" budget for
1972, including $11 billion in deficit spending.

Though these measures brought a temporary improvement in the economy,
the general decline persisted. Overall economic growth, as measured by the gross
national product (GNP), had averaged 4.1 percent per year in the 1960s; in the
1970s it dropped to only 2.9 percent, contributing to a noticeable decline in most
Americans' standard of living. At the same time galloping inflation forced consumer
prices upward. Housing prices, in particular, rose rapidly: the average cost of a
single-family home more than doubled in the 1970s, making home ownership
inaccessible to a growing segment of the working and middle classes.

Young adults faced a constricted job market in the late 1970s, as a record
number of baby boomers competed for a limited number of jobs. Unemployment peaked at around 9 percent in 1975 and hovered at 6 to 7 percent in the
late 1970s. A devastating combination of inflation and unemployment—dubbed
stagflation—bedeviled presidential administrations from Nixon to Reagan,
whose remedies (such as deficit spending and tax reduction) failed to eradicate
the double scourge.

American economic woes were most acute in the industrial sector, which entered a prolonged period of decline, or deindustrialization. Investors who had formerly bought stock in basic U.S. industries began to speculate on the stock market
or put their money into mergers or foreign companies. Many U.S. firms relocated
overseas, partly to take advantage of cheaper labor and production costs. By the end
of the 1970s the hundred largest multinational corporations and banks were earning more than a third of their overall profits abroad.

The most dramatic consequences of deindustrialization occurred in the older
industrial regions of the Northeast and Midwest, which came to be known as the
Rust Belt. There the dominant images of American industry in the mid-twentieth
century—huge factories such as Ford's River Rouge outside Detroit and the General Electric plant in Lynn, Massachusetts—were fast becoming relics. When a
community's major employer closed down and left town, the devastating effect
rippled through communities in America's heartland. Many workers moved to the

cities of the Sun Belt, continuing the dramatic growth in that region that had begun after World War II.

Deindustrialization and the changing economic conditions that provoked it posed a critical problem for the labor movement. In the heyday of labor during the 1940s and 1950s American managers had often cooperated with unions; with profits high there was room for accommodation. But as foreign competition cut into corporate profits in the 1970s, industry became less willing to bargain, and the labor movement's power declined. In the 1970s union membership dropped from 28 to 23 percent of the American workforce. Facing conflict with labor, some employers simply moved their operations abroad, where they found a cheaper, more compliant workforce. In a competitive global environment, labor's prospects seemed dim.

Reform and Reaction in the 1970s

The nation's economic problems and growing cynicism about government led to deep public anxiety and resentment. Many Americans turned inward to private satisfactions, prompting the journalist Tom Wolfe to label the 1970s the "Me Decade." Yet such a label hardly does justice to a decade in which environmentalism, feminism, lesbian and gay rights, and other social movements blossomed. Furthermore, such characterizations neglect the growing social conservatism that was in part a response to such movements. In fact, the confluence of these trends produced a pattern of shifting crosscurrents that made the 1970s a complex transitional decade.

THE NEW ACTIVISM: ENVIRONMENTAL AND CONSUMER MOVEMENTS

After 1970 many baby boomers left the counterculture behind and settled down to pursue careers and material goods. But these young adults sought personal fulfillment as well. In a quest for physical well-being, millions of Americans began jogging, riding bicycles, and working out at the gym. The fitness craze coincided with a heightened environmental awareness that spurred the demand for pesticide-free foods and vegetarian cookbooks. For spiritual support some young people embraced the self-help techniques of the human-potential, or New Age, movement; others turned to religious cults such as the Hare Krishna, the Church of Scientology, and the Unification Church of Reverend Sun Myung Moon.

A few baby boomers continued to pursue the unfinished social and political agendas of the 1960s. Moving into law, education, social work, medicine, and other fields, these former radicals continued their activism on a grassroots level. Some joined the left wing of the Democratic Party; others helped to establish community-based organizations, including health clinics, food co-ops, and day-care centers. On the local level, at least, the progressive spirit of the 1960s lived on.

Many of these 1960s-style activists helped invigorate the environmental movement, which had been reenergized by the publication in 1962 of Rachel Carson's *Silent Spring,* a powerful analysis of the impact of pesticides on the food chain. Activists brought their radical political sensibilities to the environmental movement, using sit-ins and other protest tactics developed in the civil rights and antiwar movements to mobilize mass support and infuse the movement with new life. For example, they construed the search for alternative technologies (especially solar power) as a political statement against a corporate structure that was increasingly inhospitable to human-scale technology—and to humans, as well.

Other issues that galvanized public opinion included the environmental impact of industrial projects such as the Alaska pipeline and the harmful effects of chlorofluorocarbons and increased carbon dioxide levels on the earth's atmosphere. In January 1969 a huge oil spill off the coast of Santa Barbara, California, provoked an outcry, as did the discovery in 1978 that a housing development outside Niagara Falls, New York, had been built on a toxic waste site. The abnormally high rates of illness and birth defects recorded in this Love Canal neighborhood deepened public awareness of the culpability of business in generating environmental hazards.

Nuclear energy became the subject of citizen action in the 1970s, when rising prices and oil shortages led to the expansion of nuclear power, pitting environmental concerns against the need for alternative energy sources. By January 1974 forty-two nuclear power plants were in operation, and over a hundred more were planned. Suddenly the proliferation of nuclear power plants and reactors, which had gone largely unchallenged in the 1950s and 1960s, raised public concerns about safety. Community activists protested plans for new reactors, citing inadequate evacuation plans and the unresolved problem of the disposal of radioactive waste. Their fears seemed to be confirmed in March 1979 when a nuclear plant at Three Mile Island near Harrisburg, Pennsylvania, came critically close to a meltdown of its central core reactor. A prompt shutdown of the plant brought the problem under control before radioactive material seeped into the environment, but as a member of the panel that investigated the accident admitted, "We were damn lucky." Ultimately, Three Mile Island caused Americans to rethink the question of whether nuclear power could be a viable solution to the nation's energy needs. Grassroots activism, combined with public fear of the potential dangers of nuclear energy, convinced many utility companies to abandon nuclear power, despite its short-term economic advantages.

Americans' concerns about nuclear power, chemical contamination, pesticides, and other environmental issues helped to turn environmentalism into a mass movement. On the first Earth Day, April 22, 1970, 20 million citizens gathered in communities across the country to show their support for the endangered planet. Their efforts helped to create bipartisan support for a spate of new federal legislation. In 1969 Congress passed the National Environmental Policy Act, which required the developers of public projects to file an environmental impact statement. The next year Nixon established the Environmental Protection Agency (EPA) and signed the Clean Air Act, which toughened standards for auto emissions in order to reduce smog and air pollution. Two years later Congress banned the use of the pesticide DDT. And in 1973 the Endangered Species Act expanded the protection provided by the Endangered Animals Act of 1964, granting species such as snail darters and spotted owls protected status. Thus environmental protection joined social welfare, defense, and national security as targets of federal intervention.

The environmental movement did not go uncontested. The EPA-mandated fuel-economy standards for cars provoked criticism for threatening the health of the auto industry as it struggled to keep up with foreign competitors. Corporations resented environmental regulations, but so did many of their workers, who believed that tightened standards threatened their jobs and privileged nature over human beings. "IF YOU'RE HUNGRY AND OUT OF WORK, EAT AN ENVIRONMENTALIST" read one labor union's bumper sticker. In a time of rising unemployment and deindustrialization, activists clashed head-on with proponents of economic development, full employment, and global competitiveness.

The rise of environmentalism was paralleled by a growing movement to eliminate harmful consumer products and curb dangerous practices by American corporations. After decades of inertia, in the 1960s the consumer protection movement, which had originated in the Progressive Era (see Chapter 20), reemerged under the leadership of Ralph Nader, a young lawyer whose book *Unsafe at Any Speed* (1965) attacked General Motors for putting style ahead of safety and fuel economy in its engineering. His Public Interest Research Group, a national network of consumer groups that focused on issues ranging from product safety to consumer fraud and environmental pollution, became the model for dozens of other groups that emerged in the 1970s and afterward to combat the health hazards of smoking, unethical insurance and credit practices, and other consumer problems. With the establishment of the federal Consumer Products Safety Commission in 1972 Congress acknowledged the growing need for consumer protection.

CHALLENGES TO TRADITION: THE WOMEN'S MOVEMENT AND GAY RIGHTS ACTIVISM

Feminism proved the most enduring movement to emerge from the 1960s. In the next decade the women's movement grew more sophisticated, generating an array of services and organizations, from rape crisis centers and battered women's shelters to feminist health collectives and women's bookstores. In 1972 Gloria Steinem and other journalists founded *Ms.* magazine, the first consumer magazine aimed at a feminist audience. Formerly all-male bastions, such as Yale, Princeton, and the U.S. Military Academy, admitted women undergraduates for the first time, while the proportion of women attending graduate and professional schools rose markedly. Several new national women's organizations emerged, and established groups such as the National Organization for Women (NOW) continued to grow. In 1977, 20,000

The Expanding Women's Movement

By the late 1970s the feminist movement had broadened its base, attracting women of all ages and backgrounds, such as this delegate to the 1977 National Women's Conference in Houston, Texas. As the slogan on her hat implies, though, the movement was already on the defensive against right-wing claims that it undermined traditional values. (Bettye Lane)

women went to Houston for the first National Women's Conference. Their "National Plan of Action" represented a hard-won consensus on topics ranging from violence against women to homemakers' rights, the needs of older women, and, most controversially, abortion and other reproductive issues.

Women were also increasingly visible in politics and public life. The National Women's Political Caucus, founded in 1971, actively promoted the election of women to public office. Their success stories included Shirley Chisholm, Patricia Schroeder, and Geraldine Ferraro, all of whom served in Congress, and Ella Grasso, who won election as Connecticut's governor in 1974.

Women's political mobilization produced significant legislative and administrative gains. With the passage of Title IX of the Educational Amendments Act of 1972, which broadened the 1964 Civil Rights Act to include educational institutions, Congress prohibited colleges and universities that received federal funds from discriminating on the basis of sex, a change that particularly benefited women athletes. Another federal initiative was *affirmative action.* Originally instituted in 1966 under Lyndon Johnson's administration to redress a history of discrimination against nonwhites in employment and education, affirmative action procedures—hiring and enrollment goals and recruitment training programs—were extended to women the following year and gave many women, especially educated white ones, more opportunities for educational and career advancement. In 1972 Congress authorized child-care deductions for working parents; in 1974 it passed the Equal Credit Opportunity Act, which significantly improved women's access to credit.

The Supreme Court also significantly advanced women's rights. In several rulings the Court gave women more control over their reproductive lives by reading a right of privacy into the Ninth and Fourteenth Amendments' concept of personal liberty. In 1965 *Griswold v. Connecticut* had overturned state laws against the sale of contraceptive devices to married adults, an option that was later extended to single persons. In 1973, in *Roe v. Wade,* the Court struck down Texas and Georgia statutes that allowed an abortion only if the mother's life was in danger. According to this seven-to-two decision, states could no longer outlaw abortions performed during the first trimester of pregnancy.

Roe v. Wade nationalized the liberalization of state abortion laws, which had begun in New York in 1970, but also fueled the development of a powerful anti-abortion movement. Charging that the rights of a fetus took precedence over a woman's right to decide whether or not to terminate a pregnancy, abortion opponents worked to circumvent or overturn *Roe v. Wade*. In 1976 they convinced Congress to deny Medicaid funds for abortions for poor women, one of the opening rounds in a protracted legislative and judicial campaign to chip away at the *Roe* decision.

Another battlefront for the women's movement was the proposed Equal Rights Amendment (ERA) to the Constitution. The ERA, first introduced in Congress in 1923 by the National Woman's Party, stated in its entirety, "Equality of rights under the law shall not be denied or abridged by the United States or any State on the basis of sex." In 1970 feminists revived the amendment, which passed the House but died in the Senate. In the next session it passed both houses and was submitted to the states for ratification. But though thirty-four states quickly passed the ERA between 1972 and 1974, growing opposition by conservative groups slowed its momentum (see Map 30.1). By 1982 the amendment was dead.

The fate of the ERA and the battle over abortion rights showed that by the mid-1970s the women's movement was beginning to weaken. Increasingly its members were divided over issues of race, class, age, and sexual orientation. For many non-white and working-class women, the feminist movement seemed to stand for the interests of self-seeking white career women. At the same time, the women's movement faced growing social conservatism among Americans in general. Although 63 percent of women polled in 1975 said they favored "efforts to strengthen and change women's status in society," a growing minority of both sexes expressed concern over what seemed to be revolutionary changes in women's traditional roles.

Lawyer Phyllis Schlafly, long active in conservative causes, led the antifeminist backlash. Despite the active career she had pursued while raising five children,

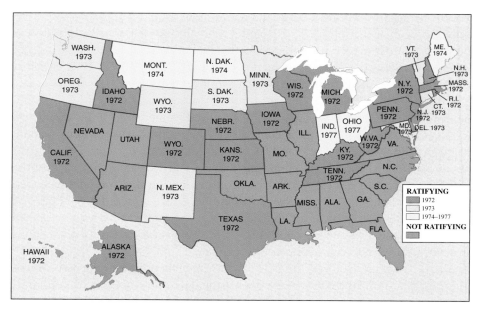

MAP 30.1
States Ratifying the Equal Rights Amendment

The Equal Rights Amendment quickly won support in 1972 and 1973 but then stalled. ERAmerica, a coalition of women's groups formed in 1976, lobbied extensively, particularly in Florida, North Carolina, and Illinois, but failed to sway the conservative legislatures in those states. After Indiana ratified in 1977, the amendment still lacked three votes toward the three-fourths majority needed to pass. Efforts to revive the ERA in the 1980s were unsuccessful.

Schlafly advocated traditional roles for women. Schlafly's STOP ERA organization claimed that the amendment would create a "unisex society" in which women could be drafted, homosexuals could be married, and separate toilets for men and women would be prohibited. (Feminists argued that those charges were groundless.) Alarmed, conservative women in grassroots networks mobilized, showing up at statehouses with home-baked bread and apple pies, symbols of their traditional domestic role. Their message, that women would lose more than they would gain if the ERA passed, resonated with many men and women, especially those who were troubled by the rapid pace of social change.

Although the feminist movement was on the defensive by the mid-1970s, women's lives showed no signs of returning to the patterns of the 1950s. Because of increasing economic pressures, the proportion of women in the paid workforce continued to rise, from 44 percent in 1970 to 51 percent in 1980. In their private lives, easier access to birth control permitted married and unmarried women to enjoy greater sexual freedom (although they also became more vulnerable to male sexual pressure). With a growing number of career options available to them, many women, particularly educated white women, stayed single or delayed marriage and child rearing. The birth rate continued its postwar decline, reaching an all-time low in the mid-1970s. At the same time, the divorce rate rose 82 percent in the 1970s, as more men and women elected to leave unhappy marriages.

Although such changes brought increased autonomy for many women, they also caused new hardships, particularly in poor and working-class families. Divorce left many women with low-paying jobs and inadequate child care. Meanwhile, more tolerant attitudes toward premarital sex, along with other social and economic factors, had contributed to rising teenage pregnancy rates. The rise in divorce and adolescent pregnancy produced a sharp increase in the number of female-headed families, contributing to the "feminization" of poverty. By 1980 women accounted for 66 percent of adults who lived below the poverty line, a development that fueled a growing wave of social reaction.

Another major focus of social activism, the gay liberation movement, achieved heightened visibility in the 1970s. Thousands of gay men and lesbians "came out," publicly proclaiming their sexual orientation (see American Voices, "A Gay Athlete Comes Out"). In New York's Greenwich Village, San Francisco's Castro, and other urban enclaves, growing gay communities gave rise to hundreds of new gay and lesbian clubs, churches, businesses, and political organizations. In 1973 the National Gay Task Force launched a campaign to include gay men and lesbians as a protected group under laws covering employment and housing rights. Such efforts were most successful on the local level; during the 1970s Detroit, Boston, Los Angeles, Miami, San Francisco, and other cities passed laws barring discrimination on the basis of sexual preference.

Like abortion and the ERA, gay rights came under attack from conservatives, who believed that granting gay lifestyles legal protection would encourage immoral behavior. When the Miami city council passed a measure banning discrimination against gay men and lesbians in 1977, the singer Anita Bryant led a campaign to repeal the law by popular referendum. Later that year voters overturned the measure by a two-to-one majority, prompting similar antigay campaigns around the country.

RACIAL MINORITIES

Although the civil rights movement was in disarray by the late 1960s, continued minority-group protests brought social and economic gains in the next decade. Native Americans realized some of the most significant changes. In 1971 the Alaska Native Land Claims Act restored 40 million acres to Eskimos, Aleuts, and other native peoples, along with $960 million in compensation. Most important, the federal government abandoned the tribal termination program of the 1950s (see Chapter 28). Under the Indian Self-Determination Act of 1974, Congress restored the tribes' right to govern themselves and gave them authority over federal programs on their reservations (see Map 30.2).

AMERICAN VOICES

A Gay Athlete Comes Out

DAVID KOPAY

F or ten years David Kopay played professional football for the San Francisco Forty-Niners, Detroit Lions, Washington Redskins, New Orleans Saints, and Green Bay Packers. In 1975, at the end of his playing career, Kopay publicly acknowledged his homosexuality, creating a national furor in the sports world.

I always knew I was a bit different, but I kept it kind of quiet. I didn't think of myself as queer. In fact I couldn't even say that word for years and years. . . .

By the time I spoke out, I really had nothing left to lose. It felt like I didn't have a choice: I just had to do it. Then one morning in 1975 I saw an article in the *Washington Star* about homosexual athletes and why they had everything to lose. There was an interview in the article with Jerry Smith [Washington Redskins tight end who died of AIDS in 1986]. . . . I was at a time and place in my own coming out where I felt that if I was going to survive, I had to speak out. It was do that or maybe go crazy.

So I called Lynn Rosellini. . . . Everybody said there was going to be a terrible backlash against me when Lynn's article was published. But there wasn't a backlash against me personally: there was a backlash against all the television shows and radio stations that I went on. And the newspapers. The *Washington Star* said they had never received more negative mail for anything they'd ever done—hundreds of horrible hate letters. . . . The letters said things like, "It doesn't belong on the sports page as a model for our young boys and girls." "How could the *Washington Star* run an article like this?" I got letters that said, "I hope you never get a coaching job. Yours in Christ. Love. . . ." Just horrible things.

I never did get a coaching job. . . . I had to make a spot for myself somehow, so I wound up working with Perry Young for a year on my book, *The Dave Kopay Story.*

I think we knew we were doing something good. . . .

A lot of kids still write. They say that the book meant so much to them. They remember that it changed them a lot or made a difference.

SOURCE: Eric Marcus, *Making History* (New York: Harper Collins, 1992), pp. 275–77.

The busing of children to achieve school desegregation proved the most disruptive social issue of the 1970s. Progress in achieving the desegregation mandated by *Brown v. Board of Education of Topeka* had been slow. In the 1970s both the courts and the Justice Department pushed for more action, not just in the South but in other parts of the country. In *Milliken v. Bradley* (1974) the Supreme Court ordered cities with deeply ingrained patterns of residential segregation to use busing to integrate their classrooms. The decision sparked intense and sometimes violent opposition. In Boston in 1974 and 1975 the strongly Irish-Catholic working-class neighborhood of South Boston responded to the arrival of African American students from Roxbury with mob action reminiscent of that in Little Rock in 1957. Threatened by court-ordered busing, many white parents transferred their children to private schools or moved to the suburbs. The resulting "white flight" exacerbated the racial imbalance busing was supposed to redress. Some black parents also opposed busing, calling instead for better schools in predominantly black neighborhoods. By the late 1970s federal courts had begun to back away from their insistence on busing to achieve racial balance.

Almost as divisive as busing was the issue of affirmative action procedures, which had expanded opportunities for blacks and Latinos. The number of African American students enrolled in colleges and universities doubled between 1970 and 1977 to 1.1 million, or 9.3 percent of the total student enrollment. A small but growing number of African Americans moved into white-collar professions in corporations and universities. Others found new opportunities in civil service occupations such as law enforcement or entered apprenticeships in the skilled construction trades. Latinos experienced similar gains in education and employment. On the whole, however, both groups enjoyed only marginal economic improvement, since

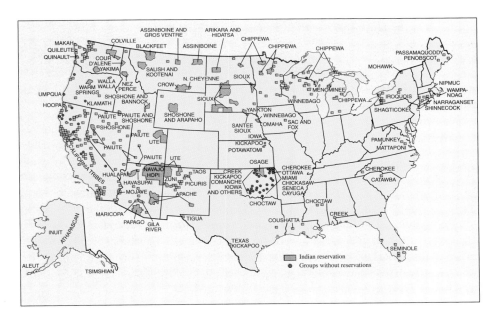

M A P 30.2
American Indian Reservations

Although Native Americans have been able to preserve small enclaves in the northeastern states, most Indian reservations are in the West. Beginning in the 1970s various nations filed land claims against federal and state governments.

An Antibusing Confrontation in Boston

Tensions over court-ordered busing ran high in Boston in 1976. When a black lawyer tried to
cross the city hall plaza during an antibusing demonstration, he became a victim of Boston's
climate of racial hatred and violence. This Pulitzer Prize–winning photograph by Stanley
Forman for the Boston *Herald American* shows a protester trying to impale the man with a
flagstaff. (Stanley Forman)

poor and working-class nonwhites bore the brunt of job loss and unemployment
in the 1970s.

Nevertheless, many whites, who were also feeling the economic pinch, came to re-
sent affirmative action programs as an infringement of their rights. White men especially complained of "reverse discrimination" against them. In 1978 Allan Bakke, a
white man, sued the University of California Medical School at Davis for rejecting him
in favor of less qualified minority candidates. The Supreme Court ruling in *Bakke v.
University of California* was inconclusive. Though it branded the medical school's strict
quota system illegal and ordered Bakke admitted, it stated that racial factors could be
considered in hiring and admission decisions, thus upholding the principle of affirmative action. But the *Bakke* decision was a setback for proponents of affirmative action, and it prepared the way for subsequent efforts to eliminate those programs.

Though activists who supported racial minorities, women, gays, consumers,
and the environment had distinct agendas, they also had much in common. They
were part of "a rights revolution"—a wide-ranging movement in the 1960s and
1970s to bring issues of social justice and welfare to the forefront of public policy.
Influenced by the Great Society's liberalism, they invariably turned to the federal
government for protection of individual rights and—in the case of environmentalists—the world's natural resources. The activists of this period made substantial

progress in widening the notion of the federal government's responsibilities, but by the end of the 1970s their movements faced growing opposition.

THE POLITICS OF RESENTMENT

Together with the rapidly growing antiabortion movement, the often vociferous public opposition to busing, affirmative action, gay rights ordinances, and the Equal Rights Amendment constituted a broad backlash against the social changes of the previous decade. Many Americans believed that their interests had been slighted by the rights revolution and resented a federal government that protected women who sought abortions or minorities who benefited from affirmative action. The economic changes of the 1970s, which left many working- and middle-class Americans with lower disposable incomes, rising prices, and higher taxes, further fueled what the conservative writer Alan Crawford has termed the "politics of resentment"—a grassroots revolt against "special-interest groups" (women, minorities, gays, and so on) and growing expenditures on social welfare. Special groups and programs, conservatives believed, robbed other Americans of educational and employment opportunities and saddled the working and middle classes with an extra financial burden.

One manifestation of the politics of resentment was a wave of local taxpayers' revolts. In 1978 California voters passed Proposition 13, a measure that reduced property taxes and eventually undercut local governments' ability to maintain schools and other essential services. Promising tax relief to middle-class homeowners and reduced funding for busing and other programs to benefit the poor— who were invariably viewed as nonwhite—Proposition 13 became the model for similar tax measures around the country in the late 1970s and 1980s.

The rising popularity of evangelical religion also fueled the conservative resurgence of the 1970s. Fundamentalist groups that fostered a "born-again" experience had been growing steadily since World War II, under the leadership of charismatic preachers such as Billy Graham. According to a Gallup poll conducted in 1976, some 50 million Americans—about a quarter of the population—were affiliated with evangelical movements. These groups set up their own school systems and newspapers. Through broadcasting networks like the Christian Broadcasting Network, founded by the Virginia preacher Pat Robertson, a new breed of televangelists such as Jerry Falwell built vast and influential electronic ministries.

Many of these evangelicals spoke out on a broad range of issues, denouncing abortion, busing, sex education, pornography, feminism, and gay rights and bringing their religious values to a wider public. In 1979 Jerry Falwell founded the Moral Majority, a political pressure group that promoted Christian "family values"—traditional gender roles, heterosexuality, family cohesion—and staunch anticommunism. The extensive media and fund-raising networks of the Christian right contributed to the organizational base for a larger conservative movement known as the New Right.

The New Right's constituency was complex. Conservatives of the early cold-war era had focused on resisting creeping socialism at home and abroad and were often identified with corporate business interests. In the 1970s they were joined not only by evangelical Christian groups but by "neoconservatives," intellectuals such as sociologist Nathan Glazier and Norman Podhoretz, editor of *Commentary* magazine, who had been associated with radical or liberal agendas in the past and now recanted their former political views vehemently. Articulate in their criticisms of affirmative action, the welfare state, and changing gender and sexual values, they helped to give conservative values a heightened respectability and reinforced much of the "politics of resentment." The New Right's diverse constituents shared a hostility toward a powerful federal government and a fear of declining social morality. Backed by wealthy corporate interests and using sophisticated computerized mass-mailing campaigns, a variety of New Right political groups mobilized thousands of followers and millions of dollars to support conservative candidates and causes.

Politics in the Wake of Watergate

It is not surprising that in the wake of Watergate many citizens had become cynical about the federal government and about politicians in general. "Don't vote. It only encourages them" read one bumper sticker during the 1976 campaign. Nixon's successors, Gerald Ford and Jimmy Carter, plagued by foreign-policy crises and continued economic woes, did little to restore public confidence. In the 1980 elections, voter apathy persisted, but Ronald Reagan's lopsided presidential victory signified a hope that the charismatic former actor could restore America's traditional values and its economic and international power.

FORD'S CARETAKER PRESIDENCY

During the two years Gerald Ford held the nation's highest office, he failed to establish his legitimacy as president. Ford's pardon of Nixon hurt his credibility as a political leader, but an even bigger problem was his handling of the economy, which was reeling from the inflation set in motion by the Vietnam War, rising oil prices, and the growing trade deficit. In 1974 the inflation rate soared to almost 12 percent, and in the following year the economy entered its deepest downturn since the Great Depression. Though many of the nation's economic problems were beyond the president's control, Ford's failure to take more vigorous action made him appear timid and powerless.

In foreign policy Ford was equally lacking in leadership. He maintained Nixon's détente initiatives by asking Henry Kissinger to stay on as secretary of state. Though Ford met with Soviet leaders hoping to hammer out the details of a SALT II (Strategic Arms Limitation Treaty) agreement, he made little progress. Ford and Kissinger also continued Nixon's policy of increasing support for the shah of Iran, ignoring the bitter opposition and anti-Western sentiment that the shah's policy of rapid modernization was provoking among the growing Muslim fundamentalist population in Iran.

JIMMY CARTER: THE OUTSIDER AS PRESIDENT

The 1976 presidential campaign was one of the blandest in years. President Ford chose as his running mate the conservative Senator Robert J. Dole of Kansas. The Democratic choice, James E. (Jimmy) Carter, governor of Georgia, shared the ticket with Senator Walter F. Mondale of Minnesota, who had ties to the traditional Democratic constituencies of labor, liberals, blacks, and big-city machines. Avoiding issues and controversy, Carter played up his role as a Washington outsider, pledging to restore morality to government. "I will never lie to you," he earnestly told voters. Carter won the election with 50 percent of the popular vote to Ford's 48 percent.

Despite his efforts to overcome the post-Watergate climate of skepticism and apathy, Carter never became an effective leader. His outsider strategy distanced him from traditional sources of power, and he did little to heal the breach. Shying away from established Democratic leaders, Carter turned to advisors and friends who had worked with him in Georgia, none of whom had national experience. When his budget director, Bert Lance, was questioned about financial irregularities at the Atlanta bank he had headed, Carter's campaign pledge to restore integrity and morality to the government rang hollow.

Inflation was Carter's major domestic challenge. When he took office, the nation was still recovering from the severe recession of 1975 and 1976. Carter embarked on a fiscal policy that eroded both business and consumer confidence. To counter inflation the Federal Reserve Board raised interest rates repeatedly; in 1980 they topped 20 percent, a historic high. A deep recession finally broke the inflationary spiral in 1982, a year after Carter left office.

The Carter administration expanded the federal bureaucracy in some cases and limited its reach in others. Carter enlarged the cabinet by creating the Departments of Energy and Education and approved new environmental protection measures, such as the $1.6 billion "Superfund" to clean up chemical pollution sites, as well as new park and forest lands in Alaska. But he continued President Nixon's efforts to reduce the scope of federal activities by reforming the civil service and deregulating the airline, trucking, and railroad industries. With deregulation prices often dropped, but the resulting cutthroat competition drove many firms out of business and encouraged corporate consolidation. Carter also failed in his effort to decontrol oil and natural gas prices as a spur to domestic production and conservation.

Carter's attempt to provide leadership during the energy crisis also faltered. He called energy-conservation efforts "the moral equivalent of war," but the media reduced the phrase to "MEOW." In early 1979 a revolution in Iran again raised oil prices, and gas lines again reminded Americans of their dependence on foreign oil.

That summer Carter's approval rating dropped to 26 percent—lower than Richard Nixon's during the worst part of the Watergate scandal.

In foreign affairs President Carter made human rights the centerpiece of his policy. He criticized the suppression of dissent in the Soviet Union—especially as it affected the right of Jewish citizens to emigrate—and withdrew economic and military aid from Argentina, Uruguay, Ethiopia, and other countries that violated human rights. Carter also established the Office of Human Rights in the State Department. Unable to change the internal policies of long-time U.S. allies who were serious violators of human rights, such as the Philippines, South Korea, and South Africa, he did manage to raise public awareness of the human-rights issue, making it one future administrations would have to address.

In Latin America Carter's most important contribution was the resolution of the lingering dispute over control of the Panama Canal. In a treaty signed on September 7, 1977, the United States agreed to turn over control of the canal to Panama on December 31, 1999. In return, the United States retained the right to send its ships through the canal in case of war, even though the canal itself would be declared neutral territory. Despite a conservative outcry that the United States was giving away more than it got, the Senate narrowly approved the treaty.

Though Carter had campaigned to free the United States from its "inordinate fear of Communism," relations with the Soviet Union soon became tense, largely because of problems surrounding arms-limitation talks. Eventually the Soviet leader Leonid Brezhnev signed SALT II (1979), but hopes for Senate ratification of the treaty collapsed when the Soviet Union invaded Afghanistan that December. In retaliation for this aggression, which Carter viewed as a threat to Middle Eastern oil supplies, the United States curtailed grain sales to the USSR and boycotted the 1980 summer Olympics in Moscow. (The Soviets returned the gesture by boycotting the 1984 summer games in Los Angeles.) When Carter left office in 1981, relations with the Soviet Union were worse than they had been when he took over.

President Carter achieved both his most stunning success and his greatest failure in the Middle East. Relations between Egypt and Israel had remained tense since the 1973 Yom Kippur War. In 1978 Carter helped to break the diplomatic stalemate by inviting Israel's prime minister Menachem Begin and Egyptian president Anwar al-Sadat to Camp David, the presidential retreat in Maryland. Two weeks of discussions and Carter's promise of additional foreign aid to Egypt persuaded Sadat and Begin to adopt a "framework for peace." The framework included Egypt's recognition of Israel's right to exist and Israel's return of the Sinai Peninsula, which it had occupied since 1967. Transfer of the territory to Egypt took place from 1979 to 1982.

Dramatically less successful was U.S. foreign policy toward Iran. Ever since the CIA had helped to install Muhammad Reza Pahlavi on the throne in 1953, the United States had counted Iran as a faithful ally in the troubled Middle East. Overlooking the repressive tactics of Iran's CIA-trained secret police, SAVAK, Carter followed in the footsteps of previous cold-war policymakers for whom access to Iranian

American Hostages in Iran

Images of blindfolded, hand-cuffed American hostages seized by Iranian militants at the American embassy in Teheran in November 1979 shocked the nation and created a foreign-policy crisis that eventually cost Jimmy Carter the presidency.
(Mingam/Liaison)

oil reserves and the shah's consistently anticommunist stance outweighed all other considerations.

Early in 1979, however, the shah's government was overthrown and driven into exile by a revolution led by fundamentalist Muslim leader Ayatollah Ruhollah Khomeini. In late October 1979 the Carter administration admitted the deposed shah, who was suffering from incurable cancer, to the United States for medical treatment. Though Iran's new leaders had warned that such an action would provoke retaliation, Henry Kissinger and other foreign-policy leaders had argued that the United States should assist the shah, both for humanitarian reasons and in return for his years of support for American policy. In response, on November 4, 1979, fundamentalist Muslim students under Khomeini's direction seized the U.S. embassy in Teheran, taking Americans there hostage in a flagrant violation of the principle of diplomatic immunity. The hostage takers demanded that the shah be returned to Iran for trial and punishment, but the United States refused. Instead, President Carter suspended arms sales to Iran, froze Iranian assets in American banks, and threatened to deport Iranian students in the United States.

For the next fourteen months the Iranian hostage crisis paralyzed Jimmy Carter's presidency. Night after night, humiliating pictures of blindfolded hostages appeared on television newscasts. The extensive media coverage, and Carter's insistence that the safe return of the fifty-two hostages was his top priority, enhanced the value of the hostages to their captors. An attempt to mount a military rescue of the hostages failed miserably in April 1980, six months into the crisis, because of helicopter equipment failures in the desert. The abortive rescue mission reinforced the public's view of Carter as a bumbling and ineffective executive.

THE REAGAN REVOLUTION

With Carter embroiled in the hostage crisis, the Republicans gained momentum by nominating former California governor Ronald Reagan. A movie actor in the late 1930s, the 1940s, and the early 1950s, Reagan had served as president of the Screen Actors Guild and had been active in the postwar anticommunist crusade in Hollywood. He had endorsed Barry Goldwater in 1964 and had begun his own political career shortly after, serving as governor of California from 1967 to 1975. After losing a bid for the Republican nomination in 1976, Reagan secured it easily in 1980 and chose former CIA director George Bush as his running mate.

In the final months of the campaign, Carter took on an embattled and defensive tone, while Reagan remained upbeat and decisive. The Republicans benefited from superior financial resources, which allowed them to make sophisticated use of television and direct-mail appeals. Reagan also had a powerful issue to exploit: the hostage stalemate. Calling the Iranians "barbarians" and "common criminals," he hinted that he would take strong action to win the hostages' return. More important, Reagan effectively appealed to the politics of resentment that flourished during the lean years of the 1970s. In a televised debate between the candidates, Reagan emphasized the economic plight of working- and middle-class Americans when he posed the rhetorical question, "Are you better off today than you were four years ago?"

In November Reagan won easily, with 51 percent of the popular vote to Carter's 41 percent. The landslide also gave the Republicans control of the Senate for the first time since 1954, though the Democrats maintained their hold on the House. Voter turnout, however, was at the lowest since the 1920s: only 53 percent of those eligible to vote went to the polls. Many poor and working-class voters stayed home. Nevertheless, the election confirmed the growth in the power of the Republican Party since Richard Nixon's victory in 1968.

The core of the Republican Party that elected Ronald Reagan remained the upper-middle-class white Protestant voters who supported balanced budgets, disliked government activism, feared crime and communism, and believed in a strong national defense. But new groups had gravitated toward the Republican vision: southern whites disaffected by big government and black civil rights gains; blue-collar workers, especially culturally conservative Catholics; young voters who identified themselves as conservatives; and residents in the West, especially those in the rapidly growing suburbs. By wooing these "Reagan Democrats," the Republican Party made deep inroads into Democratic territory, eroding that party's traditional coalition of southerners, blacks, laborers, and urban ethnics.

The New Right was another significant contributor to the Republican victory, especially the religious right, associated with groups like the Moral Majority, whose emphasis on traditional values and Christian morality dovetailed well with conservative Republican ideology. In 1980 these concerns formed the basis for the party's platform, which called for a constitutional ban on abortion, voluntary prayer in public schools, and a mandatory death penalty for certain crimes. The Republicans also demanded an end to court-mandated busing and for the first time in forty years opposed the Equal Rights Amendment. A key factor in the 1980 election, the New Right contributed to the rebirth of the Republican Party under Ronald Reagan.

On January 20, 1981, at the moment Carter turned over the presidency to Ronald Reagan, the Iranian government released the American hostages. After 444 days of captivity, the hostages returned home to an ecstatic welcome, a reflection of the public's frustration over their long ordeal. While most Americans continued to maintain "We're Number One," the hostage crisis in Iran came to symbolize the loss of America's power to control world affairs. Its psychological impact was enhanced by its occurrence at the end of a decade that had witnessed Watergate, the American defeat in Vietnam, and the OPEC embargo. To a great extent, the decline in American influence had been magnified by the unusual predominance the United States had enjoyed after World War II—an advantage that should not have been expected to last forever. The return of Japan and Western Europe to economic and political power, the control of vital oil resources by Middle Eastern countries, and the industrialization of some developing nations had widened the cast of characters on the international stage. Still, many Americans were unable to let go of the presumption of economic and political supremacy born in the postwar years. Ronald Reagan rode their frustrations to victory in 1980.

For Further Exploration

Peter N. Carroll, *It Seemed Like Nothing Happened* (1982), provides a general overview of the period. Gary Wills, *Nixon Agonistes* (rev. ed. 1990), judges Nixon to be a product of his times. For Watergate, a starting point are the books by the *Washington Post* journalists who broke the scandal, Carl Bernstein and Bob Woodward: *All the President's Men* (1974) and *The Final Days* (1976). Stanley Kutler, *Abuse of Power: The Nixon Tapes* (1997), is a collection of transcripts from the White House tapes relating to Watergate and other Nixon-era scandals. Gary Sick, a Jimmy Carter White House advisor on Iran, offers an insider's account of the hostage crisis in *All Fall Down: America's Tragic Encounter with Iran* (1986). Thomas Byrne Edsall with Mary D. Edsall, *Chain Reaction: The Impact of Race, Rights and Taxes on American Politics* (1991), examines some of the divisive social issues of the 1970s. J. Anthony Lukas, *Common Ground* (1985), tells the story of the Boston busing crisis through the biographies of three families. Barbara Ehrenreich examines the backlash against feminism in *Hearts of Men* (1984). A critical account of the New Right is *Thunder on the Right* (1980) by Alan Crawford.

For the Watergate scandal two useful sites are National Archives and Record Administration's "Watergate Trial Tapes and Transcripts" at <http://www.nara.gov/nixon/tapes/trial&transcripts.html>, which provides transcripts of the infamous tapes as well as other useful links to archival holdings concerning Richard Nixon's presidency. "Watergate" at <http://vcepolitics.com/watergate/> is a textual, visual, and auditory survey of Watergate.

T I M E L I N E

1968	Richard Nixon elected president		Freedom of Information Act strengthened
1969	Supreme Court Chief Justice Earl Warren retires, replaced by Warren Burger.		Fair Campaign Practices Act passed
		1974– 1975	Busing controversy in Boston
1970	First Earth Day		
	Environmental Protection Agency established	**1975– 1976**	Economic recession
1971	Pentagon Papers published	**1976**	Jimmy Carter elected president
1972	Watergate break-in at the Democratic National Committee's headquarters	**1977**	First National Women's Conference in Houston
	Title IX of the Educational Amendments Act		Voters overturn a Miami city council's gay rights measure.
	Congress passes Equal Rights Amendment.	**1978**	Carter brokers Camp David accords between Egypt and Israel.
	Occupational Safety and Health Administration (OSHA) and Consumer Products Safety Commission established		Proposition 13 reduces California taxes.
			Bakke v. University of California limits affirmative action.
	Nixon reelected		Discovery of the toxic waste site at Love Canal
	Ms. magazine founded		
1973	Spiro Agnew resigns; Gerald Ford appointed vice president	**1979**	Three Mile Island nuclear accident
	Roe v. Wade legalizes abortion.		Moral Majority founded
	OPEC oil embargo begins; gas shortages.		Second oil crisis triggered by revolution in Iran
	Endangered Species Act		Hostages seized at American embassy in Teheran, Iran
1974	*Milliken v. Bradley* mandates busing within cities.		USSR invades Afghanistan.
	Nixon resigns; Ford becomes president and pardons Nixon.	**1980**	Ronald Reagan elected president

Created by Australian political science professor Malcolm Farnsworth, the site's materials include a Nixon biography with speech excerpts, a Watergate chronology, an analysis of the significance of the "Deep Throat" informant, and an assessment of the Watergate legacy. Relevant links provide access to primary documents. The Oyez Project at Northwestern University at <http://oyez.nwu.edu/> is an invaluable resource for over 1,000 Supreme Court cases, with audio transcripts, voting records, and summaries. For this period, see, for example, its materials on *Roe v. Wade*, *Bakke v. University of California*, and *Griswold v. Connecticut*.

Chapter 31

A NEW DOMESTIC AND WORLD ORDER
1981–2000

The energizing slogans of the past—Making the World Safe for Democracy, the Domino Theory, the Evil Empire, the New World Order—ring hollow in light of present more sophisticated knowledge of history. When it comes to finding ways to deal with today's ambiguities and uncertainties, a new politics or a new leadership has not yet evolved.

—Haynes Johnson, 1994

On November 9, 1989, millions of television viewers worldwide watched jubilant Germans swarm through the Berlin Wall after the East German government lifted all restrictions on passage between the eastern and western sectors of the city. The Berlin Wall, which had divided the city since 1961, was the foremost symbol of communist repression and the cold-war division of Europe. Over the years more than 400 East Germans had lost their lives trying to escape to the freedom of the other side. Now East and West Berliners, young and old, danced and mingled on what remained of the structure.

When the Berlin Wall came down, it brought communism's grip over Eastern Europe down with it. With the breakup of the Soviet Union in 1991, the cold war finally ended, but new sources of conflict soon threatened world peace. In the new world order the United States was increasingly linked to a global economy that directly affected American interest rates, consumption patterns, and job opportunities. At home, Americans grappled with racial, ethnic, and cultural conflict; crime and economic inequities; the shrinking role of the federal government; and disenchantment with political leaders' failure to solve many of the nation's pressing social problems.

The Reagan-Bush Years, 1981–1993

First elected at sixty-nine, Ronald Reagan was the oldest man ever to serve as president, yet he conveyed a sense of physical vigor. By capitalizing on his skills as an actor and a public speaker and by winning the support of the emerging New Right within the Republican Party, Reagan became one of the most popular presidents of the twentieth century. George Bush paled in comparison. His one term as president often seems indistinguishable from the two terms of his predecessor, in part because Bush was overshadowed by Reagan's extraordinary charisma but also because he followed the basic policies of the previous administration. Distrustful of the federal government, both Bush and Reagan turned away from the state as a source of solutions for America's social problems, calling into question almost half a century of governmental activism. "Government is not the solution to our problem," Reagan declared. "Government is the problem."

REAGANOMICS

The economic and tax policies that emerged under Reagan, quickly dubbed Reaganomics, were based on supply-side economics theory. According to the theory, high taxes siphoned off capital that would otherwise be invested, stimulating growth. Tax cuts would therefore promote investment, causing an economic expansion that would increase tax revenues. Together with cuts in government spending, especially on entitlement programs, tax cuts would also shrink the federal budget deficit. Critics charged that conservative Republicans deliberately cut taxes to force reductions in federal funding for the social programs that they abhorred.

The Economic Recovery Tax Act passed in 1981 reduced income tax rates by 25 percent over three years. The reductions were supposed to be linked to drastic cutbacks in federal expenditures. But while cuts were made in food stamps, unemployment compensation, and welfare programs such as Aid to Families with Dependent Children (AFDC), congressional resistance kept the Social Security and Medicare programs intact. The net impact of Reaganomics was to further the redistribution of income from the poor to the wealthy.

Another tenet of Reaganomics was that many federal regulations impeded economic growth and productivity. Insisting that a safety net existed for the truly needy, the administration moved to abolish or reduce federal regulation of the workplace, health care, consumer protection, and the environment. The responsibility and cost of such regulations were transferred to the states. One of the results of this policy was the deinstitutionalization of many of the mentally ill, forcing them onto the streets.

The money saved by these means—and more—was plowed into a five-year, $1.2 trillion defense buildup. This huge increase fulfilled Reagan's campaign pledge to "make America number one again." The B-1 bomber, which President Carter had canceled, was resurrected, and development of a new missile system, the MX, was begun. Reagan's most ambitious and controversial weapons plan, proposed in 1983, was the Strategic Defense Initiative (SDI), popularly known as "Star Wars." A computerized satellite and laser shield for detecting and intercepting incoming missiles, SDI would supposedly render nuclear war obsolete.

Reagan's programs benefited from the Federal Reserve Board's tight money policies, as well as a serendipitous drop in world oil prices, which reduced the disastrous inflation rates that had bedeviled the nation in the 1970s. Between 1980 and 1982 the inflation rate dropped from 12.4 percent to just 4 percent. Unfortunately, the Fed's tightening of the money supply also brought on the "Reagan recession" of 1981 and 1982, which threw some 10 million Americans out of work. But as the recession bottomed out in early 1983 the economy began to grow, and for the rest of the decade inflation remained low. Despite rather unexceptional growth in the gross national product the Reagan administration presided over the longest peacetime economic expansion in American history.

REAGAN'S SECOND TERM

This economic growth played a role in the 1984 elections. Reagan campaigned on the theme "It's Morning in America," suggesting that a new day of prosperity and pride was dawning. The Democrats nominated former vice president Walter Mondale of Minnesota to run against Reagan. With strong ties to labor unions, minority groups, and party leaders, Mondale epitomized the New Deal coalition that had dominated the Democratic Party since Roosevelt. To appeal to women voters, Mondale selected Representative Geraldine Ferraro of New York as his running mate—the first woman to run on a major party ticket. Nevertheless, Reagan won a landslide victory, carrying the entire nation except for Minnesota and the District of Columbia. Democrats, however, held onto the House and in 1986 would regain control of the Senate.

A major scandal marred Reagan's second term when in 1986 news leaked out that the administration had negotiated an arms-for-hostages deal with the revolutionary government of Iran—the same government Reagan had denounced during the 1980 hostage crisis. In an attempt to gain Iran's help in freeing some American hostages held by pro-Iranian forces in Lebanon, the United States had covertly sold arms to Iran. Some of the profits generated by the arms sales were diverted to the Contras, counterrevolutionaries in Nicaragua, whom the administration supported over the leftist regime of the Sandinistas. The covert diversion of funds, which was both illegal and unconstitutional, seemed to have been the brainstorm of Marine Lieutenant Colonel Oliver North, a National Security Council aide at the time. One key memo linked the White House to his plan. But when Congress investigated the mounting scandal in 1986 and 1987, White House officials testified that the president knew nothing about the diversion. Ronald Reagan's defense remained simple and consistent: "I don't remember."

The scandal bore many similarities to Watergate, including the possibility that the president had acted illegally. Early in Reagan's administration, one of his

VANITY FAIR

JUNE 1985 $2.00

THE
REAGAN
STOMP

THEY COULD
HAVE DANCED
ALL NIGHT

THE
SOCIAL SWIM:
William F. Buckley, Jr.
Peter Duchin
& Brooke Hayward
Ann Getty
Mortimer's

***Festive Times at the Reagan
White House***

Since Ronald and Nancy
Reagan were both former
actors, perhaps they thought
of Fred Astaire and Ginger
Rogers (see p. 703) when
they struck this pose at a
White House state dinner
in May 1985. Some former
White House staffers now
suspect that Reagan was
already showing signs of
early Alzheimer's disease
by that point.

(Photo by Harry Benson. Cover
courtesy Vanity Fair. © 1985 by
Condé-Nast Publications, Inc.)

critics had coined the phrase "Teflon presidency" to describe Reagan's resiliency: bad news didn't stick; it just rolled off. The public seemed untroubled that the president was often confused or ill informed or that he relied heavily on close advisors, especially his wife. Even the news that Nancy Reagan was in the habit of consulting an astrologer before planning major White House events failed to shake public confidence in the president. Reagan weathered "Iran-Contragate," but the scandal did weaken his presidency.

The president proposed no bold domestic policy initiatives in his last two years in office. He had promised to place drastic limits on the federal government and to give free-market forces freer reign. Despite reordering the federal government's priorities, he failed to reduce its size or scope. And although spending for most poverty programs had been cut, Social Security and other entitlement programs remained untouched. Despite Reagan's failure to achieve his goals, his spending cuts and antigovernment rhetoric shaped the terms of political debate for the rest of the century.

One of Reagan's most significant legacies was his conservative judicial appointments. In 1981 he had nominated Sandra Day O'Connor, the first woman ever to serve on the Supreme Court. In his second term he appointed two more justices,

Antonin Scalia (1986) and Anthony Kennedy (1988), both of whom were far more conservative than the moderate O'Connor. Justice William Rehnquist, a noted conservative, was elevated to chief justice in 1986. Under his leadership the Court, often by a five-to-four margin, chipped away at the Warren Court's legacy in decisions on individual liberties, affirmative action, and the rights of criminal defendants.

Ironically, though Reagan had promised to balance the budget by 1984, his most enduring legacy was the national debt, which tripled during his two terms. The huge deficit reflected the combined effects of increased military spending, tax reductions for high-income taxpayers, and Congress's refusal to approve deep cuts in domestic programs. By 1989 the national debt had climbed to $2.8 trillion—more than $11,000 for every American citizen.

The nation was also running an annual deficit in its trade with other nations. Exports had been falling since the 1970s, when American products began to encounter increasing competition in world markets. In the early 1980s a high exchange rate for dollars made U.S. goods more expensive for foreign buyers and imports more affordable for Americans. The budget and trade deficits contributed to a major shift in 1985: for the first time since 1915 the United States became a debtor rather than a creditor nation. Since then, with phenomenal speed, the United States has accumulated the world's largest foreign debt.

THE BUSH PRESIDENCY

George H. W. Bush won the Republican nomination in 1988 and chose for vice president a young conservative Indiana senator, Dan Quayle. In the Democratic primaries the contest was between Governor Michael Dukakis of Massachusetts and the charismatic civil rights leader Jesse Jackson, whose populist Rainbow Coalition had embraced the diversity of Democratic constituencies. Dukakis received the party's nomination and chose Senator Lloyd Bentsen of Texas as his running mate.

The 1988 campaign had a harsh tone: brief televised attack ads replaced meaningful discussion of the issues. The sound bite "Read My Lips: No New Taxes," drawn from George Bush's acceptance speech at the Republican convention, became the party's campaign mantra. In a television ad featuring Willie Horton, a black man convicted of murder who had killed again while on furlough from a Massachusetts prison, Republicans, pandering to voters' racist fears, charged Dukakis with being soft on crime. Dukakis, forced on the defensive, failed to mount an effective counterattack. Bush carried thirty-eight states, winning the popular vote by 53.4 percent to 45.6 percent. Only 50 percent of eligible voters went to the polls.

Some of the more significant domestic trends of the Bush era were determined by the judiciary rather than the executive branch. Under Reagan's appointees, the Supreme Court continued to move away from liberal activism toward a more conservative stance, especially on the issue of abortion. The 1989 *Webster v. Reproductive Health Services,* which upheld the right of states to limit the use of public funds and institutions for abortions, gave states more latitude in restricting abortions. The next year the Court upheld a federal regulation barring personnel at federally funded health clinics from discussing abortion with their clients. In 1992 the Court upheld a Pennsylvania law mandating informed consent and a twenty-four-hour waiting period before an abortion could be performed. But the justices also reaffirmed the "essential holding" in *Roe v. Wade:* women had a constitutional right to abortion.

In 1990 David Souter, a little-known federal judge from New Hampshire, easily won confirmation to the Supreme Court. But the next year a major controversy erupted over President Bush's nomination of Clarence Thomas, an African American conservative with little judicial experience. Just as Thomas's confirmation hearings were drawing to a close, a former colleague, Anita Hill, testified publicly that Thomas had sexually harassed her in the early 1980s. After widely watched and widely debated televised testimony by both Thomas and Hill before the all-male Senate Judiciary Committee, the Senate confirmed Thomas by a narrow margin. In the wake of the hearings national polls confirmed the pervasiveness of sexual harassment on the job: four out of ten women said that they had been the object of unwanted sexual advances from men at work.

Bush also had relatively little control over the economic developments that soon became a key issue. His campaign promise of a "kinder, gentler administration" was

A Woman of Conscience

Accusations by University of Oklahoma law professor Anita Hill that Supreme Court nominee Clarence Thomas had sexually harassed her sparked fierce debate. Many felt that had there been more women in the Senate, Hill's charges would have been treated more seriously. After the 1992 election women's representation did in fact increase to six women in the Senate and forty-seven in the House of Representatives. (Markel/Gamma Liaison)

doomed by his predecessor's failed economic policies, especially the budget deficit. The Gramm-Rudman Act, passed in 1985, had mandated automatic cuts if budget targets were not met in 1991. Facing the prospect of a halt in nonessential government services and the layoff of thousands of government employees, Congress resorted to new spending cuts and one of the largest tax increases in history. Bush's failure to keep his "No New Taxes" promise earned him the enmity of Republican conservatives, which would dramatically hurt his chances for reelection in 1992.

Reagan's decision to shift the cost of many federal programs—including housing, education, public works, and social services—to state and local governments caused problems for Bush. In 1990 a recession began to erode state and local tax revenues. As incomes declined and industrial and white-collar layoffs increased, poverty and homelessness increased sharply. In 1991 unemployment approached 7 percent nationwide. To save money, state and local governments laid off workers even as demand for social services and unemployment compensation climbed.

Foreign Relations under Reagan and Bush

The collapse of détente during the Carter administration, after the Soviet invasion of Afghanistan, prompted Reagan's confrontational approach to what he called the "evil empire." Backed by Republican hard-liners and determined to reduce communist influence in developing nations, Reagan articulated some of the harshest anti-Soviet rhetoric since the 1950s. The collapse of the Soviet Union in 1991 removed that nation as a credible threat, but new post–cold-war challenges quickly appeared.

INTERVENTIONS IN DEVELOPING COUNTRIES AND THE END OF THE COLD WAR

Despite Reagan's rhetoric not all his international problems involved U.S.-Soviet confrontations. In 1983, after Israel invaded Lebanon, the U.S. Embassy in Beirut was bombed by anti-Israeli Muslim fundamentalists. A second bombing killed 239 Marine peacekeepers barracked in the city. Around the world terrorist assassins struck down Indira Gandhi in India and Anwar al-Sadat in Egypt. But it was the airplane hijackings and countless terrorist incidents in the Middle East that led Reagan to order air strikes against one highly visible source of terrorism, Muammar al-Qadhdhafi of Libya.

The administration reserved its most concerted attention for Central America. Halting what was seen as the spread of communism in that region became an obsession. In 1983 Reagan ordered the marines to invade the tiny Caribbean island of Grenada, claiming that its Cuban-supported communist regime posed a threat to other states in the region. Reagan's top priority, however, was to topple the leftist Sandinista government in Nicaragua. In 1981 the United States suspended aid to

Nicaragua, charging that the Sandinistas were supplying arms to rebels against a repressive right-wing regime in El Salvador. At the same time the CIA began to provide extensive covert support to the Nicaraguan opposition, the "Contras," whom Reagan called "freedom fighters." Congress, wary of the assumption of unconstitutional powers by the executive branch, responded in 1984 by passing the Boland Amendment, which banned the CIA and other intelligence agencies from providing military support to the Contras—a provision violated in the Iran-Contra affair.

Surprisingly, given Reagan's rhetoric, his second term brought a reduction in tensions with the Soviet Union. In 1985 Reagan met with the new Soviet premier, Mikhail Gorbachev, at the first superpower summit meeting since 1979. Two years later the two leaders agreed to eliminate all intermediate-range missiles based in Europe. Although a summit in Moscow in 1988 produced no further cuts in nuclear arms, the sight of the two first families attending the Bolshoi Ballet together and strolling amiably in Red Square exemplified the thaw in the cold war.

Under Bush's administration even more dramatic changes abroad brought an end to the cold war. In 1989 the grip of communism on Eastern Europe loosened and then let go completely in a series of mostly nonviolent revolutions that climaxed in the destruction of the Berlin Wall in November. Soon the Soviet Union itself began to succumb to the forces of change. The background for these dramatic upheavals was the changes set in motion by Soviet president Mikhail Gorbachev after 1985. Through his policies of *glasnost* (openness) and *perestroika* (economic restructuring), Gorbachev had signaled a willingness to tolerate significant changes. But Gorbachev, who was always more popular outside his country than at home, found that to call for the dismantling of an old system was easier than to build a new system.

On August 19, 1991, alarmed Soviet military leaders seized Gorbachev and attempted unsuccessfully to oust him. The failure of the coup broke the Communist Party's dominance over the Soviet Union. In December the Union of Soviet Socialist Republics formally dissolved itself to make way for an eleven-member Commonwealth of Independent States (CIS) (see Map 31.1). Gorbachev resigned, and Boris Yeltsin, president of the new state of Russia, the largest and most populous republic, became the preeminent leader in the region.

The suddenness of the collapse of the Soviet Union and the end of the cold war stunned America and the world. In the absence of bipolar superpower confrontations future international conflicts would arise from varied regional, religious, and ethnic differences. Suddenly the United States faced unfamiliar military and diplomatic challenges.

WAR IN THE PERSIAN GULF, 1990–1991

The first challenge surfaced in the Middle East. On August 2, 1990, Iraq, led by Saddam Hussein, invaded Kuwait, its small but oil-rich neighbor. In response President Bush sponsored a series of resolutions in the U.N. Security Council, con-

M A P 31.1
The Collapse of Communism in Eastern Europe and the Soviet Union

The end of the Soviet empire in Eastern Europe and the collapse of communism in the Soviet Union itself dramatically changed the borders of Europe and Central Asia. West and East Germany reunited, while the nations of Czechoslovakia and Yugoslavia, created by the 1919 Versailles treaty, divided into smaller states. The old Soviet Union produced fifteen new countries, of which eleven remained loosely bound in the Commonwealth of Independent States (CIS).

demning Iraq, calling for its withdrawal, and imposing an embargo and trade sanctions. When Hussein showed no signs of yielding, Bush prodded the international organization to create a legal framework for a military offensive against the man he called "the butcher of Baghdad." In November the Security Council voted to use force if Iraq did not withdraw by January 15. In a close fifty-two-to-forty-eight vote on January 12, the U.S. Senate authorized military action. Four days later President Bush announced to the nation that "the liberation of Kuwait has begun."

The forty-two-day war was a resounding success for the United Nations' coalition forces, which were predominantly American. Under the leadership of General Colin Powell, chairman of the Joint Chiefs of Staff, and the commanding general, H. Norman Schwarzkopf, Operation Desert Storm opened with a month of air strikes to crush communications, destroy armaments, and pummel Iraqi ground troops. A land offensive followed. Within days thousands of Iraqi troops had fled or surrendered, and the fighting quickly ended, although Hussein remained in power (see Map 31.2).

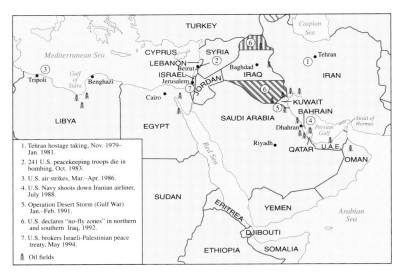

1. Tehran hostage taking, Nov. 1979–Jan. 1981.
2. 241 U.S. peacekeeping troops die in bombing, Oct. 1983.
3. U.S. air strikes, Mar.–Apr. 1986.
4. U.S. Navy shoots down Iranian airliner, July 1988.
5. Operation Desert Storm (Gulf War) Jan.–Feb. 1991.
6. U.S. declares "no-fly zones" in northern and southern Iraq, 1992.
7. U.S. brokers Israeli-Palestinian peace treaty, May 1994.
   Oil fields

MAP 31.2
U.S. Involvement in the Middle East, 1980–1994

The United States has long played an active role in the Middle East, pursuing the twin goals of protecting Israel's security and ensuring a realiable supply of low-cost oil from the Persian Gulf states. By far the largest intervention came in 1991, when, under United Nations auspices, President Bush sent 540,000 American troops to liberate Kuwait from Iraq. The United States also played a major role in the 1994 agreement allowing for Palestinian self-rule in the Gaza Strip and parts of the West Bank.

Women at War

Women played key and visible roles in the Persian Gulf War, comprising approximately 10 percent of the American troops. Increasing numbers of women are choosing military careers, despite widespread reports of sexual harassment and other forms of discrimination.

(Luc Delahaye/SIPA Press)

Operation Desert Storm's success and the few U.S. casualties (145 Americans were killed in action) produced a euphoric reaction at home. For many the American victory over a vastly inferior fighting force seemed to banish the ghost of Vietnam. "By God, we've kicked the Vietnam syndrome once and for all," Bush gloated. The president's approval rating shot up precipitously but declined almost as quickly when a new recession showed that the easy victory had masked the country's serious economic problems.

Uncertain Times

Opinion polls taken in the early 1990s showed that Americans were deeply concerned about the future. They worried about crime in the streets, increases in poverty and homelessness, the decline of the inner cities, illegal immigration, the environment, the failure of public schools, the unresolved abortion issue, and AIDS. But above all they worried about their own economic security—whether they would be able to keep their jobs in an era of global competition. By the end of the decade, a vastly improved economic picture would lessen—but not erase—Americans' concerns for the future.

THE ECONOMY

Slow growth in productivity and growing inequality in income distribution were the most salient economic trends in the 1980s and early 1990s. From 1945 to 1973 productivity grew 2.8 percent annually, allowing the standard of living to double in one generation, but in the quarter-century after 1973 productivity increased less than 1 percent annually, barely enough to double the standard of living in eighty years. Americans also faced stagnating real income. In 1991 the typical family's real income was only 5 percent higher than it had been in 1973, and that increase was achieved mainly because multiple members of a household were employed and because all of them were working more hours.

At the same time that wage stagnation was squeezing the middle class, economic inequality increased: the rich got richer, the poor got poorer, and the middle class shrank. By 1996 the United States was the most economically stratified industrial nation in the world. Statistics from the Congressional Budget Office showed that the richest 1 percent of American families reaped most of the gains of Reaganomics. This trend continued in the 1990s: a federal survey released in January 2000 reported that the earnings of the top one-fifth of Americans grew 15 percent in the preceding decade, while the bottom one-fifth grew less than 1 percent.

Even relatively well-advantaged Americans felt a sense of diminished expectations, in part from changes in the job market. Following an established pattern, the number of minimum-wage service jobs continued to grow, while the number of union-protected manufacturing jobs was shrinking. For many—one-fifth of the labor force in 1994—part-time or temporary work was the only work that was available. Moreover, in the 1980s and 1990s the downsizing trend, in which companies deliberately shed permanent workers to cut wage costs, spread to middle management. From 1980 to 1995 IBM shrank its mostly white-collar workforce from 400,000 to 220,000—a 45 percent decrease. Although most laid-off middle managers eventually found new jobs, many took a large pay cut.

These economic trends put even more pressure on women to seek paid employment. In 1994, 58.8 percent of women were in the labor force, up from 38 percent in 1962, compared with 75.1 percent of men. The stereotypical nuclear family of employed father, homemaker wife, and children characterized less than 15 percent of U.S. households. Although women continued to make inroads in traditionally male-dominated fields—medicine, law, law enforcement, the military, and skilled trades—one out of five held a clerical or secretarial job, the same proportion as in 1950. Women's pay lagged behind men's; for black and Latino women the gender gap in pay was especially wide.

At the same time, the labor movement—hurt by downsizing, foreign competition, fear of layoffs, government hostility during the Reagan-Bush years, and its own failure to organize unskilled workers—continued to decline. The number of union members dropped from 20 million in 1978 to 16.2 million in 1998, representing only 13.9 percent of the labor force. Although union membership was more than one-third female and one-fifth black, union leadership remained overwhelmingly white and male.

Another major cause of diminished economic expectations was the widespread fear that American corporations were no longer competitive in the global marketplace. Americans viewed with alarm the economic success of Germany and Japan, the growing U.S. trade deficit, and the infusion of foreign workers and investment money into the United States. To compete American corporations adopted new technologies, including microelectronics, biotechnology, computers, and robots, and by the late 1990s saw their competitiveness return. Bethlehem Steel, which invested $6 billion to modernize its operations, for example, doubled its productivity between 1989 and 1997.

These developments contributed to a brightening national economic picture. By the late 1990s the United States led the world in information technology and had expanded productivity in manufacturing. By 1997 U.S. economic growth, measured at 4 percent, was among the healthiest in the world, while one of its most serious competitors in the 1980s, Japan, limped along with only a 1.1 percent growth rate. Working Americans benefited from these developments: new jobs were added to the economy at the rate of 213,000 per month in 1997, and unemployment dropped from 7.5 percent in 1992 to barely over 4 percent in the first half of 2000. A booming stock market, which daily seemed to reach new highs, fueled the wealth and retirement savings of middle- and upper-income Americans.

But there were downsides to the picture as well. Many stock-market analysts worried that a steep drop in the stock market might create a recession. Other experts warned that the consumer spending that was fueling economic growth was tied to growing debts. The median family indebtedness in 1998 was $33,300 in 1998, up from $23,400 in 1995. An economic downturn could have serious repercussions for overextended families' ability to repay their debts. Moreover, prosperity was not equally distributed. As former Secretary of Labor Robert Reich put it, "There are still millions of people desperately trying to stay afloat. One in five children lives in poverty. Forty-four million Americans have no health insurance. The average 50-year-old without a college education hasn't seen a wage or benefit increase in 20 years. But Americans are segregated by income as never before, so it is far easier to pretend the worse off don't exist. They're out of sight."

AN INCREASINGLY PLURALISTIC SOCIETY

Ethnic and racial diversity, always a source of conflict in American culture, became a defining theme of the 1990s. Between 1981 and 1996 almost 13.5 million immigrants entered the country. The greatest number of the newcomers were Latinos. Although Mexico continued to provide the largest group of Spanish-speaking immigrants, large numbers also arrived from El Salvador and the Dominican Republic. The 1986 Immigration Reform and Control Act (Simpson-Mazzoli Act), which granted amnesty to some immigrants, primarily benefited Mexicans and other Latinos who had entered the United States illegally before 1982. The Latino population grew at a rate of 18 percent in the 1990s to reach 31 million in 1999, making it the second-largest minority group in the United States after African Americans and the second fastest-growing after Asians. Once concentrated in California, Texas, and New Mexico, Latinos now lived in urban areas throughout the country and made up about 16 percent of the population of Florida and New York (see Map 31.3). Their growing numbers have increased their significance as consumers and voters and have led advertisers and politicians alike to vie for their loyalty.

Asia was the other major source of new immigrants. This migration, which increased almost 108 percent from 1980 to 1990, consisted mainly of people from China, the Philippines, Vietnam, Laos, Cambodia, Korea, India, and Pakistan. More than 700,000 Indochinese refugees came to escape upheavals in Southeast Asia in the decade following the Vietnam War. The first arrivals, many of them well educated, adapted successfully to their new homeland. Later refugees lacked professional or vocational skills and took low-paying jobs where they could find them.

The new immigrants' impact on the country's social, economic, and cultural landscape has been tremendous. In many places they have created thriving ethnic communities, such as Koreatown in Los Angeles. In the 1980s tens of thousands of Jews fleeing religious and political persecution in the Soviet Union created Little Odessa in Brooklyn, New York. Ethnic restaurants and shops have sprung up across the country, while some 300 specialized periodicals serve immigrant readers.

In 1990 the immigration quota was expanded to 700,000 per year (modified in 1995 to 675,000), with priority given to skilled workers and relatives of current

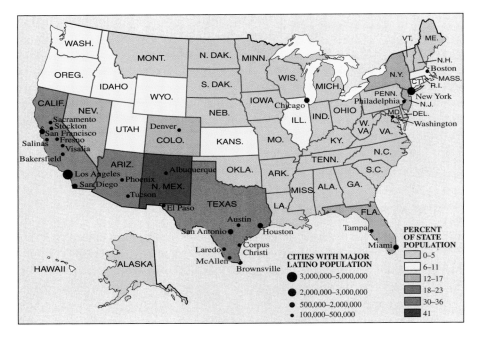

CITIES WITH MAJOR
LATINO POPULATION

● 3,000,000–5,000,000

● 2,000,000–3,000,000

● 500,000–2,000,000

• 100,000–500,000

PERCENT
OF STATE
POPULATION

0–5
6–11
12–17
18–23
30–36
41

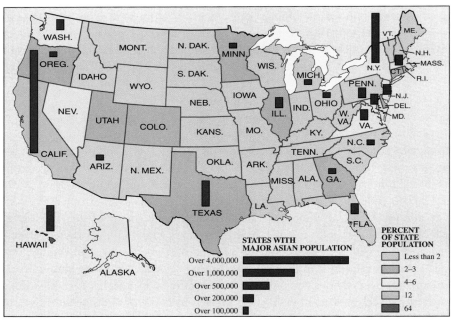

STATES WITH
MAJOR ASIAN POPULATION

Over 4,000,000

Over 1,000,000

Over 500,000

Over 200,000

Over 100,000

PERCENT
OF STATE
POPULATION

Less than 2
2–3
4–6
12
64

M A P 31.3

Latino Population and Asian American Population, 1999

In 1999 Latinos made up over 11 percent of the U.S. population, and Asian Americans 4 percent. Demographers predict that Latinos will overtake African Americans as the largest minority group early in the twenty-first century and that by the year 2050 only about half the U.S. population will be composed of non-Latino whites.

residents. But by then the new immigrants had become scapegoats for all that was wrong with the United States. Though a 1997 study by the National Academy of Science reported that immigration has benefited the nation, adding some $10 billion a year to the economy, many American-born workers felt threatened by immigrants. The unfounded assumption that immigrants were lured to the United States by generous public services influenced provisions of a 1996 welfare reform act (see page 927), which severely curtailed legal immigrants' access to welfare benefits, especially food stamps. Also in 1996 Congress enacted legislation that increased the financial requirements for sponsors of new immigrants.

The most dramatic challenges to immigrants have emerged on the state level. In the 1980s California absorbed far more immigrants than any other state: more than a third of its population growth in that decade came from foreign immigration. In 1994 California voters overwhelmingly approved Proposition 187, a ballot initiative provocatively named "Save Our State," which barred undocumented aliens from public schools, nonemergency care at public health clinics, and all other state social services. The initiative also required law enforcement officers, school administrators, and social workers to report suspected illegal immigrants to the Immigration and Naturalization Service. Though opponents challenged the constitutionality of Proposition 187, anti-immigrant feeling soon spread to other parts of the country, becoming a hotly debated issue in the 1996 election (see American Voices, "The Undocumented Worker").

Though the National Academy of Sciences report did find that "some black workers have lost their jobs to immigrants," for the most part African Americans were not adversely affected by the new immigration. But in the cities African Americans and new immigrants were forced by economic necessity and entrenched segregation patterns to fight for space in decaying, crime-ridden ghettos, where unemployment rates sometimes hit 60 percent. Overcrowded and underfunded, inner-city schools had fallen into disrepair and were unable to provide a proper education.

In April 1992 the frustration and anger of impoverished urban Americans erupted in five days of race riots in Los Angeles. The worst civil disorder since the 1960s, the violence took sixty lives and caused $850 million in damage. The riot was set off by the acquittal (on all but one charge) of four white Los Angeles police officers accused of using excessive force in arresting a black motorist, Rodney King. A graphic amateur video showing the policemen kicking, clubbing, and beating King had not swayed the predominantly white jury. Three of the officers were later convicted on federal civil rights charges.

AMERICAN VOICES

The Undocumented Worker

CUAUHTÉMOC MENDEZ

*I*n this oral history, Cuauhtémoc Mendez, an immigrant construction worker, reflects on the controversial issue of undocumented Mexican workers—an issue that helped fuel anti-immigration sentiment in the 1980s and 1990s.

In the United States, to get rid of all the illegals, you don't need a border or the Immigration. Simply, if there is no work, what would the illegals do there? . . . For the United States it is a great advantage, because Mexican labor is very cheap. The illegal produces his product much cheaper, and they can sell it cheaper to the American people. In this sense the illegal helps the United States.

He also helps Mexico. All of the *mojados* bring money back. We don't take money out of Mexico. Those of us who work in the United States help our country more than the rich who send their Mexican money out. We support our country.

Normally the Mexican who goes to the United States goes to work in jobs that many Americans don't want. In the first place, it's hard work. I'm not going to say that they can't do the work, but they don't want to work for the same price as the Mexican. It's clear there is this contradiction, this antipathy toward the Mexican who is there illegally. They look at the *mojados* as scabs. The Chicanos and Mexican-Americans look at us from this perspective because they think we are the reason they don't have jobs. But it's not true. We are there at the convenience of the owners and bosses who want cheap labor, cheaper than they can get there. It isn't our fault. We have the necessity to work. I don't think it's a sin to subsist in another country that offers the opportunity to live a little better than is possible for us in Mexico.

SOURCE: Marilyn P. Davis, *Mexican Voices, American Dreams: An Oral History of Mexican Immigration to the United States* (New York: Holt, 1990), p. 110.

The Los Angeles riot exposed the cleavages in urban neighborhoods. Trapped in the nation's inner cities, many blacks resented recent immigrants who were struggling to get ahead and often succeeding. As a result some blacks had targeted Korean-owned stores during the arson and looting. Latinos were also frustrated by high unemployment and crowded housing conditions. According to the Los Angeles Police Department, Latinos accounted for more than half of those arrested and a third of those killed during the rioting. Thus the riots were not simply a case of black rage at white injustice; they contained a strong element of class-based protest against the failure of the American system to address the needs of all poor people.

New Immigrants

In the 1980s many Korean immigrants got their start by opening small grocery stores in urban neighborhoods. Their success sometimes led to conflicts with other racial groups, such as African Americans and Latinos, who were often their customers as well as competitors.

(Kay Chernush/The Image Bank)

One of the ways federal and state governments had tried to help poor blacks and Latinos was through the establishment of affirmative action programs in government hiring, contracts, and university admissions. In 1995, however, under pressure from the Republican governor, Pete Wilson, the Regents of the University of California voted to scrap the university's twenty-year-old policy of affirmative action, despite protests from the faculty and from university presidents. In the November 1996 elections the struggle over affirmative action was intensified by California's passage of Proposition 209, which banned all preference based on race or gender. As appeals worked their way through the federal courts and black and Latino enrollments declined, the University of California sought new admissions criteria that would circumvent the restrictions imposed by Proposition 209.

One reason affirmative action became a political issue in the 1990s was that many people, including prominent conservatives like George F. Will, William Bennett, and Patrick Buchanan, saw it as a threat to core American values. Lumping affirmative action together with multiculturalism—the attempt to represent the diversity of American society and its peoples—critics feared that all this counting by race, gender, sexual preference, and age would lead to a "balkanization," or fragmentation, of American society. Attempts to revise American history textbooks along multicultural lines aroused much anger, as did efforts by universities such as Stanford to revise college curricula to include the study of non-European cultures. Conservatives also took aim at the antiracist and antisexist regulations and speech codes that had been adopted by many colleges. Arguing for the need to protect First Amendment rights, conservatives derided the attempt to regulate hate speech as "politically correct" (PC).

BACKLASH AGAINST WOMEN'S AND GAY RIGHTS

Conservative critics also targeted the women's movement. In the widely read *Backlash: The Undeclared War on American Women* (1991), the journalist Susan Faludi described a powerful reaction against the gains American women had won in the 1960s and 1970s. Spearheaded by New Right leaders and aided by the media, conservatives held the women's movement responsible for every ill afflicting modern women, from infertility to rising divorce rates; yet polls showed strong support for many feminist demands, including equal pay, reproductive rights, and a more equitable distribution of household and child-care responsibilities.

The deep national divide over abortion, one of the main issues associated with feminism, continued to polarize the country. In the 1980s and 1990s harassment and violence toward those who sought or provided abortions became common. In 1994 two workers were murdered at two Massachusetts abortion clinics, and five people were wounded in the attacks. Although only a fraction of antiabortion activists supported such extreme acts, disruptive confrontational tactics had made receiving what was still a woman's legal right more dangerous.

Gay rights was another field of battle. As gays and lesbians gained legal protection against housing and job discrimination across the country, Pat Robertson, North Carolina senator Jesse Helms, and others denounced these civil rights gains as undeserved "special rights." To conservatives gay rights threatened America's traditional family values. In 1992 Coloradans passed a referendum (overturned by the Supreme Court in 1996) that barred local jurisdictions from passing ordinances protecting gays and lesbians. Across the nation "gay bashing" and other forms of violence against homosexuals continued.

A grim backdrop to gay men's struggle against discrimination was the AIDS epidemic. Acquired immune deficiency syndrome (AIDS) was first recognized by physicians in 1981 in the gay male population, and its cause identified as the human immunodeficiency virus (HIV). At first little government funding was directed toward AIDS research or treatment; critics charged that the lack of attention to the syndrome reflected society's antipathy toward gay men. Only when heterosexuals, such as hemophiliacs who had received the virus through blood transfusions, began to be affected did AIDS begin to gain significant public attention. The death of the film star Rock Hudson from AIDS in 1985 finally broke the barrier of public apathy. Another galvanizing moment came in 1991, when the basketball great Earvin "Magic" Johnson announced that he was HIV-positive.

As early as the mid-1980s AIDS cases had begun to increase among heterosexuals, especially intravenous drug addicts and their sexual partners, as well as bisexuals. Women now constitute the group with the fastest-growing incidence of HIV infection. To date more Americans have died of AIDS than were killed in the Korean and Vietnam Wars combined. Between 1995 and 1999, however, deaths from AIDS in the United States dropped 30 percent. This decline—in part the result of new treatment strategies using a combination of drugs, or a "cocktail"—has led to cau-

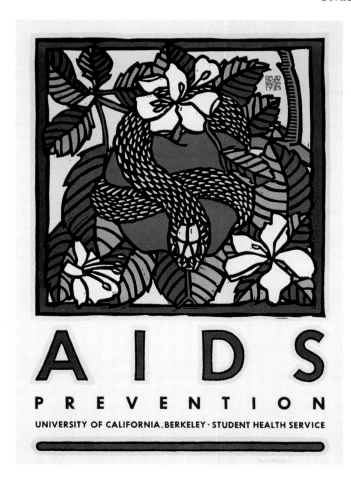

AIDS Awareness

This poster by David Lance Goines uses the image of the Garden of Eden to warn of the dangers of AIDS. By 1985, the year this poster appeared, 12,500 Americans had already died of AIDS, and the country began to confront the epidemic's human and medical costs. (David Lance Goines)

tious optimism about controlling the disease, though scientists warn that the drugs have not been effective for between 30 and 50 percent of patients. Moreover, the drugs' high costs limit their availability and make distribution particularly limited in poor nations. As AIDS deaths decline in developed countries like the United States, the epidemic reached crisis proportions in sub-Saharan Africa, which accounts for 24.5 million of the 34 million infections worldwide.

POPULAR CULTURE AND POPULAR TECHNOLOGY

Image was everything in the 1980s and 1990s—or so commentators said, pointing to rock stars Michael Jackson and Madonna and even to President Reagan. One strong influence on popular culture was MTV, a television channel that premiered in 1981 and featured short visual pieces accompanying popular songs. The MTV style—with its creative choreography, flashy colors, and rapid cuts—soon showed up in mainstream media and even political campaigns, which also adapted the 30-second sound bites common on television news shows to their own purposes. The national newspaper *USA Today,* which debuted in 1982, adapted the style, featuring eye-catching graphics, color photographs, and short, easy-to-read articles. Soon more staid newspapers followed suit.

At the same time new technology, especially satellite transmission and live "minicam" broadcasting, reshaped the television industry. Cable and satellite dishes were also increasingly available. By the mid-1990s viewers could choose from well over 100 channels, including upstarts such as Ted Turner's Cable News Network (CNN) and the Entertainment Sports Network (ESPN), an all-sports channel. Media, communications, and entertainment were big business, increasingly drawn into global financial networks, markets, and mergers.

Technology also reshaped the home in the late twentieth century. The 1980s saw the introduction of videocassette recorders (VCRs), compact disc (CD) players, cellular phones, and inexpensive fax machines. By 1993 more than three-quarters of American households had VCRs. Video was everywhere—stores, airplanes, tennis courts, operating rooms. With the introduction of camcorders, the family photo album could be supplemented by a video of a high school graduation, a marriage, or a birth.

But it was the personal computer that revolutionized both the home and office. The big breakthrough came in 1977 when the upstart Apple Computer Company offered the Apple II personal computer for $1,195—a price middle-class Americans could afford. When the Apple II became a runaway success, other companies scrambled to get into the market. IBM offered its first personal computer in the summer of 1981. Software companies such as Microsoft, whose founder Bill Gates is now the richest person in America, grew rapidly by providing operating systems and other software for the expanding personal computer market. By 1995, 37 percent of American households had at least one personal computer.

More than any other technological advance, the computer created the modern electronic office. Even the smallest business could keep all its records and do all its correspondence, billing, and other business on a single desktop machine. The very concept of the office was changing as a new class of telecommuters worked at home via computer, fax machine, and electronic mail. Today, new technologies utilizing fiberoptics, microwave relays, and satellites can transmit massive quantities of information to and from almost any place on earth, and even in outer space, via the information superhighway.

By 1999, almost 200 million people—80 million of them in the United States—used the Internet. At first scientists and other professionals, who communicated with their peers through electronic mail (e-mail), were the primary users of the Internet. But the debut of the World Wide Web in 1991 enhanced the commercial possibilities of the Internet. The web allowed companies, organizations, political campaigns, and even the White House to create their own "home pages," incorporating both visual and textual information. Businesses and entrepreneurs began to use the Internet to sell their products and services, leading critics to fear that the Net would become a big shopping mall.

Although theoretically available to all, the glories of cyberspace are still available mostly to those who can afford them: in 1997, 65 percent of Americans who used the Internet had incomes of $50,000 or more. But the trend may be changing. In 1998 only 25 percent of all households had access to cyberspace, but by 2000 the figure had grown to 50 percent. Additionally, programs to wire public schools and libraries should significantly increase access to the new technology.

The Clinton Presidency: Public Life Since 1993

If Americans hoped to make progress on the faltering economy and the deep social cleavages surrounding race, gender, and sexual orientation, they would need strong leadership. Yet low voter turnout and the strong showing of independent candidates in the 1992 presidential election signaled deep dissatisfaction with the American political system. In the ensuing years Americans' disaffection helped to continue the rollback of federal power begun by Reagan and Bush.

CLINTON'S FIRST TERM

As the 1992 election campaign got under way, the economy was the overriding issue, for the recession that had begun in 1990 showed no sign of abating. George Bush easily won renomination as the Republican candidate. To solidify the support of the New Right his running mate, J. Danforth (Dan) Quayle, spoke out strongly for "family values" and other conservative social agendas. William Jefferson (Bill) Clinton, the long-time governor of Arkansas, survived charges of marital infidelity and draft dodging, as well as questions about a dubious Arkansas real estate deal called Whitewater, to win the Democratic nomination. For his running mate he chose Albert (Al) Gore Jr., a second-term senator from Tennessee. At age forty-four Gore was a year and a half younger than Clinton, making the two men the first of the baby-boom generation to occupy the national ticket.

In the middle of the primary season the Texas billionaire H. Ross Perot, capitalizing on voters' desire for a change from politics as usual, announced he would run as an independent candidate. Although Perot dropped out of the race on the last day of the Democratic convention, he reentered it less than five weeks before the election, adding a well-financed wild card to an unusual election year.

The Democrats mounted an effective, aggressive campaign that highlighted Clinton's plans to solve domestic problems, especially in education, health care, and the economy. Gore added expertise on defense and environmental issues. Bush was hurt by the weak economy and especially by reneging on his "No New Taxes" pledge. On election day Clinton received 43 percent of the popular vote to Bush's 38 percent

Passing the Torch to the Baby Boomers

Baby boomer Bill Clinton, shown here campaigning in 1992, and his running mate Al Gore billed themselves as representing a "new generation of leadership." Born in 1946 and 1948, respectively, they came of age in the turbulent 1960s. Vietnam, not World War II or Korea, was the war that defined their generation. (Ira Wyman/Sygma)

and Perot's 19 percent. Although Perot did not win a single state, his popular vote was the highest for an independent candidate since Theodore Roosevelt's in 1912. The Democrats retained control of both houses of Congress, ending twelve years of divided government. But the narrowness of Clinton's victory and the public's perception that he did not really stand for anything did not augur well for his ability to lead the country.

The liberals who supported Clinton hoped that a Democratic presidency could erase the Reagan-Bush legacy and oversee the creation of a new Democratic social agenda. Initially, Clinton seemed to fulfill that promise. He nominated the liberal Ruth Bader Ginsberg for a seat on the Supreme Court; she was confirmed. The president also appointed Janet Reno as attorney general—the first woman to head the Department of Justice. Other trailblazing cabinet appointments included Secretary of Health and Human Services Donna E. Shalala and, in Clinton's second term, Secretary of State Madeline Albright. Clinton chose an African American, Ron Brown, as secretary of commerce, and two Latinos, Henry Cisneros and Frederico Peña, to head the Department of Housing and Urban Development (HUD) and the Department of Transportation, respectively.

Clinton's early legislative and administrative record was mixed. In early 1993 he signed into law the Family and Medical Leave Act, twice vetoed by Bush, which provided workers with up to twelve weeks of unpaid leave to tend to a newborn or an adopted child or to respond to a family medical emergency. But when Clinton tried to implement a campaign promise to lift the ban on gays serving in the armed forces, he ran into such ferocious opposition that he backed off, offering instead a weak compromise policy—"Don't ask, don't tell, don't pursue." The solution was an ineffective palliative at best, one that called into question Clinton's willingness to stand firm on issues of principle.

By the time Clinton took office, the economy had pulled out of the 1990 recession, enabling him to focus on other economic issues, especially the opening of foreign markets to U.S. goods. In 1992 President Bush had signed the North American Free Trade Agreement (NAFTA), in which the United States, Canada, and Mexico agreed to make all of North America a free-trade zone. Strongly supported by the business community, NAFTA was bitterly opposed by labor unions worried about the loss of jobs to lower-paid Mexican workers and by environmentalists concerned about the weak enforcement of antipollution laws south of the border. Nonetheless, with Clinton's support Congress narrowly passed NAFTA in November 1993. Another major development in international trade was the revision in 1994 of the General Agreement on Tariffs and Trade (GATT), which had been created at the end of World War II. The new provisions cut tariffs on many manufactured products and for the first time established regulations protecting intellectual property such as patents, copyrights, and trademarks on software, entertainment, and pharmaceuticals.

With the recession over, crime replaced the economy as a major concern among voters. In 1993 Congress passed the Brady Handgun Violence Prevention Act, over the opposition of the National Rifle Association. A much more wide-ranging piece of legislation was the Omnibus Violent Crime Control and Prevention Act (1994), which authorized $30.2 billion for stepped-up law enforcement, crime prevention, and prison construction and administration. The act also extended the death penalty to more than fifty federal crimes and banned the sale and possession of certain kinds of assault weapons. Responding to the deep anxieties Americans had about their economic security, Clinton had staked his political fortunes on his campaign promise of universal health care. Though the United States spent more on health care than any other country in the world, it remained the only major industrialized country not to provide national health insurance to all. Spiraling medical costs and rising insurance premiums had brought the health-care system to a crisis.

The president chose his wife, attorney Hillary Rodham Clinton, to head the task force that would draft the legislation—a controversial move since no first lady had ever played a formal role in policymaking. The resulting proposal was based on the idea of managed competition: market forces, not the government, would control health-care costs and expand citizen's access to health care. But even this mild form of social engineering ran into intense opposition from the well-financed pharmaceutical and insurance industries. By September 1994 congressional leaders were admitting that health reform was dead. In 1995 an estimated 40.3 million Americans—over 17 percent of the population under sixty-five—had no health insurance, and experts predicted that these statistics would climb.

Clinton seems never to have had the time to devote his full attention to pushing health reform through Congress. Three days before assuming office he had to commit his support to a missile attack President Bush had ordered on Iraq. In February foreign terrorists bombed the World Trade Center in New York City, and in April FBI agents made a misguided assault on the Branch Davidian compound in Waco, Texas. At the White House in September Israeli Prime Minister Yitzhak Rabin and Yasir Arafat, chairman of the Palestine Liberation Organization, signed an agreement allowing limited Palestinian self-rule in the Gaza Strip and Jericho. In October 1993, just after Clinton announced his health plan, twelve American soldiers were killed on a United Nations peacekeeping mission in Somalia. Constantly shifting from crisis to crisis, Clinton appeared to the American public to be vacillating, indecisive, and lacking in vision, especially in his handling of foreign affairs.

Nothing seemed more intractable than the problems that engulfed the former state of Yugoslavia, which had broken into five independent states in 1991. The province of Bosnia and Herzegovina, made up largely of Muslims and committed to a multiethnic state—Serb, Croat, and Muslim—had declared its independence in 1992. But Bosnian Serbs, supported financially and militarily by what remained of Yugoslavia, formed their own breakaway state and began a siege of the Bosnian capital, Sarajevo. In the countryside the Serbs launched a ruthless campaign of "ethnic cleansing," driving Bosnian Muslims and Croats from their homes and into concentration camps or shooting them in mass executions. More than 250,000 people were killed or reported missing after the outbreak of war in April 1992. After three years of unsuccessful efforts by the European powers to stop the carnage, President Clinton and Secretary of State Warren Christopher facilitated a peace accord in November 1995. A NATO-led peacekeeping force, backed by U.S. troops, would end the fighting, at least temporarily.

At the same time the end of cold-war superpower rivalry presented unexpected opportunities to resolve other long-standing conflicts. In Haiti the threat of a U.S. invasion in October 1993 led to the restoration of the exiled president, Jean-Bertrand Aristide, who had been ousted by a military coup in 1991. In South Africa the end of a fifty-year policy of racial separation was capped in May 1994 by the election of the rebel leader Nelson Mandela, who had spent twenty-seven years in prison for challenging apartheid, as the country's first black president. And in a move that was seen as the symbolic end to the American experience in Vietnam, the United States established diplomatic relations with Hanoi in July 1995, two decades after the fall of Saigon.

"THE ERA OF BIG GOVERNMENT IS OVER"

In the 1994 midterm elections Republicans gained fifty-two seats in the House of Representatives, which gave them a majority in the House as well as the Senate. In the House the centerpiece of the new Republican majority was the "Contract with America," a list of proposals that Newt Gingrich of Georgia, the new speaker of the house, vowed would be voted on in the first 100 days of the new session. The contract included constitutional amendments to balance the budget and set term limits for congressional office, $245 billion in tax cuts for individuals, tax incentives for small businesses, cuts in welfare and other entitlement programs, anticrime initiatives, and cutbacks in federal regulations. President Clinton, bowing to political reality, acknowledged in his State of the Union message in January 1996 that "the era of big government is over."

But the Republicans were frustrated in their commitment to cut taxes and balance the budget by the year 2002 because both practical and political considerations made many items in the budget immune to serious reductions. Interest on the national debt had to be paid. Defense spending had declined only slightly in the post–cold-war world. Since Social Security was considered untouchable, Congress looked to health care and discretionary spending as places to save.

In the fall of 1995 Congress passed a budget that cut $270 billion from projected spending on Medicare and $170 billion from spending on Medicaid over the next seven years. Other savings came from cuts in discretionary programs, including education and the environment. Clinton accepted Congress's resolve to balance the budget in seven years but, vowing to protect the nation from an "extremist" Congress, vetoed the budget itself. In the standoff that followed, nonessential departments of the government were forced to shut down twice for lack of funding, but polls showed that a majority of Americans held Congress, not the president, responsible. The budget that Clinton finally signed in April 1996 left Medicare and Social Security intact, though it did meet the Republicans' goal of cutting $23 billion from discretionary spending.

As part of the Contract with America, House Republicans were especially determined to cut welfare, a joint federal-state program that represented a fairly small part of the budget. To Republicans the program had become a prime example of misguided government priorities. The benefits of the main welfare program, Aid for Dependent Children (AFDC), were far from generous: the average annual welfare payment to families (including food stamps) was $7,740, well below the established poverty line. Still, in the 1990s both Democratic and Republican statehouses sought ways to change the behavior of welfare recipients by imposing work requirements or denying benefits for additional children born to women on AFDC. In August 1996, after vetoing two Republican-authored bills, President

Clinton, who had campaigned on a promise of welfare reform, signed into law the Personal Responsibility and Work Opportunity Act, a historic overhaul of federal entitlements. The 1996 law ended the federal guarantee of cash assistance to poor children by abolishing AFDC, required most adult recipients to find work within two years, set a five-year limit on payments to any one family, and gave states wide discretion in running their welfare programs.

The Republican takeover of Congress had one unintended consequence: it united the usually fractious Democrats behind the president. Unopposed in the 1996 primaries, Clinton was able to burnish his image as a moderate "New Democrat." His political fortunes were aided by the unpopularity of the Republican Congress following the government shutdowns. He also benefited from the continuing strength of the economy. Economic indicators released shortly before election day showed that the "misery index"—a combination of the unemployment rate and inflation—was the lowest it had been in twenty-seven years.

The Republicans settled on Senate Majority Leader Bob Dole of Kansas as their presidential candidate. Acceptable to both the conservative and the moderate wings of the party, Dole selected former representative Jack Kemp, a leading proponent of supply-side economics, as his running mate. Dole made a 15 percent across-the-board tax cut the centerpiece of his campaign, while Clinton emphasized an improved economy. Americans seemed to have made up their minds early about the candidates. With the lowest voter turnout since Calvin Coolidge won the presidency in 1924, Clinton became the first Democratic president since Franklin Roosevelt to win reelection. Republicans retained control in a majority of the nation's statehouses and in the House of Representatives and increased their majority in the Senate. Thus a key factor in Bill Clinton's second term would be the necessity, as a Democratic president working with a Republican-dominated Congress, of pursuing bipartisan policies or facing stalemate.

SECOND-TERM STALEMATES

In his 1998 State of the Union address Bill Clinton outlined an impressive program of federal spending for schools, tax credits for child care, a hike in the minimum wage, and protection for the beleaguered Social Security system. His ability to pursue this domestic agenda was seriously compromised, however, by a scandal that eventually led to his impeachment and by two international crises.

The first of these foreign crises emerged in Iraq, where Saddam Hussein was still in power despite his 1991 defeat in Operation Desert Storm and the United Nation's imposition of economic sanctions. In late 1997 Hussein ejected American members of a U.N. inspection team that was searching Iraqi sites for hidden "weapons of mass destruction," which included nuclear, biological, and chemical warfare materials. In response, the United States, with limited international support, began a military buildup in the Gulf. The threatened air strike against Iraq was averted when U.N. Secretary-General Kofi Annan brokered an agreement that temporarily put an end to the crisis. But in December 1998 the same issues led to an intense four-day joint U.S.-British bombing campaign, "Desert Fox." Neither that effort nor the missile strikes against Iraq that have continued to the present seem to have compromised the Iraqi's ability to build "weapons of mass destruction" or to have undercut Hussein's regime. At the same time international support for the United Nation's economic sanctions is eroding, fueled in part by humanitarian concerns about their impact on the Iraqi people. Growing pressure abroad and at home may force the United States to reconsider the use of economic sanctions as a diplomatic tool in Iraq.

The second major international crisis began in March 1999 in Kosovo, a province of the Serbian-dominated Federal Republic of Yugoslavia (FRY). There, NATO, strongly influenced by the United States, intervened to protect ethnic Albanians from the Serbians who were determined to drive them out of the region. Three months of bombing eventually forced the Serbians to agree to remove their troops from Kosovo and to agree to a multinational peacekeeping force. Yet, as in the Middle East, no long-term solutions were found to the problems generated by ethnic conflict. The brutal Serbian President Slobodan Milosevic was not pushed from office until 2000, the region was devastated and its people impoverished, and a year after the war most observers considered the war a "hollow triumph" for NATO and the United States. Both the Iraqi and Kosovo crises served as a potent reminder that despite its position as the most powerful nation in the world, the United States was limited in its ability to achieve its foreign-policy aims.

Although international events deflected President Clinton from his domestic agenda, far more damaging was the crisis that stemmed from a problem that had plagued him since 1992: allegations of sexual misconduct. In January 1998 attorneys representing Paula Jones, who claimed that the then governor Clinton had propositioned her when she was an Arkansas state employee, revealed that they planned to depose a former White House intern, Monica Lewinsky, about an alleged affair with President Clinton. Kenneth Starr, the independent counsel initially charged with investigating the Whitewater scandal, widened his investigation to explore whether Clinton or his aides had encouraged Lewinsky to lie in her statement. Clinton consistently denied having a sexual relationship with Lewinsky—both on national television and in deposition before a federal grand jury.

In September 1998, after Starr issued a report that concluded that the President had committed impeachable offenses, the House of Representatives began its inquiry. On December 20 the House narrowly approved two articles of impeachment against Clinton, one for perjury before a grand jury concerning his liaison with Lewinsky and a second for obstruction of justice, in which he was accused of encouraging others to lie in his behalf. Ironically, the evening of the House vote, a CBS news poll reported that 58 percent of its respondents opposed impeachment, while only 38 percent supported it.

Throughout the ensuing trial conducted by the Senate, Clinton's approval rating remained exceptionally high, perhaps because most Americans doubted the political motives of his attackers and almost certainly because a strong economy kept most citizens content with the president's performance, even if they disapproved of his personal morality. Finally, after a five-week trial and hours of televised debate, with Democrats voting solidly against impeachment and enough Republicans breaking with their party, the Senate acquitted Clinton on both charges. Like Andrew Johnson, the only other president to be impeached (see Chapter 15), Bill Clinton survived the process, but the scandal, the trial, and the profoundly partisan sentiments that surrounded it limited his ability to be an effective president and deepened public cynicism about politics and its practitioners.

For if Clinton had been hampered by the controversy, so too had Republicans. The November 1998 elections took place while the House was considering impeachment. Despite polls that indicated that Americans did not place much emphasis on the Lewinsky scandal, in many localities and on the national level Republican leaders made Clinton's moral character the focus of the campaign. The Democrats, in contrast, focused on issues like Social Security and education. They also employed vigorous get-out-the-vote drives, particularly among traditional Democratic constituencies—labor unions and African Americans. When the ballots were counted, for the first time since 1934 the party of the incumbent president gained seats—five— in a midterm election, shrinking the Republican majority in Congress to twelve. Although a variety of factors—including the improving economy—influenced voting patterns, many observers pointed to a backlash against the drive for impeachment. House leader Newt Gingrich admitted that "I totally underestimated the degree to which people would just get sick of 24-hour-a-day talk television and talk radio and then the degree to which this whole scandal became just sort of disgusting by sheer repetition." Ironically, it would be Gingrich who would be pushed from office, as the electoral debacle led to a revolt among Republicans that forced him to resign as Speaker of the House within a week of the election.

Because of the controversies surrounding Clinton and the weakened state of the Republicans, neither party was able to secure significant legislation. For the rest of Clinton's term, shoring up Social Security, addressing the high cost of medical care, and passing an effective gun-control law eluded the president and his supporters, while Republicans were stymied in their efforts to cut taxes and further roll back the federal government. The stalemate was exacerbated by politicians' focus on positioning themselves for the election of 2000. As Senator Joseph I. Lieberman, a Democrat from Connecticut, described the 106th Congress in November 1999, "This was not a session of great initiatives. . . . This was a session that was post-impeachment and preelection."

Lieberman was to become much better known when the Democratic Party nominated him as Vice President Al Gore's running mate for the 2000 presidential election. The Republicans chose Governor George W. Bush of Texas to head their ticket and Richard Cheney for their vice-presidential nominee. Although both Bush and Gore were considered moderate centrists, they had ideological differences over the role of the federal government and how best to use the large projected budget surpluses. Bush proposed a major tax cut that critics claimed would benefit primarily the wealthiest 10 percent of Americans, a partial privatization of Social Security, and the use of government-issued vouchers to pay for private education. Gore argued for using the surplus to shore up the Social Security funds, a tax break incentive for college tuition, and expansion of medicare. The two candidates disagreed on the abortion issue, with Bush opposing abortion and Gore supporting a woman's right to choose. While Pat Buchanan of the Reform Party fared poorly and was not able to make significant inroads among conservative Republicans, Ralph Nader, the Green Party representative, did appeal to many in the left wing of the Democratic Party who were disenchanted with Gore's centrist position. Nader received over two and a half million votes and detracted enough ballots from Gore in New Hampshire, New Mexico, and Florida to give those states to Bush. Nader's 97,419 votes in Florida (2 percent) contributed to making that state's presidential election a virtual tie between Bush and Gore.

As Florida hung in the balance, returns from the rest of the country showed that Gore had a lead of 337,000 in the popular vote and had won the District of Columbia and twenty states, mostly in the Northeast and Far West, with 267 electoral votes, while Bush had triumphed in twenty-nine states, mostly in the South and Midwest, with 246 electoral votes. In four states, however, fewer than 7,500 votes separated the two major candidates. In such a tight election, the results in Florida became crucial because the electoral college victory would come down to which candidate could claim that state's twenty-five electoral votes. It would take thirty-seven dramatic days to resolve the controversies surrounding the Florida vote and determine the new president, making the election one of the most remarkable in American history (see Map 31.4).

At stake were protested "butterfly ballots," which had apparently misled some Gore voters into voting for Buchanan, and "under votes," which resulted from antiquated voting machines and inattentive voters (see American Voices, "We Marched to Be Counted"). To make certain all votes were tabulated, Gore forces demanded hand recounts in several counties. How to evaluate dimpled, pregnant, and hanging "chads"—the tiny cardboard pieces punched from the ballot—became a hotly contested issue. On November 27, Florida Secretary of State Katherine Harris halted the recount process and declared Governor Bush the winner by a mere 537 votes. The struggle, however, continued. Twice Gore appealed to the Florida Supreme Court in an attempt to get a hand recount. When that court ordered the hand count to continue, Bush went to the United States Supreme Court, which then ordered it stopped. Finally on December 12, a deeply divided Supreme Court, in a 5–4 decision marked by acrimonious dissenting opinions, declared that the equal protection clause of the Fourteenth Amendment required that all ballots had to be counted in the same way and that time did not permit a statewide hand count. Justice

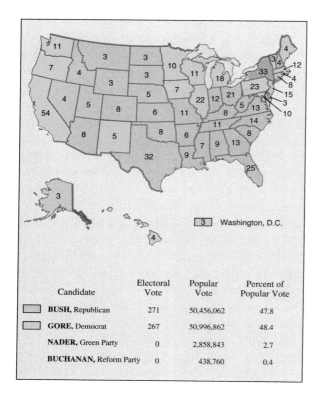

MAP 31.4
The Election of 2000

This map makes the closeness of the 2000 presidential election graphically clear. Democrat Al Gore tallied 337,576 more popular votes than his opponent. Republican George W. Bush, drawing upon solid support in the South and Midwest, won in the electoral college by only four votes, thus securing the presidency.

	Candidate	Electoral Vote	Popular Vote	Percent of Popular Vote
	BUSH, Republican	271	50,456,062	47.8
	GORE, Democrat	267	50,996,862	48.4
	NADER, Green Party	0	2,858,843	2.7
	BUCHANAN, Reform Party	0	438,760	0.4

Stephen G. Breyer in dissent angrily pointed out that the majority's opinion was clearly a political one that "runs the risk of undermining the public's confidence in the Court itself." On the following day, Vice President Gore gave his concession speech, and George W. Bush announced his victory to become the forty-third president.

MAKING SENSE OF THE LATE TWENTIETH CENTURY

The last two decades of the twentieth century brought enormous changes. In the international political arena, the end of the four-decade cold war had repercussions that are still evolving. The world appears to be returning to a situation in which power, both economic and military, is dispersed among a number of key players. The United States remains preeminent, but as the showdown in Iraq suggests, the nation's dominance in the new world order is offset by the limits to its power. Permanent peace in the Middle East or in other hot spots will undoubtedly prove elusive.

By the late 1990s the United States had dramatically improved its position in the world economy, but nonetheless decisions made beyond its borders continued to affect the daily lives of American workers, managers, and consumers. A startling 554-point drop in the stock market in November 1997—in part a reaction to se-

We Marched to Be Counted

JOHN LEWIS

E merging from the furor over apparent voting irregularities in Florida in the 2000 presidential election is a concern that uncounted and disqualified voters were more likely to be poor people, especially African Americans. John Lewis, a civil rights activist (see p. 831) who had marched from Selma to Montgomery in 1965 to demonstrate for African American voting rights in Alabama, reflects on the relationship of the 1960s Civil Rights Movement to the Florida voting controversy. Lewis is now a congressman from Atlanta.

What's happening in Florida and in Washington is more than a game for pundits. The whole mess reminds African Americans of an era when we had to pass literacy tests, pay poll taxes, and cross every *t* and dot every *i* to get to be able to vote. . . . For all the political maneuvering and legal wrangling, many people have missed an important point: the story of the 2000 election is about more than George W. Bush and Al Gore. It's about the right to vote. And you cannot understand the true implications of this campaign and the subsequent litigation without grasping how deeply many minorities feel about the seemingly simple matter of the sanctity of the ballot box.

There is a lot of troubling new talk of "political profiling"—allegations that officials tried to suppress the black vote on Election Day and may be maneuvering now to make sure it isn't counted. There are reports that officials put new voting machines in white areas but not black ones and that African Americans were asked to present two, not just one, forms of identification to be allowed to vote. These charges should be looked into. But I like to believe that no one met in some smoke-filled room and said, "We're going to keep black voters out, we're going to keep Jewish voters out." . . .

My greatest fear today is that the perception our votes were not counted may usher in a period of great cynicism. On the other hand—and I bet this is more likely—it may give people a greater sense of the importance of voting and of vigilance. The vote, after all, is the real heart of the movement. Younger people shouldn't think civil rights was just about water fountains or stirring speeches on TV. Late in the summer of 1961, after the Freedom Rides, we realized it was not enough to integrate lunch counters and buses. We had to get the vote.

SOURCE: John Lewis, "We Marched to Be Counted," *Newsweek* (December 11, 2000), p. 38.

vere economic crises in several Asian countries—served as a potent reminder of just how interconnected the global economy had become.

Finally, in politics, several important trends developed. The intense media scrutiny of President Clinton's sexual behavior was just the most dramatic example of the way in which the private morality of public officials often took on more importance than political issues. The influence of the New Right ebbed and flowed, but throughout the period it made issues like abortion, gay rights, gun control,

George W. Bush

After a hotly contested ballot-counting controversy in the state of Florida that was ultimately resolved by the U.S. Supreme Court, Texas governor George W. Bush emerged victorious in the 2000 presidential race. Observers predicted that Bush, the first president since 1888 to have lost the popular vote while winning in the electoral college, also hampered by a fifty-fifty Republican-Democrat split in the Senate, would face many obstacles in implementing his programs. (AP/Wide World Photos)

affirmative action, the death penalty, and immigration potent political flash points that continued into the next century. Finally, a significant shift occurred in the ways that Americans and their leaders seem to think about government and the political system. Low voter turnout, the popularity of third-party candidates like H. Ross Perot and Ralph Nader, and the controversies surrounding President Clinton's impeachment, point to widespread cynicism with politics as usual. The failure of Congress and the president to make significant strides toward ensuring the future of Social Security, addressing the problem of health-care coverage and costs, or tackling other social problems effectively has left many Americans disenchanted with the nation's leadership and suspicious of the federal government in particular.

Despite Americans' nervousness about an unstable world characterized by ethnic conflict, civil wars, and the proliferation of "weapons of mass destruction," despite their reservations about a global economy and nations' increased interdependency, and despite their disappointment with their own politicians, Americans were relatively confident as the twentieth century ended. Economic prosperity—as unevenly distributed as it was—deflected serious discontent. Enthusi-

T I M E L I N E

1981	Sandra Day O'Connor nominated to Supreme Court MTV premieres. Beginning of AIDS epidemic IBM markets its first personal computer.		Clarence Thomas–Anita Hill Senate hearings Susan Faludi's *Backlash: The Undeclared War on American Women*
1981–1982	Recession	1992	Los Angeles riots Bill Clinton elected president Janet Reno appointed first woman to head Department of Justice
1981–1989	National debt triples.	1993	North American Free Trade Agreement (NAFTA) ratified Family and Medical Leave Act Brady Handgun Violence Prevention Act
1982	*USA Today* debuts.		
1983	Star Wars proposed	1994	Health-care reform fails. Omnibus Crime Control and Prevention Act Republicans gain control of Congress.
1984	Geraldine Ferraro becomes first woman on major party ticket. Reagan reelected		
1985	Gramm-Rudman Act requires balanced budget.	1995	Congress passes parts of Contract with America. University of California Regents vote to end affirmative action. U.S. troops enforce peace in Bosnia.
1986	Iran-Contra scandal Immigration Reform and Control Act		
1987	Stock market collapse	1996	Clinton reelected Madeline Albright appointed first woman to head Department of State
1988	George H. W. Bush elected president		
1989	*Webster v. Reproductive Health Services* limits abortion but upholds its legality. Berlin Wall destroyed	1998	Republicans' majority in Congress shrinks.
1990–1991	Persian Gulf War	1998–1999	Bill Clinton impeached and acquitted
1990–1992	Recession	1999	United States, with NATO, intervenes in Kosovo.
1991	Dissolution of Soviet Union ends cold war.	2000	George W. Bush elected president in contested election

asm about technology, especially the potential of the Internet, encouraged many to look forward to the twenty-first century with cautious optimism. But all that can be predicted with any assurance is that the dramatic changes in domestic and world realities will shape the future of the United States and the globe in the twenty-first century and beyond.

For Further Exploration

Two valuable overviews of the period are by Haynes Johnson: *Sleepwalking Through History: America in the Reagan Years* (1992) and *Divided We Fall: Gambling with History in the Nineties* (1995). For a firsthand account of the Republican agenda, see Newt Gingrich, *To Renew America* (1995). Richard A. Posner, *An Affair of State: The Investigation, Impeachment and Trial of President Clinton* (1999), stresses the legal issues involved in Bill Clinton's impeachment and acquittal. An engaging book that uses census data to counter the emphasis on American decline in the 1980s and 1990s is Reynolds Farley, *The New American Reality: Who We Are, How We Got There, Where We Are Going* (1996). On foreign policy Stephen Ambrose and Douglas Brinkley, *Rise of Globalism* (8th ed., 1997), offers a solid assessment. A lively collection of essays debating the new immigration is Nicolaus Mills, ed., *Arguing Immigration: The Debate over the Changing Face of America* (1994). On work, women, and families, see Arlie Hochschild, *The Second Shift: Working Parents and the Revolution at Home* (1989).

"The Gulf War" at <http://www.pbs.org/wgbh/pages/frontline/gulf/> is an online documentary treatment of the Gulf War conflict. A companion to the Gulf War documentary produced by the PBS series *Frontline,* the site includes maps, a chronology, interviews with decision-makers and soldiers from the various sides of the conflict, audio clips, and a section on weapons and technology. Jurist, the Law Professors' Network, provides a "Guide to Impeachment and Censure Materials Online" at <http://jurist.law.pitt.edu/impeach.htm#Public>, which offers extensive links to materials on the constitutional issues raised by impeachment and on public opinion polls, documents, and analysis specific to the Clinton impeachment.

The Gallup Organization has been conducting public opinion surveys since 1935. Its site at <http://www.gallup.com/index.html> provides access to recent polls on politics, family, religion, crime, and lifestyle. This searchable site is an invaluable guide to contemporary American opinion. The United States Census Bureau's web page at <http://www.census.gov/population/www/> offers a rich variety of data—on health insurance, racial and ethnic composition, poverty, work environment, and marriage and family—that offer insight into the major demographic changes transforming American society.

AMERICA AND THE WORLD AT 2001:

How Historians Interpret Contemporary Events and Their Legacy to the Future

IN A PREDAWN RAID on April 23, 2000, armed U.S. Immigration and Naturalization officers forcibly removed six-year-old Elián González from the home of his Miami, Florida, relatives and flew him to the waiting arms of his father, Cuban national Juan Miguel González. Powerful images of the terrified child during the raid as well as those picturing him beaming as he embraced his father, made front-page news and lead TV stories. The raid was the most dramatic event of a seven-month saga that began when the boy was rescued floating in an inner tube after his mother tragically drowned in an attempt to flee Castro's Cuba for the United States. His relatives in Miami claimed custody, and the politically powerful expatriate Cuban leadership there spearheaded a drive to prevent the Justice Department from returning the boy to his father in Cuba. The controversy ignited a media frenzy. Pictures of Elián enjoying the fruits of a consumer culture popped up everywhere. Conservatives invoked cold-war memories of the Cuban revolution, child psychologists aired their opinions on talk shows, the boy's Cuban grandmothers arrived in the United States to plead for his return, pollsters conducted repeated public-opinion surveys, Cubans in Miami demonstrated, Cubans in Cuba demonstrated, and political candidates weighed in, all reported in minute detail by the press. Yet this *mediathon,* as *New York Times* writer Frank Rich has termed the genre of "relentless hybrid of media circus, soap opera, and tabloid journalism," ground to a halt shortly after a U.S. federal court paved the way for Elián to return to Cuba in June. The story disappeared from national attention as quickly as it had surfaced.

The Original Webmaster

Tim Berners-Lee, here represented in a mosaic composed of 2,304 websites, was the brains behind the World Wide Web. (PhotomosaicTM by Robert Silvers/www.photomosaic.com)

For the textbook writer the Elián phenomenon invokes a recurring problem: What current events should be included in the closing chapter? Which will future historians view as having long-term significance, and which will they judge to be of little consequence? The answer in the González case will depend to a large extent on its aftermath. Many observers suggest that the Cuban expatriates' militant defiance of the Justice Department heightened public awareness of the exceptional political influence that the group has exerted on U.S. foreign policy. That recognition as well as new attention to the economic plight of Cubans under the thirty-nine-year U.S. embargo against the communist regime there might bolster efforts to normalize relations with Cuba. Future historians might also analyze the González case in the context of understanding the influence of Latinos in the nation's cultural and political life. Compared to the fewer than 1 million Cuban Americans in the country, Mexican Americans (20 million) and Puerto Ricans (7.7 million) have enjoyed significantly less political clout, but that trend is changing, and the Miami situation might provide a window into a broader story about politics in a pluralistic society. For the moment, Elián's inclusion in *America: A Concise History* is in limbo. Not yet in the final chapter, his story is given temporary status in this epilogue.

Writing history is about making choices by deciding what to include and what to leave out, and nowhere is this process more difficult than in writing of recent events. The key question for future editions of *America* is determining which occurrences will be thought significant enough to warrant inclusion in a broad synthesis of American history and culture and which will be judged mere blips on society's consciousness—things that seemed all-encompassing at the time but whose long-term significance paled. What the historian can offer is some sense from the past about how to think about the present, when all of us are bombarded with headlines and breaking stories and when our own reactions to major stories and events can cloud our ability to look at them objectively. Today's headlines do not always become tomorrow's history.

In a 1992 interview former President Richard M. Nixon stated bluntly, "In my view, history is never worth reading until it's fifty years old. It takes fifty years before you're able to come back and evaluate a man or a period of time." The mere passage of time does often help participants understand events and place them in their larger historical context. For example, we know much more about the origins of the cold war now that documents from the former Soviet Union and other former communist states are surfacing that present their side of the global conflict. And fifty years after the end of World War II Swiss banks are finally accounting for money deposited by Jews later killed in Hitler's concentration camps.

Yet if textbook writers took Nixon's advice literally, they would end their books just after World War II and the onset of the cold war. Of course this isn't desirable, and the enormous outpouring of excellent scholarship that informs Part Six of *America* demonstrates that it is indeed possible to assess and interpret historically events of the fairly recent past such as the cold war, the civil rights movement, the

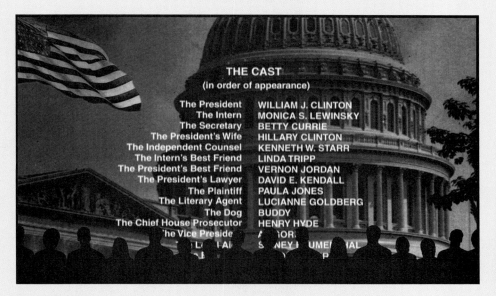

THE CAST
(in order of appearance)

The President	WILLIAM J. CLINTON
The Intern	MONICA S. LEWINSKY
The Secretary	BETTY CURRIE
The President's Wife	HILLARY CLINTON
The Independent Counsel	KENNETH W. STARR
The Intern's Best Friend	LINDA TRIPP
The President's Best Friend	VERNON JORDAN
The President's Lawyer	DAVID E. KENDALL
The Plaintiff	PAULA JONES
The Literary Agent	LUCIANNE GOLDBERG
The Dog	BUDDY
The Chief House Prosecutor	HENRY HYDE

The Impeachment Players

For more than a year the Monica Lewinsky story dominated the news, making household names of major and minor characters. Then, like a movie, it ended. Most Americans seemed relieved that the ordeal was over, telling pollsters that they were ready for Clinton and the country to move on. (Jesse Gordon/The New York Times. Reprinted with permission)

growth of suburbia, and the changing contours of the global economy. The closer that past gets to the present, the harder the task becomes. That does not mean, however, that historians have to cede the recent past or even contemporary events to journalists and television analysts.

What follows is an overview of the key areas in modern American life that we have traced throughout the book—politics, society and culture, economics, and foreign policy—at the historical moment when the twentieth century turned into the twenty-first. Think of this part of *America* as a historical document: how a group of American historians saw the challenges and promises of writing the contemporary history of their society as the year 2001 approached. Look at the choice of issues and methods to discover how historians gather and evaluate evidence, how they link individual events to larger patterns and themes, and yes, how they are often forced to revise their earlier conclusions or change their minds entirely.

POLITICS. Unlike the last edition of *America*, we have been able to provide a brief discussion of President Bill Clinton's impeachment and acquittal, but even here it is premature to assess the lasting significance of the crisis. At this stage we can only draw on our understanding of the past to pose questions about its impact. For example, will the presidency be permanently undermined by the process, only the second time in America's history that a president has been impeached, or will the institution and the country prove as resilient as they did in 1974 after Richard Nixon's resignation to avoid imminent impeachment? Has the historic balance of power between the three branches of government been permanently upset by a partisan Congress pursuing an open-ended investigation of a sitting president of the opposite political party? What will be the effects of the impeachment proceedings on citizens' attitudes toward their elected representatives and Washington in general? These are some of the larger questions that will concern historians who evaluate this era in the years to come.

Yet it is quite possible that when historians assess the Clinton presidency and the politics of governance in the 1990s, the impeachment scandal, in hindsight, will be seen as less important than the way in which President Clinton helped move the Democratic Party to a more centrist position or presided over a flourishing economy. Writing in the heat of the moment robs historians of the ability to step back, gather evidence, and listen to and weigh different viewpoints—the tools of the historian's craft. But it is not always necessary to have Richard Nixon's proverbial fifty years to gain a better historical perspective on events—sometimes just a few years will do.

A good case in point is the 1994 election, in which Republicans won control of the House of Representatives for the first time in forty years with a campaign organized around an antigovernment theme spelled out in their "Contract with America." In the last edition of *America* we interpreted the electoral results as potentially dramatic, perhaps (although we intentionally fudged a bit here) signaling the end of the rise of the state, of "big government." Two years later Bill Clinton was re-elected, and in the 1998 election Democrats picked up five seats in the House (unprecedented for a party in power in an off-year election), and the architect of the 1994 Republican victory, Speaker of the House Newt Gingrich, resigned, not Bill Clinton. Not a single Washington pundit had predicted this startling turn of events. Suddenly the "Republican revolution" of 1994 looked less like a history-altering turning point than a minor political realignment.

Often these unexpected events—election upsets, assassinations, and natural disasters—can seem to change the course of history overnight. But historians need not place themselves at the mercy of fast-breaking news; instead, they can attempt to place events in their larger context and promise to revisit their assessment later to see if it has weathered the test of time. In other cases historians can draw on their knowledge of the past to identify contemporary issues likely to emerge as defining moments when they write about this period in the future.

One such issue, a major concern at the turn of the century, is what will happen when the baby boomers (Americans born between 1945 and 1963) begin to retire and collect Social Security. Perhaps when we look back at the early twenty-first century, one of the most critical markers will be whether the budget surplus that began in 1997 was used to shore up the ailing Social Security system. Current projections show Social Security running short of money to pay all promised benefits by 2032. As a result of these gloomy predictions many Americans are losing confidence that government pensions, one of the cornerstones of the American welfare state, will actually be available for them when they retire. The historical problem has been identified, but the solution remains for the future.

Another political issue that historians will be writing about in the future is health care. As the last chapter of *America* discusses, Clinton's 1994 plan for reform of the health-care system was considered too sweeping. An incremental, market-driven approach featuring managed care seemed better suited to the needs of the country, with the result that by 1998 almost two-thirds of the population (61 percent) belonged to some kind of health maintenance organization (HMO). But no sooner had managed care become the predominant method of dispensing health care than doubts set in. Complaints about restrictions on the kinds of care and services available—often fueled by heart-wrenching stories of patients denied access to potentially life-saving treatments by their cost-conscious HMOs—became so widespread that health-care advocates and politicians proposed a "Patient's Bill of Rights" to expand patient choice and make HMOs accountable for the quality of care provided. Furthermore, managed care had failed to reach the growing proportion of Americans (more than one-sixth of the population) who had no access to health insurance at all.

Another puzzle of contemporary politics that historians will have to address is what happened to the welfare system and its beneficiaries after Congress and the states passed sweeping changes in the 1990s, especially the 1996 federal law placing a five-year lifetime limit on assistance for single mothers and a two-year limit for adults without dependent children. Current welfare recipients would theoretically reach the end of their benefits at various points between 1998 and 2001, but welfare rolls were already dropping precipitously before the federal deadlines kicked in. For example, Wisconsin, which had developed one of the most ambitious "workfare" programs to get people off welfare, saw its number of cases drop from almost 80,000 in 1994 to just over 10,000 four years later.

And yet there was no consensus on what this drop meant or what had happened to the former welfare recipients. Were they able to use state employment services to develop skills and find jobs, or did they find jobs simply because the economy was booming? What will happen if the economy slows down and is unable to absorb all those who want to work, possibly throwing them back onto welfare or, worse, onto the streets to join the many thousands of already homeless Americans? Is the goal of workfare to help people find jobs in the private sector or merely to discourage the poor from applying for public assistance in the first place? Some answers will emerge when the time limits are reached; others will take longer to become clear. Only with the completion of substantive studies of what actually happened to former welfare recipients will historians have the data to mount an assessment of the success or failure of attempts, in President Clinton's words, to "end welfare as we know it." As with Social Security and health care, this task will be crucial to

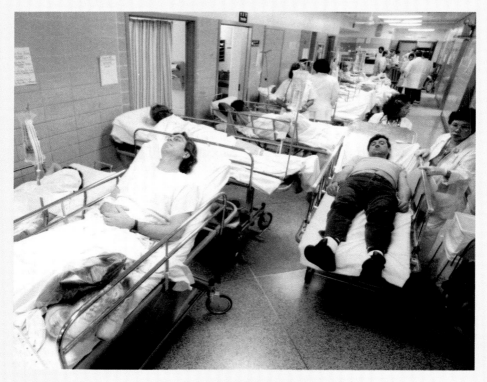

Gridlock

Although the escalating costs of medical care and prescription drugs dominate the headlines, a less well-known problem facing the country's health industry is the crisis in hospital emergency rooms. Attempts to control costs have led hospital administrators to cut back on Intensive Care Units, which have tended to shift the burden to emergency rooms, while drug overdoses, AIDS-related crises, and urban violence have increased demand. It is poor, uninsured Americans who most often turn to emergency rooms and who suffer the most from the gridlock in these facilities, such as this one at Cook County Hospital in Chicago. (Michael Melford)

understanding the evolution of the commitment of the state to public welfare, one of the major themes of the twentieth century.

Finally, historians of turn-of-the-century politics may find in this period the beginnings of changes in the political landscape. Will politicians' recognition of the gender gap in voting and its impact on elections result in a marked increase in the prominence of women in political life? Does the Democratic Party's nomination of Joseph Lieberman as the first Jewish candidate for vice president signal a new openness in the national political arena? Will the Reform Party, founded by Ross Perot, cease to be a magnet for Americans alienated from the two main parties? Will Ralph Nader's presidential campaign of 2000 mobilize Americans who are critical of corporate power and concerned about the environment? And what about

The End of Welfare as We Know It?

Californian welfare recipients attend classes at a job-training center that reformers hope will give them skills to find work that will keep them off the welfare roles. It is still too soon to evaluate the long-term impact of the state and federal welfare reforms put in place in the 1990s. (Lava Jo Regan/Saba)

the dramatic November–December protests outside the 1999 World Trade Organization meeting in Seattle, where thousands of activists—from union organizers to environmentalists to students broadly concerned about the global concentration of corporate power—surprised and disrupted the city? As one protester explained, people "can't go to the polls and talk to these big conglomerates. So they had to take to the streets and talk to them." Does Seattle represent a "blip," or does it point to a mounting tide of impassioned activism, especially on the part of the young? Or will a more conservative approach to political change—the call for campaign finance reform—be implemented, and if so, will it have any impact on removing special interests from the political process?

Another series of far-reaching questions about American politics emerges from the chaos surrounding the Florida election results in 2000. As voters learned about hanging, dimpled, and pregnant "chads," they recognized that their voting procedures were fraught with the potential for machine error. At the very least, the publicity will put pressure on local and state agencies to improve the process by which citizens cast their ballots. But will more substantial results emerge from the Supreme Court's ruling in the first of George W. Bush's challenges to the Florida recount?

Taking It to the Streets

In November 1999 more than 200 members of the Sea Turtle Restoration project, dressed in sea turtle costumes, joined thousands of protesters against the World Trade Organization that was meeting in Seattle. Whether this impassioned coalition of environmentalists, labor activists, and critics of corporate capitalism represents the beginning of a sustained and powerful movement is just one of the many open questions for the future of American politics. (Wide World)

There, the Court, whose conservative majority has consistently emphasized state and local rights, seemingly reversed its position, arguing that variability in the way in which Florida's counties conducted elections and counted ballots undermined citizens' equal protection rights under the Fourteenth Amendment. Will this serve to discredit the Court in the future? As a result of the Court's decision, legal experts predict an avalanche of lawsuits designed to implement national voting standards, which could have a far-reaching impact. Furthermore, the messiness of the Florida case reinforced Al Gore's supporters' conviction that his victory had been stolen, a belief given much emotional weight by the fact that Gore won the popular vote by over 300,000 ballots. But Bush won where it counts—in the electoral college—with 270 votes to Gore's 266 (with one abstention), making him the first president since Benjamin Harrison (over Grover Cleveland in 1888) to gain the presidency while losing the popular vote. The day after the election newly elected

New York Senator Hillary Rodham Clinton was just one of a large chorus who called for eliminating the electoral college itself. Such a change would be difficult to accomplish because it involves amending the constitution, but if implemented, it could have a profound effect on the nation's political process and its political parties.

And finally, what long-term changes will the Internet bring to the practice of politics? Many observers credited the Internet for its ability to rally thousands of people to Seattle; in the future it may facilitate extraordinary mobilization of political support. Moreover, the Web, barely a factor in public life until the mid-1990s, is challenging established sources of news information, such as television or newspapers, as a major purveyor of information about important events. While the Internet promotes a broad transmission of information, the downside to this instant news is that much of it is circulated with minimal editorial controls or checks, leading to unsubstantiated statements and more than a few rumors. One of the tasks for future historians will be to sift fact from fiction in this proliferation of new sources of information.

A related factor is the way in which the media has turned the world into a global village, allowing billions around the world to tune in and watch a story unfolding live. (CNN's on-the-spot coverage of the Persian Gulf War in 1990–1991 was a major turning point in such coverage.) This explosion of information access coincided with what one critic has called the "growing tabloidization of American culture," a frenzy for gossip that blurred the lines between public and private. What does it say about contemporary American culture that we know more about the intimate details of the president's sexual habits than about nearly anyone else's but our own? These trends, building in the late twentieth century, will be hard to derail in the twenty-first.

SOCIETY AND CULTURE.   The future of many emerging trends is unclear, but reliable projections predict a changing racial makeup for American society. The U.S. Census Bureau predicts that in the year 2050, whites will make up 52.7 percent of the American population (down from 75.7 percent in 1990), with Latinos accounting for 21.1 percent, blacks 15 percent, and Asians 10.1 percent. If projected intermarriage is factored in (Latinos and Asians marry outside their racial groups much more frequently than blacks), the estimated white "majority" will probably slip to a white "minority." At the close of the twentieth century, already one out of twenty-five married couples were interracial, and at least 3 million children were of mixed-race parentage in the country. (This latter figure does not even include the millions of Latino mestizos as well as black Americans who have either European or American Indian ancestors.) Probably the best-known example of the country's increasingly multiracial heritage is golfer Tiger Woods, who used to call himself a "Cablinasian" to reflect his mix of Caucasian, black, Native American, and Asian heritages.

More immediately, in 2005 the United States will reach another demographic milestone: according to census projections Latinos will surpass African Americans

FATHER: Chinese, Irish,
French, German, Swedish
MOTHER: Italian, Irish, Japanese

The New Face of Race

In recognition that the "old labels of black and white cannot begin to capture the subtleties" of contemporary racial identity, in September 2000 *Newsweek* presented a special report, "Redefining Race in America." With one out of twenty-five married couples now interracial unions, this family represents a significant demographic trend. (Terrence T. Miele)

as the country's largest minority group, a development of great historical import. For most of the country's history racial issues have been seen literally as "black and white." The rising numbers of Latinos and Asian Americans will push the United States to reframe the American discourse on race. Whether these two groups join forces with African Americans will have large implications for civil rights organizations and divisive national issues like affirmative action. By contrast, if Latinos and Asians are seen more as "honorary whites" in a mostly white, mixed-race majority, then the historic black-nonblack dichotomy may even intensify. Americans have often talked about their society as a melting pot, and in the twentieth century they accepted a wide range of cultures and skin colors. Deep divisions accompanied the shift, however, and such acrimony (which died down temporarily in the

Have You Registered?

In an effort to mobilize the growing Latino population's participation in the democratic process, the Southwest Voter Registration Education Project has conducted more than 1,000 voter registration and education campaigns, like this one in Travis County, Texas.
(Bob Daemmrich Photography)

late 1990s) is likely to return periodically in the next century, especially during periods of economic or social conflict.

The changing nature of the American population is also having a decided impact on America's religious life. In a trend that also will likely continue into the next century, mainline (and often liberal) Protestant denominations such as Episcopalians, Methodists, and Presbyterians have been losing members since their baby-boom-era peak in the mid-1960s. The greatest growth for Protestants since the 1970s has been in the more conservative Southern Baptist Convention, which has become the largest religious organization in the United States after the Roman Catholic Church. At the same time changes in immigration laws have increased the ranks of Catholics as well as believers of faiths that had not previously been well represented in the United States, including larger numbers of American Muslims, Buddhists, and Hindus. A multiracial society is also increasingly a multireligious one.

Conversely, in a trend with wide-reaching implications, some American-based faiths have become so multinational that they no longer depend solely on American believers. The most striking example is the Church of Jesus Christ of Latter-Day Saints, or Mormons. In 1980 three-quarters of Mormonism's 4.6 million believers lived in the United States; by 1997 the church had 10 million followers,

Muslims at Prayer

The number of mosques and Islamic centers in the United States has more than doubled in the last twenty years to a total of 1,250. These men at a prayer service at the Islamic Center of Portland, Maine, are visual testimony to the growing diversity of American religious life. (Wide World)

the majority of them overseas. The Assemblies of God, a pentecostal denomination founded in Arkansas in 1914 whose believers seek to be filled with the Holy Spirit, also had more followers abroad than in the United States, especially in Brazil. Reflecting this new complexity of American religious life, one scholar observed, "It's a fun time to be a student of religion because there are a lot of interesting changes going on. We don't know where they're going to end up." That sums up the challenge of writing the history of contemporary America.

Another contemporary trend demanding attention is environmental consciousness. On the one hand, the United States has benefited from an increasingly active environmental movement. On April 26, 1995, when Americans came together for the twenty-fifth anniversary of Earth Day, they had much to celebrate. The nation's rivers and waterways were cleaner; air pollution had been reduced by a third; and lead emissions from fuel, a cause of retardation in children, had been cut by an astounding 98 percent. The bald eagle and the California condor had come back from the brink of extinction. By 1996 more than 7,000 communities across the country had established curb-side collection recycling programs. And in addition to addressing problems in their own communities, Americans were also becoming increasingly aware that environmental protection required action not just from the United States but from the global community as a whole. An important

Los Angeles by Night

The vast expanse that is the Los Angeles metropolitan area is especially striking at night, as captured by artist Peter Alexander. Yet think of the vast amounts of energy being consumed by those city lights. (James Corcoran Gallery, Santa Monica, CA)

precedent for international action on environmental issues was set by the Montreal Protocol (1987), in which thirty-four nations agreed to phase out ozone-damaging chlorofluorocarbons (CFCs) by 1999. In June 1992 delegates to the Earth Summit in Rio de Janeiro adopted a treaty on global warming, and in 1994 the United States joined sixty-three other countries in signing the Basel Convention, which banned the export of hazardous wastes from industrialized to developing countries. In the future, U.S. environmental policy would operate more and more within an international framework.

On the other hand, turn-of-the-century Americans continued to face serious ecological problems. Despite efforts to reduce urban smog, two out of five Americans lived in areas with unhealthy air. Many rivers and lakes were still unsafe for fishing and swimming. And one out of four Americans lived within four miles of toxic waste dumps, a trend with disproportionate effect on lower-income communities, constituting what activists term *environmental racism.*

Also alarming was the nation's growing energy use at the turn of the century, which calls into question how significant a realignment actually occurred as a result of the energy crisis of the 1970s. By the late 1990s Americans were using almost as much energy per capita as they had in 1973, wiping out practically all the savings that had occurred through conservation and efficiency in between. At century's end Americans consumed more than twice as much energy per person as Europeans or Japanese. (Only Canadians, with a larger percentage of heavy industry and a colder climate, consumed more worldwide.) The short-term reason for the turnaround is clear: a worldwide decline in oil prices made it cheaper and easier for Americans to live more energy intensively. Two symptoms of the shift were the growing popularity of sports utility vehicles and the trend toward larger, more appliance-laden houses. To meet these energy needs U.S. oil imports grew from 35 percent of total consumption in 1973 to about 50 percent in the late 1990s. Even though energy experts warned that a tightening of oil supplies and higher prices was inevitable—a prediction that came true in 2000—few changed their lifestyles by reducing energy consumption.

This change in mentality about the need for conservation and environmental protection also threatened to undercut the international progress made in the 1980s and 1990s on pressing ecological issues such as acid rain and depletion of the ozone layer. Yet these problems have not gone away. More evidence for global warming emerged in August 2000, when scientists reported the discovery that the ice cap at the North Pole had melted, leaving a mile-wide expanse of water for the first time in recorded history.

Other important issues that face the United States at 2001 are, like the environment, global ones. The AIDS epidemic is another international issue. According to a United Nations study in 1997, more than 34 million people worldwide suffered from AIDS or were infected with HIV, the virus that causes AIDS. The problem was especially acute in Africa, where 24 million were infected; in Botswana, a shocking 36 percent of adults were HIV positive. Rates were lower in Asia, Eastern Europe, and South America, but the disease was spreading there as well. In the United States, by contrast, the number of AIDS deaths dropped from over 30,000 in 1995 to 20,000 four years later, the result of potent—and expensive—drugs that allowed some infected people to manage the disease. But even after extensive public health campaigns, the number of new infections did not drop in the United States.

According to *USA Today* 75 percent of Americans believe that another major and deadly disease will appear by 2025. At the same time Americans seem to expect major miracles from medical science in the next century. Fueled by consumer demands for health information and a desire to live longer, healthier lives, the news

The Human Genome Project

This gel strip, which contains DNA fragments, was one of the experimental building blocks for the Human Genome Project. Originally launched in 1990, the project announced in June 2000 that scientists had succeeded in mapping the human genetic code. While many observers exulted over the possibilities for understanding and curing diseases based on this "Book of Life," others worried over ethical questions connected to potential genetic discrimination.
(Photo Researchers)

media routinely treat advances in science and medicine as front-page news. In the June 2000 report on the "Genome Project," scientists announced that they had produced a "Book of Life" mapping the human genetic code, and commentators explored its medical implications for the treatment of disease as well as ethical questions about potential genetic discrimination. Less ambiguous was the response when the *New York Times* ran a feature story about a possible breakthrough in cancer research in 1998. Hopes soared that cancer might once and for all be conquered. "OUR BEST HOPE" ran one headline, with an accompanying article by a cancer-stricken journalist who stated, "Maybe we don't have to die." Doctors often learn about new drugs and procedures right along with their patients through newspaper accounts and drug company-sponsored advertisements; patients also surf the Internet for information about clinical trials of new treatments or experimental drugs for specific diseases. This democratization of medical knowledge empowers some consumers but at the cost of inflating hopes about untested drugs and procedures years away from marketability. And yet Americans' hope for the cure—for breast cancer, for AIDS, for Alzheimer's disease—continues unabated.

ECONOMICS.   Just as rapid-pace developments in the arenas of technology and science make it difficult for historians to assess recent events, dramatic changes in the economy in the last decade provide a good example of how quickly and unexpectedly our understanding of the nation's economic picture can be transformed. In 1989 it was widely accepted that Japan was rising and America was declining, or as the scholar Chalmers Johnson put it, "The cold war is over, and Japan won." Now the opposite appears to be true: the United States economy looks strong, almost invincible, and Asian economies are having difficulties. One seemingly safe conclusion is that when an economy is performing well, as was Japan's in the late 1980s and America's in the late 1990s, it temporarily hides all sorts of problems. As economist Laura D'Andrea Tyson observes, "In prosperous times we overstate the good and understate the bad." One of the most troubling "bad" trends is the growing disparity of wealth and opportunity that characterizes the American economy at the end of the century, with the very rich profiting the most from the recent period of prosperity.

And no matter how prosperous the United States might be, its fortunes are intimately tied to the performance of other nations' economies. The rapid growth of international corporations has eroded traditional barriers of nation states and led to increased concentration of the world's economic power, which at the very least has implications for working people who must compete in a global labor market. The late 1990s saw meltdown in Asia, with nine of Asia's thirteen major countries either in recession or depression by 1998, and the collapse of the Russian economy. As the world's economic troubles deepened, the new buzz word among politicians and economists was an updated version of the domino theory called *contagion*—the idea that if one country's economy was allowed to implode, it could set in motion an uncontrollable set of events around the world. The International Monetary Fund (IMF) and the World Bank, set up in the wake of World War II to ensure financial stability in world markets, responded by one costly rescue bailout after another of a shaky economy—Thailand, Indonesia, South Korea, and Russia. Fears surfaced that Brazil, Venezuela, or Mexico might be next.

As historians struggle to make sense of the global economic picture, they are hampered not just by the dramatic turn of events in Asia but also by the fact that many economic tenets no longer seem reliable. For example, since 1960 a widely accepted economic principle called the Phillips curve posited that there could be low inflation or low unemployment but not both. Yet the 1990s boom has seen inflation *and* unemployment drop to their lowest levels in generations. Another long-held economic tenet claimed that measures to lower the deficit would act as a drag on the economy, thereby slowing economic growth. To the contrary, in the 1990s the United States has experienced both significant deficit reduction and a period of sustained economic growth. In other words, many of the principles and tenets on which economists—and historians who rely on those economists—depend seem to have broken down. Perhaps the ups and downs of the past ten years will lead to the emergence of new economic laws, but for now we are all struggling to make sense of a complex and deeply interconnected world economy.

FOREIGN POLICY.   Just as complicated are the emerging contours of the post–cold-war world. Note that historians are still using the cold war as the organizing concept for the late twentieth century, even though it ended a decade earlier. Future textbooks will probably recognize the events of 1989 – 1991 in Eastern Europe and the Soviet Union as the defining watershed in the late twentieth century; certainly the years 1945 to 1991 would provide a logical periodization for Part Six in a future edition of America's History. Events since then—the last part of Chapter 31 and this epilogue—would in effect be the opening of a new Part Seven, as yet unnamed and (with apologies to the sports world) with themes and players to be announced later.

Despite the end of the cold war American foreign policy is still directed toward the goals that have shaped much of the twentieth century, such as desiring to contain major or potentially major nations that might appear as rivals. Thus the United States supported the expansion of NATO to include former communist bloc members Poland, Hungary, and the Czech Republic as a hedge against a resurgent Russia. Regarding China, the world's most populous country, the United States worried about China's nuclear capabilities and human-rights violations, yet the October 2000 agreement to establish Permanent Normal Trade Relations between the two nations was interpreted by U.S. leaders as a step toward promoting an American version of free-market capitalism and democracy in China. Protecting U.S. access to oil reserves worldwide remained a high priority, with the oil-rich Caspian region (wedged between Russia and Iran) emerging as the newest stage for diplomatic maneuvering.

On the eve of the twenty-first century, terrorism emerged as a central concern of U.S. foreign policy. A series of terrorist attacks, often directed at American citizens or embassies abroad but occasionally at targets in the United States (like the 1993 bombing of New York City's World Trade Center), had heightened America's sense of vulnerability. Even though the number of lives lost was relatively small (ninety-eight Americans were killed in foreign terrorist attacks between 1989 and 1998, less than are killed on average each year by lightning), driving the fear was the perception that terrorists posed a continuous, deadly, and invisible threat to American interests and installations throughout the world. As with cold-war fears of nuclear annihilation that sent schoolchildren ducking and covering under their desks, no one ever feels safe in a world where terrorists reign.

But unlike the cold war, a period when the Soviet Union was identified as America's main enemy, terrorist attacks cannot necessarily be traced to a single state or a single leader. Instead of a central headquarters like the Kremlin, loose organizations are dispersed throughout many countries. At the end of the twentieth

Terrorists Strike the USS Cole

A deadly reminder of the ever-present threat of terrorism came on October 12, 2000, when a suicide attack on the USS _Cole,_ a navy guided-missile destroyer that was refueling in the Yemeni part of Aden, blew a huge hole in the ship's hull, killing seventeen sailors. The United States immediately lay the blame on Saudi exile Osama bin Laden. In Yemen, six suspects were arrested on suspicion of complicity in the attack. (U.S. Navy/TimePix)

century the strongest threats to American interests came from militant Islamic sects committed to a messianic vision of the end of Western influence in the Arab world and the ultimate destruction of the United States. Responsibility for attacks was often difficult to pin down—was it Hezbollah, Islamic Jihad, or Osama bin Laden's followers?—and bringing terrorists to international justice even harder. Retaliation can sometimes subdue opponents or can simply provoke further terrorism in a war of attrition.

While there are few rules or guidelines for a coming war against terrorism, the world began to feel confident that nuclear proliferation had been slowed or even halted as the century drew to an end. Then in 1998 India and Pakistan each defied world opinion by testing a nuclear device. In the immediate aftermath of World War II only the largest and most advanced countries could realistically hope to develop nuclear weapons, but fifty years later the capacity is spread much more broadly. Until India and Pakistan conducted their tests, only five countries had declared nuclear-weapons capability: the United States, Russia, Britain, France, and

China, although most observers believe that Israel had such capacity as well. In addition, Iran, Iraq, North Korea, and Libya were suspected of having secret nuclear-weapons programs. Especially worrisome about the Indian and Pakistani tests was these neighboring countries' long history of a bitter acrimony in one of the world's most populous and dangerous regions. International concerns about controlling nuclear weapons deepened in October 1999 when the U.S. Senate in a partisan battle refused to ratify the Comprehensive Test Ban Treaty (CTBT), a move widely interpreted as damaging to the nation's ability to exercise political and moral leadership in the drive to contain nuclear proliferation.

Small countries as well as terrorist organizations realize that they do not require a nuclear bomb to be taken seriously: short-range nuclear missiles, germ warfare, and poison gas can be just as effective and far cheaper. (This threat is sometimes abbreviated as "NBC"—nuclear, biological, and chemical weapons—or alternatively, weapons of mass destruction.) Much of the basic material and technology is available for purchase on the thriving world arms market, in which countries like the United States, France, Britain, and the former states of the Soviet Union are major dealers. Given this traffic in arms, it is fairly easy for intermediaries in the Middle East and other developing countries to buy what they need. It is said that highly destructive cruise missiles can be bought for approximately $10,000 apiece, making them in some ways the "poor man's nukes." Their potential danger increases when combined with the capacity for chemical and biological warfare. Unlike policing who has and who doesn't have the bomb, the containment of arms proliferation and suspected chemical and biological warfare is an even more complex task, as the United States has discovered in its dealings with Iraq and Saddam Hussein in the aftermath of the 1990–1991 Gulf War.

At the same time, destructive conflicts that have little to do with high-tech weaponry and everything to do with ethnicity, religion, and territory have flared up periodically in the aftermath of the cold war and threaten to do so for the foreseeable future. In the Middle East, violent attacks and counterattacks between Israelis and Palestinians in 2000–2001 shattered a Clinton-brokered peace plan, and the 2001 election of Likud Party leader Ariel Sharon as prime minister of Israel further dimmed hopes that a resolution of the differences between the two sides could be resolved peacefully. The Balkans especially continue to challenge U.S. policymakers, NATO leaders, and United Nations peacekeeping forces. Would the Yugoslavian province of Kosovo, which U.S. special envoy Richard Holbrooke in 1998 called "the most dangerous place in Europe," become the next Bosnia? Or would the Yugoslavian republic of Montenegro? Can genocides such as those that occurred in Bosnia and Rwanda be prevented?

The contemporary world can look like a scary place indeed, but rays of hope at the end of the twentieth century included the possible resolutions of problems that have long defied peaceful solutions: the hope that the 1998 Good Friday accords may finally bring peace to Ireland, or that U.S.-Cuban relations might improve in the wake of Pope John Paul II's visit to Cuba in 1998 despite the furor over

A Hero for Our Jaded Times

Nelson Mandela is that rare contemporary hero whose stature seems destined to be confirmed posthumously by history. In a valedictory address to the United Nations in 1998, Mandela spoke of his long personal journey:

> Born as the First World War came to a close and departing from public life as the world marks half a century of the Universal Declaration of Human Rights, I have reached that part of the long walk when the opportunity is granted, as it should be to all men and women, to retire to some rest and tranquility in the village of my birth.
>
> As I sit in Qunu and grow as ancient as its hills . . . I will continue to hope that Africa's renaissance will strike deep roots and blossom forever, without regard to the changing seasons. . . .
>
> Then would history and the billions throughout the world proclaim that it was right that we dreamed and that we toiled to give life to a workable dream.

(Louise Gubb/The Image Works)

the Elián González case. The end of apartheid in South Africa and that country's determination to come to grips with its past are surely among the twentieth century's most inspiring developments, as is the emergence of democratic countries from the former Soviet satellites in Eastern Europe. Along with globalization and the challenge of forging a post–cold-war foreign policy, these potential breakthroughs are part of the story of America and the world in 2001.

DOCUMENTS

THE DECLARATION OF INDEPENDENCE

The Unanimous Declaration of the Thirteen United States of America

When in the Course of human events, it becomes necessary for one people to dissolve the political bands which have connected them with another, and to assume among the Powers of the earth, the separate and equal station to which the Laws of Nature and of Nature's God entitle them, a decent respect to the opinions of mankind requires that they should declare the causes which impel them to the separation.

We hold these truths to be self-evident, that all men are created equal, that they are endowed by their Creator with certain unalienable rights, that among these are Life, Liberty, and the pursuit of Happiness. That to secure these rights, Governments are instituted among Men, deriving their just powers from the consent of the governed. That whenever any Form of Government becomes destructive of these ends, it is the Right of the People to alter or to abolish it, and to institute new Government, laying its foundation on such principles and organizing its powers in such form, as to them shall seem most likely to effect their Safety and Happiness. Prudence, indeed, will dictate that Governments long established should not be changed for light and transient causes; and accordingly all experience hath shown, that mankind are more disposed to suffer, while evils are sufferable, than to right themselves by abolishing the forms to which they are accustomed. But when a long train of abuses and usurpations, pursuing invariably the same Object evinces a design to reduce them under absolute Despotism, it is their right, it is their duty, to throw off such Government, and to provide new Guards for their future security. —Such has been the patient sufferance of these Colonies; and such is now the necessity which constrains them to alter their former Systems of Government. The history of the present King of Great Britain is a history of repeated injuries and usurpations, all having in direct object the establishment of an absolute Tyranny over these States. To prove this, let Facts be submitted to a candid world.

He has refused his Assent to Laws, the most wholesome and necessary for the public good.

He has forbidden his Governors to pass Laws of immediate and pressing importance, unless suspended in their operation till his Assent should be obtained; and, when so suspended, he has utterly neglected to attend to them.

He has refused to pass other Laws for the accommodation of large districts of people, unless those people would relinquish the right of Representation in the Legislature, a right inestimable to them and formidable to tyrants only.

He has called together legislative bodies at places unusual, uncomfortable, and distant from the depository of their public Records, for the sole purpose of fatiguing them into compliance with his measures.

He has dissolved Representative Houses repeatedly, for opposing with manly firmness his invasions on the rights of the people.

He has refused for a long time, after such dissolutions, to cause others to be elected; whereby the Legislative powers, incapable of Annihilation, have returned to the People at large for their exercise; the State remaining in the mean time exposed to all the dangers of invasion from without and convulsions within.

He has endeavoured to prevent the population of these States; for that purpose obstructing the Laws of Naturalization of Foreigners; refusing to pass others to encourage their migrations hither, and raising the conditions of new Appropriations of Lands.

He has obstructed the Administration of Justice, by refusing his Assent to Laws for establishing Judiciary powers.

He has made Judges dependent on his Will alone, for the tenure of their offices, and the amount and payment of their salaries.

He has erected a multitude of New Offices, and sent hither swarms of Officers to harass our People, and eat out their substance.

He has kept among us, in times of peace, Standing Armies without the Consent of our legislature.

He has combined with others to subject us to a jurisdiction foreign to our constitution, and unacknowledged by our laws; giving his Assent to their Acts of pretended Legislation:

For quartering large bodies of armed troops among us:

For protecting them, by a mock Trial, from Punishment for any Murders which they should commit on the Inhabitants of these States:

For cutting off our Trade with all parts of the world:

For imposing taxes on us without our Consent:

For depriving us of many cases, of the benefits of Trial by jury:

For transporting us beyond Seas to be tried for pretended offences:

For abolishing the free System of English Laws in a neighbouring Province, establishing therein an Arbitrary government, and enlarging its Boundaries so as to render it at once an example and fit instrument for introducing the same absolute rule into these Colonies:

For taking away our Charters, abolishing our most valuable Laws, and altering fundamentally the Forms of our Governments:

For suspending our own Legislatures, and declaring themselves invested with Power to legislate for us in all cases whatsoever.

He has abdicated Government here, by declaring us out of his Protection and waging War against us.

He has plundered our seas, ravaged our Coasts, burnt our towns, and destroyed the lives of our people.

He is at this time transporting large armies of foreign mercenaries to compleat the works of death, desolation, and tyranny, already begun with circumstances of Cruelty & perfidy scarcely paralleled in the most barbarous ages, and totally unworthy the Head of a civilized nation.

He has constrained our fellow Citizens taken Captive on the high Seas to bear Arms against their Country, to become the executioners of their friends and Brethren, or to fall themselves by their Hands.

He has excited domestic insurrections amongst us, and has endeavoured to bring on the inhabitants of our frontiers, the merciless Indian Savages, whose known rule of warfare, is an undistinguished destruction of all ages, sexes, and conditions.

In every stage of these Oppressions We have Petitioned for Redress in the most humble terms: Our repeated petitions have been answered only by repeated injury. A Prince, whose character is thus marked by every act which may define a Tyrant, is unfit to be the ruler of a free people.

Nor have We been wanting in attention to our British brethren. We have warned them from time to time of attempts by their legislature to extend an unwarrantable jurisdiction over us. We have reminded them of the circumstances of our emigration and settlement here. We have appealed to their native justice and magnanimity, and we have conjured them by the ties of our common kindred to disavow these usurpations, which, would inevitably interrupt our connections and correspondence. They too have been deaf to the voice of justice and of consanguinity. We must, therefore, acquiesce in the necessity, which denounces our Separation, and hold them, as we hold the rest of mankind, Enemies in War, in Peace Friends.

We, therefore, the Representatives of the United States of America, in General Congress, Assembled, appealing to the Supreme Judge of the world for the rectitude of our intentions, do, in the Name, and by Authority of the good People of these Colonies, solemnly publish and declare, That these United Colonies are, and of Right ought to be FREE AND INDEPENDENT STATES; that they are Absolved from all Allegiance to the British Crown, and that all political connection between them and the State of Great Britain, is and ought to be totally dissolved; and that as Free and Independent States, they have full Power to levy War, conclude Peace, contract Alliances, establish Commerce, and to do all other Acts and Things which Independent States may of right do. And for the support of this Declaration, with a firm reliance on the Protection of Divine Providence, we mutually pledge to each other our Lives, our Fortunes, and our sacred Honor.

John Hancock

Button Gwinnett	**George Wythe**	**James Wilson**	**Josiah Bartlett**
Lyman Hall	**Richard Henry Lee**	**Geo. Ross**	**Wm. Whipple**
Geo. Walton	**Th. Jefferson**	**Caesar Rodney**	**Saml. Adams**
Wm. Hooper	**Benja. Harrison**	**Geo. Read**	**John Adams**
Joseph Hewes	**Thos. Nelson, Jr.**	**Thos. M'Kean**	**Robt. Treat Paine**
John Penn	**Francis Lightfoot Lee**	**Wm. Floyd**	**Elbridge Gerry**
Edward Rutledge	**Carter Braxton**	**Phil. Livingston**	**Step. Hopkins**
Thos. Heyward, Junr.	**Robt. Morris**	**Frans. Lewis**	**William Ellery**
Thomas Lynch, Junr.	**Benjamin Rush**	**Lewis Morris**	**Roger Sherman**
Arthur Middleton	**Benja. Franklin**	**Richd. Stockton**	**Sam'el Hunington**
Samuel Chase	**John Morton**	**Jno. Witherspoon**	**Wm. Williams**
Wm. Paca	**Geo. Clymer**	**Fras. Hopkinson**	**Oliver Wolcott**
Thos. Stone	**Jas. Smith**	**John Hart**	**Matthew Thornton**
Charles Carroll of Carrollton	**Geo. Taylor**	**Abra. Clark**	

THE ARTICLES OF CONFEDERATION AND PERPETUAL UNION

Between the states of New Hampshire, Massachusetts Bay, Rhode Island and Providence Plantations, Connecticut, New York, New Jersey, Pennsylvania, Delaware, Maryland, Virginia, North Carolina, South Carolina, Georgia.*

ARTICLE 1.

The stile of this confederacy shall be "The United States of America."

ARTICLE 2.

Each State retains its sovereignty, freedom and independence, and every power, jurisdiction, and right, which is not by this confederation expressly delegated to the United States, in Congress assembled.

ARTICLE 3.

The said states hereby severally enter into a firm league of friendship with each other for their common defence, the security of their liberties and their mutual and general welfare; binding themselves to assist each other against all force offered to, or attacks made upon them, or any of them, on account of religion, sovereignty, trade, or any other pretence whatever.

ARTICLE 4.

The better to secure and perpetuate mutual friendship and intercourse among the people of the different states in this union, the free inhabitants of each of these states, paupers, vagabonds, and fugitives from justice excepted, shall be entitled to all privileges and immunities of free citizens in the several states; and the people of each State shall have free ingress and regress to and from any other State, and shall enjoy therein all the privileges of trade and commerce, subject to the same duties, impositions, and restrictions, as the inhabitants thereof respectively; provided, that such restrictions shall not extend so far as to prevent the removal of property, imported into any State, to any other State of which the owner is an inhabitant; provided also, that no imposition, duties, or restriction, shall be laid by any State on the property of the United States, or either of them.

If any person guilty of, or charged with treason, felony, or other high misdemeanor in any State, shall flee from justice and be found in any of the United States, he shall, upon demand of the governor or executive power of the State from which he fled, be delivered up and removed to the State having jurisdiction of his offence.

Full faith and credit shall be given in each of these states to the records, acts, and judicial proceedings of the courts and magistrates of every other State.

---

*This copy of the final draft of the Articles of Confederation is taken from the *Journals,* 9:907–25, November 15, 1777.

ARTICLE 5.

For the more convenient management of the general interests of the United States, delegates shall be annually appointed, in such manner as the legislature of each State shall direct, to meet in Congress, on the 1st Monday in November in every year, with a power reserved to each State to recall its delegates, or any of them, at any time within the year, and to send others in their stead for the remainder of the year.

No State shall be represented in Congress by less than two, nor by more than seven members; and no person shall be capable of being a delegate for more than three years in any term of six years; nor shall any person, being a delegate, be capable of holding any office under the United States, for which he, or any other for his benefit, receives any salary, fees, or emolument of any kind.

Each State shall maintain its own delegates in a meeting of the states, and while they act as members of the committee of the states.

In determining questions in the United States, in Congress assembled, each State shall have one vote.

Freedom of speech and debate in Congress shall not be impeached or questioned in any court or place out of Congress: and the members of Congress shall be protected in their persons from arrests and imprisonments, during the time of their going to and from, and attendance on Congress, except for treason, felony, or breach of the peace.

ARTICLE 6.

No State, without the consent of the United States, in Congress assembled, shall send any embassy to, or receive any embassy from, or enter into any conference, agreement, alliance, or treaty with any king, prince, or state; nor shall any person, holding any office of profit or trust under the United States, or any of them, accept of any present, emolument, office or title, of any kind whatever, from any king, prince, or foreign state; nor shall the United States, in Congress assembled, or any of them, grant any title of nobility.

No two or more states shall enter into any treaty, confederation, or alliance, whatever, between them, without the consent of the United States, in Congress assembled, specifying accurately the purposes for which the same is to be entered into, and how long it shall continue.

No state shall lay any imposts or duties which may interfere with any stipulations in treaties entered into by the United States, in Congress assembled, with any king, prince, or state, in pursuance of any treaties already proposed by Congress to the courts of France and Spain.

No vessels of war shall be kept up in time of peace by any State, except such number only as shall be deemed necessary by the United States, in Congress assembled, for the defence of such State or its trade; nor shall any body of forces be kept up by any State, in time of peace, except such number only as, in the judgment of the United States, in Congress assembled, shall be deemed requisite to garrison the forts necessary for the defence of such State; but every State shall always keep up a well regulated and disciplined militia, sufficiently armed and accoutred, and shall provide, and constantly have ready for use, in public stores, a due number of field pieces and tents, and a proper quantity of arms, ammunition and camp equipage.

No State shall engage in any war without the consent of the United States, in Congress assembled, unless such State be actually invaded by enemies, or shall have received certain advice of a resolution being formed by some nation of Indians to invade such State, and the danger is so imminent as not to admit of a delay till the United States, in Congress assembled, can be consulted; nor shall any State grant commissions to any ships or vessels of war, nor letters of marque or reprisal, except it be after a declaration of war by the United States, in Congress assembled, and then only against the kingdom or state, and the subjects thereof, against which war has been so declared, and under such regulations as shall be established by the United States, in Congress assembled, unless such State be infested by pirates, in which case vessels of war may be fitted out for that occasion, and kept so long as the danger shall continue, or until the United States, in Congress assembled, shall determine otherwise.

ARTICLE 7.

When land forces are raised by any State for the common defence, all officers of or under the rank of colonel, shall be appointed by the legislature of each State respectively, by whom such forces shall be raised, or in such manner as such State shall direct; and all vacancies shall be filled up by the State which first made the appointment.

ARTICLE 8.

All charges of war and all other expences, that shall be incurred for the common defence or general welfare, and allowed by the United States, in Congress assembled, shall be defrayed out of a common treasury, which shall be supplied by the several states, in proportion to the value of all land within each State, granted to or surveyed for any person, as such land and the buildings and improvements thereon shall be estimated according to such mode as the United States, in Congress assembled, shall, from time to time, direct and appoint.

The taxes for paying that proportion shall be laid and levied by the authority and direction of the legislatures of the several states, within the time agreed upon by the United States, in Congress assembled.

ARTICLE 9.

The United States, in Congress assembled, shall have the sole and exclusive right and power of determining on peace and war, except in the cases mentioned in the 6th article; of sending and receiving ambassadors; entering into treaties and alliances, provided that no treaty of commerce shall be made, whereby the legislative power of the respective states shall be restrained from imposing such imposts and duties on foreigners as their own people are subjected to, or from prohibiting the exportation or importation of any species of goods or commodities whatsoever; of establishing rules for deciding, in all cases, what captures on land or water shall be legal, and in what manner prizes, taken by land or naval forces in the service of the United States, shall be divided or appropriated; or granting letters of marque and reprisal in times of peace; appointing courts for the trial of piracies and felonies committed on the high seas, and establishing courts for receiving and determining, finally, appeals in all cases of captures; provided, that no member of Congress shall be appointed a judge of any of the said courts.

The United States, in Congress assembled, shall also be the last resort on appeal in all disputes and differences now subsisting, or that hereafter may arise between two or more states concerning boundary, jurisdiction or any other cause whatever; which authority shall always be exercised in the manner following: whenever the legislative or executive authority, or lawful agent of any State, in controversy with another, shall present a petition to Congress, stating the matter in question, and praying for a hearing, notice thereof shall be given, by order of Congress, to the legislative of executive authority of the other State in controversy, and a day assigned for the appearance of the parties by their lawful agents, who shall then be directed to appoint, by joint consent, commissioners or judges to constitute a court for hearing and determining the matter in question; but, if they cannot agree, Congress shall name three persons out of each of the United States, and from the list of such persons each party shall alternately strike out one, the petitioners beginning, until the number shall be reduced to thirteen; and from that number not less than seven, nor more than nine names, as Congress shall direct, shall, in the presence of Congress, be drawn out by lot; and the persons whose names shall be so drawn, or any five of them, shall be commissioners or judges to hear and finally determine the controversy, so always as a major part of the judges who shall hear the cause shall agree in the determination; and if either party shall neglect to attend at the day appointed, without shewing reasons which Congress shall judge sufficient, or, being present, shall refuse to strike, the Congress shall proceed to nominate three persons out of each State, and the secretary of Congress shall strike in behalf of such party absent or refusing; and the judgment and sentence of the court to be appointed, in the manner before prescribed, shall be final and conclusive; and if any of the parties shall refuse to submit to the authority of such court, or to appear or defend their claim or cause, the court shall nevertheless proceed to pronounce sentence or judgment, which shall, in like manner, be final and decisive, the judgment or sentence and other proceedings begin, in either case, transmitted to Congress, and lodged among the acts of Congress for the security of the parties concerned: provided, that every commissioner, before he sits in judgment, shall take an oath, to be administered by one of the judges of the supreme or superior court of the State where the cause shall be tried, "well and truly to hear and determine the matter in question, according to the best of his judgment, without favour, affection, or hope of reward:" provided, also, that no State shall be deprived of territory for the benefit of the United States.

All controversies concerning the private right of soil, claimed under different grants of two or more states, whose jurisdictions, as they may respect such lands and the states which passed such grants, are adjusted, the said grants, or either of them, being at the same time claimed to have originated antecedent to such settlement of jurisdiction, shall, on the petition of either party to the Congress of the United States, be finally determined, as near as may be, in the same manner as is before prescribed for deciding disputes respecting territorial jurisdiction between different states.

The United States, in Congress assembled, shall also have the sole and exclusive right and power of regulating the alloy and value of coin struck by their own authority, or by that of the respective states; fixing the standard of weights and measures throughout the United States; regulating the trade and managing all affairs with the Indians not members of any of the states; provided that the legislative right of any State within its own limits be not infringed or violated; establishing and regulating post offices from one State to another throughout all the United States, and exacting such postage on the papers passing through the same as may be requisite to defray the expences of the said office; appointing all officers of the land forces in the service of the United States, excepting regimental officers; appointing all the officers of the naval forces, and commissioning all officers whatever in the service of the United States; making rules for the government and regulation of the said land and naval forces, and directing their operations.

The United States, in Congress assembled, shall have authority to appoint a committee to sit in the recess of Congress, to be denominated "a Committee of the States," and to consist of one delegate from each State, and to appoint such other committees and civil officers as may be necessary for managing the general affairs of the United States, under their direction; to appoint one of their number to preside; provided that no person be allowed to serve in the office of president more than one year in any term of three years; to ascertain the necessary sums of money to be raised for the service of the United States, and to appropriate and apply the same for defraying the public expences; to borrow money or emit bills on the credit of the United States, transmitting, every half year, to the respective states, an account of the sums of money so borrowed or emitted; to build and equip a navy; to agree upon the number of land forces, and to make requisitions from each State for in quota, in proportion to the number of white inhabitants in such State; which requisitions shall be binding; and thereupon, the legislature of each State shall appoint the regimental officers, raise the men, and cloathe, arm, and equip them in a soldier-like manner, at the expence of the United States; and the officers and men so cloathed, armed, and equipped, shall march to the place appointed and within the time agreed on by the United States, in Congress assembled; but if the United States, in Congress assembled, shall, on consideration of circumstances, judge proper that any State should not raise men, or should raise a smaller number than its quota, and that any other State should raise a greater number of men than the quota threof, such extra number shall be raised, officered, cloathed, armed, and equipped in the same manner as the quota of such State, unless the legislature of such State shall judge that such extra number cannot be safely spared out of the same, in which case they shall raise, officer, cloathe, arm, and equip as many of such extra number as they judge can be safely spared. And the officers and men so cloathed, armed, and equipped, shall march to the place appointed and within the time agreed on by the United States, in Congress assembled.

The United States, in Congress assembled, shall never engage in a war, nor grant letters of marque and reprisal in time of peace, nor enter into any treaties or alliances, nor coin money, nor regulate the value thereof, nor ascertain the sums and expences necessary for the defence and welfare of the United States, or any of them: nor emit bills, nor borrow money on the credit of the United States, nor appropriate money, nor agree upon the number of vessels of war to be built or purchased, or the number of land or sea forces to be raised, nor appoint a commander in chief of the army or navy, unless nine states assent to the same; nor shall a question on any other point, except for adjourning from day to day, be determined, unless by the votes of a majority of the United States, in Congress assembled.

The Congress of the United States shall have power to adjourn to any time within the year, and to any place within the United States, so that no period of adjournment be for a longer duration than the space of six months, and shall publish the journal of their proceedings monthly, except such parts thereof, relating to treaties, alliances or military operations, as, in their judgment, require secrecy; and the yeas and nays of the delegates of each State on any question shall be entered on the journal, when it is desired by any delegate; and the delegates of a State, or any of them, at his, or their request, shall be furnished with a transcript of the said journal, except such parts as are above excepted, to lay before the legislatures of the several states.

ARTICLE 10.

The committee of the states, or any nine of them, shall be authorized to execute, in the recess of Congress, such of the powers of Congress as the United States, in Congress assembled, by the consent of nine states, shall, from time to time, think expedient to vest them with; provided, that no power be delegated to the said committee, for the exercise of which, by the articles of confederation, the voice of nine states, in the Congress of the United States assembled, is requisite.

ARTICLE 11.

Canada acceding to this confederation, and joining in the measures of the United States, shall be admitted into and entitled to all the advantages of this union; but no other colony shall be admitted into the same, unless such admission be agreed to by nine states.

ARTICLE 12.

All bills of credit emitted, monies borrowed and debts contracted by, or under the authority of Congress before the assembling of the United States, in pursuance of the present confederation, shall be deemed and considered as a charge against the United States, for payment and satisfaction whereof the said United States and the public faith are hereby solemnly pledged.

ARTICLE 13.

Every State shall abide by the determinations of the United States, in Congress assembled, on all questions which, by this confederation, are submitted to them. And the articles of this confederation shall be inviolably observed by every State, and the union shall be perpetual; nor shall any alteration at any time hereafter be made in any of them, unless such alteration be agreed to in a Congress of the United States, and be afterwards confirmed by the legislatures of every State.

These articles shall be proposed to the legislatures of all the United States, to be considered, and if approved of by them, they are advised to authorize their delegates to ratify the same in the Congress of the United States; which being done, the same shall become conclusive.

THE CONSTITUTION OF THE UNITED STATES

We the People of the United States, in Order to form a more perfect Union, establish Justice, insure domestic Tranquility, provide for the common defence, promote the general Welfare, and secure the Blessings of Liberty to ourselves and our Posterity, do ordain and establish this Constitution for the United States of America.

ARTICLE I

Section 1

All legislative Powers herein granted shall be vested in a Congress of the United States, which shall consist of a Senate and a House of Representatives.

Section 2

The House of Representatives shall be composed of Members chosen every second Year by the People of the several States, and the Electors in each State shall have the Qualifications requisite for Electors of the most numerous Branch of the State Legislature.

No Person shall be a Representative who shall not have attained to the Age of twenty-five Years, and been seven Years a Citizen of the United States, and who shall not, when elected, be an Inhabitant of that State in which he shall be chosen.

Representatives and direct Taxes shall be apportioned among the several States which may be included within this Union, according to their respective Numbers, *which shall be determined by adding to the whole Number of free Persons, including those bound to Service for a Term of Years, and excluding Indians not taxed, three fifths of all other Persons.** The actual Enumeration shall be made within three Years after the first Meeting of the Congress of the United States, and within every subsequent Term of ten Years, in such Manner as they shall by Law direct. The Number of Representatives shall not exceed one for every thirty Thousand, but each State shall have at Least one Representative; and *until such enumeration shall be made, the State of New Hampshire shall be entitled to chuse three, Massachusetts eight, Rhode Island and Providence Plantations one, Connecticut five, New-York six, New Jersey four, Pennsylvania eight, Delaware one, Maryland six, Virginia ten, North Carolina five, South Carolina five, and Georgia three.*

When vacancies happen in the Representation from any State, the Executive Authority thereof shall issue Writs of Election to fill such Vacancies.

The House of Representatives shall chuse their Speaker and other Officers; and shall have the sole Power of Impeachment.

Section 3

The Senate of the United States shall be composed of two Senators from each State, *chosen by the Legislature thereof,*† for six Years; and each Senator shall have one Vote.

Immediately after they shall be assembled in Consequence of the first Election, they shall be divided as equally as may be into three Classes. The Seats of the Senators of the first

---

Note: The Constitution became effective March 4, 1789. Provisions in italics have been changed by constitutional amendment.

*Changed by Section 2 of the Fourteenth Amendment.

†Changed by Section 1 of the Seventeenth Amendment.

Class shall be vacated at the Expiration of the second Year, of the second Class at the Expiration of the fourth Year, and of the third Class at the Expiration of the sixth Year, so that one-third may be chosen every second Year; *and if Vacancies happen by Resignation, or otherwise, during the Recess of the Legislature of any State, the Executive thereof may make temporary Appointments until the next Meeting of the Legislature, which shall then fill such Vacancies.**

No person shall be a Senator who shall not have attained to the Age of thirty Years, and been nine Years a Citizen of the United States, and who shall not, when elected, be an Inhabitant of that State for which he shall be chosen.

The Vice President of the United States shall be President of the Senate, but shall have no Vote, unless they be equally divided.

The Senate shall chuse their other Officers, and also a President pro tempore, in the absence of the Vice President, or when he shall exercise the Office of President of the United States.

The Senate shall have the sole Power to try all Impeachments. When sitting for that Purpose, they shall be on Oath or Affirmation. When the President of the United States is tried, the Chief Justice shall preside: And no Person shall be convicted without the Concurrence of two thirds of the Members present.

Judgment in Cases of Impeachment shall not extend further than to removal from Office, and disqualification to hold and enjoy any Office of honor, Trust or Profit under the United States: but the Party convicted shall nevertheless be liable and subject to Indictment, Trial, Judgment and Punishment, according to Law.

Section 4

The Times, Places and Manner of holding Elections for Senators and Representatives, shall be prescribed in each State by the Legislature thereof, but the Congress may at any time by Law make or alter such Regulations, except as to the Places of Chusing Senators.

The Congress shall assemble at least once in every Year, and such Meeting *shall be on the first Monday in December, unless they shall by Law appoint a different Day.*†

Section 5

Each House shall be the Judge of the Elections, Returns and Qualifications of its own Members, and a Majority of each shall constitute a Quorum to do Business; but a smaller number may adjourn from day to day, and may be authorized to compel the Attendance of absent Members, in such Manner, and under such Penalties, as each House may provide.

Each House may determine the Rules of its Proceedings, punish its Members for disorderly Behavior, and, with the Concurrence of two thirds, expel a Member.

Each House shall keep a Journal of its Proceedings, and from time to time publish the same, excepting such Parts as may in their Judgment require Secrecy; and the Yeas and Nays of the Members of either House on any question shall, at the Desire of one-fifth of those Present, be entered on the Journal.

---

*Changed by Clause 2 of the Seventeenth Amendment.

†Changed by Section 2 of the Twentieth Amendment.

Neither House, during the Session of Congress, shall, without the Consent of the other, adjourn for more than three days, nor to any other Place than that in which the two Houses shall be sitting.

Section 6
The Senators and Representatives shall receive a Compensation for their Services, to be ascertained by Law, and paid out of the Treasury of the United States. They shall in all Cases, except Treason, Felony and Breach of the Peace, be privileged from Arrest during their Attendance at the Session of their respective Houses, and in going to and returning from the same; and for any Speech or Debate in either House, they shall not be questioned in any other Place.

No Senator or Representative shall, during the Time for which he was elected, be appointed to any civil Office under the Authority of the United States, which shall have been created, or the Emoluments whereof shall have been increased, during such time; and no Person holding any Office under the United States, shall be a Member of either House during his Continuance in Office.

Section 7
All Bills for raising Revenue shall originate in the House of Representatives; but the Senate may propose or concur with Amendments as on other Bills.

Every Bill which shall have passed the House of Representatives and the Senate, shall, before it becomes a Law, be presented to the President of the United States; If he approve he shall sign it, but if not he shall return it, with his Objections to that House in which it shall have originated, who shall enter the Objections at large on their Journal, and proceed to reconsider it. If after such Reconsideration two thirds of that House shall agree to pass the Bill, it shall be sent, together with the Objections, to the other House, by which it shall likewise be reconsidered, and if approved by two thirds of that House, it shall become a Law. But in all such Cases the Votes of both Houses shall be determined by Yeas and Nays, and the Names of the Persons voting for and against the Bill shall be entered on the Journal of each House respectively. If any Bill shall not be returned by the President within ten Days (Sundays excepted) after it shall have been presented to him, the Same shall be a Law, in like Manner as if he had signed it, unless the Congress by their Adjournment prevent its Return, in which Case it shall not be a Law.

Every Order, Resolution, or Vote to which the Concurrence of the Senate and the House of Representatives may be necessary (except on a question of Adjournment) shall be presented to the President of the United States; and before the Same shall take Effect, shall be approved by him, or being disapproved by him, shall be repassed by two thirds of the Senate and House of Representatives, according to the Rules and Limitations prescribed in the Case of a Bill.

Section 8
The Congress shall have Power To lay and collect Taxes, Duties, Imposts and Excises, to pay the Debts and provide for the common Defence and general Welfare of the United States; but all Duties, Imposts and Excises shall be uniform throughout the United States;

To borrow money on the credit of the United States;

To regulate Commerce with foreign Nations, and among the several States, and with the Indian Tribes;

To establish an uniform Rule of Naturalization, and uniform Laws on the subject of Bankruptcies throughout the United States;

To coin Money, regulate the Value thereof, and of foreign Coin, and fix the Standard of Weights and Measures;

To provide for the Punishment of counterfeiting the Securities and current Coin of the United States;

To establish Post Offices and post Roads;

To promote the Progress of Science and useful Arts, by securing for limited Times to Authors and Inventors the exclusive Right to their respective Writings and Discoveries;

To constitute Tribunals inferior to the supreme Court;

To define and punish Piracies and Felonies committed on the high Seas, and Offenses against the Law of Nations;

To declare War, grant Letters of Marque and Reprisal, and make Rules concerning Captures on Land and Water;

To raise and support Armies, but no Appropriation of Money to that Use shall be for a longer Term than two Years;

To provide and maintain a Navy;

To make Rules for the Government and Regulation of the land and naval Forces;

To provide for calling forth the Militia to execute the Laws of the Union, suppress Insurrections and repel Invasions;

To provide for organizing, arming, and disciplining the Militia, and for governing such Part of them as may be employed in the Service of the United States, reserving to the States respectively, the Appointment of the Officers, and the Authority of training the Militia according to the discipline prescribed by Congress;

To exercise exclusive Legislation in all Cases whatsoever, over such District (not exceeding ten Miles square) as may, by Cession of particular States, and the acceptance of Congress, become the Seat of Government of the United States, and to exercise like Authority over all Places purchased by the Consent of the Legislature of the State in which the Same shall be, for the Erection of Forts, Magazines, Arsenals, dock-Yards, and other needful Buildings;—And

To make all Laws which shall be necessary and proper for carrying into Execution the foregoing Powers, and all other Powers vested by this Constitution in the Government of the United States, or in any Department or Officer thereof.

Section 9

The Migration or Importation of such Persons as any of the States now existing shall think proper to admit, shall not be prohibited by the Congress prior to the Year one thousand eight hundred and eight but a tax or duty may be imposed on such Importation, not exceeding ten dollars for each Person.

The privilege of the Writ of Habeas Corpus shall not be suspended, unless when in Cases of Rebellion or Invasion the public Safety may require it.

No Bill of Attainder or ex post facto Law shall be passed.

No capitation, or other direct, Tax shall be laid, unless in Proportion to the Census or Enumeration herein before directed to be taken.*

---

*Changed by the Sixteenth Amendment.

No Tax or Duty shall be laid on Articles exported from any State.

No Preference shall be given by any Regulation of Commerce or Revenue to the Ports of one State over those of another: nor shall Vessels bound to, or from, one State, be obliged to enter, clear, or pay Duties in another.

No Money shall be drawn from the Treasury, but in Consequence of Appropriations made by law; and a regular Statement and Account of the Receipts and Expenditures of all public Money shall be published from time to time.

No Title of Nobility shall be granted by the United States: And no Person holding any Office of Profit or Trust under them, shall, without the Consent of the Congress, accept of any present, Emolument, Office, or Title, of any kind whatever, from any King, Prince, or foreign State.

Section 10

No State shall enter into any Treaty, Alliance, or Confederation; grant Letters of Marque and Reprisal; coin Money; emit Bills of Credit; make any Thing but gold and silver Coin a Tender in Payment of Debts; pass any Bill of Attainder, ex post facto Law, or Law impairing the Obligation of Contracts, or grant any Title of Nobility.

No State shall, without the Consent of the Congress, lay any Imposts or Duties on Imports or Exports, except what may be absolutely necessary for executing its inspection Laws: and the net Produce of all Duties and Imposts, laid by any State on Imports or Exports, shall be for the Use of the Treasury of the United States; and all such Laws shall be subject to the Revision and Control of the Congress.

No State shall, without the Consent of the Congress, lay any duty of Tonnage, keep Troops, or Ships of War in time of Peace, enter into any Agreement or Compact with another State, or with a foreign Power, or engage in War, unless actually invaded, or in such imminent Danger as will not admit of delay.

ARTICLE II

Section 1

The executive Power shall be vested in a President of the United States of America. He shall hold his Office during the Term of four Years, and, together with the Vice President, chosen for the same Term, be elected, as follows:

Each State shall appoint, in such Manner as the Legislature thereof may direct, a Number of Electors, equal to the whole Number of Senators and Representatives to which the State may be entitled in the Congress; but no Senator or Representative, or Person holding an Office of Trust or Profit under the United States, shall be appointed an Elector.

The Electors shall meet in their respective States, and vote by Ballot for two Persons, of whom one at least shall not be an Inhabitant of the same State with themselves. And they shall make a List of all the Persons voted for, and of the Number of Votes for each; which List they shall sign and certify, and transmit sealed to the Seat of the Government of the United States, directed to the President of the Senate. The President of the Senate shall, in the Presence of the Senate and House of Representatives, open all the Certificates, and the Votes shall then be counted. The Person having the greatest Number of Votes shall be the President, if such Number be a Majority of the whole Number of Electors appointed; and if there be more than one who have such Majority, and have an equal Number of Votes, then the House of Representatives shall immediately chuse by Ballot one of them for President; and if no Person have a Ma-

jority, then from the five highest on the List the said House shall in like Manner chuse the President. But in chusing the President, the Votes shall be taken by States, the Representation from each State having one Vote; a quorum for this Purpose shall consist of a Member or Members from two thirds of the States, and a Majority of all the States shall be necessary to a Choice. In every Case, after the Choice of the President, the Person having the greatest Number of Votes of the Electors shall be the Vice President. But if there should remain two or more who have equal Votes, the Senate shall chuse from them by Ballot the Vice President.*

The Congress may determine the Time of chusing the Electors, and the Day on which they shall give their Votes; which Day shall be the same throughout the United States.

No Person except a natural born Citizen, or a Citizen of the United States, at the time of the Adoption of this Constitution, shall be eligible to the Office of President; neither shall any Person be eligible to that Office who shall not have attained to the Age of thirty five Years, and been fourteen years a Resident within the United States.

In Case of the Removal of the President from Office, or of his Death, Resignation, or Inability to discharge the Powers and Duties of the said Office, the same shall devolve on the Vice President, *and the Congress may by Law provide for the Case of Removal, Death, Resignation, or Inability, both of the President and Vice President, declaring what Officer shall then act as President, and such Officer shall act accordingly, until the Disability be removed, or a President shall be elected.*†

The President shall, at stated Times, receive for his Services a Compensation, which shall neither be increased nor diminished during the Period for which he shall have been elected, and he shall not receive within that Period any other Emolument from the United States, or any of them.

Before he enter on the Execution of his Office, he shall take the following Oath or Affirmation:—"I do solemnly swear (or affirm) that I will faithfully execute the Office of President of the United States, and will to the best of my Ability, preserve, protect and defend the Constitution of the United States."

Section 2

The President shall be Commander in Chief of the Army and Navy of the United States, and of the Militia of the several States, when called into the actual Service of the United States; he may require the Opinion, in writing, of the principal Officer in each of the executive Departments, upon any Subject relating to the Duties of their respective Offices, and he shall have Power to Grant Reprieves and pardons for Offences against the United States, except in Cases of Impeachment.

He shall have Power, by and with the Advice and Consent of the Senate, to make Treaties, provided two thirds of the Senators present concur; and he shall nominate, and by and with the Advice and Consent of the Senate, shall appoint Ambassadors, other public Ministers and Consuls, Judges of the supreme Court, and all other Officers of the United States, whose Appointments are not herein otherwise provided for, and which shall be established by Law: but the Congress may by Law vest the Appointment of such inferior Officers, as they think proper, in the President alone, in the Courts of Law, or in the Heads of Departments.

---

*Superseded by the Twelfth Amendment.

†Modified by the Twenty-Fifth Amendment.

The President shall have Power to fill up all Vacancies that may happen during the Recess of the Senate, by granting Commissions which shall expire at the End of their next Session.

Section 3

He shall from time to time give to the Congress Information of the State of the Union, and recommend to their Consideration such Measures as he shall judge necessary and expedient; he may, on extraordinary Occasions, convene both Houses, or either of them, and in Case of Disagreement between them, with Respect to the Time of Adjournment, he may adjourn them to such Time as he shall think proper; he shall receive Ambassadors and other public Ministers; he shall take Care that the Laws be faithfully executed, and shall Commission all the Officers of the United States.

Section 4

The President, Vice President and all civil Officers of the United States, shall be removed from Office on Impeachment for, and Conviction of, Treason, Bribery, or other high Crimes and Misdemeanors.

ARTICLE III

Section 1

The judicial Power of the United States, shall be vested in one supreme Court, and in such inferior Courts as the Congress may from time to time ordain and establish. The Judges, both of the supreme and inferior courts, shall hold their Offices during good Behaviour, and shall, at stated Times, receive for their Services a Compensation, which shall not be diminished during their Continuance in Office.

Section 2

The judicial Power shall extend to all Cases, in Law and Equity, arising under this Constitution, the Laws of the United States, and Treaties made, or which shall be made, under their Authority;—to all Cases affecting Ambassadors, other public Ministers and Consuls;—to all Cases of admiralty and maritime Jurisdiction;—to Controversies to which the United States shall be a Party;—to Controversies between two or more States;—*between a State and Citizens of another State,**—between Citizens of different States;—between Citizens of the same State claiming Lands under Grants of different States, and between a State, or the Citizens thereof, and foreign States, Citizens or Subjects.

In all Cases affecting Ambassadors, other public Ministers and Consuls, and those in which a State shall be Party, the supreme Court shall have original Jurisdiction. In all the other Cases before mentioned, the supreme Court shall have appellate Jurisdiction, both as to Law and Fact, with such Exceptions, and under such Regulations as the Congress shall make.

---

*Restricted by the Eleventh Amendment.

The trial of all Crimes, except in Cases of Impeachment, shall be by Jury; and such Trial shall be held in the State where said Crimes shall have been committed; but when not committed within any State, the Trial shall be at such Place or Places as the Congress may by Law have directed.

Section 3

Treason against the United States, shall consist only in levying War against them, or in adhering to their Enemies, giving them Aid and Comfort. No Person shall be convicted of Treason unless on the Testimony of two Witnesses to the same overt Act, or on Confession in open Court.

The Congress shall have Power to declare the Punishment of Treason, but no Attainder of Treason shall work Corruption of Blood, or Forefeiture except during the Life of the Person attainted.

Article IV

Section 1

Full Faith and Credit shall be given in each State to the public Acts, Records, and judicial Proceedings of every other State. And the Congress may by general Laws prescribe the Manner in which such Acts, Records, and Proceedings shall be proved, and the Effect thereof.

Section 2

The Citizens of each State shall be entitled to all Privileges and Immunities of Citizens in the several States.

A Person charged in any State with Treason, Felony, or other Crime, who shall flee from Justice, and be found in another State, shall on demand of the executive Authority of the State from which he fled, be delivered up, to be removed to the State having Jurisdiction of the Crime.

*No Person held to Service or Labour in one State, under the Laws thereof, escaping into another, shall, in Consequence of any Law or Regulation therein, be discharged from such Service or Labour, but shall be delivered up on Claim of the Party to whom such Service or Labour may be due.**

Section 3

New States may be admitted by the Congress into this Union; but no new State shall be formed or erected within the Jurisdiction of any other State; nor any State be formed by the Junction of two or more States, or parts of States, without the Consent of the Legislatures of the States concerned as well as of the Congress.

The Congress shall have Power to dispose of and make all needful Rules and Regulations respecting the Territory or other Property belonging to the United States; and nothing in this Constitution shall be so construed as to Prejudice any Claims of the United States, or of any particular State.

---

*Superseded by the Thirteenth Amendment.

Section 4

The United States shall guarantee to every State in this Union a Republican Form of Government, and shall protect each of them against Invasion; and on Application of the Legislature, or of the Executive (when the Legislature cannot be convened) against domestic Violence.

ARTICLE V

The Congress, whenever two thirds of both Houses shall deem it necessary, shall propose Amendments to this Constitution, or, on the Application of the Legislatures of two thirds of the several States, shall call a Convention for proposing Amendments, which, in either Case, shall be valid to all Intents and Purposes, as Part of this Constitution, when ratified by the Legislatures of three fourths of the several States, or by Conventions in three fourths thereof, as the one or the other Mode of Ratification may be proposed by the Congress; Provided that no Amendment which may be made prior to the Year One thousand eight hundred and eight shall in any Manner affect the first and fourth Clauses in the Ninth Section of the first Article; and that no State, without its Consent, shall be deprived of its equal Suffrage in the Senate.

ARTICLE VI

All Debts contracted and Engagements entered into, before the Adoption of this Constitution, shall be as valid against the United States under this Constitution, as under the Confederation.

This Constitution, and the Laws of the United States which shall be made in Pursuance thereof; and all Treaties made, or which shall be made, under the Authority of the United States, shall be the supreme Law of the Land; and the Judges in every State shall be bound thereby, any Thing in the Constitution or Laws of any State to the Contrary notwithstanding.

The Senators and Representatives before mentioned, and the Members of the several State Legislatures, and all executive and judicial Officers, both of the United States and of the several States, shall be bound by Oath or Affirmation, to support this Constitution; but no religious Test shall ever be required as a Qualification to any Office or public Trust under the United States.

ARTICLE VII

The Ratification of the Conventions of nine States shall be sufficient for the Establishment of this Constitution between the States so ratifying the Same.

Done in Convention by the Unanimous Consent of the States present the Seventeenth Day of September in the Year of our Lord one thousand seven hundred and Eighty seven and of the Independence of the United States of America the Twelfth. In Witness whereof We have hereunto subscribed our Names.

Go. Washington

President and deputy from Virginia

New Hampshire
John Langdon
Nicholas Gilman

Massachusetts
Nathaniel Gorham
Rufus King

Connecticut
Wm. Saml. Johnson
Roger Sherman

New York
Alexander Hamilton

New Jersey
Wil. Livingston
David Brearley
Wm. Paterson
Jona. Dayton

Pennsylvania
B. Franklin
Thomas Mifflin
Robt. Morris
Geo. Clymer
Thos. FitzSimons
Jared Ingersoll
James Wilson
Gouv. Morris

Delaware
Geo. Read
Gunning Bedford jun
John Dickenson
Richard Bassett
Jaco. Broom

Maryland
James McHenry
Dan. of St. Thos. Jenifer
Danl. Carroll

Virginia
John Blair
James Madison, Jr.

North Carolina
Wm. Blount
Richd. Dobbs Spaight
Hu Williamson

South Carolina
J. Rutledge
Charles Cotesworth
    Pickney
Pierce Butler

Georgia
William Few
Abr. Baldwin

AMENDMENTS TO THE CONSTITUTION

AMENDMENT I [1791]*

Congress shall make no law respecting an establishment of religion, or prohibiting the free exercise thereof; or abridging the freedom of speech, or of the press; or the right of the people peaceably to assembley, and to petition the Government for a redress of grievances.

AMENDMENT II [1791]

A well regulated Militia, being necessary to the security of a free State, the right of the people to keep and bear Arms shall not be infringed.

AMENDMENT III [1791]

No Soldier shall, in time of peace, be quartered in any house, without the consent of the Owner, nor in time of war, but in a manner to be prescribed by law.

AMENDMENT IV [1791]

The right of the people to be secure in their persons, houses, papers, and effects, against unreasonable searches and seizures, shall not be violated, and no Warrants shall issue, but upon probable cause, supported by Oath or affirmation, and particularly describing the place to be searched, and the persons or things to be seized.

AMENDMENT V [1791]

No person shall be held to answer for a capital or otherwise infamous crime, unless on a presentment or indictment of a Grand Jury, except in cases arising in the land or naval forces, or in the Militia, when in actual service in time of War or public danger; nor shall any person be subject for the same offence to be twice put in jeopardy of life or limb; nor shall be compelled in any criminal case to be a witness against himself, nor be deprived of life, liberty, or property, without due process of law; nor shall private property be taken for public use, without just compensation.

AMENDMENT VI [1791]

In all criminal prosecutions, the accused shall enjoy the right to a speedy and public trial, by an impartial jury of the State and district wherein the crime shall have been committed, which district shall have been previously ascertained by law, and to be informed of the nature and cause of the accusation; to be confronted with the witnesses against him; to have compulsory process for obtaining witnesses in his favor, and to have the Assistance of Counsel for his defence.

---

*The dates in brackets indicate when the amendments were ratified.

AMENDMENT VII [1791]

In suits at common law, where the value in controversy shall exceed twenty dollars, the right of trial by jury shall be preserved, and no fact tried by a jury, shall be otherwise reexamined in any Court of the United States, than according to the Rules of the common law.

AMENDMENT VIII [1791]

Excessive bail shall not be required, nor excessive fines imposed, nor cruel and unusual punishments inflicted.

AMENDMENT IX [1791]

The enumeration in the Constitution, of certain rights, shall not be construed to deny or disparage others retained by the people.

AMENDMENT X [1791]

The powers not delegated to the United States by the Constitution, nor prohibited by it to the States, are reserved to the States respectively, or to the people.

AMENDMENT XI [1798]

The Judicial power of the United States shall not be construed to extend to any suit in law or equity, commenced or prosecuted against one of the United States by Citizens of another State, or by Citizens or subjects of any foreign state.

AMENDMENT XII [1804]

The Electors shall meet in their respective States and vote by ballot for President and Vice-President, one of whom, at least, shall not be an inhabitant of the same State with themselves; they shall name in their ballots the person voted for as President, and in distinct ballots the person voted for as Vice-President, and they shall make distinct lists of all persons voted for as President, and of all persons voted for as Vice-President, and of the number of votes for each, which lists they shall sign and certify, and transmit sealed to the seat of the government of the United States, directed to the President of the Senate;—the President of the Senate shall, in the presence of the Senate and House of Representatives, open all the certificates and the votes shall then be counted;—The person having the greatest number of votes for President, shall be the President, if such number be a majority of the whole number of Electors appointed; and if no person have such majority, then from the persons having the highest numbers not exceeding three on the list of those voted for as President, the House of Representatives shall choose immediately, by ballot, the President. But in choosing the President, the votes shall be taken by States, the representation from each State having one vote; a quorum for this purpose shall consist of a member or members from two-thirds of the States, and a majority of all the States shall be necessary to a choice. And if the House of Representatives shall not choose a President whenever the right of choice shall devolve upon them, before *the fourth day of March* next following, then the Vice-President shall act as President, as in the case of the death or other constitutional disability of the President.*—The person having the greatest number of votes as Vice-President, shall be the Vice-President, if such number be a majority of the whole number of Electors appointed, and if no person have a majority, then from the two highest numbers on the list, the Senate shall choose the Vice-President; a quorum for the purpose shall consist of two-thirds of the whole number of Senators, and a majority of the whole number shall be necessary to a choice. But no person constitutionally ineligible to the office of President shall be eligible to that of Vice-President of the United States.

AMENDMENT XIII [1865]

Section 1
Neither slavery nor involuntary servitude, except as a punishment for crime whereof the party shall have been duly convicted, shall exist within the United States, or any place subject to their jurisdiction.

Section 2
Congress shall have power to enforce this article by appropriate legislation.

AMENDMENT XIV [1868]

Section 1
All persons born or naturalized in the United States, and subject to the jurisdiction thereof, are citizens of the United States and of the State wherein they reside. No State shall make or enforce any law which shall abridge the privileges or immunities of citizens of the United States; nor shall any State deprive any person of life, liberty, or property, without due process of law; nor deny to any person within its jurisdiction the equal protection of the laws.

Section 2
Representatives shall be apportioned among the several States according to their respective numbers, counting the whole number of persons in each State, excluding Indians not taxed. But when the right to vote at any election for the choice of electors for President and Vice-President of the United States, Representatives in Congress, the Executive and Judicial officers of a State, or the members of the Legislature thereof, is denied to any of the male inhabitants of such State, being twenty-one years of age, and citizens of the United States, or in any way abridged, except for participation in rebellion, or other crime, the basis of representation therein shall be reduced in the proportion which the number of such male citizens shall bear to the whole number of male citizens twenty-one years of age in such State.

Section 3
No person shall be a Senator or Representative in Congress, or elector of President and Vice-President, or hold any office, civil or military, under the United States, or under any State,

---

*Superseded by Section 3 of the Twentieth Amendment.

who, having previously taken an oath, as a member of Congress, or as an officer of the United States, or as a member of any State legislature, or as an executive or judicial officer of any State, to support the Constitution of the United States, shall have engaged in insurrection or rebellion against the same, or given aid or comfort to the enemies thereof. Congress may by a vote of two-thirds of each house, remove such disability.

Section 4
The validity of the public debt of the United States, authorized by law, including debts incurred for payment of pensions and bounties for services in suppressing insurrection or rebellion, shall not be questioned. But neither the United States nor any State shall assume or pay any debt or obligation incurred in aid of insurrection or rebellion against the United States, or any claim for the loss or emancipation of any slave; but all such debts, obligations and claims shall be held illegal and void.

Section 5
The Congress shall have power to enforce, by appropriate legislation, the provisions of this article.

AMENDMENT XV [1870]

Section 1
The right of citizens of the United States to vote shall not be denied or abridged by the United States or by any State on account of race, color, or previous condition of servitude—

Section 2
The Congress shall have power to enforce this article by appropriate legislation.

AMENDMENT XVI [1913]

The Congress shall have power to lay and collect taxes on incomes, from whatever source derived, without apportionment among the several States, and without regard to any census or enumeration.

AMENDMENT XVII [1913]

The Senate of the United States shall be composed of two Senators from each State, elected by the people thereof, for six years; and each Senator shall have one vote. The electors in each State shall have the qualifications requisite for electors of the most numerous branch of the State legislatures.

When vacancies happen in the representation of any State in the Senate, the executive authority of such State shall issue writs of election to fill such vacancies: *Provided,* That the legislature of any State may empower the executive thereof to make temporary appointments until the people fill the vacancies by election as the legislature may direct.

This amendment shall not be so construed as to affect the election or term of any Senator chosen before it becomes valid as part of the Constitution.

AMENDMENT XVIII [1919]

Section 1

After one year from the ratification of this article the manufacture, sale, or transportation of intoxicating liquors within, the importation thereof into, or the exportation thereof from the United States and all territory subject to the jurisdiction hereof for beverage purposes hereby prohibited.

Section 2

The Congress and the several States shall have concurrent power to enforce this article by appropriate legislation.

Section 3

This article shall be inoperative unless it shall have been ratified as an amendment to the Constitution by the legislatures of the several States, as provided by the Constitution, within seven years from the date of submission hereof to the States by the Congress.*

AMENDMENT XIX [1920]

The right of citizens of the United States to vote shall not be denied or abridged by the United States or by any State on account of sex.

Congress shall have power to enforce this article by appropriate legislation.

AMENDMENT XX [1933]

Section 1

The terms of the President and Vice-President shall end at noon on the 20th day of January, and the terms of Senators and Representatives at noon on the 3d day of January, of the years in which such terms would have ended if this article had not been ratified; and the terms of their successors shall then begin.

Section 2

The Congress shall assemble at least once in every year, and such meeting shall begin at noon on the 3d day of January, unless they shall by law appoint a different day.

Section 3

If, at the time fixed for the beginning of the term of the President, the President elect shall have died, the Vice-President elect shall become President. If a President shall not have been chosen before the time fixed for the beginning of his term, or if the President elect shall have failed to qualify, then the Vice-President elect shall act as President until a President shall have qualified; and the Congress may by law provide for the case wherein neither a President elect nor a Vice-President elect shall have qualified, declaring who shall then act

---

*Repealed by Section 1 of the Twenty-First Amendment.

as President, or the manner in which one who is to act shall be selected, and such person shall act accordingly until a President or Vice-President shall have qualified.

Section 4
The Congress may by law provide for the case of the death of any of the persons from whom the House of Representatives may choose a President whenever the right of choice shall have devolved upon them, and for the case of the death of any of the persons from whom the Senate may choose a Vice-President whenever the right of choice shall have devolved upon them.

Section 5
Sections 1 and 2 shall take effect on the 15th day of October following the ratification of this article.

Section 6
This article shall be inoperative unless it shall have been ratified as an amendment to the Constitution by the legislatures of three-fourths of the several States within seven years from the date of its submission.

AMENDMENT XXI [1933]

Section 1
The eighteenth article of amendment to the Constitution of the United States is hereby repealed.

Section 2
The transportation or importation into any State, Territory, or possession of the United States for delivery or use therein of intoxicating liquors, in violation of the laws thereof, is hereby prohibited.

Section 3
This article shall be inoperative unless it shall have been ratified as an amendment to the Constitution by conventions in the several States, as provided in the Constitution, within seven years from the date of submission hereof to the States by the Congress.

AMENDMENT XXII [1951]

Section 1
No person shall be elected to the office of President more than twice, and no person who has held the office of President, or acted as President, for more than two years of a term to which some other person was elected President shall be elected to the office of the President more than once. But this Article shall not apply to any person holding the office of President when this Article was proposed by the Congress, and shall not prevent any person who may be holding the office of President, or acting as President, during the term within which this Article becomes operative from holding the office of the President or acting as President during the remainder of such term.

Section 2

This article shall be inoperative unless it shall have been ratified as an amendment to the Constitution by the legislatures of three-fourths of the several States within seven years from the date of its submission to the States by the Congress.

AMENDMENT XXIII [1961]

Section 1

The District constituting the seat of Government of the United States shall appoint in such manner as the Congress may direct:

A number of electors of President and Vice-President equal to the whole number of Senators and Representatives in Congress to which the District would be entitled if it were a State, but in no event more than the least populous State; they shall be in addition to those appointed by the States, but they shall be considered, for the purposes of the election of President and Vice-President, to be electors appointed by a State; and they shall meet in the District and perform such duties as provided by the twelfth article of amendment.

Section 2

The Congress shall have power to enforce this article by appropriate legislation.

AMENDMENT XXIV [1964]

Section 1

The right of citizens of the United States to vote in any primary or other election for President or Vice-President, for electors for President or Vice-President, or for Senator or Representative in Congress, shall not be denied or abridged by the United States or any State by reason of failure to pay any poll tax or other tax.

Section 2

The Congress shall have power to enforce this article by appropriate legislation.

AMENDMENT XXV [1967]

Section 1

In case of the removal of the President from office or of his death or resignation, the Vice-President shall become President.

Section 2

Whenever there is a vacancy in the office of the Vice-President, the President shall nominate a Vice-President who shall take office upon confirmation by a majority vote of both houses of Congress.

Section 3

Whenever the President transmits to the President pro tempore of the Senate and the Speaker of the House of Representatives his written declaration that he is unable to discharge the powers and duties of his office, and until he transmits to them a written declaration to the contrary, such powers and duties shall be discharged by the Vice-President as Acting President.

Section 4
Whenever the Vice-President and a majority of either the principal officers of the executive departments or of such other body as Congress may by law provide, transmit to the President pro tempore of the Senate and the Speaker of the House of Representatives their written declaration that the President is unable to discharge the powers and duties of his office, the Vice-President shall immediately assume the powers and duties of the office as Acting President.

Thereafter, when the President transmits to the President pro tempore of the Senate and the Speaker of the House of Representatives his written declaration that no inability exists, he shall resume the powers and duties of his office unless the Vice-President and a majority of either the principal officers of the executive department or of such other body as Congress may by law provide, transmit within four days to the President pro tempore of the Senate and the Speaker of the House of Representatives their written declaration that the President is unable to discharge the powers and duties of his office. Thereupon Congress shall decide the issue, assembling within forty-eight hours for that purpose if not in session. If the Congress, within twenty-one days after receipt of the latter written declaration, or, if Congress is not in session, within twenty-one days after Congress is required to assemble, determines by two-thirds vote of both Houses that the President is unable to discharge the powers and duties of his office, the Vice-President shall continue to discharge the same as Acting President; otherwise, the President shall resume the powers and duties of his office.

AMENDMENT XXVI [1971]

Section 1
The right of citizens of the United States, who are eighteen years of age or older, to vote shall not be denied or abridged by the United States or by any state on account of age.

Section 2
The Congress shall have power to enforce this article by appropriate legislation.

AMENDMENT XXVII [1992]

No law varying the compensation for services of the Senators and Representatives, shall take effect, until an election of Representatives shall have intervened.

APPENDIX

Territorial Expansion

Territory	Date Acquired	Square Miles	How Acquired
Original states and territories	1783	888,685	Treaty of Paris
Louisiana Purchase	1803	827,192	Purchased from France
Florida	1819	72,003	Adams-Onís Treaty
Texas	1845	390,143	Annexation of independent country
Oregon	1846	285,580	Oregon Boundary Treaty
Mexican cession	1848	529,017	Treaty of Guadalupe Hidalgo
Gadsden Purchase	1853	29,640	Purchased from Mexico
Midway Islands	1867	2	Annexation of uninhabited islands
Alaska	1867	589,757	Purchased from Russia
Hawaii	1898	6,450	Annexation of independent country
Wake Island	1898	3	Annexation of uninhabited island
Puerto Rico	1899	3,435	Treaty of Paris
Guam	1899	212	Treaty of Paris
The Philippines	1899–1946	115,600	Treaty of Paris; granted independence
American Samoa	1900	76	Treaty with Germany and Great Britain
Panama Canal Zone	1904–1978	553	Hay–Bunau-Varilla Treaty
U.S. Virgin Islands	1917	133	Purchased from Denmark
Trust Territory of the Pacific Islands*	1947	717	United Nations Trusteeship

*A number of these islands have recently been granted independence: Federated States of Micronesia, 1990; Marshall Islands, 1991; Palau, 1994.

The Labor Force (thousands of workers)

Year	Agriculture	Mining	Manufacturing	Construction	Trade	Other	Total
1810	1,950	11	75	—	—	294	2,330
1840	3,570	32	500	290	350	918	5,660
1850	4,520	102	1,200	410	530	1,488	8,250
1860	5,880	176	1,530	520	890	2,114	11,110
1870	6,790	180	2,470	780	1,310	1,400	12,930
1880	8,920	280	3,290	900	1,930	2,070	17,390
1890	9,960	440	4,390	1,510	2,960	4,060	23,320
1900	11,680	637	5,895	1,665	3,970	5,223	29,070
1910	11,770	1,068	8,332	1,949	5,320	9,041	37,480
1920	10,790	1,180	11,190	1,233	5,845	11,372	41,610
1930	10,560	1,009	9,884	1,988	8,122	17,267	48,830
1940	9,575	925	11,309	1,876	9,328	23,277	56,290
1950	7,870	901	15,648	3,029	12,152	25,870	65,470
1960	5,970	709	17,145	3,640	14,051	32,545	74,060
1970	3,463	516	20,746	4,818	15,008	34,127	78,678
1980	3,364	979	21,942	6,215	20,191	46,612	99,303
1990	3,186	730	21,184	7,696	24,269	60,849	118,793
1998	3,378	620	20,733	8,518	27,203	71,011	131,463

SOURCE: *Historical Statistics of the United States, Colonial Times to 1970* (1975), 139; *Statistical Abstract of the United States,* 2000, Table 672.

Changing Labor Patterns

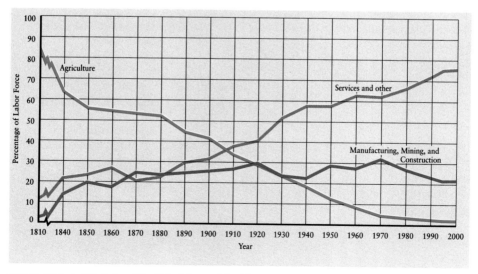

SOURCE: *Historical Statistics of the United States, Colonial Times to 1970* (1975), 139; *Statistical Abstract of the United States,* 2000, Table 672.

American Population

Year	Population	Percent Increase	Year	Population	Percent Increase
1610	350	—	1810	7,239,881	36.4
1620	2,300	557.1	1820	9,638,453	33.1
1630	4,600	100.0	1830	12,866,020	33.5
1640	26,600	478.3	1840	17,069,453	32.7
1650	50,400	90.8	1850	23,191,876	35.9
1660	75,100	49.0	1860	31,443,321	35.6
1670	111,900	49.0	1870	39,818,449	26.6
1680	151,500	35.4	1880	50,155,783	26.0
1690	210,400	38.9	1890	62,947,714	25.5
1700	250,900	19.2	1900	75,994,575	20.7
1710	331,700	32.2	1910	91,972,266	21.0
1720	466,200	40.5	1920	105,710,620	14.9
1730	629,400	35.0	1930	122,775,046	16.1
1740	905,600	43.9	1940	131,669,275	7.2
1750	1,170,800	29.3	1950	150,697,361	14.5
1760	1,593,600	36.1	1960	179,323,175	19.0
1770	2,148,100	34.8	1970	203,235,298	13.3
1780	2,780,400	29.4	1980	226,545,805	11.5
1790	3,929,214	41.3	1990	248,709,873	9.8
1800	5,308,483	35.1	2000	281,421,906	13.2

Note: These figures largely ignore the Native American population. Census takers never made any effort to count the Native American population that lived outside their political jurisdictions and compiled only casual and incomplete enumerations of those living within their jurisdictions until 1890. In that year the federal government attempted a full count of the Indian population: the Census found 125,719 Indians in 1890, compared with only 12,543 in 1870 and 33,985 in 1880.

SOURCE: *Historical Statistics of the United States, Colonial Times to 1970* (1975); *Statistical Abstract of the United States,* 1999; Bureau of the Census, 2001 <http://blue.census.gov/dmd/www/resapport/states/unitedstates.pdf>.

Presidential Elections

Year	Candidates	Parties	Percentage of Popular Vote	Electoral Vote	Percentage of Voter Participation
1789	**George Washington**	No party designations	*	69	
	John Adams†			34	
	Other candidates			35	
1792	**George Washington**	No party designations		132	
	John Adams			77	
	George Clinton			50	
	Other candidates			5	
1796	**John Adams**	Federalist		71	
	Thomas Jefferson	Democratic-Republican		68	
	Thomas Pinckney	Federalist		59	
	Aaron Burr	Democratic-Republican		30	
	Other candidates			48	
1800	**Thomas Jefferson**	Democratic-Republican		73	
	Aaron Burr	Democratic-Republican		73	
	John Adams	Federalist		65	
	Charles C. Pinckney	Federalist		64	
	John Jay	Federalist		1	
1804	**Thomas Jefferson**	Democratic-Republican		162	
	Charles C. Pinckney	Federalist		14	
1808	**James Madison**	Democratic-Republican		122	
	Charles C. Pinckney	Federalist		47	
	George Clinton	Democratic-Republican		6	
1812	**James Madison**	Democratic-Republican		128	
	De Witt Clinton	Federalist		89	
1816	**James Monroe**	Democratic-Republican		183	
	Rufus King	Federalist		34	
1820	**James Monroe**	Democratic-Republican		231	
	John Quincy Adams	Independent Republican		1	
1824	**John Quincy Adams**	Democratic-Republican	30.5	84	26.9
	Andrew Jackson	Democratic-Republican	43.1	99	
	Henry Clay	Democratic-Republican	13.2	37	
	William H. Crawford	Democratic-Republican	13.1	41	
1828	**Andrew Jackson**	Democratic	56.0	178	57.6
	John Quincy Adams	National Republican	44.0	83	
1832	**Andrew Jackson**	Democratic	54.5	219	55.4
	Henry Clay	National Republican	37.5	49	
	William Wirt	Anti-Masonic	8.0	7	
	John Floyd	Democratic	‡	11	
1836	**Martin Van Buren**	Democratic	50.9	170	57.8
	William H. Harrison	Whig		73	
	Hugh L. White	Whig		26	
	Daniel Webster	Whig	49.1	14	
	W. P. Mangum	Whig		11	
1840	**William H. Harrison**	Whig	53.1	234	80.2
	Martin Van Buren	Democratic	46.9	60	

*Prior to 1824, most presidential electors were chosen by state legislators rather than by popular vote.
†Before the Twelfth Amendment was passed in 1804, the electoral college voted for two presidential candidates; the runner-up became vice president.
‡Percentages below 2.5 have been omitted. Hence the percentage of popular vote might not total 100 percent.

Year	Candidates	Parties	Percentage of Popular Vote	Electoral Vote	Percentage of Voter Participation
1844	**James K. Polk**	Democratic	49.6	170	78.9
	Henry Clay	Whig	48.1	105	
	James G. Birney	Liberty	2.3		
1848	**Zachary Taylor**	Whig	47.4	163	72.7
	Lewis Cass	Democratic	42.5	127	
	Martin Van Buren	Free Soil	10.1		
1852	**Franklin Pierce**	Democratic	50.9	254	69.6
	Winfield Scott	Whig	44.1	42	
	John P. Hale	Free Soil	5.0		
1856	**James Buchanan**	Democratic	45.3	174	78.9
	John C. Frémont	Republican	33.1	114	
	Millard Fillmore	American	21.6	8	
1860	**Abraham Lincoln**	Republican	39.8	180	81.2
	Stephen A. Douglas	Democratic	29.5	12	
	John C. Breckinridge	Democratic	18.1	72	
	John Bell	Constitutional Union	12.6	39	
1864	**Abraham Lincoln**	Republican	55.0	212	73.8
	George B. McClellan	Democratic	45.0	21	
1868	**Ulysses S. Grant**	Republican	52.7	214	78.1
	Horatio Seymour	Democratic	47.3	80	
1872	**Ulysses S. Grant**	Republican	55.6	286	71.3
	Horace Greeley	Democratic	43.9		
1876	**Rutherford B. Hayes**	Republican	48.0	185	81.8
	Samuel J. Tilden	Democratic	51.0	184	
1880	**James A. Garfield**	Republican	48.5	214	79.4
	Winfield S. Hancock	Democratic	48.1	155	
	James B. Weaver	Greenback-Labor	3.4		
1884	**Grover Cleveland**	Democratic	48.5	219	77.5
	James G. Blaine	Republican	48.2	182	
1888	**Benjamin Harrison**	Republican	47.9	233	79.3
	Grover Cleveland	Democratic	48.6	168	
1892	**Grover Cleveland**	Democratic	46.1	277	74.7
	Benjamin Harrison	Republican	43.0	145	
	James B. Weaver	People's	8.5	22	
1896	**William McKinley**	Republican	51.1	271	79.3
	William J. Bryan	Democratic	47.7	176	
1900	**William McKinley**	Republican	51.7	292	73.2
	William J. Bryan	Democratic; Populist	45.5	155	
1904	**Theodore Roosevelt**	Republican	57.4	336	65.2
	Alton B. Parker	Democratic	37.6	140	
	Eugene V. Debs	Socialist	3.0		
1908	**William H. Taft**	Republican	51.6	321	65.4
	William J. Bryan	Democratic	43.1	162	
	Eugene V. Debs	Socialist	2.8		
1912	**Woodrow Wilson**	Democratic	41.9	435	58.8
	Theodore Roosevelt	Progressive	27.4	88	
	William H. Taft	Republican	23.2	8	
1916	**Woodrow Wilson**	Democratic	49.4	277	61.6
	Charles E. Hughes	Republican	46.2	254	
	A.L. Benson	Socialist	3.2		

Year	Candidates	Parties	Percentage of Popular Vote	Electoral Vote	Percentage of Voter Participation
1920	**Warren G. Harding**	Republican	60.4	404	49.2
	James M. Cox	Democratic	34.2	127	
	Eugene V. Debs	Socialist	3.4		
1924	**Calvin Coolidge**	Republican	54.0	382	48.9
	John W. Davis	Democratic	28.8	136	
	Robert M. La Follette	Progressive	16.6	13	
1928	**Herbert C. Hoover**	Republican	58.2	444	56.9
	Alfred E. Smith	Democratic	40.9	87	
1932	**Franklin D. Roosevelt**	Democratic	57.4	472	56.9
	Herbert C. Hoover	Republican	39.7	59	
1936	**Franklin D. Roosevelt**	Democratic	60.8	523	61.0
	Alfred M. Landon	Republican	36.5	8	
1940	**Franklin D. Roosevelt**	Democratic	54.8	449	62.5
	Wendell L. Willkie	Republican	44.8	82	
1944	**Franklin D. Roosevelt**	Democratic	53.5	432	55.9
	Thomas E. Dewey	Republican	46.0	99	
1948	**Harry S Truman**	Democratic	49.6	303	53.0
	Thomas E. Dewey	Republican	45.1	189	
1952	**Dwight D. Eisenhower**	Republican	55.1	442	63.3
	Adlai E. Stevenson	Democratic	44.4	89	
1956	**Dwight D. Eisenhower**	Republican	57.6	457	60.6
	Adlai E. Stevenson	Democratic	42.1	73	
1960	**John F. Kennedy**	Democratic	49.7	303	64.0
	Richard M. Nixon	Republican	49.5	219	
1964	**Lyndon B. Johnson**	Democratic	61.1	486	61.7
	Barry M. Goldwater	Republican	38.5	52	
1968	**Richard M. Nixon**	Republican	43.4	301	60.6
	Hubert H. Humphrey	Democratic	42.7	191	
	George C. Wallace	American Independent	13.5	46	
1972	**Richard M. Nixon**	Republican	60.7	520	55.5
	George S. McGovern	Democratic	37.5	17	
1976	**Jimmy Carter**	Democratic	50.1	297	54.3
	Gerald R. Ford	Republican	48.0	240	
1980	**Ronald W. Reagan**	Republican	50.7	489	53.0
	Jimmy Carter	Democratic	41.0	49	
	John B. Anderson	Independent	6.6	0	
1984	**Ronald W. Reagan**	Republican	58.4	525	52.9
	Walter F. Mondale	Democratic	41.6	13	
1988	**George H. W. Bush**	Republican	53.4	426	50.3
	Michael Dukakis	Democratic	45.6	111*	
1992	**William J. Clinton**	Democratic	43.7	370	55.1
	George H. W. Bush	Republican	38.0	168	
	H. Ross Perot	Independent	19.0	0	
1996	**William J. Clinton**	Democratic	49	379	49.0
	Robert J. Dole	Republican	41	159	
	H. Ross Perot	Reform	8	0	
2000	**George W. Bush**	Republican	47.9	271	N.A.
	Albert A. Gore	Democratic	48.4	266†	
	Ralph Nader	Green Party	2.7		

*One Dukakis elector cast a vote for Lloyd Bentsen.
†One Gore elector abstained.

CREDITS

CHAPTER 1

"Aztec Elders Describe the Spanish Conquest." Excerpt from *The Florentine Codex: General History of the Thiggs of New Spain,* translated by Arthur J. O. Anderson and Charles E. Dibble. Copyright © 1975 by the University of Utah Press and the School of American Research. Reprinted courtesy of the University of Utah Press.

CHAPTER 2

Excerpt from *The Unredeemed Captive: A Family Story from Early America* by John Demos. Copyright © 1994 by John Demos. Reprinted with the permission of Alfred A. Knopf, a division of Random House, Inc.

CHAPTER 4

"Runaway Servants and Slaves." Excerpt from *Blacks Who Stole Themselves: Advertisements for Runaways* in the Pennsylvania Gazette, *1728–1790* by Billy G. Smith and Richard Wojtowicz. Copyright © 1989 University of Pennsylvania Press. Reprinted with the permission of the publisher.

"The Power of a Preacher." Excerpt from *English Historical Documents Vol. IX: American Colonial Documents to 1776,* edited by Merrill Jensen. Copyright © 1955 by Oxford University Press, Inc.

CHAPTER 8

"The Battle of Tippecanoe." Excerpt from "Shabonne's Account of Tippecanoe" in *Indiana Magazine of History* 18 (December 1921): 355–59, edited by Wesley Whickar. Reprinted with permission from the Indiana Historical Society.

CHAPTER 10

"A New England Mill Worker." Excerpt from *The New England Mill Village, 1790–1860* by Gary Kulik, Roger Parks, Theodore Z. Penn, editors. Copyright © 1982 by MIT Press. Reprinted with permission of MIT Press.

CHAPTER 12

"An Illinois 'Jeffersonian' Attacks the Mormons." Excerpt from *Antebellum America: An Interpretive Anthology* by David Brion Davis, editor. Copyright © 1997 by David Brion Davis. Reprinted with permission of the author. Now published by Pennsylvania State University Press.

"A Farm Woman Defends the Grimké Sisters." Excerpt from "The Daughters of Job: Property Rights and Women's Lives in Mid-Nineteenth-Century Massachusetts" by Dianne Avery and Alfred S. Konefsky in *Law and History Review* 10 (Fall 1992): 323–56. From Box 3, folder 10, Simon Greenleaf Papers, Harvard Law School Library. Reprinted with permission of the publisher.

CHAPTER 13

"A Mexican View of the Battle of the Alamo." Excerpt from *With Santa Anna in Texas: A Personal Narrative of the Revolution* by José Enrique de la Peña, translated by Carmen Perry. Copyright © 1975 Carmen Perry. Reprinted with permission from Texas A & M University Press.

CHAPTER 27

"Resisting the Tactics of McCarthyism." Excerpt from *False Witness* by Melvyn Rader. Copyright ©1969 by Melvyn Rader. Reprinted with the permission of the University of Washington Press.

"Memories of a Cold War Childhood." Excerpt from *Born on the Fourth of July* by Ron Kovic. Copyright © 1976 by Ron Kovic. Reprinted with the permission of Pocket Books, a division of Simon & Schuster.

CHAPTER 28

"A Woman Encounters the Feminist Mystique." Excerpt from *The Fifties: A Women's Oral History* by Brett Harvey. Copyright © 1993 by Brett Harvey, editor. Copyright © 1993 by Brett Harvey. Reprinted with the permission of the author.

"A Badge of Honor." Excerpt from *Voices of Freedom: An Oral History of the Civil Rights Movement from the 1950s through the 1980s* by Henry Hampton and Steve Fayer. Copyright © 1990 by Blackside, Inc. Used by permission of Bantam Books, a division of Random House, Inc.

CHAPTER 29

"A Vietnam War Vet Remembers." Excerpt from *Winter Soldiers: An Oral History of the Vietnam Veterans against the War* by Richard Stacewicz. Copyright © 1997 by Richard Stacewicz. Reprinted with permission of Twayne Publishers, a division of Simon & Schuster.

CHAPTER 30

"Watergate Diary." Excerpt from *Washington Journal: The Events of 1973–1974* by Elizabeth Drew. Copyright © 1974 by Elizabeth Drew. Reprinted with the permission of Random House, Inc.

CHAPTER 31

"The Undocumented Worker." Excerpt from *Mexican Voices, American Dreams: An Oral History of Mexican Immigration in the United States* by Marilyn P. Davis. Copyright © 1990 by Marilyn P. Davis. Reprinted with permission of Henry Holt and Company, LLC.

INDEX

CANADA

Red River of the North

Fargo
Duluth
MINNESOTA
St. Paul
Minneapolis
L. Superior
MICHIGAN

Sioux Falls
WISCONSIN
Milwaukee
Madison
Lansing ★ Detroit
L. Michigan
L. Huron

IOWA
Des Moines
Chicago
Gary
Wisconsin R.
Mississippi R.

Omaha
Lincoln
Springfield
INDIANA
Indianapolis
Cincinnati
Wabash R.
Illinois R.
OHIO
Columbus
Wheeling
Cleveland

Topeka
Kansas City
St. Louis
Jefferson City
ILLINOIS
Louisville
Frankfort
KENTUCKY
Ohio R.
Missouri R.
WEST VIRGINIA
Charleston

Wichita
MISSOURI
Nashville
Knoxville
TENNESSEE
Cumberland R.

Oklahoma City
ARKANSAS
Memphis
Tennessee R.
NORTH CAROLINA
Charlotte
Raleigh

OKLAHOMA
Little Rock
Birmingham
Atlanta
GEORGIA
Mississippi R.
SOUTH CAROLINA
Columbia
Santee R.
Cape Fear R.
Charleston

Dallas
Fort Worth
LOUISIANA
Jackson
MISSISSIPPI
ALABAMA
Montgomery
Chattahoochee R.
Alabama R.
Jacksonville
Tallahassee

Sabine R.
Red R.
Trinity R.
Brazos R.
Houston
Antonio
Austin
Baton Rouge
New Orleans
FLORIDA

Gulf of Mexico

Miami

L. Ontario
NEW YORK
Buffalo
L. Erie
Albany
Hudson R.
Allegheny R.
PENNSYLVANIA
Harrisburg
Pittsburgh
Baltimore
MD.
Annapolis
WASHINGTON D.C.
Potomac R.
VIRGINIA
Richmond
Norfolk
Roanoke R.

MAINE
Augusta
Burlington
Montpelier
VT. N.H.
Concord
Manchester
Portland
Boston
MASS.
Providence
Hartford
CONN. R.I.
Newark
New York
Trenton
NEW JERSEY
Philadelphia
Dover
DELAWARE

APPALACHIAN MOUNTAINS

Atlantic Ocean

BAHAMAS

CUBA

Elevation

Feet	Meters
9,843	3,000
6,562	2,000
3,281	1,000
1,640	500
656	200
0	0
Below sea level	Below sea level

67° *Atlantic Ocean* 66°
San Juan ★
PUERTO RICO
Ponce
18°
Caribbean Sea
0   500
Miles

200   400
Miles

95°   90°   85°   80°   75°

160° 140° 120° 100° 80° 60° 40° 20°

80°

GREENLAND
(KALAALIT-NUNAAT)
(DEN.)

Arctic Circle
ICELAND

60°

ALASKA
(U.S.)

CANADA

UNITED
KINGDOM

IRELAND
BEL.
FRANCE

40°

UNITED STATES

PORTUGAL
SPAIN

AZORES
(PORT.)

*Atlantic
Ocean*

MOROCCO
MADEIRA IS.
(PORT.)

CANARY IS. (SP.)

Tropic of Cancer

20°

HAWAII (U.S.)

MEXICO

BAHAMAS

CUBA
DOMINICAN
REPUBLIC
PUERTO RICO (U.S.)

WESTERN
SAHARA
(MOR.)

MAURITANIA
MALI

BELIZE
JAMAICA
HONDURAS
GUATEMALA
EL SALVADOR
NICARAGUA
COSTA RICA

HAITI
ST. KITTS-NEVIS
GRENADA

ANTIGUA AND BARBUDA
DOMINICA
ST. VINCENT AND
THE GRENADINES
BARBADOS
TRINIDAD AND TOBAGO
GUYANA
SURINAME
FRENCH GUIANA (FR.)

CAPE
VERDE

SENEGAL
GAMBIA
GUINEA-BISSAU
BURKINA FASO
GUINEA
SIERRA LEONE
LIBERIA

PANAMA

VENEZUELA

COLOMBIA

0° Equator

Pacific Ocean

KIRIBATI

GALAPAGOS IS.
(ECU.)

ECUADOR

CÔTE D'IVOIRE

GHANA
EQ. GUINE.

SÃO TOMÉ
PRINCIP.

SAMOA

FRENCH
POLYNESIA

AMERICAN
SAMOA (U.S.)

20° TONGA

PERU

BRAZIL

BOLIVIA

Tropic of Capricorn

CHILE

PARAGUAY

*Atlantic
Ocean*

40°

ARGENTINA

URUGUAY

FALKLAND IS.
(U.K.)

60°

Antarctic Circle

80°

Political divisions as of January 2001

Arctic Ocean

20° 40° 60° 80° 100° 120° 140° 160°

RUSSIAN FEDERATION

NORWAY
SWEDEN
FINLAND
DEN.
EST.
RUSS.
NETH.
GER.
POLAND BELARUS
LUX.
CZ. REP.
AUS.
SLOV.
SLOV.
HUNG.
ROMANIA
B.H.
BULG.
ALB.
MAC.
SWITZ.
GREECE
MALTA
TUNISIA CYPRUS
ALGERIA
LIBYA EGYPT

LITH.

UKRAINE
MOL.

KAZAKHSTAN

MONGOLIA

GEORGIA
AZER.
ARM.
TURKEY TURKMENISTAN
LEB. SYRIA
ISRAEL
WEST
GAZA STRIP BANK IRAQ
JORDAN KUWAIT
QATAR
SAUDI
ARABIA U.A.E.

UZBEKISTAN
TAJIKISTAN

KYRGYZSTAN

CHINA

N.KOREA
S. KOREA JAPAN

IRAN
AFGHANISTAN
PAKISTAN
NEPAL BHUTAN

TAIWAN

Pacific Ocean

INDIA
BANGLADESH

MYANMAR
(BURMA) LAOS
THAILAND
CAMBODIA

NIGER
TOGO
BENIN CHAD
NIGERIA
CENTRAL
AFRICAN
REPUBLIC
CAMEROON
CONGO
GABON
DEMOCRATIC
REPUBLIC OF
THE CONGO
BURUNDI

SUDAN
ERITREA
DJIBOUTI
ETHIOPIA
SOMALIA
UGANDA
RWANDA
KENYA
TANZANIA

YEMEN
OMAN

SRI
LANKA
MALDIVES SINGAPORE

PHILIPPINES

BRUNEI

MALAYSIA

INDONESIA

NORTHERN
MARIANAS (U.S.)

GUAM (U.S.)

PALAU

FEDERATED STATES
OF MICRONESIA

PAPUA
NEW
GUINEA

EAST TIMOR

MARSHALL
ISLANDS

KIRIBATI

NAURU

SOLOMON
ISLANDS TUVALU

SEYCHELLES

Indian
Ocean

VANUATU

FIJI

ANGOLA
ZAMBIA
ZIMBABWE
NAMIBIA
BOTSWANA
SOUTH
AFRICA LESOTHO

MALAWI
COMOROS
MOZAMBIQUE
MADAGASCAR
REUNION
(FR.) MAURITIUS

SWAZILAND

AUSTRALIA

NEW
CALEDONIA
(FR.)

NEW ZEALAND

Major World Trading Blocs

APEC (Asia-Pacific Economic Cooperation)
CIS (Commonwealth of Independent States)
EU (European Union)
Membership Applicants to the EU (European Union)
NAFTA (North American Free Trade Association) and APEC
OPEC (Organization of Petroleum Exporting Countries)
Other nations

ANTARCTICA